D0895688

HANDBOOK OF PEDIATRIC PSYCHOLOGY IN SCHOOL SETTINGS

Director, Editorial:	Lane Akers
Executive Assistant:	Bonita D'Amil
Cover Design:	Kathryn Houghtaling Lacey
Textbook Production Manager:	Paul Smolenski
Full-Service Compositor:	TechBooks
Text and Cover Printer:	Hamilton Printing Company

This book was typeset in 10/12 pt. Palatino, Italic, Bold, and Bold Italic.
The heads were typeset in Palatino.

Lawrence Erlbaum Associates, Inc., Publishers
10 Industrial Avenue
Mahwah, New Jersey 07430
www.erlbaum.com

Library of Congress Cataloging-in-Publication Data

Handbook of pediatric psychology in school settings / [edited by]
Ronald T. Brown.
p. cm.
Includes bibliographical references and index.
ISBN 0-8058-3917-8 (casebound : alk. paper)
1. School psychology—United States—Handbooks, manuals, etc.
2. Child psychology—United States—Handbooks, manuals, etc. 3. School children—Mental health services—United States—Handbooks, manuals, etc.
I. Brown, Ronald T.

LB1027.55.H36 2004
371.8′01′9—dc21

2003002750

Books published by Lawrence Erlbaum Associates are printed on acid-free paper, and their bindings are chosen for strength and durability.

Printed in the United States of America
10 9 8 7 6 5 4 3 2 1

HANDBOOK OF PEDIATRIC PSYCHOLOGY IN SCHOOL SETTINGS

Edited by

Ronald T. Brown

Medical University of South Carolina

LEA

LAWRENCE ERLBAUM ASSOCIATES, PUBLISHERS

2004 Mahwah, New Jersey London

To my wonderful wife Kathy and to my son Ryan, with love

Contents

III: DISEASES ENCOUNTERED IN SCHOOL SETTINGS

IV: DEVELOPMENTAL DISORDERS AND CONDITIONS

V: HEALTH ISSUES RELATED TO DEVELOPMENT

Preface

There was a time when pediatric psychology was practiced solely in children's hospitals and in medical centers. Clearly, the field of all applied psychology has changed markedly. Health psychology has changed, in large part, because health care in the United States generally has become expensive due to increased technology and myriad other factors. As a result, there have been increasing efforts to contain and reduce costs associated with health care; particularly to limit the services provided by psychologists, psychiatrists, and other mental health care providers.

Paralleling changes in health care, there have been rapid and important developments within psychology, and there is a clear consensus that psychologists are health care providers regardless of their field of specialization or venue of practice. In fact, within the field of school psychology, there has been a burgeoning trend toward expanding school psychologists' scope of practice from that of diagnosticians to psychologists who are able to provide an array of services within a school setting. This has been fortuitous, because the changing economics of health care has dictated that children receive many psychological services within the school setting rather than in the traditional venue of the medical setting. Fortunately, the domain of practice in the field of school psychology has expanded to the practice of psychotherapy, psychopharmacology, health promotion, and prevention of disease.

With the improved outcomes of many diseases, that in previous years were given a very guarded prognosis, many pediatric psychologists have had the pleasure of seeing their clients and patients return to school. At the same time, these children have been forced to negotiate a number of other challenges in addition to physical ones, albeit no less important in their overall quality of life and well-being. In part, this has resulted in pediatric psychologists integrating part of their professional practice in school settings, whereas school psychologists have had much to contribute to health care programs, particularly in the assessment of learning and behavioral outcomes, as well as promotion of health and prevention of disease that has largely taken place in school settings. The *Handbook of Pediatric Psychology in School Settings* aims to capture the spirit of changing health care in this country and the recognition of the expanding role of psychology into health care delivery of children and adolescents. To this end, I undertook the task of assembling the present handbook that is aimed at serving both pediatric and school psychologists, physicians, as well as other professionals who are interested in chronic disease, primary care pediatrics, and health promotion and prevention as these factors impact learning, behavior, and quality of life for children in school settings.

The format for the *Handbook of Pediatric Psychology in School Settings* has been designed to reflect the state of the art of the general field. The book is divided into eight distinct sections including: (1) a section containing chapters of a general background nature to this new and exciting field; (2) a series of chapters related to prevention of disease and health promotion; (3) a set of chapters that provide a general overview of various chronic illnesses and how they might impact children's and adolescents' functioning within a school setting; (4) developmental disorders and conditions as these impact learning and behavior in the school setting; (5) specific developmental issues, including infancy and adolescence; (6) interventions for children and adolescents that are related to primary, secondary, and tertiary prevention of health-related conditions that may be implemented in a school setting; (7) a section related to special topics, including peer relationships and friendships of children with chronic conditions and a chapter dealing with the issue of organ transplantation; and (8) special issues, including career, professional, and ethical and legal issues related to this newly emerging field.

I have clearly attempted to be comprehensive in defining this new field and the topical areas relevant for review. All chapter authors necessarily suffered from page constraints because of space limitations, and the authors' tolerance with this process was deeply appreciated. For the many revisions and next drafts, I am most indebted to all of the authors who were so tolerant and patient. Clearly, the authors' tolerance has improved accuracy and readability of the chapters.

There are many individuals to whom I am indebted, including Carrie Rittle, for all of her kind and wonderful assistance with this *Handbook* throughout all stages of the publication process. I also am indebted to Martha Hagen for her superb typing of manuscripts and drafts, as well as to Emily Simerly, Ph.D., who is one of the most stellar editors with whom I have ever had the privilege of working. Their friendship and kindness over the years has been sincerely appreciated. There is no more competent and professional a team than this one. I extend my sincere appreciation to Mary Connolly, my administrative assistant, for fielding the many contacts and crisises that emerged during the tenure of this book.

I remain indebted to my wonderful wife, Kathy Sloan, for her usual patience and kind support for this work, as well as all the other projects that she has tolerated over the years while I missed many evenings at home, important family activities, and social events. Most importantly, I am grateful for our shared interests related to the care and welfare of children with various health conditions. Also, I am indebted to my son Ryan for his patience and understanding when I missed his many basketball and soccer games while tolerating the labors of my academic career.

Throughout the preparation of this *Handbook*, I have been supported financially, in part, by grants from the National Institutes of Health (Nos. CA78-957, CA90-171, and HS10-812), the Centers for Disease Control and Prevention (No. UR3/CCU418882), the Department of Education (Nos. H328C9900004 and H328C0200001), the Health Resource and Service Administration (No. 1D40 HHP 00017), the Department of Defense, the State of South Carolina, the Office of the Governor, and Shire Pharmaceuticals. In addition, I was supported financially by the College of Health Professions and the Department of Pediatrics at the Medical University of South Carolina. I am most grateful to each of these institutions, although the contents of this book are solely those of my own and the contributing authors, and do not represent the official views of these institutions.

Finally, I wish to express my sincere appreciation to Lane Akers and Bonita D'Amil of Lawrence Erlbaum Associates for their encouragement, kind support, and neverending patience in the genesis of this book.

—Ronald T. Brown, Ph.D.
Charleston, South Carolina

Contributors

Deborah L. Anderson, Ph.D.
Division of Genetics & Developmental Pediatrics
Medical University of South Carolina
Charleston, SC

Robert D. Annett, Ph.D.
Department of Pediatrics
University of New Mexico Health Science Center
Albuquerque, NM

F. Daniel Armstrong, Ph.D.
Department of Pediatrics
University of Miami School of Medicine
Miami, FL

Glen P. Aylward, Ph.D, ABPP
Department of Pediatrics
Southern Illinois University School of Medicine
Springfield, IL

Christine Barry, Ph.D.
Division of Behavioral Pediatrics and Psychology
Rainbow Babies and Children's Hospital
Cleveland, OH

Karen J. Bearman
Department of Psychology
University of Miami
Coral Gables, FL

Jessica Blom-Hoffman, Ph.D.
Department of Psychology
The Children's Hospital of Philadelphia
Philadelphia, PA

Douglas R. Bloom, Ph.D.
Learning Support Center
Texas Children's Hospital
Houston, TX

Alexandra Boeving, Ph.D.
Division of Genetics & Developmental Pediatrics
Medical University of South Carolina
Charleston, SC

Richard E. Boles, Ph.D.
Clinical Child Psychology Program
University of Kansas
Lawrence, KS

Melanie J. Bonner, Ph.D.
Department of Psychiatry
Duke University Medical Center
Durham, NC

Brandon G. Briery, Ph.D.
Department of Pediatrics
University of Miami School of Medicine
Miami, FL

Keri J. Brown, Ph.D.
Clinical Child Psychology Program
University of Kansas
Lawrence, KS

Ronald T. Brown, Ph.D., ABPP
College of Health Professions
Medical University of South Carolina
Charleston, SC

Jonathan M. Campbell, Ph.D.
Department of Educational Psychology
University of Georgia
Athens, GA

Cindy Carlson, Ph.D.
Educational Psychology
University of Texas at Austin
Austin, TX

Edward R. Christopherson, Ph.D.
Behavioral Pediatrics Division
Children's Mercy Hospital
Kansas City, MO

Claire D. Coles, Ph.D.
Department of Psychiatry and
Behavioral Sciences
Emory University School of Medicine
Atlanta, GA

Jennifer M. Coniglio
School Psychology Program
Lehigh University
Bethlehem, PA

Erin Cowell
School Psychology Program
University of Wisconsin–Madison
Madison, WI

Richard J. Cowan
Educational Psychology
University of Nebraska
Lincoln, NE

David Ray DeMaso, M.D.
Department of Psychiatry & Cardiology
Children's Hospital Boston
Boston, MA

Dennis Drotar, Ph.D.
Division of Behavioral Pediatrics
and Psychology
Rainbow Babies and Children's Hospital
Cleveland, OH

George J.DuPaul, Ph.D.
School Psychology Program
Lehigh University
Bethlehem, PA

Karen M. Eggert
Civitan International Research Center
University of Alabama at Birmingham
Birmingham, AL

Linda Ewing-Cobbs, Ph.D.
Department of Pediatrics
University of Texas Health Science
Center at Houston
Houston, TX

Elizabeth Ezell
Department of Psychiatry
Duke University Medical Center
Durham, NC

Kelly Feeney
School Psychology Program
University of Wisconsin–Madison
Madison, WI

Constance J. Fournier
Department of Educational Psychology
Texas A&M University
College Station, TX

Adrienne Fricker-Elhai
Medical University of South Carolina
Crime Victim's Center
Charleston, SC

Patrick C. Friman, Ph.D.
Department of Psychology
University of Nevada, Reno
Reno, NV

Bernard F. Fuemmeler, Ph.D.
National Cancer Institute
Cancer Prevention Fellowship Program
Bethesda, MD

Katrina K. Gilbert
Civitan International Research Center
University of Alabama at Birmingham
Birmingham, AL

Regino P. Gonzalez-Peralta, M.D.
Division of Gatroenterology
Department of Pediatrics
University of Florida
Health Science Center
Gainesville, FL

Laura Guli
Educational Psychology
University of Texas at Austin
Austin, TX

Rochelle F. Hanson, Ph.D.
Medical University of South Carolina
Crime Victim's Center
Charleston, SC

Kristina K. Hardy
Department of Psychiatry
Duke University Medical Center
Durham, NC

Jennie N. Jackson
University of Georgia
Athens, GA

W. Stephen Johnson, M.D.
Division of Adolescent Medicine and Behavioral Science
Department of Pediatrics
Vanderbilt University School of Medicine
Nashville, TN

Julie A. Kable, Ph.D.
Emory University–Briarcliff Campus
Atlanta, GA

Ernest R. Katz, Ph.D.
Department of Pediatrics
Children's Hospital, Los Angeles and The Keck School of Medicine of The University of Southern California
Los Angeles, CA

Thomas R. Kratochwill, Ph.D.
School Psychology Program
University of Wisconsin–Madison
Madison, WI

Thomas Kubiszyn
Educational Psychology
University of Texas at Austin
Austin, TX

Jason LaGory
Civitan International Research Center
University of Alabama at Birmingham
Birmingham, AL

Annette M. La Greca, Ph.D.
Department of Psychology
University of Miami
Coral Gables, FL

Max R. Langham, Jr. M.D.
Division of Pediatric Surgery
Department of Surgery
University of Florida Health Science Center
Gainesville, FL

Kathleen L. Lemanek, Ph.D.
Department of Psychology
Columbus Children's Hospital
Columbus, OH

Celia Lescano, Ph.D.
Child and Family Psychiatry
Rhode Island Hospital
Providence, RI

Avi Madan-Swain, Ph.D.
University of Alabama at Birmingham
Birmingham, AL

Patricia H. Manz, Ph.D.
Department of Education and Human Services
College of Education
Lehigh University–Mountaintop Campus
Bethlehem, PA

Staci C. Martin, Ph.D.
HIV & Aids Malignancy Branch
National Cancer Institute and
Medical Illness Counseling Center
Bethesda, MD

Joanna O. Mashunkashey
Clinical Child Psychology Program
University of Kansas
Lawrence, KS

Avani C. Modi
Department of Clinical and Health Psychology
University of Florida Health Science Center
Gainesville, FL

Hannah Moore
Department of Psychology
University of Miami
Coral Gables, FL

Sam B. Morgan, Ph.D.
Memphis State University
Department of Psychology
Memphis, TN

Bonnie K. Nastasi, Ph.D.
Associate Director of Interventions
The Institute for Community Research
Hartford, CT

Michelle R. Nebrig
School Psychology Program
Lehigh University
Bethlehem, PA

Jennie W. Neighbors
Department of Educational Psychology
University of Georgia
Athens, GA

Tonya Palermo, Ph.D.
Division of Behavioral Pediatrics and Psychology
Rainbow Babies and Children's Hospital
Cleveland, OH

William E. Pelham, Jr., Ph.D.
Center for Children and Families
State University of New York at Buffalo
Buffalo, NY

LeAdelle Phelps, Ph.D.
Department of Counseling and Educational Psychology
State University of New York at Buffalo
Buffalo, NY

Wendy Plante, Ph.D.
Child and Family Psychiatry
Rhode Island Hospital
Providence, RI

Thomas J. Power, Ph.D.
Department of Psychology
The Children's Hospital of Philadelphia
3405 Civic Center Boulevard
Philadelphia, PA

Alexandra L. Quittner, Ph.D.
Department of Clinical and Health Psychology
University of Florida Health Science Center
Gainesville, FL

William A. Rae, Ph.D.
Department of Educational Psychology
Texas A&M University
College Station, TX

Michael C. Roberts, Ph.D., ABPP
Clinical Child Psychology Program
University of Kansas
Lawrence, KS

James R. Rodrigue, Ph.D.
Department of Clinical & Health Psychology
University of Florida Health Science Center
Gainesville, FL

Amy Loomis Roux
Department of Clinical and Health Psychology
University of Florida Health Science Center
Gainesville, FL

Lisa Hagermoser Sannetti
School Psychology Program
University of Wisconsin–Madison
Madison, WI

Edward S. Shapiro, Ph.D.
Department of Education and Human Services
College of Education
Lehigh University–Mountaintop Campus
Bethlehem, PA

Susan M. Sheridan, Ph.D.
Educational Psychology
University of Nebraska
Lincoln, NE

Susan J. Simonian, Ph.D.
Department of Psychology
College of Charleston
Charleston, SC

Daniel W. Smith
Medical University of South Carolina
Crime Victim's Center
Charleston, SC

Renee A. Smith
University of Illinois at Chicago
Department of Pediatrics
Chicago, IL

Anthony Spirito, Ph.D.
Child and Family Psychiatry
Rhode Island Hospital
Providence, RI

Karen Callan Stoiber
Department of Educational Psychology
University of Wisconsin–Milwaukee
Milwaukee, WI

Kenneth J. Tarnowski, Ph.D.
Department of Psychology
Florida Gulf Coast University
Fort Meyers, FL

Lloyd A. Taylor, Ph.D.
Division of Genetics &
Developmental Pediatrics
Medical University of South Carolina
Charleston, SC

Gregory A. Waas
Northern Illinois University
Department of Psychology
DeKalb, IL

Lynn S. Walker, Ph.D.
Division of Adolescent Medicine
and Behavioral Science
Department of Pediatrics
Vanderbilt University School of Medicine
Nashville, TN

Jan L. Wallander, Ph.D.
Civitan International Research Center
University of Alabama at Birmingham
Birmingham, AL

Russell Ware
Department of Medicine
Duke University Medical Center
Durham, NC

Daniel A. Waschbusch, Ph.D.
Department of Psychology
Dalhousie University
Halifax, NS
Canada

Jane Williams, Ph.D.
UAMS, Department of Pediatrics
Little Rock, AR

Pamela L. Wolters, Ph.D.
HIV & Aids Malignancy Branch
National Cancer Institute and
Medical Illness Counseling Center
Bethesda, MD

Deborah Young-Hyman, Ph.D., CDE
National Institute of Health
Bethesda, MD

HANDBOOK OF PEDIATRIC PSYCHOLOGY IN SCHOOL SETTINGS

1

Introduction: Changes in the Provision of Health Care to Children and Adolescents

Ronald T. Brown
Medical University of South Carolina

The focus of this handbook is the delivery of pediatric psychological services in schools, but in this introduction the focus is on the broader context of pediatric psychology and health care. To understand changes in the provision of health care to children and adolescents, it is helpful first to understand the several natures of childhood illness. These aspects are both physical and psychological. Chronic illnesses are conditions involving a protracted course of treatment. Chronic illnesses can result in compromised mental, cognitive, and physical functioning and are frequently characterized by acute complications that may result in hospitalizations or other forms of intensive treatment (Thompson & Gustafson, 1996). Included in chronic illnesses are such conditions of childhood as developmental illnesses like mental retardation and diseases like cystic fibrosis. A condition that persists for more than 3 months within 1 year and necessitates ongoing care from a health care provider is considered to be chronic.

By the age of 18 years, 10% to 15% of children have experienced one or more chronic medical conditions (Tarnowski & Brown, 2000). Approximately 1 million children in this country have a chronic illness that may impair their daily functioning, and an additional 10 million children have a less serious form of chronic conditions (Thompson & Gustafson, 1996). Prevalence of chronic conditions in children has nearly doubled over the past several decades. This increased prevalence has been attributed to several factors, including advances in health care reflecting improved early diagnosis and treatment, the survival of infants of extreme prematurity or low birth weight, and new diseases like prenatal drug exposure and AIDS.

During the past two decades, the importance of psychological variables in understanding health and illness has become well established (for review, see Brown et al., 2002; Tarnowski & Brown, 2000). With medical advances and improvements in living conditions, contemporary medicine has focused on psychological determinants and sequelae of disease. In fact, the United States Public Health Service has reported that lifestyle and behavioral factors comprise seven of the leading health-risk factors in the United States (VandenBos, DeLeon, & Belar, 1991). As serious pediatric disorders (e.g., acute lymphocytic leukemia) have yielded to improved medical treatments and as some infectious diseases have been eradicated, greater attention has focused on the role of psychosocial factors. These factors mediate and moderate response to illness and are important in the prevention and management of, and adaptation to, illness. Behavioral factors can be major contributors to disease and injury onset and maintenance (e.g., smoking, lack of exercise, diet, treatment nonadherence, substance abuse) (Brannon & Feist, 1997; Brown et al., 2002).

Brown and DuPaul (1999) delineated variables that predict adaptation to illness and injury and promote health. These variables include developmental issues, socioemotional development, and environmental problems. Recent focus has been on increasing the knowledge of health-related developmental variables, including children's developmental level as it influences their conceptualization of health, injury, and illness. A child's capacity to comprehend health-related communications is critical. In addition, a child's capacity to cope with the myriad of challenges posed by chronic illness or injury may be significantly taxed by such environmental stressors as extended hospitalizations; separation from parents, siblings, and peers; and frequent painful medical procedures. Likewise, the child's illness may affect family functioning and psychological and financial resources. The environmental context in which attention to health care and management of illness or injury occurs is especially important. Family functioning and support can provide an important buffer from the short- and long-term stressors associated with hospitalization (Kazak, Segal-Andrews, & Johnson, 1995). Basic resources (e.g., access to health care, transportation, finances to secure appropriate treatment) and psychological resources (e.g., family support, coping skills) are essential ingredients in a successful formula against the challenges of a chronic illness.

CHANGES IN HEALTH CARE

Change permeates the delivery of health care services in the United States. The cost of health care has risen dramatically, in part from improved technology that better enables us to manage diseases, enhance quality of life, and reduce mortality. Third-party payers (e.g., Medicaid, private health maintenance organizations, third-party insurers) systematically attempt to limit spending and evaluate care so that services, including mental health services, are provided in the most cost-effective manner. Health care has become expensive, and efforts to contain and reduce these costs continue. If children are to receive adequate mental health care, it is important that pediatric psychologists respond appropriately. In the following sections, the areas of change are described, and arguments are made for increasing the presence of appropriately trained psychologists in schools and in primary care centers.

Focus on the Primary Care Setting

One way to contain health care costs is to limit services provided by psychologists, psychiatrists, and other mental health specialists in health care settings (e.g., hospital psychologists) or private practice. By placing the initial point of service in the primary care system and limiting referrals to specialty care providers, costs are contained (American Academy of Pediatrics, 2000), but the availability of mental health services for children and adolescents has decreased. The decrease is attributed to insurance packages that limit mental health services. Before managed care, pediatricians routinely referred their patients with emotional or behavioral disturbances or those with adjustment difficulties associated with the stressor of a chronic condition or illness to mental health providers. This made it more likely that caregivers and school personnel would have direct access to mental health professionals. Decreased availability of these services has resulted in a growing trend to fulfill mental health service needs in the primary care setting

(Brown et al., 2002) or schools (Power, Shapiro, & DuPaul, 2003). This has occurred in the midst of increased evidence on the efficacy of specific mental health services (Kazdin, Bass, Ayers, & Rodgers, 1990). Primary care providers can adequately perform some of the basic services of specialists (e.g., pharmacotherapy for the management of attention deficit hyperactivity disorder) (American Academy of Pediatrics, 2000). However, this clearly detracts from the critical needs of managing serious physical illnesses and conditions. Primary health care providers have the added burden of continuing education in disorders for which they have not been trained.

Efforts to drive down the costs of health care run concurrently with increasing mental health needs of children and adolescents and decreasing access to services (American Academy of Pediatrics, 2000). Lavigne and associates (1999) found that the percentage of emotional disorders in children has increased in recent years, particularly among preschool children. In addition, compelling evidence has emerged on psychological consequences of physical illness in children and adolescents (Cadman, Boyle, Szatmari, & Offord, 1987; Gortmaker, Walker, Weitzman, & Sobol, 1990).

Access to services for many youth in rural and disadvantaged communities is sometimes exceedingly difficult because of a shortage of mental health providers (American Academy of Pediatrics, 2000). In some locations, access to mental health care from providers other than primary care physicians or pediatricians is almost nonexistent. Data from the first wave of the Great Smoky Mountains Study of Youth, an epidemiologic investigation of psychopathology and mental health service utilization among regional children, suggest that the major system providing mental health services to children is the educational system, with 70% to 80% of children receiving services in school (Burns, Costello, Angold, Tweed, & Stangl, 1995). For most of these children, their school was the only provider of mental health services. In this study, fewer than 15% of children received mental health services in a general medical setting. Although the investigators recommended research to replicate their findings, schools clearly represent a critical venue for addressing emotional and behavioral needs of children.

There are also difficulties associated with the identification of mental health problems in the primary care setting. First, there are data to suggest that primary care providers underidentify psychological problems in pediatric populations (Brown et al., 2002). Several factors may contribute to this underidentification, including the fact that caregivers may not spontaneously report concerns of a psychological nature, because of reluctance to disclose such concerns to a primary care provider. In a survey of more than 200 mothers, 70% of the mothers had fundamental concerns about emotional and behavioral issues but fewer than one third discussed these concerns with their child's pediatrician (Hickson, Altemeir, & O'Conner, 1983). Nondisclosure of emotional and behavioral concerns is also evident in more recent surveys. Although 40% to 80% of parents have questions or concerns about their children's behavioral and emotional development, many do not raise these concerns with their pediatricians or primary care provider (Lynch, Wildman, & Smucker, 1997; Richardson, Keller, Selby-Harrington, & Parrish, 1996; Young, Davis, Schoen, & Parker, 1998).

Perrin (1999) suggested other limitations related to the identification of psychological problems in the primary care setting. First, primary care pediatricians are not generally informed about their patients' developmental and psychosocial problems. This has been attributed in part to the hesitancy of pediatricians to inquire about children's behavior, development, or family functioning. Perhaps as a result, approximately 50% of caregivers seen for well-child visits report having psychosocial concerns that go unaddressed (Sharpe, Pantell, Murphy, & Lewis, 1992).

Clearly there have been changes in the structure of health care in our country. Pediatricians and other primary care providers are now gatekeepers for subsequent mental health services; and, more important, they may underidentify psychosocial dysfunction (Costello et al.,

1988). It is a serious concern when children and adolescents go without needed mental health services.

Brown et al. (2002) identified a number of factors that play a significant role in impeding the assessment and management of emotional and behavioral disturbances in primary care settings. These barriers include training programs that do not provide pediatricians with specific education, knowledge, training, and skills to address psychosocial disturbances in their patients. Pediatricians may be undertrained in recognizing the complex problems associated with mental health issues and also may lack the necessary expertise to care for children who evidence psychopathology. With the constraints associated with managed care, physicians are often faced with time and financial pressures that restrict their ability to devote sufficient efforts toward assessment and management of their patients' psychological functioning (American Academy of Pediatrics, 2000; Perrin, 1999). The average office visit in a pediatric practice for both well- and sick-child visits is less than 15 minutes (Ferris et al., 1998), barely sufficient time to assess and manage physical needs.

Primary care physicians also may be faced with inadequate resources to manage emotional disturbances in their patients. For example, they may practice in a community where services that address emotional disturbances in children and families are inadequate (Drotar, 1995). Also, primary care providers may face cumbersome impediments when referring patients to other specialty providers (American Academy of Pediatrics, 2000). Even in the case where a child is identified by the primary care physician and referred to a mental health specialist for further evaluation and treatment, families may be reluctant for a number of reasons to follow through with recommended services. Reasons may include financial limitations, long waiting lists, and the stigma associated with labeling and receiving services at a psychiatric or mental health clinic (Armstrong, Glanville, Bailey, O'Keefe 1990). Perrin and Ireys (1984) observed that this stigma may diminish when these services are provided in pediatric offices. This would also facilitate access to mental health services.

Armstrong et al., (1990) also delineated barriers to mental health care. A general unfamiliarity with the nature and benefits of psychological services by children and their caregivers and health care providers hinders use of services. So do environmental barriers like limited office space and schedules that overlap medical appointments. Other barriers may include resources for travel and increased time demands from multiple appointments.

Another factor that may play a role in the underidentification and management of psychosocial problems in primary care settings is the extent to which the primary care provider views physical health and mental health as distinct entities. For some, the incorporation of mental health issues into one's scope of practice may require a paradigm shift. McLennan, Jansen-Williams, Comer, Gardner, and Kelleher (1999) found that psychosocial orientation was associated with a primary care provider's practice of identifying and managing emotional and behavioral disturbances. Beliefs about their inability to manage psychosocial problems and perceptions that patients would resist having psychosocial issues addressed in the primary care setting were associated with primary care providers' practice methods.

There has been some interest in determining the degree to which pediatricians regard specific treatments as acceptable and whether they actually follow treatment guidelines (Tarnowski, Kelly, & Mendlowitz, 1987). Interventions applied to severe behavioral problems (e.g., suicidal concerns) were rated as more acceptable than those interventions applied to more minor behavioral problems (e.g., temper tantrums). The severity of a child's medical condition did not contribute to the outcome of acceptability ratings. Although these findings are important in understanding the acceptability of psychological treatments among pediatric primary care providers, much more research in this area is necessary before formulating any definitive conclusions.

These issues underscore an increasing need for collaboration between psychologists and primary care pediatricians as a result of the shifts in the priority of the health care system from specialty care to primary care (Rabasca, 1999). As Roberts (1986) observed over a decade ago, roles for psychologists in primary care settings may increase. For example, many inner-city parents value working with health care providers to enhance their own knowledge of developmental and behavioral issues (Schultz & Vaughn, 1999). Only 8% of the caregivers in the Schultz and Vaughn study were in need of medical information, but nearly one half wanted specific information about developmental and behavioral issues. Other important steps in meeting the mental health needs of children include improving the detection of emotional and behavioral disturbances in primary care settings and building more integrated settings in which psychologists work alongside pediatricians and family physicians in children's primary medical homes.

Changing and Expanding the Role of Psychology in Health Care Delivery

With the growth of behavioral medicine and pediatric psychology, psychologists have had increasing numbers of opportunities to collaborate with other health care disciplines in addressing important health issues for children and adolescents. Over the years, we have witnessed the application of behavioral principles to a broad range of medical problems (for review, see Beutler, 1992). Collaborative endeavors between psychology and pediatric medicine have been important in improving health outcomes, preventing disease and injury, enhancing adaptation to illness, and reducing mortality from disease.

Traditional medicine focused largely on the treatment of disease, but recent concerns about the rising cost of health care and the cost-effectiveness of treatments may help shift the focus of health care toward preventive efforts. Psychologists are well positioned to contribute in this area. Our nation's recent emphasis on health promotion highlights the importance of psychologists' work toward the prevention of specific disorders and diseases as well as general health promotion. With the advent of evidence-based medicine, psychologists have had unique opportunities to contribute to the empirical basis of health care. Psychologists' expertise in research and evaluation have added to physical and psychological empirically based treatments. With these changes, there have been immense opportunities for psychologists to expand beyond traditional practice opportunities to exciting new domains in the delivery of health care. There are already abundant signs that psychology's influence is being felt in the medical community. For example, in primary care settings, medical utilization and costs can be reduced with psychological interventions (Sobel, 1995).

Over the years, psychologists have made significant contributions to pediatric health care (for review, see Brown et al., 2002). Dimensions include a range of disease states, diverse service activities, and psychologists' contributions to primary through tertiary prevention.

Within the range of disease entities, psychiatric or mental health disorders are conceptualized as health conditions of equivalent import to other disease categories. Psychologists have been involved in virtually all of these disease categories through research and clinical practice. For many of the diseases, interventions grounded in psychological theory are used to prevent, manage, or ameliorate the symptoms or sequelae of the disease. To participate in the management of these disorders, psychologists have developed a broad range of treatments. Empirically supported interventions ranging from weight control programs to cognitive behavior therapy and a host of other interventions improve health and well-being significantly.

As previously discussed, traditional psychological practice has emphasized a tertiary care role in the mental health arena. However, psychologists have played an integral role in public health initiatives, with researchers, service providers, and policymakers calling for the inclusions of prevention efforts in public health policy (e.g., Lorion, Myers, & Bartels, 1994). Calls for change in the delivery of health care support psychology's contributions in the areas of primary and secondary prevention activities and across a broader range of health conditions.

Primary prevention refers to efforts aimed at decreasing the prevalence of a disease or disorder by reducing its occurrence (Caplan, 1964). Thus, primary prevention addresses risk and protective factors that may influence the onset of a disease. The goals of primary prevention are to prevent specific disorders and diseases and to foster general health enhancement through education. Primary prevention has become a priority in health policy initiatives (e.g., Kaplan, 2000) and is reflected in the growth and development of programs to promote health and reduce risk factors associated with illness. Programs to promote healthy diet and exercise habits for children and adolescents in an effort to prevent or delay the onset of disease are examples of primary prevention.

Secondary prevention is aimed at reducing the prevalence or severity of a disorder through early identification and treatment (Caplan, 1964). Prevention at this level encompasses work with at-risk populations, the assessment of early disease states, and the implementation of interventions to prevent the exacerbation of symptoms. Targets for secondary prevention efforts might include individuals at high risk for adverse health outcomes due to biologic (e.g., genetic disorders), environmental (familial and sociologic risk factors), and ethnic or cultural (e.g., some diseases are more prevalent among specific ethnic groups) risk factors. Psychologists have successfully applied secondary prevention efforts with premature and low-birth-weight infants at risk for health problems and developmental and cognitive delays.

Tertiary prevention refers to efforts to minimize the sequelae of established disorders or diseases through rehabilitation. Psychologists frequently apply tertiary prevention efforts to alleviate suffering and to reduce problems that are residual to the illness or the disorder. The use of pain management for children who undergo painful and stressful medical procedures is an example of tertiary prevention.

Traditional perceptions of psychological practice generally focus on the domain of tertiary prevention. However, recognition of the importance of the timing of interventions has grown over the years with greater emphasis on disease prevention and cost reduction of long-term health care. For some, this represents a paradigm shift from treating diseases and disorders to the promotion of health and prevention of disease, necessitating recognition that potential clients are not only those who come to clinics with illnesses but also those at risk for various adverse heath outcomes (Rae-Grant, 1991).

The service provided by psychologists in health care delivery are varied and include activities such as assessment, intervention, and liaison. These activities occur at different points during the progression of a disease or illness. Timings of assessment and intervention for children are likely to assume greater importance during the next several years as the focus shifts toward preventing disease and reducing the economic burden of health costs. Services and prevention activities may be applied across a spectrum of diseases as psychology continues to make a contribution to health care.

With respect to focus of psychological services, psychologists may become involved in health care at different system levels. Service may target individual children and adolescents, families, classrooms or schools, communities, or, more broadly, federal and state policy. Psychologists have long been involved in service delivery at the individual and family level. As an example at the school level, Cunningham and colleagues (1998) implemented a student-mediated conflict resolution program in three elementary schools. They found that this school-based, student-mediation program reduced physical aggression observed on playgrounds by more than 50%.

Psychologists have also been increasingly influential in the shaping of federal and state policy. In 1995, the public policy office of the American Psychological Association (APA) published *A Psychologist's Guide to Participation in Federal Policy Making* (American Psychological Association, 1995). The volume developed partially out of APA's participation with the American Association for the Advancement of Science Congressional Fellowship program. Since 1974, 75 psychologists have been selected as APA congressional fellows and have represented the field of psychology to policymakers and scholars from other disciplines. Serving in the United States Congress, they have furthered the enactment of specific pieces of federal legislation, brought experts from across the nation to testify at congressional hearings, and enlightened policymakers about the value of psychological knowledge to many of society's most pressing concerns, including health care (Rickel & Becker-Lausen, 1997).

One example of psychology's increasing voice in public policy issues in the health arena is the work of the late Lizette Peterson and colleagues (e.g., Peterson & Stern, 1997) regarding accidental injuries, the leading cause of death among American children. In a review, Tremblay and Peterson (1999) outlined how injury prevention efforts can be enhanced using our knowledge of behavioral principles and child development. The authors argued that the training of psychologists provides unique skills with which to assess contingencies that maintain practices that place children at risk. They also argued that psychologists must work collaboratively with citizens and other professionals to mount persuasive campaigns to reduce the number of accidental injuries in children. They delineated obstacles that may have stunted federal emphasis on injury prevention and provided specific suggestions to improve public policy.

Over the years, psychologists have rendered services across many types of settings. In the past, the traditional setting has been the private office, followed by community mental health centers. Other settings have included hospitals and schools. The focus of this handbook is the delivery of pediatric psychological services in schools. The work of Cowen and colleagues (1996) focused on schools as venues for preventive efforts. The Rochester Primary Mental Health Project, first initiated in 1957, screens children en masse soon after they begin school. Children designated at risk for maladjustment participate in therapeutic activities with parents who serve as child aides. This program is notable for its active, systematic screening for early school maladjustment, its contextual relevance, and the manner in which it has joined research with clinical service and applied research findings to improve service delivery.

Cunningham, Bremmer, and Secord-Gilbert (1994) developed a community-based parent-training program in an effort to increase the availability, accessibility, and cost-effectiveness of interventions for parents of children with behavior problems. In a randomized trial comparing the community-based program to traditional, clinic-based parent training, parents of children with severe behavior problems were more likely to enroll in the community program. Also, families who participated in the community program reported greater improvements in child behavior and better maintenance of these improvements compared to families who received clinic-based services (Cunningham, Bremmer, & Boyle, 1995).

A 1998 study by APA found that most APA-licensed practitioner members were continuing to provide traditional mental health services in independent practice settings (Phelps, Eisman, & Kohut, 1998). However, newer graduates were more likely to be working in some form of medical setting, suggesting a trend to move from independent practice to multidisciplinary settings. In large part, this has been because of changes in the funding of mental health services. Clearly, the practice of psychology in private offices, mental health clinics, or hospital settings is likely to change in future years as it is necessary to enter other systems that reach children and adolescents. It is expected that there will be an increasing number of opportunities for the expansion and growth of psychologists who work with children, including participation in nontraditional health care settings like schools.

Toward an Integration of Services and Linking Systems of Care for Pediatric Populations

Psychology training programs including clinical child, pediatric, and school psychology have conventionally prepared the various specialty areas of psychology to work within a specific range of venues and have focused on specific developmental tasks of childhood and adolescence (La Greca & Hughes, 1999). As Power, Shapiro, and DuPaul (2003) observed, programs in pediatric psychology that customarily were housed in clinical child and health psychology programs have typically trained practitioners to work in health care settings and to focus specifically on assisting children to cope with the stressors of a chronic illness or to promote healthy development and reduce the risk of injuries. Training programs in school psychology traditionally have prepared psychologists to work in schools and to assess cognitive and emotional skills, particularly as they impede academic success and healthy adaptation to the school environment.

Kolbe, Collins, and Cortese (1997) noted that training in applied psychology has usually focused on the delivery of services for children and adolescents with identified psychopathology or developmental disorders. Training has included assessment and intervention in the domain of practice, with less attention to prevention of health risk and health promotion. The authors identified the leading causes of mortality and morbidity in this country and delineated six categories of behavior established during youth that contribute to these issues. They outlined specific ways in which a modern school health program might prevent such poor health behaviors and at the same time address critical health and social problems among students. Most important, they call on psychologists to improve school health programs by working with schools to improve the health of the nation's youth.

Changes in the delivery of health care in this country, particularly that the primary care provider is now the gatekeeper of services and that mental health services are being rationed within the traditional health care system, have given rise to the recommendation that there also be reforms and innovations in training (La Greca & Hughes, 1999). Training focused in one setting and restricting services to a limited range of developmental tasks makes access for the client much too difficult and also restricts employment opportunities for practicing psychologists. La Greca and Hughes decribed the overlap between child and adolescent providers of psychological services and highlighted specific competencies necessary for all psychologists who are involved in applied practice with children and adolescents. They underscored the need for greater collaboration and integration among various psychological specialties that focus on children, adolescents, and families.

Power, Shapiro, and DuPaul (2003) noted the importance of linking systems of care (i.e., the health care system and the school) to provide more accessible psychological services for children and adolescents and to promote healthy behaviors. Coupled with the major reforms in health care aimed at reducing costs and improving access to health care for children (American Academy of Pediatrics, 2000), there has been a movement to provide both pediatric and mental health psychological services in schools. This allows for the provision of more accessible primary prevention activities (e.g., nutrition education, promotion of physical exercise, violence prevention, tobacco use prevention, injury prevention) to children who may not have had easy access to these services.

Paralleling health care reform in this country are reforms in education (for review, see Power, Shapiro, & DuPaul, 2003). Adelman (1996) outlined specific barriers to instruction in the classroom that include not only emotional stressors and peer and family problems, but also health-related problems that significantly affect academic performance. Thus, a new role for schools has emerged that encompasses traditional instruction and also the removal of barriers to instruction that includes the promotion of health. Other changes in education include reforms in special education that reaffirm that rights of children and adolescents with special challenges to receive their education in the same schools as their normally developing peers. In support of this notion of education and health care reform, Short and Talley (1997) emphasized that such efforts will afford psychology the opportunity to assume prominent leadership in defining service delivery models of health care in schools.

Because of the changes in the delivery of health care and the recent emphasis on school reform, changes in models of training for applied psychologists have emerged. The most recent models in training have emphasized the importance of preparing professional psychologists to coordinate care across multiple systems (e.g., health care settings, schools) and promote prevention of health and mental health problems (La Greca & Hughes, 1999). Spirito and colleagues (2003) and Roberts and colleagues (1998) recommended that trainees have a solid foundation in developmental psychology and psychopathology; assessment of children and adolescents and the systems of which they are a part; empirically supported strategies of intervention and prevention; culturally sensitive approaches to assessment, intervention, and prevention; strategies for coordinating community-based systems of care in the community (primary care pediatric settings and schools); and ethical standards for clinical practice and research.

In recent years, a number of graduate training programs in applied psychology, predoctoral internship training sites, and postdoctoral programs have changed the structure of their programs so that they are in accord with recently articulated training models. Many programs in clinical child psychology have attempted to provide their trainees with work in the various systems where children function, including families, hospitals, and schools. Similarly, a number of training programs in school psychology have trained their students in a variety of systems, such as families and health care settings (Power, Shapiro, & DuPaul, 2003). The result has been a merger of training techniques so that they may be applied across venues (e.g., schools, hospitals, families) in the hope that children and their families have better access to care.

Power, DuPaul, Shapiro, and Parrish (1995) suggested that changes in public policy, advances in pediatric and educational practice, and the developments in educational and clinical research underscored the need for professionals who already have training in school psychology to provide services to children with chronic conditions. In delineating this role as a "pediatric school psychologist," they argued that the role for such a psychologist would be to advocate for the educational and social needs of children with chronic conditions. This would include consulting with educational and pediatric professions on the efficacy and adverse effects of pharmacological interventions (particularly as they affect children in school), the support of ongoing collaboration between pediatric and educational providers (particularly for children with complex medical conditions), and the development of health promotion programs in schools. Recommendations are made for training programs in this area, with one such innovative program at the Children's Hospital of Philadelphia described by Power, Shapiro, and DuPaul (2003).

In addition to reforms in the training of applied psychologists and the shrinking job market in tertiary health care centers, a number of traditionally trained clinical and pediatric psychologists now find themselves employed in schools where they are needed to provide services for children with chronic conditions and special challenges. These are children who previously might have received their mental health care in tertiary health care settings. With the awareness of these many changes in the delivery of mental health care, this handbook is intended both for trainees and applied professional psychologists.

STRUCTURE OF THE HANDBOOK

The handbook is divided into eight sections that reflect the areas of pediatric psychology as it is practiced in school settings. These sections include: (1) basic background issues, (2) unique issues about disease prevention and health promotion, (3) diseases encountered in schools, (4) developmental disorders and conditions, (5) health issues related to development, (6) school interventions for pediatric psychological problems, (7) special topics related to pediatric psychology in schools, and (8) professional issues in pediatric psychology as it is practiced in schools.

Background

In chapter 2, Dennis Drotar, Tonya Palermo, and Christine Barry describe methods for consultation and collaboration with schools. They recommend the development of a scientific knowledge based on detailed evaluation of school-related collaborative programs. In chapter 3, Thomas J. Power and Jessica Blom-Hoffman underscore issues related to primary and secondary prevention and discuss school as a venue for the management and prevention of health problems. Their conclusions are similar to the ones outlined in this chapter. Specifically, they argue that reforms in health care and education, coupled with the developments in the fields of medicine, psychology, and education, point to the central role of schools in the management and prevention of health problems. Edward S. Shapiro and Patricia H. Manz provide information in chapter 4 to assist the practitioner in fostering valuable and effective collaborations with schools. These are considered ultimately to integrate family and health care systems in providing school-related services for children and adolescents with chronic conditions.

Prevention and Health Promotion

In keeping with the public health focus of the handbook, Michael C. Roberts, Keri J. Brown, Richard E. Boles, and Joanna O. Mashunkashey use chapter 5 to review the literature related to key concepts and the prevention of injuries, with attention to program efforts with day care centers and elementary schools. Schools, teachers, and classmates play integral roles in children's lives, and the authors conclude that much more can be done to use the skills of psychologists effectively in prevention of injuries in schools. In chapter 6, Bernard F. Fuemmeler reviews the promotion of health behavior, with special attention to programs that have been successfully conducted in schools. He concludes that advances in the promotion of health behaviors in schools will include the long-term efficacy of such programs, the understanding of variables that predict success of health promotion programs in schools, and ongoing programmatic research that focuses on the dissemination of successful health promotion programs.

In the spirit of a public health model, Bonnie K. Nastasi examines, in chapter 7, a system of comprehensive mental health care in schools that include screening, identification, referral, direct and indirect service delivery, staff development, program evaluation, and coordination with community agencies. Such a model is anticipated to prevent serious symptoms of psychiatric disturbances and make mental health services more accessible to children in need of services. Secondary prevention efforts also are a cornerstone of public health initiatives in this country and are areas in which both pediatric and school psychologists make a viable contribution. In chapter 8, Susan J. Simonian and Kenneth J. Tarnowski review a number of informant and self-report screening instruments designed to identify behavioral and health-related problems. In chapter 9, Kathleen L. Lemanek reviews literature on adherence and argues for a partnership between psychology and the medical community, one that includes the interdisciplinary efforts of professionals in applied psychology and education, with the goal of promoting adherence to school health services.

Diseases Encountered in Schools

For this portion of the handbook, specific disease entities were selected in which pediatric psychologists have made important contributions to research. We chose diseases that are prevalent and likely to be encountered in schools. For most diseases discussed, either the disease itself or the treatment applied for its management exerts some type of influence on cognition, learning, or emotional functioning that significantly affects classroom performance.

Asthma is increasing in prevalence among school-age children, and Robert D. Annett (chapter 10) reviews literature on the cognitive factors associated with asthma, the management of this chronic disease, and the influence of the various treatment approaches on cognition and learning. In chapter 11, Deborah Young-Hyman reviews literature on the influence of type I diabetes on cognitive functioning, the influence of age at disease onset, and how this impacts cognition and learning. In addition, how specific learning impairments affect disease management is likely to be of interest to psychologists who work in schools and medical settings. In chapter 12, Renee Smith, Staci Martin, and Pam Wolters review recent and innovative advances in the prognosis for children and adolescents with HIV/AIDS. Despite these advances, the influence of the disease on physical and social functioning is significant. The general conclusion of this group is that pediatric psychologists who work in schools are in a unique position to serve as liaisons with the health care team. This liaison position allows planning, monitoring, and coordinating the care of children with HIV infection. Issues relevant to schools and the course and management of this chronic illness that are discussed include frequent absences, disclosure, behavior management, facilitation of school reentry, and prevention of the disease through safe health practices.

In chapter 13, Jane Williams provides a critical review of literature on a topic that does not receive sufficient attention in pediatric psychology literature. Seizure disorders are a frequently occurring neurological condition in childhood, and the disease and its pharmacological management significantly affect learning. Williams concludes that the influences of seizure disorders on cognitive and behavioral outcomes include medication effects, ongoing seizures, and the stigma associated with the disease. In chapter 14, Melanie J. Bonner, Kristina K. Hardy, Elizabeth Ezell, and Russell Ware summarize a wealth of literature in the area of hematological disorders, specifically sickle cell disease and hemophilia. Their review suggests that a small, albeit significant, subgroup of children experience significant difficulties in cognitive and psychosocial domains. Especially important, they provide a review of literature delineating specific risk factors and screening tools that will assist in the identification of children and adolescents at risk.

Many childhood cancers were fatal before current medical advances, but now a significant number of children can expect to live beyond the disease. In chapter 15, F. Daniel Armstrong and Brandon G. Briery review literature on long-term survivors of childhood cancer. Generally, they conclude that the challenges previously faced only in hospitals must now be recognized in classrooms. Specifically, the long-term consequences of chemotherapy and radiation therapy on learning outcome are well documented, and the emerging literature is beginning to address appropriate management of these learning problems. Psychologists working in schools need to collaborate with physicians and other health care providers. This expanded treatment team can provide services for long-term survivors of cancer, and the collaboration represents the next step in the designation of cancer as a chronic illness instead of a fatal disease.

A prevalent but underresearched disease in pediatric psychology is heart disease. This disease frequently affects neurocognitive functioning and classroom learning. In chapter 16,

David Ray DeMaso concludes that children with heart problems may manifest a number of vulnerabilities in cognition and emotional and social functioning, all of which affect adjustment in school. Recommendations are provided for the management of school children with heart disease. In chapter 17, Lynn S. Walker and Stephen Johnson provide a review of literature related to recurrent abdominal pain (RAP). Conclusions from their review are that this category of symptoms is best conceptualized and managed within the context of a biopsychosocial framework. In other words, a number of factors interact to create and maintain illness. Their conclusions will assist psychologists who work in schools to identify psychosocial risk factors and to assist in the implementation of treatments that may aid in children's coping with the symptoms of RAP.

In chapter 18, Linda Ewing-Cobbs and Douglass R. Bloom explore issues related to the neuropsychological, psychiatric, and educational sequelae of traumatic brain injury. They conclude that the consequences of traumatic brain injury reflect a complex combination of the characteristics of the injury and the child's cognitive, psychiatric, and family status before the injury. Careful assessment of functions must always be the standard of care. Interventions that effectively enhance learning and cognition and school reentry for these children appear to be in their infancy and remain a fertile ground for sound empirical research. In chapter 19, Alexandra Quittner, Avani C. Modi, and Amy Loomis Roux summarize pathophysiology literature on cystic fibrosis and review research related to individual and familial adaptation to this disease. A discussion on the management of this chronic illness is provided, as is a list of frequently noted problems encountered by children and adolescents in schools. Attention is given to clinical interventions and resources for professionals working in these settings.

Developmental Disorders and Conditions

Because children with developmental disabilities frequently receive services from psychologists in schools, a section of the handbook is devoted to developmental disabilities and genetic disorders, with a chapter on abuse and neglect. In chapter 20, LeAdelle Phelps reviews information about the field of genetics and genetic disorders. All psychologists need to have some knowledge of these issues, given the explosion of information on genetic disorders and the genetic basis for many syndromes that affect children. A review of several diverse genetic disorders is provided in this chapter, all of which are associated with learning problems. Related to the field of behavioral genetics, Julie A. Kable and Claire D. Coles use chapter 21 to review literature on prenatal alcohol exposure and fetal alcohol syndrome. The deficits associated with this syndrome significantly affect children and adolescents in school because of general intellectual impairments and specific deficits in visual-spatial perception and integration, attention, motor functioning, and working memory. The authors conclude that these children continue to remain at risk for academic achievement problems due to dysfunctional living environments.

A developmental disorder prevalent in schoolchildren is attention deficit hyperactivity disorder (ADHD). Children with this disorder almost always encounter difficulties at school. Although there is no cure for this long-course disorder, fortunately there exist a number of empirically validated treatments that can be successfully applied at school. A useful compendium of behavioral techniques is offered by William E. Pelham and Daniel A. Waschbusch in chapter 22 for the management of children with ADHD as well as typically developing children. They review behavioral strategies that are particularly effective in the classroom. Johnathan M. Campbell, Sam B. Morgan, and Jennie W. Neighbors (chapter 23) provide a review of low-incidence developmental disabilities that may be encountered in school settings, including autism spectrum disorders and mental retardation. These are on the other end of the attention continuum and are less frequently encountered in traditional classroom settings. Although there also are no cures for these developmental disabilities, increased sophistication in their early identification have improved psychologists' ability to detect both cognitive and social delays early in childhood. Early detection allows for early intervention services that markedly enhance functional capacity during later childhood. As schools continue to provide most early intervention and follow-up services for these children, there is apt to be an increased demand for psychological services in the areas of diagnosis, intervention, and assessment.

Child maltreatment has a significant effect on children in the educational setting. In chapter 24, Rochelle F. Hanson, Daniel W. Smith, and Adrienne E. Fricker observe that schools are frequently responsible for protecting and ensuring the safety of children entrusted to their care. They note that abuse is often first disclosed or discovered at school, hence the critical role of the school in assuring children's safety. They also review the literature related to school-based prevention programs and conclude that although the data on their efficacy are mixed, valuable information and preventive strategies are nonetheless learned by some children. In chapter 25, Edward R. Christophersen and Patrick C. Friman review literature related to elimination disorders. They conclude that the medical expression of elimination disorders, coupled with the emphasis on biology, necessitates that school-based psychologists become knowledgeable about physiological functioning of elimination. With the expansion of surveillance of elimination disorders in schools, treatment programs also may assist children and their parents, who often suffer a history of failed attempts at managing elimination disorders at home.

Health Issues Related to Development

This section of the handbook is devoted to neonatology, prematurity, and health issues associated with adolescence. In chapter 26, Glen P. Aylward reviews the spectrum of sequelae found among children either born prematurely or determined to be at biological risk at the time of birth. Even though many of these children function fairly well, a greater percentage of them have specific deficits. As Aylward concludes, there is an interactive effect of biological risk and environment that influences outcome. For this reason, many of these children will continue to use psychological services that are provided by schools. On the other end of the pediatric developmental spectrum, Jan L. Wallander, Karen M. Eggert, and Katrina K. Gilbert provide a review of adolescent health issues in chapter 27. These include such diverse topics as injury and violence, depression and suicide, substance use, sexual activity, and chronic illness. Recommendations are made for comprehensive, developmentally based prevention efforts whereby the school promotes the development of a range of competencies. These skills, such as social-emotional competencies, promote prevention.

Interventions in Schools

Given the importance of empirically validated interventions in applied psychology, we believe it important to include a section specifically devoted to interventions. One intervention approach that has received significant empirical corroboration is the use of behavioral management, particularly in classrooms. In chapter 28, Thomas R. Kratochwill, Erin Cowell, Kelly Feeney, and Lisa Hagermoser underscore the importance of behavioral training for pediatric psychologists. Consistent with the conclusions of Pelham and Waschbush (chapter 22), they note that behavioral approaches are important in fostering the development of academic and interpersonal skills. Such approaches may be successfully used for children with specific chronic conditions as well as their normally developing peers. Despite their undisputed efficacy, certain barriers may exist that could impede the appropriate implementation of behavioral approaches at school. Barriers include a lack of information on the values of behavioral approaches, how they might apply in school, and specific ecological factors that may impede implementation of behavioral techniques.

The use of group intervention approaches has frequently been neglected in both the pediatric and school psychology literatures, although they hold promise as empirically validated interventions and more recent requirements of economically feasible treatments. In chapter 29, Karen Callan Stoiber and Gregory A. Waas review literature related to group interventions. Their findings generally suggest that the benefits of social skills group approaches are maximized for children when they reflect the general developmental and social needs of participants, when they are implemented in an environment that most closely resembles the setting in which they are applied, and when positive peer models are included as part of the intervention. As these authors suggest, group approaches are likely to reduce risk behaviors. This promotes a public health model of pediatric psychology in schools. Another frequently used and effective intervention for a variety of childhood chronic illnesses and psychiatric disorders is pharmacotherapy. No training in pediatric or school psychology is complete without training in the area of psychopharmacology because of the influence of many medications on children's learning and behavior (for review, see Brown & Sammons, 2002). In chapter 30, George J. DuPaul, Jennifer M. Coniglio, and Michelle R. Nebrig underscore the importance of understanding the influence of pharmacological approaches on children's classroom performance. A brief overview of research examining medication effects on cognitive, affective, behavioral, and academic functioning is provided. Also reviewed is methodology for assessing children's functioning while receiving medication. Again, this is an area that will require close collaboration with psychologists who work in schools and their health care counterparts who are employed in medical settings.

In the spirit of collaboration, coordination of services, and problem solving, Susan M. Sheridan and Richard J. Cowan, in chapter 31, provide a review of the consultation literature in schools. Goals of consultation include resolving current student difficulties and prevention of future difficulties. In addition to consulting in schools, it is necessary to consult with caregivers and families. Cindy Carlson, Thomas Kubiszyn, and Laura Guli in, chapter 32, report on the importance of family relationships in predicting healthy adaptation to systems stressors of having a chronically ill child in the family. The authors conceptualize family consultation as a multistage, multisystemic, collaborative, problem-solving process between the psychologist and the family, focused on specific developmental needs of the child and the family. Resources are described that can be useful in consulting with families of children with special needs. In chapter 33, Avi Madan-Swain, Ernest R. Katz, and Jason LaGory provide a review related to school and social reintegration following a serious illness or injury. The authors define school reentry as a dynamic ongoing process requiring sustained cooperation among the medical team, the family, and the school from the time of initial hospitalization to well after the child has returned to school. The authors develop a three-phase reentry process for children and adolescents who are diagnosed with a chronic illness.

Special Topics

In the section of the handbook devoted to special topics, Annette LaGreca, Karen J. Bearman, and Hannah Moore (chapter 34) review key developmental aspects of child and adolescent peer relationships and friendships, with special attention to youth with chronic conditions. A general consensus of this review is that most children and adolescents with chronic conditions have friendships and peer relationships that are comparable to their typically developing peers, although youth with visible conditions and physical challenges as well as those with cognitive impairments have particular difficulties in social contexts. Recommendations are made for future research that details the social challenges for children and adolescents in schools and offers guidance in the development of intervention programs that may be feasibly implemented in the classroom. Given the dramatic increases in living organ donation in recent years, James

R. Rodrigue, Regino Gonzalez, and Max Langham (chapter 35) review psychological issues associated with the transplant process. Recommendations are made for ongoing evaluation throughout the period that children and adolescents are listed for transplantation and in subsequent years. Recommendations are made for close collaboration with psychologists in schools to monitor academic progress and emotional and social functioning.

Professional Issues

The practice of pediatric psychology in schools is likely to give rise to specific professional, ethical, and legal concerns that are unique to the practice of this specialty in an educational setting. In anticipation of sufficient numbers of professional pediatric psychologists trained to provide psychological services in schools, Celia Lescano, Wendy Plante, and Anthony Spirito (chapter 36) work to apply the Society of Pediatric Psychology's recommendations (Spirito et al., 2003) to specialized services in schools. Given the comprehensiveness of the training guidelines, the authors caution that this training most likely will be obtained at the postdoctoral level either through formal training at this stage or by mentorship from colleagues in health sciences centers. In chapter 37, Deborah Anderson, Lloyd A. Taylor, and Alexandra Boeving deliver career and research opportunity information for pediatric psychologists who deliver pediatric psychological services in schools. Unique professional and ethical issues exist for pediatric and school psychologists. These will be encountered in medical and school settings, and include specialized issues related to confidentiality and consent and assent. Recognizing one's training as it may limit the scope of practice in these new areas will be critical.

In the last chapter, William A. Rae and Constance J. Fournier discuss ethical and legal issues for pediatric and school psychologists. They provide important recommendations for maintaining ethical and legal standards and stress the importance of practice limitations and exercising caution in practicing within competencies. They recommend evidence-based interventions as the standard of care in clinical activities at school and conclude that pediatric and school psychologists share more similarities than differences, which can only help achieve our common goal of serving the best interests of children.

IMPLICATIONS FOR PUBLIC POLICY

We anticipate that public policy will be influenced as more children with chronic conditions attend school and as more psychologists work with the children and their families. We recognize that public policy ultimately will be expressed through federal and state legislation that will dictate appropriate allocation of resources to the programs in which these children are involved, and frequently these resources will go to schools. As Thompson and Gustafson (1996) observed, public policy typically involves the interaction of a need being demonstrated and the subsequent promulgation of legislation to get the need fulfilled.

The number of children affected by specific chronic illnesses may be small, but the numbers are more compelling when all of the chronic illnesses in combination are considered. Advocacy efforts increase and improve simply because the greater numbers of children in need tend to attract greater attention of legislators and other policymakers. Clearly, as the chapters in the handbook show, many complex services are necessary for children with chronic conditions, including medical, educational, and psychological. This is exemplified in the diversity of chapters included here, ranging from consultation with schools and families to pharmacological interventions for children. As Perrin and Ireys (1984) suggested, the organization of services for children with chronic illnesses is both diverse and fragmented. Clearly, training efforts will need to continue that focus on teaching health care providers and other medical personnel about activities that occur in school settings. Similarly, educational personnel will need to be trained on the impact of chronic disease as it influences daily functioning, academic achievement, and successful socialization, including peer relationships.

Thompson and Gustafson (1996) concluded that a major source of stress related to caring for children with chronic illnesses is economic. Many public and private services exist on federal and state levels, but the financial burden of a chronic illness for families is significant. Costs include direct costs of medication care like prescription drugs and indirect costs like transportation to clinics and hospitals and time missed from work. We hope that the major policy implication of these diverse needs of children with chronic conditions results in universal health care coverage and that advocacy among professionals and parents will be strong and vigilant in the coming years.

The Family and Medical Leave Act legislated nearly one decade ago provides approximately three months of unpaid leave for various family circumstances, like the birth or adoption of a child and serious health conditions for the employee or family members, including a child. Such legislation is helpful, especially given the complex needs of children with chronic conditions. We hope that additional advocacy legislation increases so that the financial and emotional needs of families may be met.

Thompson and Gustafson (1996) noted there has been continued legislation and programmatic efforts for children with mental retardation and those with developmental disabilities over the past four decades. The effect of this legislation has been significant and has provided for a continuum of care for children and adolescents with developmental disabilities that includes training programs for a number of professional disciplines who care for these children. Over the years, the legislation has become more generic by assisting other individuals with varied diagnoses who nonetheless need similar services. In large part, these efforts have grown from advocacy efforts across the scientific, professional, and grassroots parent organizations. These have clearly advocated for children with special challenges; and, by means of a united front, they have been responsible for legislation that has enhanced quality of life for children and families. These organizations and parents can be proud of their efforts.

Other federal programs that have emerged from significant advocacy and policy efforts by a number of organizations are the series of federal laws related to the education of children with specific challenges. Included in this legislation are public laws for early education for young children with special needs and disabilities; assistance for children with specific challenges at the preschool, elementary, and secondary school levels (Hebbeler, Smith, & Black, 1991); and specific legislation against denial of services to any children qualifying for special services. Children with specific challenges would also qualify for related services, including other support services (e.g., psychological, occupational therapy, medical, transportation) necessary for them to benefit from special education services. The category of "other health impaired" has afforded the qualification of special education services for some children with chronic conditions, particularly those with cognitive impairments. However, not all children with chronic conditions require special education services; and, because related services are intended for those in need of special education services, children with chronic illnesses frequently are not eligible for these services. Although there has been significant advocacy by the American Academy of Pediatrics, APA, and parent organizations of specific chronic illness groups, many of the needs of children with chronic illnesses have gone unmet (Thompson & Gustafson, 1996). Clearly, policy and advocacy for children with chronic illness who do not qualify for special education or related services is an important agenda for the next decade.

The many chapters prepared for this handbook by outstanding leaders in our field clearly underscore the needs of these children and their families and show the training necessary for professionals and future generations of professionals who aspire to work with children with chronic conditions who are challenged by special needs in schools. We anticipate that this dissemination of knowledge and scholarship will represent a first step in the advocacy efforts for children and their families by demonstration of clear need. In subsequent attempts it will be our professional associations and parents who will make legislators aware of these needs so that legislation may be promulgated to enhance the quality of life for these children and their families.

REFERENCES

Adelman, H. S. (1996). Restructuring education support services and integrating community resources: Beyond the full service school model. *School Psychology Review, 25*, 431–445.

American Academy of Pediatrics. (2000). Insurance coverage of mental health and substance abuse services for children and adolescents: A consensus statement (RE0090). *Pediatrics, 106*, 860–862.

APA, (1995). A psychologists guide to participation in federal policy making. Washington D.C.: Author.

Armstrong, D., Glanville, T., Bailey, E. & O'Keefe, G. (1990). Doctor-initiated consultations: A study of communication between general practitioners and patients about the need for re-attendance. *British Journal of General practice, 40*, 241–242.

Beutler, L. E. (Ed.). (1992). Behavioral medicine: An update for the 1990s [Special issue]. *Journal of Consulting and Clinical Psychology, 60*(4).

Brannon, L., & Feist, J. (1997). *Health psychology* (3rd ed.). Pacific Grove, CA: Brooks Cole.

Brown, R. T., & DuPaul, G. (1999). Promoting school success in children with chronic medical conditions: Introduction to the mini-series. *School Psychology Review, 28*(2), 175–181.

Brown, R. T., Freeman, W. S., Brown, R. A., Belar, C., Hersch, L., Hornyak, L. M., Rickel, A., Rozensky, R., Sheridan, E., & Reed, G. (2002). The role of psychology in health care delivery. *Professional Psychology: Research and Practice, 33*, 536–545.

Brown, R. T., & Sammons, M. T. (2002). Pediatric psychopharmacology: A review of new developments and recent research. *Professional Psychology: Research and Practice, 33*, 133–147.

Burns, B. J., Costello, E. J., Angold, A., Tweed, D., & Stangl, D. (1995). Children's mental health service use across service sectors. *Health Affairs, 14*, 147–159.

Cadman, D., Boyle, M., Szatmari, P., & Offord, D. R. (1987). Chronic illness, disability, and mental and social well-being: Findings of the Ontario Child Health Study. *Pediatrics, 79*, 805–813.

Caplan, G. (1964). *The principles of preventative psychiatry*. New York: Basic Books.

Costello, E. J., Burns, B. J., Costello, A. J., Edelbrock, C., Dulcan, M., & Brent, D. (1988). Service utilization and psychiatric diagnosis in pediatric primary care: The role of the gatekeeper. *Pediatrics, 82*, 435–441.

Cowen, E. L., Hightower, A. D., Pedro-Carroll, J. L., Work, W. C., Wyman, P. A., & Haffey, W. G. (1996). *School-based prevention for children at risk: The primary mental health project.* Washington, DC: American Psychological Association.

Cunningham, C. E., Bremmer, R. B., & Boyle, M. (1995). Large group community-based parenting programs for preschoolers at risk for disruptive behavior disorders: Utilization, cost effectiveness, and outcome. *Journal of Child Psychology and Psychiatry and Allied Disciplines, 36*, 1141–1159.

Cunningham, C. E., Bremmer, R., & Secord-Gilbert, M. (1994). *The community parent education (COPE) program: A school-based family systems oriented course for parents of children with disruptive behavior disorders.* Unpublished manuscript, McMaster University, Hamilton, Ontario, Canada.

Cunningham, C. E., Cunningham, L. J., Martorelli, V., Tran, A., Young, J., & Zacharias, R. (1998). The effects of primary division, student-mediated conflict resolution programs on playground aggression. *Journal of Child Psychology and Psychiatry, 39*, 653–662.

Drotar, D. (1995). *Consulting with pediatricians: Psychological perspectives*. New York: Plenum Press.

Ferris, T. G., Saglam, D., Stafford, R. S., Causino, N., Starfield, B., Culpepper, L., & Blumenthal, D. (1998). Changes in the daily practice of primary care for children. *Archives of Pediatric and Adolescent Medicine, 152*, 222–225.

Gortmaker, S. L., Walker, D. K., Weitzman, M., & Sobol, A. M. (1990). Chronic conditions, socioeconomic risks, and behavioral problems in children and adolescents. *Pediatrics, 85*, 267–276.

Hebbeler, K. M., Smith, B. J., & Black, T. L. (1991). Federal early childhood special education policy: A model for the improvement of services for children with disabilities. *Exceptional Children, 58*, 104–112.

Hickson, G. B., Altemeir, W. A., & O'Conner, S. (1983). Concerns of mothers seeking care in private pediatric offices: Opportunities for expanding services. *Pediatrics, 66*, 619–624.

Kaplan, R. M. (2000). Two pathways to prevention. *American Psychologist, 55*, 382–396.

Kazak, A. E., Segal-Andrews, A. M., & Johnson, K. (1995). Pediatric psychology research and practice: A family systems approach. In M. C. Roberts (Ed.), *Handbook of pediatric psychology* (2nd ed., pp. 84–104). New York: Guilford.

Kazdin, A. E., Bass, D., Ayers, W. A., & Rodgers, A. (1990). Empirical and clinical focus of child and adolescent psychotherapy research. *Journal of Consulting and Clinical Psychology, 58*, 729–740.

Kolbe, L. J., Collins, J., & Cortese, P. (1997). Building the capacity of schools to improve the health of the nation: A call for assistance from psychologists. *American Psychologist, 52*, 256–265.

La Greca, A. M., & Hughes, J. N. (1999). United we stand, divided we fall: The education and training of clinical child psychologists. *Journal of Clinical Child Psychology, 28*, 435–447.

Lavigne, J. V., Gibbons, R. D., Arend, R., Rosenbaum, D., Binns, H., & Christoffel, K. K. (1999). Rational service planning in pediatric primary care: Continuity and change in psychopathology among children enrolled in pediatric practices. *Journal of Pediatric Psychology, 24*, 393–403.

Lorion, R. P., Myers, T. G., & Bartels, D. A. (1994). Preventative intervention research. *Pathways for extending knowledge of child/adolescent health and pathology.* In T. H. Ollendick & R. J. Prinz (Eds.), Advances in Clinical Child Psychology, (pp. 109–139). New York: Plenum.

Lynch, T. R., Wildman, B. G., & Smucker, W. D. (1997). Parental disclosure of child psychosocial concerns: Relationship to physician identification and management. *Journal of Family Practice, 44*, 273–280.

McLennan, J. D., Jansen-Williams, L., Comer, D. M., Gardner, W. P., & Kelleher, K. J. (1999). The Physician Belief Scale and psychosocial problems in children: A report from the Pediatric Research in Office Settings and the Ambulatory Sentinal Practice Network. *Journal of Developmental and Behavioral Pediatrics, 20*, 24–30.

Perrin, E. C. (1999). Ethical questions about screening. *Journal of Developmental and Behavioral Pediatrics, 19*, 350–352.

Perrin, J. M., & Ireys, H. T. (1984). The organization of service for chronically ill children and their families. *Pediatric Clinics of North America, 31*, 235–257.

Peterson, L., & Stern, B. L. (1997). Family processes and child risk for injury. *Behavior Research and Therapy, 35*, 179–190.

Phelps, R., Eisman, E. J., & Kohut, J. (1998). Psychological practice and managed care: Results of the CAPP practitioner survey. *Professional Psychology: Research and Practice, 29*, 31–36.

Power, T. J., DuPaul, G. J., Shapiro, E. S., & Parrish, J. M. (1995). Pediatric School Psychology: The emergence of a subspecialty. *School Psychology Review, 24*(2), 244–257.

Power, T. J., Shapiro, E. S., & DuPaul, G. J. (2003). Preparing psychologists to link systems of care in managing and preventing children's health problems. *Journal of Pediatric Psychology, 28*, 147–155.

Rabasca, L. (1999, April). Looking for opportunities? Network with physicians. *APA Monitor*, 26.

Rae-Grant, N. I. (1991). Primary prevention. In M. Lewis (Ed.), *Child and adolescent psychiatry: A comprehensive textbook* (pp. 915–929). Baltimore: Williams & Williams.

Richardson, L. A., Keller, A. M., Selby-Harrington, M. L., & Parrish, R. (1996). Identification and treatment of children's mental health problems by primary care providers: A critical review of research. *Archives of Psychiatric Nursing, 10*, 293–303.

Rickel, A. U., & Becker-Lausen, E. (1997). *Keeping children from harm's way: How national policy affects psychological development.* Washington, DC: American Psychological Association.

Roberts, M. C. (1986). *Pediatric psychology: Psychological interventions and strategies for pediatric problems.* New York: Pergamon Press.

Roberts, M., Carlson, C., Erickson, M., Friedman, R., La Greca, A., Lemanek, K. et al. (1998). A model for training psychologists to provide services for children and adolescents. *Professional Psychology: Research and Practice, 29*, 293–299.

Schultz, J. R., & Vaughn, L. M. (1999). Brief Report: Learning to parent: A survey of parents in an urban pediatric primary care clinic. *Journal of Pediatric Psychology, 24*, 441–445.

Sharpe, L., Pantell, R. H., Murphy, L. O., & Lewis, C. C. (1992). Psychosocial problems during child health supervision visits: Eliciting, then what? *Pediatrics, 89*, 619–623.

Short, R. J., & Talley, R. C. (1997). Rethinking psychology in the schools: Implications of recent national policy. *American Psychologist, 52*, 234–240.

Sobel, D. S. (1995). Rethinking medicine: Improving health outcomes with cost-effective psychosocial interventions. *Psychosomatic Medicine, 57*, 234–244.

Spirito, A., Brown, R. T., D'Angelo, E., Delamater, A., Rodrigue, J., & Siegel, L. (2003). Society of Pediatric Psychology Task Force Report: Recommendations for the training of pediatric psychologists. *Journal of Pediatric Psychology, 28*, 85–98.

Tarnowski, K. J., & Brown, R. T. (2000). Psychological aspects of pediatric disorders. In M. Hersen & R. T. Ammerman (Eds.). *Advanced abnormal child psychology.* Mahwah, NJ: Lawrence Erlbaum Associates.

Tarnowski, K. J., Kelly, P. A., & Mendlowitz, D. K. (1987). Acceptability of behavioral pediatric interventions. *Journal of Consulting and Clinical Psychology, 55*, 435–436.

Thompson, R. J., & Gustafson, K. E. (1996). *Adaptation to chronic childhood illness*. Washington, DC: American Psychological Association.

Tremblay, G. C., & Peterson, L. (1999). Prevention of children's behavioral and mental health problems: New horizons for psychology. *Clinical Psychology Review, 19*, 415–434.

VandenBos, G. R., DeLeon, P. H., & Belar, C. D. (1991). How many psychologists are needed? It's too early to know! *Professional Psychology: Research and Practice, 22*, 441–448.

Young, K. T., Davis, K., Schoen, C., & Parker, S. (1998). Listening to parents: A national survey of parents with young children. *Archieves of Pediatric and Adolescent Medicine, 152*, 255–262.

PART I: Background

2

Collaboration with Schools: Models and Methods in Pediatric Psychology and Pediatrics

Dennis Drotar
Tonya Palermo
Christine Barry
Rainbow Babies and Children's Hospital and Case Western Reserve University School of Medicine

One of the hallmarks of the field of pediatric psychology is the importance of collaboration with many different professionals in patient care and research (Drotar, 1995; Hamlett & Stabler, 1995; Stabler, 1988). Schools are one of the most important settings for such collaborative activities for several reasons. Schools have a significant impact on children's psychological development (Rutter, 1979); moreover, schools are also a critical context for identification of and intervention with psychological problems that are commonly encountered in pediatric populations. Pediatric populations, especially children with chronic illness, benefit from school-based intervention that coordinates the work of pediatric psychologists and health care providers with that of school-based professionals (Brown, 1999; Edwards & Davis, 1997). Examples of such collaborative interventions include the following: developing plans to manage a child's medical treatment in school; helping to design individualized educational programs that are appropriate to specific patterns of cognitive abilities and specialized strengths and limitations; implementing interventions to limit the impact of chronic illness on a child's school attendance; managing medication of attentional problems that disrupt learning; and designing behavioral management plans for children with chronic behavioral disorders that reflect the influence of biological conditions such as autism.

The importance of pediatric psychologists' and health care providers' work with school personnel transcends clinical care. There are important areas of research in pediatric psychology and behavioral pediatrics in which collection of data from teachers and/or peers in the school setting is critical (Brown, 1999). In order to conduct research in schools in an effective manner, pediatric psychologists and pediatricians need to understand the special practical and ethical challenges involved in such research and develop strategies to manage them (Drotar et al.,

2000). As is true for clinical care, a high level of interdisciplinary collaboration is necessary to develop research with pediatric populations in school settings.

A final area of collaboration between pediatric psychologists, health care providers, and schools concerns teaching and training. Pediatric psychologists and health care providers, such as pediatricians and nurses, can make important contributions by providing training for teachers and other school staff concerning a wide range of topics including managing physical needs of children with chronic health conditions in the school setting, identifying emotional problems, or informing teachers concerning the emotional response of children with chronic health conditions to the reactions of peers. The need for such collaboration in training is by no means one-sided. Pediatric psychologists and health care providers have a great deal to learn from teachers and educators about the nature of educational programs for pediatric populations and about tailoring recommended clinical interventions to maximize children's educational opportunities in school settings. Consequently, there is considerable need to develop a shared professional agenda to guide collaborative activities among pediatric psychologists, health care providers, teachers, and other school staff.

Nevertheless, despite the potential importance of such interdisciplinary collaboration, school-based consultation and collaboration has not been a central mission of pediatric psychologists' or pediatric health care providers' professional activities. The work of many pediatric psychologists and pediatric health care providers is focused on collaborations with hospital-based staff with whom they work on a day-to-day basis. Moreover, consultation with teachers and school staff has not generally been an integral part of the professional culture of pediatric psychology training and practice, nor is it emphasized in pediatric training. The professional writings of pediatric psychologists concerning consultation and collaboration (Drotar, 1995) have focused almost exclusively on interactions and relationships with colleagues in medical settings. Moreover, with certain exceptions (Wright & Nader, 1983), schools have not been emphasized in pediatric interventions.

The purpose of this chapter is to help facilitate such work by describing relevant issues, barriers, and possibilities concerning collaboration among pediatric psychologists, pediatric health care providers, and professionals in school settings. This chapter begins with a description of a framework for consultation and collaboration and applications to the school, including influences on and models of collaboration. Second, specific examples of collaborative activities and programs that focus on two specific pediatric populations, children with sickle cell disease and children with autism, are described. Finally, the implications for future clinical practice, training, and research are discussed.

INFLUENCES ON INTERDISCIPLINARY COLLABORATIVE ACTIVITIES: APPLICATION TO SCHOOL SETTINGS

In order to understand the challenges and potential of collaboration between pediatric psychologists, health care providers, teachers, and other school personnel, it is useful to consider factors that may influence this process. Relevant factors that can affect collaboration include the goal or content of collaboration, characteristics of collaborators, outcomes of collaboration, relationship characteristics, and the stages of collaborative relationships. (See Drotar, 1993, 1995 for a more comprehensive description.)

Goals or Content of Collaboration

The nature of collaborative activities generally depends on the specific goal of the work. Most often, pediatric psychologists and at times pediatric health care providers will work with school staff and parents concerning planning for the educational and classroom support needs of an individual child. The purpose of the collaboration involves information exchange, especially advice concerning modifications in the classroom program that are necessary. Pediatric psychologists and health care providers may have information concerning the needs of children with various health conditions, medication management, and/or neuropsychological status of individual children who have been seen for medical and/or psychological evaluation and/or treatment, all of which may be very useful to teachers. On the other hand, teachers also have valuable information about how the child is responding to the social and educational demands of the school setting that can help to inform the psychologist's or pediatrician's recommendations and to develop an effective educational and psychological management plan for the child.

Characteristics of Collaborators

The nature of prior clinical experience, especially in interprofessional collaboration, will often shape the goals and expectations of potential collaborators. In addition, the kind of interprofessional collaboration that occurs among pediatric psychologists, pediatric health care providers, and teachers requires considerable skills and knowledge, many of which are not explicitly taught in training programs. For example, pediatric psychologists and pediatricians who have not had much experience working with teachers may underestimate the demands of teaching and not consider the practical relevance of their assessments or interventions to the school setting. On the other hand, teachers may not understand the potential contribution of pediatric psychologists' professional expertise in working with children with special health care needs. Moreover, teachers may not necessarily appreciate pediatricians' multifaceted roles in children's health care but may focus narrowly on their potential role in medication management.

Collaborators' current work expectations and demands also exert a powerful influence on their collaborative expectations (Drotar, 1995), and collaboration with schools is no exception. Teachers often face extraordinary work-related demands that shape their expectations of consultation and collaboration with pediatric psychologists (Sarason, 1972). For this reason, similar to pediatricians, teachers are most interested in specific suggestions that will help them in their day-to-day management of children in their classroom. They are less interested in a global assessment of a child and specific data from psychological tests or medical diagnosis unless they have very specific implications for day-to-day classroom management. Constraints on teachers and teachers' expectations raise considerable challenges for pediatric psychologists and pediatricians who work with teachers. For example, it may not be possible for the pediatric psychologist or the pediatrician to supply the kind of practical suggestions that are most useful to teachers, especially if they have not observed the child in the classroom setting and are not familiar with the specific demands of the setting (Mullins, Gillman, & Harbeck, 1992).

Situational Incentives for and Constraints on Collaboration

Situational incentives and constraints may also have powerful effects on the quality of collaboration among schools, pediatricians, and pediatric psychologists (Drotar, 1995). Many teachers operate under a highly compressed schedule in which time is a precious commodity. Psychologists and pediatric health care providers also have many competing claims on their time that limit accessibility to their teacher colleagues. Moreover, much of the important and clinically relevant collaborative work that takes place among pediatric psychologists, pediatricians, and teachers is not reimbursable by insurance. For this reason, in many settings, the nature of administrative support for pediatric psychologists' and/or pediatricians' collaboration with schools may be a key determinant of the quality of interprofessional collaboration. These constraints may lead one to ask: Is there sufficient time for collaboration? What funding can be developed to support pediatric psychologists' or pediatricians' collaboration with schools?

Importance of Professional Socialization Experience

Pediatric psychologists, pediatricians, and school staff have each been highly socialized into their respective professional roles and models of problems and use very different languages in teaching, practice, and research (Sarason, 1972). Successful collaborators are able to bridge the many gaps in language, communication, and differing models that are heavily overlearned in the course of professional training. For example, pediatric psychologists who work most effectively with teachers can translate technical expertise into recommendations that can be used by teachers in their day-to-day work with children. Pediatricians, including behavioral pediatricians, who work effectively with teachers have taken the time to learn and have had specialized training concerning the educational systems and school resources in their communities (Nader, Ray, & Gilman, 1981).

Relationship Characteristics of Collaborations

The quality of the relationships that develop among pediatric psychologists, pediatricians, and teachers is also a central characteristic of collaboration. Salient characteristics include the history and duration of this relationship. The extensiveness of one's collaborative network is another potential influence. Pediatric psychologists or health care providers who focus their work on several schools would be expected to influence their colleagues more than their counterparts who interact with a very large number of schools. Consequently, there may be some benefit for pediatric psychologists and, where possible, pediatricians to develop relationships with specific schools and teachers over the course of time. The collaborative work with teachers concerning children with autism described in this chapter illustrates the advantages of such focus.

MODELS OF COLLABORATION/CONSULTATION

Pediatric psychologists have described a range of collaborative models that have focused on clinical consultation in patient care or teaching and that are applicable to school settings. Similarly, pediatricians have also described such models (Nader et al., 1981; Wright & Nader, 1983).

Roberts (1986) described three basic models of psychological consultation in pediatric settings: (1) independent functions; (2) indirect consultation; and (3) collaborative team models. A fourth model, the systems-based approach (Mullins, Gillman, Harbeck, 1992), also merits consideration. The advantages and disadvantages of each of these models for collaboration and consultation with school staff is considered in the following sections.

Independent Functions Model

In this model, the psychologist or behavioral pediatrician functions as a specialist who provides diagnostic information and, in some instances, recommendations for management in the classroom setting of a patient referred by a teacher or pediatrician. In this model, collaboration primarily takes the form of information exchange prior to and after the referral. For example, such information can include recommendations for individual programming based on neuropsychological testing for a child who experiences cognitive and behavioral limitations following traumatic brain injury (Blosser & DePompei, 1994). As another example, a pediatric consultant may recommend individualized classroom planning to accommodate for symptoms of fatigue in a child with a chronic illness.

The primary advantage of this model is its familiarity to teachers, pediatricians, and pediatric psychologists. Moreover, this model can provide very useful information to teachers about individual children. The main disadvantages of this model of consultation involve the limited communication and relationships among professions. Moreover, the lack of opportunity for extensive dialogue between the pediatrician, psychologist, and teacher limits teaching opportunities and discussion of management alternatives.

Indirect Consultation Model

An alternative approach is the indirect psychological consultation or process-educative model. The hallmark of this model is that the psychologist or pediatrician assumes the role of informed colleague who provides advice, teaching, or protocols for ongoing management. An example of this type of collaboration would be ongoing consultation from a pediatric psychologist to a teacher concerning the classroom behavioral management of a child with pervasive developmental disorder. In this example, consultation would involve consideration of alternative strategies of behavioral management based on ongoing communication with the teacher concerning the child's progress. A pediatrician's consultation may involve advocacy with school staff to help them understand the child's medical needs (e.g., need for medication for a chronic condition such as asthma). This model has advantages over the independent functions model because it involves ongoing collaboration between an individual teacher, pediatrician, and/or pediatric psychologist. However, this model may be very difficult to implement in practice because it requires an ongoing commitment of time and energy between potential collaborators.

Collaborative Team Model

A third general model of consultation, the collaborative team model, is characterized by shared responsibility and joint decision making among the pediatric psychologist and teacher concerning the child's management (Roberts, 1986). An example of this type of collaboration would be the psychologist's regular participation in reviews of the educational and behavioral progress of children with special health care needs (physical handicaps) with a primary focus on how the program is meeting the child's needs for education and social participation. To maximize the benefits of this type of collaboration, the pediatric psychologist or pediatrician would need to spend time at regular intervals in the school and in meetings observing the children. The obvious advantage of this model is the high level of communication and mutual dialogue among potential collaborators. The major disadvantage is the level of resources required. Collaborative team models are rarely an integral part of school settings because they require special resources.

Comprehensive Program or Systems-Based Approaches

The models of consultation described thus far emphasize interactions and relationships among the individual pediatric psychologist, pediatrician, teacher, and/or educator. However, a final model, the comprehensive program or systems-based approach, is characterized by a proactive approach that may also develop a novel service designed to address the ongoing problem in systems of care (Mullins et al., 1992). Examples of this comprehensive program have been designed to address the needs of children with illnesses, such as cancer, whose treatments require children to be hospitalized and away from the school environment for long periods and in which the illness and/or treatments affect children's cognitive development and learning in important ways. One example of such a proactive approach is a program created by Katz, Rubinstein, Hubert, and Blew (1988) to ease the transition of children with cancer back into the school environment through a structured plan in which teachers and classmates are carefully apprised of the child's condition and special needs. This approach, which features the active participation of the child with cancer, has been shown to have a positive impact on the child's psychological adjustment.

Another example is Kazak and Beele's (1993) comprehensive program, described in Drotar (1995), that was designed to meet the educational needs of children with cancer at the Children's Hospital of Philadelphia (CHOP). This includes education and school consultation for teachers that is conducted by psychologists and health care providers as well as psychological assessment for selected children. The educational program includes an annual day-long program for patients, teachers, other school personnel, and patients' siblings that has been held at CHOP. This program typically consists of two panel discussions (patients, parents, and educators), a keynote address, and about 10 workshops addressing specific issues (e.g., learning problems, cancer in children at different developmental stages). A series of smaller educational programs (e.g., on parent advocacy) have also been provided.

The service programs include consultation in connection with a school reintegration program in which nurses and psychosocial staff are available to visit schools, talk with school personnel, and provide age-appropriate presentations for patients' classmates. In addition, psychological evaluations and school consultations have been provided for patients experiencing learning difficulties or concerns regarding appropriate educational placement. Finally, neuropsychological testing has also been provided regularly to several distinct groups of patients who have been targeted for evaluations, including those with relapsed leukemia who will receive cranial irradiation, children referred to bone marrow transplant (with and without total-body irradiation), and newly diagnosed patients who will receive cranial irradiation.

CLINICAL EXAMPLES OF COLLABORATION WITH TEACHERS CONCERNING PEDIATRIC POPULATIONS

In order to give readers an appreciation for what is involved in developing and sustaining collaborative work with teachers concerning specific pediatric populations, this next section describes two examples from the work of interdisciplinary teams in our setting, each of which has been designed to address the needs of pediatric populations: (1) children with sickle cell disease and (2) children with autistic spectrum disorders.

Models and Methods for Collaboration with Schools About Sickle Cell Disease

Children with sickle cell disease (SCD) are at risk for having unmet educational needs as a result of their disease complications. Moreover, because school personnel and parents may not be aware of the possible impact of SCD on learning (Bonner, Gustafson, Schumacher, & Thompson, 1999), identification and treatment of learning and school-related difficulties in children with SCD poses a significant challenge. This challenge is heightened by the routine lack of communication between the health care team members who are managing the child's disease with school staff who spend the majority of days with the child.

In order to understand the relevance of psychoeducational planning and school consultation for children with SCD, it is necessary to appreciate the impact of complications secondary to SCD on children's school performance and learning. The primary complication of SCD is vaso-occlusion. Although vaso-occlusive disease can occur in any organ, the most detrimental sequelae result from occlusion of cerebral vessels and infarction of the brain. Approximately

10% of children with SCD will experience clinical strokes, usually in early to mid-childhood (Ohene-Frempong et al., 1998). Strokes can result in motor impairment and neuropsychological deficits similar to children with other types of traumatic brain injury such as serious deficits in overall cognitive ability, memory, attention, and language functions (e.g., Wood, 1978). An even larger number of patients (25%) will experience silent cerebral infarcts, defined as an abnormal MRI without history of clinical stroke (Miller et al., 2000). Most of these children will demonstrate attention and/or executive function deficits (DeBaun, Schatz, & Siegel, 1998) and will be at risk for further neurologic progression (e.g., overt stroke) as well as for lower intelligence quotients and poor academic attainment (Armstrong et al., 1996; Craft, Schatz, Glauser, & Lee, 1993).

The indirect effects of living with SCD may also affect children's school functioning. Children with SCD may experience physical effects such as pain and fatigue, treatment-related side effects, and frequent absenteeism that impact their ability to perform optimally at school. Parents may be reluctant to send their children with SCD to school in cold weather due to transportation concerns and fears of disease exacerbations from cold weather exposure. Moreover, psychological factors such as distress and low self-esteem may impact the child's social and academic functioning at school.

Need for Psychoeducational Planning and School Consultation for Children With SCD. Although many children with SCD experience significant problems in learning and school performance, in our experience these problems often go unrecognized by parents, medical providers, and school staff. Children with SCD do not always have visible deficits. Moreover, when children with SCD fall behind in school, their problems may be attributed to their missing school rather than to cognitive deficits or other illness-related symptoms (e.g., pain and fatigue) that would be expected to interfere with their school performance and ultimately affect their academic achievement. In many instances, school problems experienced by children with SCD were not recognized by teachers, parents, or health care providers and not referred for psychological evaluation until after the child had experienced school failure or was in danger of doing so. Consequently, there was a need to develop a program that would modify the typical patterns of consultation and referral for children with SCD by an interdisciplinary team by implementing the following strategies: (1) earlier referral of larger numbers of children with SCD for psychoeducational assessment; (2) proactive academic planning; and ideally (3) prevention or amelioration of academic problems.

Purpose of the HOPE Pilot Program. Pediatric staff's concerns that school and educational issues have been an area of significant need for children with SCD coupled with their frustration by the limited follow-through of the schools to conduct psychological testing and accommodate for student's individual learning needs led to the development of this program. With funding from the hospital board of trustees, one of us (T. P.) developed a pilot program (Hematology Oncology Psycho-Educational Program or HOPE) to provide comprehensive services to our population of children with sickle cell disease at a large tertiary care medical center in the Midwest. This education, research, and service program was designed to provide children with individualized assessment and management of their educational and school-related needs and to provide education, training, and support to school personnel to advocate for these children's educational needs. The crux of the program involves applying broad screening methods to identify those children with (or at risk for) learning problems through conducting a needs-assessment interview and specialized assessment of children's cognitive and academic functioning using neuropsychological testing.

The HOPE program was designed to bridge the gap between health care and education through comprehensive psychoeducational planning and advocacy. The expected long-term benefits of the program are to provide advocacy for children with SCD over their academic careers, to promote greater awareness of these children's unique educational needs, and to provide community- and school-based education concerning methods of working with children with SCD to maximize their educational potential.

Description of Services Provided by the HOPE Program. Families are invited to participate in the program at their routine appointments in the sickle cell anemia clinic at Rainbow Babies and Children's Hospital. The sickle cell anemia clinic provides services to over 300 children with SCD in our region in a half day per week outpatient clinic. Children between the ages of 4 and 16 years are targeted for the program along with any children who have been identified by the sickle cell anemia team as having current school-related problems. Service providers include a psychologist, psychology trainee, psychometrist, and neuropsychologist who work closely with an interdisciplinary team including physicians and nurses. The HOPE program psychology trainee and psychometrist attend each clinic to conduct needs-assessment screening interviews with parents regarding their children's school-related functioning. A psychologist and neuropsychologist guide the intervention plans that are then developed. Based on the screening interview, interventions such as neuropsychological testing, review of prior school testing, school in-service about sickle cell disease, or referral for outpatient mental health services are recommended to families.

Role of Neuropsychological Testing. Children who are identified as having possible learning-related problems are targeted for neuropsychological testing. This service is offered to families at the time of the screening. The psychometrist or psychology trainee conducts the testing. The neuropsychological assessment battery includes tests of cognitive ability, verbal memory, motor skills, visual-spatial skills, academic achievement, language, adaptive behavior, and attention. Feedback regarding the test results and neuropsychological test reports are provided to the family as well as to the school and medical staff. Continuing intervention plans are discussed with the family such as planning for IEP meetings, school in-services, or other referrals.

Preliminary School Screening Results. A summary of the school screening interviews for the first 52 children entered into the HOPE program is described below (Burgess, Palermo, & Beebe, 2001). The mothers of 52 school-age children (56% male; mean age = 10.3, SD = 4.0) were interviewed regarding their child's academic, behavioral, and social functioning. Maternal reports revealed that 33% of children had been held back at least one grade, 27% were reported to be experiencing academic and behavioral difficulties, and 33% were reported to have attention problems. Only 14% of children were known to have passed their school proficiency tests. School absences (>2 wks/yr) were frequent in half of the sample, and 37% of children were reported to have difficulty participating in school activities such as gym and recess due to health.

Some children were already receiving special services at school (25% of the sample), although many parents were unsure of the type and nature of services that their children were receiving. Apart from their concerns about their children's learning, parents expressed concern about the school-related impact of the physical complications of sickle cell disease such as managing pain medication administration at school, negotiating transportation for long walks and/or exposure to cold, and dealing with frequently missed school.

Case Example. Erin is a 13-year-old female with homozygous sickle cell disease (hemoglobin SS). She was referred to the HOPE program following an inpatient hospital admission for pain during which the family informed the sickle cell team that Erin had not been in school during the current academic year. At Erin's next sickle cell clinic visit, the mother was approached for participation in the HOPE program. Concerns raised in the school screening interview included history of school failure (Erin was a sixth grader who had been held back two times), significant problems in all major academic subjects, and safety concerns including transportation problems and peer violence. Erin had not been in school for the first 3 1/2 months of the current academic year.

Erin was recommended for a neuropsychological evaluation, which began the day of the screening interview. Testing showed that Erin had deficient overall cognitive ability (Full Scale IQ = 55) and limited verbal reasoning, memory, and academic skills. Adaptive behavior was significantly delayed and attentional problems were within the clinical range. She met a diagnosis of mental retardation, severity unspecified.

Medical staff was immediately informed of the test findings due to the question of progressive deterioration or slowed rate of learning. The hematologist caring for Erin ordered a Magnetic Resonance Imaging (MRI) study, which indicated small vessel infarcts (confirming a silent cerebral infarct). Further intervention by the HOPE program included county referral for truancy and work with the family to enter Erin into a new school environment. HOPE staff conducted a school visit to discuss test findings with teachers and special education specialists (a Developmental Handicap classroom placement was recommended). Teachers were entirely unaware of Erin's deficits and were surprised to learn about the impact of SCD on her learning, having attributed her school performance to poor attitude and motivation.

Consultation and Education of School-Based Providers. Consultation and educational in-service programs for school providers are offered through the HOPE program. These programs include: (1) general education about SCD and the impact on children's learning and (2) educational programming for a specific child. General education about SCD has been offered to the public school district in collaboration with school psychologists and school nurses who serve many of the schools that our patients attend. We have worked with the local Sickle Cell Disease Association to coordinate our efforts in educating the community about SCD. Together with association staff, we have presented a general educational program that includes informational handouts for teachers and school staff about sickle cell disease. Psychologist service providers have presented specific information about neuropsychological effects.

Collaborative Issues and Challenges. The HOPE program has been successful in providing psychoeducational assessment and management services for children with SCD, many of whom have limited insurance coverage for these services. Pediatric staff have been extremely supportive of the HOPE program and have worked to integrate HOPE staff into the sickle cell clinic appointment process by allowing time at the end of the visit for the needs assessment interviews. Moreover, pediatric staff have provided valuable input concerning aspects of the child's medical condition and treatment that would be expected to affect their behavior and response to educational programs.

On the other hand, program implementation has been challenging. For example, whereas families have uniformly communicated interest in the HOPE program and have voiced concerns about their children's educational needs, many referred families have not shown up for neuropsychological testing appointments. This is a continuing challenge. We are working to try to reduce this barrier by coordinating the testing appointment with other appointments at the hospital, by exploring transportation options for families to attend appointments, and by providing more education to parents about the risk of learning problems in sickle cell disease and the importance of advocating for children's educational needs at an early age.

Our group has developed collaborations with school staff in individual cases referred to the HOPE program. We have encountered several very interested and motivated school psychologists and school nurses who have advocated for the HOPE program to conduct inservices at their schools. Based on these discussions, relevant contact people have been identified within the school districts so that education can be targeted at a broader audience. These contacts are particularly important because many of our patients attend inner-city school districts with limited resources for special education or for ongoing communication between teachers and individuals involved in special education procedures.

MODELS AND METHODS FOR CHILDREN WITH AUTISTIC SPECTRUM DISORDERS

Children with autistic spectrum disorders (ASD) are seen increasingly in pediatric practice and by pediatric psychologists, including pediatric neuropsychologists. The deficits in cognitive and social skills experienced by these children require highly specialized educational programming that addresses their specific cognitive and social deficits. However, many teachers are not aware of the nature of the psychological characteristics and deficits experienced by children with ASD and the relevant implications for educational programming.

Psychological Characteristics of ASD

Autism is a neurobiological disorder characterized by delays in social skills and communication and unusual behavioral responses (American Psychiatric Association, 1995). No matter where a child's symptoms fall on the autistic spectrum, the impact of the disorder affects the child's ability to function in the home, school, and community settings. Problematic behaviors associated with autism are often the result of the child's misperception of the environment, confusion of verbal information, and/or anxiety. Deficits in children's social understanding underlie the difficulties in communication and often lead to behavior problems (Cumine, Leach, & Stevenson, 1998). Because of their social skills deficits, children with ASD must be specifically taught social understanding.

Psychoeducational Planning and School Consultation for Children With ASD

Inferring what others mean by their communications to them is extremely problematic for children with autism. For this reason, teachers need to explicitly and concretely teach how the academic information that they are presenting in class is meaningful to the child with autism. To address this need for educational planning, one of us (C. B.) meets with a team that consists of school psychologists and teachers, parents, children with autism, occupational therapists, and speech/language pathologists to develop programs to best address the individual needs of children with autism. The team reviews difficulties in teaching social and emotional awareness to these children. For example, when most children are growing up, they do not have to be told to smile when someone praises them or to look at someone when their name is called; they perform those activities instinctively. On the other hand, children with autism need to be explicitly taught appropriate ways to request help at school, not interrupt others, listen and respond in conversation, and make appropriate facial expressions (Cumine et al., 1998).

Goals of Consultation With Teachers

One primary goal of consultation for children with ASD is to provide information to teachers on how to prevent or limit untoward reactions by the child. This is accomplished by discussing the child's specific sensory vulnerabilities and how to best organize the classroom to minimize visual and auditory distractions. Such education and information is provided to parents and staff by seminars and team meetings. In addition, the psychologist meets monthly with parents and staff to provide strategies for improving children's social and behavioral functioning, to monitor the success of these strategies, and to revise methods over time for greater effectiveness. Teachers and parents are taught how to utilize specific intervention strategies (i.e., social stories, reward charts, written social scripts) based on research findings that teachers who are directly taught intervention techniques are more satisfied and experience more success in altering children's behavior (Schroeder & Mann, 1991).

Case Study Illustrating Method of Consultation

The following case study illustrates this approach to school consultation. Hannah is an 11-year-old child who has a history of delays in social skills, pragmatic language, and gross motor coordination. In the past, Hannah had been diagnosed with attention deficit hyperactivity disorder (ADHD), inattentive type, and a learning disability in written expression. As part of the present consultation, a thorough neuropsychological assessment was conducted, including medical and developmental history, educational information, review of prior testing, grade cards, standardized test findings, and an interview regarding Hannah's functioning level in all settings, daily living skills, and past therapeutic interventions. Assessment also consisted of behavioral rating scales completed by parents and teachers, intelligence and achievement testing, and measures of memory, sensory-motor skills, perceptual ability, language, executive functions, and emotional functioning. Moreover, Hannah was observed in the school setting and several home videotapes of Hannah growing up were reviewed.

School observations revealed that Hannah was rigid, highly anxious in new settings, and insisted on following routines and rules. Although she had an excellent vocabulary with words perfectly articulated, she spoke in a formal, pedantic tone with stilted affective expression. Hannah talked obsessively about classical music and would recite factual information about all of the classical composers regardless of the listener's level of interest. Her peers thought she was odd as she talked in a robotic tone and invaded others' personal space.

Hannah had also begun to verbalize negative self-statements and somatic complaints to avoid going to school and blurted out comments in the cafeteria so that all could hear them. The school staff reprimanded Hannah for these behaviors but did not determine the factors that were responsible for her distress. After observing Hannah at lunch, it was obvious that she could not tolerate the smells and the noises in the cafeteria. Similar to many children with autism, Hannah was a picky eater with a limited repertoire of preferred foods. Moreover, she was overwhelmed by the smells, noises, and confusion at lunch.

In the classroom, Hannah was unable to take another person's perspective or understand the unwritten rules of etiquette. It was not uncommon for her to speak out loud if the teacher made a mistake (e.g., "Mrs. Smith, I am afraid that you did not do that math problem right again!"). If another student broke a rule, she would make statements such as, "Sarah is looking at Dan's paper for the answer." Hannah even attempted to set up weekly meetings with the principal to go over the list she had compiled of students whom had recently broken a school rule. Not surprisingly, these behaviors inevitably provoked angry reactions from her peers.

Previous intelligence testing indicated that Hannah's intellectual ability was in the high average range. Academically, Hannah was functioning above grade level, yet was unable to keep up with the written demands in the classroom. Moreover, she could not read her own writing or take notes, and she was poorly organized and misplaced assignments.

Hannah was diagnosed with Asperger's syndrome, which is characterized by impairments in social communication, social interaction, and social imagination (Wing, 1981). A team meeting was held with Hannah's parents, teachers, therapists, and one author (C. B.), and monthly consultation sessions were scheduled. During these consultation sessions, Hannah was observed in different school situations, interventions were implemented and modified, and C. B. met with a team of teachers to discuss progress and concerns. A series of inservices was conducted with the staff with an emphasis on how to modify the curriculum, write social stories and social scripts, and institute basic relaxation techniques with Hannah when she was stressed.

Specific goals were added to Hannah's Individual Education Plan to address deficits identified from the neuropsychological evaluation in her written expression, motor planning, social skills, and receptive language. The detailed plan included the following recommendations: (1) tutorial support in writing and in study/organizational skills; (2) teaching of keyboarding skills, which she was encouraged to use for all writing tasks by the occupational therapists; (3) provision of rest times where she could engage in calming activities to decrease her anxiety and tendency to become over stimulated by loud noises (more specifically, Hannah was permitted to enter school before the other students arrived, allowed to leave class 5 minutes before the other children, and immediately after she ate lunch she was given the opportunity to go to the library to listen to classical music as opposed to staying in the noisy cafeteria); (4) individual therapy with one of us (C. B.) to work on improving her social skills using drawings and pictorial cues to assist her through problematic social situations; (5) discussions with the guidance counselor when she felt overwhelmed; (6) social skills training by pairing her with a few empathic peer role models and a lunch group set-up on a weekly basis where she ate with the counselor and a few peers to practice social skills; (7) speech/language therapy several times per week to practice reading facial cues, carrying on conversations, and giving and receiving compliments from others; (8) behavioral modification to decrease her yelling out in the classroom (she was given a cue card that stated "raise hand before you talk" illustrated with pictures). She was also given several break times during the day to go to a quieter classroom (learning resource room) to complete her work. These interventions have enhanced the frequency of Hannah's appropriate behavior and have lessened her anxiety.

COLLABORATIVE CHALLENGES

Although many benefits are seen when neuropsychologists work as consultants in collaboration with school personnel concerning children with ASD, potential challenges to this relationship do exist. Specifically, teachers spend a considerable amount of time with children and are often skeptical about taking suggestions from a consultant. Moreover, teachers may believe that the test data the neuropsychological consultant provides will not result in meaningful, concrete intervention techniques that can be employed in the classroom. In fact, these are difficult to accomplish, and they require a high level of expertise and the time to develop and implement specific recommendations based on classroom observation on the part of the psychologist consultant. To accomplish such interventions, input from the classroom teacher and the opportunity to observe the child in the educational setting are needed to assess the functional impact of the child's problem. Thus, a crucial part of any evaluation is to obtain information from teachers and parents, as well as grade cards and actual work samples.

Another challenge faced is that the effective consultation and collaboration with school staff concerning the complex, highly individual needs of children with ASD is inevitably time consuming as it requires observation of the child in a classroom context, phone and face-to-face contact with teachers, and ongoing reviews of the child's progress. Unfortunately, almost all of these important elements of consultation and collaboration are not reimbursable by insurance. Only a few parents are willing or able to afford the costs of such consultation. Consequently, the psychologist consultant who provides such services faces a considerable dilemma: how to provide such important consultation while at the same time meeting the need to develop clinical income to cover the cost of salary.

One solution to this very difficult dilemma is for the consultant to cultivate relationships with specific school systems in which children with autistic spectrum disorders are enrolled. We have found that in some cases, if the consultant provides a service that is valued by parents and teachers and cannot be duplicated by any other professional in the community or in the school system, and the school system has sufficient resources, the services of the consultant can be paid for by a contract. To accomplish this, the consultant needs to make it clear that the services need to be reimbursed and cannot be provided otherwise.

Another challenge posed by this work involves the need to coordinate neuropsychological consultation with input from pediatric neurologists and pediatricians concerning medication management. To accomplish this goal, neuropsychologists in our setting work very closely with a pediatric neurologist who has expertise in the management of ASD. In addition, information concerning the child's psychological assessment and school-based management plan is routinely shared with the child's pediatrician.

This case study illustrates the value of school consultation for children with autistic spectrum disorders. Education is needed not only with school personnel, but also with parents, siblings, and peers of children with ASD. To use the information that is gathered from the neuropsychological exam in a productive manner, it is necessary to develop positive working relationships between psychologists and teachers and to facilitate relationships among parents, physicians, and teachers. To facilitate this working network of positive working relationships, it is necessary that teachers and parents be viewed as key members of the team during educational meetings. To accomplish this goal, begin a team meeting by asking the teachers to give their input on the child's performance in the classroom.

In addition to the consultation concerning individual children, consultation can provide school staff, parents, and, when appropriate, other children education concerning ASD with an emphasis on the individual needs of each child. The consultant can also provide resources for teaching social skills, modifying curriculum, and direct instruction in how to utilize specific intervention techniques.

One of the primary advantages of in-school consultation is the opportunity it affords to implement interventions in a timely and direct manner. This collaborative approach also emphasizes the importance of utilizing every "teachable moment" to assist the child with autism in understanding how specific events relate to each other. Intervening in the school environment as situations occur helps teachers and the child with autism understand why a behavior may be problematic and appropriate ways to respond, thus facilitating the child's acceptance by peers in the classroom.

CONCLUSIONS

We described methods and models for consultation and collaboration with schools for pediatric populations. Although they focus on very different populations with very different needs, the programs incorporate several core principles that are important to note: (1) the programs are based on interdisciplinary expertise of pediatricians and pediatric psychologists, including empirical assessments that document the child's neuropsychological and psychological strengths and weaknesses that relate specifically to their medical diagnosis; (2) the consultant develops relationships with and provides a high level of information to the school staff; and (3) the relationship with the school staff is expanded beyond a case-based or individual consultation model to a process education model that includes ongoing review of the child's progress (Roberts, 1986; Drotar, 1995).

What does it take to accomplish such consultation? The consultant needs to develop a high level of expertise with a specific population and needs to be able to communicate this expertise in ways that teachers can understand. This requires the consultant to have a mastery of the child's specific medical condition and psychological implications, the educational deficits, the specific needs of teachers, and the characteristics of school settings.

Even more than experience, expertise, and commitment, the consultant who works with teachers and school staff concerning the needs of a specific pediatric population as has been described here needs to have sufficient time to focus on this work. The time commitment that is required is formidable and, in an era of managed care, needs to be funded as well as supported by administrative leadership. Sources of funding for these programs include hospitals, local foundations, and school districts.

The present description of collaboration has several implications for training of pediatric psychologists and pediatricians concerning these activities. We believe that it is important to train the next generation of pediatric psychologists, neuropsychologists, and pediatricians to develop the level of expertise and commitment that is needed to conduct high-quality collaboration and consultation with schools that is clinically relevant to various pediatric populations. Although such training is difficult to accomplish, we have identified some methods to accomplish this. For example, graduate students in pediatric psychology have been included in the consultation program for SCD, which allows them to receive experiential training in the identification of school-related needs in the context of chronic illness as well as practical knowledge of collaboration and advocacy for children within the schools. In another experience that is part of the neuropsychology program for children with ASD, pre- and postdoctoral trainees have been involved in observing neuropsychological testing and team meetings.

Faculty in our program have also developed methods of training physicians at different levels (medical student, resident, fellow) and practicing community pediatricians to understand the educational needs of a range of pediatric populations (e.g., children with chronic illness, learning problems, and neuropsychological disorders) and the implications for medical and educational management. These methods have included electives for medical students that are included in the residents' lecture series, lectures and observational experiences during a mandatory training rotation for residents in behavior and development, supervised experiences in consultation with schools for fellows in behavioral pediatrics, and continuing education programs for pediatricians in the community. For example, the school consultation program for children with ASD is discussed with medical students and pediatric residents as part of their didactic experience in behavioral pediatrics and pediatric psychology. In addition, one of us (C. B.) worked closely with a colleague in pediatric neurology to develop a highly successful one-day conference focused on the management of autism and ASD that was attended by teachers, school psychologists, child psychiatrics, pediatricians, and speech/language pathologists.

Another training method that has been useful for both psychology and medical trainees is supervision in conducting school visits that focus on assessment and classroom management for children who present with various clinical problems that are affecting their performance and behavior in school. Such hands-on experience is especially useful in teaching trainees to understand teachers' concerns and to communicate information from medical and psychological assessments in a clear, cogent manner.

Our work has also indicated that teachers and school staff require information from pediatric psychologists and pediatricians to understand the needs of pediatric populations, especially those with chronic medical and psychological conditions. The importance of pediatricians' and pediatric psychologists' efforts in educating teachers concerning the needs of chronic illness populations has been demonstrated by a recent survey of 45 school districts in a Midwestern state. While almost all teachers indicated that they had a chronically ill student in their classroom, the majority of teachers reported that they had received no previous or current training concerning the educational-related illness issues of children with chronic illness (Cortina et al., 2001). Consequently, pediatricians, nurses, and pediatric psychologists who work in pediatric hospitals have an important opportunity to provide education for teachers concerning medical and psychological needs of children with chronic illness, the impact of illness and treatment on students' academic functioning, and relevant interventions including when and how to utilize collaborative interventions involving health care providers, school psychologists, and pediatric psychologists (Cortina et al., 2001). For example, lectures with ample opportunity for discussion of relevant questions for school professionals (e.g., teachers and school nurses) concerning the medical and psychological issues of children with chronic physical illnesses are often helpful to and well received by school staff.

We have provided a conceptual and clinical rationale for psychologists and pediatricians to collaborate with school staff concerning management of the school-related needs of pediatric populations and anecdotal evidence for its utility based on our experiences with teachers, parents, and professionals. What is needed at this point is to develop scientific knowledge that is based on detailed evaluations of such school-related collaborative programs. Data can be gathered concerning participants, baseline characteristics of academic problems, evaluation of changes in these problems, and evaluation of satisfaction of program participants (teachers, parents, and physicians). Such program evaluations may be the most feasible method to use in the context of clinical care where it is not possible to conduct randomized controlled trials of interventions. However, in some cases it may be possible for pediatric psychologists, neuropsychologists, and pediatricians to conduct comparative evaluations of the educational and academic, social, and behavioral outcomes of children with various pediatric conditions who received comprehensive school-based, consultant-initiated interventions versus those who did not receive such interventions. Controlled trials of school-based interventions with pediatric populations are the next logical step beyond program evaluation. The scarcity of data concerning school-based interventions that have been published in the *Journal of Pediatric Psychology* or *Journal of Developmental and Behavioral Pediatrics* underscores the need for such empirical studies and presents important opportunities for pediatricians and psychologists.

ACKNOWLEDGMENT

The hard work of Susan Wood in processing this manuscript is gratefully acknowledged.

REFERENCES

American Psychiatric Association. (1995). *Diagnostic and statistical manual of mental disorders*, DSM-IV. (4th ed.). Washington, DC: American Psychiatric Press.

Armstrong, F. D., Thompson, R. J., Wang, W., Zimmerman, R., Pegelow, C. H., Miller, S. Moser, F., Bello, J., Huntig, A. & Vass, K. (1996). Cognitive functioning and brain magnetic resonance imaging in children with sickle cell disease. *Pediatrics, 97*, 864–870.

Blosser, J. L., & DePompei, R. (1994). *Pediatric traumatic brain injury. Proactive intervention*. San Diego: Singular Publishing Group, Inc.

Bonner, M. J., Gustafson, K. E., Shumacher, E., & Thompson, R. J. (1999). The impact of sickle cell disease on cognitive functioning and learning. *School Psychology Review, 28*, 182–193.

Brown, R. T. (Ed.). (1999). *Cognitive aspects of chronic illness in children*. New York: Guilford.

Burgess, E. S., Palermo, T. M., & Beebe, A. (2001, April). *A psycho-educational screening program for children with sickle cell disease at risk for stroke*. Poster presented at the 8th Florida Conference on Child Health Psychology, Gainesville, FL.

Cortina, S., Clay, D. L., Harper, B. H., Cocco, K. M., Kanz, J., & Drotar, D. (2001, April). *School teachers' knowledge and experiences with childhood chronic illness* Poster. Presented at the Conference on Child Health Psychology, Gainesville, Florida.

Craft, S., Schatz, J., Glauser, T., & Lee, B. (1993). Neuropsychological effects of stroke in children with SCD. *Journal of Pediatrics, 123*, 712–717.

Cumine, V., Leach, J. & Stevenson, G. (1998). *Asperger syndrome: A practical guide for teachers*. London: David Fulton Publishers.

DeBaun, M. R., Schatz, J., & Siegel, M. J. (1998). Cognitive screening examinations for silent cerebral infarcts in sickle cell disease. *Neurology, 50*, 1678–1682.

Drotar, D. (1993). Influences on collaborative activities among psychologists and physicians: Implications for practice, research, and training. *Journal of Pediatric Psychology, 18*, 159–172.

Drotar, D. (1995). *Consulting with pediatricians*. New York: Plenum.

Drotar, D., Timmons-Mitchell, J., Williams, L. L., Palermo, T. M., Levi, R., Robinson, J. R., Riekert, K. A., & Walders, N. (2000). Conducting research with children and adolescents in clinical and applied settings: Practical lessons from the field. In D. Drotar (Ed.), *Handbook of research methods in clinical child and pediatric psychology* (pp. 261–280). New York: Kluwer Academic/Plenum Publishers.

Edwards, M., & Davis, H. (1997). *Counseling children with chronic medical conditions*. Balltimore: Paul H. Brookes.

Gagnon, El., & Smith Myles, B. (1999). *This is Asperger syndrome*. Kansas: City Kansas Autism Asperger Publishing Company.

Hamlett, K. W., & Stabler, B. (1995). In M. C. Roberts (Ed.). *Handbook of pediatric psychology* (pp. 39–54) New York: Guilford.

Katz, E. R., Rubinstein, C. L., Hubert, N. C., & Blew, A. (1988). School and social reintegration of children with cancer. *Journal of Psychosocial Oncology, 6*, 123–140.

Kazak, A., & Beele, D. (1993). *Overview of psychosocial services, The Children's Hospital of Philadelphia, Division of Oncology*. Unpublished program description, The Children's Hospital of Philadelphia, Division of Oncology, Philadelphia, PA.

Maguire, A. (2000). *Special people, special ways*. Arlington, TX: Future Horizons, Inc.

Messner, A. W. (1996). *Captain Tommy*. Stathan, NH: Potential Unlimited Publishing.

Miller, S. T., Sleeper, L. A., Pegelow, C. H., Enos, L. E., Wang, W. C., Weiner, S. J., Wethers, D. L., Smith, J., & Kinney, T. R. (2000). Prediction of adverse outcomes of children with sickle cell disease. *New England Journal of Medicine, 342*, 83–89.

Mullins, L. L., Gillman, J., & Harbeck, C. (1992). Multiple-level interventions in pediatric psychology settings: A behavioral-systems perspective. In A. M. La Greca, L. J. Siegel, J. L. Wallender, & C. E. Walker (Eds.), *Stress and coping in child health* (pp. 377–399). New York: Guilford.

Nader, P. R., Ray, L., & Gilman S. C. (1981). The new morbidity: Use of school and community health care resources for behavioral, educational, and social-family problems. *Pediatrics, 67*, 53–55.

Noll, R. B., Stith, L., Garstein, M. A., Ris, M. D., Grueneich, R., Vannatta, K., & Katlinyak, K. (2001). Neuropsychological functioning of youths with sickle cell disease: Compliance with non-chronically ill peers. *Journal of Pediatric Psychology*, 79–92.

Ohene-Frempong, K., Weiner, S., Sleeper, L., Miller, S., Embury, S., Moohr, J. W., Wethers, D. L., Pigelow, C. H. & Gill, F. M. (1998). Cerebrovascular accidents in sickle cell disease: Rates and risk factors. *Blood, 91*, 288–294.

Roberts, M. C. (1986). *Pediatric psychology: Psychological interventions and strategies for pediatric problems*. New York: Pergamon.

Roberts, M. C., & Wright, L. (1982). Role of the pediatric psychologist as consultant to pediatrician. In J. M. Tuma (Ed.), *Handbook for the practice of pediatric psychology* (pp. 251–289). New York: Wiley.

Rutter, M. (1979). *Fifteen thousand hours*. Cambridge, MA: Harvard University Press.

Sarason, S. B. (1972). *The creation of settings and the problem of change*. Boston: Allyn & Bacon.

Schroeder, C. S., & Mann, J. (1991). A model for clinical clued practice. In Schroedes, C. S. & bounder, B. N. (Eds.). *Assessment and treatment of childhood problems: A children's guide* (pp. 375–398). New York: Guilford.

Simmons, K. (1996). *Rainman*. Arlington, TX: Future Horizons, Inc.

Stabler, B. (1988). Pediatric consultation-liaison. In D. K. Routh (Ed.), *Handbook of pediatric psychology* (pp. 538–566). New York: Guilford.

Wing, L. (1981). Asperger's syndrome: A clinical account. *Journal of Psychological Medicine, 11*, 115–129.

Wood, D. (1978). Cerebrovascular complications of sickle cell anemia. *Stroke, 9*, 73–75.

Wright, G. F., & Nader, P. R. (1983). Schools as milieux. In M. D. Levine, W. B. Carey, A. C. Crooker, & R. T. Gross (Eds.), *Developmental-behavioral pediatrics* (pp. 276–283). Philadelphia: W. B. Saunders.

3

The School as a Venue for Managing and Preventing Health Problems: Opportunities and Challenges

Thomas J. Power
The Children's Hospital of Philadelphia/ University of Pennsylvania School of Medicine

Jessica Blom-Hoffman
The Children's Hospital of Philadelphia

Sociopolitical reforms and developments within the fields of psychology, education, and medicine have focused attention on the resources of the school for the provision of health services to children (Kolbe, Collins, & Cortese, 1997). Reforms in health care have emphasized the importance of improving access to care and reducing costs by shifting the locus of health-related services from secondary and tertiary care settings to community-based settings, including primary care practices and schools (Strosahl, 1998). These reforms have highlighted the need to reduce fragmentation in service delivery in the community by coordinating care for children across the health, education, child welfare, juvenile justice, and family systems (Dryfoos, 1994; U.S. Department of Health and Human Services, 1999). The school has been identified as a locus for coordinating community health services because of the existing mechanisms in schools to integrate services for children with special needs. To reduce the costs associated with providing services for individuals with identified health problems, the health reform movement has emphasized the need for health promotion for all children and prevention for children at risk for health problems (Short & Talley, 1997). In response to these developments, the school is being viewed as a unique resource for providing both intervention and prevention services for children and their families (Bickman & Rog, 1995; Kolbe et al., 1997).

Advancements in our understanding of child development have also emphasized the importance of linking systems of care and the critical role of the school. In particular, Bronfenbrenner's (1979) social–ecological model has affirmed that children develop in the context of multiple systems (e.g., family, school, neighborhood peer group, health care system, community agencies). Development is promoted when the major systems in children's lives are responsive to their needs and when each system operates to enhance the functioning of the other systems (Power & Bartholomew, 1987). For example, in order for a child with asthma to function well in school, it is often important for educators to understand effective methods of preventing and treating the child's asthma and the impact of the disease and its treatment on school attendance, academic performance, and peer functioning. In this case, optimal functioning in the school system may require close collaboration with the health care and family systems (Bender, 1999). Similarly, in order for health professionals to determine the optimal strategy for assisting a child with attention deficit hyperactivity disorder (ADHD), coordination with teachers and parents is critical to understand how the child is functioning in the school and family settings (DuPaul & Stoner, 1994). The social–ecological model affirms the importance of integrating systems of care, including the school, to promote the development of children.

A growing recognition of the limitations of the medical model of service delivery for managing and preventing health problems has highlighted the need for alternative models of care. Within psychology and related disciplines, there has been a strong movement to recognize and affirm the assets of an individual person and the resources of systems in which they function (Cowen, 2000; Frederickson, 2001; Masten, 2001). This movement is a sharp contrast to the long-standing tradition in health care that has focused on the identification and reduction of deficits within the individual. The paradigm shift toward positive psychology (see Seligman & Csikszentmihalyi, 2000) focuses on developing the assets of children and building the capacity of the systems in which children function to promote positive development and resilience in the face of adversity (Cicchetti, Rappaport, Sandler, & Weissberg, 2000; Masten & Coatsworth, 1998).

A major thrust of positive psychology, which has been termed "the science of human strength" (Seligman & Csikszentmihalyi, 2000), is to promote and maintain healthy development in contexts that serve normally developing, healthy children, such as general education settings in neighborhood schools. The mission of schools is to build children's competencies and to promote cognitive, emotional, and social development. Priorities of the educational system include enhancing children's academic success and helping them develop citizenship skills so they will be able to function independently and contribute to society in adulthood. The competency-building framework of schools is congruent with the principles of positive psychology and resilience and incongruent with a traditional, deficit-based model of psychology. The discontinuity between the positive psychology approach of general education and the traditional, deficit model used in health care may explain in part the historical fragmentation of the educational and health systems.

Schools, therefore, are now uniquely positioned to assist in the management and prevention of children's health problems (Power, Heathfield, McGoey, & Blum, 1999). This chapter identifies and discusses the opportunities provided by schools to address the health care needs of children and their families. Because schools are unusually situated to support activities related to prevention, a separate section devoted to the assets of schools related to prevention is included in addition to a section on intervention. Also, this chapter describes the limitations of the school as a venue for health programming to highlight the importance of linking multiple systems of care to develop effective prevention and intervention programs for children and their families.

HEALTH SERVICES IN SCHOOLS: OPPORTUNITIES AND CHALLENGES

School-Based Intervention Services

Schools offer numerous opportunities to provide intervention services for children with health problems. The following is a description of these assets as well as the challenges that often arise in providing school-based interventions. Table 3.1 provides a summary of these opportunities and limitations.

TABLE 3.1
Opportunities and Challenges of Conducting Health-Related Intervention and Prevention Activities in Schools

	School-Based Intervention	*School-Based Prevention*
Opportunities	⇒ Easy access to naturalistic assessment data ⇒ Venue to analyze functions of behavior ⇒ Provide multidisciplinary teams ⇒ Venue for intervening directly in children's natural environment ⇒ Access to multiple change agents ⇒ Context for developing competent healthy children ⇒ Venue to monitor interventions in the natural environment	⇒ Mission of schools is consistent with the objectives of health promotion programming ⇒ Impact large numbers of children in cost-effective ways ⇒ Provide access to large numbers of parents ⇒ Provide numerous adult and peer role models ⇒ Numerous opportunities for health messages to be integrated into ongoing instruction ⇒ Multiple opportunities to practice new skills and to receive feedback ⇒ Embedded within resource-rich communities
Challenges	⇒ Lack of expertise and resources ⇒ Not fully committed to inclusion of individuals with special needs in the general education setting ⇒ Disconnect between school and the surrounding community ⇒ School-based health and mental health professionals assigned to assessment and traditional roles ⇒ Public nature of schools makes it difficult to protect privacy	⇒ Competing instructional priorities ⇒ Lack of specially trained professionals in health promotion ⇒ School professionals are overextended ⇒ Isolation from families and surrounding community ⇒ Mental health services in schools are based on a deficit model

Opportunities. Schools provide easy access to naturalistic assessment data about how children function in real-life situations across many important domains of functioning (Power, Atkins, Osborne, & Blum, 1994). The information accessible through schools is invaluable in determining the types and severity of problems a child may be experiencing as well as the resources available to the child to cope with these problems and to succeed in school. Academic functioning can be assessed by conducting systematic observations of the child's performance in a classroom situation, by monitoring performance on tests and quizzes, by reviewing school records, and by assessing the child using materials that closely correspond to the curriculum through curriculum-based assessment (Shapiro, 1996). Adult-oriented social functioning can be assessed by systematically observing the child's behavior in relation to teachers and paraprofessionals in multiple school settings, by obtaining informant reports from school professionals, and by reviewing school disciplinary records (Walker, Colvin, & Ramsey, 1995). Peer-oriented social behavior can be assessed by directly observing a child's behavior in various school situations, by obtaining peer nominations and reports of social behavior, by acquiring teacher reports of peer-related behavior, and by reviewing records of injuries kept by the school nurse and records or peer-related disciplinary problems (Leff, Kupersmidt, Patterson, & Power, 1999). Emotional functioning can be assessed by obtaining information through the use of interviews and checklists from parents, teachers, and children themselves (Kendall et al., 1992). Further, ongoing information about the health status of the child can be obtained by reviewing the health records kept by the school nurse.

Schools not only are ideal situations for understanding a child's strengths and weaknesses across many domains of functioning but they also *provide an excellent venue for analyzing the function of behavior*, which is extremely useful in intervention planning. Researchers in the field of applied behavior analysis have delineated four major functions of behavior: (1) escaping from or avoiding situations, (2) obtaining adult or peer attention, (3) obtaining tangible reinforcers or preferred activities, and (4) acquiring sensory stimulation or automatic reinforcement (DuPaul & Ervin, 1996; McComas & Mace, 2000). By interviewing school professionals, conducting systematic direct observations of behavior, and conducting mini-experiments involving the systematic manipulation of antecedents and consequences of behavior, clinicians can identify potential functions of behavior and plan intervention strategies accordingly (Dunlap & Kern, 1993).

Schools provide multidisciplinary teams to assess problems and resources, to develop intervention plans, and to evaluate the effectiveness of interventions (Power et al., 1994). In addition to multidisciplinary teams that function to evaluate children who may have special needs to determine eligibility for special education, schools typically have pre-referral intervention teams. These intervention teams, which may be referred to as Instructional Support Teams or Mainstream Assistance Teams, function to assist children who are experiencing problems coping in the general education setting to preclude referral for special education services (Meyers & Nastasi, 1998). These teams may include school professionals from a variety of disciplines, including an administrator, general and special education teachers, a reading specialist, a guidance counselor, a school psychologist, a social worker, and a nurse.

Schools provide a venue for intervening directly in context at the point and in the moment in which children experience the greatest challenges to succeed. Research has questioned the effectiveness of interventions applied with children, particularly those who are relatively young, developmentally delayed, or impulsive, outside the contexts in which they are challenged to respond competently (Barkley, 1998; Stokes & Baer, 1977). For example, interventions to improve social skills are not likely to be effective if they do not include a well-developed plan for generalization that may involve monitoring, evaluation, and reinforcement of behavior in actual social situations (DuPaul & Eckert, 1994). For this reason, interventions directed at improving the functioning of children typically include other individuals, such as teachers, peers, and caregivers, who can assist in promoting and maintaining behavioral change at the point and in the moment in which children are likely to be most challenged. Because children attend school virtually on a daily basis, opportunities to intervene directly on an intensive, ongoing basis are available.

Schools afford access to multiple change agents who can assist in providing interventions in a culturally responsive manner. Effective schools employ professionals who are committed to understanding the community and who are responsive to the cultural values of the children and families they serve. Schools are highly accessible to families and can involve parents in a variety of ways (e.g., homework support, tutoring, assisting in the classroom) to promote the education of students and to assist with interventions when problems arise (Christenson & Sheridan, 2001). Successful schools are linked well with the community and enlist leaders and residents from the community to assist in planning and implementing school programs (Dowrick et al., 2001). In addition, schools increasingly are finding creative ways to involve peers in the process of learning through cooperative learning and reciprocal peer-tutoring activities (Fantuzzo, King, & Heller, 1992; Slavin, 1990).

Schools function to develop well-adjusted, competent, healthy children. While teacher expectations for success may vary from child to child, in general teachers expect children to perform competently and to adapt successfully. High expectations for success typically lead to self-fulfilling prophesies (Brophy, 1979). Intervention programs designed in schools for children who are experiencing problems often utilize solely a deficit-oriented approach that is aimed at the removal of problems. However, the general orientation of schools is to develop competence, which is highly compatible with a strength-based approach to assessment and intervention. This type of approach identifies areas of competence and develops skills as a protection against failure and disability (Epstein & Sharma, 1998; Nelson & Pearson, 1991). For these reasons, reforms in special education have emphasized the importance of educating children with disabilities in general education settings in which they are challenged to adapt to age-appropriate academic and social challenges and have the opportunity to learn from normally developing peers (*Individuals with Disabilities Education Act*, 1997).

Schools provide numerous opportunities and resources for evaluating intervention outcomes and for determining the impact of interventions on important domains of child functioning. The ultimate goal of most intervention programs for children with health problems is to promote successful adaptation in community settings, including family, neighborhood, and school. The school provides numerous benchmarks for determining the extent to which children are adapting successfully in the community. School-based benchmarks include academic performance, attention and behavior in the classroom, interactions with peers in multiple school settings, emotional functioning, attendance, and health status in school. Schools offer a wide range of methods and informants to collect data about functioning across many important domains (Kratochwill & Shapiro, 2000), which are invaluable in evaluating intervention outcomes.

Challenges. School professionals often lack the expertise and resources to address the special needs of children with chronic illnesses and disabilities (Clark, 1996; Power, DuPaul, Shapiro, & Parrish, 1995). Children with special needs can be highly challenging to educate, as their status can fluctuate markedly even over short periods of time, and they may require specialized methods of instruction and intervention to assist with academic and social challenges. School professionals, particularly general education teachers, may not be properly trained to address the needs of children with chronic illnesses and disabilities. Although the community may have resources to assist school professionals to work effectively with special-needs children, systems of service delivery are often fragmented, resulting in the need for school personnel and families to struggle on their own in assisting these children.

Many school systems are not fully committed to the process of inclusion. Although schools are mandated to educate children in general education settings whenever possible, some school districts and many school personnel in virtually every school district are not invested in finding creative ways for children with special needs to be educated in inclusionary settings. In many cases the resistance to inclusion is understandable, particularly in underresourced, urban settings. Educators may be so overwhelmed and frustrated with the large number of children with academic deficits and behavior problems that they cannot cope with a child with complex medical problems (Minke, Bear, Deemer, & Griffin, 1996). Unfortunately, in these situations children with special needs may be deprived of opportunities to adapt to age-appropriate academic and social challenges, thereby limiting their developmental trajectories.

Some schools are disconnected from the communities they are designed to serve. In these cases, there may be discontinuity between the educational experiences children are having at home and at school, thereby limiting the academic progress of children (Christenson & Sheridan, 2001; Comer, Haynes, Joyner, & Ben-Avie, 1996). Further, when the school and community fail to form effective linkages, schools are deprived of the wonderful resources community leaders and residents can provide in supporting children in school by serving as tutors, playground aides, and classroom assistants (Dowrick et al., 2001).

Many schools assign school-based health professionals to traditional roles and provide very little support for them to engage in intervention activities. For example, despite efforts to reform the roles of school psychologists, these professionals continue to spend a high percentage of their time engaged in testing to determine eligibility for special education (Hosp & Reschly, 2002). Similarly, guidance counselors may spend so much of their time on scheduling issues that they are only able to devote a small proportion of their time to providing counseling to students and their families.

Schools generally are public settings that promote the open exchange of ideas; these settings typically are not designed to protect privacy. The culture of the school is very different from the culture of health care systems that are designed to elicit personal information and to protect the privacy of children and families (Dryfoos, 1994; Power et al., 1994). Differences in these cultures can serve as a barrier to collaboration between educational and health professionals. Further, perceived failure to respect privacy in the school setting may prevent families from collaborating openly with school professionals about potentially important health and mental health issues.

School-Based Prevention Services

Schools are uniquely positioned to provide prevention and health promotion services to children. The following is a description of these assets as well as the challenges that often arise in providing school-based health promotion services. Table 3.1 provides a summary of the opportunities and limitations of schools with regard to providing prevention services.

Opportunities. The school's mission is consistent with the goals of health promotion programming. Schools strive to promote the development of the whole child by providing challenging, developmentally appropriate learning activities (Adelman & Taylor, 1998), and health promotion programs are designed to foster healthy development by helping children to make responsible choices. The mission of schools and the objectives of health promotion services are consistent with the framework of an asset-building, resilience-promoting, positive approach to psychology (Masten & Coatsworth, 1998; Seligman & Csikszentmihalyi, 2000).

Schools are a venue that serve almost all children. It has been estimated that 95% of children in this country attend school. Therefore, when schools make health promotion a priority, they have the potential to impact the health of most of the children in this country. Additionally, schools are organized so that children are placed into developmentally similar groupings (Ross & Harrison, 1997). This organizational structure permits information to be provided and skill-building exercises to be implemented in a developmentally appropriate manner.

Schools generally are more accessible to families than health clinics. In order for prevention programs to have a meaningful and enduring impact on children's lives, health promotion messages at school should be congruent with messages at home and should be reinforced by caregivers. When programs are developed and implemented in a manner that is sensitive to the needs and the culture of the families whose children attend the school, they are more likely to have a significant impact on children (Christenson & Sheridan, 2001). Prevention programs can include parents in a number of different ways. Ideally, parents should be included in all aspects of the program, including the needs assessment phase, the program development phase, and the implementation and outcome evaluation phases. As key stakeholders in the success and maintenance of prevention programs, parents are critical members of the health promotion team (Benson, 1997).

Schools provide numerous professionals and natural helpers to promote healthy development and to assist in the provision of services for children in need. The recent report of the Surgeon General on mental health highlighted the need to increase the supply of service providers to address the psychological health concerns of individuals and their families (U.S. Department of Health and Human Services, 1999). A similar need exists in the physical health domain. One way to address this need is to employ additional health professionals, which can be very expensive. An alternative strategy is to build upon existing resources in the school and community and to utilize mental health professionals increasingly in the role of engaging in partnerships with nonmental health staff and natural helpers to develop and evaluate prevention programs (Nastasi, 2000; Power, 2000). Schools employ a number of professionals who can assist in addressing the health needs of children, including teachers, school nurses, counselors, psychologists, food service personnel, physical education teachers, and paraprofessionals. In addition, natural helpers, such as parents and peers, can be enlisted to assist with the delivery of intervention and prevention programs (Fantuzzo, Coolahan, & Weiss, 1995). When these individuals are included at all stages of the development and implementation of capacity-building programs, they can serve to model and reinforce health-promoting behaviors for students in a number of important ways.

Schools can affirm health-promoting messages each day by integrating prevention activities into ongoing instruction. Efforts to reduce social morbidities, such as aggression, malnutrition, increasingly sedentary lifestyles, substance abuse, teen pregnancy and sexually transmitted diseases, can be incorporated into goals in the general education curriculum. When students are presented health-promoting messages in the context of history, math, science, language arts, and physical education lessons, the information may be more relevant and effective in changing behavior than when it is presented in isolation (DeVito, Krockover, & Steele, 1993; Rickard, 1995). Further, in school, students have multiple opportunities to practice health-promoting skills and to receive feedback from adults and peers. For example, when learning about healthful eating behaviors, students can practice making healthy food choices from the school cafeteria at breakfast and lunch. Additionally, adult and peer role models can provide students with feedback during mealtimes to reinforce healthy food selection skills. Similarly, students who learn about positive social skills and strategies for conflict resolution can practice their skills and receive feedback from others during recess.

Schools are embedded within resource-rich communities that have enormous potential for supporting capacity-building efforts. When schools partner with community agencies, such as faith-based organizations, local hospitals, primary care practices, police and fire departments, mental health agencies, and businesses, programs are more comprehensive and services are less fragmented (Benson, 1997). Additionally, when schools partner with families and surrounding community agencies, programs are more likely to be responsive to the needs of participants (Dowrick et al., 2001).

Challenges. Despite the many assets inherent in schools that facilitate health promotion programming, there are a number of limitations that impede schools from engaging in these efforts. First, educators often have a number of competing priorities, leaving little time for efforts to address the health needs and psychological well-being of students. Typically, mandated instructional requirements take precedence over prevention programs designed to reduce the risk for social morbidities. Ironically, the social morbidities (e.g., illness, mental health problems, parenting stress, and family–school conflict) create barriers to learning that impede schools from achieving their goal of enabling students to be successful academically (Adelman & Taylor, 1998). Efforts to mandate prevention programming in schools and creative attempts to incorporate health promotion programming into the general education curriculum (i.e., the Integrated Nutrition Project; Auld, Romaniello, Heimendinger, Hambidge, & Hambidge, 1998) can help address this barrier to the establishment of prevention programs in schools.

Schools may lack professionals with sufficient expertise required to develop and implement prevention programs in an effective, acceptable, and sustainable manner and to evaluate empirically the effects of their efforts. In addition, many school professionals are overextended and have little time, if any, to devote to programs or projects that are not mandated and are perceived as above and beyond their current responsibilities.

Despite the importance of partnering with families and community agencies, schools are often isolated from families and the communities they serve (Christenson & Sheridan, 2001). This isolation creates major obstacles for the development, implementation, and long-term maintenance of health promotion programs. In order to strengthen the connections among the school, families, and surrounding community, efforts to partner with key stakeholders from these groups are critical. These stakeholders must work together to identify needs, design programs, and decide how programs will be implemented and evaluated in an acceptable manner (Gittelsohn et al., 1999).

Although the mission of schools is to promote the development of the whole child, health services provided in schools may be based on a deficit-oriented model. When children display evidence of emerging health conditions, including symptoms of mental health disorders, school health professionals typically focus on eliminating the problems and reducing the impact of risk factors. Systems created in schools and communities to address children's health needs generally are not based on a strength-based approach to programming that builds upon assets in children and the systems in which they operate (Epstein & Sharma, 1998; Masten, 2001).

IMPLICATIONS FOR PRACTICE AND TRAINING

Although schools provide numerous opportunities to support outstanding prevention and intervention work for children with or at risk for health problems, many communities do not capitalize on these opportunities. To assist communities in capitalizing on the opportunities available in schools, there is a need for professionals, including child psychologists, who can effectively link the school, family, health care system, mental health system, and child welfare system, to manage and prevent health problems (Power et al., 1995).

Many pathways are available for the preparation of child psychologists to serve as multisystemic change agents with a focus on both prevention and intervention (Power, Shapiro, & DuPaul, 2003). For example, one pathway is for students in clinical child and pediatric psychology training programs to be prepared to link systems of care to develop comprehensive intervention programs for children with acute and chronic illnesses and to establish health promotion programs in primary care and educational settings (LaGreca & Hughes, 1999; Roberts et al., 1998; Spirito et al., 2003). Alternatively, trainees in school psychology can be prepared to coordinate systems of care that remove barriers to effective instruction (e.g., health and mental health problems, peer relation problems, home–school conflicts) for children with chronic illnesses and disabilities and to establish school-based prevention programs for all children (Nastasi, 2000; Power, et al., 1995; Ysseldyke et al., 1997). The following is a brief description of a model program for training doctoral-level school psychologists to capitalize on the opportunities available in school settings. Although this program has been designed for the preparation of school psychologists, many of its elements are applicable for the training of pediatric, clinical child, and community psychologists.

Linking the Health and Educational Systems: A Model Training Program

In 1997 a training program jointly sponsored by Lehigh University and The Children's Hospital of Philadelphia (CHOP) was established through a grant funded by the U.S. Department of Education, Office of Special Education Programs (Shapiro, DuPaul, & Power, 1997). Students in the school psychology doctoral training program at Lehigh University can elect to enter this specialty program in the third and fourth year of their studies. The goal of the Lehigh/CHOP program is to prepare school psychologists as leaders who can effectively link community-based systems of care for children with or at risk for chronic illnesses and/or mental health disorders for the purposes of removing barriers to instruction and improving educational outcomes. The program has a focus on intervention for students with or at risk for health and mental health disorders as well as health promotion for all students. Further, the program is designed to train leaders to address the needs of children and families living in underresourced, multiethnic, urban communities.

Courses for this program are taught by an interdisciplinary faculty, including professors in the departments of psychology, education, and biology at Lehigh University and faculty in the pediatric psychology and developmental-behavioral pediatrics at CHOP. In the third year of studies, coursework is focused on intervention approaches for children with identified medical conditions, and in the fourth year the focus is on prevention and health promotion. Practicum training experiences are divided equally between school and health care settings. In the school practica, students have the opportunity to learn assessment and consultation skills that are typical to school psychology practice. In addition, trainees are expected to develop school-based interventions for children with chronic illnesses and to evaluate the effectiveness of these approaches, as well as to develop prevention programs for children at risk for acquiring health and mental health disorders. In the health care practica, trainees work in a variety of primary care and specialty clinics to assist in addressing the needs of children who are experiencing problems with school adaptation (see Shapiro, DuPaul, Power, Gureasko, & Moore, 2000).

Students enrolled in this program are expected to conduct their dissertations on a topic related to intervention or prevention for children with or at risk for health problems. Course assignments, such as writing literature reviews, journal article critiques, and a grant proposal, are designed to prepare students for the dissertation process and for a career as a scientist-practitioner. Examples of the types of programmatic, clinical, research, and training activities conducted by students enrolled in this program are presented in Table 3.2.

TABLE 3.2
Examples of Program Development, Clinical, Research, and Training Activities Conducted by Students

Program Development Activities
Codeveloped pediatric obesity program
Developed ADHD program linking pediatric clinic and schools
Developed nutrition education program
Clinical Activities
Taught coping skills to families coping with Inflammatory Bowel Disease
Provided consultation to a child with sickle cell disease and feeding problems
Facilitated school-based bully prevention program for girls
Research Activities
Evaluated effectiveness of a nutrition education program
Evaluated effectiveness of an intervention to improve adherence to an asthma management regimen
Evaluated effectiveness of a playground-based violence prevention program
Training Activities
Trained school professionals about nutrition, fitness, and lead exposure
Assisted in the design of a summer institute on interventions for children with health problems in school and health care settings
Assisted in the design of a summer institute on school-based health promotion

Reprinted with permission

CONCLUSIONS

Reforms in health care and education as well as developments within the fields of psychology, education, and medicine have affirmed the critical role of the schools in the management and prevention of health problems. Schools provide numerous resources for the provision of intervention and prevention services for children with or at risk for health problems. The assets of schools include the opportunities they afford to provide services to almost all children; their accessibility to family and community members, which can facilitate family and community involvement; the large pool of professionals and natural helpers they offer to assist in developing, implementing, and evaluating intervention and prevention programs; the infrastructure created within schools to coordinate educational and mental health services for children; and the commitment of schools to foster the development of the whole child, which is highly congruent with the goals of health promotion programming. Of course, schools also have a number of limitations with regard to providing health services; these include a lack of expertise among school professionals to develop and evaluate programs to manage and prevent health problems; time constraints and conflicting priorities that may limit the ability of educators to become invested in intervention and prevention programming; and a school culture that may not actively promote family and community involvement.

To address the limitations of schools as venues for the provision of health services, professionals who can assist communities in connecting systems of care and in capitalizing on the resources of the schools are needed. A training program based at Lehigh University and The Children's Hospital of Philadelphia has been developed to prepare school psychologists to serve this critical role. Similar initiatives based in clinical child, pediatric, and community psychology training programs as well as within related disciplines (e.g., social work, nursing, guidance counseling, psychiatry, and developmental and behavioral pediatrics) are also critical to increase the pool of professionals available to capitalize on the unique resources of schools.

REFERENCES

Adelman, H. S., & Taylor, L. (1998). Mental health in schools: Moving forward. *School Psychology Review, 27*, 175–190.

Auld, G. W., Romaniello, C., Heimendinger, J., Hambidge, C., & Hambidge, M. (1998). Outcomes from a school-based nutrition education program using resource teachers and cross-disciplinary models. *Journal of Nutrition Education, 30*, 268–280.

Barkley, R. A. (1998). *Attention-deficit hyperactivity disorder: A handbook for diagnosis and treatment* (2nd ed.). New York: Guilford.

Bender, B. G. (1999). Learning disorders associated with asthma and allergies. *School Psychology Review, 28*, 204–214.

Benson, P. L. (1997). *All kids are our kids: What communities must do to raise caring and responsible children and adolescents*. San Francisco: Jossey-Bass.

Bickman, L., & Rog, D. J. (Eds.). (1995). *Children's mental health services: Research, policy, and evaluation* (Vol. 1). Thousand Oaks, CA: Sage.

Bronfenbrenner, U. (1979). *The ecology of human development*. Cambridge, MA: Harvard University Press.

Brophy, J. E. (1979). Teacher behavior and its effects. *Journal of Educational Psychology, 71*, 733–750.

Christenson, S. L., & Sheridan, S. M. (2001). *Schools and families: Creating essential connections for learning*. New York: Guilford.

Cicchetti, D., Rappaport, J., Sandler, I., & Weissberg, R. P. (Eds.). (2000). *The promotion of wellness in children and adolescents*. Washington, DC: Child Welfare League of America Press.

Clark, E. (1996). Children and adolescents with traumatic brain injury: Reintegration challenges in educational settings. *Journal of Learning Disabilities, 29*, 633–642.

Comer, J. P., Haynes, N. M., Joyner, E. T., & Ben-Avie, M. (1996). *Rallying the whole village: The Comer process for reforming education*. New York: Teachers College Press.

Cowen, E. L. (2000). Psychological wellness: Some hopes for the future. In D. Cicchetti, J. Rappaport, J. Sandler, & R. P. Weissberg (Eds.), *The promotion of wellness in children and adolescents* (pp. 477–503). Washington, DC: Child Welfare League of America Press.

DeVito, A., Krockover, G., & Steele, K. (1993). *Creative teaching: A practical approach*. New York: Harper Collins.

Dowrick, P. W., Power, T. J., Manz, P. H., Ginsburg-Block, M., Leff, S. S., & Rupnow, S. K. (2001). Community responsiveness: Examples from under-resourced urban schools. *Journal of Intervention and Prevention in the Community, 21*, 71–90.

Dryfoos, J. G. (1994). *Full-service schools: A revolution in health and social services for children, youth, and families*. San Francisco: Jossey-Bass.

Dunlap, G., & Kern, L. (1993). Assessment and intervention for children within the instructional curriculum. In J. Reichle & D. Wacker (Eds.), *Communicative alternatives to challenging behavior: Integrating functional assessment and intervention strategies* (pp. 177–203). Baltimore, MD: Brookes.

DuPaul, G. J., & Eckert, T. (1994). The effects of social skills curriculum: Now you see them, now you don't. *School Psychology Quarterly, 9*, 113–132.

DuPaul, G. J., & Ervin, R. A. (1996). Functional assessment of behaviors related to attention-deficit/hyperactivity disorder. *Behavior Therapy, 27*, 601–622.

DuPaul, G. J., & Stoner, G. (1994). *ADHD in the schools: Assessment and intervention strategies*. New York: Guilford.

Epstein, M. H., & Sharma, J. (1998). *Behavioral and Emotional Rating Scale; A strength-based approach to assessment*. Austin, TX: Pro-Ed.

Fantuzzo, J., Coolahan, K. C., & Weiss, A. D. (1997). Resiliency partnership-directed intervention: Enhancing the social competencies of preschool victims of physical abuse by developing peer resources and community strengths. In D. Cicchetti & S. L. Toth (Eds.), *Rochester symposium on developmental psychopathology (Vol. 8): Developmental perspectives on trauma: Theory, research, and intervention* (pp. 463–489). Rochester, NY: University of Rochester Press.

Fantuzzo, J. W., King, J. A., & Heller, L. R. (1992). Effects of reciprocal peer tutoring on mathematics and school adjustment: A component analysis. *Journal of Educational Psychology, 84*, 331–339.

Fredrickson, B. L. (2001). The role of positive emotions in positive psychology: The broaden-and-build theory of positive emotions. *American Psychologist, 56*, 218–226.

Gittelsohn, J., Toporoff, E. G., Story, M., Evans, M., Anliker, J., Davis, S., et al. (1999). Food perceptions and dietary behavior of American-Indian children, their caregivers, and educators: Formative assessment findings from Pathways. *Journal of Nutrition Education, 31*, 2–13.

Hosp, J. L., & Reschly, D. J. 2002. Regional differences in school psychology practice. *School Psychology Review, 31*, 11–29.

Individuals with Disabilities Education Act – Amendments of 1997. (1997). U.S. Congress, Public Law 101-476; Amended by Public Law 105-17.

Kendall, P. C., Chansky, T. E., Kane, M. T., Kim, R. S., Kortlander, E., Ronan, K. R., Sessa, F. M., & Siqueland, L. (1992). *Anxiety disorders in youth: Cognitive-behavioral interventions*. Boston: Allyn and Bacon.

Kolbe, L. J., Collins, J., & Cortese, P. (1997). Building the capacity of schools to improve the health of the nation: A call for assistance from psychologists. *American Psychologist, 52*, 256–265.

Kratochwill, T. R., & Shapiro, E. S. (2000). Conceptual foundations of behavioral assessment in schools. In E. S. Shapiro & T. R. Kratochwill (Eds.), *Behavioral assessment in schools: Theory, research, and clinical foundations* (2nd ed.; pp. 3–15). New York: Guilford.

LaGreca, A. M., & Hughes, J. N. (1999). United we stand, divided we fall: The education and training of clinical child psychologists. *Journal of Clinical Child Psychology, 28*, 435–447.

Leff, S. S., Kupersmidt, J. B., Patterson, C. J., & Power, T. J. (1999). Factors influencing teacher idenfification of bullies and victims. *School Psychology Review, 28*, 505–517.

Masten, A. S. (2001). Ordinary magic: Resilience processes in development. *American Psychologist, 56*, 227–238.

Masten, A. S., & Coatsworth, J. D. (1998). The development of competence in favorable and unfavorable environments: Lessons from research on successful children. *American Psychologist, 53*, 205–220.

McComas, J. J., & Mace, F. C. (2000). Theory and practice in conducting functional analysis. In E. S. Shapiro & T. R. Kratochwill (Eds.), *Behavioral assessment in schools: Theory, research, and clinical foundations* (2nd ed.; pp. 78–103). New York: Guilford.

Meyers, J., & Nastasi, B. K. (1998). Primary prevention as a framework for the delivery of psychological services in the schools. In T. Gutkin & C. Reynolds (Eds.), *The handbook of school psychology* (3rd ed.; pp. 764–799). New York: Wiley.

Minke, K. M., Bear, G. G., Deemer, S. A., & Griffin, S. (1996). Teachers' experiences with inclusive classrooms: Implications for the special education reform. *Journal of Special Education, 30*, 152–186.

Nastasi, B. K. (2000). School psychologists as health-care provides: A means to success for all. *School Psychology Review, 29*, 540–554.

Nastasi, B. K. (2001). School psychologists as health-care providers in the 21st century: Conceptual framework, professional identity, and professional practice. *School Psychology Review, 29*, 540–554.

Nelson, C. M., & Pearson, C. A. (1991). *Integrating services for children and youth with emotional and behavioral disorders*. Reston, VA: Council for Exceptional Children.

Power, T. J. (2000). Commentary: The school psychologist as community-focused, public health professional: Emerging challenges and implications for training. *School Psychology Review, 29*, 557–559.

Power, T. J., Atkins, M. S., Osborne, M. L., & Blum, N. J. (1994). The school psychologist as manager of programming for ADHD. *School Psychology Review, 23*, 279–291.

Power, T. J., & Bartholomew, K. L. (1987). Family-school relationship patterns: An ecological assessment. *School Psychology Review, 14*, 222–229.

Power, T. J., DuPaul, G. J., Shapiro, E. S., & Parrish, J. M. (1995). Pediatric school psychology: The emergence of a subspecialty. *School Psychology Review, 24*, 244–257.

Power, T. J., Heathfield, L., McGoey, K., & Blum, N. J. (1999). Managing and preventing chronic health problems: School psychology's role. *School Psychology Review, 28*, 251–263.

Power, T. J., Shapiro, E. S., & DuPaul, G. J. (2003). Preparing leaders in child psychology for the 21st century: Linking systems of care to manage and prevent health problems. *Journal of Pediatric Psychology, 28*, 147–155.

Rickard, K. (1995). The play approach to learning in the context of families and schools: An alternative paradigm for nutrition and fitness in the 21st century. *Journal of the American Dietetic Association, 95*, 1121–1126.

Roberts, M., Carlson, C., Erickson, M., Friedman, R., LaGreca, A., Lemanek, K., Russ, S., Schroeder, C., Vargas, L., & Wohlford, P. (1998). A model for training psychologists to provide services for children and adolescents. *Professional Psychology: Research and Practice, 29*, 293–299.

Ross, C. M., & Harrison, P. L. (1997). Ability grouping. In G. G. Bear, K. M. Minke, & A. Thomas (Eds.), *Children's needs II: Development, problems, and alternatives* (pp. 457–466). Bethesda, MD: National Association of School Psychologists.

Seligman, M. E. P., & Csikszentmihalyi, M. (2000). Positive psychology. *American Psychologist, 55*, 5–14.

Shapiro, E. S. (1996). *Academic skills problems: Direct assessment and intervention*. New York: Guilford.

Shapiro, E. S., DuPaul, G. J., & Power, T. J. (1997, August). Pediatric school psychology: A new specialty in school health reform. *The Pennsylvania Psychologist Quarterly*, 20–21.

Shapiro, E. S., DuPaul, G. J., Power, T. J., Gureasko, S., & Moore, D. (2000, November). Student perspectives on pediatric school psychology. *Communique of the National Association of School Psychologists, 29*, 6–8.

Short, R. J., & Talley, R. C. (1997). Rethinking psychology in the schools: Implications of recent national policy. *American Psychologist, 52*, 234–240.

Slavin, R. E. (1990). *Cooperative learning: Theory, research, and practice*. Englewood Cliffs, NJ: Prentice-Hall.

Spirito, A., Brown, R. T., D'Angelo, E., Delameter, A., Rodrique, J., & Siegel, L. (2003). Recommendations for the training of pediatric psychologists. *Journal of Pediatric Psychology, 28*, 85–98.

Stokes, T. F., & Baer, D. M. (1977). An implicit technology of generalization. *Journal of Applied Behavior Analysis, 10*, 349–367.

Strosahl, K. (1998). Integrating behavioral health and primary care services: The primary mental health care model. In A. Blount (Ed.), *Integrated primary care* (pp. 139–166). New York: W.W. Norton.

U.S. Department of Health and Human Services. (1999). *Mental health: A report of the Surgeon General*. Rockville, MD: U.S. Department of Health and Human Services, Substance Abuse and Mental Health Administration, Center for Mental Health Services, National Institutes of Health, National Institute of Mental Health.

Walker, H., Colvin, G., & Ramsey, E. (1995). *Antisocial behavior in school: Strategies and best practices*. Pacific Grove, CA: Brooks/Cole.

Ysseldyke, J., Dawson, P., Lehr, C., Reschly, D., Reynolds, M., & Telzrow, C. (1997). *School psychology: A blueprint for training and practice II*. Bethesda, MD: National Association of School Psychologists.

4

Collaborating with Schools in the Provision of Pediatric Psychological Services

Edward S. Shapiro
Patricia H. Manz
Lehigh University

Chronic illness is not an isolated medical condition but an experience that permeates important domains of child development and functioning. Children's cognitive, emotional, or social development can be affected, resulting in difficulties with learning, peer relationships, or coping. Positive support and involvement of salient social influences, such as schools and health care systems, can be a powerful approach for providing effective interventions for children with chronic illness and their families (Brown & DuPaul, 1999). Pediatric psychologists must develop effective skills for collaborating with social systems in designing comprehensive interventions to foster resiliency and optimize development among children with chronic illness.

Schools play a pivotal role in comprehensive intervention for children with chronic illness. Fundamental experiences are provided in schools that address the unique needs of these children in important areas, including learning, social competence, and emotional adjustment. Furthermore, schools are interconnected with families and communities, offering opportunities for these systems to collaborate in providing support and intervention.

Pediatric psychologists are advantageously positioned to facilitate effective collaboration with schools that integrates family and health care systems in intervention programming for children with chronic illness. This chapter is intended to assist pediatric psychologists in school collaboration by addressing the academic needs of chronically ill children, the resources and limitations of schools, the unique competencies of pediatric psychologists and school personnel, and guidelines for effective collaboration. Directions for future practice and training are also outlined.

IMPACT OF CHRONIC ILLNESS ON CHILDREN'S ACADEMIC ACHIEVEMENT

Children who experience chronic illness have a greater likelihood of academic difficulties and underachievement than the general population of children (Sexson & Madan-Swain, 1995). Illnesses that involve the central nervous system are commonly associated with neurocognitive impairments, resulting in mild to severe learning problems. However, epidemiological studies involving children with illnesses that do not directly impact the central nervous system demonstrate a similar prevalence of academic problems (Fowler, Davenport, & Garg, 1992; Howe, Feinstein, Reiss, Molock, & Berger, 1993). In fact, predictive relationships among type of illness and degree of academic impairment have not received consistent empirical support, underscoring the social and environmental complexities that accompany the physical experience of illness and treatment (Brown & DuPaul, 1999). In addition to direct cognitive impairment, school absenteeism and emotional status of children and families are important ecological determinants of school adjustment and achievement.

Cognitive Impairment

Illnesses or treatments that involve the central nervous system threaten the normal course of cognitive development and may produce mild to severe learning difficulties in children. Some chronic illnesses are localized within the central nervous system, such as traumatic brain injury and brain tumors. Other illnesses, such as lupus and sickle cell disease, are systemic illnesses with high risks of central nervous system impairment. The central nervous system is also vulnerable to various medical treatments for many types of chronic illnesses, such as acute lymphoblastic leukemia. For example, the treatment of cancers and brain tumors can include intrathecal chemotherapy and whole brain or localized radiation, both of which alter neurocognitive functioning (Armstrong, Blumberg, & Toledano, 1999). Medications are also associated with adverse neurocognitive effects. Antiepileptic drugs, used to manage many seizure disorders, have been shown to weaken children's attention span, psychomotor speed, and visual–motor and audio–motor integration (Handler & DuPaul, 1999). Preliminary investigation of immunosuppressants, used to facilitate acceptance of organs after transplant, indicate adverse effects on children's spatial relation abilities and are associated with underachievement in reading and writing (Kennard et al., 1999).

Children's age at the onset of illness and their premorbid level of functioning are important considerations for understanding the role illness may play in their cognitive functioning. Armstrong and Horn (1995) posited that central nervous system impairment alters the course of cognitive development such that acquired competencies are often less affected than those expected in later developmental stages. Consequently, indicators of cognitive impairment are often not immediately evident; rather they emerge as children are expected to perform advanced skills (i.e., reading, arithmetic, writing).

School Absenteeism

A primary obstacle in the academic achievement of chronically ill children is absenteeism from school. Schooling for chronically ill children is frequently interrupted by hospitalizations, doctor visits, and secondary symptoms related to the illness. For example, children with cancer are absent an average of 40 days of school during the first year of treatment (Lansky, Cairns, & Zwartjes, 1983).

Interestingly, patterns of absenteeism are not consistent among children with common diagnoses, suggesting that environmental factors may be more influential than the physical symptoms associated with the illness (Cook, Schaller, & Krischer, 1985). Parents' adjustment and manner of coping with children's illness is a primary determinant in school attendance. Parent fears of infections or medical emergencies are associated with reluctance to send children to school (Worchel-Prevatt et al., 1998). These fears may cause parents to willingly allow children to miss school in response to their children's complaints of mild discomfort. Some parents may lack confidence in the school's capacity to be responsive to their children's needs. They worry that school personnel will not provide sufficient monitoring of children's health or adequate attendance to illness-related needs. In addition to their fears that attendance at school may worsen children's illness, parents may feel a sense of hopelessness about their children's future and question the benefits of regular school attendance.

Social/Emotional Difficulties

The stress of coping with chronic illness is exacerbated by invasive medical treatments, interruption of normal life experiences and routine, and changes in physical appearance and/or functioning. It is not surprising that children with chronic illness generally show greater social and emotional difficulties than the general population of children (Sexson & Madan-Swain, 1993; Schuman & LaGreca, 1999). These difficulties can impede children's adjustment to school, inhibiting their potential for academic achievement and formation of salient interpersonal relationships with peers and educators.

In comparison to the general population of children, those with chronic illness are prone to internalizing disorders, including anxiety, depression, and poor self-esteem (Lavigne & Faier-Routman, 1992; Thompson, Gustafson & Gill, 1995). Children with chronic illness are five times more likely than healthy children to experience school phobia and separation (Henning & Fritz, 1983). Children may fear separation from their families, worry about not being able to perform physically or academically, and experience more somatic symptoms than their healthy peers (Lansky, Lowman, Vata, & Gyulay, 1975), all of which can culminate into refusal to attend school. How families cope with their children's illness and fears is a primary determinant in the progression of school phobia and separation anxiety (Lansky, Lowman, Vata, & Gyulay, 1975). Parents who worry about their children's vulnerability when apart from them and are less confident that school personnel will be sufficiently vigilant and responsive may inadvertently foster school phobia and separation anxiety through their reluctance to promote regular school attendance.

Coping with change in physical appearance and/or activity level is often associated with children's anxiety about attending school and interacting with peers (Prevatt, Heffer & Lowe, 2000; Sexson & Madan-Swain, 1993). Certain illnesses and associated treatments may have unfortunate consequences such as amputation, hair loss, or facial puffiness. Restricted activity is commonly associated with illnesses, such as asthma, HIV/AIDS, and hemophilia, as a means for preventing health complications. When in school, children's poor perceptions of body image and perceived peer rejection accentuate social isolation (Sexson & Madan-Swain, 1993). Feelings of loneliness and being different are further perpetuated if children are unable to fully participate in school activities.

Although social support enhances resiliency (Wasserstein & LaGreca, 1996), chronically ill children may experience difficulty in forming and sustaining relationships with peers (Schuman & LaGreca, 1999). One obstacle in preserving a stable peer network is the extent to which these children can participate in school contexts without interruption. Peer relationships are disrupted by frequent and/or lengthy school absences. Additionally, if upon return to school children are placed in special education classes or are restricted from certain activities, they may have less opportunity to reunite with and form new friends.

Social opportunities for chronically ill children can be affected by peers' fears and misconceptions about the illness (Prevatt, Heffer, & Lowe, 2000). When uninformed about the particular illness, other children may fear that it is contagious and respond by avoiding, teasing, or rejecting chronically ill children. Additionally, some forms of chronic illness are associated with changes in personality or behaviors that impede social interactions. For example, traumatic brain injury is associated with impulsivity, disinhibition, aggression, and poor social problem solving (Andrews, Rose, & Johnson, 1998). Personality and behavioral changes as a result of chronic illness produce a reciprocal interaction effect on peer relationships. Peers are likely to neglect or reject chronically ill children because of their atypical social behaviors, and chronically ill children are likely to cope in a socially undesirable manner (i.e., aggression, persistence).

SCHOOL CAPACITY TO MEET EDUCATIONAL NEEDS OF CHILDREN WITH CHRONIC ILLNESS

The return to school can be a time of hope and return to normalcy for children with chronic illness. Moreover, the inherent resources in schools are a necessary complement to medical care for these children. Schools offer the unique benefit of psychoeducational interventions directed toward managing academic and social difficulties and promoting achievement and developmental competencies (see Power & Blom-Hoffman chapter, this volume). Ensuring reentry and adjustment to school requires careful exploration of available resources for providing supports through special and general education programs.

Provision of Special Education Services

It is well documented that many types of chronic illness result in varying degrees of cognitive and emotional impairments that interfere with children's academic achievement (Madan-Swain, Fredrick, & Wallander, 1999; Sexson & Madan-Swain, 1993). Federal legislation ensures that children with chronic illness will receive an education that is responsive to their individual needs. The Individuals with Disabilities Act (IDEA, IDEA '97) establishes an array of educational services available for children who have disabilities so that they may attain the educational goals set for all students. IDEA and its 1997 amendments provide various avenues for meeting the needs of children for whom documentation of eligibility is yielded through a multidisciplinary evaluation process. Although there are 13 special education classifications that delineate criteria for eligibility, the classification of "Other Health Impairment" is commonly applied in instances involving children with chronic illness (Worchel-Prevatt et al., 1998). However, many of these children may also have comorbid conditions that would include more common school-based diagnostic categories such as learning disabilities or social and emotional disorders (Power, DuPaul, Shapiro, & Kazak, in press). In accordance with children's needs, an appropriate balance of special education and general education services in addition to related educational services (i.e., physical, occupational, speech therapies, transportation) are identified and implemented through individual educational plans (e.g., IEPs).

The Rehabilitation Act of 1973, Section 504 (PL 93-112), mandates that organizations receiving federal funding are accountable for ensuring that individuals with disabilities are not excluded or restricted from full participation. Under this law, schools are mandated to meet the individual educational needs of children with chronic illness even if they do not qualify for special education services under IDEA. For example, this law will provide related services such as speech therapy or special transportation to enable chronically ill children to fully participate in school. Additional legislation that applies to the integration of children with chronic illness into school includes the Handicapped Children's Protection Act of 1986 (PL 99-372) and the Preventive Health Amendments of 1992 (PL 102-531). The former provides financial compensation to families who have been involved in legal disputes with school systems and the latter requires coordination among health care and school systems in preparing educators for reentry of children with chronic health conditions.

General Education Support Services

For many children with chronic illness, the extent of cognitive or emotional impairment may not warrant intensive special education programming (Sexson & Madan-Swain, 1993). However, as a result of mild impairment or school absenteeism, these children will need educational support to achieve. Many schools offer pre-referral intervention services for students in general education as a means for preventing academic failure and later referral to special education programming (Meyers & Nastasi, 1998). Typically, a team of school professionals, representing multiple disciplines (i.e., education, counseling, nursing, school psychology), will collaborate to identify student problems, set attainable goals, and implement, monitor, and evaluate interventions.

Collaborating through this team process can result in strong outcomes for reducing the need for more intensive services. For example, Kovaleski, Tucker, and Duffy (1995) found that the number of referrals to special education was substantially reduced over a 3-year period following the implementation of a program known as Instructional Support Services. Similarly, Bickel, Zigmond, and McCall (1998), in a statewide evaluation of the Pennsylvania Instructional Support Team program, found that students referred for emotional/behavior problems had a substantial decline in decisions to place these students in special education programs following the implementation of instructional support services.

There are several approaches to pre-referral intervention. One common approach is for the classroom teacher to implement interventions that are suggested by the team. Examples include incentives for participation and engagement, alternative instructional strategies, or school–home notes. If students present weaknesses in particular content areas, the intervention may consist of individual or small-group instruction with a specialist. Schools often have educators who specialize in reading or math instruction and are available to provide direct instruction to students.

Alternative models of service delivery in schools expand resources for pre-referral intervention. Consultation is a promising method of attaining the expertise of school professionals such as psychologists, counselors, or learning consultants and providing intervention services through teachers and contexts that are familiar to the child (Sheridan, Kratochwill, & Bergan, 1996). Extending the process to include family members is an innovative consultation approach that has been shown to effectively address an array of academic, social, and behavioral concerns (Sheridan, Eagle, Cowan, & Mickelson, 2001).

Paraeducators are another valuable resource for providing pre-referral services to children with academic, behavioral, and social difficulties (Dowrick et al., 2001). Paraeducators have been effectively prepared and supported to provide reading instruction (Manz & Power, 2000; Vadasy, Jenkins, Antil, Wayne, & O'Connor, 1997), implement social skill interventions (Fantuzzo, Sutton-Smith, Atkins, Meyers, Stevenson et al., 1996), and oversee behavioral interventions and classroom management systems (Manz, Power, Coniglio, & Gureasko, 2000).

Systems of Prevention

All schools have some level of prevention services in place. At a minimal level, schools will usually have a crisis management plan that includes aspects focused on the prevention of the development of crises. For example, many schools have Student Assistance Teams or their equivalent in place. These teams focus on students who are identified as at risk for significant difficulties such as those who are found to be abusing alcohol or drugs. The teams function as mechanisms to refer and connect students to appropriate resources equipped to better handle their problems. The framework is one of trying to get students help early in the development of these types of problems.

Some schools may have extensive in-school health care clinics. These programs function as primary health care providers and have been growing in interest as well as numbers over the past decade. At times, these clinics are school-based and located directly in the building. Other school health clinics are school linked and may be located in hospital or other medical care facilities near the school (Allensworth, Lawson, Nicholson, & Wyche, 1997). In both cases, these school-based health centers serve both prevention and intervention functions.

When pediatric psychologists are consulting with schools that contain clinical operations such as school-based health centers, taking advantage of their presence is paramount to successful collaboration. Indeed, these school-based clinics can offer direct opportunity for interaction with personnel who understand and know the nature of the child's illness and its potential interaction with school-based issues and can offer excellent liaison between the medical and educational treatment programs of the child.

Pediatric Psychologists Training and Working With Schools

Pediatric psychologists are well trained to offer a knowledge perspective on the psychological impact of child illness (e.g., Drotar, 1998; LaGreca, Stone, Drotar, & Maddux, 1988). Typically, the pediatric psychologist works closely with other medical professionals to facilitate and support the treatment of children who are seriously ill or have chronic health disorders. Although there has been recent interest in the role that pediatric psychology can play in the provision of services by the primary care physician (e.g., Perrin, 1998), it is more often the case that these psychologists are working within the medical setting where a child may be receiving treatment (Roberts & McNeal, 1995).

During the time that children with chronic and serious illnesses are being treated within the medical setting, they are obviously removed from their ongoing, day-to-day interactions within the school community. Although the educational needs of a child entering the early phases of his or her medical treatment for a serious illness may not be the highest priority for the child, family, or health care providers, the importance of making sure that the child's educational needs are addressed becomes an increasing concern as the treatment of the child progresses toward resolution of his or her illness (Worchel-Prevatt et al., 1998). Indeed, the importance of facilitating an effective program that is well linked to the needs of the child in his or her reintroduction to the school community following extended absence for health reasons is critical to a healthy recovery (Sexson & Madan-Swain, 1993). Further, when the child's illness involves a condition that is chronic or even life threatening, an effective return to the school environment becomes extremely critical to the well-being of the child's family and improving the long-term life outcomes of the child.

Clearly, an effective return to the school environment and/or the meeting of the educational needs of children who are under treatment for serious medical conditions warrants a high level of effective collaboration between the school and medical personnel responsible for the child's treatment. Pediatric psychologists who are working with addressing the child's psychological needs during the medical portion of his or her treatment can play a pivotal role in facilitating an understanding of the medical needs that the child will bring when he or she is in the school environment. Offering both knowledge and skill development for school staff about the course of a medical condition and its impact on the psychological development of the child can be a key component to making sure that children are successful when they return to school.

Unfortunately, typical training in pediatric psychology does not usually offer a broad enough understanding of the complexity of the school environment. For example, Roberts and Sobel (1999) in discussing the training of child clinical psychologists pointed out that training in child clinical psychology needs to consider the broad contexts in which children live their lives.

Included among these contexts are the importance of school settings. At the same time, Roberts and Sobel (1999) noted that the majority of training programs in child clinical psychology follow the model established by adult clinical psychology and often restrict the range of training for child clinical psychology graduate students to a limited number of experiences that do not cross multidisciplinary lines into schools. Forehand (1999) echoed this view in a call for training in child clinical psychology to follow an ecological model that incorporates understanding of many subareas including study of the social context in which children and adolescents live. Obviously, schools would be a key component of study.

In training of pediatric psychologists, Roberts and McNeal (1995) noted that the common characteristics of training include clinical practice usually in a health care setting; consultation to physicians and parents and some direct interventions with child patients; use of a developmental framework on diagnosis and intervention; and an orientation toward health promotion and prevention. Certainly, while pediatric psychologists are well trained in understanding, addressing, and intervening on the psychological needs of children and the impact that illness can have on development, the knowledge base of how to effectively work with the school environment regarding these needs of children with illnesses may be lacking.

What must pediatric psychologists understand about schools to successfully impact a child with chronic illness? In the next section, each of the major domains of knowledge within schools is identified and briefly discussed. In addition, the key people and factors that need to be known to effectively collaborate with schools are also described.

DOMAINS OF KNOWLEDGE WITHIN SCHOOLS

Schools are complex environments that impact many areas of a child's development. The setting and [the adults that serve as professionals within that setting] have substantial impact on the life of children. For example, cognitive, emotional, and social needs of children are clearly linked to aspects of curriculum. Basic skills such as teaching a child to read, learning basic mathematical computation, and communicating through writing are all expected to occur within the school environment. Substantial opportunity for socialization and peer interactions are also embedded into the teaching process both formally and informally. Policy decisions of schools can have drastic and long-term effects on children, especially those who may be classified as in need of special education. Indeed, being identified as a child with special needs may result in lifelong outcomes that impact what the child will be taught, the type of job he or she will be expected to have, the nature of his or her living environment as an adult, and many other aspects of his or her ability to contribute to society (Donovan & Cross, 2002).

Events and programs that occur within the school building can have long-term consequences. For example, students at high risk for school failure who may have the opportunity to be enrolled in a prevention program focused on building competency for early school success may be successful in avoiding some of the typical poor long-term outcomes for students (Conduct Problems Prevention Research Group, 1999; Walker et al., 1998). At the same time, specific traumatic school-based events such as school shootings or other crisis situations can have long-term devastating psychological impact on these students (Goldstein & Conoley, 1997). Students exposed to chronic poor school interactions with peers are likely to show development of substantial pathology at older ages (Wasserstein & La Greca, 1996). Other children who have been exposed to long-term events such as bullying can develop very intractable problems that place them at further risk for later adolescent and adult pathology (Batsche & Knoff, 1994).

Pediatric psychologists who will be consulting with school personnel need to understand the broad array of issues that impact the lives of school-age children. At the same time, it is crucial to understand that it is not the role of the pediatric psychologist to develop expertise in each of the knowledge domains required for successfully working within school settings.

Instead, the pediatric psychologist needs to understand the importance that school personnel will place on aspects of the child's development relative to his or her medical needs.

Cognitive Development and Instructional Process

Schools have a critical responsibility to focus on the cognitive and intellectual development of children. Above all other aspects of the school environment, schools must focus on the teaching and learning process. This is the number one priority of school personnel. The understanding of curriculum development, its impact on learning, and the nature of pedagogy are the roots of understanding the school environment. When the pediatric psychologist is working with schools, a full understanding of the relationship and impact of a child's illness to the learning process is critical to impacting the child's performance. The course of a child's recovery or chronicity of his or her problems and how this links to what the child is expected to be learning need to be a priority mission of collaborating with schools.

To fully understand the relationship of the learning process and the child's illness, the pediatric psychologist must have a clear grasp of the learning expectations within the school environment. How exactly does instruction occur? What adaptations in the teaching and learning process will be possible to allow the child with an illness to effectively learn the same material? What are the demands of the curriculum and how do those demands match up against the child with the illness capacity to meet these demands? These questions are the primary frame for the pediatric psychologist's effort to work effectively within the school setting.

How best to adapt instruction and what the nature of the instructional process are difficult questions to address. Schools certainly have a mandate and legal requirement to provide the adaptations needed to maximize the potential of all students, including those with chronic illnesses. At the same time, schools also have the broader responsibility to see that all of the children attending the school, especially those without illnesses, are offered opportunities to become educated citizens. Tensions can easily arise in schools between available resources, requirements, and expectations, especially when a student with specific and extensive needs, such as a child with a chronic illness, enters a system.

Accessing Systems Within Schools

To fully work collaboratively with schools, one must understand how to gain access to the variety of systems that are typically in place to work with students who have health and other types of problems. Although the strength and quality of these systems may vary from school to school, there are basic processes in place in almost every building.

Pre-referral Support. Over the past 20 years, there has been an increasing effort in schools to provide support for students who are at risk for special education programs (Safran & Safran, 1996). Pre-referral implies that the child is being offered some level of service *prior* to being referred for evaluation for special education. Conceptually, a child who reaches the stage of problem where consideration for special education services has arisen should have had ample opportunities to resolve the problem without the need for the level of services that are brought by identification as in need of special education. Children who are offered pre-referral support services are showing academic and/or behavioral problems that are predictors of the development of significant problems likely to lead to special education classification. However, it is anticipated that with attention to these problems at their earliest presence, remediation plans can successfully prevent the need for special education.

Pre-referral services are usually accessed through an existing process within the school. Given that the nature of pre-referral services are usually developed by local school districts and sometimes are specific to the school in which services are delivered, it is important to learn the specifics of the process in the school where the student attends. Teams usually include general educators, special educators, counselors, school psychologists, reading specialists, school nurses, and other critical school personnel. Often, schools designate individuals as primary members of the team with others required to attend on an as-needed basis. For example, from 1990 to 1999, Pennsylvania required all schools servicing children between Kindergarten to sixth grade to have a pre-referral process entitled Instructional Support Teams (IST). The core members of these teams included the principal or his or her designee, the referring teacher, and an individual called the Instructional Support Teacher. The instructional support teacher was an individual specially trained to provide consultative and support services for children at risk for needing special education services. In his or her capacity, the instructional support teacher worked with general educators and other professionals to facilitate the assessment as well as intervention process. Although Pennsylvania no longer legally mandates the IST process in all schools as described here, the state does require some form of pre-referral service delivery model.

The major objective of the pre-referral process is to develop, deliver, and monitor intervention strategies that may be successful in remediating a student's difficulties. If effective, the pre-referral process can reduce the need and potential stigma that coincides with the identification of students as in need of special education services.

Use of Section 504 Plans. The Rehabilitation Act of 1973 contained a provision that allows schools to develop intervention plans specific to meeting student needs without identifying these students as eligible for special education. Known as "504 Plans," these plans are outlines of needed intervention services that schools must deliver to students. Because the legal obligations of these plans are outside of the IDEA '97, the law governing the provision of students in special education programs, the opportunities to develop, prescribe, and obtain such plans are usually not as onerous as when special education services are necessary (Zirkel & Knapp, 1993). The use of 504 Plans has been particularly valuable for students whose type of disability falls outside of traditional special education categories, such as attention deficit hyperactivity disorder. Pediatric psychologists working with schools need to understand that 504 Plans can offer opportunities to prescribe specific programs that schools are obligated to deliver. At the same time, the level and frequency of using 504 Plans may vary greatly with the level of advocacy done on the child's behalf. Because school districts do not view 504 Plans as having the full force of legal protections for either the child or school, many districts do not readily agree to the development and implementation of 504 Plans and prefer, instead, to have students identified under the legal mandate of IDEA.

IDEA '97. While the details and nuances of the law are certainly beyond the scope of this chapter, it is important that pediatric psychologists recognize that the identification of a student as having special education needs is a dramatic issue in schools, something that schools and parents do not take lightly. The process for classifying children as having special education needs involves extensive evaluation, collaboration, and discussion among many school personnel as well as parents of the child. For the purpose of this chapter, only a brief overview of how the law works is provided.

Children suspected of needing special education are referred for evaluation by a Multidisciplinary Evaluation Team (MDT). By law, the evaluation must include assessment by a certified school psychologist, but the diagnostic decision as well as the assessment is a team process. The process begins with the parents' permission to evaluate their child, with full disclosure to them about the questions being raised regarding the proper educational program for their child. Educational specialists, teachers, parents, reading specialists, guidance counselors, and school nurses can all be included in the process of data collection. Once the data are collected, a diagnostic decision is rendered by the team, shared with the parent, and, if all parties involved agree, a plan for the child's educational program based on the assessment is constructed. The plan is called the Individual Educational Plan (IEP) and is essentially the contractual agreement between the school and parent for the nature of the services to be delivered to the child. Included in the plan is an identification of the child's current level of functioning, the child's strengths, specific goals within academic and behavioral areas where the child has deficits, and the needed services to provide intervention to meet the goals. The plan is evaluated on a yearly basis with a reevaluation of the appropriateness of eligibility for special education services done usually no less than every three years. The IEP also identifies where the services will be delivered to the student. Service delivery is organized on a continuum of inclusion, ranging from providing all services within the general education classroom through full residential treatment services. In schools, the nature of services usually includes some combination of services in the regular classroom and those delivered in settings where the child is removed for a period of time from the school setting.

In consulting with schools, pediatric psychologists need to be aware of the nature of the service delivery model that the school is employing. In some cases, it may become difficult to fully provide the needed services for a child with a serious health problem within the regular education setting. At other times, the resources of the school may not permit the pull-out services needed by the student to be fully employed. Again, the key element here is that the pediatric psychologist needs to understand the nature of the way schools structure such service delivery models.

Strains of School Systems

Like any institution, schools are subject to organizational dynamics. Administrative styles of principals, school directors, and superintendents can play a substantial role in the level of support that the pediatric psychologist might have in consulting with schools about the needs of a child with an illness. For example, in some school systems with high numbers of at-risk and problem students, the addition of providing services to a student with health needs may be viewed as common practice and easily accommodated. At the same time, other schools with equal levels of difficult students may view the provision of special programs for students with health needs as pushing the schools beyond their capacity. In these later cases, adversarial relationships may develop between those advocating for the needs of the student and the district. Unfortunately, such adversial relationships usually do not result in successful outcomes for the student and leave parents, nonschool professionals, and others questioning the school's willingness to work with students with special needs.

It is important for pediatric psychologists to better understand school systems and the strains that are currently present in providing services to students with various types of difficulties. Often, professionals whose primary affiliation is outside of the school environment may be viewed as not possessing a clear understanding of the nature and limitations of the school environment. As such, pediatric psychologists who recognize the culture and priorities of school personnel are likely to receive a much more positive reception in working with schools in supporting the needs of children with chronic illnesses.

Ethics and Confidentiality of Schools

A particular challenge that can often be presented when a pediatric psychologist comes to work with a school is the issue of ethics and confidentiality within schools. The issue of confidentiality is always difficult. To what extent can thc pcdiatric psychologist talk frccly about the medical needs of the student? To what extent can the school talk freely about the educational needs of the student? What are the limits of confidentiality? Are all members of the "team" that are engaged in consultation equally aware of the confidentiality requirements?

It is essential that all personnel involved in the consultation process have confidentiality agreements established early on in the process of supporting a child. A complete understanding by all parties, including parents, on what can and cannot be revealed by the pediatric psychologist to schools and vice versa needs to be determined in writing. However, it is also important for pediatric psychologists to understand that schools do not always operate under the same sets of guidelines and ethical principles that direct psychologists. Teachers come into contact with many professionals and maintaining tight confidentiality is usually difficult. As such, the pediatric psychologist needs to discuss openly with the parent and appropriate school personnel what is and is not going to be discussed about the nature of the child's illness.

LINKING WITH SCHOOL-BASED PERSONNEL

The full understanding of school environments requires extensive study and experience. Pediatric psychology training does not usually incorporate such training. Further, to provide such training would place a burden on training programs that the length and the number of competencies necessary would be outside the capacity of a normal graduate training program. As such, it is critical for pediatric psychologists to have personnel in the schools who are trained to effectively interface between the medical and educational needs of children with illnesses.

School psychologists can be important allies in linking pediatric psychologists and schools together. For example, Woodrich and Landau (1999) identified ways that school psychologists can link with primary care physicians to better service all students in schools. Specifically, they noted the importance of using school psychologists as conduits of information between pediatricians and school personnel, establishing routine opportunities for data collection that can be offered to the pediatrician that would impact their treatment of the child, and having school psychologists work in concert with pediatricians in areas of health promotion and prevention. This list can be easily extended to the links between pediatric and school psychologists.

Recently, an attempt has been made to train professionals at the doctoral level who are equipped to offer an opportunity for linkage between meeting the school and health needs of children. Power, DuPaul, Shapiro, and Parrish (1995) first described this model of training and labeled it as training in pediatric school psychology. The individuals completing such a training program would have a strong base in schools and a full understanding of the school environment but would have sufficient cross-training in pediatric and health care settings so that they could function well as a liaison in meeting the needs of children who have health problems. The details of the training model are beyond the scope of this chapter (interested readers should see Power, Shapiro, & DuPaul, 2003) but indicate a growing recognition among the school psychology community of the importance of attaining expertise that would allow an effective link between pediatric and school psychology. Although speculative, it is possible that the future of training of doctoral school psychology will incorporate such a model.

Models of Collaboration

Although the focus of collaboration between pediatric psychologists and schools has one primary objective (i.e., maximizing potential achievement and socioemotional adjustment of children with chronic illness), the process involves strategic coordination and collaboration across multiple systems. Children's development and functioning is not a product of one contextual or relational influence; rather, it emerges from mutual exchanges with individuals and environments (Bronfenbrenner, 1979). Family and school systems are most pertinent for children's cognitive and socioemotional development and academic achievement (Pianta & Walsh, 1996). For children with chronic illness, health care systems are a unique influence in the transition and adjustment to school.

In addition to being developmentally responsive, multisystemic collaboration facilitates a continuity of care for chronically ill children. Establishing effective communication among family members and key persons from school and health care facilities can ensure that information is properly communicated. Further, processes for monitoring and evaluating children's adjustment to school and achievement will benefit by combining perspectives from persons and information from school, family, and health care contexts.

The Eco-Triadic Model of educational consultation (Shields, Heron, Rubenstein, & Katz, 1995) provides a framework for guiding pediatric psychologists in conducting multisystemic collaboration for children with chronic illness. The roles and responsibilities of pediatric psychologists reflect the two major phases of collaboration. This process begins by engaging and preparing school, family, and health care systems for children's return to school. Accordingly, pediatric psychologists serve as consultants to school personnel, family members, and health care providers. They provide needed information about chronic illness and assist each system in articulating its unique perspectives and concerns about children's return and adjustment to school. In addition, pediatric psychologists facilitate collaboration among the systems. They create avenues for exchanging information and sustaining school-based interventions for children. This can entail identification of contact persons within each system, the type of information that should be shared, and a routine for meeting or dialoguing. Moreover, pediatric psychologists may need to empower and guide individual systems for collaboration. This is particularly true for families, who may feel a lack of trust or confidence in schools' and health care providers' responsiveness to children's needs.

The second phase of multisystemic collaboration aims to support children and families during the transition and ongoing adjustment to school. Pediatric psychologists provide direct services to assist families and children in coping with the emotional and social challenges associated with school reentry. Conjoint behavioral consultation (Sheridan, Kratochwill, & Bergan, 1996) is an effective avenue for addressing concerns related to children's performance in school and families' adjustment to children's return to school. Conjoint behavioral consultation involves the full participation of families, schools, and health care providers in a four-step process of identifying and analyzing problem behaviors and developing, implementing, and evaluating interventions.

Power, DuPaul, Shapiro, and Kazak (2003) also discussed a similar model of consultation that is focused on the process of effective integration of children with chronic illnesses into the full complement of services offered in the school environment. Their model notes that the consultation process involves two phases. In the first phase, it is necessary to prepare the various contexts in which the child lives—school, medical, and family—so that each of these systems of care fully understand the child's needs and concerns. Once each of the systems of care is fully prepared, the child can be integrated into the school setting. However, the consultation process at this point requires that the various systems collaborate and coordinate their efforts to facilitate the child's success. Power, DuPaul, Shapiro, and Kazak (2003) indicated that a successful model of consultation must incorporate efforts that cross over the period prior to and after a child is reintegrated into the school setting.

IMPLICATIONS FOR TRAINING AND PRACTICE

The need for pediatric psychologists to increase their knowledge, sensitivity, and skills in school collaboration raises several important unresolved issues. First, the building of family–school–health care professional partnerships is a crucial component to successfully facilitating treatment of children with chronic illness. These partnerships are precursors to any successful intervention focused on addressing the educational issues of children with chronic illness. Given that pediatric psychologists are likely to be working with schools in the area of reentry of children with chronic and serious illness as these children heal, a full understanding of the key issues in how to establish effective partnership building is critical.

Second, pediatric psychologists need to consider the long-term and longitudinal impact of efforts to support students with illnesses who are engaged in school reentry. Often, the efforts to make sure the students are successful ends once the student is settled and appears to have made the return to school with minimal adjustment problems. However, the long-term and ongoing issues with school adjustment may not be thoroughly understood by school personnel. Pediatric psychologists are in an excellent position to remain as important and key liaisons with school personnel who can continue to support the child's long-term adjustment.

Third, schools often lack sufficient knowledge and skill in the nature, course, and outcomes of many serious childhood illnesses with which pediatric psychologists are familiar. As such, the pediatric psychologist may be in an excellent position to educate school personnel about the health issues that may impede the success of the student in question. Offering opportunities to increase knowledge among many front-line school personnel such as school psychologists, teachers, and counselors will certainly provide a potential impact point for pediatric psychologists.

Fourth, pediatric psychologists need to learn more about the school culture. It may be beneficial that part of their training program engage schools and school personnel so that they can better understand the nuances of school culture that can significantly impact any attempt to consult with the school environment. As pointed out previously, at least one training program in school psychology (at Lehigh University) has attacked this issue from the perspective of training school psychologists who are focused on developing skills to better address the medical, psychological, and educational needs of children (Power, DuPaul, Shapiro, 2003).

Finally, pediatric psychologists need to learn more about effective models of consultation within school settings. Models of the consultation process have been developed that can effectively cross the barriers that commonly occur between medical and school professionals (e.g., Conjoint Behavioral Consultation, Sheridan et al., 1996); however, the application of these models within pediatric psychology training programs is as yet unknown.

CONCLUSIONS

Pediatric psychologists are well trained to facilitate the psychological and developmental growth of children with chronic illnesses. However, the problems that children with chronic illness face must include efforts to impact on all of the systems of care that impinge on the life of these children. In particular, schools play a substantial role in the daily lives of these children and offer an ideal environment in which the child's social, emotional, and cognitive functioning can be improved. Pediatric psychologists possess knowledge and skills that if brought to the school environment can be highly influential in enhancing the healthy development of children with chronic illness. Oftentimes, these efforts are focused on children who are reentering school systems after lengthy absenteeism due to the medical treatment of their illness.

For pediatric psychologists to be effective in working with schools, it is crucial that they understand the culture, priorities, and domains of concern within school settings. Recognizing and understanding that schools are in the business of teaching and learning, that they are often overburdened with demands for services, and that resources are almost always far less than what is needed is a critical component in effectively working with school systems on behalf of children with chronic illnesses.

Schools do contain a broad array of professionals that are potential sources of collaboration between pediatric psychologists and school systems. School psychologists, counselors, special educators, nurses, and other support personnel are all well trained to understand the school culture and how to effectively tap the existing school resources available for students with chronic illnesses. However, these personnel do not possess a substantial knowledge base regarding the medical and health needs that children with chronic illnesses present. Clearly, pediatric psychologists can offer a natural bridge between addressing the medical needs of children and the lack of a strong knowledge base in this area within the schools themselves.

To effectively bridge this knowledge gap, training in pediatric psychology needs to incorporate some aspects of better understanding the school environment. In addition, learning how to use specific models of consultation in working with schools should be incorporated into the training of pediatric psychology as well. Certainly, there is great opportunity for enhancing the role that pediatric psychology can play in school collaboration.

REFERENCES

Allensworth, D., Lawson, E., Nicholson, L., & Wyche, J. (Eds). (1997). *Schools & health: Our nation's investment.* Washington, DC: National Academy Press.

Andrews, T. K., Rose, F. D., & Johnson, D. A. (1998). Social and behavioral effects of traumatic brain injury in children. *Brain Injury, 12*(2), 133–138.

Armstrong, F. D., Blumberg, M. J., & Toledano, S. R. (1999). Neurobehavioral issues in childhood cancer. *School Psychology Review, 28*(2), 194–203.

Armstrong, F. D., & Horn, M. (1995). Educational issues in childhood cancer. *School Psychology Quarterly, 10,* 292–304.

Batsche, G. M., & Knoff, H. M. (1994). Bullies and their victims: Understanding a pervasive problem in the schools. *School Psychology Review, 23,* 165–174.

Bickel, W. E., Zigmond, N., & McCall, R. (1998). *Final report: Documentation and impact of Pennsylvania's instructional support team process.* Pittsburgh: PA Bureau of Special Education and University of Pittsburgh.

Bronfenbrenner, U. (1979). *The ecology of human development experiments by nature and design.* Cambridge: Harvard University Press.

Brown, R. T. (1999). *Cognitive aspects of chronic illness in children.* New York: Guilford Press.

Brown, R. T., & DuPaul, G. J. (1999). Introduction to mini-series: Promoting school success in children with chronic medical conditions. *School Psychology Review, 28*(2), 175–182.

Conduct Problems Prevention Research Group. (1999). Initial impact of the fast track prevention trial for conduct problems: I. The high-risk sample. *Journal of Consulting and Clinical Psychology, 67,* 631–647.

Cook, B. A., Schaller, K., & Krischer, J. P. (1985). School absence among children with chronic illness. *Journal of School Health, 43,* 265–267.

Donovan, S., & Cross, C. T. (Eds.) (2002). *Minority students in special and gifted education.* Washington, DC: National Academies Press.

Dowrick, P. W., Power, T. J., Manz, P. H., Ginsburg-Block, M., Leff, S. S., & Kim-Rupnow, S. (2001). Community responsiveness: Examples from under-resourced urban schools. *Journal of Prevention and Intervention in the Community, 21*(2), 35–51.

Drotar, D. (1998). Training students for careers in medical settings: A graduate program in pediatric psychology. *Professional Psychology: Research & Practice,* 29, 402–404.

Fantuzzo, J. W., Sutton-Smith, B., Atkins, M., Meyers, R., Sterenson, H., Coolahan, K., Weiss, A. D., & Manz, P. H. (1996). Community-based resilient peer treatment of withdrawn maltreated preschool children. *Journal of Clinical and Consulting Psychology, 64*(6), 1377–1386.

Forehand, R. (1999). Clinical child and developmental-clinical programs: Perhaps necessary but not sufficient? *Journal of Clinical Child Psychology, 28,* 476–481.

Fowler, M. G., Davenport, M. G., & Garg, R. (1992). School functioning of U.S. children with asthma. *Pediatrics, 90,* 939–944.

Goldstein, A. P., & Conoley, J. C. (Eds.). (1997). *School violence intervention: A practical handbook.* New York: Guilford.

Handler, M. W., & DuPaul, G. J. (1999). Pharmacological issues and iatrogenic effects on learning. In R. T. Brown (Ed.), *Cognitive aspects of chronic illness in children* (pp. 355–385). New York: Guilford Press.

Henning, J., & Fritz, G. K. (1983). School reentry in childhood cancer. *Psychosomatics, 24,* 261–269.

Howe, G. W., Feinstein, C., Reiss, D., Molock, S., & Berger, K. (1993). Adolescent adjustment to chronic physical disorders: I. Comparing neurological and non neurological conditions. *Journal of Child Psychology and Psychiatry, 14*, 1153–1171.

Individuals with Disabilities Education Act, 20 U.S.C. Sec 1400 (1990).

Individuals with Disabilities Education Act, 20 U.S.C. ch 33, Sec 1400 (1997).

Kennard, B. D., Stewart, S. M., Phelan-McAuliffe, D., Waller, D. A., Bannister, M., Fiorvani, M., & Andrews, W. S. (1999). Academic outcome in long term survivors of pediatric liver transplantation. *Journal of Developmental and Behavioral Pediatrics, 20*, 17–23.

Kovaleski, J. F., Tucker, J. A., & Duffy, J. Jr. (1995). School reform through instructional support: The Pennsylvania initiative, part I: The instructional support team (IST). NASP *Commmuniqué, 23*, 1–8.

LaGreca, A. M., Stone, W. L., Drotar, D., & Maddux, J. E. (1988). Training in pediatric psychology: Survey results and recommendations. *Journal of Pediatric Psychology, 13*, 121–139.

Lansky, S. B., Cairns, N. U., & Zwartjes, W. (1983). School attendance among children with cancer: A report from two centers. *Journal of Psychosocial Oncology, 1*, 75–82.

Lansky, S. B., Lowman, J. T., Vata, T., & Gyulay, J. (1975). School phobia in children with malignant neoplasms. *American Journal of Disabilities of Children, 129*, 42–46.

Lavigne, J. V., & Faier-Routman, J. (1992). Psychosocial adjustment to pediatric physical disorders: A meta-analytic review. *Journal of Pediatric Psychology, 17*, 133–157.

Madan-Swain, A., Fredrick, L. D., & Wallander, J. L. (1999). Returning to school after a serious illness or injury. In R. T. Brown (Ed.), *Cognitive aspects of chronic illness in children* (pp. 312–332). New York: Guilford Press.

Manz, P. H., & Power, T. J. (2000). *Successful community partnership intervention in urban schools: Enhancement and evaluation of Reading Accelerated through Community Empowerment (Reading ACE).* Poster presented at the annual meeting of National Association of School Psychologists, New Orleans, LA.

Manz, P. H., Power, T. J., Coniglio, J., & Gureasko, S. (2000, March). *Celebrating our communities' success: Lessons in establishing effective community partnership interventions in urban schools.* Workshop presented at the annual meeting of National Association of School Psychologists Convention, New Orleans, LA.

Meyers, J., & Nastasi, B. K. (1998). Primary prevention as a framework for the delivery of psychological services in the schools. In T. Gutkin & C. Reynolds (Eds.), *The handbook of school psychology* (3rd ed., pp. 764–799). New York: Wiley.

Perrin, E. C. (1998). Collaboration in pediatric primary care: A pediatrician's view. *Journal of Pediatric Psychology, 24*, 453–458.

Pianta, R. C., & Walsh, D. J. (1996). *High-risk children in schools: Constructing sustaining relationships.* New York: Routledge.

Power, T. J., DuPaul, G. J., Shapiro, E. S., & Kazak, A. E. (2003). *Promoting children's health: Integrating school, family and community.* New York: Guilford Press.

Power, T. J., DuPaul, G. J., Shapiro, E. S., & Parrish, J. M. (1995). Pediatric school psychology: The emergence of a subspecially. *School Psychology Review, 24*, 244–257.

Power, T. J., Shapiro, E. S., & DuPaul, G. J. (in press). Preparing psychologists to link the health and educational systems in managing and preventing children's health problems. *Journal of Pediatric Psychology.*

Prevatt, F. F., Heffer, R. W., & Lowe, P. A. (2000). A review of school reintegration programs for children with cancer. *Journal of School Psychology, 38*(5), 447–467.

Roberts, M. C., & McNeal, R. E. (1995). Historical and conceptual foundations of pediatric psychology. In M. C. Roberts (Ed.), *Handbook of pediatric psychology* (2nd ed.; pp. 3–18). New York: Guilford Press.

Roberts, M. C., & Sobel, A. B. (1999). Training in clinical child psychology: Doing it right. *Journal of Clinical Child Psychology, 28*, 482–489.

Safran, S. P., & Safran, J. S. (1996). Intervention assistance programs and prereferral teams: Directions for the twenty-first century. *Remedial & Special Education, 17*, 363–369.

Schuman, W. B., & LaGreca, A. M. (1999). Social correlates of chronic illness. In R. T. Brown (Ed.), *Cognitive aspects of chronic illness in children* (pp. 289–311). New York: Guilford Press.

Sexson, S. B., & Madan-Swain, A. (1993). School reentry for the child with chronic illness. *Journal of Learning Disabilities, 26*(2), 115–125.

Sexson, S. B., & Madan-Swain, A. (1995). The chronically ill child in the school. *School Psychology Quarterly, 10*, 359–368.

Sheridan, S. M., Eagle, J. W., Cowan, R. J. M., & Mickelson, W. (2001). The effects of conjoint behavioral consultation results of a 4-year investigation. *Journal of School Psychology, 39*, 361–385.

Sheridan, S. M., Kratochwill, T. R., & Bergan, J. R. (1996). *Conjoint behavioral consultation: A procedural manual.* New York: Plenum Press.

Shields, J. D., Heron, T. E., Rubenstein, C. L., & Katz, E. R. (1995). The eco-triadic model of educational consultation for students with cancer. *Education & Treatment of Children, 18*, 184–200.

Thompson, R. Jr., Gustafson, K. E., & Gil, K. M. (1995). Psychological adjustment of adolescents with cystic fibrosis or sickle cell disease and their mothers. In J. Wallander & L. Siegal (Eds.), *Advances in pediatric psychology: II. Behavioral perspectives on adolescent health* (pp. 232–247). New York: Guilford Press.

Vadasy, P. F., Jenkins, J. R., Antil, L. R., Wayne, S. K., & O'Connor, R. E. (1997). The effectiveness of one-to-one tutoring by community tutors for at-risk beginning readers. *Learning Disability Quarterly, 20*, 126–139.

Walker, H. M., Kavanagh, K., Stiller, B., Golly, A., Severson, H. H., Feil, E. G. (1998). First step to success: An early intervention approach for preventing school antisocial behavior. *Journal of Emotional & Behavioral Disorders, 6*, 66–80.

Wasserstein, S., & La Greca, A. M. (1996). Can peer support buffer against behavioral consequences of parental discord? *Journal of Clinical Child Psychology, 25*, 177–182.

Woodrich, D. L., & Landau, S. (1999). School psychologists: Strategic allies in the contemporary practice of primary care pediatrics. *Clinical Pediatrics, 38*, 597–606.

Worchel-Prevatt, F. F., Heffer, R. W., Prevatt, B. C., Miner, J., Young-Saleme, T., Horgan, D., Lopez, M., Rae, W. A., & Frankel, L. (1998). A school reentry program for chronically ill children. *Journal of School Psychology, 36*(3), 261–279.

Zirkel, P. A., & Knapp, S. (1993). Related services for students with disabilities: What educational consultants need to know. *Journal of Educational & Psychological Consultation, 4*, 137–151.

PART II: Prevention and Health Promotion

5

Prevention of Injuries: Concepts and Interventions for Pediatric Psychology in the Schools

Michael C. Roberts
Keri J. Brown
Richard E. Boles
Joanna O. Mashunkashey
University of Kansas

OVERVIEW

Injuries are bodily "damage resulting from acute exposure to physical and chemical agents" (Haddon & Baker, 1981, p. 109). In addition to the physical pain and trauma, the scope of emotional and economic burden of childhood unintentional injuries has been well documented. Unintentional injuries are the leading cause of death and disability in children and adolescents age 1 to 19 (Guyer et al., 1999), with approximately one fourth of all children receiving medical attention for an injury each year (Kogan, Overpeck, & Fingerhut, 1995; Scheidt et al., 1995). Using injury data from The National Health Interview Survey (1987 to 1994), Danseco, Miller, and Spiler (2000) found that when the costs of medical care, future lost wages, and lost quality of life were computed, unintentional injuries in childhood accounted for an estimated $347 billion dollars annually.

To a large degree, the general public continues to view childhood injuries as "accidents," that is, injury-producing events, and often the injuries themselves are considered "twists of fate" or chance factors, basically unavoidable, and thus not subject to scientific investigation. Because of their presumed unpredictability, injury events are sometimes viewed as largely unpreventable (Zins, Garcia, Tuchfarber, Clark, & Laurence, 1994). This view is unfortunate and erroneous in that scientific methods of investigation have led to a better understanding of how injuries occur and what interventions can be made to avoid injuries or mitigate the effects of injury-potential situations. Investigators within the field of injury control now widely refer to injuries as "unintentional" or "inadvertent injuries" (to distinguish from intentional acts, such as violence). The prevailing view is that behavioral and environmental factors interact resulting in an injury to individuals (Alexander & Roberts, 2002).

KEY CONCEPTS

Active–Passive Prevention

Given the variety of professions and disciplines investigating and intervening with nonintentional injuries, a corresponding number of concepts and terms are utilized that help frame the various issues and approaches. For example, injury-control professionals often distinguish between *active* and *passive prevention.* Active prevention requires an individual to take some action on his or her own behalf every time, or at least frequently, in order to receive preventive benefit. Passive prevention often involves structural modifications to the environment to make it safer. Active prevention can be illustrated by car seat belt and child safety seat use by drivers and passengers whereas passive prevention would be evidenced through airbags or automatic seat belts in cars, improved road construction, elevated crosswalks, and berms separating pedestrians from traffic. Prevention advocates emphasize passive prevention whenever feasible because it produces benefits to everybody regardless of individual action or inaction. Sometimes structural changes are not completely passive and require at least some behavioral action to attain injury prevention. For example, childproof caps on medications and poisons are effective structural modifications to keep children separated from these hazards but are only successful when caregivers replace the caps correctly after every use. Similarly, replacing batteries in smoke detectors and putting up closeable fence-like guards across stairways and around swimming pools (and closing gates) are also examples of structural interventions requiring additional behavioral actions. Clearly, however, not all hazardous situations are amenable to modification to environmental structures. Human behavior, especially in interaction with the hazards in the environment, becomes the focal point of intervention. Although structural change is often difficult to accomplish, given the political issues and financial costs involved, influencing individual human behavior similarly may require Herculean efforts.

Targets of Prevention

Another framework for conceptualizing injury prevention interventions was presented by Roberts, Elkins, and Royal (1984) in which three targets of prevention are identified: (1) the individual child, (2) the environment and institutions, and (3) the caregivers of the child. The third target might focus on the caregiver's own behavior, the caregiver's behavior on behalf of the child, and the caregiver's behavior to change the child's behavior to be safer. Peterson and Mori (1985) elaborated on this model by developing a matrix for conceptualizing interventions according to tactics, methods, targets, and contingencies (the latter was added by Tremblay & Peterson, 1999). *Tactics* are the manner in which injury prevention is presented to the *targets* of the intervention. That is, after careful analysis of other characteristics defining the hazard, the ways the intervention is formulated may include tactics of public service announcements, information or incentive campaigns, and school- or work-based programs. *Methods* include the mechanisms by which injury risk is reduced. These methods might include active or passive prevention modalities and increasing individual consumer's motivation through effective persuasion messages to take safety actions. *Targets* refer to those parts of a hazardous situation that require modification. Targets might include the behavior of individuals (adults and children), other caregivers (teachers), and policy decision makers (legislators, agency regulators). *Contingencies* are defined in this model by Tremblay and Peterson (1999) as the "extent to which there is a direct, discernable, and relatively immediate consequence for the target's cooperation with the intervention" (p. 420). The contingencies or strength of the consequences include tangible rewards for engaging in safer behavior (e.g., chances for prizes for buckling up children in car safety seats). Alternatively, punishments such as tickets, fines, or lawsuits for failure to exhibit risk-reducing behaviors or not manufacturing safe products (e.g., fines for noncompliance with regulations or standards for safety) may be the consequences.

MAJOR APPROACHES TO UNDERSTANDING INJURIES

Public Health Approach

The traditional epidemiological model for conceptualizing injuries has been the consideration of the host, agent, and vector/vehicle (environment) (Haddon, 1972). In this approach, the host is the person (child or adult) who is injured. Such characteristics may be investigated for a predictive relationship to injury as child age and gender, maternal age, parental risk-taking, or substance use (Rivara & Mueller, 1987). The agent component of this model utilizes the concept of energy transfer in which the human host receives or loses energy. For example, mechanical energy may be the agent for car collisions, gunshot, or broken glass (Robertson, 1983). Other energy transfers may include heat (resulting in burns), lack of oxidation (resulting in drowning or asphyxiation), chemical, electrical, or radiation elements (Rivara & Mueller, 1987). The vector or vehicle component of the model involves the elements in the environment that convey or allow the agent to have its negative effects in producing an injury. Haddon's model forms a matrix of the host (human), agent, and environment when crossed with the events surrounding injuries, typically organized into preevent, the event producing the injury, and postevent (Rivara & Mueller, 1987). As noted by Wilson and Baker (1987), each of these stages can be strategic times when prevention interventions might be employed: "1. preventing events that might result in injury (preevent phase control), 2. minimizing or preventing injury should an event with injury-producing potential occur (event phase control), [and] 3. decreasing the likelihood of death or permanent damage should an injury occur (postevent phase control)" (pp. 75–76). Haddon and subsequent public health professionals have articulated general strategies to reduce damage from energy transfers ranging from initially preventing the formulation of a hazard and reducing the amount of hazard created to separating the hazard and the child in time or space and using barriers to separate the hazard and child, to making the child or environment more resistant to the hazard and countering the damage done by exposure to the hazard (Wilson & Baker, 1987; Wilson, Baker, Teret, Shock, & Garbarino, 1991). These public health models have guided a considerable number of structural and legislative actions as is detailed in the section on interventions.

Psychological Approaches

In most instances, the approaches that psychologists and other social scientists have taken to understanding injury causes focus on the individual person as opposed to the public health models that focus on aggregated or population-based orientations. These approaches have been somewhat antagonistic (Roberts, 1987), but the differences may have sharpened the contributions of both. One historical approach by public health epidemiologists was the notion that some children or adults are "accident prone" because particular identifiable population groups produced more injuries (Burnham, 1996). Although an accident-prone personality is now not supported by empirical findings, previous injuries do predict greater liability for future injuries (Jaquess & Finney, 1994; Speltz, Gonzales, Sulzbacher, & Quan, 1990). There are some characteristics of children, caregivers, and environments that consistently seem to predict hazardous behavior and higher rates of injury or other behavior problems (Matheny, 1987). For example, higher risk of injuries is associated with children with hyperactive behavior (DiScala, Lescohier, Barthel, & Li, 1998; Jaquess & Finney, 1994). Similarly, higher rates of injuries have been found when parents are stressed, younger or single, unable to properly supervise, low-income earners, and live in environments with many hazards outside the caregiver's control (Wilson et al., 1991). Even with these characteristics of individual differences, all humans are at risk for injuries. Thus, some professionals have concluded that prevention efforts need to use a universal approach, while others have argued for targeting those at higher risk. Peterson, Farmer, and Mori (1987) articulated a behavioral analytic approach to understanding injury situations that they called a *process analysis*. They noted that a carefully detailed analysis of the antecedents, the characteristics of behavior responses, and the consequences of hazardous situations can be useful for increasing precision in the conceptualization of injury-risk situations. Certainly, as is shown later, behavioral interventions have been found effective for changing a variety of behaviors to become safer.

Other psychological approaches have outlined (1) a model where adolescent parenting raises risk of childhood injuries (Gulotta & Finney, 2000), (2) a socioecological model examining the human interaction with the environment that results in injuries (e.g., Garling, 1985; Valsiner & Lightfoot, 1987), and (3) cognitive models for conceptualizing perceptions of hazards and safety decision making (Coppens, 1986; Hillier & Morrongiello, 1998; Peterson, Oliver, Brazeal, & Bull, 1995).

Summary

The complexity of children's injuries suggests that no single model will elucidate all aspects adequately to frame interventions. As noted by Roberts and Brooks (1987; Brooks & Roberts, 1990), no one discipline owns the "turf" of injuries and the various approaches complement each other. Where one discipline approach satisfactorily conceptualizes some aspects of injury, it neglects others that are nicely covered by another discipline's approach.

MAJOR APPROACHES TO INTERVENTION

In this section, we outline four general ways in which interventions are designed to prevent injuries in childhood. These approaches help frame the interventions, but often the interventions themselves derive from one or more of the approaches, thus, they overlap to some degree.

Structural Change

Changes to the environment to be safer for humans to interact are articulated in the public health model. Using Haddon's model, preventive actions such as eliminating the hazard and separating the child from the hazard are encouraged. Consequently, structural changes may include such actions as building infant cribs with slats close enough together so babies' heads cannot get through (to prevent strangulation), requiring fences around swimming pools to keep children from drowning, producing childproof containers for poisons and medications, and building walkways and berms to separate pedestrians from traffic. Also as structural/design modifications in the environment, hot water heaters with temperatures preset below what would scald a child are produced, refrigerator doors are constructed so that they do not lock, which can allow a child to escape if he or she is trapped inside, and roadways are constructed to be safer with energy-absorbing structures. Similarly, playground surfaces can be built with soft materials for falls and the equipment constructed with fewer sharp and hard surfaces. In these ways, and many others suggested by Haddon's model, changes to the environment to make it less hazardous produce fewer injuries and death. Empirical support for structural changes has been demonstrated for airbags in motor vehicles (Graham, Corso, Morris, Segui-Gomez, &

Weinstein, 1998), swimming pool fences (Pearn & Nixon, 1977), childproof caps (Walton, 1982; Clarke & Walton, 1979), and less flammable children's sleepwear (McLoughlin, Clark, Stahl, & Crawford, 1977).

Legislative and Regulatory Approaches

Many structural changes have been accomplished through the passage of laws in the U.S. Congress and state legislatures. The laws are translated into regulations by agencies to enforce the implementation. For example, some of the gains to safety noted in the previous section were accomplished through the Flammable Fabric Act of 1967, Poison Prevention Packaging Act of 1970, Refrigerator Safety Act of 1982, and other federal laws. In addition to regulating the manufacture and sales of some hazardous products, legislation also places some restrictions on individual citizens' behavior to be safer and pose fewer risks for themselves and others. For example, traffic laws and regulatory devices such as speed limits, stop signs, and stop/go lights are safety oriented. Additionally, laws regarding drunk driving and seat belts/car safety seat use also improve safety through enforcement on individuals or often only with publicity (Chorba, Reinfurt, & Hulka, 1988; Roberts, 1994; Wagenaar, Maybee, & Sullivan, 1988). Gun control and bicycle helmet laws, although less frequent in states and localities, do show changes in safety behavior (Cummings, Grossman, Rivara, & Koepsell, 1997; Dannenberg, Gielen, Beilenson, Wilson, & Joffe, 1993; Thompson, Rivara, & Thompson, 1989; Webster & Starnes, 2000).

Legal approaches through regulation for safety also derive from actions of state and federal agencies for consumer product safety, health and environmental protection, and workplace safety. In the case of the Consumer Product Safety Commission (CPSC) at the federal level, while certain products are under its review, some hazardous products are not (e.g., firearms, tobacco). While the public seemingly believes that all products for sale, especially children's toys, are reviewed and approved by the CPSC, it is a relatively weak agency and has limited powers. The Commission is prevented from investigating all products pro forma but can primarily review products when problems come to its attention (e.g., with a rise in the number of injuries and death due to a particular product). Additionally, the CPSC does not regularly invoke regulations on industry so much as it attempts to persuade manufacturers and sales units to consider safety. Over the years, for example, warning labels have been applied to unsafe products as a result of CPSC action but without clear positive effects. Labels have been overlooked, misunderstood, and ignored by consumers (Christoffel & Christoffel, 1989; Langlois et al., 1991). Despite evidence that regulation on behavior of people and industry has resulted in safety, American society has historically treasured its liberties and its representative government has been wary of imposing many regulations, especially on the private business sector (Brooks & Roberts, 1990).

Educational Approaches

A wide array of efforts has been made to change the behaviors of caregivers to be safer by providing brochures and pamphlets, instructional videos and flyers, as well as other presumed information products such as refrigerator magnets, pencils, and stickers. Some of these informational materials contain warnings about hazards and suggestions for improving the child's environment. Increasingly, safety information is being made available through public service announcements on television and on the World Wide Web. Topics of these materials have included demonstrating proper storage of poisons or guns, installing smoke detectors, implementing fire safety rules, and gauging toy safety (e.g., choking hazards). Information may be distributed through schools, shopping malls, information kiosks, and health care professionals.

Physicians, especially pediatricians, have frequently distributed injury prevention information often coupled with counseling about safety actions to take to parents (Bass et al., 1993). Although results vary, empirical evaluations do not indicate strong evidence that parents change their practices following information provision through physician advice (Hansen, Wong, & Young, 1996). Media campaigns, providing information and encouragement, generally have a similar dismal set of supporting data (Zaza et al., 2001). As noted above, a major effort in the United States in recent years has been to use warning labels on hazardous consumer products in order to provide information about proper usage to parents with unclear levels of supporting evidence. Overall, there is little evidence to support educational efforts in prevention (Durlak, 1997). At best, knowledge of hazards and risks as well as preventive actions are considered basic to more intensive efforts to effect behavior change, but information alone is unlikely to make significant improvements for child safety.

Behavioral/Psychological Approaches

Because human behavior inevitably must change in order for a completely safe interaction of the human in his or her environment, psychological principles are often engaged to influence people to change their hazardous environment or their unsafe behavior (Roberts, Fanurik, & Layfield, 1987). Additionally, psychological research into cognition, for example, aids in enhancing understanding of how adults and children perceive hazards and warnings; social and health psychology research helps develop conceptualizations for motivation.

Interventions based on reward systems have proven effective in changing parent and child behaviors, for example, for using infant safety seats and seat belts (Roberts & Broadbent, 1989) and safe playing (Embry & Malfetti, 1982). More intensive interventions relying on behavioral rehearsal also demonstrated effectiveness in improving safety behavior, such as learning to respond to fire emergencies (Hillman, Jones, & Farmer, 1986), acquiring safe behaviors for children home alone after school (Peterson, 1984), and avoiding spinal cord injuries (Richards, Hendricks, & Roberts, 1991).

Summary

The variety of approaches outlined here have differing sets of outcome data indicating success or failure in changing behavior and preventing injuries. As noted by Roberts et al. (1987), no one approach alone is likely sufficient to cover all injury-producing situations. Improvements in conceptualization and implementation of some approaches (e.g., for educational strategies) may help increase effectiveness. A comprehensive method of combining various approaches seems most likely to be effective in changing environments and behaviors.

MAJOR SETTINGS FOR INJURY CONTROL EFFORTS

In the Home

Lutzker and Rice (1984) recommended an ecobehavioral approach to preventing injuries especially those due to child abuse and neglect. Specifically, the ecobehavioral tactic regards each instance of injury as stemming from multiple interactions among child characteristics, the behavioral nature of engagement between the perpetrator and child, and environmental features related to the problem within the family (Wesch & Lutzker, 1991). Project 12-Ways, an ecobehavioral program, was created to serve families who previously have been identified as at risk for child abuse and neglect. Various services are offered by Project 12-Ways, which include problem solving, parent–child training, stress reduction, job finding, home safety, and self-control training (Wesch & Lutzker, 1991). Past evaluations have shown effective change as a result of specific components of the program (see Wesch & Lutzker, 1991) and abuse rates have dropped by 25% when the project was contrasted with a comparison group. One component of Project 12-Ways targeted home safety through a treatment package of instruction and demonstration on making hazards inaccessible to children. The multi step intervention resulted in decreasing the number of hazards in the home (Tertinger, Greene, & Lutzker, 1984). A modified program also found reductions in child-accessible home hazards (Barone, Greene, & Lutzker, 1986). Although this intensive intervention was part of an overall treatment package for child abuse per se, these studies illustrate homes can be made safer.

In the Community

Several interventions toward injury prevention have been oriented to community-level changes and shown to be effective in reducing the incidence of injury. For example, the Safe Kids/Healthy Neighborhoods injury prevention program was developed to target an increasing incidence of severe injury (i.e., injuries resulting in hospitalization or death) among school-age children in Central Harlem in New York City (Davidson et al., 1994). The coalition, comprised of 26 local organizations and city agencies, sought to provide education on the prevention of injury and violence, refurbish unsafe playgrounds, engage children in supervised activities designed to engender practical skills such as carpentry and sports, and make bicycle helmets more readily available. A surveillance of injuries from hospital records demonstrated a lowering of overall injuries. In addition, a community-wide campaign was conducted in Seattle to increase the use of bicycle helmets being worn by school-age children (DiGuiseppi, Rivara, Koepsell, & Polissar, 1989; Rivara et al., 1994). The campaign consisted of print and electronic media articles, public service announcements, informational brochures, stickers, informational and motivational activities, and discount coupons to buy helmets. After the campaign, helmet use increased significantly over a 5-year period. There was also a remarkable decrease in head injuries. The above studies demonstrate that community-wide campaigns can be effective, but must be intensive and comprehensive.

Project Burn Prevention is another example of a community-based program designed to specifically reduce burn injuries via public education (McLoughlin, Vince, Lee, & Crawford, 1982). The program was comprised of three components: (1) media promotion, (2) community-initiated interventions, and (3) school-initiated interventions (MacKay & Rothman, 1982). Educational messages focused on flame, scald, contact, and electrical burns. The project aimed to teach 13 behavioral objectives related to burns (e.g., testing bath water temperature and practicing home fire drills) by offering presentations in the community and at schools. Unfortunately, among targeted adult populations, the program showed no significant effect on knowledge of burn prevention. This finding was in part due to low attendance rates within communities. More troubling was the fact that the program showed no overall reduction of incidence or severity of burn-related injuries in school-initiated interventions (MacKay & Rothman, 1982). Clearly, education-only programs show little change in behavior, a finding repeated in other preventive programs (e.g., see the section on DARE).

Pediatric Settings

Pediatricians have long been advocates for children's safety and providers of injury counseling to parents. The American Academy of Pediatrics (AAP; Committee on Injury and Poison Prevention, 1994) emphasized that "anticipatory guidance for injury prevention should be an integral part of the medical care for all infants, children, and adolescents" (p. 566). In

1983, the AAP initiated The Injury Prevention Program (TIPP), a systematic approach to provide safety counseling to parents of children. The components of TIPP include suggested safety counseling schedules for pediatricians, parent hand-outs to reinforce safety counseling, and parent-completed Framingham Safety Surveys that help identify specific areas of risk (Krassner, 1984). Some studies have indicated that injury prevention counseling efforts in the pediatric setting have had limited effectiveness (Kelly, Sein, & McCarthy, 1987; Powell, Tanz, Uyeda, Gaffney, & Sheehan, 2000). A review of the literature completed by Bass and colleagues (1993), however, indicated some areas of beneficial outcomes for children including decreased temperature settings on water heaters and increased safety belt use. In a recent effort to increase the utility of TIPP for low-income families, researchers found that using the program in combination with enhanced resident injury-prevention training (5 hours of additional safety and counseling instruction) resulted in significantly more implementation and reported family satisfaction of injury prevention counseling during pediatric visits (Gielen et al., 2001). As one example, Cushman, James, and Waclawik (1991) evaluated the effectiveness of promoting the use of bicycle helmets in school-age children during a clinic visit. The intervention consisted of giving pamphlets and provided bicycle helmet counseling for families. The physicians were encouraged to inform parents and children about the importance of wearing helmets. At a 2-week postintervention phone call, the parents were asked whether they had purchased and their children were using helmets. The differences between the control and intervention group were not significant.

In addition to prevention counseling, some pediatric offices have initiated distribution of safety devices to families (e.g., gun locks and bicycle helmets). For example, loaner programs have been developed to provide low-income families with car safety seats. Programs to provide specially designed child safety restraint systems for children and infants who have medical needs that cannot be accommodated by regular safety seats have been reported (Bull et al., 1990). One criticism regarding the provision of injury prevention services in the medical setting includes difficulties reaching adolescent patients due to the relative infrequency of adolescent visits to family physicians or pediatricians. Merenstein, Green, Fryer, and Dovey (2001) reported that few adolescents receive counseling on injury prevention issues in the medical setting.

Day Care Centers

Several programs have attempted to prevent injuries in children who are enrolled in day care centers. These studies have been successful in increasing parental compliance with the use of child safety seats in vehicles, increasing fire safety knowledge in children, and training preschool children to identify emergency situations. For example, in a reward-based intervention study by Roberts and Turner (1986), parental compliance in using child safety seats was improved. When the child arrived at the center and was in a safety seat the child received a token. If the token was a winning token they received gift certificates for pizza, movies, and so on. The use of child safety seats increased significantly and findings showed that rewards can be used to increase parental compliance. Additional studies based in day care centers have demonstrated the utility of contingent reinforcement upon increasing use of car safety seats and seat belts (Roberts & Broadbent, 1989; Roberts & Layfield, 1987). Similarly, an intervention implemented in a day care center by Christophersen and Gyulay (1981) increased child safety restraint usage by focusing on the fact that child safety restraints improve the child's behavior while in the car.

Stuy, Green, and Doll (1993) demonstrated that the effectiveness of a health education intervention program in day care centers also increased the use of child safety seats. Included were educational presentations focusing on safety habits, stickers given to the children, and newsletters addressing safety issues sent to the parents. The child care centers adapted child safety seats as policy and the staff at the centers became intensely involved. Child as well as parent safety belt use increased.

Day care centers can be used to address other safety issues that help prevent injuries in children. For example, Jones and Kazdin (1980) developed a behavioral intervention to teach children how and when to make emergency telephone calls. Through behavioral training children were taught how to communicate effectively to an operator if an emergency occurred and how to differentiate between emergency and nonemergency situations. Similarly, a study by McConnell, Leeming, and Dwyer (1996) evaluated the effectiveness of a fire safety program called Kid Safe with a group of preschool age children. Teachers utilized a standardized program over 18 weeks to implement the Kid Safe curriculum with the results showing that the treatment group made significant gains in fire safety knowledge.

Elementary Schools

A number of interventions have utilized elementary schools as the locale for improving hazardous environments and improving safety behavior.

Playground Safety. Injuries children receive on playground equipment at schools are fairly common occurrences (Boyce, Sobolewski, Sprunger, & Schaefer, 1984; Huber, Martella, Martella, & Wood, 1996). Some interventions have been made to change the hazards of the playground equipment, while others have targeted behavior on playgrounds at schools. For example, in one intervention targeting playground injuries at elementary schools, Heck, Collins, and Peterson (2001) used teaching and rewards to decrease unsafe behaviors seen on playgrounds for first, second, and third graders. The children were taught by a safety training teacher about safe and unsafe behaviors on climbers and slides. The children were then rewarded for switching from unsafe to safe behaviors on the playground equipment. Heck and colleagues found that unsafe playground behaviors on slides decreased for all grades after safety training.

Seat Belt Safety. Roberts and Fanurik (1986) applied reward procedures in two elementary schools to increase seat belt use for children arriving at school. If all of the passengers were correctly buckled, the child received a paper slip redeemable for coloring books, stickers, and bumper stickers. Seat belt use increased significantly during the reward period. In an expanded intervention, Roberts, Fanurik, and Wilson (1988) implemented a community-wide project to increase seat belt use in 25 elementary schools. Seat belt use for children and adults increased significantly. News coverage in the community televised the events and a "Buckle Up Month" was declared. Winning posters that children had colored were featured on the nightly news with innovative rewards. The results of the study suggest that community-wide intervention can increase the use of seat belts in elementary school children (see also, Roberts, Alexander, & Knapp, 1990).

Fire Safety. As noted earlier, MacKay and Rothman (1982) also implemented a community-initiated intervention, a school-initiated intervention, and a mass media campaign to reduce the amount of children's burn injuries and measure what types of interventions are most effective. The community-initiated intervention brought about a brief reduction in burn injuries. Unfortunately, the results found no evidence that the school-initiated intervention reduced burn injuries.

Cantor and Omdahl (1999) studied exposure to dramatized accidents on television programs and educated children on safety guidelines that would prevent accidents in elementary school children. The children who viewed the dramatized injury events involving water or fire also received safety guidelines following exposure. Overall, the children's perceptions of the events were significantly different depending on which video clip they saw. Thus, these results imply that media can be an effective medium to promote safety under some circumstances.

Spinal Cord Injuries. A curriculum designed to educate preschool and elementary school children about the prevention of spinal cord injuries consisted of topics such as spinal cord injury awareness, motor vehicle safety, pedestrian safety, bike safety, playground/recreational sports safety, preventing falls, weapons safety, and water safety (Richards et al., 1991). The program was implemented and evaluated with first, third, and fifth graders. The intensive curriculum of information and activities in the school classrooms resulted in an increased knowledge in how to prevent spinal cord injuries for all grades.

Home Safety Programs. A safe at home while alone program developed by Peterson (1984) was extended to implementation in elementary school (Peterson & Thiele, 1988). Using an untrained classroom teacher to deliver manualized safety skills to a small group of elementary children, nine safety modules were taught (e.g., pedestrian safety and telephone safety). The intervention used modeling, praise, group discussion, successive approximations, and group rehearsal. The results revealed that trained children demonstrated significantly more knowledge in nearly all of the nine modules when compared to a control group.

Child Sexual Abuse Programs. Although child abuse is typically conceived as intentional injury (violence) rather than nonintentional injury, the issues of safety and protection are often the same. Additionally, schools have become a major setting of prevention intervention for child sexual abuse in particular. Harvey, Forehand, Brown, and Holmes (1988) evaluated the "Good Touch-Bad Touch" sexual abuse prevention program, a behaviorally based intervention implemented in schools. The program involved 3 half-hour group sessions during 3 days, in which children were taught to make a distinction between good, bad, and sexually abusive touching. In addition, safety rules dealing with appropriate responses to hypothetical abusive situations were included as components. The delivery of these program features occurred primarily through rehearsal, modeling, social reinforcement, and instructions. The results indicated greater knowledge on good versus bad or abusive touching, safety rules related toward sexual abuse, and more skills to help deal with situations of sexual abuse (Harvey et al., 1988). These gains were sustained at 7 weeks postintervention. Still, little is known about the actual implementation of such knowledge. Whereas didactic methods of teaching child sexual abuse can serve to increase knowledge of protective behaviors, an important consistent finding in the literature suggests that behavioral-based interventions provide greater gains in behavioral outcomes measures of protection (Miller-Perrin & Wurtele, 1988). Many other sexual abuse and molestation programs have been implemented in schools, often without empirical support (Roberts, Alexander, & Fanurik, 1990).

DARE Programs. Schools largely remain one of the most typical environments for drug prevention programs. Schools are generally used to promote the most common of all programs, DARE (Drug Abuse Resistance Education). The program is usually delivered once a week for 1 hour at a time across 17 lessons. The lessons cover drug information, decision-making skills, strengthening self-esteem, and making healthy choices. By incorporating police officers and being federally funded, DARE has become very popular, despite the lack of empirical support for its effectiveness. For example, Ennett, Tobler, Ringwalt, and Flewelling (1994) conducted a meta-analysis on eight rigorous DARE evaluations and found very small effect sizes suggesting the program did very little to change behavior, although knowledge acquisition was quite high for most studies. In a more recent follow-up study, Lynam et al. (1999) examined the impact of DARE on adults who had either received the DARE program or standard drug education courses 10 years earlier. Consistent with other evaluative studies, Project DARE failed to show any significant differences with the standard drug education curriculum. In particular, DARE had little or no effect on the use of cigarettes, alcohol, marijuana, or illicit drugs, peer pressure resistance, or self-esteem.

Driver Education. Driver education programs have been present within schools for nearly half a century. The ability of those programs to actually provide beneficial outcomes, unfortunately, has been largely untested or yielded mixed results. Recently, a review of empirical literature addressed the question of whether high school students who enrolled in a driver education course actually lowered their number of crashes or violations (Vernick, Li, Ogaitis, MacKenzie, Baker, & Gielen, 1999). Overall, the results suggest that driver education had no direct impact toward lowering crashes or reducing the number of citations. In fact, students who underwent driver education were more likely to receive a license earlier and subsequently *increase* their risk of a motor vehicle crash (Vernick et al., 1999). Thus, the most ubiquitous safety education program in schools appears to have no empirical support.

School Violence. Programs designed to reduce violence among adolescents have been implemented within schools (Farrell, Meyer, & White, 2001). Responding in Peaceful and Positive Ways (RIPP) is one example of a universal violence prevention program in which the primary goal is to "increase adolescents' capacity and motivation to respond to developmental challenges in ways that facilitate social skill acquisition and acceptance of personal responsibility" (Farrell et al., 2001, p. 452). Children in the sixth grade were recruited from public middle schools. Researchers were interested in the effects of RIPP on child knowledge, behaviors, and attitudes related to nonviolence, communication, and achievement. The results showed children in the RIPP group had a significantly lower number of disciplinary violations and in-school suspensions compared to the control group (Farrell et al., 2001). In particular, RIPP was found to be most effective when the participants displayed high pretest levels of aggression.

Another program, the Piscataway Project, was initiated in response to an elementary school's high level of multicultural insensitivity, fighting, and self-segregation (Hunter, Elias, & Norris, 2001). This longitudinal experiment occurred over 3 years in which children were evaluated on a number of violent and aggressive behaviors. In addition, children's interethnic contact and social competence were assessed. Children exposed to the program had greater social competence and scored higher on measures of rule observation, sociability–leadership, and positive interethnic contacts (Hunter et al., 2001). Unfortunately, follow-up results failed to demonstrate a maintenance of the positive impact of the program. The authors concluded one reason for the diminished findings may result from the inherent difficulty of implementing such violence programs, especially with teachers who have not endorsed the program or approach.

CONCLUSIONS

Injuries constitute the single largest threat to the health of children (and to the later adult developing from childhood), far outranking contagious diseases and chronic illness in the physical and psychological impact. Pediatric psychologists have much to offer in terms of conceptualizing for better understanding of the etiologies of injuries as well as in designing, implementing, and evaluating injury prevention programs. As can be seen in the literature presented here, a number of approaches and programs have been promulgated. Far too many injury-control efforts are implemented with good intentions and too little evaluation. Not all the injury prevention programs reviewed demonstrated success in reducing risky behavior or in improving safer behavior.

Pediatric psychologists have not been involved in injury control efforts in large numbers (cf. Finney et al., 1993). At one point, the *Journal of Pediatric Psychology* conceptualized the field as including health promotion and injury prevention (Roberts, La Greca, & Harper, 1988); occasionally articles on injury topics are published demonstrating the value of contribution and involvement in this domain. Much more could be done to effectively use the skills of psychologists. Pediatric psychology in the school setting inherently involves prevention of childhood injuries because schools, teachers, and classmates play integral roles in children's lives. Several intensive programs implemented in the schools have demonstrated that this setting and key implementers can be significant sources of injury control (Richards et al., 1991; Roberts, Layfield, & Fanurik, 1991). Other programs of intervention turn out to be less effective, mostly due to a reliance only on providing information or less intensive engagements. As noted by Peterson and Roberts (1992), schools may devote

> minimal (but highly publicized) efforts to injury prevention. For example, a fire department official typically visits most elementary schools once a year and discusses fire safety, and a member of the police department often presents information on street crossing and bicycle safety. Although educators would never consider teaching arithmetic by having a mathematician work problems before the children for one hour or teaching spelling by having an English professor discuss spelling one morning in class, these didactic methods routinely serve as most schools' "safety curriculum." (p. 1041)

In order to maximally impact the occurrence of injuries in childhood, there needs to be well-integrated comprehensive approaches, implemented across settings, on the most important injury-causing behaviors and situations. While these interventions might utilize educational efforts and media coverage to lay the groundwork, more intensive intervention will be most effective emphasizing behavioral rehearsal and contingencies with continual follow-up and booster sessions. As noted by the National Committee for Injury Prevention and Control (1989)

> Because it is rare that a single intervention will significantly reduce a complex injury problem, program designers should carefully consider a mix of legislation/enforcement, education/behavior change, and engineering/technology interventions that complement each other and increase the likelihood of success. (p. 72)

Many resources are now being developed via the World Wide Web to provide easy access for school-based pediatric psychologists interested in injury prevention. The latest version of the federal report establishing health objectives for the nation, currently entitled *Healthy People 2010*, with a chapter titled "Injury and Violence Prevention," serves as a useful source for information on injury prevention (*http://web.health.gov/healthypeople/document*). The National Center for Injury Prevention and Control (of the Centers for Disease Control) recently outlined an extensive injury research agenda for investigators to prioritize research that can lead to implementation of effective strategies (*http://www.grc.com/ncipcagenda*). Finally, evaluations of interventions to improve safety have been compiled to present "evidence of effectiveness from systematic reviews" in special supplements to the *American Journal of Preventive Medicine* (e.g., for car safety seats, Zaza et al., 2001) and on the Web (*http://www.cdc.gov/ncipc/duip*). Clearly, much more effective effort needs to be made to create a safer world for children. Pediatric psychologists in the schools, with an orientation to improving the health and development of children, can play significant roles.

REFERENCES

Alexander, K., & Roberts, M. C. (2002). Unintentional injuries in childhood and adolescence: Epidemiology, assessment and management. In L. L. Hayman, M. M. Mahon, & J. R. Turner (Eds.), *Health and behavior in childhood and adolescence: Cross-disciplinary perspectives* (pp. 145–177). New York: Springer.

Barone, V. J., Greene, B. F., & Lutzker, J. R. (1986). Home safety with families being treated with child abuse and neglect. *Behavior Modification, 10*, 93–114.

Bass, J. L., Christoffel, K. K., Widome, M., Boyle, W., Scheidt, P., Stanwick, R., & Roberts, K. (1993). Childhood injury prevention counseling in primary care settings: A critical review of the literature. *Pediatrics, 92*, 544–550.

Boyce, W. T., Sobolewski, S., Sprunger, L. W., & Schaefer, C. (1984). Playground equipment injuries in a large, urban school district. *American Journal of Public Health, 74*, 984–986.

Brooks, P. H., & Roberts, M. C. (1990). Social science and the prevention of children's injuries. *Social Policy Report, 4*(1).

Bull, M. M., Stroup, K. B., Stout, J., Doll, J. P., Jones, J., & Feller, N. (1990). Establishing special needs car seat loan program. *Pediatrics, 85*, 540–547.

Burnham, J. C. (1996). Why did the infants and toddlers die? Shifts in Americans' ideas of responsibility for accidents—from blaming mom to engineering. *Journal of Social History, 29*, 817–837.

Cantor, J., & Omdahl, B. L. (1999). Children's acceptance of safety guidelines after exposure to televised dramas depicting accidents. *Western Journal of Communication, 63*, 57–71.

Chorba, T. L., Reinfurt, D., & Hulka, B. S. (1988). Efficacy of mandatory seat-belt use legislation: The North Carolina experience from 1983 through 1987. *Journal of the American Medical Association, 260*, 3593–3597.

Christoffel, T., & Christoffel, K. K. (1989). The Consumer Product Safety Commission's opposition to consumer product safety: Lessons for public health advocates. *American Journal of Public Health, 79*, 336–339.

Christophersen, E. R., & Gyulay, J. (1981). Parental compliance with car seat usage: A positive approach with long-term follow-up. *Journal of Pediatric Psychology, 6*, 301–312.

Clarke, A., & Walton, W. W. (1979). Effect of safety packaging on aspirin ingestion by children. *Pediatrics, 63*, 687–693.

Committee on Injury and Poison Prevention. (1994). Office-based counseling for injury prevention. *Pediatrics, 94*, 566–567.

Coppens, N. M. (1986). Cognitive characteristics as predictors of children's understanding of safety and prevention. *Journal of Pediatric Psychology, 11*, 189–202.

Cummings, P., Grossman, D. C., Rivara, F. P., & Koepsell, T. D. (1997). State gun safe storage laws and child mortality due to firearms. *Journal of the American Medical Association, 278*, 1084–1086.

Cushman, R., James, W., & Waclawik, H. (1991). Physicians promoting bicycle helmets for children: A randomized trial. *American Journal of Public Health, 81*, 1044–1046.

Dannenberg, A. L., Gielen, A. C., Beilenson, P. L., Wilson, M. H., & Joffe, A. (1993). Bicycle helmet laws and education campaigns: An evaluation of strategies to increase children's helmet use. *American Journal of Public Health, 83*, 667–674.

Danseco, E. R., Miller, T. R., & Spicer, R. S. (2000). Incidence and costs of 1987–1994 childhood injuries: Demographic breakdowns. *Pediatrics, 105*, e27.

Davidson, L. L., Durkin, M. S., Kuhn, L., O'Connor, P., Barlow, B., & Heagarty, M. (1994). The impact of Safe Kids/Healthy Neighborhoods Injury Prevention Program in Harlem, 1988 through 1991. *American Journal of Public Health, 84*, 580–586.

DiGuiseppi, C. G., Rivara, F. P., Koepsell, T. D., & Polissar, L. (1989). Bicycle helmet use by children: Evaluation of a community-wide helmet campaign. *Journal of the American Medical Association, 262*, 2256–2261.

DiScala, C., Lescohier, I., Barthel, M., & Li, G. (1998). Injuries to children with attention deficit hyperactivity disorder. *Pediatrics, 102*, 1415–1421.

Durlak, J. A. (1997). *Successful prevention programs for children and adolescents*. New York: Plenum.

Embry, D. D., & Malfetti, J. L. (1982). *Reducing the risk of pedestrian accidents by preschoolers by parent training and symbolic modeling for children*. Falls Church, VA: AAA Foundation for Traffic Safety.

Ennett, S. T., Tobler, N. S., Ringwalt, C. L., & Flewelling, R. L. (1994). How effective is drug abuse resistance education? A meta-analysis of Project DARE outcome evaluations. *American Journal of Public Health, 84*, 1394–1401.

Farrell, A. D., Meyer, A. L., & White, K. S. (2001). Evaluation of Responding in Peaceful and Positive Ways (RIPP): A school-based prevention program for reducing violence among urban adolescents. *Journal of Clinical Child Psychology, 30*, 451–463.

Finney, J. W., Christophersen, E. R., Friman, P. C., Kalnins, I. V., Maddux, J. E., Peterson, L., Roberts, M. C., & Wolraich, M. (1993). Society of Pediatric Psychology Task Force: Pediatric psychology and injury control. *Journal of Pediatric Psychology, 18*, 499–526.

Garling, T. (1985). General issues at the intersection of psychology and accident prevention. In T. Garling & J. Valsiner (Eds.), *Children within environments: Toward a psychology of accident prevention* (pp. 1–10). New York: Plenum.

Gielen, A. C., Wilson, M. E., McDonald, E. M., Servint, J. R., Andrews, J. S., Hwang, W., & Wang, M. (2001). Randomized trail of enhanced anticipatory guidance for injury prevention. *Archives of Pediatric and Adolescent Medicine, 155*, 42–49.

Graham, J. D., Corso, P. S., Morris, J. M., Segui-Gomez, M., & Weinstein, M. C. (1998). Evaluating the cost-effectiveness of clinical and public health measures. *Annual Review of Public Health, 19*, 125–152.

Gulotta, C. S., & Finney, J. W. (2000). Intervention models for mothers and children at risk for injuries. *Clinical Child and Family Psychology Review, 3*, 25–36.

Guyer, B., Hoyert, D. L., Martin, J. A., Ventura, M. A., MacDorman, M. F., & Stobino, D. M. (1999). Annual summary of vital statistics 1998. *Pediatrics, 104*, 1229–1246.

Haddon, W. (1972). A logical framework for categorizing highway safety phenomena and activity. *Journal of Trauma, 12*, 193–207.

Haddon, W., & Baker, S. P. (1981). Injury control. In D. Clark & B. MacMahon (Eds.), *Preventive and community medicine* (pp. 109–140). Boston: Little, Brown.

Hansen, K., Wong, D., & Young, P. C. (1996). Do the Framingham Safety Surveys improve injury prevention counseling during pediatric health supervision visits? *Journal of Pediatrics, 129*, 494–498.

Harvey, P., Forehand, R., Brown, C., & Holmes, T. (1988). The prevention of sexual abuse: Examination of the effectiveness of a program with kindergarten-age children. *Behavior Therapy, 19*, 429–435.

Healthy People 2010. (2000). Centers for Disease Control and Prevention [Online]. Available: *http://www.health.gov/healthypeople/document*.

Heck, A., Collins, J., & Peterson, L. (2001). Decreasing children's risk taking on the playground. *Journal of Applied Behavior Analysis, 24*, 349–352.

Hillier, L. M., & Morrongiello, B. A. (1998). Age and gender differences in school-age children's appraisal of injury risk. *Journal of Pediatric Psychology, 23*, 229–238.

Hillman, H. S., Jones, R. T., & Farmer, L. (1986). The acquisition and maintenance of fire emergency skills: Effects of rationale and behavioral practice. *Journal of Pediatric Psychology, 11*, 247–258.

Huber, G., Martella, N., Martella, R., & Wood, S. (1996). A survey of the frequency of accidents/injuries for preschoolers enrolled in an inner-city Head Start program. *Education and Treatment of Children, 19*, 46–54.

Hunter, L., Elias, M. J., & Norris, J. (2001). School-based violence prevention: Challenges and lessons learned from an action research project. *Journal of School Psychology, 39*, 161–175.

Jaquess, D. L., & Finney, J. W. (1994). Previous injuries and behavior problems predict children's injuries. *Journal of Pediatric Psychology, 19*, 79–89.

Jones, R. T., & Kazdin, A. E. (1980). Teaching children how and when to make emergency telephone calls. *Behavior Therapy, 11*, 509–521.

Kelly, B., Sein, C., & McCarthy, R. L. (1987). Safety education in a pediatric primary care setting. *Pediatrics, 79*, 818–824.

Kogan, M. D., Overpeck, M. D., & Fingerhut, L. A. (1995). Medically attended nonfatal injuries among preschool-age children: National estimates. *American Journal of Preventive Medicine, 11*, 99–104.

Krassner, L. (1984). TIPP usage. *Pediatrics, 74*, 976–980.

Langlois, J. A., Wallen, B. A. R., Teret, S. P., Bailey, L. A., Hershey, J. H., & Peeler, M. O. (1991). The impact of specific toy warning labels. *Journal of the American Medical Association, 265*, 2848–2950.

Lutzker, J. R., & Rice, J. M. (1984). Project 12-Ways: Measuring outcome of a large in-home service for treatment and prevention of child abuse and neglect. *Child Abuse and Neglect, 8*, 519–524.

Lynam, D. R., Milich, R., Zimmerman, R., Novak, S. P., Logan, T. K., Martin, C., Leukefeld, C., & Clayton, R. (1999). Project DARE: No effects at 10-year follow-up. *Journal of Consulting and Clinical Psychology, 67*, 590–593.

MacKay, A. M., & Rothman, K. J. (1982). The incidence and severity of burn injuries following Project Burn Prevention. *American Journal of Public Health, 72*, 248–252.

Matheny, A. P. (1987). Psychological characteristics of childhood accidents. *Journal of Social Issues, 43*, 45–60.

McConnell, C. F., Leeming, F. C., & Dwyer, W. O. (1996). Evaluation of a fire-safety training program for preschool children. *Journal of Community Psychology, 24*, 213–227.

McLoughlin, E., Vince, C. J., Lee, A. M., & Crawford, J. D. (1982). Project Burn Prevention: Outcome and implications. *American Journal of Public Health, 72*, 241–247.

McLoughlin, E., Clark, N., Stahl, K., & Crawford, J. D. (1977). One pediatric burn unit's experience with sleepwear-related injuries. *Pediatrics, 60*, 405–409.

Merenstein, D., Green, L., Fryer, G. E., & Dovey, S. (2001). Shortchanging adolescents: Room for improvement in preventive care by physicians. *Family Medicine, 33*, 120–123.

Miller-Perrin, C. L., & Wurtele, S. K. (1988). The child sexual abuse prevention movement: A critical analysis of primary and secondary approaches. *Clinical Psychology Review, 8*, 313–329.

National Committee for Injury Prevention and Control. (1989). *Injury prevention: Meeting the challenge*. New York: Oxford University Press.

Pearn, J., & Nixon, J. (1977). Prevention of childhood drowning accidents. *Medical Journal of Australia, 1*, 616–618.

Peterson, L. (1984). The "Safe-at-Home" game: Training comprehensive safety skills in latch-key children. *Behavior Modification, 8*, 474–494.

Peterson, L., Farmer, J., & Mori, L. (1987). Process analysis of injury situations: A complement to epidemiological methods. *Journal of Social Issues, 43*(2), 33–44.

Peterson, L., & Mori, L. (1985). Prevention of child injury: An overview of targets, methods, and tactics for psychologists. *Journal of Consulting and Clinical Psychology, 53*, 586–595.

Peterson, L., Oliver, K. K., Brazeal, T. J., & Bull, C. A. (1995). A developmental exploration of expectations for and beliefs about preventing bicycle collision injuries. *Journal of Pediatric Psychology, 20*, 13–22.

Peterson, L., & Roberts, M. C. (1992). Complacency, misdirection, and effective prevention of children's injuries. *American Psychologist, 47*, 1040–1044.

Peterson, L., & Thiele, C. (1988). Home safety at school. *Child & Family Behavior Therapy, 10*, 1–8.

Powell, E. C., Tanz, R. R., Uyeda, A., Gaffney, M. B., & Sheehan, K. M. (2000). Injury prevention education using pictorial information. *Pediatrics, 105*, e16.

Richards, J. S., Hendricks, C., & Roberts, M. C. (1991). Prevention of spinal cord injury: An elementary education approach. *Journal of Pediatric Psychology, 16*, 595–609.

Rivara, F. P., & Mueller, B. A. (1987). The epidemiology and causes of childhood injuries. *Journal of Social Issues, 43*(2), 13–31.

Rivara, F. P., Thompson, D. C., Thompson, R. S., Rogers, L. W., Alexander, B., Felix, D., & Bergman, A. B. (1994). The Seattle children's bicycle helmet campaign: Changes in helmet use and head injury admissions. *Pediatrics, 93*, 567–569.

Roberts, M. C. (1987). Public health and health psychology: Two cats of Kilkenny? *Professional Psychology: Research and Practice, 18*, 145–149.

Roberts, M. C. (1994). Prevention/promotion in America: Still spitting on the sidewalk. *Journal of Pediatric Psychology, 19*, 267–281.

Roberts, M. C., Alexander, K., & Fanurik, D. (1990). Evaluation of commercially available materials to prevent child sexual abuse and abduction. *American Psychologist, 45*, 782–783.

Roberts, M. C., Alexander, K., & Knapp, L. (1990). Motivating children to use seat belts: A program combining rewards and "Flash for Life." *Journal of Community Psychology, 18*, 110–119.

Roberts, M. C., & Broadbent, M. (1989). Increasing preschoolers' use of car safety devices: An effective program for day care staff. *Children's Health Care, 18*, 157–162.

Roberts, M. C., & Brooks, P. (1987). Children's injuries: Issues in prevention and public policy. *Journal of Social Issues, 43*(2), 1–12.

Roberts, M. C., Elkins, P. D., & Royal, G. P. (1984). Psychological applications to the prevention of accidents and illness. In M. C. Roberts & L. Peterson (Eds.), *Prevention of problems in childhood: Psychological research and applications* (pp. 173–199). New York: Wiley.

Roberts, M. C., & Fanurik, D. (1986). Rewarding elementary schoolchildren for their use of safety belts. *Health Psychology, 5*, 185–196.

Roberts, M. C., Fanurik, D., & Layfield, D. (1987). Behavioral approaches to prevention of childhood injuries. *Journal of Social Issues, 43*(2), 105–118.

Roberts, M. C., Fanurik, D., & Wilson, D. R. (1988). A community program to reward children's use of seat belts. *American Journal of Community Psychology, 16*, 395–407.

Roberts, M. C., La Greca, A. M., & Harper, D. C. (1988). Editorial: *Journal of Pediatric Psychology*: Another stage of development. *Journal of Pediatric Psychology, 13*, 1–5.

Roberts, M. C., & Layfield, D. A. (1987). Promoting child passenger safety: A comparison of two positive methods. *Journal of Pediatric Psychology, 12*, 257–271.

Roberts, M. C., Layfield, D. A., & Fanurik, D. (1991). Motivating children's use of car safety devices. In M. Wolraich & D. Routh (Eds.), *Advances in developmental and behavioral pediatrics* (Volume 10, pp. 61–88). Philadelphia: Jessica Kingsley Publisher.

Roberts, M. C., & Turner, D. S. (1986). Rewarding parents for their children's use of safety seats. *Journal of Pediatric Psychology, 11*, 25–36.

Robertson, L. (1983). *Injuries: Causes, control strategies, and public policy*. Lexington, MA: Lexington.

Scheidt, P. C., Harel, Y., Trumble, A. C., Jones, D. H., Overpeck, M. D., & Bijur, P. E. (1995). The epidemiology of nonfatal injuries among US children and youth. *American Journal of Public Health, 85*, 932–938.

Speltz, M., Gonzales, N., Sulzbacher, S., & Quan, L. (1990). Assessment of injury risk in young children: A preliminary study of the Injury Behavior Checklist. *Journal of Pediatric Psychology, 15*, 373–383.

Stuy, M., Green, M., & Doll, J. (1993). Child care centers: A community resource for injury prevention. *Developmental and Behavioral Pediatrics, 14*, 224–229.

Tertinger, D. A., Greene, B. F., & Lutzker, J. R. (1984). Home safety: Development and validation of one component of an ecobehavioral treatment program for abused and neglected children. *Journal of Applied Behavior Analysis, 17*, 159–174.

Thompson, R. S., Rivara, F. P., & Thompson, D. C. (1989). A case-controlled study of the effectiveness of bicycle safety helmets. *New England Journal of Medicine, 320*, 1361–1367.

Tremblay, G. C., & Peterson, L. (1999). Prevention of childhood injury: Clinical and public policy challenges. *Clinical Psychology Review, 19*, 415–434.

Valsiner, J., & Lightfoot, C. (1987). Process structure of parent-child-environment relations and the prevention of children's injuries. *Journal of Social Issues, 43*, 61–72.

Vernick, J. S., Li, G., Ogaitis, S., MacKenzie, E. J., Baker, S. P., & Gielen, A. C. (1999). Effects of high school driver education on motor vehicle crashes, violations, and licensure. *American Journal of Preventive Medicine, 16*, 40–46.

Wagenaar, A. C., Maybee, R. G., & Sullivan, K. P. (1988). Mandatory seat belt laws in eight states: A time-series evaluation. *Journal of Safety Research, 19*, 51–70.

Walton, W. W. (1982). An evaluation of the Poison Prevention Packaging Act. *Pediatrics, 69*, 363–370.

Webster, D. W., & Starnes, M. (2000). Reexamining the association between child access preventing gun laws and unintentional shooting deaths of children. *Pediatrics, 106*, 1466–1469.

Wesch, D., & Lutzker, J. R. (1991). A comprehensive 5-year evaluation of Project 12-Ways: An ecobehavioral program for treating and preventing child abuse and neglect. *Journal of Family Violence, 6*, 17–35.

Wilson, M., & Baker, S. (1987). Structural approach to injury control. *Journal of Social Issues, 43*(2), 73–86.

Wilson, M., Baker, S. P., Teret, S. P., Shock, S., & Garbarino, J. (1991). *Saving children: A guide to injury prevention.* New York: Oxford University Press.

Zaza, S., Sleet, D. A., Thompson, R. S., Sosin, D. M., Bolen, J. C., and the Task Force on Community Preventive Services. (2001). Reviews of evidence regarding interventions to increase use of child safety seats. *American Journal of Preventive Medicine, 21*, 31–43.

Zins, J. E., Garcia, V. F., Tuchfarber, B. S., Clark, K. M., & Laurence, S. C. (1994). In R. J. Simeonsson (Ed.), *Risk, resilience, & prevention: Promoting the well-being of all children* (pp. 183–201). Baltimore: Paul H. Brookes.

6

Promotion of Health Behaviors

Bernard F. Fuemmeler
National Cancer Institute

Over the past 40 years, the health of children and adolescents has been of growing concern to health educators and to those in the behavioral sciences. Today, the health of this population is more likely to be threatened by social and behavioral factors than by disease or illness. Accidental injury, homicide, and suicide are leading causes of death among youth (U.S. Department of Health and Human Services [USDHHS, 2001]). In addition, health-compromising behaviors (i.e., smoking, eating foods high in fat) that begin in childhood are associated with a number of adult health problems (e.g., cancer, heart disease, stroke). Thus, to make a significant impact on the health of the U.S. population, efforts are warranted to promote health-enhancing behaviors among children.

Health promotion in the school setting offers the most promising venue to reach the largest number of children. About 97% of children in the United States are enrolled in school (Kann et al., 1995). These children are a ready audience for implementing programs that promote health. Although there is great variation in the type of health education provided, many states (about 80%) now require that such education be provided within the school setting (Center for Disease Control and Prevention [CDC, 2000]). This chapter provides an overview of topics relevant to the promotion of health behaviors in the school setting. The first section summarizes theories employed to guide school-based programs designed to promote health. The second section outlines predominate methods used by schools to promote health. The final section describes some specific emphases of school health programs, such as promoting a healthy diet and increasing physical activity, reducing tobacco use, and teaching sun-safe behaviors. Topics more central to adolescent health risks, such as injury, suicide, substance use, and sexual activity, are presented in chapter 27 in this text.

Programs to promote healthy behaviors among children have made many advances. Yet many children have not benefited from these interventions. This chapter summarizes the current state of the extant literature on school-based health promotion and provides a direction for future research.

THEORIES OF HEALTH PROMOTION

Investigators in developmental, social, and health psychology commonly assert that children and particularly adolescents pass through a stage of experimentation during which health-compromising or health-enhancing behaviors are adopted (Jessor, 1984). A number of theories have been proposed to help outline factors that may contribute to health-compromising or health-enhancing behaviors. Many of these theories guide interventions to reduce specific types of health-compromising behaviors such as substance abuse and risky sexual behaviors. However, other domains of health promotion have benefited from the tenants of these theories. The theories reviewed in this chapter are some of the more common theories that may be applied to promotion of health within the school setting. They include the health belief model, social cognitive theory, and problem–behavior theory.

Health Belief Model

The health belief model has been termed the "grandparent" of all theoretical models in health behavior change research (Fisher & Fisher, 2000). Originally developed in the 1950s to help explain why people fail to use preventive services, the health belief model had a number of core components, including perceived severity of disease, perceived susceptibility to disease threat, and perceived benefits and costs (or barriers) to health action (Rosenstock, 1996, 1974). Later, other components such as cues to action and perceived self-efficacy were added to further the predictive power of the model (Bandura, 1986, 1997; Rosenstock, Strecher, & Becker, 1988; Strecher, Champion, & Rosenstock, 1997). Implicit in the model is the notion that socioeconomic, demographic, and environmental factors also moderate the core components of the health belief model.

A cardinal component of the health belief model postulates that health action (e.g., seeking preventive care) is determined in part by the degree to which a person believes he or she to be vulnerable to a particular disease or illness outcome. This perception of vulnerability is a function of one's perceived severity of a particular illness and perceived susceptibility to contracting that illness. For instance, the model might propose that adolescents are likely to inquire about contraceptive devices from their school nurse if they believe that they are likely to contract a sexually transmitted disease (perceived susceptibility) and that the consequences of having such a disease would significantly affect the quality of their life (perceived severity).

The health belief model also suggests that a person's perceptions of benefits and barriers or costs of taking a particular course of action influence health-enhancing behaviors. The degree to which the belief that taking a particular health action will lead to a better health outcome or more socially desirable result contributes to the likelihood that adolescents will engage in the health-enhancing behavior. Further, perceived barriers associated with engaging in a behavior influence the likelihood of engaging in a particular behavior. Examples of barriers may include monetary costs, time constraints, physical costs, or social costs such as peer disapproval. The health belief model assumes a behavioral economic approach. This approach suggests that if the benefits are greater than the costs of engaging in a behavior, then the youngster is more likely to take action; or, visa versa, if the costs outweigh the benefits the youngster is not likely to engage in the health behavior. For instance, adolescents may decide not to seek information about contraception from the school nurse if they believe that the information provided would be unlikely to reduce chances of contracting a sexually transmitted disease and that inquiring about contraceptive devices may be stigmatizing.

Within the health belief model, perceived self-efficacy and cues to action also have been recently incorporated. Self-efficacy refers to the belief that one is capable of engaging in the preventive behaviors necessary to avert a negative health outcome (Bandura, 1994; Fisher &

Fisher, 2000). For example, this may refer to an adolescent's ability to negotiate with peers about refusing tobacco or correctly using contraceptive devices. Cues to action are events that may trigger the adoption of a health-enhancing behavior (Kohler, Grimley, & Reynolds, 1999). For instance, an adolescent may decide to stop smoking after learning an uncle has been diagnosed with lung cancer.

Although the health belief model has been examined over the past 50 years, empirical support has been equivocal (Fisher & Fisher, 2000). A recent meta-analytic review of studies on adult health practices that have examined the contribution of the health belief model components (susceptibility, severity, benefits, and barriers) found that these components only accounted for a modest proportion of variance in health behavior outcome (Harrison, Muller, Green, 1992). One critique has been that the health belief model simply lists constructs that may be associated with a health action or practice but fails to describe how and if these constructs overlap or are integrated (Fisher & Fisher, 2000; Wallston & Wallston, 1984). As a result, the model offers a better description of the conditions that lead a person to inquire about health services (i.e., sign up for physical education classes), but it fails to inform investigators about the types of intervention strategies needed to increase a particular health-promoting behavior (e.g., strategies to increase exercise time, eating a low-fat diet) (Fisher & Fisher, 2000).

The Social Cognitive Theory

The social cognitive theory (previously the social learning theory) holds that social-environmental contingencies, personal cognitive capabilities, and behavioral skills are linked and interact (Bandura 1977, 1986). As applied to the promotion of health behaviors, interventions target each of these components to influence the adoption of a new health-enhancing behavior (Perry, Story, & Lytle, 1997). Specifically, Bandura (1997) recommended four components for programs to promote health behaviors: an informational component to increase knowledge, a component to teach self-regulatory skills, a component to increase self-efficacy in self-regulatory skills, and a component to increase social support for behavior change.

With regard to the information component, the type of information to increase knowledge and facilitate motivation is critical. Information that is understandable, personally and culturally relevant, and increases one's knowledge about the particular behaviors associated with poor health outcome is more helpful than general health information (e.g., prevalence or etiology of a particular disease) (Fisher & Fisher, 2000). Teaching self-regulatory skills is also an important component. Increasing self-regulatory skills may involve recognizing cues or triggers associated with health-compromising behaviors (e.g., cues associated with overeating), developing cognitive strategies (e.g., reminding oneself of the benefits of maintaining a healthy weight), and increasing behavioral management skills (e.g., providing self-incentives or rewards for following through with one's weight management goal). Teaching self-regulatory skills could be accomplished by providing social models who themselves are successful at engaging in healthy behaviors or teaching students to negotiate with others who tempt them to revert to old behaviors. Increasing self-efficacy about the ability to apply these skills in everyday life can solidify these skills. Teaching self-efficacy may involve having children rehearse or practice the behaviors that lead to the ability to practice health-promoting behaviors (e.g., how to refuse peer pressure to smoke cigarettes). Finally, as new health-promoting behaviors begin to become established, children will need to recognize the social cues and social pressure that may lead them to revert to health-compromising behaviors. Also, identifying social systems that are supportive of health enhancing behaviors may prove beneficial.

Components of the social cognitive theory have been widely applied and tested among community- and school-based interventions designed to promote health behaviors in children and adolescents (Botvin, Eng, & Williams, 1980; Perry, Kelder, & Klepp, 1994; Perry,

Killen, Telch, Slinkard, & Danaher, 1980). An extensive body of research has documented that self-efficacy is an important mediator of health behavior (e.g., Colleti, Supnick, & Payne, 1985; Condiotte & Lichtestein, 1981; Holman & Lorig, 1992; Strecher, DeVellis, Becker, & Rosenstock, 1986; Wulfert & Wan, 1993). Thus, although the model itself is difficult to test (Fisher & Fisher, 2000), empirical support for components of the model and the usefulness of the model in designing health promotion programs is well documented. A critique of this theory is that it does not offer a method of surveying the targeted population needs and norms and assumes the homogeneity of various populations (Fisher & Fisher, 2000).

The Problem-Behavior Theory

Jessor and Jessor (1977) first developed the problem-behavior theory to guide the study of deviant behaviors among urban city youth. Since that time this model has been applied to the study of problem behaviors that ultimately affect child and adolescent health (Jessor, 1984). One major objective of the problem-behavior theory is to determine how certain sets of behaviors can function as risk or protective factors associated with health outcomes (Jessor, 1992). The model holds that health-compromising outcomes, such as lowered fitness, depression and suicide, or disease and illness, result from three major systems: the personality system, the perceived environment system, and the behavior system. Personality systems focus on those personal characteristics (e.g., low self-esteem) that place individuals at risk for health-compromising behaviors. The perceived environment system includes family, peer, and other social influences (e.g., low peer involvement, estrangement from parents) that may increase proneness to poor health outcome. Finally, the behavior system includes behaviors that are either rebellious (e.g., breaking rules) or nonconventional (e.g., lack of involvement with school or adult-directed activities), which can also be related to health-compromising outcomes.

Several investigations have demonstrated that the variables associated with these various systems of personality, perceived environment, and behavior can be useful in predicting health-compromising outcomes. Studies have examined variables as they relate to accidental and intentional injury (Sussman, Dent, Stacy, Burton, & Flay, 1994), adolescent drinking (Costa, Jessor, & Turbin, in press), risky driving (Jessor, 1987), tobacco use (Sussman et al., 1993), sexual promiscuity (Donovan & Jessor, 1985), and overall poor health practices (Sussman, Dent, Stacy, Burton, & Flay, 1995). Intervention studies, such as school-based tobacco prevention programs, have been based on the problem-behavior theory (Sussman, Dent, Burton, Stacy, & Flay, 1995). Jessor (1984) argued that because multiple systems (environment, personality, and behavior) can influence health risk, interventions designed to prevent disease or promote health-enhancing behaviors should not be limited to changing behavior alone but should also consider methods to modify other ways personality and environment influence health outcomes of children and adolescents. One critique of the problem-behavior theory is that the theory outlines factors (e.g., risk taking, being rebellious, using drugs) that are more closely linked to deviant types of health-compromising behaviors (drug use, reckless driving). However, health behaviors, such as regular exercise and eating a healthy diet, may not be examples associated with rebelliousness or risk taking. Thus, the model needs expansion to include other factors associated with these types of health-promoting behaviors (e.g., diet, exercise) (Jessor, 1997).

METHODS OF PROMOTING HEALTH IN SCHOOL SETTINGS

Promotion of health in the school setting is accomplished by various means, including the application of intervention research, comprehensive school health programs, and school-based health clinic delivery of health care (Reynolds et al., 1999). Before the 1980s, much of the health promotion efforts in schools involved a health education curriculum administered by teachers (Lynagh, Schofield, & Sanson-Fisher, 1997). However, in the absence of theoretically based curriculum, many of these programs failed to produce changes in health behavior (Green & Lewis, 1986; Thompson, 1978). Since then a greater emphasis has been applied to the development of theoretically driven intervention programs with demonstrated empirical support.

Curriculum-Based Interventions

Successful school-based interventions often include one or more of the following: theoretically grounded curriculum, engaging social systems (e.g., parent and peers), and/or efforts directed at changing community or environmental norms (Reynolds et al., 1999). As mentioned above, several behavioral health promotion theories can be used to guide curriculum development by emphasizing various components influencing behavior change. Curriculum components could include activities that provide accurate information about the consequences of health-compromising behaviors, efforts to change attitudes, efforts to increase self-efficacy, behavioral skill building, goal setting, and self-monitoring. In development of theoretically driven curriculum, investigators have emphasized the importance of conducting efficacy research in the school setting (e.g., evaluation of a program implemented by qualified and trained personnel) prior to conducting effectiveness trials in other settings (e.g., evaluating a program's success in "real-world" situations) (Flay, 1986).

To increase the scope of change or the likelihood that behaviors learned through a school-based curriculum may generalize outside of the classroom, investigators have also suggested that intervention programs targeting parents and other family members may also be necessary. Targeting parents to promote children's health has been shown to be successful when paired with a school curriculum (Luepker et al., 1996; Wojitowicz, Peveler, Eddy, Waggle, & Fitzhugh, 1992) as well as when conducted independently (Perry et al., 1988, Perry, Klepp, & Sillers, 1989).

Efforts directed at changing community and environmental norms also have been used in conjunction with curriculum-based intervention (e.g., Flay et al., 1995; Flynn, Worden, Secker-Walker, & Badger, 1992). Such efforts are directed at modifying school environments to be more supportive of health-enhancing behaviors and may come in the form of community-wide education and mass media campaigns. Fewer studies have fully evaluated this method of school-based health promotion. However, preliminary evidence has demonstrated the efficacy of such an approach in an effort to reduce tobacco use (Flynn et al., 1992) and increase seat belt use (Wojitowicz et al., 1992).

Comprehensive School Health Education

Recognition that health promotion efforts in the school setting must consider larger systems of influence such as the environment and community has resulted in the development of guidelines and suggestions from national and international organizations (American Association of School Administrators, 1990; World Health Organization, 1986). Comprehensive school health education or the health-promoting school are terms that recognize this stance (Allensworth & Kolbe, 1987; St. Leger, 1999). Advocates for comprehensive school health education suggest that in addition to developing health curriculum, school-based health services, and health-enhancing environments, comprehensive programs also need to include the development of health policy, community partnerships, providing healthy food services, offering counseling, providing physical education, and offering health promotion for staff and faculty (Allensworth & Kolbe, 1987).

Recently, the CDC has created guidelines for school health promotion and education with identified target areas. Although the guidelines are specific for each area of health promotion (e.g., tobacco, diet, physical activity), they share some common themes: developing school health policy and environmental changes (e.g., tobacco-free school, safe areas for physical activity); providing health curriculum and education to students; providing teachers and staff with training in health promotion; coordinating efforts with other components of the school program (e.g., food services, school health clinic); linking the health promotion message with families and communities; and evaluating the health program. A recent survey to assess school health programs at state, district, school, and classroom levels has found that many schools do not yet meet some of the guidelines as set forth by the CDC. Although upwards of 70% of states, districts, and schools require health promotion in physical activity, diet, and tobacco use, less than 10% of schools actually provide daily physical education throughout the school year (Burgeson, Wechsler, Brener, Young, & Spain, 2001); 75% to 98% of secondary schools have vending machines that sell high-calorie drinks, salty foods, and baked goods high in fat (Wechsler, Brener, Kuester, & Miller, 2001); only 45% of schools have tobacco-free environments that meet CDC standards (Small et al., 2001); and 29% of schools offer health education programs to families (Brener, Dittus, & Hayes, 2001). Greater efforts are needed that integrate health education and promotion programs with school policy and the community.

Efforts have been made and some programs have come close to providing a comprehensive school health program. Targets of comprehensive school health programs have included tobacco prevention (Perry et al., 1992), cardiovascular fitness (Perry et al., 1990), and programs to reduce obesity (Angelico et al., 1991), to name a few. However, outcome evaluation for comprehensive school health programs has been challenging (St. Leger, 1999). One of the major challenges has been that prevention and health promotion programs cannot be demonstrated to affect morbidity and mortality rates of health-related disease (i.e., cardiovascular disease, cancer) until much later in adulthood. Another limitation of some of these programs is that they fail to provide health promotion components for improving the health of teacher and staff, nor do they adequately emphasize the importance of developing a school policy (St. Leger, 1999). Further, these programs can require substantial state funding to be developed and implemented (Reynolds et al., 1999).

School-Based Health Clinics

Health clinics in the school setting are another venue by which the health of children and adolescents can be addressed. Although the school-based clinic was initially founded to address communicable diseases among low-income students (Reynolds et al., 1999), it's scope has broadened to address and serve larger public health–related problems among children and adolescents (e.g., substance abuse, sexually transmitted disease, psychological and emotional problems) (Dryfoos, 1994; USDHHS, 1991). The school health clinic often provides primary preventive health care and the initial treatment for injury and illness (e.g., administration of first aid, medication, health screenings, and case management of chronic illness) (Schlitt, Ricket, Montgomery, & Lear, 1994). The school health clinic may also be the first line of assessment of child abuse and children's mental health (Schlitt et al., 1994; Taylor & Adelman, 1996). The school-based clinic may also serve the health needs of the community near the school. For example, one survey found that school-based services provided 71% to 80% of medical services among 173 urban health departments (Bullerdiek, Simpson, & Peck, 1995). In addition, the school-based health clinic is often one of few institutions that provides routine medical care for children from low-income backgrounds who otherwise may lack health care coverage and access to services (U.S. Congress Office of Technology Assessment, 1994).

The benefits that school-based clinics can have on children's health and well-being are apparent. Investigators have found that the school-based health clinic can have a positive impact on improving academic performance and reducing absentee rates (McCord, Klein, Foy, & Feathergill, 1993) as well as lead to declines in the use of emergency room utilization for primary health care (Dryfoos, Brindis, & Kaplan, 1996). However, evidence demonstrating the degree to which school-based clinics have an impact on overall health status and reduction of health-compromising behaviors among students remains tentative (Kisker & Brown, 1996). For example, school-based clinics may offer some information on reproductive health; however, their presence is not likely to delay onset of intercourse or encourage consistent contraceptive use. This in part may be because of the controversy surrounding the role of the school-based clinic as a primary provider of contraceptive services and condom distribution.

SCHOOL-BASED HEALTH PROMOTION PROGRAMS

Empirical investigations of school-based programs to promote health behaviors have typically involved the evaluation of a curriculum-based intervention. Depending on the targeted health behavior, the curriculum may involve several different components. Many of these curricula share commonalties, for example, providing information about the health risks of certain behaviors; skills training in resisting peer pressure to engage in health-compromising behaviors; raising awareness of media influences; providing accurate information about the prevalence of certain health behaviors; providing positive role models; and setting behavioral goals. In addition to implementing a school-based curriculum, programs also have included broader systems by providing health education to parents, families, and the community. Although less common are health promotion programs that have the objective of changing or addressing school policy. The following section reviews school-based health promotion programs that have targeted diet and physical activity, tobacco use, and solar protection.

Diet and Physical Activity

Prevalence

Poor diet and physical inactivity are major behavioral contributors to the leading causes of death among adults older than 25 years (i.e., cardiovascular disease, strokes, and cancer) (CDC, 2000). It is estimated that these behaviors are associated with approximately 300,000 deaths each year and are second only to tobacco use as the major behavioral correlates of adult life-threatening disease (McGinnis & Foege, 1993). This is of particular concern because the dietary patterns and physical activity of childhood carry over into the adolescent and adult years (Perry et al., 1997). Likewise, physiological risk factors for cardiovascular disease and stroke, such as blood pressure, serum lipids, and lipoprotein as assessed among children, have been shown to predict adult values (Laskarezewski et al., 1979; Lauer & Clark, 1989; Lauer, Lee, & Clarke, 1988; Orchard, Donahue, Kuller, Hodge, Dash, 1983; Porkka, Viikari, & Akerblom, 1991). Thus, healthy dietary practices and regular exercise habits developed during childhood may ultimately have an impact on the degree of morbidity, suffering, and health care costs associated with adult life-threatening diseases.

With regard to dietary practices and nutritional intake, the major concern for children and adolescents is an excessive consumption of fat and sodium and insufficient intake of fruits, vegetables, and fiber. The average intake of fat (33% to 34%) and saturated fat (12%) consumed among youth exceeds the daily recommendations of 30% of calories from fat and less than 10% from saturated fat (Lewis, Crane, Moor, & Hubbard, 1994). National surveys have found that a majority of adolescent males (90%) consume more fat than the 30% recommendation (Kennedy & Goldberg, 1995). African American youth, compared to Hispanic and Caucasian youth, consume more calories from fat and are more likely to be overweight (CDC, 2000). Not only are diets of youth high in fat, they also lack fiber from fruits and vegetables. In the recent Youth Risk Behavior Surveillance study, 76% of students consumed less than the daily recommended five servings of fruits and vegetables (CDC, 2000). Also of growing concern are the unsafe weight loss methods and lack of calcium intake among young females (CDC, 2000; Kennedy & Goldberg, 1995).

In addition to poor dietary habits, findings have revealed that children's physical activity declines steadily as they approach late adolescence and young adulthood. It is estimated that about two thirds of students engage in vigorous physical activity on three or more occasions during the week, with females being less likely than males and students of racial and ethnic minority groups being less likely than Caucasians to engage in physical activity (CDC, 2000).

As a result of poor dietary habits and physical inactivity, children's risk of becoming overweight has increased. Ten percent of students have a Body Mass Index equal to or greater than the 95th percentile (Troiano & Flegal, 1998; CDC, 2000). Sixteen percent of students are at risk for becoming overweight, with males at greater risk than females and students (especially females) of racial and ethnic minority groups being at greater risk than Caucasians (CDC, 2000).

Interventions

Until relatively recently, interventions to change diet and physical activity have relied heavily on information-based curriculum. The consensus among health educators and the few outcome evaluations that have been conducted on such programs suggest that these interventions can be effective at increasing knowledge of facts related to diet and exercise but are unsuccessful at influencing the adoption of healthy behaviors (Perry et al., 1997). More recent interventions have merged information-based curriculum with the science of behavior change (i.e., use of modeling, skill building, reinforcement, etc.) and have found greater success.

Some of the larger empirically validated programs have included three main arms: a classroom-based curriculum, linkage with the community, and efforts to reach parents. Other facets have included informational media exposure and efforts to change school policy. One such program was the Know Your Body (KYB) program. This program was performed with the goal of reducing risk factors for adult onset disease by addressing tobacco use, dietary habits, and physical fitness among students in fourth through ninth grades (Walter, 1989; Walter & Wynder, 1989). The KYB program included a school-based curriculum delivered by classroom teachers. The program also involved a parent education component. The program was delivered 2 hours weekly throughout the school year and addressed knowledge, health beliefs, and decision-making skills to address social influence. The program was conducted across 15 schools and included nearly 1,000 students. Outcome analysis revealed intervention effects for health knowledge, dietary behaviors, blood cholesterol, and obesity (Walter, Hofman, Vaughan, & Wynder, 1988; Walter & Wynder, 1989).

Another mulitsite and multifaceted prevention program was the Class of 1989 Study (Perry et al., 1989). Similar to the KYB study, this program focused on reducing cardiovascular risk-factors by encouraging healthy eating, physical activity, and preventing tobacco use. However, unlike the KYB study, students in the Class of 1989 study and their families were exposed to a larger community-based health promotion program (Minnesota Heart Health Program) that involved educational campaigns to increase awareness of cardiovascular disease and prevention (Blackburn et al., 1984). The community interventions included such strategies as risk-factor screenings, media education, and restaurant and grocery store programs on food labeling. The health curriculum included a series of sessions delivered for each progressive school year starting at the sixth grade and ending at the tenth grade. Students in the program completed follow-up evaluations during the twelfth grade. Each year the curriculum emphasized developmentally appropriate messages regarding health-enhancing behaviors such as eating a balanced diet, tobacco and alcohol prevention, and physical activity. The components of the curriculum included skills training in resisting peer pressure to engage in health-compromising behaviors, providing positive role models, and goal setting. Investigators found that students who received the school-based and community health promotion programs reported healthier food choices than students in reference communities who did not receive such programs (Kelder, Perry, Lytle, & Kelp, 1995). In addition, physical activity levels were higher for female students who received the program than for those in the comparison communities (Kelder, Perry, & Klepp, 1993).

A study specifically targeting fruit, juice, and vegetable intake is The Gimme 5 Study (Barnowski et al., 2000). Participants in this investigation were 1,253 children in the fourth and fifth grade from 16 schools. Guided by the social cognitive theory (Bandura, 1977, 1986), the curriculum included skill building and behavioral interventions, such as goal setting, teaching problem solving for nonattainment, demonstrating peer support for healthy eating, and teaching children to ask for more fruits and vegetables at home. In addition, the intervention program included a weekly newsletter, a video with positive role models, and two family nights at a nearby grocery store that involved food storage and preparation tips. Findings revealed that children in the intervention reported increased consumption of vegetables, asking behaviors, and dietary knowledge.

One benchmark study and one of the largest randomized controlled school-based health promotion interventions was the Child and Adolescent Trial for Cardiovascular Health (CATCH) (Luepker et al., 1996; Perry, et al., 1992; Perry et al., 1990). This investigation included the participation of 5,100 children of diverse racial and ethnic backgrounds from 96 (56 intervention and 40 comparison) schools across 4 states. The intervention was based upon social cognitive theory (Bandura, 1977, 1986) as well as other behavioral change principles. The goal of the CATCH program was to reduce cardiovascular risk factors, through behaviors such as eating a low-fat diet, physical activity, and tobacco refusal, among children in the third, fourth, and fifth grades. The intervention included methods for modifying the school environment (e.g., recommendations for school-based food services to reduce fat and sodium, recommendations for physical education to increase moderate and vigorous physical activity), a 12–16 session classroom curriculum, and recruitment of family involvement (Perry et al., 1997). Data revealed that schools receiving the intervention, compared to those in the control group, had significantly reduced the dietary fat in school-based food services (Osganian et al., 1996) and demonstrated a significant change in children's physical activity level during their physical education classes (Luepker et al., 1996; McKenzie et al., 1996). This corresponded with students' self-reports, as students in the intervention group reported a greater decrease in the amount of dietary fat they consumed and reported engaging in more minutes of vigorous physical activity per day (McKenzie et al., 1996). Changes in psychosocial variables were also observed. Students in the intervention group reported a greater intention to change their diets, possessed more knowledge about diet, and perceived having greater social support for making healthy dietary changes (Edmundson et al., 1994). Among students in the intervention group, no significant changes in physiological risk factors were found (Luepker et al., 1996; Webber et al., 1996). Some of the limitations of the CATCH program included the lack of longitudinal follow-up data and the failure to describe methods of partnering with the broader community outside the school system (Perry et al., 1997).

Tobacco Use

Prevalence

Tobacco use, and in particular cigarette smoking, has been implicated in a number of health-related problems, such as heart disease, stroke, chronic lung disease, and cancer. It is estimated that every day about 3,000 children and adolescents take up smoking on a daily basis (Giovino et al., 1995); and on a yearly basis about 390,000 people will die each year from smoking-related illness (CDC, 1996). Like dietary habits and physical activity, tobacco use tends to track from childhood into adulthood, with nearly half of those who begin smoking as youth continuing for 16 to 20 years (Pierce & Gilpin, 1996). Decreasing tobacco use, especially among children and adolescents, will undoubtedly have a tremendous impact on the cost of health care and quality of life of many adults in the United States.

In the recent Youth Risk Behavior Surveillance report, a national survey of high school students, investigators found that 70% of students tried smoking cigarettes, one fourth reported a period of time in their lives in which they smoked on a daily basis, over one third reported smoking more than one cigarette within 30 days of the survey (i.e., current use), and nearly one fifth reported smoking more than 20 cigarettes within 30 days of the survey (i.e., current frequent use). Students who identified themselves as Caucasian or Hispanic were more likely to report current use of cigarettes (CDC, 2000). However, Caucasian students were more likely than Hispanic or African Americans to report current frequent use of cigarettes. From 1991 to 1999, investigators found a significant increase in frequent cigarette use among youth (CDC, 2000).

Interventions

A long history of investigations on the risk factors associated with tobacco use has led to the development of a number of school-based programs designed to prevent tobacco use. Several investigations have concluded that young people who use cigarettes tend to be from lower socioeconomic backgrounds, are more rebellious, have greater perceived stress, have lower self-esteem, and use other types of substances (Sussman, Dent, Burton et al., 1995). In addition, social modeling and influence strongly predict tobacco use among youth (USDHHS, 1994). Youth who smoke often have family and friends who use tobacco, lack self-efficacy to resist pressures by peers to smoke, and have misconceptions about the prevalence of tobacco use among their family and friends (Sussman, Dent, Burton et al., 1995; USDHHS, 1994).

Two programs that have produced large reductions in tobacco prevalence use in the shorter term include Project Towards No Tobacco Use (Project TNT) and the Know Your Body program (described above). Project TNT was designed specifically to reduce tobacco use among youth and was delivered over 10 sessions by trained health educators (Sussman et al., 1993; Sussman, Dent, Burton et al., 1995). The curriculum included education about the effects of smoking, social skills training to help students refuse tobacco, and methods to avoid the pressures to use tobacco (e.g., awareness of media influence, peer and family influence, correction of exaggerated notions of prevalence of tobacco use). Project TNT included 6,716 seventh graders from 48 schools in 27 school districts. Data revealed that students who received the curriculum were less likely to smoke than students who did not go through the program. Specifically, students who received the curriculum reported a significantly lower increase in weekly smoking than students in the control group. This lower increase in smoking was observed at the end of 1- and 2-year follow-up evaluations. Project KYB also demonstrated short-term effects of the smoking prevention component within the broader health promotion program. In this study smoking prevalence was shown to be lower in the group of students who received the program than among students who did not receive the program. This was confirmed by physiological indices of tobacco use (salivary cotinine) (Walter et al., 1988; Walter & Wynder, 1989).

Programs to assess the long-term effects of school-based smoking prevention programs have met with modest success. Three school-based prevention curriculum programs, including the Minnesota Smoking Prevention Program (Arkin, Roemhild, Johnson, Luepker, & Murray, 1981), the Waterloo Smoking Project (Best et al., 1984), and Project Alert (Ellickson, Bell, & McGuigan, 1993) have evaluated the long-term effects of the prevention message. These programs varied in the dose-intensity of sessions, ranging from 5 to 11 sessions and were presented in the sixth through eighth grades. All included components central to the social cognitive theory such as helping students identify social pressures to smoke, teaching skills to resist pressures to smoke, disconfirming misconceptions about smoking prevalence among peers and family, and providing information about the health risks of smoking. Outcome evaluation for these programs revealed that students who received the intervention were less likely to smoke or experiment with smoking over 1- and 2-year periods. However, by the twelfth grade the effects of these programs were no longer present.

One study that has demonstrated long-term effects is the Life Skills Training Program (LST) (Botvin, Baker, Dusenbury, Tortu, & Botvin, 1990). This program was similar to previous programs and included skills training in refusal and information about consequences of smoking as well as addressed perceived prevalence of use. The program also included general skills training, such as communication skills training and ways to make friends. The curriculum was presented over the course of 15 class periods in the seventh grade, followed by a 10-session booster in the eighth grade, and a 5-session booster in the ninth grade. In addition, five newsletters and four supportive phone calls were made to the students throughout the ninth grade. The sample included 4,466 students attending 56 schools in New York state. At the end of the ninth grade, students who received the prevention program reported a 10% lower prevalence rate than students who did not receive the program. The intervention continued to exert effects in the expected direction by the end of the twelfth grade. It is likely that the success of this program in reducing weekly smoking prevalence is due to a dose effect. Students in this study were exposed to 30 classroom sessions over 3 grades coupled with follow-up phone calls. Future studies are needed to examine the minimum number of sessions required to exert effects over the long term.

Along with the school-based curriculum, other investigations have expanded on these types of tobacco prevention programs and have included methods for targeting family and the surrounding community. Two such programs were the Class of 1989 Study (Perry et al., 1992) and the University of Vermont School and Mass Media Project (Flynn, Worden, Secker-Walker, Badger, & Geller, 1995; Worden et al., 1988). As mentioned above, students enrolled in the Class of 1989 study received informational media exposure, community education programs, and a school-based health promotion curriculum. Investigators found that students who received the school curriculum and were exposed to the community and media campaigns reported a 40% lower weekly smoking prevalence than children in the comparison communities (Perry et al., 1992). A significant difference in prevalence was maintained for 3 years following the end of the prevention program. Similar to the LST program, the Class of 1989 study involved several sessions (17) over 3 years (seventh through ninth grades); the intensity of the program may have contributed to the long-term effects, although this was not assessed. It is also likely that the community and media exposure may have contributed to the long-term effectiveness of this program. Students in the study and their families were exposed to a number of community education and organizational activities (e.g., risk-factor screenings, food-labeling education, mass media education).

The additive effect of supplementing school-based tobacco prevention programs with mass media campaigns was evaluated in the University of Vermont School and Mass Media Project

(Flynn et al., 1995). This study included a school-based tobacco prevention program presented in 15 sessions over 4 school years (Grades 5 through 8, 6 through 9, or 7 through 10). The school-based program was presented to students from four separate geographical communities from three states. In addition, 2 of the 4 communities received 4 years of television and radio broadcasting spots that had a tobacco prevention message. Investigators found that by the end of the 4 years, students who received the school and media prevention program reported 34% to 41% less smoking than children who only received the school-based program (Flynn et al., 1992). Significant effects of the intervention compared to the control were again observed 2 years following the end of the program (Flynn et al., 1994).

Solar Protection

Prevalence

Malignant melanoma and other skin cancers are some of the most common types of adult cancer in the United States with one million new cases estimated each year (Williams & Pennella, 1994; USDHHS, 1991). Although skin cancer is generally associated with a lifetime exposure to UV rays, high-intensity intermittent exposure during childhood can increase the risk of a person developing skin cancer as an adult (Truhan, 1991). Limiting exposure to ultraviolet (UV) rays by wearing sunscreen and protective clothing and reducing tanning could prevent many of these cancers and the associated mortality and morbidity.

Interventions

Only a few studies have examined the efficacy of school-based solar protection programs (Lynagh et al., 1997). Such investigations have demonstrated that school-based solar protection programs do result in greater knowledge about the dangers of the sun (Buller, Goldberg, & Buller, 1997; Fork, Wagner, & Wagner, 1992; Reding et al., 1996). Further, investigations also have demonstrated the success of school-based programs in changing attitudes about skin cancer prevention and simple behaviors, such as decreases in self-reported time tanning (Buller, Buller, Beach, & Ertl, 1996) and staying in the shade (Lombard, Neubauer, Canfield, & Winett, 1991). Hoffman, Rodrigue, and Johnson (1999) designed a 3-day, school-based solar protection program that was delivered to 99 children in the fifth grade (82 were in the control group). The program involved the following components: providing information about the risks of sun exposure and prevention behaviors; having classroom activities designed to increase peer support for sun-safe behaviors; and making a public commitment to continued practice of sun safe behaviors. Children who received the intervention reported more knowledge of skin cancer, high intentions to practice sun-safe behaviors, and a greater frequency of sunscreen use than prior to the intervention and compared to the control group.

Future studies evaluating the short- and long-term efficacy of school-based curricula designed to increase solar protection are needed. Drawing from the success of programs targeting diet, physical activity, and tobacco prevention, such investigations would benefit from a fairly intensive curriculum presented over several sessions. Incorporating components to increase peer, family, and community acceptability for sun-safe behaviors would also be warranted.

CONCLUSIONS AND FUTURE DIRECTIONS

The promotion of health behaviors in the school setting can be accomplished with some success. Studies designed to promote diet and exercise have shown that children who receive targeted interventions can decrease fat intake and increase physical activity, and in some studies these behaviors have been shown to correlate with physiological risk factors associated with cardiovascular disease. Studies designed to prevent tobacco use have been shown to reduce prevalence of monthly tobacco use from 14% to 60% among children who receive prevention programs compared to children who do not receive such programs. Delaying children's use or experimentation with tobacco can also be accomplished through well structured and planned interventions.

The success of these school-based prevention programs has been due in part to the grounding in behavioral models and theories of health promotion. The social cognitive theory is one theory that has been most used. This theory incorporates the need to address social influence and norms. This is particularly relevant to youth, as they are highly influenced by peer behaviors and social norms. The problem-behavior theory also has been influential in curriculum development. Programs that take into account how personality interacts with the environment are helpful at identifying children who may be at higher risk for developing certain types of health-compromising behaviors.

Curriculum-based programs delivered within the classroom over a period of sessions have typically been the main method of delivering the prevention message to children. Using the school-based clinic as a method of delivery of health promotion has not had much success. School health clinics typically deliver first aid and administer medications, but few (less than 40%) offer health promotion programs (Brener et al., 2001). Using a more comprehensive approach such as that outlined by the CDC has been the gold standard. However, few health education programs have been able to meet these guidelines. Few states mandate health screening or health promotion programs for their teachers and few districts offer such health programs. Also few schools and districts adopt policy that promotes healthy environments such as providing smoke-free schools, providing school lunches with low-fat meals, or limiting vending machine sales of foods high in calories, fat, and salt.

Advances in the promotion of health behaviors in the school setting will need to address three major areas. First, investigations are needed to examine the long-term effects of these programs. What we learned from the LST program (Botvin et al., 1990) in tobacco prevention is that long-term effects can be achieved if education begins early, if the "dose" is strong and presented serially over several grades, if "booster" sessions are offered after the termination of the program, and if efforts are made to reach parents and the community. In essence, long-term effects will be reached with long-term planning.

Second, greater emphasis is needed on understanding the mediators of health promotion programs. Components of health promotion programs have included a number of mediators such as health risk information; skills training in resisting peer pressure; raising awareness of media influences; correcting misconceptions about the prevalence of health-compromising behaviors; social modeling; and goal setting. Efforts to reach parents, families, and the community and change school policy also have been used. Analysis of these mediators has relied mostly on examining changes in proposed mediators by comparing the intervention to the control group. However, more stringent criteria have been proposed for posthoc mediation analysis (Holmbeck, 1997, 2002). Mediation analysis is a critical phase of program evaluation, as components of the program can be enhanced or eliminated, thereby increasing the efficacy and reducing the cost of the program.

Finally, research is needed to address diffusion and dissemination, especially to communities and populations where these programs will have the greatest impact. For example, mortality related to cardiovascular disease, stroke, and cancer are higher among African Americans than Caucasians. A greater impact on the health system in the United States can be accomplished if programs are targeted to communities most afflicted by disease related to health behaviors. Many of the health promotion programs discussed have not occurred in schools where a majority of children are African American or represent children from lower socioeconomic backgrounds. Thus, it is difficult to know if these programs will be successful if replicated in these schools. Systematic efforts to increase the availability of empirically based programs on diet, physical activity, tobacco, and solar protection and the evaluation of these efforts represent the next challenge in the science of school health promotion.

REFERENCES

Allensworth, D., & Kolbe, L. (1987). The comprehensive school health program: Exploring an expanded concept. *Journal of School Health, 57*, 409–412.

American Association of School Administrators. (1990). *Healthy kids for the year 2000: An action plan for schools*. (AASA Stock #021-00306). Arlington, VA: American Association of School Administrators.

Angelico, F., DelBen, M., Fabiani, L., Lentini, P., Pannozzo, F., Urbanati, G. C., & Ricci, G. (1991). Management of childhood obesity through a school based program of general health and nutrition education. *Public Health, 105*, 393–398.

Arkin, R. M., Roemhild, H. F., Johnson, C. A., Luepker, R. V., & Murray, D. M. (1981). The Minnesota smoking prevention program: A seventh grade health curriculum supplement. *Journal of School Health, 51*, 611–616.

Bandura, A. (1977). Self-efficacy: Toward a unifying theory of behavior change. *Psychological Review, 84*, 191–215.

Bandura, A. (1986). *Social foundations of thought and action. A social cognitive theory*. Englewood Cliffs, NJ: Prentice-Hall.

Bandura, A. (1994). Social cognitive theory and exercise control of HIV infection. In J. L. Peterson & R. J. DiClemente (Eds.), *Preventing AIDS: Theories and methods of behavioral interventions* (pp. 25–59). New York: Plenum.

Bandura, A. (1997). *Self efficacy: The exercise of control*. New York: W. H. Freeman and Company.

Barnowski, T., Davis, M., Resnicow, K., Barnowski, J., Doyle, C., Lin, L. S., Smith, M., & Wang, D. T. (2000). Gimme 5 fruit, juice, and vegetables for fun and health: Outcome evaluation. *Health Education & Behavior, 27*, 96–111.

Best, J. A., Perry, C. L., Flay, B. R., Brown, K. S., Towson, S. M. J., Kersell, M. W., Ryan, K. B., & Avernas, J. R. (1984). Smoking prevention and the concept of risk. *Journal of Applied Social Psychology, 14*, 257–273.

Blackburn, H., Luepker, R. V., Kline, F. G., Bracht, N., Carlaw, R., Jacobs, D., Mittlebark, M., Stauffer, L., & Taylor, H. L. (1984). The Minnesota heart health program: A research demonstration project in cardiovascular disease prevention. In J. D. Matarazzo, S. M. Weiss, J. A. Herd, N. E. Miller, & S. M. Weiss (Eds.), *Behavioral health: A handbook for health enhancement and disease prevention* (pp. 1171–1178). Silver Spring, MD: John Wiley.

Botvin, G. J., Baker, E., Dusenbury, L., Tortu, S., & Botvin, E. M. (1990). Preventing adolescent drug abuse through a multimodal cognitive-behavioral approach: Results of a 3-year study. *Journal of Consulting and Clinical Psychology, 58*, 437–446.

Botvin, G., Eng, A., & Williams, C. (1980). Preventing the onset of cigarette smoking through life skills training. *Preventive Medicine, 9*, 135–143.

Brener, N. D., Burstein, G. R., DuShaw, M. L., Vernon, M. E., Wheeler, L., & Robinson, J. (2001). Health Services: Results from the school health policies and programs study 2000. *Journal of School Health, 71*, 294–304.

Brener, N. D., Dittus, P. J., & Hayes, G. (2001). Family and community involvement in schools: Results from the school health policies and programs study 2000. *Journal of School Health, 71*, 340–344.

Buller, D. B., Buller, M. K., Beach, B., & Ertl, G. (1996). Sunny days, healthy ways: Evaluation of a skin cancer prevention curriculum for elementary school-aged children. *Journal of the American Academy of Dermatology, 35*, 911–922.

Buller, M. K., Goldberg, G., & Buller, D. B. (1997). Sun smart day: A pilot program for photoprotection education. *Pediatric Dermatology 41*, 257–263.

Bullerdiek, H. W., Simpson, P. S., & Peck, M. G. (1995). *What works III: Focus on school health in urban communities*. Omaha, NE: City Match.

Burgeson, C. R., Wechsler, H., Brener, N. D., Young, J. C., & Spain, C. G. (2001). Physical education and activity: Results from the school health policies and programs study 2000. *Journal of School Health, 71*, 279–293.

Center for Disease Control and Prevention. (1996). Guidelines for school health programs to promote healthy eating. *Morbidity and Mortality Weekly Report, 45*, 1–41.

Center for Disease Control and Prevention. (2000). *Youth risk behavior, surveillance-United States, 1999*. Atlanta, GA: U.S. Department of Health and Human Services, Center for Disease Control and Prevention (CDC).

Colleti, G., Supnick, J. A., & Payne, T. J. (1985). The smoking self-efficacy questionnaire (SSEQ): Preliminary scale development and validation. *Behavior Assessment, 7*, 249–260.

Condiotte, M. M., & Lichtestein, E. (1981). Self-efficacy and relapse in smoking cessation programs. *Journal of Consulting and Clinical Psychology, 49*, 648–658.

Costa, F. M., Jessor, R., & Turbin, M. S. (in press). Psychosocial risk and protective factors in adolescent problem drinking: A longitudinal approach. *Journal of Studies on Alcohol, 60*, 480–490.

Donovan, J. E., & Jessor, R. (1985). Structure of problem behavior in adolescence and young adulthood. *Journal of Consulting and Clinical Psychology, 53*, 890–904.

Dryfoos, J. G. (1994). *Full service schools: A revolution in health and social services for children, youth, and families*. San Francisco: Jossey-Bass.

Dryfoos, J. G., Brindis, C., & Kaplan, D. W. (1996). Research and evaluation in school-based health care. *Adolescent Medicine: State of the Art Reviews, 7*, 207–219.

Edmundson, E. W., Luton, S. C., McGraw, S. A., Kelder, S. H., Layman, A. K., Smyth, M. H., Bachman, K. J., Pedersen, S. A., & Stone, E. J. (1994). CATCH: Classroom process evaluation in a multicenter trial. *Health Education Quarterley (Suppl.), 2*, S27–S50.

Ellickson, P. L., Bell, R. M., & McGuigan, K. (1993). Preventing adolescent drug use: Long term results of a junior high program. *American Journal of Public Health, 83*, 856–861.

Fisher, J. D., & Fisher, W. A. (2000). Theoretical approaches to individual level change in HIV risk behavior. In J. L. Peterson & R. J. DiClemente (Eds.), *Handbook of HIV prevention* (pp. 3–55). New York: Kluwer Academic/Plenum.

Flay, B. R. (1986). Efficacy and effectiveness trials (and other phases of research) in the development of health promotion programs. *Preventive Medicine, 15*, 451–474.

Flay, B. R., Miller, T. Q., Hedeker, D., Siddiqui, O., Britton, C. F., Brannon, B. R., Johnson, C. A., Hansen, W. B., Sussman, S., & Dent, C. (1995). The television, school, and family smoking prevention and cessation project VIII. Student outcomes and mediating variables. *Preventative Medicine, 24*, 29–40.

Flynn, B. S., Worden, J. K., Secker-Walker, R. H., & Badger, G. J. (1992). Prevention of cigarette smoking through mass media intervention and school programs. *American Journal of Public Health, 82*, 827–834.

Flynn, B. S., Worden, J. K., Secker-Walker, R. H., Badger, G. J., & Geller, B. M. (1995). Cigarette smoking prevention effects of mass media and school interventions targeted to gender and age groups. *Journal of Health Education, 26*, S45–S51.

Flynn, B. S., Worden, J. K., Secker-Walker, R. H., Pirie, P. L., Badger, G. J., Carpenter, J. H., & Geller, B. M. (1994). Mass media and school interventions for cigarette smoking prevention: Effects 2 years after completion. *American Journal of Public Health, 84*, 1148–1150.

Fork, H. E., Wagner, R. F. Jr., & Wagner, K. D. (1992). The Texas peer education sun awareness project for children: Primary prevention of malignant melanoma and neomelanocytic skin cancers. *Cutis, 50*, 363–364.

Giovino, G. A., Schooley, M. W., Zhu, B. P., Chrismon, J. H., Tomar, S. L., Peddicord, J. P., Merritt, R. K., Husten, C. G., & Erikson, M. P. (1995). Surveillance for selected tobacco-use behaviors-United States, 1990–1994. *Morbidity and Mortality Weekly Report, 43*, 1–43.

Green, L., & Lewis, F. (1986). *Evaluation and measurement in health education and promotion*. Palo Alto, CA: Mayfield.

Harrison, J. A., Mullen, P. D., & Green, L. W. (1992). A meta-analysis of studies of the health belief model. *Health Education Resources, 7*, 107–116.

Hoffman, R. G., Rodrigue, J. R., & Johnson, J. H. (1999). Effectiveness of a school based program to enhance knowledge of sun exposure: Attitudes toward sun exposure and sunscreen use among children. *Children's Health Care, 28*, 69–86.

Holman, H., & Lorig, K. (1992). Perceived self-efficacy in self-management of chronic disease. In R. Schwarzer (Ed.), *Self-efficacy: Thought control of action* (pp. 305–323). Washington, DC: Hemisphere.

Holmbeck, G. N. (1997). Toward terminological, conceptual, and statistical clarity in the study of mediators and moderators: Examples from the child-clinical and pediatric psychology literatures. *Journal of Consulting and Clinical Psychology, 65*, 599–610.

Holmbeck, G. N. (2002). Post–hoc probing of significant moderational and mediational effects in studies of pediatric populations. *Journal of Pediatric Psychology, 27*, 87–96.

Jessor, R. (1984). Adolescent development and behavioral health. In J. D. Matarazzo, S. M. Weiss, J. A. Herd, N. E. Miller, & S. M. Weiss (Eds.), *Behavioral health. A handbook of health enhancement and disease prevention* (pp. 69–90). New York: Wiley.

Jessor, R. (1987). Risky driving and adolescent problem behavior: An extension of problem-behavior theory. *Alcohol, Drugs, & Driving, 3*, 3–4.

Jessor, R. (1992). Risk behavior in adolescence: A psychosocial framework for understanding and action. In D. E. Rogers & E. Ginzburg (Eds.), *Adolescents at risk: Medical and social perspectives* (pp. 19–34). Boulder, CO: Westview Press.

Jessor, R. (1997). New perspectives on adolescent risk behavior. In R. Jessor (Ed.), *New perspectives on adolescent risk behavior* (pp. 1–10). New York: Cambridge University Press.

Jessor, R., & Jessor, S. L. (1977). *Problem behavior and psychosocial development: A longitudinal study of youth*. New York: Academic Press.

Kann, L., Warren, C. W., Harris, W. A., Collins, J. L., Douglass, K. A., Collins, M. E., Williams, B. I., Ross, J. G., & Kolbe, L. J. (1995). Youth risk behavior surveillance: United States, 1993. *Morbidity and Mortality Weekly Report, 44*, 1–55.

Kelder, S., Perry, C. L., & Klepp, K. I. (1993). Community-wide exercise health promotion: Outcomes from the Minnesota heart health program and class of 1989 study. *Journal of School Health, 63*, 218–223.

Kelder, S., Perry, C. L., Lytle, L. A., & Klepp, K. I. (1995). Community-wide nutrition education: Long-term outcomes of the Minnesota heart health program. *Health Education Research, 10*, 119–131.

Kennedy, E., & Goldberg, J. (1995). What are American children eating? Implications for public policy, 1995. *Nutrition Reviews, 53*, 111–126.

Kisker, E. E., & Brown, R. (1996). Do school-based health centers improve adolescent's access to health care, health status, and risk-taking behavior? *Journal of Adolescent Health, 18*, 335–343.

Kohler, C. L., Grimley, D., & Reynolds, K. (1999). Theoretical approaches guiding the development and implementation of health promotion programs. In J. M. Raczynski & R. J. DiClemente (Eds.), *Handbook of health promotion and disease prevention* (pp. 23–49). New York: Kluwer Academic/Plenum.

Laskarezewski, P., Morrison, J. A., Groot, I., Kelly, K. A., Mellies, M. J., Khoury, P., & Glueck, C. J. (1979). Lipid and lipoprotein tracking in 108 children over a four year period. *Pediatrics, 64*, 584–591.

Lauer, R. M., & Clark, W. R. (1989). Childhood risk factors for high adult pressure: The Muscatine study. *Pediatrics, 84*, 633–641.

Lauer, R. M., Lee, J., & Clarke, W. R. (1988). Factors affecting the relationship between childhood and adult cholesterol levels: The Muscatine study. *Pediatrics, 82*, 309–318.

Lewis, C. J., Crane, N. T., Moor, B. J., & Hubbard, V. S. (1994). Healthy people 2000: Report in the 1994 nutrition progress review. *Nutrition Today, 29*, 6–15.

Lombard, D., Neubauer, T. E., Canfield, D., & Winett, R. A. (1991). Behavioral community intervention to reduce risk of skin cancer. *Journal of Applied Behavior Analysis, 24*, 677–686.

Luepker, R. V., Perry, C. L., McKinley, S. M., Nader, P. R., Parcel, G. S., Stone, E. J., Webber, L. S., Elder, J. P., Feldman, H. A., Johnson, C. C., Kelder, S. H., & Wu, M. (1996). Outcomes of a field trial to improve children's dietary patterns and physical activity: The child and adolescent trial for cardiovascular health (CATCH). *Journal of the American Medical Association, 275*, 768–776.

Lynagh, M., Schofield, M. J., & Sanson-Fisher, R. W. (1997). School health promotion programs over the past decade: A review of the literature. *Health Promotion International, 12*, 43–60.

McCord, M. T., Klein, J. D., Foy, J. M., & Feathergill, K. (1993). School-based clinic use and school performance. *Journal of Adolescent Health, 14*, 91–98.

McGinnis, J. M., & Foege, W. H. (1993). Actual causes of death in the United States. *Journal of the American Medical Association, 270*, 2207–2212.

McKenzie, T. L., Nader, P. R., Strikmiller, P. K., Yang, M., Stone, E. J., & Perry, C. L., (1996). School physical education: Effect of the child and adolescent trial for cardiovascular health. *Prevention Medicine, 25*, 423–431.

Orchard, T. J., Donahue, R. P., Kuller, L. H., Hodge, P. N., & Dash, A. L. (1983). Cholesterol screening in childhood: Does it predict adult hypercholesterolemia? The Beaver County experience. *Journal of Pediatrics, 103*, 687–691.

Osganian, V., Feldman, H., Wu, M., Luepker, R., McKenzie, T., Zive, M., Webber, L., & Parcel, G. (1996). Tracking of physiological variables in the CATCH study. *Preventive Medicine, 25*, 400–412.

Perry, C. L., Kelder, S. H., & Klepp, K. I. (1994). Community-wide cardiovascular disease prevention with young people: Long term outcomes of the class of 1989 study. *European Journal of Public Health, 4*, 188–194.

Perry, C., Killen, J., Telch, M., Slinkard, L., & Danaher, B. (1980). Modifying smoking behavior of teenagers: A school-based intervention. *American Journal of Public Health, 70*, 722–725.

Perry, C. L., Klepp, K. I., & Sillers, C. (1989). Community-wide strategies for cardiovascular health: The Minnesota heart health program youth program. *Health Education Research, 4*, 87–101.

Perry, C. L., Luepker, R. V., Murray, D. M., Kurth, C., Mullis, R., Crockett, S., & Jacobs, D. R. (1988). Parent involvement with children's health promotion: The Minnesota home team. *American Journal of Public Health , 78*, 1156–1160.

Perry, C. L., Parcel, G. S., Stone, E. J., Nader, P. N., McKinlay, S. M., Luepker, R. V., & Webber, L. S. (1992). The child and adolescent trial for cardiovascular health (CATCH): Overview of the intervention program and evaluation methods. *Cardiovascular Risk Factors, 2*, 36–44.

Perry, C. L., Stone, E. J., Parcel, G. S., Ellison, R. C., Nader, P., Webber, L. S., & Luepker, R. V. (1990). School based cardiovascular health promotion: The Child and Adolescent Trial for Cardiovascular Health (CATCH). *Journal of School Health, 60*, 406–413.

Perry, C. L., Story, M., & Lytle, L. A. (1997). Promoting healthy dietary behaviors. In R. P. Weissberg, T. P Gullotta, R. L. Hampton, B. A. Ryan, & G. R. Adams (Eds.), *Enhancing children's wellness vol. 8: Issues in children's and families' lives* (pp. 214–249). Thousand Oaks, CA: Sage.

Pierce, J. P., & Gilpin, E. (1996). How long will today's adolescent smoker be addicted to cigarettes? *American Journal of Public Health, 86*, 253–256.

Porkka, K. V., Viikari, J. S., & Akerblom, H. K. (1991). Tracking of serum HDL-cholesterol and other lipids in children and adolescents: The cardiovascular risk in young Finns study. *Preventive Medicine, 20*, 713–724.

Reding, D. J., Fischer, V., Gunderson, P., Lappe, K., Anderson, H., & Calvert, G. (1996). Teens teach skin cancer prevention. *Journal of Rural Health, 12*, 256–272.

Reynolds, K. D., Pass, M. Galvin, M., Winnail, S. D., Harrington, K. F., & DiClemente, R. J. (1999). Schools as a setting for health promotion and disease prevention. In J. M. Raczynski and R. J. DiClemente (Eds.), *Handbook of health promotion and disease prevention*. New York: Kluwer Academic/Plenum.

Rosenstock, I. M. (1974). Historical origins of the health belief model. *Health Education Monographs, 2*, 328–335.

Rosenstock I. M. (1996). Why people use health services. *Milbank Memorial Fund Quarterly, 44*, 94–124.

Rosenstock, I. M., Strecher, V. J., & Becker, M. H. (1988). Social learning theory and the health belief model. *Health Education Quarterly, 15*, 175–183.

Schlitt, J. J., Ricket, K. D., Montgomery, L. L., & Lear, J. G. (1994). *State initiatives to support school-based health center: A national survey*. Washington, DC: Making the Grade National Program Office.

Small, M. L., Jones, S. E., Barrios, L. C., Crossett, L. S., Dahlberg, L. L., Albuquerque, M. S., Sleet, D. A., Greene, B. Z., & Schmidt, E. R. (2001). School policy and environment: Results from the school health policies and programs study 2000. *Journal of School Health, 71*, 325–334.

St. Leger, L. H. (1999). The opportunities and effectiveness of the health promoting primary school in improving child health: A review of the claims and evidence. *Health Education Research, 14*, 51–69.

Strecher, V. J., Champion, V. L., & Rosenstock, I. M. (1997). The health belief model and health behavior. In D. S. Gochman (Ed.), *Handbook of health behavior research 1: Personal and social determinants* (pp. 71–91). New York: Plenum.

Strecher, V. J., DeVellis, B. M., Becker, M. H., & Rosenstock, I. M. (1986). The role of self-efficacy in achieving health behavior. *Health Education Quarterly, 13*, 73–91.

Sussman, S., Dent, C. W., Burton, D., Stacy, A. W., & Flay, B. R. (1995). *Developing school-based tobacco use prevention and cessation programs*. Thousand Oaks, CA: Sage.

Sussman, S., Dent, C. W., McAdams, L. A., Stacy, A. W., Burton, D., & Flay, B. R. (1994). Group self-identification and adolescent cigarette smoking: A 1-year prospective study. *Journal of Abnormal Psychology, 103*, 576–580.

Sussman, S., Dent, C. W., Stacy, A. W., Burton, D., & Flay, B. R. (1994). Psychosocial variables as prospective predictors of violent events among adolescents. *Health Values, 18*, 29–40.

Sussman, S., Dent, C. W., Stacy, A. W., Burton, D., & Flay, B. R. (1995). Psychosocial predictors of health risk factors in adolescents. *Journal of Pediatric Psychology, 20*, 91–108.

Sussman, S., Dent, C. W., Stacy, A. W., Sun, P., Craig, S., Simon, T. R., Burton, D., & Flay, B. R. (1993). Project towards no tobacco use: 1-year behavior outcomes. *American Journal of Public Health, 83*, 1245–1250.

Taylor, L., & Adelman, H. S. (1996). Mental health in schools: Promising directions for practice. *Adolescent Medicine: State of the Art Reviews, 7*, 303–317.

Thompson, E. L. (1978). Smoking education programs 1960–1976. *American Journal of Public Health, 68*, 250–257.

Troiano, R. P., & Flegal, K. M. (1998). Overweight children and adolescents: Description, epidemiology, and demographics. *Pediatrics, 101*, 497–504.

Truhan, A. P. (1991). Sun protection in childhood. *Clinical Pediatrics, 30*, 676–681.

United States Congress Office of Technology Assessment. (1994). Heath care reform, school-based health centers can promote access to care. (GAO/HEHS- 94-166). Washington, DC: U.S. Government Printing Office.

United States Department of Health and Human Services. (1991). Healthy people 2000: National health promotion and disease prevention objectives. (DHHS Publication No. PHS 91-50212). Washington, DC: U.S. Government Printing Office.

United States Department of Health and Human Services. (1994). Preventing tobacco use among young people. A report of the Surgeon General. Atlanta, GA: United States Department of Health and Human Services, Center for Disease Control and Prevention, National Center for Chronic Disease Prevention and Health Promotion, Office on Smoking and Health.

United States Department of Health and Human Services. (2001). Deaths: Leading causes for 1999. Atlanta, GA: United States Department of Health and Human Services, Center for Disease Control and Prevention, National Center for Health Statistics, National Vital Statistics System.

Wallston, B. S., & Wallston, K. A. (1984). Social psychological models of health behavior: An examination and integration. In A. Baum, S. E. Taylor, & J. E. Singer (Eds.), *Handbook of psychology and health* (pp. 24–53). Hillsdale: Lawrence Earlbaum Associates.

Walter, H. J. (1989). Primary prevention of chronic disease among children: The school based "Know your body" intervention trials. *Health Education Quarterly, 16*, 201–214.

Walter, H. J., Hofman, A., Vaughan R. D., & Wynder, E. L. (1988). Modification of risk factors for coronary heart disease. Five-year results of a school-based intervention trial. *New England Journal of Medicine, 318*, 1093–1100.

Walter, H. J., & Wynder, E. L. (1989). The development, implementation, evaluation, and future directions of a chronic disease prevention program for children: The "Know your body" studies. *Preventative Medicine, 18*, 59–71.

Webber, L., Nader, P., McKenzie, T., Luepker, R. V., Lytle, L. A., Nichaman, M., Edmundson, E., Osganian, V., Feldman, H., Cutler, J., & Wu, M. (1996). Cardiovascular risk factors in third to fifth grade students: Results from the child and adolescent trial for cardiovascular health. *Preventive Medicine, 25*, 432–441.

Wechsler, H., Brener, N. D., Kuester, S., & Miller, C. (2001). Food service and foods and beverages available at school: Results from the school health policies and programs study 2000. *Journal of School Health, 71*, 313–324.

Williams, M. C., & Pennella, R. (1994). Melanoma, melanocytic nevi, and other melanoma risk factors in children. *Journal of Pediatrics, 124*, 833–845.

Wojitowicz, G. C., Peveler, L. A., Eddy, J. M., Waggle, B. B., & Fitzhugh, E. C. (1992). The Midfield highs school safety belt incentive program. *Journal of School Health, 52*, 407–410.

Worden, J. K., Flynn, B. S., Geller, B. M., Chen, M., Shelton, L. G., Secker-Walker, R. H., Solomon, D. S., Solomon, L. J., Couchey, S., & Costanza, M. C. (1988). *Preventative Medicine, 22*, 325–334.

World Health Organization (WHO). (1986). The Ottawa Charter for Health Promotion. WHO Regional Office, Ottawa. Available: http://www.euro.who.int/AboutWHO/Policy/20010827_2

Wulfert, E., & Wan, C. K. (1993). Condom use: A self-efficacy model. *Health Psychology, 12*, 346–353.

7

Promotion of Mental Health

Bonnie K. Nastasi
The Institute for Community Research

Increasingly the United States and international communities have identified mental health as a public health concern and schools as a key context for providing mental health services to children and adolescents (De Jong, 2000; Doll, 1996; Nastasi, Varjas, Sarkar, & Jayasena, 1998; National Advisory Mental Health Council, 1990; U.S. Department of Health and Human Services [USDHHS], 1999, 2001a, 20001b; U.S. Public Health Service [USPHS], 1999, 2000; World Health Organization [WHO], 1997; Zill & Schoenborn, 1990). In recent reports from the U.S. Surgeon General (USDHHS, 1999, 2001a, 2001b), mental health has been characterized along a health illness continuum, thereby broadening both the focus and definition of mental health care. In contrast to the traditional medical model that has guided mental health care in the past, the Surgeon General advocates for a public health perspective focused on mental health promotion and illness prevention within the general population.

The model for school-based mental health—*School-Based Mental Health Promotion (SBMHP)* model—described in this chapter embodies a public health approach. This model stands in contrast to traditional notions of school-based special education services that are based on a medical model with emphasis on diagnosis, treatment, and etiology of health, learning, and behavioral disorders. Instead, the SBMHP model encompasses the key characteristics of the public health model advocated by the Surgeon General: (1) comprehensive service provision, ranging from prevention to treatment; (2) an ecological perspective that addresses social-cultural as well as individual factors and acknowledges the importance of person–environment interactions; (3) accessibility to services for the general population, in this instance, through school-based services available to all students; (4) science-based practice with ongoing evaluation of services; and (5) surveillance of mental health needs (e.g., through systematic school-based screening of all students).

The purpose of this chapter is to describe a model for school-based mental health promotion (i.e., the SBMHP) in which psychologists, specifically pediatric psychologists, can play a key role. Consistent with the theme of this book, the role of pediatric psychologists as school-based mental health service providers is highlighted, although the roles portrayed here extend to other psychologists working in schools. (The terms "school psychologist" and "psychologist working in schools" will be used interchangeably. For the purposes of this chapter, both terms include pediatric psychologists who work in schools.) The proposed mental health model is comprehensive in scope, reflects a developmental-ecological perspective, represents the integration of research and practice, and requires active participation of key stakeholders including professionals from diverse disciplines and nonprofessionals (e.g., community members, parents, students).

COMPREHENSIVE MENTAL HEALTH CARE

For the purposes of this discussion, mental health promotion is regarded as a component of *comprehensive health care*, which refers to the full range of services provided for a broad spectrum of health-related problems, including chronic health or health-related conditions, psychiatric disorders, and social morbidities (Nastasi, 2000). Comprehensive care covers a continuum of services, ranging from prevention to treatment, for the identified health problems and related difficulties (e.g., psychological, social, educational) in individual and family functioning. The scope of care thus necessitates the coordination of services by multiple providers (e.g., medical, psychological, social service, educational) across multiple facilities (e.g., hospitals, clinics, schools, social service agencies).

Efforts to institute comprehensive health care programs reflect recognition of (1) increasing health, mental health, educational, and social service needs of youth, particularly urban youth; (2) "agreement that *education and health are inextricably intertwined*" (Dryfoos, 1993, p. 542); (3) the fragmentation of services for youth; and (4) related demands for school and educational reform (Dryfoos, 1993, 1994, 1995). Dryfoos described these efforts as a "resurgence of a school-based services movement" (Dryfoos, 1993, p. 541), reminiscent of community action programs of the 1960s (Dryfoos, 1995), and dating back to efforts at the turn of the century to bring medical services to children in the school context (Dryfoos, 1993). Furthermore, the realization of comprehensive service delivery to children, adolescents, and families requires an integration of public education and public health and concomitant expansion of the roles of relevant professionals (Klein & Cox, 1995). The interdisciplinary nature of the work is reflected in the range of publication outlets (e.g., education, psychology, medicine, public health, social work).

A number of comprehensive health and mental health care programs have been described and tested during the past decade (Adelman & Taylor, 1998; Attkisson, Dresser, & Rosenblatt, 1995; Behar et al., 1996; DiClemente, Ponton, & Hansen, 1996; Dryfoos, 1994; Klein & Cox, 1995; Knoff, 1996; Kolbe, Collins, & Cortese, 1997; Ring-Kurtz, Sonnichsen, & Hoover-Dempsey, 1995; Roberts & Hinton-Nelson, 1996; Weissberg & Elias, 1993). These programs share several common characteristics:

> [a] integration of educational, health or mental health, and social services within and across agencies and professional disciplines; [b] attention to the various ecological contexts that influence children and adolescents, including school, family, peer group, and community; [c] services that are individually, developmentally and culturally appropriate; [d] a continuum of services ranging from prevention to treatment; [e] systematic evaluation of program process and outcome; and [f] provision of care based upon empirical evidence of the complexity of factors that influence the well-being of children and adolescents and their families. (Nastasi, 2000, p. 541)

These characteristics are consistent with a public health model of mental health advocated by the U.S. Surgeon General and the U.S. Department of Health and Human Services (USDHHS, 1999, 2001a, 2001b).

Evaluation research is generally supportive of comprehensive health and mental health programming in schools and communities, with regard to acceptability, feasibility, cost-effectiveness, accessibility, utilization, and effectiveness in promoting the well-being of children and adolescents. Researchers have found comprehensive mental health service delivery to be acceptable to stakeholders (e.g., families, teachers, community members; Behar et al., 1996; Caplan et al., 1992; Dryfoos, 1994, 1995; Saxe, Cross, Lovas, & Gardner, 1995; Walter et al., 1995) and generally feasible (Attkisson et al., 1997; Cross & Saxe, 1997; Dryfoos, 1994, 1995; Holtzman, 1997; Jordan, 1996; Saxe et al., 1995; Walter et al., 1995). Further support for feasibility of comprehensive programming comes from evidence of accessibility and utilization by intended recipients (Attkisson et al., 1997; Behar et al., 1996; Dryfoos, 1994, 1995; Hannah & Nichol, 1996; Harold & Harold, 1993; Klein & Cox, 1995; Walter et al., 1995). Furthermore, the cost-effectiveness of integrated service delivery over fragmented services has been supported (Dryfoos, 1994, 1995; Jordan, 1996), although findings on cost-effectiveness are not conclusive (Behar et al., 1996).

Most importantly, the effectiveness of comprehensive programming for enhancing the functioning of children and adolescents and reducing health and mental health risks has been documented. That is, programs have been shown to be effective in (1) facilitating early identification of high-risk students (Dryfoos, 1994, 1995); (2) reducing the need for more restrictive placements (Jordan, 1996); (3) decreasing involvement in risky behaviors and reducing morbidity and mortality (Caplan et al., 1992; Dryfoos, 1994, 1995; Hannah & Nichol, 1996; Jordan, 1996; Klein & Cox, 1995; Miller, Brehm, & Whitehouse, 1998; Schoenwald, Henggeler, Pickrel, & Cunningham, 1996); (4) enhancing health promoting behaviors (e.g., social competence and emotional well-being; Caplan et al., 1992; Cowen et al., 1996; Haynes & Comer, 1996); and (5) improving academic and school functioning (Dryfoos, 1994, 1995; Haynes & Comer, 1996; Jordan, 1996; Miller et al., 1998).

Although research suggests that comprehensive school-based services can effectively enhance well-being and reduce risk, results are not unequivocal (Behar et al., 1996; Kirby et al., 1993; Nastasi & DeZolt, 1994; Nastasi, Varjas, Bernstein, & Pluymert, 1998; Weissberg, Caplan, & Harwood, 1991) and more research is needed. For example, within multisite projects, program implementation and evaluation may be inconsistent across sites (Attkisson et al., 1997; Cross & Saxe, 1997; Saxe et al., 1995) and perceptions of successful implementation may vary across stakeholders (Attkisson et al., 1997). Inconsistency in implementation of multisite projects or replication of empirically validated programs raises questions about the feasibility of standardized programs and the need for context- or culture-specific modifications, as suggested by Cross and Saxe (1997):

> That no "right" way exists to develop systems of care, even though the systems share common elements, is not surprising given how dramatically communities differed.... The findings from MHSPY [Mental Health Services Program for Youth; 9 sites nationwide] suggest that efforts to develop generic models of systems of care may be misguided and should be viewed skeptically. (p. 67)

The conclusions of Cross and Saxe (1997) are supported by other research on organizational change and social program innovations (McLaughlin, 1976, 1990). Based on findings from a 4-year study of 293 local school-based projects directed toward educational change, McLaughlin concluded that, "*successful implementation* [of educational interventions or change projects] *is characterized by a process of mutual adaptation*" (1976, p. 340). Mutual adaptation involves continual monitoring and modification of project design and consequent changes in the participants (e.g., through professional staff development) and the context (e.g., changes in classroom structure or practices; Nastasi, Varjas, Schensul, Silva, Schensul, &

Ratnayake, 2000). Described in the next section is a model for school-based mental health promotion that encompasses key elements described earlier and integrates methods for addressing program modifications during implementation in real-life field (school) settings.

SCHOOL-BASED MENTAL HEALTH PROMOTION MODEL

The SBMHP model for development and delivery of comprehensive mental health services within schools includes seven components, characterized as *fundamental* (continuum of care, integrated services, culture specificity) and *foundational* (action research, ecological theory, participation of stakeholders, interdisciplinary collaboration). (For an earlier description of these components applied to school-based health care, see Nastasi, 2000.) The three fundamental components characterize the model of care. The continuum of care refers to the full range of mental health services, from prevention to treatment. To avoid duplication and fragmentation, efforts are made to coordinate and integrate services. Furthermore, a culture-specific approach is used to address individualization of services based upon both personal and social–cultural factors.

The four foundational components provide the conceptual, methodological, and procedural bases for development, implementation, and evaluation. The model is grounded conceptually in ecological-developmental theory (Bronfenbrenner, 1989), methodologically in action research, and procedurally in a participatory and interdisciplinary process. In the subsequent sections, each component is described and illustrated with reference to the potential role of pediatric psychologists working in schools.

Fundamental Components

The three fundamental components of the SBMHP model are viewed as essential to the provision of comprehensive mental health care. Together they reflect a continuum of integrated mental health services designed to address individual and social–cultural factors related to promoting optimal functioning.

Continuum of Care

The full continuum of mental health services ranges from prevention activities that target the general population of all students to intensive treatment for those diagnosed with specific psychiatric disorders. In this section, we examine four levels of the continuum: Level I, prevention; Level II, risk reduction; Level III, early intervention; and Level IV, treatment (Meyers & Nastasi, 1999; Nastasi, 1995, 1998). The continuum is a modification of the classic Caplanian tripartite model (Caplan, 1964). Levels I and II are encompassed in Caplan's definition of primary prevention, Level III is consistent with the secondary level, and Level IV with tertiary. The four levels differ in target population, intervention goals, intensity of services, context, and staffing.

Prevention (Level I). Prevention, or mental health promotion, activities are directed toward the general population of students. Viewed as an essential component of the school curriculum, mental health promotion involves building-level or district-wide educational programs focused on topics such as social and emotional development, social skills training, drug prevention, AIDS prevention, and violence prevention (e.g., Caplan et al., 1992; Goldstein, 1988; Goldstein, Reagles, & Amann, 1990; Knoff & Batsche, 1995; Shure, 1992; 1996; Weissberg et al., 1991). Although such programs exist in some form within most school districts in the United States, they are frequently subsumed within state-mandated drug or AIDS prevention programming and viewed as health education with the emphasis on physical rather than mental health. Such programs provide opportunities for more explicit focus on mental health promotion with the assistance of mental health professionals. Psychologists within the schools can play a key role in expanding existing health education programs to include mental health, for example, through curriculum development or selection, coteaching, and/or consultation with educators delivering the curriculum. The delivery of mental health curricula within schools provides the context for educating students about mental health and mental illness, developing strategies for coping with stress, identifying students who are at risk for or experiencing mental health problems, and providing information about mental health services within the school and community.

Level I efforts also can be directed toward changes in the school or classroom to create environments that facilitate the social–emotional development (i.e., mental health) of students. Activities are directed toward the school culture and staff as well as students. Such efforts can extend beyond the school through family and community partnerships. In a partnership model, the key stakeholders (e.g., school administrators and staff, students, parents, community members, administrators and staff from community agencies) together identify mental health concerns, gather information about student needs and relevant social–cultural or contextual factors, design system-wide programs, seek funding, educate stakeholders, and evaluate programs. At a minimum, the psychologist is a partner in this process. The psychologist also can assume a leadership role in the initiation and coordination of such efforts.

Risk Reduction (Level II). Level II activities are geared toward students who are at risk for mental health difficulties due to individual or environmental factors, for example, students who are affected by family divorce or alcoholism, students living in poverty, or students who have experienced traumatic life events (e.g., Cowen & Hightower, 1996; Cowen et al., 1996; Pedro-Carroll, 1997; Pitcher & Poland, 1992; Stolberg & Gourley, 1996). Risk reduction efforts, although preventive in focus, are more intensive than those at Level I, target specific stressors, and are delivered to selected members of the general school population (i.e., those identified as at risk). The purpose of risk reduction is to facilitate adjustment to stressors and prepare students with skills for coping with stressors that are beyond the everyday life experiences of most students. School-based Level II activities are typically delivered outside of the classroom by a mental health professional or well-trained paraprofessional supported/supervised by mental health staff. Examples of risk reduction include groups for children of divorce and crisis intervention following a school shooting. Risk reduction efforts encompass activities directed toward the individual and the environment, for example, by working with families who have experienced divorce or providing crisis intervention to adults as well as students.

Psychologists can assume multiple roles in school-based risk reduction efforts. In addition to providing direct services to students, they can assist in developing identification and referral procedures for students at risk, making referrals to community-based services, designing or selecting appropriate intervention programs, developing evaluation procedures, educating and supervising paraprofessional staff, implementing or evaluating programs, disseminating information about evidence-based programs, and educating administrators, teachers, parents, and students about indicators of risk.

Early Intervention (Level III). Early intervention efforts are directed toward students who are experiencing mild mental health difficulties, with the dual purpose of treating mild difficulties and reducing the risk of moderate to severe mental health problems (e.g., Lochman, Dunn, & Klimes-Dougan, 1993; McDougal, Clonan, & Martens, 2000). Students who receive early intervention are identified through formal or informal screening and referral. For example, students might be identified by teachers or self-identify during classroom-based prevention activities or be identified by mental health professionals through formal building-level or system-wide screening programs (e.g., screening for depression). Early intervention services are delivered individually or in small groups by mental health professionals or well-trained paraprofessionals who are supported/supervised by mental health staff. Examples of early intervention include counseling groups for students experiencing mild depression or individualized interventions for students with mild behavioral difficulties.

Psychologists working in schools can play important roles in early intervention. They can provide direct services to students at risk through individual or group interventions. They can help to develop building-level or system-wide screening, identification, and referral procedures, for example, by establishing multistage screening procedures (Laurent, Hadler, & Stark, 1994; Nastasi, 1995; Reynolds, 1986). Psychologists can provide indirect services to students through consultation with teachers and development of classroom-based interventions (e.g., behavioral management programs). In addition, they can assist administrators in developing or evaluating early intervention programs, educate staff on effective early intervention practices, and work with community agencies to provide services within the school or community. Furthermore, psychologists can play a central role in developing multidisciplinary early intervention teams to consider referrals and make recommendations.

Treatment (Level IV). Level IV activities, directed toward students who are diagnosed with specific mental health disorders (e.g., depression, conduct disorder, attention deficit hyperactivity disorder [ADHD]), involve the delivery of intensive individualized services by mental health professionals (e.g., Attkisson et al., 1997; Pelham et al., 1996; Webster-Stratton, 1993). School psychologists have historically played key roles in assessment and diagnosis of students with severe emotional disturbance, determination of eligibility for special education services, and design of appropriate educational and therapeutic programs. Psychologists can provide direct services to students through individual or group therapy or indirect services through consultation with teachers and parents regarding contextual modifications or behavior management plans (e.g., through conjoint behavioral consultation; Sheridan, Kratchowill, & Bergan, 1996). They can assist administrators in developing appropriate screening, identification, and referral procedures; locating current information about effective interventions; and evaluating special education services for students with mental health disorders. Psychologists also can assume responsibility for communication and service coordination with community providers. For example, they can work with physicians by collecting data to evaluate the effectiveness of pharmacological interventions (Brown, Dingle, & Landau, 1994). They also can work with mental health professionals in community agencies to ensure coordinated services for students with severe behavioral and emotional disorders or to facilitate transition of students from residential treatment programs (e.g., for students with substance abuse problems).

In summary, the provision of a continuum of mental health services in schools requires systematic procedures for screening, identification, referral, direct and indirect service delivery, staff development, program evaluation, and coordination with community agencies. The school psychologist is in a unique position not only to provide services but also to assist other individuals and agencies in establishing a coordinated and integrated system of mental health services. Given their expertise in research and practice related to mental health and education, school psychologists can assume leadership roles in developing, implementing, and evaluating comprehensive school-based mental health services.

Integrated Services

A common characteristic included in models of comprehensive school- or community-based mental health services is the coordination and integration of available services across disciplines and agencies. Service coordination and integration is dependent on the flexibility of the service delivery system and service providers. The purposes of integration and coordination are: (1) to avoid fragmentation and duplication of services; (2) to address the interrelationships among physical, psychological, social, and educational functioning of the child/adolescent, thereby focusing on the individual's overall functioning; and (3) to address the contextual and social–cultural factors that influence the child/adolescent's development, thereby focusing also on the ecology of the individual.

Integrated service delivery requires coordination of services within the school and between the school and community agencies. Such coordination is dependent on the willingness of professionals to engage other stakeholders (e.g., school staff, parents, students, other professionals) in decision making and service delivery and to consider alternative explanations and solutions for meeting the needs of the students and their families. School psychologists are in a key position to facilitate coordination across stakeholders.

Within the school building, it is common to find students involved in several programs with common goals related to mental health that are delivered by different staff members who do not necessarily communicate with each other. The following example addresses duplication of Level I services.

> Teaching of social problem-solving and decision-making skills may be at the core of the social skills program delivered by the classroom teacher, drug education program delivered by the physical education teacher, and reproductive health education program delivered by the school nurse. Lack of communication among school personnel responsible for these programs could result in duplication of services, limited attention to generalization of skills, and at worst, teaching of conflicting messages and strategies. (Nastasi, 2000, p. 546)

In situations such as this, the school psychologist with expertise in mental health promotion can work with school staff across disciplines (e.g., teachers and school nurse) to ensure that a consistent approach to problem solving and decision making is used across programs and to develop strategies for generalization across contexts. Similarly, the psychologist providing direct services to individual students (at Levels II, III, or IV) can work with classroom teachers and other support staff (e.g., nurse, counselor, security officers) to ensure that adults interact with the students in a consistent manner in the classroom, hallway, playground, and lunchroom. Furthermore, the psychologist can enlist parents in prevention or intervention efforts to facilitate generalization to the home setting. An excellent model for involving parents in school-based interventions is the conjoint behavioral consultation model proposed by Sheridan et al. (1996), in which the psychologist as consultant works with both parents and teachers to ensure consistent behavioral intervention at school and at home.

The coordination and integration of services across agencies can occur both informally and formally. Informally, individual service providers in schools or community agencies can initiate contact with other service providers on behalf of the student and parents in order to foster communication and consistency regarding a child's or adolescent's individual treatment. Agencies also can establish more formal mechanisms for ensuring consistent service coordination, for example, through interagency mental health teams. Such teams bring together service providers from schools and communities to plan, implement, and evaluate interagency approaches to comprehensive mental health services for children and adolescents, as the following description illustrates.

> School-based service providers include curriculum specialists, regular education teachers, special education coordinator and teachers, psychologists, social workers, medical personnel, health educators, disciplinary officers, etc. Community agencies that provide services to children, adolescents and families include mental health agencies, police departments, juvenile justice, local

> child protection agency, medical facilities, etc. The interagency team has the responsibility for developing a system for reviewing individual, organizational, and community needs; planning a system of care that includes a continuum of services from prevention to treatment; and establishing a mechanism for reviewing and monitoring individual cases (e.g., inter-agency referral team, inter-agency case management). (Nastasi, 2000, p. 546)

The concept of the interagency mental health team can be extended further to include other stakeholders such as parents, students, community leaders, and community members as partners in decision making and service delivery. A research-based approach to facilitating stakeholder involvement in design, delivery, and evaluation of comprehensive mental health services (i.e., participatory action research) is described in a later section. School psychologists can serve not only as members of interagency or school–community teams, but also can take a leadership role in establishing partnerships and facilitating team functioning.

Culture Specificity

In a recent report, the U.S. Surgeon General (USDHHS, 2001a) highlighted the role of cultural influences on mental health needs and services and recommended the development of culture-specific approaches that extend beyond the development of targeted interventions for specific racial or ethnic groups. In particular, he recommended consideration of the culture of the client/patient, culture of the provider/clinician, and the societal influences on mental health and mental health care. The Surgeon General's focus on the cultural competence of service providers is consistent with guidelines of the American Psychological Association (APA, 1993) for working with culturally, ethnically, and linguistically diverse populations. Responding to the recommendations of the Surgeon General requires rethinking current approaches to mental health services and brings into question the application of standard programs that are designed and marketed for universal use.

A broader conception of culture specificity that extends beyond racial, ethnic, and linguistic specificity has been proposed:

> Cultural specificity implies that critical elements of the intervention (e.g., intervention strategies and targeted competencies) are relevant to the targeted culture, make use of the language of the population, and reflect the values and beliefs of members of the culture. Inherent in this model is the assumption that one cannot separate person from culture and that understanding the culture is essential to understanding the individual. In addition, change efforts cannot be solely person-centered, but must address the role of culture in promoting and sustaining behavior patterns. (Nastasi, 1998, p. 169)

In this conception of culture specificity, culture is defined as the beliefs, values, language, ideas, and behavioral norms shared by the members of the culture. Given the cultural diversity within any school or classroom, a culture-specific approach requires consideration of both shared (those specific to the school and classroom) and unique (specific to neighborhood, family, ethnic group, etc.) cultural experiences of students and teachers. Services that are culture-specific thus encompass the unique and shared real-life experiences of the individuals as well as their interpretations of these experiences. A culture-specific approach to mental health services is consistent with ecological theory of human development (e.g., Bronfenbrenner, 1989), which is examined in a later section.

Designing culture-specific mental health programs requires the study of the common and unique cultures of stakeholders, with subsequent development of new programs or adaptation of existing programs (Nastasi, 2000). For example, in developing a mental health promotion program for a given school, the program staff must first examine the beliefs, norms, values, language, and experiences of the individual stakeholders (e.g., students, teachers, principal, support staff, parents). With these data, the staff members are then prepared to examine existing programs for suitability and make necessary modifications or to develop their own program. Cultural considerations are likely to affect not only the curriculum (e.g., integrating cultural experiences and local language) but also staff development efforts (e.g., to educate staff about students' cultural experiences and to address cultural biases of staff members). In addition, data about cultural variations may necessitate the development and validation of culture-specific assessment tools for screening, identification, and program evaluation. Furthermore, the development of culture-specific programs requires systematic evaluation and validation of new programs. Action research approaches (described in a subsequent section) may be particularly suitable to the design and evaluation of culture-specific programs.

As scientist-practitioners with expertise in assessment and intervention, school psychologists are in a key position to orchestrate the development and evaluation of culture-specific interventions. They can facilitate necessary data collection, identification or design of culture-specific programs, selection or development of culture-specific assessment tools, communication and shared decision making by various stakeholders, and evaluation and validation of new programs. Because of the potential for wide variation in cultural experiences across various stakeholder groups and individuals, the goal of culture-specificity is challenging and requires the consideration of alternative models for integrating research and practice. In the next section, a model of practice based in action research is examined.

FOUNDATIONAL COMPONENTS

In this section, the basic components of the SBMHP model are explored. These foundational components address the challenges of developing, implementing, and evaluating the full continuum of integrated culture-specific mental health services.

Action Research

Action research, with roots in applied anthropology, is consistent with the characterization of school psychologists as reflective practitioners who go beyond the application of extant theory and research to practice by using a research process to guide practice (Nastasi, 1998). Action research involves a recursive process that links theory, research, and practice to effect social change (Greenwood, Whyte, & Harkavy, 1993; Schensul & Schensul, 1992). Formative research, guided by existing theory and research, provides the basis for developing culture- or context-specific (local) theory and culture- or context-specific interventions (action or practice). Evaluation research focused on intervention implementation and effectiveness informs adaptations of the current intervention, subsequent approaches to practice, and general and culture-specific theory. Similarly, the reflective practitioner employs the action research process to identify and define the problem, gather data, and design and evaluate the intervention. Furthermore, engagement in this research-practice process informs subsequent professional practice. "The process is repeated in daily practice as a systematic way to apply the scientific method to school psychology practice and to make explicit the integration of theory, research, and practice" (Nastasi, 2000, p. 543).

Action research relies on systematic research methods grounded in qualitative or ethnographic inquiry (also referred to as naturalistic, postpositivistic, phenomenological; e.g., Lincoln & Guba, 1985; Schensul & LeCompte, 1999), specifically, observation, interviewing, surveys, and collection of artifacts. Such inquiry is considered critical for studying culture, developing culture-specific assessment tools and intervention strategies, and evaluating culture-specific interventions (Nastasi & Berg, 1999; Nastasi, Varjas, Bernstein, & Jayasena, 2000). The techniques of ethnographic inquiry are consistent with those traditionally used by school psychologists (e.g., classroom observations, teacher and parent interviews, student self-report measures, school records, classroom products) in addition to standardized tests. Thus, school psychologists should be well prepared to apply such methods to the development and evaluation of school-based mental health programming. The recursive nature of action research makes it particularly suitable for ongoing monitoring of program acceptability, integrity, and effectiveness, and consequent adaptations to achieve a good ecological fit of the intervention to the context (e.g., specific classroom), interventionist (teacher), and recipients (students). (For a more in-depth discussion of action research applied to intervention, see Nastasi, Varjas, S. Schensul et al., 2000.)

Ecological Theory

Extant research on children and adolescent mental health confirms the importance of an ecological perspective (Bickman & Rog, 1995; Hawkins, Catalano, & Miller, 1992; National Advisory Mental Health Council, 2001; Roberts, 1996). The role of family, peers, school, community, and society in promotion of mental health is well accepted. Although these influences are well recognized, adopting an ecological approach in practice is not easily accomplished. Bronfenbrenner's (1989) ecological-developmental theory provides a basis for research and practice related to school-based mental health. In brief, Bronfenbrenner's theory suggests that human development (in this case, mental health) is a function of an ongoing mutual accommodation of the person and the ecology in which the individual lives. The ecology of the child/adolescent is complex and includes the range of contexts in which the child/adolescent functions, such as home, school, community, and peer group. Thus, understanding and influencing mental health requires attention to the individuals (socializing agents), situations, and conditions that exist within these key contexts as well as the interactions across contexts (e.g., between family and school).

Developmental-ecological theory (Bronfenbrenner, 1989) has important implications for psychologists working in schools. For example, assessment of an adolescent's mental health problems requires attention not only to the functioning of the individual adolescent but also to potential contributions of parents, siblings, peers, school personnel, and other adults to the adolescent's current functioning and their potential role in addressing the current problems. Furthermore, any interventions directed toward the adolescent may have impact on the relevant contexts and socializing agents as well. Thus, involvement of key stakeholders from the adolescent's ecology is critical for effective diagnosis and treatment. The same logic applies to prevention programming. Efforts to promote mental health need to be directed not only to the target individuals but also to the key socializing agents and contexts that are likely to influence the individuals. The criticality of stakeholder involvement to the sustainability and institutionalization of mental health promotion and intervention efforts is discussed in the next section.

The school psychologist, with understanding of developmental-ecological aspects of mental health, can take a leading role in fostering an ecological perspective in the identification of mental health concerns and development of mental health programs. The importance of culture specificity and the psychologist's role in promoting culture-specific mental health programming was discussed in an earlier section. In addition, engaging in an action research process can help to bring attention to individual and social–cultural factors. The complexity of an ecological model also requires participation by multiple stakeholders and partnership among professionals from varied disciplines. In the next two sections, the participatory and interdisciplinary components of comprehensive mental health programming are discussed.

Participation of Stakeholders

As suggested earlier, a participatory approach is necessary for achieving culture specificity, integration, and coordination of mental health services. Participatory approaches to school and community intervention have been proposed elsewhere (Nastasi, Varjas, Bernstein, & Jayasena, 2000; Nastasi, Varjas, S. Schensul et al., 2000; Schensul, 1998). Central to a participatory process is partnership among the key stakeholders, that is, those individuals who are involved in the socialization of the child/adolescent and are likely to influence the initial success and sustainability of prevention or intervention efforts. Key stakeholders or partners in school-based mental health include students, peers, parents, school administrators, teachers, school mental health staff, community agency administrators and staff, community leaders, community members, and policymakers. Participatory action research provides the mechanism for engaging partners in the process of reflective practice. That is, stakeholders become partners in the process of identifying goals, collecting data, and designing, implementing, and evaluating programs (i.e., the action research process).

The goals of stakeholder participation are promoting ownership and empowerment of key players, and sustainability and institutionalization of prevention/intervention efforts (Nastasi, Varjas, Bernstein, & Jayasena, 2000; Nastasi, Varjas, S. Schensul et al., 2000). The assumption is that key players as partners will assume ownership of mental health promotion efforts and develop the skills and sense of efficacy necessary for continuation of program efforts after the professional consultants/interventionists withdraw their support. Realizing these goals is dependent upon the ability of consultants/interventionists to establish partnerships and provide necessary skills training and the capacity and willingness of stakeholders to develop skills and assume ownership.

The process of engaging stakeholders in comprehensive mental health services is similar to that of collaborative or participatory consultation models in school psychology (Christenson & Conoley, 1992; Nastasi, Varjas, Bernstein, & Jayasena, 2000; Nastasi, Varjas, S. Schensul et al., 2000; Rosenfield & Gravois, 1996; Sheridan et al., 1996). In facilitating development of mental health services, the school psychologist might be responsible for bringing together stakeholders to (1) identify and define the mental health concerns, (2) gather data about individual and social–cultural factors related to the target concerns, (3) discuss and interpret data, (4) develop plans for addressing the target concerns, (5) divide responsibilities for implementing and evaluating intervention efforts, and (6) analyze and disseminate evaluation data. In addition, the school psychologist might play a key role in facilitating the partnership process and providing skills training and professional development. A participatory approach to SBMHP extends beyond the involvement of nonprofessional stakeholders to include the involvement of professionals from varied disciplines, a topic explored in the next section.

Interdisciplinary Collaboration

Because of the scope and complexity of children's mental health and school-based mental health services, psychologists cannot work in isolation. Addressing the medical, psychological, educational, and sociocultural aspects of children's and adolescents' mental health requires the involvement of professionals from the respective disciplines. School psychologists have historically engaged in interdisciplinary collaboration in diagnostic-prescriptive roles related to special education placement and in consultative roles with teachers related to classroom-based interventions. Providing school-based comprehensive mental health services necessitates an extension of traditional collaborative efforts. Relevant service providers within schools include teachers, social workers, nurses, and language specialists. Members of a broader school-community team include pediatricians, psychiatrists, neurologists, social workers and other social service professionals, language specialists, and other psychologists from various community agencies such as hospitals, clinics, police departments, child protection agencies, and juvenile court. As noted earlier, the school psychologist can assume a central role in facilitating communication and collaboration of professionals in the development and implementation of mental health services.

The notion of interdisciplinary collaboration is not restricted to practice. Understanding and addressing the biological, psychological, and social–cultural aspects of mental health requires that psychologists look to other disciplines for theoretical–empirical foundations and research methodologies (Nastasi, 2000). Relevant to SBMHP are theories, methods, and findings from the fields of medicine, education, public health, anthropology, sociology, and economics. Furthermore, theory, research, and methods from developmental, health, school, clinical, educational, social, community, and organizational psychology deserve consideration. An interdisciplinary understanding of mental health requires not only study across disciplines but also partnership with professionals from these disciplines. The interdisciplinary nature of mental health also requires reconsideration of professional preparation of psychologists.

In summary, the SBMHP model represents an extension of current conceptions of psychological practice in schools as well as an extension of traditional roles of pediatric psychologists. Specifically, engaging in comprehensive school-based mental health necessitates broadening the theoretical and methodological foundations of practice, collaboration with professionals in related disciplines, and participation of key socializing agents. Realizing the potential for school-based mental health care has implications for pediatric psychology practice and professional preparation. These implications are examined in the next section.

IMPLICATIONS FOR PEDIATRIC PSYCHOLOGY PRACTICE AND PROFESSIONAL PREPARATION

Pediatric psychologists have traditionally restricted their practice to medical settings (Drotar, 1998) but in recent years have considered extending their practice to schools (Brown et al., 1994; Power, DuPaul, Shapiro, & Parrish, 1995). Power and colleagues (1995), for example, propose a subspecialty in pediatric school psychology that encompasses training and skills from both school and pediatric psychology. Discussions within the American Psychological Association and the National Institute of Mental Health have led to a proposed model of training (pre- and postdoctoral) for psychologists who provide mental health services to children and adolescents (Roberts et al., 1998). This model provides a starting point for discussion of training of pediatric psychologists working as school-based mental health service providers. The 11 training components proposed by Roberts et al. are: (1) life-span developmental psychology; (2) life-span developmental psychopathology; (3) assessment methods for children, adolescents, and families; (4) intervention strategies; (5) research methods and systems evaluation; (6) professional, ethical, and legal issues; (7) issues of diversity; (8) the role of multiple disciplines and service delivery systems; (9) prevention, family support, and health promotion; (10) social issues affecting children, adolescents, and families; and (11) specialized applied experiences in assessment, intervention, and consultation. As Power et al. (1995) suggest, pediatric school psychologists also need training regarding the ecology of schools, assessment of school-related problems, and consultation with school personnel. Furthermore, expanded training in the area of child and adolescent mental health is warranted, with particular emphasis on mental health needs and services.

The pediatric school psychologist involved in SBMHP would function as a partner and member of a mental health care team, bringing particular expertise relevant to mental health assessment, mental health promotion, and prevention and treatment of mental health problems/illness.

Engagement in the SBMHP model requires reconsideration of the applied psychologist's professional identity from that of scientist-practitioner to that of *practicing scientist* (Nastasi, 2000), who utilizes systematic inquiry (i.e., social science methods) to address the mental health needs of individual students and school systems. The pediatric school psychologist as practicing scientist would function as an action researcher to bring about cultural/systemic and personal/individual change that promote mental health of children and adolescents, for example, when consulting with teachers about the development of a behavioral intervention program for a student with ADHD, or developing a system-wide violence prevention or social skills training program, or establishing a system-wide screening program for internalizing disorders such as depression. Furthermore, interdisciplinary practice requires development of interdisciplinary models of training that extend beyond the boundaries of traditional psychology graduate programs. Fortunately, recent work within school, pediatric, and clinical psychology (Drotar, 1998; Power et al., 1995; Yung, Hammond, Sampson, & Warfield, 1998) provides the basis for integrating pediatric and school psychology training and practice.

REFERENCES

Adelman, H. S., & Taylor, L. (1998). Mental health in schools: Moving forward. *School Psychology Review, 27*, 175–190.

American Psychological Association. (1993). Guidelines for providers of psychological services to ethnic, linguistic, and culturally diverse populations. *American Psychologist, 48*(1), 45–48.

Attkisson, C. C., Dresser, K. L., & Rosenblatt, A. (1995). Service systems for youth with severe emotional disorder: System-of-care research in California. In L. Bickman & D. J. Rog (Eds.), *Children's mental health services, Volume 1: Research, policy, and evaluation* (pp. 236–280). Thousand Oaks, CA: Sage.

Attkisson, C. C., Rosenblatt, A. B., Dresser, K. L., Baize, H. R., Clausen, J. M., & Lind, S. L. (1997). Effectiveness of the California System of Care Model for Children and Youth with Severe Emotional Disorder. In C. T. Nixon & D. A. Northrup (Eds.), *Children's mental health services, Volume 3: Evaluating mental health services: How do programs for children "work" in the real world?* (pp. 146–208). Thousand Oaks, CA: Sage.

Behar, L. B., Bickman, L., Lane, T., Keeton, W. P., Schwartz, M., & Brannock, J. E. (1996). The Fort Bragg Child and Adolescent Demonstration Project. In M. C. Roberts (Ed.), *Model programs in child and family mental health* (pp. 351–372). Mahwah, NJ: Lawrence Erlbaum Associates.

Bickman, L., & Rog, D. J. (Eds.). (1995). *Children's mental health services, Volume 1: Research, policy, and evaluation*. Thousand Oaks, CA: Sage.

Bronfenbrenner, U. (1989). Ecological systems theory. In R. Vasta (Ed.), *Annals of child development* (Vol. 6, pp. 187–249). Greenwich, CT: JAI.

Brown, R. T., Dingle, A., & Landau, S. (1994). Psychopharmacology in children and adolescents. *School Psychology Quarterly, 9*, 4–25.

Caplan, G. (1964). *Principles of preventive psychiatry*. New York: Basic Books.

Caplan, M., Wiessberg, R. P., Grober, J. S., Sivo, P. J., Grady, K., & Jacoby, C. (1992). Social competence promotion with inner-city and suburban young adolescents: Effects on social adjustment and alcohol use. *Journal of Consulting and Clinical Psychology, 60*, 56–63.

Christenson, S. L., & Conoley, J. C. (1992). (Eds.), *Home-school collaboration: Building a fundamental educational resource*. Silver Spring, MD: National Association of School Psychologists.

Cowen, E. L., & Hightower, A. D. (1996). The Primary Mental Health Project: School-based preventive intervention for adjustment problems. In M. C. Roberts (Ed.), *Model programs in child and family mental health* (pp. 63–74). Mahwah, NJ: Lawrence Erlbaum Associates.

Cowen, E. L., Hightower, A. D., Pedro-Carroll, J. L., Work, W. C., Wyman, P. A., & Haffey, W. G. (1996). *School-based prevention for children at risk: The Primary Mental Health Project*. Washington, DC: American Psychological Association.

Cross, T. P., & Saxe, L. (1997). Many hands make mental health systems of care a reality: Lessons learned from the Mental Health Services Program for Youth. In C. T. Nixon & D. A. Northrup (Eds.), *Children's mental health services, Volume 3: Evaluating mental health services: How do programs for children "work" in the real world?* (pp. 45–72). Thousand Oaks, CA: Sage.

De Jong, T. (2000). The role of the school psychologist in developing a health-promoting school: Some lessons from the South African context. *School Psychology International, 21*, 339–358.

DiClemente, R. J., Ponton, L. E., & Hansen, W. B. (1996). New directions in adolescent risk prevention and health promotion research and interventions. In R. J. DiClemente, W. B. Hansen, & L. E. Ponton (Eds.), *Handbook of adolescent health risk behavior* (pp. 413–420). New York: Plenum.

Doll, B. (1996). Prevalence of psychiatric disorders in children and youth: An agenda for advocacy by school psychology. *School Psychology Quarterly, 11*, 20–47.

Drotar, D. (1998). Training students for careers in medical settings: A graduate program in pediatric psychology. *Professional Psychology: Research and Practice, 29*, 402–404.

Dryfoos, J. G. (1993). Schools as places for health, mental health, and social services. *Teachers College Record, 94*, 540–567.

Dryfoos, J. G. (1994). *Full-service schools: A revolution of health and social services for children, youth, and families.* San Francisco: Jossey-Bass.

Dryfoos, J. G. (1995). Full service schools: Revolution or fad? *Journal of Research on Adolescence, 5*, 147–172.

Goldstein, A. P. (1988). *The Prepare Curriculum: Teaching prosocial competencies*. Champaign, IL: Research Press.

Goldstein, A. P., Reagles, K. W., & Amann, L. L. (1990). *Refusal skills: Preventing drug use in adolescents*. Champaign, IL: Research Press.

Greenwood, D. J., Whyte, W. F., & Harkavy, I. (1993). Participatory action research as a process and as a goal. *Human Relations, 46*, 175–192.

Hannah, F. P., & Nichol, G. T. (1996). Memphis City Schools Mental Health Center. In M. C. Roberts (Ed.), *Model programs in child and family mental health* (pp. 173–192). Mahwah, NJ: Lawrence Erlbaum Associates.

Harold, R. D., & Harold, N. B. (1993). School-based clinics: A response to the physical and mental health needs of adolescents. *Health and Social Work, 18*, 65–74.

Hawkins, J. D., Catalano, R. F., & Miller, J. Y. (1992). Risk and protective factors for alcohol and other drug problems in adolescence and early childhood: Implications for substance abuse prevention. *Psychological Bulletin, 112*, 64–105.

Haynes, N. M., & Comer, J. P. (1996). Integrating schools, families, and communities through successful school reform: The School Development Project. *School Psychology Review, 25*, 501–506.

Holtzman, W. H. (1997). Community psychology and full-service schools in different cultures. *American Psychologist, 52*, 381–389.

Jordan, D. (1996). The Ventura Planning Model: Lessons in reforming a system. In M. C. Roberts (Ed.), *Model programs in child and family mental health* (pp. 373–390). Mahwah, NJ: Lawrence Erlbaum Associates.

Kirby, D., Resnick, M. D., Downes, B., Kocher, T., Gunderson, P., Potthoff, S., Zelterman, D., & Blum, R. W. (1993). The effects of school-based health clinics in St. Paul on school-wide birthrates. *Family Planning Perspectives, 25*, 12–16.

Klein, J. D., & Cox, E. M. (1995). School-based health clinics in the mid-1990s. *Current Opinion in Pediatrics, 7*, 353–359.

Knoff, H. M. (1996). The interface of school, community, and health care reform: Organizational directions toward effective services for children and youth. *School Psychology Review, 25*, 446–464.

Knoff, H. M., & Batsche, G. M. (1995). Project ACHIEVE: Analyzing a school reform process for at risk and underachieving students. *School Psychology Review, 24*, 579–603.

Kolbe, L. J., Collins, J., & Cortese, P. (1997). Building the capacity of schools to improve the health of the nation: A call for assistance from psychologists. *American Psychologist, 52*, 256–265.

Laurent, J., Hadler, J. R., & Stark, K. D. (1994). A multiple-stage screening procedure for the identification of childhood anxiety disorders. *School Psychology Quarterly, 9*, 239–255.

Lincoln, Y. S., & Guba, E. G. (1985). *Naturalistic inquiry*. Thousand Oaks: CA. Sage.

Lochman, J. E., Dunn, S. E., & Klimes-Dougan, B. (1993). An intervention and consultation model from a social cognitive perspective: A description of the Anger Coping Program. *School Psychology Review, 22*, 458–471.

McDougal, J. L., Clonan, S. M., & Martens, B. K. (2000). Using organizational change procedures to promote acceptability of prereferral intervention services: The School-Based Intervention Team project. *School Psychology Quarterly, 15*, 149–171.

McLaughlin, M. W. (1976). Implementation as mutual adaptation: Change in classroom organization. *Teachers College Record, 77*, 340–351.

McLaughlin, M. W. (1990). The Rand Change Agent study revisited: Macro perspectives and micro realities. *Educational Researcher, 19*(9), 11–16.

Meyers, J., & Nastasi, B. K. (1999). Primary prevention in school settings. In C. R. Reynolds & T. B. Gutkin (Eds.), *Handbook of school psychology* (3rd ed., pp. 764–799). New York: Wiley.

Miller, G. E., Brehm, K., & Whitehouse, S. (1998). Reconceptualizing school-based prevention for antisocial behavior within a resiliency framework. *School Psychology Review, 27*, 364–379.

Nastasi, B. K. (1995). Is early identification of children of alcoholics necessary for preventive intervention? Reaction to Havey & Dodd. *Journal of School Psychology, 33*, 327–335.

Nastasi, B. K. (1998). A model for mental health programming in schools and communities. *School Psychology Review, 27*, 165–174.

Nastasi, B. K. (2000). School psychologists as health care providers in the 21st century: Conceptual framework, professional identity, and professional practice. *School Psychology Review, 29*, 540–554.

Nastasi, B. K., & Berg, M. (1999). Using ethnography to strengthen and evaluate intervention programs. In J. J. Schensul & M. D. LeCompte (Eds.), *The ethnographer's toolkit. Book 7. Using ethnographic data: Interventions, public programming, and public policy* (pp. 1–56). Walnut Creek, CA: AltaMira Press.

Nastasi, B. K., & DeZolt, D. M. (1994). *School interventions for children of alcoholics*. New York: Guilford.

Nastasi, B. K., Varjas, K., Bernstein, R., & Jayasena, A. (2000). Conducting participatory culture-specific consultation: A global perspective on multicultural consultation. *School Psychology Review, 29*, 401–413.

Nastasi, B. K., Varjas, K., Bernstein, R., & Pluymert, K. (1998). Mental health programming and the role of school psychologists. *School Psychology Review, 27*, 217–232.

Nastasi, B. K., Varjas, K., Sarkar, S., & Jayasena, A. (1998). Participatory model of mental health programming: Lessons learned from work in a developing country. *School Psychology Review, 27*, 260–276.

Nastasi, B. K., Varjas, K., Schensul, S. L., Silva, K. T., Schensul, J. J., & Ratnayake, P. (2000). The Participatory Intervention Model: A framework for conceptualizing and promoting intervention acceptability. *School Psychology Quarterly, 15*, 207–232.

National Advisory Mental Health Council. (1990). *National plan for research on child and adolescent mental disorders*. Washington, DC: National Institute of Mental Health.

National Advisory Mental Health Council Workgroup on Child and Adolescent Mental Health Intervention Development and Deployment. (2001). *Blueprint for change: Research on child and adolescent mental health*. Washington, DC: National Institute of Mental Health.

Pedro-Carroll, J. (1997). The Children of Divorce Intervention Program: Fostering resilient outcomes for school-aged children. In G. W. Albee & T. P. Gullotta (Eds.), *Primary prevention works* (pp. 213–238). Thousand Oaks, CA: Sage.

Pelham, W. E. Jr., Greiner, A. R., Gnagy, E. M., Hoza, B., Martin, L., Sams, S. E., & Wilson, T. (1996). Intensive treatment for ADHD: A model summer treatment program. In M. C. Roberts (Ed.), *Model programs in child and family mental health* (pp. 193–214). Mahwah, NJ: Lawrence Erlbaum Associates.

Pitcher, G. D., & Poland, S. (1992). *Crisis intervention in the schools*. New York: Guilford.

Power, T. J., DuPaul, G. J., Shapiro, E. S., & Parrish, J. M. (1995). Pediatric school psychology: The emergence of a subspecialization. *School Psychology Review, 24*, 244–257.

Reynolds, W. R. (1986). A model for the screening and identification of depressed children and adolescents in school settings. *Professional School Psychology, 1*, 117–130.

Ring-Kurtz, S. E., Sonnichsen, S., & Hoover-Dempsey, K. V. (1995). School-based mental health services for children. In L. Bickman & D. J. Rog (Eds.), *Children's mental health services, Volume 1: Research, policy, and evaluation* (pp. 117–144). Thousand Oaks, CA: Sage.

Roberts, M. C. (Ed.). (1996). *Model programs in child and family mental health*. Mahwah, NJ: Lawrence Erlbaum Associates.

Roberts, M. C., Carlson, C. I., Erickson, M. T., Friedman, R. M., La Greca, A. M., Lemanek, K. L., Russ, S. W., Schroeder, C. S., Vargas, L. A., & Wohlford, P. F. (1998). A model for training psychologists to provide services for children and adolescents. *Professional Psychology: Research and Practice, 29*, 293–299.

Roberts, M. C., & Hinton-Nelson, M. (1996). Models for service delivery in child and family mental health. In M. C. Roberts (Ed.), *Model programs in child and family mental health* (pp. 1–22). Mahwah, NJ: Lawrence Erlbaum Associates.

Rosenfield, S. A., & Gravois, T. A. (1996). *Instructional consultation teams: Collaborating for change*. New York: Guilford.

Saxe, L., Cross, T. P., Lovas, G. S., & Gardner, J. K. (1995). Evaluation of the mental health services for youth: Examining rhetoric in action. In L. Bickman & D. J. Rog (Eds.), *Children's mental health services, Volume 1: Research, policy, and evaluation* (pp. 206–235). Thousand Oaks, CA: Sage.

Schensul, J. J. (1998). Community-based risk prevention with urban youth. *School Psychology Review, 27*, 233–245.

Schensul, J. J., & LeCompte, M. D. (Eds.). (1999). *Ethnographer's toolkit* (Volumes 1 to 7). Walnut Creek, CA: AltaMira Press.

Schensul, J. J., & Schensul, S. L. (1992). Collaborative research: Methods of inquiry for social change. In M. D. LeCompte, W. L. Millroy, & J. Preissle (Eds.), *The handbook of qualitative research in education* (pp. 161–200). San Diego, CA: Academic.

Schoenwald, S. K., Henggeler, S. W., Pickrel, S. G., & Cunningham, P. B. (1996). Treating seriously troubled youths and families in their contexts: Multisystemic therapy. In M. C. Roberts (Ed.), *Model programs in child and family mental health* (pp. 317–332). Mahwah, NJ: Lawrence Erlbaum Associates.

Sheridan, S. M., Kratochwill, T. R., & Bergan, J. R. (1996). *Conjoint behavioral consultation*. New York: Plenum.

Shure, M. B. (1992). *I Can Problem Solve: An interpersonal cognitive problem-solving program.* Champaign, IL: Research Press.

Shure, M. B. (1996). I Can Problem Solve (ICPS): An interpersonal problem solving program for children. In M. C. Roberts (Ed.), *Model programs in child and family mental health* (pp. 47–62). Mahwah, NJ: Lawrence Erlbaum Associates.

Stolberg, A. L., & Gourley, E. V., III. (1996). A school-based intervention for children of divorce: The children's support group. In M. C. Roberts (Ed.), *Model programs in child and family mental health* (pp. 75–90). Mahwah, NJ: Lawrence Erlbaum Associates.

U.S. Department of Health and Human Services. (1999). *Mental health: A report of the Surgeon General.* Rockville, MD: U.S. Department of Health and Human Services, Substance Abuse and Mental Health Administration, Center for Mental Health Services, National Institutes of Health, National Institute of Mental Health.

U.S. Department of Health and Human Services. (2001a). *Mental health: Culture, race, and ethnicity—A supplement to mental health: A report of the Surgeon General.* Rockville, MD: U.S. Department of Health and Human Services, Substance Abuse and Mental Health Services Administration, Center for Mental Health Services.

U.S. Department of Health and Human Services. (2001b). *Youth violence: A report of the Surgeon General.* Rockville, MD: U.S. Department of Health and Human Services, Center for Disease Control and Prevention, National Center for Injury Prevention and Control; Substance Abuse and Mental Health Services Administration, Center for Mental Health Services; and National Institutes of Health, National Institute of Mental Health.

U.S. Public Health Service. (1999). *The Surgeon General's call to action to prevent suicide.* Washington, DC: Department of Health and Human Services.

U.S. Public Health Service. (2000). *Report of the Surgeon General's conference on children's mental health: A national action agenda.* Washington, DC: Department of Health and Human Services.

Walter, H. J., Vaughan, R. D., Armstrong, B., Krakoff, R. Y., Tiezzi, L., & McCarthy, J. F. (1995). School-based health care for urban minority junior high school students. *Archives of Pediatric and Adolescent Medicine, 149,* 1221–1225.

Webster-Stratton, C. (1993). Strategies for helping early school-aged children with oppositional defiant and conduct disorders: The importance of home-school partnerships. *School Psychology Review, 22,* 437–457.

Weissberg, R. P., Caplan, M., & Harwood, R. L. (1991). Promoting competent young people in competence-enhancing environments: A systems-based perspective on primary prevention. *Journal of Consulting and Clinical Psychology, 59,* 830–841.

Weissberg, R. P., & Elias, M. J. (1993). Enhancing young people's social competence and health behavior: An important challenge for educators, scientists, policymakers, and funders. *Applied and Preventive Psychology, 2,* 179–190.

World Health Organization. (1997, April). *Skills for life newsletter,* No. 7. Geneva, Switzerland: World Health Organization.

Yung, B. R., Hammond, W. R., Sampson, M., & Warfield, J. (1998). Linking psychology and public health: A predoctoral clinical training program in youth violence prevention. *Professional Psychology: Research and Practice, 29,* 398–401.

Zill, N., & Schoenborn, C. A. (1990). *Developmental, learning, and emotional problems: Health of our nations children, United States, 1988.* Advanced Data: National Center for Health Statistics, Number 190 (November). Hyattsville, MD.

8

Early Identification of Physical and Psychological Disorders in the School Setting

Susan J. Simonian
College of Charleston

Kenneth J. Tarnowski
Florida Gulf Coast University

INTRODUCTION

Pediatric health and behavioral problems represent a topic of critical concern to educators and health care professionals. Approximately 6.5% to 8% of U.S. children and adolescents are impacted by one or more chronic health conditions, including asthma, juvenile diabetes, and blood-related disorders (Childstats, 2001; Newacheck & Halfon, 1998). It has been estimated that chronic illness results in millions of physician contacts and days of child school absence (Newacheck & Halfon, 1998).

Health variables can impact the academic and behavioral performance of children and adolescents in several ways. First, children with chronic illnesses are at increased risk for a number of adverse outcomes, including behavior problems and peer interaction and academic difficulties (Holden, Chmielewski, Nelson, Kager, & Foltz, 1997; Krulik, 1987). Second, recent developments and improvements in the care and management of children with a variety of chronic illnesses and disabilities have resulted in increased life expectancies and improvements in the quality of life. Third, with less frequent and lengthy hospitalizations, children with chronic illnesses are spending more time in the regular school setting. Aside from chronic childhood illnesses, general physical health can have a profound effect on the academic and behavioral functioning of children in the school setting. For example, unrecognized visual and auditory problems not only make it difficult for children to learn, but also may potentiate behavioral difficulties.

In addition to physical health variables, recent epidemiological data indicate that the prevalence of behavioral and emotional problems in children and adolescents is between 12% and 27% (Costello et al., 1988; Horwitz, Leaf, Leventhal, Forsyth, & Speechley, 1992; National Institute of Mental Health, 1990). Despite the prevalence of behavioral disturbance, data indicate that parents, in the absence of explicit provider inquiry, do not routinely present child and family mental health problems to their children's health care professionals (Goldberg, Regier, McInerny, Pless, & Roghmann, 1979; Hickson, Altemeier, & O'Connor, 1983).

It has been argued that pediatricians are ideally situated for the regular screening of psychological disorders (Simonian, in press; Simonian & Tarnowski, 2001; Tarnowski, 1991). To improve rates of identification of psychopathology, Simonian, Tarnowski, Stancin, Friman, and Atkins (1991) advocated for the use of standardized screening for psychosocial dysfunction in pediatric care settings. Although pediatricians have regular contact with younger children (i.e., multiple scheduled immunizations prior to age four), the frequency of these contacts decreases significantly as the child develops beyond infancy and young childhood. Many school-age children and adolescents utilize pediatric care only in the event of an acute illness or injury. Once a child reaches kindergarten age (i.e., five years of age), the most frequent and regular contact outside of parents is with school personnel. In addition, the school environment is unique in that children and adolescents must perform a variety of structured and unstructured tasks both individually and cooperatively with peers. Therefore, children who are at risk for behavioral difficulties are likely to evidence aberrant behavior in this setting given the nature and multitude of task demands. Children's behavior problems in school settings are associated with a number of deleterious effects. Disruptive behavior interrupts instruction and necessitates teacher intervention. In addition, child behavior problems may mediate differential levels of teacher acceptance (McComas, Hoch, & Mace, 2000). Furthermore, data indicate that children with behavior problems are often perceived negatively by peers and that peer relationship problems are relatively stable over time (Coie & Dodge, 1983).

Cost-effective identification and intervention with children with health and mental health difficulties is essential to maximizing the academic potential and social–emotional health of children and adolescents. Identification of behavior that deviates from normal developmental expectations in terms of duration, frequency, and intensity represents the foundation for all primary and secondary prevention efforts (Simonian & Tarnowski, 2001). Simonian and colleagues (1991) asserted that identification of problematic behavior should follow a two-step multimethod strategy. This model, which has proven effective in psychiatric epidemiology (Dohrenwend & Shrout, 1981), includes a first step of initial identification (i.e., brief, cost-effective screening) followed by subsequent diagnostic determination (i.e., more comprehensive assessment of identified children). Screening and assessment efforts are intricately linked to prevention models. Although the school setting has long been associated with large-scale primary prevention programs (i.e., targets the entire population to prevent the onset of a problem) for problems such as drug use and gang violence, many of these programs have evidenced disappointing results. For example, Project DARE (Drug Abuse Resistance Education), a program of education and resistance training delivered by police officers to fifth- and sixth-grade students, has not resulted in the significant overall reductions in substance abuse once envisioned (Ringwalt, Ennett, & Holt, 1991). Kauffman (1997) argued that the true value of screening is for the development of secondary prevention programs (i.e., prevents existing problems from getting worse). Lochman (1995) found that parent and teacher rating scale data were the best indicators of conduct problems for first-grade children. In addition, behavior problems in kindergarten were associated with subsequent internalizing and externalizing behavioral difficulties in children. Given the epidemiological base rate data and the associated educational context variables, the school setting emerges as an important arena for the early identification of children with behavior and health difficulties.

Within the school system, identification of problematic behavior typically begins with a teacher referral (Shapiro & Kratochwill, 2000). Psychologists working with school systems often begin the screening and assessment process via informal interview with the teacher. To supplement and enhance this information, the evaluator is likely to use screening instruments including behavioral rating scales. Of course, it is essential that screening instruments are both valid and reliable. However, recent emphasis has focused not only on the psychometric integrity of instruments but also the "goodness of fit" of these tools for use in specific settings (Simonian, in press; Simonian et al., 1991). Given the limited personnel and financial constraints inherent to public educational settings, screening instruments used in the school setting must be economical to administer and score. In addition, such instruments must be relatively brief and easy to interpret by individuals who may not have extensive training in psychometrics (e.g., guidance counselors). It has been argued that effective screening instruments have clear cutting scores with optimal levels of sensitivity and specificity (i.e., accurately discriminate between at-risk versus nonrisk children) (Myers & Winters, 2002). Furthermore, screening instruments must be culturally sensitive and appropriate for ethically diverse populations. Minority children represent one of the largest growing populations within the public school system. Castillo, Quintana, and Zamarripa (2000) estimated that 35% of the overall U.S. public school population, with up to 50% of some large urban cities, is comprised of ethnic minority children. Cultural and linguistic differences impact a number of diverse variables related to screening, including school adjustment (Boykin, 1986), mental health (Tarnowski, 1991), the conceptualization of problem behavior (Crijnen, Achenbach, & Verhulst, 1997), and help-seeking behaviors (Aponte, Rivers, & Wohl, 1995). Finally, the readability of screening instruments must be appropriate for individuals from lower socioeconomic status (SES) who may have limited educational exposure (Simonian, in press).

INFORMANT RATING SCALES

Informant rating scales represent a primary method of screening for behavior problems in school and clinical settings. In addition, these instruments often serve as a component of a more thorough, multisource, multimethod assessment, or as a method of monitoring the progress or outcome of school- and home-based interventions. These instruments are generally brief and well accepted and provide information regarding behavior across a variety of settings over a period of time. Merrell (2000) described a number of advantages associated with the use of behavioral rating scales. First, these measures often require significantly less time and professional training for use. Second, data from behavior rating scales often captures low base rate behaviors that often are not identified in time-limited classroom observations. Third, rating scales generally are psychometrically sound. Fourth, informant rating scales allow for data collection on students who cannot provide self-report data (e.g., children with developmental delays). Fifth, rating scales provide important data regarding behavior that occurs in important environments (i.e., classroom and home) from the individuals who likely are the most familiar with these behaviors.

Of course, informant rating scales are associated with a number of basic measurement problems, including response bias (e.g., halo, leniency/severity, and central tendency effects) and error variance (Martin, Hooper, & Snow, 1986). In addition, informant rating scales provide summaries of behavior as perceived by others versus direct measures of a behavior in a specific setting (Merrell, 2000).

There are a number of existing informant and self-report rating scales. The following is not meant to represent an exhaustive review of all available screening instruments. Rather, it is meant to present an overview of the psychometric considerations and practical implications associated with the use of rating scales for behavioral screening in the school setting. Many of these instruments include parent and teacher forms, thus allowing for the collection of cross-situational, multi-informant screening data. Merrell (2000) asserted that behavioral screening can be broken down into two broad categories—those that measure a broad range of social behavior problems and those that measure symptoms associated with attention deficit hyperactivity disorder (ADHD).

Broad-Spectrum Rating Scales

The Achenbach (1991a, 1991b) cross-informant rating scales have been considered a foundation for screening for externalizing and internalizing behavior problems. There is a teacher (TRF) and parent (CBCL) report form, both of which gather information about the behavioral functioning and social competencies of children ages 2–16 years indexed by sex and age. In addition, the TRF includes a number of items that directly measure school-related skills. The CBCL is administered to parents and yields a total behavior problem score, internalizing and externalizing broad-band factor scores and 8–9 narrow-band (behavior subscale) scores (e.g., attention problems, aggressive behavior, somatic complaints). Parents are asked to indicate whether over 100 behaviors have occurred during the last 2 weeks on a "never," "sometimes," or "often" basis. Data yield T-scores and percentile ranks for total and broad-band factors as well as for the individual subscales. Completion of the instrument takes approximately 20 minutes, and scoring and interpretation require some training. With computerized scoring, entering and scoring profile data take approximately 10 minutes. There exists a rather extensive database to support the validity of the CBCL (Achenbach, 1991a). The CBCL has been shown to correctly classify 82.6% of referred and nonreferred children (Achenbach & Edelbrock, 1981). The TRF, which gathers information about students ages 5–18 indexed by sex and age, is similar in format, administration, scoring, and interpretation to the CBCL. Like the CBCL, the TRF yields a total behavior problem score, internalizing and externalizing broad-band factor scores and eight narrow-band (subscale) scores (e.g., aggressive behavior, attention problems, somatic complaints). Raw data are converted to T-scores and percentiles for the total and broad-band factor scores as well as the subscale scores. Consistent with the CBCL, the TRF has extensive data to support its validity and reliability (Achenbach, 1991b). In addition, interrater reliability between multiple school-based raters ranges from .42–.72, and test-retest reliability at approximately two weeks is .84, and .74 at two months (Achenbach, 1991b). Many believe that the Achenbach cross-informant screening system is too comprehensive (i.e., cumbersome) for initial or large-scale screening efforts (Simonian, in press). Whereas it may be helpful in the identification of serious behavior dysfunction, many of the clinical items that deal with severe symptomatology (e.g., hearing voices) may not be relevant to routine screening for high base rate social, behavioral, and academic-based difficulties within the school setting (Merrell, 2000). It may be that the CBCL and the TRF are best suited for screening of specific populations (e.g., screening for ADHD symptomatology) or for use as part of a more comprehensive, cross-situational assessment of overall behavioral functioning.

The Behavior Assessment System for Children (BASC; Reynolds & Kamphaus 1992) represents a multi-informant, multidimensional system of evaluation of children's behavior. The three core components of the system include the Parent Rating Scale (PRS), the Teacher Rating Scale (TRS) and the Self-Report of Personality (SRP) (discussed under Self-Report Instruments). The BASC was designed to assist professionals in the identification of a broad range of behavior disorders in children ages 2:6 through 18:11 years, and to refine differential diagnosis, educational classification, and treatment planning (Reynolds & Kamphaus, 1992) Administration time varies by component but averages between 10 to 20 minutes, and scoring, either by hand or computer (approximately 15 to 20 minutes), requires some formal training. Reynolds and Kamphaus (1992) recommend that interpretation be conducted by individuals with at least a graduate level of education. The PRS requires parents to rate over 100 behaviors on a "never," "sometimes," "often," or "always" basis. Raw scores are converted to T-scores and percentile rankings for Externalizing and Internalizing Problems, Behavioral Symptoms Index, Adaptive Skills, and School Problems composite scores as well as for clinical (i.e., subscales) scales (e.g., aggression, anxiety, atypicality, social skills). In addition, classifications levels ranging from "very low" to "clinically significant" are provided for each T-score. A well-established literature supports adequate internal consistency and interrater reliability (.50s to .70s for the child and adolescent versions) (Reynolds & Kamphaus, 1992). Acceptable content and concurrent validity is documented as are significant correlations with the CBCL (Achenbach, 1991a; Reynolds & Kamphaus, 1992). The TRS requires teachers to rate over 100 dimensions of behavior and personality on a "never," "sometimes," "often," and "always" basis. As with the PRS, raw scores are converted to T scores and percentile rankings with classification levels provided. Internal consistency and test-retest reliability (2–8 weeks) is acceptable (i.e., ranges from .70s for scale scores to mid-.90s for composite scores). Scores from the TRS are significantly correlated to other well-established teacher rating scales (e.g., the TRF; Achenbach, 1991b; Reynolds & Kamphaus, 1992). Similar to the Achenbach cross-informant screening system (Achenbach, 1991a,b), the BASC system may be too extensive in terms of length of administration, scoring, and interpretation to be cost-effective for routine behavioral screening or intervention outcome monitoring. However, some believe that when a more thorough multidimensional, multi-informant assessment is required, the BASC represents the measure of choice (Merrell, 2000).

The Devereux Behavior Rating Scale (Naglieri, LeBuffe, & Pfeiffer, 1993) was designed expressively for the school setting for the assessment of behavioral disturbance of children, ages 5–12 and adolescents, ages 13–18 years. A separate parent version of the scale is also available. Teachers are asked to rate 40 items on a 5-point scale ranging from "never" to "very frequently." The measure yields a total score and standard score for four subscales, which are linked to the federal definition of emotional disturbance as specified in the Individuals with Disabilities Education Act (1997) (e.g., inappropriate behaviors/feelings, physical symptoms/fears). Validation studies have supported acceptable criterion-related validity, internal consistency (.90s for total score and .70–.94 for subscale scores), and one-week test-retest reliability (.69–.85) (Naglieri et al., 1993). The Devereux Behavior Rating Scale is helpful in identifying specific problem behaviors, and its brief format makes it a cost-effective screening tool for use in the school setting. In addition, this instrument may be helpful for evaluating the appropriateness of special educational placement and for tracking intervention-based progress (Merrell, 2000).

The Revised Behavior Problem Checklist (RBPC; Quay & Peterson, 1987, 1996) assesses conduct problems, socialized aggression, inattention-immaturity, anxiety-withdrawal, psychotic behavior, and motor excess in children ages 5–16 years. The measure consists of 89 items that represent behavior across generic settings (i.e., the same scale can be completed by teachers, parents, or other adults familiar with the child's behavior). Informants rate problem behaviors on a 3-point scale ranging from "not a problem" to "severe problem." Raw data are converted to T-scores based on grade level and gender for each or the six behavior domains. The measure takes approximately 10–15 minutes to administer, and scoring time is very brief. Norms are available from various clinical and nonclinical populations. However, some have argued that the normative samples are not well described and as well stratified as those for other leading rating scales (Eisert, Sturner, & Mabe, 1991; Merrell, 2000). Data support adequate internal consistency (.70–.95), interrater reliability for teachers (.52–.85) and parents (.55–.93), and two-month test-retest reliability (.49–.83) (Quay & Peterson, 1996). Convergent validity has been demonstrated with other established behavior rating scales. In addition, the RBPC has been found to be especially helpful in assessing and predicting later externalizing behaviors (i.e., conduct disorder, substance abuse, antisocial behavior).

Although it was developed specifically for screening in the pediatric primary care setting, the Pediatric Symptom Checklist (PSC; Jellinek & Murphy, 1988) may hold promise for parent-based behavioral screening in the school setting. The PSC is a 35-item instrument that screens for general behavior disturbance in children ages 6–12 years. Parents are asked to respond to descriptions of psychosocial dysfunction (e.g., angry, fidgety, refuses to share) on a 3-point scale from "never" to "often." Administration and scoring each take less than 5 minutes. Numerous studies have supported acceptable levels of agreement with more comprehensive behavior rating scales including the CBCL (Achenbach, 1991a; Jellinek & Murphy, 1988; Simonian & Tarnowski, 2001) and previous mental health history (Simonian & Tarnowski, 2001). A fairly extensive literature exists to support adequate validity and reliability (Anderson et al., 1998; Murphy et al., 1996), as well as sensitivity and specificity (Jellinek & Murphy, 1988; Simonian & Tarnowski, 2001). Although the PSC has been demonstrated to be a brief, cost-effective screening instrument (e.g., appropriate for large-scale, initial behavior screening) for use in a variety of pediatric settings, the lack of a teacher-completed format may limit its broad range utility in the school setting.

Domain-Specific Rating Scales

Perhaps one of the most well-reserached behavior syndromes for children in the school setting is attention deficit hyperactivity disorder (ADHD). It is well accepted that ADHD becomes most evident when children enter the school setting with its inherent structured time and task demands. Many children with ADHD are either academic underachievers or have a learning disability (DuPaul & Stoner, 1994). In addition, children with ADHD may exhibit other internalizing and externalizing behavioral symptomatology including oppositional behavior, aggression, anxiety, dysphoria, etc. (American Psychiatric Association, 1994). In addition comorbidity of ADHD with oppositional defiant disorder or conduct disorder is associated with increased morbidity (e.g., substance abuse, delinquency, criminality) during adolescence and adulthood (DuPaul & Stoner, 1994). Recently, a number of rating scales have been developed to assess for ADHD and related symptomatology. A summary sample of those having utility for the school setting is presented below.

The Conners Rating Scale-Revised (CRS-R; Conners, 1997) represents the most recent revision to one of the most frequently used child behavior rating scales. The measure was developed to assist in the diagnosis and treatment of ADHD in children 3–17 years of age. A number of formats (i.e., short versus long form) are available for both parent (CPRS) and teacher (CTRS) completion. All of the forms require informants to rate behaviors on a 4 point scale ranging from "not at all" to "pretty much." Although the number of items varies according to format, in general the measure takes approximately 5 minutes to administer and about the same amount of time to score. Approximately 30 years of data support the psychometric integrity of this measure as well as its sensitivity to not only ADHD but also a number of external (e.g., parental involvement) and internal (e.g., Fragile X syndrome) influences (Gianarris, Golden, & Greene, 2001). Although many have postulated that the CRS-R can be appropriate for broad-spectrum behavioral screening, data indicate that it may not be helpful in discriminating between diagnostic categories. Conners (1997) maintained that the primary focus of this screening instrument is ADHD symptomatology. However, longer versions of the instrument may assist school personnel in the identification of a wide array of externalizing behavioral symptomatology, as well as specific internalizing behaviors (i.e., passivity and social withdrawal), which are indexed by the measure.

The Attention Deficit Disorders Evaluation Scale (ADDES; McCarney, 1995) is designed for the screening of ADHD-related behavior in the classroom (56-item teacher version) and home (50-item parent version) settings. Items are linked to *Diagnostic and Statistic Manual-IV* (*DSM-IV*; American Psychiatric Association, 1994) diagnostic criteria for ADHD, with subscales to represent both inattentive and hyperactive-impulsive domains. Informants are asked to rate the frequency of behavior within specific time frames, on a 5-point scale, ranging from "does not engage in the behavior" to "one to several times per hour." Initial validation studies support adequate interrater reliability between teachers (.85) and test-retest reliability (.88–.97) (McCarney, 1995). Scores from the ADDES have been shown to correlate significantly with those from the Conners Rating Scales (Conners, 1997).

Perhaps the briefest measure specific for the screening of ADHD, the ADHD Rating Scale-IV (ADHD-IV; DuPaul, Power, Anastopoulos, & Reid, 1998, consists of only 18 items directly reflecting the 18 *DSM-IV* (APA, 1994) symptom descriptions for ADHD. Consistent with *DSM-IV* diagnostic classification, the items correspond to either the Inattention or the Hyperactivity-Impulsivity domains. Teachers and parents rate the expression of behaviors on a 4 point scale ranging from "never or rarely" to "very often." Scores for the nine items on each of the two domains are converted to percentile ranks indexed by age and gender. Data supporting the psychometric integrity of the ADHD-IV have been established through a number of empirical investigations (DuPaul, 1991; DuPaul et al., 1997; DuPaul et al., 1998). Internal consistency (.86–.96), test-retest reliability for 4 week intervals (.78–.90), and interrater agreement between parents and teachers (.40–.45) are all within an acceptable range. In addition, the two-factor structure of the instrument has been supported through factor analytic investigation (DuPaul et al., 1998). The ADHD-IV appropriately discriminates between ADHD and non-ADHD children. Given the brevity of the instrument, coupled with sound psychometric support and direct link to diagnostic criteria, the ADHD-IV appears to be a cost-effective tool for screening for ADHD symptomatology in the school setting.

A number of other self-administered scales assess for situational variability and severity of ADHD symptomatology (e.g., the ADD/H Comprehensive Teacher Rating Scale [ACTeRS; Ullmann, Sleator, and Sprague, 1988] and the School Situations Questionnaire [SSQ; Barkley, 1981]). However, issues with these instruments include lack of age-specific normative data, equivocal or limited psychometric data, and outdated diagnostic criteria (Stancin & Palermo, 1997). In addition, more comprehensive screening instruments (i.e., the CBCL [Achenbach, 1991a]; the BASC [Reynolds & Kamphaus, 1992]) may adequately screen for ADHD symptomatology as well as other forms of externalizing and internalizing behavior problems. For example, Chen, Faraone, Biederman, and Tsuang (1994) found that the Attention Problems subscale of the CBCL (Achenbach, 1991a) could effectively discriminate between the presence and absence of ADHD symptomatology in a clinical population.

Other domain-specific rating scales focus on the assessment of social skills. Deficits in social skills often are related to the presence of specific behavior disorders (e.g., social phobia, mood disorders, ADHD). Many of the instruments previously discussed include items and subscales that measure dimensions of peer interactions and social skills, including aggression. Data indicate that aggression in children is a relatively stable construct and that aggression with peers predicts not only peer rejection, but also other adverse outcomes such as delinquency, criminality, underachievement, school drop-out, and mental health problems (Kohlberg, LaCrosse, & Ricks, 1972; Kupersmidt, Coie, & Dodge, 1990; Parker & Asher, 1987). Within the last two decades, specific social behavior rating scales have been developed, many for use in the school setting (e.g., The Child Behavior Scale [Ladd & Profilet, 1996], the School Social Behavior Scales [SSBS; Merrell, 1993], the Social Skills Rating System [SSRS; Gresham & Elliott, 1990]). In general, these instruments hold promise as reliable and valid screening instruments for multiple forms of peer behavior. However, additional research on the scope and broad-range utility of these instruments for comprehensive behavioral screening is warranted. Whereas one would expect these measures to be sensitive to social skill differences associated with groups of behavioral disordered youth, additional data supporting their use for larger scale, initial screening efforts within the school system are needed.

SELF-REPORT RATING SCALES

Similar to informant-completed rating scales, self-report rating scales can focus on broad-range or domain-specific behavior problems. Youth tend to be more accurate reporters of internalizing symptomatology (i.e., sadness, suicidality), whereas parents and teachers are better reporters of externalizing behavior problems (Welner, Reich, Herjanic, Jung, & Amado, 1987; Yule, 1993). Therefore, domain-specific self-report measures tend to focus on internalizing behavior problems. The child assessment literature includes comprehensive reviews of available self-report instruments and the limitations associated with their use (e.g., Corcoran & Fisher, 2000; Eckert, Dunn, Guiney, & Codding, 2000; Kratochwill & Shapiro, 1988). Many of the disadvantages associated with the use of these measures relate primarily to the self-reporting abilities of children. Young children may not be able to accurately complete self-report instruments due to limited reading ability and an inability to self-monitor thoughts, feelings, and behaviors. In general, adolescents have been considered more competent to provide self-report information. However, factors such as limited insight, lack of emotional awareness, reading ability, learning disabilities, maturity, and experience may mediate their competency (Myers & Winters, 2002). For both children and adolescents, social desirability response biases can adversely impact the integrity of data collected. Given these caveats, there are some data to suggest that youth can provide valid and reliable self-report data. The following represents an overview of selected broad-domain and domain-specific self-report inventories.

The Youth Self-Report (YSR; Achenbach, 1991c) represents a comprehensive self-report measure of both externalizing and internalizing behavior problems. As part of the Achenbach (1991a, 1991b) cross-informant rating scales, comparisons with parent and teacher report data are possible. Children ages 11–18 years respond on a 3-point scale (i.e., "never," "sometimes," "often") to 118 behavioral descriptors. The measure takes approximately 20 minutes to administer, and some expertise is required for scoring and interpretation. The YSR provides T-scores and percentile rankings for eight behavior subscales (e.g., attention problems, social problems, aggressive behavior, somatic complaints, anxious/depressed) and four composite factors (Total Competence, Total Problem Behavior, Total Internalizing Problem, Total Externalizing Problem). Adequate validity and reliability are supported by a well-developed literature, and clinical syndromes are linked to the empirical data base (Achenbach, 1993). However, the YSR requires a fifth-grade reading level and as such may not be appropriate for use with populations with limited reading abilities (i.e., children with reading disabilities, economically disadvantaged children).

A second broad-spectrum self-report inventory is the Self-Report of Personality (SRP), a component of the comprehensive Behavior Assessment System for Children (BASC; Reynolds & Kamphaus, 1992). Children, ages 8–11 years (SRP-C), and adolescents, ages 12–18 years (SRP-A), respond in a true-false format to over 150 behavioral descriptors. The measure takes approximately 30 minutes to administer, and training is required for scoring. Authors of the BASC system recommend a graduate level of education for interpretation of the measure. The SRP-C yields T-score and percentile rankings for 12 clinical subscales (e.g., anxiety, attitude to teacher, relations with parents, social stress) and 14 clinical subscales (i.e., addition of sensation seeking and somatization scales) for the SRP-A. In addition, T-scores and percentile rankings are included for four composite scores: School Maladjustment, Clinical

Maladjustment, Personal Adjustment, and Emotional Symptoms Index. Classification levels ranging from "very low" to "clinically significant" are provided for each subscale and composite T-score. A well-established literature supports the psychometric integrity of the instrument, and the inclusion of relationship variables (i.e., relations with parent, teachers, and peers) as well as measures of sensation seeking and social stress is laudable. However, some assert that the SRP does not provide enough information regarding behavior dysfunction, such as aggression, or attentional dysfunction, which is linked to psychopathology (Eckert, et al., 2000).

The Children's Depression Inventory (CDI; Kovacs, 1981, 1992) is one of the most widely known and commonly used domain-specific self-report instruments. The CDI assesses internalizing symptomatology as related to depression in children ages 7–17 years. This 27-item multiple choice instrument requires children to endorse the frequency with which (e.g., "some of the time") they experience 27 thoughts and behaviors related to 5 behavioral domains (anhedonia, ineffectiveness, interpersonal problems, negative mood, and negative self-esteem). The instrument has acceptable levels of reliability and validity (Stancin & Palermo, 1997), but has been criticized for the lack of a national normative sample (Kavan, 1990; Knoff, 1990). The CDI was not developed as a diagnostic measure of depression (Reynolds, 1992) and hence may provide information regarding the more global constructs of dissatisfaction and distress rather than clinical depression. Due to these issues, many have recommended that school-based personnel apply this measure rather conservatively in terms of screening for depression in students (Merrell, 1999).

The Reynolds Child Depression Scale (RCDS; Reynolds, 1989) and the Reynolds Adolescent Depression Scale (RADS; Reynolds, 1987) also represent self-report instruments for depressive symptomatology. The RCDS includes clinical subscales focused in the domains of Anhedonia, Despondency-Worry, Dysphoric Mod, Generalized Demoralization-Despondency and Worry, Generalized Demoralization, Self-Worth, and Somatic-Vegetative symptoms. The RADS includes 5 clinical subscales including Anhedonia, Despondency and Worry, Generalized Demoralization, Self-Worth, and Somatic-Vegetative symptoms. Severity of depressive symptomatology is measured by total composite scores. Normative data, reliability, and validity are all acceptable, and many of the RCDS/RADS items have been found to correspond to diagnostic symptoms of clinical depression (Reynolds, 1992). Data indicate that these instruments are valuable tools as well for the measurement of intervention outcomes in treatments for depression (Reynolds & Coats, 1986).

Although the domain-specific instruments discussed here focus expressively on depressive symptomatology, there are a number of other psychometrically sound self-report rating scales that focus on a range of internalizing (e.g., Piers-Harris Children's Self-Concept Scale [PHCSCS; Piers, 1984]; Revised Children's Manifest Anxiety Scale [RCMAS; Reynolds & Paget, 1981] and externalizing behavior problems (e.g., The Self-Report Delinquency Scale (SRD; Elliott, Huizinga, & Ageton [1985]). It should also be noted that there tends to be poor concordance between informant and youth self-report data (Ines & Sacco, 1992; Welner et al., 1987). Higher concordance rates are mediated by the age of the youth reporter. However, the developmental variables underlying the agreement between adult and youth raters is not fully understood. Some have postulated that advances in social-cognitive development and verbal abilities are important factors. In addition poorer adult–youth agreement is evidenced for internal states (e.g., sadness), whereas greater agreement is evidenced for concrete, observable behaviors (e.g., school disciplinary action) (Welner et al., 1987; Yule, 1993). It is more likely that self-report instruments are best employed within the context of a more comprehensive, multimethod assessment. Given the limitations of youth self-report data, these data should be used as an adjunct to data from other sources such as teacher and parent report data, classroom observation, etc. It is unlikely that any one self-report instrument represents the measure of choice for large-scale, comprehensive behavior screening in the school setting.

HEALTH-RELATED SCREENING

Physical impairments such as hearing and vision-related problems may limit children's ability to fully process sensory information, socialize, and engage in age-appropriate recreational activities. Sattler (1998) indicated that physical limitations may interfere with the optimal development of cognitive, affective, and interpersonal skills. For example, children, with visual impairment are more likely to evidence impairments in social functioning than peers with normal vision (Sisson & Van Hasselt, 1987). Whereas psychologists working within the school setting are not necessarily trained or equipped to diagnose hearing- or vision-based disorders, they can detect behaviors (e.g., failure to respond when spoken to, difficulty following oral or written directions, squinting, poor articulation, etc.), through routine behavioral screening, that suggest such deficits. In that case, the child can be referred to an opthomologist or audiologist for complete assessment. Similarly, although physical illnesses are largely a medical issue, medical illness can have significant psychological, academic, and social sequelae. Therefore, the school setting can address health-related screening through the development of school-based health clinics. For many families, especially those from disadvantaged backgrounds, access to medical and psychological care can be limited (Tarnowski, 1991). Therefore, the integration of regular health clinics that incorporate screening for hearing, vision, and other childhood illness in the school setting will likely help to identify children who are in need of more comprehensive diagnostic assessment.

CONCLUSIONS

The present review summarizes a number of informant and self-report screening instruments. However, psychologists in the school setting, must use these instruments within the context of a systematic and empirically supported model for the identification of children with behavioral and health-related problems. Once at-risk children are identified, psychologists and other school personnel must help identify more comprehensive assessment and/or effective intervention services. There is a paucity of data regarding any form of regular screening for large numbers of children within the educational system. Psychologists can also lead research efforts on the development of case-processing algorithms and articulated treatment protocols.

Given immigration patterns within the United States, linguistic ability can vary significantly among children in the school system. Many children from homes in which English is not the dominant language may have limited English proficiency prior to entry into the public school system. Although there exists a literature regarding acquisition of English as a second language (for review see, Hamers & Blanc, 1989; Lambert, 1981), and the effects of bilingualism on education, few data exist regarding the implications of language proficiency on behavior and health-related screening.

It is also important to note that the majority of the instruments reviewed here were normed utilizing various psychiatrically impaired and controlled samples. The extrapolated use of such data for application for children and youth who present with a variety of chronic illnesses remains an uncertain enterprise. Few instruments (e.g., PSC) have been developed and normed with an explicit emphasis on the screening of children in the health care setting. Obviously, more data are needed on children who present with comorbid physical and psychological difficulties. Cautious use of instruments that do not have such supporting data is recommended for children with compromised health and behavioral and emotional difficulties.

REFERENCES

Achenbach, T. M. (1991a). *Manual for the child behavior checklist/4-18 and 1991 profile* Burlington: University of Vermont Department of Psychiatry.

Achenbach, T. M. (1991b). *Manual for the teacher report form and 1991 profile.* Burlington: University of Vermont Department of Psychiatry.

Achenbach, T. M. (1991c). *Manual for the Youth Self-Report and 1991 profile.* Burlington: University of Vermont Department of Psychiatry.

Achenbach, T. M. (1993). *Empirically based taxonomy: How to use syndromes and profile types derived from the CBCL/4-18, TRF, and YSR.* Burlington: University of Vermont Department of Psychiatry.

Achenbach, T. M., & Edelbrock, C. (1981). Behavioral problems and competencies reported by parents of normal and disturbed children aged four to sixteen. *Monographs of the Society for Research on Child Development, 46,* 188.

American Psychiatric Association. (1994). *Diagnostic and statistical manual of mental disorders. Fourth edition (DSM-IV).* Washington, DC: Author.

Anderson, D. L., Spratt, E. G., Macias, M. M., Jellinek, M. S., Murphy, J. M., Pagao, M., Griesemer, D. A., Holden, K. R., & Barbosa, E. (1998). Use of the pediatric symptom checklist in the pediatric neurology population. *Pediatric Neurology, 20,* 116–120.

Aponte, J., Rivers, R. Y., & Wohl, J. (1995). *Psychological interventions and cultural diversity.* Boston: Allyn & Bacon.

Barkley, R. A. (1981). *Hyperactive children: A handbook for diagnosis and treatment.* New York: Guilford.

Boykin, A. W. (1986). *The school achievement of minority children.* Hillsdale, NJ: Lawrence Erlbaum Associates.

Castillo, E. M., Quintana, S. M., & Zamarripa, M. X. (2000). Cultural and linguistic issues. In E. S. Shaprio & T. R. Kratochwill (Eds.), *Conducting school based assessments of child and adolescent behavior.* New York: Guilford.

Chen, W. J., Faraone, S. V., Biederman, J., & Tsuang, M. T. (1994). Diagnostic accuracy of the child behavior checklist scales for attention-deficit hyperactivity disorder: A receiver-operating characteristic analysis. *Journal of Consulting and Clinical Psychology, 62,* 1017–1025.

Childstats. (2001). Federal interagency forum on child and Family statistics [Online]. Available: http://childstats.gov.

Coie, J. D., & Dodge, K. A. (1983). Continuities and changes in children's social status: A five-year longitudinal study. *Merrill-Palmer Quarterly, 29,* 261–282.

Conners, C. K. (1997). *Conners' Rating Scales—revised.* New York: Multi Health Systems.

Corcoran, K., & Fischer, J. (2000). *Measures for clinical practice: A sourcebook* (3rd ed.). New York: Free Press.

Costello, E. J., Burns, B. J., Costello, A. J., Edelbrock, C., Dulcan, M., & Brent, D. (1988). Service utilization and psychiatric diagnosis in pediatric primary care: The role of the gatekeeper. *Pediatrics, 82,* 415–424.

Crijnen, A. A. M., Achenbach, T. M., & Verhulst, F. C. (1997). Comparisons of problems reported by parents of children in 12 cultures. Total problems, externalizing and internalizing. *Journal of the American Academy of Child and Adolescent Psychiatry, 9,* 1269–1277.

Dohrenwend, B. D., & Shrout, P. B. (1981). Toward the development of a two-stage procedure for case identification and classification in psychiatric epidemiology. *Research in Community Mental Health, 2,* 295–323.

DuPaul, G. J. (1991). Parent and teacher ratings of AD/HD symptoms: Psychometric properties in a community-based sample. *Journal of Clinical Child Psychology, 20,* 245–253.

DuPaul, G. J., Anastopoulos, A. D., Power, T. J., Reid, R., Ikeda, M., & McGoey, K. (1998). Parent ratings of attention-deficit/hyperactivity disorder symptoms: Factor structure and normative data. *Journal of Psychopathology and Behavioral Assessment, 20,* 83–102.

DuPaul, G. J., Power, T. J., Anastopoulos, A. D., & Reid, R. (1998). *ADHD Rating Scale-IV: Checklists, norms, and clinical interpretation.* New York: Guilford Press.

DuPaul, G. J., Power, T. J., Anastopoulos, A. D., Reid, R., McGoey, K., & Ikeda, M. (1997). Teacher ratings of attention-deficit/hyperactivity disorder: Factor structure and normative data. *Psychological Assessment, 9,* 436–444.

DuPaul, G. J., & Stoner, G. (1994). *ADHD in the schools: Assessment and intervention strategies.* New York: Guilford.

Eckert, T. L., Dunn, E. K., Guiney, K. M., & Codding, R. S. (2000). Self-reports: Theory and research in using rating scale measures. In E. S. Shapiro & T. R. Kratochwill (Eds.), *Behavioral assessment in schools: Theory research, and clinical foundations* (2nd ed., pp. 288–322). New York: Guilford.

Eisert, D. C., Sturner, R. A., & Mabe, P. A. (1991). Questionnaires in behavioral pediatrics: Guidelines for selection and use. *Developmental and Behavioral Pediatrics, 12,* 42–50.

Elliott, D. S., Huizinga, D., & Ageton, S. S. (1985). *Explaining delinquency and drug use.* Beverly Hills, CA: Sage.

Gianarris, W. J., Golden, C. J., & Greene, L. (2001). The Conners' Parent Rating Scales: A critical review of the literature. *Clinical Psychology Review, 21,* 1061–1093.

Goldberg, I. D., Regier, D. A., McInerny, T. K., Pless, I. B., & Roghmann, K. J. (1979). The role of the pediatrician in the delivery of mental health services to children. *Pediatrics, 63,* 898–909.

Gresham, F. M., & Elliott, S. N. (1990). *The social skills rating system.* Circle Pines, MN: American Guidance.

Hamers, J., & Blanc, M. H. (1989). *Bilinguality and bilinguism.* Cambridge, UK: Cambridge University Press.

Hickson, G. B., Altemeier, W. A., & O'Connor, S. (1983). Concerns of mothers seeking care in private practice pediatric offices: Opportunities for expanding services. *Pediatrics, 72*, 619–624.

Holden, E. W., Chmielewski, D., Nelson, C., Kager, V. A., & Foltz, L. (1997). Controlling for general and disease-specific effects in child and family adjustment to chronic childhood illness. *Journal of Pediatric Psychology, 22*, 15–28.

Horwitz, S. M., Leaf, P. J., Leventhal, J. M., Forsyth, B., & Speechley, K. N. (1992). Identification and management of psychosocial and developmental problems in community-based primary care clinics. *Pediatrics, 89*, 480–485.

Ines, T. M., & Sacco, W. P. (1992). Factors related to correspondence between teacher ratings of elementary student depression and student self-ratings. *Journal of Consulting and Clinical Psychology, 60*, 140–142.

Jellinek, M. S., & Murphy, J. M. (1988). Screening for psychosocial disorder in pediatric practice. *American Journal of Diseases of Children, 109*, 371–378.

Kauffman, J. M. (1997). *Characteristics of behavior disorders of children and youth* (6th ed.). Upper Saddle River, NJ: Prentice-Hall.

Kavan, M. G. (1990). Review of the children's depression inventory. In J. J. Kramer & J. C. Conoley (Eds.), *The supplement to the 10th mental measurements yearbook* (pp. 46–48). Lincoln, NE: Buros Institute of Mental Measurements.

Knoff, H. M. (1990). Review of the children's depression inventory. In J. J. Kramer & J. C. Conoley (Eds.), *The supplement to the 10th mental measurements yearbook* (pp. 48–50). Lincoln, NE: Buros Institute of Mental Measurements.

Kohlberg, L., LaCrosse, J., & Ricks, D. (1972). The predictability of adult mental health from childhood. In B. Wolman (Ed.), *Manual of child psychopathology* (pp. 1217–1283). New York: McGraw-Hill.

Kovacs, M. (1981). Rating scales to assess depression in school-aged children. *Acta Paedopsychiatria, 46*, 305–315.

Kovacs, M. (1992). *Children's depression inventory.* Los Angeles: Multi-Health Systems.

Kratochwill, T. R., & Shapiro, E. S. (1988). Introduction: Conceptual foundations of behavioral assessment. In E. S. Shapiro & T. R. Kratochwill (Eds.), *Behavioral assessment in the schools* (pp. 384–454). New York: Guilford.

Krulik, T. (1987). Loneliness and social isolation in school-age children with chronic life-threatening illness. In T. Krulik, B. Holaday, & I. M. Martinson (Eds.), *The child and family facing life-threatening illness* (pp. 133–161). New York: Lippincott.

Kupersmidt, J. B., Coie, J. D., & Dodge, K. A. (1990). The role of poor peer relationships in the development of disorder. In S. R. Asher & J. D. Coie (Eds.), *Peer rejection in childhood* (pp. 274–305). New York: Cambridge University Press.

Ladd, G. W., & Profilet, S. M. (1996). The Child Behavior Scale: A teacher-report-measure of young children's aggressive, withdrawn, and prosocial behaviors. *Developmental Psychology, 32*, 1008–1024.

Lambert, W. E. (1981). Bilingualism and language acquisition. *Annals of the New York Academy of Science, 379*, 9–22.

Lochman, J. E. (1995). Screening of child behavior problems for prevention programs at school entry. *Journal of Consulting and Clinical Psychology, 63*, 549–559.

Martin, R. P., Hooper, S., & Snow, J. (1986). Behavior rating scale approaches to personality assessment in children and adolescents. In H. Knoff (Ed.), *The assessment of child and adolescent personality* (pp. 309–351). New York: Guilford.

McCarney, S. B. (1995). *Attention Deficit Disorders Evaluation Scale–school version.* Columbia, MO: Hawthorne Educational Services.

McComas, J. J., Hoch, H., & Mace, F. C. (2000). Functional analysis. In E. S. Shaprio & T. R. Kratochwill (Eds.), *Conducting school-based assessments of child and adolescent behavior* (pp. 78–101). New York: Guilford.

Merrell, K. W. (1993). *School Social Behavior Scales.* Austin, TX: PRO-ED.

Merrell, K. W. (1999). *Behavioral, social, and emotional assessment of children.* Mahwah, NJ: Lawrence Erlbaum Associates.

Merrell, K. W. (2000). Informant reports: Theory and research in using child behavior rating scales in school settings. In E. S. Shapiro & T. R. Kratochwill (Eds.), *Behavioral assessment in schools: Theory research, and clinical foundations* (2nd ed.; pp. 233–256). New York: Guilford.

Murphy, J. M., Reede, J., Jellinek, M. S., & Bishop, S. (1992). Screening for psychosocial dysfunction in inner-city children. Further validation of the Pediatric Symptom Checklist. *Journal of the American Academy of child and Adolescent Psychiatry, 31*, 221–232.

Murphy, J. M., Ichinose, C., Hicks, R. C., Kingdon, D., Crist-Whitzel, J., Jordan, P., Feldman, G., & Jellinek, M. S. (1996). Utility of the Pediatric Symptom Checklist as a psychosocial screen to meet the federal Early and Periodic Screening, Diagnosis, and Treatment (EPSDT) standards: A pilot study. *Journal of Pediatrics, 129*, 864–869.

Myers, K., & Winters, N. C. (2002). Ten-year review of rating scales I: Overview of scale functioning, psychometric properties, and selection. *Journal of the American Academy of Child and Adolescent Psychiatry, 41*, 114–122.

Naglieri, J. A., LeBuffe, P. A., & Pfeiffer, S. I. (1993). *Devereux Behavior Rating Scale-school form.* San Antonio, TX: Psychological Corporation.

National Institute of Mental Health. (1990). *National plan for research on child and adolescent mental disorders.* Rockville, MD: National Institute of Mental Health.

Newacheck, P. W., & Halfon, N. (1998). Prevalence and impact of disabling chronic conditions in childhood. *American Journal of Public Health, 88*, 610–617.

Parker, J. G., & Asher, S. R. (1987). Peer relations and later personal adjustment: Are low-accepted children at risk? *Psychological Bulletin, 102*, 357–389.

Piers, E. V. (1984). *Revised manual for the Piers-Harris Children's Self-Concept Scale.* Los Angeles: Western Psychological Services

Quay, H. C., & Peterson, D. R. (1987). *Manual for the revised child behavior checklist.* Unpublished manuscript, University of Miami.

Quay, H. C., & Peterson, D. R. (1996). *Manual for the revised child behavior checklist—PAR version.* Odessa, FL: Psychological Assessment Resources.

Reynolds, C. R., & Kamphaus, R. W. (1992). *Behavior assessment system for children.* Circle Pines, MN: American Guidance Service.

Reynolds, C. R., & Richmond, B. O. (1981). *The Revised Children's Manifest Anxiety Scale.* Austin, TX: Pro-Ed.

Reynolds, C. R., & Paget, K. D. (1981). Factor analysis of the Revised Children's Manifest Anxiety Scale for blacks, whites, males, and females with a national normative sample. *Journal of Consulting and Clinical Psychology, 44*, 352–359.

Reynolds, W. M. (1987). *Professional manual for the Reynolds Adolescent Depression Scale.* Los Angeles: Western Psychological Services.

Reynolds, W. M. (1989). *Professional manual for the Reynolds Child Depression Scale.* Odessa, FL: Psychological Assessment Resources.

Reynolds, W. M. (1992). Depression in children and adolescents. In W. M. Reynolds (Ed.), *Internalizing disorders in children and adolescents* (pp. 149–254). New York: Wiley.

Reynolds, W. M., & Coats, K. I. (1986). A comparison of cognitive-behavior therapy and relaxation training for the treatment of depression in adolescents. *Journal of Consulting and Clinical Psychology, 54*, 653–660.

Ringwalt, C., Ennett, S. T., & Holt, K. D. (1991). An outcome evaluation of Project Dare (Drug Abuse Resistance Education). *Health Education Research, 6*, 327–337.

Sattler, J. M. (1998). Clinical and forensic interviewing of children and families: Guidelines for the mental health, education, pediatric, and child maltreatment fields. San Diego, CA: Jerome M. Sattler, Publisher, Inc.

Shapiro, E. S., & Kratochwill, T. R. (2000). Conducting a multidimensional behavioral assessment. In E. S. Shapiro & T. R. Kratochwill (Eds.), *Conducting school based assessment of child and adolescent behavior* (pp. 1–20). New York, Guildford Press.

Simonian, S. J. (in press). Screening and identification in pediatric primary care. *Behavior Modification.*

Simonian, S. J., & Tarnowski, K. J. (2001). Utility of the pediatric symptom checklist for behavior screening of disadvantaged children. *Journal of Child Psychiatry and Human* Development, *31*, 269–278.

Simonian, S. J., Tarnowski, K. J., Stancin, T., Friman, P. C., & Atkins, M. (1991). Disadvantaged children and families in pediatric primary care settings II: Screening for behavior disturbance. *Journal of Clinical Child Psychology, 20*, 360–371.

Sisson, L. A., & Van Hasselt, V. B. (1987). Visual impairment. In V. B. Hasselt & M. Hersen (Eds.), *Psychological evaluation of the developmentally and physically disabled* (pp. 115–153). New York: Plenum.

Stancin, T., & Palermo, T M. (1997). A review of behavioral screening practices in pediatric settings: Do they pass the test? *Developmental and Behavioral Pediatrics, 18*, 183–193.

Tarnowski, K. J. (1991). Disadvantaged children and families in pediatric primary care settings I: Broadening the scope of integrated mental health service. *Journal of Clinical Child Psychology, 20*, 351–359.

Ullmann, R. K., Sleator, E. K., & Sprague, R. L. (1988). A new rating scale for diagnosis and monitoring of ADD children. *Psychopharmacological Bulletin, 20*, 160–165.

Welner, Z., Reich, W., Herjanic, B., Jung, K. G., & Amado, H. (1987). Reliability, validity, and parent child agreement studies of the diagnostic interview for children and adolescents (DICA). *Journal of the American Academy of Child and Adolescent Psychiatry, 26*, 649–653.

Yule, W. (1993). Developmental considerations in child assessment. In T. H. Ollendick & M. Hersen (Eds.), *Handbook of child and adolescent assessment,* Vol. 167 (pp. 15–25). Boston: Allen & Bacon.

9

Adherence

Kathleen L. Lemanek
Columbus Children's Hospital
Ohio State University College of Medicine

The optimal care of children with chronic diseases should be based on a comprehensive program that involves multiple professionals (Drotar, 2001; Hobbs & Perrin, 1985). Such an approach generally includes family members, mental health professionals, and health care providers. While attention has been directed toward increasing family involvement in the comprehensive care of children, the involvement of the school has not been consistently sought (Drotar, 2001). There are, however, models available that incorporate school personnel in the delivery of medical, social, and mental health services to children in educational settings (Gardner, 1992). If implemented, these models are supposed to increase the efficiency of treatment, reduce their costs, and decrease the likelihood of professional burnout (Thousand & Villa, 1992). Within these model services are either termed school-linked or school-based services, where schools provide primary, secondary, or tertiary interventions to address a range of problems (D'Amato & Dean, 1989). School-linked health services refer to medical, social, and mental health services that are available to students outside the school building (Gardner, 1992). In contrast, school-based health services provide a range of medical services directly in the school building, usually by a part-time or full-time school nurse (Gardner, 1992).

Preventive care or services provided by the schools typically involve giving scheduled immunizations, physical examinations, and nutritional advice, as well as prevention of suicides, injuries, and school violence (Shaw, Kelly, Joost, & Parker-Fisher, 1995). Such high-risk behaviors as alcohol and drug abuse, smoking, accidents, sexually transmitted diseases, and eating disorders are the focus of secondary care or services (Berlin, 1990; Shaw et al., 1995). Acute care provided in school clinics to students with injuries and somatic complaints, such as stomachaches and headaches, could be considered secondary interventions (Shaw et al., 1995). Tertiary intervention or chronic care highlights providing special educational services to children with chronic diseases based on the Individuals with Disabilities Act (1990; PL 101-476; 94-142) (Shaw et al., 1995). In general, these services are applied in varying degrees to children with disorders that impose physical, cognitive, and emotional or social impairments in school settings (Shellenberger & Couch, 1984). These disorders may pertain to developmental disabilities, such as autism and mental retardation, or chronic diseases, such as asthma, cancer, diabetes, or epilepsy, as well as those requiring rehabilitation, such as traumatic brain injuries (Shellenberger & Couch, 1984). Consultation, counseling, home-based school collaboration, crisis intervention, and family therapy are suggested methods of intervention to address these problems (Shellenberger & Couch, 1984).

In theory the benefits of a comprehensive approach to the care of children should outweigh the costs of such services. Unfortunately, barriers limit such an approach from being delivered in practice. Drotar (2001) listed several such barriers including cost-containment of medical procedures, separation of mental health from health care coverage, and reduced allowance for hospitalizations. Within the school system, such barriers pertain to systemic and individual resistance related to reimbursement and professional identity, minimal time due to mandatory assessments for special educational services, and training issues (i.e., different jargon, socialization, knowledge of roles and functions) (Dobos, Dworkin, & Bernstein, 1994; Parsons & Meyers, 1987; Thousand & Villa, 1992; West, 1990).

Funding and federal statutes, in fact, encourage and require schools to participate to some degree in the health care of children and adolescents (Gerry & Certo, 1992). Examples of these statutes include the Agency for Health Care Policy and Research Programs (PL 102-410) and the Preventative Health Amendment (PL 102–531). While legislatures assign a priority to the collaboration between medicine and education in the school setting, teachers seem unclear as to their involvement in the medical care of children and adolescents (Gerry & Certo, 1992). In addition, for school personnel there are competing demands from government initiatives in education that focus on tests and performance and from the medical community and families that request services for an increasing number of students enrolled with chronic diseases (Mukherjee, Lightfoot, & Sloper, 2000).

Adherence to acute and chronic medical regimens affect whether children and adolescents attend school and, once in school, their level of functioning. Because of the importance of adherence to the functioning of children and adolescents, this chapter emphasizes the literature related to adherence to both acute and chronic medical regimens. Adherence is defined and prevalence rates are given for acute and chronic diseases. The consequences of nonadherence, correlates of adherence, and assessment methods are summarized. Interventions designed to improve adherence are described, in addition to the evidence for their empirical support. The chapter then focuses on the relevance of this review to the school setting. The data on adherence in school settings is almost nonexistent. However, studies pertaining to the functioning of children with acute and chronic diseases in school, especially the latter, is discussed in relation to issues of adherence. The chapter concludes with suggestions for areas of future research and practice.

DEFINITION OF ADHERENCE

The definition of adherence proposed by Robert Haynes in 1979 is still the one most often used in clinical practice and research. He defined adherence as "the extent to which a person's behavior (terms of medications, following diets, or executing lifestyle changes) coincides with medical or health advice" (Haynes, 1979, pp. 2–3). This definition not only delineates a range of adherent behaviors (e.g., taking medications, following diets) but also suggests whether adherence agrees with medical recommendations (Rapoff & Barnard, 1991). Adherent behaviors for acute medical regimens typically include medication taking for various infections, receiving scheduled immunizations, and keeping appointments. Regimen components for chronic diseases are more diverse than for short-term regimens and often additive in terms of the number of individual tasks patients are expected to complete. The most common regimen components for chronic diseases consist of taking medications, following dietary and exercise recommendations, and monitoring symptoms (e.g., glucose levels, peak expiratory flow rate).

La Greca and Schuman (1995) outlined three approaches to operationalize adherent behavior. The first approach categorizes patients as either adherent or nonadherent according to specific criteria or cutoff scores. The second approach generates an overall index of adherence by combining multiple indicators of adherence. In the third approach, adherence is viewed as a continuum where adherence rates are calculated for specific behaviors. La Greca and Schuman considered this third approach as optimal due to its ability to compare rates of adherence across individuals and studies.

PREVALENCE OF NONADHERENCE

On average, the prevalence of nonadherence to acute medical regimens is at least 33% (Rapoff, 1999) and between 50% and 55% for chronic medical regimens (Dunbar-Jacob et al., 2000; Litt & Cuskey, 1980). These rates of nonadherence have remained fairly consistent over time, continuing to make nonaderence "the best documented but least understood health-related behavior" (Becker & Maiman, 1975, p. 11). The fact that prevalence estimates for nonadherence to acute medical regimens and to chronic medical regimens vary depending on a range of factors contributes to this limited understanding. These factors include what patients are sampled, what behaviors are measured, what measures are employed, and what criteria are used to classify patients as nonadherent (Rapoff, 1999; Rapoff & Barnard, 1991). For example, Dunbar-Jacob and colleagues (2000) cited nonadherence rates for appointment keeping from 8.5% to 63.4% in their review of adherence in chronic disease across the life span. In terms of chronic diseases, nonadherence rates for pediatric asthma have ranged from 34% (Wood, Casey, Kolski, & McCormick, 1985) to 98% (Sublett, Pollard, Kadlec, & Karibo, 1979) when examining serum assays for therapeutic levels of theophylline. With respect to medications administered through metered-dose inhalers, nonadherence rates range from 40% to 55%, based on either canister weights (Zora, Lutz, & Tinkelman, 1989) or a Nebulizer chronolog (Coutts, Gibson, & Paton, 1992).

CONSEQUENCES OF NONADHERENCE

The documented consequences of nonadherence center on costs related to individual symptom management, health care utilization, and clinical outcomes. One negative consequence of nonadherence is increased morbidity and mortality. Increased morbidity is reflected in exacerbation of symptoms, serious medical complications, and greater school absences. For example, nonadherence may lead to heart, kidney, or liver transplant failures or to reemergence of such infectious diseases as tuberculosis (Rapoff, 1999). The limiting effects of symptoms on daily activities, social relationships, and school attendance also are evident across diseases (Dunbar-Jacob et al., 2000; Rapoff, 1999). Asthma management may account for anywhere from 2% to 30% of a family's income, excluding costs related to lost work time and home alterations required as part of the treatment program (Creer, Renne, & Chai, 1982). Finally, while asthma-related deaths are low compared to the number of deaths from other illnesses (e.g., cancer), the mortality rate may be as high as 1% to 2% (Rubinstein, Hindi, Moss, Blessing-Moore, & Lewiston, 1984).

Adverse clinical outcomes are associated with nonadherence for both individual patients and for classes of patients. For individual patients, poor clinical outcomes may be attributed to ineffective medical regimens that necessitate prescription of stronger medications or scheduling of additional procedures (Rapoff, 1999). Conversely, assumptions are made that link regimen failures to nonadherence, which precludes examination of other potential reasons for such failures and, therefore, effective treatments (Rapoff, 1999). Nonadherence also may influence decisions regarding clinical drug trials in terms of the adequacy of specific medications to manage diseases (Rapoff, 1999; Rapoff & Barnard, 1991).

A third impact of nonadherence is on increased health care costs, with estimates of $100 billion annually (Berg, Dischler, Wagner, Raia, & Palmer-Shevlin, 1993; Lewis, 1997). These costs are related to money spent on unused or unclaimed medications, needless laboratory tests, and unnecessary clinic appointments, emergency room visits, and/or hospitalizations (Dunbar-Jacob et al., 2000; Lemanek, 1990; Rapoff, 1999). Because of the range of negative consequences of nonadherence, research has attempted to identify factors related to nonadherence.

CORRELATES OF NONADHERENCE

Identified factors related to nonadherence to medical regimens can be placed into one of three categories: (1) regimen characteristics, (2) disease characteristics, and (3) patient/family characteristics (Creer & Levstek, 1996; La Greca & Schuman, 1995). These characteristics are correlated with adherence or nonadherence and identified through correlational/regression analyses or analyses of group differences (Rapoff, 1999). Although not being based on theoretical models, they serve to target "at-risk" individuals and those characteristics that are amenable to modification (Rapoff, 1999).

The first category of risk factors is related to patient and family characteristics, such as demographics, knowledge and health beliefs, and parent monitoring or supervision (Dunbar-Jacob et al, 2000; La Greca & Schuman, 1995; Rapoff, 1999). All aspects of children's and adolescents' cognitive, physical, social, and emotional functioning influence successful management of and adherence to medical regimens. These domains of functioning are then modified by peer and cultural contextual factors (Dunbar-Jacob et al., 2000). Demographic characteristics center on developmental and chronological age and economic status of the family. In general, lower socioeconomic status in general, and parent education levels in particular, are associated with nonadherence in pediatric asthma, cystic fibrosis, diabetes, and renal disease (Rapoff, 1999). Because of the cognitive demands of adhering to medical regimens, developmental level rather than chronological age should be considered in examining children and adolescents' abilities to manage their chronic disease. However, with few exceptions, extreme age ranges (i.e., very young and adolescents) show decreased adherence for such diseases as asthma, diabetes, cancer, and cystic fibrosis (La Greca & Schuman, 1995; Lemanek, 1990; Rapoff & Barnard, 1991).

Dunbar-Jacob et al. (2000) delineated those cognitive skills required in simply taking medication, which includes attending to health care professional's instructions, encoding the treatment plan, recalling it from long-term memory, integrating new information into daily activities, monitoring adherent behavior, and updating "working memory." These skills are conceptualized as reflecting higher executive functions. As such, children and adolescents who have problems paying attention, understanding verbal instructions, or remembering immediate and long-term tasks should show poorer adherence than those without these problems (Dunbar-Jacob et al., 2000). However, the relationship between age or cognitive functioning and adherence is complex and not well delineated (Dunbar-Jacob et al., 2000). For example, school-age children's cognitive view that recovery from illness results from strict adherence to rigid health rules is conducive to medical adherence (La Greca & Schuman, 1995). In contrast, preschool-age children's belief that illness is a consequences of bad behavior and adolescents' feelings of invincibility hinder adherence to medical regimens. In addition, children and adolescents' increasing contacts with peers at school and emphasis on peer acceptance may pose barriers to adherence (La Greca & Schuman, 1995). To counter any cognitive deficits, Dunbar-Jacob and colleagues (2000) suggested the use of external supports either through mechanical devices or human support.

Parents' and children's active knowledge of their disease and treatment and skills in implementing management tasks are associated with adherence with respect to such diseases as asthma, diabetes, and hemophilia (La Greca & Schuman, 1995; Rapoff, 1999). La Greca and Schuman (1995) stipulated that active knowledge of one's disease involves not only having specific facts about the disease, but also understanding the individual regimen tasks, the ability to execute these tasks correctly, and the capability to make changes when problems arise. Similarly, Rapoff (1999) proposed a distinction between "knowing that" (knowledge) and "knowing how" (skills). The former involves knowing about something or knowledge and the latter consist of skills or knowing how to do something. While knowledge is necessary for skill development, adequate knowledge about one's disease and treatment does not necessarily lead to adherence to the regime or skill in executing it. These skill deficits become most notable when executing parts of tasks and making decisions when problems arise, such as food restrictions during social activities and timing of outdoor excursions (Rapoff, 1999; Rapoff & Barnard, 1991).

Any personal or family factor that interferes with being able to attend to, comprehend, remember, or complete medical tasks impedes adherence. In general, adherence to medical regimens is more challenging for those patients with additional behavioral or psychiatric problems, either before or after disease onset (La Greca & Schuman, 1995; Rapoff & Barnard, 1991). Personal factors that are associated with lower adherence include emotional maladjustment (e.g., depression), behavior problems (e.g., noncompliance), low self-esteem or feelings of ineffectiveness, and poor problem-solving skills in such diseases as diabetes, cystic fibrosis, juvenile rheumatoid arthritis, and cancer (La Greca & Schuman, 1995; Rapoff, 1999).

A bidirectional influence appears to exist between family functioning and adherence as it relates to families' ability to cope with and adjust to children's and adolescents' disease (La Greca & Schuman, 1995; Rapoff & Barnard, 1991). A primary source of support for children and adolescents are their families in terms of tangible resources (i.e., instrumental support) and acceptance or praise (i.e., emotional support) (La Greca & Schuman, 1995). Family discord, disorganization, and parent pathology (e.g., anxiety) interfere with adequate support and supervision and, therefore, relate to poor treatment management (Dunbar-Jacob et al., 2000; Rapoff, 1999). In turn, inconsistent supervision or monitoring by physicians and parents is related to nonadherence in children and adolescents with different chronic diseases, such as asthma, diabetes, and cancer (Dunbar-Jacob et al., 2000; La Greca & Schuman, 1995; Rapoff, 1999).

The second category of risk factors is those related to the disease. Disease characteristics consist of asymptomatic periods, younger age at illness onset, and illness severity as perceived by the family. Decreased adherence is evident when patients are not experiencing symptoms (Dunbar-Jacob et al, 2000; Rapoff, 1999). With short-term regimens, symptom reduction may occur after 3 to 4 days and patients may then discontinue some or all of the medication. With chronic diseases, such as asthma and juvenile rheumatoid arthritis, periods of remission and exacerbation are more apparent. Patients also may adapt to a steady state of symptomatic discomfort, such as with sickle cell disease (Rapoff & Barnard, 1991). In general, the duration/course of such chronic diseases as asthma, diabetes, and renal disease is related to adherence (Johnson, Freund, Silverstein, Hansen, & Malone, 1990; La Greca & Schuman, 1995; Lemanek, 1990). Adherence declines over the length of treatment and is particularly problematic with earlier age of onset (Dunbar-Jacob et al., 2000; Rapoff & Barnard, 19991). However, if positive effects are obtained by following regimen components (e.g., pain relief or symptom reduction), adherence is a more likely outcome. The literature indicates that adolescents who engage in nonadherent behaviors without experiencing negative consequences are more likely to repeat these behaviors or nonadherent episodes (Dunbar, 1983; La Greca & Hanna, 1983). Finally, the beliefs of children and parents regarding: (1) seriousness of disease, (2) increased susceptibility to complications, and (3) benefits of regimen appear to promote adherence (Rapoff, 1999; Rapoff & Barnard, 1991). These beliefs may be related to the degree of parental supervision and vigilance about following regimen components, which are, in fact, correlates of adherence (Rapoff & Barnard, 1991).

Regimen factors are the third category of risk factors and include complexity of the regimen, presence of adverse side effects of the medication or the regimen, and unstable efficacy of the regimen. In terms of regimen complexity, having to take multiple medications on different schedules decreases adherence. In addition, high-demand regimens that require lifestyle changes are more difficult to follow than those that focus on medication taking alone. For example, regimens that involve dietary modifications (e.g., diabetes, obesity) alter family eating habits. Regimens that demand frequent hospital-based procedures or emergency room visits (e.g., sickle cell disease, cancer) interfere with family routines and activities (Dunbar-Jacob et al., 2000; Rapoff & Barnard, 1991). Negative side effects of regimens also relate to poor adherence with respect to changes in appearance (e.g., chemotherapy, steroid medications) and interference with social activities or participation in athletics (La Greca & Schuman, 1995; Lemanek, 1990). This relationship is observed even for life-threatening conditions, such as chest physiotherapy for patients with cystic fibrosis and immunosuppressive medications for patients with renal transplants (Rapoff, 1999; Rapoff & Barnard, 1991). Finally, the relationship and the communication between families and their providers are associated with adherence to such diseases as asthma and diabetes (Lemanek, 1990; Rapoff, 1999). Examples of these factors include perceptions of the medical provider as being warm and empathic, convenience of medical care, and explaining and repeating instructions using limited jargon.

THEORIES OF ADHERENCE

How adherence is conceptualized for clinical practice or research will affect the assessment measures chosen, the experimental designs used, and the statistical analyses conducted, as well as how the data are interpreted. However, the literature on adherence is primarily based on correlational studies rather than those using a particular theoretical perspective. La Greca and Schuman (1995) and Rapoff (1999) summarized and critiqued the essential components of various theoretical perspectives on adherence and health care behaviors. As noted by La Greca and Schuman, it is a formable challenge for theories to account for the complexity and individuation of diseases and medical regimens, along with the mediating effects of changing developmental challenges in childhood and adolescence. The theories delineated to varying degrees by La Greca and Schuman (1995) and Rapoff (1999) include the Children's Health Belief Model (Bush & Iannotti, 1990), Social Cognitive Theory (Bandura, 1997; O'Leary, 1992), Theory of Reasoned Action/Planned Behavior (Montano, Kasprzk, & Taplin, 1997), Transtheoretical Model of Change (Prochaska, Redding, & Evers, 1997), and Applied Behavior Analysis (Rapoff, 1996). The Health Belief Model and the Transtheoretical Model of Change appear to be the models examined most in pediatric and adult populations, although the literature on pediatric populations is scant.

The Health Belief Model was developed by Becker and his colleagues (e.g., Becker, Drachman, & Kirscht, 1972) to attempt to explain nonadherence to preventive health regimens (e.g., dietary restrictions for high blood pressure). This model was then extended to adherence to prescribed regimens (e.g., dietary restrictions for high blood pressure). This model was then extended to adherence to prescribed regimens (Janz & Becker, 1984) and pediatric populations (Bush & Iannotti, 1990). Sets of variables are proposed as predictors of adherence (e.g., perceived susceptibility), as barriers to adherence (e.g., perceived financial cost), and as moderators (e.g., age, caretaker's perceived benefits of medication). Although data on the relationship between parents' beliefs about susceptibility, severity, and benefits support the Health Belief Model, information from adolescents do not consistently show such a relationship (e.g., Bond, Aiken, & Somerville, 1992; Tamaroff, Festa, Adesman, & Walco, 1992). The Health Belief Model also is criticized for the difficulties in operationalizing the proposed concepts and beliefs and translating specific findings into treatment strategies (La Greca & Schuman, 1995; Rapoff, 1999).

The Transtheoretical Model of Behavior Change originally addressed systems of psychotherapy (Prochaska, 1979) and then targeted high-risk behaviors (e.g., smoking) and health-promoting behaviors (e.g., Prochaska, DiClemente, & Norcross, 1992). This model postulates five stages that individuals move through to change health behaviors, including precontemplative, contemplative, preparation, action, and maintenance. The constructs of decisional balance and self-efficacy are moderating variables that influence how and when individuals progress, relapse, and recycle through these five stages. The fluidity of the stages and the lack of application to and support with pediatric populations are criticisms of this model (La Greca & Schuman, 1995; Rapoff, 1999).

In practice and research, adherence is viewed as a static rather than a continuous process (La Greca & Schuman, 1995). Conceptualizing adherence as a process that will change from initial diagnosis through subsequent regimen modifications suggests repeated measurement periods. Repeated assessment will then signal when intervention strategies are necessary to promote and/or maintain adherence. Considering adherence as a process also concerns the recruitment of families for participation in clinical or research projects. Families who are nonadherent do not participate or drop out prematurely, thus creating a selection bias (La Greca & Schuman, 1995; Rapoff & Barnard, 1991). To obtain more accurate estimates of adherence, Sackett (1979) suggested using "inception cohorts," which entails recruiting all newly diagnosed patients who have been prescribed a specific regimen; all patients would then be followed whether or not they drop out of treatment. An alternative strategy is to target children and adolescents with low adherence and poor treatment outcomes as they are likely to benefit most from adherence interventions (Rapoff & Barnard, 1991). The variable results on the effectiveness of individual treatment strategies and multicomponent programs within and across chronic illnesses cited below may be partly attributable to such recruitment methods.

ASSESSMENT METHODS OF ADHERENCE

Multiple methods are available to assess adherence, including drug assays, behavioral observations, automated measurement, pill counts, parent and provider estimates, and patient and parent reports (La Greca & Schuman, 1995; Lemanek, 1990; Rand & Wise, 1994; Rapoff, 1999). These methods can be conceptualized along a continuum of direct depending on the accuracy with which they determine the amount of medication ingested (Epstein & Cluss, 1982; Rand & Wise, 1994). Each method has advantages and disadvantages, which negate the reliance on only one method of adherence in any clinical or research program. Currently, there is no "gold standard" for assessing adherence. Rapoff (1999) proposed that the gold standard for assessing medication adherence be continuous use of automated measures and periodic assays to confirm actual ingestion. In addition, the gold standard for nonmedication regimens could be a combination of periodic structured telephone interviews on task completion and periodic observation of task completion by caregivers. While objective measures of adherence (e.g., blood and urine assays, direct observations) provide a more accurate estimate of adherence than indirect measures (e.g., interviews and ratings), the clinical utility and feasibility of more direct measures need to be considered in future basic and clinical research efforts (Rapoff, 1999; Rapoff & Barnard, 1991).

The following summary of direct and indirect methods of assessment is based on reviews provided by La Greca and Schuman (1995), Lemanek (1990), Rand and Wise (1994), and Rapoff (1999). Drug assays directly measure drug levels, metabolic products of drugs, or markers (i.e., inert substances or low-dose medications) in serum, urine, or saliva. Although pharmacological treatments (e.g., theophylline, insulin, phenobarbital) are generally assessed through this method, markers of dietary treatments (e.g., phenylalamine) and prophylaxis penicillin can be measured. Drug assays are considered one of the most reliable, objective, and valid techniques for assessing adherence (La Greca & Schuman, 1995; Rand & Wise, 1994). However, drug assays are influenced by individual variation in metabolism and in drug absorption rates (see Lemanek, 1990; Rapoff, 1999). Absorption of medications depends on how doses are administered (i.e., orally, parenterally [intravenous, intramuscular, or subcutaneous], or by inhalation) and the route of administration (i.e., lungs, transdermally, or mucosal routes [nose, mouth, or rectum]) (Rapoff, 1999). Some of the advantages of this type of measurement are its quantifiable nature and its direct effect on adjusting dosages. Disadvantages include the high cost of conducting the assays, their invasive nature (e.g., multiple finger sticks), and the inability to assess daily variations in adherence.

Behavioral observations typically involve self- and/or other monitoring of the presence or occurrence of specific adherent behaviors. Observation of and recording of nonmedication regimens and multicomponent regimens, such as blood or urine glucose testing, factor replacement therapy, and metered-dose inhaler use, are common, as well as checklists to assess the skills in completing these tasks (La Greca & Schuman, 1995; Rapoff, 1999). On occasion, parents and/or siblings record such observations or check patients' observations for accuracy (e.g., Rapoff, Lindsley, & Christophersen, 1984). In this study, parents observed and recorded their daughter's daily adherence to medication, splint wearing, and prone lying for management of systemic-onset juvenile rheumatoid arthritis. This method produces data that allow for quantifiable, repeated assessment of skills as they develop or deteriorate over time. In contrast, direct observations, especially those that are repeated, can be obtrusive and can cause reactivity in terms of overcompliance during periods of observation. In addition, records can be falsified and observations are not clinically practical for some treatment regimens, such as desferol treatments throughout the night or glucose testing in the middle of the night.

Automated measures are essentially microprocessor-based devices that record and store information on the date and the time medications are dispensed or other regimen components are completed. Monitors are available to record dispensing of tablets or liquid medication from standard vials, bottles, blister packages, or eyedroppers. Data from metered-dose inhalers, peak flow meters, and reflectance glucose meters also can be recorded on available devices. Examples of these devices are the Medication Event Monitoring System (MEMS) for use with pill bottles (Aprex Corporation), the MDILog for metered-dose inhalers (Medtrac Technologies, Inc.), and ThAIRapy vest for chest physiotherapy (American Biosystems). Adherence to regimen components, such as diets and exercise, can be obtained through diaries on palm-top computers. Automated measurement can be unobtrusive, provide continuous data, and furnish details about the exact date and time of each dose. Disadvantages of this method include the fact that devices do not measure whether the medication was actually ingested or used correctly, and they are costly, which restricts their use on a clinic basis. Furthermore, while data can be downloaded to a desktop computer for analysis, mechanical failures cannot be accounted for or controlled (Rapoff, 1999).

If automated measures are not available, pharmacy records for medications may approximate such measurement. Prescription tallies are especially useful for measuring long-term regimens in an unobtrusive manner (Rand & Wise, 1994). As noted by Rand and Wise (1994), prescription records tend to be used in epidemiological or survey studies from computerized database systems.

One indirect method of assessment is pill counts where medications in the form of pills, liquids, or inhaler canisters are counted or weighed. The most common formula for calculating adherence based on this method is number of pills removed divided by the number of pills prescribed $\times 100 =$ the percentage of doses taken. In general, with this method of assessment one needs to know how much medication patients have at the beginning and at the end of the assessment period (Rand & Wise, 1994). Pill counts can be obtained for both short-term regimens (e.g., otitis media; Finney, Friman, Rapoff, & Christophersen, 1985) and long-term regimens (e.g., rheumatic disease; Pieper, Rapoff, Purviance, & Lindsley, 1989). This method is feasible in most settings, is inexpensive, and is used to validate another indirect method, patient/parent and provider estimates. However, this method is known to overestimate adherence because it does not actually measure whether the medication was taken (versus thrown out or sprayed into the air), at the correct time, and in the proper dose.

Two other indirect measures of adherence are health care provider estimates and patient and parent reports. Global assessment of patients' likely adherence may be the most common method used by health care providers (Rand & Wise, 1994). In general, Likert type scales (e.g., 4 = almost always adherent; 0 = rarely adherent) or dichotomous judgements (i.e., yes or no) are completed to provide global ratings of children's and adolescents' adherence to their regimens. For example, Smith, Seale, Ley, Mellis, and Shaw (1994) used a 5-point Likert scale to obtain parent and physician ratings of control and symptoms in children with asthma. Advantages of this method include its feasibility (i.e., fast and free) and identification of nonadherent patients. However, this method tends to underestimate nonadherence since the basis for these estimates vary across patients over time (Rapoff, 1999). In these ratings or estimates, providers may or may not ask patients directly about their level of adherence. Ratings or estimates also may be partly based on personal characteristics (e.g., socioeconomic status), behavior problems (e.g., oppositional behaviors), and treatment outcomes (e.g., symptom reduction).

Patient and parent reports are frequently employed and take the form of interviews, structured questionnaires, and daily diaries that produce global ratings or specific ratings (e.g., 1 = very nonadherent; 5 = very adherent). This method is useful in that children, adolescents, and their parents may record specific adherent behaviors or regimen tasks over a designated period of time. One example of this method is the 24-hour recall interview where patients record their daily management tasks for two days during the week and one day during the weekend for a two-week interval. The accuracy of information increases when recall periods are minimized and when objective versus subjective information is requested (e.g., adherence lasts 24 hours versus since last office visit) (La Greca & Schuman, 1995). This interview method is commonly used in practice and research with children and adolescents with diabetes (see Johnson, 1991, for details) or with cystic fibrosis (e.g., Quittner & Opipari, 1994). A variation of this method, the Family Asthma Management System Scale, is available for children with asthma and their parents to assess adherence and general management (Klinnert, McQuaid, & Gavin, 1997). An example of daily diaries is asthma diaries that request information about preventive and as-needed medications, events that trigger symptoms or asthma attacks, and symptom severity. Questionnaires tend be disease-specific, such as behavior modification principles and procedures for self-managing diabetes (e.g., Gross, 1982) or problem checklists for children with asthma (Creer et al., 1989). Advantages of this method include its ease, low cost, and information about the day-to-day variations in adherence, such as appropriate use, overuse, or erratic use. Disadvantages consist of reporting bias or "faking good" by patients, so that adherence is overestimated.

In addition to measures of adherence, measures of treatment outcome/health status are often employed in clinical and research programs (Johnson, 1994). Specific examples of treatment outcome or health status cited by Rapoff (1999) include either clinical signs or symptoms. Clinical signs are secured during physical examinations or observation of patients with instrumentation (e.g., blood pressure) or without instrumentation (e.g., palpation of lymph nodes). Symptoms focus on information obtained from reports of children and adolescents (e.g., pain or fatigue) usually through interviews or diaries. Laboratory tests (e.g., blood chemistry profile) and diagnostic tests (e.g., MRI) provide information about the biological states of specific diseases (Rapoff, 1999).

Health status or quality of life measures assess individual's perceptions of physical symptoms (e.g., pain), functional status (e.g., activities of daily living), psychological functioning (e.g., mood, adjustment), social functioning (e.g., quality and quantity of social contacts), and cognitive functioning (e.g., academic performance) (Spieth & Harris, 1996). Examples of general quality of life measures include the Functional Status Inventory II (R) (Stein & Jessop, 1990) and the Health-Related Quality of Life Measure (Apajasalo et al., 1996). Disease-specific quality of life questionnaires are available for such diseases as cancer (e.g., Pediatric Cancer Quality of Life Inventory-32; Varni, Katz, Seid, Quiggins, Friedman-Binder, & Castro, 1998), asthma (e.g., Childhood Asthma Questionnaire; Christie, French, Sowden, & West, 1993), and juvenile rheumatoid arthritis (e.g., Juvenile Arthritis Functional Assessment Report; Howe et al., 1991). Unfortunately, there is not a one-to-one correspondence between adherence and treatment outcome or health status due to individual responsiveness to treatment (La Greca & Schuman, 1995). Advantages of measures of treatment outcome focus on both health care providers' and patients' ability to monitor treatment progress over time and during routine clinical visits. However, treatment outcome measures do not directly measure adherence since treatment decisions may be based on inaccurate information.

With all of these methods of assessment, questions are raised by clinicians and researchers regarding the specific data to collect and the types of analyses to conduct. Rapoff (1999) described the parameters of adherence behaviors that can be examined, including frequency, duration, rate per unit of time, and percentage of opportunities to engage in the behavior. Various formulas are available to calculate adherence depending on the parameter of behavior being measured. Unfortunately, standards or criteria for judging levels or percentages of adherence versus nonadherence is arbitrary and not universal (La Greca & Schuman, 1995; Rapoff, 1999). For example, criteria for "good" adherence may be 80% of the overall regimen or 100% for individual tasks.

Adherence affects the design of research studies in that it is treated as both an outcome and an explanatory variable (Dunbar-Jacob et al., 2000). In terms of outcome variable, the units of analysis outlined by Rapoff (1999) are applicable, in addition to the use of longitudinal analytic techniques for managing these units and repeated assessments. With respect to adherence as an explanatory variable, data from measures are used to judge treatment efficacy (Friedman, Furberg, & Demets, 1996). An intent-to-treat approach is used in these studies versus one that addresses treatment actually received. Results of studies using these different approaches bear directly on treatments recommended in clinical settings with individual patients.

The clinical and treatment utility of assessment methods is a final assessment issue and relates to whether assessments contribute to beneficial treatment outcome (Rapoff, 1999). Increased consistency between type of assessment measure (e.g., blood assay) and behavior or task being measured (e.g., medications) may, in fact, improve the clinical and treatment utility of measures (La Greca & Schuman, 1995; Rapoff, 1999). However, there are no current guidelines for directly matching assessment measures and regimen requirements or tasks for individual illnesses, which limits obtaining information on the treatment utility of specific methods.

Rapoff and colleagues (Rapoff & Barnard, 1991; Rapoff, 1999) encouraged the development of reliable and valid clinical outcome measures, such as interviews and questionnaires on functional status. Whether for clinical practice or research, parents and youth should be considered active participants in the adherence process, whose opinions regarding goals of treatment and specific recommendations influence subsequent adherence (La Greca & Schuman, 1995; Rapoff & Barnard, 1991). This lack of direct relationship between adherence and treatment outcome poses problems in judging the effectiveness of interventions.

TREATMENT STRATEGIES FOR ADHERENCE

Treatment strategies encompass a range of techniques to improve adherence to both short-term and long-term regimens. These strategies can be grouped into one of three categories: (1) educational, (2) organizational, and (3) behavioral (Dunbar-Jacob et al., 2000; Roter et al., 1998). Additional reviews that provide descriptions of these strategies and reference specific studies can be found in La Greca and Schuman (1995); Lemanek, Kamps, and Chung (2001); and Rapoff (1999).

Educational strategies focus on educating children and parents about their disease, regimen requirements, and self-management skills through supplemental verbal or written instructions. Rapoff (1999) stated that it is critical for children and parents to know WHY (i.e., rationale for regimen) and WHAT TO DO (i.e., regimen requirements), which stems from the distinction between "knowing that" and "knowing how." A skills-training approach should be followed when educating children and families about specific regimens. Even with verbal and written instructions, it is essential for health care providers to model the necessary skills to complete components of the regimen. Patients should then rehearse or practice these skills, with feedback being given by providers on how well each skill or task was performed. This sequence of training should end with reeducation about the components done incorrectly or requiring further practice. A skills-training approach is especially critical for learning and maintaining components of complex regimens. Educational strategies appear necessary for improving adherence, especially to short-term medication regimens (e.g., 10-day course of penicillin). However, it is not sufficient to achieve adherence for more chronic diseases and complex regimens. For example, most adherence interventions for pediatric asthma include an educational component as part of a multicomponent program that is provided either in the home (da Costa, Rapoff, Lemanek, & Goldstein, 1997) or during clinic visits (Smith, Seale, Ley, Shaw, & Bracs (1986) using such forms as leaflets, videotapes, books, or slide shows.

Organizational strategies attempt to modify aspects of the health care system to foster a patient-friendly clinical setting. Examples of organizational strategies include (1) increasing continuity of care by seeing the same health care provider, (2) decreasing wait time for clinical appointments, (3) increasing the frequency of follow-up visits, and (4) improving parent satisfaction with the care of their child. Providing supervision and support are strategies that promote a patient-friendly setting by focusing on the physician–patient relationship. Specific examples of these strategies consist of health care professionals (i.e., physicians, nurses, psychologists) increasing their attention by discussing the medical and the psychological aspects of diseases on an individual basis, calling patients to remind them of future appointments, and assisting patients to reduce barriers to adherence (e.g., obtaining transportation or day care). Support and information about care and services also can be provided during stressful hospital periods, such as admissions, before preoperative medications are given, and when returning from the recovery room (La Greca & Schuman, 1995; Rapoff & Barnard, 1991).

Other strategies focus on recommendations that target identified risk factors, such as simplifying regimens (e.g., reduce the number of medications or schedules), shaping adherence (e.g., schedule task requirements to fit in with daily routines such as at breakfast, at lunch, during after-school activity, at dinner, and at bedtime), and minimizing adverse side effects (e.g., changing medications or dose). Organizational strategies, especially enhanced medical supervision, are used to improve adherence in such diseases as asthma (e.g., Smith et al., 1986), diabetes (e.g., Delamater et al., 1990), and juvenile rheumatoid arthritis (e.g., Rapoff, Purviance, & Lindsley, 1988). In general, organizational strategies are effective in improving short-term regimens, but they are not as successful when used alone with long-term regimens.

Behavioral strategies are considered one of most effective approaches for improving adherence with long-term regimens. These strategies can be divided into stimulus control techniques, self-control techniques, or reinforcement control techniques (Rapoff, 1999). Stimulus-control techniques include visual cues or reminders, such as calendars, postcards, and telephone calls. Cues and reminders may be particularly helpful for short-term regimens, during the initial phase of a long-term regimen, and when efforts are directed at increasing children's and adolescents' responsibilities for their own care (La Greca & Schuman, 1995). Stimulus-control techniques are used to increase appointment keeping (e.g., O'Brien & Lazebnik, 1998), medication taking (e.g., Finney et al., 1985), and urine/blood glucose testing (e.g., Lowe & Lutzker, 1979).

Self-monitoring is a self-control technique and may include monitoring of medications taken, the severity of symptoms, and exercises completed. These two types of strategies appear to improve adherence with those regimens that involve only one or few treatment components, such as asthma (e.g., Smith et al., 1994) and otitis media (e.g., Mattar, Marklein, & Yaffe, 1975). However, in isolation they do not increase adherence rates in more complex regimens, such as diabetes (e.g., Wysocki, Green, & Huxtable, 1989).

Reinforcement control methods consist of providing incentives for various regimen components, such as medication use, symptom reduction, and regimen completion. Contracts and token economies are most common where rewards and sanctions are delivered for regimen adherence, as well as increased supervision by parents or other family members. Specific aspects of incentive programs focus on earning points for adhering to regimen components, losing points for nonadherence to general instructions and to specific regimen components, and exchanging points for daily and weekly privileges. Reinforcement-based procedures are designed for children with a variety of diseases, such as asthma (e.g., da Costa et al., 1997), diabetes (e.g., Wysocki et al., 1989), juvenile rheumatoid arthritis (e.g., Rapoff et al., 1984), and hemophilia (e.g., Greenan-Fowler, Powell, & Varni, 1987). Within this category of interventions are methods to enhance parenting practices or skills, especially in those families where discord or emotional or behavior problems exist in any family member. Specific parenting practices center on increasing monitoring by parents, strengthening consistent limit setting, and decreasing coercive interactions, as well as training in problem-solving skills. Especially in the diabetes literature, training focuses on conflict resolution skills training, general management and disease-related regimen tasks, and disease-related stress (e.g., Delamater et al., 1990; Gross, Magalnick, & Richardson, 1985; Snyder, 1987).

A multicomponent intervention plan is essential to promote adherence to complex regimens, including such components as educating parents and children, increasing supervision by parents, fostering self-monitoring by children, and dispensing reinforcement for parents and children. Programs and studies using multicomponent treatment interventions for such diseases as asthma and diabetes tend to emphasize group designs, where self-management skills are taught through discussion, modeling, role playing, goal setting, and contracting (e.g., Anderson, Wolf, Burkhart, Cornell, & Bacon, 1989; Baum & Creer, 1986; Schafer, Glasgow, & McCaul, 1982).

EVALUATION OF ADHERENCE INTERVENTIONS

In general, future research and practice is critical to determine what procedures work "best," with which children, and under whose instruction. For all adherence interventions, treatment integrity is pertinent to these questions and needs to be examined as well. Manuals with protocol checklists or monitoring done by video- or audiotaping are recommended to determine if protocols are adequately followed by therapists, patients, and families in a consistent manner (Rapoff, 1999).

In 1994, The American Psychological Association (APA) developed a task force called Effective Psychosocial Interventions: A Lifespan Perspective to highlight interventions that had empirical data to support their effectiveness. Criteria were developed to evaluate the degree of empirical support for specific interventions: (1) *Well-established treatment* is an intervention tested in at least two randomized group designs and showing superiority over a psychological placebo or alternative treatment with adequate statistical power (about 30 per group). A large series of well-designed single-case experiments that compare the intervention to another treatment can be used as well. Further criteria for well-established treatments were treatments must be manualized, samples must be adequately described, and effects must be demonstrated by two independent research groups. (2) *Probably efficacious treatments* require two or more group intervention studies displaying superiority over a waiting list control group or one study meeting criteria for a well-established intervention. (3) *Promising interventions* had the following criteria: support from one well-controlled study and at least one other less well-controlled study, or a small number of single case-design experiments, or two or more well-controlled studies by the same investigator (Chambless et al., 1996). Additional modifications to the Chambless criteria were proposed for interventions designed for medical regimens: a specified treatment protocol could replace a manual, the number of participants for chronic illness groups could be smaller than 30, and two multiple baseline designs by independent investigators could be evidence for a well-established treatment (Spirito, 1999).

The Chambless and Society of Pediatric Psychology (SPP) criteria were applied to treatments for nonadherence in pediatric asthma, JRA, and diabetes (Lemanek et al., 2001). This review of treatment studies on regimen adherence indicates that operant-based or behavioral strategies are probably efficacious with respect to specific treatment components. Other individual strategies, such as education or self-monitoring, and multicomponent programs are, at best, promising interventions. Single-subject experimental designs appear to offer the most consistent results and allow for tailoring treatments to individual patients. However, single-subject experimental designs will need to be conducted for individual chronic illnesses, especially as the Chambless/SPP criteria requires comparisons with psychological placebos and alternating treatments. A range of single-subject designs is available, such as concurrent schedule strategy and extensions of the A-B-A design, that can examine effects of psychological placebos and interactions (Hersen & Barlow, 1981). Single-subject designs would be the initial phase in "a phased studies approach" recommended by La Greca and Varni (1993). These designs would lead to single-site group studies and then multisite randomized controlled group designs. However, investigators will need to be creative and knowledgeable about the range of options available, without limiting themselves to use of withdrawal or reversal designs.

The inconsistency in assessment measures, treatment protocols, and research designs within and across illness groups has ultimately limited the development and validation of well-established treatments to improve adherence to short-term regimens and long-term regimens. In general, future research on regimen adherence will need to examine both the empirical and clinical effectiveness of any adherence intervention. Rather than continuing to attempt large-scale group designs in single centers, patient-focused research should be considered as an alternative research strategy (Howard, Moras, Brill, Martinovich, & Lutz, 1996). Traditional outcome research tries to answer the following two questions: (1) Does it work under experimental conditions based on randomized clinical trials (efficacy questions)? and (2) Does it work in practice based on quasi-experimental designs (effectiveness question)? In contrast, patient-focused research seeks to answer the question Does it work for this patient? by continuously assessing the treatment progress of each patient. This approach also focuses on choosing appropriate outcome measures to assess progress and choosing different interventions optimal for each phase of treatment. In terms of adherence, behavioral strategies may be the initial intervention examined to improve adherence to medications. Other strategies can then be introduced and assessed for their effectiveness in promoting more complex regimens and general self-management skills in individual children and adolescents.

ADHERENCE IN THE SCHOOLS

The treatment literature on adherence to pediatric regimens is minimal due to the conceptual and methodological challenges inherent in providing comprehensive services and conducting research projects in clinics and/or in homes. The number and type of challenges present may seem to increase exponentially once the school setting is added to this system of care. However, future clinical and research efforts directed at improving adherence in children and adolescents should include measures of quality of life and health outcome (Dunbar-Jacob et al., 2000; La Greca & Bearman, 2001; Rapoff, 1999). For children and adolescents, one domain considered within quality of life measures is the school setting, where academic performance and peer relationships are assessed. Clinical practice and research in adherence to pediatric regimens also need to emphasize the day-to-day management of the disease, along with "matching" the type of intervention and regimen task or treatment-related behavior (La Greca & Bearman, 2001; La Greca & Schuman, 1995). In effect, patients and their families' ability to manage day-to-day tasks should be enhanced through effective collaboration between health care providers, school personnel, and families (Shaw et al., 1995). Thus far, the literature on the assessment and treatment of adherence to medical regimens in the school setting is basically nonexistent when compared to the total number of studies and reports in general. The fact that children and adolescents spend the majority of their days in school with a range of school personnel and other students would seem to offset potential challenges to obtaining assessment data and implementing interventions for individual students or groups of students. However, specific aspects of children' and adolescents' disease management may need to be targeted because of the current care systems in which most school personnel and medical professionals operate.

There are several aspects of disease management that are affected by adherence and could be addressed in the schools. One aspect involves shared knowledge about individual diseases and their medical management, as well as effects on specific students. Teachers report needing increased information about how to deal with school absences, taking part in school activities, peer relationships, explaining medical conditions to other pupils, and having someone to talk to about health-related worries (Mukherjee et al., 2000). In addition, research indicates that teachers feel ill-informed about the range of medical conditions, how to deal with emergencies, and to what degree to "push" a child to keep up with academic and physical activities at school (Lynch, Lewis, & Murphy, 1992). Although teachers are reporting feeling anxious about teaching and responding adequately to the needs of children with chronic diseases, parents are expecting schools to become more involved in their children' health care (Yaffe, 1998).

Yaffe (1998) suggested that all professionals working with children with chronic diseases should move beyond the traditional boundaries of classrooms, clinics, and hospital settings. To accomplish this goal, regular communication between health care professionals, families, and school personnel should be established, along with the role of liaison being well-defined (Lynch et al., 1992). Another strategy adopted by several communities is to develop programs that integrate students with health care needs into the school setting (Yaffe, 1998). One person, such as a school health officer, is essential to coordinate, implement, and oversee the program. The roles of all team members need to be defined (e.g., physician to educate school staff about medical treatments and response to medical emergencies), the goals of the program need to be delineated (e.g., to provide mandated immunization screenings), and illnesses or diseases should be identified (e.g., immunization reviews, asthma or diabetes management) (Yaffe, 1998).

A second aspect of adjustment relates to school attendance, where missed days can negatively impact students' academic achievement and peer relationships (Fowler, Johnson, & Atkinson, 1985; Sturge, Garralda, Boissin, Dore, & Woo, 1997). However, only about 20% of students with chronic disease need 80% of the services, a pattern similar to that found in general population samples (Sturge et al., 1997). Adjustment in school seems to be partly related to the emphasis by clinic and center staff on school attendance and education, as well as considering problems in school attendance as reflecting maladjustment to the disease (Sturge et al., 1997). Many communities also are developing school reentry programs to integrate students with various chronic diseases (e.g., cancer, cardiac conditions) back into the school system. Generally, successful programs focus on preparing the child and the family, preparing the school personnel, preparing the class, and ensuring continued follow-up after the initial return to school (Sexson & Madan-Swain, 1993). Unfortunately, there are limited data on the process of school reentry from a multidisciplinary approach (Sexson & Madan-Swain, 1993). However, these suggestions for improved education, supervision, and communication are consistent with educational and organizational strategies identified in the treatment literature on adherence to medical regimens.

Services or care for students with chronic diseases can be conceptualized as primary, secondary, or tertiary, similar to services for other students. An example of primary service or care pertains to scheduled immunizations for children and adolescents. Although 84% of physicians surveyed preferred that immunizations be administered at their practice, 71% considered schools and 63% considered teen clinics as satisfactory alternatives (Schaffer, Humiston, Shone, Averhoff, & Szilagyi, 2001). Barriers that may prevent immunizations (e.g., record scattering, financial costs) need to be reduced to ensure continuity of care, another organizational strategy used to increase adherence rates.

Two examples of secondary services for children and adolescents with chronic diseases are high-risk behaviors and nutritional therapy. Adolescents with chronic diseases may engage in high-risk behaviors that jeopardize their health care. Britto and colleagues (1998) showed that 21% of adolescents with cystic fibrosis and 30% of adolescents with sickle cell disease had smoked. In addition, 28% and 51%, respectively, had engaged in sexual intercourse. Those adolescents with more severe conditions had the same frequency of high-risk behaviors than those with milder conditions. These authors expressed the view that schools can provide routine screenings of such behaviors in children and adolescents with chronic conditions if not done by medical professionals. Dietary changes can potentially decrease risks for some diseases (e.g., cardiovascular) and are critical for management of other diseases (e.g., diabetes) (Brownell & Cohen, 1995; Schlundt, Rowe, Pichert, & Plant, 1999). The data on school weight-loss programs involving peers and teachers is mixed (Brownell & Cohen, 1995). With dietary changes, education appears to be necessary but not sufficient to produce lasting changes because of the complex relationship among psychological, cultural, environmental, and behavioral factors (Brownell & Cohen, 1995). However, parents (and perhaps school personnel) as either role models in their own weight-loss program or as "helpers" appear to be critical in modifying dietary habits (Israel, Solotar, & Zimand, 1990). With specific reference to children and adolescents with chronic diseases, dietary restrictions and/or nutrition therapy may foster the development of irrational beliefs and attitudes about food and body weight, as well as compulsive behaviors (Schlundt, et al., 1999). Programs within the schools on eating disorders would be applicable for these students, along with additional educational sessions about the disease process for school personnel.

Tertiary services can focus on self-management programs for such medical conditions as asthma and chronic headaches. For example, in Persaud et al. (1996), school nurses taught 36 children with asthma self-management principles and skills in 20-minute individual sessions over 8 weeks. Results revealed less anxiety during exacerbations in both the control group and the treatment group, as well as increased nurses' knowledge of peak expiratory flow rates. Although no changes in emergency room visits or school absences were found, the program was considered a practical, low-cost approach to increasing self-management skills. Evans and colleagues (1993) studied 239 children with asthma who participated in "Open Airways," an asthma self-management program provided in the schools. Basic information about asthma was taught in six 60-minute sessions using practicing of skills, role playing, decision making, and physical and artistic activities. Increased self-management skills, self-efficacy scores, and academic grades were found through participation in this program. Another school program involved adolescents with recurrent tension or migraine headaches, who met for 5 weeks of relaxation training (Larsson, Melin, Lamminen, & Ullstedt, 1993). Headache frequency, headache-free days, headache duration, and peak headache intensity changed following participation in a self-help relaxation group compared to either a problem-discussion group or a self-monitoring group. Treatment effects were more evident 5 months following treatment than directly after treatment.

CONCLUSIONS

The role of psychology in health care is varied but highlights applying psychological techniques and principles to health promotion, primary prevention, collateral treatment of general medical illness, and physical rehabilitation (VandenBos, DeLeon, & Belar, 1991). Collaboration between psychologists and medical professionals is essential to coordinate delivery of optimal medical, social, and mental health services (Drotar, 2001; Shaw et al., 1995). Shaw et al. (1995) described the essential elements of collaboration based on behavioral principles and empirical evidence. These elements include (1) patient-defined and medically diagnosed problems defined; (2) specific problem targeted, realistic goals set, and an action plan determined; (3) services to teach skills to carry out plans and provide emotional support; and (4) active and sustained follow-up where patients are contacted at specified intervals to monitor health status, identify complications, and check or reinforce progress. The educational, organizational, and behavioral strategies identified in the literature to improve adherence to medical regimens are consistent with these elements of collaboration. In addition, the focus of this collaboration and of adherence interventions is to enhance the day-to-day disease management of children and adolescents with chronic diseases.

In addition to changes in clinical practice and research initiatives, the health care system will need to be altered due to the effects of managed care on the professions of psychology and medicine (Hersch, 1995; Shaw et al., 1995). For example, cost-control mechanisms, such as increased copayment and deductibles, caps on sessions, and exclusion of certain diagnoses and treatment approaches, are barriers to optimal service delivery in any setting. VandenBos and colleagues (1991) advocated for "equal partnership" between psychology and medicine at all levels of care for children and adolescents. However, technical assistance, practice guidelines, and incentives, along with clinical information systems, research, and community involvement, are required components of a plan to improve the health care system and service delivery. In effect, a multicomponent intervention plan is needed that incorporates education, organization, reinforcement, and skills training to enhance adherence to the philosophy and practice of comprehensive services for children and adolescents with chronic diseases.

REFERENCES

Agency for Health Care Policy and Research Programs, Pub. L. No. 106 Stat. 2095. (1993).

Anderson, B. J., Wolf, F. M., Burkhart, M. T., Cornell, R. G., & Bacon, G. E. (1989). Effects of peer-group intervention on metabolic control of adolescents with IDDM: Randomized outpatient study. *Diabetes Care, 3*, 179–183.

Apajasalo, M., Rautonen, J., Holmbery, C., Simkkonen, J., Aalberg, V., Pihko, H., Siimes, M. A., Kaitila, I., Mäkelä, A., Rantakari, K., Anttila, R., & Rautonen, J. (1996). Quality of life in early adolescence: A sixteen-dimensional health-related measure (16D). *Quality of Life Research, 5*, 205–211.

Bandura, A. (1997). *Self-efficacy: The exercise of control*. New York: Freeman.

Baum, D., & Creer, T. L. (1986). Medication compliance in children with asthma. *Journal of Asthma, 23*, 49–59.

Becker, M. H., Drachman, R. H., & Kirscht, J. P. (1972). Predicting mothers' compliance with pediatric medical regimens. *Journal of Pediatrics, 81*, 843–854.

Becker, M. H., & Maiman, L. A. (1975). Sociobehavioral determinants of compliance with health and medical care recommendations. *Medical Care, 13*, 10–24.

Berg, J. S., Dischler, J., Wagner, D. J., Raia, J., & Palmer-Shevlin, N. (1993). Medication compliance: A health care problem. *The Annals of Pharmacotherapy, 27*(Suppl.), 2–21.

Berlin, I. N. (1990). The role of the community mental health center in prevention of infant, child, and adolescent disorders: Retrospective and prospects. *Community Mental Health Journal, 26*, 89–106.

Bond, G. G., Aiken, L. S., & Somerville, S. C. (1992). The health belief model and adolescents with insulin-dependent diabetes mellitus. *Health Psychology, 11*, 190–198.

Britto, M. T., Garrett, J. M., Dugliss, M. A. J., Daeschner, C. W., Johnson, C. A., Leigh, M. W., Majure, J. M., Schultz, W. H., & Konrad, T. R. (1998). Risky behavior in teens with cystic fibrosis or sickle cell disease: A multicenter study. *Pediatrics, 101*, 250–256.

Brownell, K. D., & Cohen, L. R. (1995). Adherence to dietary regimens 1: An overview of research. *Behavioral Medicine, 20*, 149–154.

Bush, P. J., & Iannotti, R. J. (1990). A children's health belief model. *Medical Care, 28*, 69–86.

Chambless, D. L., Sanderson, W. C., Shoham, V., Bennet-Johnson, S., Pope, K. S., Crits-Christoph, P., Baker, M., Johnson, B., Woody, S. R., Sue, S., Beutler, L., Williams, D. A., & McCurry, S. (1996). An update on empirically validated therapies. *Clinical Psychologist, 49*, 5–18.

Christie, M. J., French, D., Sowden, A., & West, A. (1993). Development of child-centered disease-specific questionnaires for living with asthma. *Psychosomatic Medicine, 55*, 541–548.

Coutts, J. A., Gibson, N. A., & Paton, J. Y. (1992). Measuring compliance with inhaled medication in asthma. *Archives of Diseases in Children, 67*, 332–333.

Creer, T. L., & Levstek, D. (1996). Medication compliance and asthma: Overlooking the trees for the forest. *Journal of Asthma, 33*, 203–211.

Creer, T. L., Renne, C. M., & Chai, H. (1982). The application of behavioral techniques to childhood asthma. In D. C. Russo & J. W. Varni (Eds.), *Behavioral pediatrics: Research and practice* (pp. 27–66). New York: Plenum.

Creer, T. L., Wigal, J. K., Tobin, D. L., Kotses, H., Snyder, S. E., & Winder, J. A. (1989). The revised asthma problem behavior checklist. *Journal of Asthma, 26*, 17–29.

da Costa, I. G., Rapoff, M. A., Lemanek, K., & Goldstein, G. L. (1997). Improving adherence to medication regimens for children with asthma and its effect on clinical outcome. *Journal of Applied Behavior Analysis, 30*, 687–691.

D'Amato, R. C., & Dean, R. S. (1989). *The past, present, and future of school psychology in nontraditional settings*. Hillsdale, NJ: Lowrence Erlbaum Associates.

Delamater, A. M., Bubb, J., Davis, S. G., Smith, J. A., Schmidt, L., White, N. H., & Santiago, J. V. (1990). Randomized prospective study of self-management training with newly diagnosed diabetic children. *Diabetes Care, 13*, 492–498.

Dobos, A. E., Dworkin, P. H., & Bernstein, B. A. (1994). Pediatricians' approaches to developmental problems: Has the gap narrowed? *Journal of Developmental & Behavioral Pediatrics, 15*, 34–38.

Drotar, D. (2001). Promoting comprehensive care for children with chronic health conditions and their families: Introduction to the special issue. *Children's Services: Social Policy, Research, and Practice, 4*, 157–163.

Dunbar, J. (1983). Compliance in pediatric populations: A review. In P. J. McGrath & P. Firestone (Eds.), *Pediatric and adolescent behavioral medicine: Issues in treatment* (pp. 210–230). New York: Springer.

Dunbar-Jacob, J., Erlen, J. A., Schlenk, E. A., Ryan C. M., Sereika, S., & Doswell, W. M. (2000). Adherence in chronic disease. *Annual Review of Nursing Research, 18*, 48–90.

Epstein, L. H., & Cluss, P. A. (1982). A behavioral medicine perspective on adherence to long-term medical regimens. *Journal of Consulting and Clinical Psychology, 50*, 950–971.

Evans, D., Clark, N. M., Feldman, C. H., Rips, J., Kaplan, D., Levison, M. J., Wasilewski, Y., Levin, B., & Mellins, R. B. (1993). A health education program to improve asthma management. In J. J. Cohen & M. C. Fish (Eds.), *Handbook of school-based interventions: Resolving student problems and promoting healthy educational environments* (pp. 475–476). San Francisco: Jossey-Bass.

Finney, J. W., Friman, P. C., Rapoff, M. A., & Christophersen, E. R., (1985). Improving compliance with antibiotic regimens for otitis media: Randomized clinical trial in a pediatric clinic. *American Journal of Diseases in Children, 139*, 89–95.

Fowler, M. G., Johnson, M. P., & Atkinson, S. S. (1985). School achievement and absence in children with chronic health conditions. *Journal of Pediatrics, 106*, 683–687.

Friedman, L. M., Furberg, C. D., & Demets, D. L. (1996). *Fundamentals of clinical trials* (3rd ed.). St Louis: Mosby-Year Book.

Gardner, S. L. (1992). Key issues in developing school-linked, integrated services. *Future of Children, 2*, 85–94.

Gerry, M. H., & Certo, N. J. (1992). Current activity at the federal level and the need for service integration. *Future of Children, 2*, 118–126.

Greenan-Fowler, E., Powell, C., & Varni, J. W. (1987). Behavioral treatment of adherence to therapeutic exercise by children with hemophilia. *Archives of Physical Medicine & Rehabilitation, 68*, 846–849.

Gross, A. M. (1982). Self-management training and medication compliance in children with diabetes. *Child & Family Behavior Therapy, 4*, 47–55.

Gross, A. M., Magalnick, L. J., & Richardson, P. (1985). Self-management training with families of insulin-dependent diabetic children. A controlled long-term investigation. *Child & Family Behavior Therapy, 7*, 35–50.

Haynes, R. B. (1979). Introduction. In R. B. Haynes, D. W. Taylor, & D. C. Sackett (Eds.), *Compliance in health care* (pp. 1–7). Baltimore: Johns Hopkins University Press.

Hersch, L. (1995). Adapting to health care reform and managed care: Three strategies for survival and growth. *Professional Psychology: Research and Practice, 26*, 16–26.

Hersen, M., & Barlow, D. H. (1981). *Single case experimental designs: Strategies for studying behavior change*. New York: Pergamon.

Hobbs, N., & Perrin, J. M. (1985). *Issues in the care of children with chronic illness*. San Francisco: Jossey-Bass.

Howard, K. I., Moras, K., Brill, P. L., Martinovich, Z., & Lutz, W. (1996). Evaluation of psychotherapy. Efficacy, effectiveness, and patient progress. *American Psychologist, 51*, 1059–1064.

Howe, S., Levinson, J., Shear, E., Hartner, S., McGirr, G., Schulte, M., & Lovell, D. (1991). Development of a disability measurement tool for juvenile rheumatoid arthritis: The juvenile arthritis functional assessment report for children and their parents. *Arthritis & Rheumatism, 34*, 873–880.

Individuals with Disabilities Act of 1990, Pub. L. No. 101–476, 136 Stat. 1103. (1990).

Israel, A. C., Solotar, L. C., & Zimand, E. (1990). An investigation of two parental involvement roles in the treatment of obese children. *International Journal of eating Disorders, 9*, 557–564.

Janz, N. K., & Becker, M. H. (1984). The health belief model: A decade later. *Health Education Quarterly, 11*, 1–47.

Johnson, S. B. (1991). Compliance with complex medical regimens: Assessing daily management of childhood diabetes. In R. J. Prinz (Ed.), *Advances in behavioral assessment of children and families* (vol. 5, pp. 113–137). Bristol, PA: Jessica Kingsley.

Johnson, S. B. (1994). Health behavior and health status: Concepts, methods, and applications. *Journal of Pediatric Psychology, 19*, 129–141.

Johnson, S. B., Freund, A., Silverstein, J., Hansen, C. A., & Malone, J. (1990). Adherence-health status relationships in childhood diabetes. *Health Psychology, 9*, 606–631.

Klinnert, M. D., McQuaid, E. L., & Gavin, L. A. (1997). Assessing the family asthma management system. *Journal of Asthma, 34*, 77–88.

La Greca, A. M., & Bearman, K. J. (2001). Commentary: If "An apple a day keeps the doctor away," Why is adherence so darn hard? *Journal of Pediatric Psychology, 26*, 279–281.

La Greca, A. M., & Hanna, N. C. (1983). Health beliefs of children and their mothers: Implications for treatment [Abstract]. *Diabetes, 32*(Suppl.), 66.

La Greca, A. M., & Schuman, W. B. (1995). Adherence to prescribed medical regimens. In M. C. Roberts (Ed.), *Handbook of pediatric psychology* (2nd ed., pp. 55–83). New York: Guilford.

La Greca, A. M., & Varni, J. W. (1993). Editorial: Intervention in pediatric psychology: A look toward the future. *Journal of Pediatric Psychology, 18*, 667–697.

Larsson, B., Melin, L., Lamminen, M., & Ullstedt, F. (1993). Self-help relaxation for chronic headaches. In J. J. Cohen & M. C. Fish (Eds.), *Handbook of school-based interventions: Resolving student problems and promoting healthy educational environments* (pp. 476–478). San Francisco: Jossey-Bass.

Lemanek, K. (1990). Adherence issues in the medical management of asthma. *Journal of Pediatric Psychology, 15*, 437–458.

Lemanek, K. L., Kamps, J., & Chung, N. B. (2001). Empirically supported treatments in pediatric psychology: Regimen adherence. *Journal of Pediatric Psychology, 26*, 253–275.

Lewis, A. (1997). Non-compliance: A $100 billion problem. *Remington Report, 5*, 14–15.

Litt, I. F., & Cuskey, W. R. (1980). Compliance with medical regimens during adolescence. *Pediatric Clinics of North America, 27*, 3–15.

Lowe, K., & Lutzker, J. R. (1979). Increasing compliance to a medical regimen with a juvenile diabetic. *Behavior Therapy, 10*, 57–64.

Lynch, E. W., Lewis, R., & Murphy, D. (1992). Educational services for children with chronic illnesses: Perspectives of educators and families. *Exceptional Children, 59*, 210–220.

Mattar, M. F., Marklein, J., & Yaffe, S. J. (1975). Pharmaceutic factors affecting pediatric compliance. *Pediatrics, 55*, 101–108.

Montano, D. E., Kasprzyk, K. D., & Taplin, S. H. (1997). The theory of reasoned action and the theory of planned behavior. In K. Glanz, F. Lewis, & B. K. Rimer (Eds.), *Health behavior and health education: Theory, reseach, and practice* (2nd ed., pp. 85–112). San Francisco: Jossey-Bass.

Mukherjee, S., Lightfoot, J., & Sloper, P. (2000). The inclusion of pupils with a chronic health condition in mainstream school: What does it mean for teachers? *Educational Research, 42*, 59–72.

O'Brien, G., & Lazebnik, R. (1998). Telephone call reminders and attendance in an adolescent clinic. *Pediatrics, 101*, E6.

O'Leary, A. (1992). Self-efficacy and health: Behavioral and stress-physiological mediation. *Cognitive Therapy and Research, 16*, 229–245.

Parsons, R. D., & Meyers, J. (1987). *Developing consultation skills*. San Francisco: Jossey-Bass.

Persaud, D. I., Barnett, S. E., Weller, S. C., Baldwin, C. D., Niebuhr, V., & McCormick, D. P. (1996). As asthma self-management program for children, including instruction in peak flow monitoring by school nurses. *Journal of Asthma, 33*, 37–43.

Pieper, K. B., Rapoff, M. A., Purviance, M. R., & Lindsley, C. B. (1989). Improving compliance with prednisone therapy in pediatric patients with rheumatic disease. *Arthritis Care and Research, 2*, 132–135.

Preventive Health Amendment, Pub. L. No. 102-531, 106 Stat. 3469. (1993).

Prochaska, J. O. (1979). *Systems of psychotherapy: A transtheoretical analysis*. Homewood, IL: Dorsey.

Prochaska, J. O., DiClemente, C. C., & Norcross, J. C. (1992). In search of how people change: Applications to addictive behaviors. *American Psychologist, 47*, 1102–1114.

Prochaska, J. O., Redding, C. A., & Evers, K. E. (1997). The transtheoretical model and stages of change. In K. Glanz, F. M. Lewis, & B. K. Rimer (Eds.), *Health behavior and health education: Theory, research, and practice* (2nd ed., pp. 60–84). San Francisco: Jossey-Bass.

Quittner, A. L., & Opipari, L. C. (1994). Differential treatment of siblings: Interview and diary analysis comparing two family contexts. *Child Development, 65*, 800–814.

Rand, C. S., & Wise, R. A. (1994). Measuring adherence to asthma medication regimens. *American Journal of Critical Care Medicine, 149*, 569–576.

Rapoff, M. A. (1996, Summer). Why comply? Theories in pediatric medical adherence research. *Progress Notes. Newsletter of the Society of Pediatric Psychology, 20*, 3–4.

Rapoff, M. A. (1999). *Adherence to pediatric medical regimens*. New York: Kluwer Academic/Plenum.

Rapoff, M. A., & Barnard, M. U. (1991). Compliance with pediatric medical regimens. In J. A. Cramer & B. Spiker (Eds.), *Patient compliance in medical practice and clinical trials* (pp. 73–98). New York: Raven Press.

Rapoff, M. A., Lindsley, C. B., & Christophersen, E. R. (1984). Improving compliance with medical regimens: Case study with juvenile rheumatoid arthritis. *Archives of Physical Medicine and Rehabilitation, 65*, 267–269.

Rapoff, M. A., Purviance, M. R., & Lindsley, C. B. (1988). Improving medication compliance for juvenile rheumatoid arthritis and its effect on clinical outcome: A single-subject analysis. *Arthritis Care and Research, 1*, 12–16.

Roter, D. L., Hall, J. A., Merisca, R., Nordstrom, B., Cretin, D., & Svarstad, B. (1998). Effectiveness of interventions to improve patient compliance: A meta-analysis. *Medical Care, 36*, 1138–1161.

Rubenstein, S., Hindi, R. D., Moss, R. B., Blessing-Moore, J., & Lewiston, N. J. (1984). Sudden death in adolescent asthma. *Annals of Allergy, 53*, 311–318.

Sackett, D. L. (1979). Methods for compliance research. In R. B. Haynes, D. W. Taylor, & D. L. Saclett (Eds.), *Compliance in health care* (pp. 323–333). Baltimore: Johns Hopkins University Press.

Schafer, L. C., Glasgow, R. E., & McCaul, K. D. (1982). Increasing the adherence of diabetic adolescents. *Journal of Behavioral Medicine, 5*, 353–362.

Schaffer, S. J., Humiston, S. G., Shone, L. P., Averhoff, F. M., & Szilagyi, P. G. (2001). Adolescent immunization practices. A national survey of US physicians. *Archives of Pediatric and Adolescent Medicine, 155*, 566–571.

Schlundt, D. G., Rowe, S., Pichert, J. W., & Plant, D. D. (1999). What are the eating cognitions of children whose chronic diseases do and do not require attention to diet? *Patient Education and Counseling, 36*, 279–286.

Sexson, S. B., & Madan-Swain, A. (1993). School reentry for the child with chronic illness. *Journal of Learning Disabilities, 26*, 115–125.

Shaw, S. R., Kelly, D. P., Joost, J. C., & Parker-Fisher, S. J. (1995). School-linked and school-based health services: A renewed call for collaboration between school psychologists and medical professionals. *Psychology in the Schools, 32*, 190–201.

Shellenberger, S., & Couch, K. W. (1984). The school psychologist's pivotal role in promoting the health and well-being of children. *School Psychology Review, 13*, 211–215.

Smith, N. A., Seale, J. P., Ley, P., Mellis, C. M., & Shaw, J. (1994). Better medication compliance is associated with improved control of childhood asthma. *Archives of Chest Diseases, 49*, 470–474.

Smith. N. A., Seale, J. P., Ley, P., Shaw, J., & Bracs, P. U. (1986). Effects of intervention on medication compliance in children with asthma. *Medical Journal of Australia, 144*, 119–122.

Snyder, J. (1987). Behavioral analysis and treatment of poor diabetic self-care and antisocial behavior: A single-subject experimental study. *Behavior Therapy, 18*, 251–263.

Spieth, L. E., & Harris, C. V. (1996). Assessment of health-related quality of life in children and adolescents: An integrative review. *Journal of Pediatric Psychology, 21*, 175–193.

Spirito, A. (1999). Introduction. *Journal of Pediatric Psychology, 24*, 87–90.

Stein, R. E. K., & Jessop, D. J. (1990). Functional status II ®: A measure of child health status. *Medical Care, 28*, 1041–1055.

Sturge, C., Garralda, M. E., Boissin, M., Dore, C. J., & Woo, P. (1997). School attendance and juvenile chronic arthritis. *British Journal of Rheumatology, 36*, 1218–1223.

Sublett, J. L., Pollard, S. J., Kadlec, G. J., & Karibo, J. M. (1979). Non-compliance in asthmatic children: A study of theophylline levels in a pediatric emergency room population. *Annals of Allergy, 43*, 95–97.

Tamaroff, M. H., Festa, R. S., Adesman, A. R., & Walco, G. A. (1992). Therapeutic adherence to oral medication regimens by adolescents with cancer. II. Clinical and psychological correlates. *Journal of Pediatrics, 120*, 812–817.

Thousand, J. S., & Villa, R. A. (1992). Collaborative teams: A powerful tool in school restructuring. In R. A. Villa, J. S. Thousand, W. Stainback, & S. Stainback (Eds.), *Restructuring for caring and effective education* (pp. 73–108). Baltimore: Paul H. Brookes.

VandenBos, G. R., DeLeon, P. H., & Belar, C. D. (1991). How many psychological practitioners are needed? It's too early to know! *Professional Psychology: Research and Practice, 22*, 441–448.

Varni, J. W., Katz, E. R., Seid, M., Quiggins, D. J. L., Friedman-Bender, A., & Castro, C. M. (1998). The Pediatric Cancer Quality of Life Inventory (PCQL). I. Instrument development, descriptive statistics, and cross-informant variance. *Journal of Behavioral Medicine, 21*, 179–204.

West, J. F. (1990). Educational collaboration in the restructuring of schools. *Journal of Educational and Psychological Consultation, 1*, 23–40.

Wood. P. R., Casey, R., Kolski, G. D., & McCormick, M. C. (1985). Compliance with oral theophylline therapy in asthmatic children. *Annals of Allergy, 54*, 400–404.

Wysocki, T., Green, L. B., & Huxtable, K. (1989). Blood glucose monitoring by diabetic adolescents: Compliance and metabolic control. *Health Psychology, 8*, 267–284.

Yaffe, M. J. (1998). Developing and supporting school health programs. Role for family physicians. *Canadian Family Physician, 44*, 821–829.

Zora, J. A., Lutz, C. N., & Tinkelman, D. G., (1989). Assessment of compliance in children using inhaled beta adrenergic agonists. *Annals of Allergy, 62*, 406–409.

PART III: Diseases Encountered in School Settings

10

Asthma

Robert D. Annett
University of New Mexico

Pediatric asthma is the most common illness impacting on children's school performance, being considered by some to be the leading cause of childhood disability (Newacheck & Halfon, 2000). What makes this disease even more special is that the disease itself is invisible, though it can have a noticeable impact on a child's school performance with reports indicating that there are more than 10 million missed school days per year attributable to asthma. While the disease itself is "invisible," the obvious effects of the disease are seen in school activities such as sporting events, school trips, physical education, and play activities. Other effects of this disease include how nocturnal asthma symptoms affect sleep architecture and subsequently school performance. In addition, the medications used to manage asthma can also have an impact on school performance. Children who have well-controlled asthma do, in fact, have the capability to engage in the entire range of children's activities and are not likely to have disrupted sleep (Bender & Annett, 1999).

There are a variety of common school problems that a student with asthma is likely to encounter, including: (1) problems associated with absenteeism, (2) avoidance of school activities, (3) delayed treatment for symptoms occurring within the school setting, (4) medication adverse side effects, and (5) effects of poorly controlled asthma upon sleep architecture and subsequent school performance.

The goal of this chapter is to provide school and pediatric psychologists with information on important characteristics of pediatric asthma such as the natural history, epidemiology, pathophysiology, and management of the disease. Although the chapter cannot provide a comprehensive review of these areas, the objective of this review is to provide relevant information that can be utilized in psychological assessment within the school setting to understand the relationship between asthma and psychological functioning, which in turn can guide the psychologist in school-based interventions.

NATURAL HISTORY

Asthma symptoms are most likely to present in children before the age of 5 years. In fact, before entering school, 50% to 80% of children who will develop asthma demonstrate the cardinal symptoms of airflow obstruction including coughing, wheezing, shortness of breath, and/or rapid breathing and chest tightness. A host of factors are associated with the development of asthma symptoms, including allergies (Nelson et al., 1996; Sears, Burrows, Herbison, Holdaway, & Flannery, 1993), genetic factors (Roorda, 1996; Roorda et al., 1993), perinatal exposure to tobacco smoke (Beeber, 1996; Chen, Rennie, & Dosman, 1996; Ehrlich et al., 1996; Gortmaker, Walker, Jacobs, & Ruch-Ross, 1982), viral respiratory infections (Busse & Gern, 1997; Martinez, 1995), male gender (Lanphear, Aligne, Auinger, Weitzman, & Byrd, 2001; Newacheck & Halfon, 2000), smaller lung airways (Schaubel et al., 1996), and low birth weight (Sears, Holdaway, Flannery, Herbison, & Silva, 1996).

Although a host of factors have been associated with the development of asthma in early childhood, there are additional factors that place a child at risk for continued asthma symptoms into the school-age years. These include a family history of asthma, the presence of allergies, and exposure to tobacco smoke. These factors contribute to the expression of the classic asthma symptoms of wheezing, shortness of breath, rapid breathing, and chest tightness. During school-age years, these symptoms can lead to associated behavioral symptoms including fatigue, irritability, missed school days, and avoidance of activities such as sleepovers and sports.

Asthma is the most frequently occurring chronic illness in children in the United States, affecting between 4 and 5 million children (Centers of Disease Control and Prevention, 1996; Sears, 1997). The prevalence and morbidity and mortality rates for children with asthma have increased during the past two decades (Centers of Disease Control and Prevention, 1996; Weiss, Gergen, & Wagener, 1993; Weitzman, Gortmaker, Sobol, & Perrin, 1992), with the rate increasing by 75% in the interval from 1980 to 1993 (Centers of Disease Control and Prevention, 1996). This has occurred at considerable cost, with annual estimates of medical costs alone being as much as 6.2 billion dollars (O'Neill, 1996). Indirect costs of treating asthma, such as workdays lost by the parent caring for the acutely ill child, remain largely unknown.

Asthma is a complex disease to manage within a school setting as the natural history of the illness is variable, with episodic exacerbations and periods of few symptoms. Further complicating the management of a child's asthma is the role played by allergies. Allergies and pediatric asthma are related in a complex manner. Epidemiological research has suggested that as many as 60% to 80% of children with asthma have allergies (Warner, 1978), though the relationship is not necessarily causal. In fact, only children with specific allergies may have asthma. Allergies to dust mites, dog and cat danders, as well as several types of molds increase the risk for asthma in children. Exposure to these environmental allergens can result in decreases in airflow and associated airway hyperresponsiveness that can persist for long periods of time (Nelson, 1999).

For children with asthma who are of school age, it has been estimated that over 50% miss more than 6 days of school per year due to asthma, with up to 15% missing more than 20 days per year (Eggleston et al., 1998). These facts indicate that children with asthma are missing more than 10 million school days per year, a rate that is greater than 3 times the rate of school absence for children without asthma. Children living in poverty are suggested to have an even higher rate of school absence due to asthma (Goodman, Stukel, & Chang, 1998; Mielck,

Reitmeir, & Wjst, 1996). The relationship between asthma management at school and asthma morbidity has not been established, nor have there been comprehensive studies to examine whether the presence of school-based guidelines can reduce morbidity associated with this disease. However, it has been suggested that the development of school-based guidelines for medication management could greatly reduce asthma morbidity (Milgrom, et al., 1996).

PATHOGENESIS

Asthma is an inflammatory disease of the airway and lung. Although it is not possible to review the pathophysiology of pediatric asthma in detail due to the space limitations of this chapter, it is important for the psychologist working in the school setting to understand that there is an inflammatory process occurring within the lung and upper airway. This process has been reviewed in detail elsewhere (Castro, Smith, & Strunk, 1999), though it is important to understand that the child's airway hyperresponsiveness results in airflow limitation and consequent respiratory symptoms including coughing, wheezing, shortness of breath, rapid breathing, and chest tightness. In order to be diagnosed with asthma, these symptoms must be at least partially reversible, meaning that with medications and environmental controls the symptoms can abate. In addition, alternative causes for airflow obstruction must be excluded by the physician caring for the child.

As a result of airflow limitation and its associated symptoms, asthma severity can range across four categories of severity, from mild intermittent to severe persistent (see National Heart, Lung, and Blood Institute, 1997). In general, the preponderance of children with asthma have mild asthma. Taylor and Newacheck (1992) examined reported symptoms in the 1988 National Health Interview Survey to estimate the incidence of different severities of asthma and concluded that 59% of children have mild asthma, 32% have moderate asthma, and 10% have severe asthma.

MANAGEMENT

Medical treatment for the child with asthma consists of both medical and educational interventions. These procedures are typically combined into an asthma management plan. In a review of asthma management approaches, Bartlett (1983) described five criteria essential to the success of asthma education: (1) development of patient responsibility for asthma symptom control; (2) full disclosure of information pertaining to the illness; (3) training the caregiver and child in decision-making skills; (4) use of peer educators; and (5) training health care professionals to encourage self-help attitudes and behaviors among their patients. Yet the implementation of these asthma management approaches may rest on fundamental rapport between the parent of the child with asthma and the physician guiding treatment. There is some evidence that rapport is not always easily established (Cohen & Wamboldt, 2000).

The medical management of pediatric asthma generally involves a stepwise approach that helps the child and family gain control of acute asthma symptoms and maintain control. From the standpoint of asthma medications, the amount utilized is indicated by the severity of the child's asthma symptoms, with the objective of these medications being a reduction in airway inflammation. The two general approaches to asthma medication interventions include gaining rapid control of asthma symptoms through either aggressive medication interventions or dosing medications to the current state of the child. In the aggressive approach to therapy, the health care provider prescribes higher dosages of asthma medications in order to help the child gain control of symptoms, with the goal being a decrease in asthma therapy as symptom severity

TABLE 10.1
Frequently Used Medications Used to Treat Children With Asthma

	Long-Term Control Medications	*Medications for Acute Relief From Symptoms*
	• Taken to treat acute symptoms (coughing, wheezing, difficulty breathing, chest tightness) and to prevent exercise-induced bronchospasm	• Taken daily and chronically (for long periods of time) to maintain control of persistent asthma and to prevent exacerbations
Medications:	• Cromones Cromolyn Nedocromil sodium • Inhaled corticosteroids Beclomethasone Budesonide Fluticasone Flunisolide • Oral/Systemic corticosteroids Prednisone Prednisolone Methylprednisone • Leukotriene modifiers Monolukast Zileuton Zafirlukast • Long-acting $beta_2$-agonists Salmeterol Levealbuterol • Sustained-release theophylline	• Short-acting inhaled or oral $beta_2$-agonists Albuterol Pirbuterol Bitolterol Terbutaline • Oral corticosteroids (short course) Predisone Prednisolone Methylprednisone • Anticholinergics Ipratropium bromide

decreases. With the other approach, therapy with medications is initiated based on the current assessment of the child's asthma symptoms and increasing the amount of medication until symptom control is achieved. In either approach, medications are selected based on child symptom severity and the device employed to administer medications, which is chosen based on the child or caregiver's ability to correctly use it. Long-term control medications and quick-relief medications are the two general classes of asthma medications utilized with pediatric populations. A listing of these medications is presented in Table 10.1.

Medications used to treat pediatric asthma are typically selected according to the child's symptom severity. The National Heart Lung and Blood Institute (1997) provided clinical guidelines for the care of pediatric asthma symptoms that include both medications for long-term control and quick relief of symptoms. Long-term control medications are generally referred to as anti-inflammatory or long-acting bronchodilator medications. Short-acting bronchodilator medications am employed for immediate relief of symptoms and are often recommended for the child with asthma who is about to participate in a sport or other form of exercise in order to prevent the acute exacerbation of symptoms.

The medical management of the child's asthma symptoms also includes training in the use of a peak flow meter, pulmonary function testing to determine airway reactivity, and selection of the medications believed to be of most benefit to the child's acute and chronic symptoms. Asthma has associated changes in the child's lung physiology that chiefly include increased airflow resistance, increased airway responsiveness to allergenic and nonspecific stimuli, and variability in airway tone (Eigen, 1999). Critical for the child with asthma is learning how to evaluate the function of his or her own lungs, which is simply accomplished with a peak flow monitor. The peak flow monitor is a handheld device that provides the child with an opportunity to view their lung function, which they are typically asked to assess on a twice-daily basis. Peak flow readings are set within a clinic setting so that by taking readings from the peak flow meter twice per day, the child and caregiver can determine the level of lung function. Levels of lung function are identified on the peak flow meter as normal, a "yellow zone," and a "red zone." A peak flow reading that is greater than 80% of the predicted normal value is considered normal, whereas readings in the yellow or red zones would necessitate some action from the child and caregivers. The action plan developed in the clinical setting provides information to the child and caregivers about when to administer additional medication, seek medical help through the primary care physician, or go to the emergency department of the local hospital.

Within the clinic setting, pulmonary function testing, often referred to as lung function testing, is a critical component to the ongoing management of the child's asthma. The purpose of this testing is to examine the degree of airway obstruction as well as the reversibility of airway obstruction to bronchodilator medications. Thus the child completes lung function testing two times within the context of a clinic visit, with medication being utilized to examine the degree of airway response to asthma medication.

Educational interventions primarily focus on the precipitants of an asthma "attack," though this intervention also includes teaching basic asthma facts, explaining the role of medications, teaching the child/parent to monitor asthma symptoms, teaching environmental control measures, and teaching when/how to take rescue medications. The precipitants for an asthma attack, often referred to as "triggers," can include viral upper respiratory infections, exposure to environmental irritants and allergens, tobacco/wood smoke, house-dust mites, animal proteins, cockroaches, fungi/molds, exercise, aggravating conditions not appropriately treated (e.g., rhinitis, sinusitis, gastroesophageal reflux), stress, and strong emotional expressions. Within a comprehensive asthma management program, educational strategies are based on the child's developmental level or more specifically, grade level in school, with action plans developed and written down for the child/family.

In addition to the preceding activities that occur within the clinic setting, management of asthma within the school setting should involve the development of a school action plan. In this plan the clinic educator identifies relevant school personnel who should be trained to participate and assist in the care of a child with asthma. Training then consists of education about asthma characteristics, common "triggers," the child's use of a peak flow meter, and information on asthma medications. Of particular concern to school personnel and the child with asthma is the availability of asthma medications. That is, for a child who may need to use medication on a long-term basis, there may be stereotypes that develop that could adversely affect the child. For example, it is important for school personnel to understand that asthma medications are not addictive, that these medications remain effective when used daily, that allowing the child to freely use his or her asthma medication reduces the impact of the disease upon school function, and that while these mediations are generally useful, there may be cognitive toxicities for the child. Cognitive toxicities associated with some asthma medications typically include nervousness, nausea, drowsiness, jitteriness, or increased behavioral activity. When these are experienced by the child at school, it is imperative that the caregivers and subsequently the treating physician be notified. In severe exacerbations at school, it may be necessary to notify the treating physician directly and to have the child brought to an emergency room.

RELATIONSHIP OF ASTHMA AND PSYCHOSOCIAL FUNCTIONING

Asthma has been linked to childhood disability, in fact being identified as the leading cause of childhood disability (Newacheck & Halfon, 2000). In an examination of data from the 1994–1995 National Health Interview Survey, data for 62,171 children were examined for the presence and degree of disability, restricted days of activity, school absences, and use of medical care services measured as outcomes. Overall, approximately 1.4% of children were reported as experiencing some type of disability due to asthma. Risk factors for experiencing disability due to asthma included being an adolescent, African American, male, living in a low-income family, and from a single parent family. Asthma resulted in 20 days of restricted activity for children, including 10 days of school absence. Although the psychological cost of asthma can only be inferred from these findings, there are obvious social costs to children with asthma that have implications for their psychological functioning.

Overall, a number of factors such as symptom severity, psychosocial variables, natural history of asthma symptoms, sociodemographic factors, and the culture in which the child resides can influence child health status. These factors can either have direct effects or indirect effects upon the child's health status. For example, more severe asthma can have numerous medical complications requiring frequent visits to a specialty clinic, which in turn has an impact on the child's school performance. Earlier onset of asthma symptoms has been linked directly with increased risk of behavioral difficulties including night awakenings, depressed mood, and increased fearfulness (Mrazek, Schuman, & Klinnert, 1998). Shasha, Lavigne, Lyons, Pongracic, and Martini (1999) assessed the prevalence of behavioral problems (with the Child Behavior Checklist [CBCL]; Achenbach, 1991) in a large group of children with at least a one-year history of asthma who were receiving care within a tertiary care pediatric clinic. Their findings revealed that almost 30% of the children exceeded the 9th percentile on one or more of the major CBCL broad-band domains (e.g., internalizing). Approximately one half of these children had received mental health services in the year before data collection, suggesting that children with asthma have an increased risk of behavioral and emotional problems. In addition to these findings, degree of acculturation has been associated with adherence with treatment for asthma in children (Pachter & Weller, 1993).

Asthma severity alone can have implications for the child's psychosocial adaptation. McLean, Perrin, Gortmaker, and Pierre (1992) examined a group of 6–14-year-old children with asthma on a variety of measures including the CBCL. Children with more severe asthma received significantly higher problem scores, as rated by the caregiver, than those with moderate asthma and demonstrated lower levels of psychosocial adaptation. Similarly, children with mild and severe asthma received lower adjustment scores than children with moderate asthma, again suggesting an association between asthma severity and psychosocial adaptation (Perrin, MacLean & Perrin, 1989). Others have suggested that children with asthma have a higher incidence of psychiatric problems than children without disease (Graham, Rutter, Yule, & Pless, 1967; Kashani, Konig, Shepperd, Wilfley, & Morris, 1988; McNichol, Williams, Allan, & McAndrew, 1973; Mrazek, 1992; Vila et al., 1999). A disturbing finding has been that children with more severe asthma, depressive features, high levels of family conflict, and poor symptom awareness skills are at increased risk for asthma-related mortality (Strunk, Mrazek, Fuhrmann, & LaBrecque, 1985). In contrast to these findings, an examination of a large population of children with mild and moderate asthma found the frequency of childhood behavior problems to be no different than in the general population (Bender et al., 2000). Obviously, there are many dynamic factors contributing to control of a complex disease such as asthma. In particular, the demands placed on the child and family for changing behavior through environmental modifications and taking medications places additional burdens on children and families, likely contributing to stressors and possible difficulties with psychological adjustment.

These preceding studies suggest that there is a reciprocal relationship between asthma and psychological functioning, though it is highly dependent on control of the disease and psychological adjustment of the child and family. Disease-related factors such as the demands of the medication regimen, cognitive toxicity profile associated with asthma medication, and the child/family's ability to make environmental modifications all have an impact on the child's ability to function with asthma in a school setting. Research related to asthma outcomes suggests that there are presumed reciprocal influences between disease processes, the natural environment, and individual differences of children with the disease (Creer, Stein, Rappaport, & Lewis, 1992).

The school environment and particularly a teacher's reactions to the child may influence psychological functioning of the child with asthma. The teacher may hold different expectations for academic performance and psychosocial adaptation leading to further complications for the child's adjustment, although research in this area does not indicate differences in teacher-reported social competence in children with asthma and matched controls (Nassau & Drotar, 1995). Teachers do not typically have training in the management of asthma and may have misconceptions regarding the disease (Bevis & Taylor, 1990; Brookes & Jones, 1992). Expectations may be based on the teacher's past experiences with children with asthma or with other features of the disease, such as frequent absences from school because of illness or direct consequences of the disease such as mood-related difficulties (e.g., withdrawn behavior). Conversely, a teacher may not even know that a child has asthma or recognize the symptoms and how these symptoms may impact school performance.

Poorly managed asthma can have negative implications for the child's school performance and psychosocial adaptation (Bender, 1999). This may be most apparent in the child's avoidance of physical activity, fatigue, and consequent arousal difficulties, making learning a substantial challenge. Manifestations of poorly managed asthma can also include days missed from school because of disease exacerbations. Days missed from school may interfere with the child acquiring new knowledge, subsequently presenting learning challenges for the child. For the child with severe asthma, prolonged home treatment or hospitalizations for asthma can interfere with learning. Under these circumstances, the child's learning needs may best be addressed by the implementation of a home-school program where a teacher comes into the child's home to provide educational services during a prolonged absence. For children who are not absent for an extended period of time, catch-up support after return to school may be necessary and can be implemented through the development of a 504 Plan (Rehabilitation Act of 1973; 29 U.S.C. 794). It has been estimated that 1.4% of all school-age children experience some disability due to asthma, resulting in as many as 20 days of missed school per year (Newacheck & Halfon, 2000). The risk for disability associated with asthma is increased in adolescents, minority children, males, and children from low-income families (Gutstadt et al.,1989; Newacheck & Halfon, 2000). Children with a chronic illness such as asthma are likely to benefit from increased teacher knowledge about asthma as well as increased teacher involvement. When children experience this increased level of support, their academic progress is most likely to continue in a manner consistent with their peers (Lightfoot, Wright, & Sloper, 1999).

Cognitive and Behavioral Effects Associated With Medication

There are differing viewpoints on the association between asthma medications and children's psychological functioning. Reviews of this literature (Creer & Bender, 1993, 1995) revealed mixed results ranging from findings suggesting that medications have associated adverse to beneficial effects on a child's memory and behavior. Only one class of medication, corticosteroids, have been demonstrated to be associated with alterations in psychological functioning. In particular, oral steroids at high dosages have been associated with cognitive toxicity, most clearly manifest as irritability in the child. This is likely due to the dosage and that orally administered steroids have a greater degree of systemic absorption in comparison with inhaled steroids. Effects on neuropsychological functioning, such as memory, have been identified as transient (Bender & Milgrom, 1995), though individual case studies have suggested that there are unique circumstances where inhaled steroids may be associated with neurobehavioral dysfunction (Koenig, 1988). There is clearly s dose-response relationship when examining cognitive outcomes associated with asthma medications, with higher dosages being associated with greater impact on neuropsychological functioning (e.g., memory). In addition, there appear to be age-associated effects with asthma medications such as those described by Nelson and Schwartz (1987) who reported age-related cognitive toxicities of asthma medications, including insomnia and hyperactivity, as occurring in up to 33% of children under 4 years of age and as low as 5% of school-age children.

Undertreatment of asthma may result in adverse events that produce neuropsychological compromise. Specifically, lack of treatment or ineffective treatment can result in a respiratory crisis. Although primarily case reports exist to examine this adherence-related problem (e.g., Bierman, Pierson, Shapiro & Simons, 1975), there are studies of the natural history of respiratory arrests from pediatric asthma indicating that when respiratory failure does occur from asthma, there can be associated morbidity from hypoxic brain injury (Newcomb & Akhter, 1988). Other attempts to examine the possibility of brain damage associated with asthma have not demonstrated a significant association (Bender, Belleau, Fukuhara, Mrazek, & Strunk, 1987). In contrast, literature reviews on the effects of asthma medications and psychological functioning (Annett & Bender, 1994) reveal that few controlled trials have examined the neurobehavioral tonicities of asthma medications used with children. Case reports have been identified to suggest some cause for concern regarding the effects of asthma medications and children's psychological functioning (Koenig, 1988), yet these concerns have not been supported in controlled trials.

Three types of asthma medications are commonly employed with children: corticosteroids, xanthenes, and beta agonists. Corticosteroids are a type of anti-inflammatory medication employed to decrease airway responsiveness. These medications are administered with a metered dose inhaler (MDI) and thus inhaled directly into the lung, though there are also oral steroids that are typically administered in a "burst" over several days in response to a serious asthma exacerbation. It is believed that there is little systemic absorption of the inhaled steroid into the body, and thus decreased chance of steroids impacting on central nervous system functioning and development. However, this is not without controversy (Geddes, 1992). Reviews of this literature (Annett & Bender, 1994) suggest that administration of oral steroids to children with asthma results in subtle changes in neuropsychological functioning (e.g., attention, verbal and visual memory and executive functions), though this appears to be ameliorated within 24 to 48 hours after medication administration. These changes appear to be limited to children's mood and memory functioning and are specific to the administration of oral steroids (e.g., prednisone).

Xanthenes are the second category of asthma medication employed with children, though the prevalence of their use appears to have declined in recent years. These agents are similar in nature to caffeine and act as a central nervous system stimulant. By far the most controversial of these medication has been theophylline, which has been reported to be instrumental in children with asthma becoming overactive (*The American Asthma Report*, 1989). When examined in randomized controlled trials, the adverse side effects of theophylline can best be described as similar to those of caffeine, a closely related member of the xanthene class. Studies in the 1980s found that theophylline was associated with adverse effects on neuropsychological functioning (Furukawa et al., 1984b; Springer, Goldenberg, Ben Dov, & Godfrey, 1985) and school performance (Rachelefsky et al., 1986). However, when controlled trials have addressed this issue, findings appear to suggest no detrimental effects on neuropsychological processes such as attention and memory functioning in children with asthma (Rappaport et al., 1989; Schlieper, Adcock, Beaudry, Feldman, & Leikin, 1991).

Children who have been treated with theophylline in a structured asthma treatment program have been compared with controls on standardized group achievement tests (e.g., Iowa Tests of Basic Skills). Findings have indicated that there are no between-group differences in the area of academic achievement (Lindgren et al., 1992). It is noteworthy that when parent beliefs were studied, 28% of parents believed that learning problems for their child were the result of either asthma or asthma medications. When treatment with theophylline has been compared with an inhaled corticosteroid employing neuropsychological measures of attention and memory, no significant effects have been reported (Bender, Ikle, DuHamel, & Tinkelman, 1998). It seems safe to conclude that results from controlled trials suggest that theophylline does not have demonstrable adverse effects on learning for children with asthma.

The third type of asthma medications are the beta agonists. The action of this class of medications is to promote bronchodilation. Anti-inflammatory medications, including cromolyn, promote bronchodilation. These medications typically are administered through an MDI so that the child breathes in the medication. A well-known adverse side effect of bronchodilator medications is tremors, though there are few reported toxicities associated with psychological or neuropsychological functioning in children (Furukawa et al., 1984a).

Though not used in the management of pediatric asthma, antihistamine medications are often utilized in the management of allergies, which commonly co-occur with asthma. A small body of research is available on the relative benefits of sedating and nonsedating antihistamines on adult cognitive performance (Kay, 2000; Kay et al., 1997). Yet little scientific evidence exists about the effects of these common allergy medications on children's cognitive functioning. Symptoms associated with allergies in children can include malaise, irritability, and fatigue, as well as diminished learning (Simons, 1996). In fact, in one study examining sedating and nonsedating antihistamines in children, Vuurman and colleagues concluded that children with allergic rhinitis learned less well than children without allergic rhinitis (Vuurman, van Veggel, Uiterwijk, Leutner, & O'Hanlon, 1993). Additionally, these investigators found that a sedating antihistamine (diphenhydramine hydrochloride) impeded children's learning of factual information as well as ability to apply a learning strategy, while a nonsedating antihistamine (loratadine) resulted in improved learning in children with allergies.

Asthma, Smoking, and Psychological Functioning

Perhaps one of the most deleterious effects in the control of asthma symptoms in children is exposure to smoke, through both second-hand smoke and direct smoking. Tobacco smoke exposure is a significant trigger for asthma, producing increased airway responsiveness and inflammation (Menon, Stankus, Rando, Salvaggio, & Lehrer, 1991). It is well known that there is a strong association between maternal cigarette smoking and subsequent child neurobehavioral dysfunction (Butler & Goldstein, 1973; Denson, Nanson, & McWaters, 1975; Dunn, McBurney, Ingram, & Hunter, 1977; Naeye & Peters, 1984; Rantakallio, 1983; Sexton, Fox, & Hebel, 1990; Weitzman, Gortmaker, & Sobol, 1992). Parental smoking has an equally strong association with the onset and persistence of asthma symptoms in children (Floreani & Rennard, 1999; Joad, 2000; Kay, Mortimer, & Jaron, 1995). Simply being exposed to second-hand tobacco smoke can result in increased wheezing, decreased lung function in children, and school absence (Mannino, Moorman, Kingsley, Rose, & Repace, 2001).

There can be adverse psychologic consequences of smoking, particularly among adolescents. For example, adolescent smoking has been associated with depression, anxiety, attention deficit hyperactivity disorder, and a variety of other psychiatric problems (Brown, Lewinsohn, Seeley, &Wagner, 1996; Millberger, Biederman, Faraone, Chen, & Jones, 1997). Adolescent smoking also has been shown to differ across ethnic groups. Different prevalence rates have been observed, with cigarette smoking being highest among Native American adolescent males and females (42% and 39%, respectively), followed by White adolescent males and females (33% and 33%), Hispanic adolescent males/females (28% and 19%), Asian American adolescent males and females (21% and 14%), and African American adolescent males and females (12% and 9%), having the lowest percentage of adolescent smokers (U.S. Dept of Health and Human Services, 1998). More importantly, some experts suggest that the prevalence of smoking is even higher among adolescents with asthma, placing them at additional risk for psychiatric difficulties (Forero, Bauman, Young, Booth, & Nutbeam, 1996).

Taken as a whole, these findings suggest that children and adolescents with asthma are at increased risk for problems in psychological functioning if there are smokers within the home or if the children themselves smoke, and this risk may increase depending on the ethic group of the individual. Encouraging smoking parents of children with asthma to smoke outside of the home may serve to lessen these risks (Bahceciler, Barlan, Nuhoglu, & Basaran, 1999).

Nocturnal Asthma and Psychological Functioning

Many children with asthma experience a worsening of symptoms at night and during sleep. In the general population, as many as 25% of children experience some type of sleep disruption (Lozoff, Wolf, & Davis, 1985; Paavonen et al., 2000; Richman, 1981), with speculation suggesting that sleep disturbances that begin in infancy persist into childhood (Mindell, 1997). However, among individuals with asthma, little data exist about the frequency of sleep disruption related to asthma symptoms, with one survey indicating that 11% of the sample reported nightly awakenings related to asthma (Storms, Bodman, Nathan, & Byer, 1994). Mindall (1997) identified and described three categories of sleep disorders in children: insomnia, excessive daytime sleepiness, and parasomnias. Each of these may be complicated by the child having asthma symptoms. In more severe cases, actual obstruction of the airway known as obstructive sleep apnea, may be associated with asthma symptoms. From 1.6% to 3.4% of children under 6 years of age have obstructive sleep apnea (Gislason & Benediktsdottir, 1995).

Children with lung disease such as asthma experience a significant decline in lung function during the night, which may be coupled with a heightened degree of airway responsiveness. These changes can result in awakenings that are the hallmark of disrupted sleep architecture. Consequences may be inadequate sleep and resultant excessive daytime sleepiness. For children, daytime sleepiness is not simply manifest in behaviors such as falling asleep at school. Behaviors such as increased irritability, problems with attention/concentration, and fatigue can be the presenting symptoms of disrupted sleep architecture associated with nocturnal asthma symptoms. Children are typically unaware of the occurrence of these arousals, which have a duration of 2 to 20 seconds. Several contributing factors have been suggested for daytime sleepiness, including sleep fragmentation and oxygen desaturation. Sleep fragmentation, characterized by multiple brief arousals from sleep, has been associated with alterations in neuropsychological performance, including problems with arousal, attention, and memory (Bonnet, 1985, 1993). Children are thought to be especially vulnerable to these neuropsychological effects to sleep fragmentation (Bonnet, 1994). When there is greater airway obstruction, oxygen desaturation can result in acute hypoxia, which in turn is suspected of resulting in daytime sleepiness (Sink, Bliwise, & Dement, 1986).

The child with nocturnal asthma symptoms may be at increased risk of having disrupted sleep (Bender & Annett, 1999), with the associated adverse side effects including arousal difficulties during the school day (Stores, Ellis, Wiggs, Crawford, & Thomson, 1998. There also appears to be an association between nocturnal asthma and asthma severity, though this finding has most often been demonstrated in adults (Fix et al., 1997). A review of the literature in this area has generally concluded that nocturnal asthma symptoms are associated with a host of morbidities

(D'Ambrosio & Mohsenin, 1998). For example, children with nocturnal asthma symptoms have been found to have more psychological problems as well as poorer performance on tests of memory and concentration relative to their normally developing peers (Stores et al., 1998). Remarkably, when asthma is better controlled there are fewer nocturnal asthma symptoms, and interestingly a resolution of the problems in psychological functioning. In contrast with this report are the findings of Sadeh, Horowitz, Wolach-Benodis, and Wolach (1998) who compared the sleep quality of children with asthma to that of a normally developing comparison control group. Findings indicated that the children with asthma had poorer sleep quality, as manifest in lower percentages of quiet sleep on a wrist actigraph. These studies suggest that a child's having asthma results in increased risk of disturbed sleep and the consequent neurobehavioral outcomes associated with disrupted sleep. Disturbances in sleep, including sleep fragmentation, often result in daytime sleepiness with resulting problems in arousal. For a child with asthma-related sleep disturbances, daytime sleepiness can result in arousal-associated inattentiveness and other problems in memory and learning.

Disturbance in a child's sleep often has been associated with psychological problems. For example, sleep disturbance was included as one of the criteria for attention deficit disorder in the *Diagnostic and Statistical Manual of Mental Disorders, Third Edition* (*DSM-III*; American Psychiatric Association, 1980), with it being dropped as a criterion in subsequent editions. However, sleep problems remain an associated feature of a host of psychological problems for children (Ball & Koloian, 1995; Dahl & Pugh-Antich, 1990). What is clear at present is that children with nocturnal asthma are known to have increased school absences (Diette et al., 2000) and diminished school performance (Gozal, 1998). Diette and colleagues surveyed parents of 438 children (ages 5–17 years) with asthma that were enrolled in a managed care health plan. They found that 40% of the children were reported to have had an episode of nocturnal asthma awakenings in the previous 4 weeks. Children with nocturnal awakenings from asthma differed from their peers who had no awakenings from asthma in the number of school days missed, with the frequency of school days missed increasing with the number of nights of reported nocturnal asthma symptoms. Other associated findings included more severe asthma symptoms and greater use of quick-relief medication. Parents also reported that nighttime awakenings from asthma were strongly associated with poor academic progress. Not all children actually awaken from asthma symptoms, thus it is critical that research in this area determine both the child's and the parent's perspective on the presence of nocturnal asthma symptoms, as well as the extent to which sleep awakenings occur as a result of asthma symptoms.

Family Functioning and Asthma

Family functioning and asthma health outcomes are strongly interconnected. For younger children, asthma is typically managed by a caregiver, meaning that symptom identification and management (administering of daily or rescue medications) is the responsibility of the caregiver. Yet as a child enters school age, the typical expectation is for the child to assume greater responsibility for his or her asthma care. By the time a child reaches adolescence he or she should be able to assume complete responsibility for the identification and management of asthma symptoms. The process whereby the caregiver relinquishes control of asthma management and the child assumes greater responsibility for treatment is a complex one that depends to a great degree on the quality of the parent–child relationship. Families with problems in the parent–child relationship, disorganization, psychiatric illness, and poor child supervision can be expected to have marked difficulties in assisting children assume greater responsibility for their care.

Impairments in family functioning are most likely to contribute to medication nonadherence and can also contribute to impediments in the child learning to identify asthma symptoms. In one study examining treatment adherence, problems with administration of prophylactic treatment were associated with increased need for treatment in hospital emergency departments and the need for treatment with oral steroid medications (Milgrom et al., 1996). Parent concern about medication cognitive toxicity has been reported to be as significant a worry as the asthma symptoms themselves (Townsend et al., 1991). At times, children may be undertreated for their asthma symptoms. Medication undertreatment has been associated with problems with family communication and organization (Bender, 1995), whereas greater levels of nonadherence have been associated with family conflict (Wamboldt, Wamboldt, Gavin, Roesler, & Brugman, 1995). The most dangerous combination of factors for the child with asthma is when there is severe marital conflict, severe parent–child conflict, conflict between medical care providers and the family, substance abuse, depressive symptoms in the child, and lack of identification of asthma symptoms. Under these circumstances the child is at risk for death related to asthma. This disturbing finding was reported by Strunk, Mrazek, Fuhrmann, and LaBrecque (1985) who examined 21 cases of children who later died from their asthma.

For children with asthma, stressors within the family that are not asthma related can place additional burden on the successful management of the disease (McLean et al., 1992). Bussing, Halfon, Benjamin, and Wells (1995) examined a large group of children with asthma, a substantial number of whom had comorbidity of another chronic medical condition. These investigators found that children with asthma that was comorbid with another chronic health problem were even at greater risk for adjustment difficulties. In our own study of children with mild and moderate asthma, a strong association was found between psychological adaptation of the child and the emotional climate of the family (Bender et al., 2000). Secure family relationships, social support, and the parents' reports of the impact of the disease on family functioning were the strongest predictors of child psychological adjustment. Not surprisingly, and consistent with other literature related to chronic illness in children, severity of asthma itself was not predictive of children's psychological adjustment.

ROLE FOR PEDIATRIC PSYCHOLOGISTS IN SCHOOL SETTINGS

For the pediatric psychologist working in a school setting there are a variety of roles that can be fulfilled in the care of children with asthma. While these roles may differ based on the developmental level of the child, there are some general functions that the pediatric psychologist may fulfill. Perhaps most fundamental of these roles occurs in the general clinical evaluation of a child with possible emotional, behavioral, or learning problems. For children receiving a comprehensive clinical workup, it is important to determine whether fundamental observations of child neurobehavioral difficulties, such as problems with attention, concentration, focusing, restlessness, irritability, anxiety, or withdrawal, have an etiology that includes poor control of asthma symptoms. For example, the child with asthma who has clinically significant attention problems should be queried about sleep and the quality of his or her sleep, as disrupted sleep associated with nocturnal asthma symptoms may lead to symptoms of inattention during schoolwork activities.

For children with particularly severe asthma, cognitive and academic functioning may be severely compromised by events in the child's past medical history as well as by current management. For example, a child being treated in our Pediatric Pulmonary Center has a birth history of prematurity and associated chronic lung disease. She currently has severe asthma, for which treatment with nebulized Albuterol occurs on a daily basis. This child has compromised learning capabilities, with her current treatment and its associated adverse side effect of bilateral tremor further interfering with simple functions such as legible handwriting. In presenting evaluation findings to the child's teachers, it is critical to help them understand how neurocognitive processes and treatment factors (i.e., medications and associated hand tremor) may compromise learning. Approaches to improved academic performance and self-competence need to incorporate interventions to address memory and learning capabilities, as well as emotional functioning.

Other clinical activities for the pediatric psychologist occur as children with asthma are required to take on increasing responsibility for their care. While younger school-age children often rely on adult supervision for the identification of symptoms and directions for management of their disease, increasing responsibility for asthma care shifts directly to children as they progress through school. Shifting responsibility for symptom awareness and management to the child increases the risk for problems of adherence. Children with asthma clearly differ in terms of symptom awareness and particularly breathlessness, or dyspnea (Rietveld & Prins, 1998). Dyspnea is likely the child's first symptom that provides a clue to asthma exacerbation. Without any assistance, however, children with asthma demonstrate poor awareness of dyspnea. Yet with training and practice in the use of a peak flow meter, children can improve their awareness of dyspnea, which is the first step in a management and intervention plan.

Important self-management behaviors for children have been characterized within four broad areas: prevention, intervention, compensatory behaviors, and management of environmental factors (McNabb, Wilson-Pessano, & Jacobs, 1986). Clearly there is more to the management of asthma than simply taking one's medications! The competencies a child needs to develop include a host of behaviors ranging from avoiding specific allergens that are known to be associated with exacerbations of asthma to accepting responsibility for the management of his or her asthma. Yet these competencies occur within a context of the family and school. Research available indicates that problems within the home setting, such as increased levels of family dysfunction, result in decreased child competencies in asthma management (Christiaanse, Lavigne, & Lerner, 1989). For the pediatric psychologist working within the school setting, a substantial role in improved child self-management can occur through a careful examination of the complicating family environment surrounding the child with asthma. A child with a history of poor adherence with a regimen of inhaled corticosteroids is at increased risk for psychological morbidity (Cluley, 2001). More specifically, increased risk of psychological problems have been associated with more severe asthma, high use of steroid medications to control asthma symptoms, and hospitalization for asthma. This configuration of factors in a clinical history should certainly raise the concern of the pediatric psychologist and ultimately spur the development of a comprehensive plan of intervention, including collaboration with the school nurse and primary care physician. Findings have revealed that when a positive relationship exists between the primary care physician and the child with asthma, there is less risk of adherence problems (Gavin, Wamboldt, Sorokin, Levy, & Wamboldt, 1999).

Certainly one of the areas of clinical care of children with which pediatric psychologists are involved is child advocacy. For the child with asthma, advocacy within the school setting may be needed in two areas. First, cooperative efforts are needed with school nurses in providing information to teachers, playground supervisors, and athletic coaches about a child's asthma management plan, such as the need for peak flow monitoring and treatment. Cultural and health beliefs of school personnel can play a decided role in how they react to the child experiencing an acute asthma episode. There are indications that school personnel may actually interfere with a child's management of acute asthma symptoms because they lack knowledge about asthma (McNabb et al., 1986). This potential problem could be remedied by increasing knowledge of asthma emergency plans within the child's school setting, particularly given the finding of recent research indicating that relatively few children have an asthma emergency plan on file at their local school (Sapien & Allen, 2000). The second manner in which advocacy for the child may occur is in the area of school policy. Frequently children are not allowed to carry medications with them or administer medications independently. For some children with asthma, experiencing an acute exacerbation of symptoms necessitates the immediate administration of rescue medications. Children who have demonstrated an ability to act responsibly should be allowed to carry their own medications, especially during field trips, sports activities, and whenever the school office is closed. In order for the child to assume these responsibilities, changes may be necessary in school policies on administration of medications as well as careful monitoring of the child's ability to assume a reasonable degree of responsibility for his or her care.

The National Asthma Education Program has supported both of these methods of child advocacy (see *Managing Asthma: A Guide for Schools*, 1991). Specifically what is recommended is the development of a school-wide management plan for children with asthma. This should include recognition of school policies and procedures for the administration of medications, specific actions for school staff members to perform in an asthma management program, and a general action plan for child asthma episodes. More specific details are necessary for individual students with asthma such as a list of medications the student receives, a specific plan of action for school personnel in the event of an acute asthma episode, and emergency procedures and telephone numbers.

CONCLUSIONS

Asthma is quite prevalent in school-age children, and the disease ranges in severity from intermittently mild to severe. Clearly, routine and proper use of medications to control symptoms can make life for the child with asthma completely normal, including full participation in the range of activities of interest. However, treatment demands for the child and family are likely to result in reciprocal problems in maintaining adherence to a treatment regimen.

Effective management for asthma is complex because of the varying course of the illness, associations with other heath-related problems (e.g., allergies, sleep-related breathing problems), challenges of maintaining good adherence with taking medications, and problems of symptom awareness. Family, cultural, and environmental factors need to be appreciated and assessed as they can be areas that help the child/family effectively manage asthma or may represent barriers to effective treatment. Difficulties in management of symptoms, family functioning, and children's adjustment difficulties can result in alterations that are apparent in the child's school functioning. These alterations range widely from potential problems with arousal, attention, and learning to internalizing and externalizing behavior problems.

Pediatric psychologists in school settings have important contributions to make in the management of this chronic disease. The ability to assess the host of complicating factors, including family functioning, child emotional functioning, and neuropsychological factors underlying academic performance, can result in interventions to improve the child's psychosocial adaptation, academic performance, as well as the general knowledge about asthma treatment within a school setting. The complexities associated with pediatric asthma, particularly when the child has experienced adverse effects from the disease, require the expertise and collaborative efforts of a variety of professionals, including physicians, nurses, teachers, and psychologists. This team of health professionals, working together, can improve the overall well-being of children with asthma and work to assist families in adjusting to the differing demands of the illness.

REFERENCES

Achenbach, T. M. (1991). *Manual for the child behavior checklist/4-18 and 1991 profile*. Burlington: University of Vermont, Department of Psychiatry.

The American asthma report. (1989). New York: Research and Forecasts, Inc.

American Psychiatric Association. (1980). *Diagnostic and statistical manual of mental disorders* (3rd ed.). Washington, DC: American Psychiatric Association.

Annett, R. D., & Bender, B. G. (1994). Neuropsychological dysfunction in asthmatic children. *Neuropsychology Review, 4*, 91–116.

Bahceciler, N. N., Barlan, I. B., Nuhoglu, Y., & Basaran, M. M. (1999). Parental smoking behavior and the urinary cotinine levels of asthmatic children. *Journal of Asthma, 36*, 171–175.

Ball, J. D., & Koloian, B. (1995). Sleep patterns among ADHD children. *Clinical Psychology Review, 15*, 681–691.

Bartlett, E. E. (1983). Educational self-help approaches in childhood asthma. *Journal of Allergy and Clinical Immunology, 72*, 545–554.

Beeber, S. J. (1996). Parental smoking and childhood asthma. *Journal of Pediatric Health Care, 10*, 58–62.

Bender, B. G. (1995). Psychological effects of chronic disease in children: Focus on chronic rhinitis and asthma. In *The chronic airways disease connection: Redefining rhinitis. Consensus conference proceedings, Part I* (pp. 10–12). Los Angeles: UCLA Office of Continuing Medical Education.

Bender, B. G. (1999). Learning disorders associated with asthma and allergies. *School Psychology Review 28*, 204–214.

Bender, B. G., & Annett, R. D. (1999). Pediatric neuropsychological outcomes in nocturnal asthma. *Chronobiology International, 16*, 695–710.

Bender, B. G., Annett, R. D., Bucher-Bartelson, B., DuHamel, T., Rand, C., & Struck, R. (2000). Relationship between disease status and psychological adaptation in the Childhood Asthma Management Program. *Archives of Pediatrics and Adolescent Medicine, 154*, 706–713.

Bender, B. G., Belleau, L., Fukuhara, J. T., Mrazek, D. A., & Strunk, R. C. (1987). Psychomotor adaptation in children with severe chronic asthma. *Pediatrics, 79*, 723–727.

Bender, B. G., Ikle, D. N., DuHamel, T., & Tinkelman, D. (1998). Nenropsychological and behavioral changes in asthmatic children treated with beclomethasone dipropionate versus theophylline. *Pediatrics, 101*(3 Pt. 1), 355–360.

Bender, B. G., & Milgrom, H. (1995). Neuropsychiatric effects of medications for allergic diseases. *Journal of Allergy and Clinical Immunology, 95*, 523–528.

Bevis, M., & Taylor, B. (1990). What do school teachers know about asthma? *Archives of Diseases of Childhood, 65*, 622–625.

Bierman, C., Pierson, W., Shapiro, G., & Simons, E. (1975). Brain damage from asthma in children. *Journal of Allergy and Clinical Immunology, 55*, 126.

Bonnet, M. H. (1985). Effect of sleep disruption on sleep, performance, and mood. *Sleep, 8*, 11–19.

Bonnet, M. H. (1993). Cognitive effects of sleep and sleep fragmentation. *Sleep, 16*, S65–S67.

Bonnet, M. H. (1994). Sleep deprivation. In M. H. Kryger, T. Roth, & W. C. Dement (Eds.), *Principles and practice of sleep medicine* (pp. 50–67). Philadelphia Saunders.

Brookes, J., & Jones, K. (1992). Schoolteachers' perceptions and knowledge of asthma in primary school children. *British Journal of General Practice, 42*, 504–507.

Brown, R. A., Lewinsohn, P., Seeley, J. R., & Wagner, E. F. (1996). Cigarette smoking, major depression, and other psychiatric disorders among adolescents. *Journal of the American Academy of Child and Adolescent Psychiatry, 35*, 1602–1610.

Busse, W. W., Gern, J. E. (1997). Viruses in asthma. *Journal of Allergy and Clinical Immunology, 100*, 147–150.

Bussing, R., Halfon, N., Benjamin, B., & Wells, K. B. (1995). Prevalence of behavior problems in US children with asthma. *Archives of Pediatrics & Adolescent Medicine, 149*, 565–572.

Butler, N. R., & Goldstein, H. (1973). Smoking in pregnancy and subsequent child development. *British Medical Journal, 4*, 573–575.

Castro, M., Smith, T. F., & Strunk, R. C. (1999). Pathophysiology. In S. Murphy & H. W. Kelly (Eds.), *Pediatric asthma* (pp. 71–116). New York: Marcel Dekker, Inc.

Centers of Disease Control and Prevention. (1996). Asthma mortality and hospitalization among children and young adults, 1980–1993. *MMWR Morbidity and Mortality Weekly Report, 45*, 350–353.

Chen, Y., Rennie, D. C., & Dosman, J. A. (1996). Influence of environmental tobacco smoke on asthma in nonallergic and allergic children. *Epidemiology, 7*, 536–539.

Christiaanse, M. E., Lavigne, J. V., & Lerner, C. V. (1989). Psychosocial aspects of compliance in children and adolescents with asthma. *Journal of Developmental and Behavioral Pediatrics, 10*, 75–80.

Cluley, S. (2001). Psychological disorder in asthma is associated with poor control and poor adherence to inhaled steroids. *Respiratory Medicine, 95*, 37–139.

Cohen, S. Y., & Wamboldt, F. S. (2000). The parent-physician relationship in pediatric asthma care. *Journal of Pediatric Psychology, 25*, 69–77.

Creer, T. L., & Bender, B. G. (1993). Asthma. In R. J. Gatchel & E. B. Blanchard (Eds.), *Psychophysiological disorders* (pp. 151–203). Washington, DC: American Psychological Association.

Creer, T. L., & Bender, B. G. (1995). Recent trends in asthma research. In A. J. Goreczney (Ed.), *Handbook of health and rehabilitation psychology* (pp. 31–35). New York: Plenum.

Creer, T. L., Stein, R. E., Rappaport, L., & Lewis, C. (1992). Behavioral consequences of illness: Childhood asthma as a model. *Pediatrics, 90* (5 Pt 2), 808–815.

D'Ambrosio, C. M., & Mohsenin, V. (1998). Sleep in asthma. *Clinics in Chest Medicine, 19*, 127–137.

Dahl, R. E.. & Pugh-Antich, J. (1990). Sleep disturbance in child and adolescent psychiatric disorders. *Pediatrician 17*, 32–37.

Denson, R., Nanson, J., & McWaters, J. (1975). Hyerkinesis and maternal smoking. *Canadian Psychiatric Association Journal, 20*, 183–187.

Diette, G. B., Markson, L., Skinner, E. A., Nguyen, T. T., Algatt-Bergstrom, P., & Wu, A.W. (2000). Nocturnal asthma in children affects school attendance, school performance, and parents' work attendance. *Archives of Pediatrics And Adolescent Medicine, 154*, 923–928.

Dunn, R, McBurney, A., Ingram, S., & Hunter, C. (1977). Maternal cigarette smoking during pregnancy and the child's subsequent development: II. Neurological and intellectual maturation to the age of 6 1/2 years. *Canadian Journal of Public Health, 68*, 43–50.

Eggleston, P. A., Malveaux, F. J., Butz, A. M., Huss, K., Thompson, L., Kolodner, K., & Rand, C. S. (1998). Medications used by children with asthma living in the inner city. *Pediatrics, 101*, 349–354.

Ehrlich, R. I., DuToit, D., Jordaan, E., Zwarenstein, M., Potter, P., Volmink, J. A., & Weinberg, E. (1996). Risk factors for childhood asthma and wheezing. Importance of maternal and household smoking. *American Journal of Respiratory and Critical Care Medicine, 154*, 300–307.

Eigen, H. (1999). Pulmonary function testing. In S. Murphy and H. W. Kelly (Eds.), *Pediatric asthma* (pp. 133–150). New York: Marcel Dekker, Inc.

Fix, A., Sexton, M., Langenberg, P., Santanello, N., Hyndman, S., & Williams, R. (1997). The association of nocturnal asthma with asthma severity. *Journal of Asthma, 34*, 329–336.

Floreani, A. A., & Rennard, S. I. (1999). The role of cigarette smoke in the pathogenesis of asthma and as a trigger for acute symptoms. *Current Opinion in Pulmonary Medicine, 5*, 38–46.

Forero, R., Bauman, A., Young, L., Booth, M., & Nutbeam, D. (1996). Asthma, health behaviors, social adjustment, and psychosomatic symptoms in adolescence. *Journal of Asthma, 33*, 157–164.

Furukawa, C. T., Shapiro, G. G., Bierman, C. W., Kraemer, M. J., Ward, D. J., & Pierson, W. E. (1984a). A double-blind study comparing the effectiveness of cromolyn sodium and sustained release theophylline in childhood asthma. *Pediatrics, 74*, 453–459.

Furukawa. C. T., Shapiro, G. G., DuHamel, T., Weimer, L., Pierson, W. E., & Bierman, C. W. (1984b). Laming and behavior problems associated with theophylline therapy. *Lancet, 1*, 621.

Gavin, L. A., Wamboldt, M. Z., Sorokin, N., Levy, S. Y., & Wamboldt, F. S. (1999). Treatment adherence and its association with family functioning, adherence, and medical outcome in adolescents with severe, chronic asthma. *Journal of Pediatric Psychology, 24*, 355–365.

Geddes, D. M. (1992). Inhaled corticosteroids: Benefits and risks. *Thorax, 47*, 404–407.

Gislason, T., & Benediktsdottir, B. (1995). Snoring, apneic episodes, and nocturnal hypoxemia among children 6 months to 6 years old. An epidemiologic study of lower limit of prevalence. *Chest, 107*, 963–966.

Goodman, D. C., Stukel T. A., & Chang, C. H. (1998). Trends in pediatric asthma hospitalization rates: Regional and socioeconomic differences. *Pediatrics, 101*, 208–213.

Gortmaker, S. L., Walker, D. K., Jacobs, F. H., & Ruth-Ross, H. (1982). Parental smoking and the risk of childhood asthma. *American Journal of Public Health, 72*, 574–579.

Gozal, D. (1998). Sleep-disordered breathing and school performance in children. *Pediatrics, 102*, 616–620.

Graham, P. J., Rutter, M. L., Yule, W., & Pless, I. B. (1967). Childhood asthma: A psychosomatic disorder? Some epidemiological considerations. *British Journal of Social Medicine, 21*, 78–85.

Gutstadt, L. B., Gillette, J. W., Mrazek, D. A., Fukuhara, J. T., LaBrecque, J. F., & Strunk, R. C. (1989). Determinants of school performance in children with chronic asthma. *American Journal of Diseases of Children, 143*, 471–475.

Joad, J. P. (2000). Smoking and pediatric respiratory health. *Clinics in Chest Medicine, 21*, 37–46.

Kashani, J. H., Konig, P., Shepperd, J. A., Wilfley, D., & Morris, D. A. (1988). Psychopathology and self-concept in asthmatic children. *Journal of Pediatric Psychology, 13*, 509–520.

Kay, G. G. (2000). The effects of antihistamines on congnition and performance. *Journal of Allergy and Clinical Immunology, 105* (6 pt 2), S622–S627.

Kay, G. G. Berman, B., Mockoviak, S. K., Morris, C. E., Reeves, D., Starbuck, V., Sukenik, E., & Harris, A. G. (1997). Initial and steady-state effects of diphenhydramine and loratadine on sedation, cognition, mood, and psychomotor performance. *Archives of Internal Medicine, 157*, 2350–2356.

Kay, J., Mortimer, M. J., & Jaron A. G. (1995). Do both paternal and maternal smoking influence the prevalence of childhood asthma? A study into the prevalence of asthma in children and the effects of parental smoking. *Journal of Asthma, 32*, 47–55.

Koenig, P. (1988). Inhaled corticosteroids—their present and future role in the management of asthma. *Journal of Allergy and Clinical Immunology*, 82, 297–306.

Lanphear, B. P., Aligne, C. A., Auinger, P., Weitzman, M., & Byrd, R. S. (2001). Residential exposures associated with asthma in US children. *Pediatrics, 107*, 505–511.

Lightfoot, J., Wright, S., & Sloper, P. (1999). Supporting pupils in mainstream school with an illness or disability: Young people's views. *Child: Care, Health & Development, 25*, 267–283.

Lindgren, S., Lokshin, B., Stromquist, A., Weinberger, M., Nassif, E., McCubbin, M., & Frasher R. (1992). Does asthma treatment with theophylline limit children's academic performance? *The New England Journal of Medicine, 327*, 926–930.

Lozoff, B., Wolf, A., & Davis, N. S. (1985). Sleep problems seen in pediatric practice. *Pediatrics, 75*, 477–483.

Managing Asthma: A Guide for Schools. (1991). U.S. Department of Health and Human Services, Public Health Service, National Institutes of Health. NIH Publication No. 91–2660.

Mannino, D. M., Moorman, J. E., Kingsley, B., Rose, D., & Repace, J. (2001). Health effects related to environmental tobacco smoke exposure in children in the United States: Data from the third national health and nutrition examination. *Archives of Pediatrics & Adolescent Medicine, 155*, 36–41.

Martinez, F. D. (1995). Viral infections and the development of asthma. *American Journal of Respiratory and Critical Care Medicine, 151*, 1644–1647.

McLean, W. E., Perrin, J. M., Gortmaker, S., & Pierre, C. B. (1992). Psychological adjustment of children with asthma: Effects of illness severity and recent stressful life events. *Journal of Pediatric Psychology, 17*, 159–171.

McNabb, W. L., Wilson-Pessano, S. R., & Jacobs, A. M. (1986). Critical self-management competencies for children with asthma. *Journal of Pediatric Psychology, 11*, 103–117.

McNichol, K. N., Williams, H. E., Allan, J., & McAndrew, I. (1973). Spectrum of asthma in children-III, psychological and social components. *British Medical Journal, 4*, 16–20.

Menon, P. K., Stankus, R. P., Rando, R. J., Salvaggio, J. E., & Lehrer, S. B. (1991). Asthmatic responses to passive cigarette smoke: Persistence of reactivity and effect of medication. *Journal of Allergy and Clinical Immunology, 88*, 861–869.

Mielck, A., Reitmeir, P., & Wjst, M. (1996). Severity of childhood asthma by socioeconomic status. *International Journal of Epidemiology, 25*, 388–393.

Milgrom, H., Bender, B., Ackerson, L., Bowry, P., Smith, B., & Rand, C. (1996). Noncompliance and treatment failure in children with asthma. *Journal of Allergy and Clinical Immunology, 98*, 1051–1057.

Millberger, S., Biederman, J., Faraone, S. V., Chen, L., & Jones, J. (1997). ADHD is associated with early initiation of cigarette smoking in children and adolescents. *Journal of the American Academy of Child and Adolescent Psychiatry, 36*, 37–44.

Mindell, J. A. (1997). Children and sleep. In M. R. Pressman & W. C. Orr (Eds.), *Understanding sleep: The evaluation and treatment of sleep disorders* (pp. 427–440). Washington, DC: American Psychological Association.

Mrazek, D. A. (1992). Psychiatric complications of pediatric asthma. *Annals of Allergy, 69*, 285–293.

Mrazek, D. A., Schuman, W. B., & Klinnert, M. (1998). Early asthma onset: Risk of emotional and behavioral difficulties. *Journal of Child Psychology & Psychiatry & Allied Disciplines, 39*, 247–254.

Naeye, R. L., & Peters, E. C. (1984). Mental development of children whose mothers smoked during pregnancy. *Obstetrics and Gynecology, 64*, 601–607.

Nassau, J. H., & Drotar, D. (1995). Social competence in children with IDDM and asthma: Child, teacher, and parent reports of children's social adjustment, social performance, and social skills. *Journal of Pediatric Psychology, 20*, 187–204.

National Heart, Lung, and Blood Institute. (1997). *Expert panel report 2: Guidelines for the diagnosis and management of asthma*, NIH Publication No. 97–4051.

Nelson, H. S. (1999). The role of allergy. In S. Murphy & H. W. Kelly (Eds.), *Pediatric asthma* (pp. 117–132) New York: Marcel Dekker, Inc.

Nelson, L., & Schwartz, J. (1987). Theophylline-induced age-related CNS stimulation. *Pediatric Asthma, Allergy and Immunology, 1*, 175–183.

Nelson, R. P. Jr., DiNicolo, R., Fernandez-Caldas, E., Seleznick, M. J., Lockey, R. F., & Good, R. A. (1996). Allergen-specific IgE levels and mite allergen exposure in children with acute asthma first seen in an emergency department and in nonasthmatic control subjects. *Journal of Allergy and Clinical Immunology, 98*, 258–263.

Newacheck, P. W., & Halfon, N. (2000). Prevalence, impact, and trends in childhood disability due to asthma. *Archives of Pediatrics & Adolescent Medicine, 154*, 287–293.

Newcomb, R. W., & Akhter, J. (1988). Respiratory failure from asthma. A marker for children with high morbidity and mortality. *American Journal of Diseases of Children, 142*, 1041–1044.

O'Neill, M. (1996). Helping school children with asthma breathe easier: Partnerships in community-based environmental health education. *Environmental Health Perspectives, 104*, 464–466.

Paavonen, E. J., Aronen, E. T., Moilanen, I., Piha, J., Rasanen, E., Tamminen, T., & Almqvist F. (2000). Sleep problems of school-aged children: A complementary view. *Acta Paediatrica, 89*, 223–228.

Pachter, L. M., & Weller, S. C. (1993). Acculturation and compliance with medical therapy. *Journal of Developmental & Behavioral Pediatrics, 14*, 163–168.
Perrin, J. M., MacLean, W. E., & Perrin, E. C. (1989). Parental perceptions of health status and psychologic adjustment of children with asthma. *Pediatrics*, 83, 26–30.
Rachelefsky, G. S., Wo, J., Adelson, J., Mickey, M. R., Spector, S. L., Katz, R. M., Siegel, S. C., & Rohr, A. S. (1986). Behavior abnormalities and poor school performance due to oral theophylline use. *Pediatrics, 78*, 1133–1138.
Rantakallio, P. (1983). A follow-up study up to the age of 14 of children whose mothers smoked during pregnancy. *Acta Paediatrica Scandinavica, 72*, 747–753.
Rappaport, L., Coffman, H., Guare, R., Fenton, T., DeGraw, C., & Twarog, F. (1989). Effects of theophylline on behavior and learning in children with asthma. *American Journal of Diseases of Children, 143*, 369–372.
Richman, N. (1981). A community survey of characteristics of one to two year olds with sleep disruptions. *Journal of the American Academy of Child Psychiatry, 20*, 281–291.
Rietveld, S., & Prins, P. J. M. (1998). Chidren's perceptions of physical symptoms: The example of asthma. In T. H. Ollendick & R. J. Prinz (Eds.), *Advances in clinical child psychology* (pp. 153–182). New York: Plenum.
Roorda, R. J. (1996). Prognostic factors for the outcome of childhood asthma in adolescence. *Thorax, 51*, S7–S12.
Roorda, R. J., Gerritsen, J., Van Aalderen, W. M., Schouten, J. P., Veltman, J. C., Weiss, S. T., & Knol, K. (1993). Risk factors for the persistence of respiratory symptoms in childhood asthma. *American Review of Respiratory Disease, 148*, 1490–1495.
Sadeh, A., Horowitz, I., Wolach-Benodis, L., & Wolach, B. (1998). Sleep and pulmonary function in children with well-controlled, stable asthma. *Sleep, 21*, 379–384.
Sapien, R. E., & Allen, A. (2000). School preparation for the asthmatic student. *Journal of Asthma, 37*, 719–724.
Schaubel, D., Johansen, H., Dutta, M., Desmeules, M., Becker, A., & Mao, Y. (1996). Neonatal characteristics as risk factors for preschool asthma. *Journal of Asthma, 33*, 255–264.
Schlieper, A., Adcock, D., Beaudry, P., Feldman, W., & Leikin, L. (1991). Effect of therapeutic plasma concentrations of theophylline on behavior, cognitive processing, and affect in children with asthma. *Journal of Pediatrics, 118*, 449–455.
Sears, M. R. (1997). Epidemiology of childhood asthma. *Lancet, 350*, 1015–1020.
Sears, M. R., Burrows, B., Herbison, G. P., Holdaway, M. D., & Flannery, E. M. (1993). Atopy in childhood. II. Relationship to airway responsiveness, hay fever, and asthma. *Clinical and Experimental Allergy, 23*, 949–956.
Sears, M. R., Holdaway, M. D., Flannery, E. M., Herbison, G. P., & Silva, P. A. (1996). Parental and neonatal risk factors for atopy, airway hyper-responsiveness, and asthma. *Archives of Diseases of Childhood, 75*, 392–398.
Sexton, M., Fox, N., & Hebel, J. (1990). Prenatal exposure to tobacco: II. Effects on cognitive functioning at age three. *International Journal of Epidemiology, 19*, 72–77.
Shasha, M., Lavigne, J. V., Lyons, J. S., Pongracic, J., & Martini, D. R. (1999). Mental health and service use among children with asthma: Results from a tertiary care center. *Children's Services: Social Policy, Research, and Practice, 2*, 225–243.
Sink, J., Bliwise, D. L., & Dement, W. C. (1986). Self-reported excessive daytime somnolence and impaired respiration in sleep. *Chest, 90*, 177–180.
Simons, F. E. (1996). Learning impairment and allergic rhinitis. *Allergy Asthma Proceedings, Jul-Aug. 17*, 185–189.
Springer, C., Goldenberg, B., Ben Dov, I., & Godfrey, S. (1985). Clinical, physiologic, and psychologic comparison of treatment by cromolyn or theophylline in childhood asthma. *Journal of Allergy and Clinical Immunology, 76*, 64–69.
Stores, G., Ellis, A. J., Wiggs, L., Crawford, C., & Thomson, A. (1998). Sleep and psychological disturbance in nocturnal asthma. *Archives of Disease in Childhood, 78*, 413–419.
Storms, W. W., Bodman, S. F., Nathan, R. A., & Byer, P. (1994). Nocturnal asthma symptoms may be more prevalent than we think. *Journal of Asthma, 31*, 313–318.
Strunk, R. C., Mrazek, D. A., Fuhrmann, G. S., & LaBrecque, J. F. (1985). Physiological and psychological characteristics associated with deaths due to asthma in childhood: A case-controlled study. *Journal of the American Medical Association, 254*, 1193–1198.
Taylor, W. R., & Newacheck, P. W. (1992). Impact of childhood asthma on health. *Pediatrics, 90*, 657–662.
Townsend, M., Feeny, D. H., Guyatt, G. H., Furlong, W. J., Seip, A. E., & Dolovich, J. (1991). Evaluation of the burden of illness for pediatric asthmatic patients and their parents. *Annals of Allergy, 67*, 403–408.
U.S. Department of Health and Human Services. (1998). *Tobacco Use Among US Racial/Ethnic Minority Groups—African Americans, American Indians and Alaska Natives, Asian Americans and Pacific Islanders, and Hispanics: A Report of the Surgeon General.* Atlanta, GA: U.S. Department of Health and Human Services, Centers for Disease Control and Prevention, National Center for Chronic Disease Prevention and Health Promotion, Office on Smoking and Health.

Vila, G., Nollet-Clemencon, C., Vera, M., Robert, J. J., de Blic, J., Jouvent, R., Mouren-Simeoni, M. C., & Scheinmann, P. (1999). Prevalence of DSM-IV disorders in children and adolescents with asthma versus diabetes. *Canadian Journal of Psychiatry, 44*, 562–569.

Vuurman, E. F. P. M., van Veggel, L. M. A., Uiterwijk, M. M. C., Leutner, D., & O'Hanlon, J. F. (1993). Seasonal allergic rhinitis and antihistamines effects on children's learning. *Annals of Allergy, 71*, 121–126.

Wamboldt, F. S., Wamboldt, M. Z., Gavin, L. A., Roesler, T. A., & Brugman, S. M. (1995). Parental criticism and treatment outcome in adolescents hospitalized for severe chronic asthma. *Journal of Psychosomatic Research, 39*, 995–1005.

Warner, J. O. (1978). Mites and asthma in children. *British Journal of Diseases of the Chest, 72*, 79–87.

Weiss, K. B., Gergen, P. J., & Wagener, D. K. (1993). Breathing better or wheezing worse? The changing epidemiology of asthma morbidity and mortality. *Annual Review of Public Health, 14*, 491–513.

Weitzman, M., Gortmaker, S., & Sobol, A. (1992). Maternal smoking and behavior problems in children. *Pediatrics, 90*, 342–349.

Weitzman, M., Gortmaker, S., Sobol, A. & Perrin, J. M. (1992). Recent trends in the prevalence and severity of childhood asthma. *Journal of the American Medical Association, 268*, 2673–7.

11

Diabetes and the School-Age Child and Adolescent: Facilitating Good Glycemic Control and Quality of Life

Deborah Young-Hyman
National Institutes of Health

INTRODUCTION

Approximately 1 of every 550–600 school-age children in the United States has Type 1 diabetes, with an overall prevalence of 1.7 children and adolescents less than 20 years of age per 1,000 individuals affected (Libman, Songer, & LaPorte, 1993; Rewers, LaPorte, King, & Tuomilehto, 1988). In the next 10 years, because of increased rates of obesity in children and adolescents in Western cultures, many more children and adolescents can be expected to be diagnosed with Type 2, weight-related diabetes (American Diabetes Association, 2000; Troiana, Flegal, Kuczmarski, Campbell, & Johnson, 1995). Although Type 1 (insulin requiring) and Type 2 diabetes necessitate somewhat different treatment strategies, both require lifestyle-based interventions, and health is dependent on the achievement of good glycemic (blood glucose) control (Diabetes Control and Complications Trial Research Group, 1993; U.K. Prospective Diabetes Study Group, 1998b). The goal of diabetes care is to ensure physical health and to preserve quality of life for the child and family while facilitating the accomplishment of normal developmental tasks of childhood.

Control of blood sugar requires constant monitoring of glucose status, adjustments to food, exercise, and medications, and communication among individuals involved in the child's care, including the child. The child's immediate and long-term health, the role and tasks each individual assumes in the process of daily diabetes management, and the integration of this care regimen into the child's daily activities are the subject of this chapter.

Children and adolescents spend more time in school than any other venue outside their home. Thus, educators and school administrators are often thrown into a role for which they have not been prepared or educated but assume out of necessity. This chapter will acquaint school personnel with the forms of diabetes, treatment regimens, self-care behaviors that are required for management, and what we know about how children function cognitively and psychosocially when they have this condition. The role of educators and their interactions with the children, families, and health care providers will be discussed, with suggestions about methods of communication and management that lessen each individual's burden and ensure the health and safety of the child. The information is evidence based, but a great deal more research must be conducted to identify strategies for enhancing successful health and education for these children.

DESCRIPTION OF CONDITIONS IN WHICH GLUCOSE METABOLISM IS ALTERED

Diabetes mellitus is a heterogeneous group of disorders in which the unifying mechanism is a disruption of glucose metabolism that results in excessive sugar in the blood. The disruption in glucose metabolism may be caused by an autoimmune-produced failure of the pancreatic β-cells to produce insulin (Type 1 diabetes), or an inability of the β-cells in the pancreas to keep up with need or to produce insulin secondary to prolonged "overuse" (Type 2 diabetes), or an inability to keep up with insulin need because of pregnancy. In some Type 1 cases, injury and illness can damage the pancreas (Expert Committee on the Diagnosis and Classification of Diabetes Mellitus, 2002). Both types of diabetes are heritable. The percentage of children who have parents who have Type 1 diabetes is quite low (Cantor et al., 1995). The percentage of children inheriting the polygenic propensity to develop Type 2 diabetes varies by ethnicity and also is significantly moderated by the cultural, food, and exercise environment in which the child is raised (Barnet, Eff, Leslie, & Pike, 1981; Tuomilehto et al., 2001).

Type 1 diabetes is usually diagnosed during childhood with a peak during adolescence (Cantor et al., 1995). Type 1 diabetes requires exogenous replacement of insulin, coordinated with food intake and exercise patterns. Replacement insulin allows food to be metabolized into energy to feed cells, maintain life, and allow growth during childhood and adolescence. Inadequate insulin and nutrition can lead to stunted growth and delayed development (Skyler, 1998). Complete lack of exogenous insulin will lead to death by starvation, a situation that rarely occurs in Western cultures (Dorman & LaPorte, 1985).

In the past, Type 2 diabetes was considered a disease of old age. This condition is secondary to decreased insulin sensitivity associated with overproduction of insulin and is associated with overweight, old age, or both, and weight-related resistance at the cellular level (Expert Committee on the Diagnosis and Classification of Diabetes Mellitus, 2002). Increasing numbers of children and teens are being diagnosed with Type 2 diabetes associated with genetic predisposition, sedentary lifestyle, and overweight (Bryne et al., 1996; Vaxillaire et al., 1995). One in five school children is overweight or obese in the United States (Third National Health and Nutrition Examination Survey [NHANES III] Centers for Disease Control and Prevention [CDC]), and it is expected that if overweight continues to increase at the rates occurring over the past 20 years, the number of children diagnosed with Type 2 diabetes will increase significantly (Flegal & Trioano, 2000). Minority children—especially African Americans, American Indians, and Latinos—are at particular risk for developing Type 2, weight-related diabetes. Genetic make-up and sociocultural environments contribute to increasing rates of Type 2 diabetes (Strauss & Pollack, 2001). In some cases, children with Type 1 diabetes may also have insulin resistance, sometimes called *type* $1\frac{1}{2}$ (Banerji & Lebovitz, 1989).

Type 2 diabetes is substantially different from Type 1 diabetes in that children with Type 2 diabetes will most likely still be making insulin, but will be sugar toxic as a result of their body's inability to keep up with insulin production and increasing insulin resistance because of adiposity (Bogardus, Lillioja, Mott, Hollenbeck, & Reaven, 1985; Turner, Holman, Matthews, Hockaday, & Peto, 1979). These children will not become extremely sick, as those without endogenous insulin, the hallmark of Type 1 diabetes. As a result, Type 2 diabetes has not traditionally been seen as serious a disease as Type 1. This is a gross underestimation of the morbidity associated with Type 2 diabetes. Children with Type 2 diabetes will suffer the same ill effects of glucose toxicity and complications associated with Type 1 diabetes unless the disease is well controlled (Klein, 1995). We know that glucose toxicity creates the complications and morbidity associated with diabetes (Harris, 1993). This damaging process of metabolic deterioration can and does begin in childhood when children are overweight and have other risk factors of the insulin resistance syndrome (Sinha et al., 2002; Young-Hyman, Schlundt, Herman, DeLuca, & Counts, 2001), a syndrome that predisposes to cardiovascular risk and the development of Type 2 diabetes (Reaven, 1997).

Thus, whether a child has Type 1 or Type 2 diabetes, careful management to restore glucose levels to the normal range is essential for growth and long-term health. In addition, poorly controlled glucose levels can negatively affect growth and development, cognitive processing, and potentially long-term cognitive abilities.

It is important to understand that children with diabetes can and do remain healthy if good glycemic control is achieved and maintained. There is inter- and intraindividual variation in the ease with which this goal is accomplished. However, methods for treating diabetes have progressed to the point that technology and regimens are available to enable patients to keep glucose values within the nondiabetic range. We also know that eliminating or reducing the risk for the complications caused by glucose toxicity is an attainable goal (Diabetes Control and Complications Trial Research Group, 1993). This level of glucose control requires constant vigilance and a high degree of organization and motivation by the child and family to undertake rigorous diabetes self-management tasks. Diabetes cannot, however, be managed by a child and his/her family without assistance. A team approach that involves the child, the family, health care professionals, and all those who come into contact with the child, including educators and coaches, is required.

COURSE OF DIABETES

The onset of Type 1 diabetes is usually marked by a constellation of symptoms, including high blood sugar, excessive thirst and urination, weight loss, and blurred vision (National Diabetes Data Group, 1979). In the past, many children became very ill with ketoacidosis, a condition wherein fat and muscle tissue are broken down to provide energy for the body, caused by the lack of insulin to metabolize the food consumed (Atkinson & Maclaren, 1994). Children who progress into ketoacidosis can lapse into a life-threatening coma. Most children are now being diagnosed before severe ketoacidosis occurs. Type 1 diabetes requires immediate life-saving treatment with insulin replacement and a lifestyle-based management plan. Once insulin replacement is initiated, most children quickly regain their health, weight, and muscle mass (Peterson, Korsgaard, Keckert, & Nielsen, 1978).

Most children with Type 1 diabetes will go through a period called the *honeymoon phase*, which can last up to 1½ years. During this time, their pancreas continues to produce some insulin, and blood sugars are relatively easy to control. Once β-cells do not produce any insulin, blood sugars become more difficult to control, and the honeymoon phase is over (Kukreja & Maclaren, 1999). Awareness of the honeymoon phase is important because children and caregivers can be lulled into an expectation that blood sugar is predictable and easy to control. When the honeymoon phase is over and families have difficulty controlling blood glucose levels using the skills and tactics they have previously learned, they often believe they have failed and that diabetes has taken over their lives. Renewed effort and education by the treatment team usually results in the family achieving a new equilibrium with the disease, but the end of the honeymoon phase often marks a period of frustration and anger over blood sugar levels that are difficult to control (Rubin & Peyrot, 1992).

A second period of difficult-to-control blood sugars, caused by the hormones involved in secondary sexual development, occurs when children enter puberty. Insulin resistance is associated with the increase in these hormones and usually lasts through the adolescent's greatest growth period (Amiel, Sherwin, Simonson, Lauritano, & Tamborlane, 1986; Blethan, Sargeant, Whitlow, & Santiago, 1981; Cutfield, Bergman, Menon, & Sperling, 1990). Thus, hormonally induced insulin resistance and increased insulin needs caused by enlarged muscle mass make determination of total insulin needs a difficult task during this period of adolescence; and good glucose control is a difficult goal to achieve. Once full sexual maturation is reached, insulin resistance subsides and insulin requirements become more stable. However, when combined with a variable adolescent lifestyle and expectations that adolescents will assume greater responsibility for their diabetes management, this period often is associated with a deterioration in blood glucose control (Ingersoll, Orr, Herrold, & Golden, 1986).

The onset of Type 2 diabetes is more insidious and, in children and adolescents, is often diagnosed incidental to a routine well-child visit, a sports physical, or when the child or adolescent becomes ill with another systemic process. Diagnosis of Type 2 diabetes more frequently occurs during adolescence rather than childhood, associated with insulin resistance, overweight status, and genetic predisposition (Bloch, Clemons, & Sperling, 1987).

The management of Type 2 diabetes requires immediate initiation of lifestyle interventions targeting weight loss and increasing activity level (American Diabetes Association, 1998b). Children and adolescents with Type 2 diabetes may be started on oral medications that enhance insulin action or affect the metabolism of sugars or fats (Jones, Arslanian, Peterokova, Jong-Soon, & Tomlinson, 2002). Medications to facilitate weight reduction, however, are still experimental in the child population (McDuffie et al., 2002). Insulin is used in individuals with Type 2 diabetes who are unable to attain glucose values in the normal range using oral medications, a weight-reduction plan, and exercise. Type 2 diabetes can be controlled if the child or adolescent is able to lose enough weight such that their insulin needs are met with endogenous insulin. However, most children or adolescents who develop Type 2 diabetes will have to adopt lifestyle changes that must be maintained and will become the essential tools in their diabetes management throughout life.

TREATMENT REGIMENS AND GOALS

Treatment of diabetes, whether Type 1 or Type 2, consists of balancing the use of medications and lifestyle interventions. The goal of diabetes care in children is not just the attainment of good glycemic control, but preservation of quality of life for the child and family, normal growth and development, and attainment of usual developmental tasks. As a result, each developmental stage brings unique issues to diabetes management.

Insulin replacement is required in Type 1 diabetes. Most treatment regimens for children with Type 1 diabetes consist of a minimum of two injections of insulin a day; a minimum of two, ideally four or more, blood glucose tests a day; and a dietary plan (currently based on carbohydrate counting) that promotes growth and healthy weight gain. Moderate aerobic activity of at least 30 min most days also is recommended (American Diabetes Association, 2002c). A variety of insulins are made that have varying lengths of action, thereby permitting a child to follow his/her usual schedule rather than interrupting their daily routine to achieve medication administration. The peak action of insulin ranges from 20 min to a long-acting insulin that has no peak, but acts continuously for 20–24 hr (Becker, 1998).

Combinations of insulin are prescribed based on a child's age, weight, and activity level. Most school-age children and adolescents must take combination injection of short- and long-acting insulin before they go to school in the morning and often take an injection of short-acting insulin at lunch time. A second or third injection, consisting of both long- and short-acting insulin, usually takes place before dinner. Whenever insulin is given, food intake is essential to avoid a hypoglycemic (low-blood sugar) episode. School-age children and adolescents have to coordinate their insulin administration, snacks and meals, exercise, and glucose tests with their academic schedule. For example, if a child has lunch at 10:30 a.m., which occurs in some schools, that child must alter his/her insulin regimen and nutrition plan to match their academic schedule. The child must leave class early to test blood and administer a shot, or he/she must lose part of their lunch period to accomplish these tasks. Young school-age children with diabetes must also eat snacks twice a day to prevent hypoglycemia.

Medication and meals must be timed with daily activities to promote optimal glucose control (Tamborlane, Gatcomb, Held, & Ahern, 1994). To avoid hypoglycemia, the child with diabetes must also coordinate exercise (usually gym, club, or school sports activities) with insulin peaks and food intake. Extra food often carbohydrates, are needed when exercise immediately precedes lunch or occurs at the end of the school day. An extra blood glucose test and snack frequently are recommended to ensure blood sugar levels will not be too low or too high before participation in sports. Children frequently have different insulin schedules for school and nonschool days. (For a complete description of the medical management of Type 1 diabetes, see the American Diabetes Association, 1998a).

Oral medications, insulin, or both may be prescribed for adolescents and children with Type 2 diabetes; however, whenever possible, oral hypoglycemics will be used (Jones et al., 2002). When oral medication is prescribed, Orlistat, an agent that blocks fat metabolism, may also be prescribed to enhance weight reduction and improve lipid status; but this agent is still considered experimental (McDuffie et al., 2002). When insulin is prescribed for adolescents with Type 2 diabetes, it is because normal blood sugars have not been attained using a regimen of oral hypoglycemics, a nutrition plan that promotes weight reduction, and an exercise plan that enhances metabolic efficiency. Because children and adolescents with Type 2 diabetes usually are making their own insulin, when extra exogenous insulin is necessary, combination insulin, which has both long- and short-acting insulin, is often used; and only two injections a day are prescribed. Adolescents with Type 2 weight related diabetes are always placed on a nutrition plan to promote weight loss, and an exercise plan to enhance metabolic efficiency, whether on insulin or oral hypoglycemic agents.

Blood glucose monitoring is required for all individuals with diabetes and serves the purpose of giving immediate feedback regarding glycemic levels in response to food intake, exercise, and medication effects. Blood glucose testing is accomplished using a lancet-like device that pricks the finger. The drop of blood is then placed on a strip that is inserted into a blood glucose monitoring machine that reads the glucose level in the blood (American Diabetes Association, 1993). Most meters have memories that can be downloaded by computer, or results are transcribed in a log book to track patterns of blood glucose. These blood sugar results are used to make modifications to medications and food intake in relation to activity level. Effective use of blood glucose monitoring is a cornerstone of glycemic control and a primary tool in diabetes management (American Diabetes Association, 1998a,b). At this time, newer devices that constantly measure glucose in the interstitial fluid have not been calibrated or recommended for children (Garg et al., 1999). The hope is that noninvasive blood glucose testing methods will replace the more painful lancet-like device (Tamada et al., 1999). In addition to the routine of two to four daily blood tests, children are expected to test their blood whenever they suspect low or high blood sugar and before, during, and after exercise so that corrective action can be taken when necessary. For Type 1 diabetes, whenever the child or adolescent records a blood sugar ≥250 mg/dl, they must also check blood or urine for ketones. This indicates that blood sugar is high and that insulin action has been inhibited to the extent that alternative sources of fuel, such as fat cells, are breaking down. Medical attention must be received to avoid the possibility of diabetic ketoacidosis (American Diabetes Association, 2002d).

Nutrition and exercise plans are important therapeutic agents for all diabetes care regimens. There is no such thing as a diabetic diet. Rather, the nutrition plans given to children with diabetes provide adequate calories for growth and development, recommend 30% or less fat intake a day with an emphasis on polyunsaturated fats, recommend at least 10–20% protein, and are based on the child's typical eating patterns and food preferences (American Diabetes Association, 2002b). Adolescents with Type 2 diabetes are typically prescribed a reduced calorie and saturated-fats plan to lose weight. The principles of nutrient allocation and food choices are the same for both Type 1 and Type 2 nutrition plans. Efforts are made to allow the children latitude and flexibility (Daly, 1994). It is often a challenge for children with diabetes to obtain and choose appropriate healthy eating choices at school. As a result, the most frequently recommended course of action is for families to pack their child's lunch to ensure the recommended carbohydrate, low fat allocation.

In many cases, it is not necessary to prescribe an exercise plan for children and adolescents with Type 1 diabetes if they are involved in school, extracurricular, or club sports. Most youngsters, especially adolescents with Type 2 diabetes, are sedentary and will need encouragement and structure to initiate activities or increase their level of fitness. Data from the Third National Health and Nutrition Examination Survey by the CDC indicates that the average American child engages in 3–4 hr of sedentary activity a day (independent of school) and less than 1 hr of moderate or high aerobic activity (Anderson, Crespo, Bartlett, Cheskin, & Pratt, 1998). However, overweight and obese children and adolescents (i.e., those prone to Type 2 weight-related diabetes) are less active than their ideal-weight peers (Goran, Reynolds, & Lindquist, 1999; Trost, Kerr, Ward, & Pate, 2001). Type 2 diabetes disproportionately effects lower socioeconomic status and minority children (Dabelea, Pettitt, Jones, & Arslanian, 1999), making resources for regular exercise more difficult to access. Many urban schools are decreasing physical education programs because of declining financial resources, and urban environments are often not safe for children to engage in outdoor activities. To facilitate the fitness level of these overweight children and adolescents, attempts need to be made to engage community resources such as church groups and community centers to support physical activity groups and sports teams (Young-Hyman, 2002). Effective exercise plans must be individualized to the preferences and lifestyle of the child.

INTENSIVE MANAGEMENT

The Diabetes Control and Complications Trial (DCCT) clinical trial showed that achieving near-normal blood sugar significantly reduces or prevents long-term complications associated with Type 1 diabetes (Diabetes Control and Complications Trial Research Group, 1993). Resultantly, intensive management of blood sugar has become the bench mark for diabetes care, unless there are extenuating circumstances, such as the presence of severe complications (e.g., gastroparesis), the patient is elderly, or the patient is a young child who cannot reliably report symptoms of hypoglycemia (American Diabetes Association, 2002a). These findings also have been extended to Type 2 diabetes (Lebovitz, 1994; Nicolleral, 2000; U.K. Prospective Diabetes Study Group, 1998a,b). The goal of intensive diabetes management is to achieve near-normal blood sugar to prevent the complications associated with glucose toxicity (Diabetes Control and Complications Trial Research Group, 1995).

Increasingly, children and adolescents with Type 1 diabetes are using the insulin pump. The pump delivers insulin via a catheter insert below the skin of the stomach or other suitable area, such as the buttocks. The constant subcutaneous insulin infusion pump mimics the delivery action of the pancreas in that it delivers a basal rate of insulin at all times, and bolus insulin is programmed for delivery every time food is consumed. The insulin pump requires matching food intake with an appropriate amount of insulin every time food is ingested, and blood glucose testing up to 8–10 times a day (Farkas-Hirsch, 1998). Intensive management also can be accomplished in Type 1 diabetes using multiple daily injections with associated blood tests every time insulin is administered.

Intensive management in general brings greater responsibility for, and intensity of, diabetes management tasks. Use of an insulin pump allows greater flexibility in lifestyle, including timing of meals and reduction in insulin dosing when exercise is anticipated. Many families are expressing interest in this method of insulin delivery because of their desire for flexibility of lifestyle (Weisberg-Benchell, Antisdel-Lomaglio, & Seshadri, 2003), reduction of nocturnal hypoglycemia, hypoglycemia unawareness (Hirsch, 2001), and overall better control. Continuous glucose monitoring also improves glycemic outcomes in children (Boland et al., 2001), although this methodology has not yet received Federal Drug Administration approval for children and thus is considered experimental. Indications for use of intensive management and pump use in children include better control of fluctuations in blood glucose, reduction of repeated severe hypoglycemia and nocturnal hypoglycemia, and desire for increased lifestyle flexibility (Farkas-Hirsch, 1998).

There are no established guidelines regarding which children will make good candidates for pump use. The following are conditions that must be met to use an insulin pump. The child or a designated caregiver must learn how to program the pump and match insulin dose to food intake using a carbohydrate-to-insulin ratio; learn how to problem-solve pump failures; keep records of insulin dose, food intake, and blood sugar results; establish communication with health care providers; and identify someone who would be willing to assist the child with pump use throughout the day (Farkas-Hirsch & Levandoski, 1988). There are a number of pumps on the market with different features. There is no one right pump for a child, and the companies that make pumps provide literature to help children and families master pump skills and use (Fredrickson & Graff, 2000; Fredrickson, Rubin, & Rubin, 2001).

Pumps are now being used for children starting in infancy, when parents assume complete responsibility for pump use and a child safety lock is activated so that the young child cannot inadvertently administer insulin. Pump therapy can be used in the nursery school-age child if a parent is willing to come to the school to bolus insulin at snack time and meals, or a teacher assumes responsibility for this task. Children are usually started on the pump if they master the criteria listed above, at about age 12 or older, depending on cognitive maturity, ability to take responsibility, and family support (Bode, Tamborlane, & Davidson, 2002). In addition to mastering pump-related tasks, children and adolescents must be willing to be open about having diabetes, because tubing can often be seen outside of clothing, the beeper-sized pump often is worn outside clothing, and bolusing of insulin takes place at all meals and snacks. Children and adolescents also must be willing to maintain a high degree of communication with their parents, health care providers, and school personnel (Boland, Grey, Oesterle, Fredrickson, & Tamborlane, 1999); and, in all cases, a high degree of motivation and demonstration of mastery of pump skills and diabetes-related problem solving must be evidenced (American Diabetes Association, 1998a).

COMPLICATIONS

Complications associated with diabetes are both short and long term. Usually the term *complications* refers to the secondary disease processes that occur as a result of prolonged glucose toxicity. These include micro- and macrovascular disease, autonomic and other neuropathies, kidney failure, and retinopathy (Colwell, 1998; Porte & Schwartz, 1996). These complications usually begin after 15 years disease duration; however they can also be a result of poor glycemic control earlier in the disease course (Krolewski, Laffel, Krolewski, Quinn, & Warram, 1995).

Adolescents with a long duration of Type 1 diabetes, who have been in poor glucose control, may begin to experience some of these complications, especially worsening of kidney function (Warram, Gearin, Laffel, & Krolewski, 1996) and early-stage retinopathy (Flack, Kaar, & Laatikainen, 1996). Because the hormones that produce secondary sexual development also produce reduced insulin sensitivity, there may be worsening or onset of medical complications during adolescence, particularly the early stages of retinopathy and degeneration in kidney function (Amiel et al., 1986).

There is evidence that children with early-onset diabetes (before age 7) and longer duration are at greater risk for learning difficulties (Rovet, Ehrlich, & Hoppe, 1987), decrements in tested intelligence (Holmes & Richman, 1985), and clinically significant and nonsignificant changes in cognitive function (Deary, 1993). In adults, these deficits may be transient or permanent (Draelos et al., 1995). A study by Holmes, O'Brien, and Greer (1995) documented "generally lower achievement scores," although IQ scores fell within the normal range. A prospective evaluation of the verbal skills of newly diagnosed children for up to 8 years found deterioration in the Wechsler Intelligence Scale for Children-Revised Vocabulary subtest (Kovacs, Goldson, & Iyengar, 1992). A recent study by McCarthy, Lindgren, Mengeling, Tsalikian, and Engvall, (2002) documented that decrements in neurocognitive function did not have associated decrements in academic accomplishments. However, prior work by Holmes et al. (1995) did document lower academic achievement scores.

Mild hypoglycemia (a common adverse event) that often occurs at school, also is associated with deterioration of mental efficiency in children with insulin-dependent diabetes (Ryan et al., 1990). Cognitive deficits have been documented in children and adults who have had repeated episodes of mild, moderate, and severe hypoglycemia (Deary et al., 1993; Gold, Deary, MacLeod, Thomson, & Frier, 1995), and associated with hypoglycemic seizures in young children with Type 1 diabetes (Rovet et al., 1987). Holmes, Hayford, Gonzalez, and Weydert (1987) found distinct differences in cognitive processing at varying levels of blood glucose, although whether these glucose-associated changes in cognitive processing are predictive of future academic achievement has not been thoroughly examined. Holmes et al. noted that children with diabetes were reported to have more behavior problems than their same-aged peers. For a review of the association between childhood diabetes and neurocognitive function, the reader is referred to Rovet and Fernandes (1999) and Frier (2001).

Few descriptive or controlled studies that have assessed the cognitive function of children and adolescents with Type 2 diabetes are available. In one study by Perlmuter, Tun, Sizer, McGlinchey & Nathan (1987), children and adults were found to have cognitive deficits similar to those found in elderly persons. Deficits clustered around new learning and memory tasks. Because children with Type 2 diabetes do not typically experience severe hypoglycemia and peripheral neuropathy because they have not had disease duration long enough, it is possible that the deficits are associated with glucose toxicity, microvascular changes, or both.

As diabetes care and our ability to manage blood glucose has improved significantly over the past 15 years, the prevalence of neurocognitive deficits associated with poor glycemic control is not known in the current cohort of children and adolescents with Type 1 or Type 2 diabetes. It can be expected that the overall prevalence of cognitive dysfunction from poor glycemic control and complications such as severe hypoglycemia will decrease. The findings provided by McCarthy and colleagues (2002) support this hypothesis. As the prevalence of Type 2 diabetes increases in the young, more studies will be needed to document whether the types of cognitive dysfunction in these youth are similar to those seen in children and adolescents with Type 1 diabetes and whether they are transient or respond to improvements in glucose control. Both in the case of Type 1 and Type 2 diabetes, glycemic status during school hours needs to be carefully monitored to prevent both hypoglycemia and chronic hyperglycemia.

ADVERSE EVENTS

Complications that children and adolescents are more likely to experience are short term and tied to daily fluctuations in blood glucose. These episodes are more appropriately termed *adverse events*, because they are transient and correctable. Hypoglycemia is the condition in which the level of glucose falls below normal levels (blood glucose value <50 mg/dl; American Diabetes Association, 1998a), affecting the individual's ability to process information, including interruption in short-term memory, decrements in motor control (weakness), and other autonomic and adrenergic symptoms (e.g., trembling, difficulty concentrating, tiredness, headache, sweating, dry mouth, and hunger; American Diabetes Association, 1998a).

Mild hypoglycemia, being "low," is a common adverse event associated with both poor glycemic control and intensive diabetes management (attempting to keep blood sugars in the non-diabetic range). Hypoglycemia occurs because the amount of insulin, food, and activity do not match, creating a sugar deficit in the body (Santiago, Levandoski, & Bubb, 1994). Common causes of hypoglycemia in children are lack of appetite, resulting in insufficient food intake, and excessive activity without compensatory food intake.

Mild hypoglycemia can be effectively and quickly managed by giving the child or adolescent sugar (usually 10–15 g of fast-acting carbohydrate) and checking sugar levels to ensure that blood sugar returns to, and stays, within the normal range (80–120 mg/dl). Repeated treatment with fast-acting carbohydrates and then complex carbohydrates and protein may be necessary to bring blood sugar back to the normal range (Becker & Ryan, 2000; Herbel & Boyle, 2000).

Children with diabetes are taught to recognize the symptoms of hypoglycemia and to treat it immediately. But individuals with diabetes may not recognize when they are low or others may first recognize hypoglycemia (Cox, Gonder-Frederick, Antoun, Cryer, & Clark, 1993; Widom & Simonson, 1990). Although there is an accepted blood glucose level-related definition of hypoglycemia, patients who are in very good glycemic control may not experience these symptoms at a blood glucose of 50 mg/dl. After a long duration of diabetes, it is also common to lose awareness of hypoglycemic symptoms, termed *hypoglycemia unawareness* (Mokan et al., 1994). It is critical that people in the child's environment be trained to recognize the symptoms of hypoglycemia and to keep treatment available. If left untreated, mild hypoglycemia can progress to severe hypoglycemia that involves loss of consciousness and seizures, and can result in death. Severe hypoglycemia is preventable and death from this condition is not common in children (Becker & Ryan, 2000). Adults in the child's environment need to recognize when a child is not aware of his or her symptoms, or is showing signs of altered consciousness, lethargy, weakness, or slurred speech. These symptoms can be indications of severe hypoglycemia and immediate management with sugar administered orally is indicated (if the child is conscious enough to swallow) or an injection of glucagon (by the school nurse or other qualified personnel) or intravenous sugar may be necessary (Herbel & Boyle, 2000). In any case, if hypoglycemia occurs the child should not be left alone, treatment should happen immediately, and a supervising adult should obtain emergency assistance (if the child is unable to participate in treatment).

Fear of hypoglycemia can be an iatrogenic consequence of treatment with exogenous insulin. Administration of exogenous insulin is based on a calculation using the current blood glucose value, the expected food intake, and the expected activity level (Hirsch, Farkas-Hirsch, & Skyler, 1990). If calculations are incorrect or the child or adolescent undereats or exercises more than anticipated, hypoglycemia can be expected. The main symptoms of hypoglycemia involve a sense that one is losing control of body and thought processes, a phenomenon many children and parents seek to avoid (Polonsky, Davis, Jacobson, & Anderson, 1992); so children and families may purposely keep sugar levels high to avoid a low blood sugar reaction (Green, Wysocki, & Reineck, 1990; Marrero, Guare, Vandagriff, & Fineberg, 1997). This avoidance has been coined *fear of hypoglycemia* (Cox, Irvine, Gonder-Frederick, Nowacek, & Butterfield, 1987). Children can be trained to identify the symptoms of mild hypoglycemia and provided with monitoring, coping, and corrective strategies that allay their anxiety and manage hypoglycemic events. A program called Blood Glucose Awareness Training has successfully increased patient awareness of hypoglycemic symptoms and decreased the incidence of severe hypoglycemia (Cox et al., 1989, 2001).

Another common adverse event associated with diabetes is hyperglycemia or high blood sugar. As with hypoglycemia, high blood sugars can be associated with poor diabetes management and control, but they can also be associated with other stressors and illnesses. Although low blood sugar can be associated with stress (e.g., caused by reduced appetite without lowering insulin dose), the experience of stress produces adrenergic hormones that impede the action of insulin (Cox, Taylor, Nowacek, Holley-Wilcox, & Pohl, 1984; Shamoon, Hendler, & Sherwin, 1980). For example, when a child is having a test, entering into a sports competition, or participating in a school play, the hormones produced in response to the stressor may raise blood sugar. This, in turn, can interfere with performance of tasks and mental acuity. The individual can feel sluggish and lack energy (Draelos et al., 1995). Results of various studies are mixed regarding the effects of hyperglycemia on cognitive processing. A controlled study of the effects of laboratory-produced acute hyperglycemia on cognitive function in adolescents with diabetes did not show cognitive decrements (Gschwend, Ryan, Atchison, Arslanian, & Becker, 1995). Neurocognitive tests of mental efficiency were used (i.e., simple and choice visual reaction time and trail making). The association of these tests to the children's performance on academic tasks is not known, thus the clinical significance of these effects cannot be determined. It may be that transient hyperglycemia is not detrimental; but, as with other diabetes-related complications, long-term effects of glucose toxicity may contribute to cognitive changes in children and adolescents.

Stress reactivity is highly idiosyncratic (Surwit, Schneider, & Feinglos, 1992), and the only way to determine a child's response to a particular stressful situation is to test their blood glucose level. Attempts to examine the association between hyperglycemia and stress in a laboratory setting have not been successful (Delamater et al., 1988; Gilbert, Johnson, Silverstein, & Malone, 1988), although it is not ethically possible to create intense prolonged stress in the laboratory that might more accurately mimic life stressors and result in chronic high blood sugar. Children often find it more difficult to recognize high blood sugar than low blood sugar, and misidentify high for low blood sugar, especially in a stressful situation. Stress can also interfere with the performance of diabetes care tasks, including dietary disinhibition (not keeping to the prescribed meal plan; Balfour, White, Schiffrin, Dougherty, & Dufresne, 1993; Hanson & Pichert, 1986). Some stress is unavoidable, but providing the child with coping strategies can head off or mitigate the effects of stress on glycemic control. If a child is known to be stress reactive and blood sugars typically rise in response to stressful situations, in conjunction with extra monitoring of blood glucose, extra insulin and fluids may be administered. Other steps to recognize and cope with the stressful situation should be taken (Rubin, 2001).

Another adverse event, ketoacidosis, can occur or recur with Type 1 diabetes if children are in poor glycemic control, become ill with an infection, or omit taking insulin. Ketoacidosis does not usually have a rapid onset, with the exceptions of such conditions as the onset of a virulent infection. Children and adolescents may come to school not knowing they are ketotic. Children may come to school with high blood sugars associated with a cold or flu, or may have omitted an insulin dose. If treated appropriately, these children do not necessarily progress into ketoacidosis; however, there are times when, despite parents' and health care providers' best efforts, children do require hospitalization for this condition.

In almost all cases, ketoacidosis can be prevented or short circuited if families are taught sick-day management (unless the child is intentionally omitting insulin), have easy access to health care providers, and feel free to communicate when sugars start to become out of control. The key in preventing high blood sugar from becoming ketoacidosis is immediate treatment, usually by administering extra fast-acting insulin, noncaloric fluids, and frequently monitoring blood sugar (Butkiewicz, Leibson, O'Brien, Palumbo, & Rizza, 1995). In the past, children were usually admitted to the hospital to treat ketoacidosis. If possible, the preference now is to try to manage the acidosis at home in conjunction with a physician or diabetes nurse educator. If the family is unable to bring the child's glucose down to a reasonable level and eliminate ketones from the urine, the family is asked to bring the child to the nearest emergency room where intravenous fluids and insulin are administered. Attempts are usually made to manage this condition on an outpatient basis unless the child disorients, the fluid and electrolyte balance is disrupted, and the child is obviously very weakened. In these cases, the children are so sick that they are severely dehydrated, have lost a significant amount of weight, and are close to or comatose (American Diabetes Association, 2002d). In these cases the child is always admitted to the hospital.

Children and adolescents are prone to both high and low blood sugars because of the daily fluctuations in their routines, the weather, their activity level, their hormones, their mood, usual childhood illnesses, their growth, and their general health status. These normal life circumstances underscore the need to expect children and adolescents with diabetes to achieve the same set of academic and social standards as those without diabetes. Glucose management strategies can incorporate contingencies for all of the adverse events (and complications) that can (and do) occur. Families can be educated about strategies to manage fluctuations in blood glucose on a daily basis. In most cases, including minor childhood illnesses, children and adolescents need not miss school to manage diabetes effectively. Children and adolescents who miss a great deal of school because of diabetes-related illness may be evidencing poor adjustment to their illness or significant psychosocial stressors that may or may not be disease related. Although Vetiska, Glaab, Perlman, and Daneman (2000) found children with diabetes missed more school days than peers or siblings, children with diabetes who missed more school also had siblings who missed school more frequently. The authors suggest that family functioning may be more predictive of school attendance than the presence or absence of the diagnosis of diabetes.

ADHERENCE TO SELF-CARE REGIMENS

Studies assessing the effect of adherence to diabetes self-care regimens on glycemic control in children have produced varying results. In her review of the adherence literature, Johnson (1992) attends to the issue of how adherence is defined and whether we use the correct indices to measure adherence. Adherence and compliance have been used interchangeably to indicate children's or adolescents' accomplishment of diabetes care tasks. Johnson correctly points out that the word adherence suggests following a prescribed treatment regimen, although compliance suggests the accomplishment of tasks necessary for medical management. This latter definition more appropriately fits the paradigm of diabetes care because treatment is individualized and diabetes care tasks can vary significantly from child to child and change repeatedly over time.

The reasons studies on adherence may have failed to predict glycemic control are varied and may be because of issues of study design or lack of appreciation for the complexity of the determinants of diabetes care behavior. Other factors that may have contributed to the failure to predict glycemic control are the failure to assess who was actually assigned the diabetes care task in the family (Anderson, Auslander, Jung, Miller, & Santiago, 1990) and whether expectations for task mastery were assessed in the child, family caregivers, and health care providers (Hanson et al., 1988; Wysocki et al., 1992). In addition, families often do not understand the diabetes care regimen they have been prescribed (Page, Verstraete, Robb, & Etzwiler, 1981), or the clinician has not been clear about the prescription. Surveys of physician versus parental expectations about children's ability to master and be responsible for self-care behavior show clear discrepancies between parental and professional opinions (Marteau, Johnson, Baum, & Bloch, 1987; Wysocki, Meinhold, Cox, & Clarke, 1990).

It is quite possible that differences of opinion between parents and caregivers about whether the child is capable or responsible for diabetes management tasks translates into confusion for the child and the family about who should be doing what. Anderson and colleagues' (1990) work on responsibility taking in diabetes care suggests that it is the gap between what is expected and carried out that predicts glycemic control. This same negative association was found between glycemia and conflict, with diabetes-related family conflict predicting poorer glycemic control (Rubin, Young-Hyman, & Peyrot, 1989). As a responsible caregiver in the child's environment, it is important to be aware of the child's current diabetes care regimen, to know which tasks the child is capable of and expected to carry out independently, and to aid the child in complying with the prescribed tasks that occur at school. Clear guidelines for the role of school personnel need to be established, whether it be in a supervisory or instrumental capacity.

A number of factors have been identified that seem to be robustly associated with either better adherence or better control, although the relationships between adherence and control appear to be multi-dimensional (Pendley et al., 2002; Wysocki et al., 1999). Parental involvement predicts greater compliance with diabetes self-care tasks; however, greater compliance is not always associated with better glycemic control in both children and adolescents (Anderson, Ho, Brackett, Finkelstein, & Laffel, 1997; Hansen, Henggler, & Burghen, 1987; Jacobson et al., 1990; Johnson, 1995; La Greca et al., 1995; Wysocki et al., 1999). Conversely, in a prospective controlled trial of skills training with newly diagnosed children with Type 1 diabetes, Delamater et al. (1990) demonstrated that those who received skills training achieved better glycemic control, but did not show differences in adherence to self-care behaviors. In a more recent trial of coping skills training combined with parental involvement, Grey, Davidson, Boland, and Tamborlane (2001) showed improvement in hemoglobin values (a 3-month measure of glycemic control). Thus, it seems that skills training, parental support, and problem solving are necessary elements of maintaining management behavior (adherence to self-care tasks) and improving glycemic outcomes. Grey et al. (2001) suggested that diabetes-related quality of life may be a mediating variable that affects level of glucose control despite high levels of adherence to care tasks.

There is also evidence to suggest that although adherence to regimen tasks may be good during the period after diagnosis, regardless of the age of the child, deterioration in adherence can be expected (Jacobson et al., 1990). A number of investigators have documented that length of illness is a more robust predictor of deterioration in diabetes control than the age of the child (Johnson, Freund, Silverstein, Hansen, & Malone, 1990; La Greca, 1990). It may be that the longer the child or adolescent has diabetes, the poorer their diabetes-related quality of life (Ingersoll & Marrero, 1991), which may mediate adherence to care tasks.

Some attention has been devoted to the role of peers in adherence with diabetes self-management tasks. Pendley and colleagues (2002) assessed perception of parental and peer support and *peer-associated* care behavior on glycemic control delivered through an intervention. Actual participation by peers in the intervention was associated with improved glycemic control, but perceptions of either peer or parental support was not associated with glycemic control. Anderson, Wolf, Burkhart, Cornell, and Bacon (1989) assessed the effects of a diabetic peer-based intervention to enhance compliance with, and use of, self-monitoring of blood glucose. After 18 months, the adolescents who were exposed to a peer-based, problem-solving group not only made more use of the information gathered by testing blood glucose, but their overall control was better than those assigned to a control group. Many teens do not wish their parents to be actively involved in care tasks, and sometimes parents completely withdraw from self-management tasks by the time their child is about 15 years of age (Ingersoll et al., 1986). These results suggest that, at least during adolescence, use of peer-based participation in care to enhance adherence to diabetes care tasks may improve control when parental participation is waning. Anecdotally, teens with diabetes report less annoyance and more acceptance of peer based reminders regarding self-care behaviors (Young-Hyman, 2003).

DEVELOPMENTAL ISSUES AND PSYCHOSOCIAL FACTORS CONTRIBUTING TO DISEASE ADJUSTMENT

Diabetes, whether it be Type 1 or Type 2, is a self-managed disease. The day-to-day management is performed by the patient or parent or both, with guidance from the health care team. As a result, the developmental level and maturity of the child, and parent and health care provider expectations play a large role in determining which tasks the child will perform and which tasks will be performed by adults (Wysocki et al., 1992). Many children can test blood sugar by 7–8 years of age and self-administer insulin with supervision by 10 years of age (Kohler, Hurwitz, & Milar, 1982). Children who have had diabetes since early childhood may be able to test blood, self-inject, and calculate insulin dosage with supervision by the age of 12 years (Hanson & Onikul-Ross, 1990). High school-aged adolescents can accurately perform diabetes care tasks without supervision.

There is no hard and fast rule for when these tasks should be mastered, but independence in diabetes self-care tasks with parental oversight is encouraged. The need for parental involvement in a monitoring capacity is necessary because the behaviors not carried out are predictive of poor glycemic control (Anderson et al., 1990). It therefore becomes important for educators and health care providers at schools to be aware of who is actually assigned a diabetes care task rather than assuming lack of compliance when a child is in poor control. Absence of a clear directive about who is to assume responsibility for care tasks, especially during late childhood and adolescence when responsibility for care is shifting, may become evident. School personnel may be in the position of helping families clarify assumption of responsibility for self-management tasks or for aiding the monitoring process.

Parents often expect their teens to be independent in diabetes care; however, poor adherence to diabetes care self-management tasks during the adolescent years is common (Anderson et al., 1997; Ingersoll et al., 1986). Transition of care from parents to children, especially during adolescence, is one of the most difficult issues to navigate in diabetes care. A constellation of factors result in deterioration of glucose control during adolescence. Parents may become less strict in their rule-oriented approach to diabetes care and provide less supervision to their teens (Hanson, DeGuire, Schinkel, & Henggeler, 1992). Children eat more independent of their family and spend less time in family activities, thereby making parental supervision less feasible.

A number of investigators have assessed psychological correlates of adjustment to diabetes. Psychological sequela associated with the onset of diabetes has been prospectively studied in children. Studies by Jacobson and colleagues (1986), Kovacs, Feinberg, Paulauskas, Finkelstein, and Pollack (1985), Kovacs, Finkelstein et al. (1985), and Kovacs, Brent, Steinberg, Paulauskas, and Reid (1986) suggest that, contrary to often-held beliefs, most children with newly diagnosed diabetes do not suffer lower self-esteem, have increased behavioral symptoms or lessened social functioning, and responded to the diagnosis with relatively mild feelings of sadness and some social withdrawal. Some children do respond with more severe psychological distress, but most were shown to be within normal limits on measures of adjustment

9 months after diagnosis. When children are distressed, early intervention is effective in reducing psychological distress (Laron et al., 1979).

A higher than experted prevalence (2.4 times more likely in girls aged 12–19) of eating disorders has been documented in children with diabetes. (Nissim et al., 2002; Rodin, 2000; Marcus & Wing, 1990). However, the development of, onset, and cause and effect relationships between having diabetes and an eating disorder have not been established. Prospective studies that assess eating behavior at diagnosis (either Type 1 or Type 2) will help to elucidate the unique roles of diagnosis, treatment and emotional distress.

In a prospective study of the social relationships of children and adolescents with diabetes compared with a cohort without diabetes, Jacobson et al. (1996) suggested similar patterns of social relationships, including dating and friendship patterns, intimacy, and feelings of loneliness. Patterns were found to be similar between the two groups, suggesting that having diabetes need not hamper relationship aspects of social adjustment. Similarly, Tebbi, Bromberg, Sills, Cukierman, and Piedmonte (1990) found employment issues not to be a problem among young adults with diabetes.

Diabetes-related quality of life has also received attention in recent years as clinicians recognize that an individual's diabetes care should not be at the expense of usual developmental and life tasks, or cause such disruption of family functioning or allocation of resources to cause emotional distress. In a review of the literature concerning psychosocial problems and interventions in diabetes, Rubin and Peyrot (1992) note that psychosocial problems in individuals with diabetes are not especially different than other individuals, but that individuals who do show evidence of psychological distress are at increased risk for reduced physical and emotional well-being. Anderson and colleagues (2000) found that 8- to 16-year-old children who had Type 1 diabetes of relatively recent duration (1 month–5 years) reported similar overall quality of life to normative data on the Pediatric Quality of Life Inventory (Varni, Seid, & Rode, 1999). Parents who saw their child as having more normative health had healthier children, as indicated by a long-term measure of glycemic control. Although the study was conducted with an adult cohort with Type 2 diabetes, fewer symptoms and better glycemic control were associated with a greater sense of well-being (Van der Does et al., 1996). The review of the literature by Rubin and Peyrot and the results of the DCCT (Diabetes Control and Complications Trial Research Group, 1996) suggest that good health maintenance is associated with good quality of life in individuals with diabetes, regardless of age and the intensity of treatment.

Other factors contributing to adjustment to the illness are the social competence of the child and family members. Social competence and family support have been found to be mediators of the link between stress and metabolic control in adolescents with insulin-dependent diabetes mellitus (Hanson et al., 1987). Coping style has been suggested as a mechanism by which the effects of stress on blood sugar is mediated (Aiken, Wallander, Bell, & Cole, 1992; Delamater, Bubb, Kurtz, White, & Santiago, 1987; Peyrot & McMurray, 1992). Likewise, when children are trained in self-care/self-management strategies, their health outcomes improve (Delamater et al., 1990). Conversely, children with Type 1 diabetes whose mothers found it difficult to cope with the daily demands of caring for the disease were in poorer metabolic control and had poorer adherence to care regimens than did mothers who had good coping skills (Kovacs, Finkelstein et al., 1985; Kovacs et al., 1990).

EFFECT OF SPORTS AND EXERCISE ON GLYCEMIC CONTROL

Participation in school-related and club-based sports not only helps control blood sugar levels, but also improves insulin sensitivity, therefore lowering the requirement for antihyperglycemic agents, such as insulin or metformin (Landt, Campaigne, James, & Sperling, 1985). Seasonal variation in sports activities plays a major role in the management of blood sugar. At issue are not only the need to change insulin, medication, and nutrition regimens in response to changes in physical activity, but also the need to assist the child in being comfortable with the diabetes care regimen in the sports venue (Kistler, 1995). Educating education and coaching personnel to understand their role in the child's care and appreciate that exercise is not harmful but, in fact, a therapeutic agent, will aid in the child's integration into sports without undue fear of ostracism and by reducing fear of hypoglycemia.

Although it is recommended that children and adolescents remain involved in routine sports activities throughout the year, few can and do maintain the same level of physical activity throughout all seasons (Sallis et al., 1992). As a result, insulin in particular and nutrition plans must be altered to meet caloric needs and prevent hypoglycemia each time a different physical activity is initiated. Children with Type 1 diabetes whose gym class occurs before lunch or at the end of the school day will need to test blood and have a snack before participation to prevent hypoglycemia. An adolescent, for example, who plays indoor soccer in the winter, but baseball in the spring, may need to increase insulin and decrease caloric intake as that transition is made. However, if the child is intensely invested in baseball and is stress reactive (i.e., a Type A personality), insulin might need to increase before games to compensate for the child's stress response (Stabler et al., 1987). Insulin, medication requirements, and food intake will need to be altered whenever a change in physical activity takes place.

Also at issue is the time and commitment to competitive sports because participation requires children and adolescents with Type 1 diabetes to increase the monitoring of their glycemic status before, during, and after vigorous exercise; to formulate a nutrition plan that takes into account intense activity level and duration and the need for extra calories; and to involve coaches and parents in monitoring for signs of hypoglycemia (Wasserman & Zinman, 1994). Club and school sports team practice often occurs during evening snack and meal-time hours, making routine administration of insulin and meal timing difficult. This may result in the need for the child to bring diabetes care supplies to the sports venue; test blood sugar before, during, and after the game; and possibly eat at intervals during the sports activity. Elite athletes with diabetes are known to test blood sugar frequently during exercise, adopt very specific nutrition regimens that contain multiple meals, and have fast-acting sugar with them at all times to compensate for their caloric expenditure (Golberg, 1995; Sherman, Ferrara, & Schneider, 1995).

The goal of intensive monitoring of glycemic status during sports is to prevent both mild and severe hypoglycemia in individuals with Type 1 diabetes. Prolonged rigorous activity not only has an influence on current glycemic status, but also can result in hypoglycemia hours after exercise has ended (Zinman, 1984). Children and adolescents often become self-conscious about the possibility of having a hypoglycemic reaction because of loss of control over their behavior and performance. Children may not recognize their symptoms because of the context or excitement attached to the activity, or because of competing sensations. Their blood sugar may also drop so quickly that others recognize their symptoms before they do, making them feel embarrassed (Cox et al., 1993). With proper monitoring, there is no reason a child cannot successfully compete in their chosen sports activity.

As cited previously, children with Type 2 diabetes are often more sedentary than their ideal-weight peers (Goran et al., 1999; Trost et al., 2001) and often do not have the opportunity to participate in sports at home (Young-Hyman, 2002). The sports and exercise activities that take place at school can become a therapeutic tool to reduce insulin resistance for children and adolescents with Type 2 diabetes. Providing a supervised exercise venue for children and adolescents through the gym and collegiate sports programs at school can potentially fill this important gap in diabetes care. Not only is it important to provide the venue, but supervision to ensure active participation is equally important. Children and adolescents who have Type 2 diabetes are not prone to hypoglycemia unless they are prescribed insulin. Education staff who supervise sports activities need to know what type of diabetes a child has, and what medication is prescribed to monitor glycemic status adequately. For a complete review of guidelines regarding diabetes and exercise, see Ruderman and Devlin (1995).

THE DIABETES CARE TEAM

Many children with Type 1 diabetes are seen by a pediatric endocrinologist or an endocrinologist who specializes in diabetes, whereas children and adults with Type 2 diabetes are often managed by their primary care physician (Glasgow et al., 2001). Aided by the success of the DCCT (Diabetes Control and Complications Trial Research Group, 1995), a multidisciplinary care team is now strongly advocated and recommended in the clinical practice guidelines of the American Diabetes Association (2003). This team is patient and family centered, and includes the physician, a nurse educator, a dietician, and a mental health care provider. Other family members, educators, coaches, or interested family friends who are willing to learn diabetes management skills and to aid the child in their care are strongly encouraged. Medical specialists—such as a neurologist, ophthamologist, or a podiatrist—are called on once a year for check-ups. Routine evaluations that range from the eye doctor—to a psychosocial evaluation for quality of life and other adjustment issues, to check-ups to monitor medical needs and glucose control—are spelled out in the clinical practice guidelines offered by the American Diabetes Association (2003).

Diabetes care is constantly changing, and a case can be made that the general practitioner does not have sufficient time to remain current with the changes in medications, technologies, and philosophies in treatment and nutrition necessary to provide children with state-of-the-art care to achieve the tightest blood glucose control possible. However, despite the clear indications for specialty care for children with Type 1 and Type 2 diabetes, the current shortage of pediatric endocrinologists suggests that most care will continue to take place in the primary care venue for the foreseeable future (Marrero, Moore, Fineberg, Langefeld, & Clark, 1991). The primary care or pediatric physician need not have these team members under one roof; yet, input from, and communication between, these individuals is dictated by the clinical practice guidelines. Members of the team need agreed-on mechanisms of accountability and feedback among themselves. A monitoring mechanism is also important so that if appointments are missed or adverse events or other illnesses occur, information is available for timely management decisions and to maintain educational progress.

As with other chronic disease management paradigms, care must be ongoing, integrated into the child's lifestyle, and the medical regimen constantly changing to meet developmental and psychosocial needs of the child or adolescent (Clark et al., 2001). Feedback to health care providers from all individuals involved in the child's care is necessary to maintain health (Glasgow et al., 2001).

ROLE OF SCHOOL PERSONNEL

Federal law requires that resources be available at school to accommodate the needs of children with disabilities. Diabetes is considered a disability according to Section 504 of the Rehabilitation Act of 1973 and the Individuals with Disabilities Act of 1991. These laws require an individual evaluation and plan for every child with diabetes so that these children can participate fully in all school activities in their usual school environment, with as little disruption to the school and child's academic routine. These laws also apply to day-care facilities but not to privately funded educational institutions. Regardless of whether these recommendations are mandated by law or voluntarily adopted by the school, the necessity for the family and school personnel to arrive at a school management plan is essential for the child's safety, well-being, and academic achievement.

The first step in formulating a diabetes health care plan is education of school personnel and sharing of the child's usual diabetes care routine and treatment regimen. Although few systematic studies of school personnel have been conducted, most school personnel know little about the disease and its management (Lindsey, Jarrett, & Hillman, 1987). In addition, parents lack confidence in school personnel's ability to manage diabetes (Siminerio, Clougherty, Gillilard, Icelly, 2000; Siminerio & Koerbel, 1999). It is the responsibility of the parents and health care providers to provide access to diabetes education to all those who come in contact with the child in the course of the school day. Personnel include teachers, administrators, coaches, health suite and transportation personnel, cafeteria, and day-care employees.

Essential elements of a diabetes care plan and education of the school personnel include glucose monitoring (timing and indications for extra tests) and record keeping, insulin dosing and administration (if prescribed during school hours), recognition and treatment of symptoms of hypo- and hyperglycemia (and administration of glucagon for treatment of severe hypoglycemia), testing for ketones, and the handling of meals and snacks (including content, amount, and timing). It is the parents' responsibility to provide all supplies necessary for diabetes care based on the child's current regimen; the contact numbers for health care providers; emergency numbers for parents or guardians; and specific information about the child's insulin regimen, testing schedule, and nutrition plan. Also, it is essential that there are designated individuals at school who are trained to aid and monitor the child in their diabetes care tasks, including testing, insulin administration, and eating routines; ensure immediate availability of supplies (fast-acting carbohydrates) to treat hypoglycemia; and ascertain permission for the child to complete diabetes care tasks without disruption to his/her schedule or to seek medical help if he/she feels it necessary. Because routine medical visits are necessary, the child should not be penalized in any way for school time missed for this purpose. Advance planning can prevent falling behind in assignments or medical visits that coincide with tests. To date, there have been no controlled studies that have evaluated optimal diabetes management plans at school versus usual management.

Multiple factors affect the ease with which diabetes management is conducted at school. As with all diabetes care, the age and self-management skills of the child determine how much independence can be anticipated; however, governmental agencies, such as the local school board, often have policies in place that provide oversight about who can aid the child in diabetes care, where blood testing can be conducted, how blood products must be handled, and whether a child can carry out most diabetes care tasks in the classroom. Often, the school principal will establish the guidelines. As mentioned early in this chapter, the key to successful diabetes control is communication among caregivers, and it may be necessary to involve health care providers and school administrators to implement the most efficacious educational plan.

Optimally, diabetes care tasks are best accomplished in the classroom if the child is comfortable being open about his/her care behaviors. The goal is to lose a minimum of education time and academic achievement and objectives. Time out of the classroom to test blood or eat a snack can significantly disrupt the learning process either because the child simply does not have access to information taught in his/her absence, or because focus is lost when interrupting attention to the educational task. Care tasks, such as eating snacks and testing, are less disruptive in the younger grades when snacks are routinely eaten, school time is shorter, and tasks can bracket the school day. Providing education to classmates and teachers so that care behavior is not seen as unusual or frightening often facilitates smooth classroom functioning and may facilitate permission for care to take place in the classroom. Show-and-tell demonstrations of diabetes care tasks are suggested for younger children.

When a midday injection is prescribed, regardless of age, children or adolescents must either go to the health suite or the principal's office to have their injection supervised by school personnel because of legal liability and safety. As more and more children practice intensive management, health suite personnel become integral resources in the child's diabetes care. Health suite personnel may assume the monitoring function for school hours and communicate test results to parents so that adjustments to insulin dosage and meal plans can be made. It is not unusual for a school nurse to take a pump training class to aid pupils who use insulin infusion pumps and to conduct support groups for their students with diabetes.

Management becomes more complex as children enter middle and high school, where classrooms and teachers change and more teachers must be educated about the symptoms of hypoglycemia and its treatment. Children and adolescents become more reticent to take time away from class or lunch to test blood. Self-consciousness about the social stigma of having diabetes and being different may increase even when a child has seemingly adjusted well in the past (Jacobson et al., 1997). Adolescents may reject the need to have help or be monitored by an adult at school when carrying out their usual diabetes care tasks or when they experience hypoglycemia. It may be effective to establish a form of communication whereby the adolescent reports blood glucose results or treatment of hypoglycemic symptoms. In middle and upperstood sports participation is more systematically incorporated into the curriculum, and coaching personnel need to be educated about the symptoms of hypoglycemia and its treatment.

DISPELLING MYTHS ABOUT DIABETES

Children and adolescents who have diabetes need not be restricted from any usual childhood activities. This includes eating all types of foods in moderation; (American Diabetes Association Nutrition Guidelines) and, with planning, participating in strenuous sports (e.g., gymnastics, lacrosse, football, rugby, or ice hockey; American Diabetes Association Exercise Guidelines), or undertaking career paths that are demanding and require advanced education. There are a few professions, such as the armed forces, that are closed to individuals who have been previously diagnosed with diabetes; however, as long as adequate monitoring of blood sugar takes place and corrective steps are taken to keep sugar in a safe range, expectations should not be altered regarding the achievement of usual childhood activities and developmental tasks (Delamater, 2002).

To counter feelings of separateness, techniques that enhance cognitive and athletic abilities, aspirations, and self-esteem that incorporate diabetes are encouraged (Delamater, 2002). Stressful situations are not to be avoided, but managed in the same fashion that other situations that affect blood sugar are problem solved (Rubin & Peyrot, 1992). Medical advances have enabled adults with well-controlled diabetes to be functional sexually and reproductively, thus removing a barrier that has caused some individuals to be hesitant to enter into intimate relationships (Jacobson, Hauser, Cole et al., 1997; Jacobson, Hauser, Willett et al., 1997; Pasui & McFarland, 1997). Adolescents with diabetes are counseled that, if they control their blood sugars and remain in good health, it is a reasonable expectation that they can be biological parents.

Control of blood glucose and healthy living provides the corner stones on which a child or adolescent with diabetes can maintain his/her health. Although diabetes brings the burden of constant care (Polansky, 1999) and the requirements of care are constantly changing, it is the expectation of good health and quality of life that provides motivation to undertake rigorous blood glucose management.

It seems clear that children and adolescents with diabetes can be expected to thrive medically, academically, and socially if given the skills, guidance, and structure within which to carry out their complex and ever-changing self-care regimen. This is not to imply that this is an easy or burden-free task, rather that with education, resources, and attention, supports can be put in place to enable the child or adolescent to be successful in diabetes management. Not all children and families will be equally successful in this endeavor, but health care providers and school personnel can provide a safety net to monitor and support the child.

REFERENCES

Aiken, J., Wallander, J., Bell, D., & Cole J. (1992). Daily stress variability, learned resourcefulness, regimen adherence, and metabolic control in Type 1 diabetes mellitus: Evaluation of a path model. *Journal of Consulting and Clinical Psychology, 60*, 113–118.

American Diabetes Association. (1993). ADA consensus statement: Self-monitoring of blood glucose. *Diabetes Care, 16*(Suppl. 2), 60–65.

American Diabetes Association. (1998a). *Medical management of Type 1 diabetes* (3rd ed.). Alexandria, VA:

American Diabetes Association. (1998b). *Medical management of Type 2 diabetes* (4th ed.). Alexandria, VA: Philip Raskin, Ed.

American Diabetes Association. (2000). Type 2 diabetes in children and adolescents (consensus statement). *Diabetes Care, 23*, 381–389.

American Diabetes Association. (2002a). Implications of the Diabetes Control and Complications Trial. *Diabetes Care, 25*(Suppl. 1), S25–S27.

American Diabetes Association. (2002b). Evidence-based nutrition principles and recommendations for the treatment and prevention of diabetes and related complications. *Diabetes Care, 25*(Suppl. 1), S50–S59.

American Diabetes Association. (2002c). Diabetes mellitus and exercise. *Diabetes Care, 25*(Suppl. 1), S64–S68.

American Diabetes Association. (2002d). Hyperglycemic crises in patients with diabetes mellitus. *Diabetes Care, 25*(Suppl. 1), S100–S108.

American Diabetes Association. (2003). Clinical Practice Recommendations: Standards of medical care for patients with diabetes mellitus. *Diabetes Care, 26*(Suppl. 1), 533–550.

Amiel, S., Sherwin, R., Simonson, D., Lauritano, A., & Tamborlane, W. (1986). Impaired insulin action in puberty: A contributing factor to poor glycemic control in adolescents with diabetes. *New England Journal of Medicine, 315*, 215–219.

Anderson, B., Auslander, W., Jung, K., Miller, P., & Santiago J. (1990). Assessing family sharing of diabetes responsibility. *Journal of Pediatric Psychology, 15*, 477–492.

Anderson, B. J., Ho, J., Brackett, J., Finkelstein, D., & Laffel, L. (1997). Parental involvement in diabetes management tasks: Relationships to blood glucose monitoring, adherence and metabolic control in young adolescents with insulin-dependent diabetes mellitus. *Journal of Pediatrics, 130*, 257–265.

Anderson B., Mansfield A., Fisher A., Goebel Fabbri A., & Laffel L. (2000). Measuring quality of life (QOL) in youth with short duration Type 1 diabetes. Diabetes, *49*(Suppl), A318.

Anderson, B. J., Wolf, F. M., Burkhart, M. T., Cornell, R. G., & Bacon, G. E. (1989). Effects of peer-group intervention on metabolic control of adolescents with IDDM. Randomized outpatient study. *Diabetes Care 12*(3), 179–183.

Anderson, R. E., Crespo, C. J., Bartlett, S. J., Cheskin, L. J., & Pratt M. (1998). Relationship of physical activity and television watching with body weight and level of fatness among children: Results from the Third National Health and Nutrition Examination Survey. *Journal of the American Medical Association, 279*, 938–942.

Atkinson, M. A., & Maclaren, N. K. (1994). The pathogenesis of insulin dependent diabetes. *New England Journal of Medicine, 331*, 1428–1436.

Balfour, L., White, D., Schiffrin, A., Dougherty, G., & Dufresne, J. (1993). Dietary disinhibition, perceived stress and glucose control in young Type 1 diabetic women. *Health Psychology, 12*, 33–38.

Banerji, M., & Lebovitz H. (1989). Insulin sensitive and insulin resistant variants in IDDM. *Diabetes, 38*, 784–792.

Barnet, A. H., Eff, C., Leslie, R. D. G., & Pike, D. A. (1981). Diabetes in identical twins. *Diabetologia, 20*, 87–93.

Becker, D. (1998). Individualized insulin therapy in children and adolescents with Type 1 diabetes. *Acta Paediatrica, 425*(Suppl.), 20–24.

Becker, D. J., & Ryan, C. M. (2000). Hypoglycemia: A complication of diabetes therapy in children. *Trends in Endocrinology and Metabolism, 11*(5), 198–202.

Blethen, S., Sargeant, D., Whitlow, M., & Santiago, J. (1981). Effect of pubertal stage and recent blood glucose control on plasma somatomedin C in children with insulin-dependent diabetes mellitus. *Diabetes, 30*, 868–872.

Bloch, C. A., Clemons, P. S., & Sperling, M. A. (1987). Puberty decreases insulin sensitivity. *Journal of Pediatrics, 110*, 481–487.

Bode, B. W., Tamborlane, W. V., & Davidson, P. C. (2002). Insulin pump therapy in the 21st century. Strategies for successful use in adults, adolescents, and children with diabetes. *Postgraduate Medicine, 111*(5), 69–77.

Bogardus, C., Lillioja, S., Mott, D. M., Hollenbeck, C., & Reaven, G. (1985). Relationship between degree of obesity and in vivo insulin action in man. *American Journal of Physiology, 248*, E286–E291.

Boland, E., Monsard, T., Delucia, M., Brandt, C. A., Ferenando, S., & Tamborlane, W. V. (2001). Limitations of conventional methods of self-monitoring of blood glucose: Lessons learned from 3 days of continuous glucose sensing in pediatric patients with Type 1 diabetes. *Diabetes Care, 24*(11), 1858–1862.

Boland, E. A., Grey, M., Oesterle, A., Fredrickson, L., & Tamborlane, W. V. (1999). Continuous subcutaneous insulin infusion: A new way to lower risk of severe hypoglycemia, improve metabolic control, and enhance coping in adolescents with Type 1 diabetes. *Diabetes Care, 22*, 1779–1784.

Bryne, M. M., Sturis, J., Menzel, S., Yamagata, K., Fajans, S. S., Dronsfield, M. J., Bain, S. C., Hattersley, A. T., Velho, G., Froguel, P., Bell, G. I., & Polonsky, K. S. (1996). Altered insulin secretory response to glucose in diabetic and nondiabetic subjects with mutations in the diabetes susceptibility gene MODY3 on chromosome 12. *Diabetes, 45*, 1503–1510.

Butkiewicz, E. K., Leibson, C., O'Brien, P. C., Palumbo, P. J., & Rizza, R. A. (1995). Insulin therapy for diabetic ketoacidosis. *Diabetes Care, 18*, 1187–1190.

Cantor, A. B., Krischer, J. P., Cuthbertson, D. D., Schwartz, D. A., Quattrin, T., & McClaren, N. K. (1995). Age and family relationship accentuate the risk of IDDM in relatives of patients with insulin dependent diabetes. *Journal of Clinical Endocrinology and Metabolism, 80*, 3739–3743.

Clark, C. M., Jr., Fradkin, J. E., Hiss, R. G., Lorenz, R. A., Vinicor, F., & Warren-Boulton, E. (2001). The National Diabetes Education Program, changing the way diabetes is treated: Comprehensive diabetes care. *Diabetes Care, 24*(4), 617–618.

Colwell, J. A. (1998). Prevention of diabetes complications. *Clinical Cornerstone, 1*(3), 58–71.

Cox, D. J., Gonder-Frederick, L., Antoun, B., Cryer, P. E., & Clark, W. (1993). Perceived symptoms in the recognition of hypoglycemia. *Diabetes Care, 16*, 519–527.

Cox, D. J., Gonder-Frederick, L. A., Lee, J. H., Julian, D. M., Carter, W. L., & Clarke, W. L. (1989). Effects and correlates of glucose awareness training among patients with IDDM. *Diabetes Care, 12*, 313–318.

Cox, D. J., Gonder-Frederick, L. A., Polonsky, W. H., Schlundt, D. G., Kovatchev, B. P., & Clark, W. L. (2001). Blood glucose awareness training (BGAT-2): Long-term benefits. *Diabetes Care, 24*, 637–642.

Cox, D., Irvine, A., Gonder-Frederick, L., Nowacek, G., & Butterfield, J. (1987). Fear of hypoglycemia: Quantification, validation and utilization. *Diabetes Care, 10*, 617–621.

Cox, D., Taylor, A., Nowacek, G., Holley-Wilcox, P., & Pohl, S. (1984). The relationship between psychological stress and insulin-dependent diabetic blood glucose control: Preliminary investigations. *Health Psychology, 3*, 63–75.

Cutfield, W., Bergman, R., Menon, R., & Sperling, M. (1990). The modified minimal model: Application to measurement of insulin sensitivity in children. *Journal of Clinical Endocrinology and Metabolism, 70*, 1644–1650.

Dabelea, D., Pettitt, D. J., Jones, K. L., & Arslanian, S. A. (1999). Type 2 diabetes mellitus in minority children and adolescents. An emerging problem. *Endocrinology and Metabolism Clinics of North America, 28*(4), 709–729.

Daly, A. (1994). Nutrition management. In H. E. Lebovitz (Ed.), *Therapy for diabetes mellitus and related disorders* (2nd ed., pp. 95–101). Alexandria, VA: American Diabetes Association.

Diabetes Control and Complications Trial Research Group. (1993). The effect of intensive treatment of diabetes on the development and progression of long-term complications in IDDM. *New England Journal of Medicine, 16*, 1517–1520.

Diabetes Control and Complications Trial Research Group. (1995). Implementation of the treatment protocols in the Diabetes Control and Complications Trial. *Diabetes Care, 18*, 361– 376.

Diabetes Control and Complications Trial Research Group. (1996). Influence of intensive diabetes treatment on quality-of-life outcomes in the Diabetes Control and Complications Trial. *Diabetes Care, 19*, 195–203.

Deary, I., Crawford, J., Hepburn, D. A., Langan, S. J., Blackmore, L. M., & Frier B. M. (1993). Severe hypoglycemia and intelligence in adults patients with insulin-treated diabetes. *Diabetes, 42*, 341–344.

Deary, I. J. (1993). Effects of hypoglycemia on cognitive function. In B. Frier & M. Fisher (Eds.), *Hypoglycemia and diabetes: Clinical and physiological aspects* (pp. 80–92). London. Edwin Arnold.

Delamater, A. (2002). Working with children who have Type 1 diabetes. In R. R. Rubin & B. J. Anderson (Eds.), *Practical psychology for diabetes clinicians* (2nd ed., pp. 127–137). Alexandria, VA: American Diabetes Association.

Delamater, A., Bubb, J., Kurtz, S., Kuntz, J., Smith, J., White, N., & Santiago, J. (1988). Physiologic responses to acute psychological stress in adolescents with Type 1 diabetes mellitus. *Journal of Pediatric Psychology, 13*, 69–86.

Delamater, A., Bubb, J., Kurtz, S., White, N., & Santiago, J. (1987). Stress and coping in relation to metabolic control of adolescents with Type 1 diabetes. *Journal of Developmental and Behavioral Pediatrics, 8*, 136–140.

Delamater, A. M., Bubb, J., Davis, S. G., Smith, J. A., Schmidt, L., White, N. H., & Santiago, J. V. (1990). Randomized prospective study of self-management training with newly diagnosed diabetic children. *Diabetes Care, 13*, 492–498.

Dorman, J., & LaPorte, R. (1985). Mortality in insulin dependent diabetes. In National Diabetes Data Group, *Diabetes in America* (pp. 1–9). U.S. Department of Health and Human Services, PAS, NIH. Bethesda, MD.

Draelos, M. T., Jacobson, A. M., Weinger, K., Widom, B., Ryan, C. M., Finkelstein, D. M., & Simonson, D. C. (1995). Cognitive function in patients with insulin dependent diabetes mellitus during hyperglycemia and hypoglycemia. *American Journal of Medicine, 98*, 135–144.

Expert Committee on the Diagnosis and Classification of Diabetes Mellitus (2002). Report of the Expert Committee on the Diagnosis and Classification of Diabetes Mellitus. *Diabetes Care, 25*(Suppl. 1), S5–S20.

Farkas-Hirsch, R. (Ed.). (1998). Insulin infusion pump therapy. In*Intensive diabetes management* (2nd ed., pp. 99–120). Alexandria, VA: American Diabetes Association.

Farkas-Hirsch, R., & Levandoski, L. (1988). Implementation of continuous subcutaneous insulin infusion therapy: An overview. *Diabetes Educator, 14*, 401–406.

Flack, A., Kaar, M. L., & Laatikainen, L. (1996). A prospective, longitudinal study examining the development of retinopathy in children with diabetes. *Acta Paediatrica, 85*(3), 313–319.

Flegal, K. M., & Trioano, R .P. (2000). Changes in the distribution of body mass index of adults and children in the US population. *International Journal of Obesity, 24*, 807–818.

Fredrickson, L., & Graff, M. R. (2000). *Pumper in the school: Insulin pump guide for school nurses, school personnel and parents.* Sylmar, CA: MiniMed.

Fredrickson, L., Rubin, R. R., & Rubin, S. (2001). *Optimal pumping: A guide to good health with diabetes.* Sylmar, CA: MiniMed.

Frier, B. M. (2001). Hypoglycemia and cognitive function in diabetes. *International Journal of Clinical Practice 123*(Suppl.), 30–37.

Garg, S. K., Potts, R. O., Ackerman, N. R., Fermi, S. J., Tamada, J. A., & Chase, H. P. (1999). Correlation of fingerstick blood glucose measurements with GlucoWatch biographer glucose results in young subjects with Type 1 diabetes. *Diabetes Care, 22*(10), 1708–1714.

Gilbert, B., Johnson, S., Silverstein, J., & Malone, J. (1989). Psychological and physiological responses to acute laboratory stressors in insulin-dependent diabetes mellitus adolescents and non-diabetic controls. *Journal of Pediatric Psychology, 14*, 577–591.

Glasgow, R. E., Hiss, R. G., Anderson, R. M., Friedman, N. M., Hayward, R. A. Marrero, D. G., Taylor, C. B., & Vinicor F. (2001). Report of the health care delivery work group: Behavioral research related to the establishment of a chronic disease model for diabetes care. *Diabetes Care, 24*(1), 124–130.

Golberg, N. J. (1995). The elite diabetic athlete. In N. Ruderman & J. T. Devlin (Eds.), *The health professional's guide to diabetes and exercise* (pp. 271–272). Alexandria, VA: American Diabetes Association.

Gold, A. E., Deary, I. J., MacLeod, K. M., Thomson, K. G., & Frier, B. M. (1995). Cognitive function during insulin induced hypoglycemia in humans: Short term cerebral adaptation does not occur. *Psychological Pharmacology, 119*, 325–333.

Goran, M. I., Reynolds, K. D., & Lindquist, C. H. (1999). Role of physical activity in the prevention of obesity in childhood. *International Journal of Obesity, 23*(suppl.), S18–S33.

Green, L., Wysocki, T., & Reineck, B. (1990). Fear of hypoglycemia in children and adolescents with diabetes. *Journal of Pediatric Psychology, 15*, 633–641.

Grey, M., Davidson, M., Boland, E. A., & Tamborlane, W. V. (2001). Clinical and psychosocial factors associated with achievement of treatment goals in adolescents with diabetes mellitus. *Journal of Adolescent Health, 28*(5), 377–385.

Gschwend, S., Ryan, C., Atchison, J., Arslanian, S., & Becker, D. (1995). Effects of acute hyperglycemia on mental efficiency and counterregulatory hormones in adolescents with insulin-dependent diabetes mellitus. *Journal of Pediatrics, 126*, 178–184.

Hanson, C. L., DeGuire, M. J., Schinkel, A. M., & Henggeler, S. W. (1992). Comparing social learning and family systems correlates of adaptation in youths with IDDM. *Journal of Pediatric Psychology, 17*, 555–572.

Hanson, C. L., & Onikul-Ross, S. R. (1990). Developmental issues in the lives of youths with insulin-dependent diabetes mellitus. In S. B. Morgan & T. M. Okwumabua (Eds.), *Child and adolescent disorders: Developmental and health psychology perspectives* (pp. 201–240). Hillsdale, NJ: Erlbaum.

Hanson, S., Henggler, S. W., & Burghen, G. A. (1987). Social competence and parental support as mediators of the link between stress and metabolic control in adolescents with insulin-dependent diabetes mellitus. *Journal of Consulting and Clinical Psychology, 55*, 529–533.

Hanson, S., Henggler, S., Harris, M., Mitchell, K., Carle, D., & Burghen, G. (1988). Associations between family members' perceptions of the health care system and the health of youths with insulin-dependent diabetes mellitus. *Journal of Pediatric Psychology, 13*, 543–554.

Hanson, S., & Pichert J. (1986). Perceived stress and diabetes control in adolescents. *Health Psychology, 5*, 439–452.

Harris, M. I. (1993). Undiagnosed NIDDM: Clinical and public health issues. *Diabetes Care, 16*, 642–652.

Herbel, G., & Boyle, P. J. (2000). Hypoglycemia: Pathophysiology and treatment. *Endocrinology and Metabolism Clinics of North America, 29*(4), 725–743.

Hirsch, I. B. (2001). Hypoglycemia and hypoglycemia awareness syndrome. *Diabetes Technology and Therapeutics 2*(Supppl. 1), S81–S87.

Hirsch, I. B., Farkas-Hirsch, R., & Skyler, J. S. (1990). Intensive insulin therapy for treatment of Type 1 diabetes. *Diabetes Care, 13*, 1265–1283.

Holmes, C. S., Hayford, J. T., Gonzalez, J. L., & Weydert, J. A. (1987). Intellectual deficits associated with early onset of insulin-dependent diabetes mellitus in children. *Diabetes Care, 10*, 510–515.

Holmes, C. S., O'Brien, B., & Greer, T. (1995). Cognitive functioning and academic achievement in children with insulin-dependent diabetes mellitus (IDDM). *School Psychology Quarterly, 10*, 329–345.

Holmes, C. S., & Richman, L. C. (1985). Cognitive profiles of children with insulin-dependent diabetes. *Journal of Developmental and Behavioral Pediatrics, 6*, 323–326.

Ingersoll, G., Orr, D., Herrold, A., & Golden M. (1986). Cognitive maturity and self-management among adolescents with insulin-requiring diabetes mellitus. *Journal of Pediatrics, 108*, 620–623.

Ingersoll, G. M., & Marrero, D. G. (1991). A modified quality-of-life measure for youths: Psychometric properties. *Diabetes Educator, 17*(2), 114–118.

Jacobson, A., Hauser, S., Lavori, P., Wolfsdorf, J., Herskowitz, R., Milley, J., Bliss, R., Gelfand, E., Wertlieb, D., & Stein, J. (1990). Adherence among children and adolescents with insulin dependent diabetes mellitus over a four year longitudinal follow-up: The influence of patient coping and adjustment. *Journal of Pediatric Psychology, 15*, 511–526.

Jacobson, A. M., Hauser, S.T., Cole, C., Willet, J. B., Wolfsdorf, J. I., Dvorak, R., & Wolpert, H. (1996). Social relationships among young adults with insulin-dependent diabetes mellitus; ten year follow-up of an onset cohort. *Diabetic Medicine, 14*, 73–79.

Jacobson, A. M., Hauser, S. T., Cole, C., Willett, J. B., Wolfsdorf, J. I., Dvorak, R., Wolpert, H., Herman, L., & de Groot, M. (1997). Social relationships among young adults with insulin-dependent diabetes mellitus: Ten-year follow-up of an onset cohort. *Diabetic Medicine, 14*(1), 73–79.

Jacobson, A. M., Hauser, S. T., Wertlieb, D., Wolfsdorf, J. I., Orleans, J., & Vieyra, M. (1986). Psychological adjustment of children with recently diagnosed diabetes mellitus. *Diabetes Care, 9*, 323–329.

Jacobson, A. M., Hauser, S. T., Willett, J. B., Wolfsdorf, J. I., Dvorak, R., Herman, L., & de Groot, M. (1997). Psychological adjustment to IDDM: 10-year follow-up of an onset cohort of child and adolescent patients. *Diabetes Care, 20*(5), 811–818.

Johnson, S. B. (1992). Methodological issues in diabetes research: Measuring adherence. *Diabetes Care, 11*, 1658–1667.

Johnson, S. B. (1995). Managing insulin dependent diabetes mellitus: A developmental perspective. In J. Wallander & L. Siegal (Eds.), *Advances in pediatric psychology. II. Perspectives in adolescent health* (pp. 265–288). New York: Guilford.

Johnson, S. B., Freund, A., Silverstein, J., Hansen, C., & Malone, J. (1990). Adherence-health status relationships in childhood diabetes. *Health Psychology, 9*, 606–631.

Jones, K. L., Arslanian, S., Peterokova, V. A., Jong-Soon, P., & Tomlinson, M. J. (2002). Effect of metformin in pediatric patients with Type 2 diabetes. *Diabetes Care, 25*, 89–94.

Kistler, J. (1995). Exercise in special patient groups: Children and adolescents in the health professionals guide to diabetes and exercise. N. Ruderman and J. Devlin (Eds), American Diabetes Association, Alexandria VA, 217–222.

Klein, R. (1995). Hyperglycemia and microvascular and macrovascular disease in diabetes. *Diabetes Care, 18*, 258–268.

Kohler, E., Hurwitz, L. S., & Milan, D. (1982). A developmentally staged curriculum for teaching self-care to the child with insulin-dependent diabetes mellitus. *Diabetes Care, 5*, 300–304.

Kovacs, M., Brent, D., Steinberg, T. F., Paulauskas, S., & Reid, J. (1986). Children's self-reports of psychologic adjustment and coping strategies during first year of insulin-dependent diabetes mellitus. *Diabetes Care, 9*, 472–479.

Kovacs, M., Feinberg, T. L., Paulauskas, S., Finkelstein, R., & Pollack, M. (1985). Initial coping responses and psychosocial characteristics of children with insulin-dependent diabetes mellitus. *Journal of Pediatrics, 106*, 827–834.

Kovacs, M., Finkelstein, M., Feinberg, R., Crouse-Novak, M., Paulauskas, S., & Pollack, M. (1985). Initial psychological responses of parents to the diagnosis of insulin-dependent diabetes mellitus in their children. *Diabetes Care, 8*, 568–575.

Kovacs, M., Goldson, D., & Iyengar, S. (1992). Intellectual development and academic performance of children with insulin-dependent diabetes mellitus: A longitudinal study. *Developmental Psychology, 28*, 676–684.

Kovacs, M., Iyengar, S., Goldston, D., Obrosky, D., Steward, J., & Matrsh, J. (1990). Psychological functioning among mothers of children with insulin-dependent diabetes mellitus: A longitudinal study. *Journal of Consulting and Clinical Psychology, 58*, 189–195.

Krolewski, A. S., Laffel, L. M., Krolewski, M., Quinn, M., & Warram, J. H. (1995). Glycosylated hemoglobin and the risk of microalbuminuria in patients with insulin-dependent diabetes mellitus. *New England Journal of Medicine, 332*(19), 1251–1255.

Kukreja, A., & Maclaren, N. K. (1999). Autoimmunity and diabetes. *Journal of Clinical Endocrinology and Metabolism, 84*(12), 4371–4378.

La Greca, A. M. (1990). Issues in adherence with pediatric regimens. *Journal of Pediatric Psychology, 15*, 423–436.

La Greca, A. M., Auslander, W. F., Greco, P., Spetter, D., Fisher, E. B., Jr., & Santiago, J. V. (1995). Get by with a little help from my family and friends: Adolescents' support for diabetes care. *Journal of Pediatric Psychology, 20*(4), 449–476.

Landt, K. W., Campaigne, B. N., James, F. W., & Sperling, M. A. (1985). Effects of exercise training on insulin sensitivity in adolescents with Type 1 diabetes. *Diabetes Care, 8*, 461–465.

Laron, Z., Galatzer, A., Amir, S., Gil, R., Karp, M., & Mimouni, M. (1979). A multidisciplinary, comprehensive, ambulatory treatment scheme for diabetes mellitus in children. *Diabetes Care, 2*, 342–348.

Lebovitz, H. E. (1994). The DCCT and its implications for NIDDM. *Clinical Diabetes, 12*, 3.

Libman, I., Songer, T., & LaPorte, R. (1993). How many people in the U.S. have IDDM? *Diabetes Care, 16*, 841–842.

Lindsey, R., Jarrett, L., & Hillman K. (1987). Elementary schoolteachers' understanding of diabetes. *Diabetes Educator, 13*, 312–314.

Marcus, M. D., & Wing, R. R. (1990). Eating disorders and diabetes. In C. S. Holmes (Ed.), *Neuropsychological and behavioral aspects of diabetes* (pp. 102–121). New York: Springer-Verlag.

Marrero, D. G., Guare, J. C., Vandagriff, J. L., & Fineberg, N. S. (1997). Fear of hypoglycemia in the parents of children and adolescents with diabetes: Maladaptive or healthy response?. *Diabetes Educator, 23*(3), 281–286.

Marrero, D. G., Moore, P. S., Fineberg, N. S., Langefeld, C. D., & Clark, C. M., Jr. (1991). The treatment of patients with insulin-requiring diabetes mellitus by primary care physicians. *Journal of Community Health, 16*(5), 259–267.

Marteau, T., Johnson, M., Baum, J., & Bloch, S. (1987). Goals of treatment: A comparison of doctors and parents of children with diabetes. *Journal of Behavioral Medicine, 10*, 33–48.

McCarthy, A. M., Lindgren, S., Mengeling, M. A., Tsalikian, E., & Engvall, J. C. (2002). Effects of diabetes on learning in children. *Pediatrics, 109*, E9.

McDuffie, J. R., Calis, K. A., Uwaufi, G. I., Sebring, N. G., Fallon, E. M., Hubbard, V. S., & Yanovski, J. A. (2002). Three-month tolerability of Orlistat in adolescents with obesity-related comorbid conditions, *Obesity Research, 10*(7), 642–650.

Mokan, M., Mitrakou, A., Veneman, T., Ryan, C., Korytkowski, M., Cryer, P., & Gerich, J. (1994). Hypoglycemia unawareness in insulin dependent diabetes mellitus. *Diabetes Care, 17*, 1397–1403.

National Diabetes Data Group. (1979). Classification and diagnosis of diabetes mellitus and other categories of glucose intolerance. *Diabetes, 28*, 1039–1057.

Nicolleral, J. A. (2000). Implications of the United Kingdom Prospective Diabetes Study (UKPDS) results on patient management. *Diabetes Educator, 26*(Suppl.), 8–10.

Nissim, R., Rodin, G., Daneman D., Rydall, A., Colton, P., Maharaj, S., & Jones, J. (2002). Eating disturbances in adolescent girls with Type 1 diabetes mellitus. *Harepuah 141*(10): 902–907.

Page, P., Verstraete, D., Robb, J., & Etzweiler, D. (1981). Patient recall of self-care recommendations in diabetes. *Diabetes Care, 4*, 96–98.

Pasui, K., & McFarland, K. F. (1997). Management of diabetes in pregnancy. *American Family Physician, 55*(8), 2731–2738, 2742–2744.

Pendley, J. S., Kasmen, L. J., Miller, D. L., Donze, J., Swenson, C., & Reeves, G. (2002). Peer and family support in children and adolescents with Type 1 diabetes. *Journal of Pediatric Psychology, 27*, 429–438.

Perlmuter, L. C., Tun, P., Sizer, N. McGlinchey, R. E., Nathan, D. M. (1987). Age and diabetes related changes in verbal fluency. *Experimental Aging Research, 13*, 9–14.

Peterson, H. D., Korsgaard, B., Keckert, T., & Nielsen, E. (1978). Growth, body weight and insulin requirement in diabetic children. *Acta Pediatrica Scandinavia, 67*, 453–457.

Peyrot, M., & McMurray, J. (1992). Stress buffering and glycemic control: The role of coping styles. *Diabetes Care, 15*, 842–846.

Polansky, W. H. (1999). *Diabetes burnout: What to do when you just can't take it anymore.* Alexandria VA: American Diabetes Association.

Polonsky, W. H., Davis, C. L., Jacobson, A. M., & Anderson, B. J. (1992). Correlates of hypoglycemic fear in Type I and Type II diabetes mellitus. *Health Psychology, 11*(3), 199–202.

Porte, D. Jr., Schwartz, M. W. (1996). Diabetes complications: Why is glucose potentially toxic? *Science, 272(5262)*, 699–700.

Reaven, G. M. (1997). Syndrome X. Past, present and future. In B. Draznin & R. Rizza (Eds.), *Clinical research in diabetes and obesity, Volume II: Diabetes and obesity* (pp. 357–382). Totowa, NJ: Humana Press.

Rewers, M., LaPorte, R., King, H., & Tuomilehto, J. (1988). Trends in the prevalence and incidence of diabetes: Insulin dependent diabetes mellitus in childhood. *World Health Statistical Quarterly, 41*, 179–189.

Rodin, G. (2000). Eating disorders more common among girls with diabetes. British Medical Journal, 320, 1563–1566.

Rovet, J. F., Ehrlich, R. M., & Hoppe, M. (1987). Intellectual deficits associated with early onset of insulin-dependent diabetes mellitus in children. *Diabetes Care, 10*, 10–15.

Rovet, J., & Fernandes C. (1999). Insulin-dependent diabetes mellitus. In R. Brown (Ed.), *Cognitive aspects of chronic illness in children* (pp. 142–171). New York: Guilford.

Rubin, R. R. (2001). Facilitating self-care in people with diabetes. *Diabetes Spectrum, 14*, 55–57.

Rubin, R. R., & Peyrot, M. (1992). Psychosocial problems and interventions in diabetes. *Diabetes Care, 15*, 1640–1657.

Rubin, R., Young-Hyman, D., & Peyrot M. (1989). Parent-child responsibility and conflict in diabetes care. *Diabetes, 38*(1), 7A.

Ruderman, N., & Devlin, J. T. (Eds.). (1995). *The health professional's guide to diabetes and exercise.* Alexandria, VA: American Diabetes Association.

Ryan, C. M., Atchison, J., Puczynski, S., Puczynski, M., Arslanian, S., & Becker, D. (1990). Mild hypoglycemia associated with deterioration of mental efficiency in children with insulin-dependent diabetes mellitus. *Journal of Pediatrics, 117*, 32–37.

Sallis, J. F., Simons Morton, B. G., Stone, E. J., Corbin, C. B., Epstein, L. H., Faucette, N. et al. (1992). Determinants of physical activity and interventions in youth medicine and science in sports and medicine. *Medical Science Sports Exercise, 24*, 5248–5257.

Santiago, J. V., Levandoski, L. A., & Bubb, J. (1994). Hypoglycemia in patients with Type 1 diabetes. In H. E. Lebovitz, (Ed.), *Therapy for diabetes mellitus and related disorders* (2nd ed., pp. 170–177). Alexandria, VA: American Diabetes Association.

Shamoon, H., Hendler, R., & Sherwin, R. (1980). Altered responsiveness to cortisol, epinephrine, and glucagon in insulin-infused juvenile-onset diabetes: A mechanism for diabetic instability. *Diabetes, 29*, 284–291.

Sherman, W. M., Ferrara, C., & Schneider, B. (1995). Nutritional strategies to optimize athletic performance. In N. Ruderman & J. T. Devlin (Eds.), *The health professional's guide to diabetes and exercise* (pp. 91–98). Alexandria, VA: American Diabetes Association.

Siminerio, L., Clougherty M., Gillilard A., & Icelly, K. (2000). Evaluating children with diabetes and their parents preparedness and involvement in diabetes care for the school. Diabetes *49*(Suppl): A719.

Siminerio, L., & Koerbel, G. (1999). Evaluating the effectiveness of a diabetes educations program for school personnel diabetes. *48*(Suppl. 1), A713.

Sinha, R., Fisch, G., Teague, B., Tamborlane, W. V., Banyas, B., Allen, K. Savoye, M., Rieger, V., Taksali, S., Barbetta, G., Sherwin, R. S., & Caprio, S. (2002). Prevalence of impaired glucose tolerance among children and adolescents with marked obesity. *New England Journal of Medicine, 346*(11), 802–810.

Skyler, J. S. (Ed.). (1998). *Medical management of Type 1 diabetes* (3rd ed.) Alexandria, VA: American Diabetes Association.

Stabler, B., Surwit, R. S., Lane, J. D., Morris, M. A. et al. (1987). Type A behavior pattern and blood glucose control in diabetic children. *Psychosomatic Medicine, 49*, 313–316.

Strauss, R. S., & Pollack, H. A. (2001). Epidemic increase in childhood overweight 1986–1998. *Journal of the American Medical Association, 286*, 2845–2848.

Surwit, R., Schneider, M., & Feinglos, M. (1992). Stress and diabetes mellitus. *Diabetes Care, 15*, 1413–1422.

Tamada, J. A., Garg, S., Jovanovic, L., Pitzer, K. R., Fermi, S., & Potts, R. O. (1999). Noninvasive glucose monitoring: Comprehensive clinical results. Cygnus Research Team. *Journal of the American Medical Association, 282,* 1839–1844.

Tamborlane, W. V., Gatcomb, P. M., Held, N. A., & Ahern, J. (1994). Type 1 diabetes in children. In H. E. Lebovitz (Ed.), *Therapy for diabetes mellitus and related disorders* (pp. 46–60). Alexandria VA: American Diabetes Association.

Tebbi, C., Bromberg, C., Sills, I., Cukierman, J., & Piedmonte, M. (1990). Vocational adjustment and general well-being of young adults with IDDM. *Diabetes Care, 13*, 98–103.

Troiana, R. P., Flegal, K. M., Kuczmarski, R. J., Campbell, S. M., & Johnson, C. L. (1995). Overweight prevalence and trends for children and adolescents. *Archives Pediatric and Adolescent Medicine, 149*, 1085–1091.

Trost, S. G., Kerr, L. M., Ward, D. S., & Pate, R. R. (2001). Physical activity and determinants of physical activity in obese and non-obese children. *International Journal of Obesity Related Metabolic Disorders, 25*, 822–829.

Tuomilehto, J., Lindstrom, J., Eriksson, J. G., Valle, T. T., Hamalainen, H., Illanne-Parikka, P., Keinanen-Kiukaaniemi, S., Laakso, M., Louheranta, A., Rastas, M., Salminen, V., & Uusitupa, M. (2001). Prevention of Type 2 diabetes mellitus by changes in lifestyle among subjects with impaired glucose tolerance. *New England Journal of Medicine, 344*, 1343–1350.

Turner, R. C., Holman, R. R., Matthews, D., Hockaday, T. D. R., & Peto, J. (1979). Insulin deficiency and insulin resistance interaction in diabetes: estimation of their relative contribution by feedback analysis from basal plasma insulin and glucose concentrations. *Metabolism, 28*, 1086–1096.

U.K. Prospective Diabetes Study Group. (1998a). Effect of intensive blood-glucose control with metformin on complications in over-weight patients with Type 2 diabetes (UKPDS 34). *Lancet, 317*, 703–713.

U.K. Prospective Diabetes Study Group. (1998b). Intensive blood-glucose control with sulphonylureas or insulin compared with conventional treatment and risk of complications in patients with Type 2 diabetes (UKPDS 33). *Lancet, 352*(9131), 837–853.

Van der Does, F. E. E., De Neeling, J. N. D., Snoek, F. J., Kostense, P. J., Grootenhuis, P. A., Bouter, L. M., & Heine, R. J. (1996). Symptoms and well-being in relation to glycemic control in Type 2 diabetes. *Diabetes Care, 19*, 204–210.

Varni, W., Seid, M., & Rode, C. (1999). The Peds QL: Measurement model for the Pediatric Quality of Life Inventory. *Medical Care, 37*, 126–139.

Vaxillaire, M., Boccio, V., Philippi, A., Vigouroux, C., Terwilliger, J., Passa, P., Beckman, J. S., Velho, G., Lathrop, G. M., & Froguel, P. (1995). A gene for maturity onset diabetes of the young (MODY) maps to chromosome 12q. *Nature Genetics, 9*, 418–423.

Vetiska, J., Glaab, L., Rerlaman, K., & Daneman, D. (2000). School attendance of children with Type 1 diabetes. *Diabetes Care, 23*(11), 1706–7.

Warram, J. H., Gearin, G., Laffel, L., & Krolewski, A. S. (1996). Effect of duration of Type I diabetes on the prevalence of stages of diabetic nephropathy defined by urinary albumin/creatinine ratio. *Journal of the American Society of Nephrology, 7*(6), 930–937.

Wasserman, D. H., & Zinman B. (1994). Exercise in individuals with IDDM (Technical Review). *Diabetes Care, 17*, 924–937.

Widom, B., & Simonson, D. C. (1990). Glycemic control and neuropsychololgic function during hypoglycemia in patients with insulin dependent diabetes mellitus. *Annals of Internal Medicine, 112*, 904–912.

Weisberg-Benchell, J., Antisdel-Lomaglio, J., & Seshadri, R. (2003). Insulin pump therapy: A meta-analysis. *Diabetes Care, 26*(4), 1079–1087.

Wysocki, T., Meinhold, P. A., Abrams, K. C., Barnard, M. U., Clarke, W. L., Bellando, B. J., & Bourgeois, M. J. (1992). Parental and professional estimates of self-care independence of children and adolescents with IDDM. *Diabetes Care, 15*, 43–52.

Wysocki, T., Meinhold, P., Cox, D. J., & Clarke, W. L. (1990). Survey of diabetes professionals regarding developmental changes in diabetes self-care. *Diabetes Care, 13*, 65–68.

Wysocki, T., Miller, K. M., Greco, P., Harris, M. A., Harvey, L. M., Taylor, A., Danda, C. E., McDonell, K., & White, N. H. (1999). Behavior therapy for families of adolescents with diabetes: Effects on directly observed family interactions. *Behavior Therapy, 30*, 507–525.

Young-Hyman, D. (2002). Identification and intervention with youth at risk for Type 2 diabetes. In R. R. Rubin & B. J. Anderson (Eds.), *Practical diabetes* (2nd ed., pp. 171–179). Alexandria, VA: American Diabetes Association.

Young-Hyman, D. L., Schlundt, D. G., Herman, L., De Luca, F., & Counts, D. R. (2001). Evaluation of the insulin resistance syndrome in 5– to 10-year-old overweight/obese African American children. *Diabetes Care, 24*(8), 1359–1364.

Zinman, B. (1984). Comparison of the acute and long-term effects of exercise on glucose control in Type 1 diabetes. *Diabetes Care, 7*, 515.

12

Pediatric and Adolescent HIV/AIDS

Renee A. Smith
University of Illinois at Chicago

Staci C. Martin
HIV and AIDS Malignancy Branch, National Cancer Institute and Medical Illness Counseling Center

Pamela L. Wolters
HIV and AIDS Malignancy Branch, National Cancer Institute and Medical Illness Counseling Center

INTRODUCTION

With the advent of more numerous and effective treatment options, infection with human immunodeficiency virus (HIV) is changing from a terminal disease to a chronic illness. In the pediatric population, this is evidenced by decreasing morbidity and mortality, and the survival of infants and children with vertically acquired HIV infection into adolescence and young adulthood. HIV infection is a disease that may affect all aspects of an infected child's life. It not only impacts the child's health and physical growth, but the effects of HIV on the developing central nervous system (CNS) may result in neurocognitive deficits and behavioral impairments. As a result, the child's learning and school performance may be compromised. Furthermore, social-emotional development, peer relationships, and family functioning may be affected from the psychological stressors of living with HIV disease and having one or more infected family members. Since the impact of HIV infection on the child and family will be increasingly long-term and multifaceted, the use of psychological and educational services may be helpful to the management of this chronic illness over time. In particular, pediatric psychologists who are specifically trained in the psychological aspects of chronic illness, can help children and their families manage both neurocognitive and psychosocial effects of HIV disease. In addition, most children and adolescents with HIV attend public schools (Cohen et al., 1997), which increasingly have school-based health clinics, including mental health services, to improve access to health care. Thus, pediatric psychologists who work in the school setting are in a unique position to help youth with HIV disease by providing psychological services in this convenient and nonthreatening environment.

This chapter reviews topics related to pediatric and adolescent HIV infection that are of primary importance to pediatric psychologists working with this population. The first section summarizes the effects of HIV on the developing CNS, the behavioral and psychological aspects of the disease, and medical management of HIV-positive children. The second section discusses a variety of psychological services that may be helpful for children and families living with the disease and suggests opportunities for pediatric psychologists working with youth infected with HIV in school settings.

PEDIATRIC HIV INFECTION IN THE UNITED STATES

Epidemiology

As of December 31, 2001 the Centers for Disease Control and Prevention (CDC) reported 9,074 children less than 13 years of age and 4,428 adolescents from 13 to 19 years of age with acquired immune deficiency syndrome (AIDS) in the United States (CDC, 2002). Children and adolescents comprise approximately 2% of all individuals with AIDS in this country, and 82% are from African American and Hispanic minority groups (CDC, 2002). These data only include cases of AIDS and do not take into account children thought to be infected with HIV, but who have not yet experienced an AIDS-defining illness. It is estimated that about 4,000 children, 6,000 adolescents, and as many as 21,000 young adults—many of whom likely contracted the virus as adolescents—are infected with HIV, but do not yet have AIDS (CDC, 2002).

Transmission

Ninety-one percent of children with AIDS under 13 years of age acquired HIV disease through vertical transmission, that is, from an HIV-positive mother, most often infected through intravenous drug use or from sexual contact with an infected partner (CDC, 2002). Vertical transmission may occur in utero by transplacental passage, during the intrapartum period by exposure to maternal secretions, or through breast feeding (Friedland & Klein, 1987). Treatment with the antiretroviral (ARV) agent zidovudine (ZDV; also known as AZT) during pregnancy and labor and to the newborn reduces the vertical transmission rate from 25% to approximately 6–10% (Aleixo, Goodenow, & Sleasman, 1997; Connor et al., 1994; Simpson, Shapiro, & Andiman, 2000). Factors associated with the probability that a mother infected with HIV will transmit the virus to her infant include the mother's immunologic status (Mayaux et al., 1995; Pitt et al., 1997) and viral load (Aleixo et al., 1997; Blanche et al., 1997; Garcia et al., 1999), maternal genetics (John et al., 2000), biologic characteristics of the virus (Douglas, 1994), and obstetric factors related to the delivery (Douglas, 1994; Landesman et al., 1996; Mayaux et al., 1995).

In adolescents, HIV infection is most frequently acquired through sex and intravenous drug use (CDC, 2002). Adolescents are considered to be at particular risk for contracting HIV infection due to the high rates of risk-taking behavior found in this age group (Biglan et al., 1990), including sexual activity. In fact, 51% of females with AIDS 13–19 years old have contracted HIV through heterosexual contact (CDC, 2002).

Clinical Course

The course of HIV disease varies among different subgroups of children. Several studies have indicated a bimodal distribution in the onset of AIDS symptoms and a distinction between rapid and slow disease progression (Auger et al., 1988; Blanche, Tardieu, & Duliege, 1990; Galli et al., 1995). Approximately 20% of children with HIV infection exhibit an early onset of symptoms, usually within the first year of life. This subgroup has rapid disease progression and a higher incidence of opportunistic infections, encephalopathy, and a shorter survival time. In contrast, another subgroup has a later onset of symptoms and slow disease progression, without opportunistic infections or encephalopathy in the early years of life (Auger et al., 1988; Blanche et al., 1990). Symptoms associated with early onset and faster disease progression include low birth weight (The Italian Registry, 1994; Galli et al., 1995; Tovo et al., 1992), delayed neurodevelopment (Cooper et al., 1998; Pearson et al., 2000), and severe immunosuppression (Galli et al., 1995). Although the factors associated with rapid versus slow disease progression in children with vertical HIV infection are inconclusive, potential mediators include host immune response, timing of infection (Diaz et al., 1998; Shearer et al., 1997), host genetic factors (Misrahi et al., 1998; Buseyne et al., 1998), viral strain, and effects of ARV therapy (Diaz et al., 1998; Pizzo et al., 1990). Recent advances in ARV therapy have resulted in greater differentiation between those with rapid versus slow disease progression, with fewer morbidities, and later onset of symptoms for all children (Cooper, Charurat, Burns, Blattner, & Hoff, 2000).

ANTIRETROVIRAL TREATMENT

Advancements in science have facilitated significant progress in the medical management of children with HIV, including the development of new drugs and use of combination therapies and other supportive medications. Treatment goals have evolved from simply prolonging survival to also promoting normal growth and development, preventing infections, and improving quality of life.

The main goal of ARV therapy is to inhibit replication of HIV, which serves to lower viral load and reduce its damage to the immune system and other body organs. There are three classes of ARV drugs that are grouped according to the mechanism by which they attack the virus. The three classes are known as nucleoside reverse transcriptase inhibitors, nonnucleoside reverse transcriptase inhibitors, and protease inhibitors (PIs). Current treatment guidelines recommend that these agents be used in combination to target the virus at various steps in its life cycle. Combination regimens that include PIs are termed highly active antiretroviral therapies (HAART). Historically, standard practice has been to initiate therapy as soon as a child has a confirmed diagnosis of HIV, but if the child is more than 1 year of age and is asymptomatic (i.e., no clinical signs, low viral load, and high CD4 cell counts), some health care professionals choose to defer initiation of treatment until symptoms appear (HIV/AIDS Treatment Information Service, 2001).

Deterioration in virologic, immunologic, or clinical functioning (including neurodevelopmental status) may warrant a change in treatment regimen. Significant improvements in cognitive and behavioral functionings have been consistently demonstrated with the initiation of ARV therapy (Brouwers et al., 1990; Butler et al., 1991; Pizzo et al., 1988). Some ARV drugs are more effective for treating CNS disease than others, because they differ with respect to their ability to penetrate the CNS (Enting et al., 1998) and thus, inhibit HIV replication in specific types of brain cells affected by HIV. Pizzo et al. (1988) were the first to report the positive effects of ZDV on the cognitive status of symptomatic children with HIV disease. Subsequent studies have demonstrated improvement in general cognitive abilities (Butler et al., 1991; Brady et al., 1996; Pizzo et al., 1990), as well as behavioral and adaptive functioning (Brivio, Tornaghi, Musetti, Marchisio, & Principi, 1991; Moss et al., 1994; Wolters, Brouwers, Moss, & Pizzo, 1994), using AZT alone and in combination with other drugs. The effectiveness of more recently developed PIs and other HAART regimens on CNS functioning has not been well investigated and the results of current studies are mixed. Initial reports suggest that, although the use of these combinations may result in fewer mutations to the virus and slower disease progression, the relatively poor CNS penetration of PIs may limit their ability to ameliorate the effects of HIV-associated CNS disease in children (Mueller, Nelson et al., 1998a). However, other studies have found a beneficial effect of HAART on neuropsychological functioning (Civitello et al., 2000; Mueller, Sleasman, et al., 1998b).

Adherence to complex HAART regimens is vitally important, but often extremely difficult for children and families. For those who are unable to adhere to the regimen, not only does disease progression become a risk, but resistance to a particular drug or class of drugs becomes a grave possibility. When a dose is missed or taken off-schedule, it allows the virus to replicate more readily and increases the likelihood of mutations that are then resistant to that specific agent, as well as other medications. Resistance has been shown to occur with as little as 5–10% of missed doses (Paterson et al., 2000).

Adverse side effects of ARV drugs can manifest immediately or up to several months after the initiation of treatment. These effects may range from mild to severe and include rash, headache, nausea, fever, peripheral neuropathy (pain in the extremities), pancreatitis (inflammation of the pancreas causing abdominal pain), and increased or decreased activity level. CNS adverse side effects from some ARVs have been documented in adults, with lower incidence in children, and include mood disorders, increased activity level, and other psychiatric symptoms (Taketomo, Hodding, & Kraus, 1999; Vertex, 2001). These adverse medication side effects may have an impact on a child's ability to learn and/or perform in the school setting.

NEUROPSYCHOLOGICAL ASPECTS OF PEDIATRIC AND ADOLESCENT HIV/AIDS

Neuropathogenesis

Evidence suggests that the neurodevelopmental abnormalities associated with HIV-related CNS disease are caused primarily by the indirect effects of the virus on the CNS rather than by the direct killing of neurons (Epstein & Gendelman, 1993; Lipton, 1992). Neurons are not as vulnerable to infection with HIV as are the macrophages and microglia within the CNS. Once infected, these phagocytes become immune activated and secrete a variety of neurotoxic products that affect neural function and cause CNS inflammation. Some of these neurotoxins may compromise vital astrocyte function as well. Several viral products also have been found to contribute to neuronal injury. In addition, the blood–brain barrier can be damaged by chronic inflammation and contribute to neuronal injury by allowing entry of toxic secreting immune competent cells from the periphery (Epstein & Gelbard, 1999; Swindells, Zheng, & Gendelman, 1999). Finally, the number of HIV-infected cells and the virulence of HIV strains within the CNS are also likely to be related to the degree of interference with CNS processes (Tersmette et al., 1989; Tornatore, Meyers, Atwood, Conant, & Major, 1994).

Adult studies suggest that HIV may enter the CNS shortly after systemic HIV infection (Davis et al., 1992). In children, the exact timing of HIV entry into the CNS is not clear and may vary across individuals, but has been found as early as 15 weeks gestation in fetal CNS tissue (Lyman et al., 1990). The timing of productive HIV CNS infection and periods of highest HIV replication during the development of the brain may significantly influence the neuropathogenesis (Civitello, Brouwers, DeCarli, & Pizzo, 1994; DeCarli, Civitello, Brouwers, & Pizzo, 1993) and impact the pattern and severity of neurodevelopmental abnormalities (Brouwers et al., 1995).

Neuroimaging Findings

Computed tomography (CT) and magnetic resonance imaging (MRI) brain scans of children with HIV infection have shown that global cerebral atrophy is the most common abnormality (Chamberlain, Nichols, & Chase, 1991; DeCarli et al., 1993). Severity of abnormality on CT scans has been associated with degree of neurodevelopmental impairment, including general cognition (Brouwers et al., 1995), language (Wolters, Brouwers, & Moss, 1995), and behavior (Brouwers et al., 1995). More recent research suggests that magnetic resonance spectroscopy (MRS), a technique assessing the level of specific metabolites in the brain, may offer more predictive utility as a neurodiagnostic tool in the HIV population (Arendt, 1995; Suwanwela et al., 2000). For example, MRS has been able to detect subtle changes in spectra from the basal ganglia region and white matter of children with HIV (Pavlakis et al., 1995). Thus, MRS appears to be useful in the early detection of HIV-related neurochemical changes in the CNS. However, more studies are needed to examine the utility of MRS among pediatric HIV patients for monitoring CNS changes related to disease progression and ARV treatment.

Secondary HIV-Related CNS Manifestations

The immune system's impaired ability to fight infections may result in secondary manifestations of HIV, such as neoplastic disease or stroke, that may affect the CNS and cause significant neuropsychological impairment. Although the overall prevalence of HIV-related secondary morbidities has decreased with the advent of HAART those that cause CNS manifestations are typically observed more frequently in older children and adolescents.

Strokes and headaches are among the most common cerebrovascular complications in children with HIV. Strokes may lead to focal neurological deficits, such as hemiparesis (Dickson, Llena, & Weidenheim, 1990), whereas headaches may be an early symptom of any number of secondary HIV-related CNS manifestations. In contrast to adults with AIDS, opportunistic and bacterial infections of the CNS, such as toxoplasmosis, cytomegalovirus, and JC virus (Berger et al., 1992), occur in less than 10% of children with HIV infection (Civitello, Brouwers, & Pizzo, 1993; Krasinski, 1994). Primary CNS lymphoma and systemic lymphoma metastatic to the CNS are rare in children with HIV (Dickson et al., 1990) yet can produce rapid neurological deterioration and must be distinguished from the symptoms of HIV encephalopathy.

Clinical Presentation of HIV-Related CNS Disease in Children

The clinical presentation of HIV-related CNS disease in children varies with respect to onset, prevalence, and severity of impairment in different subgroups (Belman, 1994). Infants and young children exhibit the most frequent and severe neurodevelopmental impairments (Chase, Vibbert, Pelton, Coulter, & Cabral, 1995; Englund et al., 1996), which have been identified as early as four months of age (Chase et al., 2000). In adolescence, however, the prevalence and severity of HIV CNS disease is significantly less (Englund et al., 1996). Children with vertically-acquired infection tend to have more severe CNS manifestations than children who were infected via blood or blood products, even during the neonatal period (Mintz, 1994). In addition, children who are naïve to ARV (Englund et al., 1996) or being treated with monotherapy (McKinney et al., 1998) appear to be at greater risk for developing HIV CNS disease than children who are being treated with combination ARV, such as HAART (Tardieu & Boutet, 2002). Other factors associated with more severe CNS manifestations in children include high plasma viral loads (Cooper et al., 1998; Lindsey et al., 2000; Tardieu et al., 2000), more impaired immune function early in life (Cooper et al., 1998; Mayaux et al., 1996; Tardieu et al., 2000), and genetic factors in the child (Just et al., 1995; Sei et al., 2001). Finally, HIV-infected children may have other medical and environmental risk factors, such as preterm birth, maternal substance abuse, exposure to toxic substances (i.e. lead), other CNS infections, and impoverished socioeconomic and environmental conditions, that can negatively affect development.

Despite these variations in the clinical presentation of pediatric HIV-related CNS disease, three main patterns have been identified: encephalopathy, CNS compromise, and apparently unaffected (Working Group of the American Academy of Neurology AIDS Task Force, 1991; Wolters & Brouwers, 1998). Children with *encephalopathy* exhibit global impairments in all areas of development, and demonstrate the more severe form of CNS impairment with some specific functions differentially affected. Encephalopathy can take a progressive or static course. The progressive course is characterized by a pervasive loss of previously attained skills and abilities, resulting in a decline in standardized scores on repeated neurodevelopmental testing. The static course is defined by a slower rate of developmental gain compared with same-age peers such that scores on standardized assessments are below average but remain stable over time (Belman, 1994; Brouwers, Belman, & Epstein, 1994). The current prevalence of HIV encephalopathy in children with AIDS is estimated to be approximately 13 to 23 percent with the highest rates in infants and toddlers (Blanche et al., 1997; Cooper et al., 1998; Lobato, Caldwell, Ng, & Oxtoby, 1995; Tardieu et al., 2000).

Children with HIV-related *CNS compromise* typically demonstrate adequate functioning in school and day-to-day functioning, but exhibit significant decline in one or more areas on cognitive testing or selective neurodevelopmental functions (Wolters & Brouwers, 1998), such as expressive language, perceptual-motor skills (Epstein, 1986), and motor function (Belman et al., 1988). Children are classified as *apparently not affected* when responses on standardized cognitive assessments are within normal limits for age, and there is no evidence of HIV-related significant deficits in daily living or social skills. Some children with HIV may exhibit impaired cognitive functioning, or brain scan or neurological abnormalities that are unrelated to HIV disease. Assessment of medical, developmental and family history may reveal other risk factors known to compromise development. These children are classified as having *non-HIV-related CNS impairment.* Frequently, children may have both HIV and non-HIV-related impairments. Determining the etiology of these deficits is important for making treatment decisions.

Domains of Neuropsychological Impairment

In children with HIV encephalopathy, the effects of HIV on the CNS tend to be generalized and cognitive functioning is affected severely and globally (Brouwers et al., 1995; Brouwers, Wolters, & Civitello, 1998). However, in children with less advanced disease, general cognitive function may be preserved while selected domains may be differentially affected by HIV, for which further evaluation is recommended. The effects of HIV on different domains of functioning are described below.

Language. Children with symptomatic HIV disease frequently exhibit speech and language abnormalities (Epstein, 1986; Pressman, 1992; Wolters, Brouwers, & Moss, 1995), which may appear prior to declines in general cognitive function and even when being treated with ARV therapy (Wolters, Brouwers, Civitello, & Moss, 1997). In both encephalopathic and non-encephalopathic children, expressive language is significantly more impaired than receptive language (Wolters, Brouwers, & Moss, 1995). Furthermore, uninfected siblings score higher than HIV-infected children on both receptive and expressive language, suggesting that the deficit is related to HIV and not environmental factors (Wolters, Brouwers, Moss, & Pizzo, 1995). The differential deficit in expressive language also may reflect a more general HIV-associated impairment of expressive behavior (Moss, Wolters, Brouwers, Hendricks, & Pizzo, 1996).

Attention. Children with HIV disease frequently exhibit attentional deficits, but it is unclear whether an increased prevalence of attentional problems exists in these children compared with uninfected peers and whether these problems are directly attributable to HIV (Havens,

Whitaker, Feldman, & Ehrhardt, 1994; Loveland et al., 1994; Whitt et al., 1993). The various components of attention (divided, focused, sustained) may be differentially affected in pediatric HIV infection. Studies assessing attention using continuous performance tasks, however, have found that children with HIV infection exhibit deficits in sustained attention that are not found in uninfected control groups (Watkins et al., 2000). These impairments may result in academic and learning problems. Such attention deficits may respond to stimulant medication.

Memory. Early studies assessing memory function in pediatric HIV disease have yielded mixed results with memory deficits generally found in children with vertically-acquired HIV infection (Boivin et al., 1995; Levenson, Mellins, Zawadzki, Kairam, & Stein, 1992) but not in those with transfusion-acquired disease (Cohen et al., 1991; Loveland et al., 1994; Whitt et al., 1993). More recently, however, declines in memory function have been found in HIV-infected hemophiliacs with low CD4 counts (Loveland et al., 2000). In addition, children with HIV CNS disease have exhibited significantly poorer performance on verbal learning and recall measures compared to children without CNS disease, who scored in the average range. However, these two groups had similar scores on a recognition task (Klaas, Wolters, Martin, Civitello, & Zeichner, 2002; Perez, Wolters, Moss, Civitello, & Brouwers, 1998), suggesting a retrieval deficit.

Academic Achievement. Children with HIV infection are at risk for developing academic difficulties related to the neurocognitive effects of HIV and secondary factors, such as frequent school absences and fatigue. Studies of HIV-infected children with hemophilia generally have reported mean academic achievement scores in the average range, which were lower than expected based on their intelligence test scores (Loveland et al., 2000; Loveland et al., 1994; Sirois & Hill, 1993; Smith et al., 1997). For hemophiliacs with low CD4 counts, achievement scores in reading, reading comprehension, and spelling declined over time (Loveland et al., 2000). In a study of school-age children with vertically-acquired HIV infection, two-thirds demonstrated normal academic achievement as well as normal cognitive function (Tardieu et al., 1995). The children with normal academic skills had better immune function than the children having academic difficulties. In a more recent study, HIV-infected children and their uninfected siblings both had mean reading, spelling, and math scores in the low-average range despite average scores on tests of general cognitive function (Blanchette, Smith, King, Fernandes-Penney, & Read, 2002), suggesting that secondary factors may influence academic performance. Thus, current research indicates that the majority of school-age children with HIV infection exhibit average to low average academic performance; however, they may not be learning at a level commensurate with their intellectual function. A combination of the effects of HIV on the CNS as well as secondary factors may contribute to the generally mild academic difficulties of children with HIV disease.

Motor Functioning. Infants less than 1 year of age are at much greater risk for developing motor impairments than school-age children (Chase et al., 2000; Englund et al., 1996). Children with encephalopathy exhibit the most severe motor involvement and may lose previously attained motor milestones (Belman, 1994). In addition, oral-motor functioning may be impaired, which can contribute to articulation problems, expressive language deficits, and feeding and swallowing difficulties (Pressman, 1992). Gross motor functions, especially running speed and agility, tend to be more impaired than fine motor skills (Parks & Danoff, 1999). In children with less severe CNS disease, impairments may be seen in gross motor strength and fine motor speed (Blanchette et al., 2002). Significant motor deficits may limit communication, interfere with cognitive development, and complicate the assessment of cognitive abilities. Thus, when evaluating cognitive function, specific tests and subtests should be selected to minimize the impact of motor impairments.

BEHAVIORAL AND PSYCHOSOCIAL ASPECTS OF PEDIATRIC AND ADOLESCENT HIV/AIDS

Although HIV is a chronic illness, there are important differences that challenge generalizations with other chronic illnesses, such as the multigenerational nature of the illness, the potential CNS sequelae, and the social stigma associated with HIV. These differences warrant study and discussion to identify their unique contributions to the child and family's ability to adapt to living with HIV. Although relatively little research exists in this area, compared with other chronic illnesses, preliminary findings suggest that children and families affected by HIV face numerous and pervasive risk factors associated with the direct and indirect effects of the disease (Wiener, Moss, Davidson, & Fair, 1992), which may lead to behavioral and psychosocial dysfunction.

Direct behavioral and psychiatric effects are associated with HIV-related encephalopathy. These abnormalities tend to be more severe in younger children and may improve with ARV treatment (Moss et al., 1994; Wolters et al., 1994). Indirect behavioral effects of HIV impact psychosocial functioning through environmental factors commonly associated with this disease (Wiener et al., 1992), such as poverty, parental illness, and pre- and postnatal drug exposure. Discerning the etiology of behavior and psychiatric problems is often difficult, since a bidirectional relationship likely exists between the direct and indirect effects of HIV. Some of the environmental factors associated with HIV may be more potent mediators of psychiatric and behavioral problems than HIV itself (Campbell, 1997; Mellins & Ehrhardt, 1994). Consideration of previous and current medical and social issues in a child's life is vital in determining possible causes and effective intervention strategies. The following two sections review the direct and indirect behavioral and psychosocial consequences of HIV in children and adolescents, and their potential mediators.

Behavioral Functioning and Psychological Adjustment

Depression. Depressive symptoms are not uncommon in children with HIV (Hooper et al., 1993; Pao et al., 2000), and may be related to the direct and/or indirect behavioral effects of the virus. For example, apathy and psychomotor slowing can be indicators of either depression or HIV-related encephalopathy (Stolar & Fernandez, 1997). Research evidence of direct behavioral effects includes an association between more severe abnormality on CT brain scans, and higher scores on the "depressed" subscale from a Q-sort behavior rating scale (Brouwers et al., 1995).

Depression may also be the result of the indirect effects of HIV, including living in poverty (Murrain & Barker, 1997), parental drug use, and parental illness or death. Additionally, the stigma surrounding HIV may lead to rejection by peers, feelings of isolation, and in severe cases, suicidal ideation (Prinstein, Boergers, Spirito, Little, & Grapentine, 2000). Although suicidal ideation and rates of completed suicides have been associated with HIV infection in adults (Cote, Biggar, & Dannenberg, 1992; Judd & Mijch, 1996), less is known about these behaviors in children and adolescents. In teenagers, passive suicidal behavior or depressive symptoms may manifest as nonadherence to their medical regimen, or participation in high-risk behaviors, such as mixing alcohol or drugs with HIV medications.

Externalizing Behavior/Conduct Problems. Preliminary research has suggested that the prevalence of hyperactive behaviors is higher in children with HIV, compared with uninfected children, but the results are inconsistent and inconclusive because of small sample sizes and lack of appropriate control groups. It is also not clear to what degree such behaviors may be related to direct CNS effects and/or environmental stressors. In one study, 12% of HIV-infected patients scored in the clinical range of hyperactivity on the Conners Parent Rating

Scale (CPRS; Conners, 1989), compared with only 5% of children from the normative sample (Bose, Moss, Brouwers, Pizzo, & Lorion, 1994). Havens, Whitaker, Feldman, and Ehrhardt (1994) found no difference in the rates of disruptive behaviors between children with HIV and two control groups, yet the scores of all three groups were elevated well above the levels of the normative sample. In a comparison of HIV-infected children and their uninfected siblings, parents rated the siblings as having more conduct problems than the infected children on the CPRS. The scores of both groups were significantly higher than those from the same-age normative group (Moss, Wolters, Brouwers, & Perez, 2000). Another study compared caregiver ratings of behavior among children infected with HIV and children uninfected but exposed to the virus. Results indicated no significant differences on any subscale of the CPRS, although scores from both groups were higher than those from the normative sample (Mellins et al., 2003). The results of these studies suggest that such externalizing behavior problems may be associated with environmental factors rather than the direct effects of HIV on the CNS.

Conduct problems in adolescents with HIV may have dangerous implications as high-risk behaviors, such as intravenous drug use and unprotected sex may result in transmission of the virus. Remafedi (1998) found that an alarming 83% of HIV-positive adolescents surveyed did not consistently use condoms during sexual encounters.

Adaptive Behavior. Deficits in adaptive functioning are part of the pattern of neurobehavioral effects associated with HIV-related CNS disease. On the Vineland Adaptive Behavior Scale, parents reported impairments in expressive language, socialization, daily living skills, and motor function (Wolters et al., 1994) with encephalopathic children scoring lower than nonencephalopathic children. The Vineland scores of both groups however, improved significantly after 6 months of ZDV therapy. In addition, abnormal findings on CT brain scans (i.e., calcifications and ventricular enlargement) have been associated with nonsocial or withdrawn behavior in HIV-positive children (Brouwers et al., 1995).

Indirect behavioral effects of HIV, such as frequent hospitalizations and the tendency for parents to assign caregiving responsibilities (i.e., for an ill family member) to their children with HIV, may also impact adaptive functioning by limiting the amount of time these children are able to spend engaging in age-appropriate activities (Gewirtz & Gossart-Walker, 2000). Among children with HIV infection, poor social self-concept and lower social competence (Bose et al., 1994; Moss, Bose, Wolters, & Brouwers, 1998) may be mediated by peer rejection (Bose et al., 1994). Finally, parental guilt also may contribute to socialization difficulties. Parents of children with HIV often hesitate to correct or punish inappropriate social behavior because of their feelings of guilt about the child being sick, especially in cases of vertical transmission. As a result, children are not given the feedback needed to form appropriate interpersonal skills (Harper, 1991).

Anxiety. A recent study by Pao and colleagues (2000) identified a high prevalence of anxiety disorders among HIV-positive adolescents, including specific phobias, social phobias, and other anxiety-related symptoms. Furthermore, increased levels of anxiety in HIV-positive children with hemophilia have been associated with lower CD4 counts (Nichols et al., 2000). Other factors, including pain, secrecy surrounding the diagnosis, and fear of becoming sick or dying, also may contribute to a child's level of anxiety.

Mediating Psychosocial Factors

Family Stressors. Families with a chronically ill child are at risk for psychological dysfunction. For families with HIV, those illness-related stressors are complicated by stigma, isolation, secrecy, and multiple loss. Additionally, these stressors often exist in the background of environmental strains, such as poverty, violence, drug use, and/or unstable housing (Mellins & Ehrhardt, 1994; Sherwen & Boland, 1994).

Biological mothers are particularly vulnerable to the various stressors in their families' lives. A high prevalence of comorbid drug abuse, depression, chronic stress, and self-criticism (Havens et al., 1994; Morrison et al., 2002; Rotheram-Borus, Robin, Reid, & Draimin, 1998) has been found in biological mothers of HIV infected children. The ability for families to adapt to these stressors depends on many factors, including characteristics of individual family members, family coping styles, family support, and other available resources.

Approximately 50% of children with HIV live with an extended family member, typically a maternal aunt or grandmother (Mellins & Ehrhardt, 1994; Shable, et al., 1995). Although stress for nonbiologic primary caregivers is not as high as for biological mothers, they may still face the stigma and isolation that biological parents experience, as well as the challenge of caring for an infected child (Sherwen, Boland, & Gilchrist, 1993). Siblings of children with HIV are also at increased risk for psychological dysfunction and poor school performance (Fanos & Wiener, 1994). Siblings may share some of the same anxieties as the infected child regarding death of an infected family member, isolation, unanswered questions about family illness, and pressures in keeping silent about the family's infection status (Fanos & Wiener, 1994). They may also harbor anger and resentment for having to share caregiving responsibilities with their parent(s) for their infected sibling (Mellins & Ehrhardt, 1994).

Adolescence. As perinatally infected children age, new psychosocial issues surrounding adaptation and coping with HIV arise. Adolescence is typically a time of increasing independence and a heightened focus on issues such as body image, sexuality, and peer acceptance. The normal process of exploring sexuality is challenged in adolescents with HIV as fears about transmission of the virus emerge. Adolescents must deal with decisions regarding disclosure of their diagnosis to their potential partner as well as be educated about and practice safe sex. Questions about how they will inform their partner and anticipation of possible rejection increase the stress associated with sexuality. Some adolescents infected with HIV avoid sexual intimacy because they are uninformed or unclear about transmission possibilities (Lewis, Haiken, & Hoyt, 1994). Others may choose not to disclose their HIV status to their partner and consequently risk transmission.

Adolescents who acquired HIV through homosexual activities are often faced with discrimination and open hostility if their homosexuality is known or even suspected by peers. One study reported that 70% of teachers and school administrators surveyed had witnessed homophobic language in school (Remafedi, 1993).

Peer acceptance may also be challenged in adolescents with HIV because of physical abnormalities. Youths with perinatally acquired HIV are typically smaller in height, weight, and head circumference (Moye et al., 1996), and may experience dermatologic conditions as well as distorted body shapes (e.g., distended abdomens) from the effects of some medications.

Disclosure. Because of the fear of stigmatization associated with HIV infection, many parents choose to maintain the secrecy of the family's infection status with friends, extended family members, schools, and even the infected child. It is estimated that only 15–30% of children under 10 years of age have been fully informed of their infection status (Funck-Brentano et al., 1997; Ledlie, 1999). However, findings from pediatric cancer patients suggest that sharing information about a child's illness is beneficial to the patient by decreasing emotional distress and increasing responsibility for the child's own health care. Benefits to the family also include increased trust, communication and intimacy, and a greater ability to cope and support one another (Lipson, 1994; Siegel & Gorey, 1994). Parents may decide not to share the diagnosis with a child because of the following fears: the child will share the information indiscriminately and suffer ostracism as a consequence; the information will lead to questions regarding transmission, including parental sexual behavior, drug use, and death; the parents may feel unprepared about how to tell their child; and the child may respond negatively to the information, leading to depression or suicide (Funck-Brentano et al., 1997; Ledlie, 1999; Lipson, 1994). Cultural norms for sharing information with children also may contribute to parental nondisclosure (Wiener & Vasquez, 1999a).

Disclosure of one's HIV status to others is often done with the hopes of gaining social support (Gillman & Newman, 1996), although for many families this only leads to discrimination and further social isolation (Lesar & Meldonado, 1997). Some evidence suggest that families of children with HIV utilize social support as a means of coping significantly less often than they rely on other means of coping (Martin et al., 2001). Benefits of self-disclosure from an infected child to a friend have been linked with positive outcomes, including improved immune functioning (Sherman, Bonanno, Wiener, & Battles, 2000). Disclosure to schools may be particularly difficult as families depend on the school as an important resource and an indicator of normalcy in a child's life (Rehm & Franck, 2000). Families who disclose to the school often tell the health or administrative personnel rather than the child's teacher, in hopes of avoiding differential treatment of the child (Cohen et al., 1997).

Individual states vary with regard to policy of disclosing an HIV diagnosis to school personnel. Current guidelines acknowledge the importance of confidentiality, and advise the disclosure of a child's status only with consent of the family and age-appropriate assent of the child (American Academy of Pediatrics, 2000). In a few states, physicians are required to report HIV-positive children by name to the state's Department of Public Health. The Health Department, in turn, is required to report the child's infection status to the school principal.

Adherence. Adherence to medication for pediatric chronic diseases is notoriously poor (Parrish, 1986) and for children with HIV, additional barriers exist for optimal adherence. Documented rates of adherence in children with HIV is roughly 40–50% (Belzer, Fuchs, Luftman, & Tucker, 1999; Reddington et al., 2000; Watson & Farley, 1999). For young children, adherence rates are more closely associated with caregiver factors, including caregiver health (Singh et al., 1996), beliefs regarding the efficacy of the medication, and social circumstances (Reddington et al., 2000). As children age and become more independent, parents often assign them more responsibility for their own health care, including their medication. Challenges in adherence for older children are associated with maintaining secrecy or normalcy in the school setting (Reddington et al., 2000) and with peers (Rehm & Franck, 2000). Some research suggests that older children with HIV are more likely to be nonadherent if the school has not been informed of their diagnosis, and if the child's regimen requires a midday dose that may cause others to question the purpose of the medications (Reddington et al., 2000). Additionally, the adolescent's sense of indestructibility and focus on immediate actions and consequences may allow them to rationalize nonadherence to a difficult regimen when they are asymptomatic (HIVATIS, 2001). Other reasons for nonadherence may include lack of education about HIV and/or medications, distrust of medical professionals, denial or fear of HIV, lack of social support, and involvement in a chaotic or high-risk lifestyle.

Grief and Bereavement. Most HIV-infected children eventually face the premature loss of at least one significant family member (Aronson, 1996) or peer. The stress of this loss may be compounded by the child's concern for his/her own mortality and that of other family members, and may result in an anticipatory grief process (Wiener & Vasquez, 1999b). Only 15% of families of children with HIV consist of both the mother and father living in the home (Schable et al., 1995). In a large number of cases, HIV-infected youth are raised by single mothers. In these situations, fathers are often incarcerated or uninvolved in the child's life, thus leaving the child with no biological parent if the mother with HIV becomes ill and dies. Thus, the death of a mother leads to a transition in caregiving for the child, typically a grandmother or maternal aunt (Forehand et al., 1999). This transition may be particularly difficult for the child if full disclosure did not occur prior to the mother's death, leaving the child with unanswered questions regarding the illness and no parent to offer social/emotional support (Fanos & Wiener, 1994). The child may also feel unable to seek out social support from friends because of the need to maintain secrecy about HIV. Even family members are often unwilling to discuss issues related to the person's death.

Chronic Absences. Although only about 3% of children with HIV are unable to attend school at all (Cohen et al., 1997), repeated absences are relatively common and may be due to clinic visits, hospitalizations, or acute illness. For younger children, missing school may lead to social isolation and delays in cognitive development (American Academy of Pediatrics, 1989). For older children, absences may be questioned by school personnel and peers, a situation that may eventually eliminate school as a place of social support (Rehm & Franck, 2000) and the only setting in which the child with a chronic illness is not viewed as a patient (Sexson & Madan-Swain, 1993).

When children are hospitalized for an acute infection or the child's disease progresses to the point that attending school is not an option, home or in-hospital instruction may be implemented. When re-entry to school occurs, children may experience adjustment problems directly or indirectly related to HIV disease. Direct effects, such as CNS compromise or fatigue (Thompson & Gustafson, 1996), may create learning problems or require an adjusted schedule, whereas indirect effects may include psychological stress stemming from the burden of making up missed schoolwork, missing out on shared social experiences, and explaining absences to peers.

Pain. Pain in children with HIV may be recurrent or chronic (Oleske & Czarniecki, 1999). In a recent study, 52% of infected children reported having pain that affected the quality of their lives (Boland, 2000). Children may experience pain because of medical procedures, side effects from medications, or direct effects of the disease process. Unmanaged pain can affect daily functioning via depression, impaired attention, or decreased activity. Pain management should therefore not be viewed solely as end-stage care, but as palliative care to improve quality of life (Frager, 1997).

ROLE OF THE PEDIATRIC PSYCHOLOGIST IN THE SCHOOL SETTING

Integration of health services in the school setting is increasingly important as the number of children with chronic illness attending school continues to increase with advancements in medical treatments and technology. Schools are more frequently offering health services, including immunizations, physicals, acute care, mental health interventions, and specialized therapies (physical, occupational, and speech/language). The benefits of these services within the school include self-referral, greater accessibility, enhanced compliance, and increased use of preventive care and mental health services (American Academy of Pediatrics, 2001). For children with HIV who have limited access to health services, and have significant physical and mental health needs, these school-based health clinics may offer a consistent and convenient source of support in adhering to often complex care. The integration of a pediatric psychologist in the school setting enriches the quality of mental health services that schools can offer children who otherwise may not have access to such services. The pediatric psychologist working in the school setting may have many roles in the care of a child with HIV, including assessment of direct and indirect effects of HIV; intervention in numerous psychosocial issues; consultation with school staff and parents; liaison between the school and health care team; education regarding HIV awareness and prevention; and research.

Assessment

Psychological assessment is a critical task for psychologists working with HIV-infected children in the school setting. Because of the many potential psychosocial, developmental, and biomedical risk factors faced by children with HIV, it is important that the assessment be comprehensive, with an interdisciplinary approach, to try to discern the direct and indirect behavioral effects of HIV and to develop appropriate medical, psychological, and educational interventions. In addition, assessments need to be scheduled on an ongoing basis to monitor for changes in CNS functioning because of the progressive nature of HIV disease. Recommendations for the routine assessment of children with HIV are as follows: children less than 2 years of age should be assessed every 3–6 months; children from 2–8 years of age should be assessed every year; and children greater than 8 years of age should be assessed every 2 years (Wolters & Brouwers, in press). Frequency of assessments should be increased if the child is known or suspected to have neurodevelopmental impairment. To avoid duplicate or too frequent testing, it is important to facilitate coordination of testing and sharing of information with the medical facility.

Psychologists play a key role in developing an appropriate interdisciplinary assessment team that may include parents; teachers; special educators; social workers; school nurse; speech/language, occupational, and/or physical therapists. Members of the child's health care team—such as the child's physician, nurse, child life specialist, and/or hospital education specialist—may provide valuable input as well. The role of the assessment team and the information shared may vary based on the child's needs and on the extent of disclosure that the family has made with the school and child.

The psychologist also will determine the specific test battery used to evaluate the wide range of domains vulnerable to the direct and indirect effects of HIV. The various assessments must be sufficiently sensitive to detect subtle changes, particularly for older children. Areas vulnerable to direct effects of HIV include cognition, expressive and receptive language, attention, memory, achievement skills, motor skills, social-emotional status, and adaptive behavior. Assessment of indirect effects that may influence the child's functioning should include consideration of disclosure issues, psychiatric symptoms, and social relationships. Environmental factors to be assessed should include housing, family financial support, nutrition, and transportation. For a list of standardized measures deemed appropriate for assessing children with HIV, see Wolters and Brouwers (in press).

Standardized assessments are critical for monitoring change, but in some circumstances additional unstandardized testing is appropriate and even recommended. If a child is developmentally delayed to the extent that she/he does not obtain minimum raw scores to register in the appropriate age norm index, a more developmentally appropriate test may be used, or administration of standardized tests may be altered. Unstandardized assessments may be more suitable to assess indirect effects that may not be normed on a comparable population or that may be unique to HIV. For example, knowledge around disclosure or transmission prevention may be best measured by semistructured interview, whereas emotional lability and social skills may be assessed by direct observation or anecdotal observation records. A battery containing both standardized and unstandardized measures from a number of different informants (parents, teachers, health care team, etc.) offers a more informative and comprehensive profile of the child's functioning across settings.

Psychologists in the school also will assist with integrating assessment results into the planning of special educational or therapeutic services, short-term classroom objectives, and daily adaptive living and social activities, and with implementing methods for assessing progress in these areas. Since the timing of HIV-related CNS impairment and concomitant developmental delay is often unpredictable, informal monitoring in between formal assessments is important, as is the need for flexible classroom and therapeutic objectives.

Intervention

Limited financial resources, distrust of medical professionals, fear of being stigmatized as mentally ill, and inconvenience may prevent parents and youth from seeking mental health services in a conventional setting. Working within the schools offers psychologists access to students in need of services and a nonthreatening and convenient environment in the community for children and families to obtain psychological services on a regular basis. School-based clinics have been found to receive significantly more visits for counseling regarding psychosocial issues than pediatric outpatient clinics in tertiary care medical settings (McHarney-Brown & Kaufman, 1991).

Family Adaptation. Earlier sections in this chapter describe the overwhelming difficulties that are common among family members of children with HIV. The emotional impact of the infected child's illness may be complex, and each family member may find different ways of coping. In addition, such difficulties may be left unattended because of a family's unwillingness to seek out psychological services. Weekly family therapy sessions held at the child's school may help the psychologist to circumvent that problem. For parents who are willing, support groups can be helpful in the coping process. In addition, many families of HIV-positive children often rely on organized religion and spirituality as a means of coping and support.

Adolescent Issues. Pediatric psychologists working in the junior high and high-school setting should be aware of issues related to homosexuality and risk behaviors for HIV, such as substance abuse. Counseling for substance abuse, as well as for HIV testing, should be available to adolescents as part of a comprehensive HIV prevention program.

Psychologists may be able to lessen prejudiced attitudes toward homosexuality through educational interventions geared toward creating a more accepting atmosphere. Encouraging results were obtained from one training program that provided education for school professionals on topics including prevention of HIV in homosexual adolescents (Remafedi, 1993). Participants reported an improvement of their awareness of homosexuality among teenagers, and performed significantly better than controls on a measure of knowledge about AIDS and adolescent homosexuality. More tolerant attitudes among teenagers toward people with AIDS have been demonstrated following educational interventions (Brown, Reynolds, & Lourie, 1997; Siegel, DiClemente, Durbin, Krasnovsky, & Saliba, 1995), but whether these attitude changes translate into lasting behavioral changes is questionable.

Behavior Management. Psychologists working with HIV-positive children with behavior problems can borrow from techniques commonly used with healthy children. Daily report cards from teachers, frequent reinforcement for desired behavior, and consistent consequences for misbehavior should be used as needed. It should be emphasized to both parents and teachers that, the same rules and principles of reinforcement generally apply eventhough certain behavior problems might result from the CNS effects of the virus. Being excessively lenient with children who are HIV-positive will only serve to maintain inappropriate behaviors and teach them that their illness can serve as an excuse for breaking the rules. Psychologists should educate teachers regarding the direct and indirect effects of HIV on behavior, and the importance of working together to determine the etiology of behavior problems. Sudden changes in behavior may warrant consultation with the health care team for consideration of possible HIV-related CNS disease and changes in ARV treatment. In addition, children should be given the opportunity to discuss any feelings of frustration, anger, or fear regarding their condition. Although children usually do not make an overt connection between their behavioral problems and these confusing emotions, allowing them an appropriate outlet to express their feelings may help ameliorate some of the behavioral difficulties.

Disclosure. When the time comes for a child with HIV to learn about their diagnosis, psychologists can be extremely helpful in navigating the disclosure process. Some psychologists working with HIV-infected children offer formal disclosure programs consisting of weekly sessions aimed at helping the child understand the diagnosis. During these sessions, the psychologist reviews information with the child on topics such as the immune system, modes of transmission, treatment, and prognosis. Such disclosure programs (S. Martin, personal communication, March 2001) also assess the child's emotional reactions throughout the entire disclosure process and help them to integrate the knowledge of their virus into a healthy self-concept. Formal disclosure programs typically last from 8 to 12 sessions, depending on the developmental level of the child and the extent of family involvement, but the process of disclosure continues well after the child learns of the HIV diagnosis. Education regarding the virus and the child's health—as well as issues surrounding peer acceptance, sexuality, and death—should be discussed as the child's developmental ability to process this information allows for an increased understanding of these concepts.

Often disclosure work must start with the parents, because they are often reluctant to tell their child about the fact that they have HIV. Psychologists may be able to assist parents in coping with feelings of grief and guilt stemming from the knowledge that their child inherited a life-threatening illness, particularly in cases of vertical transmission. Once these feelings are processed in a supportive, nonjudgmental context, parents may be more willing to engage in open communication with their child.

Even when disclosure has been successfully completed within the immediate family, parents often remain opposed to the idea of disclosing to the school, and in many cases, there is no legitimate need for anyone at the school to be informed of the child's diagnosis. However, disclosure may be warranted in certain situations. For example, if adherence is a significant problem in the home, the child may benefit from having the school nurse administer medication at school. Every school should have a policy in place for serving children with HIV infection. Guidebooks are available to assist school personnel in developing such policies (National Association for the State Boards of Education or [NASBE] 2001).

It is extremely important for children learning about their diagnosis to be provided with developmentally appropriate information. Thus, the psychologist involved in disclosure work may wish to obtain information from teachers regarding the child's academic performance and any behavioral problems that exist. Sometimes only partial information needs to be given to children, depending on their capacity to understand and process illness-related concepts. A child's impulsivity should be taken into account before disclosing the name of their illness, because impulsive children may "blurt out" the information to others without understanding the potential consequences. Psychologists can work with teachers to prepare them for such an occurrence. For example, teachers should be ready to address the situation with the infected child, and should watch for and address any discriminative or hostile reactions from peers. Educational sessions in the classroom may be warranted to teach children accurate information about HIV and to ensure that any misconceptions are corrected. Psychologists may also need to address concerns from other children's parents, and even school employees, if a child's status becomes public. Thus, educational programs should not be limited to children and adolescents.

Adherence. Some parents of HIV-positive children are often so overwhelmed with environmental and psychosocial stressors that overseeing their child's medical regimen is not a priority. Administration of medications at school can be particularly beneficial in these cases. For example, when school nurses are involved in administering medications, they can be a reliable source of information for the psychologist concerning any problems with adherence and can work with the psychologist to implement behavioral strategies for improving adherence. As children become older and gain a better understanding of their condition, they may be reluctant to take their medications at school, because they are often anxious about peers finding out their diagnosis. Ideally, older children and teenagers would be able to shift to a medication regimen that would require two doses per day, thus eliminating the requirement of a midday dose. If this is not possible, the psychologist may be able to collaborate with medical staff, school personnel, and the child to coordinate a workable medication schedule that will fit in easily with the child's class schedule and allow for discreet trips to the nurse's office.

Grief and Bereavement. When children with HIV experience the loss of a parent, family member, or friend with HIV, they may not be given the opportunity to process their grief fully because of a family's unwillingness to discuss issues related to the loved one's death. Psychologists working in the schools may be able to provide grief-focused therapy that the child may otherwise never receive. Therapeutic sessions may involve answering the child's questions about death, allowing the child to express his/her grief, and helping the child find ways of remembering his/her loved one, such as making a scrapbook of memories or writing a poem. The psychologist should also be prepared to address the child's concerns about his/her health status and any issues that the child may have about death.

Chronic Absences. Regular school attendance is an important factor in maintaining healthy psychosocial functioning in children with HIV. Unfortunately, frequent clinic visits, hospitalizations, and acute illnesses make it difficult for children with HIV to attend school on a regular basis. Psychologists may provide assistance during extended absences by developing creative ways for the child to stay in contact with friends and teachers, and to keep up with missed schoolwork including handwritten letters or electronic mail, audiotapes, or videotapes of projects and presentations made by classmates.

Facilitation of School Re-entry. Following extended absences, psychologists should advocate for school re-entry to occur as soon as reasonably possible, because the school environment offers children a chance to participate in age-appropriate social and academic activities that are an integral part of emotional and cognitive development. Feelings of anxiety and guilt about their child's health may prevent parents from taking a stand on school attendance, but pediatric psychologists can reassure parents of the importance of engaging in routine. Depending on the child's disclosure status, psychologists can prepare staff and students for school re-entry by educating them about possible limitations and adaptations that may be necessary because of the child's health status. Areas of particular vulnerability that should be monitored include the child's ability to attend, energy level, and peer relations.

Vocational Planning. With new HAART therapies, children infected with HIV during infancy or early childhood are living into adulthood. Thus, families need to think about future vocational plans. Psychologists can help the adolescent and caregivers prepare for life after high school by developing plans for attending college or vocational school. These plans should be made with consideration of the teenager's academic needs, including the continuation of special educational services if necessary.

Pain Management. Physical symptoms and depression can influence each other in a cyclical manner. Thus, both medical and psychological variables need to be addressed when physical symptoms, such as pain, are reported (Ostrow et al., 1989). Psychologists can assist with pain management by teaching children strategies for actively coping with their pain at home and at school. More severe pain warrants referral to a physician for pain medication.

Psychopharmacology. Psychotropic medication can be of tremendous benefit for HIV-positive children and adolescents suffering from symptoms of depression and other psychological disorders. However, factors such as adverse side effects, adherence, drug interactions, and drug–illness interactions should be taken into consideration (Cohen & Jacobson, 2000). The most common needs for medication in this population are likely related to symptoms of depression and attention deficit hyperactivity disorder (ADHD). Findings suggest that selective serotonin reuptake inhibitors (SSRIs) and tricyclic antidepressants (TCAs) are both moderately effective for the management of depressive symptoms, although more side effects are associated with tricyclic antidepressants (Elliott & Roy-Byrne, 1998). Monoamine oxidase inhibitors (MAOIs) are generally not recommended for use with this population because of their potential interactions with HIV drugs and possible serious adverse side effects. Stimulants are commonly prescribed for a confirmed comorbid diagnosis of ADHD and are not known to interact with the existing HIV drugs. It should be noted that clinical trials of psychotropic medications for HIV-positive individuals have included primarily adults, while studies involving children and adolescents are sorely needed.

Prevention. Since teenagers are often faced with opportunities for engaging in high-risk behaviors, such as drug use and sex, pediatric psychologists can play an important role in the prevention of HIV by providing educational programs geared toward increasing knowledge of HIV and AIDS. Self-esteem building and assertiveness training should be an integral part of prevention programs to assist adolescents in preparing for and successfully negotiating the risky situations that can lead to transmission of HIV. Similar programs for HIV-positive students can be a valuable tool for teaching these teenagers how to decrease the risk of transmitting the virus to others, while learning techniques for communicating with peers and sexual partners about their virus.

One educational program involved teaching minority teenagers about HIV and AIDS, instructions regarding proper use of condoms, and communication and assertiveness skills for managing risky sexual encounters. Participants assigned to the treatment group demonstrated greater knowledge about contracting HIV/AIDS than did the control group. Participants also demonstrated improved assertiveness and communication skills during role-plays that involved risky sexual situations. However, no actual behavior changes were demonstrated after completion of the program (Kipke, Boyer, & Hein, 1993).

Among elementary-school children, impulsive and aggressive behaviors are particularly problematic, because these behaviors may lead to accidents involving blood and open wounds. Although there have been no known cases of HIV transmission in the school setting, the use of universal precautions is a required practice among all childcare workers, including teachers, to prevent exposure to blood or body fluids. However, contact with fluids may occur among children before any teachers become aware of the situation. Thus, psychologists may be called on to provide preventive anger management therapy for children with aggression in an effort to decrease the likelihood of high-risk situations or the spread of HIV.

Consultation

The pediatric psychologist working in the school may be the most appropriate person to take a lead role in offering consultation services regarding HIV/AIDS to schools and medical settings. Disease-related developmental challenges, educational and rehabilitation planning, school disclosure, and legal and policy issues related to the education of children with HIV are among the topics for which psychologists may be able to provide consultation services. As previously discussed, consultation services may also be offered with regard to home schooling placement and school re-entry.

The role of liaison between school and medical settings is an important one in forming a mutually beneficial relationship between the two settings, and in facilitating participation of health team members in educational planning meetings. This relationship should be established and maintained as early in the school year as possible, with consent from the parents and with extreme regard for confidentiality. Schools may benefit from information provided by the medical team via the psychologist, including health updates during a child's extended absence; and medication changes, including possible adverse side effects, timing of medication doses, and diet restrictions. Likewise, the school may offer the medical setting information regarding unexplained changes in the child's behavior or academic performance that may stem from the direct or indirect effects of HIV or the child's medications. The two institutions can collaborate in determining the frequency and content of neurodevelopmental testing and share information attained from those measures.

Teaching/Education

Educating students and school staff about HIV is a critically important role for all psychologists working in schools, regardless of the number of HIV-positive students who attend school. HIV awareness programs can help to overcome societal stigma and fear of this disease. Developmentally appropriate information regarding HIV-related issues and universal precautions should be taught in health or sexuality courses, or as part of special health seminars at several points during a child's middle school and high school experience. Education about HIV is particularly important for adolescents who may be involved in high-risk behaviors that could lead to infection with the virus. Educational programs should also be offered to all school personnel—including principals, teachers, counselors, and administrative and janitorial staff—regarding HIV confidentiality, universal precautions, and caregiver risk. All rooms should have guidelines posted providing universal precaution procedures.

Research Directions

For pediatric psychologists working with HIV-infected youth, school-based clinics offer the opportunity to reach many more children whose families may otherwise never access mental health services. Future lines of research should aim toward the development and evaluation of structured psychotherapeutic programs within school clinics.

Research has outlined specific neurocognitive deficits that are common among children and adolescents with HIV. Future research is needed to develop effective interventions targeting these areas of weakness (e.g., speech/language therapy for expressive language deficits, cognitive-behavioral therapy for attention deficits. These interventions should be made available through the school so that children can receive services on a regular basis.

Educational programs designed to teach students about various AIDS-related issues (e.g., routes of transmission, risk behaviors) show promise in terms of their ability to increase knowledge of HIV and improve attitudes toward people with the disease. Research examining such programs will need to demonstrate efficacy with regard to enduring behavioral changes. Finally, effective prevention programs need to be implemented in more schools across the country to reach the many students who could benefit from these interventions.

SUMMARY

Advances in HIV therapy have resulted in important changes in the AIDS epidemic. To date, the most significant changes for pediatric HIV disease include a lower incidence of maternal–child transmission, a lower prevalence of severely debilitating disease, a longer survival time, and an improved quality of life. Despite these advances, many children, adolescents, and families will experience the pervasive and sometimes devastating impact that HIV can have on their physical and/or psychological well-being. Comprehensive health care, including psychological services, is needed to address the direct and indirect effects of HIV and help the child and family successfully adapt to living with this disease.

Pediatric psychologists working in the school setting are in a unique position to act as a liaison with the health care team to help plan, monitor, and coordinate the comprehensive care of students with HIV infection. Psychologists can also provide a range of direct psychological services in a convenient and nonthreatening school environment to improve access to health care for youth infected with or at risk for HIV.

REFERENCES

Aleixo, L. F., Goodenow, M. M., & Sleasman, J. W. (1997). Zidovudine administered to women infected with human immunodeficiency virus type 1 and to their neonates reduces pediatric infection independent of an effect on levels of maternal virus. *Journal of Pediatrics, 130*(6), 906–914.

American Academy of Pediatrics, Committee on Pediatric AIDS. (2000). Disclosure of illness status to children and adolescents with HIV infection. *Pediatrics, 103*, 164–166.

American Academy of Pediatrics, Committee on School Health. (2001). School health centers and other integrated school health services. *Pediatrics, 107*(1), 198–201.

American Academy of Pediatrics, Task Force on Pediatric AIDS. (1989). Infants and children with acquired immunodeficiency syndrome: Placement in adoption and foster care. *Pediatrics, 83*, 609–612.

Arendt, G. (1995). Imaging methods as a diagnostic tool in neuro-AIDS. A review. *Bildgebung, 62*, 310–319.

Aronson, S. (1996). The bereavement process in children of parents with AIDS. *Psychoanalytic Study of the Child, 51*, 422–435.

Auger, I., Thomas, P., De Gruttola, V., Morse, D., Moore, D., Williams, R., Truman, B., & Lawrence, C. E. (1988). Incubation periods for pediatric AIDS patients. *Nature, 336*, 575–577.

Belman, A. L., Diamond, G., & Dickson, D. (1988). Pediatric acquired immunodeficiency syndrome: Neurologic syndromes. *American Journal of Diseases of Children, 142*, 29–35.

Belman, A. L. (1994). HIV-1 associated CNS disease in infants and children. In R. W. Price & S. W. Perry (Eds.), *HIV, AIDS and the Brain* (pp. 289–310). New York, New York: Raven Press.

Belman, A. L., Diamond, G., Dickson, D., Horoupian, D., Llena, J., Lantos, G., & Rubinstein, A. (1988). Pediatric acquired immunodeficiency syndrome: neurologic syndromes. *American Journal of Diseases of Children, 142*(1), 29–35.

Belzer, M., Fuchs, D., Luftman, G., & Tucker, D. (1999). Antiretroviral adherence issues among HIV-positive adolescents and young adults. *Journal of Adolescent Health, 25*(5), 316–319.

Berger, J. R., Scott, G., Albrecht, J., Belman, A. L., Tornatore, C., & Major, E. O. (1992). Progressive multifocal leukoencephalopathy in HIV-1 infected children. *AIDS, 6*, 837–841.

Biglan, A., Metzler, C. W., Wirt, R., Ary, D., Noell, J., Ochs, L., French, C., & Hood, D. (1990). Social and behavioral factors associated with high-risk sexual behavior among adolescents. *Journal of Behavioral Medicine, 13*(3), 245–261.

Blanche, S., Newell, M., Mayaux, M., Dunn, D., Teglas, J., Rouzioux, C., & Peckham, C. (1997). Morbidity and mortality in European children vertically infected by HIV-1. *Journal of Acquired Immune Deficiency Syndromes and Human Retrovirology, 14*, 442–450.

Blanche, S., Tardieu, M., & Duliege, A. (1990). Longitudinal study of 94 symptomatic infants with perinatally acquired human immunodeficiency virus infection. Evidence for a bimodal expression of clinical and biological symptoms. *American Journal of Diseases of Children, 144*, 1210–1215.

Blanchette, N., Smith, M. L., King, S., Fernandes-Penney, A., & Read, S. (2002). Cognitive development in school-age children with vertically transmitted HIV infection. *Developmental Neuropsychology, 2*, 223–241.

Boland, M. G. (2000). Caring for the child and family with HIV disease. *Pediatric Clinics of North America, 47*(1), 189–202.

Boivin, M., Green, S., Davies, A., Giordani, B., Mokili, J., & Cutting, W. (1995). A preliminary evaluation of the cognitive and motor effects of pediatric HIV infection in Zairian children. *Health Psychology, 14*(1), 13–21.

Bose, S., Moss, H., Brouwers, P., Pizzo, P., & Lorion, R. (1994). Psychologic adjustment of human immunodeficiency virus-infected school-age children. *Developmental and Behavioral Pediatrics, 15*(3), S26–S33.

Brady, M. T., McGrath, N., Brouwers, P., Gelber, R., Fowler, M. G., Yogev, R., Hutton, N., Bryson, Y. J., Metchell, C. D., Fikrig, S., Borkowsky, W., Jimenez, E., McSherry, G., Rubinstein, A., Wilfert, C. M., McIntosh, K., Elkins, M. M., Weintrub, P. S., & Pediatric AIDS Clinical Trials Group. (1996). Randomized study of the tolerance and efficacy of high-versus-low dose zidovudine in human immunodeficiency virus-infected children with mild to moderate symptoms (AIDS clinical trials group 128). *The Journal of Infectious Diseases, 173*, 1097–1106.

Brivio, L., Tornaghi, R., Musetti, L., Marchisio, P., & Principi, N. (1991). Improvement of auditory brainstem responses after treatment with zidovudine in a child with AIDS. *Pediatric Neurology, 7*, 53–55.

Brouwers, P., Belman, A. L., & Epstein, L. (1994). Central nervous system involvement: Manifestations, evaluation, and pathogenesis. In P. A. Pizzo & C. M. Wilfert (Eds.), *Pediatric AIDS: The challenge of HIV infection in infants, children and adolescents* (2nd ed., pp. 433–455). Baltimore: Williams & Wilkins.

Brouwers, P., DeCarli, C., Civitello, L., Moss, H., Wolters, P., & Pizzo, P. (1995, January). Correlation between computed tomographic brain scan abnormalities and neuropsychological function in children with symptomatic human immunodeficiency virus disease. *Archives of Neurology, 52*, 39–44.

Brouwers, P., Moss, H., Wolters, P., Eddy, J., Balis, F., Poplack, D., & Pizzo, P. A. (1990). Effect of continuous-infusion zidovudine therapy on neuropsychologic functioning in children with symptomatic human immunodeficiency virus infection. *The Journal of Pediatrics, 117*(6), 980–985.

Brouwers, P., Wolters, P., & Civitello, L. (1998). *Central nervous system manifestations and assessment* (3rd ed.). Baltimore: Williams & Wilkins.

Brown, L. K., Reynolds, L. A., & Lourie, K. J. (1997). A pilot HIV prevention program for adolescents in a psychiatric hospital. *Psychiatric Services, 48*(4), 531–533.

Buseyne, F., Janvier, G., Teglas, J. P., Ivanoff, S., Burgard, M., Bui, E., Mayaux, M. J., Blanche, S., Rouzioux, C., Riviere, Y. (1998). Impact of heterozygosity for the chemokine receptor CCr5 32-bp-deleted allele on plasma viral load and CD4 T lymphocytes in perinatally human immunodeficiency virus-infected children at 8 years of age. *The Journal of Infectious Diseases, 178*, 1019–1023.

Butler, K. M., Husson, R. N., Balis, F. M., Brouwers, P., Eddy, J., El-Amn, D., Gress, J., Hawkins, M., Jarosinski, P., Moss, H., Poplack, D., Sanacroce, S., Venzon, D., Wiener, L., Wolters, P., & Pizzo, P. A. (1991). Dideoxyinosine in children with symptomatic human immunodeficiency virus infection. *New England Journal of Medicine, 324*(3), 137–144.

Campbell, T. (1997). A review of the psychological effects of vertically acquired HIV infection in infants and children. *British Journal of Health and Psychology, 2*, 1–13.

Center for Disease Control and Prevention. [CDC]. (2002). *HIV/AIDS surveillance report* (Vol. 13, pp. 1–45). Atlanta, GA:

Chamberlain, M. C., Nichols, S. L., & Chase, C. H. (1991). Pediatric AIDS: Comparative cranial MRI and CT scans. *Pediatric Neurology, 7*, 357–362.

Chase, C., Vibbert, M., Pelton, S., Coulter, D., & Cabral, H. (1995, August). Early neurodevelopmental growth in children with vertically transmitted human immunodeficiency virus infection. *Archives of Pediatric Adolescent Medicine, 149*, 850–855.

Chase, C., Ware, J., Hittelman, J., Blasini, I., Smith, R., Llorente, A., Anisfeld, E., Diaz, C., Fowler, M. G., Moye, J., & Kaligh, L. I. (2000). Early cognitive and motor development among infants born to women infected with human immunodeficiency virus. Women and Infants Transmission Study Group. *Pediatrics, 106*(2), E25.

The *Italian Registry* for HIV Infection in Children (1994). Features of children perinatally infected with HIV-1 surviving longer than 5 years. *Lancet, 343*, 191–195.

Civitello, L., Brouwers, P., DeCarli, C., & Pizzo, P. (1994). Calcification of the basal ganglia in children with HIV infection. *Annals of Neurology, 36*, 506.

Civitello, L., Wolters, P., Serchuck, L., Wood, L., Janelevich, S., Yarchoan, R., & Brouwers, P. (2000). Long-term effect of protease inhibitors on neuropsychological function and neuroimaging in pediatric HIV disease. *Annals of Neurology, 48*, 513.

Civitello, L. A., Brouwers, P., & Pizzo, P. A. (1993). Neurological and neuropsychological manifestations in 120 children with symptomatic human immunodeficiency virus infection [Abstract]. *Annals of Neurology, 34*, 481.

Cohen, J., Reddington, C., Jacobs, D., Meade, R., Picard, D., Singleton, K., Smith, D., Caldwell, M. B., DeMaria, A., & Hsu, H. W. (1997). School-related issues among HIV-infected children. *Pediatrics, 100*(1), e8.

Cohen, M. A. A., & Jacobson, J. M. (2000). Maximizing life's potentials in AIDS: A psychopharmacologic update. *General Hospital Psychiatry, 22*, 375–388.

Cohen, S. E., Mundy, T., Kaarassik, B., Lieb, L., Ludwig, D. D., & Ward, J. (1991). Neuropsychological functioning in children with HIV-1 infection through neonatal blood transfusion. *Pediatrics, 88*(1), 58–68.

Conners, C. K. (1989). *Conners' rating scales: Conners' Teacher Rating Scales and Conners' Parent Rating Scales.* Los Angeles, CA: Western Psychological Services.

Connor, E. M., Sperling, R. S., Gelber, R., Kiselev, P., Scott, G., O'Sullivan, M. J., VanDyke, R., Bey, M., Shearer, W., Jacobson, R. L., Jiminez, E., O'Neill, E., Bazin, B., Delfraisy, J. F., Culnane, M., Coombs, R., Elkins, M., Moye, J., Stratton, P., & Balsley, J. (1994). Reduction of maternal-infant transmission of human immunodeficiency virus type 1 with zidovudine treatment. *New England Journal of Medicine, 331*(18), 1173–1180.

Cooper, E. R., Charurat, M., Burns, D. N., Blattner, W., & Hoff, R. (2000). Trends in antiretroviral therapy and mother-infant transmission of HIV. The Women and Infants Transmission Study Group. *Journal of Acquired Immune Deficiency Syndrome, 24*, 45–47.

Cooper, E. R., Hanson, C., Diaz, C., Mendez, H., Abboud, R., Nugent, R., Pitt, J., Rich, K., Rodriguez, E. M., & Smeriglio, V. (1998). Encephalopathy and progression of human immunodeficiency virus disease in a cohort of children with perinatally acquired human immunodeficiency virus infection. Women and Infants Transmission Study Group. *Journal of Pediatrics, 132*, 808–812.

Cote, T., Biggar, R., & Dannenberg, A. (1992). Risk of suicide among persons with AIDS. *JAMA, 268*(15), 2066–2068.

Davis, L., Hjelle, B. L., Miller, V. E., Palmer, C. L., Llewellyn, A. L., Merlin, T. L., Young, S. A., Mills, R. G., Wachsman, W., & Wiley, C. A. (1992). Early viral brain invasion in iatrogenic human immunodeficiency virus infection. *Neurology, 42*, 1736–2739.

DeCarli, C., Civitello, L. A., Brouwers, P., & Pizzo, P. A. (1993). The prevalence of computed tomographic abnormalities of the cerebrum in 100 consecutive children symptomatic with the human immune deficiency virus. *Annals of Neurology, 34*(2), 198–205.

Diaz, C., Hanson, C., Cooper, E. R., Read, J. S., Watson, J., Mendez, H. A., Pitt, J., Rich, K., Smeriglio, V., & Lew, J. F. (1998). Disease progression in a cohort of infants with vertically acquired HIV infection observed from birth: The Women and Infants Transmission Study (WITS). *Journal of Acquired Immune Deficiency Syndrome Human Retrovirology, 18*(3), 221–228.

Dickson, D. W., Llena, J. F., & Weidenheim, K. M. (1990). Central nervous system pathology in children with AIDS and focal neurologic signs – stroke and lymphoma. In P. Kozlowski (Ed.), *Brain behavior and pediatric AIDS* (pp. 147–157). Basel, Switzerland: Karger.

Douglas, S. D. (1994). Immunological and virological clues for mother-to-child transmission of HIV-1 and HIV-2. *Journal of the American Medical Association, 272*(6), 487–488.

Elliott, A. J., & Roy-Byrne, P. P. (1998). Major depressive disorder and HIV-1 infection: A review of treatment trials. *Seminars on Clinical Neuropsychiatry, 3*(2), 137–150.

England, J. A., Baker, C. J., Raskino, C., McKinney, R., Lifschitz, M., Petrie, B., Fowler, M. G., Connor, J., Mendez, H., O'Donnell, K., Wara, D., & the AIDS Clinical Trials Group Protocol 152 Study Team. (1996). Clinical and laboratory characteristics of a large cohort of symptomatic, human immunodeficiency virus-infected infants and children. *Pediatric Infectious Disease Journal, 15*, 1025–1036.

Enting, R. H., Hoetelmans, R. M. W., Lange, J. M. A., Burger, D. M., Beijnen, J. H., Portegies, P. (1998). Antiretroviral drugs and the central nervous system. *AIDS, 12*, 1941–1955.

Epstein, L. G. (1986). Neurologic manifestations of HIV infection in children. *Pediatrics, 78*, 678–687.

Epstein, L. G., & Gelbard, H. A. (1999). HIV-1–induced neuronal injury in the developing brain. *Journal of Leukocyte Biology, 65*(4), 453–457.

Epstein, L. G., & Gendelman, H. E. (1993). Human immunodeficiency virus type 1 infection of the nervous system: Pathogenetic mechanisms. *Annals of Neurology, 33*(5), 429–436.

Fanos, J., & Wiener, L. (1994). Tomorrow's survivors: Siblings of human immunodeficiency virus-infected children. *Journal of Developmental & Behavioral Pediatrics, 15*(3), S43–S48.

Forehand, R., Pelton, J., Chance, M., Armistead, L., Morse, E., Morse, P. S., & Stock, M. (1999). Orphans of the AIDS epidemic in the United States: Transition-related characteristics and psychosocial adjustment at 6 months after mother's death. *AIDS Care, 11*, 715–722.

Frager, G. (1997). Palliative and terminal care of children. *Child and Adolescent Psychiatric Clinics of North America, 6*, 889–909.

Friedland, G., & Klein, R. (1987). Transmission of the human immunodeficiency virus. *New England Journal of Medicine, 317*(18), 1125–1135.

Funck-Brentano, I., Costagliola, D., Seibel, N., Straub, E., Tardieu, M., & Blanche, S. (1997, October). Patterns of disclosure and perceptions of the human immunodeficiency virus in infected elementary school-age children. *Archives of Pediatric and Adolescent Medicine, 151*, 978–985.

Galli, L., de Martino, M., Tovo, P., Gabiano, C., Zappa, M., Giaquinto, C., Tulisso, S., Vierucci, A., Guerra, M., Marchisio, P., Plebani, A., Zuccotti, G. V., Martino, A., Dallacasa, P., Stegagno, M., & the Italian Register for HIV Infection in Children (1995). Onset of clinical signs in children with HIV-1 perinatal infection. *AIDS, 9*, 455–461.

Garcia, P. M., Kalish, L. A., Pitt, J., Minkoff, H., Quinn, T. C., Burchett, S. K., Kornegay, J., Jackson, B., Moye, J., Hanson, C., Zorrilla, C., & Lew, J. F. (1999). Maternal levels of plasma human immunodeficiency virus type 1 RNA and the risk of perinatal transmission. Women and Infants Transmission Study Group. *New England Journal of Medicine, 341*, 394–402.

Gewirtz, A., & Gossart-Walker, S. (2000). Home-based treatment for children and families affected by HIV and AIDS. *Child and Adolescent Psychiatric Clinics of North America, 9*(2), 313–330.

Gillman, R. R., & Newman, B. S. (1996). Psychosocial concerns and strengths of women with HIV infection: An empirical study. *Family Society: Journal of Contemporary Human Services, 2*, 131–141.

Harper, D. C. (1991). Paradigms for investigating rehabilitation and adaptation to childhood disability and chronic illness. *Journal of Pediatric Psychology, 16*(5), 533–542.

Havens, J., Whitaker, A., Feldman, J., & Ehrhardt, A. (1994). Psychiatric morbidity in school-age children with congenital human immunodeficiency virus infection: A pilot study. *Developmental and Behavioral Pediatrics, 15*(3), S18–S25.

HIV/AIDS Treatment Information Service [HIVATIS]. (2001). Guidelines for the use of antiretroviral agents in pediatric HIV infection [On-line]. Available: http://www.hivatis.org/guidelines/Pediatric/Aug08_01/pedaug08_01.pdf [2001]

Hooper, S., Whitt, J. K., Tennison, M., Burchinal, M., Gold, S., & Hall, C. (1993, May). Behavioral adaptation to human immunodeficiency virus-seropositive status in children and adolescents with hemophilia. *American Journal of Diseases of Children, 147*, 541–545.

John, G. C., Rousseau, C., Dong, T., Rowland-Jones, S., Nduati, R., Mbori-Ngacha, D., Rostron, T., Kreiss, J. K., Richardson, B. A., Overbaugh, J. (2000). Maternal SDF-1 3' A Polymorphism is associated with increased perinatal human immunodeficiency virus type 1 transmission. *Journal of Virology, 74*, 5736–5739.

Judd, F. K., & Mijch, A. M. (1996). Depressive symptoms in patients with HIV infection. *Australian New Zealand Journal of Psychiatry, 30*(1), 104–109.

Just, J., Abrams, E., Louie, L., Urbano, R., Wara, D., Nicholas, S., Stein, Z., & King, M. C. (1995). Influence of host genotype on progression to acquired immunodeficiency syndrome among children infected with human immunodeficiency virus type 1. *The Journal of Pediatrics, 127*, 544–549.

Kipke, M. D., Boyer, C., & Hein, K. (1993). An evaluation of an AIDS risk reduction education and skills training (ARREST) program. *Journal of Adolescent Health, 14*(7), 533–539.

Klaas, P., Wolters, P. L., Martin, S., Civitello, L., & Zeichner, S. (2002). Verbal learning and memory in children with HIV [Abstract]. *Journal of the International Neuropsychological Society, 8*, 187.

Krasinski, K. (1994). Bacterial infections. In P. A. Pizzo & C. M. Wilfert (Eds.), *Pediatric AIDS* (2nd ed., pp. 241–253). Baltimore: Williams & Wilkins.

Landesman, S. H., Kalish, L. A., Burns, D. N., Minkoff, H., Fox, H. E., Zorrilla, C., Garcia, P., Fowler, M. G., Mofenson, L., Tuornala, R. (1996). Obstetrical factors and the transmission of human immunodeficiency virus type 1 from mother to child. The Women and Infants Transmission Study. [comment] *New England Journal of Medicine, 334*(25):1617–1623.

Ledlie, S. (1999). Diagnosis disclosure by family caregivers to children who have perinatally acquired HIV disease: When the time comes. *Nursing Research, 48*(3), 141–149.

Lesar, S., & Meldonado, Y. A. (1997). The impact of children with HIV infection on the family system. *Family Society: Journal of Contemporary Human Services, 3*, 272–279.

Levenson, R., Mellins, C., Zawadzki, R., Kairam, R., & Stein, Z. (1992). Cognitive assessment of human immunodeficiency virus-exposed children. *American Journal of Diseases in Children, 146*, 1479–1483.

Lewis, S., Haiken, H., & Hoyt, L. (1994). Living beyond the odds: A psychosocial perspective on long-term survivors of pediatric human immunodeficiency virus infection. *Developmental and Behavioral Pediatrics, 15*(3), S12–S17.

Lindsey, J. C., Hughes, M. D., McKinney, R. E., Cowles, M. K., Englund, J. A., Baker, C. J., Burchett, S. K., Kline, M. W., Kovacs, A., & Moye, J. (2000). Treatment-mediated changes in human immunodeficiency virus (HIV) Type I RNA and CD4 cell counts as predictors of weight growth failure, cognitive decline, and survival in HIV-infected children. *The Journal of Infectious Diseases, 182*, 1385–1393.

Lipson, M. (1994). Disclosure of diagnosis to children with human immunodeficiency virus or acquired immunodeficiency syndrome. *Developmental and Behavioral Pediatrics, 15*(3), S61–S65.

Lipton, S. A. (1992). Models of neuronal injury in AIDS: Another role for the NMDA receptor? *Trends in Neuroscience, 15*, 75–79.

Lobato, M. N., Caldwell, M. B., Ng, P., & Oxtoby, M. J. (1995). Encephalopathy in children with perinatally acquired human immunodeficiency virus infection. *The Journal of Pediatrics, 126*(5 – Part I), 710–715.

Loveland, K. A., Stehbens, J., Contant, C., Bordeaux, J., Sirois, P., Bell, T., & Hill, S. (1994). Hemophilia growth and development study: Baseline neurodevelopmental findings. *Journal of Pediatric Psychology,* (19), 223–239.

Loveland, K., Stehbens, J., Mahoney, E., Sirois, P., Nichols, S., Bordeaux, J., Watkins, J., Amodei, N., Hill, S. D., & Donfield, S. M. (2000). Declining immune function in children and adolescents with hemophilia and HIV infection: effects on neuropsychological performance. *Journal of Pediatric Psychology, 25*(5), 309–322.

Lyman, W. D., Kress, Y., Kure, K., Rashbaum, W. K., Rubinstein, A., & Soeiro, R. (1990). Detection of HIV in fetal central nervous system tissue. *AIDS, 4*(9), 917–920.

Martin, S., Wolters, P. L., Klaas, P., Perez, L., Moss, H. A., & Wood, L. V. (2001). Relationship between family coping styles and children's medical and psychological functioning in pediatric HIV disease. Paper presented at the NIMH Conference on the Role of Families in Preventing and Adapting to HIV/AIDS, Los Angeles, CA.

Mayaux, M. J., Blanche, S., Rouzioux, C., LeChenadec, J., Chambrin, V., Firtion, G., Allemon, M., Vilmer, E., Vigneron, N. C., Tricoire, J., Guillot, F., Courpotin, C., & the French Pediatric HIV Infection Study Group (1995). Maternal factors associated with perinatal HIV-1 transmission: The French cohort study: 7 years of follow-up observation. *Journal of Acquired Immune Deficiency Syndromes and Human Retrovirology, 8*, 188–194.

Mayaux, M. J., Burgard, M., Teglas, J.-P., Cottalorda, J., Krivine, A., Simon, F., Puel, J., Tamalet, C., Dormont, D., Masquelier, B., Doussin, A., Rouzioux, C., & Blanche, S. (1996). Neonatal characteristics in rapidly progressive perinatally acquired HIV-1 disease. *JAMA, 275*(8), 606–610.

McHarney-Brown, C., & Kaufman, A. (1991). Comparison of adolescent health care provided at a school-based clinic and at the hospital-based pediatric clinic. *Southern Medical Journal, 84*, 1340–1342.

McKinney, R. E., Johnson, G. M., Stanley, K., Yong, F. H., Keller, A., O'Donnell, K. J., Brouwers, P., Mitchell, W. G., Yogev, R., Wara, D. W., Wiznia, A., Mofenson, L., McNamara, J., & Spector, S. A. (1998). A randomized study of combined zidovudine-lamivudine versus didanosine monotherapy in children with symptomatic therapy-naive HIV-1 infection. The Pediatric AIDS Clinical Trials Group Protocol 300 Study Team. *Journal of Pediatrics, 133*(4), 500–508.

Mellins, C. A., & Ehrhardt, A. A. (1994). Families affected by pediatric AIDS: Sources of stress and coping. *Developmental and Behavioral Pediatrics, 15*, S54–S60.

Mellins, C. A., Smith, R., O'Driscoll, P., Magder, L., Chase, C., Blasini, I., Llorente, A., Matzen, E., & Moye, J. (2003). High rates of behavioral problems in perinatally HIV-infected children are not linked to HIV disease. *Pediatrics, 111*(2), 384–393.

Mintz, M. (1994). Clinical comparison of adult and pediatric NeuroAIDS. *Advances in Neuroimmunology, 4*, 207–221.

Misrahi, M., Teglas, J. P., N'Go, N., Burgard, M., Mayaux, M. J., Rouzioux, C., Delfraissy, J. F., Blanche, S. (1998). CCR5 chemokine receptor variant in HIV-1 mother-to-child transmission and disease progression in children. *Journal of the American Medical Association, 279*, 277–280.

Morrison, M. F., Petitto, J. M., Have, T. T., Gettes, D. R., Chiappini, M. S., Weber, A. L., Brinker-Spence, P., Bauer, R. M., Douglas, S. D., & Evans, D. L. (2002). Depressive and anxiety disorders in women with HIV infection. *American Journal of Psychiatry, 159*(5), 789–796.

Moss, H., Bose, S., Wolters, P., & Brouwers, P. (1998). A preliminary study of factors associated with psychological adjustment and disease course in school-age children infected with the human immunodeficiency virus. *Journal of Developmental-Behavioral Pediatrics, 19*(1), 18–25.

Moss, H., Brouwers, P., Wolters, P. L., Wiener, L., Hersh, S. P., & Pizzo, P. A. (1994). The development of a Q sort behavior rating procedure for pediatric HIV patients. *Journal of Pediatric Psychology, 20*, 79–90.

Moss, H. A., & Wolters, P. L. (1996). Impairment of expressive behavior in pediatric HIV-infected patients with evidence of CNS disease. *Journal of Pediatric Psychology, 21*(3), 379–400.

Moss, H. A., Wolters, P. L., Brouwers, P., & Perez, L. (2000). *Parental report on maladaptive behavior in children with HIV infection and in their uninfected siblings.* Unpublished manuscript.

Moss, H. A., Wolters, P. L., Brouwers, P., Hendricks, M. L., & Pizzo, P. A. (1996). Impairment of expressive behavior in pediatric HIV-infected patients with evidence of CNS disease. *Journal of Pediatric Psychology, 21*(3), 379–400.

Moye, J., Jr., Rich, K. C., Kalish, L. A., Sheon, A. R., Diaz, C., Cooper, E. R., Pitt, J., & Handelsman, E. (1996). Natural history of somatic growth in infants born to women infected by human immunodeficiency virus. Women and Infants Transmission Study Group. *Journal of Pediatrics, 128*(1), 58–69.

Mueller, B. U., Nelson, R. P., Sleasman, J., Zuckerman, J., Heath-Chiozzi, M., Steinberg, S., Katz, T. K., Higham, C., Aker, D., Edgerly, M., Jarosinski, P., Serchuck, L., Whitcup, S. M., Pizzuit, D., & Pizzo, P. A. (1998a). A phase I/II study of the protease inhibitor Ritonavir in children with HIV infection. *Pediatrics, 101*(3), 335–343.

Mueller, B. U., Sleasman, J., Nelson, R. P., Smith, S., Deutsch, P. J., Ju, W., Steinberg, S. M., Balis, F. M., Jaronsinski, P. F., Brouwers, P., Mistry, G., Winchell, G., Zwerski, S., Sei, S., Wood, L. V., Zeichner, S., & Pizzo, P. A. (1998b). A phase I/II study of the protease inhibitor Indinavir in children with HIV infection. *Pediatrics, 102*(1), 101–109.

Murrain, M., & Barker, T. (1997). Investigating the relationship between economic status and HIV risk. *Journal of Healthcare for the Poor & Underserved, 8*(4), 416–423.

National Association for the State Boards of Education. (2001). *Someone at school has AIDS* Alexandria, VA: Nasbe Publishing.

Nichols, S., Mahoney, E., Sirois, P., Bordeaux, J., Stehbens, J., Loveland, K., Amodei, N. (2000). HIV-associated changes in adaptive, emotional, and behavioral functioning in children and adolescents with hemophilia: Results from the Hemophilia Growth and Development Study. *Journal of Pediatric Psychology, 25*(8), 545–556.

Oleske, J. M., & Czarniecki, L. (1999). Continuum of palliative care: lessons from caring for children infected with HIV-1. *Lancet, 354*(9186), 1287–1291.

Ostrow, D. G., Monjan, A., Joseph, J., VanRaden, M., Fox, R., Kingsley, L., Dudley, J., & Phair, J. (1989). HIV-related symptoms and psychological functioning in a cohort of homosexual men. *American Journal of Psychiatry, 146*(6), 737–742.

Pao, M., Lyon, M., D'Angelo, L., Schuman, W., Tipnis, T., & Mrazek, D. (2000, March). Psychiatric diagnoses in adolescents seropositive for the human immunodeficiency virus. *Archives of Pediatric Adolescent Medicine, 154,* 240–244.

Parks, R. A., & Danoff, J. V. (1999). Motor performance changes in children testing positive for HIV over 2 years. *The American Journal of Occupational Therapy, 53*(5), 524–528.

Parrish, J. M. (1986). Parent compliance with medical and behavioral recommendations. In J. M. Parrish, N. Krasnegor, J. Arasteh, & M. Cataldo (Eds.), *Child health behavior: a behavioral pediatrics* (pp. 453–501). New York: Wiley.

Paterson, D. L., Swindells, S., Mohr, J., Brester, M., Vergis, E. N., Squier, C., Wagener, M. M., & Singh, N. (2000). Adherence to protease inhibitor therapy and outcomes in patients with HIV infection. *Annals of Internal Medicine, 133*, 21–30.

Pavlakis, S., Dongfeng, L., Frank, Y., Bakshi, S., Pahwa, S., Barnett, T., Porricolo, M., Gould, R., Nozyce, M., & Hyman, R. (1995). Magnetic resonance spectroscopy in childhood AIDS encephalopathy. *Pediatric Neurology, 12*(4), 277–282.

Pearson, D. A., McGrath, N. M., Nozyce, M., Nichols, S. L., Raskino, C., Brouwers, P., Lifschitz, M. C., Baker, C. J., & Englund, J. A. (2000). Predicting HIV disease progression in children using measures of neuropsychological and neurological functioning. Pediatric AIDS clinical trials 152 study team. *Pediatrics, 106*(6), E76.

Perez, L. A., Wolters, P. L., Moss, H. A., Civitello, L. A., & Brouwers, P. (1998). Verbal learning and memory in children with HIV infection [Abstract]. *Journal of Neurovirology, 4*, 362.

Pitt, J., Brambilla, D., Reichelderfer, P., Landay, A., McIntosh, K., Burns, D., Hillyer, G. V., Mendez, H., & Fowler, M. G. (1997). Maternal immunologic and virologic risk factors for infant human immunodeficiency virus type 1 infection: Findings from the Women and Infants Transmission Study. *Journal of Infectious Diseases, 175*, 567–575.

Pizzo, P., Butler, K., Balis, F., Brouwers, P., Hawkins, M., Eddy, J., Einloth, M., Falloon, J., Husson, R., Jaronski, P., Gress, J., Moss, H., Poplack, D., Santacroce, S., & Wiener, L. (1990). Dideoxycytidine alone and in alternating schedule with zidovudine in children with symptomatic human immunodeficiency virus infection. *The Journal of Pediatrics, 117*, 799–808.

Pizzo, P., Eddy, J., Falloon, J., Balis, F., Murphy, R., Moss, H., Wolters, P., Brouwers, P., Jaronsinski, P., Rubin, M., Broder, S., Yarchoan, R., Brunetti, A., Maha, M., Nusinoff-Lehrman, S., & Poplack, D. (1988). Effect of continuous intravenous infusion of zidovudine (AZT) in children with symptomatic HIV infection. *The New England Journal of Medicine, 319*(14), 889–896.

Pressman, H. (1992). Communication disorders and dysphagia in pediatric AIDS. *ASHA, 34*, 45–47.

Prinstein, M., Boergers, J., Spirito, A., Little, T., & Grapentine, W. L. (2000). Peer functioning, family dysfunction, and psychological symptoms in a risk factor model for adolescent inpatients' suicidal ideation severity. *Journal of Clinical Child Psychology, 29*(3), 392–405.

Reddington, C., Cohen, J., Baldillo, A., Toye, M., Smith, D., Kneut, C., DeMaria, A., Bertolli, J., & Hsu, H. W. (2000). Adherence to medication regimens among children with human immunodeficiency virus infection. *Pediatric Infectious Diseases, 19*(12), 1148–1153.

Rehm, R., & Franck, L. (2000). Long-term goals and normalization strategies of children and families affected by HIV/AIDS. *Advanced Nursing Science, 23*(1), 69–82.

Remafedi, G. (1993). The impact of training on school professionals' knowledge, beliefs, and behaviors regarding HIV/AIDS and adolescent homosexuality. *Journal of School Health, 63*, 153–157.

Remafedi, G. (1998). The University of Minnesota Youth and AIDS Projects' Adolescent Early Intervention Program. *Journal of Adolescent Health, 23S*, 115–121.

Rotheram-Borus, M. J., Robin, L., Reid, H. M., & Draimin, B. (1998). Parent-adolescent conflict and stress when parents are living with AIDS. *Family Process, 37*, 83–94.

Schable, B., Diaz, T., Chu, S. Y., Caldwell, M. B., Conti, L., Alston, O. M., Sorvillo, F., Checko, P. J., Hermann, P., Davidson, A. J. (1995). Who are the primary caretakers of children born to HIV-infected mothers? Results from a multistate surveillance project. *Pediatrics, 95*(4), 511–515.

Sexson, S., & Madan-Swain, A. (1993). School reentry for the child with chronic illness. *Journal of Learning Disabilities, 26*(2), 115–125.

Sei, S., Boler, A. M., Nguyen, G. T., Stewart, S. K., Yang, Q., Edgerly, M., Wood, L. V., Brouwers, P., & Venzon, D. J. (2001). Protective effect of CCR5 delta32 heterozygosity is restricted by SDF-1 genotype in children with HIV-1 infection. *AIDS, 15*, 1343–1352.

Shearer, W. T., Quinn, T. C., LaRussa, P., Lew, J. F., Mofenson, L., Almy, S., Rich, K., Handelsman, E., Diaz, C., Pagano, M., Smeriglio, V., & Kalish, L. A. (1997). Viral load and disease progression in infants infected with human immunodeficiency virus type 1. Women and Infants Transmission Study Group. *New England Journal of Medicine, 336*(19), 1337–1342.

Sherman, B., Bonanno, G., Wiener, L., & Battles, H. (2000). When children tell their friends they have AIDS: Possible consequences for psychological well-being and disease progression. *Psychosomatic Medicine, 62*(2), 238–247.

Sherwen, L., & Boland, M. (1994). Overview of psychosocial research concerning pediatric human immunodeficiency virus infection. *Developmental and Behavioral Pediatrics, 15*(3), S5–S11.

Sherwen, L., Boland, M., & Gilchrist, M. (1993). Stress, coping and perception of child vulnerability in female caretakers of HIV infected children: A preliminary report. *Pediatric AIDS and HIV Infection: Fetus to Adolescent, 4*, 358–366.

Siegel, D., DiClemente, R., Durbin, M., Krasnovsky, F., & Saliba, P. (1995). Change in junior high school students' AIDS-related knowledge, misconceptions, attitudes, and HIV-preventive behaviors: Effects of a school-based intervention. *AIDS Education Prevention, 7*(6), 534–543.

Siegel, K., & Gorey, E. (1994). Childhood bereavement due to parental death from acquired immunodeficiency syndrome. *Developmental and Behavioral Pediatrics, 15*(3), S66–S70.

Simpson, B. J., Shapiro, E. D., & Andiman, W. A. (2000). Prospective cohort study of children born to human immunodeficiency virus-infected mothers, 1985 through 1997: Trends in the risk of vertical transmission, mortality and acquired immunodeficiency syndrome indicator diseases in the era before highly active antiretroviral therapy. *Pediatric Infectious Disease Journal, 19*(7), 618–624.

Singh, N., Squier, C., Sivek, C., Wagener, M., Nguyen, M., & Yu, V. (1996). Determinants of compliance with antiretroviral therapy in patients with human immunodeficiency virus: Prospective assessment with implications for enhancing compliance. *AIDS Care, 8*(3), 261–269.

Sirois, P., & Hill, S. D. (1993). Developmental change associated with human immunodeficiency virus infection in school-age children with hemohilia. *Developmental Neuropsychology, 9*, 177–197.

Smith, M. L., Minden, D., Netley, C., Read, S., King, S., & Blanchette, V. (1997). Longitudinal investigation of neuropsychological functioning in children and adolescents with hemophilia and HIV infection. *Devlopmental Neuropsychology, 13*(1), 69–85.

Stolar, A., & Fernandez, F. (1997). Psychiatric perspective of pediatric human immunodeficiency virus infection. *Southern Medical Journal, 90*(10), 1007–1016.

Suwanwela, N., Phanuphak, P., Phanthumchinda, K., Suwanwela, N., Tantivatana, J., Ruxrungtham, K., Suttipan, J., Wangsuphachart, S., & Hanvanich, M. (2000). Magnetic resonance spectroscopy of the brain in neurologically asymptomatic HIV-infected patients. *Magnetic Resonance Imaging, 18*, 859–865.

Swindells, S., Zheng, J., & Gendelman, H. E. (1999). HIV-associated dementia: New insights into disease pathogenesis and therapeutic interventions. *AIDS Patient Care & STDs, 13*(3), 153–163.

Taketomo, C. K., Hodding, J. H., & Kraus, D. M. (1999). *Pediatric dosage handbook: Including neonatal dosing, drug administration & extemporaneous preparations* (6th ed.). Cleveland, OH: Lexi-Comp.

Tardieu, M., & Boutet, A. (2002). HIV-1 and the Central Nervous System, *Current Topics in Microbiology and Immunology* (Vol. 265, pp. 183–195). Berlin: Springer Verlag.

Tardieu, M., Chenadec, J. L., Persoz, A., Meyer, L., Blanche, S., & Mayaux, M. J. (2000). HIV-1-related encephalopathy in infants compared with children and adults. *Neurology, 54*, 1089–1095.

Tardieu, M., Mayaux, M. J., Seibel, N., Funck-Brentano, I., Straub, E., Teglas, J., & Blanche, S. (1995). Cognitive assessment of school-age children infected with maternally transmitted human immunodeficiency virus type 1. *Pediatrics, 126*(3), 375–379.

Tersmette, M., Lange, J. M., de Goede, R. E., de Wolf, F., Eeftink-Schattenkerk, J. K., Schellekens, P. T., Coutinho, R. A., Huisman, J. G., Goudsmit, J., & Miedema, F. (1989). Association between biological properties of human immunodeficiency virus variants and risk for AIDS and AIDS mortality. *Lancet, 1*(8645), 983–985.

Thompson, R. J., & Gustafson, K. F. (1996). *Adaptation to chronic childhood illness.* Paper presented at the American Psychological Association, Washington, DC.

Tornatore, C., Meyers, K., Atwood, W., Conant, K., & Major, E. O. (1994). Temporal patterns of human immunodeficiency virus type 1 transcripts in human fetal astrocytes. *Journal of Virology, 68*, 93–102.

Tovo, P. A., de Martino, M., & Gabiano, C. (1992). Prognostic factors and survival in children with perinatal HIV-1 infection. *Lancet, 339*, 1249–1253.

Vertex. (2001). Complete prescribing information for Agenerase capsules (Amprenavir) [On-line]. Available: http://www.atom-by-atom.com

Watkins, J. M., Cool, V. A., Usner, D., Stehbens, J. A., Nichols, S., Loveland, K. A., Bordeaux, J. D., Donfield, S., Asarnow, R. F., & Nuechterlein, K. H. (2000). Attention in HIV-infected children: results from the Hemophilia Growth and Development Study. *Journal of the International Neuropsychological Society, 6*(4), 443–454.

Watson, D., & Farley, J. (1999). Efficacy of and adherence to highly active antiretroviral therapy in children infected with human immunodeficiency virus type 1. *Pediatric Infectious Disease Journal, 18*(8), 682–689.

Whitt, J. K., Hooper, S. R., Tennison, M. B., Robertson, W., Gold, S., Burchinal, M., Wells, R., McMillan, C., Whaley, R., Combest, J., & Hall, C. (1993). Neuropsychologic functioning of human immunodeficiency virus-infected children with hemophilia. *Journal of Pediatrics, 122*, 52–59.

Wiener, L., Moss, H., Davidson, R., & Fair, C. (1992). Pediatrics: The emerging psychosocial challenges of the AIDS epidemic. *Child and Adolescent Social Work Journal, 9*(5), 381–407.

Wiener, L. S., & Vasquez, M. J. P. (1999a). Issues of disclosure in HIV and AIDS. In S. L. Zeichner & J. S. Read (Eds.), *Handbook of pediatric HIV care* (pp. 582–586). Philadelphia: Lippincott Williams & Wilkins.

Wiener, L. S., & Vasquez, M. J. P. (1999b). Psychosocial factors associated with childhood bereavement and grief. In S. L. Zeichner & J. S. Read (Eds.), *Handbook of pediatric HIV care* (pp. 587–601). Philadelphia: Lippincott Williams & Wilkins.

Wolters, P. L., & Brouwers, P. (in press). Evaluation of neurodevelopmental deficits in children with HIV-1 infection. In H. E. Gendelman, I. Grant, I. Everall, S. Lipton, & S. Swindells (Eds.), *The Neurology of AIDS, 2nd Edition*. Oxford: Oxford University Press.

Wolters, P., Brouwers, P., & Moss, H. (1995). Pediatric HIV disease: Effect on cognition, learning, and behavior. *School Psychology Quarterly, 10*(4), 305–328.

Wolters, P., Brouwers, P., Moss, H., & Pizzo, P. (1994). Adaptive behavior of children with symptomatic HIV infection before and after zidovudine therapy. *Journal of Pediatric Psychology, 19*(1), 47–61.

Wolters, P. L., & Brouwers, P. (1998). Evaluation of neurodevelopmental deficits in children with HIV infection. In H. E. Gendelman, S. A. Lipton, L. Epstein, & S. Swindells (Eds.), *The neurology of AIDS* (pp. 425–442). New York: Chapman & Hall.

Wolters, P. L., & Brouwers, P. (1999). Neurodevelopmental function and assessment of children with HIV-1 infection. In S. L. Zeichner & J. S. Read (Eds.), *Handbook of pediatric HIV care* (pp. 210–227). Philadelphia: Lippincott Williams & Wilkins.

Wolters, P. L., Brouwers, P., Civitello, L., & Moss, H. A. (1997). Receptive and expressive language function of children with symptomatic HIV infection and relationship with disease parameters: A longitudinal 24 month follow-up study. *AIDS, 11*(9), 1135–1144.

Wolters, P. L., Brouwers, P., Moss, H. A., & Pizzo, P. A. (1995). Differential receptive and expressive language functioning of children with symptomatic HIV disease and relation to CT scan brain abnormalities. *Pediatrics, 95*, 112–119.

Working Group of the American Academy of Neurology AIDS Task Force (1991). Nomenclature and research case definitions for neurologic manifestations of human immunodeficiency virus-type 1 infection. *Neurology, 41*, 778–785.

13

Seizure Disorders

Jane Williams
University of Arkansas for Medical Sciences

INTRODUCTION

As a fever indicates infection within the body, seizures are the outwardly visible sign of abnormal brain activity. They are quite common, and the lifetime risk of having at least one seizure is 8% (Berg & Shinnar, 1994). The occurrence of seizures is greatest during infancy, childhood, and adolescence. Seizure disorders are the most common neurological condition of childhood. During the first two decades of life, the cumulative risk of a seizure disorder is nearly 1%. Seizure onset peaks for children in the first 2 years of life and at puberty. Prevalence of seizures is 3.94–5 per 1,000 in children from birth to adolescence, with a slightly greater occurrence in males (Berg & Shinnar, 1994; Eriksson & Koivikko, 1997a; Hiemenz, Hynd, & Jimenez, 1999).

Seizures involve both changes in the electrical activity in the brain and changes in behavior. Changes in brain activity are typically reflected on electroencephalograph (EEG) recordings. An EEG recording will reveal abnormal patterns, known as epileptiform activity, in 60–70% of individuals who have seizures. Typical EEG patterns are noted for different seizure types and syndromes that aid in the classification and treatment of seizures. Children can have abnormal brain activity on the EEG, but must have accompanying changes in behavior to be classified as having a seizure (Williams & Sharp, 1999).

The occurrence of seizure-type behaviors in children may result from epileptiform brain activity, physiologic events, or psychogenic events (Gates & Erdahl, 1993). Physiologic and psychogenic events do not involve abnormal brain activity and often need to be ruled out as part of the diagnostic work-up for seizures. Physiologic events include syncope (fainting), migraine, tics, movement disorders, parasomnia, or reflux. Some of the behaviors associated with these disorders are very similar to seizure-type behavior changes. Psychogenic events, also known as pseudoseizures or nonepileptic seizures (NES), involve seizure-type behaviors that are generally attributed to maladaptive coping in reaction to stressful life events, reinforcement of avoidant or oppositional behavior, or untreated affective disorders, particularly anxiety and depression. The occurrence rate of NES in children is unknown, but Ritter and Kotagal (2000) contend that 25% of children referred to pediatric neurologists have NES. Children can have both epileptic seizures and NES.

HETEROGENEITY OF SEIZURES

Seizures differ on multiple dimensions, including etiology, type, syndrome, chronicity, and treatment response. In addition to these dimensions, there are multiple physical and psychosocial influences that affect the functioning and prognosis of the child with seizures. Part of the confusion in understanding seizures and the inconsistency in research findings have resulted from treating them as homogeneous events.

Etiology

Seizures have a wide variety of etiologies. Acute symptomatic seizures result from immediate, known causes (i.e., head trauma, sleep deprivation, chemical imbalance, infections, etc.) and generally do not recur. For example, during early childhood, acute symptomatic seizures associated with fever are common. Febrile seizures occur in 2–5% of children, do not typically warrant treatment, and generally resolve by the age of 5 years (Baumann, 2001; Williams & Sharp, 1999).

Afebrile seizures without an acute cause are considered unprovoked. When more than one unprovoked seizure occurs, the diagnosis of epilepsy is made. Unprovoked seizures with a known neurological cause—such as asphyxia at birth, brain tumors, prenatal brain malformations, and cerebral vascular insults—are referred to as remote symptomatic epilepsy. Developmental brain abnormalities are a common cause of remote symptomatic epilepsy in infants and young children. Central nervous system infections (e.g., encephalitis, meningitis) in children, and moderate-to-severe head injuries in adolescents are important causes of remote symptomatic epilepsy. Mild head trauma is rarely a cause of seizures.

Unprovoked seizures without an identified underlying cause are referred to as idiopathic or cryptogenic epilepsy. The vast majority (70%) of children have idiopathic seizures in which no cause is known (Annegers, 1996). The term "cryptogenic" is sometimes used as a descriptor of seizures as it implies that an underlying cause exists but cannot be identified (Williams & Sharp, 1999). There is considerable evidence supporting a genetic contribution to the etiology of epilepsy, especially for idiopathic primary generalized epilepsy and benign focal epilepsies of childhood (Treiman & Treiman, 1996).

Seizure Types

Seizures are divided into two general categories based on the location of the electrical discharge within the brain. Partial seizures are those that begin within a focal region of the brain, and their clinical expression frequently reflects the function of the area involved. For example, confusion and unresponsiveness occur in seizures with a temporal lobe onset or visual phenomena occur with occipital lobe onset. They are often preceded by an aura or warning, such as a strange feeling or fear, nausea, foul odor, or unusual taste. Partial seizures may be simple or complex. Simple partial seizures have no alteration of consciousness, whereas complex partial seizures involve an alteration of consciousness. During a complex partial seizure, the individual commonly appears confused and may exhibit automatisms, such as lip smacking, facial grimacing, mumbling or humming, fumbling hand movements, or picking at clothing.

Speech may be altered or arrested if the dominant hemisphere is involved. These seizures last a few seconds to a few minutes and are accompanied by confusion and fatigue after the event. In some children, the electrical activity may spread from the original focus and results in a secondary generalized convulsion (Williams & Sharp, 1999).

The second category involves simultaneous electrical activity within the "whole brain," including both cerebral hemispheres and their subcortical connections and structures. These are referred to as generalized seizures. Primary generalized seizures have an abrupt onset without an aura and generally involve a loss of consciousness. Generalized seizures may be convulsive or nonconvulsive. The most common convulsive seizure is the tonic-clonic seizure (formerly known as grand mal). The tonic phase is characterized by stiffening of the trunk and extremities, and the clonic phase involves rhythmic, repetitive jerking movements. These seizures last less than 5 min and are followed by unresponsiveness and fatigue. Other convulsive generalized seizure types include tonic (without the clonic phase), clonic (without the tonic phase), and clonic-tonic-clonic.

Generalized nonconvulsive seizure types include atonic, myoclonic, and absence seizures. Atonic seizures are characterized by an extremely abrupt loss of muscle tone that produces a sudden fall and frequently results in repetitive injuries to the child. Myoclonic seizures are single symmetrical jerks of the head and upper extremities that may occur in a series or cluster, often after awakening. Absence seizures (previously known as petit mal) are brief staring episodes that involve a sudden cessation of activity. The child may simply stare blankly or have a rapid eye flutter. Often, the child appears inattentive. Absence seizures last only seconds, and there is no confusion or fatigue after the seizure (ictal) event. Children can also have atypical absence seizures that are generally accompanied by other types of generalized seizures, making seizure control difficult (Williams & Sharp, 1999).

About 10–20% of individuals with epilepsy have mixed seizure types, making specific classification of seizures difficult.

Syndromes

There are several specific epileptic syndromes that occur in childhood and generally follow a rather predictable developmental course. Epileptic syndromes are based on clinical features, such as predominant seizure type, EEG patterns, evolutional features, and response to antiepileptic drugs (AEDs). These syndromes run the gamut from benign to those that significantly interfere with cognitive and social development.

Benign focal epilepsy of childhood has an onset generally between 3 and 10 years of age. Seizures are typically infrequent and spontaneously resolve before late adolescence. In the most common type, benign rolandic epilepsy, the seizures occur at night and involve unilateral clonic activity of the face and upper extremity. A typical EEG involving centrotemporal spikes is noted, and the child is often not treated unless seizures occur during the day, are frequent, or involve secondary generalization. A less frequently occurring type, benign occipital epilepsy, involves visual symptoms, such as partial loss of vision, visual hallucinations, illusions, or flashing stars. They are typically induced by eye closure (Williams & Sharp, 1999). Questions have recently been raised about whether benign epilepsy of childhood is as benign as previously believed. Findings have been inconsistent concerning cognitive effects in these children. Most studies do not suggest intellectual or academic decline, although one study identified weaknesses in memory and executive function when the children with seizures were compared with controls (Croona, Kihlgren, Lundberg, Eeg-Olofsson, & Eeg-Olofsson, 1999). However, longitudinal assessment of children with benign epilepsy of childhood suggests that these weaknesses may be transient and directly related to the presence of abnormal brain activity noted on EEG recordings (Deonna et al., 2000).

Childhood absence epilepsy has an onset generally between 4 and 8 years, is characterized by a pattern of 3-per-second spike and wave discharge on the EEG, is usually easily treated, and has a remission rate of approximately 80%. Generalized tonic-clonic seizures may develop in 35–40% of these children, but they tend to be infrequent and occur more during adolescence.

Juvenile absence epilepsy has a peak onset near puberty. Unlike childhood absence epilepsy, the majority of these adolescents will experience generalized convulsive seizures, as well as absence seizures, and persistence of these seizures into adulthood is more common.

Juvenile myoclonic epilepsy (JME) has an onset between late childhood and early adolescence. It involves myoclonic jerks of the upper extremities and usually is associated with morning wakening. There is no loss of consciousness, although 90–95% of these patients will have generalized tonic-clonic seizures. There is no associated cognitive decline, and it has a good intellectual prognosis. Resolution of these seizures is infrequent. JME is a common condition, accounting for 10% of all epilepsies, and it is genetically inherited in an autosomal dominant fashion (Williams & Sharp, 1999).

Infantile spasms or West syndrome has an onset in infancy and generally involves clusters of myoclonic seizures. The seizures, which involve a pattern of hypsarrhythmia (random high-voltage slow waves and spikes that spread to all cortical areas) on the EEG, generally cease between the second and fourth years of life. However, other seizure types later develop in 25–60% of the children. Etiology may be symptomatic or cryptogenic, with a high incidence (80%) of mental retardation in symptomatic cases (Williams & Sharp, 1999).

Lennox-Gastaut syndrome involves mixed seizure types, including atypical absence, atonic, and myoclonic. The onset is generally between 2 and 8 years of age, and the EEG contains background slowing and slow spike-wave discharges. Etiology may be symptomatic or cryptogenic, the seizures tend to be difficult to control, status epilepticus (prolonged seizure) is common, and few children with Lennox-Gastaut are intellectually normal. Mental retardation is often progressive. Care of the child tends to be complex because of hyperactivity and falls associated with the atonic seizures (Camfield & Camfield, 2002; Williams & Sharp, 1999).

Landau-Kleffner syndrome is a rare disorder that is characterized by a sudden or gradual onset of auditory agnosia in a previously normally developing child. Onset is between 2 and 11 years, and often speech stops completely. Behavioral changes, including hyperactivity and temper outbursts, are often present. The EEG is abnormal with a variety of seizure types. Seizures may occur before, during, or after the development of aphasia and are present in 70% of the children. Seizures remit by the mid-teenage years, but the language and behavior problems generally persist (Camfield & Camfield, 2002; Williams & Sharp, 1999).

Continuous-spike-wave-in-slow-sleep is another rare disorder of childhood that involves continuous spike and wave activity during nonrapid-eye-movement (NREM) sleep. Age of onset is between 4 and 14 years, with discontinuation of the abnormal EEG pattern and seizures during adolescence. The majority of children experience neuropsychological regression associated with the emergence of the abnormal EEG pattern, and the cognitive course is variable (Camfield & Camfield, 2002; Williams & Sharp, 1999).

Chronicity

The prognosis of seizure disorders is diverse. In the past, epilepsy was thought of as a lifelong condition. Presently, the prognosis for seizure control, remission, and medication withdrawal is excellent for the majority of children with epilepsy (Hauser & Hesdorffer, 1996). Between 70 and 80% of the children will experience long-term and frequently permanent remission either on or off medications (Berg & Shinnar, 1994). This is especially true when the etiology is idiopathic, and for children with normal neurological examination, EEG, and intelligence. The majority of those who enter remission will do so during the first year after diagnosis (Hauser &

Hesdorffer, 1996), and anticonvulsant treatment can generally be safely discontinued within 2 years of remission (Berg & Shinnar, 1994).

For 17 to 20% of the children with epilepsy, seizures are considered severe and often become intractable (Eriksson & Koivikko, 1997a). Uncontrolled, chronic seizures are most often correlated with symptomatic etiology (e.g., neurological insult), early onset of epilepsy (i.e., less than 1 year of age), and other neuroimpairments (e.g., mental retardation or cerebral palsy). Children with epileptic syndromes, such as West or Lennox-Gastaut, or those with multiple seizure types, are at greater risk for intractable seizures (Berg & Shinnar, 1994; Eriksson & Koivikko, 1997a).

Treatment

Treatment is initiated for seizures when the benefits outweigh the risks of medication use. In most cases, treatment begins when seizures are prolonged or significantly recurrent. Monotherapy, the use of one AED to control seizures, is preferred. Monotherapy is more efficacious, avoids drug interactions, improves adherence, and results in fewer physical and cognitive adverse side effects. Polytherapy is used when individual AEDs have failed to control seizures (Hiemenz et al., 1999; Williams, & Sharp, 1999).

Children are highly variable in their response to any AED. This diversity in response, as well as differences in metabolism and elimination of drugs, complicates the dosing of AEDs in children. Extended clinical trials with different medications at varying doses may be necessary to obtain seizure control (Hiemenz et al., 1999). This process can become very discouraging and frustrating for parents and can impact AED compliance, as well as the physician–parent relationship.

Most children are effectively treated with AEDs, with up to 80% having complete seizure control. As different AEDs have been found to be more efficacious with different seizure types/syndromes, the correct classification of seizures and epilepsy syndromes contributes to the selection of an appropriate AED. Table 13.1 contains common AEDs used in pediatric practice, the generic name, the types of seizures or syndromes that are managed with each AED, side effects, and symptoms of toxicity (Sharp & Wilder, 2000). Some of these drugs are more traditional and generally selected first as the primary AED, whereas other newer AEDs are used more often as adjunctive drugs that are added on to manage difficult-to-control seizures.

For the 20% of pediatric patients whose seizures are not controlled with AEDs, other options are considered. Technological advances have resulted in increased surgical intervention for medically refractory seizures in childhood. The most common procedure is aimed at controlling complex partial seizures through removal of a localized seizure focus. Focal resections of seizures, that are determined to originate in the temporal lobe, involve removal of the anterior temporal lobe although extratemporal resections also are performed. The majority of children who undergo a temporal lobectomy are seizure-free or have greatly reduced seizure frequency after surgery. No marked changes in cognition and improvement in quality of life have been reported (Williams & Sharp, 1999). Hemispherectomy, in which one cerebral hemisphere is removed or disconnected, is used to control partial seizures. Children who undergo a hemispherectomy generally have a pre-existing hemiplegia with seizures arising from damage in the contralateral hemisphere. Control of partial seizures has been reported in 80–90% of the children, and improvement in behavior and cognition has been found. When the surgery is performed before 10 years of age, aphasia does not occur, but problems with nonverbal spatial abilities have been reported (Cross, 2002; Williams & Sharp, 1999). A corpus callosotomy involves two-thirds division or complete division of the corpus callosum. It is used to control intractable generalized seizures by preventing the rapid spread of seizures from one hemisphere

TABLE 13.1
Common Pediatric Antiepileptic Drugs

Generic Name	*Seizure Type/Syndrome*	*Side Effects*	*Toxicity*
Carbamazepine (Carbatrol) (Tegretol)	Partial onset, benign focal epilepsy	Drowsiness, rash	Dizziness, blurred vision, nausea, sedation, diplopia
Felbamate (Felbatol)	Lennox-Gastaut, partial onset, PGC + Absence	Anorexia, insomnia, nausea, emesis	Aplastic anemia, hepatic failure
Gabapentin (Neurontin)	Partial onset, benign focal epilepsy	Somnolence, ataxia, dizziness	None
Lamotrigine (Lamictal)	Lennox-Gastaut, Partial onset, PGC; Absence, PGC + Absence, JME	Rash, CNS depression	Rash
Valproic acid (Depakote) (Depakene)	Absence, PGC, Absence, PGC + Absence, Lennox-Gastaut JME, partial onset	Somnolence, nausea, tremor, abdominal pain, weight gain, hair loss	CNS depression, hepatic failure, pancreatitis, thrombocytopenia
Topiramate (Topamax)	Lennox-Gastaut, partial onset, PGC, JME, PGC + Absence	Somnolence, ataxia, fatigue, dizziness, psychomotor slowing, speech disturbance	CNS depression, increased renal stones
Phenobarbital	Partial onset	Sedation, dizziness, ataxia, hyperactivity	Somnolence, confusion, CNS depression, hypotension, respiratory depression
Ethosuximide (Zarontin)	Absence	Abdominal pain, nausea, emesis	CNS depression
Phenytoin (Dilantin)	Partial onset, benign focal epilepsy, PGC	Gingival hyperplasia, nystagmus, ataxia	Lethargy, nausea, emesis, ataxia, nystagmus, rash
Tigabine (Gabatril)	Partial onset	Dizziness, fatigue, somnolence, knee buckling	Somnolence, CNS depression, confusion

PGC = primary generalized convulsive; CNS = central nervous system; JME = juvenile myoclonic epilepsy.

to the other. Atonic seizures stop in 80% of the cases, thereby eliminating injuries from falls. Because many of these children have seizures that are multifocal in origin, the goal is often improved control rather than complete seizure cessation. The majority of children who undergo a corpus callosotomy have various degrees of mental retardation and behavioral difficulties. Although cognitive abilities do not generally increase after surgery, improvements in behavior, attention, and performance of daily activities are reported (Williams & Sharp, 1999).

Vagus nerve stimulation, which involves implantation of a small programmable device below the clavicle, has been used as an adjunct therapy in children with medically refractory seizures. The device stimulates the vagus nerve and has been found to reduce the number and intensity of seizures and increase alertness in children.

In addition to surgical intervention, the ketogenic diet has been used to increase seizure control in children with drug-resistant epilepsy. The ketogenic diet generally consists of greater than 80% of total calories supplied as fat, with a relatively equal amount of remaining calories from protein and carbohydrates. One-third of the children experience complete seizure control, whereas about one-half of those without complete control have a significant reduction in seizure frequency or required AED dosage (Williams & Sharp, 1999).

COGNITIVE AND BEHAVIORAL FUNCTIONING

Cognition

The IQ distribution of children with seizure disorders is similar to the general pediatric population (Hauser & Hesdorffer, 1990a). Exceptions to this finding are children who have significant neurological abnormalities or epileptic syndromes, such as Lennox-Gastaut, that are associated with moderate-to-severe cognitive delay. When cognitive impairment is present, the profile tends to be diffuse and generalized (Schoenfeld et al., 1999).

There is a higher occurrence of seizures in children diagnosed with developmental disorders, such as mental retardation (9–31%) and autism (11–35%). There is no causative link between seizures and these conditions; rather common underlying antecedents result in their co-occurrence (Hauser & Hesdorffer, 1990b).

It has been postulated that children with complex partial seizures are more vulnerable to memory difficulties, especially when the temporal lobe and hippocampus are involved. Some studies have suggested memory deficits related to hemispheric specialization with decreased verbal memory in children with left temporal lobe epilepsy and decreased visual memory in children with right temporal lobe epilepsy (Cohen, 1992). However, other studies have failed to demonstrate focus-specific memory deficits, because children have been found to exhibit memory problems whose seizures were outside the temporal lobe (Jambaque, Dellatolas, Dulac, Ponsot, & Signoret, 1993). Children with intractable seizures have not been found to have specific memory deficits based on laterality and site of seizure focus (Smith, Elliott, & Lach, 2002). Children with epilepsy may experience more diffuse memory problems with less lateralized patterns than noted in adults with epilepsy (Williams, in press).

There are some indications that children with frontal lobe epilepsy may demonstrate some specific cognitive findings associated with seizure location. When compared with children with temporal lobe or generalized seizures, children with frontal lobe epilepsy demonstrated deficits in planning and impulse control. No differences were noted in conceptual shift or recent memory. In younger children, more problems with coordination and rigidity were noted (Hernandez et al., 2002).

Risk of Learning Disabilities

Children with epilepsy have a higher risk of learning disabilities (Dodson, 1993), although specific subtypes have not been consistently identified (Williams & Sharp, 1999). The greatest academic risk for children with epilepsy appears to be educational underachievement (Aldenkamp & Mulder, 1999; Seidenberg & Berent, 1992). Academic weaknesses do not appear to be confined to any one area, because underachievement has been found in a variety of subjects, including math, spelling, writing to dictation, reading, reading comprehension, and general knowledge (Aldenkamp, Overweg-Plandsoen, & Diepman, 1999; Williams & Sharp, 1999). The risk for school failure appears highest in children with symptomatic epilepsy, and several studies have suggested normal achievement in children with low-severity epilepsy (Austin, Huberty, Huster, & Dunn, 1999; Williams et al., 1996). However, in a prospective study of children with normal intelligence and idiopathic epilepsy, a greater than expected rate (34%) of grade retention and special education placement (19%) were found, compared with sibling controls. This prospective study might suggest a higher risk of educational failure for children with epilepsy than for children in the general population (Bailet & Turk, 2000). In a longitudinal study of epilepsy from childhood to adulthood, educational problems persisted even in individuals who were medication and seizure free (Sillanpaa, Jalava, Kaleva, & Shinnar, 1998).

In addition to the impact of seizures and medications, there are multiple factors that have been associated with this academic vulnerability. These include cognitive functions, environmental variables, personality and motivation of the child, family adjustment, and social variables (Seidenberg & Berent, 1992). In a recent study that examined self-esteem, socioeconomic status, attention, and memory in children with epilepsy, attention was the primary factor associated with achievement scores when intelligence was controlled (Williams et al., 2001).

Researchers have consistently found a disruption of attentional skills that appears to be present even when the child is not diagnosed with comorbid attention deficit hyperactivity disorder (ADHD). In a comprehensive neuropsychological study assessing memory, attention, language, achievement, fine motor skills, executive function, visual motor integration, and behavior, the neurocognitive skills of children with epilepsy were within expectations for their measured intelligence with the exception of attention skills (Williams, Griebel, & Dykman, 1998). In a recent study using the Test of Variables of Attention (Greenberg, Leark, Dupuy, Corman, & Kindschi, 1988) to assess attention skills in children with complex partial seizures with or without ADHD, findings revealed significant problems with attention regardless of the diagnosis of ADHD (Semrud-Clikeman & Wical, 1999). These findings suggest that children with epilepsy are at risk for attention problems that may contribute to academic underachievement.

Along with attention, memory problems are not uncommon in children with epilepsy (Blennow, Heijbel, Sandstedt, & Tonnby, 1990; Dam, 1990). It is unclear whether these problems result from decreased initial encoding of information from inattention or from impaired retrieval and consolidation. Computerized testing during EEG recordings suggest disruption of working memory, even during brief subclinical epileptiform discharges (Kasteleijn-Nolst-Trenite, Smit, Velis, Willemse, & van Emde Boas, 1990). Although these memory effects may be transitory, continuing abnormal activity may adversely affect the child's acquisition of academic skills (Binnie, Channon, & Marston, 1990).

Need for Special Education

There is an increased likelihood for children with epilepsy to need special education. However, heterogeneity again must be considered when examining this risk. In a study by Zelnik, Sa'adi, Silman-Stolar, and Goikhman (2001), children with idiopathic epilepsy had a benign outcome with good seizure control and enrollment in regular classes. The need for special education placement was associated with remote symptomatic seizures, poor seizure control, young age at onset, underlying brain lesions, and mixed EEG patterns. Similarly, when IQ and achievement were examined, Bulteau et al. (2000) found that children with idiopathic generalized or focal epilepsy had higher IQ scores and higher probability of mainstream schooling than those with symptomatic or cryptogenic generalized epilepsies or epileptic syndromes that were undetermined.

BEHAVIORAL AND EMOTIONAL FUNCTIONING

As with cognition, children with epilepsy are at increased risk for behavioral and emotional difficulties compared with the general population or children with other chronic illnesses (Bolter, 1986; Caplan et al., 1998). However, some studies suggest that children with idiopathic seizures and normal neuropsychological abilites are not at a higher risk for psychiatric disturbance than a nonneurological patient population (Fiordelli, Beghi, Boglium, & Crespi, 1993; Kokkonen, Kokkonen, & Saukkonen, 1998). The increased risk appears to be most associated with additional neurological impairment, intractable seizures, and family dysfunction (Dunn, in press).

The most common comorbid behavioral disturbance in children with epilepsy is ADHD. Barkley (1990) estimated that 20–30% of children with epilepsy have ADHD. In a retrospective study of children with intractable seizures, 35% had been diagnosed with ADHD (Hempel, Frost, Ritter, & Farnham, 1995). In contrast to ADHD, there does not appear to be an increased risk for externalizing disorders, including oppositional defiant disorder or conduct disorder, in children with uncomplicated epilepsy (Dunn, in press; Schoenfeld et al., 1999).

In terms of mood disturbance, increased symptoms of depression and anxiety have been reported. In a study (Ettinger et al., 1998) of children and adolescents with epilepsy, who had not been previously diagnosed with a mood disorder, 26% had significantly elevated scores on the Children's Depression Inventory (Kovacs, 1992) and 16% met criteria for clinically significant levels of anxiety on the Revised Children's Manifest Anxiety Scale (Reynolds & Richmond, 1985).

Psychosis in children with epilepsy is rare. At initial diagnosis, some children with occipital lobe seizures will have phenomena similar to visual hallucinations, but this resolves following treatment with anticonvulsants. Differences in psychiatric frequency based on seizure type or side of laterality of EEG findings have not been supported in recent studies (Caplan et al., 1998).

MULTIPLE INFLUENCES ON COGNITION AND BEHAVIOR

Ongoing Seizures

Frequent seizures, even when short in duration and involving subtle symptoms, are associated with decreased alertness and short-term memory. In a study that examined cognitive performance in children with nonconvulsive seizures, a significant association was found between the number of seizures experienced and impaired alertness, whereas the duration of the seizure was associated with memory impairment (Aldenkamp et al., 2000). These findings would suggest that children with ongoing seizures may be at increased risk for learning and memory difficulties (Aldenkamp, Overweg-Plandsoen, & Ahrends, 1999).

Although there is no evidence to suggest that seizures themselves cause brain damage (Berg & Shinnar, 1994), some research indicates that children who have intractable seizures over a long period of time may demonstrate a decline in intelligence scores (Bjornaes, Stabell, Hendriksen, & Loyning, 2001). Schoenfeld et al. (1999) found that age of onset of recurrent seizures was the strongest and most consistent predictor of later cognitive functioning.

Status epilepticus, defined as a single seizure lasting at least 30 min or intermittent seizures lasting for 30 min or longer, may pose a threat for altered cognitive or neurological functioning in children. However, neurological changes have been more associated with a symptomatic etiology and prolonged status (lasting more than 2 hr). Cerebral damage is thought to result from infectious or metabolic causes rather than being secondary to the status epilepticus itself (Eriksson & Koivikko, 1997b).

Frequency of seizures has been found to be one of the strongest predictors of behavioral and emotional difficulties in children with seizure disorders (Schoenfeld et al., 1999). When children with new onset seizures were followed for 24 months, a trend was found for behavioral improvement in children whose seizures had not recurred, and behavioral difficulties remained unchanged for those who had further seizures (Dunn, Austin, Harezlak, Perkins, & Ambrosius, 2001).

Medication Effects

Findings concerning cognitive and behavioral adverse side effects of AEDs have been marked by inconsistent and contradictory results. The most consistent cognitive effects of AEDs appear to be impaired attention, vigilance, and psychomotor speed (Meador, 2002). Studies suggest that the majority of children taking AEDs do not experience clinically relevant adverse effects (Bourgeois, 1998). In studies of children with new-onset idiopathic seizures, deleterious effects from AED therapy on cognitive skills and neuropsychological functioning in the initial 6–12 months of treatment have not been found (Mandelbaum & Burack, 1997; Williams et al., 1998). In an AED discontinuation study, the only significant improvement noted was in psychomotor speed, and the investigators suggested that there was little evidence supporting adverse effects of AEDs on higher order cognitive function (Aldenkamp et al., 1993).

Of the more traditional AEDs, carbamazepine (Tegretol) and valproic acid (Depakote) generally appear to exert less cognitive toxicity when compared with phenytoin (Dilantin) and phenobarbital (Hiemenz et al., 1999). Some studies have suggested a progressive encephalopathy and mental retardation occur with continuing treatment with phenytoin (Dilantin), whereas phenobarbital has been found to lower concentration and motor speed (Hiemenz et al., 1999). Behaviorally, carbamazepine (Tegretol) has been found to have an overall calming effect that may be helpful in children with comorbid behavioral difficulties. Phenobarbital, on the other hand, may produce increased levels of activity in up to 70% of children treated with this AED (Crumrine, 2002).

Of the newer AEDs, gabapentin (Neurontin) and lamotrigine (Lamictal) seem to have a low potential for intellectual impairment, whereas topiramate (Topamax) appears related to cognitive problems in a subgroup of patients (Bourgeois, 2002). Behaviorally, vigabatrin (Gabatril) has been associated with behavior disturbances in children, especially in those with mental retardation or a history of behavior problems, and gabapentin (Neurontin) has been associated with explosive outbursts of aggressiveness and oppositional behavior (Bourgeois, 1998).

When cognitive and behavioral effects have been found, they are often associated with higher AED doses, higher plasma concentrations, and polytherapy (Williams et al., 1998). Children with pre-existing behavioral disorders may be more vulnerable to intensification of behavioral difficulties, and children with mental retardation may be more susceptible to cognitive loss after AED treatment (Williams et al., 1998).

It appears that no single AED causes problems in *every* patient, and no AED can be assumed to *never* cause any cognitive or behavioral impairment. However, the widespread belief held by some physicians and parents that AEDs will invariably have an adverse affect on a child's cognitive abilities is not supported by currently available research (Bourgeois, 2002).

Sleep

Children with epilepsy have been found to experience high rates of sleep disorders, particularly poor quality sleep and anxiety about sleeping (Stores, Wiggs, & Campling, 1998). The issue of sleep in children with seizure disorders is often not adequately considered, but can impact both cognition and behavior for two primary reasons. First, sleep disruption can contribute to increased seizure frequency. Second, poor sleep hygiene can have a negative impact on learning because of reduced concentration. Disrupted sleep in children with epilepsy can be present even on seizure-free nights. This may involve delayed sleep onset, increased frequency and duration of awakenings, and increased NREM sleep. Sleep abnormalities are more prominent in children with generalized seizures and those with frequent seizures. When epilepsy and sleep disorders coexist, treatment for the sleep disorder may contribute to improved seizure control (Mendez & Radtke, 2001).

Stigma

Stigma involves beliefs about epilepsy that result in the child being perceived, and often treated, differently from others. The parents, siblings, extended family members, teachers, peers, or culture may hold these beliefs. Stigma has both direct and indirect effects on children with epilepsy and their families.

Cultures vary in their beliefs about epilepsy. Many cultures have negative attitudes and fear about seizure disorders. Dominant cultural religious teachings may include the belief that epilepsy involves demonic possession and results from punishment or a curse. As part of these beliefs, the child is seen as intrinsically bad. There are some cultures that view epilepsy more positively and believe that these individuals have special powers of influence or vision. In either belief system, the individual with epilepsy is perceived as different. Stigma within the school environment may lead to decreased academic expectations by teachers, exclusion from activities, and negative interactions with classmates.

Stigma can have a particularly detrimental effect during adolescence. Feelings associated with stigma may directly impact the adolescent's medication compliance. In a study that examined predictive factors of good AED adherence, one significant predictor was the belief that epilepsy was not a threat to the adolescent's social well-being (Kyngas, 2001). Changes in physical appearance, such as increased facial hair resulting from treatment with phenytoin or weight gain from valproic acid, can impact peer relationships, as well as the adolescent's sense of self. Depression in adolescents has been associated with negative attitudes about having epilepsy and a decreased internal locus of control (Hermann & Whitman, 1992).

Stigma may influence parental perception about the child's behavior. In a pilot study, parents, who believed that having epilepsy would stigmatize and limit their child, reported higher levels of behavior problems for their children than parents who did not have these beliefs (Carlton-Ford, Miller, Nealeigh, & Sanchez, 1997). Negative beliefs about the possible association between epilepsy and decreased cognitive ability may lower parental expectations concerning school performance. Decreased expectations can impact the child's effort, the child's attitude about his/her abilities, and the child's academic accomplishments.

Unfortunately, stigma may lead to secrecy, especially for the school-age child, thus reducing the amount of positive education about epilepsy that can take place (Ziegler, Erba, Holden, & Dennison, 2000).

Misinformation

Misinformation not only contributes to the stigma associated with epilepsy, but also can directly contribute to adjustment problems for the child with seizures. Believing in myths, such as swallowing your tongue during a seizure, may result in significant anxiety about having seizures. Studies have shown that children frequently lack basic knowledge about their disorder. In one study, children were found to have the necessary cognitive development, but lacked the factual information to understand epilepsy. Only 40% of the children in the third through fifth grades and 36% of the children in the sixth through eighth grades stated that the brain was involved in their seizures (Sanger, Perrin, & Sandler, 1993). When children lack information, they may develop misperceptions about seizures that affect their psychosocial development. For example, an uninformed child may misattribute the cause of a seizure to whatever they are doing at the time of the seizure occurrence. If the child was involved in exercise and attributes the seizure to overexertion, the child may cease athletic activities.

As with the child, lack of information or misinformation may result in overprotectiveness and limitations on the child's activities by the parents. It has been suggested that parental restriction of activities may be directly linked to the level of information that has been provided for parents (Suurmeijer, 1994). One study found that parents who believed that information given by the physician was adequate imposed one to two fewer restrictions than parents who rated information as inadequate (Suurmeijer, 1994).

Misinformation by others can also lead to a restriction of activities. For example, photosensitivity has been reported in 2–5% of adults with epilepsy with a somewhat higher proportion in children and adolescents. In a recent study concerning the link between video games and seizure occurrence, the sample interviewed indicated that all individuals with epilepsy are at risk from playing video games at a substantially greater proportion than suggested by the estimated real risk. Without accurate information, individuals may not be allowed to participate in activities even when they are not at increased risk for seizures (Millett, Fish, & Thompson, 1997).

Within the school environment, lack of information about epilepsy may cause children to be sent home inappropriately after a seizure (Johnson & Thomas, 1999). Few teachers receive formal instruction in childhood illnesses and often have little knowledge of different types of seizure disorders (Bannon, Wildig, & Jones, 1992). If a seizure is not a generalized tonic-clonic, often the behavior is misinterpreted, and the child is punished. With absence seizures, the teacher may have a tendency to consider the child inattentive rather than consider the presence of a seizure disorder. In a survey of teachers, the majority (64%) indicated that they did not feel confident when teaching children with epilepsy (Bannon, Wildig, & Jones, 1992).

Anxiety

When parents witness a child's first seizure, it is often a terrifying and confusing experience, especially if the seizure is prolonged. They relate feelings of helplessness and fright. Parents of children with new onset seizures have been found to worry about unlikely and rare events, including underlying brain tumors, brain damage resulting from seizures, and death during a seizure (Austin, Dunn, Huster, & Rose, 1998; Shore et al., 1998). Because the majority of children have seizures without a known cause, these worries tend to be intensified by the lack of an identified etiology. Even with the passage of time, parents retain the fear of seizure occurrence. When children have breakthrough seizures, such as when growth spurts require increases in medication, the old anxieties are rekindled.

Children, like their parents, may have increased vulnerability for anxiety because of the unique nature of seizures. These events are unpredictable and involve loss of control, which make them frightening for children.

Family Adaptation

Epilepsy can result in a restriction of activities for the family with more time and attention focused on the child with seizures. Increased stressors for the family include repeated physician visits, costly anticonvulsants, possible adverse side effects of medications, loss of parental work time, school absences for the child, and changes in social activities. Siblings often complain of feeling neglected. Although these stressors are present for all families, the intensity of these changes is generally directly related to frequent or intractable seizures. Severity of epilepsy has been associated with impaired emotional status and decreased social adaptation in families (Thomas & Bindu, 1999).

In attempting to adapt to chronic epilepsy, family relationships may be altered. In a study that compared maternal responses toward children with seizures and sibling controls, mothers showed significantly more emotional overinvolvement and a tendency for more hostility toward their children with epilepsy. Although the overinvolvement was not associated with child misbehavior, the hostility and high levels of criticism were related to ratings of child behavioral deviance (Hodes, Garralda, Rose, & Schwartz, 1999). Likewise, children with epilepsy who reported that their parents used an overcontrolling approach to parenting were more likely to endorse higher levels of behavior problems for themselves (Carlton-Ford et al., 1997).

Family adaptation may particularly impact the adolescent's emotional functioning. In a study that examined depression in adolescents with epilepsy, satisfaction with family relationships and the youth's attitude toward having seizures were the factors most significantly associated with depression scores (Dunn, Austin, & Huster, 1999). Problems with family adaptation can impede psychosocial development in the older adolescent with epilepsy, particularly concerning independence, driving, sexuality, and employment.

ROLE OF THE PEDIATRIC PSYCHOLOGIST

The role of the pediatric psychologist in working with children with epilepsy and their families is multifaceted. It may include assessment, therapy, and/or consultation with the medical caregivers. Providing education, monitoring the child's academic and emotional functioning, advocating for the needs of the child and family, being an intermediary between the school and physician, and interacting across disciplines are not uncommon activities. Each of these roles and responsibilities requires knowledge of the disorder and effective interventions.

Assessment

Cognitive assessment of children with epilepsy can be helpful if questions have been raised about the child's capacity. Some parents may have unrealistic expectations of their child and tend to blame decreased academic performance on seizures. They often expect that seizure control will result in significantly higher performance. If the child's ability is within the lower ranges, this expectation may not be realistic and result in undue stress on the child.

However, in assessing children with seizure disorders, it is important to evaluate beyond general cognition. A more in-depth neuropsychological assessment is frequently needed to determine cognitive strengths and weaknesses. In particular, the evaluation needs to include assessment of attention, memory, and processing speed. Direct measures of the child's attentional abilities as well as parent and teacher ratings of behavior need to be administered, because children with epilepsy often have difficulty with inattention that may be subthreshhold for a diagnosis of ADHD. The memory assessment should include working memory, retrieval, consolidation, and recognition skills. Tests should involve both rote and complex information. Speed of information processing and psychomotor speed, which are especially sensitive to the effects of medication toxicity and/or polytherapy, need to be assessed.

Children with epilepsy are highly diverse in their patterns of cognitive strengths and weaknesses. During the neuropsychological assessment, further evaluation of visual motor integration skills, executive functioning, language, fine motor coordination, perceptual skills, and/or sensory integration may be needed. Delays in these skills may signal the need for intervention, and identification of strengths may pinpoint stronger processing modalities. When assessing any child with epilepsy, one should use caution in interpreting the results, particularly if the child has any signs of cognitive toxicity because of their medication, has seizures in close proximity to the time of the assessment, or is on polytherapy.

Monitoring Achievement

It is important to monitor the academic progress of any child diagnosed with a seizure disorder, especially those with poorly controlled seizures or those on polytherapy. Tracking scores from standardized achievement test batteries for regression or lack of progress in achievement skills could signal the need for an individual psychoeducational assessment or neuropsychological evaluation. Under the Individual with Disabilities Education Act, children with epilepsy may qualify for classroom modifications or special education services in the category of Other Health Impaired if their seizures or treatment are having a deleterious effect on academic performance.

Monitoring Behavior

Children with epilepsy need to be monitored for behavioral and/or emotional difficulties, especially those with frequent seizures. Assessment of depression, anxiety, and ADHD symptoms with the children, as well as obtaining collateral information from parents and teachers through interviews and rating scales, can determine the presence of comorbid conditions and signal the need for intervention. A number of instruments have been developed to assess quality of life in families who have a child with epilepsy. Measurement of quality of life provides helpful information concerning the perceived impact of epilepsy on the family. As part of the evaluation, it is important to gain a level of understanding about the beliefs and perceived stigma reported by the child, parent, and teacher concerning epilepsy. In addition, parents need to be questioned about the child's sleep hygiene because of its critical impact on both behavior and learning.

Education

Working in coordination with the school nurse, the pediatric psychologist can assist with training of school personnel concerning the management, educational, and psychosocial implications of seizures. Active knowledge acquired through experience with an individual child appears to be the most effective way to gain understanding about epilepsy (Johnson & Thomas, 1999). The psychologist can target the needs of a specific child for teacher and classroom intervention. Educational presentations within the classroom using age-appropriate materials may decrease peers' negative feelings and misinformation about seizures.

Education of school staff is important concerning how seizures are handled. Seizures are generally very short in duration, but children are frequently tired and need a short rest after a complex partial or generalized tonic-clonic seizure. Allowing the child to rest in the health room and return to class is generally the most productive way to handle seizure occurrence. Sending children home may reinforce the stigma associated with seizures, as well as increase the child's anxiety about their health status. Although parameters for intervention vary, seizures that last between 5 and 15 min need to be addressed medically.

Correcting misinformation can be helpful to parents and teachers when they are trying to make decisions about activities for the child with seizures. As noted in the prior example concerning video games, the parent can be encouraged to contact their physician concerning any photosensitivity noted during their child's EEG. If their child is not photosensitive, undue concern about participation can be eliminated (Millett et al., 1997). Providing educational materials for parents and teachers can reduce anxiety and assist with management issues. Excellent resources for these materials include the Epilepsy Foundation of America (www.efa.org) or the state or local epilepsy associations.

Support Groups

Providing a support group for children with epilepsy is important, especially for children with newly diagnosed seizures who have a need for information concerning their seizure disorder. In a study that assessed psychosocial care at 3 and 6 months after diagnosis, children remained concerned about management issues, especially how to handle seizures at school and protection from injury. They expressed a strong need to talk with peers who also had seizures (McNelis, Musick, Austin, Dunn, & Creasy, 1998). Psychoeducational groups can focus on management issues, as well as psychosocial concerns. The group process has the potential to decrease feelings of stigma through activities, such as role playing, or discussions about how to respond when being treated differently because of their seizure disorder. It also provides an opportunity to talk about the advantages and disadvantages of disclosure issues, and how to inform friends. Psychoeducational groups for children have been found to increase medical compliance and feelings of competence (Ziegler et al., 2000). In an intervention program that contained both cognitive and affective components, children in the intervention group had greater knowledge in management of seizures and of unnecessary restrictions on their social and play activities. They also demonstrated improved perceptions of their social competency (Lewis, Salas, de la Sota, Chiofalo, & Leake, 1990).

Family Interventions

When quality of life has been measured, parents of children with epilepsy are more likely to rate epilepsy as having an adverse effect than parents of children with diabetes. This was especially true when seizures were poorly controlled, the child had an additional disability, and/or the epilepsy began early in life (Hoare, Mann, & Dunn, 2000). When comorbid conditions are present, especially involving behavioral disorders, parents may need assistance with behavioral management strategies. In families in which a child has intractable seizures, parents often focus on seizure control, believing that educational intervention and psychosocial opportunities can wait until the seizures are controlled. In working with these families, it is important to maintain hope for seizure control, but to encourage activities that contribute to the child's cognitive, educational, and psychological development. Family therapy may be particularly needed when issues concerning independence or medical compliance during adolescence are involved or if family communication is conflictual and nonsupportive.

Individual Therapy

Elementary-age children often need supportive therapy to deal with issues of competence and control. It may be helpful for them to have a therapist to process disclosure issues, as well as how they want to have their seizures handled within the school environment. These children are often aware of auras they experience with the onset of their partial seizures, and the therapist can work with the child on informing school personnel of typical preseizure behavior (Hiemenz et al., 1999). Because these children spend much of their time in the school environment, they are often responsible for managing their condition and frequently are called on to teach others about seizures. Providing the child information about epilepsy during therapy sessions gives them increased feelings of control and less anxiety. Research has suggested that knowledge about epilepsy can influence the child's ability to cope. Issues that may involve stigma, such as peer relationships and academic ability, need to be addressed. Because some children with epilepsy experience academic difficulties, encouraging activities outside of the school environment that enhance feelings of self-esteem and personal control may be helpful.

Adolescents are particularly vulnerable to the psychosocial effects of epilepsy and are at greater risk for depression. Lack of an internal locus of control, negative attitudes toward having epilepsy, and problems with family communication have been frequently associated with occurrence of depression. Targeting these issues may be important in the therapeutic process

(Dunn et al., 1999). In addition, supportive therapy may be needed to address activities involving independence, such as driving, employment, living alone, and college or vocational choices.

Children and adolescents with NES may present for therapeutic intervention. These children and adolescents often experience decreased school performance before the onset of NES and frequently miss excessive amounts of school because of continuing symptoms. Avoidance of aversive activities, such as school attendance or interacting with peers, may be maintaining their symptoms (Williams & Grant, 2000). For those children whose NES symptoms are strongly associated with stressful life events or an anxiety disorder, relaxation techniques—including muscle relaxation, hypnosis, and desensitization—may be effective. Anxiolytic agents or antidepressants in combination with therapy have been useful in the management of these children (Andriola & Ettinger, 1999). Assessment for possible learning problems or disabilities is important, because school failure has been associated with NES. When school attendance is decreased, behavioral interventions may be effective in reducing school avoidance.

Consultation with Medical Providers

The pediatric psychologist can be a valuable asset in the coordinated care of children with epilepsy by providing a communication link with medical care providers, teachers, and parents. The psychologist can work with teachers concerning behavioral observations of children with possible seizures, because the school environment is often the first place that absence seizures are suspected in young children. Observations in the classroom can also assist with medical management through recognition of seizure patterns, adjustment of medication, and monitoring the effects of anticonvulsants on classroom performance or for possible toxicity (Johnson & Thomas, 1999). This information can be directly relayed to the medical care provider.

Consultation with the medical care provider concerning comorbid conditions is critical. Children with comorbid ADHD can be safely treated for both conditions simultaneously. Methylphenidate has been used safely and effectively to decrease ADHD symptoms in children with epilepsy (Gross-Tsur, Manor, van der Meere, Joseph, & Shalev, 1997; Semrud-Clikeman & Wical, 1999).

SUMMARY AND CONCLUSIONS

Seizure disorders are the most common neurological condition in childhood and have the potential to affect both cognitive and emotional functioning. Seizure disorders are highly heterogeneous and differ on multiple dimensions, including etiology, type, syndrome, chronicity, and treatment response. The majority of children with seizure disorders respond well to treatment and experience permanent remission of their seizures. However, some children will develop intractable seizures and require significant medical, educational, and psychosocial interventions. For all children with seizure disorders, there are multiple influences on cognitive and behavioral outcomes, including ongoing seizures, medication effects, sleep disruption, stigma associated with having epilepsy, misinformation, anxiety for the parents and child, and difficulty with family adaptation to the disorder.

Because of the complexity of seizure disorders and the multiple medical, psychosocial, and treatment issues involved, the pediatric psychologist can play a critical role in the total care of these children. Their involvement may include assessment, monitoring achievement and behavior, providing education for the parents, child, and teacher, developing support groups, providing family and individual therapy, and consulting with medical providers. Addressing issues that affect the "whole" child may ensure a more positive prognosis for long-term psychosocial adjustment.

REFERENCES

Aldenkamp, A. P., Alpherts, W. C. J., Blennow, G., Elmqvist, D., Heifbel, J., Nilsson, H. L., Sandstedt, P., Tonnby, B., Wahlander, L., & Wosse, E. (1993). Withdrawal of antiepileptic medication in children: Effects on cognitive function. The multicenter Holmfried study. *Neurology, 43*, 41–50.

Aldenkamp, A. P., Arends, J., Overweg-Plandsoen, T. C. G., van Bronswijk, K. C., Schyns-Soeterboek, A., Linden, I., & Diepman, L. (2000). Acute cognitive effects of nonconvulsive difficult-to-detect epileptic seizures and epileptiform electroencephalographic discharges. *Journal of Child Neurology, 16*, 119–123.

Aldenkamp, A. P., & Mulder, O. G. (1999). Psychosocial consequences of epilepsy. In A. Goreczny & M. Hersen (Eds.), *Handbook of pediatric and adolescent health psychology* (pp. 105–114). Boston: Allyn & Bacon.

Aldenkamp, A. P., Overweg-Plandsoen, W. C. G., & Arends, J. (1999). An open, nonrandomized clinical comparative study evaluating the effect of epilepsy on learning. *Journal of Child Neurology, 14*, 795–800.

Aldenkamp, A. P., Overweg-Plandsoen, W. C. G., & Diepman, L. A. M. (1999). Factors involved in learning problems and educational delay in children with epilepsy. *Child Neuropsychology, 5*(2), 130–136.

Andriola, M. R., & Ettinger, A. B. (1999). Pseudoseizures and other nonepileptic paroxysmal disorders in children and adolescents. *Neurology, 53*(2), S89–S95.

Annegers, J. F. (1996). The epidemiology of epilepsy. In E. Wyllie (Ed.), *The treatment of epilepsy: Principles and practice* (2nd ed., pp. 154–172). Baltimore, MD: Williams & Wilkins.

Austin, J., Dunn, D., Huster, G., & Rose, D. (1998). Development of scales to measure psychosocial care needs of children with seizures and their parents. *Journal of Neuroscience Nursing, 30*(3), 155–160.

Austin, J. K., Huberty, T. J., Huster, G. A., & Dunn, D. W. (1999). Does academic achievement in children with epilepsy change over time? *Developmental Medicine & Child Neurology, 41*, 473–479.

Bailet, L. L., & Turk, W. R. (2000). The impact of childhood epilepsy on neurocognitive and behavioral performance: A prospective longitudinal study. *Epilepsia, 41*(4), 426–431.

Bannon, M. J., Wildig, C., & Jones, P. W. (1992). Teachers perceptions of epilepsy. *Archives of Disease in Childhood, 67*, 1467–1471.

Barkley, R. A. (1990). *Attention deficit hyperactivity disorder: A handbook for diagnosis and treatment.* New York: Guilford.

Baumann, R. J. (2001). Prevention and management of febrile seizures. *Paediatric Drugs, 3*(8), 585–592.

Berg, A. T., & Shinnar, S. (1994). The contributions of epidemiology to the understanding of childhood seizures and epilepsy. *Journal of Child Neurology, 9*(2), 19–26.

Binnie, C. D., Channon, S., & Marston, D. (1990). Learning disabilities in epilepsy: Neurophysiological aspects. *Epilepsia, 31*, S2–S8.

Bjornaes, H., Stabell, K., Henriksen, O., & Loyning, Y. (2001). The effects of refractory epilepsy on intellectual functioning in children and adults: A longitudinal study. *Seizure, 10*(4), 250–259.

Blennow, G., Heijbel, J., Sandstedt, P., & Tonnby, B. (1990). Discontinuation of antiepileptic drugs in children who have outgrown epilepsy: Effects on cognitive function. *Epilepsia, 31*, S50–S53.

Bolter, J. F. (1986). Epilepsy in children: Neuropsychological effects. In J. E. Obrzut & G. W. Hynd (Eds.), *Child neuropsychology* (pp. 59–81). Orlando, FL: Academic Press.

Bourgeois, F. D. (1998). Antiepileptic drugs, learning, and behavior in childhood epilepsy. *Epilepsia, 39*(9), 913–921.

Bourgeois, F. D. (2002). Differential cognitive effects of antiepileptic drugs. *Journal of Child Neurology, 17*(2), 2S28–2S33.

Bulteau, C., Jambaque, I., Viguier, D., Kieffer, V., Dellatolas, G., & Dulac, O. (2000). Epileptic syndromes, cognitive assessment and school placement: A study of 251 children. *Developmental Medicine & Child Neurology, 42*, 319–327.

Camfield, P., & Camfield, C. (2002). Epileptic syndromes in childhood: Clinical features, outcomes, and treatment. *Epilepsia, 43*, 27–32.

Caplan, R., Arbelle, S., Magharious, W., Guthrie, D., Komo, S., Shields, W. D., Chayasirisobhon, S., & Hansen, R. (1998). Psychopathology in pediatric complex partial and primary generalized epilepsy. *Developmental Medicine & Child Neurology, 40*, 805–811.

Carlton-Ford, S., Miller, R., Nealeigh, N., & Sanchez, N. (1997). The effects of perceived stigma and psychological over-control on the behavioural problems of children with epilepsy. *Seizure, 6*, 383–391.

Cohen, M. (1992). Auditory/verbal and visual/spatial memory in children with complex partial epilepsy of temporal lobe origin. *Brain and Cognition, 20*, 315–326.

Croona, C, Kihlgren, M., Lundberg, S., Eeg-Olofsson, O., & Eeg-Olofsson, K. E. (1999). Neuropsychological findings in children with benign childhood epilepsy with centrotemporal spikes. *Developmental Medicine & Child Neurology, 41*, 813–818.

Cross, J. H. (2002). Epilepsy surgery in childhood. *Epilepsia, 43*, 65–70.

Crumrine, P. K. (2002). Antiepileptic drug selection in pediatric epilepsy. *Journal of Child Neurology, 17*(2), 2S2–2S8.

Dam, M. (1990). Children with epilepsy: The effect of seizures, syndromes, and etiological factors on cognitive functioning. *Epilepsia, 31*, S26–S29.

Deonna, T., Zesiger, P., Davidoff, V., Maeder, M., Mayor, C., & Roulet, E. (2000). Benign partial epilepsy of childhood: A longitudinal neuropsychological and EEG study of cognitive function. *Developmental Medicine & Child Neurology, 42*, 595–603.

Dodson, W. E. (1993). Epilepsy and IQ. In W. E. Dodson & J. M. Pellock (Eds.), *Pediatric epilepsy: Diagnosis and therapy* (pp. 373–385). New York: Demos.

Dunn, D. (in press). Neuropsychiatric aspects of epilepsy in children. *Epilepsy and Behavior.*

Dunn, D. W., Austin, J. K., Harezlak, J., Perkins, S., & Ambrosius, W. T. (2001). Do behavioral problems vary by recurrence of seizures? *Epilepsia, 42*(7), 159.

Dunn, D. W., Austin, J. K., & Huster, G. A. (1999). Symptoms of depression in adolescents with epilepsy. *Journal of the American Academy of Child & Adolescent Psychiatry, 38*(9), 1132–1138.

Eriksson, K. J., & Koivikko, M. J. (1997a). Prevalence, classification, and severity of epilepsy and epileptic syndromes in children. *Epilepsia, 38*, 1275–1282.

Eriksson, K. J., & Koivikko, M. J. (1997b). Status epilepticus in children: Aetiology, treatment, and outcome. *Developmental Medicine & Child Neurology, 39*, 652–658.

Ettinger, A. B., Weisbrot, D. M., Nolan, E. E., Gadow, K. D., Vitale, S. A., Andriola, M. R., Lenn, N. J., Novak, G. P., & Hermann, B. P. (1998). Symptoms of depression and anxiety in pediatric epilepsy patients. *Epilepsia, 39*(6), 595–599.

Fiordelli, E., Beghi, E., Boglium, G., & Crespi, V. (1993). Epilepsy and psychiatric disturbance: A cross-sectional study. *British Journal of Psychiatry, 163*, 446–450.

Gates, J., & Erdahl, P. (1993). Classification of non-epileptic events. In J. Rowan & J. Gates (Eds.), *Non-epileptic seizures* (pp. 21–30). Stoneham, MA: Butterworth-Heinemann.

Greenberg, L., Leark, R. A., Dupuy, T. R., Corman, C. L., & Kindschi, C. L. (1988). *Test of variables of attention.* Los Alamitos, CA: Universal Attention Disorders, Inc.

Gross-Tsur, V., Manor, O., van der Meere, J., Joseph, A., & Shalev, R. S. (1997). Epilepsy and attention deficit hyperactivity disorder: Is methylphenidate safe and effective? *Journal of Pediatrics, 130*, 670–674.

Hauser, W. A., & Hesdorffer, D. C. (1990a). *Epilepsy: Frequency, causes, and consequences.* New York: Demos.

Hauser, W. A., & Hesdorffer, D. C. (1990b). *Facts about epilepsy.* New York: Demos.

Hauser, W. A., & Hesdorffer, D. C. (1996). The natural history of seizures. In E. Wyllie (Ed.), *The treatment of epilepsy: Principles and practice* (2nd ed., pp. 173–178). Baltimore, MD: Williams & Wilkins.

Hempel, A. M., Frost, M. D., Ritter, F. J., & Farnham, S. (1995). Factors influencing the incidence of ADHD in pediatric epilepsy patients. *Epilepsia, 36*, 122.

Hermann, B., & Whitman, S. (1992). Psychopathology in epilepsy. *American Psychologist, 47*, 1134–1138.

Hernandez, M. T., Sauerwein, H. C., Jambaque, I., DeGuise, E., Lussier, F., Lortie, A., Dulac, O., & Lassonde, M. (2002). Deficits in executive functions and motor coordination in children with frontal lobe epilepsy. *Neuropsychologia, 40*, 384–400.

Hiemenz, J. R., Hynd, G. W., & Jimenez, M. (1999). Seizure disorders. In R. T. Brown (Ed.), *Cognitive aspects of chronic illness in children* (pp. 238–261). New York: Guilford.

Hoare, P., Mann, H., & Dunn, S. (2000). Parental perception of the quality of life among children with epilepsy or diabetes with a new assessment questionnaire. *Quality of Life Research, 9*, 637–644.

Hodes, M., Garralda, M. E., Rose, G., & Schwartz, R. (1999). Maternal expressed emotion and adjustment in children with epilepsy. *Journal of Child Psychology & Psychiatry & Allied Disciplines, 40*(7), 1083–1093.

Jambaque, I., Dellatolas, G., Dulac, O., Ponsot, G., & Signoret, J. L. (1993). Verbal and visual memory impairment in children with epilepsy. Neuropsychologia, *31*, 1321–1337.

Johnson, M., & Thomas, L. (1999). Schools responses to pupils with epilepsy. *Support for Learning, 14*, 13–21.

Kasteleijn-Nolst-Trenite, D. G. A., Smit, A. M., Velis, D. N., Willemse, J., & van Emde Boas, W. (1990). On-line detection of transient neuropsychological disturbances during EEG discharges in children with epilepsy. *Developmental Medicine & Child Neurology, 32*, 46–50.

Kokkonen, E., Kokkonen, J., & Saukkonen, A. (1998). Do neurological disorders in childhood pose a risk for mental health in young adulthood? *Developmental Medicine & Child Neurology, 40*, 364–368.

Kovacs, M. (1992). *Children's depression inventory*. North Tonawanda, NY: Multi-Health Systems, Inc.

Kyngas, H. (2001). Predictors of good compliance in adolescents with epilepsy. *Seizure, 10*, 549–553.

Lewis, M. A., Salas, I., de la Sota, A., Chiofalo, N., & Leake, B. (1990). Randomized trial of a program to enhance the competencies of children with epilepsy. *Epilepsia, 31*, 101–109.

Mandelbaum, D. E., & Burack, G. D. (1997). The effect of seizure type and medication on cognitive and behavioral functioning in children with idiopathic epilepsy. *Developmental Medicine & Child Neurology, 39*, 731–735.

McNelis, A., Musick, B., Austin, J., Dunn, D., & Creasy, K. (1998). Psychosocial care needs of children with new-onset seizures. *Journal of Neuroscience Nursing, 30*(3), 161–165.

Meador, K. J. (2002). Cognitive outcomes and predictive factors in epilepsy. *Neurology, 58*(8), S21–S26.

Mendez, M., & Radtke, R. A. (2001). Interactions between sleep and epilepsy. *Journal of Clinical Neurophysiology, 18*(2), 106–127.

Millett, C. J., Fish, D. R., & Thompson, P. J. (1997). A survey of epilepsy-patient perceptions of video-game material/electronic screens and other factors as seizure precipitants. *Seizure, 6*, 457–459.

Reynolds, C. R., & Richmond, B. O. (1985). *Revised children's manifest anxiety scale*. Los Angeles, CA: Western Psychological Services.

Ritter, F. J., & Kotagal, P. (2000). Non-epileptic seizures in children. In J. Gates & J. Rowan (Eds.), *Non-epileptic seizures, second edition* (pp. 95–110). Woburn, MA: Butterworth-Heinemann.

Sanger, M. S., Perrin, E. C., & Sandler, H. M. (1993). Development in children's causal theories of their seizure disorders. *Developmental and Behavioral Pediatrics, 14*, 88–93.

Schoenfeld, J., Seidenberg, M., Woodard, A., Hecox, K., Inglese, C., Mack, K., & Hermann, B. (1999). Neuropsychological and behavioral status of children with complex partial seizures. *Developmental Medicine & Child Neurology, 41*, 724–731.

Seidenberg, M., & Berent, S. (1992). Childhood epilepsy and the role of psychology. *American Psychologist, 47*, 1130–1133.

Semrud-Clikeman, M., & Wical, B. (1999). Components of attention in children with complex partial seizures with and without ADHD. *Epilepsia, 40*(2), 211–215.

Sharp, G. B., & Wilder, B. J. (2000). *Epilepsy and the use of antiepileptic drugs (reference guide)*. Cincinnati, OH: USA: Shire Richwood, Inc.

Shore, C., Austin, J., Musick, B., Dunn, D., McBride A., & Creasy, K. (1998). Psychosocial care needs of parents of children with new-onset seizures. *Journal of Neuroscience Nursing, 30*(3), 169–174.

Sillanpaa, M., Jalava, M., Kaleva, O. & Shinnar, S. (1998). Long-term prognosis of seizures with onset in childhood. *New England Journal of Medicine, 338*, 1715–1722.

Smith, M. L., Elliott, I. M., & Lach, L. (2002). Intelligence, memory, attention and academic skills in children with intractable epilepsy: Comparison of surgical and non-surgical candidates. *Epilepsia, 43*(6), 631–637.

Stores, G., Wiggs, L., & Campling G. (1998). Sleep disorders and their relationship to psychological disturbance in children with epilepsy. *Child: Care, Health & Development, 24*(1), 5–19.

Suurmeijer, Th. P. B. M. (1994). Quality of care and quality of life from the perspective of patients and parents. *International Journal of Adolescent Medicine and Health, 7*, 289–302.

Thomas, S. V., & Bindu, V. B. (1999). Psychosocial and economic problems of parents of children with epilepsy. *Seizure, 8*, 66–69.

Treiman, D. M., & Treiman, L. J. (1996). Genetic aspects of epilepsy. In E. Wyllie (Ed.), *Treatment of epilepsy: Principles and practice,* (2nd ed., pp. 151–164). Baltimore, MD: Williams & Wilkins.

Williams, J. (in press). Learning and behavior in children with epilepsy. *Epilepsy and Behavior*.

Williams, J., Bates, S., Griebel, M. L., Lange, B., Mancias, P., Pihoker, C. M., & Dykman, R. (1998). Does short-term antiepileptic drug treatment in children result in cognitive or behavioral changes? *Epilepsia, 39*(10), 1064–1069.

Williams, J., & Grant, M. (2000). Characteristics of pediatric NES patients: A retrospective study. In J. Gates & J. Rowan (Eds.), *Non-epileptic seizures* (2nd ed., pp. 197–206). Woburn, MA: Butterworth-Heinemann.

Williams, J., Griebel, M. L., & Dykman, R. A. (1998). Neuropsychological patterns in pediatric epilepsy. *Seizure, 7*, 223–228.

Williams, J., Phillips, T., Griebel, M., Sharp, G., Lange, B., Edgar, T., & Simpson, P. (2001). Factors associated with academic achievement in children with controlled epilepsy. *Epilepsy and Behavior, 2*, 217–223.

Williams, J., & Sharp, G. B. (1999). Epilepsy. In K. O. Yeates, M. D. Ris, & H. G. Taylor (Eds.), *Pediatric neuropsycholgy* (pp. 47–73). New York: Guilford Press.

Williams, J., Sharp, G. B., Bates, S., Griebel, M., Lange, B., Spence, G. T., & Thomas, P. (1996). Academic achievement and behavioral ratings in children with absence and complex partial epilepsy. *Education and Treatment of Children, 19*, 143–152.

Ziegler, R. G., Erba, G., Holden, L., & Dennison, H. (2000). The coordinated psychosocial and neurologic care of children with seizures and their families. *Epilepsia, 41*(6), 732–743.

Zelnik, N., Sa'adi, L., Silman-Stolar, Z., & Goikhman, I. (2001). Seizure control and educational outcome in childhood-onset epilepsy. *Journal of Child Neurology, 16*, 820–824.

14

Hematological Disorders: Sickle Cell Disease and Hemophilia

Melanie J. Bonner
Kristina K. Hardy
Elizabeth Ezell
Russell Ware
Duke University Medical Center

INTRODUCTION

The hematological system depends on several types of cells and proteins for normal childhood development. To function properly, a complex system of red and white blood cells (neutrophils and lymphocytes), circulating blood platelets, and coagulant/anticoagulant proteins must work together. Problems in one or more components of this system can result in hematological diseases, some that are congenital and others that are acquired. In children, hematological disorders can be classified by cell of origin, clinical manifestations, whether the disorder is quantitative or qualitative, or by other parameters (Thompson, Gustafson, & Ware, 1998). This chapter will focus on two common hematological disorders: sickle cell disease and hemophilia. Although most children with these disorders function well, some are at risk for direct neurocognitive effects and indirect behavioral and psychosocial effects. These effects can impact a child's performance in the classroom, considering the significant amount of time children spend in educational settings. Given the potential impact of these disorders on school functioning, including academic skills and social development, pediatric psychologists can serve as a valuable resource to school personnel who are responsible for educating all children, including those with chronic illness. Indeed, the expertise of the pediatric psychologist can significantly enhance the quality of life of patients with hematological disorders through assessments and interventions that address cognitive and academic functioning, school attendance, pain control, and peer relations.

This chapter begins with a biomedical description of both disorders, followed by recent research findings pertaining to the neurocognitive and psychosocial correlates of these diseases. In the final section, recommendations that highlight the potential role of the pediatric psychologist will be offered.

BIOMEDICAL FACTORS

Hemophilia and sickle cell disease refer to a collection of inherited hematological disorders rather than single disease entities. Medical advances in recent years have resulted in improved treatment of these diseases, such that prognosis has improved measurably over time. The sections herein summarize the biomedical aspects of these diseases, including pathogenesis, pathophysiology, and medical treatment.

Hemophilia

Hemophilia is a group of inherited hematological diseases marked by the deficiency of one of several clotting factors, most commonly Factor VIII or Factor IX. Both of these deficiencies are recessive, X-linked traits and are thus carried by females and expressed in males. Patients with hemophilia are unable to produce normal fibrin clots and therefore are vulnerable to spontaneous and prolonged bleeding. Such bleeding episodes are very painful and most commonly occur in joints and muscles. The degree of coagulation factor deficiency determines the severity of the disease, ranging from mild to severe. In mild cases, hemorrhage occurs only after a surgical procedure, whereas spontaneous bleeding may occur in severe cases. With repeated bleeding episodes, patients may experience severe damage to a particular joint, which can result in chronic pain, limited range of motion, and physical deformity. Although rare, patients with moderate-to-severe hemophilia are also at risk for intracranial hemorrhaging (Hoots & Cecalupo, 1994).

Patients with hemophilia generally require comprehensive, long-term care, including family education, prevention, medical management, pain management, physical rehabilitation, and supportive psychological services (Huszti & Rosko, 1994; Thompson et al., 1998). Medical management of bleeding episodes typically involves intravenous infusion of the deficient coagulation factor, thereby facilitating the formation of blood clots. Prompt factor replacement is especially important among patients who experience severe hemorrhaging, as delays in treatment can result in destruction of joints. For this reason, patients and their families are often taught to administer factor replacement at home. Some treatment regimens also include routine factor replacement infusions as a prophylactic measure. Although a synthetic replacement compound is available for patients with mild Factor VIII deficiency, most factor concentrates are derived from human blood products that retain a slight risk of viral transmission despite being purified. Indeed, before the availability of purification procedures and human immunodeficiency virus (HIV) screening for blood donors, more than 90% of patients with hemophilia who received blood products were infected with HIV (Brookmeyer & Goedert, 1989).

The spread of HIV/acquired immune deficiency syndrome (AIDS) disrupted previous increases in life expectancy among hemophilia patients. Although improved medical management of hemophilia (e.g., factor replacement therapy) was initially associated with increased survival, mortality subsequently worsened. Specifically, the estimated median life expectancy for patients with hemophilia fell from nearly 68 years in the 1970s to 49 years in the 1980s (Jones & Ratnoff, 1991). More recent estimates reveal improved outcomes for patients with hemophilia, with the median age of death increasing from 40 years during the 1980s to 46 years during the late 1990s (Chorba, Holman, Clarke, & Evatt, 2001). Thus, although the introduction of HIV and AIDS among patients with hemophilia has greatly compounded the medical and psychosocial stressors inherent in coping with this chronic illness, improved treatment for HIV/AIDS has begun to result in better outcomes for patients with hemophilia.

Sickle Cell Disease

Sickle cell disease (SCD) is a group of inherited disorders affecting approximately one in every 400–500 African-American newborns in the United States (Tarnowski & Brown, 2000), making it a significant public health concern (Thompson et al., 1998). Although most common in persons of African descent, SCD also affects other ethnic groups, including persons of Mediterranean, Caribbean, South and Central American, Arabian, and East Indian descent.

SCD results from an autosomal recessive genetic deficit and is classified by genotype. Persons affected with SCD demonstrate abnormal genes for hemoglobin S, which produce a change in the shape of red blood cells from their normal disk shape to a sickle shape. These abnormally shaped cells obstruct normal blood flow and production of new red blood cells, resulting in chronic anemia. The most common type of SCD is the homozygous condition, sickle cell anemia (Hb SS) that is caused by two abnormal genes for hemoglobin S and is associated with earlier and more frequent and severe symptoms than other types (Charache, Lubin, & Reid, 1989). Other common types include sickle cell hemoglobin C, and sickle beta-thalassemia (HbS beta-thalassemia). Persons who inherit only one abnormal gene have the sickle cell trait, which is associated with a predominance of normal hemoglobin and is not a disease.

In addition to anemia, persons with SCD commonly experience obstructions in blood flow (vaso-occlusions) that can occur anywhere in the body and result in tissue and organ damage. The most common problem associated with vaso-occlusions is a painful episode called a *crisis* that may result in pain in the musculoskeletal system, abdomen, and/or lower back. Pain crises may be precipitated by dehydration, infections, injury, and extreme cold, with the frequency and severity of the pain episodes varying within and between patients.

Vaso-occulsions also can occur in the brain, putting children with SCD at increased risk for neurological diseases, including stroke. Stroke occurs in 7–17% of children with SCD (Type Hb SS) and is a significant cause of morbidity. These strokes may be clinically detectable or may reflect microvascular infarcts without overt symptoms, called *silent* strokes. If untreated, recurrent strokes are common (Platt et al., 1994).

Although SCD continues to be associated with a reduced life expectancy (median age of survival = 42 years for males and 48 years for females; Charache, 1994; Platt et al., 1994), treatment for the disease has improved significantly since 1972 when Congress passed the National Sickle Cell Anemia Control Act (Cohen, 1998; Ris & Grueneich, 2000). Moreover, the initiation of the Cooperative Study of Sickle Cell Disease (CSSCD) in 1979 (Gaston & Rosse, 1982), a large, multicenter study, resulted in a better understanding of the natural history of the disease and the efficacy of specific treatment interventions.

More recent clinical, molecular, and genetic advances have further improved the care of patients with SCD (Hagar & Vichinsky, 2000). For example, given the potentially serious effects of stroke, neuroradiological procedures have been evaluated to determine their effectiveness in identifying at-risk patients. The Stroke Prevention Trial in Sickle Cell Anemia (STOP) included a consortium of 14 clinical centers that participated in a randomized clinical trial using transcranial Doppler ultrasonography (TCD) to evaluate patients for stroke risk. TCD is a noninvasive procedure that identifies areas of the brain with higher than normal blood flow velocity, an index of stroke risk (Adams et al., 1998). Patients deemed *high risk* were randomized to receive either chronic transfusions to reduce the percentage of HbS or standard care. Transfusion treatment resulted in significant reduction in stroke, which lead to early termination of the trial. Given the positive results, the National Heart, Lung, and Blood Institute issued a Clinical Alert recommending transfusion treatment for children with SCD aged 2–16 who demonstrate stroke risk on the basis of TCD (Adams, 2000). Thus, these findings highlight the efficacy of both an evaluation procedure (TCD) and a treatment (chronic blood transfusions). Although encouraging, both TCD and transfusions are not without risks.

Specifically, although the STOP study demonstrates the utility of TCD in identifying patients at risk for stroke, a recent study found discrepant findings when TCD and magnetic resonance imaging (MRI) data were compared (Wang et al., 2000). Comparisons of the two neurodiagnostic tests were made in 78 children with no history of overt stroke who participated in both the CSSCD and STOP trials. MRI data from the CSSCD study were classified as either *silent infarct* or *normal*, and TCD data were classified as *normal, conditional*, or *abnormal*. Discordant results were found for 23 of the patients. The researchers concluded that these neurodiagnositic procedures identify different aspects of pathophysiology of central nervous system (CNS) injury in children with SCD, and that more sensitive and specific indicators of early CNS pathology, including neuropsychological testing, are needed.

Additionally, although prophylactic blood transfusion therapy has been shown to reduce stroke risk and holds promise of decreased major symptoms of acute chest syndrome and severe pain crises, there are risks associated with this therapy, including reactions, infections, and iron overload (Hagar & Vichinsky, 2000). This suggests the need for alternative therapies (Ware, Zimmerman, & Schultz, 1999). For example, clinical trials are underway to assess the efficacy of hydroxyurea (HU), an antineoplastic drug that stimulates the production of fetal hemoglobin (HbF), which is a determinant in the clinical severity of patients with SCD.

A few small studies have demonstrated the short-term safety and efficacy of HU in children with SCD (Hoppe et al., 2000; Rogers, 1997; Vichinsky, 1997). The efficacy has also been demonstrated by results from the Pediatric Hydroxyurea Study Group, a large, multicenter Phase I/II trial (Kinney et al., 1999). Participants included 84 children with SCD aged 5–15, 52 of whom were treated with the maximum tolerated HU dose for a year. Most children experienced significant hematological improvements with minimum toxicity and no life-threatening events.

Additionally, HU may be an alternative to blood transfusions for children with recurrent stroke. In a recent study, transfusion therapy was prospectively discontinued in 16 pediatric patients with SCD who had experienced a previous stroke (Ware et al., 1999). The preliminary findings suggested that pediatric patients tolerate and benefit from HU. Only three patients had recurrent stroke; however, these occurred before maximal HU effects could be achieved. Additionally, phlebotomy was well-tolerated and significantly reduced iron overload. Thus, HU appears to be an efficacious and safe treatment for pediatric patients resulting in improved HbF levels and stroke prevention. Long-term trials are now needed to help determine the tolerance of HU and its impact on morbidity, mortality, and quality of life.

Finally, use of bone marrow transplantation holds promise for some patients with SCD (Hoppe & Walters, 2001; Nietert, Abboud, Silverstein, & Jackson, 2000; Walters et al., 2000). In one recent study, 50 children who had symptomatic SCD received matched sibling marrow transplants. Of that sample, 26 were followed for at least 2 years posttransplant to evaluate clinical efficacy and adverse effects. For the majority of patients (22 of 26), SCD symptoms resolved including an absence of further episodes of pain, stroke, or acute chest syndrome. Moreover, stability in physiological functions and CNS studies was found. An adverse effect on ovarian functioning was documented in 5 of 7 females who were at least 13 years of age. Although encouraging overall, patient variables, suitable donors, and other medical risks limit the scope of this treatment option (Hagar & Vichinsky, 2000; Walters, 1999).

Summary

Much progress has been made in the treatment of hemophilia and SCD, lending hope for improved outcomes. Given this, the range of potential effects of these diseases and their treatment on cognition, adjustment, and quality of life needs to be investigated to help determine the long-term sequelae of these chronic conditions (Frank, Allison, & Cant, 1999). Because children spend much of their time in school, particular attention to the impact of these diseases on cognitive and academic functioning is needed.

COGNITIVE AND ACADEMIC FACTORS

Studies of the cognitive and academic functioning of children with hemophilia and SCD have revealed inconsistent findings regarding the nature, extent, and severity of deficits. Although methodological problems likely account for some of these inconsistencies as described herein, the findings suggest that children with these diseases are at risk for problems.

Hemophilia

Children and adolescents with hemophilia appear to be at risk for subtle neurocognitive difficulties, as well as academic underachievement. Most studies have documented average overall cognitive functioning among this population, with a normal distribution (Olch, 1971). However, at least one study provided evidence of cognitive weaknesses among children with hemophilia. For example, Whitt et al. (1993) found subtle neurocognitive deficits among patients with hemophilia with regard to motor performance, attention, and speeded visual processing. In addition, a number of studies have documented discrepancies in children's cognitive and academic functioning (e.g., Colegrove & Huntzinger, 1994; Sirois & Hill, 1993; Smith et al., 1997; Woolf et al., 1989). For example, Woolf and colleagues (1989) found that 6 of 22 children displayed academic achievement more than two grade levels below expectation in math and/or reading. Similarly, Smith and colleagues (1997) documented math and spelling achievement at the low end of the average range among children whose mean Full-Scale IQ was in the High-Average range. This pattern of findings suggests that children and adolescents with hemophilia are at risk for academic underachievement and learning difficulties. Of note, the severity of children's hemophilia has not been found to correlate with academic achievement scores (Woolf et al., 1989).

In addition to the risk posed by hemophilia itself, many patients face the risk of neurocognitive sequelae of HIV infection (Hoots & Cecalupo, 1994). Given the prevalence of HIV infection among pediatric patients with hemophilia, a multicenter study has begun to evaluate the long-term functioning of such patients with and without HIV infection. The Hemophilia Growth and Development Study (HGDS) is a longitudinal investigation that has studied the physical, neurocognitive, and psychosocial functioning of boys with moderate-to-severe hemophilia since 1989. At baseline, 333 boys (6–18 years old) were included in the study, approximately 60% of whom were HIV-seropositive (HIV+; Loveland et al., 1994).

Results from the HGDS at baseline revealed overall cognitive functioning at age-expected levels, with no differences emerging among children with and without HIV infection (Loveland et al., 1994). In addition, academic skills were lower than expected among both HIV+ and HIV- hemophilia patients, given their mean IQ scores. In follow-up studies with this sample, Sirois et al. (1998) found that lowered neuropsychological functioning was associated with hemophilia-related morbidity (e.g., coordination and gait abnormalities) rather than HIV status. Moreover, a pattern of age-expected cognitive abilities but significantly weaker academic skills among patients with hemophilia, regardless of HIV status, remained true at a 4-year follow-up assessment (Loveland et al., 2000). Such a discrepancy in cognitive and academic functioning is consistent with results from earlier studies and indicates that reduced academic performance is likely related to hemophilia and its effects rather than to the presence of HIV. Indeed, in a 4-year follow-up study, differences in neuropsychological functioning between patients with hemophilia with and without HIV were apparent only among children with the largest declines in immune functioning. Specifically, these patients with HIV+ showed significantly lower functioning in nonverbal intelligence and memory, perceptual/performance skills, academic achievement (reading and spelling), and language (Loveland et al., 2000).

It also has been suggested that academic difficulties among patients with hemophilia may result from school absences related to medical treatment or from bleeding episodes (Colegrove &

Huntzinger, 1994; Huszti & Rosko, 1994; Varni & Wallander, 1988). Indeed, Woolf et al. (1989) found that their sample of 26 boys with hemophilia had nearly three times as many absences as the national average for children with chronic illness. However, school absences were not significantly related to academic achievement, consistent with findings from other studies (e.g., Mayes et al., 1996; Olch, 1971). Woolf et al. (1989) argue that increased school attendance alone likely will not suffice to address these students' difficulties; rather, special educational services are probably indicated in many cases.

Sickle Cell Disease

Early studies of SCD resulted in equivocal findings regarding cognitive effects of the disease. Although most studies identified some cognitive impairment, the type and severity of the deficiencies varied, likely as a function of methodological weaknesses. Specifically, some studies used general intellectual functioning as the outcome measure, whereas others used both general and specific measures of neuropsychological functioning, as well as academic skills (for reviews, see Bonner, Gustafson, Schumacher, & Thompson, 1999; Brown, Armstrong, & Eckman, 1993; Lemanek, Buckloh, Woods, & Butler, 1995). Additionally, most studies are cross-sectional in design and the type of control group used has been variable (e.g., sibling control, chronic illness control, normal control). Moreover, until recently, most studies did not include neuroradiological outcome data, making it difficult to evaluate the impact of SCD in children with no history of overt stroke. Finally, many early studies did not consider the potentially important impact of sociodemographic factors on outcome (Brown, Armstrong et al., 1993). Despite these methodological weaknesses, it has become apparent that children with SCD are at increased risk for neurocognitive impairment. Findings from relevant studies are reviewed herein, including those that used samples with no evidence of overt clinical stroke, those with documented clinical stroke, and those with subclinical or silent stroke.

Studies have consistently revealed deficits in the cognitive functioning of children with SCD. The nature and severity of these deficits varies as a function of several factors including the presence of cerebral infarction. However, there is evidence that, even in the absence of stroke, SCD is associated with cognitive deficits (for a review, see Schatz, Finke, Kellet, and Kramer, 2002).

Early studies by Fowler and associates (1988) and Swift and colleagues (1989) found that, compared with healthy and comparison sibling controls, children with SCD performed lower on tests of intellectual functioning and academic achievement. Deficits in intellectual functioning were also reported by Wasserman, Willmas, Fairclogh, Mulhern, and Wang (1991), though no differences in academic achievement were found when compared with healthy peers.

Brown, Buchanan et al. (1993) compared the cognitive and academic functioning of 70 children, aged 2–17 to nondiseased siblings. Although there was no evidence of overt stroke, children with SCD performed more poorly than the control group on measures of sustained attention. Moreover, consistent with Fowler et al. (1988), significant differences in achievement scores were also found on a reading subtest when compared with nondiseased siblings. Additionally, overall intellectual and academic functioning were related to socioeconomic status and hemoglobin level. This study highlighted the potential impact of SCD on the frontal region of the brain, given that this area of the brain is strongly associated with attention. The study also underscores the importance of assessing sociodemographic factors in addition to biomedical risk factors.

Recently, Noll et al. (2001) compared children with SCD who had no history of overt clinical stroke with case controls. This study extended previous investigations by using a control group of nonchronically ill peers matched for age, gender, race, and demographics. This enabled the researchers to be sensitive to sociodemographic and developmental factors while addressing the problem of using sibling controls, given the potential impact of chronic illness on other family members. Findings revealed significant deficits in neuropsychological functioning in the SCD sample, including lower performance on verbal, attention, and overall neurocognitive functioning.

Studies investigating the impact of overt clinical stroke have revealed expected findings with the pattern of stroke influencing the pattern of neuropsychological deficits. For example, children who suffered a diffuse cortical stroke exhibited impairments in spatial ability, whereas children with anterior lesions exhibited deficits in attention (Craft, Schatz, Glauser, Lee & DeBaun, 1993). Cohen and associates (1997) found that children with left-hemisphere stroke demonstrated expected impairments in verbal intellectual functioning (Mean Verbal IQ = 66.50), as well as weaknesses in language and immediate auditory/verbal memory when compared with children who suffered right-hemisphere stroke. Additionally, when compared with normally developing children, children with left-hemisphere stroke evidenced problems with attention and hyperactivity. Children who suffered right-hemisphere stroke experienced nonverbal/spatial impairment (Mean Verbal IQ = 82.17; Mean Performance IQ = 66.67).

Similarly, Schatz et al. (1999) demonstrated that children with SCD who suffered anterior cerebral infarcts evidenced deficits on measures of attention and executive functioning. White, Salorio, Schatz, and DeBaun (2000) found differences in verbal working memory in children depending on the region of the brain affected. Children with anterior infarcts demonstrated an overall word span consistent with that of controls, but the typical effect of word length on span was reduced.

Of importance, research has suggested that the 11–20% of all children with SCD who have no evidence of neurological disease on clinical examination have cerebral infarction (silent stroke) that is detectable on MRI (Hindmarsh, Brozovic, Brook, & Davies, 1987; Kinney et al., 1999; Pavlakis et al., 1988). Thus, the potentially high rate of false negatives on clinical examination is concerning from the standpoint that silent strokes may contribute to neuropsychological morbidity and put children at greater risk for clinical stroke.

Findings from an ongoing, longitudinal study from the Cincinnati Children's Hospital Medical Center highlights the importance of neuroimaging data when evaluating the neuropsychological functioning of children with SCD (for a review, see Ris & Grueneich, 2000). Thirty-two children with SCD with no evidence of clinical stroke on neurological examination demonstrated lower scores on measures of Full-Scale IQ, composite measures of verbal skills, attention and memory skills, and impulsivity when compared with matched normal classroom controls. Neuropsychological functioning was not associated with disease type or severity (Ris, Grueneich, & Kalinyak, 1995). Of importance, however, findings from MRI and MRI perfusion studies obtained on 22 of the children revealed that 10 children (45% of the sample) demonstrated abnormalities, including structural abnormalities involving the white matter and hypoperfusion in the frontal lobes. As expected, the presence of these abnormalities was related to the clinical severity of the disease. Moreover, these MRI abnormalities were associated with greater variability (test scatter, discrepancies in scores) in neuropsychological test performance, but not with IQ or composite scores. This study may help explain some of the inconsistencies in neuropsychological findings from earlier studies that did not include neuroimaging measures.

Only a few additional studies have evaluated the correlation between silent stroke and neuropsychological functioning. One study used a sample of children selected from a subset of the CSSCD (Armstrong et al., 1996). This subset included 194 children with SCD aged 6–12 years, 135 of whom had type Hb SS. The subjects completed both an MRI study and a neuropsychological evaluation, including measures of intellectual functioning, academic achievement, motor speed and coordination, and parent-reported behavioral adjustment. Results revealed that 17% of the sample experienced CNS abnormalities, with 12.4% of those categorized as silent stroke. In children with type Hb SS, 22.2% evidenced abnormal MRIs, with 15.6% consistent with silent stroke. As expected, children with overt evidence of stroke exhibited the most significant neuropsychological impairments. Although children with silent stroke did not demonstrate problems as severe or pervasive, they did perform significantly worse than children with no MRI abnormalities on tests of arithmetic, vocabulary, and visual-motor speed and coordination.

More recently, Brown and colleagues (2000) compared children with clinical stroke to those with silent stroke and no stroke on neuropsychological and MRI measures. Participants were 63 children and adolescents with SCD who had been referred for learning problems and/or adjustment difficulties. The results revealed that children with a history of clinical stroke or silent stroke performed more poorly on tasks requiring sustained attention when compared with the no stroke group. Moreover, these groups exhibited a high frequency of damage in the frontal lobes on MRI. Of note, no significant differences were revealed on measures of IQ, academic achievement, and visual-motor processing. The researchers cited a possible *floor effect* on these general measures, given that the children in this study were specifically referred because of academic problems. Indeed, 40% of the sample were receiving special education services, including those without CNS pathology. This study reveals the importance of including specific measures of attention and concentration when evaluating children with SCD considered at risk for CNS involvement. Indeed a meta-analytic study of cognitive functioning in children with SCD suggested that measures of specific abilities appear more sensitive to cognitive decrements than IQ scores (Schatz, Finke, Kellett, and Kramer, 2002).

Although the findings regarding academic achievement have been inconsistent, it appears that SCD has the most significant impact on reading abilities. However, studies of other aspects of school functioning (e.g., absenteeism, special education services, grade point average) have generally found no differences between children with SCD and controls. Indeed, although children with SCD have more frequent absences than their healthy peers, Brown, Buchanan, et al. (1993) found no relationship between absenteeism and academic achievement scores.

More recently, education attainment was evaluated in children with SCD and silent stroke (Schatz, Brown, Pascual, Hsu, & DeBaun, 2001). Nineteen children with SCD (type Hb SS) and silent infarcts on MRI were evaluated on measures of neurocognitive functioning and academic achievement, as well as parent interview to assess academic history (e.g., grade retention, special education services). Comparison groups included 45 children with overt stroke and 18 siblings without SCD. Results revealed that, for children with silent stroke, nearly 60% were retained or required special education services at the time of study enrollment, compared with 27% of children without silent stroke and only 6% of siblings without SCD. Children in the silent stroke group were followed for an additional 3 years, resulting in additional cases of attainment difficulties for a total of 74%. A similar pattern was found for measures of academic achievement and neuropsychological performance, with the silent stroke group showing the most significant deficits. Moreover, neuropsychological deficits were most likely if the silent infarct involved the frontal lobes. These findings suggest that educational outcomes should be considered as another indicator of silent stroke. Additionally, location of the lesion serves as a specific risk factor.

Summary

Overall, the findings from these studies suggest the utility of neuropsychological testing as a valuable, noninvasive screening tool when identifying children in need of more extensive neurological and radiological evaluations (Brown, Davis et al., 2000). Of importance, evaluation should extend beyond general (e.g., IQ) or composite measures to identify accurately the range of deficiencies that might be present. Ideally, such testing would be a standard of care for all children with SCD, beginning early in life to establish baseline levels of functioning from which to monitor development. Indeed, although the studies are few, findings from studies of preschool-age children suggest that developmental testing should begin in infancy to help determine at what point in development children with SCD first experience neuropsychological sequelae (Bonner et al., 1999). Findings from a 5–year longitudinal developmental follow-up study by Thompson, Gustafson, Bonner, and Ware (2002) at the Duke–UNC Comprehensive Sickle Cell Center suggest that whereas early development is markedly normal, there is greater variability with age.

Although extremely important to assess, neuropsychological functioning does not account for all of the variance in school functioning. For example, several studies have found correlations between neuropsychological difficulties and sociodemographic variables. Moreover, school functioning can also be impacted by psychosocial variables. Such findings lend support for the addition of psychosocial assessment in the comprehensive care of children with hematological disorders.

PSYCHOSOCIAL FACTORS

Despite the increased risk for psychosocial problems in children with chronic illness, relatively few studies have been conducted (LaGreca, 1990, 1992), and fewer still pertain to children with hemophilia and SCD. Additionally, most investigations of behavioral and emotional functioning rely on parent report measures rather than clinical or diagnostic interviews. Moreover, when evaluating the important role of peer relations in children with chronic illness, studies tend to rely on parent and teacher reports of social competence rather than using peer sociometric ratings that are standard in the developmental literature. As such, the distinction between acceptance by the peer group at large and the quality of individual friendships is largely ignored, and perception of the social skills of children with chronic illness by the peers themselves is relatively undocumented. Despite these problems, evidence from a few studies suggests some general and unique psychosocial stressors experienced by some children with hemophilia and SCD that put them at risk for adjustment-related difficulties. The following sections summarize the literature to date on the psychosocial variables that have emerged as important and also highlight the resiliency found in this population.

Hemophilia

Relatively few empirical studies have assessed the psychosocial adjustment of pediatric patients with hemophilia. Of those that have been conducted, most are limited by small sample sizes and nonstandardized measures.

Emotional Functioning. Several early studies suggested that hemophilia was associated with increased risk for children's depressive symptoms (Klein & Nimorwicz, 1982) and internalizing symptoms (Wallander & Varni, 1986). In addition, the spread of HIV/AIDS among this population has heightened the emotional challenges involved in coping with a chronic illness. Not surprisingly, Bussing and Burket (1993) found a higher rate of anxiety disorders among boys with hemophilia who were also HIV+, compared with patients with hemophilia who were HIV-. However, findings remain mixed, because several other studies have not revealed elevated levels of depression or anxiety symptoms among children with hemophilia (Logan et al., 1990; Mayes et al., 1996; Overby, Lo, & Litt, 1989). The presence of HIV could, however, complicate the development of adolescents' sexual identity, given the social stigma of HIV, fear of disclosure, and the fear of sexual transmission (Forsberg, King, Delaronde, & Geary, 1997).

Finally, stress management appears to be especially important among patients with hemophilia. As with any chronic illness, children with hemophilia face a number of disease related stressors. For example, these children often endure painful bleeding episodes, hospitalizations, school absences, and restricted physical activity (Varni & Wallander, 1988). Not only do such stressors likely affect children's emotional adjustment, but also there is some evidence to suggest that stress may contribute to spontaneous bleeding episodes. Indeed, Perrin, MacLean, and Janco (1988) reviewed a number of relevant case reports and empirical studies, concluding that stress is likely related to bleeding among children with hemophilia.

Behavioral Functioning. Given the numerous stressors that patients with hemophilia may face, it is not surprising that they also might experience behavioral and emotional difficulties. An early study revealed that children with hemophilia displayed significantly higher levels of defiance and hostility than a group of healthy controls, according to maternal reports (Meijer, 1980). In addition, Wallander and Varni (1986) found that children with hemophilia were at increased risk for both internalizing and externalizing behavior problems. Mayes and colleagues (1996) also reported elevated levels of attention problems among hemophilia patients, according to teacher reports on behavior rating scales. However, research findings remain mixed, because a number of studies have revealed behavioral functioning among pediatric patients with hemophilia within the normal range (Colegrove & Huntzinger, 1994; Sirois & Hill, 1993).

The HGDS has provided a more recent investigation of psychosocial factors associated with hemophilia and HIV. Loveland et al. (1994) investigated adaptive behaviors (e.g., communication, daily living skills) among children and adolescents with hemophilia. They found that, although these patients displayed mean adaptive behavior scores in the average range regardless of their HIV status, their scores were lower than expected, given their relatively higher mean IQ scores. A 4-year follow-up study of this sample indicated lowered levels of adaptive behaviors only among children who were HIV+, with the greatest declines in immune functioning (Nichols et al., 2000). Specifically, children with lower immune functioning showed below-average communication skills on the Vineland Adaptive Rating Scales (Nichols et al., 2000). In addition, behavior problems as reported by parents (e.g., attention, conduct) decreased over time for all children with hemophilia (Nichols et al., 2000).

Social Functioning. A number of social stressors commonly accompany hemophilia. For example, children with hemophilia can sometimes suffer social isolation because of medically related school absences and/or parental protectiveness (Huszti & Rosko, 1994). In addition, patients and their families often fear public misconceptions about hemophilia and are therefore wary of disclosing their hemophilia diagnosis (Huszti & Rosko, 1994; Oremland, 1986). Such fears are only exacerbated with the additional diagnosis of HIV infection or AIDS.

Hemophilia also poses restrictions on children's physical activity, given the risks of uncontrolled bleeding secondary to injury. Children with hemophilia therefore have somewhat reduced opportunities for social interaction via team sports involving physical contact. However, hemophilia patients are encouraged to engage in physical activity that poses little risk to joints (e.g., swimming). With the advent of prophylactic factor replacement therapies, more children with mild cases of hemophilia may be able to engage in a wider variety of sports; however, caution is recommended. With damage to their joints resulting from bleeds, children with hemophilia often become dependent on their parents' help with daily tasks. However, degree of physical impairment has not been found to be related to these children's psychosocial adjustment (e.g., Wallander & Varni, 1986).

Finally, although overall social competence among patients with hemophilia has been estimated in the normal range, school absences have been associated with lower teacher ratings of social competence for boys with hemophilia (Colegrove & Huntzinger, 1994).

Sickle Cell Disease

Although most children with SCD do *not* manifest adjustment problems, both direct and indirect effects of SCD may impede development across emotional, behavioral, and social domains. Physical restrictions and painful crises may limit or delay opportunities to participate in developmentally critical processes, such as gaining independence from parents, interacting with peers, and forming an integrated sense of self-identity (e.g., Robinson, 1999; Sexson & Dingle, 1997). Difficulties in these areas are likely to impact further a child's academic progress and adaptive functioning in the school setting. Moreover, even those who cope successfully with SCD may face periods of difficulty as they encounter new developmental tasks and transitions. In a recent longitudinal study, investigators found that individuals' adjustment to SCD is relatively unstable, such that good adjustment at one time point did not necessarily predict adaptive functioning at another, and vice versa (Thompson, Gustafson, Gil, Kinney, & Spock, 1999). Thus, it is important to be aware of risk factors associated with poor adjustment.

Before reviewing the literature in this area, it is also important to note that social and cultural factors have been largely neglected in the research conducted to date (Barbarin & Christian, 1999). Within the systems framework, these factors are considered essential components that interact with biomedical aspects of the disease to predict adjustment outcomes. Because the population of individuals affected with SCD is predominantly African-American, the omission of sociocultural factors in this research makes it difficult to tease apart those factors specific to SCD that contribute to the prevalence, severity, and origins of psychosocial adjustment problems among individuals with the disease. Indeed, there is little evidence for disease-specific adjustment problems affecting this population (Barbarin & Christian, 1999; Schuman & LaGreca, 1999). Rather, adjustment difficulties exhibited by individuals with SCD are typically similar to those experienced by children with a variety of chronic illnesses and are thought to reflect processes common to coping with any ongoing stressor (Thompson & Gustafson, 1996).

Emotional Functioning. In addition to experiencing problems with academic or social competence, children with SCD may also be at greater risk for emotional adjustment problems than are their non-ill peers. Informed primarily by parent- and child-report data, investigations have found estimates of psychological problems occurring in one-third to almost two-thirds of samples (Barbarin, Whitten, & Bond, 1994; Cepeda, Yang, Price, & Shah, 1997; Thompson, Gil, Burbach, Keith, & Kinney, 1993; Thompson, Gustafson, & Gil, 1995), with internalizing problems (particularly anxiety-based disorders) occurring more frequently than externalizing problems. Depressive symptomatology also has been found to be elevated in children with SCD relative to healthy peers (Lemanek et al., 1995; Midence, Fuggle, & Davies, 1993). In one recent study, however, young children with SCD were found to have *fewer* psychological problems than comparison controls matched for age, race, gender, and socioeconomic status (Barbarin, 1999). Of importance, the investigator noted that scores on the Child Behavior Checklist internalizing and externalizing scales for the entire sample approached the clinical range. These findings, based on parent- and self-report data, were interpreted as reflecting the difficulties faced by African-American children from financially disadvantaged communities. It was concluded that children with SCD with similar backgrounds may face adjustment difficulties related to environmental challenges more so than their illness.

Other investigators have examined factors that contribute to healthy adjustment in children with SCD. Recent studies have noted that positive adjustment was predicted by an internal health locus of control, high self-esteem, and good social assertiveness (Brown, Lambert, et al., 2000; Burlew, Telfair, Colangelo, & Wright, 2000).

Several studies have examined the role of demographic, medical, and environmental factors on the development of psychological symptoms in children with SCD. For example, the frequency of internalizing problems appears to increase with the age of the child, with adolescents at the greatest risk (Barbarin, 1999; Midence et al., 1993). In addition, poverty may be a separate factor contributing to emotional adjustment problems in children with SCD. From a sample of 327 children and adolescents with SCD, Barbarin, Whitten, Bond, and Conner-Warren (1999) found that children and parents experiencing financial hardship reported more psychological symptoms and more difficulty coping with the disease on a day-to-day basis than did families without financial distress. Finally, the effect of illness severity on the prevalence and extent of symptoms also has been studied, with inconsistent results. However, given that painful crises occur in most children with SCD, methods of coping with pain have been assessed to determine which styles of coping are associated with healthy adjustment and optimal functioning.

Researchers have demonstrated that children and adolescents with high levels of coping attempts maintained greater levels of social, school, and home activities than those with *negative thinking* or *passive adherence* coping styles (Gil et al., 1993). Recent studies conducted by Gil and colleagues (1997, 2001) assessed pain coping skills in 46 children and adolescents with SCD aged 8–17. Subjects were divided into two groups: those who received brief pain coping skills training and those who received standard medical care alone. Posttreatment assessment findings indicated that those who had received pain coping skills had fewer negative thoughts and less tendency to report pain in response to focal pressure (Gil et al., 1997). After analyzing daily pain diaries kept by the subjects, the investigators found that participants in the pain coping skills training group used more active coping strategies than those in the control group. Moreover, children who received instruction in pain coping skills also demonstrated fewer school absences, fewer contacts with health professionals, and experienced less disruption in their routines at a 1-month follow-up assessment (Gil et al., 2001). The authors conclude that continued practice and daily use of coping skills may contribute to successful home management of painful crises in children with SCD, which in turn may allow children greater participation in social, home, and school activities.

Behavioral Functioning. SCD-related pain may interfere with several aspects of children's school functioning. If pain is experienced during school hours, children's attention, concentration, and motivation may be negatively affected. Because medications used to treat SCD pain often cause children to feel drowsy or lethargic, children receiving such treatment may have less energy and mental alertness for academic tasks. Additionally, because analgesics do not completely control pain in the majority of patients (Beyer, 2000), painful crises may disrupt school attendance. Indeed, children with SCD tend to miss many more days of school than their non-ill peers (Shapiro et al., 1995) and to reduce their participation in school activities when pain is experienced (Gil et al., 2000). In one study, investigators found that children with SCD missed 21% of days in the school year. However, the average length of each absence, 2.7 days, was relatively short (Shapiro et al., 1995). The authors conclude that these frequent, brief absences may be overlooked by school systems, who tend to provide homebound services only to children missing a week or more of school at a time. Another investigation examined absenteeism in children with high (at least four in a 21-month period) and low (no more than one in a 21-month period) rates of hospitalization (Eaton, Haye, Armstrong, Pegelow, & Thomas, 1995). Although the group with a high rate of hospitalizations missed more days of school overall, it was noted that the rate of school absence was quite high for both groups. The authors found that there were no differences between the groups on grades and standardized measures of achievement; however, both groups were achieving below grade level.

In addition to interfering with children's school attendance and participation in activities, SCD also may increase children's risk for behavior problems. Indeed, a variety of behavior problems have been identified in samples of children with SCD across home and school settings. Although parent, teacher, and self-ratings of externalizing problems tend to be higher in children with SCD than for healthy children, problems are not typically of clinical significance (e.g., Lemanek et al., 1995). However, age and gender effects have been found such that adolescents and males appear to be at greatest risk for externalizing behavior difficulties (Lemanek et al., 1995; Schuman, Armstrong, Pegelow, & Routh, 1993). It has been hypothesized that adolescents may be at greater risk for adjustment problems than younger children because of SCD's interference with developmental tasks during this period (e.g., Barbarin, 1999; Lemanek, Steiner, & Grossman, 1999). For example, adolescents with SCD may experience delays in physical maturation and in achieving independence from their parents.

Social Functioning. The importance of competent peer relations and social acceptance for healthy adjustment has been well-documented in the developmental literature (see Hartup, 1996; Parker & Asher, 1987; Rose & Asher, 2000). Whereas a number of studies suggest that children with chronic illness generally do not differ from their healthy peers with respect to prevalence of problematic peer relations (e.g., Lemanek, Horwitz, & Ohene-Frempong, 1994; Noll, Ris, Davies, Bukowski, & Koontz, 1992; Rodrigue, Streisand, Banko, & Kedar, 1996; Thompson et al., 1993), extant research also suggests that individuals with diseases affecting the CNS are at greatest risk for social adjustment problems (Nassau & Drotar, 1997). Specifically, numerous factors associated with the direct and indirect affects of SCD on physical, cognitive, and psychosocial functioning may put children at increased risk for problematic peer relations.

Nassau and Drotar (1997) noted that the cognitive difficulties exhibited by some children with SCD secondary to stroke or other disease processes also interfere with competency in the social domain. Specifically, nonverbal skills deficits may make it difficult for children to perceive or comprehend important subtle features of many social interactions. Problems associated with inattention and impulsivity may make children less desirable as playmates because of their inability to follow the rules or organization of group activities. Finally, poor academic functioning has been associated with peer rejection in the developmental literature (see Asher & Parker, 1989; Wentzel & Asher, 1995).

In addition to factors related to biomedical aspects of the disease, children may be at increased risk for social adjustment problems from factors related to functional limitations, medical compliance, and school absenteeism. Indeed, several investigators have found that children with SCD spend less time with peers participating in social activities and have fewer friends than non-ill peers (Lemanek et al., 1995; Schuman et al., 1993). A study conducted by Noll et al. (1996) on 34 children with SCD (aged 8–14) also found social adjustment problems in this population. Specifically, children with SCD were perceived as less sociable and less well-accepted by peers than matched healthy classmates. Moreover, girls with SCD were less well-liked and chosen less often as best friends. Males, in contrast, were perceived as less aggressive than their non-ill classmates. Of note, there were no other differences between the children with SCD and their healthy peers on social adjustment measures, and illness severity was not related to problems with social competence. Similarly, Barbarin (1999) found that, despite few psychological adjustment problems, children and adolescents with SCD were rated by themselves and their parents as less socially competent than matched controls. Thus, despite inconsistent findings to date, there is evidence to suggest that some children with SCD may experience peer relations difficulties, perhaps as a result of reduced participation in organizations and activities (Barbarin, 1999). However, this is an area in need of more extensive study using updated methodology.

Increasingly, investigators are considering healthy adjustment to chronic illness within the framework of a systems model in which socioecological factors play a large role (e.g., Belsky, 1984; Thompson et al., 1993, 1994). As such, recent research has focused on family factors that contribute to psychosocial adjustment in children with SCD, including family cohesion (Hurtig & Park, 1989), family relations and social support (Burlew, Evans, & Oler, 1989; Burlew et al. 2000), level of family conflict (Thompson, Armstrong et al., 1999), and parenting style and distress (Thompson et al., 2002).

Summary

The findings from studies of psychosocial functioning in children with hemophilia and SCD have been limited. However, those that have emerged suggest that contextual variables can influence children's functioning in the important social context of school. Given this, these children may benefit from intervention services aimed at improving their adjustment and peer relations. These interventions may need to be delivered at the level of the child (individual therapy to improve social skills, pain coping, behavioral control, or emotional functioning) or more broadly to include the child's peer group and family members.

ROLE OF THE PEDIATRIC PSYCHOLOGIST

In the section that follows, recommendations for pediatric psychologists who work with school systems are offered. This work can take a variety of forms, including assessment, consultation and education, and/or direct intervention with students. Specific recommendations for teachers and other school staff are summarized elsewhere (Bonner et al., 1999). It is expected that the collaboration of pediatric psychologists and school staff will contribute greatly to the outcomes of children with hemophilia and SCD.

1. Pediatric psychologists can help school personnel facilitate positive academic and psychosocial adjustment by providing education about the diseases for teachers and students. This includes helping to demystify the diseases and providing information about common symptoms and treatment expectations (e.g., children with SCD need to be well hydrated).
2. In unfortunate cases in which disease management requires extensive or frequent hospitalizations, pediatric psychologists can help facilitate the child's transition back to school. This is particularly important in cases of physical or cognitive morbidity. Although there are currently no standard school re-entry programs for children with SCD or hemophilia, successful programs used with the cancer population (Katz, Rubinstein, Hubert, & Blew, 1988) could be adapted to address concerns of school staff, as well as questions and fears that classmates have.
3. Pediatric psychologists can also help school personnel set appropriate performance expectations for the student. For example, teachers may erroneously attribute all behavioral or learning problems to the illness or conversely may fail to challenge the student to potential

because of concerns about the disease (Sexson & Dingle, 1997). Alternatively, teachers may not appreciate true weaknesses if the child appears normal, as in the case of silent stroke in SCD. In such cases, the teacher may hold unrealistically high expectations for the child's performance, which are met with frustration by the child. Given the known risks, children with SCD and hemophilia should be monitored for cognitive and academic deficits. Any changes in educational programming should then be based on a careful evaluation of needs, not on the medical diagnosis alone. To facilitate this, pediatric psychologists can design neuropsychological protocols that supplement the standard educational assessments that are completed with children exhibiting academic difficulties. In particular, specific measures of attention and executive functioning can be added to form the basis for additional educational recommendations. Given that school-based assessments typically focus on broad academic achievement that may mask more specific deficits that negatively impact learning, the collaborative role of a pediatric psychologist could help address the child's needs more fully.

4. In addition to disease education and curriculum planning, pediatric psychologists can also address peer relations. When children with SCD or hemophilia experience limitations from their cognitive or physical abilities, their opportunities to successfully engage with peers may be reduced. A pediatric psychologist, working closely with school staff, can help address issues of peer acceptance and friendship. This may include teaching children with SCD and hemophilia prosocial skills and social problem solving if assessment reveals they are deficient. Or, this may involve finding creative ways for children to be involved with their peer group. For example, if the child is unable to participate in contact sports (e.g., because of bleeding risk in hemophilia or hemiparesis secondary to stroke in SCD), he/she may be assigned a role that is integral to the success of the team (e.g., coaching assistant).

5. Peer relations may also be impacted by attempts of school staff and/or parents to *protect* children with a chronic disease (Ross, 1984; Sexson & Dingle, 1997). Given the increased management of chronic illness in the outpatient setting and in the school context, school personnel may be involved with medical care (administering medication, monitoring symptoms). Teachers may see these children as particularly vulnerable and exempt them from both learning and social activities that may be valuable to their development. Additionally, expectations for behavioral control may differ if teachers perceive these children to be overly stressed from their illness. Certainly, some children will be stressed and will require intervention, however, the source of stress may not be the illness per se. A pediatric psychologist could help school staff sort these issues such that opportunities for normal social, emotional, and behavioral development are enhanced.

6. Pediatric psychologists can also design collateral parent interventions to address the potential stress of the disease on parenting and family functioning. Parent intervention may include education such that they can participate in school-based educational programs about hemophilia or SCD, thereby empowering them to manage the disease and advocate for their child.

7. Finally, the role of the treating physician should be considered. Indeed, successful school functioning requires that medical personnel communicate effectively with school personnel and support the child's regular attendance. For example, when a child with SCD or hemophilia reports repeated incidents of pain that result in high absenteeism, careful medical assessment and psychological assessment are indicated to help identify the factors contributing to the pain. Specifically, the pain may be exacerbated by poor coping skills or stress associated with undiagnosed learning problems. Thus, a pediatric psychologist can serve as a liaison between medical and school personnel when questions of adjustment and performance are raised.

CONCLUSION

This chapter suggests that hematological disorders are potential stressors to which the child and his/her family need to adapt and highlights the need for an integrated biopsychosocial approach to care (Thompson et al., 1998). Significant progress has been made in the medical domain to improve the outcomes of children with SCD and hemophilia, including earlier diagnosis, prophylactic medicine, and better symptom management. Furthermore, in the case of SCD, the addition of radiological measures has resulted in better detection of children who have suffered a subclinical stroke and those who are at risk so that appropriate treatments can ensue. Finally, the use of new therapies (e.g., HU in SCD), in-home treatments (factor replacement in hemophilia), and potential curative measures (bone marrow transplants in SCD) hold promise for further improving the lives of children with these genetic diseases.

Recent research also has advanced our understanding of the range of physiological and psychological parameters in SCD and hemophilia, and how they are related to functional outcomes. Although the majority of children with these diseases exhibit normal development, a small but significant group experiences difficulties in the cognitive and/or psychosocial domains. Indeed, recent studies have identified important risk factors and screening tools that need to be considered. Moreover, much of the management of SCD and hemophilia occurs in outpatient settings such that these children can attend school regularly and participate in other social functions. Therefore, consideration of these diseases in the family and school contexts is critical.

Pediatric psychologists must work with the medical team and school staff to address issues of quality of life in children with hemophilia and SCD through careful assessment and intervention. As revealed in the previous section, pediatric psychologists are uniquely qualified to participate in the comprehensive care of these children, given their training and expertise in psychological, neuropsychological, and academic assessment, and how assessment findings relate to disease parameters. As such, pediatric psychologists are important contributors to the development and evaluation of hematology treatment programs, and aim to provide comprehensive care to their patients.

REFERENCES

Adams, R. J. (2000). Lessons from the Stroke Prevention Trial in Sickle Cell Anemia (STOP) study. *Journal of Child Neurology, 15*, 344–349.

Adams, R. J., McKie, V. C., Brambilla, D., Carl, E., Gallagher, D., Nichols, F. T., Roach, S., Abbound, M., Berman, B., Driscoll, C., Files, B., Hsu, L., Hurlet, A., Miller, S., Olivieri, N., Pegelow, C., Scher, C., Vichinsky, E., Wang, W., Woods, G., Kutlar, A., Wright, E., Hagner, S., Tighe, F., Lewin, J., Cure, J., Zimmerman, R.A., & Waclawiw, M.A. (1998). Stroke prevention trial in sickle cell anemia. *Controlled Clinical Trials, 19*, 110–129.

Armstrong, F. D., Thompson, R. J., Jr., Wang, W., Zimmerman, R. A., Pegelow, C. H., Miller, S., Moser, F., Bello, J., Hurtig, A., & Vass, K. (1996). Cognitive functioning and brain magnetic resonance imaging in children with sickle cell disease. *Pediatrics, 97*, 864–870.

Asher, S. R., & Parker, J. G. (1989). Significance of peer relationship problems in childhood. In B. H. Schneider, & G. Attili, (Eds.), *Social competence in developmental perspective. NATO advanced science institutes series. Series D: Behavioural and social sciences* (Vol. 51, pp. 5–23). Dordrecht, the Netherlands: Kluwer Academic Publishers.

Barbarin, O. A. (1999). Do parental coping, involvement, religiosity, and racial identity mediate children's psychological adjustment to sickle cell disease. *Journal of Black Psychology, 25*, 391–426.

Barbarin, O. A., & Christian, M. (1999). The social and cultural context of coping with sickle cell disease: I. A review of biomedical and psychosocial issues. *Journal of Black Psychology, 25*, 277–293.

Barbarin, O. A., Whitten, C. F., & Bond, S. (1994). Estimating rates of psychosocial problems in urban and poor children with sickle cell anemia. *Health & Social Work, 19*, 112–119.

Barbarin, O. A., Whitten, C. F., Bond, S., & Conner-Warren, R. (1999). The social and cultural context of coping with sickle cell disease: II. The role of financial hardship in adjustment to sickle cell disease. *Journal of Black Psychology, 25*, 294–315.

Belsky, J. (1984). The determinants of parenting: A process model. *Child Development, 55*, 83–96.

Beyer, J. E. (2000). Judging the effectiveness of analgesia for children and adolescents during vaso-occlusive events of sickle cell disease. *Journal of Pain and Symptom Management, 19*, 63–72.

Bonner, M. J., Gustafson, K. E., Schumacher, E., & Thompson, R. J., Jr. (1999). The impact of sickle cell disease on cognitive functioning and learning. *School Psychology Review, 28*, 182–193.

Brookmeyer, R., & Goedert, J. J. (1989). Censoring in an epidemic with an application to hemophilia-associated AIDS. *Biometrics, 45*, 325–335.

Brown, R. T., Armstrong, F. D., & Eckman, J. R. (1993). Neurocognitive aspects of pediatric sickle cell disease. *Journal of Learning Disabilities, 26*, 33–45.

Brown, R. T., Buchanan, I., Doepke, K., Eckman, J. R., Baldwin, K., Goonan, B., & Schoenherr, S. (1993). Cognitive and academic functioning in children with sickle cell disease. *Journal of Clinical Child Psychology, 22*, 207–218.

Brown, R. T., Davis, P. C., Lambert, R., Hsu, L., Hopkins, K., & Eckman, J. (2000). Neurocognitive functioning and magnetic resonance imaging in children with sickle cell disease. *Journal of Pediatric Psychology, 25*, 503–513.

Brown, R. T., Lambert, R., Devine, D., Baldwin, K., Casey, R., Doepke, K., Ievers, C. E., Hsu, L., Buchanan, I., & Eckman, J. (2000). Risk-resistance adaptation model for caregivers and their children with sickle cell syndromes. *Annals of Behavioral Medicine, 22*, 158–169.

Burlew, K., Evans, R., & Oler, C. (1989). The impact of a child with sickle cell disease on family dynamics. *Annals of the New York Academy of Sciences, 565*, 161–171.

Burlew, K., Telfair, J., Colangelo, L., & Wright, E. C. (2000). Factors that influence adolescent adaptation to sickle cell disease. *Journal of Pediatric Psychology, 25*, 287–299.

Bussing, R., & Burket, R. C. (1993). Anxiety and intra-familial stress in children with hemophilia after the HIV crisis. *Journal of the American Academy of Child and Adolescent Psychiatry, 32*, 562–567.

Cepeda, M. L., Yang, Y., Price, C., & Shah, A. (1997). Mental disorders in children and adolescents with sickle cell disease. *Southern Medical Journal, 90*, 284–287.

Charache, S. (1994). Natural history of disease: Adults. In S. H. Embury, R. P. Hebbel, N. Mohandas, & M. H. Steinberg (Eds.), *Sickle cell disease: Basic principles and clinical practice*. New York: Raven Press.

Charache, S., Lubin, B., & Reid, C. D. (1989). *Management and therapy of sickle cell disease* (NIH Publication No. 89–2117). Washington, DC: National Institutes of Health.

Chorba, T. L., Holman, R. C., Clarke, M. J., & Evatt, B. L. (2001). Effects of HIV infection on age and cause of death for persons with hemophilia A in the United States. *American Journal of Hematology, 66*, 229–240.

Cohen, A. R. (1998). Sickle cell disease: New treatments, new questions [Editorial]. *The New England Journal of Medicine, 339*, 42–44.

Cohen, M. J., Branch, W. B., McKie, V. C., & Adams, R. J. (1997). Neuropsychological impairment in children with sickle cell anemia and cerebrovascular accidents. *Clinical Pediatrics, 33*, 517–524.

Colegrove, R. W., & Huntzinger, R. M. (1994). Academic, behavioral, and social adaptation of boys with hemophilia/HIV disease. *Journal of Pediatric Psychology, 19*, 457–473.

Craft, S., Schatz, J., Glauser, T., Lee, B., & DeBaun, M. (1993). Neuropsychological effects of stroke in children with sickle cell anemia. *Journal of Pediatrics, 123*, 712–717.

Eaton, M. L., Haye, J. S., Armstrong, F. D., Pegelow, C. H., & Thomas, M. (1995). Hospitalizations for painful episodes: Association with school absenteeism and academic performance in children and adolescents with sickle cell anemia. *Issues in Comprehensive Pediatric Nursing, 18*, 1–9.

Forsberg, A. D., King, G., Delaronde, S. R., & Geary, M. K. (1997). Maintaining safer sex behaviors in HIV infected adolescents with hemophilia. The Hemophilia Behavioral Evaluative Intervention Project Committee. *AIDS Care, 8*, 629–640.

Fowler, M. G., Whitt, J. K., Lallinger, R. R., Nash, K. B., Atkinson, S. S., Wells, R. J., & McMillan, C. (1988). Neuropsychologic and academic functioning of children with sickle cell anemia. *Developmental and Behavioral Pediatrics, 9*, 213–220.

Frank, N. C., Allison, S. M., & Cant, M. E. C. (1999). Sickle cell disease. In R. T. Brown (Ed.), *Cognitive aspects of chronic illness in children* (pp. 172–189). New York: Guildford Press.

Gaston, M., & Rosse, W. F. (1982). The Cooperative Study of Sickle Cell Disease: Review of study design and objectives. *American Journal of Pediatric Hematology/Oncology, 4*, 197–201.

Gil, K. M., Anthony, K. K., Carson, J. W., Redding-Lallinger, R., Daeschner, C. W., & Ware, R. E. (2001). Daily coping practice predicts treatment effects in children with sickle cell disease. *Journal of Pediatric Psychology, 26*, 163–173.

Gil, K. M., Porter, L. S., Ready, J., Workman, E., Sedway, J., & Anthony, K. K. (2000). Pain in children and adolescents with sickle-cell disease: An analysis of daily pain diaries. *Children's Health Care, 29*, 225–241.

Gil, K. M., Thompson, R. J., Jr., Keith, B. R., Tota-Faucette, M., Noll, S., & Kinney, T. R. (1993). Sickle cell disease pain in children and adolescents: Change in pain frequency and coping strategies over time. *Journal of Pediatric Psychology, 18*, 621–637.

Gil, K. M., Wilson, J. J., Edens, J. L., Workman, E., Ready, J., Sedway, J., Reading-Lallinger, R., & Daeschner, W. C. (1997). Cognitive coping skills training in children with sickle cell disease. *International Journal of Behavioral Medicine, 4*, 365–378.

Hagar, R. W., & Vichinsky, E. P. (2000). Major changes in sickle cell disease. *Advances in Pediatrics, 47*, 249–272.

Hartup, W. W. (1996). The company they keep: Friendships and their developmental significance. *Child Development, 67*, 1–13.

Hindmarsh, P. C, Brozovic, M., Brook C. G., & Davies, S. C. (1987). Incidence of overt and covert neurological damage in children with sickle cell disease. *Postgraduate Medical Journal, 63*, 751–753.

Hoots, K., & Cecalupo, A. (1994). Hemophilia: Medical issues. In R. A. Olson, L. L. Mullins, J. B. Gillman, & J. M. Chaney (Eds.), *The sourcebook of pediatric psychology* (pp. 145–149). Boston: Allyn & Bacon.

Hoppe, C., Vichinsky, E., Quirolo, K., van Warmerdam, J., Allen, K., & Styles, L. (2000). Use of hydroxyurea in children 2–5 with sickle cell disease. *Journal of Pediatric Hematology/Oncology, 22*, 330–334.

Hoppe, C. C., & Walters, M. C. (2001). Bone marrow transplantation in sickle cell anemia. *Current Opinion in Oncology, 13*, 85–90.

Hurtig, A. L., & Park, K. B. (1989). Adjustment and coping in adolescents with sickle cell disease. *Annals of the New York Academy of Sciences, 565*, 172–182.

Huszti, H. C., & Rosko, C. K. (1994). Hemophilia: Psychological issues. In R. A. Olson, L. L. Mullins, J. B. Gillman, & J. M. Chaney (Eds.), *The sourcebook of pediatric psychology* (pp. 150–159). Boston: Allyn & Bacon.

Jones, P. K., & Ratnoff, O. D. (1991). The changing prognosis of classic hemophilia (factor VIII "deficiency"). *Annals of Internal Medicine, 114*, 641–648.

Katz, E. R., Rubenstein, C. L., Hubert, N. C., & Blew, A. (1988). School and social reintegration of children with cancer. *Journal of Psychosocial Oncology, 6*, 123–140.

Kinney, T. R., Sleeper, L. A., Wang, W. C., Zimmerman, R. A., Pegelow, C. H., Ohene-Frempong, K., Wethers, D. L., Bello, J. A., Vichinsky, E. P., Moser, F. G., Gallagher, D. M., DeBaun, M. R., Platt, O. S., & Miller, S. T. (1999). Silent cerebral infarcts in sickle cell anemia: A risk factor analysis. *Pediatrics, 103*, 640–645.

Klein, R. H., & Nimorwicz, P. (1982). The relationship between psychological distress and knowledge of disease among hemophilia patients and their families: A pilot study. *Journal of Psychosomatic Research, 26*, 387–391.

LaGreca, A. M. (1990). Social consequences of pediatric conditions: Fertile area for future investigation and intervention. *Journal of Pediatric Psychology, 15*, 285–307.

LaGreca, A. M. (1992). Peer influences in pediatric chronic illness: An update. *Journal of Pediatric Psychology, 17*, 775–784.

Lemanek, K. L., Buckloh, L., Woods, G., & Butler, R. (1995). Diseases of the circulatory system: Sickle cell disease and hemophilia. In M. Roberts (Ed.), *Handbook of pediatric psychology* (pp. 286–309). New York: Guilford Press.

Lemanek, K. L., Horwitz, W., & Ohene-Frempong, K. (1994). A multi-perspective investigation of social competence in children with sickle cell disease. *Journal of Pediatric Psychology, 19*, 443–456.

Lemanek, K. L., Steiner, S. M., & Grossman, N. J. (1999). Too little, too late: Primary vs. secondary interventions for adolescents with sickle cell disease. *Adolescent Medicine, 10*, 385–400.

Logan, F. A., MacLean, C. A., Howie, C. A., Gibson, B., Hann, I. M., & Parry-Jones, W. L. (1990). Psychological disturbance in children with hemophilia. *British Medical Journal, 301*, 1253–1256.

Loveland, K. A., Stehbens, J., Contant, C., Bordeaux, J. D., Sirois, P., Bell, T. S., & Hill, S. (1994). Hemophilia Growth and Development Study: Baseline neurodevelopmental findings. *Journal of Pediatric Psychology, 19*, 223–239.

Loveland, K. A., Stehbens, J. A., Mahoney, E. M., Sirois, P. A., Nichols, S., Bordeaux, J. D., Watkins, J. M., Amodei, N., Hill, S. D., Donfield, S., & Hemophilia Growth and Development Study. (2000). Declining immune function in children and adolescents with hemophilia and HIV infection: Effects on neuropsychological performance. *Journal of Pediatric Psychology, 25*, 309–322.

Mayes, S. D., Handford, H. A., Schaefer, J. H., Scogno, C. A., Neagley, S. R., Michael-Good, L., & Pelco, L. E. (1996). The relationship of HIV status, type of coagulation disorder, and school absenteeism to cognition, educational performance, mood, and behavior of boys with hemophilia. *The Journal of Genetic Psychology, 157*, 137–151.

Meijer, A. (1980). Psychiatric problems of hemophilic boys and their families. *International Journal of Psychiatry in Medicine, 10*, 163–172.

Midence, K., Fuggle, P., & Davies, S. (1993). Psychosocial aspects of sickle cell disease in childhood and adolescence: A review. *British Journal of Clinical Psychology, 32*, 271 – 280.

Nassau, J. H., & Drotar, D. (1997). Social competence among children with central nervous system-related chronic health conditions: A review. *Journal of Pediatric Psychology, 22*, 771–793.

Nichols, S., Mahoney, E. M., Sirois, P. A., Bordeaux, J. D., Stehbans, J. A., Loveland, K. A., Amodei, N., & the Hemophilia Growth and Developmental Study (2000). HIV-associated changes in adaptive, emotional, and behavioral functioning in children and adolescents with hemophilia: Results from the Hemophilia Growth and Development Study. *Journal of Pediatric Psychology, 25*, 545–556.

Nietert, P. J., Abboud, M. R., Silverstein, M. D., & Jackson, S. M. (2000). Bone marrow transplantation versus periodic prophylactic blood transfusions in sickle cell patients with high risk for ischemic stroke: A decision analysis. *Blood, 95*, 3057–3064.

Noll, R. B., Ris, M. D., Davies, W. H., Bukowski, W. M., & Koontz, K. (1992). Social interactions between children with cancer or sickle cell disease and their peers: Teacher ratings. *Journal of Developmental and Behavioral Pediatrics, 13*, 187–193.

Noll, R. B., Stith, L., Gartstein, M. A., Ris, M. D., Grueneich, R., Vannatta, K., & Kalinyak, K. (2001). Neuropsychological functioning of youths with sickle cell disease: Comparison with non-chronically ill peers. *Journal of Pediatric Psychology, 26*, 79–92.

Noll, R. B., Vannatta, K., Koontz, K., Kalinyak, K., Bukowski, W. M., & Davies, W. H. (1996). Peer relationships and emotional well-being of youngsters with sickle cell disease. *Child Development, 67*, 423–436.

Olch, D. (1971). Effects of hemophilia upon intellectual growth and academic achievement. *Journal of Genetic Psychology, 119*, 63–74.

Oremland, E. K. (1986). Communication over chronic illness: Dilemmas of affected school-aged children. *Children's Health Care, 14*, 218–223.

Overby, K. J., Lo, B., & Litt, I. F. (1989). Knowledge and concerns about acquired immunodeficiency syndrome and their relationship to behaviors among adolescents with hemophilia. *Pediatrics, 83*, 204–210.

Parker, J. G., & Asher, S. R. (1987). Peer relations and later personal adjustment: Are low-accepted children at risk? *Psychological Bulletin, 102*, 357–389.

Pavlakis, S. G., Bello, J., Prohovnik, I., Sutton, M., Ince, C., Mohr, J. P., Piomelli, S., Hilal, S., & DeVivo, D. C. (1988). Brain infarction in sickle cell anemia: Magnetic resonance imaging correlates. *Annals of Neurology, 23*, 125–130.

Perrin, J. M., MacLean, W. E., & Janco, R. L. (1988). Does stress affect bleeding in hemophilia? A review of the literature. *The American Journal of Pediatric Hematology/Oncology, 10*, 230–235.

Platt, O., Brambilla, D. J., Rosse, W. F., Milner, P. F., Castro, O., Steinberg, M. H., & Klue, P. P. (1994). Mortality in sickle cell disease: Life expectancy and risk factors for early death. *New England Journal of Medicine, 339*, 1639–1644.

Ris, M. D., & Grueneich, R., (2000). Sickle cell disease. In K. O. Yeates, M. D. Ris, & H. G. Taylor (Eds.), *Pediatric Neuropsychology* (pp. 320–335). New York: Guilford Press.

Ris, M. D., Grueneich, R., & Kalinyak, K. (1995). Neuropsychological risk in children with sickle cell disease [Abstract]. *Journal of the International Neuropsychological Society, 1*, 360.

Robinson, M. R. (1999). There is no shame in pain: Coping and functional ability in adolescents with sickle cell disease. *Journal of Black Psychology, 25*, 336–355.

Rodrigue, J. R., Streisand, R., Banko, C., & Kedar, A. (1996). Social functioning, peer relations, and internalizing and externalizing problems among youths with sickle cell disease. *Children's Health Care, 25*, 37–52.

Rogers, Z. R. (1997). Hydroxyurea therapy for diverse pediatric populations with sickle cell disease. *Seminars in Hematology, 34*, 42–47.

Rose, A. J., & Asher, S. R. (2000). Children's friendships. In C. Hendrick, & S. S. Hendrick (Eds.), *Close relationships: A sourcebook* (pp. 47–57). Thousand Oaks, CA: Sage Publications, Inc.

Ross, J. W. (1984). Resolving nonmedical obstacles to successful school re-entry for children with cancer. *Journal of School Health, 54*, 84–86.

Schatz, J., Brown, R. T., Pascaul, J. M., Hsu, L., & DeBaun, M. R. (2001). Poor school and cognitive functioning with silent cerebral infarcts and sickle cell disease. *Neurology, 56*, 1109–1111.

Schatz, J., Craft, S., Koby, M., Siegel, M. J., Resar, L., Lee, R., Chu, U. F., Launius, G., Dadash-Zedeh, M., & DeBaun, M. R. (1999). Neuropsychologic deficits in children with sickle cell disease and cerebral infarction: The role of lesion location and volume. *Child Neuropsychology, 5*, 92–103.

Schatz, J., Finke, R. L., Kellet, J. M., & Kramer, J. H. (2002). Cognitive functioning in children with sickle cell disease: A meta analysis. *Journal of Pediatric Psychology, 27*, 739–748.

Schuman, W., Armstrong, S., Pegelow, C., & Routh, D. (1993). Enhanced parenting knowledge and skills in mothers of preschool children with sickle cell disease. *Journal of Pediatric Psychology, 18*, 575–591.

Schuman, W. B., & LaGreca, A. M. (1999). Social correlates of chronic illness. In R. Brown (Ed.), *Cognitive aspects of chronic illness in children* (pp. 289–311). New York: Guilford Press.

Sexson, S. B., & Dingle, A. D. (1997). Medical problems that might present with academic difficulties. *Child & Adolescent Psychiatric Clinics of North America, 63*, 509–522.

Shapiro, B. S., Dinges, D. F., Orne, E. C., Bauer, N., Reilly, L. B., Whitehouse, W. G., Ohene-Frempong, K., & Orne, M. T. (1995). Home management of sickle cell-related pain in children and adolescents: Natural history and impact on school attendance. *Pain, 61*, 139–144.

Sirois, P. A., & Hill, S. D. (1993). Developmental change associated with HIV infection in school-aged children with hemophilia. *Developmental Neuropsychology, 9*(3–4), 177–197.

Sirois, P. A., Usner, D. W., Hill, S. D., Mitchell, W. G., Bale, J. F., Jr., Loveland, K. A., Stehbens, J. A., Donfield, S. M., Maeder, M. A., Amodei, N., Contant, C. F., Nelson, M. D., Jr., Willlis, J. K., & the Hemophilia Growth and Development Study (1998). Hemophilia Growth and Development Study: Relationships between neuropsychological, neurological, and MRI findings at baseline. *Journal of Pediatric Psychology, 23*, 45–56.

Smith, M. L., Minden, D., Netley, C., Read, S. E., King, S. M., & Blanchette, V. (1997). Longitudinal investigation of neuropsychological functioning in children and adolescents with hemophilia and HIV infection. *Developmental Neuropsychology, 13*, 69–85.

Swift, A. V., Cohen, M. J., Hynd, G. W., Wisenbaker, J. M., McKie, K. M., Makari, G., & McKie, V. (1989). Neuropsychological impairment in children with sickle cell anemia. *Pediatrics, 84*, 1077–1085.

Tarnowski, K., & Brown, R. T. (2000). Psychological aspects of pediatric disorders. In M. Hersen & R. Ammerman (Eds.), *Advanced abnormal child psychology* (2nd ed., pp. 131–152). Hillsdale, NJ: Erlbaum.

Thompson, R. J., Jr., Armstrong, F. D., Kronenberger, W. G., Scott, D., McCabe, M. A., Smith, B., Radcliffe, J., Colangelo, L., Gallagher, D., Islam, S., & Wright, E. (1999). Family functioning, neurocognitive functioning, and behavior problems in children with sickle cell disease. *Journal of Pediatric Psychology, 24*, 491–498.

Thompson, R. J., Jr., Gil, K. M., Burbach, D. J., Keith, B. R., Gustafson, K. E., George, L. K., & Kinney, T. R. (1994). Psychological adjustment of children with sickle cell disease: Stability and change over a 10–month period. *Journal of Consulting and Clinical Psychology, 62*, 856–860.

Thompson, R. J., Jr., Gil, K. M., Burbach, D. J., Keith, B. R., & Kinney, T. R. (1993). Role of child and maternal processes in the psychological adjustment of children with sickle cell disease. *Journal of Consulting and Clinical Psychology, 61*, 468–474.

Thompson, R. J., Jr., & Gustafson, K. (1996). *Adaptation to chronic childhood illness*. Washington, DC: American Psychological Association.

Thompson, R. J., Jr., Gustafson, K., Bonner, M. J., Ware, R. E. (2002). Neurocognitive development of young children with sickle cell disease through three years of age. *Journal of Pediatric Psychology*.

Thompson, R. J., Jr., Gustafson, K., & Gil, K. M. (1995). Psychological adjustment of adolescents with cystic fibrosis or sickle cell disease and their mothers. In J. Wallander & L. Siegal (Eds.), *Advances in pediatric psychology: II. Behavioral perspectives on adolescent health* (pp. 232–247). New York: Guilford Press.

Thompson, R. J., Jr., Gustafson, K. E., Gil, K. M., Kinney, T. R., & Spock, A. (1999). Change in the psychological adjustment of children with cystic fibrosis or sickle cell disease and their mothers. *Journal of Clinical Psychology in Medical Settings, 6*, 373–392.

Thompson, R. J., Gustafson, K. E., & Ware, R. E. (1998). Hematologic disorders. In R. T. Ammerman & J. V. Campo, (Eds.), *Handbook of pediatric psychology and psychiatry—Volume II: Disease, injury, and illness* (pp. 298–312). Boston: Allyn and Bacon.

Varni, J. W., & Wallander, J. L. (1988). Pediatric chronic disabilities: Hemophilia and spina bifida as examples. In D. K. Routh (Ed.), *Handbook of pediatric psychology* (pp. 190–221). New York: Guilford Press.

Vichinsky, E. P. (1997). Hydroxyurea in children: Present and future. *Seminars in Hematology, 34*, 22–29.

Wallander, J. L., & Varni, J. W. (1986, March). *Psychosocial factors, adaptation, and bleeding episodes in hemophilic children*. Paper presented at the meeting of the Society of Behavioral Medicine, San Francisco.

Walters, M. C. (1999). Bone marrow transplantation for sickle cell disease: Where do we go from here? *Journal of Pediatric Hematology/Oncology, 21*, 467–474.

Walters, M. C., Storb, R., Patience, M., Leisenring, W., Taylor, T., Sanders, J. E., Buchanan, G. E., Rogers, Z. R., Dinndorf, P., Davies, S. C. Roberts, I. A., Dickerhoff, R., Yeager, A. M., Hus, L., Kurtzberg, J., Ohene-Frempong, K, Bunin, N., Bernaudin, F., Wong, W. Y., Scott, J. P., Margolis, D., Vichinsky, E., Wall, D. A., Wayne, A. S., Pegelow, C., Redding-Lallinger, R., Wiley, J., Klemperer, M., Mentzer, W. C., Smith, F. O., & Sullivan, K. M. (2000). Impact of bone marrow transplantation for symptomatic sickle cell disease: An interim report. *Blood, 95*, 1918–1924.

Wang, W. C., Gallagher, D. M., Pegelow, C. H., Wright, E. C., Vichinsky, E. P., Abboud, M. R., Moser, F. G., & Addams, R. J. (2000). Multi-center comparison of magnetic resonance imaging and transcranial Doppler ultrasonography in the evaluation of the central nervous system in children with sickle cell disease. *Journal of Pediatric Hematology/Oncology, 22*, 335–339.

Ware, R. E., Zimmerman, S. A., & Schultz, W. H. (1999). Hydroxyurea as an alternative to blood transfusions for the prevention of recurrent stroke in children with sickle cell disease. *Blood, 94*, 3022–3066.

Wasserman, A. L., Willmas, J. A., Fairclogh, D. L., Mulhern, R. K., & Wang, W. (1991). Subtler neuropsychological deficits in children with sickle cell disease. *American Journal of Pediatric Hematology/Oncology, 13*, 14–20.

Wentzel, K. R., & Asher, S. R. (1995). The academic lives of neglected, rejected, popular, and controversial children. *Child Development, 66*, 754–763.

White, D. A., Salorio, C. F., Schatz, J., & DeBaun, M. (2000). Preliminary study of working memory in children with stroke related to sickle cell disease. *Journal of Clinical and Experimental Neuropsychology, 22*, 257–264.

Whitt, J. K., Hooper, S. R., Tennison, M. B., Gold, S. H., Burchinal, M., Wells, R., McMillan, C., Whaley, R. A., Combest, J., & Hall, C. D. (1993). Neuropsychological functioning of HIV-infected children with hemophilia. *Journal of Pediatrics, 122*, 52–59.

Woolf, A., Rappaport, L., Reardon, P., Cibrowski, J., D'Angelo, E., & Bessette, J. (1989). School functioning and disease severity in boys with hemophilia. *Journal of Developmental and Behavioral Pediatrics, 10*, 18–85.

15

Childhood Cancer and the School

F. Daniel Armstrong
Brandon G. Briery
University of Miami School of Medicine

INTRODUCTION

In the United States, approximately 8,500 children each year are diagnosed with some form of cancer before the age of 15 (Parker, Tong, Bolden, & Wingo, 1997). Of these, approximately 30% have some form of leukemia, and an additional 20% are diagnosed with a tumor of the central nervous system (CNS; Robison, 1997). Overall, survival rates for all types of childhood cancer are now approaching 70%, although not all childhood cancers have as good a success rate of cure (Parker et al., 1997). Nonetheless, it is estimated that, by the year 2010, more than 1 of 1,000 adults will be a survivor of childhood cancer (Hawkins & Stevens, 1996). As treatment has improved, many children with cancer are able to return to school, although many will experience long-term cognitive and growth late effects that will affect academic performance, social competence, and long-term quality of life (Armstrong & Mulhern, 1999; Humpl, Fritsche, Bartels, & Gutjahr, 2001; Packer, Meadows, Rorke, Goldwein, & D'Angio, 1987).

Childhood cancer presents professionals in the school setting with a number of challenges and opportunities. Unfortunately, because childhood cancer is such a rare event, many school personnel—including teachers, counselors, school psychologists, and administrators—are unfamiliar with what it means for a child to have cancer, what is involved in treatment, what long-term outcomes to expect, and how these will impact the child's academic performance and progress. In the following sections, we will provide basic background information about childhood cancer, its treatment, acute school-related issues, and long-term effects on learning. We will also present an overview of different educational and medical approaches that may help alleviate some of the late effects of treatment.

CHILDHOOD CANCER: THE DISEASE

Childhood cancer is often misunderstood to be a uniform disease, but it is actually a constellation of multiple diseases involving different organ systems that are treated differently, are associated with diverse adverse side effects, and have different long-term outcomes. Within diseases, there are subclassifications that differ on the basis of genetics, clinical presentation, risk factors, and overall prognosis. Some types of cancer may involve a single organ, treatment that is relatively mild and of short duration, and have excellent long-term prognosis. Other types may involve disseminated disease in multiple organs, intensive treatment over a long period of time that produces significant side effects, and have poor-to-moderate long-term prognosis. As we have learned more about childhood cancer and the ways to treat it, we have become increasingly aware of the importance of focusing on issues related to specific types of cancer that are treated in similar ways.

Cancer is a noncontagious disease that may involve any organ or organ system of the body. Although there is significant evidence pointing to environmental and genetic determinants of cancer in adults (e.g., smoking linked to lung cancer, BRAC1 gene linked to breast cancer), such evidence does not exist for most types of childhood cancer. Some specific genetic patterns have been identified for limited types of cancer (e.g., neuroblastoma, retinoblastoma), and children with other genetic disorders may have a higher risk for cancer (e.g., Down's syndrome and acute lymphoblastic leukemia; Robison, 1997). It is likely that there are many factors that contribute to the development of childhood cancer, and not a single cause. Fully identifying these factors is a difficult challenge, because, fortunately, cancer in children is a rare event.

As noted earlier, there are many types of childhood cancer, and these usually do not include the most common types of cancer seen in adults (e.g., breast cancer, lung cancer, prostate cancer).

Leukemia

The most common type of childhood cancer is leukemia, a malignancy of the white blood cells, and the solid tumor form of leukemia, lymphoma, that involves the white blood cells in the lymphatic system. Leukemias and lymphomas account for approximately 30% of all childhood cancers (Margolin & Poplack, 1997). Treatment of leukemia and lymphoma primarily involves the use of chemotherapy (drugs used to treat cancer) administered over a period of 2–3 years duration. Because leukemia cells are capable of crossing the blood-brain barrier, aggressive treatment to prevent CNS disease is provided. This typically involves injecting chemotherapy drugs directly into the spinal fluid of the CNS (intrathecal chemotherapy), but may also involve radiation treatment of the brain and spinal cord. Treatment of leukemia usually involves about 1 year of regular hospitalizations for chemotherapy or treatment of infections that occur because of adverse side effects of treatment. The last 2 years of treatment typically involve outpatient treatment and a relatively normal lifestyle. Overall survival after diagnosis and treatment of acute lymphoblastic leukemia (ALL), the most common form in children, ranges from 70 to 80%. In cases in which initial treatment is ineffective and the leukemia returns (relapses), children with leukemia and lymphoma may be successfully treated with bone marrow transplantation (Margolin & Poplack, 1997; Sanders, 1997).

CNS Tumors

The second most common form of cancer is a tumor of the CNS, or a brain tumor. Brain tumors account for approximately 20% of all childhood cancers. Brain tumors may be slow growing (low-grade) or rapidly growing and metastatic, meaning that the tumor cells spread throughout the CNS. Previously, low-grade tumors were called benign tumors, but this is a misnomer. Low-grade tumors may be fatal if they grow in a section of the brain that makes them inoperable, but where tumor growth may nonetheless affect critical biologic and neurologic regulation mechanisms. The most common approach to treatment of a brain tumor is neurosurgery, followed by combinations of brain radiation therapy and chemotherapy. Bone marrow transplantation may also be a consideration. There are many different types of brain tumors in children, each treated differently, and each having a different long-term outcome. Treatment duration is also dependent on the specific type of tumor, with some treatment only involving surgery, and others involving up to 3 years of treatment with chemotherapy and radiation. Overall survival of a childhood brain tumor is also tumor specific, ranging from less than 20% five-year survival for some tumors to better than 85% five-year survival for others (Heideman, Packer, Albright, Freeman, & Rorke, 1997).

Other Solid Tumors

The remaining childhood cancers are generally classified as solid tumors, but each of these tumors involves a different organ system, behaves differently, is treated differently, and has a different outcome. The more common solid tumors include those involving bone (osteogenic sarcoma and Ewing's sarcoma), muscle (rhabdomyosarcoma), eye (retinoblastoma), peripheral nervous system (neuroblastoma), kidney (Wilm's tumor), and soft tissues (sarcomas). Treatment of these tumors may involve surgical removal or amputation, chemotherapy lasting from 6 weeks to 3 years, and possibly radiation therapy. The risk of tumor recurrence varies by disease, and overall survival rates range from 20% to greater than 90% (Robison, 1997; Robison, Mertens, & Neglia, 1991). Thus, depending on the type and extent of the tumor, the child treated for a solid tumor may miss a few weeks of school, or may require a specialized education plan that addresses the need for frequent hospitalizations over a prolonged period of time.

CHILDHOOD CANCER: TREATMENT AND TREATMENT EFFECTS

Children treated for cancer experience a number of acute and long-term consequences of disease and treatment that may affect emotional, social, and academic functioning in the school setting. It is important for school personnel to be aware of the common adverse effects associated with cancer treatment, but also to be alerted to unique effects associated with the treatment of specific types of cancer. Some of these effects are transient, but some may be lifelong, and the nature and magnitude of the effects may change over time.

The most recognized effects of cancer treatment are those that alter the appearance of children. Loss of hair, use of prosthetic limbs because of amputation, bloating and puffiness secondary to treatment with steroids, and weight loss or weight gain are obvious physical signs to the child's parents, peers, and teachers that the child is being treated for cancer. Fortunately, most of these adverse effects are of short duration (e.g., hair will grow back after chemotherapy ends, weight will return to normal, and overall physical appearance will return to normal), except in those cases of amputation or hair loss secondary to radiation for a brain tumor. Less obvious are those side effects that are associated with nonvisible aspects of treatment, including cognitive impairments, fatigue, loss of emotional well-being, sterility, and increased susceptibility to lifethreatening infections. Once again, these less obvious side effects may be of short-term duration, but may also represent sources of disability that will persist throughout the child's life (Armstrong, 2001; Armstrong, Blumberg, & Toledano, 1999; Humpl et al., 2001; Margolin & Poplack, 1997; Packer et al., 1987).

Acute Side Effects of Treatment

A number of chemotherapeutic agents produce adverse effects that interfere with the child's ability to learn and perform in school. The primary biologic mechanism of chemotherapy is that the medication disrupts cell development and causes rapidly dividing cells to die. Unfortunately, current chemotherapies are not cell-specific. Thus, any cell that is rapidly dividing may be harmed by exposure to chemotherapy. It is this process that produces low red blood cell counts (hemoglobin), which are often associated with fatigue; low white blood cell counts (lymphocytes), which increase susceptibility to infection; and low platelet counts, which increase susceptibility to bleeding. Other cells in the body that are highly sensitive to the effects of chemotherapy include hair and cells lining the esophagus, stomach, and intestinal tract. Damage to these cells produces the characteristic alopecia, or hair loss, associated with cancer treatment, as well as nausea and vomiting (Balis, Holcenberg, & Poplack, 1997).

Other chemotherapeutic agents have specific acute side effects that directly affect performance in the classroom. Vincristine, one of the most common chemotherapeutic agents used with children, affects the peripheral nervous system, resulting in jaw pain, constipation, tingling in fingers and toes, and slowing of motor coordination. Children treated with vincristine frequently experience difficulties with written assignments and fine motor tasks. These difficulties are transient, and typically resolve when use of the medication is stopped. Another common chemotherapy, prednisone, is a type of steroid. Children treated with prednisone often experience rapid weight gain, an insatiable appetite, and episodic mood swings that may include extreme negative (e.g., frustration and even rage) and extreme positive (e.g., giggling, accelerated activity) emotions (Armstrong & Mulhern, 1999; Balis et al., 1997). Educators and school psychologists working with children with cancer in the classroom should make an effort to learn about the treatments that the child is receiving, understand likely consequences of these treatments, and develop educational plans that are sensitive to the acute effects of treatment.

Long-term Effects of Treatment

Acute treatment effects are the most obvious signs that a child has been treated for cancer. However, the most debilitating effects may be those that begin to emerge in the years after successful treatment, particularly for children with diseases that involve the CNS. The children at greatest risk for these long-term treatment effects are those treated for leukemia, tumors of the CNS, tumors of the face and head that are treated with localized radiation, and children treated with bone marrow transplantation (Armstrong, 2001; Armstrong et al., 1999; Fletcher & Copeland, 1988; Moore, Copeland, Ried, & Levy, 1992; Moore et al., 2000).

There are four major factors that are associated with long-term consequences of treatment. These include (a) the location and invasiveness of tumors in the brain, (b) complications of neurosurgery, (c) radiation to the brain and spinal cord, and (d) chemotherapy that affects brain development or impairs sensory functioning (Armstrong & Mulhern, 1999).

Tumor and Surgical Consequences. Late effects associated with tumor characteristics and complications of neurosurgery are often unique to a specific child. These depend on what structures of the brain are involved; whether surgery damages healthy brain tissue in the process of removing the cancerous tissue, and whether there are complications of surgery, such as unexpected bleeding. Some tumors routinely result in disabilities that are predictable. For instance, tumors of the optic pathway usually result in significant visual impairment, if not lifelong blindness. Other tumors may result in serious health-related consequences, such as severe problems in appetite regulation and the onset of juvenile diabetes in children treated for tumors called craniopharyngiomas (Danoff, Cowchock, & Kramer, 1983). Unintended surgical consequences may result in partial paralysis, loss of strength in lower limbs, seizures, hyperactivity, and other significant physical disabilities that will require multiple adaptations for disabilities in the classroom (Bordeaux et al., 1988; Danoff, Cowchock, Marquette, Mulgrew, & Kramer, 1982; Doxey, Bruce, Sklar, Swift, & Shapiro, 1999; Mulhern, Hancock, Fairclough, & Kun, 1992; Packer et al., 1987).

Radiation Late Effects. Radiation therapy involves the delivery of high-intensity radiation beams to the area of the tumor, or, in the case of tumors with a very high likelihood of spreading across the brain and spinal cord, to the entire brain and spinal cord. Radiation is a very effective treatment for many tumors, including those of the CNS. However, radiation is most effective for tumors that divide rapidly, because the radiation destroys the cells at the time of cell division. Radiation therapy is sometimes used to treat tumors that are called *low-grade* (or, inappropriately, *benign*), but children may experience more toxicity from this treatment than benefit (Kun, 1997).

For a long time, it was believed that radiation treatment destroyed brain tissue. This was based on the observation that many children treated with whole-brain radiation experience significant declines in IQ, often 20–50 Full-Scale IQ points (Danoff et al., 1982; Dennis, Spiegler, Hetherington, & Greenberg, 1996; Johnson et al., 1994; Kun, Mulhern, & Crisco, 1983; Moore Ater, & Copeland, 1992; Mulhern, 1994; Packer et al., 1989). However, in recent years, it has been observed that normal brain cells grow slowly. Existing brain cells therefore appear relatively unaffected by radiation, but very small blood vessels in the brain do appear to be damaged by radiation (Steen et al., 2001). At the same time, cells, connections between nerves in the brain, and the covering that surrounds nerve cells (myelin) that should develop in the years after treatment appear to either fail to develop or develop far more slowly than expected (Armstrong & Mulhern, 1999; Kun et al., 1983; Mulhern, 1994; Mulhern et al., 1999, 2001). The biologic mechanisms are important to understand when we consider the late cognitive, academic, and social consequences of childhood cancer, because both microvascular damage (calcification of blood vessels that prevent blood supply to areas of the developing brain) and disrupted development of brain structures can be associated with an emerging pattern of specific cognitive and academic problems. For educators, this often means that the learning challenges faced by these children will emerge over time, will be subtle and specific rather than global, and may only be seen years after the obvious, acute signs of cancer treatment have disappeared (Armstrong et al., 1999; Kun et al., 1983; Mulhern, 1994).

As noted earlier, several factors have been associated with the severity and scope of late cognitive and academic effects of radiation therapy. These include (a) the age of the child at the time of treatment, (b) the age of the child at assessment and the duration of time between treatment and current assessment of neuropsychological functioning, (c) the dose and location of radiation therapy, and (d) other chemotherapeutic agents used in conjunction with radiation therapy (Armstrong & Mulhern, 1999; Mulhern, 1994).

Age at Diagnosis. Younger children, particularly those under age 4, appear to be at the greatest risk for both more severe cognitive late effects and more global cognitive late effects, likely because they have more brain development programmed to occur after the delivery of treatment than do older children (Chapman et al., 1995; Duffner et al., 1995; Gajjar et al., 1994; Kaleita, Reaman, MacLean, Sather, & Whitt, 1999; Mulhern, 1994; Mulhern et al., 2001; Packer et al., 1989; Smedler & Bolme, 1995; Wilson et al., 1991).

Age at Time of Assessment and Time Since Diagnosis. Late effects of cancer treatment emerge over time (Anderson, Smibert, Ekert, & Godber, 1994; Armstrong et al., 1999; Brown et al., 1996; Cetingul et al., 1999; Espy et al., 2001; Mulhern, 1994; Mulhern & Kun,

1985; Packer et al., 1987; Radcliffe et al., 1992; Radcliffe, Bunin, Sutton, Goldwein, & Phillips, 1994). Thus, changes in patterns of scores can be anticipated, and specific patterns of difficulties can be anticipated at different ages, based on what skills are developmentally appropriate for the child's age. The pattern of neuropsychological findings for a child treated at age 4 and evaluated at age 6 is likely to be quite different from that of a child treated at age 4 and evaluated at age 12. Stability of functioning, often expected in children with congenital or genetic developmental disabilities, cannot be anticipated for children with acquired brain injury resulting from radiation therapy. Significant brain development and skill acquisition can be expected to occur between ages 6 and 12, and disruptions in brain structures associated with this development are likely to produce quite different patterns of cognitive outcomes. In general, the child treated at age 4 and evaluated at age 12 years is likely to have significantly more areas of difficulty than if evaluated at age 6 years.

Dose and Intensity of Treatment. The effects of radiation therapy are more pronounced as the dose of radiation increases. Recent approaches to radiation therapy have attempted to reduce the dose of radiation required to treat the tumor; reduce the intensity of the radiation by providing smaller doses more frequently (hyperfractionated radiation); or provide more focused radiation to the side of the tumor, sparing noncancerous brain tissue (conformal radiation). All of these approaches still have potential negative effects on growth and development after treatment, but it is hoped that the strategies will reduce the severity of the long-term outcomes (Kun, 1997). An interaction between the dose of radiation and the age of the child at the time of radiation has been identified, with reductions in cognitive impairment noted as age increases and radiation dose is lowered (Moore, Kramer, Wara, Halberg, & Ablin, 1991; Mulhern, Kepner, et al., 1998).

Other Chemotherapeutic Agents. For children treated for brain tumors, treatment sometimes includes both radiation therapy and chemotherapy. Chemotherapy is often used before radiation therapy is administered to shrink a tumor and maximize the benefits of radiation therapy. One of the most common chemotherapeutic drugs used in the treatment of brain tumors in children is cisplatin. Although highly effective in treating brain tumors, cisplatin, in combination with radiation therapy, is known to result in high-frequency hearing loss. Children treated with cisplatin and radiation therapy are monitored carefully for hearing loss, and when this is noted, these children are treated with another medication that limits hearing loss (Balis et al., 1997; Freilich, Kraus, Budnick, Bayer, & Finlay, 1996). Once high-frequency hearing loss occurs, it is a permanent disabling condition that often requires hearing aids and other accommodations for children with hearing impairment.

In the 1970s and 1980s, radiation treatment was used as prophylaxis, or preventive therapy, for leukemia that spread to the CNS. For children with leukemia, additional chemotherapy was injected directly into the cerebrospinal fluid of the CNS (called intrathecal chemotherapy), and the most common drug used for this treatment was methotrexate. In a series of studies in the 1980s, it was clearly demonstrated that children who were treated with radiation therapy, combined with intrathecal methotrexate, had a significantly greater risk of cognitive impairment than those children treated with methotrexate alone or radiation alone (Armstrong & Mulhern, 1999; Mulhern, 1994). In addition, a strong gender relationship between methotrexate and radiation therapy exists, with girls having significantly poorer cognitive outcomes than boys (Waber, Gioia, et al., 1990; Waber, Urion, et al., 1990; Waber, Tarbell, Kahn, Gelber, & Sallan, 1992). Unfortunately, protocols that did not include intrathecal methotrexate had significantly poorer overall survival, so its inclusion continues to be seen as an essential component of optimal therapy.

Chemotherapy Late Effects. For many years, it was assumed that the major source of cognitive impairment in children treated for cancer was radiation therapy. In the mid-1980s, treatment protocols for very young children with brain tumors began to use chemotherapy to delay radiation therapy, and protocols for children with acute leukemia were designed to replace radiation therapy with intrathecal chemotherapy (methotrexate, hydrocortisone, and cytosine arabinoside) alone. For young children with brain tumors, the benefits of delaying radiation by using chemotherapy were substantial, and this practice altered the treatment of brain tumors in young children for the next 15 years (Duffner et al., 1995). For children with leukemia, however, the benefits were not as striking. The use of intrathecal chemotherapy for CNS prophylaxis was effective in preventing growth delays and endocrine problems, but acute neurologic events and long-term learning problems continued to be noticed for a number of children treated for ALL (Brown et al., 1992, 1996, 1998; Brown & Madan-Swain, 1993; Brown, Sawyer, Antoniou, Toogood, & Rice, 1999; Mahoney et al., 1998). The late cognitive effects of chemotherapy treatment for ALL resemble those seen in children in the past who were treated with cranial radiation therapy.

COGNITIVE LATE EFFECTS

Over the past 30 years, numerous studies have been conducted that examined the effects of radiation therapy and chemotherapy on cognitive functioning in children treated for brain tumors and ALL. The studies will not be reviewed in detail, because several recent papers and chapters have provided reviews of this literature (Armstrong et al., 1999; Armstrong & Mulhern, 1999; Moore et al., 2000; Mulhern, 1994). From this research, however, some consistent findings have emerged that should be integrated into the evaluation of cognitive late effects, and considered when developing educational intervention plans.

Common Cognitive Late Effects

Early research on cognitive late effects focused primarily on changes in IQ scores over time. This research was helpful in identifying the pattern of global cognitive impairment that emerged slowly in the years after treatment, but was limited in its contribution to understanding specific *changes in* brain development and the development of effective educational, medication, and prevention approaches to intervention.

Several investigators proposed a specific effects model to better understand the CNS effects of treatment of leukemia (Cousens, Ungerer, Crawford, & Stevens, 1991; Fletcher & Copeland, 1988). The specific effects model suggested that the effects of CNS treatment can be global for some children, but usually more specifically affects nonverbal abilities; with much less an effect, if any, on verbal abilities. The cognitive late effects that are of specific concern are concentration and the ability to sustain attention, processing speed, short-term memory, and sequencing ability (Cousens et al., 1991). Subsequently, a series of studies suggested difficulties with a variety of memory abilities; slowed fine motor speed and accuracy; and difficulties with social cue perception, executive functioning, and social and behavioral adjustment (Armstrong & Mulhern, 1999; Brown et al., 1999; Espy et al., 2001; Fossen, Abrahamsen, & Storm-Mathisen, 1998; Hetherington, Dennis, & Spiegler, 2000; Hill et al., 1998; Mulhern, 1994; Sands, van Gorp, & Finlay, 1998).

The observation that specific cognitive effects are likely to be noted in children treated for CNS cancer has led to consideration of a model suggesting developmental emergence of late effects over years after treatment (Armstrong et al., 1999; Armstrong & Horn, 1995). This model is based on an understanding of normal brain development combined with the issues of timing of treatment and timing of assessment that were discussed earlier. Simply, the model suggests that cognitive abilities associated with brain structures that have developed before treatment with radiation and/or chemotherapy will be only minimally affected by treatment. Cognitive abilities associated with brain structures that develop after treatment are more likely to be affected and will represent the specific effects proposed by Cousens et al. (1991), in addition to others who have been identified in subsequent investigations. Furthermore, the specific effects seen will depend on individual responses to treatment and the age of the child at the time cognitive abilities are evaluated. Thus, some children may have protective factors, for example, genetics, that will result in their experiencing minimal late cognitive effects. For other children, the late effects that are detected will depend on the age at which the child was treated (establishing which structures have already developed and are likely to be unaffected, and those that are still developing and likely to be most affected), how long it has been since the treatment, and how old child is at the time of the assessment.

Consideration of these three factors is essential to understanding the late cognitive effects of children treated for cancer. The age at the time of treatment establishes baseline functioning. Although some loss of functioning may occur, particularly for children with invasive tumors or those who receive surgery, fundamental abilities that developed before the age of treatment appear to remain intact. For many children, these are verbal abilities, particularly verbal abilities that involve processing of auditory information and communication using speech. The older the child is at the time of treatment, the fewer the abilities that are likely to be affected.

Time since treatment is a second critical feature. Cognitive effects of CNS treatment are often not detected until 1–3 years after treatment is completed. Two factors are believed to influence this finding.

The first is the rate of brain growth after treatment. CNS treatment does not appear to produce immediate, detectable brain injury. Instead, it appears to disrupt the development of myelin and neural connections that emerged over time as the child grows (Reddickaij et al., 2000; Steen et al., 2001; Surtees, Clelland, & Hann, 1998). Evidence of cognitive impairment will not appear until this developmental process reaches the point in which children not exposed to treatment will have acquired skills, whereas those exposed to treatment will not. For example, the child receiving radiation therapy at age 6 may not differ from a healthy child at age 6 on tasks of simple addition and subtraction. However, by age 8, brain development essential to the memorization of multiplication tables will have taken place in the child not exposed to radiation, but not in the child exposed to radiation. It is at this point that the effects of radiation therapy become developmentally obvious.

The second factor involves the developmental complexity of the tasks the child needs to perform at the time of assessment. Not only is the brain developing in the years after treatment, but also the complexity of information and ability needed to perform successfully increases. For instance, a child may demonstrate age-appropriate reading skills in the first, second, and third grades, only to have significant difficulties in reading in the fifth grade. Most frequently, this does not represent deterioration in reading skills. Instead, it likely represents an interaction between slower development of the brain combined with significantly greater complexity of reading tasks. For instance, type size decreases and the concentration of written text on pages increases as the child ages, but brain development for the child exposed to CNS treatment is not progressing at the same rate as this increasing task complexity. The child may still have the ability to decode the words on the page. However, the process of decoding may become so complex and affected by slowed processing speed, difficulty with sustained attention, and difficulty with visual-motor integration that comprehension of reading deteriorates. This, in turn, may result in emerging delays in reading ability, comprehension ability, and vocabulary acquisition, ultimately leading to progressive school failure over time.

Common Areas of Cognitive Impairment

Children who are treated for tumors of the CNS, and some treated for ALL, are at increased risk to experience specific neurocognitive impairments that affect the way they learn and perform in school. These include slowed processing speed (Bordeaux et al., 1988; Brown et al., 1998; Butler, Hill, Steinherz, Meyers, & Finlay, 1994; Cousens et al., 1991; Schatz, Kramer, Ablin, & Matthay, 2000), difficulties with sustained attention (Anderson et al., 1994; Appleton, Farrell, Zaide, & Rogers, 1990; Brouwers, Riccardi, Poplack, & Fedio, 1984; Butler, 1998; Butler et al., 1994; Christie et al., 1994; Moore, Ater, & Copeland, 1992; Mulhern & Kun, 1985), difficulties with visual-motor integration (Bordeaux et al., 1988; Butler et al., 1994; Copeland et al., 1985, 1988; Cousens et al., 1991; Espy et al., 2001; Harten et al., 1984; Kingma et al., 2001; MacLean et al., 1995; Moore et al., 1991, 1992; Mulhern et al., 1989; Mulhern, Wasserman, Fairclough, & Ochs, 1988; Packer et al., 1989; Sands et al., 1998; Smedler & Bolme, 1995; Waber, Urion, et al., 1990), some specific memory difficulties (Ciesielski et al., 1994; Copeland et al., 1985; Dennis et al., 1991; Dennis, Hetherington, & Spiegler, 1998; Kingma et al., 2001; Packer et al., 1989; Rodgers, Britton, Morris, Kernahan, & Craft, 1992; Schatz et al., 2000; von der Weid, 2001; Waber et al., 1992), and academic problems in math (Anderson et al., 1994; Brown et al., 1992, 1996; Copeland et al., 1985; Espy et al., 2001), and sometimes in reading (Brown et al., 1996, 1999; Smibert, Anderson, Godber, & Ekert, 1996). In the classroom, these neurocognitive impairments often result in children (a) failing to complete assignments on time (processing speed); (b) having episodes of inattention that affect learning; (c) having difficulty with handwriting that affects performance on essays, written tests, and other writing assignments; (d) having qualitatively different performance on oral as opposed to written tests; (e) having difficulty learning information that is nonmeaningful, involves symbols and sequences, and is primarily visual; (f) having difficulty with math calculations, but not necessarily math concepts; (g) demonstrating the capability to recognize and read words, but declining comprehension of what they read as material becomes more complex; and (h) having difficulty with organization and planning. Recognizing these more common cognitive outcomes permits the school psychologist to better plan an assessment strategy that addresses the child's strengths and weaknesses and leads to an effective intervention strategy.

ASSESSMENT STRATEGY

Children treated for CNS cancer present school psychologists and other educators responsible for educational planning and providing appropriate educational services with a number of challenges. Conventional approaches to evaluation and determination of educational needs are often based on static concepts of learning disabilities that rely heavily on discrepancies between intellectual functioning and academic achievement (Shaw, Cullen, McGuire, & Brinckerhoff, 1995). Learning deficits are also often considered stable. For children treated for cancer, these assumptions may be inaccurate and may lead to psychological assessments that do not provide information helpful to the child or the school system (Armstrong et al., 1999).

Assessment of the child treated for CNS cancer should be carefully planned. Inclusion of age-appropriate measures of intellectual functioning and academic achievement may be necessary to meet local, state, or federal guidelines for evaluation of children eligible for special education, but these will often provide insufficient data to appropriately plan for the education of the child with CNS cancer-related difficulties. For these children, the evaluation should also include tests of specific functional abilities likely to be affected by radiation or chemotherapy over time, as well as tests of specific functional abilities that are unlikely to be affected, representing strengths of the child in the educational setting (Armstrong et al., 1999; Mulhern, Armstrong, & Thompson, 1998). Furthermore, the evaluation should be planned to anticipate areas of functioning that may not be detected as impaired at the time of the evaluation, but can be expected to demonstrate impairment at some later point in time. Finally, evaluation of the child with CNS cancer should be considered a process, with planned re-evaluations every 18–24 months, or as clinically indicated, to appropriately track the developmental emergence of new areas of difficulty. In these situations, changes in performance should involve examination of both standard score changes (which often decline over time) and raw score changes (which usually increase over time, but not at the rate anticipated).

Each psychologist, center, and school system will have tests that are commonly used, and that define local standards of assessment. Test versions change, and new tests are frequently published. For this reason, we will not recommend specific tests to be included in an assessment battery, but will instead discuss the kinds of tests that should be considered, consistent with both previous recommendations (Mulhern, Armstrong, & Thompson, 1998) and current understanding of recent empirical findings.

Most evaluations will include a test of global intellectual functioning, and measures of reading and math achievement. These are usually included to meet state and federal guidelines for entry into special education services, and for this reason will be included in the assessment of the child with cancer. However, in addition to these basic tests, the assessment battery for the child treated for a CNS tumor or ALL should include:

1. A computerized test of attention and concentration that permits examination of both errors of omission (likely to be detected) and errors of commission (infrequently identified in this population). This measure will also provide a sensitive index of response time, or processing speed, that can be quite helpful.
2. Standardized tests of memory that include assessment of auditory memory, visual memory, sequential memory, and delayed recall.
3. Standardized tests of processing speed involving visual-motor abilities.
4. Standardized tests of planning, organization, and problem-solving ability.
5. Standardized tests of language ability, including expressive and receptive language, verbal fluency, and listening comprehension skills. These tests are helpful in identifying the child's strengths and often lead to interventions that can be beneficial in the classroom.
6. Standardized tests of behavioral adjustment (including internalizing behavior difficulties) and parent report of adaptive behavior.

In addition to these core areas, the results of several current studies may ultimately suggest inclusion of measures of social cue perception and social problem-solving skills in the assessment strategy.

INTERVENTION APPROACHES

School-based intervention for children with cancer may involve a number of activities, depending on the specific type of cancer, intensity of treatment, course of treatment, and anticipated late effects. Intervention strategies may include school reintegration programs, special education support, specialized cognitive rehabilitation, use of medications, and environmental modification and use of assistive technology. For some children, social skills support may be indicated, and, for some classrooms, bereavement support for classmates and teachers may be needed if the child should die.

School Reintegration

For all children, regardless of specific diagnosis, the development of a school integration or re-entry intervention that provides information to teachers and classmates may be highly effective in reducing emotional concerns and social withdrawal of the child with cancer. This type of program may also significantly reduce the discomfort experienced by other children in the classroom, reduce teasing because of changes in physical appearance, and improve the behavioral adjustment of the child with cancer in the school setting (Blakeney, 1995; Fryer, Saylor, Finch, & Smith, 1989; Katz & Varni, 1993; Katz, Varni, Rubenstein, Blew, & Hubert, 1992; Richardson, Nelson, & Meeske, 1999; Sexson & Madan-Swain, 1993; Varni, Katz, Colegrove, & Dolgin, 1993). School reintegration programs are usually coordinated with the medical team involved in the child's treatment, and often include presentations to the child's classmates about his/her cancer and treatment, as well as regular and ongoing communication between the school and medical team.

Education and Advocacy

Children with cancer may be eligible for special education services under the Individuals with Disabilities Education Act (IDEA) for identified developmental or learning delays, or under 504 Regulations for children with chronic health conditions. Unfortunately, parents of children with cancer have encountered many difficulties obtaining appropriate services, largely because the patterns of difficulties are unfamiliar to many school personnel involved in determining eligibility for services. Whereas school-reintegration programs facilitate a child's return to school, and many school personnel are more than willing to provide accommodations to address emotional needs, long-term educational needs have not been well identified and addressed. Recently, educational materials that address learning issues in children with cancer have been developed to help parents, school personnel, and physicians better understand the late-learning effects of treatment. At least one program provides advocacy training for parents, teaching them how to (a) communicate with teachers, (b) understand their child's rights under federal and state law, and (c) monitor the educational support provided to their child in the school (Richardson et al., 1999).

Direct Intervention

As empirical evidence has accumulated to support our understanding of the late effects of childhood cancer, several strategies have emerged that directly address some of these deficits. These have included pharmacologic intervention, cognitive rehabilitation, and compensatory intervention. As these are relatively new strategies, solid data on long-term outcomes are not yet available, but aspects of these interventions may prove beneficial for children experiencing cognitive late effects of cancer treatment.

Pharmacologic Intervention. Several recent reports suggest that the use of methylphenidate, or other stimulant medications commonly used to treat attention deficit hyperactivity disorder, may be beneficial in addressing attention and concentration problems in children with cancer (DeLong, Friedman, Friedman, Gustafson, & Oakes, 1992; Meyers, Weitzner, Valentine, & Levin, 1998; Thompson et al., 2001). Clinical trials evaluating the effectiveness and safety of these medications in children treated for CNS tumors are underway. Before widespread use of stimulant medications is recommended, evaluation of the safety of the medication in children who have received substantial CNS treatment is necessary. It is possible that dose–response relationships will be different for these children, and that their sensitivity to both beneficial and undesired effects of the medications may be different from that experienced by children who have not received intensive CNS treatment.

Cognitive Rehabilitation. Another promising approach to intervention is based on a rehabilitation model involving repetitive exposure to behavioral tasks that strengthen neural pathways and promote recovery of function. Using computer-based learning tasks, children are exposed to mass-practice trials involving multiple skills over a period of 6 months to 1 year. At this point in time, this intervention is still at an experimental level. Preliminary data suggest that children's attention is improved after the intervention, but no significant impact on other cognitive or academic abilities has yet been identified (Butler & Rizzi, 1995; Butler, 1998). This strategy is promising, but may ultimately find its greatest utility when applied to children at the time they receive CNS treatment than at the time functional deficits are identified.

Compensatory Intervention. For children who have developed neurocognitive impairments after CNS treatment, rehabilitation options may be limited. An alternative strategy relies on accommodation in the school setting and use of assistive technology to help children compensate for the deficits that follow CNS treatment. This approach identifies those functional abilities that are likely to be unaffected by rehabilitative approaches (e.g., memory, processing speed, visual-motor integration tasks). Accommodations and technological supports are then provided that allow children to work around the areas of deficits while continuing to develop areas of strength (Armstrong et al., 1999; Armstrong & Horn, 1995). Because the research on late effects of CNS treatment supports the observation that functions associated with early development (e.g., language and other verbal abilities) are less affected than those associated with later development (e.g., visual-motor integration, processing speed, attention regulation, executive functioning, and memory), the compensatory intervention model focuses on heavy reliance on language-based learning and performance, with minimization of emphasis on visual and motor learning and performance. Essentially, the education model shifts from reading and writing to listening and speaking.

The primary components of the compensatory intervention model include:

1. Providing children with access to books on to tape for all reading requirements. Although the word decoding skills of children continue to develop after CNS treatment, comprehension often declines as reading tasks become more complex. However, comprehension of auditory information continues to progress in the face of increasing language complexity.
2. Using oral assessment, as opposed to written testing, for all evaluation of knowledge acquisition and learning progress. Writing is a skill that is negatively impacted by slower processing speed, difficulties with memory, and impairment in visual-motor integration. The quality of written work may be far more a reflection of handwriting ability than of conceptualization and creativity. Unfortunately, the quality of the child's thinking may be lost in the process of writing the ideas on paper, leading to a negative evaluation of the child's progress. This often results in (a) efforts to remediate a problem that may not be amenable to intervention because of delayed neural structural development or (b) failure to provide opportunities that permit the child to continue learning progress in those areas unrelated to the CNS deficits.
3. Using computers to shape reading skills systematically for daily living tasks and for tests that must be read (e.g., some state standardized testing). Computers can be used to enlarge or change fonts, and the amount and complexity of text viewed on a screen can be limited to improve recognition and comprehension.
4. Exploring the use of voice recognition technology to help children dictate written work.

5. Using calculators to help children compensate calculation deficits related to memory deficits after CNS treatment.
6. Limiting the amount of time a child spends on an assignment by reducing the volume of work expected. This is particularly important for home-based assignments. Children treated for CNS cancer often require 2–4 times more time to complete homework assignments than children who are typically developing.
7. Eliminating time expectations for all evaluations.
8. Using audiotaping or FM transmitted speech-to-text (e.g., FM transmission of teacher lectures to voice recognition by child's laptop) for classroom notes and lectures.
9. Teaching keyboard skills instead of handwriting skills.

Most of these accommodations do not require expensive human resources, yet provide children with the opportunity to learn and demonstrate their learning efficiently.

Prevention. The best approach to cognitive and learning impairments in children treated for cancer is to prevent these impairments from occurring. Close collaboration between medical teams, hospital-based pediatric psychologists, school psychologists, and classroom teachers is important to develop prevention strategies for these children. Collaborations between behavioral scientists and pediatric subspecialists have led to changes in the intensity and way that treatment is provided, This collaboration has resulted in improved outcomes for many children (Duffner et al., 1995; Duffner, Cohen, Thomas, & Lansky, 1985; Horowitz et al., 1988; Horowitz & Poplack, 1991). New approaches to treatment are currently being evaluated, including substituting less toxic chemotherapeutic agents, reducing radiation therapy doses, and identifying medications that prevent brain injury when chemotherapy is administered. Similarly, in the educational setting, interventions that are provided within windows of development, often before obvious deficits are detected, may offer substantial long-term benefits to this group of children.

BEREAVEMENT IN THE CLASSROOM

Treatment for children with cancer has greatly improved the chances that children with cancer will be long-term survivors, but cancer nonetheless remains the most frequent disease-related cause of death in children in the United States (Centers for Disease Control and Prevention, 2002). A great deal of attention has been focused on how such bereavement issues can be addressed within the context of the family, including focusing on their effects on parents and siblings of the deceased child (Dongen Melman & Sanders Woudstra, 1986; Gibbons, 1988; Martinson & Papadatou, 1994; Mulcahey & Young, 1995; Sourkes, 1987). However, little attention has been given to the effects of bereavement within the classroom, on school personnel, and on peers of the deceased child.

Developmental issues during adolescence influence the significance of the loss of a friend, and because friends play a central role in dealing with various psychosocial tasks, the death of a friend may put at risk or delay successful completion of those tasks (Oltjenbruns, 1996). Children and adolescents who have experienced significant losses are at greater risk for a number of problems, including medical illness (Schmale & Iker, 1991), psychiatric illness (Valente, Saunders, & Street, 1988), and risk of suicide as adults (Adams, Overholser, & Lehnert, 1994). Other acute problems have been associated with loss of a peer, including "shock, numbness, sadness, anger, insomnia, loneliness, fright, survivor guilt, nightmares, suicide ideation, fears of own death, drug abuse, and school problems" (Ringler & Hayden, 2000, p. 210). In a study of high school-aged adolescents (ages 14–19 years) who had lost a peer, 98% reported receiving help from other peers, 97% reported receiving help from parents, and 75% reported receiving help from teachers. Adolescents who had lost a peer generally reported wanting support from both other peers and from parents for a period of 1–3 months. These adolescents reported that generally teachers provided support for a few days, but that they wanted teacher support for a few weeks after the death of their peer. They also reported that other peers were the most helpful to them during this time (Ringler et al., 2000). Similarly after the loss of a peer, many adolescents only felt comfortable talking with peers who had also been close to the deceased (O'Brien, Goodenow, & Espin, 1991).

For these reasons, it is important to ensure that children and adolescents are allowed to deal with bereavement adequately and appropriately. Consideration of developmental issues and the adolescent's need to spend time with other peers in processing what has happened are important components of bereavement support. When the death of a peer is eminent (e.g., when all treatment options have been exhausted and/or when a family decides to seek only palliative care for a child), it may be helpful to prepare peers for the upcoming event by giving them an opportunity to say goodbye. This may be done in person, over the telephone, or through a card or e-mail. After the death of the child, it can be helpful to allow time for peers to remember their former classmate. A number of memorial strategies may be helpful, including class or individual projects, constructing memorials, or group discussions about the peer who died. Developmental considerations and individual choice are important aspects of these strategies. No single strategy will be helpful for all of the children, and providing individuals with choices (including the option to not participate) should be included in any classroom bereavement intervention. It may also be helpful to bring in a psychosocial professional skilled in bereavement issues to provide one or more group therapy sessions for the child's peers. Once again, it is essential to recognize that children and adolescents may have difficulty expressing their reactions to the bereavement situation, and that each may experience the death in a different way. As a result, a combination of approaches may be necessary to ensure that the needs of each individual in the classroom has his or her needs fully met. If it is unclear how best to accomplish this, consultation with a psychosocial professional skilled in bereavement issues is recommended, even if group therapy sessions are not planned.

CONCLUSIONS

Once uniformly believed to be a fatal disease, childhood cancer is now highly treatable, with the majority of children expected to be long-term survivors into adulthood. For the school psychologists and other educational personnel, the challenges once faced primarily in the hospital setting are increasingly those that must be faced in the educational setting. Close communication between the school and the medical setting is essential to facilitate return and reintegration of children after treatment. The long-term consequences of cancer therapy, particularly chemotherapy and radiation therapy focusing on the CNS, are emerging as major concerns for the surviving population. Education of school personnel about the kinds of impairments likely to be experienced is needed at administrative and classroom instruction levels. Elimination of barriers to access to educational services under special education laws is essential. Development and evaluation of approaches to prevention, acute intervention, and long-term educational planning and accommodation remain a challenge for parents, physicians, and educators. In those cases in which treatment is unsuccessful and the child dies, strategies for assisting siblings and classmates in the school setting need to be evaluated and implemented. In each of these cases, the school psychologist can play a critical role by facilitating communication between hospital and school, providing educational opportunities for school-based personnel, and ensuring that appropriate services are provided for children who are survivors.

ACKNOWLEDGMENTS

This chapter was prepared with the support of the Maternal and Child Health Bureau (Leadership Education in Neurodevelopmental Disabilities Program [T73MC00013–10]), the National Institute of Child and Human Development (HD-07510-04), the Children's Medical Services of Florida (Contract COQ3), the Administration for Developmental Disabilities (University Center for Excellence in Developmental Disabilities Education, Research and Service [90DD0408]), and a grant from the Health Foundation of South Florida.

REFERENCES

Adams, D. M., Overholser, J. C., & Lehnert, K. L. (1994). Perceived family functioning and adolescent suicidal behavior. *Journal of the American Academy of Child and Adolescent Psychiatry, 33*, 498–507.

Anderson, V., Smibert, E., Ekert, H., & Godber, T. (1994). Intellectual, educational, and behavioural sequelae after cranial irradiation and chemotherapy. *Archives of Diseases of Children, 70*, 476–483.

Appleton, R. E., Farrell, K., Zaide, J., & Rogers, P. (1990). Decline in head growth and cognitive impairment in survivors of acute lymphoblastic leukaemia. *Archives of Diseases of Children, 65*, 530–534.

Armstrong, F. D. (2001). Acute and long-term neurodevelopmental outcomes in children following bone marrow transplantation. *Frontiers in Bioscience, 6*, G6–G12.

Armstrong, F. D., Blumberg, M. J., & Toledano, S. R. (1999). Neurobehavioral issues in childhood cancer. *School Psychology Review, 28*, 194–203.

Armstrong, F. D., & Horn, M. (1995). Educational issues in childhood cancer. *School Psychology Quarterly, 10*, 292–304.

Armstrong, F. D., & Mulhern, R. K. (1999). Acute lymphoblastic leukemia and brain tumors. In R. T. Brown (Ed.), *Cognitive aspects of chronic illness in children* (pp. 47–77). New York: Guilford Publications.

Balis, F. M., Holcenberg, J. S., & Poplack, D. G. (1997). General principles of chemotherapy. In P. A. Pizzo & D. G. Poplack (Eds.), *Principles and practice of pediatric oncology* (3rd ed., pp. 215–272). Philadelphia: Lippincott-Raven.

Blakeney, P. (1995). School reintegration. *Journal of Burn Care Rehabilitation, 16*, 180–187.

Bordeaux, J. D., Dowell, R. E., Jr., Copeland, D. R., Fletcher, J. M., Francis, D. J., & van Eys, J. (1988). A prospective study of neuropsychological sequelae in children with brain tumors. *Journal of Child Neurology, 3*, 63–68.

Brouwers, P., Riccardi, R., Poplack, D., & Fedio, P. (1984). Attentional deficits in long-term survivors of childhood acute lymphoblastic leukemia (ALL). *Journal of Clinical Neuropsychology, 6*, 325–336.

Brown, R. T., & Madan-Swain, A. (1993). Cognitive, neuropsychological, and academic sequelae in children with leukemia. *Journal of Learning Disabilities, 26*, 74–90.

Brown, R. T., Madan-Swain, A., Pais, R., Lambert, R. G., Sexson, S., & Ragab, A. (1992). Chemotherapy for acute lymphocytic leukemia: cognitive and academic sequelae. *Journal of Pediatrics, 121*, 885–889.

Brown, R. T., Madan-Swain, A., Walco, G. A., Cherrick, I., Ievers, C. E., Conte, P. M., Vega, R., Bell, B., & Lauer, S. J. (1998). Cognitive and academic late effects among children previously treated for acute lymphocytic leukemia receiving chemotherapy as CNS prophylaxis. *Journal of Pediatric Psychology, 23*, 333–340.

Brown, R. T., Sawyer, M. G., Antoniou, G., Toogood, I., & Rice, M. (1999). Longitudinal follow-up of the intellectual and academic functioning of children receiving central nervous system-prophylactic chemotherapy for leukemia: A four-year final report. *Journal of Developmental and Behavioral Pediatrics, 20*, 373–377.

Brown, R. T., Sawyer, M. B., Antoniou, G., Toogood, I., Rice, M., Thompson, N., & Madan-Swain, A. (1996). A 3-year follow-up of the intellectual and academic functioning of children receiving central nervous system prophylactic chemotherapy for leukemia. *Journal of Developmental and Behavioral Pediatrics, 17*, 392–398.

Butler, R. W. (1998). Attentional processes and their remediation in childhood cancer. *Medical and Pediatric Oncology, 30*(Suppl. 1), 75–78.

Butler, R. W., Hill, J. M., Steinherz, P. G., Meyers, P. A., & Finlay, J. L. (1994). Neuropsychologic effects of cranial irradiation, intrathecal methotrexate, and systemic methotrexate in childhood cancer. *Journal of Clinical Oncology, 12*, 2621–2629.

Butler, R. W., & Rizzi, L. P. (1995). The remediation of attentional deficits secondary to treatment for childhood cancer. *Progress Notes, Society of Pediatric Psychology, 19*(5), 13.

Centers for Disease Prevention and Control, Office of Statistics and Programming, National Center for Injury Prevention and Control (2002). *10 leading causes of death, United States, 1988, all races, both sexes*. Atlanta: National Center for Health Statistics. http://webapp.cdc.gov/cgi-bin/broker.exe.

Cetingul, N., Aydinok, Y., Kantar, M., Oniz, H., Kavakli, K., Yalman, O., Erermis, S., Celebisoy, N., Akyurekli, O., Oztop, S., & Nisli, G. (1999). Neuropsychologic sequelae in the long-term survivors of childhood acute lymphoblastic leukemia. *Pediatric Hematology Oncology, 16*, 213–220.

Chapman, C. A., Waber, D. P., Bernstein, J. H., Pomeroy, S. L., LaVally, B., Sallan, S. E., & Tarbell, N. (1995). Neurobehavioral and neurologic outcome in long-term survivors of posterior fossa brain tumors: Role of age and perioperative factors. *Journal of Child Neurology, 10*, 209–212.

Christie, D., Battin, M., Leiper, A. D., Chessells, J., Vargha-Khadem, F., & Neville, B. G. (1994). Neuropsychological and neurological outcome after relapse of lymphoblastic leukaemia. *Archives of Diseases of Children, 70*, 275–280.

Ciesielski, K. T., Yanofsky, R., Ludwig, R. N., Hill, D. E., Hart, B. L., Astur, R. S., & Snyder, T. (1994). Hypoplasia of the cerebellar vermis and cognitive deficits in survivors of childhood leukemia. *Archives of Neurology, 51*, 985–993.

Copeland, D. R., Dowell, R. E., Jr., Fletcher, J. M., Bordeaux, J. D., Sullivan, M. P., Jaffe, N., Frankel, L. S., Ried, H. L., & Cangir, A. (1988). Neuropsychological effects of childhood cancer treatment. *Journal of Child Neurology, 3*, 53–62.

Copeland, D. R., Fletcher, J. M., Pfefferbaum-Levine, B., Jaffe, N., Ried, H., & Maor, M. (1985). Neuropsychological sequelae of childhood cancer in long-term survivors. *Pediatrics, 75*, 745–753.

Cousens, P., Ungerer, J. A., Crawford, J. A., & Stevens, M. M. (1991). Cognitive effects of childhood leukemia therapy: A case for four specific deficits. *Journal of Pediatric Psychology, 16*, 475–488.

Danoff, B. F., Cowchock, F. S., & Kramer, S. (1983). Childhood craniopharyngioma: Survival, local control, endocrine and neurologic function following radiotherapy. *International Journal of Radiation Oncology, Biology, and Physiology, 9*, 171–175.

Danoff, B. F., Cowchock, F. S., Marquette, C., Mulgrew, L., & Kramer, S. (1982). Assessment of the long-term effects of primary radiation therapy for brain tumors in children. *Cancer, 49*, 1580–1586.

DeLong, R., Friedman, H., Friedman, N., Gustafson, K., & Oakes, J. (1992). Methylphenidate in neuropsychological sequelae of radiotherapy and chemotherapy of childhood brain tumors and leukemia. *Journal of Child Neurology, 7*, 462–463.

Dennis, M., Hetherington, C. R., & Spiegler, B. J. (1998). Memory and attention after childhood brain tumors. *Medical and Pediatric Oncology, Suppl. 1*, 25–33.

Dennis, M., Spiegler, B. J., Fitz, C. R., Hoffman, H. J., Hendrick, E. B., Humphreys, R. P., & Chuang, S. (1991). Brain tumors in children and adolescents. II. The neuroanatomy of deficits in working, associative and serial-order memory. *Neuropsychologia, 29*, 829–847.

Dennis, M., Spiegler, B. J., Hetherington, C. R., & Greenberg, M. L. (1996). Neuropsychological sequelae of the treatment of children with medulloblastoma. *Journal of Neurooncology, 29*, 91–101.

Dongen Melman, J. E., & Sanders Woudstra, J. A. (1986). Psychosocial aspects of childhood cancer: A review of the literature. *Journal of Child Psychology and Psychiatry and Allied Disciplines, 27*, 145–180.

Doxey, D., Bruce, D., Sklar, F., Swift, D., & Shapiro, K. (1999). Posterior fossa syndrome: Identifiable risk factors and irreversible complications. *Pediatric Neurosurgery, 31*, 131–136.

Duffner, P. K., Cohen, M. E., Thomas, P. R., & Lansky, S. B. (1985). The long-term effects of cranial irradiation on the central nervous system. *Cancer, 56*, 1841–1846.

Duffner, P. K., Kun, L. E., Burger, P. C., Horowitz, M. E., Cohen, M. E., Sanford, R. A., Krischer, J. P., Mulhern, R. K., James, H. E., & Rekate, H. L. (1995). Postoperative chemotherapy and delayed radiation in infants and very young children with choroid plexus carcinomas. The Pediatric Oncology Group. *Pediatric Neurosurgery, 22*, 189–196.

Espy, K. A., Moore, I. M., Kaufmann, P. M., Kramer, J. H., Matthay, K., & Hutter, J. J. (2001). Chemotherapeutic CNS prophylaxis and neuropsychologic change in children with acute lymphoblastic leukemia: A prospective study. *Journal of Pediatric Psychology, 26*, 1–9.

Fletcher, J. M., & Copeland, D. R. (1988). Neurobehavioral effects of central nervous system prophylactic treatment of cancer in children. *Journal of Clinical and Experimental Neuropsychology, 10*, 495–537.

Fossen, A., Abrahamsen, T. G., & Storm-Mathisen, I. (1998). Psychological outcome in children treated for brain tumor. *Pediatric Hematology Oncology, 15*, 479–488.

Freilich, R. J., Kraus, D. H., Budnick, A. S., Bayer, L. A., & Finlay, J. L. (1996). Hearing loss in children with brain tumors treated with cisplatin and carboplatin-based high-dose chemotherapy with autologous bone marrow rescue. *Medical and Pediatric Oncology, 26*, 95–100.

Fryer, L. L., Saylor, C. F., Finch, A. J., Jr., & Smith, K. E. (1989). Helping the child with cancer: What school personnel want to know. *Psychological Review, 65*, 563–566.

Gajjar, A., Mulhern, R. K., Heideman, R. L., Sanford, R. A., Douglass, E. C., Kovnar, E. H., Langston, J. A., Jenkins, J. J., & Kun, L. E. (1994). Medulloblastoma in very young children: Outcome of definitive craniospinal irradiation following incomplete response to chemotherapy. *Journal of Clinical Oncology, 12*, 1212–1216.

Gibbons, M. B. (1988). *Coping with childhood cancer: A family perspective. Family interventions throughout chronic illness and disability* (Vol. 7, pp. 74–103). New York: Springer Publishing Co., Inc., Springer Series on Rehabilitation.

Harten, G., Stephani, U., Henze, G., Langermann, H. J., Riehm, H., & Hanefeld, F. (1984). Slight impairment of psychomotor skills in children after treatment of acute lymphoblastic leukemia. *European Journal of Pediatrics, 142*, 189–197.

Hawkins, M. M., & Stevens, M. C. (1996). The long-term survivors. *British Medical Bulletin, 52*, 898–923.

Heideman, R. L., Packer, R. J., Albright, L. A., Freeman, C. R., & Rorke, L. B. (1997). Tumors of the central nervous system. In P. A. Pizzo & D. G. Poplack (Eds.), *Principles and practice of pediatric oncology* (3rd ed., pp. 633–698). Philadelphia: Lippincott-Raven.

Hetherington, R., Dennis, M., & Spiegler, B. (2000). Perception and estimation of time in long-term survivors of childhood posterior fossa tumors. *Journal of the International Neuropsychology Society, 6*, 682–692.

Hill, J. M., Kornblith, A. B., Jones, D., Freeman, A., Holland, J. F., Glicksman, A. S., Boyett, J. M., Lenherr, B., Brecher, M. L., Dubowy, R., Kung, F., Maurer, H., & Holland, J. C. (1998). A comparative study of the long term psychosocial functioning of childhood acute lymphoblastic leukemia survivors treated by intrathecal methotrexate with or without cranial radiation. *Cancer, 82*, 208–218.

Horowitz, M. E., Kun, L. E., Mulhern, R. K., Kovnar, E. H., Sanford, R. A., Hockenberger, B. M., Greeson, F. L., Langston, J. W., Fairclough, D. L., & Jenkins, J. J., III. (1988). Feasibility and efficacy of preirradiation chemotherapy for pediatric brain tumors. *Neurosurgery, 22*, 687–690.

Horowitz, M. E., & Poplack, D. G. (1991). Development of chemotherapy treatment for pediatric brain tumors. *Neurology Clinics, 9*, 363–373.

Humpl, T., Fritsche, M., Bartels, U., & Gutjahr, P. (2001). Survivors of childhood cancer for more than twenty years. *Acta Oncology, 40*, 44–49.

Johnson, D. L., McCabe, M. A., Nicholson, H. S., Joseph, A. L., Getson, P. R., Byrne, J., Brasseux, C., Packer, R. J., & Reaman, G. (1994). Quality of long-term survival in young children with medulloblastoma. *Journal of Neurosurgery, 80*, 1004–1010.

Kaleita, T. A., Reaman, G. H., MacLean, W. E., Sather, H. N., & Whitt, J. K. (1999). Neurodevelopmental outcome of infants with acute lymphoblastic leukemia: A Children's Cancer Group report. *Cancer, 85*, 1859–1865.

Katz, E. R., & Varni, J. W. (1993). Social support and social cognitive problem-solving in children with newly diagnosed cancer. *Cancer, 71*, 3314–3319.

Katz, E. R., Varni, J. W., Rubenstein, C. L., Blew, A., & Hubert, N. (1992). Teacher, parent, and child evaluative ratings of a school reintegration intervention for children with newly diagnosed cancer. *Children's Health Care, 21*, 69–75.

Kingma, A., van Dommelen, R. I., Mooyaart, E. L., Wilmink, J. T., Deelman, B. G., & Kamps, W. A. (2001). Slight cognitive impairment and magnetic resonance imaging abnormalities but normal school levels in children treated for acute lymphoblastic leukemia with chemotherapy only. *Journal of Pediatrics, 139*, 413–420.

Kun, L. E. (1997). General principles of radiation therapy. In P. A. Pizzo & D. G. Poplack (Eds.), *Principles and practice of pediatric oncology* (3rd ed., pp. 289–321). Philadelphia: Lippincott-Raven.

Kun, L. E., Mulhern, R. K., & Crisco, J. J. (1983). Quality of life in children treated for brain tumors. Intellectual, emotional, and academic function. *Journal of Neurosurgery, 58*, 1–6.

MacLean, W. E., Jr., Noll, R. B., Stehbens, J. A., Kaleita, T. A., Schwartz, E., Whitt, J. K., Cantor, N. L., Waskerwitz, M., Ruymann, F., & Novak, L. J. (1995). Neuropsychological effects of cranial irradiation in young children with acute lymphoblastic leukemia 9 months after diagnosis. The Children's Cancer Group. *Archives of Neurology, 52*, 156–160.

Mahoney, D. H., Jr., Shuster, J. J., Nitschke, R., Lauer, S. J., Steuber, C. P., Winick, N., & Camitta, B. (1998). Acute neurotoxicity in children with B-precursor acute lymphoid leukemia: An association with intermediate-dose intravenous methotrexate and intrathecal triple therapy—A Pediatric Oncology Group study. *Journal of Clinical Oncology, 16*, 1712–1722.

Margolin, J. F., & Poplack, D. G. (1997). Acute lymphoblastic leukemia. In P. A. Pizzo & D. G. Poplack (Eds.), *Principles and practice of pediatric oncology* (3rd ed., pp. 409–462). Philadelphia: Lippincott-Raven.

Martinson, I. M., & Papadatou, D. (1994). Care of the dying child and the bereaved. In R. K. Mulhern & D. J. Bearison (Eds.), *Pediatric psychooncology: Psychological perspectives on children with cancer* (pp. 193–214). New York: Oxford University Press.

Meyers, C. A., Weitzner, M. A., Valentine, A. D., & Levin, V. A. (1998). Methylphenidate therapy improves cognition, mood, and function of brain tumor patients. *Journal of Clinical Oncology, 16*, 2522–2527.

Moore, B. D., Copeland, D. R., Ried, H., & Levy, B. (1992). Neurophysiological basis of cognitive deficits in long-term survivors of childhood cancer. *Archives of Neurology, 49*, 809–817.

Moore, B. D., III, Ater, J. L., & Copeland, D. R. (1992). Improved neuropsychological outcome in children with brain tumors diagnosed during infancy and treated without cranial irradiation. *Journal of Child Neurology, 7*, 281–290.

Moore, I. M., Espy, K. A., Kaufmann, P., Kramer, J., Kaemingk, K., Miketova, P., Mollova, N., Kaspar, M., Pasvogel, A., Schram, K., Wara, W., Hutter, J., & Matthay, K. (2000). Cognitive consequences and central nervous system injury following treatment for childhood leukemia. *Seminars in Oncology Nursing, 16*, 279–290.

Moore, I. M., Kramer, J. H., Wara, W., Halberg, F., & Ablin, A. R. (1991). Cognitive function in children with leukemia. Effect of radiation dose and time since irradiation. *Cancer, 68*, 1913–1917.

Mulcahey, A. L., & Young, M. A. (1995). A bereavement support group for children: Fostering communication about grief and healing. *Cancer Practice, 3*, 150–156.

Mulhern, R. K. (1994). Neuropsychological late effects. In D. Bearison & R. K. Mulhern (Eds.), *Pediatric psycho-oncology: Psychological perspectives on children with cancer* (pp. 99–121). New York: Oxford Press.

Mulhern, R. K., Armstrong, F. D., & Thompson, S. J. (1998). Function-specific neuropsychological assessment. *Medical and Pediatric Oncology, 30*(Suppl. 1), 34–40.

Mulhern, R. K., Hancock, J., Fairclough, D., & Kun, L. (1992). Neuropsychological status of children treated for brain tumors: A critical review and integrative analysis. *Medical and Pediatric Oncology, 20*, 181–191.

Mulhern, R. K., Horowitz, M. E., Kovnar, E. H., Langston, J., Sanford, R. A., & Kun, L. E. (1989). Neurodevelopmental status of infants and young children treated for brain tumors with preirradiation chemotherapy. *Journal of Clinical Oncology, 7*, 1660–1666.

Mulhern, R. K., Kepner, J. L., Thomas, P. R., Armstrong, F. D., Friedman, H. S., & Kun, L. E. (1998). Neuropsychologic functioning of survivors of childhood medulloblastoma randomized to receive conventional or reduced-dose craniospinal irradiation: A Pediatric Oncology Group study. *Journal of Clinical Oncology, 16*, 1723–1728.

Mulhern, R. K., & Kun, L. E. (1985). Neuropsychologic function in children with brain tumors: III. Interval changes in the six months following treatment. *Medical and Pediatric Oncology, 13*, 318–324.

Mulhern, R. K., Palmer, S. L., Reddick, W. E., Glass, J. O., Kun, L. E., Taylor, J., Langston, J., & Gajjar, A. (2001). Risks of young age for selected neurocognitive deficits in medulloblastoma are associated with white matter loss. *Journal of Clinical Oncology, 19*, 472–479.

Mulhern, R. K., Reddick, W. E., Palmer, S. L., Glass, J. O., Elkin, T. D., Kun, L. E., Taylor, J., Langston, J., & Gajjar, A. (1999). Neurocognitive deficits in medulloblastoma survivors and white matter loss. *Annals of Neurology, 46*, 834–841.

Mulhern, R. K., Wasserman, A. L., Fairclough, D., & Ochs, J. (1988). Memory function in disease-free survivors of childhood acute lymphocytic leukemia given CNS prophylaxis with or without 1,800 cGy cranial irradiation. *Journal of Clinical Oncology, 6*, 315–320.

O'Brien, J. M., Goodenow, C., & Espin, O. (1991). Adolescents' reactions to the death of a peer. *Adolescence, 31*, 585–595.

Oltjenbruns, K. A. (1996). Death of a friend during adolescence: Issues and impacts. In C. A. Corr (Ed.), *Handbook of adolescent death and bereavement* (pp. 196–215). New York: Springer Publishing Co., Inc.

Packer, R. J., Meadows, A. T., Rorke, L. B., Goldwein, J. L., & D'Angio, G. (1987). Long-term sequelae of cancer treatment on the central nervous system in childhood. *Medical and Pediatric Oncology, 15*, 241–253.

Packer, R. J., Sutton, L. N., Atkins, T. E., Radcliffe, J., Bunin, G. R., D'Angio, G., Siegel, K. R., & Schut, L. (1989). A prospective study of cognitive function in children receiving whole-brain radiotherapy and chemotherapy: 2-year results. *Journal of Neurosurgery, 70*, 707–713.

Parker, S. L., Tong, T., Bolden, S., & Wingo, P. A. (1997). Cancer statistics, 1997. *CA Cancer, 47*, 5–27.

Radcliffe, J., Bunin, G. R., Sutton, L. N., Goldwein, J. W., & Phillips, P. C. (1994). Cognitive deficits in long-term survivors of childhood medulloblastoma and other noncortical tumors: Age-dependent effects of whole brain radiation. *International Journal of Developmental Neuroscience, 12*, 327–334.

Radcliffe, J., Packer, R. J., Atkins, T. E., Bunin, G. R., Schut, L., Goldwein, J. W., & Sutton, L. N. (1992). Three- and four-year cognitive outcome in children with noncortical brain tumors treated with whole-brain radiotherapy. *Annals of Neurology, 32*, 551–554.

Reddickaij, W. E., Russell, J. M., Glass, J. O., Xiong, X., Mulhern, R. K., Langston, J. W., Merchant, T. E.. Kun, L. E., & Gajjar, A. (2000). Subtle white matter volume differences in children treated for medulloblastoma with conventional or reduced dose craniospinal irradiation. *Magnetic Resonance Imaging, 18*, 787–793.

Richardson, R. C., Nelson, M. B., & Meeske, K. (1999). Young adult survivors of childhood cancer: Attending to emerging medical and psychosocial needs. *Journal of Pediatric Oncology Nursing, 16*, 136–144.

Ringler, L. L., & Hayden, D. C. (2000). Adolescent bereavement and social support: Peer loss compared to other losses. *Journal of Adolescent Research, 15*, 209–230.

Robison, L. L. (1997). General principles of the epidemiology of childhood cancer. In P. A. Pizzo & D. G. Poplack (Eds.), *Principles and practice of pediatric oncology* (3rd ed., pp. 1–10). Philadelphia: Lippincott-Raven.

Robison, L. L., Mertens, A., & Neglia, J. P. (1991). Epidemiology and etiology of childhood cancer. In D. J. Fernback & T. J. Vietti (Eds.), *Clinical pediatric oncology* (pp. 11–28). St. Louis: Mosby Year Book.

Rodgers, J., Britton, P. G., Morris, R. G., Kernahan, J., & Craft, A. W. (1992). Memory after treatment for acute lymphoblastic leukaemia. *Archives of Diseases of Children, 67*, 266–268.

Sanders, J. (1997). Bone marrow transplantation in pediatric oncology. In P. A. Pizzo & D. G. Poplack (Eds.), *Principles and practice of pediatric oncology* (3rd ed., pp. 357–373). Philadelphia: Lippincott-Raven.

Sands, S. A., van Gorp, W. G., & Finlay, J. L. (1998). Pilot neuropsychological findings from a treatment regimen consisting of intensive chemotherapy and bone marrow rescue for young children with newly diagnosed malignant brain tumors. *Children's Nervous Systems, 14*, 587–589.

Schatz, J., Kramer, J. H., Ablin, A., & Matthay, K. K. (2000). Processing speed, working memory, and IQ: A developmental model of cognitive deficits following cranial radiation therapy. *Neuropsychology, 14*, 189–200.

Schmale, A. H., & Iker, H. (1991). Hopelessness as a predictor of cervical carcinoma. *Social Science and Medicine, 5*, 95–100.

Sexson, S. B., & Madan-Swain, A. (1993). School reentry for the child with chronic illness. *Journal of Learning Disabilities, 26*, 115–25, 137.

Shaw, S. F., Cullen, J. P., McGuire, J. M., & Brinckerhoff, L. C. (1995). Operationalizing a definition of learning diabilities. *Journal of Learning Disabilities, 28*, 586–597.

Smedler, A. C., & Bolme, P. (1995). Neuropsychological deficits in very young bone marrow transplant recipients. *Acta Paediatrica, 84*, 429–433.

Smibert, E., Anderson, V., Godber, T., & Ekert, H. (1996). Risk factors for intellectual and educational sequelae of cranial irradiation in childhood acute lymphoblastic leukaemia. *British Journal of Cancer, 73*, 825–830.

Sourkes, B. M. (1987). Siblings of the child with a life-threatening illness. *Journal of Children in Contemporary Society, 19*, 159–184.

Steen, R. G., Koury, B. S. M., Granja, C. I., Xiong, X., Wu, S., Glass, J. O., Mulhern, R. K., Kun, L. E., & Merchant, T. E. (2001). Effect of ionizing radiation on the human brain: White matter and gray matter T1 in pediatric brain tumor patients treated with conformal radiation therapy. *International Journal of Radiation Oncology, Biology, and Physiology, 49*, 79–91.

Surtees, R., Clelland, J., & Hann, I. (1998). Demyelination and single-carbon transfer pathway metabolites during the treatment of acute lymphoblastic leukemia: CSF studies. *Journal of Clinical Oncology, 16*, 1505–1511.

Thompson, S. J., Leigh, L., Christensen, R., Xiong, X., Kun, L. E., Heideman, R. L., Reddick, W. E., Gajjar, A., Merchant, T., Pui, C. H., Hudson, M. M., & Mulhern, R. K. (2001). Immediate neurocognitive effects of methylphenidate on learning-impaired survivors of childhood cancer. *Journal of Clinical Oncology, 19*, 1802–1808.

Valente, S. M., Saunders, J., & Street, R. (1988). Adolescent bereavement following suicide: An examination of relevant literature. *Journal of Counseling and Development, 67*, 174–177.

Varni, J. W., Katz, E. R., Colegrove, R., Jr., & Dolgin, M. (1993). The impact of social skills training on the adjustment of children with newly diagnosed cancer. *Journal of Pediatric Psychology, 18*, 751–767.

von der Weid, N. (2001). Late effects in long-term survivors of ALL in childhood: Experiences from the SPOG late effects study. *Swiss Medicine Weekly, 131*, 180–187.

Waber, D. P., Gioia, G., Paccia, J., Sherman, B., Dinklage, D., Sollee, N., Urion, D. K., Tarbell, N. J., & Sallan, S. E. (1990). Sex differences in cognitive processing in children treated with CNS prophylaxis for acute lymphoblastic leukemia. *Journal of Pediatric Psychology, 15*, 105–122.

Waber, D. P., Tarbell, N. J., Kahn, C. M., Gelber, R. D., & Sallan, S. E. (1992). The relationship of sex and treatment modality to neuropsychologic outcome in childhood acute lymphoblastic leukemia. *Journal of Clinical Oncology, 10*, 810–817.

Waber, D. P., Urion, D. K., Tarbell, N. J., Niemeyer, C., Gelber, R., & Sallan, S. E. (1990). Late effects of central nervous system treatment of acute lymphoblastic leukemia in childhood are sex-dependent. *Developmental Medicine and Child Neurology, 32*, 238–248.

Wilson, D. A., Nitschke, R., Bowman, M. E., Chaffin, M. J., Sexauer, C. L., & Prince, J. R. (1991). Transient white matter changes on MR images in children undergoing chemotherapy for acute lymphocytic leukemia: Correlation with neuropsychologic deficiencies. *Radiology, 180*, 205–209.

16

Pediatric Heart Disease

David Ray DeMaso
Children's Hospital Boston

INTRODUCTION

Pediatric heart disease consists of a wide spectrum of heart disorders ranging from those that spontaneously resolve to those that are life-threatening. The incidence of congenital pediatric heart disease is reported to be between 5 and 8 in 1,000 live births (Clark, 1995). There are also a number of heart disorders that are acquired later in life. Innovative medical and surgical techniques have allowed countless numbers of even the most seriously ill youngsters to not only survive, but also to resume healthy and active lives. The purpose of this chapter is to provide a *practical* approach to understanding and managing children and adolescents with heart disease in a school setting. The approach is grounded in a developmentally based biopsychosocial model that can be used to guide the design and implementation of individual, social, and academic interventions for these youngsters. The content of this chapter is based on a review of the literature, along with the author's two decades of clinical and research work with the Department of Cardiology at Children's Hospital Boston.

MEDICAL OVERVIEW

Pediatric heart disease consists of a varied and complex range of physical disorders that entire cardiology textbooks are devoted to describing (Chang, Hanley, Wernovsky, & Wessel, 1998; Fyler, 1992; Emmanouilides, Riemenschneider, Allen, & Gutgesell, 1995). The spectrum of heart diseases has a wide variation in clinical effects ranging from subtle problems with few consequences on an individual's life to death. The age at which most children are identified with cardiac defects can vary from in utero diagnosis to recognition in adult life. Practically, they can be divided into the following interrelated groupings of heart disease: left-to-right shunts,

TABLE 16.1
Interrelated Groupings of Pediatric Heart Disease

Group	*Selected Types of Heart Lesions*
Left-to-right shunts	Atrial septal defects
	Ventricular septal defects
	Patent ductus arteriosus
Complex cyanotic	Tetralogy of Fallot
	Transposition of the great arteries
	Truncus arteriosus
	Total anomalous pulmonary venous return
	Tricuspid atresia
	Ebstein's anomaly
	Single ventricle physiology or anatomy
	Double outlet right ventricle
Obstructive	Coarctation of the aorta
	Aortic valve stenosis
	Mitral valve stenosis
	Pulmonary valve stenosis
Acquired heart disease	Cardiomyopathy, dilated, restrictive, or hypertropic
	Myocarditis, infectious or autoimmune
Arrhythmias	Bradyarrhythmias
	Tachyarrhythmias

complex cyanotic lesions, obstructive heart lesions, acquired heart disease, and arrhythmias (see Table 16.1).

Left-to-Right Shunt Lesions

Before birth, the fundamental site of gas exchange in the fetal circulation is across the placenta. Shunts (foramen ovale and ductus arteriosus) are present in the fetal circulation to allow for placental gas exchange. At birth, major circulatory changes occur with closure of the shunts and establishment of the lungs as the site of gas exchange. In some children, these shunts or holes dividing the right and left sides of the heart remain open, resulting in the following types of congenital heart defects: atrial septal defects, ventricular septal defects, and patent ductus arteriosus. Together, these defects represent between 37–46% of congenital heart lesions, with ventricular septal defect being the most common (25–30%; Bernstein, 2000). The circulatory pressures required to pump the blood to the body (left side) are higher than those required to pump blood to the lungs (right side), thus creating in effect a left to right shunt of blood away from the body to the lungs. Less severe variations of these lesions can close spontaneously, whereas more severe variants may require special cardiac medication, catheterization, or surgery for closure. With correction, these children generally do quite well with no significant physical limitations.

Complex Cyanotic Lesions

The cyanotic or right-to-left shunt lesions represent a more severe and complex group of congenital pediatric heart disease. Although a detailed description of each specific lesion is beyond the scope of this chapter, these defects involve structural changes in the cardiovascular system that result in blood being shunted away from the lungs (right side) toward the body (left side). As a result, these youngsters have lower levels of oxygen in their blood causing cyanosis, as evidenced by the blueness of their lips and finger nails. The most common types include tetralogy of Fallot, transposition of the great arteries, truncus arteriosus, total anomalous pulmonary venous return, tricuspid atresia, Ebstein's anomaly, single ventricle physiology, and double outlet right ventricle. Together, these defects account for 15–28% of the common pediatric heart defects, with tetralogy of fallot being the most frequent at 5–7% (Bernstein, 2000). These defects generally require surgical correction at or near birth. They often require subsequent follow-up surgeries in later childhood or adolescence. The past two decades have seen significant surgical advances that have made corrective surgeries available for many of these youngsters. Nevertheless, some of these children do not survive beyond infancy, and others can only receive palliative interventions leaving them with limited physical endurance and shortened lifespan.

Obstructive Lesions

This group of lesions consists of obstructions to either the left (to the body) or right (to the lungs) ventricular blood flows. The common congenital left outflow defects, coarctation of the aorta and aortic valve stenosis, have an occurrence frequency of 9–14%. Pulmonary valve stenosis has a 5–7% frequency (Bernstein, 2000). Mitral valve (left outflow obstructions) disease can also occur, although it can have either a congenital or acquired (i.e., inflammatory) etiology. All of these defects can occur as single lesions, but they also are frequently associated with other congenital heart lesions. These defects generally require cardiac catheterization and/or surgical corrections. With correction, these children generally do well physically with no significant physical limitations (other than the common recommendation against competitive athletics for the severe valve defects).

Acquired Heart Diseases

Cardiomyopathies are diseases of the heart muscle. They are characterized by heart failure where the pump function of the heart is incapable of providing sufficient oxygen to the body. Myocarditis represents an inflammation of the heart with generally either an infectious (i.e., viral, bacterial, fungal, etc.) or autoimmune etiology (i.e., systemic lupus erythematosus, rheumatoid arthritis, acute rheumatic, Kawasaki syndrome, etc.). Spontaneous improvement and full recovery are possible, although progress to persistent heart failure may occur in severe cases. Dilated cardiomyopathy, in which the heart enlarges and pumps poorly, is the most common cause of heart failure in children without other known cardiac defects. Hypertropic cardiomyopathy, which has a hereditary component, is the leading cause of sudden death in children and young adults. All of these disorders of the heart muscle are associated with an increased incidence of arrhythmias (irregular beating of the heart). Management of these disorders is to provide heart muscle support by medications that enhance the functioning of the heart. For some youngsters, the severity of the cardiomyopathy may lead to cardiac transplantation despite maximal medical therapy.

Arrhythmias

Arrhythmias or irregular heart rhythms can occur in children with structurally normal hearts. They are related to disturbances in the electrical conduction system of the heart. Bradyarrhythmias (slow heart rate) and tachyarrhythmias (fast heart rates) are the primary rhythms of concern. Only in rare cases does an irregular heartbeat indicate serious heart disease. Those that occur at birth or early infancy generally correct themselves by age 1. A second peak age of occurrence is between 8 and 12 years. It is less common at other ages. Children with all of the previously described heart defects are more likely to have serious arrhythmias. Although serious ventricular dysrhythmias are uncommon in children, they do occur in older teenagers and young adults with congenital heart disease, as well as those with various cardiomyopathies. Successful treatment of these disorders has included pharmacological agents, implanted pacemakers and implantable defibrillators, radiofrequency catheter ablation of ectopic heart muscle foci and pathways during cardiac catheterization, and, in extreme cases, heart transplantation.

Depending on the specific type of pediatric heart disease, children and adolescents may manifest a wide range of symptoms. They may exhibit no symptoms with normal functioning to those with reduced exercise tolerance and limited physical activity. With more medically severe illnesses, children may complain of fatigue, shortness of breath, and cough while having growth failure or cyanosis. These youngsters may also have associated medical problems. For example, neurological sequelae (e.g., seizures or learning disorders) from cardiac surgery are not uncommon (Rappaport et al., 1998). The hemodynamic burden of pregnancy in complex heart defects carries a high risk to both mother and fetus.

Chest pain and syncope (fainting episode) are uncommon symptoms of cardiac disease in children, occurring only occasionally. By far, the most frequent cause of chronic chest pain concerns cases in which there is no heart disease and fall into two overlapping groups, idiopathic and psychogenic (Veasy, 1995). Arrhythmias are more likely to cause chest discomfort or heart awareness (i.e., fluttering, skipping beat, or turning sensation). Simple syncope generally results from vasovagal nerve stimulation, causing decreased blood pressure. It is precipitated by pain, fear, excitement, and extended periods of standing still, particularly in a warm environment. Loss of consciousness in association with exercise is rarely from simple fainting or epilepsy; in every case, a cardiac cause (e.g., arrhythmias) must be considered.

The specific grouping or cardiac diagnosis does not always accurately reflect the degree of medical severity. The Cardiologist's Perception of Medical Severity scale has been used with reliability as a measure of global disease severity (DeMaso et al., 1991, 2000).This scale has the following rating range: (1) no or insignificant disorder; (2) mild disorder—lesion requires no operative intervention, only long-term follow-up; (3) moderate disorder—patient is asymptomatic, but has had or will need operation, easy repair; (4) marked disorder—patient quite symptomatic, has had or will need major difficult repair; and (5) severe disorder—uncorrectable cardiac lesions or only complex palliative repair possible.

The cause of most congenital pediatric heart disease is generally unknown. Genetics play some role, as evidenced by a higher risk of recurrence if a parent or sibling is affected, as well as the higher incidence of heart defects in identifiable single gene defects (e.g., Marfan's or Noonan's syndrome). In addition, heart disease has a greater incidence in trisomy 18, trisomy 21 (Down's syndrome), Turner's syndrome, and chromosome 22q11 deletions (DiGeorge or Velocardiofacial syndromes). Less than 2% of congenital heart problems may result from adverse environmental or maternal conditions (e.g., phenyketonuria, diabetes mellitus, systemic lupus erythematosus, or congenital rubella). The cause of acquired pediatric heart disease is generally the result of bacterial and/or viral infections damaging the heart (e.g., rheumatic heart disease, subacute bacterial endocarditis, or viral myocarditis). Kawasaki syndrome is an acquired disease that affects the coronary arteries causing in some cases life-threatening aneurysms.

The assessment and management of the specific pediatric heart diseases require children to undergo a variety of technologically advanced procedures beyond the routine history and physical examination by a cardiologist. The child routinely undergoes a standard chest radiograph (or x-ray). The child may also undergo an echocardiogram that produces an ultrasound image of the heart that may provide necessary information so that a cardiac catheterization, which is more invasive, is unnecessary. The electrocardiogram (ECG) to explore the electrical activity of the heart remains a routine test. In the assessment of an arrhythmia, the child may wear a Holter monitor, which is a small continuous ECG recording device. In some circumstances, the child takes a stress or exercise test in which he/she walks on a treadmill while an ECG is recorded. Less often, cardiac computed tomography or magnetic resonance imaging may be used in some youngsters.

Cardiac catheterizations are used for diagnostic evaluations, therapeutic manipulations, and electrophysiological studies. Catheterizations, which are performed by cardiologists, remain a vital procedure given the increasingly large repertoire of transcatheter interventions as well as the increasingly aggressive approach to the treatment of complex structural heart defects (Bridges & Freed, 1995). Cardiac catheterization involves the insertion of catheters into the heart through peripheral blood vessels (i.e., neck or groin). On average, the procedure lasts 2–3 hr. Generally, the patient is given a sedating medication (i.e., Versed or midazolam) rather than using general anesthesia. The child lies on a hard table surrounded by cardiology and nursing staff that use radiographic technology to monitor the catheterization process. Depending on the clinical status of the child, as well as the aim of the procedure, cardiac catheterization may be done on an outpatient basis or an overnight stay in the hospital.

Over the last three decades with the advances in cardiac surgery, the number of children with pediatric heart disease surviving to adulthood has increased dramatically. The left-to-right shunt lesions were the first lesions to receive total surgical corrections, and the complex cyanotic heart defects generally received palliative repairs. Newer corrective repairs (e.g., arterial-switch operation in transposition of the great arteries) are now available for many complex defects. For lesions that cannot be corrected, innovative palliative repairs (e.g., Fontan procedures) are increasingly used that more closely approximate normal blood circulation. The past 15 years has also witnessed a trend for the primary surgical repairs to occur in the neonatal and infancy periods. These surgical advances have been supported by the development of enhanced cardiopulmonary bypass techniques, whereby blood flow to the heart and lungs can be interrupted transiently to allow surgical repair (i.e., low-flow cardiopulmonary bypass) or time for heart/lung recovery, as well as to gain added time and opportunity to procure a heart for transplantation (i.e., extracorporeal membrane oxygenation).

It is increasingly common for the toddler, school-aged child, or adolescent to come in 1–2 days before surgery to have their admission blood work done, as well as to meet with the cardiac surgeon and/or cardiologist. The patient then returns home or to a hotel room (if coming from a distance) until they are admitted to the hospital for surgery. After their surgery, children are monitored in a cardiac intensive care unit for several days. After they are stabilized, they are moved to a general cardiology unit for approximately 1–2 weeks before their discharge home. The length of stay is variable, depending on the particular heart lesion and hospital course, although there has been a clear trend toward shorter hospital stays.

With approximately 90% one-year and 75% three-year survival rates for patients between the ages of 2 and 17 years (Transplant Patient DataSource, 2000), heart transplantation has become a standard treatment option for end-stage pediatric heart disease. Improvements in both the surgical and medical management of heart transplantation have enabled many patients to survive who in the past would have died. After transplantation, these children and adolescents experience a chronic illness requiring long-term immunosuppression for the continued threat of organ rejection.

COGNITIVE AND EMOTIONAL FUNCTIONING

With the improved survival rates of children with pediatric heart disease, interest in the cognitive and emotional functionings of these children has grown significantly. Studies of cognitive development have found that the complex heart defects have the potential for adverse effects on the cognitive functioning of these children (DeMaso, Beardslee, Silbert, & Fyler, 1990). The complex cyanotic cardiac lesions have been associated with developmental and neurological abnormalities in as many as 25% of survivors (Ferry, 1987). Studies have produced conflicting results regarding emotional adjustment ranging from major psychopathology to healthy coping (DeMaso et al., 1991). In general, early studies of emotional functioning suggest a negative impact, whereas more recent studies support healthy adjustment. The latter is likely from improved prognosis associated with the disease.

Cognitive Functioning

Studies using a number of different standardized intelligence tests (e.g., Bayley Scales, Cattel, McCarthy, Stanford Binet, Wechsler Preschool and Primary Scale of Intelligence, Wechsler Intelligence Scale for Children-Revised) have shown lower mean IQ scores for children with complex cyanotic lesions when compared with children with left-to-right shunts or physically healthy children (DeMaso et al, 1990; Kramer, Awiszus, Sterzel, van Halteren, & Clabsen, 1989; Linde, Rasof, & Dunn, 1967; Morris, Krawiecki, Wright, & Walter, 1993; Newburger, Silbert, Buckley, & Fyler, 1984; O'Dougherty, Wright, Garmezy, Loewenson, & Torres, 1983; O'Dougherty, Wright, Loewenson, & Torres, 1985; Silbert, Wolff, Mayer, Rosenthal, & Nadas, 1969). However, it is important to note that these lower mean IQ scores were consistently within the normal range of intelligence.

Most of the aforementioned studies predated the primary surgical repair of pediatric heart disease in infancy. The trend for early surgical correction was strongly supported by the findings of Newburger et al. (1984) and O'Dougherty et al. (1983), in which significant inverse correlations were found between IQ scores and chronological age at surgical repair for transposition of the great arteries. Nevertheless, Bellinger et al. (1999) have continued to find that children who have received repairs of transposition of the great arteries at less than 3 months of age continue to demonstrate IQ means that are below the population mean, although within the normal range of intelligence.

Several studies have shown that children with complex cyanotic disease are particularly vulnerable in the areas of motor, speech, and language function. Early studies by Silbert et al. (1969) and Newburger et al. (1984) found that cyanotic children had significantly lower scores on perceptual-motor and gross motor tasks when compared with acyanotic children. More recently, Bellinger et al. (1999) and Newburger et al. (1993) in a longitudinal follow-up study of children with transposition of the great arteries who underwent an arterial-switch operation, found that visual-motor integration, motor function, and oromotor control were below expectations. Expressive language abilities have been found to be delayed relative to the chronological age by Bellinger, Rappaport, Wypij, Wernovsky, & Newburger (1997) and Bellinger et al. (1999).

Studies have evaluated the neurodevelopmental outcomes after the Fontan repair of complex heart defects. Uzark et al. (1998) found that cognitive development of children with single ventricle anatomy was within the normal range. They also found that visual-motor integration deficits were more prevalent. Wernovsky et al. (2000) reported similar findings with cognitive outcome and academic function within the normal range, although the performance of their cohort was lower than that of the general population. Goldberg et al. (2000) noted that neurodevelopmental outcome after the Fontan procedure was unremarkable in the preschool and early school years, with Wechsler Intelligence scores generally in the normal range. They also noted that children with single ventricle anatomy had significantly lower scores than did a nonsingle ventricle comparison group, although it was noted that neither group scored significantly different from the standard population.

In a literature review, Todaro, Fennell, Sears, Rodrigue, and Roche (2000) reported that, after heart transplantation, children functioned within the normal range on most measures of cognitive functioning, although a complicated transplant course may place the child at increased risk for cognitive difficulties. O'Brien, Blume, Stafford, DeMaso, and Bastardi (2001) found that 80% of the heart transplant patients required special school services for some period of time posttransplant. In this study, those with pre-existing complex cyanotic heart defects were particularly vulnerable for school academic problems.

In summary, children and adolescents with pediatric heart disease are at risk for adverse cognitive functioning. Inadequate oxygenation during early development most likely underlies this vulnerability as evidenced by the improvement in cognitive functioning found when cardiac surgeries were conducted at earlier ages (Newburger et al., 1984; O'Dougherty et al., 1983). Nevertheless, even with more advanced surgical repairs at younger ages, those youngsters with complex cyanotic heart lesion remain at significantly greater risk for motor and language delays (Bellinger et al., 1995; Bellinger et al., 1999; Newberger et al., 1993). Many of these delays will likely have direct impact on these children's academic performance and as such require assessment and intervention.

Emotional Functioning

The literature suggests that infants with congenital heart disease have temperament and attachment characteristics that may be more problematic than healthy infants (Goldberg, Simmons, Newman, Campbell, & Fowler, 1991; Marino & Lipshitz, 1991). These characteristics may set the stage for parent–infant interactional problems during feedings. However, the medical contributions of fatigue, breathing trouble, or oromotor problems may also play important roles for children in which feeding becomes problematic.

The literature pertaining to emotional outcomes of children and adolescents with various cardiac disorders continues to be somewhat limited and often contradictory. Many of the early studies reported a negative impact on emotional functioning (Aurer, Senturia, Shopper, & Biddy, 1979; Green & Levitt, 1962; Myers-Vando, Steward, Folkins, & Hines, 1979), whereas the more recent studies have found that many children demonstrated generally healthy adjustment (DeMaso et al., 1990, 1991). There are few studies of the long-term impact of pediatric heart disease into adulthood, although the available studies do report emotional vulnerabilities (Baer, Freedman, & Garson, 1984; Brandhagen, Feldt, & Williams, 1991; Garson, Williams, & Redford, 1974; Horner, Lieberthson, & Jellinek, 2000).

The contradictory results across studies are related to several factors (DeMaso et al., 1990). First, the measures of emotional adjustment vary markedly across studies. Many studies have used small samples without comparison control groups, along with little consistency across studies with respect to type of pediatric heart lesion. There were wide age ranges of children examined without acknowledging the effects of age-related developmental differences.

From a clinical standpoint, the type or severity of pediatric heart disease does not readily predict the children's level of emotional functioning. DeMaso et al. (1990) found that the diagnosis of a cyanotic heart defect did not necessarily predict emotional difficulties in young children. Poorer overall psychological functioning was accounted for in these children primarily by the degree of IQ and CNS impairment rather than the heart defect itself. Severity of cardiac illness is less critical to successful adaptation than the quality of the mother–child relationship (DeMaso et al., 1991; DeMaso, Twente, Spratt, & O'Brien, 1995; Linde, Rasof, & Dunn, 1966). In contrast, Spurkland, Bjornstad, Lindberg, and Seem (1993) noted that adolescents with cyanotic heart disease had higher rates of emotional difficulties, compared with those with left-to-right shunts. They specifically highlighted depression and anxiety as vulnerable areas.

The literature pertaining to the emotional functioning of patients with cardiac arrhythmias has been essentially limited to adults. Depression and anxiety have been the two common symptoms experienced by these patients (Fricchione & Vlay, 1986). DeMaso et al. (2000) found that children and adolescents facing recurrent arrhythmias resembled a healthy population without elevated rates of anxiety or depression. They also found that those children who underwent a curative ablation (removal ectopic electrical heart pathways during cardiac catheterization) had better functioning than those who did not show improvement after the procedure. Alpern, Uzark, and Dick (1989) found a relatively healthy psychological adaptation for children requiring pacemakers through the effective use of denial. Barrett, Van der Feen, Spieth, Berul, and DeMaso (2001) presented preliminary findings that adolescents with implantable cardioverter defibrillators appeared to be reassured about their health, but also simultaneously harbored feelings of anxiety about the device's impact on their health. Most of the adolescents recommended the device, yet believed that its placement did not necessarily enhance overall the quality of their life.

Todaro et al. (2000) reviewed the psychological outcomes of pediatric heart transplantation. They found that most transplant recipients demonstrated adequate psychological adjustment within 1 year posttransplantation. Although based on only a few studies, 20–24% of these youngsters experienced significant symptoms of psychological distress (e.g., anxiety, depression, behavior problems) during the first year posttransplant. However, DeMaso et al. (1995) found that 78% of patients at a mean time of 2 years since transplant had good psychological functioning. Thus, adjustment difficulties after transplantation seem to be transitory.

In summary, emotional functioning of children and adolescents with pediatric heart disease is generally not in psychopathology range. These youngsters definitely have the capacity for healthy psychological functioning. From a clinical standpoint, a pediatric heart lesion by itself is not necessarily associated with poorer adaptation. Those children who are at higher risk generally have other risk factors that need to be taken into account (e.g., cognitive or family functioning). Those patients with complex lesions and associated risk factors may be at greater risk for adjustment difficulties as they enter into adolescence and early adulthood.

SOCIAL OVERVIEW

Family Functioning

Pediatric heart disease can require recurrent invasive procedures and hospitalizations, and often involves a degree of prognostic uncertainty, all of which can be stressful for families (Peterson & Harbaugh, 1995). Although the acute, life-threatening nature of pediatric heart disease has decreased for many patients, parents continue to have concerns about their children's illness and management, and the effects of both on their children's daily functioning, development, and quality of life.

Sparacino et al. (1997) explored concerns expressed by parents of adolescents and young adults with pediatric heart disease and identified seven areas of concern: dilemmas of normality, disclosure dilemmas, challenge of uncertainty, illness management dilemmas, social integration versus isolation, impact on family, and coping. Using a larger sample of mothers of younger children, Van Horn, DeMaso, Gonzalez-Heydrich, and Dahlmeier Erickson (2001) extended these findings by reliably grouping maternal concerns into five categories: medical prognosis, quality of life, psychosocial functioning, effects on family, and financial issues.

Van Horn et al. (2001) also compared these concerns during hospitalization and 2–3 weeks after hospitalization, finding that distress about most concerns decreased after discharge, as did mother's anxiety and depressed mood.

As noted previously, maternal adjustment has been linked to emotional adaptation among children with pediatric heart disease (DeMaso et al., 1990, 1991, 1995), as well as other chronic physical conditions (Banez and Compas, 1990). Davis, Brown, Bakeman, and Campbell (1998) found that daily stressors and increased palliative coping techniques (i.e., self-blame, avoidance, emotion-focused, and wishful thinking) were negatively related to maternal adjustment. As with other physical illnesses, maternal adjustment was unrelated to the type and severity of pediatric heart disease (Davis et al., 1998). Maternal anxiety and distress have been associated with mother-reported behavior problems and child-reported symptoms (Thompson, Gustafson, George, & Spock, 1994; Thompson, Gustafson, Hamlett, & Spock, 1992). Maternal depressed mood has been linked to behavior problems among children with chronic physical conditions (Walker, Ortiz-Valdes, & Newbrough, 1989). Mothers reporting anxiety and depressed mood may express more emotional and behavioral concerns about their children than those who do not report these symptoms.

DeMaso et al. (1991) and Van Horn et al. (2001) found mothers to have accurate and realistic perceptions of children's heart lesions, because their ratings of medical severity were highly correlated with those of cardiologists. Cardiologists generally recommend to parents that children and adolescents set their own limitations. Even for those with severe heart lesions, the patients are judged in general to be the best at gauging the level of physical activities that they can engage in and will stop when "they need to stop." However, as noted previously, patients with severe valve lesions often have activity limitations.

Social Functioning

Schuman and LaGreca (1999) outlined several conclusions that could be drawn from the literature on the social correlates of pediatric chronic illness. First, chronic illness may be a risk factor for adjustment problems in the domain of peer relations. Second, physical limitations, lifestyle modifications, altered physical appearances, and cognitive impairments in chronic pediatric illness appear to increase the risk of peer relationship problems. Third, peers may be a source of support and acceptance, facilitating adaptation. Finally, intervention programs are being developed to address the challenges faced by children with chronic disease.

There are few studies examining specifically the social functioning of youngsters with pediatric heart disease. Casey, Sykes, Craig, Power, & Mulholland (1996) found teachers rated school-aged children with complex heart disease more withdrawn than those children with an innocent heart murmur. They also found family strain to be a critical factor in the school adjustment in these children, more so than the physical limitations. Youssef (1988) reported that the added burdens of low IQ, low self-esteem, and high depression in pediatric heart disease increased the risk of poor school adjustment.

For many children facing pediatric heart disease, there appears to be no interference in social functioning. For some, like other children facing a chronic pediatric illness, they must face the challenge of being unable to and/or being restricted from the physical activities (e.g., sports) or of having significant cognitive impairments that can be such an important part of peer interactions. Those that are successful tend to develop alternative interest and/or are able tolerate their restrictions.

Children with complex cyanotic heart lesions face the visible stigma of the blueness of their lips and fingernails. Related to their decreased oxygenation, there also can be a thickening of the ends of their fingers and toes called clubbing. Although this color is often noticed and commented on by peers and adults across the age range, clinically it appears to become particularly noted by the child around the ages of 9–10 years when peer group issues are so important. They may hear statements such as, "Did you just eat a grape Popsicle" or "Its Captain Grape" or "What's wrong with you?"

The beach or the locker room is another environment that impacts on the child with pediatric heart disease. A scar from surgery may become an object of concern and questioning by peers. This is more commonly an issue for the adolescent facing the normal developmental issue of body image. For younger children, the issue is generally more of a concern for the parent with the child taking a "cue" from the parent as to how to respond.

Heart transplant recipients face significant visual stigmata as a result of their need for immunosuppression. Moon facies, truncal obesity, acne, facial hair growth, excessive gum growth, pubertal stage delay, and weight gain are common observable side effects seen in heart transplantation. These adverse side effects tend to be the most pronounced in the first year after a heart transplant as the antirejection regimen is established. The changes may be enough to make the child look totally different and almost unrecognizable in severe cases. By the second year, although they can never be completely stopped, the medications may be reduced to a level in which the effects are small or completely resolved.

Campis, DeMaso, & Twente (1995) found in school-age children with craniofacial disfigurement that maternal adjustment and maternal perceptions of the mother–child relationships were more potent predictors of children's emotional adjustment than the severity of the facial deformity. These same children and their mothers resembled a normal population in terms of overall psychological functioning. There is little reason to expect that the visual stigmata associated with pediatric heart disease should have any more impact than in a craniofacial disfigured population. For example, DeMaso et al. (1995) found no correlations between posttransplant adjustment and observable side effects in children who had received heart transplantation. Nevertheless, pending future study, children with pediatric heart disease with physical limitations, altered physical appearances, and/or cognitive impairments should be considered at risk for impaired social functioning.

MANAGEMENT IN THE SCHOOL SETTING

In summary, pediatric heart disease consists of a range of specific heart lesions with varying medical severity and impact. As outlined previously, children and adolescents with these disorders may present with a number of vulnerabilities in the cognitive, emotional, and social realms that have direct relevance to the school setting. It is also evident that these youngsters have the capacity for healthy functioning. Understanding the developmentally based biopsychosocial aspects of pediatric heart disease provides the foundation for the management of children and adolescents in the school setting. The following recommendations can prove useful to approaching the academic needs of the youngster facing pediatric heart disease.

1. *Treat as "children with cardiac illness" not "cardiac children."* As with all physical illnesses, it is important to view a child or adolescent as having a pediatric heart problem, rather than responding as if the illness defines who they are. This approach is critical in supporting a youngster's identity, as well as how they are viewed in the school setting. In doing so, a child or adolescent should be treated as *normally* as possible within the constraints of their illness.

2. *Clarify the specific type of heart disease.* Pediatric heart disease represents a wide range of heart disorders, ranging from the very mild with no significant disability to the severe with disabling effects (see Table 16.1). Clarification of the specific heart disease provides critical understanding for the school setting. This information can be obtained from the child's parent(s), and can be further clarified through parental permission by speaking with the child's pediatrician and/or cardiologist. In addition, this information can guide the school in providing reasonable accommodations to a child's physical limitations (e.g., allowing more time to change classes, placing all classes on same floor, etc.)

3. *Be alert for potential school fear.* Parents of children with pediatric heart disease occasionally will report that the school is afraid of their child. Understanding the type of heart disease is one approach to reducing this worry. The school nurse, psychologist, or counselor can work with the parents to provide the necessary psychoeducation for the teacher and other staff around the illness.

4. *Pediatric heart disease is not adult heart disease.* It can be important to clarify that pediatric heart disease is different than adult heart disease that is characterized by myocardial infarctions or heart attacks that are frequently because of blockages of the coronary arteries of the heart. As described previously, chest pain is an uncommon symptom of pediatric cardiac disease. Chest discomfort or awareness (i.e., fluttering, skipping beat, or turning sensation) related to arrhythmias is a much more likely pediatric heart disease complaint and is not the symptom of a heart attack.

5. *Be alert to learning problems.* Children with complex cyanotic heart lesions are at significant risk for motor and language problems (Bellinger et al., 1997, 1999; Newburger et al., 1984; Silbert et al., 1969; Uzark et al., 1998). There is a strong association between behavioral problems and expressive learning delays (Bellinger et al., 1997). Psychological testing should be considered for any youngster with academic, emotional, or behavioral problems.

6. *Consider support for coping.* Many of these children and adolescents face the need for continued invasive procedures. There may be opportunities to help with preadmission hospital or procedural preparation, as well as the return to school. Preparatory interventions include cognitive strategies (e.g., hospital preadmission programs) designed to provide families with educational information regarding their illnesses combined with the modeling of and permission for adverse affective responses (e.g., fear, anger). Although difficult to measure, all interventions have been generally viewed as helpful to families (Campbell, Kirkpatrick, Berry, & Lamberti, 1995; Kain, Mayes, & Caramico, 1996; Rasnake & Linschied, 1989; Schmidt, 1990; Van Horn & DeMaso, 2001; Vernon & Thompson, 1993). After cardiac surgery, these children often need a graduated transition back into the school. The provision of tutoring or assistance with homework, in which children may have fallen behind on, can be immensely helpful. Individual counseling or peer groups can be helpful for children and adolescents struggling with longer term issues related to their heart problem.

7. *Consider classroom education.* A child's classroom can benefit from educational information regarding the heart illness, particularly if the child needs to be hospitalized during the school year. This should be done only if the child wants this to occur. Parental permission and review of "what will be said" is critical. This recommendation is generally most useful for younger children. In these younger age situations, parental participation is often a consideration. Older children tend not to want to highlight differences among their peers, particularly in the classroom.

8. *Pediatric heart disease Web sites.* There are a number of active Web sites devoted to pediatric heart disease containing content ranging from factual information to narratives describing the experience (see Table 16.2).

TABLE 16.2
Selected Web Sites Related to Pediatric Heart Disease

American Heart Association Easy-to-read medical information and pictures on congenital heart defects and children.	www.americanheart.org/children
Baby Hearts Press Provides books and information for parents, teens, children, nurses, doctors, social workers, and other medical caregivers in language that is easy to understand and read.	www.babyheartspress.com
Children's Health Information Network Provides medical information, support groups, and Internet links for families of children with heart conditions.	www.tchin.org
Children's Hospital Boston Learn about pediatric heart problems, as well as other pediatric conditions by searching "Child Health A to Z."	www.childrenshospital.org
Experience Journal Provides narrative stories and videos of families and clinicians facing pediatric heart disease, along with a hospital preparation manual entitled, *Helping Your Child with a Medical Experience, a Practical Parent Guide*.	www.experiencejournal.com
Family Village A global community integrating information, resources, and communication opportunities for the chronically ill and their families.	www.familyvillage.com
Kids with Heart Provides support, education, and information for families of children and adults with congenital heart defects and acquired heart disease.	www.execpc.com/~kdswhrt/
Little Hearts A support network for parents of children with congenital heart defects.	www.littlehearts.net
PediHeart Check out the Kidzone and Parent's Place to learn about the heart, ask questions, and meet other families.	www.pediheart.org
Trio Nonprofit organization committed to provide support, awareness, education, and advocacy to those involved with organ transplants.	www.trioweb.org

REFERENCES

Alpern, D., Uzark, K., & Dick, M., II. (1989), Psychosocial responses of children to cardiac pacemakers. *Journal of Pediatrics, 114*, 494–501.

Aurer, E. T., Senturia, A. G., Shopper, M., & Biddy, R. (1971). Congenital heart disease and child adjustment. *Psychiatric Medicine, 2*, 210–219.

Baer, P. E., Freedman, D. A., & Garson, A., Jr. (1984). Long-term psychological follow-up of patients after corrective surgery for tetralogy of Fallot. *Journal of the American Academy of Child and Adolescent Psychiatry, 23*, 622–625.

Banez, G. A., & Compas, B. E. (1990). Children's and parents' daily stressful events and psychosocial symptoms. *Journal of Abnormal Child Psychology, 18*, 591–605.

Barrett, K., Van der Feen, J. R., Spieth, L., Berul, C., & DeMaso, D. R. (2001, April) *Worries in adolescents with implantable cardioverter defibrillators: A pilot study*. Poster session presented at the annual meeting of the North American Society of Pacing and Electrophysiology, Boston, MA.

Bellinger, D. C., Jonas, R. A., Rappaport, L. A., Wypij, D., Wernovsky, G., Kuban, K. C. K., Barnes, P. D., Holmes, G. L., Hickey, P. R., Strand, R. D., Walsh, A. Z., Helmers, S. L., Constantinou, J. E., Carrazana, E. J., Mayer, J. E., Hanley, F. L., Castaneda, A. R., Ware, J. H., & Newburger, J. W. (1995). Developmental and neurologic status of children after heart surgery with hypothermic circulatory arrest or low-flow cardiopulmonary bypass. *New England Journal of Medicine, 332*, 549–555.

Bellinger, D. C., Rappaport, L. A., Wypij, D., Wernovsky, G., & Newburger, J. W. (1997). Patterns of developmental dysfunction after surgery during infancy to correct transposition of the great arteries. *Journal of Developmental and Behavioral Pediatrics, 18*, 75–83.

Bellinger, D. C., Wypij, D., Kuban, K. C. K., Rappaport, L. A., Hickey, P. R., Wernovsky, G., Jonas, R. A., & Newburger, J. W. (1999). Developmental and neurological status of children at 4 years of age after heart surgery with hypothermic circulatory arrest or low-flow cardiopulmonary bypass. *Circulation,100*, 526–532.

Bernstein, D. (2000). The cardiovascular system. In R. E. Behrman, R. M. Kliegman, & H. B. Jenson (Eds.), *Nelson textbook of pediatrics* (16th ed., pp. 1337–1456). Philadelphia: W. B. Saunders.

Brandhagen, D. J., Feldt, Z. R. H., & Williams, D. E. (1991). Long-term psychologic implications of congenital heart disease. *Mayo Clinic Proceedings*, 66, 474–479.

Bridges, N. D., Freed, M. D. (1995). Cardiac catheterization. In G. C. Emmanouilides, T. A. Riemenschneider, H. D. Allen, & H. P. Gutgesell (Eds.), *Moss and Adams heart disease in infants, children, and adolescents* (5th ed., Vol. I, pp. 310–329). Baltimore: Williams & Wilkins.

Campbell, L. A., Kirkpatrick, S. E., Berry, C. C., & Lamberti, J. J. (1995). Preparing children with congenital heart disease for cardiac surgery. *Journal of Pediatric Psychology, 20*, 313–328.

Campis, L. B., DeMaso, D. R., & Twente, A. W. (1995). The role of maternal factors in the adaptation of children with craniofacial disfigurement. *Cleft Palate-Craniofacial Journal, 32*, 55–61.

Casey, F. A., Sykes, D. H., Craig, B. G., Power, R., & Mulholland, H. C. (1996). Behavioral adjustment of children with surgically palliated complex congenital heart disease. *Journal of Pediatric Psychology, 21*, 335–352.

Chang, A. C., Hanley, F. L., Wernovsky, G., & Wessel, D. L. (Eds.). (1998). *Pediatric cardiac intensive care*. Baltimore: Williams & Wilkins.

Clark, E. B. (1995). Epidemiology of congenital cardiovascular malformations. In G. C. Emmanouilides, T. A. Riemenschneider, H. D. Allen, & H. P. Gutgesell (Eds.), *Moss and Adams heart disease in infants, children, and adolescents* (5th ed., Vol. I, pp. 60–70). Baltimore: Williams & Wilkins.

Davis, C. C., Brown, R. T., Bakeman, R., & Campbell, R. (1998). Psychological adaptation of mother of children with congenital heart disease: Stress, coping, and family functioning. *Journal of Pediatric Psychology, 23*, 219–228.

DeMaso, D. R., Beardslee W. R., Silbert A. R., & Fyler D. C. (1990). Psychological functioning in children with cyanotic heart defects. *Journal of Developmental and Behavioral Pediatrics, 11*, 289–293.

DeMaso, D. R., Campis, L. K., Wypij, D., Bertram, S., Lipshitz, M., & Freed, M. (1991). The impact of maternal perceptions and medical severity on the adjustment of children with congenital heart disease. *Journal of Pediatric Psychology, 16*, 137–149.

DeMaso, D. R., Spratt, E. G., Vaughan, B. L., D'Angelo, E. J., Van der Feen, J. R., & Walsh, E. (2000). Psychological functioning in children and adolescents undergoing radiofrequency catheter ablation. *Psychosomatics, 41*,134–139.

DeMaso, D. R., Twente, A. W., Spratt, E. G., & O'Brien, P. (1995). The impact of psychological functioning, medical severity, and family functioning in pediatric heart transplantation. *Journal of Heart Lung Transplantation, 14*, 1102–1108.

Emmanouilides, G. C., Riemenschneider, T. A., Allen, H. D., & Gutgesell, H. P. (Eds.). (1995). *Moss and Adams heart disease in infants, children, and adolescents* (5th ed., Vol. I, pp. xxx–xxx). Baltimore: Williams & Wilkins.

Ferry, P. (1987). Neurologic sequelae of cardiac surgery in children. *American Journal of Diseases of Children, 141*, 309–312.

Fyler, D. C. (Ed.). (1992). *NADAS' pediatric cardiology*. Philadelphia: Hanley & Belfus.

Fricchione, G. L., & Vlay, S. C. (1986). Psychiatric aspects of patients with malignant ventricular arrhythmias. *American Journal of Psychiatry, 143*, 1518–1526.

Garson, A., Williams, R. B., & Redford, T. (1974). Long term follow up of patients with tetralogy of Fallot: Physical health and psychopathology. *Journal of Pediatrics, 85*, 429–433.

Goldberg, C. S., Schwartz, E. M., Brunberg, J. A., Mosca, R. S., Bove, E. L., Schork, M. A., Stetz, S. P., Cheatham, J. P., & Kulik, T. J. (2000). Neurodevelopmental outcome of patients after the Fontan operation: A comparison between children with hypoplastic left heart syndrome and other functional single ventricle lesions. *Journal of Pediatrics, 137*, 646–652.

Goldberg, S., Simmons, R. J., Newman, J., Campbell, K., & Fowler, R. S. (1991). Congenital heart disease, parental stress, and infant-mother relationships. *Journal of Pediatrics, 119*, 661–666.

Green M., & Levitt, E. (1962). Constriction of body image in children with congenital heart disease. *Pediatrics, 29*, 438–443.

Horner, T., Lieberthson, R., & Jellinek, M. (2000). Psychosocial profile of adults with complex congenital heart disease. *Mayo Clinic Proceedings, 75*, 31–36.

Kain, Z. N., Mayes, L. C., & Caramico, L. A. (1996). Preoperative preparation in children: A cross-sectional study. *Journal of Clinical Anesthesia, 8*, 508–514.

Kramer, H. H., Awiszus, D., Sterzel, U., van Halteren, A., & Clabsen, R. (1989). Development of personality and intelligence in children with congenital heart disease. *Journal of Child Psychology and Psychiatry, 30*, 299–308.

Linde, L. M., Rasof, B., & Dunn, O. J. (1966). Attitudinal factors in congenital heart disease. *Pediatrics, 38*, 92–101.

Linde, L. M., Rasof, B., & Dunn, O. J. (1967). Mental development in congenital heart disease. *Journal of Pediatrics, 71*, 198–203.

Marino, B. L., & Lipshitz, M. (1991). Temperament in infants and toddlers with cardiac disease. *Pediatric Nursing, 17*, 445–448.

Morris, R. D., Krawiecki, N. S., Wright, J. A., & Walter, L. W. (1993). Neuropsychological, academic, and adaptive functioning in children who survive in-hospital cardiac arrest and resuscitation, *Journal of Learning Disabilities, 26*, 46–51.

Myers-Vando, R., Steward, M. S., Folkins, C. H., & Hines, P. (1979). The effects of congenital heart disease on cognitive development, illness causality concepts, and vulnerability. *American Journal of Orthopsychiatry, 49*, 617–625.

Newburger, J. W., Jonas, R. A., Wernovsky, G., Wypij, D., Hickey, P. R., Kuban, K. C. K., Farrell, D. M., Holmes, G. L., Helmers, S. L., Constantinou, J., Carrazana, E. J., Barlow J. K., Walsh, A. Z., Lucius, K. C., Share, J. C., Wessel, D. L., Hanley, F. L., Mayer, J. E., Castaneda, A. R., & Ware, J. H. (1993). A comparison of the perioperative neurologic effects of hypothermic circulatory arrest versus low-flow cardiopulmonary bypass in infant heart surgery. *New England Journal of Medicine, 329*, 1057–1064.

Newburger, J. W., Silbert, A. R., Buckley, L. P., & Fyler, D. (1984). Cognitive development and age of repair of transposition of the great arteries in children. *New England Journal of Medicine, 310*, 1495–1499.

O'Brien, P., Blume, E. D., Stafford, K., DeMaso, D. R., & Bastardi, H. (2001, May). *School performance following pediatric heart transplantation*. Poster session presented at the 3rd World Congress of Pediatric Cardiology and Cardiac Surgery, Toronto, Canada.

O'Dougherty, M., Wright, F. S., Garmezy, N., Loewenson, R. B., & Torres, R. (1983). Later competence and adaptation in infants who survive severe heart defects. *Child Development, 54*, 1129–1142.

O'Dougherty, M., Wright, F. S., Loewenson, R. B., & Torres, R. (1985). Cerebral dysfunction after chronic hypoxia in children. *Neurology, 35*, 42–46.

Peterson, C., & Harbaugh, B. L. (1995). Children's and adolescents' experiences while undergoing cardiac catheterization. *Maternal–Child Nursing Journal 23*, 15–25.

Rappaport, L. A., Wypij, D, Bellinger, D. C., Helmers, S. L., Holmes, G. L., Barnes, P. D., Wernovsky, G., Kuban, K. C. K., Jonas, J. A., & Newburger, J. W. (1998). Relation of seizures after cardiac surgery in early infancy to neurodevelopmental outcomes. *Circulation, 97*, 773–779.

Rasnake, L. K., & Linscheid, T. R. (1989). Anxiety reduction in children receiving medical care: Developmental considerations. *Journal of Developmental Behavior Pediatrics, 10*, 169–175.

Schmidt, C. K. (1990). Pre-operative preparation: Effects on immediate pre-operative behavior, post-operative behavior and recovery in children having same-day surgery. *Maternal–Child Nursing Journal, 19*, 321–330.

Schuman, W. B, & LaGreca, A. M, (1999). Social correlates of chronic illness. In R. T. Brown (Ed.), *Cognitive aspects of chronic illness in children* (pp. 289–311). New York: The Guilford Press.

Silbert A., Wolff, P. H., Mayer, B., Rosenthal, A., & Nadas, A. S. (1969). Cyanotic heart disease and psychological development. *Pediatrics, 143*, 192–200.

Sparacino, P. A., Tong, E. M., Messias, D. K., Foote, D., Chesla, C. A., Gilliss, C. L. (1997). The dilemmas of parents of adolescents and young adults with congenital heart disease. *Heart Lung, 26*, 187–195.

Spurkland, I., Bjornstad, P. G., Lindberg, H., & Seem, E. (1993). Mental Health Functioning in adolescents with congenital heart disease: A comparision between adolescents born with severe heart defect and atrial septal defect. *Acta Paediatr, 82*, 71–76.

Thompson, R. J., Gustafson, K. E., George, L. K., & Spock, A. (1994). Change over a 12-month period in the psychological adjustment of children and adolescents with cystic fibrosis. *Journal of Pediatric Psychology 19*, 189–204.

Thompson, R. J., Gustafson, K. E., Hamlett, K. W., & Spock, A. (1992). Psychological adjustment of children with cystic fibrosis: The role of child cognitive processes and maternal adjustment. *Journal of Pediatric Psychology, 17*, 741–755.

Todaro, J. F., Fennell, E. B., Sears, S. F., Rodrigue, J. R., & Roche, A. K. (2000). Review: Cognitive and psychological outcome of pediatric heart transplantation. *Journal of Pediatric Psychology, 25*, 567–576.

Transplant Patient DataSource. (2000, February 16). *United network for organ sharing* [On-line]. Available: http://207.239.150.13/tpd/

Uzark, K., Lincoln, A., Lamberti, J. J., Mainwaring, R. D., Spicer, R. L., & Moore, J. W. (1998). Neurodevelopmental outcomes in children with Fontan repair of functional single ventricle. *Pediatrics, 101*, 630–633.

Van Horn, M., & DeMaso, D. R. (2001). *Helping your child with medical experiences: A practical parent guide* [On-line]. Available: www.experiencejournal.com

Van Horn, M., DeMaso, D. R., Gonzalez-Heydrich, J., & Dahlmeier Erickson, J. (2001). Illness-related concerns of mothers with congenital health disease. *Journal of American Academy Child and Adolescent Psychiatry, 40*, 847–854.

Veasy, L. G. (1995). Chest pain in children. In G. C. Emmanouilides, T. A. Riemenschneider, H. D. Allen, & H. P. Gutgesell (Eds.). *Moss and Adams heart disease in infants, children, and adolescents* (5th ed., Vol. I, pp. 653–657). Baltimore: Williams & Wilkins.

Vernon, D. T., & Thompson, R. H. (1993). Research on the effect of experimental interventions on children's behavior after hospitalization: A review and synthesis. *Journal of Developmental Behavior Pediatrics, 14*, 36–44.

Walker, L. S., Ortiz-Valdes, J. A., & Newbrough, J. R. (1989). The role of maternal employment and depression in the psychological adjustment of chronically ill, mentally retarded and well children. *Journal of Pediatric Psychology, 14*, 357–370.

Wernovsky, G., Stiles, K. M., Gauvreau, K., Gentles, T. L., duPlessis, A. J., Bellinger, D. C., Walsh, A. Z., Burnett, J., Jonas, R. A., Mayer, J. E., Jr., & Newburger, J. W. (2000). Cognitive development after the Fontan operation. *Circulation, 102*, 883–889.

Youssef, N. M. (1988). School adjustment of children with congenital heart disease. *Maternal–Child Nursing Journal, 17*, 217–302.

17

Recurrent Abdominal Pain and Functional Gastrointestinal Disorders in the School Setting

Lynn S. Walker
W. Stephen Johnson
Vanderbilt University School of Medicine

INTRODUCTION

Schools are frequently confronted with children who complain of stomachaches and ask to leave school early. Many of these children return to school after a brief illness and have no further complaints. Others, however, complain of stomachaches repeatedly for months on end and may miss a great deal of school. Dealing with these students creates a dilemma—how can schools be responsive to the children's illness, yet ensure that their educational needs are met? The goals of this chapter are to review the empirical literature on children with recurrent abdominal pain (RAP) and to provide guidelines for helping these children in the school setting.

RAP affects 10–15% of school-aged children (Apley, 1975) and is the most common recurrent pain complaint of childhood (McGrath, 1990). Children with RAP may have multiple clinic visits, extensive medical evaluations, and considerable school absence. RAP is more common in girls than boys, is most prevalent during middle childhood, and is frequently associated with other symptoms, such as vomiting and headaches (Stone & Barbero, 1970; Walker, Garber, & Greene, 1991). One-third to one-half of children with RAP report abdominal pain and related symptoms as adults (Apley & Hale, 1973; Christensen & Mortensen, 1975; Stickler & Murphy, 1979; Walker, Garber, Van Slyke, & Greene, 1995; Walker, Guite, Duke, Barnard, & Greene, 1998).

Five years after their initial medical evaluation, adolescents and young adults with a history of RAP still have significantly more school and work absence and greater illness-related impairment in daily activities than their peers (Walker et al., 1995). Schools can play a significant role in decreasing this long-term impairment. Drawing on the clinical and empirical literature on RAP, we will suggest ways that schools can help children with RAP learn to cope with their symptoms while maintaining their academic performance and peer relationships. Development of these coping skills during childhood will help children with RAP maximize their productivity and quality of life as adults.

When RAP was first identified by Apley and Naish in the 1950s (Apley & Naish, 1958), it was not known whether it was associated with organic disease. Since then, empirical investigations have shown that fewer than 5% of children evaluated for RAP in primary care settings have organic disease (Christensen & Mortensen, 1975; Stickler & Murphy, 1979; Walker et al., 1995). Instead, the vast majority of cases of RAP reflect functional gastrointestinal disorders (FGIDs).

To understand FGIDs, we must first grasp the meaning of the term "functional." Functional symptoms are those that occur in the absence of documented inflammation, disease, or anatomical abnormality. They are caused by variations in functioning that are within the repertoire of responses inherent in organs free of disease (Fleisher, 1994). Even though results of physical examinations and laboratory tests are not abnormal, functional symptoms are "real." The subjective experience of functional abdominal pain, for example, is just as real and can be just as incapacitating as if diagnostic tests had revealed underlying peptic ulcer disease. The absence of identifiable pathology means that traditional medical interventions, such as medication and surgery, often are not helpful. The lack of a standard, effective treatment for functional symptoms may lead to tremendous frustration for the patient, family, medical professionals, and school staff.

A simple example of a functional symptom is a cramp in the calf muscle (Fleisher & Feldman, 1999). It creates a great deal of pain and is definitely not "all in your head." However, a physician examining the leg would find no disease or physical damage. The pain is real, but it is caused by a fatigue-induced muscle spasm that is a normal event for a healthy leg muscle. Some functional symptoms, such as blushing, are usually associated with a particular emotional state. Others, such as nausea at the sight of blood, are associated with a particular environmental circumstance. Still other functional symptoms may be associated with multiple factors. For example, physiology, emotions, environmental circumstances, and behavior may interact in producing or maintaining tension headaches. In many instances, functional symptoms are inconsequential; but, in others, they become recurrent or chronic, resulting in significant impairment in daily activities.

DEFINITIONS OF RAP AND FGIDs

RAP is defined as episodes of abdominal pain that occur repeatedly over a period of 3 months or longer and are severe enough to interfere with children's daily activities (Apley, 1975). RAP can be viewed as a broad category that includes several FGIDs, listed in Table 17.1, in which abdominal pain is a key feature (Von Baeyer & Walker, 1999). FGIDs are defined as conditions in which chronic or recurrent gastrointestinal symptoms are present in the absence of any identifiable pathology (Drossman, 1994). Although FGIDs by definition are not associated with organic disease, they are thought to have a physiological basis.

TABLE 17.1
Functional Gastrointestinal Disorders Often Associated with Recurrent Abdominal Pain

Functional Gastrointestinal Disorders
Irritable bowel syndrome
Functional constipation
Functional dyspepsia
Functional abdominal pain

Considerable research has aimed to understand the biology underlying FGIDs. Three early investigations described altered intestinal motor activity in pediatric patients with RAP (Dimson, 1971; Kopel, Kim, & Barbero, 1967; Pineiro-Carrero, Andres, Davis, & Mathias, 1988). Recently, research has focused on the possibility that FGIDs, particularly irritable bowel syndrome (IBS), are associated with visceral hyperalgesia (i.e., a low threshold for perceiving sensations in the gastrointestinal tract; Naliboff et al., 1997; Mertz, Naliboff, Munakata, Negar, & Mayer, 1995; Van Ginkel, Voskuijl, Benninga, Taminiau, & Boeckxstaens, 2001). These studies suggest that, whereas most people usually would not even be aware of distention in their intestines related to the movement of food or gas, individuals with FGIDs may consciously perceive even the slightest distention and experience it as painful. The mechanism for this hypersensitivity is not understood, and might include altered threshold of pain receptors in the gastrointestinal tract, an altered modulation in the conduction of sensory input from the gastrointestinal tract to the brain, or an altered threshold for symptom consciousness at the level of the central nervous system (Milla, 2001).

At present, no biological markers exist for FGIDs; in other words, no blood assays or diagnostic procedures can document the diagnosis of a FGID. Instead, these disorders are defined by particular patterns of symptoms that occur in the absence of any evidence of disease. A multinational team of experts has specified symptom criteria (the "Rome criteria") necessary for a diagnosis of each of the FGIDs that occur in childhood (Rasquin-Weber et al., 1999). The symptom criteria for FGIDs that are often associated with recurrent episodes of abdominal pain are described below.

Irritable Bowel Syndrome

A substantial proportion of children with RAP may meet the criteria for IBS. In one study, irritable bowel-like symptoms were present in the majority of children and adolescents presenting to a gastroenterology clinic with abdominal pain (Hyams et al., 1995). In IBS, abdominal pain is associated with changes in bowel habits, including: (a) change in stool frequency at the onset of abdominal pain, (b) change in stool form (constipation, diarrhea) at the onset of abdominal pain, and (c) pain relief by defecation (Rasquin-Weber et al., 1999). Additional symptoms of IBS may include visible abdominal distention, passage of mucus, and the sensation of incomplete bowel movement. Results of a public school survey suggested that IBS may affect as many as 6% of middle-school students and 14% of high school students (Hyams, Burke, Davis, Rzepski, & Andrulonis, 1996).

Functional Constipation

Constipation is often associated with abdominal pain and is the underlying mechanism for RAP in some children. Constipation in children is quite common and almost always functional in nature. Parents may not recognize that their child is constipated until they bring the child to the clinic for evaluation of abdominal pain. At that time, a physical examination or x-ray may reveal excessive stool in the colon. Because stool retention may occur even in children who appear to have several bowel movements a week, the problem may go undiagnosed for months.

Functional Dyspepsia

Functional dyspepsia (also known as "nonulcer dyspepsia") refers to pain or discomfort in the upper abdomen that is not associated with identifiable disease. It is classified into two subcategories: (a) ulcer-like dyspepsia, in which pain centered in the upper abdomen is the predominant symptom; and (b) dysmotility-like dsypepsia, in which an unpleasant nonpainful sensation (e.g., nausea, fullness) in the upper abdomen is the predominant symptom (Rasquin-Weber et al., 1999).

Functional Abdominal Pain

Functional abdominal pain is diagnosed when the patient has insufficient criteria for other functional gastrointestinal disorders that would explain the abdominal pain. It is defined as persistent abdominal pain in the absence of disease and without a recognizable pattern to the pain or accompanying symptoms (Rasquin-Weber et al., 1999). Unlike the other FGIDs, functional abdominal pain is not associated with eating or defecation. It may be recurrent or continuous and usually affects daily functioning.

THE BIOPSYCHOSOCIAL MODEL IN ASSESSMENT AND TREATMENT

The biopsychosocial model of illness is a particularly useful framework for understanding and treating functional gastrointestinal disorders. George Engel is credited with defining the biopsychosocial model as an alternative to the conventional biomedical model of illness (Engel, 1977, 1980). To understand the difference between the biomedical and biopsychosocial models is to understand the difference between disease and illness. Disease connotes objectively demonstrable tissue damage and organ malfunction. Illness connotes the patient's subjective sense of feeling unwell, suffering, or being disabled (Eisenberg, 1977). The biomedical model reduces illness to a single etiology—disease. It requires that physicians focus the medical evaluation on "ruling out disease" by conducting various diagnostic tests. If no disease, biochemical abnormality, or inflammation is found, it is assumed that the patient is well. Thus, the biomedical approach limits the role of physicians to the diagnosis and treatment of disease. This approach fails when applied to patients whose illness is because of functional symptoms that cannot be traced to disease.

The biopsychosocial model, in contrast, regards disease as only one of several potential causes of illness. As shown in Fig. 17.1, factors that may contribute to illness include environmental factors (e.g., stress, diet, social relationships), psychological factors (e.g.,

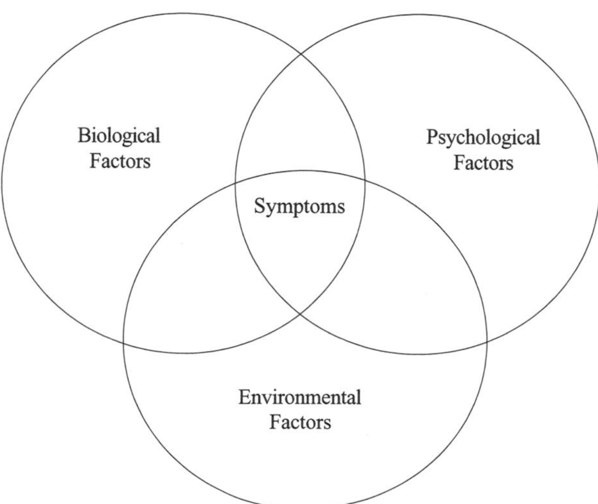

FIG. 17.1. A biopsychosocial model of functional gastrointestinal symptoms.

emotions, cognitions, behavior, and attention), and biological factors not limited to disease (e.g., physiological arousal, genes). Furthermore, all of these factors are thought to interact with each other in a dynamic process of mutual influence. For example, in a child with visceral hypersensitivity, certain foods might precipitate abdominal pain that, in turn, could lead to anxiety that lowers the child's pain threshold, thereby increasing pain and eliciting parent concern that focuses the child's attention on the pain. Increased attentional focus on the pain, in turn, could interfere with the child's performance at school, leading to further increases in anxiety, decreases in pain threshold, and increased symptoms and disability.

Treatment of the FGIDs associated with RAP varies greatly, depending on whether the physician takes a biomedical or biopsychosocial approach. A strictly biomedical approach may entail a lengthy medical evaluation, including laboratory tests and procedures to rule out various diseases. When no organic basis for the child's symptoms is found, families may be told, "Nothing is wrong," and "There's no reason this child can't attend school and other activities." If the child's symptoms continue despite reassurance regarding the absence of disease, the physician may conclude that the symptoms are psychogenic and may make a mental health referral. Referral for mental health services is likely to be made only as a last resort, when the biomedical practitioner has nothing else to offer.

A biopsychosocial approach, in contrast, assumes from the start that multiple factors contribute to the etiology and maintenance of FGIDs, and must be addressed for treatment to be successful (Drossman, 1996; Hyams & Hyman, 1998). Practitioners from multiple disciplines (including medicine, psychology, nutrition, and social work) may be involved early in the evaluation process. Treatment is likely to have several components, (listed in Table 17.2). First, in addition to reassurance regarding the absence of disease, results of the medical evaluation should include an explanation of functional symptoms and how pain can occur without disease (for case examples, see Schwankovsky & Hyman, 1999; Zeltzer, 1995). Prescription and nonprescription medications and other preparations may be recommended for symptom relief. For example, stool softeners and osmotic laxatives, such as milk of magnesia, may be used to treat patients with constipation. Patients with functional dyspepsia may be treated with medications that speed movement of food from the stomach to the intestine. Some antidepressant medications modify pain sensations arising in the gastrointestinal tract so that they do not reach the brain; these drugs may be used to relieve abdominal pain, regardless of whether a patient also has symptoms of depression.

Frequently, dietary changes also are a component of treatment for children with FGIDs, particularly for those with constipation, diarrhea, or bloating. For example, treatment of functional constipation and IBS may entail a high fiber diet and a decrease in dairy products. Treatment of functional dyspepsia may call for elimination of caffeinated beverages, spicy foods, and fatty foods that could aggravate dyspeptic symptoms. Symptoms of gas and bloating may be reduced by eliminating carbonated beverages, beans, and other foods.

TABLE 17.2
Components of a Biopsychosocial Approach

Medical evaluation to rule out disease
Reassurance and explanation of functional symptoms
Prescription or nonprescription medications for symptom relief
Dietary changes
Social/environmental interventions
Behavioral interventions

Environmental interventions, often involving school or school attendance, also may be suggested in the treatment of FGIDs. For example, a family may be asked to rearrange their morning schedule so that a child with functional constipation is not too rushed to use the bathroom before school. Similarly, an adolescent with IBS who fears having a bowel accident on the drive to school might be encouraged to identify a convenience store along the route where he or she could use the bathroom if necessary. In addition to changes in routine, environmental stressors that exacerbate symptoms may be eliminated. For example, a child whose symptoms worsened significantly after assignment to an advanced class might be reassigned to the regular class.

Finally, a biopsychosocial approach often uses behavioral interventions in conjunction with other treatments. Nonpharmacological pain management techniques, such as hypnosis or pain distraction strategies, are helpful for some children. Children may be referred for stress management because stress may affect digestion, gastrointestinal motility, and pain threshold. Various forms of individual and family therapy may be beneficial if family factors or emotional distress are thought to precipitate or exacerbate the child's symptoms.

ISSUES SPECIFIC TO THE SCHOOL SETTING

The biopsychosocial model suggests that understanding and helping children with FGIDs requires attention to multiple factors and collaboration among the school, family, and health care professionals. Within the school setting, a team approach similar to the Multidisciplinary Team used to address academic problems is especially helpful in supporting children with FGIDs. In the following section, the authors draw on their clinical experience and the empirical literature to describe issues specific to the school setting that are relevant to RAP (see Table 17.3). Interventions that address these issues are described. Additional information and practical suggestions for coping with FGIDs associated with RAP are available from the International Foundation for Functional Gastrointestinal Disorders in Milwaukee, WI (P.O. Box 170864, Milwaukee, WI 53217-8076; www.iffgd.org).

Communications about the Child's Illness

Functional symptoms are difficult even for a physician to explain, so it is not surprising that some children with RAP do not know what to say when asked the reason for their absence from school. Children who have been told that the medical evaluation showed "nothing was

TABLE 17.3
Issues Specific to the School Setting

Communication about the child's illness
Unintentional reinforcement of the child's symptoms and disability
Use of the school bathroom
Child emotional distress
Pain episodes at school
Return to school after extensive absence
Diet and eating habits at school
Make-up work after school absence
Performance anxiety
Relationship between school and parents
Life stress
Threat of school failure

wrong" may be embarrassed and may worry what others will think of them. They can save face by being helped to explain their condition in a way appropriate to their age. For example, a younger child might simply say, "The doctor said something is wrong with my stomach. It's getting better, but it still bothers me sometimes."

Despite the absence of identifiable organic disease, the pain is legitimate and may be as severe and disabling as in conditions with organic causes for abdominal pain (Walker, Garber, & Greene, 1993). Children are quick to recognize comments by classmates and others that imply they are "faking" the pain. Such remarks create shame and embarrassment that may adversely affect their ability to cope with the symptoms, ultimately resulting in symptom exacerbation and further school absence. School professionals can help by intervening when it appears that classmates or others are responding in ways that invalidate the child's experience. Communcations that acknowledge the pain and encourage coping efforts are more helpful.

Unintentional Reinforcement of the Child's Symptoms and Disability

Although symptoms of RAP should not be invalidated or minimized, they also should not elicit such a high level of concern that the symptoms are unintentionally intensified and reinforced. Attention to somatic sensations tends to heighten one's experience of those symptoms (Pennebaker, 1982). Thus, when children are asked how they feel, any symptoms they have will be drawn into greater conscious awareness. Furthermore, frequent expressions of concern by others may increase children's perceptions of the severity of those symptoms. To avoid frequent interactions that draw attention to the pain, teachers and psychologists might set up a single "check-in" time during the day to review the child's pain episodes, if any, and discuss how to cope with the pain.

In addition to focusing children's attention on their symptoms, expressions of concern from others may be associated with privileges or relief from responsibility that appeal to some children and thereby unintentionally reinforce symptoms. In a study of pediatric patients with RAP, they perceived their parents as giving them significantly more attention and relief from responsibility when they were sick than was reported by other children (Walker et al., 1993). At school, children who do not have other means of recognition for being "special" may value attention resulting from their illness. For example, those who are not doing well in school (or fear that they will not do well) may value staying home from school or being given extra time for an assignment when they are ill. In these cases, it is especially important to develop alternatives to the sick role that will bring the child special attention and recognition. This could include both immediate gestures, such as allowing the child to be a hall monitor, as well as more long-term plans to promote development of the child's overall sense of competence.

Using the School Bathroom

Children with RAP may need to use the bathroom more frequently than other children, particularly if their abdominal symptoms are associated with functional constipation or IBS. Using the toilet may bring symptom relief for children with IBS and is imperative for those with functional constipation whose treatment regimen includes laxatives. Many children, however, are reluctant to use their school bathrooms. Their reluctance may be caused by several factors, including: (a) lack of privacy because doors on the toilet stalls have been removed, cannot be latched, or do not fully hide the occupant from view; (b) poor sanitation in the bathrooms; (c) lack of toilet paper; (d) fear that classmates will know they are defecating by the sound or smell; (e) fear that using the bathroom will take too long and they will be reprimanded for being late to class; and (f) fear of verbal or physical assault by classmates while in the bathroom. Children may be embarrassed to volunteer information about these issues and, furthermore, may not recognize that their concerns are legitimate. Thus, parents and teachers usually need to ask direct questions and observe children's behavior to assess the extent to which difficulties using the school bathroom contribute to children's physical and emotional distress.

It is important to facilitate children's use of the bathroom to avoid further symptom exacerbation. Some children benefit from being allowed to leave the classroom to use the bathroom whenever necessary, without first asking permission. This puts use of the bathroom under children's control. Of course, this arrangement should be reconsidered if a child appears to be using it to avoid classroom activities. In many cases, just knowing that they can use the bathroom whenever necessary relieves children's anxiety and allows them to cope more effectively with their symptoms. In some cases, arrangements can be made for children to use a private bathroom or to go to the bathroom when other children are not present. Finally, some schools may need to take steps to improve the conditions of the children's bathrooms.

Child Emotional Distress

The earliest clinical descriptions characterized children with RAP as "anxious, timid, fussy, and over-conscientious, taking the ordinary difficulties of life (especially of school life) too much to heart" (Apley & Naish, 1958, p. 170). Subsequent empirical investigations have demonstrated that children with RAP exhibit significantly higher levels of internalizing symptoms, such as anxiety and depression, than their well peers (Walker & Greene, 1989; Walker et al., 1993; Wasserman, Whitington, & Rivara, 1988). Nonetheless, their internalizing symptoms are significantly lower than those of children seen at an outpatient psychiatric clinic (Walker et al., 1993).

Most empirical investigations of RAP have been based on pediatric patients in tertiary care settings whose symptoms were of long duration and intractable to primary care treatment. Thus, emotional distress in these patient samples may have been higher than that of children in the community with RAP. It is likely that most children with RAP identified in school settings will not have a serious psychiatric disorder. Instead, the majority are likely to exhibit moderate levels of internalizing symptoms that reflect separation anxiety, reactions to stress, or difficulty coping with their gastrointestinal symptoms. In many cases, these problems can be managed by professionals within the school setting without referral to external mental health service providers. Indeed, waiting to address the problem until an appointment can be obtained with a professional outside the school may allow time for symptoms and disability to escalate to the point that children's academic progress is significantly compromised.

Separation anxiety merits particular mention, because it is often associated with RAP and may contribute to considerable school absence. One of the symptom criteria for separation anxiety is, "repeated complaints of physical symptoms (such as headaches, stomachaches, nausea, or vomiting) when separation from major attachment figures occurs or is anticipated" (American Psychiatric Association, 1994). Children with separation anxiety frequently complain of stomachaches in the morning before school in anticipation of separation from their parents. Some of these children are allowed to stay home, and others attend school despite their symptoms but call their parents to bring them home before the end of the day. The children's symptoms tend to resolve when they are at home. This pattern of morning stomachaches and school absence often begins after a period of particular closeness between children and their parents, for example, after a vacation or illness. A medical evaluation should be obtained for these children as soon as possible so that the family and school can address the underlying problem of separation anxiety without worrying that they have overlooked a serious disease.

Pain Episodes at School

Some children with RAP worry that they will have a pain episode at school and be unable to manage it. These children may have poor skills for coping with pain and at times may exhibit such exaggerated distress that they are rushed to the emergency room. Their distress arises from a habit of focusing their attention on minor physical sensations and becoming fearful that these sensations will increase in intensity. Fear, in turn, magnifies the noxious sensory experience. These children are caught in a vicious cycle of anticipation of pain, increased anxiety and physiological arousal, lowered pain threshold, and increased distress (cf. Zeltzer, Bush, Chen, & Riveral, 1997).

The school and family should agree on a plan regarding what the child should do if he or she experiences pain during school hours. In general, it is counterproductive for children to call home or leave school early when they experience a pain episode, because this will reinforce their pain complaint and passive coping. Instead, children should be allowed to rest for a while in the office, clinic, or library until they feel well enough to return to class or it is time to leave school.

In some cases, physicians recommend homebound instruction for children with RAP. This practice tends to foster children's passive coping with pain and implicitly communicates that children are too sick to carry on regular activities. Empirical evidence suggests that children with RAP who use passive pain coping strategies, such as withdrawing from activities and social interaction, are more likely to maintain their symptoms over time than are children who do not engage in such passive strategies (Walker, Smith, Garber, & Van Slyke, 1997). Thus, children who are removed from the school setting may become entrenched in the sick role, failing to learn skills that would help them cope with their symptoms. Because functional gastrointestinal symptoms may last a lifetime, it is critical that children learn to minimize the impact of symptoms on their activities. Although homebound instruction may reduce children's distress in the short-term, it can be counterproductive in the long-term.

Return to School after Extensive Absence

Some degree of school absence is to be expected for children with FGIDs, if only to obtain medical consultation. As their school absence increases, however, some children may lose confidence in their ability to manage the demands of school. If required to return to school for full days, some of these children will fail repeatedly. In cases such as these, it is best that children's initial return to school be for a limited period of time, as few as one or 2 hr a day, with a token reward system to reinforce daily attendance. Most children will agree that they can manage being at school for a very short period of time even if they experience pain. This abbreviated attendance will help build their confidence that they can survive a pain episode at school. A gradual return to school also may help children and parents overcome separation anxiety. In our experience, most children allowed to make a gradual return to school are able to attend full time within 3–4 weeks.

Diet and Eating Habits at School

Diet and eating habits have the potential to exacerbate symptoms of RAP (Barr, Levine, & Watkins, 1979; Friedman, 1991; Hunter, 1991). The nature of the impact of diet on symptoms varies according to whether RAP is associated with underlying IBS, functional dyspepsia, constipation, or functional abdominal pain. Nonetheless, for all children with RAP, the scheduling of school lunch and the type of food available are important factors to consider in planning symptom management.

In many schools, the lunch period is as brief as 20 min. This is unfortunate, because rapid ingestion of food can cause abdominal pain. Furthermore, if bathroom visits also are scheduled during the lunch period, children may not have time to use the toilet, resulting in further abdominal discomfort. Extension of the lunch period would benefit many children who already experience RAP and might help prevent the development of similar symptoms in other children.

The type of foods and beverages children consume for lunch also may play a role in triggering or perpetuating functional gastrointestinal symptoms. Drinking carbonated beverages, chewing gum, and sucking on candy can increase gas, creating abdominal pain. Certain carbohydrates, such as beans, also increase intestinal gas. Caffeine, contained in chocolate and in many carbonated beverages, causes abdominal distress in some children. Sorbitol, a chemical found in many dietetic foods and beverages, creates substantial abdominal distress in some children (Hyams, 1982). Dairy products produce abdominal pain in some children with lactose intolerance (Barr et al., 1979). Foods with a high fat content slow the digestive process and may increase symptoms of bloating. The child's physician or a dietician may be able to suggest foods or beverages that could be eliminated on a trial basis and then reintroduced to assess their impact on individual children's symptoms.

Make-up Work after School Absence

Children with RAP who have missed school may become so overwhelmed by the extent of make-up work confronting them that the prospect of returning to school creates unmanageable anxiety and exacerbates their abdominal symptoms. They may worry that they simply cannot do the work, that it will consume all their free time, or that they have missed so much class that they will not understand the work and will fail.

Concerns about make-up work are best addressed with a structured plan developed before the children's return to school. Children will find make-up work more manageable if it is broken into small components with a schedule that emphasizes steady progress rather than final products. For example, children who are overwhelmed by a list of due dates for various assignments might agree that they could work on their assignments for 30 min a day until they are finished, particularly if a parent or teacher agrees to help them. In the case of children who have a particularly heavy load of make-up work, it often makes sense to excuse them from less essential assignments. This will improve their morale and increase the likelihood of their success in catching up with their classmates.

Performance Anxiety

Some children's symptoms are worse before a test, athletic event, or other competitive activity. If the focus of anxiety is fairly circumscribed, children may benefit from simple coping strategies that can be suggested by the teacher or psychologist. Many programs that teach children coping skills for anxiety control are based on cognitive-behavioral theory and entail replacing debilitating self-statements with adaptive self-statements (Grace, Spirito, Finch, & Ott, 1993). For example, children may be taught to redirect their thoughts and images so that these enhance rather than undermine their success. One of these strategies is to "Be a good coach." Most children will agree that good coaches inspire confidence by making statements such as "I know you can do it!" and "Get in there and give it your best!" In contrast, children with performance anxiety often are not good coaches for themselves. They are likely to think, "What if I fail?" and, "I don't know if I can do it." Teachers and other school professionals can help children become aware of the "what ifs" and negative statements they make to themselves, and substitute these with "good coaching, " such as saying to themselves, "I know I can do it" and "I'm going to do my best."

In some cases, performance anxiety is just one aspect of generalized anxiety that is manifest in many domains of the child's life. These children should be referred to a mental health professional for individual treatment.

Relationship Between School and Parents

Empirical studies have found no significant differences between families of children with RAP and families of well children on measures of family functioning that assess general characteristics, such as family cohesion and parent marital satisfaction (McGrath et al., 1983; Walker et al., 1993; Wasserman et al., 1988). However, the theoretical literature suggests that families of children with RAP may differ from other families in domains that are not adequately assessed by standard measures of family functioning (Walker, 1999; Walker, McLaughlin, & Greene, 1988). For example, families of children with RAP have been described as overprotective and highly enmeshed (i.e., with a high degree of closeness that interferes with children's individuation and autonomy). Empirical evidence to support this view is lacking, perhaps because overprotection and enmeshment are difficult to assess with existing questionnaire measures and difficult to distinguish from healthy levels of protection and family cohesion (Walker, 1999).

Nonetheless, one characteristic consistently differentiates families of children with RAP from other families: the incidence of illness—including gastrointestinal and nongastrointestinal disorders—is greater in families of RAP patients than in families of well children (Walker et al., 1991, 1993; Wasserman et al., 1988). This observation has led to speculation that social modeling of pain behavior may contribute to RAP. For example, children may learn pain behavior vicariously by observing that a parent who complains of abdominal pain receives special attention from other family members (cf. Levy, Whitehead, Von Korff, & Feld, 2000). In addition, high levels of family illness could serve to heighten concern regarding children's symptoms, leading parents to seek extensive medical evaluations and unintentionally reinforce children's symptom complaints with attention and relief from responsibility.

Clinical observations suggest that many parents of children with RAP view their children as vulnerable and try to protect them from various threats, particularly potential health-related threats, that are of less concern to caregivers of other children. Unlike parents who encourage or even insist that their children go to school when they have a stomachache, parents of children with RAP usually consider a stomachache to be a legitimate reason for staying home from school. In some instances, children get caught in a conflict between parents and teachers regarding their school attendance. Teachers believe that the child is well enough to go to school and that the parents should force the child to attend. However, parents believe that their child is in too much pain to attend school and that the teacher is unreasonable and uncaring. As the school increases pressure for attendance, parents may increase their protectiveness, resulting in increased child dependency and reluctance to attend school.

It is important to recognize that parental protectiveness, even at a level that seems exaggerated, is grounded in good intentions. Labeling their behavior "overprotective" implicitly blames parents and may create an adversarial relationship. It is important to search for common goals in which the school and parents can both agree. For example, many parents will agree that good parents not only protect their children by keeping them home from school when ill, but also help them learn how to cope with illness. The school may be able to join the parents in developing ways to facilitate their children's coping by making modifications in the children's school schedule, developing contingency plans for when the child has a pain episode at school, and so on. Above all, school staff should take care to communicate that they take the child's symptoms seriously and regard the pain as real.

Life Stress

Life stress may play an important role in precipitating or maintaining symptoms of RAP. A recent diary study demonstrated that, in comparison with their peers, patients with RAP reported significantly more daily stressors (Walker, Smith, Garber, Van Slyke, & Claar, 2001). The majority of these stressors occurred during school hours and included difficulty understanding homework, worrying about a test, concern about a grade, and not liking a particular class. Both patients with RAP and other children reported increased anxiety and sadness on days that they experienced stressful events. However, RAP patients differed from their peers in that they also reacted to stressful events with abdominal pain and other somatic symptoms. Thus, it appears that children with RAP may have a particular type of stress reactivity that is manifest in somatic symptoms.

Longitudinal studies have found that RAP patients who experience many negative life events are more likely to maintain their symptoms over time, compared with those with few negative life events (Walker & Greene, 1991). This is particularly true for children who, based on their own perceptions and teachers' ratings, lack competence in social skills (Walker, Garber, & Greene, 1994). These children may have difficulty obtaining support from others. Children with high social competence, in contrast, are more likely to obtain support in coping with stress and also are more likely to be involved in peer activities that distract them from their physical symptoms. An implication of this finding is that for children with RAP, interventions to help increase social competence may indirectly enhance their ability to cope with symptoms.

Teaching Style

Some parents of children with RAP cite the child's relationship with a teacher as a factor contributing to their children's pain episodes (Claar & Walker, 1999). A common scenario involves a sensitive child who in the past has had warm, maternal, and nurturant teachers, but this year has a more matter-of-fact, business-like teacher who maintains strict discipline. The child may interpret the teacher's manner as disapproval and may worry about getting in trouble. The resulting increase in anxiety may contribute to increased abdominal symptoms. Sometimes the problem is alleviated when the teacher is made aware of the child's perceptions and makes an extra effort to make the child feel special. In other cases, the child must be helped to understand and cope with the teacher's personality and teaching style. A change of teacher should be a last resort, because this tends to reinforce children's belief that they cannot cope and may create additional stressors associated with adjustment to a new classroom.

Threat of School Failure

Some children with RAP have had such extensive school absence that they risk failing and being required to repeat the school year. It may be difficult to ascertain whether school failure is from illness-related school absence or a learning problem, attention deficit/hyperactivity disorder, failure to complete assignments, or placement in a class that is too advanced. Regardless of the reason, children who believe that they have already failed the school year have little incentive to cope with their symptoms and return to school. Thus, the potential reasons for failure should be carefully evaluated, and every effort should be made to remedy these and facilitate the child's return to school as soon as possible, even if only a few weeks of the school year remain.

SUMMARY AND CONCLUSIONS

RAP is the most common recurrent pain complaint of childhood. RAP is a broad category that includes several FGIDs, in which abdominal pain without organic disease is the primary feature. RAP and associated FGIDs are best understood and treated within a biopsychosocial framework that recognizes that multiple factors interact in creating and maintaining illness. Psychologists who work within school settings are in a strategic position to contribute to assessment of psychosocial factors that contribute to RAP and to help implement interventions that assist children in coping with their symptoms.

ACKNOWLEDGMENTS

The authors appreciate comments from Roy Hutton, Susan Lewis, and David MacMillan on an earlier version of this chapter.

REFERENCES

American Psychiatric Association (1994). *Diagnostic and statistical manual of mental disorders* (4th ed.). Washington, DC: Author.

Apley, J. (1975). *The child with abdominal pains*. London: Blackwell.

Apley, J., & Hale, B. (1973). Children with recurrent abdominal pain: How do they grow up? *British Medical Journal, 7*, 7–9.

Apley, J., & Naish, N. (1958). Recurrent abdominal pain: A field survey of 1,000 school children. *Archives of Diseases of Childhood, 33*, 165–170.

Barr, R. G., Levine, M. D., & Watkins, J. (1979). Recurrent abdominal pain in children due to lactose intolerance: A prospective study. *New England Journal of Medicine, 300*, 1449–1452.

Christensen, M. F., & Mortensen, O. (1975). Long-term prognosis in children with recurrent abdominal pain. *Archives of Diseases of Children, 50*, 110–114.

Claar, R. L., & Walker, L. S. (1999). Maternal attributions for the causes and remedies of their children's abdominal pain. *Journal of Pediatric Psychology, 24*, 345–354.

Dimson, S. B. (1971). Transit time related to clinical findings in children with recurrent abdominal pain. *Pediatrics, 47*, 666–674.

Drossman, D. A. (1996). Gastrointestinal illness and the biopsychosocial model. *Journal of Clinical Gastroenterology, 22*, 252–254.

Drossman, D. A. (Ed.). (1994). *The functional gastrointestinal disorders. Diagnosis, pathophysiology, and treatment: A multinational consensus* (pp. 1–23). Boston: Little, Brown.

Eisenberg, L. (1977). Disease and illness. *Culture, Medicine, and Psychiatry, 1*, 9–23.

Engel, G. L. (1977). The need for a new medical model: A challenge for biomedicine. *Science, 196*, 129–136.

Engel, G. L. (1980). The clinical application of the biopsychosocial model. *American Journal of Psychiatry, 137*, 535–544.

Fleisher, D. R. (1994). Integration of biomedical and psychosocial management. In P. E. Hyman & C. DiLorenzo (Eds.), *Pediatric gastrointestinal motility disorders* (pp. 13–31). New York: Academy Professional Information Services.

Fleisher, D. R., & Feldman, E. J. (1999). The biopsychosocial model of clinical practice in functional gastrointestinal disorders. In P. E. Hyman (Ed.), *Pediatric functional gastrointestinal disorders* (pp. 1–20). New York: Academy Professional Information Services.

Friedman, G. (1991). Diet and the irritable bowel syndrome. *Gastroenterology Clinics of North America, 20*, 313–324.

Grace, N., Spirito, A., Finch, A. J., & Ott, E. S. (1993). Coping skills for anxiety control in children. In A. J. Finch, W. M. Nelson, & E. S. Ott (Eds.), *Cognitive-behavioral procedures with children and adolescents: A practical guide* (pp. 257–288). Needham Heights, MA: Allyn & Bacon.

Hunter, J. O. (1991). Food intolerance and the irritable bowel syndrome. In N. W. Read (Ed.), *Irritable bowel syndrome* (pp. 203–219). Oxford: Blackwell.

Hyams, J. (1982). Chronic abdominal pain caused by sorbitol malabsorption. *Journal of Pediatrics, 100*, 772–773.

Hyams, J. S., Burke, G., Davis, P. M., Rzepski, B., & Andrulonis, P. A. (1996). Abdominal pain and irritable bowel syndrome in adolescents: A community-based study. *Journal of Pediatrics, 129*, 220–226.

Hyams, J. S., & Hyman, P. E. (1998). Recurrent abdominal pain and the biopsychosocial model of medical practice. *Journal of Pediatrics, 133*, 473–478.

Hyams, J. S., Treem, W. R., Justinich, C. J., Davis, P., Shoup, M., & Burke, G. (1995). Characterization of symptoms in children with recurrent abdominal pain: Resemblance to irritable bowel syndrome. *Journal of Pediatric Gastroenterology and Nutrition, 20*, 209–214.

Kopel, F. B., Kim, I. C., & Barbero, G. J. (1967). Comparison of rectosigmoid motility in normal children, children with recurrent abdominal pain, and children with ulcerative colitis. *Pediatrics, 39*, 539–545.

Levy, R. L., Whitehead, W. E., Von Korff, M. R., & Feld, A. D. (2000). Intergenerational transmission of gastrointestinal illness behavior. *American Journal of Gastroenterology, 95*, 451–456.

McGrath, P. A. (1990). *Pain in children: Nature, assessment, and treatment*. New York: Guilford.

McGrath, P. A., Goodman, J. T., Firestone, P., Shipman, P., & Peters, S. (1983). Recurrent abdominal pain: A psychogenic disorder? *Archives of Diseases of Childhood, 58*, 888–890.

Mertz, H., Naliboff, B., Munakata, J., Negar, N., & Mayer, E. A. (1995). Altered rectal perception is a biological marker of patients with irritable bowel syndrome. *Gastroenterology, 109*, 40–52.

Milla, P. J. (2001). Irritable bowel syndrome in childhood. *Gastroenterology, 120*, 287–307.

Naliboff, B. D., Munakata, J., Fullerton, S., Gracely, R. H., Kodner, A., Harraf, F., & Mayer, E. A. (1997). Evidence for two distinct perceptual alterations in irritable bowel syndrome. *Gut, 41*, 505–512.

Pennebaker, J. W. (1982). *The psychology of physical symptoms*. New York: Springer-Verlag.

Pineiro-Carrero, V. M., Andres, J. M., Davis, R. H., & Mathias, J. R. (1988). Abnormal gastroduodenal motility in children and adolescents with recurrent functional abdominal pain. *Journal of Pediatrics, 113*, 820–825.

Rasquin-Weber, A., Hyman, P. E., Cucchiara, S., Fleisher, D. R., Hyams, J. S., Milla, P. J., & Staiano, A. (1999). Childhood functional gastrointestinal disorders. *Gut, 45*, 60–68.

Schwankovsky, L., & Hyman, P. E. (1999). Responses to questions and statements of children, adolescents, and parents. In P. E. Hyman (Ed.), *Pediatric functional gastrointestinal disorders* (pp. 12.1–12.17). New York: Academy Professional Information Services.

Stickler, G. B., & Murphy, D. B. (1979). Recurrent abdominal pain. *American Journal of Diseases of Children, 133*, 486–489.

Stone, R. T., & Barbero, G. J. (1970). Recurrent abdominal pain in childhood. *Pediatrics, 45*, 732–738.

Van Ginkel, R., Voskuijl, W. P., Benninga, M. A., Taminiau, J. M., & Boeckxstaens, G. E. (2001). Alterations in rectal sensitivity and motility in childhood irritable bowel syndrome. *Gastroenterology, 120*, 31–38.

Von Baeyer, C., & Walker, L. S. (1999). Children with recurrent abdominal pain: Research criteria for selection of subjects. *Journal of Developmental and Behavioral Pediatrics, 20*, 307–313.

Walker, L. S. (1999). The evolution of research on recurrent abdominal pain: History, assumptions, and a conceptual model. In P. J. McGrath & G. A. Finley (Eds.), *Progress in pain research and management* (Vol. 13, pp. 141–172). Seattle, WA: International Association for the Study of Pain Press.

Walker, L. S., Garber, J., & Greene, J. W. (1991). Somatization symptoms in pediatric abdominal pain patients: Relation to chronicity of abdominal pain and parent somatization. *Journal of Abnormal Child Psychology, 19*, 379–394.

Walker, L. S., Garber, J., & Greene, J. W. (1993). Psychosocial characteristics of recurrent childhood pain: A comparison of children with recurrent abdominal pain, organic illness, and psychiatric disorders. *Journal of Abnormal Psychology, 102*, 248–258.

Walker, L. S., Garber, J., & Greene, J. W. (1994). Somatic complaints in pediatric patients: A prospective study of the role of negative life events, child social and academic competence, and parental somatic complaints. *Journal of Consulting and Clinical Psychology, 62*, 1213–1221.

Walker, L. S., Garber, J., Van Slyke, D. A., & Greene, J. W. (1995). Long-term health outcomes in patients with recurrent abdominal pain. *Journal of Pediatric Psychology, 20*, 233–245.

Walker, L. S., & Greene, J. W. (1989). Children with recurrent abdominal pain and their parents: More somatic complaints, anxiety, and depression than other patient families? *Journal of Pediatric Psychology, 14*, 231–243.

Walker, L. S., & Greene, J. W. (1991). Negative life events and symptom resolution in pediatric abdominal pain patients. *Journmal of Pediatric Psychology, 16*, 341–360.

Walker, L. S., Guite, J. W., Duke, M., Barnard, J. A., & Greene, J. W. (1998). Recurrent abdominal pain: A potential precursor of irritable bowel syndrome in adolescents and young adults. *Journal of Pediatrics, 132*, 1010–1015.

Walker, L. S., McLaughlin, F. J., & Greene, J. W. (1988). Functional illness and family functioning: A comparison of healthy and somaticizing adolescents. *Family Process, 27*, 317–325.

Walker, L. S., Smith, C. A., Garber, J., & Van Slyke, D.A. (1997). Development and validation of the Pain Response Inventory for children. *Psychological Assessment, 9*, 392–405.

Walker, L. S., Smith, C. A., Garber, J., Van Slyke, D. A., & Claar, R. (2001). The relation of daily stressors to somatic and emotional symptoms in children with recurrent abdominal pain. *Journal of Consulting and Clinical Psychology, 69*, 85–91.

Wasserman, A. L., Whitington, P. F., & Rivara, F. P. (1988). Psychogenic basis for abdominal pain in children and adolescents. *Journal of the American Academy of Child and Adolescent Psychiatry, 27*, 179–184.

Zeltzer, L. K. (1995). Challenging case: Recurrent abdominal pain. *Journal of Developmental and Behavioral Pediatrics, 16*, 277–281.

Zeltzer, L. K., Bush, J. P., Chen, E., & Riveral, A. (1997). A psychobiologic approach to pediatric pain: Part 1. History, physiology, and assessment strategies. *Current Problems in Pediatrics, 27*, 255–258.

18

Traumatic Brain Injury: Neuropsychological, Psychiatric, and Educational Issues

Linda Ewing-Cobbs
University of Texas Health Science Center at Houston

Douglas R. Bloom
Texas Children's Hospital

INTRODUCTION

In this chapter, we will briefly discuss the epidemiology and pathophysiology of traumatic brain injury (TBI), common neuropsychological deficits, as well as academic, social, and psychiatric issues. Educational strategies for transition from hospital to school, and issues regarding long-term educational management, are addressed. The focus of the chapter is on issues pertaining to school-age children and adolescents sustaining moderate-to-severe TBI.

EPIDEMIOLOGY OF TBI

TBI is a major pediatric public health concern. TBI is the most common cause of death (case fatality rate ranging from 3 to 14/100 cases) and acquired brain insult (incidence of 180/100,000 hospitalized cases) in American children. Approximately 17,000 of these children become disabled by TBI annually; severe lifetime disabilities are incurred by 2–5% (Kraus, 1995). The cause of injury varies with age. Major causes of pediatric TBI included falls (35%), recreational activities (29%), and motor vehicle accidents (24%; Kraus, Fife, Cox, Ramstein, & Conroy, 1986).

The quality of outcome after TBI varies with the severity of the initial injury. Outcomes range from death to persistent vegetative state to variable cognitive and physical consequences. Assessment of the severity of injury is most frequently based on the Glasgow Coma Scale score (Teasdale & Jennett, 1974), which ranges from 3 to 15 and evaluates three components of consciousness: eye opening, motor response, and verbal response. Scores from 3 to 8 reflect a severe injury producing coma, operationally defined as the absence of eye opening, inability to follow one stage commands, and failure to utter recognizable words. Moderate TBI is defined by Glasgow Coma Scale scores from 9 to 12; mild TBI is defined by scores from 13 to 15, indicating that patients are alert, have spontaneous eye opening, and have verbal responses ranging from confused to oriented. The duration of coma and posttraumatic amnesia (period of confusion and failure to encode new information in ongoing memory) is also commonly used to estimate the severity of TBI and shows strong relationships with long-term outcome measures (Massagli, Michaud, & Rivara, 1996; McDonald et al., 1994).

Severe TBI, which is present in 5–8% of children treated at hospitals (Kraus, 1995), produces residual neurological deficit in 50% (DiScala, Osberg, Gans, Chin, & Grant, 1991; Massagli, Jaffe, et al., 1996). Disabilities reflect deficits in multiple areas of functioning, including intelligence, memory, attention, adaptive behavior, motor, executive function, and psychiatric domains. Based on a conservative estimate of nearly 20,000 American children and adolescents incurring new persisting disabilities each year, the prevalence of educational disability secondary to TBI is quite high (Ylvisaker et al., 2001).

Pathophysiology of TBI

Recent neuroimaging and neuropathology studies have clarified the mechanisms of injury and the nature of posttraumatic abnormalities. TBI may be produced by either contact or noncontact forces. Contact forces occur when the head strikes or is struck by an object. Contact forces may cause focal brain injury at the site of impact, as well as injuries distant from the impact site. Noncontact injuries result from movement of the head and brain related to cranial acceleration or deceleration irrespective of whether there is direct contact (e.g., in high-speed motor vehicle accidents where the speed and direction in which a passenger's head is moving may change abruptly). Noncontact injuries are caused by two mechanisms: (1) the brain may move relative to the skull and underlying membranes, causing rupture of veins located between the brain and membranes; and (2) the movement of the brain may produce direct damage to neurons by compression and/or shearing effects (Ommaya, Goldsmith, & Thibault, 2002). Most severe TBI cases involve a combination of contact and noncontact forces that produce diffuse and focal injury. Focal brain injuries consist of visible macroscopic lesions, including contusions (bruising of the surface of the brain), intracerebral hematomas (collections of blood within the brain tissue), and extra-axial hematomas (collections of blood that lie between layers of membranes between the brain and skull). Focal lesions produce deficits related to direct tissue damage, as well as to remote effects, such as mass effect (shifting of the brain to the left or right because of swelling or pressure effects from collections of blood that causes compression of tissue), herniation, and compression of brainstem structures (Luerssen, 2001). Diffuse brain injuries, which are initiated by distortion of the brain after acceleration or deceleration motion, may produce extensive disruption of neurologic function. Diffuse axonal injury and alterations in neurotransmitter function contribute to chronic impairment of neuronal networks (Hayes & Dixon, 1994). Widespread microscopic lesions in the cerebral white matter have been implicated as the primary pathophysiological substrate for diffuse injuries. These white matter injuries yield clinical syndromes varying from mild concussion to prolonged coma. The forces produced by acceleration/deceleration motion initiate a process of delayed axonal injury that produces heterogeneous axonal changes ranging from temporary disturbances of ionic homeostasis to complete shearing of axons (Gennarelli, Thibault, & Graham, 1998). TBI also initiates release of a cascade of excitotoxic neurotransmitters that can cause additional widespread neuronal injury and chronic alteration in cellular functions (Povlishock, 2000). Recent animal models of TBI identified time-linked biphasic changes in physiological processes. The biphasic hypothesis posits an acute phase of excessive neuronal excitation and elevated cerebral metabolism after TBI, which is followed by a chronic state of depressed cholinergic function and decreased cerebral metabolism (Hamm, Temple, Buck, Deford, & Floyd, 2000). Secondary brain injury occurs when healthy cells are compromised because of other local or systemic stresses, including cerebral edema/swelling, increased intracranial pressure, and hypoxic-ischemic injury produced by reduced blood flow and oxygen delivery (Novack, Dillon, & Jackson, 1996). Recent investigations have implicated genetic vulnerability to neuronal injury, such as related to the apolipoprotein E epsilon 4 allele, as impacting initial morbidity and eventual outcome (Samatovicz, 2000).

In children and adolescents with moderate-to-severe TBI, mass lesions are frequently visualized on magnetic resonance imaging (MRI) scans. In a series of TBI patients consecutively admitted to an acute pediatric trauma unit, 71% had hemispheric lesions. Subsequent MRI studies disclosed focal areas of abnormal signal intensity in 75% of children; lesions most frequently occurred in the dorsolateral frontal, orbitofrontal, and frontal lobe white matter (Levin et al., 1997). Diffuse injury is often manifested as cerebral atrophy on long-term structural imaging scans (Bigler, 2001; Levin, Benavidez et al., 2000).

NEUROPSYCHOLOGICAL OUTCOME STUDIES

Intellectual Outcomes

Prospective longitudinal studies of intellectual recovery after severe TBI in children ages 5–15 years of age at the time of injury typically report initial reduction in both Verbal and Performance IQ scores; 6 months to 1 year after TBI, the Performance IQ score remains impaired relative to the Verbal IQ score and a relatively stable pattern of intellectual functioning is obtained. By 1 year after TBI, the mean IQ scores for mild, moderate, and severe TBI groups were in the average range (Chadwick, Rutter, Brown, Shaffer, & Traub, 1981a; Jaffe et al., 1993). Patterns of posttraumatic IQ scores are quite heterogeneous (Donders, 1993) and have substantial variability from interrelationships with other variables, such as preinjury IQ, socioeconomic status, and family functioning (Max et al., 1999; Taylor, Yeates, Wade, Drotar, & Klein, 1999; Yeates et al., 1997).

Attention and Memory

Although attentional deficits are common during the early stages of recovery from TBI (Chadwick, Rutter, Shaffer, & Shrout, 1981b; Jaffe et al., 1992), some investigators have not identified persisting injury severity group differences at least 1 year after the injury (Chadwick et al., 1981b; Kinsella et al., 1995; Perrot, Taylor, & Montes, 1991). Long-term follow-up studies ranging from 6 months to 8 years after TBI have noted persisting impairment on measures of psychomotor speed and accuracy, divided attention, focused attention, shifting attention, and sustained attention (Dennis, Wilkinson, Koski, & Humphreys, 1995; Ewing-Cobbs et al., 1998d; Kaufmann, Fletcher, Levin, Miner, & Ewing-Cobbs, 1993; Knights et al., 1991; Levin et al., 1993; Murray, Shum, & McFarland, 1992). In contrast, severity group differences are not consistently identified on attentional indices reflecting encoding verbal information, such as on the Digit Span subtest or Freedom from Distractibility Index (Donders, 1993; Kaufmann et al., 1993; Warschausky, Kewman, & Selim, 1996).

Children with severe TBI consistently showed a significantly slower rate of learning and a reduction in the amount of information acquired on verbal list learning tests than children with lesser injuries (Di Stefano et al., 2000; Jaffe et al., 1993; Kinsella et al., 1997; Levin et al., 1988, 1993; Roman et al., 1998; Yeates, Blumenstein, Patterson, & Delis, 1995). Patients with severe TBI did not consistently show differences in verbal learning characteristics, such as clustering words in terms of their meaning or in consistency of recall over trials (Jaffe et al., 1993; Yeates et al., 1995). Anderson and colleagues (1997) identified impairments persisting for 1 year after severe TBI on a story recall task, but not on a test of everyday memory. The few studies of visual memory indicated impairment after severe TBI on visual recognition memory (Levin et al., 1988) and spatial span tasks, but not on a spatial learning task.

Discourse

Although children infrequently show persisting aphasia after severe TBI, impairments in discourse are prominent (Dennis & Lovett, 1990). Discourse tasks assess the use of language in social contexts. Long-term deficits in discourse have been characterized by difficulty in the areas of interpreting ambiguous sentences and metaphors, drawing inferences, and developing sentences using specific parts of speech (Dennis & Barnes, 1990). Story retelling tasks revealed sparse narratives characterized by a significant loss of information, difficulties correctly sequencing the narrative, as well as loss of story structure that contributed to impoverished and disjointed content (Chapman et al., 1992, 2001; Chapman, Levin, Wanek, Weyrauch, & Kufera, 1998; Ewing-Cobbs, Brookshire, Scott, & Fletcher, 1998a). In addition to deficits in gist recall, deficits in inferencing (Barnes & Dennis, 2001) and summarization (Chapman, 1998) further compromise the communicative, social, and academic skills of children with severe TBI.

Executive Functions

Executive functions refer to a group of related but separable higher order cognitive abilities, including planning, impulse control, working memory, maintenance of mental set, attentional control (Roberts & Pennington, 1996), metacognition, as well as development and implementation of strategies for problem solving (Pennington, 1994). Metacognitive skills enable children to assess their knowledge, monitor their cognitive activities, and deploy strategies to solve problems. Dennis and colleagues identified impaired metacognitive skills involving knowledge appraisal and knowledge management; poorer performance was noted in children younger than 7 years at the time of injury, as well as in children with lower Glasgow Coma Scale scores, frontal lobe contusions with coma, bilateral brain contusions, and/or left-sided brain contusions (Dennis, Barnes, Donnelly, Wilkinson, & Humphreys, 1996).

Longitudinal studies by Levin and colleagues (1993, 1994, 1996, 2001) revealed significant relationships between performance on executive function tasks, severity of injury, and age. In general, younger (6- to 10-year-old) children with severe TBI demonstrated more consistent impairment than older (11- to 16-year-old) children with TBI on tasks evaluating concept formation-problem solving, semantic clustering on verbal memory responses, planning, verbal fluency, design fluency, and response inhibitory control. Severely injured older children and adolescents showed impairment relative to normal control children only on measures of concept formation-problem solving, verbal fluency, design fluency, and planning.

These neuropsychological outcome studies highlight the persistent deficits commonly present after TBI that interfere with educational progress. Difficulties in the areas of abstraction, dysregulation of attention and behavior, decreases in the rate of learning new information, disruption of metacognitive processes, and difficulty producing and processing oral and written discourse create significant academic and social challenges.

PSYCHIATRIC AND SOCIAL ISSUES

Lifetime and Novel Psychiatric Disorders

Studies of lifetime (pre- and postinjury onset) and novel (postinjury onset) psychiatric disorders identified high rates of both pre-existing and novel disorders that impact educational interventions. The rate of lifetime and novel disorders varies with the severity of TBI. Max and colleagues (1997b) estimated that 52% of a prospective cohort exhibited lifetime psychiatric disorders. Both Max et al. (1998a) and Brown, Chadwick, Shaffer, Rutter, and Traub (1981) reported a higher rate of pre-existing disorders in children with mild TBI (38% and

31%, respectively) than children with more severe TBI (25% and 14%, respectively). Novel psychiatric disorders develop most commonly after severe TBI (Bloom et al., 2001; Brown et al., 1981; Gerring et al., 1998; Max et al., 1998b).

Novel Disorders

Attention deficit hyperactivity disorder (ADHD) and internalizing disorders are the most frequent lifetime disorders, as well as novel disorders arising after TBI. Bloom and colleagues (2001) identified that 44% of their sample met either full criteria for an ADHD subtype or demonstrated prominent cognitive symptoms of ADHD yielding a diagnosis of ADHD not otherwise specified. Symptoms persisted in all children with novel ADHD. Depressive disorders and anxiety disorders, which were the second and third most common novel disorders, typically resolved. Gerring and colleagues (1998) found that 15% of children with no preinjury history of ADHD, who had sustained moderate-to-severe TBI, developed secondary ADHD. Importantly, 19% of children sustaining moderate-to-severe TBI met full diagnostic criteria for ADHD before their injuries. Max et al. (1998b) reported that the most frequent diagnoses following severe TBI were organic personality disorder (54%), major depressive disorder (25%), and ADHD (21%).

Social Adjustment and Adaptive Behavior

In relation to preinjury levels, children often experience a significant decrease in adaptive behavioral competency and a decline in participation in social activities after moderate-to-severe TBI (Asarnow, Satz, & Light, 1991; Fletcher et al., 1996; Fletcher, Ewing-Cobbs, Miner, Levin, & Eisenberg, 1990). Administration of social problem-solving tasks revealed variable levels of competency in different studies. Children sustaining brain injuries from a variety of etiologies showed age-appropriate ability to generate positive strategies for managing social situations and were as adept as peers for selecting appropriate strategies from alternatives (Lewis, Morris, Morris, Krawiecki, & Foster, 2000). In contrast, other investigators noted that TBI children had more difficulty than matched peers generating multiple solutions to peer situations, especially peer entry situations (Warschausky, Cohen, Parker, Levendosdy, & Okun, 1997). Children with severe TBI showed difficulty managing conflict, coordinating play with peers, and maintaining intimacy in their closest friendships (Bohnert & Parker, 1997).

Risk Factors for Adjustment Difficulties

Psychosocial adversity—such as parental marital conflict, parental psychiatric disorder, and/or the child's preinjury behavioral characteristics—are important factors in predicting new posttraumatic psychiatric disturbance (Brown et al., 1981). Max and colleagues (1997a) reported that preinjury family dysfunction was a significant predictor of new psychiatric disturbances throughout the entire 2-year follow-up interval. A history of family psychiatric disorder was a significant predictor through the first postinjury year, whereas injury severity was a significant predictor through the first 6 months and from 1 to 2 years postinjury. Butler, Rourke, Fuerst, and Fisk (1997) noted that children with a pattern of severe, persistent deficits, on a wide array of intelligence, neuropsychological, and academic instruments may be at increased risk for problems related to social isolation, withdrawal, and emotional lability.

Preinjury family environmental factors are significant predictors of cognitive and behavioral outcome at 12 months after injury above and beyond that explained by level of injury severity (Rivara et al., 1994; Yeates et al., 1997). Preinjury family environment was found to buffer the impact of deficits, such as poor memory in severe TBI children from high functioning families and exacerbate the effect of injury in low functioning families. Severely injured children from poorly functioning families tended to have a less rapid recovery and greater deficits at 12 months after TBI than children from more functional families (Yeates et al., 1997). Postinjury problems were reported by parents and teachers that related to poor academic performance, behavior problems, trouble adapting to demands of everyday living, and stressful parent–child relationships, compared with siblings (Perrot et al., 1991).

INTERVENTIONS FOR BEHAVIORAL AND EXECUTIVE SYSTEM DYSFUNCTION

As previously noted, there is significant overlap in characteristic symptoms of TBI and ADHD in nearly half of the children with moderate-to-severe TBI. The comorbidity rates of the two conditions range from 19% preinjury to 15% postinjury (Gerring et al., 1998) to 44% for lifetime rates (Bloom et al., 2001). Bloom and colleagues noted that preinjury symptoms were consistent with ADHD Hyperactive-Impulsive or Combined Types; however, postinjury symptoms reflected predominantly cognitive rather than behavioral symptoms of ADHD (Bloom et al., 2001). Both ADHD and TBI are characterized by marked dysregulation of executive functions. Therefore, the intervention literature evaluating approaches to ADHD will be briefly reviewed.

Pharmacological intervention with stimulant medication has been the most frequently used intervention for ADHD. Recent findings from a multicenter, randomized clinical trial of children with ADHD indicated that pharmacological intervention alone and in combination with intensive behavioral intervention was superior to behavioral interventions alone or routine community care (Jensen et al., 2001b). Investigation of treatment efficacy for ADHD subtypes revealed that children with comorbid anxiety disorders responded equally well to behavioral and medication treatments. Children with ADHD only or ADHD with comorbid externalizing disorders responded best to medication treatments with or without behavioral treatments, and children with multiple comorbid disorders responded optimally to combined medication and behavioral treatments (Jensen et al., 2001a). Despite significant short-term effects, including positive effects on classroom performance and decreases in disruptive behavior, treatment with stimulant medication has not shown measurable effects in areas such as academic achievement (Pelham & Gnagy, 1999). In a recent review of the efficacy of a variety of behavioral interventions for ADHD, Pelham and Gnagny (1999) concluded that programs using clinical behavior therapy, contingency management, or a combination of these approaches were efficacious; cognitive behavioral approaches were not. Barkley and colleagues (2000) reported similar findings from extensive studies of intensive interventions for young children with disruptive behaviors and identified few enduring therapeutic effects of treatment (Shelton et al., 2000). Although externalizing disorders respond well to comprehensive treatments—including parent training, school intervention, child intervention, and medication—it is unknown which interventions are most efficacious for children with comorbid disorders, including learning disabilities and brain injury. Although stimulant medication shows promise for treatment of secondary ADHD (Hornyak, Nelson, & Hurvitz, 1997), issues involving the dosage of medication, intensity of behavioral interventions, timing of onset of different treatment components, duration of treatment, and generalization remain unclear.

Cognitive-behavioral therapy consists of several techniques involving teaching cognitive mediational strategies to assist children in guiding their behavior. Meta-analysis of variables that moderate efficacy of cognitive-behavior therapy revealed that the single most important moderator of outcome was the child's cognitive developmental level. Durlak, Fuhrman, and Lampman (1991) noted that studies of children ages 11–13 yielded an effect size almost twice that of children ages 5–11. Gains were quite impressive, and posttreatment effects were durable across an average follow-up of 4 months, particularly in children ages 7–11. Intervention produced meaningful improvements in children's adjustment. Robinson and colleagues (1999) noted that meta-analysis of school-based cognitive behavior modification interventions for adolescents with ADHD supported the efficacy of these techniques for reducing hyperactivity, impulsivity, and aggression; treatment effects were generally maintained over time. Cohen and Schleser (1984) characterized the cognitive skills underlying therapeutic change to include attention and memory, language, conditional thinking, understanding and using rules, social perception, discrimination learning, and metacognition. It is unclear whether these techniques are best suited for internalizing versus externalizing disorders, or how the cognitive and metacognitive deficits associated with TBI may impact outcome.

In a recent review of empirically supported psychological and behavioral therapies in pediatric TBI, Warshausky, Kewman, and Kay (1999) noted that most reviews have discussed behavioral interventions for externalizing features or strategies for cognitive skill acquisition with less emphasis on interventions for psychological distress. Although operant conditioning has yielded positive results in decreasing aggressive behavior, maintenance of behavior has been inconsistent. Despite the lack of empirical studies, Warshausky and colleagues (1999) advocated for studies of treatment of internalizing conditions, particularly those using cognitive-behavioral therapies; coping skills training, particularly for adolescents; and school-based intervention emphasizing social skills training.

In the absence of research to guide selection of interventions, the types of interventions that are most efficacious will likely depend on (1) the child's preinjury adjustment and presence of comorbid disorders, (2) availability of family support systems, (3) presence of psychosocial adversity, (4) severity of injury and postinjury levels of functioning, and (5) age. For children sustaining the most severe injuries who may have impaired inhibition and limited abstraction, operant conditioning and contingency management techniques are well-suited to managing specific behavioral issues. Younger children and/or children with preinjury histories of significant externalizing disorders may also require more structured environmental manipulations to decrease undesired behaviors and shape more desirable behaviors. Older children and adolescents may benefit from a larger array of interventions, including social skills training and other cognitive-behavioral techniques. Both individual and group interventions may be effective. Group interventions may enhance awareness of deficits and provide ecologically valid contexts for development of social skills. Standard interventions will likely need to be adjusted to accommodate posttraumatic disruption of attention, reduced efficiency of learning and memory, diminished problem-solving capacity, impaired inhibition and/or initiation, impaired awareness of deficits, and reduced pragmatic language skills. Programs may need to be simplified, taught more systematically with emphasis on step-by-step progression, incorporate substantial repetition and practice of skills, address issues of importance to children and their families, and be structured to maximize generalization. Children from families with multiple psychosocial stressors may require more intensive and extended services incorporating a family component to realize meaningful gains. Supportive psychotherapy is often helpful in assisting children to manage issues related to bereavement for the many short-term and long-term personal and familial losses incurred as a result of their accidents.

ASSESSMENT AND EDUCATIONAL ISSUES

Neuropsychological Assessment

Assessment is an integral part of transition and long-term planning. Because of the rapid rate of recovery in the first year after TBI, assessments need to be performed more often than the traditional 3-year interval. Assessments should be updated several times during the first year, and then completed annually for the first 3 years after the injury.

To meet federal guidelines for assessment of children with potential disabilities, the comprehensive individual assessment must encompass word decoding, reading comprehension, written language, mathematical reasoning and calculation, oral expression, and listening comprehension. Children also must be assessed in areas of suspected disabilities. For children with TBI, evaluations must also include standardized assessments of motor, visual-motor, attention, memory, discourse, and executive functions. The executive function deficits often associated with TBI contribute to deficits in academic performance (Ewing-Cobbs & Bloom, 1999). Because psychoeducational and neuropsychological evaluations are very structured and are conducted in quiet settings with individualized administration, the influence of executive system dysfunction may be masked by the structure inherent in the testing environment. Executive dysfunction commonly produces either disinhibition or impaired initiation. To identify executive dysfunction, it is essential that comprehensive assessments include school observation and work samples. Assessments must include contextually valid observations in situations that contain more realistic levels of stress, expectations for independent production of work, distracting conditions, and time pressures. Observation in the classroom setting is essential to see if the child can independently orient to instructions, initiate appropriate activity, organize materials, follow directions, complete tasks within a time limit, and maintain appropriate behavior. Observation during less structured free time or recess is helpful for evaluation of the level of social competence, self-management skills, and peer acceptance. Although certain abilities and skills are often disrupted by severe TBI, an individualized assessment plan for each child should incorporate evaluation of possible comorbid disorders, as well as strengths. Ylvisaker and colleagues (2001) note that assessment should be flexible and identify possible gaps in knowledge at lower levels and preserved strengths at higher levels; traditional basal and ceiling conventions may need to be adjusted. Because outcomes are often less favorable in younger children than in older children and adolescents in a variety of areas, careful attention to assessment of diverse abilities in young children is essential (Anderson, Catroppa, Morse, Haritou, & Rosenfeld, 2000; Ewing-Cobbs, Fletcher, Levin, Francis, Davidson, & Miner, 1997; Levin & Ewing-Cobbs, 2001).

Educational Issues

After severe TBI, children experience changes in their physical, cognitive, and emotional status that impact all aspects of daily living. Moreover, many children experience loss of significant others in the accident and must often adjust to changes within themselves, as well as to significant changes in their home and school environments. Multimodal interventions that extend for several years are often required to maximize the child's recovery from the injury, adjustment to posttraumatic social and psychological changes, differences in learning competencies, as well as self-management issues. Because of increasingly restrictive and/or limited access to rehabilitation services, the schools have become the primary agent of intervention for many children with TBI. This shift in service provision from rehabilitation specialists to educational specialists necessitates additional training and education for education professionals. Although the incidence of TBI is very high, it is uncommon for many children identified with TBI to be enrolled in any given public school, which decreases the ability of educational professionals to obtain experience assessing neuropsychological strengths and weaknesses for the comprehensive individualized assessment; to contribute to development of individualized education plans that address the child's learning and behavioral in/competencies; to ascertain need for rehabilitation interventions, including speech/language, occupational, and physical therapies; to provide related psychological services; and to assist with monitoring and revision of the educational plan. Increased training of educators and school psychologists is essential to improve service delivery to youth with TBI. Walker, Boling, and Cobb (1999) recently reported on a national survey of training of school psychologists in neuropsychology and brain injury. They identified striking limitations in the availability of full-time faculty with expertise in developmental neuropsychology, few programs requiring a complete course in neuropsychology, and minimal instructional emphasis on interventions and educational placement issues.

Academic Skill Issues

Successful return to an academic setting is related to several cognitive and behavioral factors, such as level of academic skill development, processing speed, attention, and self-management skills. Although academic scores often recover to the average range in school-aged children and adolescents after moderate-to-severe TBI, these average scores are not paralleled by average academic performance. Ewing-Cobbs and colleagues (1998b) followed children and adolescents for 2 years after mild/moderate and severe TBI; only 21% of severely injured children and adolescents were promoted each year and received a regular educational curriculum despite generally average achievement scores.

Studies comparing Wide Range Achievement Test (Jastak & Wilkinson, 1984) scores in different content areas revealed that reading recognition scores were relatively spared, whereas arithmetic scores were the most vulnerable to disruption by TBI (Berger-Gross & Shackelford, 1985; Ewing-Cobbs et al., 1998b). The sensitivity of the arithmetic subtest may be due in part to the demands of the task for both speed and power; the reading recognition and spelling subtests are untimed. The few studies assessing reading comprehension suggested mild reduction in scores related to the severity of injury (Barnes, Dennis, & Wilkinson, 1999; Ewing-Cobbs, Fletcher, Levin, Iovino, & Miner, 1998b).

In contrast to the generally good recovery of academic achievement test scores, indices of academic performance often show persistent deficits. Donders (1994), Kinsella et al. (1995), and Ewing-Cobbs et al. (1998b) identified that children with severe TBI were significantly more likely to receive special educational services than children with milder injuries 1–2 years after the injury. Comparison of group-administered academic achievement test scores from school records revealed that significant declines were noted in language and reading comprehension areas from 1 to 2 years before the injury to 3 years after TBI (Stallings, Ewing-Cobbs, Francis, & Fletcher, 1995). Other indices of academic performance, such as classroom grades, declined in severely injured children (Jaffe, Polissar, Fay, & Liao, 1995). Parent ratings of academic competence indicated that severe TBI was associated with significant declines from preinjury academic performance (Ewing-Cobbs et al., 1998b; Fay et al., 1994; Rivara et al., 1994; Taylor et al., 1999). Achievement scores and ratings of academic competence remained lower in children with severe TBI, in comparison with those with mild/moderate TBI for 2–5 years, suggesting persistent academic deficits (Ewing-Cobbs et al., in press).

Educational Intervention Issues

Early initiatives geared toward educating the TBI student were predicated on the assumption that grouping students with a common disability in classrooms would improve service delivery. As Cooley and Singer (1991) noted, categorical service delivery models have been displaced by service models that emphasize educational intervention in the mainstream classrooms. Once again, there is little to no empirical research to guide educational programming for TBI students. Cohen (1991) detailed strategies for adapting educational programs to accommodate the cognitive and behavioral deficits often accompanying TBI. Because TBI frequently reduces learning efficiency, educational intervention approaches based on Direct Instruction (Engleman & Carnine, 1991) instructional theories may be useful. Direct Instruction is a behavioral approach that uses task analysis, modeling, shaping of responses, reinforcement of correct responses, and continuous assessment to maximize learning. Learning is enhanced by preteaching component skills and general case problem-solving strategies, providing sufficient practice to ensure errorless mastery of each step, and cumulative review of all skills to maximize integration of new skills with previously learned information. Glang, Singer, Codey, and Tish (1992) presented case studies that illustrated the successful use of Direct Instruction approaches to remediate both cognitive and metacognitive deficits following TBI. They noted that limitations of this technique included the extensive training required for teachers to master all aspects of the approach; the in-depth knowledge of the technique required to allow teachers to individualize the approach for TBI students; and the difficulty of placing TBI students in instructional groups because of their variability in progress. Despite these caveats, the Direct Instruction approach clearly has promise for educational intervention after TBI and has an empirical basis of successful implementation in diverse groups of disabled learners (Ylvisaker & Feeney, 1998).

The errorless learning approach (Wilson, Baddeley, & Evans, 1994) may also hold promise for educational intervention for subgroups of TBI students. This approach has been used to teach children with learning disabilities and intellectual deficiency, as well as adults with severe memory disorders after TBI (Walsh & Lamberts, 1979). These populations have shown learning advantages under errorless learning conditions, where they are not allowed to make potentially distracting errors, in comparison with traditional trial-and-error learning. It is unclear which types of learning disorders will respond best to this strategy. Students with severe memory impairment and/or intellectual deficiency may learn more efficiently using errorless learning; more able students may learn better using a trial-and-learning approach due to generation of responses and accessing deeper levels of processing. Additional research is clearly needed to characterize the relative advantages of errorless learning for various types of academic material for different subgroups of TBI children.

Secondary School Issues

Education of secondary students with TBI presents additional challenges caused in part by the increased cognitive and social demands placed on students in secondary settings, as well as normal developmental changes toward increased autonomy that are often quite challenging because of the frequent dysregulation of executive functions after severe TBI. A model service delivery program for secondary students was recently presented (Sohlberg, Todis, & Glang, 1998). The Student Centered Education Management and Advocacy (SCEMA) model is a team-based program emphasizing collaboration of the student, family, educators, and medical personnel to design, implement, and evaluate the effectiveness of a compensatory cognitive system developed specifically to address the organizational challenges of individual TBI students. This model is based on the principles of Direct Instruction. Implementation of the SCEMA model, which is undergoing empirical evaluation, yielded the following qualitative themes: (1) school personnel often lack information about acquired brain injury, (2) instructional assistants require training and supervision, (3) school-based teams are resourceful, and (4) interventions need to be regarded as long-term works in progress rather than a quick fix. The SCEMA process has been questioned for the lack of empirical data and proof of efficacy (McDonald, 1998), relative passivity of the student in learning compensatory strategies (Ylvisaker & Feeney, 1998), underemphasis on issues involved in application of the SCEMA model during different stages of recovery from TBI, and limited assessment of higher order abilities tapping executive functions, such as discourse (Chapman, 1998). Ylvisaker and DeBonis (2000) emphasized the importance of placing interventions in the context of everyday routines that can be supported by others in the child's environment to create habits of self-regulatory cognitive activity and promote generalization.

TRANSITIONING TO SCHOOL

With the implementation of the Individuals with Disabilities Education Act (IDEA, 1990), TBI was recognized as a separate category of special education disability. Before this, special education eligibility for students with TBI had to be justified under disability categories for students with chronic health issues (i.e., other health impaired), or mapped onto special education categories for students with dissimilar disabilities and educational needs, such as learning disabilities, mental retardation, or emotional disturbance. Under IDEA, a TBI was defined from an educational perspective as an acquired brain injury (not the result of congenital or degenerative etiologies or birth trauma) caused by an external physical force resulting in total or partial functional disability or psychosocial impairment, or both in one or more areas of cognition, language, memory, attention, reasoning, abstract thinking, judgment, problem-solving, sensory, perceptual and motor abilities, psychosocial behavior, physical functions, information processing, and speech. This was an important change, because it recognized the difference in etiology, course, symptom patterns, and educational needs of students who had sustained TBI as distinct from those of students with developmental disabilities, such as learning disabilities or mental retardation, or students with emotional disturbance. Because symptom patterns differ depending on the developmental timing, severity, and location of brain injury, there is considerable variation in the pattern of competencies, deficits, and educational needs that result from moderate-to-severe TBI that need to be addressed in the process of school re-entry.

School Re-entry after TBI

Students sustaining a moderate-to-severe TBI face significant challenges in the transition from the acute care or rehabilitation hospital to home and school. Recovery from TBI-related cognitive, behavioral, and psychosocial impairment is often prolonged and frequently incomplete so that significant adjustments in expectations by the family and school, as well as the student, are required. When the child returns to the home and school settings, significant frustration and failure may result if these factors are not adequately considered and appropriate modifications in expectations not implemented.

An effective transition from the hospital to the school and community requires ongoing cooperation, flexibility, communication, and collaboration between physicians and intervention team specialists in the hospital and rehabilitation settings, educational professionals, and members of the child's family (Feeney & Ylvisaker, 1995; Savage & Mishkin, 1994). The child's school should be contacted soon after the injury so that they may receive accurate information regarding the child's current status, and tentative timelines and potential needs if possible, so that planning for the child's transition to the home and school settings can be initiated (Telzrow, 1990; Ylvisaker et al., 1995). It is beneficial to designate case managers early in this process in the hospital and educational settings. Case managers can be particularly helpful in facilitating communication between the hospital, school, and family; identifying needed services or supports for the child; providing information to professionals in the other settings regarding the child's course of recovery, including the extent of cognitive and other impairments; providing staff in-service or instructional media regarding TBI and the important role that teachers, principals, and other education professionals will play during the child's recovery period; and coordinating task assignments among the professional staff within their settings to carry out a smooth, efficient transition. It is also beneficial for educators (e.g., teachers, administrators) to visit the hospital to make contact with the child and the family, and communicate directly with hospital staff regarding factors relevant to the child's educational needs. The experience and insights of medical and rehabilitation professionals who have worked with a variety of children with TBI can be particularly important in providing accurate information and assistance to teachers and other school professionals who may have had little or no previous experience with students who have sustained a TBI. Visits to the child's school by medical professionals and rehabilitation specialists can help identify potential physical barriers to the child at the school, identify appropriate educational programs and resources available in the school, and assist the school in other aspects of short- and long-term planning efforts relevant to the child's return to school.

With regard to when a student may be ready for a return to school, Cohen (1986) identified several competencies that the child or adolescent should demonstrate. These include the ability to sustain attention for 10–15 min; tolerate 20–30 min of classroom stimulation, such as distractions or noise; be able to function within a group of two or more students; communicate meaningfully; follow simple directions; and have sufficient recovery to demonstrate learning potential. If a child does not demonstrate these competencies, temporary alternatives to classroom placement, such as additional interventions in the rehabilitation setting, homebound services, or significantly shortened school day with corresponding reduction in educational expectations, may be considered until additional recovery has occurred.

A number of factors should be considered in planning for the return to school of children and adolescents who have sustained TBI. These students frequently return to school with significant impairment in learning and memory, attention, executive functions, speed of information processing, or other cognitive or motor functions that can profoundly impact academic learning and performance. In addition, factors such as reduced stamina for physical or and mental activities, behavioral disinhibition, increased distractibility in group settings, reduced motivation, denial or unawareness of deficits, and lower tolerance for academic and social frustrations also frequently interfere with a smooth school re-entry and need to be considered in transition planning (Lehr, 1990). The returning student may appear to have fully recovered on the basis of physical appearance and discharge from medical care. However, cognitive recovery generally occurs at a slower rate and is often incomplete. As time since injury lengthens and there are few if any outward manifestations of injury, failure to complete schoolwork or chores may be attributed to a lack of motivation, laziness, or oppositional behavior when in fact the child continues to be affected by cognitive impairment, reduced stamina and frustration tolerance, emotional reactions (e.g., anxiety, depression) related to increasing awareness in the child or adolescent that they are not the same as before, and the cumulative effects of problems with learning and memory, inattention, and executive functions on academic learning. Therefore, it is crucially important that teachers and parents are aware of this fact so that the cause of the problems can be accurately identified and appropriate interventions provided. Appropriate educational modifications need to be implemented, such as homebound instruction, attendance at school for a half day (or less) initially, scheduled rest breaks during the school day, small group or individual instruction, slower pace of instruction, reduced length of tests or daily assignments, testing that relies more on recognition memory than recall, or selective requirements for makeup assignments that facilitate instructional objectives and follow direct instruction of material.

Factors in the child's preinjury history (e.g., academic performance levels, prior history of an attentional or learning disorder, behavioral adjustment) interact with the TBI to influence the child's postinjury behavior and academic performance. Being aware of these factors would help educators more accurately understand the contribution of the TBI, as well as preinjury factors, on current behavior and performance. Although the impact of TBI is often uncertain in the individual child, an accurate understanding of the child's background, as well as an understanding of the nature and severity of the current injury and its consequences on cognitive functioning and behavior, will assist school professionals in appropriately planning for the child's needs on school re-entry. Therefore, more frequent assessments using both standardized and functional (i.e., related to real-world tasks and expectations) assessment procedures in addition to more frequent educational program reviews are required to monitor changes during periods of rapid recovery to revise educational plans based on the current stage of recovery and corresponding educational needs (D'Amato & Rothlisberg, 1996; Savage & Mishkin, 1994). Information regarding the child's TBI and the educational implications of the injury need to be effectively communicated to the child's teachers in each succeeding grade to increase understanding of the child's needs so that appropriate expectations and educational interventions will be provided. This may include introduction of additional educational services, such as resource room instruction; and personal or career counseling, vocational programs, such as work-study programs, involvement of vocational rehabilitation specialists in high school planning meetings, or review of accommodations available at colleges that students wish to attend. At the same time, there can be significant benefit from efforts to help students learn how to cope and adjust to real-world situations and settings where intensive supports such as those they received during their school years are either unavailable or cannot be expected. Ylvisaker et al. (1995) recommend a systematic, planned withdrawal of support as part of an educational program in the years after TBI. This may not only assist students in becoming more independent, but also increase their insight and awareness of their strengths and weaknesses, help them develop strategies for circumventing obstacles, increase their awareness of the possibility and consequences of failure, and assist them in revising intervention plans so that they are geared toward realistic future goals.

When the student returns to the classroom after TBI, Ylvisaker and colleagues (1995) emphasized that academic, behavioral, or cognitive interventions are most likely to be maintained when they are provided in familiar everyday settings, such as the child's regular classroom within the context of established daily routines. Furthermore, traditional behavior management techniques, wherein consequences are provided for rule infractions, may not be as effective with students who have sustained frontal lobe injury, because they often experience difficulty regulating their behavior. Instead, Ylvisaker and associates recommend modifying antecedent conditions that potentially produce behavioral difficulties. Examples include preventing negative behavior by eliminating potential frustrations, such as unreasonable demands, ensuring that the child understands and attends to the task, preceding difficult tasks with easier tasks that ensure success, and desensitizing the student to situations that arouse anxiety (Ylvisaker et al., 1995).

D'Amato and Rothlisberg (1996) emphasized prevention of learning or behavioral difficulties by modifying intervention methods to incorporate interventions to incorporate structure, organization, and development of strategies (S.O.S.). These modifications are applicable when working with students with TBI who demonstrate adequate basic academic skills, but exhibit difficulty in the application of these skills to everyday academic and daily activities from injury-related impairment in organizational skills, problem solving, memory, attention, and difficulties with social relationships. They define structure as referring to the extent of physical organization necessary for optimal learning with a safety net in place in situations where structure is reduced. In context, this might include such factors as providing clear academic and behavioral expectations for the child; developing a consistent, predictable routine; providing a learning environment that is quiet and relatively free of distractions through the use of study carrels, headphones, or special learning areas when necessary; modifying the school day or work assignments in accordance with the student's stamina; organizing teaching methods in a manner that provides structure and substance to learning activities; and allowing the child to work with the same teacher throughout the school year and possibly for more than 1 year to facilitate continuity of teacher and educational programming. D'Amato and Rothlisberg (1996) noted that increased structure helps bring the child a sense of order and stability out of the confusion created by the impact of the injury. D'Amato and Rothlisberg (1996) and Telzrow (1990) refer to organization as environmental cues and aids that facilitate learning acquisition and retrieval of previous learning. These might include assistance in relearning strategies for learning, such as how to locate information, determining what is important, planning a structured approach to completing each stage of a task, revising plans when a plan fails, and continuing the task to completion with revisions when needed (D'Amato & Rothlisberg, 1996; Savage & Mishkin, 1994). Providing students with a clear schedule of upcoming activities; using daily planners or organizers; providing the students with objective sheets, including key words and concepts; and using multimodal instructional cues are some of the means by which organization can be enhanced for students with TBI in presenting instructional information. Modifications to increase organization in work assignments—such as compensating for poor note-taking skills by allowing tape recording of instructional lessons or allowing duplication of class notes, allowing extended deadlines, or providing alternate means of assessing performance—may also be helpful. For older students, transitional programs emphasizing career education and job training with opportunities to increase career awareness and to practice vocational skills in a structured setting with observation and feedback can be extremely valuable (Sachs & Redd, 1993). Activities such as structured modeled performance, job coaching, or on-the job training help prepare students for transitions to vocational settings. D'Amato and Rothlisberg (1996) also recommend that teachers instruct students in learning strategies that are appropriate to age and capabilities to assist them in using problem-solving procedures that increase learning efficiency. These might include compensatory approaches in which students use stronger skills and work around areas of impairment; teaching alternative means for solving problems or completing work; using appropriate models and feedback to facilitate academic and social learning; and directly teaching academic or social skills with the use of cues, clear expectations, and ample opportunities to practice the skills in a variety of contexts. It is hoped that this brief review of school re-entry and transition issues demonstrates that the student who sustains a TBI requires multidisciplinary collaboration and consistent communication among professionals within the medical, rehabilitation, and school settings, as well as the family. Consequently, there needs to be a shared knowledge base and extensive, ongoing planning and problem solving starting shortly after injury and continuing as long as required to meet the multidimensional needs of students who suffer a TBI.

CONCLUSION

The neuropsychological consequences of TBI reflect a complex combination of the characteristics of the injury and the child's status before the injury in cognitive, psychiatric, and family domains. Variables related to the injury itself—such as the duration of impaired consciousness, severity of diffuse brain injury, and the presence of focal/multifocal brain lesions—interact with the child's preinjury characteristics and the child's developmental level at the time of injury to produce heterogeneous deficits and recovery characteristics. Even though group studies have documented that many children have difficulties in executive functions, speed of information processing, oral and written discourses, attention, and memory, the pattern and severity of deficits will vary considerably from child to child. Despite significant alteration in intellectual and executive functions, children may score well on tests that assess previously learned skills or knowledge and tests of specific abilities, such as word decoding. Assessment must incorporate ecologically valid assessment not only of the child's knowledge base, but also of their ability to learn and apply knowledge in new contexts. Therefore, careful assessment of each child's functioning in varied cognitive, psychiatric, and social domains is essential.

The literature examining psychiatric and educational interventions for children with TBI is in its infancy. Future studies should characterize benefits of pharmacological intervention, different psychotherapeutic approaches, and behavioral interventions for children at different developmental levels with differing posttraumatic symptoms and various levels of functioning. Research on educational interventions should characterize optimal strategies for school re-entry of children of differing ages and functional levels, examine instructional theories that may suggest strategies that optimize learning new skills and generalization of concepts, and evaluate techniques to promote social integration.

ACKNOWLEDGMENTS

Preparation of this chapter was supported in part by the National Institutes of Health Grants R01 NS 29462, R01 NS 21889, R01 HD 27597, and by the U.S. Department of Education Grants H133B990014 and H133B40002.

REFERENCES

Anderson, V. A., Catroppa, C., Morse, S., Haritou, F., & Rosenfeld, J. (2000). Recovery of intellectual ability following traumatic brain injury in childhood: Impact of injury severity and age at injury. *Pediatric Neurosurgery, 32*, 282–290.

Anderson, V., Morse, S. A., Klug, G., Catroppa, C., Haritou, F., Rosenfeld, J., & Pentland, L. (1997). Predicting recovery from head injury in young children: A prospective analysis. *Journal of the International Neuropsychological Society, 3*, 568–580.

Asarnow, R. F., Satz, P., & Light, R. (1991). Behavioral problems and adaptive functioning in children with mild and severe closed head injury. *Journal of Pediatric Psychology, 16*, 543–555.

Barkley, R. A., Shelton, T., Crosswait, C., Moorehouse, M., Fletcher, K., Barrett, S., Jenkins, L., & Metevia, L. (2000). Multi-method psycho-educational intervention for preschool children with disruptive behavior: Preliminary results at post-treatment. *Journal of Child Psychology and Psychiatry, 41*, 319–332.

Barnes, M. A., & Dennis, M. (2001). Knowledge-based inferencing after childhood head injury. *Brain and Language, 76*, 253–265.

Barnes, M. A., Dennis, M., & Wilkinson, M. (1999). Reading after closed head injury in childhood: Effects on accuracy, fluency, and comprehension. *Developmental Neuropsychology, 15*, 1–24.

Berger-Gross, P., & Shackelford, M. (1985). Closed head injury in children: Neuropsychological and scholastic outcomes. *Perceptual and Motor Skills, 61*, 254.

Bigler, E. (2001). Quantitative magnetic resonance imaging in traumatic brain injury. *Journal of Head Trauma Rehabilitation, 16*, 117–134.

Bloom, D. R., Levin, H., Ewing-Cobbs, L., Saunders, A., Song, J., Fletcher, J., & Kowatch, R. (2001). Lifetime and novel psychiatric disorders after pediatric traumatic brain injury. *Journal of the American Academy of Child and Adolescent Psychiatry, 40*, 572–579.

Bohnert, A., & Parker, J. (1997). Friendship and social adjustment of children following a traumatic brain injury: An exploratory investigation. *Developmental Neuropsychology, 13*, 477–486.

Brown, G., Chadwick, O., Shaffer, D., Rutter, M., & Traub, M. (1981). A prospective study of children with head injuries: III. Psychiatric sequelae. *Psychological Medicine, 11*, 63–78.

Butler, K., Rourke, B. P., Fuerst, D. R., & Fisk, J. L. (1997). A typology of psychosocial functioning in pediatric closed-head injury. *Child Neuropsychology, 3*, 98–133.

Chadwick, O., Rutter, M., Brown, G., Shaffer, D., & Traub, M. (1981a). A prospective study of children with head injuries: II. Cognitive sequelae. *Psychological Medicine, 11*, 49–61.

Chadwick, O., Rutter, M., Shaffer, D., & Shrout, P. E. (1981b). A prospective study of children with head injuries: IV. Specific cognitive deficits. *Journal of Clinical Neuropsychology, 3*, 101–120.

Chapman, S. (1998). Bridging the gap between research and education reintegration: Direct instruction on processing connected discourse. *Aphasiology, 12*, 1081–1088.

Chapman, S., Culhane, K. A., Levin, H. S., Harward, H., Mendelsohn, D., Ewing-Cobbs, L., Fletcher, J. M., & Bruce, D. A. (1992). Narrative discourse after closed head injury in children and adolescents. *Brain and Language, 43*, 42–65.

Chapman, S. B., Levin, H. S., Wanek, A., Weyrauch, J., & Kufera, J. (1998). Discourse after closed head injury in young children. *Brain and Language, 61*, 420–449.

Chapman, S. B., McKinnon, L., Levin, H. S., Song, J., Meier, M. C., & Chiu, S. (2001). Longitudinal outcome of verbal discourse in children with traumatic brain injury: Three-year follow-up. *Journal of Head Trauma Rehabilitation, 16*, 441–455.

Cohen, R. A. & Schleser, R. (1984). Cognitive development and clinical interventions. In W. E. Craighead (Ed.), *Cognitive behavior therapy with children* (pp. 45–68). New York: Plenum Press.

Cohen, S. (1986). Education reintegration and programming for children with head injuries. *Journal of Head Trauma Rehabilitation, 1*, 22–29.

Cohen, S. (1991). Adapting educational programs for students with head injuries. *Journal of Head Trauma Rehabilitation, 6*, 56–63.

Cooley, E., & Singer, G. (1991). On serving students with head injuries: Are we reinventing a wheel that doesn't roll? *Journal of Head Trauma Rehabilitation, 6*, 47–55.

D'Amato, R., & Rothlisberg, B. (1996). How education should respond to students with traumatic brain injury. *Journal of Learning Disabilities, 29*, 670–683.

Dennis, M., & Barnes, M. A. (1990). Knowing the meaning, getting the point, bridging the gap, and carrying the message: Aspects of discourse following closed head injury in childhood adolescence. *Brain and Language, 39*, 428–446.

Dennis, M., Barnes, M. A., Donnelly, R. E., Wilkinson, M., & Humphreys, R. P. (1996). Appraising and managing knowledge: Metacognitive skills after childhood head injury. *Developmental Neuropsychology, 12*, 77–103.

Dennis, M., & Lovett, M. W. (1990). Discourse ability in children after brain damage. In Y. Joanette & H. H. Brownell (Eds.), *Discourse ability and brain damage: Theoretical and empirical perspectives.* (pp. 199–223) New York: Springer Verlag.

Dennis, M., Wilkinson, M., Koski, L., & Humphreys, R. P. (1995). Attention deficits in the long term after childhood head injury. In S. H. Broman & M. E. Michel (Eds.), *Traumatic head injury in children* (pp. 165–187). New York: Oxford University Press.

Di Stefano, G., Bachevalier, J., Levin, H. S., Song, J., Scheibel, R. S., & Fletcher, J. (2000). Volume of focal brain lesions and hippocampal formation in relation to memory function after closed head injury in children. *Journal of Neurology, Neurosurgery, and Psychiatry, 69*, 210–216.

DiScala, C., Osberg, J. S., Gans, B. M., Chin, L. J., & Grant, C. C. (1991). Children with traumatic head injury: Morbidity and postacute treatment. *Archives of Physical Medicine and Rehabilitation, 72*, 662–666.

Donders, J. (1993). WISC-R subtest patterns in children with traumatic brain injury. *Clinical Neuropsychologist, 7*, 430–442.

Donders, J. (1994). Academic placement after traumatic brain injury. *Journal of School Psychology, 32*, 53–65.

Durlak, J., Fuhrman, T., & Lampman, C. (1991). Effectiveness of cognitive-behavior therapy for maladapting children: A meta-analysis. *Psychological Bulletin, 110*, 201–214.

Engleman, S., & Carnine, D. (1991). *Theory of Instruction: Principles and application.* Eugene, OR: ADI Press.

Ewing-Cobbs, L., Barnes, M. A., Fletcher, J., Levin, H. S., Swank, P. R., & Song, J. (in press). Modeling of longitudinal academic achievement scores after pediatric traumatic brain injury. *Developmental Neuropsychology*.

Ewing-Cobbs, L., & Bloom, D. R. (1999). Traumatic brain injury. In R. Brown (Ed.), *Cognitive aspects of chronic illness in children* (pp. 262–285). New York: The Guilford Press.

Ewing-Cobbs, L., Fletcher, J. M., Levin, H. S., Francis, D. J., Davidson, K., & Miner, M. E. (1997). Longitudinal neuropsychological outcome in infants and preschoolers with traumatic brain injury. *Journal of the International Neuropsychological Society, 3*, 581–591.

Ewing-Cobbs, L., Brookshire, B., Scott, M. A., & Fletcher, J. M. (1998a). Children's narratives following traumatic brain injury: Linguistic structure, cohesion, and thematic recall. *Brain and Language, 61*, 395–419.

Ewing-Cobbs, L., Fletcher, J. M., Levin, H. S., Iovino, I., & Miner, M. E. (1998b). Academic achievement and academic placement following traumatic brain injury in children and adolescents: A two-year longitudinal study. *Journal of Clinical and Experimental Neuropsychology, 20*, 769–781.

Ewing-Cobbs, L., Levin, H. S., & Fletcher, J. (1998c). Neuropsychological sequelae after pediatric traumatic brain injury: Advances since 1985. In M.Ylvisaker (Ed.), *Traumatic brain injury rehabilitation: Children and adolescents* (2nd ed., pp. 11–26). Newton, MA: Butterworth-Heinemann.

Ewing-Cobbs, L., Prasad, M., Fletcher, J. M., Levin, H. S., Miner, M. E., & Eisenberg, H. M. (1998d). Attention after pediatric traumatic brain injury: A multidimensional assessment. *Child Neuropsychology, 4*, 35–48.

Fay, G. C., Jaffe, K. M., Polissar, N. L., Liao, S., Rivara, J., & Martin, K. M. (1994). Outcome of pediatric traumatic brain injury at three years: A cohort study. *Archives of Physical Medicine and Rehabilitation, 75*, 733–741.

Feeney, T. J., & Ylvisaker, M. (1995). Choice and routine: Antecedent behavioral interventions for adolescents with severe traumatic brain injury. *Journal of Head Trauma Rehabilitation, 10*, 67–86.

Fletcher, J. M., Ewing-Cobbs, L., Miner, M. E., Levin, H. S., & Eisenberg, H. M. (1990). Behavioral changes after closed head injury in children. *Journal of Consulting and Clinical Psychology, 58*, 93–98.

Fletcher, J. M., Levin, H. S., Lachar, D., Kusernik, L., Harward, H., Mendelsohn, D., & Lilly, M. A. (1996). Behavioral adjustment after pediatric closed head injury: Relationships with age, severity, and lesion size. *Journal of Child Neurology, 11*, 283–290.

Gennarelli, T. A., Thibault, L. E. , & Graham, D. (1998). Diffuse axonal injury: An important form of traumatic brain damage. *Neuroscientist, 4*, 202–215.

Gerring, J., Brady, K., Chen, A., Vasa, R., Gardos, M., Bandeen-Roche, K., Bryan, R., & Denckla, M. (1998). Premorbid prevalence of ADHD and development of secondary ADHD after closed head injury. *Journal of the American Academy of Child and Adolescent Psychiatry, 37*, 647–654.

Glang, A., Singer, G., Cooley, E., & Tish, N. (1992). Tailoring direct instruction techniques for use with elementary students with brain injury. *Journal of Head Trauma Rehabilitation, 7*, 93–108.

Hamm, R., Temple, M., Buck, D., Deford, S., & Floyd, C. (2000). Cognitive recovery from traumatic brain injury: Results of posttraumatic experimental interventions. In H. S. Levin & J. Grafman (Eds.), *Cerebral reorganization of function after brain damage* (pp. 49–67). New York: Oxford University Press.

Hayes, R. L., & Dixon, C. E. (1994). Neurochemical changes in mild head injury. *Seminars in Neurology, 14*, 25–31.

Hornyak, J., Nelson, V., & Hurvitz, E. (1997). The use of methyphenidate in paediatric traumatic brain injury. *Pediatric Annals, 1*, 15–17.

Hymel, K. P., Rumack, C. M., Hay, T. C., Strain, J. D., & Jenny, C. (1997). Comparison of intracranial computed tomographic (CT) findings in pediatric abusive and accidental head trauma. *Pediatric Radiology, 27*, 743–747.

Individuals with Disabilities Education Act. (1990). IDEA-PL 101–476.

Jaffe, K. M., Gayle, C. F., Polissar, N. L., Martin, K. M., Shurtleff, H., Rivara, J. B., & Winn, H. R. (1992). Severity of pediatric traumatic brain injury and early neurobehavioral outcome: A cohort study. *Archives of Physical Medicine and Rehabilitation, 73*, 540–547.

Jaffe, K. M., Gayle, C. F., Polissar, N. L., Martin, K. M., Shurtleff, H., Rivara, J. B., & Winn, H. R. (1993). Severity of pediatric traumatic brain injury and neurobehavioral recovery at one year: A cohort study. *Archives of Physical Medicine and Rehabilitation, 74*, 587–595.

Jaffe, K. M., Polissar, N. L., Fay, G. C., & Liao, S. (1995). Recovery trends over three years following pediatric traumatic brain injury. *Archives of Physical Medicine and Rehabilitation, 76*, 17–26.

Jastak, S., & Wilkinson, G. (1984). *The Wide Range Achievement Test Revised administration manual*. Wilmington, DE: Jastak Associates.

Jensen, P., Hinshaw, D. B., Kraemer, H., Lenora, N., Newcorn, J., Abikoff, H., March, J., Arnold, L., Cantwell, D., Conners, C., Elliot, G., Greenhill, L., Hechtman, L., Hoza, B., Pelham, W., Severe, J., Swanson, J. M., Wells, K., Wigal, T., & Vitiello, B. (2001a). ADHD comorbidity findings from the MTA study; comparing comorbid subgroups. *Journal of the American Academy of Child and Adolescent Psychiatry, 40*, 147–158.

Jensen, P., Hinshaw, S., Swanson, J. M., Greenhill, L., Conners, C., Arnold, L., Abikoff, H., Elliot, G., Hechtman, L., Hoza, B., March, J., Newcorn, J., Severe, J., Vitiello, B., Wells, K., & Wigal, T. (2001b). Findings from the NIMH multimodal treatment study of ADHA (MTA): Implications and applications for primary care providers. *Journal of Developmental and Behavioral Pediatrics, 22*, 60–73.

Kaufmann, P. M., Fletcher, J. M., Levin, H. S., Miner, M. E., & Ewing-Cobbs, L. (1993). Attentional disturbance after pediatric closed head injury. *Journal of Child Neurology, 8*, 348–353.

Kinsella, G., Prior, M., Sawyer, M., Murtagh, D., Einsenmajer, R., Anderson, V., Bryan, D., & Klug, G. L. (1995). Neuropsychological deficit and academic performance in children and adolescents following traumatic brain injury. *Journal of Pediatric Psychology, 20*, 753–767.

Kinsella, G. J., Prior, M., Sawyer, M., Ong, B., Murtagh, D., Eisenmajer, R., Bryan, D., Anderson, V., & Klug, G. (1997). Predictors and indicators of academic outcome in children 2 years following traumatic brain injury. *Journal of the International Neuropsychological Society, 3*, 608–616.

Knights, R. M., Iran, L. P., Ventureyra, E. C., Bentirogrio, C., Stoddart, C., Winogron, W., & Bawden, H. N. (1991). The effects of head injury in children on neuropsychological and behavioral functioning. *Brain Injury, 5*, 339–351.

Kraus, J. F. (1995). Epidemiological features of brain injury in children: Occurrence, children at risk, causes and manner of injury, severity, and outcomes. In S. H. Broman & M. E. Michel (Eds.), *Traumatic head injury in children* (pp. 22–39). New York: Oxford University Press.

Kraus, J. F., Fife, D., Cox, P., Ramstein, K., & Conroy, C. (1986). Incidence, severity, and external causes of pediatric brain injury. *American Journal of Diseases in Children, 140*, 687–693.

Lehr, E. (1990). School management. In E. Lehr (Ed.), *Psychological management of traumatic brain injuries in children and adolescents*. Rockville, MD: Aspen.

Levin, H. S., Benavidez, D., Verger-Maestre, K., Perachio, N., Song, J., Mendelsohn, D., & Fletcher, J. (2000). Reduction of corpus callosum growth after severe traumatic brain injury in children. *Neurology, 54*, 647–653.

Levin, H. S., Culhane, K. A., Mendelsohn, D., Lilly, M., Bruce, D., Fletcher, J. M., Chapman, S. B., Harward H., & Eisenberg, H. M. (1993). Cognition in relation to magnetic resonance imaging in head-injured children and adolescents. *Archives of Neurology, 50*, 897–905.

Levin, H. S., & Ewing-Cobbs, L. (2001). Outcome for brain-injured children. In D. G. McLone, A. Marlin, D. Reigel, R. Scott, M. Walker, P. Steinbok, & W. Cheek (Eds.), *Pediatric neurosurgery* (4th ed., pp. 654–659). Philadelphia: W. B. Sanders Company.

Levin, H. S., Fletcher, J. M., Kufera, J. A., Harward, H., Lilly, M., Mendelsohn, D., Bruce, D., & Eisenberg, H. M. (1996). Dimensions of cognition measured by the Tower of London and other cognitive tasks in head-injured children and adolescents. *Developmental Neuropsychology, 12*, 17–34.

Levin, H. S., High, W. M., Ewing-Cobbs, L., Fletcher, J. M., Eisenberg, H. M., Miner, M. E., & Goldstein, F. C. (1988). Memory functioning during the first year after closed head injury in children and adolescents. *Neurosurgery, 22*, 1043–1052.

Levin, H. S., Mendelsohn, D., Lilly, M., Fletcher, J. M., Chapman, S. B., Harward, H., Kusnerik, L., Bruce, D., & Eisenberg, H. M. (1994). Tower of London performance in relation to magnetic resonance imaging following closed head injury in children. *Neuropsychology, 8*, 171–179.

Levin, H. S., Mendelsohn, D., Lilly, M., Yeakley, J., Song, J., Scheibel, R. S., Harward, H., Fletcher, J. M., Kufera, J., Davidson, K., & Bruce, D. (1997). Magnetic resonance imaging in relation to functional outcome of pediatric closed head injury: A test of the Ommaya-Gennarelli model. *Neurosurgery, 40*, 432–441.

Levin, H. S., Song, J., Ewing-Cobbs, L., Chapman, S. B., & Mendelsohn, D. (2001). Word fluency in relation to severity of closed head injury, associated frontal brain lesions, and age at injury in children. *Neuropsychologia, 39*, 122–131.

Lewis, J., Morris, M., Morris, R., Krawiecki, N., & Foster, M. (2000). Social problem solving in children with acquired brain injuries. *Journal of Head Trauma Rehabilitation, 15*, 930–942.

Luerssen, T. G. (2001). Acute traumatic cerebral injury. In D. G. McLone, A. Marlin, D. Reigel, R. Scott, M. Walker, P. Steinbok, & W. Cheek (Eds.), *Pediatric neurosurgery* (4th ed., pp. 601–617). Philadelphia: W. B. Sanders Company.

Massagli, T. I., Jaffe, K. M., Fay, G. C., Polissar, N. L., Liao, S., & Rivara, J. B. (1996). Neurobehavioral sequelae of severe pediatric traumatic brain injury: A cohort study. *Archives of Physical Medicine and Rehabilitation, 77*, 223–231.

Massagli, T. L., Michaud, L. J., & Rivara, F. P. (1996). Association between injury indices and outcome after severe traumatic brain injury in children. *Archives of Physical Medicine and Rehabilitation, 77*, 125–132.

Max, J. E., Arndt, S., Castillo, C. S., Bond, M., Bokura, H., Robin, D. A., Lindgren, S. D., Smith W., Sato, Y., & Mattheis, P. J. (1998a). Attention-deficit hyperactivity symptomatology after traumatic brain injury: A prospective study. *Journal of the American Academy of Child and Adolescent Psychiatry, 37*, 841–847.

Max, J. E., Koele, S. L., Lindgren, S. D., Robin, D. A., Smith, W. L., Sato, Y., & Arndt, S. (1998b). Adaptive functioning following traumatic brain injury and orthopedic injury: A controlled study. *Archives of Physical Medicine and Rehabilitation, 79*, 893–899.

Max, J. E., Roberts, M., Koele, S. L., Lindgren, S. D., Robin, D. A., Arndt, S., Smith W., & Sato, Y. (1999). Cognitive outcome in children and adolescents following severe traumatic brain injury: Influence of psychosocial, psychiatric, and injury-related variables. *Journal of the International Neuropsychological Society, 5*, 58–68.

Max, J. E., Robin, D. A., Lindgren, S. D., Smith, W. L., Sato, Y., Mattheis, P. J., Stierwalt, J. A. G., & Castillo, C. S. (1997a). Traumatic brain injury in children and adolescents: Psychiatric disorders at two years. *Journal of the American Academy of Child Adolescent Psychiatry, 36*, 1278–1284.

Max, J. E., Smith, W., Sato, Y., Mattheis, P. J., Castillo, C. S., Lindgren, S. D., Robin, D. A., & Stierwalt, J. A. G. (1997b). Traumatic brain injury in children and adolescents: Psychiatric disorders in the first three months. *Journal of the American Academy of Child and Adolescent Psychiatry, 36*, 94–102.

McDonald, C. M., Jaffe, K. M., Fay, G. C., Polissar, N. L., Martin, K. M., Liao, S., & Rivara, J. B. (1994). Comparison of indices of traumatic brain injury severity as predictors of neurobehavioral outcome in children. *Archives of Physical Medicine and Rehabilitation, 75*, 328–337.

McDonald, S. (1998). The SCEMA scheme: A worthy project as yet underspecified, overestimated and unproven. *Aphasiology, 12*, 1076–7080.

Murray, R., Shum, D., & McFarland, K. (1992). Attentional deficits in head-injured children: An information processing analysis. *Brain and Cognition, 18*, 99–115.

Novack, T. A., Dillon, M. C., & Jackson, W. T. (1996). Neurochemical mechanisms in brain injury and treatment: A review. *Journal of Clinical and Experimental Neuropsychology, 18*, 685–706.

Ommaya, A. K., Goldsmith, W., & Thibault, L. (2002). Biomechanics and neuropathology of adult and pediatric head injury. *British Journal of Neurosurgery, 16*, 220–242.

Pelham, W., & Gnagy, E. (1999). Psychosocial and combined treatments for ADHD. *Mental Retardation and Developmental Disabilities Research Reviews, 5*, 225–236.

Pennington, B. F. (1994). The working memory function of the prefrontal cortices: Implications for developmental and individual differences in cognition. In M. M. Haith, J. Benson, R. Roberts, & B. F. Pennington (Eds.), *Future oriented processes in development* (pp. 243–289). Chicago: University of Chicago Press.

Perrot, S. B., Taylor, H. G., & Montes, J. L. (1991). Neuropsychological sequelae, familial stress, and environmental adaptation following pediatric head injury. *Developmental Neuropsychology, 7(1)*, 69–86.

Povlishock, J. (2000). Pathophysiology of neural injury: Therapeutic opportunities and challenges. *Clinical Neurosurgery, 46*, 113–126.

Rivara, J. B., Jaffe, K. M., Polissar, N. L., Fay, G. C., Martin, K. M., Shurtleff, H. A., & Liao, S. (1994). Family functioning and children's academic performance and behavior problems in the year following traumatic brain injury. *Archives of Physical Medicine and Rehabilitation, 75*, 369–379.

Roberts, R. J., & Pennington, B. F. (1996). An interactive framework for examining prefrontal cognitive processes. *Developmental Neuropsychology, 12*, 105–126.

Robinson, T., Smith, S., Miller, M., & Brownell, M. (1999). Cognitive behavior modification of hyperactivity/impulsivity and aggression. A meta-analysis of school-based studies. *Journal of Educational Psychology, 91*, 195–203.

Roman, M., Delis, D. C., Willerman, L., Demandura, T., de la Pena, J., Loftis, C., Walsh, J., & Kracun, M. (1998). Impact of pediatric traumatic brain injury on components of verbal memory. *Journal of Clinical and Experimental Neuropsychology, 20*, 245–258.

Sachs, P., & Redd, C. (1993). The Americans with Disabilities Act and individuals with neurological impairments. *Rehabilitation Psychology, 38*, 87–101.

Samatovicz, R. (2000). Genetics and brain injury: Apolipoprotein E. *Journal of Head Trauma Rehabilitation, 15*, 869–874.

Savage, C., & Mishkin, L. (1994). A neuroeducational model for teaching students with acquired brain injuries. In R. Savage & G. Wolcot (Eds.), *Educational dimensions of acquired brain injury.* Austin, TX: ProEd.

Shelton, T., Barkley, R. A., Crosswait, C., Moorehouse, M., Fletcher, K., Barrett, S., Jenkins, L., & Metevia, L. (2000). Multimethod psychoeducational intervention for preschool children with disruptive behavior: Two-year post-treatment follow-up. *Journal of Abnormal Child Psychology, 28*, 253–266.

Sohlberg, M., Todis, B., & Glang, A. (1998). SCEMA: A team-based approach to serving secondary students with executive dysfunction following brain injury. *Aphasiology, 12*, 1047–1092.

Stallings, G. A., Ewing-Cobbs, L., Francis, D., & Fletcher, J. (1995). Achievement test scores in head-injured children before and after injury. *Journal of International Neuropsychological Society, 1*, 156.

Taylor, H. G., Yeates, K., Wade, S., Drotar, D., & Klein, S. (1999). Influences on first-year recovery from traumatic brain injury in children. *Neuropsychology, 13*, 76–89.

Teasdale, G., & Jennett, B. (1974). Assessment of coma and impaired consciousness: A practical scale. *Lancet, 2*, 81–84.

Telzrow, C. (1990). Management of academic and educational problems in traumatic brain injury. In E. Bigler (Ed.), *Traumatic brain injury* (pp. 251–272). Austin, TX: ProEd.

Walker, N., Boling, M., & Cobb, H. (1999). Training of school psychologists in neuropsychology and brain injury: Results of a national survey of training programs. *Child Neuropsychology, 5*, 137–142.

Walsh, B., & Lamberts, F. (1979). Errorless learning and picture fading as techniques for teaching sight words to TMR students. *American Journal of Mental Deficiency, 83*, 473–479.

Warschausky, S., Cohen, E. H., Parker, J., Levendosdy, A., & Okun, A. (1997). Social problem-solving skills of children with traumatic brain injury. *Pediatric Rehabilitation, 1*, 77–81.

Warschausky, S., Kewman, D., & Kay, J. (1999). Empirically supported psychological and behavioral therapies in pediatric rehabilitation of TBI. *Journal of Head Trauma Rehabilitation, 14*(4), 373–383.

Warschausky, S., Kewman, D., & Selim, A. (1996). Attentional performance of children with traumatic brain injury: A quantitative and qualitative analysis of digit span. *Archives of Clinical Neuropsychology, 11*, 147–153.

Wilson, B., Baddeley, A., & Evans, J. (1994). Errorless learning in the rehabilitation of memory impaired people. *Neuropsychological Rehabilitation, 4*, 307–326.

Yeates, K., Taylor, H. G., Drotar, D., Wade, S., Klein, S., Stancin, T., & Schatschneider, C. (1997). Preinjury family environment as a determinant of recovery from traumatic brain injuries in school-age children. *Journal of the International Neuropsychological Society, 3*, 617–630.

Yeates, K. O., Blumenstein, E., Patterson, C. M., & Delis, D. C. (1995). Verbal learning and memory following pediatric closed-head injury. *Journal of the International Neuropsychological Society, 1*, 78–87.

Ylvisaker, M., & DeBonis, D. (2000). Executive function impairment in adolescence: TBI and ADHD. *Topics in Language Disorders, 20*, 29–57.

Ylvisaker, M., & Feeney, T. J. (1998). Serving adolescents with acquired brain injury: Comments on SCHEMA. *Aphasiology, 12*, 1066–1075.

Ylvisaker, M., Feeney, T. J., Maher-Maxwell, N., Mesere, N., Greary, P., & DeLorenzo, J. (1995). School re-entry following severe traumatic brain injury: Guidelines for educational planning. *Journal of Head Trauma Rehabilitation, 10*, 25–41.

Ylvisaker, M., Todis, B., Glang, A., Urbanczyk, M., Franklin, C., DePompei, R., Feeney, T. J., Maxwell, N., Pearson, S., & Tyler, J. (2001). Educating students with TBI: Themes and recommendations. *Journal of Head Trauma Rehabilitation, 16*, 76–93.

19

Psychosocial Challenges and Clinical Interventions for Children and Adolescents with Cystic Fibrosis: A Developmental Approach

Alexandra L. Quittner
Avani C. Modi
Amy Loomis Roux
University of Florida

INTRODUCTION

Children with chronic illnesses are faced with a number of ongoing stressors that affect many dimensions of their lives. They often encounter changes in their physical, social, and emotional functioning, and must cope with the added burden of clinic visits and daily medical treatments (Drotar, 2000; Quittner & DiGirolamo, 1998). Parents also experience increased demands on their time, energy, and resources, as well as shifts in the enactment of their primary social roles (e.g., parental, marital; Quittner & DiGirolamo, 1998). This chapter reviews the current literature on family adaptation to cystic fibrosis (CF)—a serious, life-shortening, chronic illness that poses difficult challenges for children, teens, and parents. Since the discovery of the defective gene for CF in 1989, significant changes have occurred in the understanding and management of the disease, and these changes are highlighted in this review. A developmental approach is used emphasizing how psychosocial challenges and adjustment change from the preschool to school age to the adolescent period. This emphasis reflects the importance of developmental influences, such as the growth of cognitive abilities over time, the necessity of achieving developmental milestones, and the impact that social and emotional maturation are likely to have on the day-to-day management of a chronic illness.

The chapter is organized as follows: (1) a brief overview of the pathophysiology of CF, with attention to new epidemiological data; (2) a review of research on individual and family adjustment to CF, focusing on those issues likely to be addressed by psychologists in school settings; (3) a discussion of disease management, including the difficulties of adhering to complex, daily medical regimens; and (4) an outline of interventions that have been designed to address these psychosocial issues. We end with a comprehensive list of common problematic situations encountered by children and adolescents with CF in school settings, with specific suggestions for clinical interventions and resources that may be helpful to professionals in these settings.

THE CHANGING EPIDEMIOLOGY OF CF

CF is one of the most common terminal, genetic diseases of Caucasian populations, affecting approximately 1 in 3,400 live births (FitzSimmons, 1993; Kosorok, Wei, & Farrell, 1996). However, it is more rare in other ethnic populations. For example, CF affects only 1 in 17,000 African Americans and 1 in 90,000 Asians. CF is an autosomal recessive disease that occurs because of a mutation in the gene that regulates the exchange of salt and water across the cell membranes (Collins, 1992). The defective gene must be present in both parents to produce an affected child. The most common genetic defect is Delta F508, however, several hundred different mutations of the gene have been identified, which has significantly slowed efforts to introduce population screening.

CF affects three primary organ systems: respiratory, gastrointestinal, and integumentary (i.e., skin; Welsh, Tsui, Boat, & Beaudet, 1995). The lungs of patients with CF develop thick, sticky mucus secretions that lead to poor airway clearance, frequent lung infections, and chronic inflammation. The major objective of medical treatment is to clear the airways of mucus and reduce the chronic cycle of inflammation, infection, and lung damage. Despite aggressive treatments to clear mucus from the lungs and reduce infection, lung disease progresses, and respiratory failure is the primary cause of death, accounting for more than 85% of the mortality in CF (FitzSimmons, 1993).

CF also affects the digestive system. During fetal development, the pancreas is blocked, which prevents the release of enzymes needed to digest food. As a consequence, individuals with CF experience malabsorption, digestive difficulties, and poor growth and development. To counter these problems, children with CF must consume more calories than similar-aged children (125–150% of the Recommended Daily Allowance) and must take pancreatic replacement enzymes with all meals and snacks. Despite these efforts, children with CF are often shorter and thinner than their peers, and there is growing evidence that poor nutritional status affects the body's ability to fight infection and preserve lung function (Littlewood, 1992).

Finally, CF affects all the mucus-producing glands in the body (i.e., integumentary), including the sweat glands, mammary glands, and reproductive organs. It is possible for women with CF to become pregnant and have children, but it is more difficult because of the thickness of vaginal secretions and the additional stress pregnancy can place on the lungs and pancreas (Gilljam et al., 2000; Kent & Farquharson, 1993). Furthermore, the majority of males with CF are sterile as a result of the blockage of the vas deferens during fetal development.

Life expectancy for individuals with CF has increased dramatically over the past 30 years (FitzSimmons, 1993; Fogarty, Hubbard, & Britton, 2000). In the 1960s, few children with CF reached adolescence; and in 1974, the international median age of survival was only 8 years. Today, children who are born with CF can expect to live into adulthood, with a median survival age of approximately 31 years (FitzSimmons, 1993; Morgan et al., 1999). Several factors have led to this increase in life span, including earlier diagnosis, aggressive treatment of the disease, use of pancreatic enzyme replacements, and new antibiotics to treat lung infections (Morgan et al., 1999). A gender difference in survival has also been noted, with males living an average of 3 years longer than females. Although a number of reasons for this difference have been explored (e.g., nutritional status, pulmonary functioning, airway microbiology), this *gender gap* in survival has not yet been explained (Rosenfeld, Davis, FitzSimmons, Pepe, & Ramsey, 1997).

The discovery of the defective gene for CF has also increased our understanding of the pathophysiology of CF, which has led to the development of new treatments. There are now medications that help to thin sticky mucus (Dornase alpha) and new ways to deliver antibiotics deep into the lungs. Gene therapy is beginning to be tested in human trials and may ultimately hold the greatest promise, however, its therapeutic use is still several years away.

As CF has changed from being an exclusively pediatric disease to one that continues into adulthood, new psychosocial issues have emerged. Adolescents with CF must plan for the typical developmental transitions of young adulthood, including attending college, seeking employment, and developing long-term relationships. For many parents, allowing their teenagers to become independent is difficult because of the need to do daily treatments, attend regular clinic appointments, and exercise good judgment in managing the disease (e.g., staying away from cigarette smoke). Sexuality and fertility issues are now being addressed by the health care team, and recent studies indicate that women with CF can deliver healthy babies (Gilljam et al., 2000). Greater attention should be paid to these developmental issues to promote successful transitions to adulthood.

INDIVIDUAL PSYCHOLOGICAL ADAPTATION

Although earlier diagnosis and more aggressive treatment have significantly increased life span, CF continues to be a progressive disease that places a significant burden on children and families, and ultimately shortens life span. The rigors of daily treatments, frequent hospitalizations, and the unpredictable course of the disease place demands on the resources of the individual with CF and their family members (DiGirolamo, Quittner, Ackerman, & Stevens, 1997; Quittner et al., 1998). Given this increased stress, it has long been suspected that the risk for psychological maladjustment in individuals with CF may be quite high. Thus, a great deal of attention has focused on the psychological adaptation of children and adolescents with CF. Early descriptive studies of psychological adjustment in these children and adolescents reported significant emotional and behavioral problems (Simmons et al., 1987). However, more recent research, using improved methodologies, has indicated that whereas children and adolescents with CF do face a number of specific stressors, the majority adapt well to these challenges and very few have clinically diagnosable psychological disorders (Quittner & DiGirolamo, 1998; Thompson, Gustafson, George, & Spock, 1994). In this section, research on the emotional and behavioral adjustment of individuals with CF will be reviewed using a developmental approach, beginning with infancy and toddlerhood and moving forward chronologically through adolescence.

Infants and Preschoolers

Few studies have examined the psychological adjustment of infants, toddlers, and preschoolers with CF, in part because of the methodological challenges of measuring adjustment in young children. For the most part, studies have relied on parental reports of behavior problems and emotional symptomatology, with observational reports of parent–child interactions being the exception.

Studies of early attachment of mothers and infants with CF have found no differences during the first 2 years of life in the attachment patterns of those with and without CF (Goldberg, Washington, Morris, Fischer-Fay, & Simmons, 1990). However, parent–child attachment patterns in the first few years of life have been associated with important health outcomes (e.g., nutritional status). Infants exhibiting insecure attachment at 1 year of age demonstrated significant declines in weight for height percentiles through age 3, but infants who were securely attached at age 1 increased their weight for height percentiles through age 4. These findings suggest that the presence of chronic illness in a young child may affect early parent–child relationships. Additional research is needed to understand this relationship better.

In the preschool period, no differences in parent-reported behavior problems were found between groups with and without CF (Goldberg et al., 1997). However, 36% of children with

CF scored in the clinical range on at least one of the three scales of the Child Behavior Checklist (CBCL), which was used to assess emotional and behavioral problems, compared with 25% of children in the group without CF. A parent's own level of stress was the most consistent predictor of behavior problems in children between 1 and 4 years of age, whereas greater illness severity predicted higher total behavior problem scores in children 3 years of age and older. It is noteworthy that serious questions have been raised about the use of the CBCL for children with chronic illnesses (Drotar, Stein, & Perrin, 1995), because some of the items reflect symptoms that are associated with having a chronic illness (e.g., fatigue, aches and pains, nausea, lacks energy). In contrast to the findings with the CBCL, Cowen et al. (1985) used the Preschool Behavior Questionnaire (Behar & Stringfield, 1974) and found that *healthy* children had more parent-reported behavior problems than children with CF, although children with CF demonstrated significantly more hostile-aggressive behaviors than their healthy peers.

Although preschoolers with CF generally do not demonstrate elevated levels of problem behaviors as measured by standardized checklists, a number of studies have identified behavior problems associated with illness-specific situations. For example, mealtimes are often cited as problematic by parents of young children with CF (Quittner et al., 1996). Stark et al. (1995, 2000) examined mealtime behaviors in preschoolers with CF and found that they are more likely than peers without CF to exhibit behavior problems, such as food refusal, dawdling, and noncompliance toward commands to eat during mealtimes. Given the nutritional demands of preschoolers with CF, including both enzymes and increased calorie consumption, behavior problems during mealtimes represent a special challenge for families.

In sum, only a few studies have focused on the psychological adjustment of preschoolers with CF, with most examining behavior problems using standardized measures. There is little evidence of elevated behavior problems on these generic checklists. However, managing mealtimes and medication routines appear to place significant stress on parents and may warrant increased attention (Powers & Mitchell, 2001).

School-Aged Children

Studies examining psychological adjustment in school-age children with CF have reported conflicting results. Although early studies generally found that school-age children with CF were at increased risk for psychological problems—such as depression, anxiety, and poor social adjustment (Mrazek, 1985)—more recent studies have failed to support these findings (Drotar et al., 1981; Thompson, Gustafson, et al., 1994; Thompson, Hodges, & Hamlett, 1990). More recent studies have found that children with CF have rates of behavior problems similar to the general population. This inconsistency is likely because of improved methods of assessment, which have moved from being largely descriptive to more empirically and theoretically driven (Thompson, Gustafson et al., 1994). Newer models have included factors that are predictive of psychosocial adjustment, such as age and illness severity. Still, these studies have continued to search for symptoms of psychopathology in children with CF, concentrating on the identification of internalizing and externalizing behavior disorders.

Several studies have reported an increased incidence of internalizing behavior problems in school-age children with CF. Simmons et al. (1987) examined a sample of 6- to 11–year-olds with CF using the CBCL and found that 23% had significant behavior problems, with a higher profile of internalizing problems, especially for males. Children with CF in this study were generally reported to have good self-concept and social competence. Thompson et al. (1990) also suggested that internalizing behavior problems were slightly more common in children with CF than in healthy children.

Social functioning and peer relationships are also important aspects of psychological adjustment. Although social competence and peer interactions in children with CF have not been extensively studied, peer support and acceptance have been identified in qualitative studies as critically important to the psychological adjustment of children with CF (Christian & D'Auria, 1997). The physical consequences of CF, such as chronic cough, decreased physical endurance, and interruption of play and school activities to complete treatments, may place children with CF at risk for difficulties with peer interactions (Christian & D'Auria, 1997). Using a retrospective interview technique that asked 20 adolescents with CF to look back on their childhood, Christian and D'Auria (1997) found that, during middle childhood, many adolescents reported negative responses from peers regarding their CF diagnosis. They also frequently had difficulty telling their friends about their CF diagnosis, and many reported a desire to hide their illness from peers (e.g., not taking medications in front of peers, at school, etc.).

Very few studies have directly examined school functioning in children with CF. The studies that have addressed this issue have found both cognitive ability and academic achievement to be normal in children with CF and not affected by disease severity (Thompson, Gustafson, Meghdadpour, et al., 1992). Thompson, Gustafson, Meghdadpour, et al. (1992) examined intellectual and academic functioning in 76 children and adolescents with CF, and found that whereas IQ and academic achievement were normally distributed, 22% of the sample was functioning more than 1 year below grade level in reading and 14% in math. This is likely because of illness-related absences and hospitalizations. The difficulties of making up schoolwork have been documented in other studies of adolescents with CF (DiGirolamo et al., 1997) and are an important area for intervention.

Adolescents

Although school-age children with CF typically enjoy relatively stable health status, the disease frequently progresses from mild or moderate in childhood to severe in adolescence and young adulthood. As a result, the physical manifestations of CF become more noticeable (e.g., clubbing of fingers, increased cough), and adolescents may have more pulmonary exacerbations, requiring frequent and lengthy hospitalizations. Just as the need for increasingly intense management of the illness arises, adolescents are facing the developmental challenges of establishing independence (Mador & Smith, 1988). For example, adolescents may begin to view their treatment regimen as interfering with preferred social activities. Despite facing these additional stressors, most teens evidence remarkably good adjustment (Cowen et al., 1985; Mador & Smith, 1988; Smith, Gad, & O'Grady, 1983; Thompson, Gustafson, et al., 1994).

There is some evidence that as individuals with CF get older, they experience more psychological problems. Pearson, Pumariega, and Seilheimer (1991) found an increase in symptoms of depression and anxiety in adolescents with CF, but not in younger children. Sawyer, Rosier, Phelan, and Bowes (1995) reported that female adolescents with CF were less well adjusted in terms of self-concept than their healthy peers, especially with regard to body image. Lower self-concept scores, however, were not related to disease severity. Zeltzer, Kellerman, Ellenberg, Dash, and Rigler (1980) also found that female adolescents with CF were especially concerned about the impact of their illness on their physical appearance. Interestingly, Quittner, Buu, Watrous, and Davis (2000) reported that female adolescents with CF were less likely to view being thin as problematic on a quality-of-life measure, whereas males often noted concern about being underweight.

Whereas the majority of studies examining psychological adjustment have used standardized behavior checklists, DiGirolamo et al. (1997) examined stressors in adolescents with CF using a context-specific measure of stressful situations. Interviews and daily diaries were used to elicit problematic situations from adolescents, with the greatest number of problems mentioned in domains related to school, medications and treatment, and the parent–teen relationship. Adolescents who rated their problems as more difficult also endorsed more symptoms of depression and lower perceptions of social competence on standardized measures of social and emotional functioning.

Social competence and peer relationships gain importance during the adolescent period. Although few studies have focused on these areas, qualitative studies have found that peer relationships play an integral part in adolescents' adjustment to CF (D'Auria, Christian, Henderson, & Haynes, 2000). For example, in analyses of interview data from 15 teens with CF, increased illness severity was perceived as placing limits on social activities, and frequent and lengthy school absences were viewed as contributing to feelings of being left out of peer relationships at school (D'Auria et al., 2000). Adolescents also reported feeling different from healthy peers and stated that even long-term friends had difficulty understanding their illness. Many adolescents noted the importance of having other friends with CF; however, concerns about transmission of multiresistant bacteria have severely limited opportunities for social interactions (Saiman et al., 1996). Friends have been found to be important sources of emotional and tangible support, and virtually the only source of companionship support (Graetz, Shute, & Sawyer, 2000). Adolescents in this study also indicated they were reluctant to disclose their CF diagnosis to friends and did not want to be distinguished or identified by their illness.

Taken together, results of studies examining psychosocial adjustment in children and adolescents with CF indicate that whereas children and adolescents with CF face specific stressors related to their illness, most are able to adapt successfully. To increase sample size, many of these studies have grouped school-age and adolescent children together, often obscuring the specific challenges of these developmental periods. Future studies should examine psychosocial adjustment separately in school-age children and adolescents, and emphasize factors associated with positive adjustment, such as social support and family relationships.

FAMILY ADAPTATION

Parental Adaptation

The impact of CF on family functioning has been the focus of numerous studies over the past 20 years. Parents of children with CF must not only help their children manage the illness, but also they themselves must cope with the demands of the treatment regimen and the emotional distress related to the diagnosis and lifelong nature of the disease. Rolland (1984, 1988) has written extensively about the phases of a chronic illness in relation to family functioning, dividing a disease such as CF into three phases: diagnosis, chronic, and terminal. Each of these phases presents a unique set of challenges for the family, such as learning about the condition and its treatment, coping with pulmonary exacerbations, and dealing with declining health. As families move through these phases, they may experience new crises, periods of stabilization, and the need to reorganize family roles and responsibilities (Quittner, DiGirolamo, Michel, & Eigen, 1992).

Impact of Diagnosis. Numerous studies have shown that the diagnosis phase is one of the most difficult periods for families. Parents typically know very little about CF and must take in a tremendous amount of new information about the disease and its treatment. Soon after diagnosis, they are introduced to the health care team and must develop relationships with a new group of people during a period of high stress (Quittner, DiGirolamo, et al., 1992). Finally, parents may experience guilt about transferring the CF gene to their child, feelings of uncertainty about their child's future, and increased depression about the loss of a perfect child (Myer, 1988).

One study examining global parenting stress during the diagnosis phase found similar levels of stress in these parents and a normative sample (Goldberg, Morris, Simmons, & Fowler, 1990). However, parents of children with CF reported significantly higher levels of demandingness. Note that the use of global measures of adaptation has been criticized for their lack of sensitivity to the specific concerns of parents of chronically ill children (Quittner & DiGirolamo, 1998).

Using a more situation-specific measurement approach, Quittner, DiGirolamo, et al. (1992) found that mothers of infants recently diagnosed with CF experienced higher levels of strain and depression, compared with fathers. High levels of strain were attributed to the unequal division of care-taking responsibilities, with mothers spending more time doing daily medical treatments and child care than fathers. Fathers in this study also reported high levels of stress in relation to finances and emotional attachment to their child.

Interestingly, working outside the home may serve to buffer the stress associated with caring for a chronically ill child (Quittner, DiGirolamo, et al., 1992; Walker, Ortiz-Valdes, & Newbrough, 1989). The mechanism of protection is not clear, but could be related to receiving additional social support from peers at work and/or a more equal division of responsibilities in the home. Taken together, studies of parental adaptation soon after diagnosis indicate that parents are at increased risk for role strain and depression. Support from the health care team, as well as spouses, family members, and coworkers, may be particularly important during this time.

Preschool. Cowen et al. (1985) found that parents of healthy preschoolers report more child-related problems than do parents of children with CF. Researchers attribute this difference to parents of children with CF minimizing the normal stresses of the developmental period. For example, parents of preschool children with CF find mealtimes to be quite difficult, most likely because of the increased caloric intake prescribed for children with CF (Eiser, Zoritch, Hiller, Havermans, & Billig, 1995). This type of illness-related stress may be more problematic than typical child care tasks, such as bedtime routines, because they can have a significant impact on the child's health. Other factors that may contribute to poor maternal well-being include problems with treatment adherence, child adjustment problems, sibling externalizing behaviors, and lack of maternal support (Foster, Bryon, & Eiser, 1998). Identifying these stressors is important because poor maternal well-being can have a significant impact on the family unit, including marital strain, differential treatment of siblings, and a disruption in parenting practices (Hauenstein, 1990; Quittner & Opipari, 1994). Given these findings, health care professionals should address not only the needs of the child, but also the needs of caregivers.

School-Age. As children with CF grow older and start school, parents continue to report higher levels of stress and depression, in comparison with parents of children with other chronic conditions (Thompson, Gil, et al., 1994; Walker, Ford, & Donald, 1987). Illness-related stress and lower levels of family support contributed to poor maternal adjustment (Thompson, Gustafson, Hamlett, & Spock, 1992). It is important to note that maternal adjustment was related to stressors specific to the illness and not to the normal stresses of parenting during this developmental period.

The coping strategies used by parents of children with CF may play a large role in their adaptation patterns. Studies suggest that maladaptive coping strategies include denial and escape-avoidance (Mullins et al., 1991; Myer, 1988). However, strategies that have helped parents of children with CF effectively cope typically involve seeking knowledge about the illness, religion, and use of social support (Thompson, Gustafson, Hamlett, et al., 1992). Patterson, Budd, Goetz, and Warwick (1993) suggest that a balanced coping style, in which the family attends to their own needs and the needs of the child with CF, can be quite effective in helping families reduce stress and discord. Using a behavior-analytic model, Quittner and colleagues (1996) have advocated the evaluation of coping responses using an inventory of both CF-specific and normal developmental issues, the Role-Play Inventory of Situations and Coping Strategies. This measure holds promise for generating profiles of competence for parents of children with CF, allowing clinicians to target specific areas of intervention.

Adolescence. As children begin to move through the period of adolescence and young adulthood, parental adaptation may change. Adolescence can be described as a time of intense emotions and turbulence as the child strives for independence and autonomy. For parents, it can be difficult to relinquish medication management to the adolescent (DiGirolamo et al., 1997). Other problematic situations that have been reported by parents regarding their adolescents with CF include clinic and hospital visits (problems with medical procedures and long hospital stays), peer relationships (treated differently or hurt by friends), and physical activities (physical endurance and sports). In general, few studies have been conducted examining psychological adaptation of parents of adolescents with CF, and greater attention should be focused on the family system during this developmental period.

Marital Adjustment

Children with CF require an intensive and time-consuming medical regimen that often involves parental time and assistance. As a result, caring for a child with CF can be taxing and burdensome for parents. The stress associated with caregiving can have a significant impact on family roles and marital satisfaction (Quittner, Opipari, Regoli, Jacobsen, & Eigen, 1992).

Several studies have suggested that having a child with CF can affect a couple's functioning. Turk (1964) found that parents of children with CF reported decreased time for their partner, less interest in intimacy, and problems with communication. Couples have also reported increased guilt about passing the defective gene on to their child and higher stress because of caregiver burden (Whyte, 1992). In terms of impact on the marriage, 10–25% of parents of children with CF have reported problems with their marital relationship (Phillips, Bohannon, Gayton, & Friedman, 1985). Increased stress and ineffective communication between couples, along with the financial burden of caring for a child with a chronic illness, can lead to separation and divorce. Denning, Gluckson, and Mohr (1976) found a 9.5 times greater divorce rate among families of children with CF, compared with the general population. However, it is important to note that several of these studies lacked a matched comparison group and standardized assessment measures. Thus, these results should be interpreted with caution.

Role strain related to caregiving has been associated with higher levels of depression in mothers, after accounting for situation-specific parenting stress and marital satisfaction (Quittner, DiGirolamo, et al., 1992). A more recent study examining marital satisfaction and role strain using well-validated assessment measures showed that couples of children with CF reported greater role strain resulting from role conflicts, caretaking tasks, and exchanges of affection, compared with couples with a healthy child (Quittner, Espelage, et al., 1998). Time spent in recreation has also been found to be a significant predictor of role strain, suggesting that respite services and additional support early on may be critical for preserving positive family functioning (Quittner, Opipari, et al., 1992). These results indicate that health care professionals should be sensitive to the caregiving strains experienced by parents of children with CF. By providing these parents with information on respite care, such as camps or caregiving services, health care professionals can facilitate quality time spent between husbands and wives of children with CF.

Sibling Adjustment

There is growing recognition that sibling relationships are an important component of the family system and are likely to be affected by stressors on the family unit (Brody, et al., 1992; Dunn, Stocker, & Plomin, 1990; McHale & Pawletko, 1992). Siblings spend a great deal of time together, and the sibling relationship serves as the foundation for the development of peer relationships, the provision and receipt of social support, and a model for the resolution of conflicts (Brody et al., 1992; Csikszentmihalyi & Larson, 1984; Dunn, 2000). As a result of their unique role and the lifelong duration of their relationship, siblings can be strongly affected by the presence of a brother or sister with a chronic illness (McHale & Gamble, 1989; Quittner & Opipari, 1994).

Growing up with a brother or sister who has a chronic illness, such as CF, may alter the lives of siblings in several ways: parents may have less time and attention to devote to the healthy sibling (Crocker, 1981; Quittner & Opipari, 1994); siblings may be expected to assume greater responsibility for household chores and caretaking tasks, particularly if they are female; and siblings may experience increased anxiety during health crises, such as hospitalizations (McHale & Pawletko, 1992). Thus, siblings may be at risk for poor adaptation, including behavioral and emotional difficulties (e.g., jealousy, aggression, withdrawal; Cadman, Boyle, Szatmari, & Offord, 1988; Derouin & Jessee, 1996; Tritt & Esses, 1988). To date, however, the majority of research has focused on the psychological adjustment of the child with the chronic illness, with less attention directed toward other siblings in the home.

Current research examining the psychological adjustment of healthy siblings of children with chronic illnesses has provided conflicting results (Breslau & Prabucki, 1987; Breslau, Weitzman, & Messenger, 1981; Harder & Bowditch, 1982; Taylor, 1980). For instance, siblings of children with CF have been shown to express significant worries about their ill sibling's health (Menke, 1987). Researchers reported that 72% of mothers stated that healthy siblings have minor problems, including feelings of jealousy and overprotection of the child with CF (Phillips et al., 1985). Parents also reported that the healthy sibling receives less attention, with 26–33% of children complaining about inattention (Phillips et al., 1985).

Quittner and Opipari (1994) examined differential treatment of siblings of children with CF. Participants in this study were 40 mothers, 20 of whom had a younger child with CF and a healthy, older child, and 20 of whom had age-matched, healthy children. Although mothers of children with CF reported that they spent equal time with their older and younger children, daily telephone diaries indicated that they spent more individual time with their younger child with CF in comparison with their healthy older child. Furthermore, they rated their time with their younger siblings as more positive than time spent with their older, healthy children. This type of differential treatment was not found in the comparison group. These results were later replicated in school-aged children using a similar design, with additional evidence that the extent of differential treatment was related to poorer behavioral and emotional adjustment in the healthy sibling (Quittner & Opipari, 1994).

Siblings of children with CF also have reported positive ways in which their brother/sister's illness has affected their lives. These include strengthening family roles and relationships within the family, attending special events for the sibling with CF, and allowing adolescent siblings to be more independent (Derouin & Jessee, 1996). Similarly, Harder and Bowditch (1982) reported that families with a child with CF show evidence of increased cohesion and personal growth. Increased maturity in the healthy sibling may be fostered by the sibling being well informed and involved in their chronically ill sibling's daily life (Taylor, 1980). For this reason, the family can play an important role in helping siblings adjust to having a brother/sister with CF. As one 17–year-old sibling stated, "Talk about what's going on, or you'll feel like you're going to explode. Ask a lot of questions. You always think things are worse than they really are" (Derouin & Jessee, 1996).

Siblings of children with CF often worry about the potential early death of their brother/sister. The loss of a sibling can also have significant effects on other family members. Fanos and Nickerson (1991) found that siblings of children with CF who were interviewed in adulthood had a global sense of guilt regarding their sibling's death, increased anxiety, vulnerability, fear of intimacy, and sleep difficulties. Sibling responses were often affected by their developmental level at the time of their brother/sister's death. For example, siblings who were between the ages of 13–17 at the time of their brother/sister's death had significantly more anxiety, depression, and guilt, compared with siblings who were 9–12 years of age or over the age of 18. Results from this study suggest that surviving adolescent siblings may have considerable difficulty coping with the death of their brother/sister. This is an area in which intervention from health care professionals and school psychologists may play a critical role in facilitating the grieving process. Support groups, such as Grief Busters, have been established in several communities to give siblings who have lost a brother or sister a forum in which to express their feelings, meet children who have experienced a similar traumatic event, and seek assistance from trained professionals.

ADHERENCE TO MEDICAL REGIMENS

One of the most significant challenges for children with CF and their families is adherence to the daily treatment regimen, which is critical to long-term management of the disease. It involves several components, including pancreatic enzymes taken with each meal and snack, use of aerosolized medications to open the airways, airway clearance to remove thick, sticky mucus, and ingestion of several medications to replace vitamins and control infections. Completing all of these treatments typically takes several hours each day, with recent studies documenting generally poor rates of adherence and increased family conflict in relation to treatment-related tasks (Quittner, Drotar, et al., 2000).

Several studies of adherence have reported that, on average, only one-half of the children and teens with CF are adhering to their treatment regimen, which is comparable with adherence rates for children with other chronic conditions (Coutts, Gibson, & Paton, 1992; Rapoff, 1999). The consequences of poor adherence can be serious, including increased hospitalizations, school absenteeism, the emergence of resistant bacteria, and reduced health-related quality of life (LaGreca & Shuman, 1995; Quittner, Espelage, Ievers-Landis, & Drotar, 2000; Rapoff & Christophersen, 1982). Several factors have been shown to influence rates of adherence, such as the characteristics of the treatment regimen, developmental age, knowledge of the treatment regimen, and family functioning (Becker, Drachman, & Kirscht, 1972; Ievers-Landis & Drotar, 2000; Patterson et al., 1993).

Factors Influencing Adherence

The factors that have been shown to influence adherence include the characteristics of the treatment regimen (e.g., complexity, efficacy), developmental age of the child, knowledge of the treatment regimen, and family functioning (see Table 19.1). Passero, Remor, and Solomon (1981) reported that patients have higher rates of adherence for appointment keeping (78%) and antibiotics/vitamins (90%), compared with diet (20%) and chest physiotherapy (CPT) (40%), thus indicating that adherence is more difficult for the time-intensive and complex portions of the treatment regimen.

The age of the child, along with his/her responsibility in completing treatment tasks, can affect adherence. For example, adherence to dietary recommendations was found to decline significantly between infancy and school age, with older children cooperating less with the

TABLE 19.1
Factors Associated with Poorer Adherence

Characteristics of treatment regimen	More complex tasks (diet, airway clearance) More time-consuming Side effects (puffiness, stomach aches) Uncertain efficacy
Developmental age	Adolescence
Knowledge	Incomplete information Inaccurate information Poor understanding of treatment needs
Family functioning	Greater parental stress Parent–child conflict Inadequate parental monitoring

dietary regimen (Gudas, Koocher, & Wypij, 1991). Several studies have suggested that adolescents have the lowest rates of adherence, with more problems noted for females than males (Czajkowski & Koocher, 1986). This has been attributed to normal adolescent needs for greater independence and parental shifting of responsibility to the teen. Drotar and Ievers (1994) suggest that the sudden shift in responsibility for the medical management of CF to the older child may not be adaptive and should be closely monitored by physicians and parents.

Inadequate knowledge may also contribute to poor rates of adherence in children with CF. Research has found that parents of children with CF may not accurately remember information provided to them by their physicians, and physicians may not communicate the information clearly (Gudas, Koocher, & Wypij, 1991). Mothers of children with CF reported being unaware that their children should take pancreatic enzymes with snacks and meals (Henley & Hill, 1990). Similarly, Ievers et al. (1999) found that 20% of mothers of children with CF were unable to report the prescribed frequency of their child's airway clearance treatment, whereas 33% could not accurately recall the prescribed frequency of nebulized medications. Inadequate knowledge has also been found when asking children about their medical regimen (Henley & Hill, 1990). For example, 22% of children believed that chest physiotherapy was unnecessary when the patient is feeling well. These studies, taken together, indicate that accurate and complete information about the prescribed treatment regimen is critical to good adherence, and that health care professionals should devote more attention to communicating this information during routine clinic visits.

Finally, poor family functioning also has been associated with lower rates of adherence. Patterson, McCubbin, and Warwick (1990) found that family stress and conflict, as well as parental availability and positive family coping, were associated with better pulmonary functioning and nutritional status. These findings were consistent over a 10–year period, suggesting that family variables may play a key role in adherence for children and adolescents with CF. Similarly, higher levels of marital strain, stress, and problems with communication have been shown to impact adherence negatively (Geiss, Hobbs, Hammersley-Maercklein, & Henley, 1992; Patterson et al., 1993; Quittner et al., 1998). For this reason, interventions focusing on family communication patterns and interactions may be beneficial (Quittner, Drotar, et al., 2000; see Interventions and Consultation section).

In summary, with the advent of new technologies and medications, it is likely that the life span of individuals with CF will increase. As a result, the issue of adherence becomes a crucial component to improved quality of life. Parents and children with CF face several barriers to treatment adherence, and these issues are likely to change through the course of the child's development. As a result, it is important to tailor interventions to the individual needs of the family.

MEASURING THE IMPACT OF CHRONIC ILLNESS ON QUALITY OF LIFE

It is important to assess how a chronic illness, such as CF, affects the child or teen across several different areas. Although traditional measures of health status, such as pulmonary and nutritional indicators, are critical, they do not capture the broader impact of the disease on the patient's physical, social, and emotional functioning (Quittner, 1998). This may be particularly true for chronic, rather than acute, diseases in which an important goal of treatment is to improve patient well-being. Measures of health-related quality of life (HRQOL) provide this broader assessment of functioning and can yield unique information about the consequences of the illness and the effects of new treatments.

Over the past two decades, significant progress has been made in defining and measuring HRQOL (Drotar, 1998; Spilker, 1996). There is now broad consensus that HRQOL: (1) is a multidimensional construct with several core dimensions, including physical functioning and symptoms, social functioning, and psychological and emotional state; (2) should be patient rather than physician-centered; and (3) reflects the individual's subjective evaluation of his or her daily functioning and psychological well-being (Schipper, Clinch, & Olweny, 1996; Spilker, 1996).

Recent efforts have been made to develop disease-specific measures of HRQOL for CF, which have been shown to be more sensitive than generic (general) measures (see Quittner, 1998, for a review). Two CF-specific HRQOL measures have now been developed: The Cystic Fibrosis Questionnaire (CFQ; Modi & Quittner, in press; Quittner, Buu, et al., 2000) and the Cystic Fibrosis Quality of Life questionnaire (CFQoL; Gee, Abbott, Conway, Etherington, & Webb, 2000). In contrast to the CFQoL, the CFQ was developed for a broader age range. Three versions of the CFQ were constructed: (1) CFQ–Child for children ages 6–13, (2) CFQ–Parent for the parents of children age 6–13, and (3) CFQ–Adolescent/Adult for adolescents and adults over the age of 14. The CFQ assesses functioning in a variety of key domains, including physical functioning, vitality, emotional state, body image, treatment burden, and several symptom scales (see Table 19.2).

Using HRQOL Measures

There are several ways in which psychologists working in school settings may be able to use HRQOL measures. First, these measures may provide a quick and easy method of assessing how a school-aged child or adolescent is functioning physically, emotionally, and socially. There are preliminary norms available that can indicate if a child is having difficulty in a specific area. For example, some children may feel more socially isolated because of their disease, which would be illustrated by lower scores on the CFQ Social Scale.

Second, it may be useful to administer a measure such as the CFQ each year to determine if there are changes in functioning that should be addressed by the psychologist or health care team. Adolescents, for example, may experience more pulmonary exacerbations as they get older, which may lead to increased coughing, low energy levels, and poorer physical functioning. A profile of the teen's scores can be calculated across the 12 domains and compared with their profile from the year before (see Fig. 19.1). If a significant decline in functioning

TABLE 19.2
Cystic Fibrosis Questionnaire (CFQ) Scales

	CFQ: Child Version	*CFQ: Parent Version*	*CFQ: Teen/Adult Version*
QOL dimensions			
Physical functioning	X	X	X
Vitality		X	X
Emotional state	X	X	X
Social limitations	X		X
Role limitations/school performance		X	X
Body image	X	X	X
Eating disturbances	X	X	X
Treatment burden	X	X	X
Symptom scales			
Respiratory symptoms	X	X	X
Digestive symptoms	X	X	X
Weight		X	X
Health perceptions		X	X

QOL = quality of life.

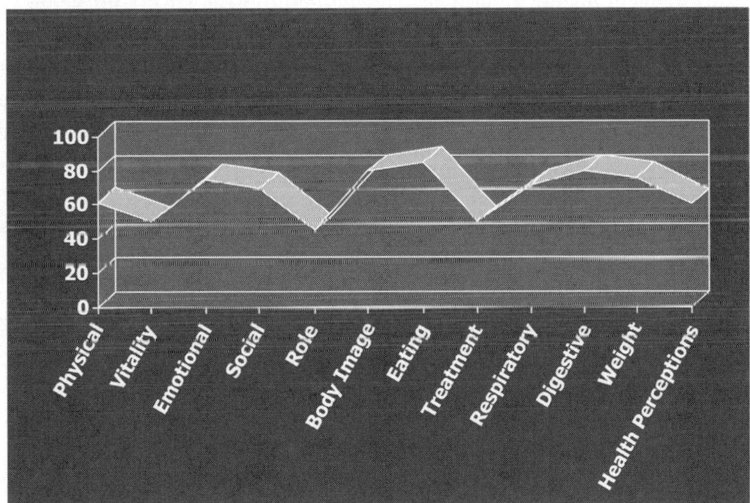

FIG. 19.1. Profile of a child's scores on the Cystic Fibrosis Questionnaire. Higher scores indicate better health-related quality of life.

is observed, it might alert the psychologist to the need for some type of intervention to accommodate the teen's change in health (e.g., reduced number of classes, study or rest period during the day).

Finally, because there is both child and parent versions of the CFQ available, a psychologist can compare family members' perceptions of how that child is functioning. Parents may not always be aware of the difficulties their child is encountering, either because the child is reluctant to disclose their emotions or because parents have not had the opportunity to observe their child's interactions with peers. For example, children may be reluctant to reveal feelings of sadness or fear to their parents, in part, to protect them from added stress. Having a chance to assess both the parent and child perspectives may provide a means of bridging these sensitive issues.

TRANSITIONING INTO ADULTHOOD

Recent advances in medical treatments and earlier diagnosis have led to dramatic increases in life expectancy for individuals with CF (FitzSimmons, 1993; Fogarty et al., 2000). Median survival age is currently 31 years, and approximately 38% of individuals with CF are over 18 years of age (Cystic Fibrosis Foundation, 2000; FitzSimmons, 1993: Morgan et al., 1999). A majority of infants who are born with CF today can expect to live into their 40s. Thus, CF is no longer a pediatric disease, but one that continues into adulthood.

Those who survive into adulthood will face unique challenges, including the transition from pediatric to adult pulmonary clinics, greater responsibility for management of the disease and its treatments, and the normal processes of planning for the future. To facilitate this transition, health care professionals and others in the teen's social network (e.g., parents, teachers) will need to anticipate these developmental changes and try to foster independence. For example, early consideration should be given to the different types of careers and educational opportunities that will be possible for adults with CF.

Many young adults with CF continue education beyond high school and move on to earn college and advanced degrees. One important decision is whether the young adult is able to leave home and manage his/her treatments independently. Because adolescence is a time to develop one's own identity and strive for autonomy, young adults with CF still have trouble managing their treatment and self-care because they want to fit in with their peers (Baker & Coe, 1993; Webb, 1995). However, if health status declines because of poor adherence, they may need their parents for assistance, which thwarts their efforts to become independent. Ideally, good disease management should be established in adolescence so that it does not become problematic in adulthood.

Because CF is a progressive disease that leads to decreased lung functioning over time, adolescents and young adults with CF may experience more symptoms and physical limitations. Awareness of having a chronic and fatal illness increases during adolescence; however, it is not until adulthood that more mature views about long-term health and the role of adherence begin to form (Admi, 1996). As adolescents gain greater autonomy over their illness, parental roles in managing the disease decrease. It is critical for health care professionals to recognize this transition and facilitate the patient's self-management.

In the last 20 years, adult CF clinics have been developed to address the health care needs of adolescents and adults with CF. However, patients who have been seen by their pediatric pulmonologist since childhood often have difficulty with the transition from pediatric to adult clinics (Flume, Anderson, Hardy, & Gray, 2001). Transitioning to an adult pulmonary team may be difficult because it signifies a transition toward independent living, which involves greater self-care and decreased involvement by both parents and physicians who have played a significant role in managing the disease (Nasr, Campbell, & Howatt, 1992). The pediatric team can play an important role in preparing the patient for transfer (i.e., holding joint transition clinics), including establishing a transition program (Nasr et al., 1992). Establishing rapport and promoting a supportive environment can positively impact the transition process, and teens will continue to need support from family members (Webb, 1995). In general, adolescents and young adults with CF are faced with a variety of unique issues that they did not deal with earlier in life, and the health care team, with the aid of family members, can make an enormous difference in facilitating this stage of growth and development.

INTERVENTIONS AND CONSULTATION

Interventions to Increase Knowledge and Coping Skills

Given the challenges of adapting to a chronic illness, such as CF, it is surprising that so few clinical or school-based interventions have been developed and evaluated. The few interventions that have been described in the literature have focused primarily on adherence to medical treatments, knowledge about CF, and psychosocial issues, such as coping skills and social support. In this section, we review interventions aimed at increasing knowledge of the disease and its management, and programs that have targeted broader psychosocial issues.

In terms of programs designed to increase knowledge and disease management, Bartholomew and colleagues (Bartholomew et al., 1991, 1997; Parcel et al., 1994) have developed a comprehensive, self-paced educational program entitled the "Cystic Fibrosis Family Education Program." This program consists of instructional modules for respiratory care, nutrition, communication, and coping skills that are written at different developmental levels for patients (e.g., preschool, school-age, and adolescent) and their primary caregivers. The health care team distributes the written materials and spends time during a regular clinic visit reviewing the relevant sections. Participants then take the books home, read through them, and complete specific learning activities. Using a pretest–posttest nonequivalent groups design, results indicated that the program led to increases in knowledge for both children and caregivers, increases in self-efficacy and problem-solving for those who were low in those characteristics at the pretest, and positive changes on a self-management questionnaire. No significant differences were found for parenting stress, family adaptation, adaptive behavior, and HRQOL. This is not surprising given the program's focus on providing information and helpful suggestions. In sum, this program showed considerable promise as a psychoeducational intervention.

The Starbright Foundation has recently developed an educational CD-ROM program, entitled "Fitting CF Into Your Life Everyday," with the aim of providing children with accurate information about their disease and preparing them to take greater responsibility for their medical regimens. The CD-ROM consists of three modules: (1) Eating, (2) Breathing, and (3) CF Questions and Answers. The program takes about 15 min to complete; has colorful, animated graphics; and is highly interactive. A study is currently being conducted to evaluate the effectiveness of this CD-ROM program as an educational tool for patients with CF. The study is examining whether use of the CD-ROM leads to increased knowledge about CF and improved strategies for coping with frequent and difficult situations. It will also assess secondary outcomes, such as consumer satisfaction with the CD-ROM program and changes in HRQOL. An important question of particular importance is whether children with CF would share the CD-ROM with their classmates. This would be one positive way of educating peers about CF. If the final results indicate that the program is beneficial, psychologists may want to use this as a resource in their schools (Davis, Quittner, Stack & Yang, 2003; Quittner, Davis, & Larson, 2001).

In terms of interventions with a psychosocial focus, a recent Internet support program for teens with CF was evaluated at Johns Hopkins University (Johnson, Ravert, & Everton, 2001). The goals of this program were to provide a support site for adolescents with CF, improve access and communication with the health care team, and facilitate peer interactions among teens with CF. This type of intervention is particularly timely, because group meetings among patients with CF (e.g., camps, family education days) have been discouraged because of the spread of multiresistant organisms. Participants logged onto the site an average of 4 times per month and directed questions to the health care team and to peers with CF. In a small sample of teens ($n = 18$), half of the participants e-mailed each other at least once per week, and 77% e-mailed peers every other week. There were no significant changes on a CF knowledge quiz, but participants' reported a perception that their knowledge had increased. Furthermore, they also perceived that they had more friends they could relate to at the end of the study. Although the sample size was small, this type of support group is promising and should be evaluated in a larger, multisite trial.

Finally, a home visiting program was developed for families experiencing substantial psychosocial stress (Bryon, Burton, Tostevin, & Madge, 2000). These families were not attending clinic visits on a regular basis and their children's health status was erratic. The home visiting program consisted of at least four home visits by the nurse and psychologist over a 6-month period to address psychosocial issues (e.g., adherence to medical treatments) and health status. Preliminary findings indicate that the intervention led to increases in parental well-being, improved clinic attendance and follow-through on needed hospitalizations, and more stable health status. More detailed information about the nature of the intervention and the size of the study sample are needed; however, this intervention appeared to be effective with a high-risk group. Furthermore, home visiting programs have been used successfully with other pediatric chronic illnesses, such as asthma (Sherman, Baumstein, & Hendeles, 2001) and may be an effective way of intervening with families who live a long distance from the medical center.

Adherence Interventions

Few interventions have been developed to promote adherence in children and adolescents with CF, and even less attention has been paid to evaluating the impact of these interventions. To date, these interventions have included psychoeducational programs, behavioral therapy, and family systems therapy. The CF Family Education Program is one type of psychoeducational program that has been evaluated in the literature and is discussed previously. This program led to increases in knowledge for caregivers and children, greater self-efficacy for children, and positive changes in self-management behaviors (Bartholomew et al., 1997). These findings indicate that psychoeducational programs may promote better management of CF.

Behavioral interventions have also been conducted with families of children with CF. Behavioral strategies include the use of positive reinforcement (i.e., sticker charts and goal setting) and ignoring. (Stark, Bowen, Tyc, Evans, and Passero (1990) have conducted several studies evaluating a behavioral intervention designed to increase caloric intake in school-aged children. Results indicated that calorie consumption increased approximately 1,000 calories per day for the five children in the study and that these increases were significantly greater than those of the control group. Follow-up studies revealed maintenance of these effects over a 2-year period (Stark et al., 1993). A larger, multisite trial is currently comparing this behavioral intervention to a nutritional education program (Stark & Quittner, 1996–2001).

Intervention programs are also being conducted with a family focus (Quittner, Drotar, et al., 2000). Currently, Quittner and colleagues are conducting a multisite controlled trial of interventions designed to promote adherence in adolescents with CF. There are three different groups: standard medical care, family learning program (FLP), and behavioral family systems therapy (BFST). The FLP program includes 10 sessions providing specific information about the effects of CF on different body systems and the purpose of each type of medical treatment. The sessions engage teens and parents in activities that encourage hands-on learning, active participation, and homework assignments that reinforce information learned during the session. The BFST group also participates in 10 sessions that are focused on problem solving, communication, cognitive restructuring, and discussion of functional roles and beliefs

(Robin & Foster, 1989). Previous studies using a family-centered approach have been effective with adolescents with diabetes and eating disorders (Robin & Seigel, 1999; Wysocki et al., 2000). Results of this intervention trial for families of children with CF will provide important information regarding the efficacy of treatment interventions for adherence.

In sum, only a few interventions for children and adolescents with CF have been developed and evaluated to determine their efficacy. The interventions described previously have generally produced positive changes; however, they have been limited by small sample sizes, limited descriptions of the intervention program, and a focus on increasing knowledge rather than changing the key behaviors related to good disease management (e.g., problem-solving skills, communication among family members). A systematic review of psychosocial interventions for CF is now underway through the Cochrane Library to identify interventions that have demonstrated efficacy using rigorous standards (Quittner & Glascoe, 2001). Once complete, this review may help to stimulate further development of interventions that show substantial promise.

SCHOOL CONSULTATION FOR CHILDREN AND ADOLESCENTS WITH CYSTIC FIBROSIS

Although children and adolescents with CF are not at increased risk for cognitive or academic problems, other challenges at school may arise. When school difficulties do occur for children and adolescents with CF, they are more likely to concern management of CF at school, absenteeism, and interaction with peers (DiGirolamo et al., 1997). In this section, the consultation role of the psychologist in a school setting will be discussed, with particular attention to problematic situations that have been documented for children and adolescents with CF (DiGirolamo et al., 1997; Quittner et al, 1996). These problematic situations will be described using a developmental approach, beginning with preschool and continuing through elementary and secondary school (see Table 19.3).

As consultants to the school system, psychologists are often called on to offer expertise and work collaboratively with teachers and other school personnel to solve classroom problems (Erchul & Martens, 1997). The psychologist can collaborate with educational professionals (teachers, school nurses, and guidance counselors) conducting assessments and designing and implementing intervention plans for children with chronic illnesses (Power, Heathfield, McGoey, & Blum, 1999). As a consultant, the psychologist can foster successful school adaptation and reduce barriers to education for students with CF. Although the psychologist in the school system may have intermittent contact with individual children, teachers, on the other hand, are in daily contact with children, and may need assistance in dealing with children with chronic illnesses in their classroom. In many cases, school difficulties faced by children with CF can be best addressed by helping teachers and other school personnel implement school-based interventions for common problematic situations. By being aware of problems commonly faced by children and adolescents with CF at different stages of development, psychologists can be better prepared to help teachers and other school personnel.

Preschool

For preschool-age children with CF, problems frequently arise around eating. Children with CF have a variety of special needs related to nutrition, including increased calorie consumption and adherence to enzyme medications. Mealtime is one of the most frequently cited problems by families of children with CF (Quittner et al., 1996). As discussed earlier, preschoolers with

TABLE 19.3
Common School Difficulties for Children and Adolescents with Cystic Fibrosis (CF)

Educational Level	*Common Problems*	*Interventions*
Preschool	Eating difficulties; adherence to enzymes/other medications	Behavior charts to reinforce eating and adherence (i.e., sticker charts)
	Digestive and bathroom problems	Opportunities to use restrooms outside the classroom; use of spray air sanitizers
Elementary school	Explaining CF to peers	Peer education (classroom presentations, books, STARBRIGHT CD-ROM)
	Teasing by peers	Enhance skills to cope with teasing
	Explaining CF to teachers	Frequent parent–teacher contact and teacher education
	Managing CF at school	Medication management form for teacher with a description of the treatment regimen
Middle/high school	Frequent/lengthy school absences	Set up plans before hospitalizations, including bringing missed assignments to hospital, extending deadlines, and arranging tutoring if needed
	Concerns about body image/physical appearance	Enhance self-esteem via support and/or individual psychotherapy
	Adherence to treatment	Behavior management strategies, family/individual psychotherapy; facilitate taking medications at school
	Participating in school activities	Modify sports activities; encourage participation in different types of activities (i.e., band, debate, etc.)
	Declining health; death and dying issues	Encourage students to visit in the hospital, e-mail, telephone; provide information to teachers and peers about teen's condition (with parental consent); establish links between school and student

CF are more likely than non-CF peers to exhibit a number of problematic behaviors at meals (Spieth et al., 2001; Stark et al., 1995, 2000). Children in the preschool environment may have up to two meals per day at school; so, managing the complex nutritional needs of a child with CF can be difficult for preschool teachers. Given the challenges that many parents experience, it seems reasonable to expect that preschool teachers may find it hard to encourage a child with CF to eat the necessary amount of calories and to make sure they take their enzymes before eating. In both of these situations, behavior charts (such as sticker charts) and positive reinforcement can help in increasing consumption of calories and adherence to enzymes and other medications.

In addition to difficulties with eating and medication, preschool children may also experience difficulties related to using the bathroom. Children with CF, even when taking enzymes correctly, may have digestive problems and more frequent, foul-smelling stools. Bathrooms in the preschool setting are usually located in the classroom, which provides little privacy, and may increase teasing from peers. In this case, teachers can help alleviate this problem by allowing the child with CF to use a bathroom that is outside the classroom and by discouraging teasing.

The psychologist can play an important role in facilitating communication between teachers and parents of children with CF. Effective communication is an essential component of school success for young children with chronic illnesses, including CF (Fauvre, 1988). In many cases, development of a written educational plan, which includes management of nutritional and other medical needs for the child at school, will help teachers and parents feel more comfortable. It may also be helpful to provide the child's preschool teacher with a pamphlet about CF and a medical management form, which provides greater detail than normal school health records. In some cases, parents have found it helpful to write a letter to the teacher that includes a detailed description of the child's illness and treatment, as well as accommodations needed at school (Fauvre, 1988). Effective communication between the family and school will remain important throughout the child's school career; establishing good communication during the preschool years can be very beneficial.

Elementary School

In elementary school, children with chronic illnesses, including CF, begin to realize that their illness makes them different from their peers. Whereas preschoolers perceive their illness and treatment as potentially common to all children, elementary school children become aware that other children do not have CF and are not required to perform treatments. Peers may also become aware of these differences and ask difficult questions. Thus, in elementary school, children with CF begin to face the challenges of telling others about their disease. They may have trouble answering questions from peers about visible signs of CF, such as taking pills or coughing at school. School-aged peers may express fears about contagion and worry that they can *catch* the disease (Sexson & Madan-Swain, 1993). In many cases, simply educating peers about CF can alleviate many of these problems (Benner & Marlowe, 1991; Treiber, Schramm, & Mabe, 1986).

School-based interventions aimed at increasing peer knowledge about specific chronic illnesses can be helpful in fostering more positive attitudes toward a peer with a chronic illness (Benner & Marlowe, 1991; Treiber et al., 1986). Although educational programs about CF specifically have not been developed and evaluated, programs focusing on other childhood illnesses (such as cancer) have been effective in promoting peer knowledge (Benner & Marlowe, 1991; Treiber et al., 1986). There are several ways information about CF could be presented to elementary school-aged peers, including age-appropriate books or presentations by the child's parents or members of the medical team (see Resource, Table 19.4). In addition, an educational CD-ROM program recently developed by the Starbright Foundation may help children with CF explain their illness to peers (see Fig. 19.2; Davis et al., 2003; Quittner et al., 2001). In some cases, the child with CF may want to present information about his or her illness to classmates; however, it is important to check with the child and his or her family about their comfort level before planning an educational presentation to classmates.

Increasing teacher knowledge about CF is also important. Many parents of elementary school children with CF would like the teacher to know more about CF and its treatment, but are not sure how to provide teachers with this information (Lynch, Lewis, & Murphy, 1993; Ryan & Williams, 1996). Similarly, many teachers would like information about a chronic illness that affects a student in their class, but are not aware of good sources of reliable, accurate information (Johnson, Lubker, & Fowler, 1988; Lynch et al., 1993). Teachers also report being unsure how to set realistic expectations for the student and are concerned about how to handle the reactions of classmates (Davis, 1989). A number of good resources are

TABLE 19.4
Book References for Parents, Teachers, and Peers of Children with Cystic Fibrosis (CF)

Book	*Author*	*Source*	*Appropriate Age Group*			
			Toddler	*Preschool*	*School-age*	*Adolescent*
Taking Cystic Fibrosis to School	Cynthia Henry	Bookstore			X	
CF and Me	Susan Tumiel Smith	McNeil Pharmaceutical		X	X	
Big PATS or Little Pats?	Susan Tumiel Smith	McNeil Pharmaceutical	X			
Mallory's 65 Roses	Diane Shader Smith	Scandipharm		X	X	
Cystic Fibrosis in the Classroom	Amanda Young	Scandipharm		X	X	
Miguel and Sarah: Close friends with Cystic Fibrosis	Andrea Dowell & Kathie Rokke	Malkerson Library		X	X	
CF and Your Tomorrow: A Guide to Surviving and Thriving with Cystic Fibrosis	Deirdre Ann Croal	Solvay Pharmaceuticals				X
Cystic Fibrosis: A guide for Patient and Family (2nd ed.)	David M. Orenstein	Bookstore				X
Cystic Fibrosis Family Education Program (set of books for different age groups in different areas)	Cystic Fibrosis Education Project at Baylor College of Medicine and Texas Children's Hospital	CF Center	X	X	X	X

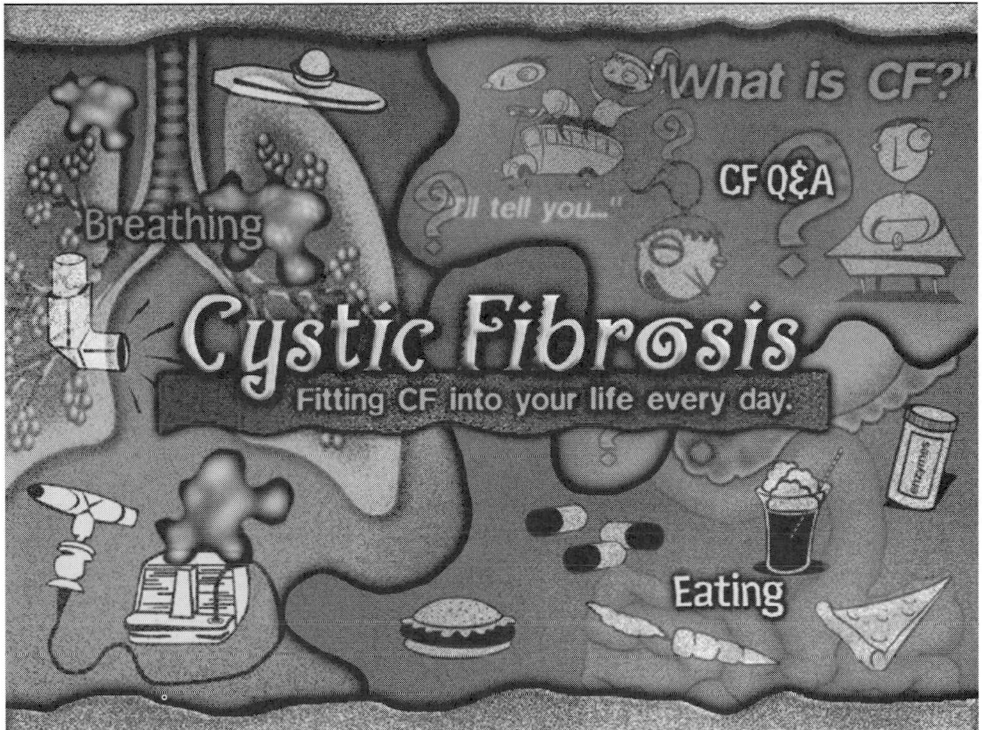

FIG. 19.2. A screen from the STARBRIGHT Explorer Series program, Fitting CF into Your Life Everyday. Copyright © 2001 by the STARBRIGHT Foundation and its licensors. All rights reserved.

available that can provide teachers with information about CF (Fig. 19.2), including those developed by the CF Foundation and pharmaceutical companies (see Tables 19.5 and 19.6).

In addition to educating peers and teachers about CF, school difficulties for children with CF can also be alleviated by making simple accommodations to the classroom environment. For example, a child with CF may require more frequent visits to the restroom than other students, so the teacher could allow the child to leave the classroom for bathroom breaks without special permission. In addition, some children with CF may require medical treatment while they are at school (e.g., taking inhaled medications, chest physiotherapy, etc.). The timing of treatments should be planned to minimize disruption of the child's school activities. Often, children with CF are concerned that they will stand out or feel different because of their illness, so efforts should be made not to draw attention to the child's medical condition when making classroom accommodations.

Middle and High School

As children with CF progress into adolescence, hospital visits often become more frequent and lengthy. It is not uncommon for an adolescent with CF to miss 2 weeks of school for a routine hospitalization (i.e., *tune up*). Frequent or prolonged absences from school can result in feelings of isolation, and teens who have missed a lot of school may feel out of the loop when they return (D'Auria et al., 2000). Thus, school absenteeism is a major problem, and adequate planning, including how to make up schoolwork, can be particularly important. It may be helpful for adolescents, teachers, and parents to establish a plan for dealing with all upcoming absences at the beginning of a new school year to minimize stress. Efforts should

TABLE 19.5
Multimedia Resources for Parents, Teachers, and Peers of Children with Cystic Fibrosis (CF)

		Appropriate Age Group			
Multimedia	*Source*	*Toddler*	*Preschool*	*School-age*	*Adolescent*
Fitting Cystic Fibrosis into Your Life Everyday—CD ROM	STARBRIGHT Explorer Series www.starbright.org				X
Adventures of Mr. Enzyme—video and comic books	McNeil Pharmaceutical		X	X	X
Walking Hand in Hand	Alexandra Quittner, Ph.D.—University of Florida	X	X	X	X
AC and Awesome E's	Solvay Pharmaceuticals			X	

TABLE 19.6
Web Sites

		Appropriate Age Group			
Web Sites	*Source*	*Toddler*	*Preschool*	*School-age*	*Adolescent*
Cystic Fibrosis Foundation	www.cff.org			X	X
Links2go	www.links2go.net/topic/Cystic_Fibrosis			X	X
Boomer Esiason's Site	www.esiason.org			X	X

also be made by school personnel to maintain contact with the adolescent while he or she is hospitalized to encourage peer contact and alleviate feelings of isolation.

Another issue that may be problematic for adolescents with CF is their body image and concerns about physical appearance. Adolescents with CF tend to be smaller and thinner than their peers and may experience delays in the onset of puberty. They may also evidence physical manifestations of the disease, such as clubbing of the fingers and a barrel chest. These visible differences may elicit teasing from peers. In this situation, teens with CF may benefit from support aimed at enhancing their self-esteem or individual psychotherapy.

As mentioned earlier, adolescents with CF often have difficulty adhering to their treatment regimen. This can be complicated by the school environment. For example, in many schools, students are required to go to the office to obtain their medication. For children and teens with CF, going to the office every day to get their enzymes before lunch poses several problems. First, they may miss worktime in the classroom. Second, because lunchtime is quite limited, they may also miss out on time to eat their full lunch, as well as time to socialize. Finally, having to walk down to the office marks them as different from their peers and invites questions. It may be possible to increase an adolescent's adherence to his or her medications simply by making it more convenient and less disruptive to take medications during the school day.

Because of breathing difficulties, fatigue, and problems tolerating heat, some adolescents find it difficult to participate in school-related activities, such as physical education classes and extracurricular sports. However, because participation in these kinds of activities is important to both the psychological and physical development of adolescents with CF, efforts should be made to encourage their participation, making accommodations whenever possible. In addition, school personnel who supervise these activities should be aware of the adolescent's diagnosis and given appropriate information about the disease's possible effects. Finally, although earlier diagnosis and advances in medical treatment have dramatically increased the life expectancy of individuals with CF, it remains a progressive and ultimately terminal illness. Therefore, adolescents with CF, as well as their classmates and teachers, may be faced with death and dying issues. Education professionals often feel unprepared to deal with a terminally ill student, and psychologists are often called on to help the school community through this difficult situation. A number of steps can be taken to prepare teachers and students for this type of loss, including providing information about the disease and its progression, answering questions about the student's prognosis honestly, and establishing links between the school and the teen. One of the most important issues is to prevent the teen's social isolation. Encouraging peers to e-mail, call, or visit the teen in the hospital can help prevent this isolation.

FUTURE DIRECTIONS

Substantial advances have been made in our understanding and treatment of CF, with concomitant improvements in survival and quality of life. However, these positive developments have also required children and adolescents with CF to adhere to arduous, time-consuming medical treatments that disrupt daily activities and increase strain on the family. Several promising clinical interventions have recently been developed to address disease management and adherence issues, and further research is needed to determine if they are effective (Quittner, Espelage, et al., 2000).

Another area of future research concerns how to implement interventions that have been shown to be effective in highly controlled laboratory conditions in the context of usual clinical care. Termed *translational* research, these studies seek to implement effective interventions in medical settings (i.e., effectiveness research). This is an important step, because having access to these interventions in clinical and community settings increases their dissemination and accessibility to a wide range of families. Quittner and Johnson (2001) recently received funding from the National Institutes of Health to evaluate a clinic-based adherence promotion trial for children with CF and diabetes that is conducted in the context of usual medical care.

Schools are another ideal context for implementing clinical interventions. Children and adolescents spend a great deal of time at school and often encounter specific challenges in that setting, such as the need for medications, frequent school absences, and stigma and teasing by peers. Psychologists in these settings may serve as the key resource for assisting children with these issues and facilitating communication between home and school. Adolescents who are experiencing declines in their health status may also need emotional and social support as they try to cope with the terminal nature of their disease. Having a professional to talk to outside the family and medical team may provide the adolescent with an important source of support, and psychologists may be particularly effective in assisting teachers and peers at school in coping with impending loss.

Adolescents and young adults who reach the terminal stage of the illness may also consider the option of lung transplantation (Kotloff & Zuckerman, 1996). Recent advances in transplantation medicine have improved the survival statistics for patients with CF. Current data indicate that 60–90% of CF patients survive 1 year and approximately 50% survive for 5 years posttransplantation (Cystic Fibrosis Foundation, 2000). Despite improved prognosis, having a transplant brings with it a number of new medical responsibilities and challenges (e.g., antirejection drugs, frequent medical monitoring), as well as new psychosocial issues (e.g., body hair, *moon* face, scarring; Zuckerman & Kotloff, 1998). Little is currently known about the relationship between disease management behaviors pretransplant and how the patient will adhere to the regimen posttransplant (Quittner & Hoffman, 2000–2001). More research is also needed to determine the variables that predict the best adaptation to both the immediate surgery and long-term follow-up.

Finally, rapid developments in genetic screening and gene therapy may also hold promise for patients with CF and their families. Identification of the major gene for CF, and subsequent mapping of several hundred mutations, will make it possible at some point to screen the general population for the presence of the defective gene. These tools are also being used in prenatal screening for families who have had an affected child, but the rates of utilization of these services indicate that parents are reluctant to consider termination of pregnancy. Newborn screening programs for the general population have also produced mixed results, with evidence of improvements in nutritional outcomes, as well as increased parental stress (Baroni, Anderson, & Mischler, 1997; Doull, 2001). Serious concerns about how to protect the confidentiality of genetic information and its potentially negative impact on health insurance and employment remain obstacles to the implementation of these screening programs nationwide.

In sum, medical advances in the diagnosis and treatment of CF have highlighted more dramatically the importance of addressing key psychosocial issues, such as adherence, social and emotional adjustment, and developmental transitions to adulthood. Psychologists in school and medical settings are in a unique position to develop, evaluate, and implement interventions to address these issues. These interventions hold substantial promise and are likely to make a significant difference in the lives of children with CF and their families.

ACKNOWLEDGMENTS

We thank Melissa A. Davis, Wendy Hofer, and Amy Perwien who provided valuable comments on our earlier drafts of this manuscript.

REFERENCES

Admi, H. (1996). Growing up with a chronic health condition: A model of an ordinary lifestyle. *Quantitative Health Research, 6*(2), 163–183.

Baker, K. L., & Coe, L. M. (1993). Growing up with a chronic condition: Transition to young adulthood for the individual with cystic fibrosis. *Holistic Nursing Practice, 8*(1), 8–15.

Baroni, M. A., Anderson, Y. E., & Mischler, E. (1997). Cystic fibrosis newborn screening: Impact of early screening results on parenting stress. *Pediatric Nursing, 23*(2), 143–151.

Bartholomew, L. K., Czyzewski, D. I., Parcel, G. S., Swank, P. R., Sockrider, M. M, Mariotto, M. J., Schidlow, D. V., Fink, R. J., & Seilheimer, D. K. (1997). Self-management of cystic fibrosis: Short-term outcomes of the Cystic Fibrosis Family Education Program. *Health Education & Behavior, 24*(5), 652–666.

Bartholomew, L. K., Parcel, G. S., Seilheimer, D. K., Czyzewski, D., Spinelli, S. H., & Congdon, B. (1991). Development of a health education program to promote the self-management of cystic fibrosis. *Health Education Quarterly, 18*(4), 429–443.

Becker, M. H., Drachman, R. H., & Kirscht, J. P. (1972). Predicting mother's compliance with pediatric medical regimens. *Journal of Pediatrics, 81*, 843–854.

Behar, L., & Stringfield, S. (1974). A behavior rating scale for the preschool child. *Developmental Psychology, 10*(5), 601–610.

Benner, A. E., & Marlowe, L. S. (1991). The effect of a workshop on childhood cancer on students' knowledge, concerns, and desire to interact with a classmate with cancer. *Children's Health Care, 20*(2), 101–107.

Breslau, N., & Prabucki, K. (1987). Siblings of disabled children: Effects of chronic stress in the family. *Archives of General Psychiatry, 44*, 1040–1046.

Breslau, N., Weitzman, M., & Messenger, K. (1981). Psychological functioning of siblings of disabled children. *Pediatrics, 67*, 344–353.

Brody, G. H., Stoneman, Z., & McCoy, J. K. (1992). Associations of maternal and paternal direct and differential behavior with sibling relationships: Contemporaneous and longitudinal analyses. *Child Development, 63*(1), 82–92.

Bryon, M., Burton, J., Tostevin, M., & Madge, S. (2000). A home visiting programme to improve health status and psychosocial functioning of families with a child with cystic fibrosis [Abstract]. *Pediatric Pulmonology, Pediatric Pulmonology, 30*(Suppl. 20), 336.

Cadman, D., Boyle, M., Szatmari, P., & Offord, D. R. (1988). The Ontario Child Health Study: Social adjustment and mental health of siblings of children with chronic health problems. *Journal of Developmental and Behavioral Pediatrics, 9*, 117–121.

Christian, B. J., & D'Auria, J. P. (1997). The child's eye: Memories of growing up with cystic fibrosis. *Journal of Pediatric Nursing, 12(1)*, 3–12.

Collins, F. S. (1992). Cystic fibrosis: Molecular biology and therapeutic implications. *Science, 256*(5058), 774–779.

Coutts, J. A., Gibson, N. A., & Paton, N. Y. (1992). Measuring compliance with inhaled medication in asthma. *Archives of Disabled Children, 67*, 332–333.

Cowen, L., Corey, M., Kennan, N., Simmons, R., Arndt, E., & Levison, H. (1985). Family adaptation and psychosocial adjustment to cystic fibrosis in the preschool child. *Social Sciences Medicine, 20*(6), 553–360.

Crocker, A. (1981). The involvement of siblings of children with handicaps. In A. Milunsky (Ed.), *Coping with crisis and handicap* (pp. 219–223.). New York: Plenum Press.

Csikszentmihalyi, M., & Larson, R. (1984). *Being adolescent: Conflict and growth in the teenage years*. New York: Basic Books.

Cystic Fibrosis Foundation. (2000, September). *Patient registry 1999 annual report*. Bethesda, MD: Author.

Czajkowski, D. R., & Koocher, G. P. (1986). Predicting medical compliance among adolescents with cystic fibrosis. *Health Psychology, 5*(3), 297–305.

D'Auria, J. P., Christian, B. J., Henderson, Z. G., & Haynes, B. (2000). The company they keep: The influence of peer relationships on adjustment to cystic fibrosis during adolescence. *Journal of Pediatric Nursing, 15*(3), 175–182.

Davis, K. G. (1989). Educational needs of the terminally ill student. *Issues in Comprehensive Pediatric Nursing, 12*, 235–245.

Davis, M. A., Quittner, A. L., Stack, C. M., & Yang, M. (2003). Controlled evaluation of the STARBRIGHT CD-ROM program for children and adolescents with cystic fibrosis. Manuscript submitted for publication.

Denning, C. R., Gluckson, M. M., & Mohr, I. (1976). Psychological and social aspects of cystic fibrosis. In J. A. Mangos & R. C. Talamo (Eds.), *Cystic fibrosis: Projections into the future* (pp. 127–151). New York: Stratton.

Derouin, D., & Jessee, P. O. (1996). Impact of a chronic illness in childhood: Siblings' perceptions. *Issues in Comprehensive Pediatric Nursing, 19*, 135–147.

DiGirolamo, A. M., Quittner, A. L., Ackerman, V., & Stevens, J. (1997). Identification and assessment of ongoing stressors in adolescents with a chronic illness: An application of the Behavior Analytic Model. *Journal of Clinical Child Psychology, 26*, 53–66.

Doull, I. J. (2001). Recent advances in cystic fibrosis. *Archives of Disease in Childhood, 85*(1), 62–66.

Drotar, D. (1998). *Measuring health-related quality of life in children and adolescents: Implications for research and practice*. Mahwah, NJ: Lawrence Erlbaum Associates.

Drotar, D. (Ed.). (2000). *Promoting adherence to medical treatment in chronic childhood illness: Concepts, methods and interventions*. Mahwah, NJ: Erlbaum Associates.

Drotar, D., Doershuk, C., Stern, R., Boat, T., Boyer, W., & Matthews, L. (1981). Psychosocial functioning of children with CF. *Pediatrics, 67*, 338–343.

Drotar, D., & Ievers, C. (1994). Age differences in parent and child responsibilities for management of cystic fibrosis and insulin-dependent diabetes mellitus. *Journal of Developmental and Behavioral Pediatrics, 15*(4), 265–272.

Drotar, D., Stein, R. E. K., & Perrin, E. C. (1995). Methodological issues in using the Child Behavior Checklist and its related instruments in clinical child psychology research. *Journal of Clinical Child Psychology, 24*(2), 184–192.

Dunn, J. (2000). State of the art: Siblings. *Psychologist, 13*(5), 244–248.

Dunn, J., Stocker, C., & Plomin, R. (1990). Assessing the relationship between young siblings: A research note. *Journal of Child Psychology and Psychiatry, 31*(6), 983–991.

Eiser, C., Zoritch, B., Hiller, J., Havermans, T., & Billig, S. (1995). Routine stresses in caring for a child with cystic fibrosis. *Journal of Psychosomatic Research, 39*(5), 641–646.

Erchul, W. P., & Martens, B. K. (1997). *School consultation: Conceptual and empirical bases of practice*. New York: Plenum Press.

Fanos, J. H., & Nickerson, B. G. (1991). Long-term effects of sibling death during adolescence. *Journal of Adolescent Research, 6*(1), 70–82.

Fauvre, M. (1988). Including young children with "new" chronic illnesses in an early childhood education setting. *Young Children, 43*(6), 71–77.

FitzSimmons, S. C. (1993). The changing epidemiology of cystic fibrosis. *Journal of Pediatrics, 122*, 1–9.

Flume, P. A., Anderson, D. L., Hardy, K. K., & Gray, S. (2001). Transition programs in cystic fibrosis centers: Perceptions of pediatric and adult program directors. *Pediatric Pulmonology, 31*(6), 443–450.

Fogarty, A., Hubbard, R., & Britton, J. (2000). International comparison of median age at death from cystic fibrosis. *Chest, 117*, 1656–1660.

Foster, C. L., Bryon, M., & Eiser, C. (1998). Correlates of well-being in mothers of children and adolescents with cystic fibrosis. *Child Care, Health, and Development, 24*(1), 41–56.

Gee, L., Abbott, J., Conway, S. P., Etherington, C., & Webb, A. K. (2000). Development of a disease specific health related quality of life measure for adults and adolescents with cystic fibrosis. *Thorax, 55*(11), 946–954.

Geiss, S. K., Hobbs, S. A., Hammersley-Maercklein, G., Kramer, J. C., & Henley, M. (1992). Psychosocial factors related to perceived compliance with cystic fibrosis treatment. *Journal of Clinical Psychology, 48*(1), 99–103.

Gilljam, M., Antoniou, M., Shin, J., Dupuis, A., Corey, M., & Tullis, D. E. (2000). Pregnancy in cystic fibrosis. *Chest, 118*, 85–91.

Goldberg, S., Janus, M., Washington, J., Simmons, R. J., MacLusky, I., & Fowler, R. S. (1997). Prediction of preschool behavioral problems in healthy and pediatric samples. *Journal of Developmental and Behavioral Pediatrics, 18*, 304–313.

Goldberg, S., Morris, P., Simmons, R. J., & Fowler, R. S. (1990). Chronic illness in infancy and parenting stress: A comparison of three groups of parents. *Journal of Pediatric Psychology, 15*(3), 347–358.

Goldberg, S., Washington, J., Morris, P., Fischer-Fay, A., & Simmons, R. J. (1990). Early diagnosed chronic illness and mother-child relationships in the first two years. *Canadian Journal of Psychiatry, 35*, 726–733.

Graetz, B. W., Shute, R. H., & Sawyer, M. G. (2000). An Australian study of adolescents with cystic fibrosis: Perceived supportive and nonsupportive behaviors from families and friends and psychological adjustment. *Journal of Adolescent Health, 26*, 64–69.

Gudas, L. J., Koocher, G. P., & Wypij, D. (1991). Perceptions of medical compliance in children and adolescents with cystic fibrosis. *Journal of Developmental and Behavioral Pediatrics, 12*, 236–242.

Harder, L., & Bowditch, B. (1982). Siblings of children with cystic fibrosis: Perceptions of the impact of the disease. *Children's Health Care, 10*(4), 116–120.

Hauenstein, E. (1990). The experiences of distress in parents of chronically ill children: Potential or likely outcome? *Journal of Clinical Child Psychology, 19*, 356–364.

Henley, L. D., & Hill, I. D. (1990). Errors, gaps, and misconceptions in the disease-related knowledge of cystic fibrosis patients and their families. *Pediatrics, 85*(6), 1008–1014.

Ievers, C. E., Brown, R. T., Drotar, D., Caplan, D., Pishevar, B., & Lambert, R. G. (1999). Knowledge of physician prescriptions and adherence to treatment among children with cystic fibrosis and their mothers. *Journal of Developmental and Behavioral Pediatrics, 2*, 335–343.

Ievers-Landis, C. E., & Drotar, D. (2000). Parental and child knowledge of the treatment regimen for childhood chronic illnesses: Related factors and adherence to treatment. In D. Drotar (Ed.), *Promoting adherence to medical treatment in childhood chronic illness: Concepts, methods and interventions*. Mahwah, NJ: Lawrence Erlbaum Associates.

Johnson, K. B., Ravert, R. D., & Everton, A. (2001). Hopkins Teen Central: Assessment of an internet-based support system for children with cystic fibrosis. *Pediatrics, 107*(2), E24.

Johnson, M. P., Lubker, B. B., & Fowler, M. G. (1988). Teacher needs assessment for the educational management of children with chronic illnesses. *The Journal of School Health, 58*(6), 232–235.

Johnson, S. B., & Quittner, A. L. (2001). *Clinic-based adherence intervention for diabetes and cystic fibrosis*. National Institutes of Health grant, Rockville, MD: NIH.

Kent, N. E., & Farquharson, D. F. (1993). Cystic fibrosis in pregnancy. *Canadian Medical Association Journal, 149*(6), 805–806.

Kosorok, M. R., Wei, W. H., & Farrell, P.M. (1996). The incidence of cystic fibrosis. *Statistics in Medicine 15*(5), 449–462.

Kotloff, R. M., & Zuckerman, J. B. (1996). Lung transplantation for cystic fibrosis: Special considerations. *Chest, 109*, 787–798.

LaGreca, A. M., & Schuman, W. B. (1995). Adherence to prescribed medical regimens. In M. C. Roberts (Ed.), *Handbook of pediatric psychology* (2nd ed., pp. 55–83). New York: Guilford.

Littlewood, J. M. (1992). Cystic fibrosis: Gastrointestinal complications. *British Medical Bulletin, 48*(4), 847–859.

Lynch, E. W., Lewis, R. B., & Murphy, D. S. (1993). Educational services for children with chronic illnesses: Perspectives of educators and families. *Exceptional Children, 59*(3), 210–220.

Mador, J. A., & Smith, D. H. (1988). The psychosocial adaptation of adolescents with cystic fibrosis: A review of the literature. *Journal of Adolescent Health Care, 10*, 136–142.

McHale, S. M., & Gamble, W. (1989). Sibling relationships of children with disabled and non-disabled brothers and sisters. *Developmental Psychology, 25*, 421–429.

McHale, S. M., & Pawletko, T. M. (1992). Differential treatment of siblings in two family contexts. *Child Development, 63*, 68–81.

Menke, E. (1987). The impact of a child's chronic illness on school-aged siblings. *Children's Health Care, 15*(3), 132–140.

Modi, A. C., & Quittner, A. L. (in press). Validation of a disease-specific measure of health-related quality of life for children with cystic fibrosis. *Journal of Pediatric Psychology.*

Morgan, W. J., Butler, S. M., Johnson, C. A., Colin, A. A., FitzSimmons, S. C., Geller, D. E., Konstan, M. W., Light, M. J., Rabin, H. R., Regelmann, W. E., Schidlow, D. V., Stokes, D. C., Wohl, M. E. B., Kaplowitz, H., Wyatt, M. M., & Stryker, S. (1999). Epidemiological study of cystic fibrosis: Design and implementation of a prospective, multicenter, observational study of patients with cystic fibrosis in the U.S. and Canada. *Pediatric Pulmonology, 28*, 231–241.

Mrazek, D. A. (1985). Cystic fibrosis: A systems analysis of psychiatric consequences. *Advances in Psychosomatic Medicine, 14*, 119–135.

Mullins, L. L., Olson, R. A., Reyes, S., Bernardy, N, Huszti, H. C., & Volk, R. J. (1991). Risk and resistance factors in the adaptation of mothers of children with cystic fibrosis. *Journal of Pediatric Psychology, 16*(6), 701–715.

Myer, P. A. (1988). Parental adaptation to cystic fibrosis. *Journal of Pediatric Health Care, 2*, 20–28.

Nasr, S. Z., Campbell, C., & Howatt, W. (1992). Transition program from pediatric to adult care for cystic fibrosis patients. *Journal of Adolescent Health, 13*(8), 682–685.

Parcel, G. S., Swank, P. R., Mariotto, M. J., Bartholomew, L. K., Czyzewski, D. I., Sockrider, M. M., & Seilheimer, D. K. (1994). Self-management of cystic fibrosis: A structural model for educational and behavioral variables. *Social Sciences Medicine, 38*(9), 1307–1315.

Passero, M. A., Remor, B., & Solomon, J. (1981). Patient-reported compliance with cystic fibrosis therapy. *Clinical Pediatrics, 20*, 264–268.

Patterson, J. M., Budd, J., Goetz, D., & Warwick, W. J. (1993). Family correlates of a 10–year pulmonary health trend in cystic fibrosis. *Pediatrics, 91*(2), 383–389.

Patterson, J. M, McCubbin, H. I., & Warwick,W. J. (1990). The impact of family functioning on health changes in children with cystic fibrosis. *Social Sciences and Medicine, 31*(2), 159–164.

Pearson, D. A., Pumariega, A. J., & Seilheimer, D. K. (1991). The development of psychiatric symptomatology in patients with cystic fibrosis. *Journal of the American Academy of Child and Adolescent Psychiatry, 30*(2), 290 297.

Phillips, S., Bohannon, W., Gayton, W., & Friedman, S. (1985). Parent interview findings regarding the impact of CF on families. *Developmental and Behavioral Pediatrics, 6*, 122–127.

Power, T. J., Heathfield, L. T., McGoey, K. E., & Blum, N. J. (1999). Managing and preventing chronic health problems in children and youth: School psychology's expanded mission. *School Psychology Review, 28*(2), 251–263.

Powers, S. W., & Mitchell, M. J. (2001, August). *Improving dietary adherence and health status in children with cystic fibrosis.* Paper presented at the meeting of the American Psychological Association, San Francisco, CA.

Quittner, A. L. (1998). Measurement of quality of life in cystic fibrosis. *Current Opinion in Pulmonary Medicine, 4*, 326–331.

Quittner, A. L., Buu, A., Watrous, M., & Davis, M. A. (2000). *The Cystic Fibrosis Questionnaire (CFQ): User's manual.* Washington, DC: Cystic Fibrosis Foundation.

Quittner, A. L. Davis, M. A., & Larson, E. (2001, August). *Evaluation of a CD-ROM for young adolescents with cystic fibrosis.* Paper presented at the annual meeting of the American Psychological Association, San Francisco, CA.

Quittner, A. L., & DiGirolamo, A. M. (1998). Family adaptation to childhood disability and illness. In R. T. Ammerman & J. V. Campo (Eds.), *Handbook of pediatric psychology and psychiatry* (Vol. 2, pp. 70–102). Boston, MA: Allyn & Bacon Publishing Co.

Quittner, A. L., DiGirolamo, A. M., Michel, M., & Eigen, H. (1992). Parental response to cystic fibrosis: A contextual analysis of the diagnosis phase. *Journal of Pediatric Psychology, 17*(6), 683–704.

Quittner, A. L., Drotar, D., Ievers-Landis, C., Seidner, D., Slocum, N., & Jacobsen, J. (2000). Adherence to medical treatments in adolescents with cystic fibrosis: The development and evaluation of family-based interventions. In D. Drotar (Ed.), *Promoting adherence to medical treatment in childhood chronic illness: Interventions and methods.* Mahwah, NJ: Lawrence Erlbaum Associates Inc.

Quittner, A. L., Espelage, D. L., Ievers-Landis, C., & Drotar, D. (2000). Measuring adherence to medical treatments in childhood chronic illness: Considering multiple methods and sources of information. *Journal of Clinical and Psychology in Medical Settings, 7*, 41–54.

Quittner, A. L., Espelage, D. L., Opipari, A. C., Carter, B., Eid, M., & Eigen, H. (1998). Role strain in couples with and without a child with a chronic illness: Associates with marital satisfaction, intimacy, and daily mood. *Health Psychology, 17*, 112–124.

Quittner, A. L., & Glascoe, E. (2001, June). *Using the Cochrane Systematic Review to evaluate psychological interventions for cystic fibrosis.* Paper presented at the European Cystic Fibrosis Meeting, Vienna, Austria.

Quittner, A. L., & Hoffman, S. (2000–2001). *Evaluating and treating adherence problems in adolescents before and after heart or lung transplantation.* Children's Miracle Network grant.

Quittner, A. L., & Johnson, S. B. (2001). *Clinic-based adherence intervention for diabetes and cystic fibrosis.* National Institutes of Health grant Rockville, MD.

Quittner, A. L., & Opipari, L. C. (1994). Differential treatment of siblings: Interviews and diary analyses comparing two family contexts. *Child Development, 65*, 800–814.

Quittner, A. L., Opipari, L. C., Regoli, M. J., Jacobsen, J., & Eigen, H. (1992). The impact of caregiving and role strain on family life: Comparisons between mothers of children with cystic fibrosis and matched controls. *Rehabilitation Psychology, 37*, 289–304.

Quittner, A. L., Tolbert, V. E., Regoli, M. J., Orenstein, D., Hollingsworth, J. L., & Eigen, H. (1996). Development of the Role-play Inventory of Situations and Coping Strategies (RISCS) for parents of children with cystic fibrosis. *Journal of Pediatric Psychology, 21*, 209–235.

Rapoff, M. A. (1999). *Adherence to pediatric medical regimens.* New York: Kluwer Academic/Plenum Publishers.

Rapoff, M. A., & Christophersen, E. R. (1982). Compliance of pediatric patients with medical regimens: A review and evaluation. In R. B. Stuart (Ed.), *Adherence, compliance, and generalization in behavioral medicine* (pp. 79–124). New York: Brunner/Mazel.

Robin, A. L., & Foster, S. L. (1989). *Negotiating parent adolescent conflict: A behavioral-family systems approach.* New York: Guilford Press.

Robin, A. L., Seigel, P. T. (1999). Family therapy with eating-disordered adolescents. In. S. W. Russ & T. Ollendick (Eds.), *Handbook of psychotherapies with children and families. Issues in clinical child psychology* (pp. 301–325). New York: Kluwer Academic/Plenum Publishers.

Rolland, J. S. (1984). Toward a psychosocial typology of chronic and life-threatening illness. *Family Systems Medicine, 2*, 245–262.

Rolland, J. S. (1988). A conceptual model of chronic and life-threatening illness and its impact on families. In C. Chilman & E. Nunnally (Eds.) *Families in trouble: Volume 2. Chronic illness and disability* (pp. 17–68). Thousand Oaks, CA: Sage Publications, Inc.

Rosenfeld, M., Davis, R., FitzSimmons, S., Pepe, M., & Ramsey, B. (1997). Gender gap in cystic fibrosis mortality. *American Journal of Epidemiology, 145*(9), 794–803.

Ryan, L. L., & Williams, J. K. (1996). A cystic fibrosis handbook for teachers. *Journal of Pediatric Health Care, 10*(4), 174–179.

Saiman, L., Maher, F., Niu, W. W., Neu, H. C., Shaw, K. J., Muler, G., & Prince, A. (1996). Antibiotic susceptibility of multiply resistant *Pseudomonas aeruginosa* isolated from patients with cystic fibrosis, including candidates for transplantation. *Clinical Infectious Disease, 23*(3), 532–537.

Sawyer, S. M., Rosier, M. J., Phelan, P. D., & Bowes, G. (1995). The self-image of adolescents with cystic fibrosis. *Journal of Adolescent Health, 16*, 204–208.

Schipper, H., Clinch, J. J., & Olweny, C. L. (1996). Quality of life studies: Definitions and conceptual issues. In B. Spilker (Ed.), *Quality of life and pharmacoeconomics in clinical trials* (2nd ed., pp. 11–23). Philadelphia: Lippincott-Raven.

Sexson, S. B., & Madan-Swain, A. (1993) School reentry for the child with chronic illness. *Journal of Learning Disabilities, 26*(2), 115–125, 137.

Sherman, J. M., Baumstein, S., & Hendeles, L. (2001). Intervention strategies for children poorly adherent with asthma medications: One center's experience. *Clinical Pediatrics, 40*(5), 253–258.

Simmons, R. J., Corey, M., Cowen, L., Keenan, N., Robertson, J., & Levison, H. (1987). Behavioral adjustment of latency age children with cystic fibrosis. *Psychosomatic Medicine, 49*(3), 291–301.

Smith, M. S., Gad, M. T., & O'Grady, L. (1983). Psychosocial functioning, life change, and clinical status in adolescents with cystic fibrosis. *Journal of Adolescent Health Care, 4*(4), 230–234.

Spieth, L. E., Stark L. J., Mitchell, M. J., Schiller M., Cohen L. L., Mulvihill, M., & Hovell, M. F. (2001). Observational assessment of family functioning at mealtime in preschool children with cystic fibrosis. *Journal of Pediatric Psychology, 26*(4), 215–224.

Spilker, B. (1996). Introduction. In B. Spilker (Ed.), *Quality of life and pharmacoeconomics in clinical trials* (2nd ed., pp. 1–10). Philadelphia: Lippincott-Raven.

Stark, L. J., Bowen, A. M., Tyc, V. L., Evans, S., & Passero, M. A. (1990). A behavioral approach to increasing calorie consumption in children with cystic fibrosis. *Journal of Pediatric Psychology, 15*(3), 309–326.

Stark, L. J., Jelalian, E., Mulvihill, M. M., Powers, S. W., Bowen, A. M., Spieth, L. E., Keating, K., Evans, S., Creveling, S., Harwood, I., Passero, M. A., & Melbourne, M. F. (1995) Eating in preschool children with cystic fibrosis and healthy peers: behavioral analysis. *Pediatrics, 95*(2), 210–215.

Stark, L. J., Jelalian, E., Powers, S. W., Mulvihill, M. M., Opipari, L. C., Bowen, A., Harwood, I., Passero, M. A., Lapey, A., Light, M., & Hovell, M. F. (2000). Parent and child mealtime behavior in families of children with cystic fibrosis. *The Journal of Pediatrics, 136*(2), 195–200.

Stark, L. J., Knapp, L, Bowen, A. M., Powers, S. W., Jelalian, E., Evans, S., Passero, M. A., Mulvihill, M. M., & Hovell, M. (1993). Behavioral treatment of calorie consumption in children with cystic fibrosis: Replication with two-year follow-up. *Journal of Applied Behavior Analysis, 26*, 435–450.

Stark, L. J., & Quittner, A. L., (June 1996–May 2001). *Behavioral treatment of weight gain in cystic fibrosis* (PHS R01 #DK50092). National Institutes of Health grant. Rockville, MD: Author.

Taylor, S. (1980). The effect of chronic childhood illness upon well siblings. *Maternal-Child Nursing Journal, 9*, 109–116.

Thompson, R. J., Gil, K., Gustafson, K. E., George, L. S., Keith, B. R., Spock, A., & Kinney, T. R. (1994). Stability and change in the psychological adjustment of mothers of children and adolescents with cystic fibrosis and sickle cell disease. *Journal of Pediatric Psychology, 19*, 171–188.

Thompson, R. J., Gustafson, K. E., George, L. K., & Spock, A. (1994). Change over a 12-month period in the psychological adjustment of children and adolescents with cystic fibrosis. *Journal of Pediatric Psychology, 19*(2), 189–203.

Thompson, R. J., Gustafson, K. E., Hamlett, K.W., & Spock, A. (1992). Stress, coping, and family functioning in the psychological adjustment of mothers of children and adolescents with cystic fibrosis. *Journal of Pediatric Psychology, 17*, 573–585.

Thompson, R. J., Gustafson, K. E., Meghdadpour, S., Harrell, E., Johndrow, D. A., & Spock, A. (1992). The role of biomedical and psychosocial processes in the intellectual and academic functioning of children and adolescents with cystic fibrosis. *Journal of Clinical Psychology, 48*(1), 3–10.

Thompson, R. J., Hodges, K., & Hamlett, K. W. (1990). A matched comparison of adjustment in children with cystic fibrosis and psychiatrically referred and nonreferred children. *Journal of Pediatric Psychology, 15*(6), 745–759.

Treiber, F. A., Schramm, L., & Mabe, P. A. (1986). Children's knowledge and concerns towards a peer with cancer: A workshop intervention approach. *Child Psychiatry & Human Development, 16*(4), 249–260.

Tritt, S. G., & Esses, L. M. (1988). Psychosocial adaptation of siblings of children with chronic medical illnesses. *American Journal of Orthopsychiatry, 58*, 211–220.

Turk, J. (1964). Impact of cystic fibrosis on family functioning. *Pediatrics, 34*, 67–71.

Walker, L. S., Ford, M. B., & Donald, W. D. (1987). Cystic fibrosis and family stress. Effects of age and severity of illness. *Pediatrics, 79*, 239–245.

Walker, L. S., Ortiz-Valdes, J. A., & Newbrough, J. R. (1989). The role of maternal employment and depression in the psychological adjustment of chronically ill, mentally retarded, and well children. *Journal of Pediatric Psychology, 14*, 357–370.

Webb, A. K. (1995). Communicating with young adults with cystic fibrosis. *Postgraduate Medical Journal, 71*(837), 385–389.

Welsh, M. J., Tsui, L.-C., Boat, T. F., & Beaudet, A. L. (1995). Cystic fibrosis. In C. Scriver, A. L. Beaudet, W. E. Sly, & D. Valle (Eds.), *The metabolic and molecular bases of inherited disease set* (7th Ed., pp. 3799–3876). New York: McGraw-Hill.

Whyte, D. A. (1992). A family nursing approach to the care of a child with a chronic illness. *Journal of Advanced Nursing, 17*, 317–332.

Wysocki, T., Harris, M. A., Greco, P., Bubb, J., Danda, C. E., Harvey, L. M., McDonell, K., Taylor, A., & White, N. H. (2000). Randomized, controlled trial of behavior therapy for families of adolescents with insulin-dependent diabetes mellitus. *Journal of Pediatric Psychology, 25*(1), 23–33.

Zeltzer, L., Kellerman, J., Ellenberg, L., Dash, J., & Rigler, D. (1980). Psychologic effects of illness in adolescence. II: Impact of illness in adolescents—crucial issues and coping styles. *Journal of Pediatrics, 97*(1), 132–138.

Zuckerman, J. B., & Kotloff, R. M. (1998). Lung transplantation for cystic fibrosis. *Clinics in Chest Medicine, 19*(3), 534–554.

PART IV: Developmental Disorders and Conditions

20

Genetic Disorders in Children

LeAdelle Phelps
State University of New York at Buffalo

OVERVIEW

More than 200 genes have been identified as causing hereditary diseases; new genes are isolated at a rate of 1 per month (Singer & Berg, 1997; Thompson, Hellack, Braver, & Durica, 1997). Some childhood disorders originate solely from prenatal or postnatal environmental events (e.g., deaf-blindness in the offspring caused by the pregnant mother contracting rubella, exposure to toxic chemicals such as PCBs [polychlorinated biphenyls], or sustainment of a traumatic head injury) but many are clearly related to a defective gene transmitted through the generations (e.g., albinism, hemophilia, sickle cell anemia, Tay-Sachs). Still other conditions appear to result from genetic susceptibility coupled with prenatal or postnatal stressors (e.g., stuttering, Giles de la Tourette's syndrome). To facilitate an understanding of genetic conveyance, principles of hereditary transmission are presented and illustrated. A glossary is provided at the end of the chapter to facilitate an understanding of common genetic terms.

There are 23 pairs of human chromosomes; 22 are autosomes (non-sex related) and the 23rd pair determines sex (XX for female, XY for male). All of the chromosomes, with the exception of the male-determining Y, contain thousands of genes that are the basic units of heredity. Each gene consists of chemicals called nucleotides, which are designated by the letters A (adenine), C (cytosine), G (guanine), and T (thymine). The sequence of these nucleotides determines which specific protein is produced. Initial changes in the normal sequence of the nucleotides occur through sudden spontaneous mutations. The outcomes may be deletions, alterations, or faulty repetitions of the A, C, G, and T sequence, thus modifying the intended protein. This transformed protein causes the appearance of clustered symptoms that define a specific disorder or syndrome.

Spontaneous mutations occur during conception and early cell division. Some are so damaging that they cause the developing embryo to abort spontaneously. In fact, approximately 50% of all miscarriages are a result of chromosomal abnormalities (Harper, 1998). A few mutations may actually be beneficial to the carrier, but most result in detrimental outcomes. Because the mutation occurs in every cell of the body, it is present in the carrier's eggs or sperm and is thus passed down through the generations.

There are two types of spontaneous mutations: (1) point mutations, which are changes within a specific gene, and (2) chromosome alterations, which result in the deletion (monosomy or only one copy) or addition (trisomy or three copies) of an entire chromosome (Adolph, 1996). Because a modification in the number of chromosomes is exceedingly pernicious and usually results in immediate miscarriage of the embryo, most known genetic disorders result from point mutations. For example, only eight chromosome alterations have been observed in live births. Of these, only five are known to survive infancy with any degree of regularity: (1) Turner (XO), a monosomy (the "O" indicating an absence of the second chromosome); (2) Jacobs (XYY), a trisomy with an additional copy of the Y chromosome; (3) Klinefelter (XXY), a trisomy with two copies of the X chromosome; (4) Triple-X (XXX), a trisomy with three X chromosomes; and (5) Down syndrome (21,21,21), indicating a trisomy of the 21st chromosome (Singer & Berg, 1997). It should be noted that at least one X chromosome is always required; YO and YY embryos never develop.

The relationship between the genetic makeup (genotype) and the developmental outcomes or expression of these genes (phenotype) can be complex and is determined by an interplay of the genotype and the environment. For example, there may exist multiple alleles or forms of a given gene (e.g., A, a^1, a^2; in this case, there are three variants for the same gene). This results in a wide range of phenotype expression from mild penetrance to the full constellation of symptoms. Likewise, some characteristics are the result of the interplay of several genes and environmental factors. This phenomenon is referred to as multifactorial or polygenic transmission (Thompson et al., 1997).

Modern cytogenetic techniques can distinguish all 23 pairs of human chromosomes. In addition, sections of each chromosome can be studied with genetic analysis so refined as to identify the exact location or band of a genetic error. In giving the location, the involved arm of the chromosome is identified with the long arm given the designation of "q" whereas the letter "p" indicates the short arm. The letter "t" indicates that there has been a translocation of genetic material between two involved chromosomes, "+" indicates the addition of chromosomal material, and "−" indicates deletion. In an agreed-on international nomenclature, a genetic code would first list the number of chromosomes, next the sex chromosomes, and finally the genetic malformation. For example, the code

`46, XY, t(4, 22) (q32, q12)`

would indicate that the person in question has the normal number of chromosomes (23 pair), is male, and has a translocation of genetic data on chromosomes 4 and 22 with band 32 of the long arm (q32) of chromosome 4, and band 12 of the long arm of chromosome 22 affected. The designation of

`47, XY, +21`

would indicate a male with Down syndrome (i.e., one extra chromosome [47], which is a trisomy of chromosome 21). Finally, a female with cri-du-chat, caused by a deletion of the short arm of chromosome 5, would have a code of

`46, XX, 5p−`

GENETIC TRANSMISSION

There are numerous processes in which genetic conveyance can occur. The most common will be reviewed with illustrations to promote understanding.

Mendelian Transmission

The Austrian monk Gregor Mendel first identified simple patterns of inheritance in his classic pea plant experiments. As with Mendel's peas, many human traits are controlled by a single pair of genes, one inherited from each parent. Mendel assigned letters of the alphabet to represent such various hereditary traits. The first letter of the trait's name is used most frequently (e.g., "C" for cystic fibrosis, "H" for Huntington's disease).

Dominant Traits. Mendel's experiments illustrated that some traits are expressed whenever a dominant gene is present. He chose the word *dominant* because the gene's presence always determines the outcome. Applying the letter system mentioned above, Mendel used a capital letter (e.g., "H") to designate the presence of a dominant gene. The dominant gene may be inherited from either parent, and only one copy is necessary for the disorder to be evident. In such cases, children have a 50% probability of inheriting the disorder (see Fig. 20.1). If both parents have the disorder and each carries a single copy of the dominant gene, 75% of the offspring are affected (refer to Fig. 20.2). When both parents carry two copies of the dominant gene (HH), every child displays the disorder. Table 20.1 lists common autosomal dominant disorders.

Recessive Traits. Mendel used a lowercase letter (e.g., "c") to indicate a recessive gene. The term *recessive* was selected because the trait is never expressed when in combination with a dominant gene. The term *homogeneous* is applied when the two copies are identical in either dominance (CC) or recessiveness (cc). When the pair consists of one dominant gene and one recessive gene (Cc), the pattern is referred to as *heterogeneous*. Finally, the term *carrier* indicates a person "carries" one copy of the recessive gene; however, he or she shows no evidence of the disorder, because the dominant gene (C) is normal and both copies must be recessive (cc) for trait expression.

In recessive inheritance, the disorder is apparent in offspring only in the following circumstances: (1) both parents are carriers (Cc; see Fig. 20.3); (2) one parent is affected (cc) and the

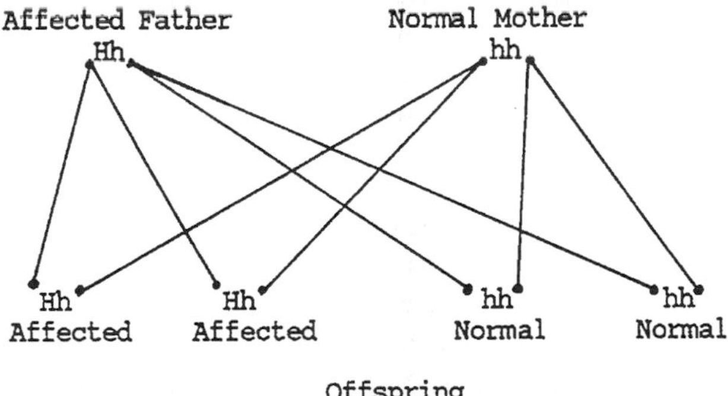

Defective gene (H) is dominant over its normal counterpart (h). As a result, offspring have a 50% chance of inheriting the disorder when one parent is affected.

FIG. 20.1. Dominant inheritance using Huntington's as a model when only one parent is affected.

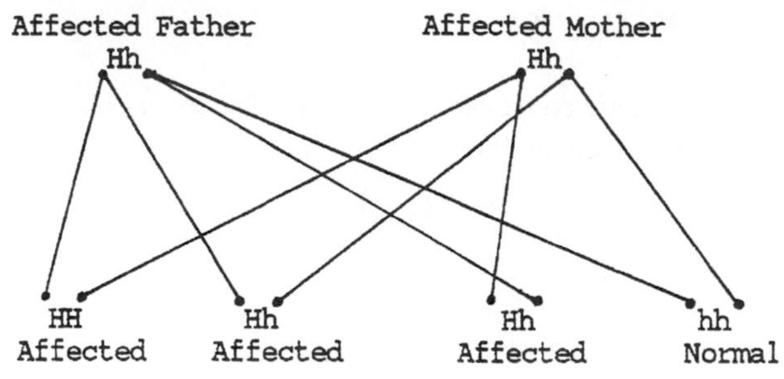

Defective gene (H) is dominant over its normal counterpart (h). Offspring have a 75% chance of inheritance when both affected parents are heterogeneous for the disorder.

FIG. 20.2. Dominant inheritance using Huntington's as a model when both parents are affected.

TABLE 20.1
Common Autosomal Dominant, Autosomal Recessive, and X-Linked Disorders

Autosomal Dominant	*Autosomal Recessive*	*X- Linked*
Achondroplasia	Albinism	Aldrich syndrome
Apert syndrome	Bardet-Biedl syndrome	Alport syndrome
Huntington's disease	Congenital adrenal hyperplasia	Cerebral sclerosis, diffuse
Malignant hyperpyrexia	Cystic fibrosis	Color blindess (several types)
Marfan syndrome	Familial dysautonomia	Duchenne muscular dystrophy
Mystonic muscular dystrophy	Hurler syndrome	Hemphilia (A and B)
Neurofibromatosis	Louis-Bar syndrome	Lesch-Nylan syndrome
Treacher Collins syndrome	Phenylketonuria (PKU)	Male pattern baldness
Tuberous sclerosis	Tay-Sachs disease	Night blindness, congenital

Notes: Adolph, 1996; Harper, 1998; McKusick, 1998; Singer & Berg, 1997; Thompson, Hellack, Braver, & Durica, 1997.

other is a carrier (Cc; see Fig. 20.4); or (3) both parents are affected (cc). In such cases, the probability of inheritance is 25%, 50%, or 100% respectively. Examples of autosomal recessive disorders are listed in Table 20.1

X-Linked Disorders

Because the Y (male) chromosome is very small and carries little genetic information beyond gender typing, no serious diseases are conveyed via the Y chromosome and all gender-related transmissions are found on the X (female) chromosome. Recall that females carry two copies of the X chromosome (XX), whereas the males have only one (XY). Over 100 X-linked disorders or traits have been identified (McKusick, 1998). The large majority of these conditions are classified as X-linked recessive with the female (X^a X) functioning as a carrier. For the male (X^a Y), the presence of the gene is always apparent because there is no second X chromosome

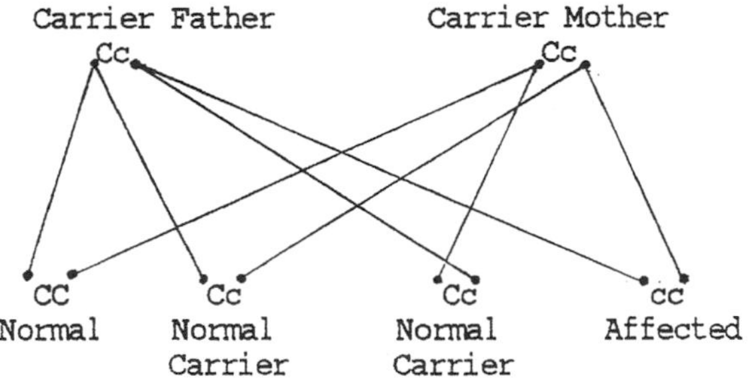

Offspring

Normal gene (C) is dominant over defective counterpart (c). Thus, two copies (cc) are necessary before the disorder becomes evident.

FIG. 20.3. Recessive inheritance using cystic fibrosis as a model when both parents are normal carriers.

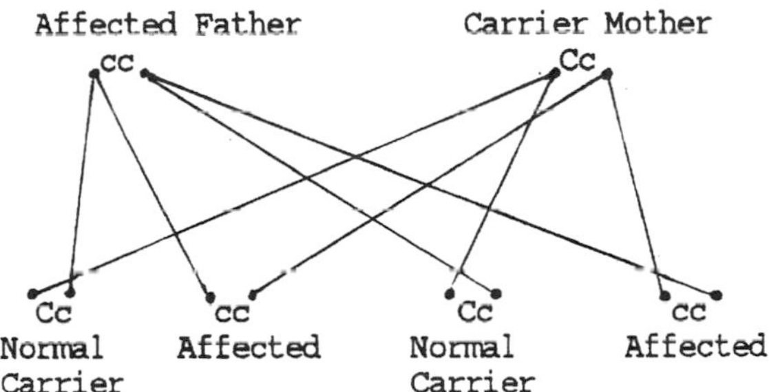

Offspring

Normal gene (C) is dominant over defective counterpart (c). Offspring have a 50% chance of inheritance when one parent is homogeneous and the other is a heterogeneous carrier.

FIG. 20.4. Recessive inheritance using cystic fibrosis as a model when one parent is affected and one parent is a normal carrier.

to negate the effects. Therefore, the disorders are primarily recessive for females and dominant for males. Because the female has two copies of the X chromosome, she is affected only if the disorder is X-linked dominant, which is extremely rare, or if she carries a copy of the defective gene on each X chromosome, which also is rare. The most common pattern is for the mother to be a carrier and pass the disorder to one half of her sons; none of the daughters shows the abnormality, yet one half are carriers (refer to Fig. 20.5). Only when the father has the disorder and the mother is a carrier can an affected daughter be produced (see Fig. 20.6). Thus, X-linked abnormalities produce significantly different gender outcomes. Refer to Table 20.1 for a listing of the more common X-linked disorders.

Entire Chromosome Additions (Trisomy) or Deletions (Monosomy)

Trisomies occur when an entire chromosome is replicated and results in three rather than two copies. Autosomal chromosome trisomies are rare with only four resulting in occasional live births: trisomy 21 (1.5 per 1,000 births; referred to as Down syndrome), trisomy 18 (0.12 per

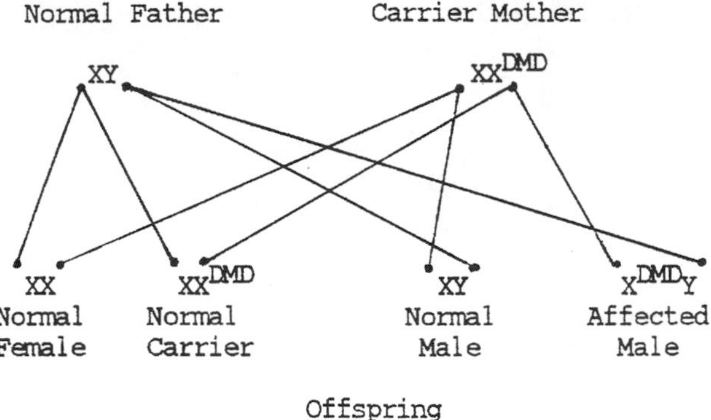

One half of all male offspring will display the disorder; one half of females will be carriers. Thus, significant gender disparity is common in X-linked recessive traits.

FIG. 20.5. X-linked recessive inheritance using Duchenne's muscular dystrophy as a model when the mother is a normal carrier.

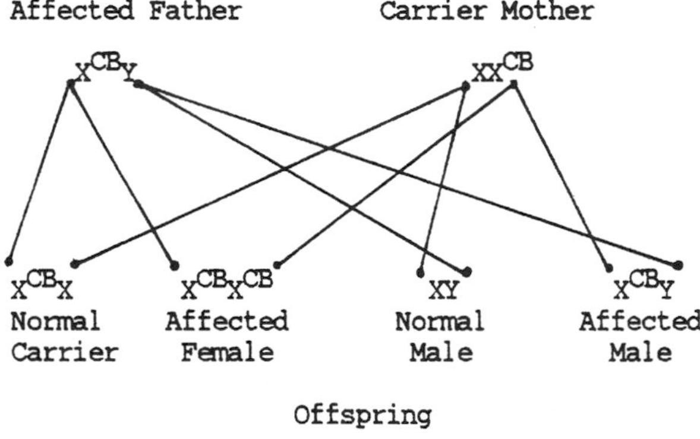

Only when the father has the disorder and the mother is either a carrier or similarly affected can a daughter display the abnormality.

FIG. 20.6. X-linked recessive inheritance using color blindness as a model when the father is affected and mother is a normal carrier.

1,000 births), trisomy 13 (0.07 per 1,000 births), and trisomy 22 (0.05 per 1,000 births). Limb defects, cleft lip and/or palate, internal organ dysfunction, renal disease, and perinatal infant mortality are common outcomes of trisomies 13, 18, and 22. Only infants with Down syndrome survive into childhood. The risk of all four of these autosomal chromosome additions increases with maternal age (Cassidy & Allanson, 2001).

There are three sex chromosome trisomies: XXY (Klinefelter syndrome), which occurs in 1.5 per 1,000 live births, XYY (Jacobs syndrome; 1.5 per 1,000 live births), and XXX (Triple-X; 0.65 per 1,000 live births). The outcome of these syndromes varies. For example, reduced intelligence is apparent only in Triple-X syndrome, XYY results in severe acne, and XXY males are sterile with atrophied testes (Harper, 1998).

Monosomies are extremely rare in live births with the only reported form being XO (Turner syndrome) with an occurrence of 0.4 in 1,000 live births (Harper, 1998). As mentioned previously, the "O" indicates the absence of the second sex chromosome. Females with Turner's are sterile, usually of normal intelligence with minimal behavior problems, but have the physical anomalies of short stature, neck webbing, and cardiac defects (Cassidy & Allanson, 2001).

Microrepetitions and Deletions

Some disorders are a result of faulty repeats of the genetic code within only a small portion of a particular chromosome. Fragile X syndrome is perhaps the best example of this phenomenon. It is caused by a repeat expansion of the nucleotides (CGG) that occur in the fragile X mental retardation 1 gene (FMR1) at the Xq27.3 site (i.e., band 27.3 of the long arm of the X chromosome). A small expansion (i.e., 50–200 repeats) is usually not associated with noticeable outcomes. Between 200–230 repeats usually result in moderate symptomatology whereas 250–2000 repeats result in the full constellation of Fragile X features (i.e., mental retardation, facial dysmorphology, attention deficit hyperactivity disorder (ADHD), autistic-like behaviors; Cassidy & Allanson, 2001). Thus, depending on the extent of the faulty repetition, the spectrum of clinical involvement can be very broad. Likewise, there is often considerable variability in outcome between the genders with the heterozygous female (one X copy is normal whereas the other copy carries the repeat) showing little to no effects, whereas the male ($X^{FMR1}Y$) may be very affected depending on the number of repeats.

Also evident are deletions of genetic material. Phenotypic features may be less severe in microdeletions than when the entire chromosome is lost. Examples of genetic disorders associated with microdeletions include cri du chat (5p-), Prader-Willi syndrome (15q11 through 13-), Smith-Magenis syndrome (17p11.2-), and Williams syndrome (7q11.23-).

Multiple Gene Paths

Some disorders can result from several genetic pathways. DiGeorge syndrome is one such example. To date, cases of autosomal dominance, autosomal recessive, and partial deletions on chromosome 22 have been identified (Driscoll, 1994). Likewise, albinism has an autosomal recessive type (most common), autosomal dominant (less common), and an X-linked type (rare). Just as with Fragile X syndrome, outcomes in albinism can also vary, with some persons having albinism yet displaying few, if any, of the primary symptoms. Such outcomes have historically been referred to as *nonpenetrant* or *partial penetrance*. Finally, different genetic pathways can result in similar outcomes. For example, there are numerous types of muscular dystrophies with the type and outcome based on the genetic involvement. Autosomal dominant cases result in myotonic dystrophy, autosomal recessive in congenital muscular dystrophy, and X-linked in Duchenne and Becker muscular dystrophies.

GENETIC TESTING

The Human Genome Project was conceived in the mid-1980s and officially launched October 1, 1990. The intent of the extensive endeavor was to map the entire human genome by the year 2005. Private companies, the most notable being Celera Genomics, were also working independently to map the entire set of human DNA. On June 26, 2000, Francis Collins, head of the Human Genome Project, and Craig Venter, head of Celera Genomics, jointly announced that they had completed a "rough draft" of the entire human genome (Ridley, 2001). This development further propelled the possibility for genetic testing prior to pregnancy, identification of genetic disorders in utero, and the assessment of risk status for diseases common in a family before symptom onset (i.e., ovarian cancer, Alzheimer's). For example, in addition to tracking simple Mendelian genetic disorders such as Huntington's, cystic fibrosis, or Tay-Sachs disease, some testing firms assess a person's susceptibility to future diseases on the basis of genetic markers that indicate risk status.

Because each cell contains two copies of every gene, analysis for anomalous genes is as easy as giving a blood or inner cheek swab sample. For example, the p53 gene on chromosome 17 is implicated in 52 different types of cancers. Approximately 90% of cervix cancers and 30–40% of breast cancers are related to the 17p53 band (Teichler-Zallen, 1997). A sampling of other genes and gene markers identified during the last 5 years include Type II diabetes, total baldness, obsessive-compulsive disorder, a severe form of ADHD, Lou Gehrig's disease, color blindness, basal cell carcinoma, prostrate cancer, Usher syndrome, bipolar disorder, progressive myoclonus epilepsy, schizophrenia, and several sites for both early onset and late onset Alzheimer's. In short, Celera Genomics and the Human Genome Project have been so successful that every chromosome has been identified and detailed DNA markers for numerous disorders have been mapped to a varying degree of accuracy.

Current national debate focuses on genetic testing of unborn fetuses, the right to terminate a pregnancy on the basis of a genetic anomaly, and health insurance denials or terminations on the basis of positive genetic findings (Harper, 1998). Ranging from tests that identify diseases decades before the onset of symptoms to cures using gene replacement through immature embryo tissue, the ethical quandaries abound (Murray, Rothstein, & Murray, 1996).

Prenatal testing is a relatively simple process for many disorders. The dilemma of what to do with the information, however, may be quite difficult. Weeks 15–16 of gestation is the earliest time that a satisfactory amniocentesis sample can be reliably obtained (Harper, 1998). Thus, if a couple has decided to terminate the pregnancy if the results are positive, the procedure may have to occur as late as 18 weeks' gestation. Yet it is not uncommon for the parents' attitude to change during pregnancy, especially once fetal movement has occurred.

Consider, for example, the case of Sharon and David Zali (pseudonym). David had witnessed two of his siblings endure excruciating childhood deaths from cystic fibrosis. Determined that he would preclude his offspring from suffering these agonies, he insisted that he and his wife, Sharon, be tested for the recessive cystic fibrosis gene before conceiving a child. Each donated a cheek swab sample for genetic analysis. Notification came 5 days later; both were carriers. Now the decisions became difficult. There is a 25% chance that conception will result in an affected fetus (refer to Fig. 20.3). The couple contemplated reproductive options including sperm donation from a noncarrier, adoption, and going childless. After considerable debate and reflection, they elected to conceive, identify the cystic fibrosis status of the fetus as early as possible, and terminate the pregnancy if necessary.

It took David and Sharon 8 months to get pregnant. Genetic testing could not occur for 3 1/2 months because amniocentesis prior to that time would risk miscarriage and is not reliable. When the time came, cell samples were removed from the placenta, not the fetus. (Because the placenta is developed entirely from fetal cells, placental analysis provides an accurate diagnosis with little possibility of injury to the developing fetus.)

The couple waited 7 days for the news that, for them, meant life or death. Yet, unwittingly they had bonded with the unborn child. The months of striving for pregnancy, the weeks of morning sickness, and the hours spent in outpatient surgery completing placental sampling had exacted a transformation. Before being notified of the genetic status of their child, the couple concluded that they could not abort the pregnancy, come what may. Because in utero gene therapy for cystic fibrosis is still in the experimental stage (Larsen, Morrow, Happel, & Sharp, 1997), choices are limited. For the Zalis, the laws of probability paid off; their first baby was a healthy carrier. They became pregnant a second time and elected not to undergo amniocentesis. Given their inability to terminate the first pregnancy, they doubted that they could abort the second. Unfortunately, the second child inherited a defective gene from both parents and has cystic fibrosis.

As with other current sociopolitical quandaries (e.g., unlimited access to abortion, medically assisted suicide for terminally ill patients), the implications of deciphering the human genome are momentous. Whether one views genetic testing and possible in utero gene therapy or termination of the pregnancy as tinkering with destiny or the welcome relief from disabling disorders, there is no turning back. As genetic testing increases in sophistication and we are able to identify potential carriers of devastating diseases, clear roles for psychologists and other mental health practitioners will emerge, particularly in assisting families with appropriate decision making.

REVIEW OF SEVERAL DIVERSE GENETIC DISORDERS

A brief synopsis of several genetic disorders that dominant pediatric health-related services follows. Data regarding etiology, prevalence, and psychosocial implications are discussed.

Down Syndrome

Down syndrome (DS) occurs in approximately 1 of every 800–1,000 live births (Gerlai, 2000). Caused by an extra copy of chromosome 21 (trisomy 21), the genetic disorder is highly related to the age of the mother. For example, the chances of having a child with DS are about 1 in 400 at age 35, 1 in 110 at age 40, and 1 in 35 at age 45 (National Down Syndrome Society, 1995). The common features of DS include: (1) mental retardation, (2) flat facial profile, (3) epicanthal folds (small skin creases in the inner corners of the eye), (4) muscle hypotonia, (5) abnormal shape of the ear, (6) simian crease (deep ridge across the center of the palm), (7) dysplastic middle phalanx of the fifth finger (one flexion furrow instead of two), (8) excessive space between the large and second toes, (9) enlargement of the tongue in relationship to size of the mouth, and (10) hyperflexibility Other health-related difficulties associated with DS include cardias defects, Alzheimer's-type dementia, leukemia, hypothyroidism, and cervical spine instability (Prasher & Cunningham, 2001).

Because of the brain structures affected by DS (hippocampus, cerebellum, and specific neocortex cell layers; Nadel, 1995), cognitive competencies, motor dexterity, and language development are affected. Although the degree of mental retardation can vary from severe to borderline, most children with DS score in the mild to moderate range on IQ tests (Prasher & Cunningham, 2001). Because of cervical spine instability, musculoskeletal concerns are evident (Merrick, 2000). Expressive language skills are fairly limited (Fowler, 1995). Historically, academic expectations for persons affected with DS were low. More recently, however, there is increasing recognition that acquisition of modest reading and math skills is possible (Fowler, Doherty, & Boynton, 1995).

Klinefelter Syndrome

Caused by two or more X chromosomes in a male (XXY, XXXY), Klinefelter syndrome occurs in approximately 1.3 to 1.5 per 1,000 live births (Ratcliffe, 1999). Because the disorder produces no obvious symptoms, the majority of males with Klinefelter's are never identified. The most common features include lack of facial, body, and pubic hair; obesity; and diminished penile length and testicular volume (Smyth, & Bremner, 1998). Often first diagnosed in adolescence or adult life, males seek medical assistance because of hypogonadism, infertility, or enlargement of the breasts.

Most children and adolescents with Klinefelter syndrome score within the normal range on IQ tests with better performance on nonverbal tasks and somewhat lower presentation on language-based competencies (Patwardhan, Eliez, Bender, Linden, & Reiss, 2000). The primary treatment for this disorder is testosterone replacement therapy started at age 11 or 12 (Smyth & Bremner, 1998). Because the disorder is often not diagnosed by that age, replacement therapy completed at a later date is still considered appropriate with beneficial outcomes including increased facial and pubic hair, more masculine deposition of body fat, increased strength, and improved libido. Unfortunately, testicular size, breast enlargement (gynecomastia), and sterility are not positively affected by testosterone replacement (Patwardhan et al., 2000).

Lesch-Nyhan Disease

Lesch-Nyhan disease is caused by a mutation on the X chromosome that occurs in approximately 1 in 380,000 live births (Matthew, Solan, & Barabas, 1995). It results in the almost complete absence of the enzyme hypothine guanine phosphoribosl transferase (HGPRT) with the consequence of an enormous overproduction of uric acid in body fluids (Little & Rodemaker, 1998). Outcomes include below average cognitive functioning, spastic cerebral palsy, choreoathetosis (rapid jerky involuntary muscle movements), and severe aggressive self-mutilation (Matthew et al., 1995). The self-biting may be so severe as to lead to loss of tissue around the lips and partial amputation of the tongue (Mikhail & King, 2001). Biting is frequently controlled only when the primary teeth are extracted early in development.

All children with this disease have such severe cerebral palsy and involuntary muscle movements that they are unable to stand or walk without assistance (Breese, Mueller, & Schroeder, 1987). Because of the motor and self-mutilation difficulties, most individuals with Lesch-Nyhan require some form of physical restraint at all times (Page & Nyhan, 1990). Medications such as gabapentin are frequently necessary to reduce the aggressive and self-injurious behaviors to a manageable limit (McManaman & Tam, 1999).

Mucopolysaccharide Disorders

The mucopolysaccharides (MPS) are rare (1 in 100,000 live births) metabolic disorders transmitted by autosomal recessive (Hurler, Scheie, Hurler-Scheie, Sanfilippo syndromes) or sex-linked recessive (Hunter syndrome) inheritance. The genetic defect causes a deficiency of lysomal enzymes, which results in cellular malfunctioning in the connective tissue (Kachur & Del Maestro, 2000). There are numerous variants of MPS with classification based on the specific enzyme deficiency. For example, MPS Type I (Hurler, Scheie, Hurler-Scheie) is caused by an inadequacy of the enzyme iduronidase and results in progressive curvature of the spine, hand deformities, contractions of the joints, and unusual facial features such a large head, flattening of the bridge of the nose, wide nostrils, thick lips, and a large protruding tongue (Brown & Trivette, 1998). Because of joint stiffness, mobility is limited. Cardiac complications are common with death usually occurring in the first decade of life because of cardiorespiratory failure (Wraith, 1995).

MPS II (Hunter) is related to iduronate sulphate sulphatase deficiency (Wraith, 1995). The primary features of Hunter syndrome include distortion of facial bones with a depressed nasal bridge and enlarged head, joint stiffness, claw-like hand deformity, and dwarfism (Brown & Trivette, 1998). Progressive neurodegeneration results in a vegetative existence with death usually in adolescence (Wraith, 1995).

MPS III (Sanfilippo) is related to four separate enzyme defects, identified as A, B, C, or D (Jacob-Timm & Daniels, 1998). Although there is considerable heterogeneity of outcomes, the general spectrum of effects include early normal cognitive development followed by progressive mental retardation, severe behavior problems, respiratory difficulties, and seizures. As with Type II, progressive brain damage results in immobility and death in the teenage years (Wraith, 1995).

Neurofibromitosis

Neurofibromitosis type 1 (NF1) is an autosomal (chromosome 17) dominant disorder with an appropriate incidence of 1 in 3,000 (Fete, 2000). The condition results in café au lait maculas (spots of pigmentation similar to birthmarks), neurofibromas (visible benign tumors of various sizes on and under the skin), focal brain lesions frequently observed in the basal ganglia, cerebellum, brain stem, and subcortical white matter, freckling in areas not exposed to sunlight such as the armpit or groin area, and Lisch nodules (slightly raised benign tumors of the iris; Phelps, 1998).

Neurofibromitosis type 2 (NF2) is a distinct dominant disorder caused by a missing gene located on the long arm of chromosome 22 (Fete, 2000). NF2 affects only 1 in 50,000 persons. The disorder results in benign neuromas on the eighth cranial nerve with corollary hearing loss, balance disturbances, pain, headaches, and tinnitus (ringing or buzzing sounds in the ears). The tumors usually appear in the second or third decade of life.

Noonan Syndrome

Characterized by short stature, congenital heart disease, pulmonary stenosis, delayed puberty, webbing of the neck (extra skin on the back of the neck), downward slanting eyes with drooping eyelids, and ocular hypertelorism (wide spaces between the eyes), Noonan syndrome is caused by autosomal dominant inheritance (Noonan, 1999). An incidence of 1:1,000 live births is expected. Developmental and cognitive delays are common outcomes (van der Burgt et al., 1999).

Perhaps the most notable concern with Noonan is cardiovascular abnormality. A recent study reported over 80% of patients with Noonan's had cardiac defects, making it essential that any child with suspected Noonan syndrome undergo a complete cardiovascular evaluation (Sharland, Burch, McKenna, & Patton, 1999). The other primary consideration with Noonan is the short stature. Studies have indicated positive outcomes with human growth hormone therapy (Cotterill, McKenna, & Brady, 1996; Kirk et al., 2001).

Phenylketonuria

Phenylketonuria (PKU) is transmitted by autosomal recessive inheritance and occurs in 1:15,000 live births (Carey & Lesen, 1998). Screening for PKU involves a blood test that measures phenylalanine accumulation. Outcomes include moderate to severe mental retardation, hyperactivity, aggressiveness, and motor difficulties (Stermerdink et al., 1995).

The treatment for PKU consists primarily of dietary supplements and restrictions. Food intake must provide enough proteins and other essential nutrients to ensure optimal growth and development while maintaining a low concentration of phenylalanine in the blood. Use of synthetic foods and low-protein dietary supplements are necessary because it is impossible to devise a diet from natural foods that lowers phenylalanine yet provides essential nutrients (Fisch et al., 1995). Dietary compliance is often a significant problem for children and adolescents who may have little appreciation for the necessity of a rigid, mundane diet when surrounded by the varied and appealing foods consumed by other family members and friends.

Prader-Willi Syndrome

The etiology of Prader-Willi syndrome (PW) is autosomal recessive involving multiple genes on chromosome 15 (15q11-q13 deletion or mutation). With an approximate incidence of 1 in 15,000 live births, it is characterized by mental retardation, short stature, hyperphagia (a compulsion to eat incessantly), behavioral difficulties (temper tantrums, lability, aggression), and compulsivity (hoarding of nonfood items, repetitive skin picking, verbal perseverations; Cassidy & Allanson, 2001; Dykens, Leckman, & Cassidy, 1996).

Without appropriate dietary and behavioral interventions, children with Prader-Willi will quickly become morbidly obese (State & Dykens, 2000). The hyperphagia is very resistant to treatment, with parents reporting children with Prader-Willi eating dog food, garbage, frozen meat, jars of peanut butter, containers of salt, and cubes of butter (Daniel & Gridley, 1998). Treatment with human growth hormone, locking of food storage cabinets and refrigerator, regular exercise, and highly controlled, planned dietary intake (portion controls, calorie counts) have been successful in reducing the morbid obesity and notable cardiovascular risk (Martin et al., 1998).

Williams Syndrome

Caused by a rare (1:20,000 births) microdeletion on chromosome 7 (7q11.23–), Williams syndrome (WS) results in craniofacial dysmorphology (full checks, facial asymmetry, epicanthal folds, short turned-up nose, star-shaped iris pattern, protruding upper lip, and a relative lack of a philtrum or groove on the upper lip) and mild to moderate retardation (Schmitt, 2001). Yet there is considerable variability in skill functioning, with profoundly impaired visual-spatial competencies but relatively intact language abilities (Schultz, Grelotti, & Pober, 2001). The behavioral phenotype includes excessive sociability with strangers, impulsivity, hyperactivity, yet heightened anxiety (Schmitt, 2001).

The long-term outlook for children with WS is similar to that of other disorders resulting in low cognitive functioning. For example, Udwin (1990) reported that most adults with WS had considerable behavioral and social deficiencies, necessitating daily supervision and, thus, limited independent functioning. Poor motor skills and restricted cognitive competencies resulted in most of these adults living in supervised housing and being employed in managed workshop facilities.

CONCLUSIONS

The last decade has resulted in an explosion of knowledge regarding genetic disorders. It is now possible to accurately identify the genetic basis for many syndromes that affect children. Although in utero gene replacement is still at the experimental stage, analysis of one's genetic code and identification of anomalous chromosomes and genes is not. In the past, risk status was determined by an extensive family history with probable outcomes stated in general probabilities. Now one need only donate a cheek swab sample to receive a definitive answer as to the presence of a particular gene or chromosomal anomaly. In addition, susceptibility to future diseases on the basis of genetic markers is also a possibility. With this wealth of information comes greatly enhanced family planning and treatment options. Yet it also carries the burden of weighty decision making and sociopolitical quandaries. It is anticipated that as this field continues to develop, psychologists will have a role in working with families and children that are designated at risk or who, in fact, are affected with genetic anomalies.

GLOSSARY

Allele: One of several alternative structural forms of a gene.

Autosomal: Non-sex related chromosome.

Carrier: A person who "carries" one copy of the recessive gene; however, he or she shows no evidence of the disorder, because the dominant gene (C) is normal and both copies must be recessive (cc) for trait expression.

Congenital: Present at birth.

Dominant: A gene requiring only one copy to show expression of the characteristic or disorder.

Etiology: Source or origin of a disorder.

Genotype: Genetic makeup of the individual.

Heterogeneity (heterogeneous, adj.): A pair of genes that are dissimilar.

Heterozygous: Possessing different genes for a given characteristic.

Homogeneity (homogeneous, adj.): A pair of genes that are similar.

Homozygous: Possessing two of the same genes for a given characteristic.

Monosomy: One member of a chromosomal pair is missing (e.g., XO wherein O stands for the missing sex chromosome).

Multifactorial: Characteristics are result from several genes and environmental factors affecting one another.

Nucleotide: Consists of a sugar, a phosphate, and one of four types of bases: adenine (A), guanine (G), cytosine (c), or thymine (T).

Partial Penetrance: Only some of the characteristics of a given disorder are expressed even though the person carries the gene for the anomaly.

Penetrance: Proportion of genotype expressed in the phenotype.

Phenotype: Outward appearance of a genetic characteristic.

Point mutations: Alterations within a specific gene.

Polygenic: Caused by several genes interacting with one another.

Recessive: A gene requiring two copies to show expression of the characteristic or disorder.

Trisomy: Presence of three copies of a specific chromosome.

REFERENCES

Adolph, K. W. (1996). *Human molecular genetics.* San Diego: Academic Press.

Breese, G. R., Mueller, R. A., & Schroeder, S. R. (1987). The neurochemical basis of symptoms in the Lesch-Nyhan syndrome. In E. Schopler & G. B. Mesibov (Eds.), *Neurobiological issues in autism* (pp. 145–160). New York: Plenum.

Brown, M. B., & Trivette, P. S. (1998). Mucopolysaccharide disorders. In L. Phelps (Ed.), *Health-related disorders in children and adolescents: A guidebook for understanding and educating* (pp. 442–452). Washington, D.C.: American Psychological Association.

Carey, K. T., & Lesen, B. M. (1998). Phenylketonuria. In L. Phelps (Ed.), *Health-related disorders in children and adolescents: A guidebook for understanding and educating* (pp. 519–523). Washington, D.C.: American Psychological Association.

Cassidy, S. B., & Allanson, J. E. (2001). *Management of genetic syndromes.* New York: Wiley.

Cotterill, A. M., McKenna, W. J., & Brady, A. F. (1996). The short-term effects of growth hormone therapy on height velocity and cardiac ventricular well thickness in children with Noonan's syndrome. *Journal of Clinical Endocrinology and Metabolism, 81*, 2291–2297.

Daniel, L. L., & Gridley, B. E. (1998). Prader-Willi syndrome. In L. Phelps (Ed.), *Health-related disorders in children and adolescents: A guidebook for understanding and educating* (pp. 524–540). Washington, D.C.: American Psychological Association.

Driscoll, D. A. (1994). Genetic basis of DiGeorge and veloccardiofacial syndromes. *Current Opinions in Pediatrics, 6*, 702–706.

Dykens, E. M., Leckman, J. F., & Cassidy, S. B. (1996). Obsessions and compulsions in Prader-Willi syndrome. *Journal of Child Psychology and Psychiatry, 37*, 995–1002.

Fete, M. (2000). Neurofibromatosis: Phenotype, natural history, and pathogenesis. *Neurology, 55*, 325–327.

Fisch, R. O., Chang, P. N., Weisberg, S., Goldberg, P., Guttler, F., & Tsai, M. Y. (1995). PKU patients decades after diet. *Journal of Inherited Metabolic Disease, 18*, 347–353.

Fowler, A. E. (1995). Linguistic variability in persons with Down syndrome: Research and implications. In L. Nadel & D. Rosenthal (Eds.), *Down syndrome: Living and learning in the community* (pp. 121–131). New York: Wiley.

Fowler, A. E., Doherty, B. J., & Boynton, L. (1995). The basic reading skills of young adults with Down syndrome. In L. Nadel & D. Rosenthal (Eds.), *Down syndrome: Living and learning in the community* (pp. 182–196). New York: Wiley.

Gerlai, R. T. (2000). Down to less than 300 genes: The DNA sequence of human chromosome 21 and Down syndrome. *Trends in Neuroscience, 23*, 332.

Harper, P. S. (1998). *Practical genetic counseling* (5th ed.). Oxford: Butterworth-Heinemann Press.

Jacob-Timm, S., & Daniels, J. A. (1998). Sanfilippo syndrome. In L. Phelps (Ed.), *Health-related disorders in children and adolescents: A guidebook for understanding and educating* (pp. 571–577). Washington, D.C.: American Psychological Association.

Kachur, E., & Del Maestro, R. (2000). Mucopolysaccharidoses and spinal cord compression. *Neurosurgery, 47*, 223–229.

Kirk, J. M., Betts, P. R., Butler, G. E., Donaldson, M. D., Dunger, D. B., & Johnston, D. I. (2001). Short stature in Noonan syndrome: Response to growth hormone. *Archives of Disease in Childhood, 84*, 440–443.

Larsen, J. E., Morrow, S. L., Happel, L., & Sharp, J. F. (1997). Reversal of cystic fibrosis phenotype in mice by gene therapy in utero. *Lancet, 349*, 619–620.

Little, S. G., & Rodemaker, J. E. (1998). Lesch-Nyhan Disease. In L. Phelps (Ed.), *Health-related disorders in children and adolescents: A guidebook for understanding and educating* (pp. 386–391). Washington, D.C.: American Psychological Association.

Martin, A., State, M., Koenig, K., Schultz, R., Dykens, E. M., Cassidy, S. B., & Leckman, J. F. (1998). Prader-Willi syndrome. *The American Journal of Psychiatry, 155*, 1265–1273.

Matthew, W. S., Solan, A., & Barabas, G. (1995). Cognitive functioning in Leach-Nyhan syndrome. *Developmental Medicine and Child Neurology, 37*, 715–722.

McKusick, V. A. (1998). *Mendelian inheritance in man* (12th ed.). Baltimore, MD: Johns Hopkins University Press.

McManaman, J., & Tam, D. A. (1999). Gabapentin for self-injurious behavior in Lesch-Nyhan syndrome. *Pediatric Neurology, 20*, 381–382.

Merrick, J. (2000). Musculoskeletal concerns in Down's syndrome. *International Journal of Adolescent Medical Health, 12*, 53–59.

Mikhail, A. G., & King, B. H. (2001). Self-injurious behavior in mental retardation. *Current Opinion in Psychiatry, 14*, 457–461.

Murray, T. H., Rothstein, M. A. K., & Murray, R. F. (Eds.). (1996). *The human genome project and the future of health care*. Bloomington: Indiana University Press.

Nadel, L. (1995). Neural and cognitive development in down syndrome. In L. Nadel & D. Rosenthal (Eds.), *Down syndrome: Living and learning in the community* (pp. 107–114). New York: Wiley.

National Down Syndrome Society. (1995). *Questions and answers about down syndrome*. New York: National Down Syndrome Society.

Noonan, J. A. (1999). Noonan syndrome revisited. *The Journal of Pediatrics, 135*, 667–668.

Page, T., & Nyhan, W. L. (1990). Biochemical correlates of auto-aggressive behavior: Inferences from Lesch-Nyhan syndrome. In S. I. Deutch, A. Weizman, & R. Weizman (Eds.), *Applications of basic neuroscience to child psychiatry* (pp. 297–311). New York: Plenum Medical Book Company.

Patwardhan, A. J., Eliez, S., Bender, B., Linden, M. G., & Reiss, A. L. (2000). Brain morphology in Klinefelter syndrome: Extra X chromosome and testosterone supplementation. *Neurology, 54*, 2218–2223.

Phelps, L. (1998). Neurofibromatosis. In L. Phelps (Ed.), *Health-related disorders in children and adolescents: A guidebook for understanding and educating* (pp. 459–462). Washington, D.C.: American Psychological Association.

Prasher, V., & Cunningham, C. (2001). Down syndrome. *Current Opinion in Psychiatry, 14*, 431–436.

Ratcliffe, S. (1999). Long term outcome of sex chromosome abnormalities. *Archives of Disease in Childhood, 80*, 192–195.

Ridley, M. (2001, January). The year of the genome, the end of the great mystery, the real beginning of biology. *Discover*, 50–53.

Schmitt, J. E. (2001). Williams syndrome: Recent developments. *Current Opinion in Psychiatry, 14*, 451–456.

Schultz, R. T., Grelotti, D. J., & Pober, B. (2001). Genetics in childhood disorders XXVI: Williams syndrome and brain-behavior relationship. *Journal of the American Academy of Child and Adolescent Psychiatry, 40*, 606–609.

Sharland, M., Burch, M., McKenna, W. M., & Patton, M. A. (1999). A clinical study of Noonan syndrome. *Archives of Disease in Childhood, 67*, 178–183.

Singer, M., & Berg, P. (1997). *Exploring genetic mechanism*. Sausalito, CA: University Science Books.

Smyth, C. M., & Bremner, W. J. (1998). Klinefelter syndrome. *Archives of Internal Medicine, 158*, 1309–1314.

State, M. W., & Dykens, E. M. (2000). Genetics of childhood disorders: XV, Prader-Willi syndrome: Genes, brain, and behavior. *Journal of the American Academy of Child and Adolescent Psychiatry, 39*, 797–800.

Stermerdink, B. A., van der Meere, J. J., van der Molen, M. W., Kalverboer, A. F., Hendriks, M. M., Huisman, J., & van er Schot, L. W. (1995). Information processing in patients with early and continuously treated PKU. *European Journal of Pediatrics, 154*, 739–746.

Teichler-Zallon, D. (1997). *Does it run in the family? A consumer's guide to DNA testing for genetic disorders*. New Brunswick, NJ: Rutgers University Press.

Thompson, J. N., Hellack, J. J., Braver, G., & Durica, D. S. (1997). *Primer of genetic analysis: A problems approach* (2nd ed.). Cambridge: Cambridge University Press.

Udwin, O. (1990). A survey of adults with Williams syndrome and idiopathic infantile hypercalcaemia. *Developmental Medicine and Child Neurology, 13*, 232–244.

van der Burgt, I., Thoonen, G., Roosenboom, N., Assman-Hulsmans, C., Gabreels, F., & Otten, B. (1999). Patterns of cognitive functioning in school-aged children with Noonan syndrome associated with variability in phenotypic expression. *Journal of Pediatrics, 135*, 707–713.

Wraith, J. E. (1995). The mucopolysaccharidoses: A clinical review and guide to management. *Archives of Disease in Childhood, 72*, 263–267.

21

Teratology of Alcohol: Implications for School Settings

Julie A. Kable
Claire D. Coles
*Emory University School of Medicine and
The Marcus Institute, a Division of Kennedy-Krieger
Institute at Emory University*

Fetal alcohol syndrome (FAS) was brought to the attention of professionals and the public more than 25 years ago (Jones & Smith, 1973; Jones, Smith, Ulleland, & Streissguth, 1973). Since that time, there has been extensive study, both in animal models and in clinical studies, of the teratogenic effects of prenatal alcohol exposure on the development of offspring, confirming original observations and extending our understanding of this disorder. Estimates of the incidence of this disorder in the general population of the United States, using prospective active surveillance studies, range from .50 to .97 cases per 1,000 with clinically based estimates being higher particularly among high risk groups (Abel, 1998). Thus, although it is not widely recognized as such, prenatal alcohol exposure is one of the leading causes for birth defects and cognitive disorders and the implications for academic functioning are significant.

While many debates continue regarding the subtleties of the neurobehavioral profile (U.S. Department of Health and Human Services, 2000), there is no longer any question that this disorder has significant long-term consequences both for affected individuals and for their families. Initially, because of a teratogenic perspective, much empirical research was focused on the neurocognitive consequences of exposure with limited attention to the clinical and social outcomes. However, with better identification of this disorder, parents and clinicians became increasingly aware of the behavioral, adaptive, and social consequences and began to ask for appropriate methods for treatment and habilitation of affected individuals (Center for Disease Controls and Prevention (CDC), 1998; DeVries, 1999; Weinberg, 1997). The problem of "secondary disabilities" in those who were not appropriately treated was well described by Streissguth, Barr, Kogan, and Bookstein (1996) and has energized research on educational, mental health, and social/environmental interventions needed to habilitate individuals with FAS.

Using animal models and human birth cohorts, considerable attention has been devoted to the identification and description of the specific effects associated with a given substance of abuse (e.g., alcohol, cocaine, heroin); however, the reality for most alcohol-affected children is a history of prenatal exposure to many different substances. For example, women who drink at excessive levels during their pregnancy are more likely to smoke, use marijuana, and use cocaine during their pregnancy as well (Day & Robles, 1989; Giunta & Streissguth, 1988; Hingson et al., 1982; Jacobson et al., 1991; Kuzma & Kissinger, 1981). In addition to being polysubstance users, these women usually differ in terms of their physical and medical status was well as in lifestyle from those who do not abuse drugs and alcohol during pregnancy (Coles & Platzman, 1993; Giunta & Streissguth, 1988; Jacobson et al., 1991; Jacobson, Fein, Jacobson, Schwartz, & Dowler, 1984; Kuzma & Kissinger, 1981; Stratton, Howe, & Battaglia, 1996), including nutritional adequacy of their diets (Day & Richardson, 1994; Dreosti & Joschko, 1995). These issues are challenging to researchers attempting to identify the specific teratogenic actions of a particular drug as well as to clinicians working with individual clients. Understanding the practical consequences of prenatal exposure and maternal substance abuse to the child in academic settings requires identification of the teratogenic effects of the drug as well as pathogenic effects of the environment and its interaction with the initial physical insult. This chapter provides information on the neurodevelopmental consequences of heavy prenatal alcohol exposure while bearing in mind the impact of the adverse lifestyle that these children often experience. Information from prospective longitudinal studies as well as aggregated case samples are provided to describe the typical physical and neurodevelopmental profiles of children with FAS but clinicians are encouraged to keep in mind that children with FAS can be very diverse in their presentation. For this reason, individualized assessments are needed to address the child's unique social, educational, physical, and adaptive needs.

MAKING THE DIAGNOSIS OF FAS

Prenatal exposure to alcohol is associated with a spectrum of negative outcomes, including dysmorphology, growth retardation, microcephaly, and cognitive impairment (Jones and Smith, 1973; Stratton et al., 1996; Streissguth, 1997). The individual with all these deficits can be diagnosed with fetal alcohol syndrome (FAS). The diagnostic code used for this disorder is "761.71:NOXIOUS INFLUENCE AFFECTING FETUS VIA PLACENTA OR BREAST MILK, I.E. ALCOHOL, FETAL ALCOHOL SYNDROME" (ICD-9-CM, 1997, p. *181*).

Although there is some variability in the outcomes for individuals, both longitudinal and clinical studies of alcohol-affected children have confirmed a set of core diagnostic features. These include physical characteristics like facial dysmorphology and growth retardation, as well as global cognitive delays of variable severity. Some of the physical characteristics show some diminution as a result of developmental change over time but the cognitive impact appears to be persistent and to be aggravated by caregiving instability and the impoverished and disorganized environments often associated with maternal substance abuse (Coles & Platzman, 1993; Streissguth et al., 1996).

In 1996, the Institute of Medicine (Stratton et al., 1996) suggested diagnostic criteria for FAS using a five-category system (see Table 21.1) with two ways of characterizing those who meet the criteria for the full diagnosis of FAS, one way (Partial FAS; pFAS) to describe individuals with prenatal alcohol exposure who do not meet criteria for the full diagnosis, and two categories to delineate alcohol-related physical (Alcohol-Related Birth Defects; ARBD) and neurodevelopmental effects associated with maternal alcohol exposure (Alcohol-Related Neurodevelopmental Disorders; ARND). Individuals diagnosed as FAS must have some of the specific facial anomalies associated with prenatal alcohol exposure, evidence of growth retardation, and evidence of central nervous system (CNS) or developmental abnormalities. CNS compromise is evidenced by decreased head circumference at birth, evidence of structural brain abnormalities, and neurological hard or soft signs. The diagnosis is then made with or without confirmed evidence of maternal alcohol exposure. Although these criteria are helpful in

TABLE 21.1

Diagnostic Criteria for Fetal Alcohol Syndrome (FAS) and Alcohol-Related Effects

Fetal Alcohol Syndrome

1. FAS with confirmed maternal alcohol exposure
   - A. Confirmed maternal alcohol exposure[a]
   - B. Evidence of a characteristic pattern of facial anomalies that includes features such as short palpebral fissures and abnormalities in the premaxillary zone (e.g., flat upper lip, flattened philtrum, and flat midface)
   - C. Evidence of growth retardation, as in at least one of the following:
     - –low birth weight for gestational age
     - –decelerating weight over time not because of nutrition
     - –disproportional low weight to height
   - D. Evidence of CNS neurodevelopmental abnormalities, as in at least one of the following:
     - –decreased cranial size at birth
     - –structural brain abnormalities (e.g., microcephaly, partial or complete agenesis of the corpus callosum, cerebellar hypoplasia)
     - –neurological hard and soft signs (as age appropriate), such as impaired fine motor skills, neurosensory hearing loss, poor tandem gait, poor eye-hand coordination

2. FAS without confirmed maternal alcohol exposure

   B, C, and D as above

3. Partial FAS with confirmed maternal alcohol exposure

   Confirmed maternal alcohol exposure

   Evidence of some components of the pattern of characteristic facial anomalies

   Either C or D or E
   - C. Evidence of growth retardation, as in at least one of the following:
     - –low birth weight for gestational age
     - –decelerating weight over time not because of nutrition
     - –disproportional low weight to height
   - D. Evidence of CNS neurodevelopmental abnormalities, as in:
     - –decreased cranial size at birth
     - –structural brain abnormalities (e.g., microcephaly, partial or complete agenesis of the corpus callosum, cerebellar hypoplasia)
     - –neurological hard and soft signs (as age appropriate), such as impaired fine motor skills, neurosensory hearing loss, poor tandem gait, poor eye-hand coordination
   - E. Evidence of a complex pattern of behavior or cognitive abnormalities that are inconsistent with developmental level and cannot be explained by familial background or environment alone, such as learning difficulties; deficits in school performance; poor impulse control; problems in social perception; deficits in higher level receptive and expressive language; poor capacity for abstraction or metacognition; specific deficits in mathematical skills; or problems in memory, attention, or judgment

Alcohol-Related Effects

Clinical conditions in which there is a history of maternal alcohol exposure [a,b] and where clinical or animal research has linked maternal alcohol ingestion to an observed outcome. There are two categories, which may co-occur. If both diagnoses are present, then both diagnoses should be rendered:

4. Alcohol-related birth defects (ARBD)

List of congenital anomalies, including malformation and dysplasias

Cardiac	Atrial septal defects	Aberrant great vessels
	Ventricular septal defects	Tetralogy of Fallot
Skeletal	Hypoplastic nails	Clinodactyly
	Shortened fifth digits	Pectus excavatum and carinatum
	Radioulnar synostosis	Klippel-Feil syndrome
	Flexion contractures	Hemivertebrae
	Camptodactyly	Scoliosis

(Continued)

TABLE 21.1
(Continued)

Renal	Aplastic, dysplastic hypoplastic kidneys Horseshoe kidneys	Ureteral duplications Hydronephrosis
Ocular	Strabismus	Refractive problems secondary to small globes
	Retinal vascular anomalies	
Auditory	Conductive hearing loss	Neurosensory hearing loss
Other	Virtually every malformation has been described in some patient with FAS. The etiologic specificity of most of these anomalies to alcohol teratogenesis remains unclear.	

5. Alcohol-related neurodevelopmental disorder (ARND)
Presence of:
  A. Evidence of CNS neurodevelopmental abnormalities, as in any one of the following:
    –decreased cranial size at birth
    –structural brain abnormalities (e.g., microcephaly, partial or complete agenesis of the corpus callosum, cerebellar hypoplasia)
    –neurological hard and soft signs (as age appropriate), such as impaired fine motor skills, neurosensory hearing loss, poor tandem gait, poor eye-hand coordination

and/or:
  B. Evidence of a complex pattern of behavior or cognitive abnormalities that are inconsistent with developmental level and cannot be explained by familial background or environment alone, such as learning difficulties; deficits in school performance; poor impulse control; problems in social perception; deficits in higher level receptive and expressive language; poor capacity for abstraction or metacognition; specific deficits in mathematical skills; or problems in memory, attention, or judgment

[a] A pattern of excessive intake characterized by substantial, regular intake or heavy episodic drinking. Evidence of this pattern may include frequent episodes of intoxication, development of tolerance or withdrawal, social problems related to drinking, legal problems related to drinking, engaging in physically hazardous behavior while drinking, or alcohol-related medical problems such as hepatic disease.

[b] As further research is completed and as, or if, lower quantities or variable patterns of alcohol use are associated with ARBD or ARND, these patterns of alcohol use should be incorporated into the diagnostic criteria.

Source: Reprinted from IOM report Stratton et al., 1996.

defining domains of impact, this diagnostic system still left ambiguity regarding the presence or absence of a given diagnostic feature (e.g., 5th or 10th percentile for weight and head circumference; the number of facial features needed).

As a result of ambiguity in the diagnostic criteria, and indeed in the presentation of individuals, researchers and clinicians have operationalized these criteria differently in categorizing individuals as FAS. For functional reasons, diagnostic systems often have differing goals. Some are designed to establish "yes/no" on a given criteria while others are designed to capture severity of impact. One example of the later approach is the physical dysmorphia checklist (Fernhoff, Smith, & Falek, 1980), which generates a weighted cumulative score of dysmorphic features related to alcohol teratogenesis. This checklist was first used as an outcome measure in an exposure study (Coles, Smith, Fernhoff, & Falek, 1985) but is now used in a clinical environment as well to confirm diagnosis. This checklist does not include information about neurocognitive status or maternal alcohol use. Similar systems are used by many dysmorphologists in diagnosing FAS (e.g., May et al., 2001; Robinson, 2001).

Growth, dysmorphia, as well as neurodevelopmental functioning and gestational alcohol exposure are all quantified in a manualized diagnostic system developed by a group of Seattle researchers (Astley & Clarren, 1996, 2001). Rating severity in each of these areas from 1 to 4 allows the quantification of the diagnosis with codes that translate into ICD-10 diagnostic categories (World Health Organization, 1994). To date, none of the diagnostic systems systematically addresses ethnic and racial differences in presentation or how symptomatology changes over the course of development.

Not all alcohol-exposed individuals exhibit full FAS. In fact, only about 40% of those born to alcoholic mothers can be so classified (Abel, 1995). Various attempts have been made to describe effectively those children with the alcohol-related physical and neurodevelopmental impairments who have a history of prenatal alcohol exposure but who do not have sufficient damage to meet full criteria for FAS. Alcohol Related Neurodevelopmental Disorder (ARND) is one of the more recent contributions (Stratton et al., 1996) to what has been referred to jokingly as the "alphabet soup" of labels attached to these children. Previous attempts have included Fetal Alcohol Effects (FAE; Hanson, Streissguth, & Smith, 1978), Possible Fetal Alcohol Effects (PFAE; Clarren & Smith, 1978), Partial FAS (pFAS; Stratton et al., 1996), Alcohol-Related Birth Defects (ARBD; Sokol & Clarren, 1989; Stratton et al., 1996—two different meanings), Alcohol-abuse related malformations (ARMS; Abel, 1998), and Alcohol-Abuse-Related Birth Defects (ARBES; Abel, 1998). All of these terms share the goal of describing children who have some effects but not the full syndrome but may differ in the scope of alcohol-related sequalae that they attempt to capture. The conditions described range from those meeting criteria on only one or two of the areas needed for the full syndrome diagnosis to those involving subtle neurodevelopmental consequences associated with moderate prenatal alcohol exposure. Faced with these diverse outcomes, investigators have recently begun to view FAS as a multifaceted spectrum disorder. At the most extreme end of the spectrum are individuals who meet full criteria for fetal alcohol syndrome (May, 1995; Streissguth & O'Malley, 2001). Children who do not meet criteria but who have a history of prenatal alcohol exposure may be thought of as being in the spectrum of FAS with varying degrees of symptomatology in the areas of growth, dysmorphology, and neurodevelopmental compromise.

However the outcomes are described, it is clear that the impact of prenatal exposure is a wide range of physical anomalies and neurodevelopmental deficits. As a result, adequate evaluation of a child for FAS and alcohol-related disabilities requires a team of professionals rather than a single discipline. This team must include medical professionals to evaluate growth and physical status, as well as general health, and to make a differential diagnosis from other conditions associated with growth deficits and dysmorphology. This kind of diagnosis is made, most appropriately, by a clinical geneticist, or "dysmorphologist." Neurocognitive development and psychoeducational status require assessment by psychologists and/or educational specialists. Often multidisciplinary clinics who make this differential diagnosis also include social workers and/or case managers to assist with record collection, identifying the social needs of the child, and selecting appropriate community resources for the family. Specific areas of disability may also necessitate evaluations by other professionals, such as occupational, physical, and speech and language therapists. A recent publication (Barnwell & Morse, 1999) cataloged diagnostic clinics established to provide such services across the United States.

Socioenvironmental Issues and the Diagnosis of FAS

FAS has been reported in many different countries (*Germany*—Spohr & Steinhausen, 1984; *Scotland*—O'Beattie, Day, Cockburn, & Garg, 1983; *Scandinavia*—Olegard et al., 1979; *Japan*—Tanaka, Masataka, & Suzuki, 1981; *Canada*—Bray & Anderson, 1989; *South Africa*—May et al., 2001; *Russia*—Robinson, 2001) and among different ethnic groups in the United States (*Native Americans*—May, Hymbaugh, Aase, & Samet, 1983; *African Americans*-Sokol et al., 1986; and *White*—Streissguth, Aase, Clarnen, Randels, LaDue & Smith, 1991). The widespread recognition of this disorder supports the idea that alcohol-related teratogenesis can occur in any individual who is exposed to sufficient alcohol prenatally. Despite this diversity, further examination of these data also suggests that FAS is identified more frequently among individuals in lower economic groups than among the more economically advantaged (Abel, 1995).

For instance, the Centers for Disease Control and Prevention's Atlanta Metropolitan Birth Defects Survey found that FAS was identified in .3 per 1,000 births in an inner-city hospital serving predominantly an African American and low-income population, but was .003 per 1,000 in a suburban hospital serving a predominantly white, middle-class population that was geographically only a few miles away (CDC, 1993). Similar patterns have been reported elsewhere in different countries (*France*—Crepin, Dehaene, & Samille, 1989; Dehaene et al., 1981; *Scotland*—O'Beattie et al., 1983; *Canada*—Bray & Anderson, 1989) and within different minority groups in the United States (*African Americans*—Sokol et al., 1986; Bingol et al., 1987; *Hispanics*—Bingol et al., 1987; and *Native Americans*—May et al., 1983).

The increased prevalence of FAS in economically disadvantaged groups raises a number of questions about the nature and etiology of this disorder as well as about the criteria for diagnosis. Socioeconomic status (SES) or ethnic status may artificially mark different patterns of alcohol use, differences in genetic susceptibility to alcohol, and/or other lifestyle factors associated with poverty that may influence maternal drinking or the impact of the exposure. A second possibility for these findings is that there are some biases inherent in the process of identification of those with FAS. These may include bias in ascertainment, a higher probability that low SES individuals will be identified with this disorder, or bias inherent in the criteria of FAS. For example, research on performance on cognitive tests suggests that the probability of being identified as cognitively impaired is significantly greater among low SES groups (McLoyd, 1998), suggesting that identification of FAS would be significantly higher among low SES groups when applying uniform criteria across groups to identify neurodevelopmental compromise. Finally, there may be multiple, unmeasured factors associated with minority status or poverty that potentiate the teratogenic effects of prenatal exposure. The international studies currently being carried out in South Africa (May et al., 2001) and in Moscow, Russia (Marintcheva et al., 2001; Robinson, 2001) may help to resolve some of these issues. Because of the high incidence and social conditions in these countries, matching alcohol-affected children to appropriate controls within different SES groups will be possible and may allow evaluation of specific effects of alcohol.

EXPOSURE LEVELS

The question of how much prenatal alcohol exposure is needed to produce a child with FAS and what the level is at which no observable effects are found (NOEL) has proven to be difficult to answer. Use by pregnant women is difficult to measure accurately as levels of alcohol consumption tend to be variable from day to day and week to week, even among heavy alcohol users (Abel, 1998). This makes it difficult to quantify levels of alcohol exposure at specific points in pregnancy, which is needed to resolve these questions. As a result, arguments continue in the field as to whether average daily ounces of alcohol is sufficient to capture exposure levels or whether frequency of binging ($\geq$5 drinks per day) behavior is a better predictor of alcohol teratogenesis (Stratton et al., 1996). Even among the heaviest of female drinkers, the rate of children born with full FAS is less than 40% (Abel, 1995). Dosage level interacts with period of fetal development and the mother's physical status and metabolic system to produce the observed outcomes. Maternal age, smoking behavior, obstetric history, and disease status, particularly liver disease, all increase the probability of having a child with FAS. Despite extensive research, there has been no specified "safe" level of alcohol exposure identified and most physicians recommend that women do not drink throughout the pregnancy to prevent any subtle teratogenic effects.

PHYSICAL SEQUALAE ASSOCIATED WITH FAS

Facial Dysmorphia

The facial anomalies associated with heavy prenatal alcohol exposure are one of the defining features of this disorder (see Fig. 21.1). The facial anomalies are believed to be the result of disturbances in cellular migration during the organogenesis period of development (U.S. Department of Health and Human Services, 2000). These disturbances result in dysmorphic features along the midline of the face. Short palpebral fissures, flat midface, short nose, flat philtrum, and thin upper lip have been recognized as the discriminating facial features of FAS (Streissguth, 1997), while epicanthal folds, low nasal bridge, ear anomalies, and micrognathia (i.e., small chin) have been identified as commonly associated features of the disorder. Assessment of these anomalies is best conducted by a pediatric dysmorphologist as many of these features vary as a function of race and age and can be associated with various other genetic syndromes or medical conditions that require specialized training to be able to appropriately discriminate. Assessment of these facial anomalies over the course of the life span has suggested that individuals with FAS may be more difficult to identify when they reach puberty (Streissguth, 1997). Longitudinal research is needed on the continuity of each of the different facial anomalies with different ethnic groups to discern which features are most stable over the course of development to provide guidelines for making the diagnosis in older children and adults.

Weight and Growth

Children with FAS, by definition, have growth problems with overall body weight typically being below the 5th or 10th percentile relative to age norms at the time of diagnosis. Most children with FAS do not have feeding problems but in the more extreme cases, children

FIG. 21.1. Facial dysmorphia associated with prenatal alcohol exposure. In comparison to a typically developing child, portrayed on the left, the alcohol-affected child on the right shows the facial dysmorphia characteristic of fetal alcohol syndrome (FAS). Note the microcephaly (small head size), low-set, rotated ears, and the underdevelopment of the midface. This underdevelopment includes a flattened nasal bridge, absent philtrum, thin upper lip without a bow, epicanthal folds, and the shortened palpebral fissues (eye openings) that give the child a "wide-eyed" appearance.

with FAS may require enteral feedings to supplement oral intake of food. There is some evidence to suggest that these children may demonstrate accelerated weight gain over the course of their development (Streissguth, 1997; Streissguth et al., 1991) and concern has been raised about applying the criteria of either the 5th or 10th percentile uniformly across the life span. These concerns are based on results of longitudinal studies of children who were diagnosed with FAS that have identified individuals who no longer meet the physical growth criteria when they are adolescents or adults (i.e., Coles, Platzman, Lynch, & Friedes, 2002; Streissguth, 1997) despite continuing to have the neurodevelopmental impairments associated with prenatal alcohol exposure. In a Seattle cohort, the average weight-to-height ratio percentile for a group of adolescents and adults with FAS was 48% as compared to 1–15% found in studies of younger children (Streissguth, 1997). However, only 16% of this older sample had height within normal limits, suggesting that these individuals experienced disproportionate changes in their height and weight growth over time. Consequently, the individual's height percentile rather than weight may best capture physical growth problems when making the diagnosis among adolescents and adults. It may also be appropriate to use "historical growth retardation" rather than current weight/height in older children for diagnostic purposes.

Cardiology

Cardiac abnormalities have been found in children who have FAS. The most common are septal heart defects with defects in the ventricles occurring more often than in the atria. Other problems identified have included tetratology of Fallot and pulmonary stenosis. An estimated 30% of clinically referred children with FAS have some cardiac abnormalities but often these are benign and/or transient (Streissguth, 1997; Clarren & Smith, 1978; Smith et al., 1981; Streissguth, Clarren, & Jones, 1985).

Other Physical Anomalies

A variety of other congenital anomalies have been identified in children who have FAS, including deformities of the skeletal (Smith et al., 1981; Spohr & Steinhausen, 1987; Streissguth, 1997), ocular (Stromland, 1990), and auditory (Church, 1987, 1996) systems. Because of limited research, these anomalies have not been as well characterized in alcohol-affected children as are other signs and have not been incorporated into the diagnostic system. It has been recommended that all children with FAS be evaluated by an opthmalogist and an audiologist to identify any sensory impairments that they may be experiencing (Abel, 1998).

NEURODEVELOPMENTAL OUTCOMES ASSOCIATED WITH PRENATAL ALCOHOL EXPOSURE

Neurodevelopmental outcomes associated with heavy prenatal alcohol exposure are complex and multifaceted. In theory, observed outcomes result from prenatal damage to the brain as well as the negative life experiences these individuals may encounter throughout their development. Streissguth and colleagues (1996) described the primary and secondary disabilities observed in clinically referred individuals with a FAS/E diagnosis. Primary disabilities result from the direct effects of prenatal exposure and are thought to include reduced intellectual capacity and poor academic achievement. Secondary disabilities are the effects of poor environmental supports and the lack of interventions needed to help the individual to succeed in the environment. Using Streissguth's model, mental health problems, disrupted school experience, being in trouble with the law, confinement, inappropriate sexual behavior, drug use, and dependent living were categorized as secondary disabilities. Although there may be different ways of conceptualizing these types of disabilities, this distinction suggests that many of the negative life experiences and functional disabilities that children with FAS and/or FAE experience may be ameliorated with appropriate intervention strategies designed to foster positive adaptation to the environment.

Effects on Brain Structure

Using animal models, autopsies of deceased children with FAS, and data from magnetic resonance imaging and single photon emission computed tomography (SPECT), reductions in brain volume (Clarren, 1986; Mattson, Jernigan, & Riley, 1994; Mattson, Riley et al., 1994, 1996; Riikonen, Salonen, Partanen, & Verho, 1999), malformations of gray and white matter brain tissue (Riikonen et al., 1999), disruption in cellular migration during brain development (Lancaster, 1994), and reductions in volume or complete absence of specific brain structures (i.e., agenesis of the corpus callosum) (Mattson & Riley, 1996; Riikonen et al., 1999) have been related to prenatal alcohol. Paralleling the midline disturbances in facial formation, there is evidence to suggest that midline regions of the brain are also malformed. The corpus callosum, the structure linking the two hemispheres of the brain that provides communication between the two regions, has been found to be thinned or missing in some children with FAS (Johnson, Swayze, Sato, & Andreasen, 1996; Mattson, Riley et al., 1992, 1996; Riley et al., 1995; Riikonen et al., 1999; Swayze et al., 1997). The cerebellum, which is located posteriorally and is involved heavily in arousal regulation and motor activity, has been found to have reduced volume (Clarren, 1986; Harris-Collazo, Kwok, Mattson, Jernigan, & Riley, 1998; Mattson & Riley, 1996; Riikonen, 1994; Robin & Zackai, 1994), particularly in the vermis (Sowell et al., 1996), the area connecting the two halves of the cerebellum and linked to the execution of motor activities. Reductions in the size of the basal ganglia, an area also involved in motor movement, have been found among children with FAS after controlling for overall brain size with the caudate nucleus portion of this region showing the greatest loss volume as well (Harris-Collazo et al., 1998; Mattson, Riley et al., 1992, 1994, 1996). Alterations in the structure of the cells that make up the hippocampus have been found to be related to prenatal alcohol exposure in animal models (West & Pierce, 1984) and have been found in some human studies (Riikonen et al., 1999) using magnetic resonance imaging in children with FAS but not in other studies (Harris-Collazo et al., 1998).

Effects on Motor Functioning

Alcohol effects on psychomotor functioning have been observed regularly in infants and toddlers (Coles, 1993; Coles & Platzman, 1992; Coles et al., 1985; Jacobson, Jacobson, Sokol, Martier, & Ager, 1993; Smith, Coles, Lancaster, Fernhoff, & Falek, 1986, Smith, Lancaster, Moss-Wells, Coles, & Falek, 1987) while problems in motor functioning during later stages of development are less well documented (Aronson, Kyllerman, Sabel, Sandin, & Olegard, 1985; Janzen, Nanson, & Block, 1995; Kyllerman et al., 1985). Descriptive studies of clinical cases of children with FAS almost always note deficits in motor skills and coordination (Mattson & Riley, 1998). Among quasi-experimental research designs with children with FAS, deficits in visual-motor integration (Coles et al., 1991; Conry, 1990; Mattson, Carlos, & Riley, 1993) and fine-motor strength and coordination are often noted (Barr, Streissguth, Darby, & Sampson, 1990; Conry, 1990; Mattson et al., 1993). Kyllerman and colleagues (1985) found that children (mean age 70 months) born to women who abuse alcohol had lower motor development scores and did more poorly on motor coordination tests than did a nonexposed comparison sample matched on sex, age, birth, and gestational age. Children with FAS have also been found to show deficits in balance (Marcus, 1987; Roebuck, Mattson, & Riley, 1998; Roebuck, Simmons, Mattson, & Riley, 1998), increased clumsiness (Steinhausen, Nestler, & Spohr, 1982), abnormal gait (Conn-Blowers, 1991; Marcus, 1987), and tremors (Aronson et al., 1985; Marcus, 1987). Roebuck and colleagues (Roebuck, Simmons, Mattson, & Riley, 1998; Roebuck, Simmons, Richardson, Mattson, & Riley, 1998) posit that damage to the cerebellum from heavy prenatal alcohol exposure may contribute to difficulties with using visual and somatosensory system cues to maintain balance. Performance when visual and somatosensory cues were systematically altered suggested that children with FAS were overly reliant on somatosensory cues (Roebuck, Simmons, Mattson, & Riley, 1998). Using electromyography (EMG), these researchers concluded that this deficit was the result of damage to the CNS rather than damage to the peripheral nervous system controlling the muscles or the vestibular system (Roebuck, Simmons, Richardson et al., 1998).

Although there is some clinical and experimental evidence of motor impairments in children with FAS, research in this area has been relatively limited. Additional attention to this area of functioning appears warranted particularly because these deficits have significant impact on early development, affecting both physical status and social functioning. Later in development, such deficits may limit activities in classrooms and on playgrounds and, in adult, occupational placements. Research would benefit from multidisciplinary collaboration, including the input of occupational and physical therapists.

Effects on Neurocognitive Function

Global intellectual deficits are the primary neurodevelopmental outcome of maternal alcohol abuse. This pattern is consistent with the results of other early neurological insults that, contrary to the adult pattern, tend to be more global than specific. Deficits in general intellectual functioning (that is, on intelligence or ability tests) have been observed in samples composed of children diagnosed with FAS and those drawn from longitudinal studies of heavy maternal alcohol use. In reviews of the literature, children meeting the diagnostic criteria for FAS may show a relatively broad range of intellectual functioning with sample estimates ranging from severe intellectual deficiency to average levels of functioning (e.g., Mean Intelligence Quotients (IQs) range from 20 to 120; Mattson & Riley, 1998; and from 16 to 105; Streissguth, Herman, & Smith, 1978). However, the mean level of performance on standardized measures of intellectual functioning have typically been in the borderline to the mildly intellectual deficient range (IQs of 65 to 75) in large retrospective and prospective studies of children with FAS (Mattson & Riley, 1998; Stratton et al., 1996). Only about 50% of children diagnosed with FAS meet criteria for mental retardation, which is an IQ of less than 70 on most standardized tests of intelligence (Abel, 1998).

In addition to the global deficits that are usually observed, there are several specific areas that appear to be impacted by prenatal exposure and may contribute to the functional deficits, behavioral problems, and academic failures that are often reported (Spohr, Willms, & Steinhausen, 1993; Streissguth et al., 1991). In addition to the motor problems discussed above, functions that have been examined and appear to be affected by prenatal alcohol exposure include specific deficits in visual-spatial processing, arousal and regulation of attention, working memory, planning and organizational skills, mathematical achievement, and behavioral regulation.

Visuospatial Processing

Evidence for a specific deficit in visual-spatial perception (Coles et al., 2002; Spohr, Willms, & Steinhausen, 1993; Ueckerer & Nadel, 1996) similar to that associated with nonverbal learning disabilities (NVLD; Rourke, 1995) has been found. In a review of published articles on the cognitive functioning of individual cases with FAS, Mattson and Riley (1998) found that mean Verbal Intelligence Quotient (VIQ) was 61.00 (SD = 12.82) and the mean Performance Intelligence Quotient (PIQ) was 55.33 (SD = 13.45), a pattern similar to that seen in individuals with NVLD. In addition, children with NVLD have been found to have abnormalities in their white matter development and malformations of the corpus callosum that are similar to the brain abnormalities associated with heavy prenatal alcohol exposure (Riley et al., 1995). Deficits in visual memory (Carmichael-Olson, Feldman, Streissguth, Sampson, & Bookstein, 1998; Kaemingk & Paquette, 1999; Platzman, Freides, Lynch, & Falek, 2000), visual perceptual skills (Aronson & Hagberg, 1998; Aronson et al., 1985; Morse, Adams, & Weiner, 1992; Steinhausen et al., 1982), visual-motor integration (Janzen et al., 1995; Kaemingk & Paquette, 1999; Mattson, Riley, Gramling, Delis, & Jones, 1998) and spatial memory (Ueckerer & Nadel, 1998) have been reported. A specific deficit in visual processing, which is independent of the global intellectual deficit, is suggested by findings from a cohort of alcohol-exposed individuals who were seen during adolescence (Coles et al., 2002). In this study, auditory and visual sustained attention were compared and dysmorphic (i.e., pFAS and FAS) adolescents were less efficient in processing visual than auditory information. Sensitivity to the visual stimuli was significantly lower in alcohol-affected youth, suggesting that the neurocognitive impact of prenatal alcohol exposure may be more significant for tasks that involve visual than auditory processing.

Not all studies on the effect of the teratogenic effects of prenatal alcohol exposure have found a specific or consistent impairment in visual or spatial processing of information and some report that auditory information processing is more impaired (e.g., Connor, Streissguth, Sampson, Bookstein, & Barr, 1999; Janzen et al., 1995; Kerns, Don, Mateer, & Streissguth, 1997). Certainly, there may be real differences as a function of exposure in different groups of individuals; however, methodological differences between studies and in analysis strategies also may be contributing to the variability in results across studies. Mattson and Riley (1998) reviewed retrospective and prospective longitudinal studies and individual case studies and suggested that evidence for relative deficits in visual or verbal learning was equivocal. However, in their review, they compared studies of children diagnosed with FAS/FAE and studies of children with low to moderate alcohol exposure, where no such diagnosis has been made. Such children may have different pattern of deficits than those who meet criteria for the full spectrum disorder. Studies of individuals with a diagnosis of FAS also vary in the extent to which they attempt to equate the discriminative power of the tasks by modality (auditory or visual) and whether they control for an overall level of intellectual functioning in their analysis. The effect of SES on cognitive scores may also contribute to difficulties with interpreting results across studies. For example, in both the Kerns and colleagues (1997) and the Conry (1990) samples, low SES children diagnosed with FAS had verbal IQs that were lower than performance IQs; however, in both studies, SES factors may have contributed to the lower performance on verbal IQ. Conry (1990), who included a low SES contrast group, concluded, after examining discrepancy scores, that "alcohol involvement appeared to have greater effects on visual/spatial problem solving than on verbal effects" (p. 654).

Clarification of modality-specific processing deficits will require the implementation of rigorous methodological procedures, including appropriate comparison samples to control for the SES factors influencing cognitive development and equating the discriminative power of tasks utilized for the comparisons (Chapman & Chapman, 1973). In addition, samples with moderate exposure may or may not demonstrate such differences because the effect may only be manifested at the severe end of alcohol exposure. If this is so, children diagnosed with the full syndrome will be needed to clarify the pattern of neurodevelopmental compromise.

Arousal and Attention Deficits

The regulation of attentional skills in children prenatally exposed to alcohol has been of recent interest (Coles, 2000; Kopera-Frye, Carmichael-Olson, & Streissguth, 1997). Regulation of attention is a fundamental prerequisite for learning (Mackintosh, 1975) and, therefore, has the potential to mediate a number of long-term neurodeveopmental outcomes associated with prenatal exposure to alcohol. Many children with FAS have been noted to have difficulties with regulation of arousal that may be associated with attention deficit hyperactivity disorder (Kopera-Frye et al., 1997; Nanson & Hisock, 1990; Oesterheld & Wilson, 1997; Streissguth et al., 1986; Streissguth, Bookstein, Sampson, & Barr, 1995; Streissguth, Sampson et al., 1994) or other alterations in attention (Coles et al., 1997; Streissguth, Martin, Barr, & Sandman, 1984).

Investigations into the impact of prenatal alcohol exposure employing prospective longitudinal designs have produced inconsistent results regarding regulation of attentional skills. Streissguth and her colleagues (1984) found that prenatal exposure to alcohol resulted in more errors and slower reaction times on a task of vigilance and sustained attention in a sample of preschool children with a history of moderate alcohol exposure. In the same cohort, observations of children's behavior by trained observers and ratings of their behavior by parents suggested that prenatal alcohol exposure was associated with being less attentive, less compliant, and more fidgety (Landesman-Dwyer & Ragozin, 1981). These results, however, have not been supported in other prospective cohorts (e.g., Boyd, Ernhart, Greene, Sokol, & Martier, 1991; Coles et al., 1997). Brown and colleagues (1991) also found an association between maternal alcohol use and regulation of attention but suggested that the postnatal environment associated with maternal substance abuse may have accounted for these findings. Using a four-factor, multidimensional model of attentional regulation (Mirsky, 1989), 7-year-old children prenatally exposed to alcohol have been found to differ significantly from children with attention deficit hyperactivity disorder in the nature of their impairment. Alcohol-affected children were found to have more difficulties with encoding of information and in their problem-solving flexibility (Coles et al., 1997) but had no difficulties with their ability to focus or sustain attention while the ADHD children showed a contrasting pattern.

To further explore these issues, as well as to examine specific elements of attention in infants, Kable and Coles (2000) identified deficits in early attentional regulation in alcohol-exposed 6-month-olds. Using a habituation paradigm, 158 infants were presented with both auditory and visual stimuli and cardiac responses (i.e., heart rate) to the stimuli were recorded. By measuring the deceleration in heart rate (HR) during the first three habituation trials, the efficiency of the infant's encoding of environmental events could be estimated. Infants who were identified as being at risk based on a cumulative risk index for prenatal alcohol exposure (Coles, Kable, Drews-Botsch, & Falek, 2000) took longer to respond to the stimuli, indicating that their learning was slower and less efficient than that of other infants. This finding is consistent with the very limited number of previous studies of prenatal alcohol exposure and infant information processing (Jacobson, Jacobson, & Sokol, 1994; Jacobson et al., 1993). In addition to slower processing, infants of women whose drinking behaviors were identified as high risk were rated as having higher arousal levels across the three trials, suggesting that the mediation of arousal by the attentional system was not as well developed when compared to the contrast group of infants. Whereas the interaction between attention and arousal has been the subject of much debate in and of itself (e.g., Coull, 1998; Mesulam, 1981; Posner & Petersen, 1990), these results suggest that the attention-arousal system, as indexed by the cardiac responses, may be compromised and that this compromise may be associated with less efficient processing of information. The role that these relative deficits play in subsequent, more complex cognitive development and attentional regulation skills has not yet been explored.

Executive Function Skills

Executive functioning is a construct that has been referred to as, "Perhaps the most appealing, yet least understood, aspect of cognition and metacognition" (Borkowski & Burke, 1996, p. 235). This aspect involves higher order cognitive processes that range from attentional regulation, working memory skills, planning and organizational thinking, and problem solving (Lyon, 1996; Morris, 1996). From an information processing perspective, Borkowski and Burke (1996) posited that attention, memory, and executive function are interrelated processes that impact cognitive functioning and the ability to carry out goal attainment behaviors. Both clinical descriptions of children with FAS and longitudinal studies of children with heavy alcohol exposure have investigated these skills. Investigators have varied in their theoretical approaches with some aggregating measures to obtain a general estimate of executive functioning (e.g., Connor, Sampson, Bookstein, Barr, & Streissguth, 2000; Sampson et al., 1997) and others choosing to explore the skills as a collection of higher order cognitive processes (e.g., Kerns et al., 1997; Mattson, Goodman, Caine, Delis, & Riley, 1999; Mattson, Riley, Gramling, Delis, & Jones, 1998; Schonfeld, Mattson, Lang, Delis, & Riley, 2001). Because of the various ways in which executive functioning is understood, we will review studies related to several aspects of this construct.

Memory is a subject in itself and only some aspects of memory fall under the rubric of executive functioning. Children with FAS have been found to exhibit deficits in their memory skills but the impairments appear to be influenced by the modality of the task as well as specific cognitive demands of the task. Using the McCarthy Scales of Children's Abilities (McCarthy, 1972), Janzen and colleagues (1995) found that preschool children with FAS did not differ in memory functioning from a contrast group recruited from day-care settings. In another study comparing learning and recall in tasks presented visually or in narrative format, adolescents with FAS were found to have poorer recall of visual elements when compared to a comparison sample matched for SES but showed no differences in the memory for auditorially presented story elements or in their short-term memory for strings of digits (Platzman et al., 2000). In contrast, memory deficits have consistently been found on a verbal learning task that involves list learning of orally presented words in several categories (i.e., clothes, fruits, and toys) (Kerns et al., 1997; Mattson et al., 1998; Schonfeld et al., 2001). The task consists of an initial list that is presented for five trials with a second list presented to identify the effects of interference on recalls obtained after short and long delays (California Verbal Learning Test; Delis, Kramer, Kaplan, & Ober, 1987). Kerns and colleagues (1997), using a sample of adolescent and young adults with FAS, grouped as "Average IQ" or "Below Average IQ," reported that the greatest difference between groups was not on the initial learning trial but on the fifth learning trial, suggesting that individuals with FAS were not able to use semantic memory strategies appropriately to maintain a comparable learning slope over the course of repeated trials. This lack of use of more sophisticated memory strategies was demonstrated by the finding that individuals with FAS were less likely than controls to demonstrate semantic clustering during recall despite having comparable primacy effects and serial clustering scores.

Active working memory, which involves mental manipulation of elements stored in short-term memory, also has been noted as one of the aspects of executive functioning. It involves the capacity to store and process meaningful units at a given moment in time and has been referred to as a "mental scratch pad" (Ashcraft, Kirk, & Hopko, 1998). Many cognitive tasks commonly used in neurodevelopmental batteries have components that require use of active working memory skills because higher order processing or problem solving requires that several units of information be maintained simultaneously. Using a visual expectancy paradigm

(Haith, Hazan, & Goodman, 1988; Jacobson et al., 1992) as a measure of working memory capacity during infancy, Wass and Haith (1999) found that 3-month-old infants exposed prenatally to alcohol had more difficulties with maintaining and manipulating 3 pieces of information in memory simultaneously than did a contrast group, suggesting a reduction in working memory capacity. On this same task, alcohol-exposed infants were found to have difficulties with shifting from one rule to another and with mastering complex spatial sequences. With older individuals, using several neurodevelopmental tasks of executive functioning skills, Kodituwakku, Handmaker, Cutler, Weathersby, and Handmaker (1995) concluded that deficits in the ability to manage goals in working memory were the underlying mechanism responsible for much of the cognitive impairment seen in children with FAS.

Of course, deficits in working memory will have an impact on everyday functioning as well as outcome of cognitive tasks. For instance, children with FAS consistently demonstrate relative deficits in performance on the arithmetic subtest from the Wechsler series (Wechsler, 1989, 1991) of intelligence tests, which relies heavily on active working memory skills (Platzman et al., 2000; Streissguth, 1997) by requiring individuals to maintain numbers and operations in short-term memory and then manipulate them accordingly to generate the appropriate answer.

Children with FAS also have been described as having impairments in planning, organization, and problem-solving aspects of executive functioning (Streissguth, 1997). Two tasks that have been used to assess these skills are progressive planning tasks (e.g., Tower of London; Shallice, 1982) and tasks assessing learning and reversal or shifts in discriminative stimuli (e.g., Wisconsin Card Sort Task; Heaton, Chelune, Talley, Kay, & Curtiss, 1993), both originally used to measure the effects of frontal lobe damage (Shallice, 1982). Progressive planning tasks require the individual to replicate a visually presented design that requires the rearranging of circular disks or balls that are placed on vertical pegs. The task requires the child to retain a sequence of moves in working memory to effectively problem solve. Initially the task is simple and requires little planning but as task complexity increases, the amount of strategic planning needed to successfully complete the task also increases.

The Wisconsin Card Sort and similar tasks require the individual to identify or sort on specific characteristics of stimuli (i.e., color or shape) presented to them with feedback provided to facilitate learning. Once the correct solution (category) has been identified, a different solution is required and the feedback is altered accordingly. This task requires the individual to inhibit learned responses and to shift sets or rules learned from the previous experience. Using both types of tasks, children with FAS have been found to have deficits in overall performance and to make perseveration errors (repetitions of responses that are nonreinforced) (Coles et al., 1997; Kerns, et al, 1997; Kodituwakku, et al., 1995), suggesting that they have difficulties with incorporating environmental feedback to correct a response. Children with FAS typically have more difficulties in their ability to learn the shifts, particularly reversal shifts (Coles et al., 1997; Kerns et al., 1997; Kodituwakku et al., 1995).

Kodituwakku, May, Clericuzio, and Weers (2001) used another paradigm to discriminate emotion-related learning from conceptual set shifting to further document neurodevelopmental impairments associated with FAS. In this study, conceptual set shifting was measured using the Wisconsin Card Sort Test and contrasted with a different task (Rolls, Hornak, Wade, & McGrath, 1994) that assessed visual-discrimination reversal learning and extinction of reward-response associations. This second task was used to measure emotion-related learning. After controlling for their conceptual set shifting and intellectual abilities, school-age, alcohol-exposed children performed more poorly on the emotion-related learning as demonstrated by fewer reversals and more variability in extinction than the reference sample. Furthermore, these measures of emotion-related learning and conceptual shifting were good predictors of parent reported behavioral problems.

Academic Achievement Deficits

Repeating grades, school failure, and dropping out of school have all been identified as negative outcomes associated with FAS (Autti-Ramo, 2000; Streissguth et al., 1996). However, for alcohol-exposed as well as other children, academic problems are determined by complex interactions between the child's neurodevelopmental status, environmental supports for academic success, and emotional stability. Overall academic difficulties are predicted by the individual's general intellectual ability but there may be specific areas of academic weakness in the child with FAS. Relative to their general intellectual impairments, children with FAS have been found to have particular problems with mathematics (Spohr & Steinhausen, 1984; Streissguth et al., 1994).

Deficits in math achievement associated with prenatal alcohol exposure have been identified regularly in both longitudinal and clinical studies of alcohol-affected children (Goldschmidt, Richardson, Stoffer, Geva, & Day, 1996; Kodituwakku et al., 1995; Mattson, Riley, Delis, Stern, & Jones, 1996; Streissguth et al., 1994). In their description of their middle-class, longitudinal cohort, Streissguth and colleagues (1993) reported that arithmetic disabilities were related to prenatal alcohol exposure, particularly with a history of "massed" or heavy drinking. These investigators also note that this experimental finding is in accordance with experience with their older clinically referred patients (Streissguth et al., 1991) and relate these early arithmetic deficits to later difficulties with problem solving, generalization, and abstract thinking. In a different population, Coles and her colleagues (Coles et al., 1991, 1997, 2002) found that low-income, African American school children were specifically impaired in this academic area, despite controlling for global delays, and that the same group of children showed deficits in visuomotor functioning (Beery, 1997) and visual-spatial processing. Jacobson (1999) noted similar deficits and attributed these deficits to impairments in working memory and executive functioning.

In a heterogeneous sample (both urban and suburban populations) of alcohol-exposed, low-birthweight children followed at 4 1/2 years, Kable, Coles, Drews-Botsch, and Falek (1999) identified specific deficits in preacademic mathematical skills that were associated with maternal alcohol and other drug use. Preschoolers (mean age = 4. 5 years) participated in a longitudinal study of maternal drinking and intrauterine growth retardation. The Test of Early Mathematics Ability, 2nd ed. (TEMA; Ginsburg & Baroody, 1990), was used to assess mathematical concept development. A cumulative risk index for maternal drinking behaviors (Coles et al., 2000) was used to assess the degree of alcohol-related neurodevelopmental risk to the child. Higher scores on this checklist, reflecting heavier alcohol consumption, were significantly related to poorer performance on items assessing a number of early math skills, including cardinality, constancy, finger display of numbers to 5, counting to 21, counting backward from 10, and visual recognition of numbers. These data were interpreted to suggest that children had difficulties with working memory, visual perception, and executive functioning skills, which were impacting on their ability to learn mathematical concepts and processes.

In adulthood, individuals with FAS have difficulties with computation and solving problems requiring estimation of magnitude (Kopera-Frye, Dehaene, & Streissguth, 1996), suggesting that difficulties with mathematics persist across the life span.

There are a number of precursors to mathematic ability as well as identified cognitive deficits that may account for these findings, including problems in attention, executive functioning and working memory, as well as difficulties with visual-spatial processing (Rourke, 1995). Children with nonverbal learning disability historically have had a relative deficit in their math achievement. Geary (1993), a leading researcher in the area of math development, posited that a visuospatially based deficit is one of the three subtypes of developmental dyscalculia (math disability). Geary suggested that children who have difficulties in visual processing misinterpret spatial symbols and show deficits in spatial representation that underlie fundamental math concepts (Geary, 1994). Ashcraft (1995) further argued that math disability results from working memory deficits but acknowledged that these problems may be related. As both the areas of working memory and visual-spatial processing have been found to be compromised in children who are alcohol-affected, it is not surprising that they have relative deficits in their mathematical achievement.

In children with FAS, evidence of structural brain damage in areas associated with mathematical thinking has been found. Using SPECT, Riikonen and colleagues (1999) found hypoperfusion in the left parietooccipital region in a clinical sample of children with FAS. This region has been associated with mathematical and logical thinking skills (Dehaene, 1997). In the future, functional imaging of these areas of the brain during mathematical problem solving may provide additional answers as to how these damaged areas affect performance of mathematical tasks.

Emotional and Behavioral Regulation

Behavioral regulation and attention problems in alcohol-affected children are commonly reported by parents and professionals (Kodituwakku et al., 1995; Kopera-Frye, Carmichael-Olson, & Streissguth, 1997, Mattson & Riley, 2000; Oesterheld & Wilson, 1997; Roebuck, Mattson, & Riley, 1999; Steinhausen, Willms, & Spohr, 1993), and such behaviors may interfere with performance in academic settings. However, the association between behavioral problems and prenatal alcohol exposure, while often identified, may not be causal in nature. Children with FAS can experience a host of environmental factors that also may contribute to behavioral regulation difficulties. Caregiving disruptions of various kinds are the norm, rather than the exception, when dealing with young, alcohol-affected children who present in clinical settings. Many children with FAS come from minority or low-income families and often are identified through the foster care system. Janzen, Nanson, and Block (1995) found that clinically referred preschool children with FAS had significantly more behavioral problems than did typically developing children recruited from daycare facilities. However, in another clinical sample, behavioral problems, although frequent, were found to be independent of an alcohol-related diagnosis (Autti-Ramo, 2000).

In a sample of children (mean age = 4.5 years) who were referred to a FAS specialty clinic for a diagnostic evaluation, 54.7% of the children diagnosed with FAS (n = 109) were identified as being too active, 30.5% had difficulties with temper tantrums, and 41.1% were described as having problems with aggression (Coles & Kable, 2002). However, the corresponding percentages for a group of children referred to the same clinic who were found to have no evidence of dysmorphia or growth problems and no history of prenatal alcohol exposure was 53.1%, 25.0%, and 43.8%, respectively. Among children diagnosed with FAS at this clinic, 15.6% were on psychoactive medications and 8.3% were on multiple psychotropic medications, but the comparison sample of children with no evidence of dysmorphia and growth problems and no history of alcohol exposure had 34.4% on psychoactive medications and 9.4% on multiple psychotropic medications. Further examination of groups categorized as FAS, partial FAS (pFAS), alcohol-exposed, or no documented exposure or effects indicates no direct relationship between alcohol teratogenesis and behavioral and emotional outcome (Coles & Kable, 2002). These results suggest that problems with emotional and behavioral regulation, while common to children with FAS, may be associated as much with clinical status or adverse experiences as with prenatal exposure.

Streissguth and colleagues (1996) surveyed adults with FAS or FAE and found that 94% had a history of mental health problems with the most common diagnoses being attention deficit hyperactivity disorder and depression. Although daunting to contemplate, it may be premature to interpret these outcomes as the direct results of teratogenic exposure to alcohol as the survey does not include a comparison sample. These results do, however, reflect the mental health outcomes associated with the combined effects of a damaged brain functioning within a compromised environment over the course of a lifespan.

GENERAL TREATMENT GUIDELINES

There are, as yet, no generally accepted treatment protocols designed specifically for individuals affected by prenatal alcohol exposure. Debate continues about the core neurocognitive deficits and the implications for education and treatment guidelines. However, in 1996, the Institute of Medicine (IOM; Stratton et al., 1996) reviewed the consequences of alcohol exposure as well as the barriers to treatment and intervention that are often experienced by individuals and families and provided a number of recommendations to address these concerns. These suggestions included the need for regional centers for diagnosis and specialized treatment as well as treatment that is designed to meet the special, often complex needs of alcohol-affected individuals and their families. Also suggested was that clinical practice guidelines and educational material should be developed to assist in the training of professionals who work with alcohol-affected individuals. The IOM directed that attention should be paid to postnatal environmental factors and emotional development of affected children within the family context and pointed to the need for further research to provide a solid foundation for the implementation of these guidelines. The basic research required for the development of treatment guidelines that should ameliorate core deficits associated with FAS is not yet in place (CDC, 1998), although, since the IOM report, several projects have been initiated with this goal in mind (CDC, 2002).

One of the important challenges for educators working with alcohol-affected individuals are problems matching their characteristics to the requirements of existing systems. Working within existing systems can be difficult because affected children and adolescents may not fit comfortably into treatment and educational categories (Coles & Platzman, 1992). Many function in the low average to borderline range intellectually (Coles & Platzman, 1993), limiting the availability of specific educational services. This is particularly a problem early in life and may result in denial of the services that could prevent the occurrence of the secondary disabilities, like emotional and behavioral disorders and academic failure, that are so devastating for affected individuals and their families. In addition, because alcohol-affected individuals are impacted both cognitively and physically and also may experience a host of negative postnatal environmental experiences, services and supports must cover a wider spectrum than is the case for some other disabilities.

Socioenvironmental Supports

Most clinically referred children with FAS have problematic medical and caregiving histories (as well as problems associated with coming from disadvantaged backgrounds) that must be addressed. Successful intervention is possible only when the needs and goals of the family as well as those of the child are taken into account and when caregivers are actively involved in the solution to these problems. As a result of the complicated social–environmental contexts and backgrounds that the children with FAS often have experienced, some attention must be paid to stabilizing their environments and to their emotional and behavioral status before they will be able to benefit from typical educational supportive services. Case management, medication management, educational management, and behavioral regulation training services are often needed before a child can obtain optimal benefit from any educational intervention that is implemented. A multidisciplinary team is often needed to provide the various services necessary for these individuals.

Caregiver Advocacy Training

The child's caregiver is the primary support throughout development. If the caregiver is an alcoholic who is still using, assuring appropriate treatment of the child may be very difficult and may require that the parent's needs be addressed first. However, many alcohol-affected individuals are being cared for by foster and adoptive families and in this situation, a different approach is possible. Caregiver education regarding neurodevelopmental consequences of alcohol and training regarding implementation of appropriate treatments is vital for fostering generalization of learning and educational principles. An intervention model that views caregivers as cotherapists and the primary agents of therapeutic change may be most effective (Briesmeister & Schaefer, 1998) in facilitating generalization and empowering caregivers with the knowledge and techniques needed to facilitate their child's long-term adjustment. Caregivers should receive education regarding FAS, how to communicate with pertinent professionals regarding their child's needs and to assist in goal planning for their child. Caregivers should learn about their child's rights within the educational system and should be encouraged to advocate for their children in the context of educational, political, social, and legal systems.

Educational Placement

Many children who are diagnosed with FAS do not fit into existing category schemas used by most school systems. As their ability scores are often in the "borderline" range (IQ 70 to 85), children have difficulties with meeting traditional requirements of either intellectual impairment or learning disability (a score greater than 1.5 standard deviations below cognitive functioning) despite having numerous neurodevelopmental impairments that interfere with these children's academic success. Classification of other health impairment (OHI), based on the neurological damage associated with prenatal exposure, is often used to establish individualized educational plans for those who do not meet traditional requirements.

Cognitive Habilitation

Cognitive habilitation refers to the facilitation of brain development by environmental events and experiences. Previous work in cognitive rehabilitation with children who have brain damage associated with severe head traumas and/or tumors has suggested that in order to effectively alter cognitive functioning, interventions must be contextualized within the environment of the individual (Ylvisaker, 1998) as interventions designed to treat the underlying cognitive structures of a task have shown little generalization beyond the specific task parameters specified in the intervention. In developing interventions to habilitate children who have brain damage from prenatal alcohol exposure, one must select a functional skill that is impacted by the brain damage and construct an intervention to remediate the deficits (e.g., visual-spatial processing and working memory) within the context of that functional skill. This means that in order to alter the brain development of children with FAS, interventions must be construed within the context of their lives, impacting on their social, educational, physical, and adaptive behavioral functioning.

Educational Supports

An active learning approach to instruction is recommended to facilitate learning in children with FAS where the specific content of the instruction is individualized based on the child's preexisting skills. One approach with potential for this group involves implementing a "plan-do-review" phase to learning and problem solving. This approach was utilized with other groups of children in the High/Scope Perry Preschool Project and found to have positive long-term consequences on academic achievement and educational attainment (Luster & McAdoo, 1996; Weikart & Schweinhart, 1992). This approach has also been found to be beneficial in cognitive rehabilitation programs for children with acquired brain damage (Ylvisaker, 1998). The use of visual materials and visual aids is also recommended to compensate for the deficit in visual-spatial skills and working memory associated with fetal alcohol exposure.

In a current intervention study directed at the remediatation of math deficits (Coles & Kable, 2002), each child receives instruction in developmentally appropriate mathematical problem solving using step-wise sequential procedures that are illustrated and/or written for the child. Graphical visual organizing aids are used to facilitate understanding of mathematical concepts and memory aids and strategies are used if needed. Each child is encouraged to frequently utilize nonverbal-visual-spatial skills and to use organizational strategies to solve problems. Assistance to the child in interpreting and organizing visual information is provided as needed. Common sources of error in school-related tasks are identified (faulty sequence, omission, perseveration, object substitution or misuse) and strategies to reorient and correctly identify are communicated to parents and teachers. Modifications are made for visual-motor difficulties as needed and consultations with occupational therapists are recommended to assist with this.

Auxiliary Therapeutic Supports

Children with FAS often need auxiliary therapy services to manage developmental and behavioral problems. Speech and language therapies often are recommended to facilitate language development and to deal with oral-motor problems. Occupational and physical therapies are often needed to address motor functioning impairments and to assist with adapting educational experiences as needed. Psychiatrists, psychologists, counselors, and social workers may be involved with the target child or their families to address various mental health issues that are common among the children with FAS but have not been demonstrated to be the direct result of the teratogenic effects of alcohol.

CONCLUSIONS

FAS is a disorder characterized by a three defining features, including growth delays, physical dysmorphia, and neurodevelopmental compromise. Heavy prenatal alcohol exposure is associated with a host of negative neurodevelopmental sequalae that interfere with children's adaptation to their social, educational, physical, and behavioral functioning. Such deficits include general intellectual impairments as well as specific deficits in visual-spatial perception and integration, motor functioning, attention and arousal regulation, working memory skills, and planning and organizational skills. Academically, they often demonstrate relative deficits in mathematical thinking and problem solving. In addition to the teratogenic effects of prenatal alcohol exposure, the caregiving instability and impoverished environments that children with FAS often experience appear to negatively impact academic, social, and behavioral adjustments. Although intervention research is limited with children who have FAS, guidelines for developing such interventions were discussed. A model of cognitive habilitation was proposed as well as recommendations for implementing appropriate socioenvironmental, parental, educational, and therapeutic supports.

REFERENCES

Abel, E. L. (1995). An update on incidence in fetal alcohol syndrome: FAS is not an equal opportunity birth defect. *Neurotoxicology and Teratology, 17*, 427–443.

Abel, E. L. (1998). *Fetal alcohol abuse syndrome*. New York: Plenum.

Aronson, M., & Hagberg, B. (1998). Neuropsychological disorders in children exposed to alcohol during pregnancy: A follow-up study of 24 children to alcoholic mothers in Goteborg, Sweden. *Alcoholism: Clinical Experimental Research, 22*, 321–324.

Aronson, M., Kyllerman, M., Sabel, K. G., Sandin, B., & Olegard, R. (1985). Children of alcoholic mothers. Developmental, perceptual and behavioural characteristics as compared to matched controls. *Acta Paediatrica Scandinavica, 74*(1), 27–35.

Ashcraft, M. H. (1995). Cognitive psychology and simple arithmetic: A review and summary of new directions. *Mathematical Cognitive, 1*, 3–34

Ashcraft, M. H., Kirk, E. P., & Hopko, D. (1998). On the cognitive consequences of mathematics anxiety. In C. Donlan (Ed.), *The development of mathematical skills* (pp. 175–196). East Sussex, UK: Psychology Press/Taylor & Francis.

Astley, S. J., & Clarren, S. K. (1996). *Diagnostic guide for fetal alcohol syndrome and related conditions: FAS diagnostic and prevention network*. Seattle: University of Washington.

Astley, S. J., & Clarren, S. K. (2001). Measuring the facial phenotype of individuals with prenatal alcohol exposure: correlations with brain dysfunction. *Alcohol and Alcoholism, 36*(2), 147–159.

Autti-Ramo, I. A. (2000). Twelve-year follow-up of children exposed to alcohol in utero. *Developmental Medicine and Child Neurology, 42*, 406–411.

Barnwell, C., & Morse, B. A. (1999). *Fetal alcohol syndrome/fetal alcohol effects: Resources for maternal and child health programs*. Boston, MA: Fetal Alcohol Education Program.

Barr, H. M., Streissguth, A. P., Darby, B. L., & Sampson, P. D. (1990). Prenatal exposure to alcohol, caffeine, tobacco, and aspirin: Effects on fine and gross motor performance in 4-year-old children. *Developmental Psychology, 26*, 339–348.

Beery, K. E. (1997). *Developmental test of visual-motor integration (4th ed.)*. Parsippany, NJ: Modern Curriculum Press.

Bingol, N., Schuster, C., Fuchs, M., Iosub, S., Turner, G., Stone, R. K., & Gromisch, D. S. (1987). The influence of socioeconomic factors on occurrence of fetal alcohol syndrome. *Advances in Alcoholism and Substance Abuse: Special Issue: Children of Alcoholics, 6*, 105–118.

Borkowski, J. G., & Burke, J. E. (1996). Theories, models and measurements of executive functioning: An information processing perspective. In G. R. Lyon & N. A. Krasnegor (Eds.), *Attention, memory, and executive function* (pp. 235–263). Baltimore: Paul Brookes Publishing Co.

Boyd, T. A., Ernhart, C. B., Greene, T. H., Sokol, R. J., & Martier, S. (1991). Prenatal alcohol exposure and sustained attention in the preschool years. *Neurotoxicology and Teratology, 13*, 49–55.

Bray, D. L., & Anderson, P. D. (1989). Appraisal of the epidemiology of fetal alcohol syndrome among Canadian native people. *Canadian Journal of Public Health, 80*, 42–45.

Briesmeister, J. M., & Schaefer, C. E. (Eds.). (1998). *Handbook of parent training: Parents as co-therapists for children's behavior problems* (2nd ed.). New York: Wiley.

Brown, R. T., Coles, C. D., Smith, I. E., Platzman, K. A., Silverstein, J., Erickson, S., & Falek, A. (1991). Effects of prenatal alcohol exposure at school age: II. Attention and behavior. *Neurotoxicology and Teratology, 13*(4), 369–376.

Carmichael-Olson, H., Feldman, J. J., Streissguth, A. P., Sampson, P. D., & Bookstein, F. L. (1998). Neuropsychological deficits in adolescents with fetal alcohol syndrome: Clinical findings. *Alcoholism: Clinical and Experimental Research, 22*, 1998–2012.

Centers for Disease Control and Prevention. (1993). Fetal alcohol syndrome—United States, 1979–1991. *MMWR, 173*, 575.

Centers for Disease Control and Prevention. (1998). Intervening with children affected by prenatal alcohol exposure. Proceedings of a Special Focus Session Interagency Coordinating Committee on Fetal Alcohol Syndrome, September 10–11, Chevy Chase, MD.

Centers for Disease Control and Prevention. (2002). Currently funded projects. In National Center on Birth Defects and Developmental Disabilities [Online]. Available: http://www.cdc.gov/ncbddd/funding.htm.

Chapman, L. J., & Chapman, J. P. (1973). Problems in the measurement of cognitive deficit. *Psychological Bulletin, 79*(6), 380–385.

Church, M. W. (1987). Chronic in utero alcohol: Exposure affects auditory function in rats and in humans. *Alcohol, 4*, 231–239.

Church, M. W. (1996). The effects of prenatal alcohol exposure on hearing and vestibular function. In E. L. Abel (Ed.), *Fetal alcohol syndrome: From mechanism to prevention* (pp. 85–111). Boca Raton, FL: CRC Press.

Clarren, S. K. (1986). Neuropathology in fetal alcohol syndrome. In J. R. West (Ed.), *Alcohol and brain development* (pp. 158–166). New York: Oxford University Press.

Clarren, S. K., & Smith, D. W. (1978). The fetal alcohol syndrome. *New England Journal of Medicine, 298*, 1063–1067.

Coles, C. D. (1993). Impact of prenatal alcohol exposure on the newborn and the child. *Clinical Obstetrics and Gynecology, 36*(2), 255–266.

Coles, C. D. (2000). *Prenatal alcohol exposure and attention*. Paper presented at the Fetal Alcohol Syndrome Study Group at the 23rd Annual Scientific Meeting of the Research Society on Alcoholism, Denver, CO.

Coles, C. D., Brown, R. T., Smith, I. E., Platzman, K. A., Erickson, S., & Falek, A. (1991). Effects of prenatal alcohol exposure at school age: I. Physical and cognitive development. *Neurotoxicology and Teratology, 13*(4), 357–367.

Coles, C. D., & Kable, J. A. (2002). [Socio-cognitive habilitation]. Unpublished manuscript.

Coles, C. D., Kable, J. A., Drews-Botsch, C., & Falek, A. (2000). Early identification of risk for effects of prenatal alcohol exposure. *Journal of Studies on Alcohol, 61*(4), 607–616.

Coles, C. D., & Platzman, K. A. (1992). Fetal alcohol effects in preschool children: Research, prevention, and intervention. Identifying the Needs of Drug-Affected Children: Public Policy Issues, OSAP Prevention Monograph #11, 59–86.

Coles, C. D., & Platzman, K. A. (1993). Behavioral development in children prenatally exposed to drugs and alcohol. *International Journal of the Addictions, 28*(13), 1393–1433.

Coles, C. D., Platzman, K. A., Lynch, M. A., & Freides, D. (2002). Auditory and visual sustained attention in adolescents prenatally exposed to alcohol. *Alcohol: Clinical and Experimental Research, 26*(2), 263–271.

Coles, C. D., Platzman, K. A., Raskind-Hood, C. L., Brown, R. T., Falek, A., & Smith, I. E. (1997). A comparison of children affected by prenatal alcohol exposure and attention deficit, hyperactivity disorder. *Alcoholism: Clinical and Experimental Research, 21*(1), 150–161.

Coles, C. D., Smith, I. E., Fernhoff, P. M., & Falek, A. (1985). Neonatal neurobehavioral characteristics as correlates of maternal alcohol use during gestation. *Alcoholism: Clinical and Experimental Research, 9*(5), 1–7.

Conn-Blowers, E. A. (1991). Nurturing and educating children prenatally exposed to alcohol: The role of the counsellor. *International Journal for the Advancement of Counseling, 14*(2), 91–103.

Connor, P. D., Sampson, P. D., Bookstein, F. L., Barr, H. M., & Streissguth, A. P. (2000). Direct and indirect effects of prenatal alcohol damage on executive function. *Developmental Neuropsychology, 18*(3), 331–354.

Connor, P. D., Streissguth, A. P., Sampson, P. D., Bookstein, F. L., & Barr, H. M. (1999). Individual differences in auditory and visual attention among fetal alcohol-affected adults. *Alcoholism: Clinical and Experimental Research, 23*(8), 1395–1402.

Conry, J. (1990). Neuropsychological deficits in fetal alcohol syndrome and fetal alcohol effects. *Alcoholism: Clinical and Experimental Research, 14*(5), 650–655.

Coull, J. T. (1998). Neural correlates of attention and arousal: Insights from electrophysiology, functional neuroimaging and psychopharmacology. *Progress in Neurobiology, 55*, 343–361.

Crepin, G., Dehaene, P., & Samaille, C. (1989). Aspects cliniques, evolutifs epidemiologiques de l'alcoolisme foetal: Un fleau tourjours d'actualite. *Bulletin de L'Academe National du Medcine, 173*, 575–582.

Day, N. L., & Richardson, G. A. (1994). Comparative teratogenicity of alcohol and other drugs. *Alcohol Health and Research World, 18*(1), 42–48.

Day, N. L., & Robles, N. (1989). Methodological issues in the measurement of substance use. *Annals of the New York Academy of Sciences, 562*, 8–13.

Dehaene, S. (1997). *The number sense: How the mind creates mathematics* (pp. 207–228). Oxford: Oxford University Press.

Dehaene, P., Crepin, G., Delahousse, G., Querleu, D., Walbaum, R., Titran, M., & Samaille-Villette, C. (1981). Aspects epidemiologique du syndrome d'alcoolisme foetal: 45 observations en 3 ans. *La Nouvelle Press Medicale, 10*, 2639.

Delis, D. C., Kramer, J. H., Kaplan, E., & Ober, B. A. (1987). *California verbal learning test*. San Antonio, TX: Psychological Corp.

DeVries, J. (1999, Fall). Early intervention, part II. *F.A.S. Times: Fetal Alcohol Syndrome/Family Resource Institute Newsletter*, 1–2.

Dreosti, I. E., & Joschko, M. A. (1995). Diet- and drug-related factors and the expression of the fetal alcohol syndrome. *Developmental Brain Dysfunction, 8*(2–3), 1033–1108.

Fernhoff, P. M., Smith, I. E., & Falek, A. (1980). *Dysmorphia checklist*. Document available through the Maternal Substance Abuse and Child Development Project, Division of Psychiatry, Emory University School of Medicine, Atlanta, GA.

Geary, D. C. (1993). Mathematical disabilities: Cognitive, neuropsychological, and genetic components. *Psychological Bulletin, 114*(2), 345–362.

Geary, D. C. (1994). *Children's mathematical development: Research and practical applications*. Washington, D.C.: American Psychological Association.

Ginsburg, H. P., & Baroody, A. J. (1990). *Test of early mathematics ability*. Austin, TX: PRO-ED, Inc.

Giunta, C. T., & Streissguth, A. P. (1988). Patients with fetal alcohol syndrome and their caretakers. *Social Casework: The Journal of Contemporary Social Work*, 453–459.

Goldschmidt, L., Richardson, G. A., Stoffer, D. S., Geva, D., & Day, N. (1996). Prenatal alcohol exposure and academic achievement at age six: A nonlinear fit. *Alcoholism: Clinical & Experimental Research, 20*(4), 763–770.

Haith, M. M., Hazan, C., & Goodman, G. S. (1988). Expectation and anticipation of dynamic visual events by 3.5-month-old babies. *Child Development, 59*(2), 467–479.

Hanson, J. W., Streissguth, A. P., & Smith, D. W. (1978). The effects of moderate alcohol consumption during pregnancy on fetal growth and morphogenesis. *Journal of Pediatrics, 92*, 457–460.

Harris-Collazo, M. R., Kwok, W., Mattson, S. N., Jernigan, S. N., & Riley, E. P. (1998). Quantitative magnetic resonance imaging analysis of fetal alcohol syndrome. *Journal of the International Neuropsychological Society, 4*(1), 48.

Heaton, R. K., Chelune, G. J., Talley, J. L., Kay, G. G., & Curtiss, G. (1993). *Wisconsin card sort testing manual: Revised and expanded.* Odessa, FL: Psychological Assessment Resources.

Hingson, R., Alpert, J. J., Day, N., Dooling, E., Kayne, H., Morelock, S., Oppenheimer, E., & Zuckerman, B. (1982). Effects of maternal drinking and marijuana use on fetal growth and development. *Pediatrics, 70*(4), 539–546.

International classification of diseases 9th revision clinical modification, volumes 1 and 2 (ICD-9-CM) (5th ed.). (1997). Salt Lake City, UI: Medicode Publications, Inc.

Jacobson, S. W. (1999). *Cognitive processing deficits associated with poor mathematical performance in alcohol-exposed school-aged children.* Paper presented at the 22nd Annual Scientific Meeting of the Research Society on Alcoholism, Santa Barbara, CA.

Jacobson, S. W., Fein, G. G., Jacobson, J. L., Schwartz, P. M., & Dowler, J. K. (1984). Neonatal correlates of prenatal exposure to smoking, caffeine, and alcohol. *Infant Mental Health Journal, 7*, 253–265.

Jacobson, S. W., Jacobson J. L., O'Neill, J. M., Padgett, R. J., Frankowski, J. J., & Bihun, J. T. (1992). Visual expectation and dimensions of infant information processing. *Child Development, 63*(3), 711–724.

Jacobson, S. W., Jacobson, J. L., & Sokol, R. J. (1994). Effects of fetal alcohol exposure on infant reaction time. *Alcoholism: Clinical and Experimental Research, 18*(5), 1125–1132.

Jacobson S. W., Jacobson J. L., Sokol, R. J., Martier, S. S., & Ager, J. W. (1993) . Prenatal alcohol exposure and infant information processing ability. *Child Development, 64*(6), 1706–1721.

Jacobson, S. W., Jacobson, J. L., Sokol, R. J., Martier, S. S., Ager, J. W., & Kaplan, M. G. (1991). Maternal recall of alcohol, cocaine, and marijuana use during pregnancy. *Neurotoxicology and Teratology, 13*, 535–540.

Janzen, L. A., Nanson, J. L., & Block, G. W. (1995). Neuropsychological evaluation of preschoolers with Fetal Alcohol Syndrome. *Neurotoxicology & Teratology, 17*(3), 273–279.

Johnson, V. P., Swayze, V. W. II, Sato, Y., & Andreasen, N. C. (1996). Fetal alcohol syndrome: Craniofacial and central nervous system manifestations. *American Journal of Medical Genetics, 61*(4), 329–339.

Jones, K. L., & Smith, D. W. (1973). Recognition of the fetal alcohol syndrome in early infancy. *Lancet, 2*, 989.

Jones, K. L., Smith, D. W., Ulleland, C. N., & Streissguth, A. P. (1973). Pattern of malformation in offspring of chronic alcoholic mothers. *Lancet, 1*, 1267–1271.

Kable, J. A., & Coles, C. D. (2000). *The impact of prenatal alcohol exposure on attentional regulation during infancy.* Poster session presented at Scientific Meeting of the Research Society on Alcoholism, Denver, CO.

Kable, J. A., Coles, C. D., Drews-Botsch, C., & Falek, A. (1999). *The effects of maternal drinking prenatally on patterns of pre-academic mathematical concept development.* Paper presented at the 22nd Annual Scientific Meeting of the Research Society on Alcoholism, Santa Barbara, CA.

Kaemingk, K., & Paquette, A. (1999). Effects of prenatal alcohol exposure on neuropsychological functioning. *Developmental Neuropsychology, 15*(1), 111–140.

Kerns, K. A., Don, A., Mateer, C. A., & Streissguth, A. P. (1997). Cognitive deficits in nonretarded adults with fetal alcohol syndrome. *Journal of Learning Disabilities, 30*(6), 685–693.

Kodituwakku, P. W., Handmaker, N. S., Cutler, S. K., Weathersby, E. K., & Handmaker, S. D. (1995). Specific impairments in self-regulation in children exposed to alcohol prenatally. *Alcoholism: Clinical & Experimental Research, 19*(6), 1558–1564.

Kodituwakku, P. W., May, P. A., Clericuzio, C. L., & Weers, D. (2001). Emotion-related learning in individuals prenatally exposed to alcohol: An investigation of the relation between set shifting, extinction of responses, and behavior. *Neuropsychologia, 39*, 699–708.

Kopera-Frye, K., Carmichael-Olson, H., & Streissguth, A. P. (1997). Teratogenic effects of alcohol on attention. In J. A. Burack & J. T. Enns (Eds.), *Attention, development and psychopathology* (pp. 171–204). New York: Guildford.

Kopera-Frye, K., Dehaene, S., & Streissguth, A. P. (1996). Impairments of number processing induced by prenatal alcohol exposure. *Neuropsychologia, 34*(12), 1187–1196.

Kuzma, J. W., & Kissinger, D. G. (1981). Patterns of alcohol and cigarette use in pregnancy. *Neurobehavioral Toxicology and Teratology, 3*, 211–221.

Kyllerman, M., Aronson, M., Sabel, K. G., Karlberg, E., Sandin, B., & Olegard, R. (1985). Children of alcoholic mothers. *Acta Paediatr Scand, 74*, 20–26.

Lancaster, F. (1994). Alcohol and white matter development. *Alcoholism: Clinical and Experimental Research, 18*, 644–647.

Landesman-Dwyer, S., & Ragozin, A. S. (1981). Behavioral correlated of prenatal alcohol exposure: A four-year follow-up study. *Neurobehavioral Toxicology and Teratology, 3*, 187–193.

Luster, T., & McAdoo, H. (1996). Family and child influences on educational attainment: A secondary analysis of the high/scope Perry Preschool data. *Developmental Psychology, 32*(1), 26–39.

Lyon, G. R. (1996). The need for conceptual and theoretical clarity in the study of attention, memory, and executive function. In G. R. Lyon & N. A. Krasnegor (Eds.), *Attention, memory, and executive function* (pp. 3–10). Baltimore: Paul Brookes Publishing Co.

Mackintosh, N. J. (1975). A theory of attention: Variations in the associability of stimuli with reinforcement. *Psychology Review, 82*(4), 276–298.

Marcus, J. C. (1987). Neurological findings in the fetal alcohol syndrome. *Neuropediatrics, 18*(3), 158–160.

Marintcheva, G., Riley, E. P., Mattson, S. N., Coles, C. D., Konovalova, V., & Matveeva, A. (2001). Neuropsychological test performance in Russian children with FAS compared to controls matched for age, sex, IQ, and living environment. Paper presented at Research Society on Alcoholism, 24th Annual Scientific Meeting, June 27, 2001, Montreal, Quebec, Canada.

Mattson, S. N., Carlos, R., & Riley, E. P. (1993). The behavioral teratogenicity of alcohol is not affected by pretreatment with aspirin. *Alcohol, 10*(1), 51–57.

Mattson, S. N., Goodman, A. M., Caine, C., Delis, D. C., & Riley, E. P. (1999). Executive functioning in children with heavy prenatal alcohol exposure. *Alcoholism: Clinical & Experimental Research, 23*(11), 1808–1815.

Mattson, S. N., Jernigan, T. L., & Riley, E. P. (1994). MRI and prenatal alcohol exposure: Images provide insight into FAS. *Alcohol Health Research World, 18*(1), 49–52.

Mattson, S. N., & Riley, E. P. (1996). Brain anomalies in fetal alcohol syndrome. In E. L. Abel (Ed.), *Fetal alcohol syndrome: From mechanism to prevention* (pp. 51–68). Boca Raton, FL: CRC Press.

Mattson, S. N., & Riley, E. P. (1998). A review of the neurobehavioral deficits in children with fetal alcohol syndrome or prenatal exposure to alcohol. *Alcoholism: Clinical & Experimental Research, 22*(2), 279–294.

Mattson S. N., & Riley, E. P. (2000). Parent ratings of behavior in children with heavy prenatal alcohol exposure and IQ-matched controls. *Alcoholism: Clinical & Experimental Research, 24*(2), 226–231.

Mattson, S. N., Riley, E. P., Delis, D. C., Stern, C., & Jones, K. L. (1996). Verbal learning and memory in children with fetal alcohol syndrome. *Alcoholism: Clinical & Experimental Research, 20*(5), 810–816.

Mattson, S. N., Riley, E. P., Gramling, L., Delis, D. C., & Jones, K. L. (1998). Neuropsychological comparison of alcohol-exposed children with or without physical features of fetal alcohol syndrome. *Neuropsychology, 12*(1), 146–153.

Mattson, S. N., Riley, E. P., Jernigan, T. L., Ehlers, C. L., Delis, D. C., Jones, K. L., Stern, C., Johnson, K. A., Hesselink, J. R., & Bellugi, U. (1992). Fetal alcohol syndrome: A case report of neuropsychological, MRI and EEG assessment of two children. *Alcoholism: Clinical & Experimental Research, 16*(5), 1001–1003.

Mattson, S. N., Riley, E. P., Jernigan, T. L., Garcia, A., Kaneko, W. M., Ehlers, C. L., & Jones, K. L. (1994). A decrease in the size of the basal ganglia following prenatal alcohol exposure: A preliminary report. *Neurotoxicology Teratology 16*(3), 283–289.

Mattson, S. N., Riley, E. P., Sowell, E. R., Jernigan, T. L., Sobel, D. F., & Jones, K. L. (1996). A decrease in the size of the basal ganglia in children with fetal alcohol syndrome. *Alcoholism: Clinical & Experimental Research, 20*(6), 1088–1093.

May, P. A. (1995). A multiple-level, comprehensive approach to the prevention of fetal alcohol syndrome (FAS) and other alcohol-related birth defects (ARBD). *The International Journal of Addictions, 30*(12), 1549–1602.

May, P. A., Brooke, L., Gessage, J. P., Croxford, J., Adnams, C., Jones, K. L., Robinson, L., & Viljoen, D. (2001). Epidemiology of fetal alcohol syndrome in a South African Community in the Western Cape Province. *American Journal of Public Health, 90*(12), 1905–1912.

May, P. A., Hymbaugh, K. J., Aase, J. M., & Samet, J. M. (1983). Epidemiology of fetal alcohol syndrome among American Indians of the southwest. *Social Biology, 30*, 374–387.

McCarthy, D. (1972). *The McCarthy scales of children's abilities*. New York: Psychological Corporation.

McLoyd, V. C. (1998). Socioeconomic disadvantage and child development. *American Psychologist, 53*(2), 185–204.

Mesulam, M. M. (1981). A cortical network for directed attention and unilateral neglect. *Archives of Neurology, 10*, 304–325.

Mirsky, A. F. (1989). The neuropsychology of attention: Elements of a complex behavior. In E. Peregman (Ed.), *Integrated theory and practice in clinical neuropsychology*. Hillsdale, NJ: Lawrence Erlbaum Associates.

Morris, R. D. (1996). Relationships and distinctions among the concepts of attention, memory, and executive function: A developmental perspective. In G. R. Lyon & N. A. Krasnegor (Eds.), *Attention, memory, and executive function* (pp. 11–16). Baltimore: Paul Brookes Publishing Co.

Morse, B. A., Adams, J., & Weiner, L. (1992). FAS: Neuropsychological manifestations. *Alcoholism: Clinical and Experimental Research, 16*, 380.

Nanson, J. L., & Hiscock, M. (1990). Attention deficits in children exposed to alcohol prenatally. *Alcoholism: Clinical and Experimental Research, 14*(5), 656–661.

O'Beattie, J., Day, R. E., Cockburn, F., & Garg R. A. (1983). Alcohol and the fetus in the west of Scotland. *British Medical Journal, 287*, 17–20.

Oesterheld, J. R., & Wilson, A. (1997). ADHD and FAS. *Journal of the American Academy Child and Adolescent Psychiatry, 36*, 1163.

Olegard, R., Sabel, K. G., Aronsson, M., Sadin, B., Johansson, P. R., Carlsson, C., Kyllerman, M., Iversen, K., & Hrbek, A. (1979). Effects on the child of alcohol abuse during pregnancy: Retrospective and prospective studies. *Acta Paediatr Scand. Supppl. 275*, 112–121.

Platzman, K. A., Friedes, D., Lynch, M. E., & Falek, A. (2000). *Narrative and visual-spatial memory in adolescents prenatally exposed to alcohol.* Poster session presented at the Annual Meeting of the Research Society on Alcoholism, Denver, CO.

Posner, M. I., & Petersen, S. E. (1990). The attention system of the human brain. *A Rev. Neurosci., 13*, 25–42.

Riikonen, R. S. (1994). Difference in susceptibility to teratogenic effects of alcohol in discordant twins exposed to alcohol during the second half of gestation. *Pediatric Neurology, 11*(4), 332–336.

Riikonen, R., Salonen, I., Partanen, K., & Verho, S. (1999). Brain perfusion SPECT and MRI in foetal alcohol syndrome. *Developmental Medicine & Child Neurology, 41*, 652–659.

Riley, E. P., Mattson, S. N., Sowell, E. R., Jernigan, T. L., Sobel, D. F., & Jones, K. L. (1995). Abnormalities of the corpus callosum in children prenatally exposed to alcohol. *Alcoholism: Clinical & Experimental Research 19*(5), 1198–1202.

Robin, N. H., & Zackai, E. H. (1994). Unusual craniofacial dysmorphia due to prenatal alcohol and cocaine exposure. *Teratology, 50*(2), 160–164.

Robinson, L. (2001). *Incidence and manifestation of fetal alcohol syndrome in special orphanages and boarding schools in Moscow, Russia.* Paper presented at Symposium, Alcohol Problems in Russia: Results of Four Research Initiatives Developed Under the U.S./Russian Bilateral Commission for Science and Technology, M. M. Murry (Chair), Research Society on Alcoholism, 24th Annual Scientific Meeting, June 26, Montreal, Quebec, Canada.

Roebuck, T. M., Mattson, S. N., & Riley, E. P. (1998). A review of the neuroanatomical findings in children with fetal alcohol syndrome or prenatal exposure to alcohol. *Alcoholism: Clinical & Experimental Research, 22*(2), 339–344.

Roebuck, T. M., Mattson, S. N., & Riley, E. P. (1999). Behavioral and psychosocial profiles of alcohol-exposed children. *Alcoholism: Clinical & Experimental Research, 23*(6), 1070–1076.

Roebuck, T. M., Simmons, R. W., Mattson, S. N., & Riley, E. P. (1998). Prenatal exposure to alcohol affects the ability to maintain postural balance. *Alcoholism: Clinical & Experimental Research, 22*(1), 252–258.

Roebuck, T. M., Simmons, R. W., Richardson, C., Mattson, S. N., & Riley, E. P. (1998). Neuromuscular responses to disturbance of balance in children with prenatal exposure to alcohol. *Alcoholism: Clinical & Experimental Research, 22*(9), 1992–1997.

Rolls, E. T., Hornak, J., Wade, D., & McGrath, J. (1994). Emotion-related learning in patients with social and emotional changes associated with frontal lobe damage. *Journal of Neurology, Neurosurgery, and Psychiatry, 57*, 1518–1524.

Rourke, B. P. (Ed.). (1995). *Syndrome of nonverbal learning disabilities: Neurodevelopmental manifestations.* New York: Guilford.

Sampson, P. D., Kerr, B., Carmichael-Olson, H., Streissguth, A. P., Hunt, E., & Barr, H. (1997). The effects of prenatal alcohol exposure on adolescent cognitive processing: A speed-accuracy tradeoff. *Intelligence, 24*(2), 329–353.

Schonfeld, A. M., Mattson, S. N., Lang, A., Delis, D. C., & Riley, E. P. (2001). Verbal and nonverbal fluency in children with heavy prenatal alcohol exposure. *Journal of Studies on Alcohol, 62*(2), 239–246.

Shallice, T. (1982). Specific impairments in planning. In D. E. Broadbent & L. Weiskrantz (Eds.), *The neuropsychology of cognitive function* (pp. 199–209). London: The Royal Society.

Smith, I. E., Coles, C. D., Lancaster, J., Fernhoff, P. M., & Falek, A. (1986). The effect of volume and duration of prenatal ethanol exposure on neonatal physical and behavioral development. *Neurobehavioral Toxicology & Teratology, 8*, 375–381.

Smith, I. E., Lancaster, J. S., Moss-Wells, S., Coles, C. D., & Falek, A. (1987). Identifying high risk pregnant drinkers: Biological and behavioral correlates of continuous heavy drinking during pregnancy. *Journal of Studies on Alcohol, 48*, 304–309.

Smith, D. F., Sandor, G. G., MacLeod, P. M., Tredwell, S., Wood, B., & Newman, D. E. (1981). *Neurobehavioral Toxicology and Teratology, 3*, 145–152.

Sokol, R. J., Ager, J., Martier, R. S., Debanne, S., Ernhart, C., Kuzma, J., & Miller, S. I. (1986). Significant determinations of susceptibility to alcohol teratogenicity. *Annuals of the New York Academy Science, 47*, 87–102.

Sokol, R. J., & Clarren, S. K. (1989). Guidelines for use of terminology describing the impact of prenatal alcohol on the offspring. *Alcoholism: Clinical & Experimental Research, 13*(4), 597–598.

Sowell, E. R., Jernigan, T. L., Mattson, S. N., Riley, E. P., Sobel, D. F., & Jones, K. L. (1996). Abnormal development of the cerebellar vermis in children prenatally exposed to alcohol, size reduction in lobules I-V. *Alcoholism: Clinical & Experimental Research, 20*(1), 31–34.

Spohr, H-L., & Steinhausen, H. C. (1984). Clinical, psychopathological, and developmental aspects in children with the fetal alcohol syndrome (FAS). In *CIBA Foundation Symposium 105: Mechanisms of alcohol damage in utero* (pp. 197–217). London: CIBA Foundation. Pitman Publishers.

Spohr, H. L., & Steinhausen, H. C. (1987). Follow-up of children with Fetal Alcohol Syndrome. *Neuropediatrics, 18*, 13–17.

Spohr, H. L., Willms, J., & Steinhausen, J. C. (1993). Prenatal alcohol exposure and long-term developmental consequences. *Lancet, 32*, 990–1006.

Steinhausen, H. C., Nestler, V., & Spohr, H. L. (1982). Development and psychopathology of children with the Fetal Alcohol Syndrome. *Developmental and Behavioral Pediatrics, 3*(2), 49–54.

Steinhausen, H. C., Willms, J., & Spohr, H. L. (1993). Long-term psychopathological and cognitive outcome of children with fetal alcohol syndrome. *J. Am. Acad. Child Adolesc. Psychiatry, 32*(5), 990–994.

Stratton, K., Howe, C., & Battaglia, F. (Eds.). (1996). *Fetal alcohol syndrome: Diagnosis, epidemiology, prevention and treatment*. Washington, D.C.: National Academy Press.

Streissguth, A. P. (1997). *Fetal alcohol syndrome: A guide for families and communities*. Baltimore: Paul Brookes Publishing Co.

Streissguth, A. P., Aase, J. M., Clarren, S. K., Randels, S. P., LaDue, R. A., & Smith, D. F. (1991). Fetal alcohol syndrome in adolescents and adults. *Journal of the American Medical Association, 265*, 1961–1967.

Streissguth, A. P., Barr, H. M., Carmichael-Olson, H., Sampson, P. D., Bookstein, F. L., & Burgess, D. M. (1994). Drinking during pregnancy decreases word attack and arithmetic scores on standardized tests: Adolescent data from a population-based prospective study. *Alcoholism: Clinical & Experimental Research, 18*(2), 248–254.

Streissguth, A. P., Barr, H. M., Kogan, J., & Bookstein, F. L. (1996). *Understanding the occurrence of secondary disabilities in clients with fetal alcohol syndrome (FAS) and fetal alcohol effects (FAE). Final report.* Seattle: University of Washington Publication Service.

Streissguth A. P., Barr, H. M., Sampson, P. D., Parrish-Johnson, J. C., Kirchner, G. L., & Martin, D. C. (1986). Attention, distraction and reaction time at age 7 years and prenatal alcohol exposure. *Neurobehavioral Toxicology & Teratology, 8*(6), 717–725.

Streissguth, A. P., Bookstein, F. L., Sampson, P. D, & Barr, H. M. (1993). *The enduring effects of prenatal alcohol exposure on child development: Birth through seven years, a Partial Least Squares Solution.* Ann Arbor: University of Michigan Press.

Streissguth, A. P., Bookstein, F. L., Sampson, P. D., & Barr, H. M. (1995). Attention: Prenatal alcohol and continuities of vigilance and attentional problems from 4 through 14 years. *Development and Psychopathology, 7*, 419–446.

Streissguth A. P., Clarren, S. K., & Jones, K. L. (1985). Natural history of the fetal alcohol syndrome: A 10-year follow-up of eleven patients. *Lancet, 2(8446)*, 85–91.

Streissguth, A. P., Herman, C. S., & Smith, D. W. (1978). Intelligence, behavior and dysmorphogenesis in the Fetal Alcohol Syndrome: A report on 20 patients. *Journal of Pediatrics, 92*(3), 363–367.

Streissguth, A. P., Martin, D. C., Barr, H. M., & Sandman, B. M. (1984). Intrauterine alcohol and nicotine exposure: Attention and reaction time in 4-year-old children. *Developmental Psychology, 20*(4), 533–541.

Streissguth, A. P., & O'Malley, K. (2001). Neuropsychiatric implications and long-term consequences of fetal alcohol spectrum disorders. *Seminars in Clinical Neuropsychiatry, 5*(3), 177–190.

Streissguth A. P., Sampson, P. D., Carmichael-Olson, H., Bookstein, F. L., Barr, H. M., Scott, M. Feldman, J., & Mirsky, A. (1994). Maternal drinking during pregnancy: Attention and short-term memory in 14-year-old offspring: A longitudinal prospective study. *Alcoholism: Clinical & Experimental Research, 18*(1), 202–218.

Stromland, K. (1990). Contribution of ocular examination to the diagnosis of foetal alcohol syndrome in mentally retarded children. *Journal of Mental Deficiency Research, 34*, 429–435.

Swayze, V. W. II, Johnson, V. P., Hanson, J. W., Piven, J., Sato, Y., Giedd, J. N., Mosnik, D., & Andreasen, N. C. (1997). Magnetic resonance imaging of brain anomalies in fetal alcohol syndrome. *Pediatrics, 99*(2), 232–240.

Tanaka, H., Masataka, A., & Suzuki, N. (1981). The fetal alcohol syndrome in Japan. *Brain Development, 3*, 305–311.

Ueckerer, A., & Nadel, L. (1996). Spatial locations gone awry: Object and spatial memory deficits in children with fetal alcohol syndrome. *Neuropsychologia, 34*, 209–223.

U.S. Department of Health and Human Services. (2000). Prenatal exposure to alcohol. In Tenth Special Report to the U.S. Congress on Alcohol and Health: Highlights from Current Research, 283–322.

Wass, T. S., & Haith, M. M. (1999). *Executive function deficits in 3-month-old human infants exposed to alcohol in utero.* Poster session presented at the Annual Meeting of the Research Society on Alcoholism, Santa Barbara, CA.

Wechsler, D. (1989). *Wechsler preschool and primary scale of intelligence—Revised.* San Antonio, TX: Psychological Corporation.

Wechsler, D. (1991). *Wechsler intelligence scale for children* (3rd ed.). San Antonio, TX: Psychological Corporation.

Weikart, D. P., & Schweinhart, L. J. (1992). High/scope preschool program outcomes. In J. McCord & R. E. Tremblay (Eds.), *Preventing antisocial behavior: Interventions from birth through adolescence* (pp. 67–86). New York: Guilford.

Weinberg, N. Z. (1997). Cognitive and behavioral deficits associated with parental alcohol use. *Journal of the American Academy of Child and Adolescent Psychiatry, 36*, 1177–1186.

West, J. R., & Pierce, D. R. (1984). The effect of in utero ethanol exposure on hippocampal mossy fibers: An HRP study. *Brain Research. Developmental Brain Research, 15*(2), 275–279.

World Health Organization. (1994). *ICD-10: International statistical classification of diseases and related health problems* (10th rev.). Geneva, Switzerland: World Health Organization.

Ylvisaker, M. (1998). *Traumatic brain injury rehabilitation*. Albany, NY: Butterworth-Heinmann.

22

Assessment and Treatment of Attention Deficit Hyperactivity Disorder (ADHD) in Schools

William E. Pelham, Jr.
State University of New York at Buffalo

Daniel A. Waschbusch
Dalhousie University

INTRODUCTION

The defining features of attention deficit hyperactivity disorder (ADHD) are inattention, impulsivity, and hyperactivity (American Psychiatric Association, 1994). Children with ADHD express some combination of these symptoms to such a high degree that they experience clinically significant impairment, including peer rejection, academic difficulties, classroom behavior problems, and conflicts with parents and teachers. Children with ADHD often become adolescents and adults who experience low employment and socioeconomic status, poor academic achievement, and high rates of automobile accidents, family problems, antisocial behavior, and perhaps mood problems. ADHD is one of the more common disorders of childhood. Estimates from epidemiological studies suggest that between 1 and 7% of elementary-age children meet criteria for ADHD and that ADHD accounts for a large percentage of referrals to mental health clinics. Collectively, these findings argue that ADHD is associated with serious negative consequences for both the child and for those in the child's environment and is therefore a serious community health concern (Hinshaw, 1994a).

Typically, school behavior and performance constitute some of the main areas of impairment experienced by children with ADHD. Children with ADHD are often first referred for assessment and treatment when they first enter school. There are many reasons for this trend, such as the fact that they spend a considerable amount of time in school relative to other activities and that school entry typically coincides with the first demands to sit still, listen, attend, organize, and comply for an extended period of time (Barkley, 1990). The scope of research documenting that children with ADHD have serious problems in school is enormous and a comprehensive review of this evidence is beyond the scope of this chapter. In brief, both objective measures of school performance, such as observations of behavior (e.g., Atkins, Pelham, & Licht, 1985), and subjective measures of school performance, such as teacher ratings of behavior (e.g., DuPaul et al., 1997; Pelham, Gnagy, Greenslade, & Milich,

1992), consistently show that children with ADHD have more negative school experiences than do children without ADHD. For example, in one elementary school sample (Waschbusch & Northern Partners in Action for Children and Youth, 2002), 25 of 202 students had substantially higher than average rates of classroom rule violations (defined as 1.5 standard deviations above the mean). Of these 25 children, 18 (72%) met criteria for ADHD according to their teachers.

This pattern—that children with ADHD have serious difficulties at school—is important for a number of reasons. First, school difficulties in elementary school tend to be stable over time and predictive of poor outcomes later in life (Birch & Ladd, 1998; Brophy, 1979; Kellam, Ling, Merisca, Brown, & Ialongo, 1998; Pianta, Steinberg, & Rollins, 1995). Second, school problems often reflect other adjustment difficulties, such as peer relationship problems and academic delays, which are themselves associated with negative developmental outcomes (Beitchman & Young, 1997; Parker & Asher, 1987). Third, the school difficulties expressed by children with ADHD may negatively influence their non-ADHD peers, as suggested by an early study that found that non-ADHD children in classrooms with ADHD children tend to perform worse than non-ADHD children in classrooms without ADHD (Campbell & Paulauskas, 1979).

These findings indicate that children with ADHD have serious difficulties in school and that school difficulties are associated with serious negative outcomes in the short and long term. Clearly, accurate assessment and treatment of the school difficulties of children with ADHD is important for both education and mental health professions. In fact, the U.S. Office of Education has formally recognized ADHD as a handicapping condition since 1991 (under the Individuals with Disabilities Education Act and Section 504 of the 1973 Rehabilitation Act) and has directed all state officers of education to ensure that local school districts establish procedures for the screening and identification of ADHD children and the provision of special educational and psychological services to those children in need. As a result of this directive, school districts across the United States have established procedures for identifying and intervening with children with ADHD. In addition, professional guidelines for identification and treatment of ADHD have been developed by numerous professional organizations.

The purpose of this chapter is to provide an overview of the assessment and treatment of ADHD in school settings. Our discussion of assessment in schools focuses on both the defining features of ADHD as well as its associated problems, and our discussion of treatments for ADHD in schools covers different levels of interventions, including school-wide, classroom-based, and individually targeted interventions. Pharmacological interventions are not discussed; readers interested in school-based pharmacological assessment and treatment of ADHD are referred to other sources (Pelham, 1993; Pelham & Waschbusch, 1999). In addition, this chapter emphasizes assessment and treatment of elementary-age children because this is the most common age of referral for children with ADHD (American Psychiatric Association, 1994) and because there is a paucity of research on adolescent ADHD (Smith, Waschbusch, Willoughby, & Evans, 2000), including a shortage of school-based interventions for this group (but see Evans, Pelham, & Grudberg, 1995, for an exception).

Although some of the assessment and treatment procedures we describe are specific to ADHD, the majority of information is applicable to many children with behavior and learning problems—not just ADHD children. Thus, the techniques we discuss can easily be implemented in regular elementary classrooms. This point is worth noting because the current emphasis on inclusion with regard to special education students has highlighted the wisdom of utilizing programs such as school-wide and classroom-wide interventions that facilitate the process of inclusion by focusing on problems of special students in the regular classroom while at the same time offering benefit to the majority of the classmates of such pupils.

ASSESSMENT

One of the first steps in any successful intervention is to conduct a comprehensive and accurate assessment. Assessment of ADHD in school settings is important because it provides a foundation on which effective treatment is built. Research suggests that somewhat different treatments should be used for children who are assessed as having ADHD as compared to children who are assessed as having anxiety, depression, or other adjustment difficulties (Lonigan, Elbert, & Johnson, 1998). Identifying ADHD may have considerable implications for the child's experience at school. In particular, a child who is identified as having ADHD may become eligible for additional resources from the school, such as one-on-one time with a teacher aide or support from a special education teacher, whereas children with other difficulties may not. Thus, accurate assessment of ADHD in school settings is a critical step in effectively treating ADHD in schools (Atkins & Pelham, 1991).

Components of an accurate assessment of ADHD in school settings include: (1) evaluating the defining features of ADHD (i.e., inattention, impulsivity, and hyperactivity) and (2) evaluating the functional deficits (or associated features) associated with ADHD. Each component is important. Assessing the defining features of ADHD is important because it provides a link to a considerable body of knowledge on treatments for ADHD and because it can help determine whether the child is eligible to receive treatment (i.e., whether insurance companies or school districts will pay for treatment). This type of assessment is usually based on the clinical psychology and psychiatry literatures as formulated in the *Diagnostic and Statistical Manual of Mental Disorders*, curently in its fourth edition (American Psychiatric Association, 1994). At the same time, assessing the defining features of ADHD (i.e., diagnosing ADHD) typically does not provide sufficient information to allow for effective treatment. In contrast, assessment of the functional deficits associated with ADHD does typically lead to the development of an effective treatment. Assessments of functional deficits are usually based on the applied behavior analysis literature (Kazdin, 2001; Martin & Pear, 1996; Pelham & Fabiano, 2000).

To conduct a diagnostic assessment or assessment of functional problems, any number of specific measurement methods can be used, including rating scales, interviews, and observations. These can be administered to parents, teachers, and children, or all of these A review of these methods is presented next. The methods we focus on were selected because they are empirically supported and appropriate for school settings and because they are widely used and well known.

Assessment of Defining Features

Rating Scales. Rating scales are one of the most, if not the most, widely used measures of children's adjustment. We focus here on teacher ratings, with reference to parent ratings when appropriate. Teacher ratings offer a number of advantages as an assessment method. First, teacher ratings are among the least expensive assessments to gather in terms of both cost and time. Second, teachers have a unique perspective on children's adjustment that few others share. This unique perspective arises from the fact that teachers work with a large number of children and thus build a considerable "normative base" about child development, combined with the fact that teachers have extended involvement with individual children. Third, teacher-rated instruments have been developed to measure a large variety of constructs, providing researchers and clinicians ready-made measures for almost any area of children's development and adjustment, including ADHD.

Two types of teacher ratings have been developed for assessing ADHD. The first type is based on the clinical psychology literature and consists of the symptoms of ADHD, as specified in the current DSM diagnostic nomenclature. Typically, these items are rated on Likert scales anchored by the degree to which they are present in a child (e.g., "not at all present" to "very much present"). These types of teacher ratings of ADHD can be used to provide an estimate of whether a particular child meets symptomatic criteria consistent with an ADHD diagnosis. Examples include the Disruptive Behavior Disorder (DBD) Rating Scale (Pelham et al., 1992), the Swanson Nolan and Pelham-IV (Swanson, 1996), the Child and Adolescent Disruptive Behavior Inventory (Burns et al., 1997), the ADHD rating scale (DuPaul, 1991), the Vanderbilt Rating Scale (Wolraich, Feurer, Hannah, Baumgaertel, & Pinnock, 1998), and many others. These DSM-based ratings are also widely used with parents and are typically normed for parents as well as teachers. Some of these must be purchased, while others can be downloaded at no charge (e.g., the DBD Rating scale at www.summertreatmentprogram.com).

A second type of teacher rating for evaluating ADHD selects items using empirical methods, such as factor analysis or receiver operating characteristics. The main advantage to these types of rating scales is increased confidence in the psychometric properties of the scales. One of the most widely used and well-known empirically based rating scales for ADHD is the IOWA Conners Rating Scale. The IOWA, which stands for Inattentive-Overactive With Aggression, was developed to address research findings that the original Abbreviated Conners Teacher Rating Scale (Conners, 1969), which was a rationally developed scale, confounded ADHD behaviors with conduct problem behaviors. To address this concern Milich and colleagues (Loney & Milich, 1982; Milich, Landau, Kilby, & Whitten, 1982; Milich, Landau, & Loney, 1981; Milich, Loney, & Landau, 1982), used a variety of methods to select items from the original Conners that best distinguish inattention/overactive behavior from oppositional/defiant behavior. This led to the creation of the current IOWA, which has two scales—an inattention/overactivity (I/O) scale and an oppositional/defiant (O/D) scale—each of which are five items. The IOWA Conners has been empirically demonstrated to discriminate ADHD behaviors from conduct problem behaviors (Loney, Langhorne, & Paternite, 1978; Milich, Loney et al., 1982). Further research has validated the IOWA (Atkins et al., 1985; Atkins, Pelham, & Licht, 1989), provided normative information (Pelham, Milich, Murphy, & Murphy, 1989), and demonstrated sensitivity to treatment effects (Pelham et al., 2001). As a result of these efforts, the teacher IOWA Conners has become one of the most widely used measures of ADHD. This is demonstrated by its widespread use in studies included in recent comprehensive reviews of treatment of ADHD in childhood and adolescence (Pelham, Wheeler, & Chronis, 1998; Smith et al., 2000) and in a comprehensive review of the comorbidity between ADHD and conduct problems (Waschbusch, 2002). The parent version of the IOWA Conners has also been shown to be sensitive to treatment effects (Pelham et al., 2001), but unfortunately, normative information for the parent version of the IOWA Conners has not been established and is sorely needed.

Interviews. Another measure of ADHD symptoms is an interview with an adult in the child's life. Parent interviews are always employed in clinic settings. Typically these are unstructured clinical interviews designed to gather information about the child's history and presenting problems. Less commonly used but widely recommended are structured clinical interviews with parents that ask in a structured manner questions regarding DSM symptoms and are designed to yield DSM diagnoses. Several of these are available for downloading over the Internet, some without charge (www.summertreatmentprogram.com; www.wpic.pitt.edu/ksads) and others for a fee (www.c-disc.com). Interviews with teachers are often utilized in school settings, but these are typically focused on the child's referring problems rather than deriving a diagnosis (see discussion in functional assessments below).

The advantage of a structured interview regarding symptoms over a rating scale is that the mental health professional is able to probe the adult's knowledge of the child, which may lead to a more accurate (that is, valid) determination of whether the behavior in question meets diagnostic criteria. The degree to which the interview allows for exchange between the adult and the interviewer (within the structure of the interview) and clinical judgment on the part of the clinician is the aspect of the interview that putatively produces enhanced validity of diagnosis. The main disadvantage of the teacher-structured interviews is that they require considerably more time (for both the teacher and the mental health professional) to complete than do rating scales, especially if they allow for exchange between the adult and the interviewer. For example, it is not uncommon for a diagnostic interview to take 60 to 90 minutes to complete, whereas rating scales typically take 10 or 15 minutes. Unless it is demonstrated that such interviews in fact yield more accurate diagnoses than rating scales—and that has not yet been demonstrated—then rating scales would be preferred in most school settings based on time/cost considerations alone.

At the same time, these disadvantages may be partially overcome in the near future by technological advances. For example, structured protocols for interviewing teachers have been developed, including ones that can be administered over the telephone or over the Internet. For example, preliminary research has been conducted on a teacher-completed version of the Diagnostic Interview Schedule for Children, including an Internet version (see *www.c-disc.com*). These advances may eventually lead to an interview that can be completed by a teacher in his or her own school, with follow-up probes and queries based on computer algorithms. This would eliminate substantial costs associated with conducting school-based interviews, including costs of mental health specialists' travel time to and from a school and the time they need to conduct the interviews, and would free that time for the specialists to complete other tasks.

Observations. Observations of the child's behavior in his or her classroom, on the playground, or both can also be an important aspect of assessing ADHD. The main advantage of using observational methods in school is obtaining direct information about ADHD behaviors without the subjective filter of teacher perception. This can be important because teachers may have a tendency to view children with oppositional problems *alone* as having *both* oppositional problems *and* ADHD, even though objective measures would suggest that they do not have ADHD (Abikoff, Courtney, Pelham, & Koplewicz, 1993; Stevens, Quittner, & Abikoff, 1998). Observational methods have long been used effectively to assess ADHD. One review of this work suggests that classroom observations of attention, activity, and vocalizations are especially effective in discriminating ADHD and non-ADHD children (Platzman, Stoy, Brown, & Coles, 1992).

Numerous coding schemes have been developed to evaluate classroom behavior (Abikoff, Gittelman-Klein, & Klein, 1977; Barkley, 1990; Pelham, Gnagy, & Greiner, 1994). One example of an empirically sound observation system for use in both classroom and playground settings is the Classroom Observations of Conduct and Attention Deficit Disorder (COCADD), developed by Atkins, Pelham, and colleagues (Atkins et al., 1985; Atkins, Pelham, & Licht, 1988, 1989). The COCADD system consists of 64 codes (32 for classroom activities, 32 for playground activities) that assess behavioral categories (position, physical–social orientation, vocal activities, nonvocal activities, play activities). These categories are combined into seven global classroom scores (overactive, distracted, verbally disruptive, off task, verbally aggressive, physically aggressive, and stealing/cheating) and five playground scores (verbal disruptive, verbal aggressive, physical aggressive, stealing/cheating, and highly active play). Research suggests the categories can be evaluated with adequate reliability and validity and that they yield important information about ADHD and other disruptive behavior that is unique from information obtained from teacher ratings (Atkins et al., 1988; Atkins, Pelham, & Licht, 1989). A simplified version of this scheme has been used in numerous clinical investigations and has been shown to be sensitive to treatment effects (e.g., Carlson, Pelham, Milich, & Dixon, 1992; Pelham et al., 1993; Pelham et al., 2001). Because this observational scheme and others typically assess a wide range of classroom behaviors beyond DSM symptoms of ADHD, they often yield information beyond that obtained through standardized symptom rating scales.

Assessment of Functional Deficits

Teacher Ratings. Similar to the assessment of ADHD symptoms, teacher ratings are a useful measure of the functional deficits associated with ADHD. As noted above, teacher ratings have been developed for a wide variety of constructs, but among the more useful and most overlooked for assessing functional deficits associated with ADHD are ratings of impairment. Impairment is a critical aspect of assessment of ADHD because inattention, impulsivity, and hyperactivity are very common behaviors exhibited by elementary-age children. What distinguishes normative levels of these behaviors (i.e., levels found in typically developing children) from pathological levels found in children with ADHD is the degree to which these behaviors cause children "real-life" difficulties or impairment in daily life functioning. In other words, whereas typically developing children do not experience significant impairment from their inattention, hyperactivity, or impulsivity, children with ADHD do (i.e., impairment in daily life functioning is required in addition to symptoms for a DSM diagnosis of ADHD). Clearly, assessing impairment is a crucial component of evaluating and understanding ADHD. Indeed, the prevalence of ADHD and the level of correspondence between different informants of ADHD symptomatology is seriously influenced by whether impairment criteria are applied (Bird et al., 1990; Weissman, Warner, & Fendrich, 1990).

Assessing problems in daily functioning and the events associated with them—that is conducting a functional analysis of target behaviors—has long been a hallmark of behavioral assessment and intervention for childhood disorders (see Ervin, Ehrhardt, & Poling, 2001; and Gresham, Watson, & Skinner, 2001, for a review). Despite the importance of impairment to understanding ADHD, it is only recently that standardized methods of assessing impairment as conceptualized in the DSM have been developed. Two recently developed measures are the Columbia Impairment Scale (Bird et al., 1993) and the children's Impairment Rating Scale (Fabiano et al., 2002)

The Columbia Impairment Scale consists of 13 items that tap 4 areas of functioning: interpersonal relations, broad psychopathological domains, functioning in job or school, and use of leisure time. Preliminary research suggests that this scale is easy to use, takes little time, and has good reliability. However, the Columbia Impairment Scale has only been developed for use with parents and not with teachers.

The Children's Impairment Rating Scale (CIRS) consists of six items that tap six areas of functioning: peer/sibling relationships, teacher/parent–student relationships, academic progress, classroom/home behavior, self-esteem, and overall adjustment. For each item, the rater is asked to put an "x" on a line to reflect the degree to which the child has a problem in that domain and needs treatment or special services. Like the Columbia Impairment Scale, the CIRS is easy to use, takes little time to complete (less than 5 minutes), can be scored by simply looking at the lines, and has excellent reliability and validity demonstrated across a wide age range and variety of treatments. The CIRS has other advantages as well; most noteworthy are the availability of normative data for both parent and teacher versions and the incorporation of key domains of functioning. In addition, the CIRS has a section that allows teachers and parents the opportunity to write a brief description of the child's impairment and need for treatment in each domain. Such qualitative information is often informative yet unavailable through other instruments.

If a more extensive assessment of problems and improvement in daily life functioning is desired, then a series of Improvement Rating Scales has been developed for teachers, parents, and other staff members (Pelham et al., 2000). These scales employ a standardized improvement scale ("very much worse" to "very much improved") to evaluate 33 different target behaviors that reflect functional impairment as well as adaptive behaviors in school and home settings for children with disruptive behavior problems. The advantage of the longer scales is that they assess a wider range of target behaviors than does the CIRS (e.g., rule following, using materials and possessions appropriately, name calling and teasing, good sportsmanship, cooperation).

Ratings of other constructs, such as co-occurring (or comorbid) psychopathology, may also be useful because children with ADHD have a high rate of co-occurring disorders (Pliszka, Carlson, & Swanson, 1999). Indeed, children with ADHD have higher than chance rates of conduct problems (Waschbusch, 2002), learning disabilities (Hinshaw, 1992), and possibly internalizing disorders (Russo & Beidel, 1994). The Teacher Report Form (TRF; for teachers) and the Child Behavior Checklist (CBCL; for parents) are widely used and effective for this purpose (Achenbach, 1991a, 1991b). The TRF and the CBCL have strong psychometric properties and extensive normative information and are therefore useful for screening whether children with ADHD have comorbid psychopathologies. However, it should be noted that simply establishing the presence of a comorbid disorder does not typically convey useful information regarding treatment—evaluation of functional impairments is more useful to the child, teacher, and family (Pelham & Fabiano, 2001).

Teacher Interview. Interviewing teachers to determine the functional deficits experienced by children with ADHD is universally recommended in writings on school intervention methods (Walker, Colvin, & Ramsey, 1995; Wielkiewicz, 1995), and numerous interviews and forms have been developed for this purpose (Sterling-Turner, Robinson, & Wilczynski, 2001). For the MTA study (Wells et al., 2000) Pelham and Kotkin developed a semistructured interview for use in a school psychologist's/consultant's initial meeting with teachers (available for downloading at www.summertreatmentprogram.com). The interview provides a structure for evaluating the child's referring problems and the possible controlling environmental variables (antecedents and consequences), as well as the classroom management practices that the teacher has employed with the target child and with other children. The teacher's evaluation of the effectiveness (if tried) of various interventions with the child and classroom is assessed, as well as the teacher's preferences regarding possible interventions that might be employed in the classroom and his or her opinion regarding the possible functions of the target behaviors (e.g., to gain peer attention, self-stimulation, to avoid tasks, etc.).

Such an interview is the first step in performing a functional analysis that sets the stage for intervention. After gathering information regarding impairments, identifying and operationalizing target behaviors, and formulating hypotheses regarding the functions of the target behaviors, the consultant can assist the teacher in manipulating antecedents or consequences in the classroom setting to investigate whether the teacher's guesses regarding functions were correct. If such manipulations confirm the function of a given target behavior (e.g., peer attention is maintaining classroom clowning), then an intervention can be developed (e.g., a class-wide positive consequence for ignoring class clowning). Thus, initial information regarding functional impairments and adaptive functioning is used to yield an intervention. Numerous examples of the successful use of these types of functional analyses with ADHD children in classroom settings are available (Boyajian, DuPaul, Handler, Eckert, & McGoey, 2001; Northup & Gulley, 2001; Sterling-Turner et al., 2001).

Peer Ratings and Sociometrics. It has long been known that peer problems are among the most salient and pervasive problems experienced by children with ADHD (Milich & Landau, 1982, 1989; Pelham & Bender, 1982). For this reason, as well as the fact that peer problems are a strong predictor of negative long-term adjustment (Parker & Asher, 1987), evaluating peer problems is one of the most important components of an ADHD evaluation. Unfortunately, it is also one of the most difficult to assess sufficiently. Parent and teacher ratings and observations of peer behaviors are easy to obtain, but evidence suggests that they are of limited usefulness because they accurately identify only children who are especially popular but not children who are rejected—the very children of most interest in evaluating ADHD (Bukowski & Hoza, 1989; Landau & Milich, 1984). To accurately identify the socially rejected child, it is necessary to use peer report to evaluate peer relationships, a measurement strategy referred to as sociometrics (Coie, Dodge, & Coppotelli, 1982; Coie, Dodge, & Kupersmidt, 1990).

Peer nominations are one type of sociometric. Peer nominations require children to nominate some number of other children (usually three) for different categories of interest. For example, each child in a classroom may be asked to nominate three classmates that they like a lot, three classmates that they don't like at all, three classmates that hit or fight a lot, and so on. Alternatively, a child may be asked whether a descriptive statement applies to each other child in the class (e.g., Pupil Evaluation Inventory, see Pekarik, Prinz, Liebert, Weintraub, & Neale, 1976). Peer nominations can be used to obtain a measure of how much children like or dislike a particular child (social preference), how much they notice or don't notice a particular child (social impact), and to determine whether the child's peer status is best described as popular, rejected, neglected, controversial, or average—categories that have distinct behavioral and developmental correlates (Coie et al., 1982).

A second type of sociometric is peer ratings. Peer ratings require children to rate every other child in their classroom on one or more dimension of interest. For example, each child might rate every other child on a measure of liking, aggression, attention, and so on. The advantages of this methodology are that every child provides data on every other child and that children can provide a range of information about other children (e.g., nonaggressive, a little aggressive, a lot aggressive, etc.).

There is considerable evidence supporting the reliability and validity of peer sociometrics, and they are widely considered the gold standard measure of peer relationships (Coie et al., 1990; Coie & Kupersmidt, 1983; Coie, Terry, Lenox, Lochman, & Hyman, 1995). Despite these advantages, sociometrics are difficult to obtain because they are typically viewed as unacceptable by parents, teachers, and principals. Some of the common objections raised by parents and teachers are that sociometric evaluations take away from time spent on academics, cause the children distress, and lead children to dislike peers that they otherwise would not dislike. Researchers have found that many of these concerns are without empirical merit and methods have been developed for minimizing these potential difficulties (Bell-Dolan, Foster, & Sikora, 1989; Bell-Dolan & Wessler, 1994; Hayvern & Hymel, 1984). Despite this, sociometrics are viewed as unacceptable by schools more often than not.

Other Measures. Various other measures may be useful for the evaluation of ADHD in school settings. Report cards can be useful for determining whether the child has a history of classroom behavior or academic problems (as indicated by teacher comments, for example), suggesting a long-standing problem, or if instead the difficulties are newly emerging. Classroom rule violations and office referrals can be used in a similar fashion. Scores on standardized tests can provide important screening information for determining whether more comprehensive assessment is required for co-occurring learning disabilities, which are commonly found in children with ADHD (Hinshaw, 1994b) and seem to be especially highly related to attention problems (Goldstein, 1987; Manguin & Loeber, 1996).

Summary

What assessment procedures should be employed by a school psychologist in diagnosing and assessing ADHD? A good guideline is provided by the American Academy of Pediatrics (2001). Their guidelines, as well as the discussion above, argue that the *sine qua non* of ADHD diagnosis and evaluation is standardized teacher (and parent) rating scales. If time and resources permit, standardized, structured interviews might be useful in amplifying information obtained from rating scales. Given the additional costs they entail, however, it would appear most efficient to use them in situations where rating scales fail to provide clear information—for example, if different teachers or parents and teachers provide conflicting ratings. Following DSM guidelines, parent and teacher information should be combined to yield a diagnosis, with either parent or teacher endorsement of a given symptom defining symptom presence, and the total number of symptoms endorsed compared to DSM requirements. Direct observations are expensive to gather and require considerable training to conduct reliably, so arguably their role should be to clarify discrepant information from rating scales.

We should note that there are some commonly employed assessment procedures that are *not* useful for diagnosis/evaluation of ADHD. These include subscales on IQ tests such as the Freedom from Distractibility Index on the Wechsler scales and such cognitive measures as continuous performance tasks. Careful research has failed to support the validity of such indices for the diagnosis and assessment of ADHD, and they are not recommended for use in school or clinical settings (American Academy of Pediatrics, 2001). The same conclusion holds for the extensive list of neuropsychological tests that have been advocated for diagnosis of ADHD (Barkley, 1991; Nichols & Waschbusch, under review). In other words, standardized tests are useful only to rule in or out other difficulties—not to diagnose ADHD—and neuropsychological and other cognitive tests are not useful in diagnosis.

Finally, identification of target behaviors, assessment of impairment in daily life functioning, with an accompanying functional analysis of the associated environmental determinants, and evaluation of a child's adaptive strengths—all with the intent of providing information relevant for intervention—are far more important for the child and family than assigning a DSM diagnosis. School psychologists and others who assess children should spend the minimum time necessary to develop a diagnosis for an ADHD child and invest the bulk of their time and effort assessing the child's impairment and adaptive functioning and developing interventions.

INTERVENTION

The only school-based interventions that are evidence based for ADHD are behavioral interventions (American Academy of Pediatrics, 2001; DuPaul & Eckert, 1997; Pelham, Wheeler & Chronis, 1998). Behavioral strategies can be implemented in a variety of ways in school settings. There are three intervention approaches that have been described for addressing mental health problems, including ADHD: universal, targeted, and clinical interventions (Offord, Kraemer, Kazdin, Jensen, & Harrington, 1998). The cardinal difference between these approaches is who the intervention targets. In universal interventions, all children in a particular geographic area receive the intervention; individual families or children are not singled out for the intervention. In targeted interventions, individual families or children receive the intervention based on their risk for developing difficulties; that is, they have not yet expressed the disorder but are believed to be prone to do so. In clinical interventions, individual children or families receive the intervention because they are perceived to be actively expressing the disorder.

These levels of intervention are useful for classifying school interventions. School-wide interventions can be considered universal level because all children in an entire school receive the intervention. Classroom-wide interventions can be considered targeted level because classrooms are usually selected for interventions based on risk factors (e.g., high rates of disruptive behaviors, teachers with poor behavior management skills, etc.). Individual interventions can be considered clinical level because children are usually referred for an individual intervention after they express problematic school behavior.

With respect to ADHD, each of these types of school interventions is firmly based in behavior modification. The philosophy behind behavior modification is in many ways very simple: encourage good behavior and discourage negative behavior. As others have written, behavior modification advocates believe that the key to improving the behavior of children (including those with ADHD) in school settings (and in other settings) is to ignore (as much as possible) minor annoyances and misbehaviors and spend as much time as possible attending to students when they are behaving appropriately (Wielkiewicz, 1995). This approach may seem philosophically simple, but putting this philosophy into practice can be difficult. Fortunately, a number of specific intervention programs and techniques—including school-wide interventions, classroom interventions, and individual interventions—have been developed and often manualized to assist schools in the implementation of this philosophy. Sometimes such interventions involve only positive interventions, while other times they involve providing consequences for both increasing positive behaviors and decreasing negative behaviors.

School-Wide Interventions

One of the most efficient school intervention systems for ADHD is a school-wide intervention. A school-wide intervention is implemented across an entire school rather than with a single child or a single classroom. There are numerous advantages to school-wide approaches for treating ADHD. First, school-wide interventions make treatment accessible to all families regardless of their economic means. Second, school-wide interventions are extremely cost-effective, as a large number of children receive great benefit from a relatively small amount of effort from psychologists, psychiatrists, or other mental health professionals. Third, school-wide interventions are among the most comprehensive and self-sustaining mental health treatment approaches that have been developed for schools. Fourth, school-wide programs serve important preventive functions. In particular, children whose behavior problems are emerging but are not yet sufficiently salient to have brought them to the attention of professionals (for example, kindergarteners) receive treatment in school-wide programs and might thereby avoid the development of more serious problems. Finally, children whose behavior and/or learning problems in regular classroom settings might be so severe that they would need to be placed in special education (e.g., ADHD children) might be able to avoid that outcome with school-wide intervention because their regular classroom teachers would be better equipped to implement appropriate programs with them.

These facts argue that school-wide approaches are an ideal approach to treating ADHD, but it is also important to note that school-wide programs likely benefit those students who do *not* have behavior or learning problems. That is, school-wide interventions include components that are designed to increase rates of prosocial behavior and lower rates of antisocial behavior, increase independence and personal responsibility, develop negotiation skills, and improve the reading level and arithmetic skills of all students, not just those who are having difficulties in these areas.

There are numerous approaches to school-wide interventions that have been developed (Walker et al., 1995), often subsumed under the label "positive behavioral support programs" (see: http://www.pbis.org/). We describe one school-wide intervention that we have developed, called the School Wide Intervention Model (SWIM). SWIM is adapted from a well-developed summer program for children with ADHD that the first author (W. E. P.) and colleagues have implemented and researched over the past 20 years (Pelham, Gnagy, & Greiner, 1998; Pelham, Greiner et al., 1996; Pelham et al., 2000). The behavioral intervention techniques that have proven effective in the summer camp were adapted for use in regular school settings, as described in the SWIM manual (Pelham, Wilson & Kipp, 2000a) and video (Pelham, Wilson & Kipp, 2000b)

The overall purpose of the SWIM program is to develop and maintain a positive learning environment that prevents misbehavior and recognizes adaptive behavior. More specifically, the fundamental goals of SWIM include: (1) creating a positive school climate that facilitates all students' success; (2) providing all school staff with the necessary behavioral training and support to make successful all students, especially those at risk; (3) recognizing and reinforcing students for being "good" students and implementing effective discipline to those who inhibit the educational process; (4) facilitating inclusion of students with behavioral difficulties by preventing and remediating problem areas; (5) improving and increasing communications between home and school; (6) offering to parents strategies and ideas on effective preventing and handling common situations at home concerning children's behavior; (7) increasing the academic achievements of all students; (8) improving problem-solving, social, and conflict resolution skills of all students; and (9) building and enhancing staff unity and support. The SWIM program works to achieve these goals using an intervention philosophy that encourages and recognizes "positive" behavior and prevents misbehavior. The specific treatment components outlined in the next paragraphs are the means through which this philosophy is put into practice and are based on well-validated treatment approaches, including social reinforcement, effective commands, use of incentives (rewards), and response-cost procedures.

The first step in adopting the SWIM model, as in any school-wide program, is getting the school community (school board, administration, teachers, parents) to "buy in" to the concept of developing and adopting a school-wide program. This process can be initiated by any of the constituencies, but the involvement of all is necessary. Typically a working group is established to garner support for a school-wide program and to shepherd the process of reaching consensus to develop a program. Once agreement to develop a program has been reached, then a working group (or subgroups) is established to develop the specifics of the program, including whether to adopt an existing program (e.g., the SWIM program), modify an existing program, or develop from scratch an intervention unique to the school.

Following the decision to implement a school-wide program, the first step is to train the staff in the basics of classroom behavior management. In the SWIM program, as in other school-wide models (e.g., Walker et al., 1995; Walker & Walker, 1991; Wielkiewicz, 1995), the most basic (and in many ways most important) treatment component is that teacher–child interactions are shaped using contingent social reinforcement (e.g., praise and ignoring), consistent and effective commands, and effective verbal reprimands. Observational studies in school settings have shown that two out of every three teacher–child interactions in elementary school involve negative attention for inappropriate behavior (Walker et al., 1995). The goal of retraining teachers in contingent, positive attention is to at least reverse this ratio so that the vast majority of teacher–child interactions are positive. These procedures are described during an in-service training that takes place before the beginning of the school year and is attended by the entire school staff: recess monitors, lunchroom workers, bus drivers, principals, teachers, teaching assistants, school psychologists, and the like. The staff is taught the basics of the program, with an emphasis on how to recognize students' positive behaviors and to call specific attention and approval to these behaviors. The school staff is also taught how to give effective commands such that students are most likely to comply with adult requests (Walker & Walker, 1991). Role playing with feedback is used to practice these skills. The importance of mastering these techniques is emphasized by tying them to the goal of improving interactions between the teachers and children and to the goal of improving the school climate.

In addition to emphasizing social reinforcement, the school staff develops school-wide rules, procedures for systematically rewarding children who follow the rules, and procedures for delivering consistent minor negative consequences for children who do not follow rules. By developing school-wide rules children come to learn that the same behavioral expectations are in effect anywhere and anytime they are in the school or near the school (i.e., on the playground, getting on and off the bus, walking to and from school, etc.). Students quickly realize that they always have the same rules to follow whether they are in music, their homeroom, the bathroom, the lunchroom, hallways, recess, and so on. To facilitate the student's acquisition and compliance with rules, school-wide rules are posted and monitored ubiquitously. Rules that we have used successfully in SWIM include: (1) Be Respectful of Others; (2) Remain in Assigned Seat or Area; (3) Raise Hand to Speak or Ask for Help; (4) Work Quietly; (5) Use Materials and Possessions Appropriately; (6) Follow Adult Directions; and (7) Complete Assigned Tasks. School-wide contingencies (negative consequences for rule violations and positive consequences for rule following—see the next paragraph) are tied to these rules.

In addition to increased teacher attention for positive behavior, daily positive home-school notes and class privileges are implemented to recognize and reward good behavior. If a student follows the rules with two or fewer violations, completes homework, and obtains a parent/guardian signature on his or her assignment sheet, he or she earns the privilege of taking home a positive note at the end of each day. Ideally, parents back up the school-wide program by giving their children privileges at home contingent on receipt of a positive daily note. If parents are unable or unwilling to reinforce their child's positive accomplishments, the student can be reinforced at school and school personnel can meet with the parents to evaluate whether additional home interventions (e.g., individual meetings with teacher, referral to a parenting course, etc.) may be useful.

Social recognition for positive behavior is also employed. Students who earn a daily positive note for two consecutive days become "Behavior Honor Roll Students." Behavior Honor Role students are recognized through public recognition and special privileges. The public recognition includes posting their pictures on a "Wall of Fame" and letting them wear a special button. The special privileges can be small but meaningful, such as allowing the honor role children to act as line leader, messenger, paper passer, homework stamper, bathroom monitor, and so on. The Behavior Honor Role program is an important component of the SWIM model because it encourages children to exhibit positive behavior for extended periods of time.

In addition to home notes and public recognition, Friday enrichment activities are implemented that are contingent on having had a good week at school. Friday enrichment activities serve as a reward (in addition to frequent social reinforcement) for maintaining good behavior. Typical Friday enrichment activities include guest speakers, recreational games, and arts and crafts. These activities are held at the end of each week for the last 30–45 minutes of the day. Students earning four out of five daily positive notes during the week are able to participate in the Friday enrichment activity, while children who have earned fewer than four positive daily notes spend that time in a classroom completing seat-work assignments that they did not complete during the week. Thus, children are taught that prosocial behavior is noticed and appreciated, whereas failure to follow school rules and complete work has consequences.

In addition to the positive behavioral interventions described earlier, the SWIM program, as in other school-wide programs, includes systematic negative consequences for certain behaviors that cannot be ignored. These are typically in the form of a time-out program, depending on school district policies and regulations. Time-out, which is short for "time-out from positive reinforcement," is used for serious negative behaviors. In the SWIM program, time-out is used for three types of behaviors: repeated noncompliance (e.g., continually breaking classroom rules), intentional aggression, and intentional destruction of property. Other types of negative behaviors (single instances of talking out of turn, getting out of the seat, interrupting, etc.) have their own consequences (e.g., loss of points) but do not result in a time-out. This is to ensure that time-out does not become overused as the default response to every negative behavior, but instead remains the response to some of the most serious negative behaviors that children exhibit.

Time-out in the SWIM program consists of removing children from ongoing activities and assigning them to a time-out area within the student's classroom for a specified length of time. It is important to ensure that the child does not receive attention from peers or adults during the time-out. The length of time typically varies depending on the child's age—ranging from 5 minutes for younger children (those in kindergarten/primary or first grade) to 20 minutes for older elementary children. As shown in Fig. 22.1, time-out should vary contingent on the child's behavior during the time-out, with reductions in time served for appropriate behavior in time-out and increases for continued inappropriate behavior (Fabiano et al., under review). The advantage of this modification to the typical time-out procedure—reductions in time-out contingent on appropriate behavior during time-out are rarely described in the behavioral treatment literature—is that the child is rewarded (i.e., the reduction in length) for exhibiting self-control while in a time-out. As shown in Fig. 22.1, if children serve time-outs appropriately in the classroom, they are not sent to the principal's office. In the SWIM program, as in many

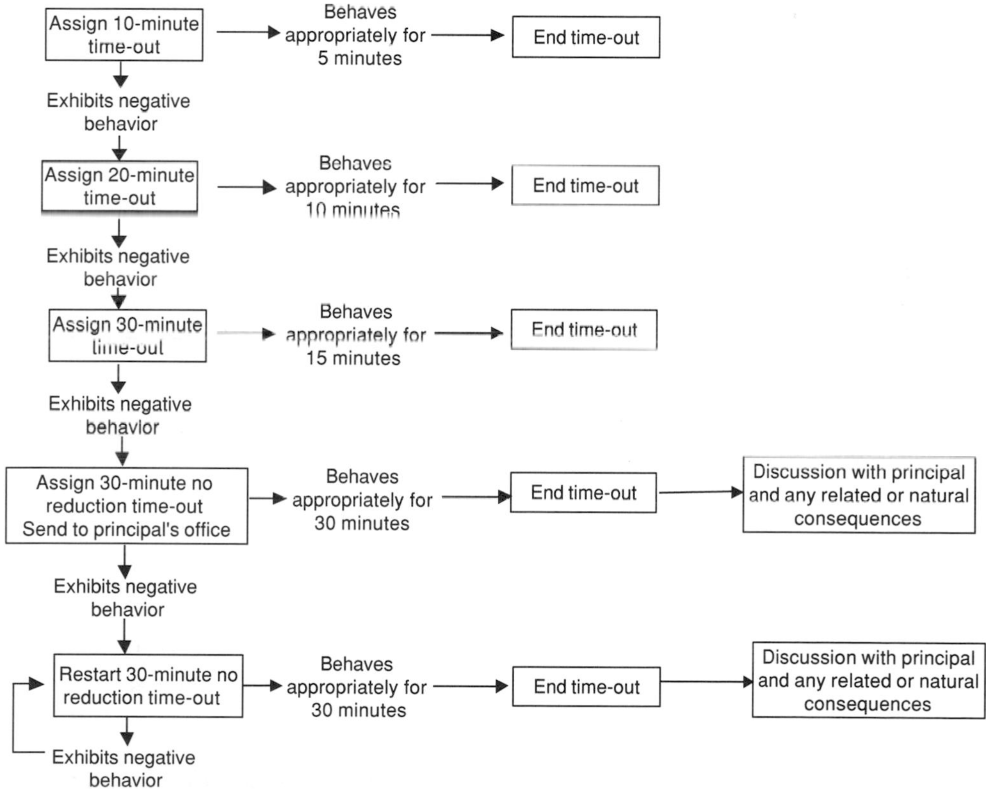

Notes: The times included in the figure should be adjusted for children's age. We recommend starting with 5 minutes (with comparable increases and reductions throughout) for K-1 children, 10 minutes (as shown above) for Grades 2-4, and 20 minutes for Grades 5 and above.

FIG. 22.1. Sample school-based time-out flow chart.

other similar programs, children are sent to the principal's office for continually being disruptive or noncompliant in the classroom. Depending on the school district's policies and decisions, students can be sent to the principal's office for behaviors such as major fighting, swearing, and the like.

In addition to the focus on behavior in the school setting, an important component of a good school-wide program is a procedure to improve homework completion. Thus, homework assignment sheets are used in the SWIM program and consist of weekly record sheets on which children record schoolwork assignments (including a description of the project and a due date). Homework assignment sheets provide children an explicit means of organizing their school assignments, tests, projects, and upcoming activities—an important function for children with ADHD who are by definition disorganized, as well as for most other elementary-age children. Furthermore, homework assignment sheets are a daily communication tool between school and home because parents sign off on the assignment sheet each night, with their signature indicating that homework has been completed and that important papers (e.g., permission slips, notices, etc.) have been seen and/or reviewed. Children are reinforced at school for returning completed homework and signed homework assignment sheets. Adaptations can be made for children who repeatedly complete their homework but have parents who fail to sign the assignment sheet, such as having the principal or teacher sign the sheet instead. This can also be an indicator that a meeting with parents may be useful.

Finally, students who are consistently not successful in earning daily positive notes, honor role, and other reinforces are identified and referred to a Student Support Team (SST) whose main mission is to make every student successful. The SST can serve as an intermediary team that evaluates and intervenes with children who are identified by their classroom teacher as having difficulties but who have not received formal evaluation or intervention. The composition of the SST frequently includes a core group of teachers who are committed to improving the school, along with the principal or vice principal, special education (or resource) teachers, and a school psychologist or other similar professionals. Typically, the SST develops classroom and/or individually targeted programs to supplement the school-wide components (see descriptions of such programs in the section Classroom-wide Interventions). These individual programs should comply with section 504 of the 1973 Rehabilitation Act, which requires such programs for ADHD children to be implemented in regular classroom settings, except in exceptional circumstances.

Preliminary research on the SWIM model suggests that it is an effective program for improving the school climate (Pelham et al., 2002). In one elementary school, the SWIM program has been implemented for eight years. At the end of the first year, parents, teachers, and students were asked to complete ratings that measured their opinions about the program. As shown in Table 22.1, teachers and parents rated the program as both effective and well accepted. Ratings from the students were also positive, with 85% of students indicating that the program helped them in school. Suspension and expulsion records showed dramatic positive changes from the year prior to program implemention to the first year of intervention.

Research from another pilot research project also suggests that the SWIM program is effective in improving classroom and school behavior (Waschbusch & Northern Partners in Action for Children and Youth, 2002). In this project, six schools that were interested in participating in an intervention study were matched geographically then randomly assigned to either a school intervention condition or a control school condition.[1] Each of the three intervention schools implemented a different type of behaviorally based intervention, one of which was a slightly modified version of SWIM. A number of measures were gathered to

[1] An additional school joined the project after assignment to condition and was included as a control school.

TABLE 22.1
Percentages of Teachers and Parents Who Responded "Yes" to Each Question about the School Wide Intervention Model (SWIM)

	Year 1		*Year 2*	
Item	*Teacher*	*Parent*	*Teacher*	*Parent*
Rules and point system helped the children's behavior	100%	90%	88%	75%
Homework assignment sheet helped the children academically	100%	92%	87%	83%
Homework assignment sheet helped communication between parents and teacher	100%	88%	100%	81%
Daily Report Card helped communication between parents and teacher	100%	87%	87%	76%
The children liked the behavior management system	100%	87%	63%	72%
You would like the system to continue next year	100%	94%	100%	92%
Children's attitudes toward school have improved	100%	85%	63%	66%
The system has been effective for your [child's] classroom	100%	95%	88%	76%
The system has been effective for the whole school	100%	95%	100%	76%
The system has been effective for this child	93%	92%	92%	82%
The system has allowed you to give more time and effort to instruction versus behavior management	89%	–	69%	–
Your students would like the system to continue next year	100%	–	69%	–

evaluate these models, including office referrals for disruptive behavior. As shown in Fig. 22.2, students in the SWIM school showed a decreased number of office referrals over the course of the school year, whereas the same trend is not as evident in the Control school.[2] Frequency of classroom rule violations (see Fig. 22.3), which were gathered in the SWIM school as part of the treatment, also decreased over the course of the school year for both disruptive (defined as children with ADHD, oppositional defiant disorder, or conduct disorder) and nondisruptive children, and this was true regardless of whether the child received an individualized (targeted) intervention to supplement the SWIM intervention. This data suggests that the SWIM model is effective at improving the classroom behavior not only of disruptive children but also of typically developing, nondisruptive children.

[2] As can be seen in Fig. 22.2, office referrals showed a substantial increase at the end of the school year in both schools. Based on qualitative interviews with school staff, we believe that this is related to a labor dispute between the school board and the teacher's union that was ongoing at the time. Others examining disruptive behavior schools in the same geographical area and at the same time have noted similar findings.

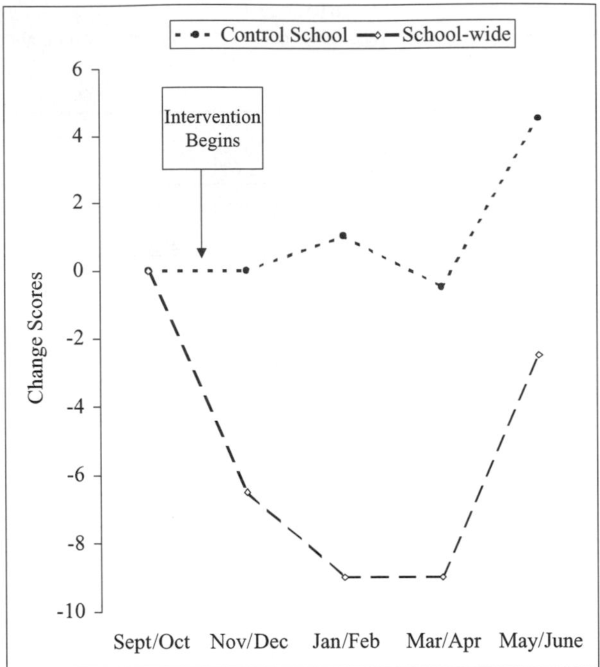

FIG. 22.2. Change in office referrals in school-wide intervention and control school.

Classroom-Wide Interventions

Classroom interventions are procedures designed to improve the functioning of an entire group of children, with a classroom of students being the typical grouping unit for school settings. Generally, classroom interventions are warranted any time that student learning or functioning is inhibited because of group behavior. Examples of when classroom interventions might be warranted include: (1) when a peer group is reinforcing each other's negative, disruptive behavior; (2) when a peer group is targeting one or two other children for excessive teasing or bullying; or (3) when a large proportion of the class is exhibiting unacceptable behavior, such as constant talking at inappropriate times, using materials or equipment inappropriately, or continual tardiness in completing homework or other activities.

Like other behavioral interventions, classroom interventions can be designed to increase positive behavior or decrease negative behavior, with the most effective interventions likely to be when both approaches are used. Numerous sources describe classroom programs that can be used with ADHD children (DuPaul & Stoner, 1994; Pfiffner, 1996; Rief, 1993; Walker et al., 1995; Wielkiewicz, 1995). We discuss several types of classroom-wide programs.

One effective classroom intervention for decreasing negative group behavior is a group contingency program. A group contingency is when an entire group of children experiences a consequence—positive or negative—because of the behavior of one or more members of that group. Reasons for implementing a group contingency may vary from serious problematic behavior, such as aggression toward a peer, to less major infractions, such as violating classroom rules. In a commonly used example, children in a kindergarten could earn free time at the end of the school day or a popcorn party when they have filled up a jelly-bean jar (with beans put in for individual instances of positive behavior and taken out for individual instances of negative behavior). Alternatively, an older class could earn a special Friday activity if they as a group have fewer than a given number of rule violations. A well-known modification of a

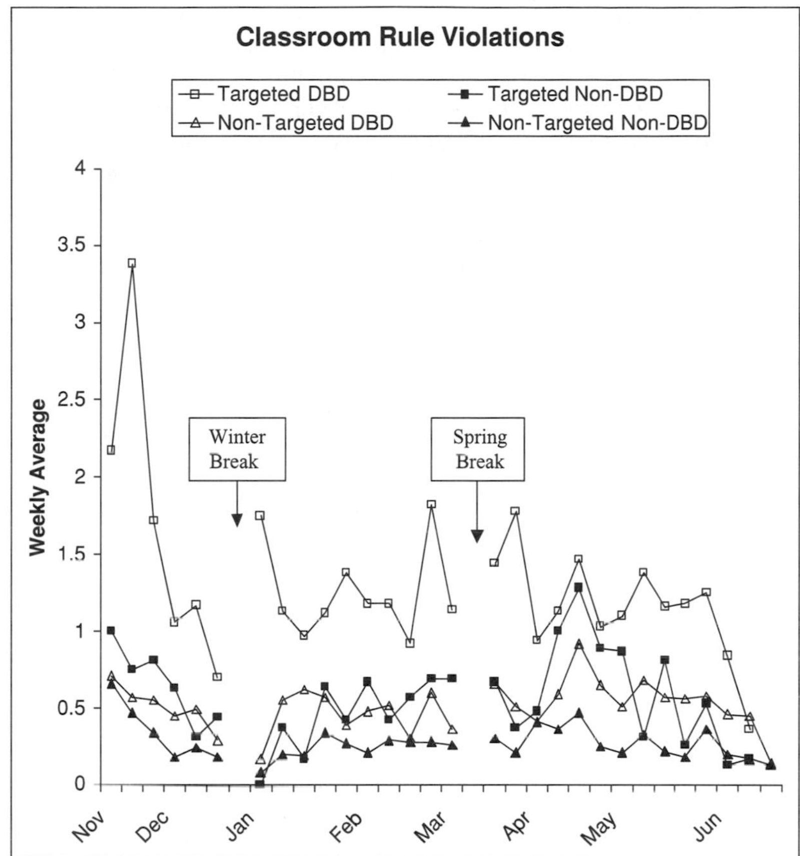

Notes: DBD = disruptive behavior disorder (ADHD, ODD, and/or CD). "Targeted" indicates child that was identified for receiving individualized intervention for disruptive behavior.

FIG. 22.3. Weekly average frequency of classroom rule violations over time in school wide intervention.

classwide-group contingency is the "Good Behavior Game," in which the class is divided into teams (e.g., rows or tables) that compete against one another by having the lowest number of group rule violations and sharing a group reward (Barrish, Wolf, & Saunders, 1969; Kellam et al., 1998).

Group contingencies are effective not only in classroom settings, but also for negative behaviors in unstructured settings such as at lunch, during recess, and on school busses. For example, a classroom of students may be prohibited from using certain recess equipment or lose part of their recess time because equipment was not returned properly; alternatively, the students could be given extra recess time when they use the equipment appropriately. Group contingencies can be used in settings where multiple classes interact, such as the lunchroom. Classes within the lunchroom could earn group rewards of some type for following, as a group, lunchroom rules (Fabiano et al., in press).

Group contingency programs can be a very effective technique for reducing negative classroom behavior because they (in part) draw on peer group pressure to shape children's behavior. However, for this same reason, schools must be cautious about implementing group contingencies in situations where they would be inappropriate. In general, group contingencies should only be used for problems that result from difficulties in *group* functioning. Problems that are generally impelled by an individual (e.g., the entire class is late for music because one student could not find his instrument) are not appropriate for group contingencies and may in fact cause the child to suffer serious negative consequences from his or her peers. In such instances, an individualized program that targets the student's specific behavior should be implemented rather than a class contingency. Group contingencies are also not appropriate to address a conflict between individuals (e.g., a few students arguing over a game). Situations such as these are better resolved between the particular students who are involved (Cunningham & Cunningham, 1995, 1998).

Class-wide interventions can also be combined with individual contingencies. For example, a point system can be used such that individual children earn and lose points, but the results determine a group-based reward (Wielkiewicz, 1995). When reward and response-cost systems are combined in such a point system, it is quite effective at changing the behavior of ADHD children (Carlson et al., 1992; Pelham et al., 1993). A simple example of a response-cost system that can be implemented class-wide is a class lottery (Witt & Elliott, 1982). The system is easy to implement, costs nothing, is relevant to almost every classroom, works for almost any student, takes only a few minutes of teacher time per day, and is usually effective in improving classroom rule following in a short period of time. In a classroom lottery system, the teacher uses naturally occurring rewards to reinforce rule following in the classroom. The rewards are the classroom jobs that are typically given noncontingently in most elementary classrooms (e.g., line leader, lunch money collector, paper collector, paper distributer, board cleaner, lottery drawer), of which there are usually 5 to 10 desired jobs. The teacher scans the classroom at preselected but unannounced times five times each day to see who is following the rules. Scan times should focus on any parts of the day that are especially problematic, but the times should be unpredictable from the children's perspective. When the scheduled times arrive, teachers scan the classroom for 10 or 15 seconds to evaluate which children are violating classroom rules, and those children's names are recorded on the board and announced to the class. At the end of the day, children who followed rules above a preselected criterion level (e.g., four out of five scans initially and five out of five scans later) put their names in a hat to be drawn either by a child who is the lottery leader or by the teacher. When a child's name is drawn, he or she chooses a class job for the following day. Because there should be 5 to 10 jobs, children learn that if they follow the rules they have a substantial chance at earning the reward every day. If the teacher conducts the draw, he or she can control who gets the reward. For example, if a child who has serious behavior problems has a rare successful day, the teacher can read his or her name regardless of who is actually drawn to ensure that the child is reinforced for his or her behavior that day.

Individual Interventions

Some students, typically children with ADHD and other disruptive behavior disorders (e.g., oppositional defiant disorder and conduct disorder), require individualized programs even after school-wide and classroom-wide procedures are implemented. Individual programs are more intensive, comprehensive, and structured interventions that are directed at individual students who are actively displaying disruptive behavior in the school. As we have argued elsewhere (Pelham & Waschbusch, 1999), one of the most effective individual interventions for the treatment of ADHD is a daily report card (DRC; O'Leary, Pelham, Rosenbaum, & Price, 1976).

The DRC serves as a means of identifying, monitoring, and changing the student's classroom problems and does so with minimal time and effort required from the school. The DRC operates by providing the child clear goals and guidelines for his or her behavior, providing active and ongoing feedback to the child about his or her performance in reaching these goals, and motivating the child to achieve the goals. The motivating component of the DRC is usually provided by transmitting information about the child's behavior between the school and the student's parent(s) on a daily basis. The student's parent(s) are then expected to appropriately reinforce their child's behavior, either by providing rewards in the home when their child earns a positive DRC or providing a prudent negative consequence when their child performs especially poorly. For these reasons, the DRC is often sufficient to normalize the child's classroom behavior, especially when it is implemented in the context of other interventions.

There are also other advantages to using a DRC, including that it: (1) costs little, (2) takes little teacher time to implement (3) often reduces the amount of time teachers spend on addressing disruptive behavior, (4) typically increases the consistency of adults response to disruptive behavior, (5) provides regular communication between home and school, (6) is highly motivating to the student (assuming the parents select the right reinforcement and response-cost strategy to back up the DRC), (7) provides the child clear goals and structure, (8) provides frequent feedback and frequent rewards to the child, both of which are necessary for ADHD children, and (9) provides a simple, naturalistic measure of how the child is doing across numerous areas of functioning that can be used to track the child's progress and response to interventions (e.g., Pelham et al., 2001).

Like other interventions, implementing a DRC can be relatively complex. To make the process easier, the procedures for developing and implementing have been described in detail (Jacob & Pelham, 1999), and a stand-alone, parent-and teacher-friendly packet has been developed that can be downloaded free of charge from www.summertreatmentprogram.com. Briefly, the development takes place in a meeting between the teacher and parents with the assistance of a school-based or consultant coordinator if needed. After ensuring agreement that the child needs a DRC, the group developing the DRC seeks to determine specific areas of functioning that are in need of improvement (typically peer relationships, daily academic productivity and accuracy, classroom rule following, and compliance with teacher requests), what specific goals can be defined, how the goals will be operationalized into measurable DRC criteria, how the DRC will be monitored and evaluated, who will describe the DRC to the child, and what steps will be taken to ensure the continued effectiveness of the DRC over time. An example of a DRC for an ADHD child is shown in Fig. 22.4. It illustrates several

Child's Name: ____________ Date: ____________

	Special	Language Arts	Math	Reading	SS/Science
Follows class rules with no more than 3 rule violations per period.	Y N	Y N	Y N	Y N	Y N
Completes all assignments within the designated time.	Y N	Y N	Y N	Y N	Y N
Completes assignments at 80% accuracy.	Y N	Y N	Y N	Y N	Y N
Complies with teacher requests (no more than 3 instances of noncompliance per period).	Y N	Y N	Y N	Y N	Y N
No more than 3 instances of teasing per period.	Y N	Y N	Y N	Y N	Y N

OTHER

Follows lunch rules (no more than 2 violations).	Y N
Follows recess rules (no more than 3 violations).	Y N

Total Number of Yes Answers ____________
Total Number of No Answers ____________
Percentage ____________

Teacher's Initials: ______
Comments:

FIG. 22.4. Sample daily report card.

important points about DRCs: (1) Attainable goals are established—that is, perfect behavior is not required but instead small improvements are shaped from the child's initial level of functioning. (2) Goals are described explicitly. (3) Tracking is based on behavior counts not on global ratings of performance. (4) Feedback is given multiple times per day by whomever is with the child in each setting.

The successful completion of this discussion should include working with the child's parent(s) to develop a detailed home-based reward system that serves as the main motivator to the child to perform well on the daily report card. When these steps are followed and a DRC is established and implemented correctly, it can be a highly effective means of assessing and treating classroom behavior and academic problems, as shown in numerous studies conducted over the past 25 years (Chronis et al., 2001; Fabiano et al, in press; Kelly, 1990; O'Leary et al., 1976; O'Leary & Pelham, 1978; Pelham, 1993; Pelham et al., 2001; Pelham et al., 1988; Pelham, Schnedler, Bologna, & Contreras, 1980; Waschbusch, Kipp, & Pelham, 1998). Details of how to set up a daily report card, including a sample template and sample goals, and procedures for establishing a home reward system can be downloaded for free from www.summertreatmentprogram.com.

Contingency management procedures are also frequently used as an individual intervention in classroom settings. The efficacy of school-based contingency management has been well established by case studies (Abramowitz, Eckstrand, O'Leary, & Dulcan, 1992; Atkins, Pelham, & White, 1989; DuPaul, Guevremont, & Barkley, 1992; Hoza, Pelham, Sams, & Carlson, 1992; Kelly & McCain, 1995; Schell et al., 1986) and group studies (Carlson et al., 1992; Pelham et al., 1993). One effective and easy to use contingency management (also called response-cost) program that has been implemented with ADHD children in regular classroom settings employs a system in which the child and teacher have flip cards with numbers in descending order from 20 to 0 (Rapport, Murphy, & Bailey, 1980). Children are told they will be given 20 minutes of free time if they work consistently during the designated time, but that each time the teacher catches them off task, they will lose a minute of play time. This will be signaled by flipping a card, reducing the number by one. Children monitor their progress by matching the flip card number on the teacher's desk with their own flip card. This response-cost system has been shown to have beneficial effects on both classroom work and classroom behavior (Rapport et al., 1980). In one study, the effects of this response-cost treatment were equal to and sometimes greater than those obtained with substantial doses of methylphenidate (Ritalin) (Rapport, Murphy, & Bailey, 1982).

Selecting an Intervention

As we have just described, there are multiple ways to effectively treat ADHD in a school setting. Given this fact, an important question is how to select the appropriate approach. In our opinion, the best answer to this question is that one should not choose between them but should instead choose all of them because each level of intervention has different strengths and weaknesses (Offord et al., 1998). Thus, to most effectively treat ADHD in a school context, schools should implement a school-wide intervention, followed by classroom and individual interventions for those children who do not show an adequate response to the school-wide procedures.

Unfortunately, clinicians are often constrained by time, money, or other factors and are forced to select a single intervention. In such situations, it is important to keep in mind that the intervention should match the needs of the child, which is in turn determined by the assessment. School-wide and classroom interventions are likely to be most beneficial when there are a considerable number of disruptive children or when peer variables appear to be an especially important contributor to the disruptive behavior (e.g., the child with ADHD is experiencing high rates of being teased or high rates of peer reinforcement for negative behavior). In contrast, individual interventions are likely to be needed when the disruptive behavior is more severe, when the problem behavior is not clearly addressed by classroom rules (e.g., being easily distracted or showing low concentration), or when teachers or principals are reluctant to initiate a large-scale intervention.

Office referrals might also be useful in determining which intervention approach should be used. One study examined office referral data collected from 11 elementary schools over a number of years to determine when to use the different types of interventions (Sugai, Sprague, Horner, & Walker, 2000). The following guidelines were suggested:

1. *Universal interventions* (such as school-wide programs) should be implemented when the ratio of office referrals per student is above 0.5, or when more than 20% of the student body is referred to the office at least once in a given school year.
2. *Targeted interventions* (such as classroom program) should be implemented when schools have 10 or more children with 10 or more office referrals.
3. *Individual interventions* should be implemented when there are more than 0.5% of the student body who have 10 or more office referrals, or when the 5% of the student body with the most office referrals accounts for 60% or more of all referrals.

Although further examination of the validity of these recommendations is needed, such databased recommendations promise to be very helpful to teachers, principals, and mental health workers. Similar databased recommendations using parent and teacher ratings and classroom rule violations would also be useful.

Two final points about intervention should be noted. First, we have discussed only a small portion of the possible interventions that can be used to assist children with ADHD in schools. There are many other components that can be added to any or all of the above interventions. Social skills programs (e.g., Webster-Stratton, 1991), peer conflict mediation programs (e.g., Cunningham & Cunningham, 1998), parenting groups (e.g., Cunningham, Bremner, & Boyle, 1995), and peer tutoring (e.g., DuPaul & Henningson, 1993; Fuchs, Locke, & Fuchs, 1995) programs are just a few examples of other approaches that have some empirical support. Second, a growing body of evidence indicates that ADHD is a chronic problem (Weiss & Hechtman, 1993), suggesting that long-term treatments are likely to be needed to provide meaningful improvement. Indeed, common sense suggests that school interventions should be implemented and evaluated over years, rather than over months, given that the problems associated with ADHD are typically present for years, rather than months. Unfortunately, this can be a challenge because effective interventions require an investment of time, energy, and other resources on behalf of everyone involved. Maintaining this level of involvement is made even more difficult by the fact that positive effects of school interventions are sometimes apparent only after long periods of time (i.e., years) (Kellam et al., 1998; McConaughy, Kay, & Fitzgerald, 2000), leading to a serious delay of gratification.

CONCLUSIONS

Children with attention deficit hyperactivity disorder (ADHD) frequently have difficulties in school settings. This chapter described a number of evidence-based procedures for assessing ADHD in schools, including the assessment of both the defining features of ADHD (inattention, impulsivity, hyperactivity) and, more importantly, the assessment of functional deficits (i.e., impairment and deficient adaptive skills) that by definition accompany ADHD. Interventions that can be effective for assisting children with ADHD in schools were also discussed and specific examples were described. These include school-wide interventions (e.g., school-wide rules and rewards, an honor role system, time-out, etc.), classroom interventions (e.g., group contingencies and classroom lotteries), and individual interventions (a daily report card). At each of these levels, functional analytic methods should be used to develop and modify interventions, using the procedures discussed herein. Although each of these techniques on its own is evidence based and likely to be useful, it is arguable that children with ADHD are most efficiently, cost-effectively, and otherwise best served by an approach that includes each of these different levels of intervention.

REFERENCES

Abikoff, H. B., Courtney, M., Pelham, W. E., & Koplewicz, H. S. (1993). Teachers' ratings of disruptive behaviors: The influence of halo effects. *Journal of Abnormal Child Psychology, 21*, 519–533.

Abikoff, H. B., Gittelman-Klein, R., & Klein, D. (1977). Validation of a classroom observation code for hyperactive children. *Journal of Consulting and Clinical Psychology, 45*, 772–783.

Abramowitz, A. J., Eckstrand, D., O'Leary, S. G., & Dulcan, M. K. (1992). ADHD children's responses to stimulant medication and two intensities of a behavioral intervention. *Behavior Modification, 16*, 193–203.

Achenbach, T. M. (1991a). *Manual for the child behavior checklist (ages 4–18) and 1991 profile*. Burlington: Department of Psychiatry, University of Vermont.

Achenbach, T. M. (1991b). *Manual for the teacher's report form & 1991 profile*. Burlington: Department of Psychiatry, University of Vermont.

American Academy of Pediatrics. (2001). *Clinical practice guideline: Diagnosis and evaluation of a child with attention-deficit/hyperactivity disorder. Pediatrics, 105*, 1158–1170.

American Psychiatric Association. (1994). *Diagnostic and statistical manual of mental disorders* (4th ed.). Washington, DC: American Psychiatric Association.

Atkins, M. S., & Pelham, W. E. (1991). School-based assessment of attention deficit-hyperactivity disorder. *Journal of Learning Disabilities, 24*, 197–204.

Atkins, M. S., Pelham, W. E., & Licht, M. H. (1985). A comparison of objective classroom measures and teacher ratings of attention deficit disorders. *Journal of Abnormal Child Psychology, 13*, 155–167.

Atkins, M. S., Pelham, W. E., & Licht, M. H. (1988). The development and validation of objective classroom measures for the assessment of conduct and attention deficit disorders. In R. J. Prinz (Ed.), *Advances in behavioral assessment of children and families* (Vol. 4, pp. 3–33). Greenwich, CT: JAI.

Atkins, M. S., Pelham, W. E., & Licht, M. H. (1989). The differential validity of teacher ratings of inattention/overactivity and aggression. *Journal of Abnormal Child Psychology, 17*, 423–435.

Atkins, M. S., Pelham, W. E., & White, K. J. (1989). Hyperactivity and attention deficit disorders. In M. Hersen (Ed.), *Psychological aspects of developmental and physical disabilities: A casebook* (pp. 137–156). Beverly Hills, CA: Sage.

Barkley, R. A. (1990). *Attention deficit hyperactivity disorder: A handbook for diagnosis and treatment*. New York: Guilford.

Barkley, R. A. (1991). The ecological validity of laboratory and analogue assessment methods of ADHD symptoms. *Journal of Abnormal Child Psychology, 19*, 149–178.

Barrish, H. H., Wolf, M. M., & Saunders, M. (1969). Good behavior game: Effects of individual contingencies for group consequences on disruptive behavior in a classroom. *Journal of Applied Behavior Analysis, 2*, 119–124.

Beitchman, J. H., & Young, A. R. (1997). Learning disorders with a special emphasis on reading disorders: A review of the past 10 years. *Journal of the American Academy of Child and Adolescent Psychiatry, 36*, 1020–1032.

Bell-Dolan, D. J., Foster, S. L., & Sikora, D. M. (1989). Effects of sociometric testing on children's behavior and loneliness in school. *Developmental Psychology, 25*, 306–311.

Bell-Dolan, D. J., & Wessler, A. E. (1994). Ethical administration of sociometric measures: Procedures in use and suggestions for improvement. *Professional Psychology: Research and Practice, 25*, 23–32.

Birch, S. H., & Ladd, G. W. (1998). Children's interpersonal behaviors and the teacher-child relationship. *Developmental Psychology, 34*, 934–946.

Bird, H. R., Shaffer, D., Fisher, P., Gould, M. S., Staghezza, B., Chen, J. Y., et al. (1993). The columbia impairment scales (CIS): Pilot findings on a measure of global impairment for children and adolescents. *International Journal of Methods in Psychiatric Research, 3*, 167–176.

Bird, H. R., Yager, T. J., Staghezza, B., Gould, M. S., Canino, G., & Rubio-Stipec, M. (1990). Impairment in the epidemiological measurement of childhood psychopathology in the community. *Journal of the American Academy of Child and Adolescent Psychiatry, 29*, 796–803.

Boyajian, A. E., DuPaul, G. J., Handler, M. W., Eckert, T. L., & McGoey, K. E. (2001). The use of classroom-based brief functional analysis with preschoolers at-risk for attention-deficit hyperactivity disorder (ADHD). *School Psychology Review, 30*, 278–293.

Brophy, J. E. (1979). Teacher behavior and its effects. *Journal of Educational Psychology, 71*, 733–750.

Bukowski, W. M., & Hoza, B. (1989). Popularity and friendship: Issues in theory, measurement and outcome. In T. J. Berndt & G. W. Ladd (Eds.), *Peer relationships in child development* (pp. 15–45). New York: Wiley.

Burns, G. L., Walsh, J. A., Patterson, D. R., Holte, C. S., Sommers-Flanagan, R., & Parker, C. M. (1997). Internal validity of the disruptive behavior disorder symptoms: Implications from parent ratings for a dimensional approach to symptom validity. *Journal of Abnormal Child Psychology, 25*, 307–319.

Campbell, S. B., & Paulauskas, S. (1979). Peer relations in hyperactive children. *Journal of Child Psychology and Psychiatry, 20*, 233–246.

Carlson, C. L., Pelham, W. E., Milich, R., & Dixon, M. J. (1992). Single and combined effects of methylphenidate and behavior therapy on the classroom behavior, academic performance and self-evaluations of children with attention deficit-hyperactivity disorder. *Journal of Abnormal Child Psychology, 20*, 213–232.

Chronis, A. M., Fabiano, G. A., Gnagy, E. M., Wymbs, B. T., Burrows-MacLean, L., & Pelham, W. E. (2001). Comprehensive, sustained behavioral and pharmacological treatment for attention-deficit/hyperactivity disorder: A case study. *Cognitive & Behavioral Practice, 8*, 346–358.

Coie, J. D., Dodge, K. A., & Coppotelli, H. (1982). Dimensions and types of social status: A cross-age perspective. *Developmental Psychology, 18*, 557–570.

Coie, J. D., Dodge, K. A., & Kupersmidt, J. B. (1990). Peer group behavior and social status. In S. R. Asher & J. D. Coie (Eds.), *Peer rejection in childhood* (pp. 17–59). New York: Cambridge University Press.

Coie, J. D., & Kupersmidt, J. B. (1983). A behavioral analysis of emerging social status in boys' groups. *Child Development, 54*, 1400–1416.

Coie, J. D., Terry, R., Lenox, K., Lochman, J., & Hyman, C. (1995). Childhood peer rejection and aggression as predictors of stable patterns of adolescent disorder. *Development and Psychopathology, 7*, 697–713.

Conners, C. K. (1969). A teacher rating scale for use in drug studies with children. *American Journal of Psychiatry, 126*, 884–888.

Cunningham, C. E., Bremner, R., & Boyle, M. (1995). Large group community-based parenting programs for families of preschoolers at risk for disruptive behavior disorders: Utilization, cost effectiveness, and outcome. *Journal of Child Psychology and Psychiatry, 36*, 1141–1159.

Cunningham, C. E., & Cunningham, L. J. (1995). Reducing playground aggression: Student-mediated conflict resolution. *The ADHD Report*, 9–11.

Cunningham, C. E., & Cunningham, L. J. (1998). Student-mediated conflict resolution programs. In R. A. Barkley (Ed.), *Attention-deficit hyperactivity disorder: A handbook for diagnosis and treatment* (2nd ed., pp. 491–509). New York: Guilford.

DuPaul, G. J. (1991). Parent and teacher ratings of ADHD symptoms: Psychometric properties in a community-based sample. *Journal of Clinical Child Psychology, 20*, 245–253.

DuPaul, G. J., & Eckert, T. L. (1997). The effects of school-based interventions for Attention Deficit Hyperactivity Disorder: A meta-analysis. *School Psychology Review, 26*, pp. 5–27.

DuPaul, G. J., Guevremont, D. C., & Barkley, R. A. (1992). Behavioral treatment of attention-deficit hyperactivity disorder in the classroom: The use of the attention training system. *Behavior Modification, 16*, 204–225.

DuPaul, G. J., & Henningson, P. N. (1993). Peer tutoring effects on the classroom performance of children with attention deficit hyperactivity disorder. *School Psychology Review, 22*, 134–143.

DuPaul, G. J., Power, T. J., Anastopoulos, A. D., Reid, R., McGoey, K. E., & Ikeda, M. J. (1997). Teacher ratings of attention deficit hyperactivity disorder symptoms: Factor structure and normative data. *Psychological Assessment, 9*, 436–444.

DuPaul, G. J., & Stoner, G. (1994). *ADHD in the schools: Assessment and intervention strategies*. New York: Guilford.

Ervin, R. A., Ehrhardt, K. E., & Poling, A. (2001). Functional assessment: Old wine in new bottles. *School Psychology Review, 30*, 173–179.

Evans, S. W., Pelham, W. E., & Grudberg, M. V. (1995). The efficacy of notetaking to improve behavior and comprehension of adolescents with attention deficit hyperactivity disorder. *Exceptionality, 5*, 1–17.

Fabiano, G., & Pelham, W. E. (in press). Improving the effectiveness of established classroom interventions for attention deficit hyperactivity disorder: A case study. *Journal of Emotional and Behavioral Disorders.*

Fabiano, G., Pelham, W. E., Gnagy, E. M., Chronis, A. M., Onyango, A. N., Williams, A., Burrows-MacLean, L., Coles, E. K., & Meichenbaum, D. L. (under review). An evaluation of three time out procedures for child with attention-deficit hyperactivity disorder.

Fabiano, G., Pelham, W. E., Gnagy, E. M., Waschbusch, D., Lahey, B. B., Chronis, A. M., Onyango, A. N., & Kipp, H. L. (2002). The children's Impairment Rating Scale (CIRS): A practical impairment measure for children with ADHD.

Fuchs, D., Locke, W. R., & Fuchs, L. S. (1995). Effects of peer-mediated reading instruction on the on-task behavior and social interactions of children with behavior disorders. *Journal of Emotional and Behavioral Disorders, 3*, 92–99.

Goldstein, H. S. (1987). Cognitive development in low attentive, hyperactive, and aggressive 6 through 11 year old children. *Journal of the American Academy of Child and Adolescent Psychiatry, 26*, 214–218.

Gresham, F. M., Watson, T., & Skinner, C. H. (2001). Functional behavioral assessment: Principles, procedures, and future directions. *School Psychology Review, 30*, 156–172.

Hayvern, M., & Hymel, S. (1984). Ethical issues in sociometric testing: Impact of sociometric measures on interaction behavior. *Developmental Psychology, 20*, 844–849.

Hinshaw, S. P. (1992). Academic underachievement, attention deficits, and aggression: Comorbidity and implications for intervention. *Journal of Consulting and Clinical Psychology, 60*, 893–903.

Hinshaw, S. P. (1994a). *Attention deficits and hyperactivity in children* (Vol. 29). Thousand Oaks, CA: Sage.

Hinshaw, S. P. (1994b). Externalizing behavior problems and academic underachievement in childhood and adolescence: Causal relationships and underlying mechanisms. *Psychological Bulletin, 111*, 127–155.

Hoza, B., Pelham, W. E., Sams, S. E., & Carlson, C. (1992). An examination of the "dosage" effects of both behavior therapy and methylphenidate on the classroom performance of two ADHD children. *Behavior Modification, 16*, 164–192.

Jacob, R., & Pelham, W. E. (1999). Behavior therapy. In H. Kaplan & B. Sadock (Eds.), *Comprehensive textbook of psychiatry* (7th ed.; pp. 2080–2127). New York: Williams & Wilkins.

Kazdin, A. E. (2001). *Behavior modification in applied settings*. Belmont, CA: Wadsworth/Thomson Learning.

Kellam, S. G., Ling, X., Merisca, R., Brown, C. H., & Ialongo, N. (1998). The effect of the level of aggression in the first grade classroom on the course and malleability of aggressive behavior into middle school. *Development and Psychopathology, 10*, 165–185.

Kelly, M. L. (1990). School-home notes: Promoting children's classroom success. New York: Guilford.

Kelly, M. L., & McCain, A. P. (1995). Promoting academic performance in inattentive children: The relative efficacy of school-home notes with and without response cost. *Behavior Modification, 19*, 357–375.

Landau, S., & Milich, R. (1984). A comparison of teacher and peer assessment of social status. *Journal of Consulting and Clinical Psychology, 13*, 44–49.

Loney, J., Langhorne, J. E. Jr., & Paternite, C. E. (1978). An empirical basis for subgrouping the hyperkinetic/MBD syndrome. *Journal of Abnormal Psychology, 87*, 431–441.

Loney, J., & Milich, R. (1982). Hyperactivity, inattention, and aggression in clinical practice. In M. Wolraich & D. K. Routh (Eds.), *Advances in developmental and behavioral pediatrics* (Vol. 3; pp. 113–147). Greenwich, CT: JAI.

Lonigan, C., Elbert, J. C., & Johnson, S. B. (1998). Empirically supported psychosocial interventions for children: An overview. *Journal of Clinical Child Psychology, 27*, 138–145.

Manguin, E., & Loeber, R. (1996). Academic performance and delinquency. *Crime and Justice, 20*, 145–264.

Martin, G., & Pear, J. (1996). *Behavior modification: What it is and how to do it* (5th ed.). Upper Saddle River, NJ: Prentice-Hall.

McConaughy, S. M., Kay, P. J., & Fitzgerald, M. (2000). How long is long enough? Outcomes for a school-based prevention program. *Exceptional Children, 67*, 21–34.

Milich, R., & Landau, S. (1982). Socialization and peer relations in hyperactive children. In K. Gadow & I. Bailer (Eds.), *Advances in learning and behavioral disabilities* (Vol. 1; pp. 283–339). Greenwich, CT: JAI.

Milich, R., & Landau, S. (1989). The role of social status variables in differentiating subgroups of hyperactive children. In J. Swanson & L. Bloomingdale (Eds.), *Attention deficit disorders: IV. Current concepts and emerging trends in attentional and behavioral disorders of childhood* (pp. 1–16). London: Pergamon.

Milich, R., Landau, S., Kilby, G., & Whitten, P. (1982). Preschool peer perceptions of the behavior of hyperactive and aggressive children. *Journal of Abnormal Child Psychology, 10*, 497–510.

Milich, R., Landau, S., & Loney, J. (1981, August). *The interrelationships among hyperactivity, aggression, and impulsivity*. Paper presented at the 89th Annual Convention of the American Psychological Association, Los Angeles.

Milich, R., Loney, J., & Landau, S. (1982). Independent dimensions of hyperactivity and aggression: A validation with playroom observation data. *Journal of Abnormal Psychology, 91*, 183–198.

Nichols, S., & Waschbusch, D. A. (under review). Ecological validity of inattention and impulsivity: What have we learned in the past decade?

Northup, J., & Gulley, V. (2001). Some contributions of functional analysis to the assessment of behaviors associated with attention deficit hyperactivity disorder and the effects of stimulant medication. *School Psychology Review, 30*, 227–238.

Offord, D. R., Kraemer, H. C., Kazdin, A. E., Jensen, P. S., & Harrington, R. (1998). Lowering the burden of suffering from child psychiatric disorder: Trade-offs among clinical, targeted, and universal interventions. *Journal of the American Academy of Child and Adolescent Psychiatry, 37*, 686–694.

O'Leary, K. D., Pelham, W. E., Rosenbaum, A., & Price, G. H. (1976). Behavioral treatment of hyperkinetic children: An experimental evaluation of its usefulness. *Clinical Pediatrics, 15*, 510–515.

O'Leary, S. G., & Pelham, W. E. (1978). Behavior therapy and withdrawal of stimulant medication with hyperactive children. *Pediatrics, 61*, 211–217.

Parker, J. G., & Asher, S. R. (1987). Peer relations and later personal adjustment: Are low-accepted children at risk? *Psychological Bulletin, 102*, 357–389.

Pekarik, E. G., Prinz, R. J., Liebert, D. E., Weintraub, S., & Neale, J. M. (1976). The pupil evaluation inventory: A sociometric technique for assessing children's social behavior. *Journal of Abnormal Child Psychology, 4*, 83–97.

Pelham, W. E. (1993). Pharmacotherapy for children with attention-deficit hyperactivity disorder. *School Psychology Review, 22*, 199–227.

Pelham, W. E., & Bender, M. E. (1982). Peer relationships in hyperactive children: Description and treatment. In K. Gadow & I. Bailer (Eds.), *Advances in learning and behavioral disabilities* (Vol. 1; pp. 365–436). Greenwich, CT: JAI.

Pelham, W. E., Billheimer, S., Newman, B., Wilson T., Myers, D., Myers, C., Palmer, A., Whichard, S. M., & Myers, M. (2002). *A school-wide intervention for inclusion in an elementary school.* Unpublished manuscript, State University of New York at Buffalo, Buffalo, New York.

Pelham, W. E., Carlson, C., Sams, S. E., Vallano, G., Dixon, M. J., & Hoza, B. (1993). Separate and combined effects of methylphenidate and behavior modification on boys with attention deficit-hyperactivity disorder in the classroom. *Journal of Consulting and Clinical Psychology, 61*, 506–515.

Pelham, W. E., & Fabiano, G. A. (2000). Behavior modification. *Child and Adolescent Psychiatric Clinics of North America, 9*, 671–683.

Pelham, W. E., & Fabiano, G. A. (2001). Treatment of attention-deficit hyperactivity disorder: The impact of comorbidity. *Journal of Clinical Psychology and Psychotherapy, 8*, 315–329.

Pelham, W. E., Gnagy, E. M., Greenslade, K. E., & Milich, R. (1992). Teacher ratings of DSM-III-R symptoms for the disruptive behavior disorders. *Journal of the American Academy of Child and Adolescent Psychiatry, 31*, 210–218.

Pelham, W. E., Gnagy, E. M., & Greiner, A. R. (1994). *Children's summer day treatment program 1994 research assistant manual.* Pittsburgh: University of Pittsburgh Medical Center.

Pelham, W. E., Gnagy, E. M., & Greiner, A. R. (1998). *Children's summer day treatment program manual.* Buffalo, NY: CTADD

Pelham, W. E., Gnagy, E. M., Greiner, A. R., Hoza, B., Hinshaw, S. P., Swanson, J. M., Simpson, S., Shapiro, C., Bukstein, O., Baron-Myak C. (2000). Behavioral vs. behavioral and pharmacological treatment in ADHD children attending a summer treatment program. *Journal of Abnormal Child Psychology, 28*, 507–525.

Pelham, W. E., Greiner, A. R., Gnagy, E. M., Hoza, B., Martin, L., Sams, S. E., et al. (1996). Intensive treatment for ADHD: A model summer treatment program. In M. Roberts & A. LaGreca (Eds.), *Model programs for service delivery for child and family mental health* (pp. 193–212). Hillsdale, NJ: Lawrence Erlbaum Associates.

Pelham, W. E., Hoza, B., Pillow, D. R., Gnagy, E. M., Kipp, H. L., Greiner, A. R., et al. (2002). Effects of methylphenidate and expectancy on children with ADHD: Behavior, academic performance, and attributions in a Summer Treatment Program and regular classroom setting. *Journal of Consulting and Clinical Psychology, 70*, 320–335.

Pelham, W. E., Milich, R., Murphy, D. A., & Murphy, H. A. (1989). Normative data on the IOWA Conners teacher rating scale. *Journal of Clinical Child Psychology, 18*, 259–262.

Pelham, W. E., Schnedler, R. W., Bender, M. E., Nilsson, D. E., Miller, J., Budrow, M. S., et al. (1988). The combination of behavior therapy and methylphenidate in the treatment of attention deficit disorders: A therapy outcome study. In L. Bloomingdale (Ed.), *Attention deficit disorders III: New research in attention, treatment, and psychopharmacology* (pp. 29–48). London: Pergamon.

Pelham, W. E., Schnedler, R. W., Bologna, N., & Contreras, A. (1980). Behavioral and stimulant treatment of hyperactive children: A therapy study with methylphenidate probes in a within-subject design. *Journal of Applied Behavior Analysis, 13*, 221–236.

Pelham, W. E., & Waschbusch, D. A. (1999). Behavioral intervention in ADHD. In H. C. Quay & A. E. Hogan (Eds.), *Handbook of disruptive behavior disorders* (pp. 255–278). New York: Plenum.

Pelham, W. E., Wheeler, T., & Chronis, A. M. (1998). Empirically supported psychosocial treatment for attention deficit hyperactivity disorder. *Journal of Clinical Child Psychology, 27*, 190–205.

Pelham, W. E., Wilson, T., & Kipp, H. (2000a). *Schoolwide intervention model: Program manual.* Buffalo, NY: CTADD.

Pelham, W. E., Wilson, T., & Kipp, H. (2000b). *Schoolwide intervention model: Program video.* Buffalo, NY: CTADD.

Pfiffner, L. J. (1996). All about ADHD: The complete practical guide for classroom teachers. New York: Scholastic Professional Books.

Pianta, R. C., Steinberg, M., & Rollins, K. (1995). The first two years of school: Teacher-child relationships and deflections in children's classroom adjustment. *Development and Psychopathology, 7*, 295–312.

Platzman, K. A., Stoy, M. R., Brown, R. T., & Coles, C. D. (1992). Review of observational methods in attention deficit hyperactivity disorder (ADHD): Implications for diagnosis. *School Psychology Review, 7*, 155–177.

Pliszka, S. R., Carlson, C. L., & Swanson, J. M. (1999). *ADHD with comorbid disorders*. New York: Guilford.

Rapport, M. D., Murphy, A., & Bailey, J. S. (1980). The effects of a response cost treatment tactic on hyperactive children. *Journal of School Psychology, 18*, 98–111.

Rapport, M. D., Murphy, A., & Bailey, J. S. (1982). Ritalin vs. response cost in the control of hyperactive children: A within-subject comparison. *Journal of Applied Behavior Analysis, 15*, 205–216.

Rief, S. F. (1993). How to reach and teach ADD/ADHD children. West Nyack, NY: Center for Applied Research in Education.

Russo, M. F., & Beidel, D. C. (1994). Comorbidity of childhood anxiety and externalizing disorders: Prevalence, associated characteristics, and validation issues. *Clinical Psychology Review, 14*, 199–221.

Schell, R. M., Pelham, W. E., Bender, M. E., Andree, J., Law, T., & Robbins, F. (1986). The concurrent assessment of behavioral and psychostimulant interventions: A controlled case study. *Behavioral Assessment, 8*, 373–384.

Smith, B. H., Waschbusch, D. A., Willoughby, M. T., & Evans, S. (2000). The efficacy, safety, and practicality of treatments for adolescents with attention-deficit/hyperactivity disorder (ADHD). *Clinical Child and Family Psychology Review, 3*, 243–267.

Sterling-Turner, H. E., Robinson, S. L., & Wilczynski, S. M. (2001). Functional assessment of distracting and disruptive behavior in the school setting. *School Psychology Review, 30*, 211–226.

Stevens, J., Quittner, A. L., & Abikoff, H. (1998). Factors influencing elementary school teachers' ratings of ADHD and ODD behaviors. *Journal of Clinical Child Psychology, 27*, 406–414.

Sugai, G., Sprague, J. R., Horner, R. H., & Walker, H. M. (2000). Preventing school violence: The use of office discipline referrals to assess and monitor school-wide discipline interventions. *Journal of Emotional and Behavioral Disorders, 8*, 94–101.

Swanson, J. M. (1996). *The SNAP-IV teacher and parent rating scale* [Online]. Available: http://www.adhd.net/.

Walker, H. M., Colvin, C., & Ramsey, E. (1995). *Antisocial behavior in school: Strategies and best practices*. Pacific Grove, CA: Brooks/Cole.

Walker, H. M., & Walker, J. E. (1991). *Coping with noncompliance in the classroom: A positive approach for teachers*. Austin, TX: Proed.

Waschbusch, D. A. (2002). A meta-analytic examination of comorbid hyperactive/impulsive/inattention problems and conduct problems. *Psychological Bulletin, 128*, 118–150.

Waschbusch, D. A., Kipp, H. L., & Pelham, W. E. (1998). Generalization of behavioral and psychostimulant treatment of attention deficit/hyperactive disorder (ADHD): Discussion and case study examples. *Behavior Research and Therapy, 36*, 675–694.

Waschbusch, D. A., & Northern Partners in Action for Children and Youth. (2002). *Behavior, education, support and treatment (BEST) program: A semi-randomized, controlled comparison of school interventions*. Unpublished manuscript, Dalhousie University, Halifax, Nova Scotia, Canada.

Webster-Stratton, C. (1991). Annotation: Strategies for helping families with conduct disordered children. *Journal of Child Psychology and Psychiatry and Allied Disciplines, 32*, 1047–1062.

Weiss, G., & Hechtman, L. T. (1993). *Hyperactive children grown up: ADHD in children, adolescents, and adults*. New York: Guilford.

Weissman, M. M., Warner, V., & Fendrich, M. (1990). Applying impairment criteria to children's psychiatric diagnosis. *Journal of the American Academy of Child and Adolescent Psychiatry, 29*, 789–795.

Wells, K. C., Pelham, W. E., Kotkin, R. A., Hoza, B., Abikoff, H. B., Abramowitz, A., et al. (2000). Psychosocial treatment strategies in the MTA study: Rationale, methods, and critical design issues. *Journal of Abnormal Child Psychology, 28*, 483–506.

Wielkiewicz, R. M. (1995). *Behavior management in the schools: Principles and procedures* (2nd ed.). Boston: Allyn and Bacon.

Witt, J. C., & Elliott, S. N. (1982). The response cost lottery: A time efficient and effective classroom intervention. *Journal of School Psychology, 20*, 155–161.

Wolraich, M. L., Feurer, I. D., Hannah, J. N., Baumgaertel, A., & Pinnock, T. Y. (1998). Obtaining systematic teacher reports of disruptive behavior disorders utilizing DSM-IV. *Journal of Abnormal Child Psychology, 26*, 141–152.

23

Autism Spectrum Disorders and Mental Retardation

Jonathan M. Campbell
University of Georgia

Sam B. Morgan
University of Memphis

Jennie N. Jackson
University of Georgia

AUTISM SPECTRUM DISORDERS

Psychologists working in school settings today more than in previous years will experience increased contact with children with autism, pervasive developmental disorders (PDD), and mental retardation (MR). There are at least two reasons that may account for this increased contact. First, the incidence of autism and related PDDs appears to have risen in the past 20 years. Recent epidemiological studies suggest that autism and PDDs are not as rare as once believed, with some prevalence estimates as high as about 6 in 1,000 (Chakrabarti & Fombonne, 2001). To reflect this trend, the *Diagnostic and Statistical Manual of Mental Disorders*, Fourth Edition, Text Revision (*DSM-IV-TR*) prevalence rates for autism were revised from 2 to 5 per 10,000 to 2–20 per 10,000 with 5 per 10,000 reported as the median prevalence rate (American Psychiatric Association [APA], 2000). A second reason that school professionals are encountering more children with autism, PDD, and MR today is that these children are included more frequently in regular classroom programs than previously. The responsibility for providing appropriate programs now extends beyond special education personnel to include virtually everyone working in the school setting. School professionals should therefore be knowledgeable about autism, PDD, and MR in order to facilitate acceptance of these children and to help in implementing effective educational and intervention programs.

The literature on autism, PDD, and MR has reached proportions that would intimidate even the most dedicated scholars. Within the limited space of this chapter, we hope to provide a brief review of certain areas that we consider important to those working in school settings and to point the reader to sources that offer more detailed information regarding this population. To this end, this chapter briefly summarizes the defining characteristics, proposed causal mechanisms, diagnosis, treatment, and outcomes for children diagnosed with autism, PDD, and MR.

Definition of Autism and Pervasive Developmental Disorders

In clinical settings, the most widely used diagnostic criteria for autism are those set forth in the *DSM-IV-TR*, which refers to autism as "autistic disorder" and classifies it as a pervasive developmental disorder (APA, 2000, p. 69). These criteria specify three categories of symptoms, often referred to as the "autistic triad," that a child must show before 3 years of age:

Qualitative Impairments in Social Interaction. These impairments include those features that Kanner (1943) conveyed with the term *autistic aloneness*. Children with autism generally do not develop normal attachments and peer relationships, spontaneously share enjoyment and interests with other people, nor engage in social and emotional "give-and-take" with others.

Qualitative Impairments in Communication. These impairments refer to what Kanner (1943) described as the failure of these children to use "language for the purpose of communication (p. 241)." Children with autism are delayed in speaking or do not develop speech at all. They show salient problems in initiating or sustaining conversation with others, and their speech is stereotyped, repetitive, or idiosyncratic. They exhibit marked deficits in engaging in varied, spontaneous make-believe play, or social imitative play.

Restricted, Repetitive, Stereotyped Behavior, Interests, and Activities. Kanner (1943) also noted that children with autism showed "an anxiously obsessive desire for the maintenance of sameness (p. 243)" and a fascination and facility with objects. Children with autism abnormally preoccupy themselves with stereotyped and restricted interests and with parts of objects. They inflexibly adhere to specific routines or rituals that have no apparent function and/or engage in stereotyped and repetitive motor mannerisms, such as hand-flapping and rocking.

For reasons still unknown, autism appears in boys four times more often than in girls, although girls with autism tend to be more severely impaired (Lord & Schopler, 1987). Autism occurs in all ethnic and racial groups and in families at all educational and economic levels.

In addition to autism or "autistic disorder," *DSM-IV-TR* describes three additional subtypes of PDD: Asperger's disorder, Rett's disorder, and childhood disintegrative disorder. These disorders, along with autistic disorder, are increasingly known as "autism spectrum disorders." All children with PDD show severe impairments, typically in communication and social interactions, that emerge in early childhood and deviate from their overall developmental level. They usually engage in repetitious, stereotyped behaviors, interests, and activities, such as those described with autistic children. Most children with PDD, except for those with Asperger's disorder, function within the mentally retarded range. Also, most children with PDD are male by a great margin, except for those with Rett's disorder, which has only been reported in females. For complete discussions of Rett's disorder and childhood disintegrative disorder, the reader is referred to Van Acker (1997) and Volkmar, Klin, Marans, and Cohen (1997).

Asperger's disorder is the PDD category most related to autism, both historically and in common features (Klin, Volkmar, & Sparrow, 2000). It was first described by Austrian physician Hans Asperger in 1944, one year after Leo Kanner first defined infantile autism as a clinical disorder (Asperger, 1944). Despite this coincidence in time and the overlap in symptoms with autism, Asperger's disorder has only recently been recognized in the United States as a distinct disorder (Campbell & Morgan, 1998). The disorder occurs more commonly than autism, with some prevalence estimates as high as 3–4 children in 1,000. Like autism, Asperger's disorder is found about four times more frequently in boys than girls.

The symptoms of Asperger's disorder are less evident than in typical autism and may not become apparent until the child reaches 3 or 4 years of age. According to *DSM-IV-TR*, the two essential features of the disorder are: (1) qualitative impairments in social interaction, such as gaze aversion, failure to develop normal peer relations, and lack of social or emotional reciprocity; and (2) restricted and stereotyped patterns of behavior, such as intense, persistent preoccupations with narrow interests or objects, rigid adherence to nonfunctional routines, and/or stereotyped motor mannerisms. Unlike children with autism, children with Asperger's disorder show no significant delay in language and cognitive development. However, they may be delayed in motor milestones and often show motor clumsiness (Iwanaga, Kawasaki, Tsuchida, 2000). The long-term prognosis for individuals with Asperger's disorder is better than the prognosis for most individuals with autism. Most can achieve independent adjustment in adulthood, although problems in social interaction often persist (Klin et al., 2000). Although *DSM-IV-TR* includes Asperger's disorder as a distinct diagnostic entity, controversy exists as to whether individuals with Asperger's disorder are different from high functioning individuals with autism (Schopler, Mesibov, & Kunce, 1998).

Because many children fail to fully meet the diagnostic criteria for a specific PDD, *DSM-IV-TR* includes the category of "PDD not otherwise specified" (PDD-NOS; APA, 2000; Towbin, 1997). These children show severe impairment in reciprocal social interaction that is typically associated with impairment in communication skills or with the presence of stereotypic behaviors, interests, and activities. PDD-NOS, which includes atypical autism, is also considered to be an autism spectrum disorder.

Biological Factors in Autism

Although no consistent cause of autism has been determined, little evidence exists to support early theories of psychosocial causation of autism, such as pathogenic parenting (e.g., Bettelheim, 1967); however, numerous studies suggest that the disorder is clearly related to biological factors. For example, twin studies have demonstrated a substantial genetic predisposition toward autism, with identical twins showing a much higher concordance rate for autism than fraternal twins (Bailey et al., 1995). Other research has demonstrated that autism is associated with a number of diverse neuropathological conditions, which include phenylketonuria (PKU), congenital rubella, tuberous sclerosis, lead intoxication, congenital syphilis, Fragile X, and convulsive disorders (Dykens & Volkmar, 1997). Most children with autism fail to show the gross anomalies of brain structure or histology found in severely mentally retarded children. In addition, autism is usually not associated with generalized brain damage or hazards known to cause brain damage (Rutter & Schopler, 1987).

The organic dysfunction underlying autism is apparently subtler and less discernible than that found in MR in general. A great deal of research on possible neuroanatomical anomalies in autism is now being conducted with refined neuroimaging methods, but the findings thus far are somewhat inconsistent. Courchesne (1995), for example, found that two areas in the cerebellum are smaller than normal in one subgroup of individuals with autism and larger than normal in another subgroup. Overall, there is general consensus that autism is the result of central nervous system dysfunction that results in a cluster of behavioral end products (e.g., Volkmar, 2001). The mechanisms associated with the pathophysiology in autism are numerous (e.g., genetics and neurochemical) and may well work in combination to produce the behavioral symptoms observed in autism spectrum disorders.

Cognitive and Language Impairment in Autism

Although the level of functional intelligence varies widely in children with autism, the vast majority function within the retarded range. About 60% of children with autism have IQs below 50, 20% have IQs between 50 and 70, and only 20% have IQs of 70 or higher (Ritvo &

Freeman, 1977). Research also has shown that the everyday adaptive functioning of individuals with autism is typically more impaired than intellectual functioning (Carpentieri & Morgan, 1996).

Also reflective of a basic cognitive impairment is the language retardation found in the preponderance of autistic persons. At least 28% of children with autism are mute (Lotter, 1978), and about 35% to 40% fail to develop functional or communicative language at all during their lifetimes (Mesibov, Adams, & Klinger, 1997). Those who develop speech show a wide range of individual differences in ability to communicate, with most demonstrating substantial retardation in language development, especially in pragmatics. Language delays usually appear at an early age; in fact, speech delay represents the most frequent early presenting complaint by parents of children with autism (Ornitz & Ritvo, 1976). Early language deficits tend to persist. Individuals with autism generally perform well below average on language tasks, especially those requiring verbal comprehension. Moreover, language skills are usually well below developmental age estimated from nonverbal ability tests (Carpentieri & Morgan, 1994).

Intellectual functioning and language development assume even greater importance in light of the finding that they represent the most potent predictors of eventual adjustment. Onset of meaningful speech before age 5 or 6 appears to be crucial to later adjustment (Kanner, Rodriguez, & Ashenden, 1972; Rutter, Greenfeld, & Lockyer, 1967). The child who develops functional speech by this age has a better chance of attaining marginal or good adjustment when compared to a child with no language. The measured intelligence of the young child with autism also serves as a strong predictor of later adaptation. The higher the IQ, the closer the child will approach normal adaptation. An IQ below 40 is predictive of poor outcome; conversely, an IQ above 60 or 70 greatly increases the chances of educational progress and social adjustment (DeMyer et al., 1973; Rutter & Lockyer, 1967). Moreover, children with higher language skills and IQs show a much better response to behavioral treatment programs (Rogers, 1998).

The picture of cognitive functioning in children with autism is sometimes complicated by the presence of "splinter" skills or, more rarely, savant skills. These isolated abilities, which may be strikingly higher than the child's general level of functioning, include motor and spatial skills, rote memory, and hyperlexia (Treffert, 1988). Savant skills, which only occur in about 10% of persons with autism, may include exceptional talents in music or art, but in most cases are demonstrated in individuals who are significantly impaired in general intellectual and adaptive functioning.

What Is the Basic Cognitive Deficit in Autism?

Because autism and MR both involve substantial cognitive impairment, what distinguishes children with autism from peers with MR who are of comparable mental age but not autistic? Children with MR tend to demonstrate social responsiveness that is lacking in children with autism. For example, children with Down syndrome, often severely impaired in symbolic and conceptual skills, usually form emotional attachments and relate affectionately to the people in their world (Bieberich & Morgan, 1998). This discrepancy between children with autism and those with MR suggests peculiar deficits that do not arise from general retardation, that is, deficits that impair not only cognitive functioning but also social and affective responsiveness.

A number of hypotheses have addressed the question of the basic cognitive defect in autism. As early as 1971, Lovaas and his colleagues proposed that a basic feature in autism is "stimulus overselectivity," due to an inability to shift attention (Lovaas, Schreibman, Koegel, & Rehm, 1971), and subsequent research provided support for this theory (e.g., Wilhelm & Lovaas, 1976). Based on findings indicating cerebellar and parietal anomalies in autism, Courchesne

(1995) proposed that individuals with autism exhibit deficits in regulation of three attention operations: orienting, shifting, and distributing attention to, between, and across locations of potential importance. According to Courchesne, these functions are needed to apprehend and engage in everyday nonsocial and social situations. Another hypothesis suggests a deficit in executive functioning as mediated by the frontal lobes resulting in deficiencies in self-regulation (Adrien et al., 1995; McEvoy, Rogers, & Pennington, 1993). Despite likely differences in underlying neurological anomalies, as suggested by these hypotheses, problems in self-regulation have emerged as basic deficiencies in autism and other forms of PDD.

One of the more intriguing hypotheses offered to explain the cognitive deficit specific to autism invokes the concept of "theory of mind" (Baron-Cohen, Leslie, & Frith, 1985). Theory of mind refers to one's ability to understand that others have thoughts, beliefs, and intentions that differ from one's own. Research has provided some support for the hypothesis that children with autism show "theory of mind" deficits; that is, they show specific difficulty in inferring that others have beliefs or intentions that differ from their own (Ozonoff & McEvoy, 1994).

Diagnostic Assessment of Autism Spectrum Disorders

Although the *DSM-IV-TR* presents a fairly detailed, up-to-date set of criteria for the diagnosis of autistic disorder, it provides no quantitative rating system for assessing the symptoms of autism and differentiating the disorder from related disorders, such as MR. The Childhood Autism Rating Scale (CARS; Schopler, Reichler, & Renner, 1988) has emerged as one of the most reliable and valid rating scales for identifying children with autism (Morgan, 1988a). Other recently developed scales that appear to be useful in the diagnostic assessment of autism spectrum disorders and in the early screening for such disorders include the Autism Diagnostic Interview–Revised (Lord, Rutter, & Le Couteur, 1994), Autism Diagnostic Observation Schedule-Generic (ADOS-G; Lord et al., 2000), Checklist for Autism in Toddlers (CHAT; Baron-Cohen, Allen, & Gillberg, 1992), the Parent Interview for Autism (PIA; Stone & Hogan, 1993), and the Screening Tool for Autism in Two-Year-Olds (STAT; Stone, Coonrod, & Ousley, 2000). The ADOS-G can be used in the diagnosis of not only autism but also PDD-NOS (Lord et al., 2000). The CHAT is designed to provide an early screening measure for autism in children as young as 18 months (Baron-Cohen et al., 1992). Similarly, the STAT is a screening tool for very young children with autism (Stone et al., 2000). Early screening measures, such as the CHAT, are likely to be used more frequently in coming years due to the increased emphasis on early detection of autism and other forms of PDD.

Psychoeducational Assessment

To aid in educational planning for the child with autism, many instruments are available to assess intelligence, developmental attainment, patterns of abilities and deficits, academic achievement, and adaptive skills. Traditional intelligence scales can be helpful in estimating the autistic child's current level of intellectual functioning and profile of abilities. Further, research has shown that early IQ scores are highly predictive of response to treatment and long-term functioning in persons with autism (Lotter, 1978; Rogers, 1998). In higher functioning children, the Stanford-Binet Intelligence Scales (Thorndike, Hagen, & Sattler, 1986) and the Wechsler Intelligence Scale for Children-Third Revision (WISC-III; Wechsler, 1991) can be used in assessing intellectual functioning. Nonverbal tests of intellectual functioning, such as the Leiter International Performance Scale-Revised (Roid & Miller, 1997), can also be used, especially with the nonverbal, or severely verbally impaired child. For very young or very low functioning children, infant scales, such as the Bayley Scales of Infant Development-Second Edition (Bayley, 1993), can yield reliable and valid measures of developmental level.

Often the "untestable" child can be found to perform if the items are appropriate to his or her developmental level (Alpern, 1967).

In assessing the adaptive skills of children with autism, the Vineland Adaptive Behavior Scales (Vineland; Sparrow, Balla, & Cicchetti, 1984) appear to be especially useful. Standard scores based on age are derived in four domains: Communication, Daily Living Skills, Socialization, and Motor Skills. These scores then serve as the basis for an overall standard score, the Adaptive Behavior Composite. Because the Vineland yields an overall score and specific domain scores, the child's general adaptive level can be determined as well as a profile of adaptive functioning. This information can then be used in treatment and educational programs. Studies have indicated that children with autism show a characteristic profile, with Socialization and Communication domains being the most impaired (e.g., Carpentieri & Morgan, 1996). The Vineland is also useful because supplementary norms for individuals with autism have been published (Carter et al., 1998).

The Psychoeducational Profile-Revised (PEP-R; Schopler, Reichler, Bashford, Lansing, & Marcus, 1990) is a measure designed specifically for gaining assessment information for use in individualized education and treatment of the autistic child. The PEP-R assesses developmental functioning in 10 areas: imitation, perception, gross motor, fine motor, eye-hand integration, cognitive performance, expressive language, self-help skills, social skills, and behavior problems. In combination with other assessment information, the PEP-R profile is used to design appropriate teaching strategies and specific teaching programs. An adolescent and adult form of the PEP-R, the AAPEP, has also been developed to assess the following six areas: vocational behaviors, work-related socialization, vocational skills, self-help skills, independent work skills, and leisure activities (Mesibov, Schopler, Schaffer, & Landrus, 1988).

Intervention, Treatment, and Long-Term Outcome

Despite claims made by ardent proponents of certain treatments, no treatment has resulted in a "cure" for autism, although certain interventions have been shown to be more effective than others in helping autistic persons adapt. (For a recent series of articles on behavioral, psychoeducational, and pharmacological treatments, see the *Journal of Autism & Developmental Disorders, 30,* no. 5.). The most effective treatment involves well-structured behavioral and educational programs that are started early and pervade the child's life (Schreibman, 2000). Such programs require early diagnosis of autism, early counseling of parents, strong parental involvement in the child's treatment, and individualized special education.

Professionals working in settings where autism is diagnosed have the responsibility of explaining to parents what the diagnosis means (for a more thorough discussion of this topic, see Morgan, 1984). The extreme complexity of autism presents a special set of problems in such counseling. The diagnosis of autism, of course, should not be conveyed to the parents unless a thorough assessment has determined that the child meets the classification criteria.

Pharmacological Treatments. As most evidence points to the physical causation of autism, increased efforts have been made to find an effective biochemical treatment. Although a number of drugs have been tried, none has been successful in significantly reducing the core symptoms of autism. For example, neuroleptics (e.g., haloperiodol), beta blockers, clonidine, tricyclic antidepressants (e.g., clomipramine), and opiate antagonists (e.g., naltrexone) have been reported to be useful in reducing secondary symptoms, such as self-injury, stereotypic behavior, aggression, and sleep disturbances (Campbell, Green, & Deutsch, 1985; Volkmar, 2001). A recent well-controlled clinical investigation reported that the hormone secretin produced only transient changes in speech and behavior in some children but generally resulted in few clinically meaningful changes when compared to placebo injections (Chez et al., 2000).

Psychosocial Interventions. Treatment programs based on psychodynamic theory have shown little success with autistic children (Schreibman, 1988). There is little doubt that treatment based on behavioral principles has been much more effective with autistic children than any other approach. (For a recent review of empirically supported treatments, see Rogers, 1998.)

The behavioral treatment program that has reported the highest success rates for children with autism is that developed by Lovaas and his associates. Lovaas (1987) presented the results of a well-controlled study that evaluated the effectiveness of his program. Children with autism began the program at about the age of 3 and continued for 3 years. Well-trained therapists worked with each child for an average of 40 hours per week in the child's home, school, and community. In addition, parents were thoroughly trained in treatment procedures so that intervention took place for most of the child's waking hours. Lovaas (1987) found that 9 of 19 children (47%) enrolled in intensive treatment performed at normal intellectual and educational levels by first grade, whereas only 1 (2%) child in the control group achieved this level. By late childhood and adolescence, McEachlin, Smith, and Lovaas (1993) found that 47% of the original sample of children in the intensive treatment group continued to be in regular educational placements without any evidence of learning problems, whereas all of the children in the control group were in special educational placements. Furthermore, the mean IQ for the intensive group (84.5) was 30 points higher than that for the control group (54.9). Comparable differences were found for adaptive behavior scores.

In an evaluation of behavioral treatments based on published studies, Rogers (1998) noted that all programs reported positive results but not as positive as those of Lovaas. She specified several variables related to treatment outcome. First, younger children (i.e., less than 5 years of age) respond more positively than older children. Second, children with higher pretreatment IQs and language skills show a better response. As newer diagnostic categories have emerged within the autism spectrum, these guidelines have appeared to hold true. For example, children diagnosed with Asperger's disorder showed more improved social skills and fewer autistic behaviors than those diagnosed with autism over a 2-year period (Szatmari et al., 2000). Third, all of the treatment studies involved 20 or more hours of therapy, with the best results coming from the program offering the most hours of treatment. Rogers points out, however, that the only study specifically examining effect of hours of treatment found no difference between an average of 21 hours and an average of 32 hours per week. Thus, more research is needed on the optimal number of treatment hours per week.

One problem often reported with behavioral treatment programs is the child's failure to generalize learned responses to different situations. To address this problem, Koegel, Koegel, and McNerney (2001) outlined a treatment model that focuses on core pivotal areas of the disorder. They hypothesized that the lack of motivation to respond to complex stimuli is a core problem area and that treatment should be aimed at motivating the child to initiate large numbers of social interactions that provide naturally occurring learning opportunities. Such motivation, they proposed, is needed to reduce the core and peripheral features associated with autism.

In order for treatment programs to be effective, parents must be included. There is no doubt that treatments that employ parents as therapists are superior to treatments taking place only in the clinic (Schreibman, 2000). One of the most obvious advantages of incorporating the parents into treatment is that it greatly enhances generalization. For specific techniques of parent training, the reader is referred to Koegel and Koegel (1996) and Lovaas (1981). Although parent training is often included in treatment, an important but often neglected aspect of intervention concerns the impact of children with autism on parents and family members. Parents and siblings of autistic children may experience special stressors, and an autistic child may have a disruptive influence on the family system (Morgan, 1988b; Sanders & Morgan,

1997). To meet these needs, supportive counseling for individual family members and therapy for the family as a whole should be included in treatment.

As a part of any comprehensive treatment program, special education instruction is essential for the vast majority of children with autism. The passage in 1975 of the Education for All Handicapped Children's Act served as a much-needed stimulus for the development of appropriate educational programs for individuals with autism. Most important, children with autism are now being integrated as much as possible into regular classroom programs.

As the individual with autism approaches adulthood, more and more attention in special education programs should be given to assessment and training of vocational skills that will allow the individual better adjustment as an adult. A related concern is the development of community group homes that can serve as an alternative to institutional placement for adults with autism (Schopler & Mesibov, 1983).

The most effective intervention programs for children with autism and their families are broad-based and extend into the home, school, and community. The Treatment and Education of Autistic and Related Communication Handicapped CHildren (TEACCH) program in North Carolina represents a model community approach that provides comprehensive treatment and educational services to children with autism and their families (Schopler, 1998). Unfortunately, most communities fall short of offering comprehensive services of this type.

Long-Term Outcome. The question that eventually enters the minds of most people interested in children with autism is: What will happen when they grow up? Answers to this question come from available information on individuals with autism who have already reached adolescence and adulthood. Any conclusions that we draw from such data, however, must be tentative and subject to revision. Many of the individuals studied, especially those who are now adults, did not have the benefit of intensive early treatment or special education programs that are now available to children in many communities.

The current prognosis for children with autism as adolescents and adults is generally poor. Based on results of follow-up studies, as many as 75% of individuals with autism continue to function within the mentally retarded range as adults, being generally unable to lead independent lives (DeMyer, Hingtgen, & Jackson, 1981; Lotter, 1978). As noted previously, two of the strongest predictors of positive outcome are early communicative speech and higher measured intelligence (Kanner et al., 1972; Lotter, 1978). Other factors related to later adjustment include degree of neuropathology, severity of early symptoms, and appropriateness of early play behavior (Morgan, 1990). Most important, if the parents are willing to commit themselves to a systematic behavioral program for the child at an early age, then chances of later adaptation are increased (Schreibman, 2000).

MENTAL RETARDATION

Definitions and Classification Systems

Guidelines published by the *DSM-IV-TR* (APA, 2000) and the American Association for Mental Retardation (AAMR; Luckasson et al., 1992) define MR as the presence of significantly subaverage intellectual functioning and concurrent delays in adaptive skills with an onset prior to the age of 18. Within each diagnostic system, adaptive skill areas include a wide range of functioning such as communication, self-help, social skills, work, and home living, among others. The *DSM-IV-TR* includes subcategories of MR that describe an individual's level of impairment based on intellectual functioning: Mild (IQ of 50–55 to about 70), Moderate (IQ of 35–40 to 50–55), Severe (IQ of 20–25 to 35–40), and Profound (IQ < 20–25) (APA, 2000). In contrast, the 1992 AAMR guidelines delineate four categories (i.e., Intermittent, Limited, Extensive, and Pervasive) to describe an individual's need for intervention services within areas of delay. The AAMR categories were proposed in order to reduce reliance on IQ for classifying disability level, as well as to provide descriptions of an individual's needs for intervention services.

Prevalence rates of MR are frequently reported to range from 1 to 3% for school-age children, although rates fluctuate considerably depending on definitions of MR, methods used to detect individuals with MR, and the size of the study population. In a recent review, the average reported prevalence rate for severe MR (i.e., IQ < 50) was 3.8 per 1,000 and the average reported prevalence rate for mild MR (i.e., IQ from 50 to 70) was 29.8 per 1,000 or roughly 3% (Roelveld, Zielhuis, & Gabreëls, 1997). Males are more frequently diagnosed with MR than females at a rate of approximately 1.2:1 in the severe range of MR and 1.4:1 in the mild range of MR (Murphy, Boyle, Schendel, Decoufle, & Yeargin-Allsopp, 1998; Roelveld et al., 1997).

Etiology and Causal Mechanisms

MR is associated with a large number of conditions, including genetic disorders (e.g., Down syndrome, Fragile X syndrome), prenatal or early environmental insults (e.g., fetal alcohol syndrome, lead poisoning), health-related conditions (e.g., tuberous sclerosis), and psychiatric disorders (e.g., autism, Rett's disorder) (Murphy et al., 1998). Over 500 genetic disorders have been identified that are associated with MR, with Down syndrome and Fragile X syndrome often reported as the two most frequent genetic causes (Flint & Wilkie, 1996; Moldavsky, Lev, & Lerman-Sagie, 2001). Down syndrome occurs in about 1 in every 800–1,000 births (Ramirez & Morgan, 1998) whereas Fragile X syndrome occurs in approximately 1 in 1,000 males and 1 in 2,000 females (Murphy et al., 1998). Outside of the realm of congenital causes, fetal alcohol syndrome is considered to be one of the leading causes of MR in the United States, occurring in about 1 per 1,000 births (Murphy et al., 1998). In approximately 30% to 40% of all individuals diagnosed with MR, no etiology can be determined (APA, 2000). In individuals with IQ scores of less than 50, approximately 40–70% receive a diagnosis; however, in individuals with IQ scores in the mild range of MR (50–70), a diagnosis is rendered in only about 20–24% of cases (Flint & Wilkie, 1996; Murphy et al., 1998). In cases where no clear etiology exists, MR is typically thought to be the result of multiple causal factors, such as polygenic inheritance and environmental risks (e.g., Flint & Wilkie, 1996; Roeveld et al., 1997).

Characteristics

Despite sharing common deficits in intellectual functioning and adaptive skills, individuals with MR exhibit a wide range of cognitive and behavioral features. As evidenced by the diagnostic criteria described earlier, individuals with MR vary according to the severity of intellectual impairments as well as unique strengths and liabilities within the realm of adaptive skills (Luckasson et al., 1992). For example, one individual with mild MR may exhibit impaired adaptive skills in the areas of functional academics and self-care whereas another individual with severe MR may show impairments across the entire range of adaptive areas.

Diagnostic heterogeneity is coupled with etiological heterogeneity. As noted above, MR is present in a number of disorders with varied etiologies and behavioral phenotypes (Moldavsky et al., 2001). In this section three of the most common syndromes associated with MR—Down syndrome, Fragile X, and fetal alcohol syndrome—are briefly described in order to illustrate the heterogeneity of cognitive and behavioral phenotypes present across individuals with MR. The following descriptions are brief, and the interested reader is referred to the appropriate references for more thorough discussion of each disorder.

Down Syndrome. Down syndrome is caused by the presence of extra genetic material from the 21st chromosome. Approximately 95% of individuals with Down syndrome have an extra 21st chromosome and are identified as having the "trisomy 21" subtype (Ramirez & Morgan, 1998). Approximately 3–4% of individuals with Down syndrome are classified as "translocation" subtypes, due to a portion of chromosome 21 being attached to other chromosomes. The "mosaicism" subtype of Down syndrome refers to the presence of normal and trisomic cells within the individual and occurs in about 1–2% of cases. Among others, common physical characteristics associated with Down syndrome include muscle hypotonia, flat facial profile, an upward slant to the eyes (i.e., oblique palpebral fissures), and hyperflexibility (Moldavsky et al., 2001; Ramirez & Morgan, 1998). Individuals with Down syndrome often suffer from moderate to severe MR, show expressive language delays with relative strengths in pragmatical versus grammatical language abilities, and exhibit relative strengths in visual over auditory/verbal memory (Chapman & Hesketh, 2000). Down syndrome is associated with a greater risk of developing a range of serious health problems, such as hearing deficits, heart defects, leukemia, hypothyroidism, and gastrointestinal disorders (Ramirez & Morgan, 1998). The stereotypic representation of individuals with Down syndrome is an affectionate child with an easy temperament. In general, individuals with Down syndrome show lower levels of maladaptive behaviors and psychiatric disorders when compared to peers with MR (Chapman & Hesketh, 2000). However, parents and teachers have reported higher rates of depression when compared to peers with MR, and more behavioral problems when compared to the general population (Chapman & Hesketh, 2000; Ramirez & Morgan, 1998).

Fragile X Syndrome. Fragile X syndrome is considered the most common form of inherited MR caused by an expanded repetition of the normally occurring CGG (cytosine/guanine/guanine) genetic sequence on the long arm of the X chromosome (Mazzocco, 2000). The abnormal genetic repetition inhibits the Fragile X MR-1 (FMR-1) gene from producing a protein that results in cognitive, affective, physical, and behavioral difficulties observed in Fragile X syndrome (Moldavsky et al., 2001). Full mutation (CGG repetitions of greater than 200) and premutation (CGG repetitions of about 50 to about 200) subtypes have been identified with the premutation subtype generally resulting in less severe symptoms. Although significant phenotypic variability exists within each group, in general, females are less affected than males (Mazzocco, 2000). The majority of males with Fragile X syndrome have MR compared to only 50% of females with the full mutation (Klaiman & Phelps, 1998). Characteristic physical features in boys with Fragile X include hyperextensible finger joints, flat feet, large ears, narrow face, and macroorchidism (i.e., enlarged testicles; Moldavsky et al., 2001). In general, the presence of physical characteristics is less prevalent in girls with Fragile X (Klaiman & Phelps, 1998). Males with Fragile X syndrome frequently exhibit social deficits ranging from autistic-like features (such as poor eye contact, stereotyped behavior, and perseverative speech), pragmatic language deficits, and social anxiety. Approximately 7–25% of children with Fragile X syndrome also meet criteria for autistic disorder (Mazzocco, 2000; Moldavsky et al., 2001). Boys with Fragile X syndrome frequently show sensory hypersensitivity across tactile, visual, and auditory channels. Hyperactivity and distractibility are also common with up to 70% of boys meeting full criteria for attention deficit hyperactivity disorder (Moldavsky et al., 2001). Females with Fragile X syndrome often show a pattern of shyness, social anxiety, poor eye contact, and social avoidance. Hyperactivity, inattention, and distractibility are frequently present in girls with Fragile X syndrome (Klaiman & Phelps, 1998).

Fetal Alcohol Syndromes. Prenatal exposure to alcohol can result in the presence of fetal alcohol syndrome or other disorders of less severity, such as partial fetal alcohol syndrome and alcohol-related neurodevelopmental disorder (Hagerman, 1999). Fetal alcohol syndrome is characterized by the presence of prenatal and/or postnatal growth delay, abnormalities of the face and head (e.g., microcephaly), and central nervous system dysfunction (Astley & Clarren, 2001b). The characteristic facial phenotype includes small eyes, smooth philtrum (i.e., indistinct groove between upper lip and nose), and a thin upper lip (see Astley & Clarren, 2001a). In addition to the physical features described above, children with fetal alcohol syndrome are more likely to suffer from chronic otitis media, visual problems (e.g., strabismus), cardiac problems, skeletal malformations, and immune system deficits (Smith & Graden, 1998). In addition to MR, children with fetal alcohol syndrome often exhibit problems with sustained attention, overactivity, and deficient social skills. Their conversational style has been characterized as active, overinquisitive, and intrusive (Smith & Graden, 1998). Adults with fetal alcohol syndrome show an increased risk for psychopathology and social problems, such as incarceration, attention deficit disorders, depression, alcohol and drug dependence, and suicide (Hagerman, 1999). It is unclear what contribution social factors play in these outcomes, as children with fetal alcohol syndrome may continue to reside with parents who continue to abuse alcohol.

Assessment

Intelligence and Adaptive Behavior. As outlined in the definition of MR, diagnosis requires documentation of significant subaverage performance on an individually administered test of intellectual ability, such as the WISC-III (Wechsler, 1991). Significant delays in adaptive behavior must also be documented across several domains. As with autism, the Vineland (Sparrow et al., 1984) is widely used to measure adaptive behavior in individuals with MR. Other measures include the American Association on Mental Retardation (AAMR) Adaptive Behavior Scales (Nihira, Leland, & Lambert, 1993) and the Scales of Independent Behavior, Revised (Bruininks, Woodcock, Weatherman, & Hill, 1996). The 1992 AAMR guidelines describe diagnosis of MR as the first step in a three-step process of appropriate assessment of an individual with MR. In addition to measuring intellectual functioning and adaptive skills across several areas, the AAMR recommends assessment of the individual's psychological functioning, physical health, and current environmental placement in order to provide the most appropriate level of support and intervention (Luckasson et al., 1992).

Psychological and Emotional Assessment. Individuals with MR can suffer from the full range of psychopathology, often at rates higher than reported in the general population (Luckasson et al., 1992); therefore, assessment of emotional functioning is essential. Historically, psychological disorders appear to have been underdiagnosed in individuals with MR due to *diagnostic overshadowing*, that is, the tendency to deemphasize behavioral disturbances associated with psychopathology due to the presence of MR (Luckasson et al., 1992). Psychological and emotional assessment of individuals with MR presents problems due to cognitive limitations and associated language delays; therefore, a focus on behavioral signs of mental illness as opposed to verbally reported symptoms is recommended. As with typically developing children, assessment of psychological functioning includes a parent or caregiver interview, interview with the individual with MR, and appropriate behavioral rating scales (Szymanski & King, 1999). A few measures of psychopathology exist for assessment of individuals with MR, such as the Reiss Scales (Reiss & Valenti-Hein, 1994).

Health, Physical, and Etiological Considerations. Assessment of physical health is important for making recommendations to improve adaptation. As illustrated earlier in the chapter, individuals with MR are at greater risk for developing a host of physical problems when contrasted with the general population, such as epilepsy, cerebral palsy, and cardiac abnormalities. The AAMR guidelines also assert that the assessment of physical health is important to establish the etiology of MR, if possible. Etiological information is important because it (1) increases professionals' awareness of associated health problems, (2) may lead to prescriptive intervention (e.g., dietary restriction for PKU), (3) helps to guide prevention efforts, and (4) allows for individuals to be grouped together for research, administrative, and clinical purposes (Luckasson et al., 1992).

Environmental Considerations. Aspects of the environment significantly influence behavioral adaptation in terms of facilitating or hindering independence, community integration, and overall well-being. For example, providing access to medical services improves an individual's physical health, and allowing an individual control of possessions improves independence and self-efficacy. For these reasons, the AAMR provides recommendations for the analysis of environments across educational programs, living environments, and employment settings (Luckasson et al., 1992). The purpose of the analysis is to identify factors within each environment that facilitate or inhibit adaptation. Incorporated within the context of other information, analysis of an individual's environment allows for the most appropriate recommendations for support systems and intervention.

Prevention and Intervention

Prevention. MR is not curable but can be prevented. Within the MR literature, the last four decades have seen an increase in prevention research, resulting in the discovery of new causes of MR, new methods of early diagnosis, and new modes of prevention (Alexander, 1998). Prevention of MR can now begin before conception. For example, new technology allows parents to be tested to determine if they are carrying a gene that might indicate a higher risk for their child developing MR or another developmental disability. While pregnant, there are several ways women can help prevent MR. Reducing risk by 50–75%, dietary supplementation of folic acid lowers the likelihood of neural tube defects, a cause of MR (Alexander, 1998). Early diagnosis with screening techniques, such as ultrasound imaging, amniocentesis, and maternal serum alpha-fetoprotien screening, allows parents to prepare for parenting a child with a disability or consider experimental treatment (Alexander, 1998). Blood tests conducted in the first few days after birth can detect diseases such as PKU and congenital hypothyroidism, both of which lead to the development of MR if left untreated. Regular immunizations for newborns and infants also have been associated with reduced prevalence rates of MR (Alexander, 1998).

When compared to medical risk factors, environmental and sociocultural contributions to MR are often more complex and difficult to alter. Within this realm, successful prevention efforts have been grounded in legal mandates and social policy. For example, a 98% decrease in rates of MR due to lead poisoning has been associated with legislation limiting the use of lead in items such as paint and gasoline (Alexander, 1998). Legislation requiring seat belt use, airbags, and bike helmets also has been associated with reductions in the incidence of MR due to head injury (Alexander, 1998).

Lack of stimulation contributes to diminished brain development and poor cognitive functioning in individuals (Alexander, 1998). Provision of an enriched and stimulating environment has been shown to reduce the risk of poor cognitive development, particularly within the first 5 years of life, a crucial developmental period for children (Alexander, 1998; Guralnick, 1998). Early intervention programs such as Head Start appear to provide young children with a stimulating environment for improved cognitive development. Research suggests that intervention programs that provide greater amounts of intensive and direct individualized services to children appear to have the greatest benefits in altering the child's earlier experiences (Ramey & Ramey, 1999).

Behavioral Intervention. The predominant approach to treating children and adults with MR involves the use of behavioral methods to increase adaptive skills and decrease maladaptive behaviors. Behavioral techniques, such as task analysis, shaping, chaining, and prompting, are frequently used in combination to teach adaptive skills in a systematic manner (Miltenberger, 2001). Once adaptive skills are reliably performed within one setting, intervention focuses on teaching the individual to perform the skills in other settings, a process known as generalization. Within educational settings, up to 15% of individuals with MR exhibit problem behaviors such as self-injury, self-stimulation, and/or aggression (Emerson et al., 2001). Reviews have indicated that problem behaviors can be reduced significantly through behavioral intervention, with positive and punishment-based interventions producing equivalent results (Scotti, Evans, Meyer, & Walker, 1991). Behavioral interventions that include a functional analysis and attempt to generalize behavioral changes result in improved treatment outcomes (Scotti et al., 1991).

Psychopharmacological Intervention. Similar to psychotropic treatment in autism, a wide range of psychopharmacological agents has been used to manage cognitive, behavioral, and psychiatric difficulties in individuals with MR. In the case of Fragile X, for example, stimulants, selective serotonin reuptake inhibitors (SSRIs), mood stabilizers, and atypical antipsychotics have been used to treat symptoms of hyperactivity, anxiety, agitation, and aggression (Hagerman, 1999). Similar guidelines have been offered in the management of behavioral difficulties in individuals with other causes of MR, such as fetal alcohol syndrome. At present, significant overlap exists in the psychopharmacological treatment recommendations across syndromes; however, identification of "psychopharmacological phenotypes" has been identified as a future goal within psychiatry (Hagerman, 1999). Successful psychopharmacological phenotyping would lead to the use of medications that work best for various syndromes. Controlled research examining the clinical efficacy of the use of psychotropic medications with individuals with MR is lacking (e.g., Hagerman, 1999) and has resulted in critical reviews regarding the use of psychotropic medications with individuals with MR (e.g., Matson et al., 2000).

Outcomes

Employment. Employment opportunities for individuals with MR have grown within the last few decades because of federal policies, such as the Americans with Disabilities Act (ADA), that promote employment for individuals with disabilities and prohibit discrimination (McDermott, Martin, & Butkus, 1999). After the ADA was passed, Blanck (1998) found that the employment rate for individuals with MR rose 2% from 1986 to 1991, and approximately 30–40% of adults with MR were employed in 1994 and 1995. McDermott et al. (1999) found that 10% of individuals with MR were employed, working in grocery stores, fast food restaurants, large department stores, and other service settings, earning about $105 per week, on average.

In the past, individuals with MR typically began to work in sheltered workshops soon after high school, learning skills consistent with remaining on task and maintaining stamina (McDermott et al., 1999). As a result of sheltered workshops being highly structured and overprotective, skills learned in the workshop transferred little to other job situations (Kiernan, 2000). The sheltered workshop did not allow the worker to become self-sufficient or develop peer networks with people other than those with a disability. The restrictions associated with sheltered workshops led to the development of supported employment opportunities. Supported employment involves placing individuals with MR in real job settings with a range of supports, such as on-site training (McDermott et al., 1999). Seventy percent of the individuals in supported employment settings have been diagnosed with MR (Mank, Cioffi, & Yovanoff, 1997).

Living. In 1998, there were approximately 3.24 million people with MR and other developmental disabilities living in the United States, about 1.2% of the population (Braddock, Emerson, Felce, & Stancliffe, 2001). Of this population, 13% were living in supervised residential services, 60% were living with family caregivers, 13% were living on their own, and 15% were living with a spouse (Braddock et al., 2001). The deinstitutionalization movement, which advocated the closing of numerous state-funded mental hospitals in order to integrate patients into the community, resulted in an expansion of community-based services. Lakin, Prouty, Polister, and Anderson (2000) found that as of June 1999, three fourths of individuals with MR and other developmental disorders were living in residential facilities of 15 or fewer occupants.

The Independent Living Movement (ILM) has also had an impact on the living situations of individuals with MR (Keigher, 2000). The goal of the ILM movement is to maximize independence and self-sufficiency for individuals with MR and other disabilities (Keigher, 2000). With an emphasis on increasing independence, the ILM movement espouses the belief that persons with disabilities should contribute to making important decisions about work and living arrangements with the help of family and friends, if necessary.

Mortality. Researchers have found that mortality rates among individuals with MR increase with the severity of their disabilities and disabling conditions (Hayden, 1998). Respiratory diseases are among the most common causes of death for people with MR (Chaney & Eyman, 2000; Hayden, 1998). The best predictor for developing respiratory difficulties in individuals with MR is nonambulation. The three most common causes of death among individuals with MR are cardiovascular disease, respiratory disease, and neoplasms (i.e., a new growth of tissue serving no physiological function), affecting men and women equally (Patja, Molsa, & Iivanainen, 2001). Researchers have concluded that health promotion in the community to fight and prevent infections and cardiac disease is crucial in reducing these causes of death for people with MR. Suicide has been found to be a rare occurrence among people with MR in comparison to the general population (Patja, Iivanainen, Raitasuo, & Lonnqvist, 2001). On average, individuals with MR commit suicide at a rate that is 33% lower than that of the general population; however, the risk factors are similar for both groups. Similar to adults in the general population who commit suicide, most individuals with MR who commit suicide suffer from untreated depression and poor social support (Patja, Iivanainen et al., 2001).

School-Related Issues

IDEA Guidelines and Individualized Education Program. The reauthorization of the Individuals with Disabilities Education Act (IDEA, 1997) continued legal mandates designed to improve education for children with disabilities. IDEA requires educational systems to set educational goals and standards consistent with those of children without disabilities, to the appropriate extent (Autin, 1999). The IDEA also mandates that children with disabilities be educated in the least restrictive environment with appropriate educational supports. In addition, children with MR are entitled to equal opportunity for participation in extracurricular activities, such as recreation, groups, counseling services, and athletics. According to IDEA guidelines, public educators must have a statement of transition needs established for children with disabilities by the age of 14 for the purposes of transition from school to community living (Patton, Polloway, & Smith, 2000).

The IDEA mandates that every student with MR have an Individualized Education Program (IEP). The IEP is created by a multidisciplinary team composed of educational professionals, parents or guardians, and the individual with MR, if possible. The team evaluates the strengths and weaknesses of the student and establishes formal educational goals and objectives within the IEP. IDEA guidelines identify six elements that should be included in an IEP: (1) levels of performance, (2) annual goals, (3) short-term objectives, (4) specific special education and other services to be provided and the amount of time spent in general classrooms, (5) projected dates of beginning the program and the duration of services needed, and (6) criteria and schedules for determining goal achievement (Thomas, 1996). Essential information, such as findings from formal assessments and medical conditions, should be retained in an individual's IEP as goals and objectives are revised by the team.

Inclusion. Inclusion, the practice of educating children with special needs within general classroom settings, is a controversial educational practice. Research reports and expert opinions differ regarding the benefits and risks of the inclusion model for educating children with special needs and typically developing peers. Chesley and Calaluce (1997) argued that inclusive educational practices may not focus on teaching necessary functional and vocational skills to individuals with MR. For normally functioning children, functional and vocational skills do not require formal educational intervention; therefore, integrating such curriculum into general classroom education does not benefit typically developing peers. Rather than advocating for immediate inclusion, Chesley and Calaluce (1997) argued that children with MR benefit most from early intensive training in more restrictive settings prior to placement in inclusive settings. The authors acknowledged the potential social benefits of inclusion for children with MR, such as improving social skills; however, they emphasized that cognitive and vocational preparation should not be sacrificed for this social interaction.

The position against inclusion is countered by recent research findings that demonstrate the benefits of inclusion. For example, children with MR placed in inclusive classrooms showed better social and academic attainment over children with MR in special education classes (Freeman & Alkin, 2000). In addition, complete integration of students with MR has been found to be more beneficial than partial integration in the domains of social and academic attainment (Freeman & Alkin). These authors suggest that improvement in social competence was the result of increased opportunity to interact with typical peers. Freeman and Alkin (2000) concluded that although children with MR might not reach the social and academic attainment of typically developing peers, inclusion can be more beneficial than traditional special education.

Successful inclusion of children with MR into general classrooms depends on a variety of factors, including class size, selection of appropriate curriculum, and the provision of needed assistance in the classroom (Demchak, 1997). A large group format for instruction is often not beneficial for children with MR due to their academic limitations when compared to their typical peers. Therefore, tailoring curriculum to the needs of children with MR is essential for inclusion to be beneficial.

Curriculum. Curriculum developed for individuals with MR should be based on the individual needs of the student and tailored to his or her unique abilities, cognitive strengths, and personal goals (Luckasson et al., 1992). Most programs with formal curricula designed for students with MR focus on increasing life skills and planning for future community living within the context of community-based instruction (Thomas, 1996). Although most curricula designed for students with MR share similar goals, such as increasing communication and/or leisure skills, meaningful differences exist. Hickson, Blackman, and Reis (1995) described curriculum for students with MR as either developmental or functional. Developmental curriculum focuses on the elements, standards, and sequence of typical development. In the developmental model, curriculum is designed to remediate undeveloped skills of children with MR. For example, developmental intervention for delays in speech and language functioning might focus on the remediation of basic skills needed for communication, such as improved articulation. In contrast, functional curriculum focuses on the essential skills needed for independent living for individuals with MR. For example, functional intervention might target improvement of adaptive areas, such as ordering meals or telephone skills, without improving basic deficits in speech and language functioning. It is important to note that developmental and functional curriculum can be combined and used together for teaching and instruction.

CONCLUSIONS

This chapter provided an overview of developmental disabilities that psychologists are likely to encounter in school settings. Despite improved understanding of the causal mechanisms involved in the etiology of autism, PDD, and MR, no curative treatments exist. However, early assessment techniques have improved our ability to detect cognitive and social delays in toddlerhood, thus allowing for the implementation of early intervention services for children with autism spectrum disorders and MR. After diagnosis, children with autism spectrum disorders and MR are best served within the context of an array of coordinated services, including professionals working within the school system. As school systems provide an increasing amount of services for children with autism spectrum disorders and MR, psychologists working in school settings are likely to find expanded opportunities to provide assessment, intervention, and consultation services to these children and their families.

When working with children with autism, PDD, and/or MR it is important to remember that these children vary widely with respect to their cognitive abilities, adaptive skills, social interests, and social relatedness. In our opinion, children with autism, PDD, and/or MR will be best served by psychologists who: (1) tailor interventions based on the strengths of the child, (2) assist in advocating on behalf of the child's needs, and (3) help school professionals and family members plan for the child's future. Psychologists who assist families with establishing a diagnosis and securing services as early as possible provide children with autism spectrum disorders and MR the best opportunity for optimal adjustment in the future.

REFERENCES

Adrien, J. L., Martineau, J., Barthelemy, C., Bruneau, N., Garreau, B., & Savage, D. (1995). Disorders of regulation of cognitive activity in children with autism. *Journal of Autism and Developmental Disorders, 25*, 249–263.

Alexander, D. (1998). Prevention of mental retardation: Four decades of research. *Mental Retardation and Developmental Disabilities, 4*, 50–58.

Alpern, G. D. (1967). Measurement of "untestable" autistic children. *Journal of Abnormal Psychology, 72*, 278–296.

American Psychiatric Association. (2000). *Diagnostic and statistical manual of mental disorders* (4th ed.-Text Revision). Washington, D.C.: American Psychiatric Association.

Asperger, H. (1944). Die "autistichen psychopathen" in Kindesalter. *Archiv fur Psychiatrie and Nervenkrankheiten, 117*, 76–136.

Astley, S. J., & Clarren, S. K. (2001a). FAS DPN Image Analysis laboratory: Overview [Online]. Retrieved September 7, 2001, from University of Washington, Fetal Alcohol Syndrome Diagnostic and Prevention Network Web site. Available: http://depts.washington.edu/fasdpn/imganalysis.html

Astley, S. J., & Clarren, S. K. (2001b). Measuring the facial phenotype of individuals with prenatal alcohol exposures: Correlations with brain dysfunction.[Electronic version]. *Alcohol and Alcoholism, 36*, 147–159.

Autin, D. (1999). Inclusion and the new IDEA. *The Exceptional Parent, 29*, 66–68.

Bailey, A., Le Couteur, A., Gottesman, I., Bolton, P., Simonoff, E., Yuzda, E., et al. (1995). Autism as a strongly genetic disorder: Evidence from a British twin study. *Psychological Medicine, 25*, 63–77.

Baron-Cohen, S., Allen, C., & Gillberg, C. (1992). Can autism be diagnosed at 18 months? The needle, the haystack, and the CHAT. *British Journal of Psychiatry, 161*, 839–843.

Baron-Cohen, S., Leslie, A. M., & Frith, U. (1985). Does the autistic child have a theory of mind? *Cognition, 21*, 37–46.

Bayley, N. (1993). *Bayley scales of infant development* (2nd ed.). San Antonio: Psychological Corporation.

Bettelheim, B. (1967). *The empty fortress: Infantile autism and the birth of self.* New York: The Free Press.

Bieberich, A., & Morgan, S. B. (1998). Affective expression in children with autism or Down syndrome. *Journal of Autism and Developmental Disorders, 28*, 333–338.

Blanck, P. (1998). *The Americans with Disabilities Act and the emerging workforce: Employment of people with mental retardation*. Washington, D.C.: American Association on Mental Retardation.

Braddock, D., Emerson, E., Felce, D., & Stancliffe, R. J. (2001). Living circumstances of children and adults with mental retardation or developmental disabilities in the United States, Canada, England and Wales, and Australia. *Mental Retardation and Developmental Disabilities Research Reviews, 7*, 115–121.

Bruininks, R. H., Woodcock, R. W., Weatherman, R. F., & Hill, B. K. (1996). *Scales of independent behavior, Revised.* Chicago, IL: Riverside Publishing Company.

Campbell, J. M., & Morgan, S. B. (1998). Asperger's disorder. In L. Phelps (Ed.), *Health-related disorders in children and adolescents* (pp. 68–73). Washington, D.C.: American Psychological Association.

Campbell, M., Green, W. H., & Deutsch, S. I. (1985). *Child and adolescent psychopharmacology*. Beverly Hills, CA: Sage.

Carpentieri, S., & Morgan, S. B. (1994). Patterns of cognitive functioning on the Stanford-Binet, Fourth Edition: A comparison of autistic and retarded children. *Journal of Autism and Developmental Disorders, 24*, 215–223.

Carpentieri, S., & Morgan, S. B. (1996). Adaptive and intellectual functioning in autistic and non-autistic retarded children. *Journal of Autism and Developmental Disorders, 26*, 611–620.

Carter, A. S., Volkmar, F. R., Sparrow, S. S., Wang, J., Lord, C., Dawson, G., et al. (1998). The Vineland adaptive behavior scales: Supplementary norms for individuals with autism. *Journal of Autism and Developmental Disorders, 28*, 287–302.

Chakrabarti, S., & Fombonne, E. (2001). Pervasive developmental disorders in preschool children. *Journal of the American Medical Association, 285*, 3093–3099.

Chaney, R. H., & Eyman, R. K. (2000). Patterns of mortality over 60 years among persons with mental retardation in a residential facility. *Mental Retardation, 38*, 289–293.

Chapman, R. S., & Hesketh, L. J. (2000). Behavioral phenotype of individuals with Down syndrome. *Mental Retardation and Developmental Disabilities Research Reviews, 6*, 84–95.

Chesley, G. M., & Calaluce, P. D. (1997). The deception of inclusion. *Mental Retardation, 35*, 488–490.

Chez, M. G., Buchanan, C. P., Bagan, P. T., Hammer, M. S., McCarthy, K. S., Ovrutskaya, I., et al. (2000). Secretin and autism: A two-part clinical investigation. *Journal of Autism and Developmental Disorders, 30*, 87–94.

Courchesne, E. (1995). Infantile autism. Part 1: MR imaging abnormalities and their neurobehavioral correlates. *International Pediatrics, 10*, 141–154.

Demchak, M. (1997). *Teaching students with severe disabilities in inclusive settings*. Washington, D.C.: American Association on Mental Retardation.

DeMyer, M. K., Barton, S., DeMyer, W. E., Morton, J. A., Allen, J., & Steele, R. (1973). Prognosis in autism: A follow-up study. *Journal of Autism and Childhood Schizophrenia, 3*, 109–128.

DeMyer, M. K., Hingtgen, J. N., & Jackson, R. K. (1981). Infantile autism reviewed: A decade of research. *Schizophrenia Bulletin, 7*, 388–451.

Dykens, E. M., & Volkmar, F. R. (1997). Medical conditions associated with autism. In D. J. Cohen & F. R. Volkmar (Eds.), *Handbook of autism and pervasive developmental disorders* (2nd ed.; pp. 388–410). New York: Wiley.

Emerson, E., Kiernan, C., Alborz, A., Reeves, D., Mason, H., Swarbrick, R., et al. (2001). The prevalence of challenging behaviors: A total population study. *Research in Developmental Disabilities, 22*, 77–93.

Flint, J., & Wilkie, A. O. M. (1996). The genetics of mental retardation. *British Medical Bulletin, 52*, 453–464.

Freeman, S. F., & Alkin, M. C. (2000). Academic and social attainment of children with mental retardation in general education and special education settings. *Remedial and Special Education, 21*, 3–18.

Guralnick, M. J. (1998). Effectiveness of early intervention for vulnerable children: A developmental perspective. *American Journal on Mental Retardation, 102*, 319–345.

Hagerman, R. J. (1999). Psychopharmacological interventions in Fragile X syndrome, fetal alcohol syndrome, Prader-Willi syndrome, Angelman syndrome, Smith-Magenis syndrome, and velocariofacial syndrome. *Mental Retardation and Developmental Disabilities Research Reviews, 5*, 305–313.

Hayden, M. F. (1998). Mortality among people with mental retardation living in the United States: Research review and policy application. *Mental Retardation, 36*, 345–359.

Hickson, L., Blackman, L. S., & Reis, E. M. (1995). *Mental retardation: Foundations of educational programming.* Boston: Allyn and Bacon.

Individuals with Disabilities Education Act Amendments of 1997, Public Law 105-17, 20 U.S.C. Chapter 33, Section 1415 et seq. (EDLAW, 1997).

Iwanaga, R., Kawasaki, C., & Tsuchida, R. (2000). Brief report: Comparison of sensory-motor and cognitive function between autism and Asperger syndrome in preschool children. *Journal of Autism and Developmental Disorders, 30*, 169–174.

Kanner, L. (1943). Autistic disturbances of affective contact. *Nervous Child, 2*, 217–250.

Kanner, L., Rodriguez, A., & Ashenden, B. (1972). How far can autistic children go in matters of social adaptation? *Journal of Autism and Childhood Schizophrenia, 2*, 9–33.

Keigher, S. (2000). Emerging issues in mental retardation: Self-determination versus self-interest. *Health and Social Work, 25*, 163–168.

Kiernan, W. (2000). Where we are now: Perspectives on employment of persons with mental retardation. *Focus on Autism and Other Developmental Disabilities, 15*, 90–96.

Klaiman, R. S., & Phelps, L. (1998). Fragile X syndrome. In L. Phelps (Ed.), *Health-related disorders in children and adolescents* (pp. 299–308). Washington, D.C.: American Psychological Association.

Klin, A., Volkmar, F. K., & Sparrow, S. S. (Eds.). (2000). *Asperger syndrome*. New York: Guilford.

Koegel, R. L., & Koegel, L. K. (1996). *Teaching children with autism: Strategies for initiating positive interactions and improving learning opportunities*. Baltimore: Paul H. Brookes.

Koegel, R. L., Koegel, L. K., & McNerney, E. K. (2001). Pivotal areas in intervention for autism. *Journal of Clinical Child Psychology, 30*, 19–32.

Lakin, K. C., Prouty, R., Polister, B., & Anderson, L. (2000). Over three quarters of all residential service recipients in community settings as of June 1999. *Mental Retardation, 38*, 378–379.

Lord, C., Risi, S., Lambrecht, L., Cook, E. H., Leventhal, B. L., DiLavore, P. C., et al.(2000). The autism diagnostic observation schedule-generic: A standard measure of social and communication deficits associated with the spectrum of autism. *Journal of Autism and Developmental Disorders, 30*, 205–223.

Lord, C., Rutter, M., & Le Couteur, A. (1994). Autism diagnostic interview-revised: A revised version of a diagnostic interview for caregivers of individuals with possible pervasive developmental disorders. *Journal of Autism and Developmental Disorders, 24*, 659–685.

Lord, C., & Schopler, E. (1987). Neurobiological implications of sex differences in autism. In E. Schopler & G. B. Mesibov (Eds.), *Neurobiological issues in autism* (pp. 191–211). New York: Plenum.

Lotter, V. (1978). Follow-up studies. In M. Rutter & E. Schopler (Eds.), *Autism: A reappraisal of concepts and treatment* (pp. 475–505). New York: Plenum.

Lovaas, O. I. (1981). *Teaching developmentally disabled children: The me book*. Austin, TX: Pro-Ed.

Lovaas, O. I. (1987). Behavioral treatment and normal educational and intellectual functioning in young autistic children. *Journal of Consulting and Clinical Psychology, 55*, 3–9.

Lovaas, O. I., Schreibman, L., Koegel, R., & Rehm, R. (1971). Selective responding by autistic children to multiple sensory input. *Journal of Abnormal Psychology, 77*, 211–222.

Luckasson, R., Coulter, D. L., Polloway, E. A., Reiss, S., Schalock, R. L., Snell, M. E., et al. (Eds.). (1992). *Mental retardation: Definitions, classification, and systems of support*. Washington, D.C.: American Association on Mental Retardation.

Mank, D., Cioffi, A., & Yovanoff, P. (1997). Analysis of the typicalness of supported employment jobs, natural supports, and wage and integration outcomes. *Mental Retardation, 35*, 185–197.

Matson, J. L., Bamburg, J. W., Mayville, E. A., Pinkston, J., Bielecki, J., Kuhn, D., et al. (2000). Psychopharmacology and mental retardation: A 10-year review (1990–1999). *Research in Developmental Disabilities, 21*, 263–296.

Mazzocco, M. M. (2000). Advances in research on the Fragile X syndrome. *Mental Retardation and Developmental Disabilities Research Reviews, 6*, 96–106.

McDermott, S., Martin, M., & Butkus, S. (1999). What individual, provider, and community characteristics predict employment of individuals with mental retardation? *American Journal on Mental Retardation, 104*, 346–355.

McEachlin, J. J., Smith, T., & Lovaas, O. I. (1993). Long-term outcome for children with autism who received early intensive behavioral treatment. *American Journal on Mental Retardation, 97*, 359–372.

McEvoy, R. E., Rogers, S. J., & Pennington, B. F. (1993). Executive function and social communication deficits in young autistic children. *Journal of Child Psychology and Psychiatry, 34*, 563–578.

Mesibov, G. B., Adams, L. W., & Klinger, L. G. (1997). *Autism: Understanding the disorder*. New York: Plenum.

Mesibov, G., Schopler, E., Schaffer, B., & Landrus, R. (1988). *Individualized assessment and treatment for autistic and developmentally disabled children: Vol. 4. The Adolescent and Adult Psychoeducational Profile (AAPEP)*. Austin, TX: Pro-Ed.

Miltenberger, R. C. (2001). *Behavior modification: Principles and procedures* (2nd ed.). Belmont, CA: Wadsworth/Thomson Learning.

Moldavsky, M., Lev, D., & Lerman-Sagie, T. (2001). Behavioral phenotypes of genetic syndromes: A reference guide for psychiatrists. *Journal of the American Academy of Child and Adolescent Psychiatry, 40*, 749–761.

Morgan, S. B. (1984). Helping parents understand the diagnosis of autism. *Journal of Developmental and Behavioral Pediatrics, 5*, 78–85.

Morgan, S. (1988a). Diagnostic assessment of autism: A review of objective scales. *Journal of Psychoeducational Assessment, 6*, 139–151.

Morgan, S. B. (1988b). The autistic child and family functioning: A developmental-family systems perspective. *Journal of Autism and Developmental Disorders, 18*, 263–280.

Morgan, S. B. (1990). Early childhood autism: Current perspectives on definition, assessment, and treatment. In S. B. Morgan & T. M. Okwumabua (Eds.), *Child and adolescent disorders: Developmental and health psychology perspectives* (pp. 3–45). Hillsdale, NJ: Lawrence Erlbaum Associates.

Murphy, C. C., Boyle, C., Schendel, D., Decoufle, P., & Yeargin-Allsopp, M. (1998). Epidemiology of mental retardation in children. *Mental Retardation and Developmental Disabilities Research Reviews, 4*, 6–13.

Nihira, K., Leland, H., & Lambert, N. (1993). *AAMR adaptive behavior scale, residential and community, second edition.* Austin, TX: PRO-ED.

Ornitz, E. M., & Ritvo, E. R. (1976). The syndrome of autism: A critical review. *American Journal of Psychiatry, 133*, 609–621.

Ozonoff, S., & McEvoy, R. (1994). A longitudinal study of executive function and theory of mind development in autism. *Development and Psychopathology, 6*, 415–431.

Patja, K., Iivanainen, M., Raitasuo, S., Lonnqvist, J. (2001). Suicide mortality in mental retardation: A 35-year follow-up study. *Acta Psychiatrica Scandinavica, 103*, 307–311.

Patja, K., Molsa, P., & Iivanainen, M. (2001). Cause-specific mortality of people with intellectual disability in a population-based, 35-year follow-up study. *Journal of Intellectual Disability Research, 45*, 30–40.

Patton, J. R., Polloway, E. A., & Smith, T. E. (2000). Educating students with mild mental retardation. *Focus on Autism and Other Developmental Disabilities, 15*, 80–89.

Ramey, S. L., & Ramey, C. T. (1999). Early experience and early intervention for children "at risk" for developmental delay and mental retardation. *Mental Retardation and Developmental Disabilities, 5*, 1–10.

Ramirez, S. Z., & Morgan, V. (1998). Down syndrome. In L. Phelps (Ed.), *Health-related disorders in children and adolescents* (pp. 68–73). Washington, D.C.: American Psychological Association.

Reiss, S., & Valenti-Hein, D. (1994). Development of a psychopathology rating scale for children with mental retardation. *Journal of Consulting and Clinical Psychology, 62*, 28–33.

Ritvo, E. R., & Freeman, B. J. (1977). National Society for Autistic Children definition of the syndrome of autism. *Journal of Pediatric Psychology, 2*, 146–148.

Roelveld, N., Zielhuis, G. A., & Gabreëls, F. (1997). The prevalence of mental retardation: A critical review of recent literature. *Developmental Medicine and Child Neurology, 39*, 125–132.

Rogers, S. J. (1998). Empirically supported comprehensive treatments for young children with autism. *Journal of Clinical Child Psychology, 27*, 168–179.

Roid, G., & Miller, L. (1997). *Leiter international performance scale-revised.* Wood Dale, IL: Stoelting.

Rutter, M., Greenfeld, D., & Lockyer, L. (1967). A five to fifteen year follow-up study of infantile psychosis: II. Social and behavioral outcome. *British Journal of Psychiatry, 113*, 1183–1189.

Rutter, M., & Lockyer, L. (1967). A five to fifteen year follow-up study of infantile psychosis. I. Description of the sample. *British Journal of Psychiatry, 113*, 1169–1182.

Rutter, M., & Schopler, E. (1987). Autism and pervasive developmental disorders: Concepts and diagnostic issues. *Journal of Autism and Developmental Disorders, 17*, 159–188.

Sanders, J. L., & Morgan, S. B. (1997). Family stress and adjustment as perceived by parents of children with autism or Down syndrome: Implications for intervention. *Child and Family Behavior Therapy, 19*, 15–32.

Schopler, E. (1998). Prevention and management of behavior problems: The TEACCH approach. In E. Sanavio (Ed.), *Behaviour and cognitive therapy today: Essays in honour of Hans Eysenck.* Amsterdam: Elsevier Science.

Schopler, E., & Mesibov, G. (Eds.). (1983). *Autism in adolescents and adults.* New York: Plenum.

Schopler, E., Mesibov, G., & Kunce, L. J. (Eds.). (1998). *Asperger syndrome or high-functioning autism?* New York: Plenum.

Schopler, E., Reichler, R. J., Bashford, A., Lansing, M., & Marcus, L. (1990). *Individualized assessment and treatment for autistic and developmentally disabled children: Vol. 1. The psychoeducational profile-revised (PEP-R).* Austin, TX: Pro-Ed.

Schopler, E., Reichler, R. J., & Renner, B. R. (1988). *The childhood autism rating scale (CARS).* Los Angeles: Western Psychological Services.

Schreibman, L. (1988). *Autism.* Beverly Hills: Sage.

Schreibman, L. (2000). Intensive behavioral/psychoeducational treatments for autism: Research needs and future directions. *Journal of Autism and Developmental Disorders, 30*, 373–378.

Scotti, J. R., Evans, I. M., Meyer, L. H., & Walker, P. (1991). A meta-analysis of intervention research with problem behavior: Treatment validity and standards of practice. *American Journal on Mental Retardation, 96*, 233–256.

Smith, J. J., & Graden, J. L. (1998). Fetal alcohol syndrome. In L. Phelps (Ed.), *Health-related disorders in children and adolescents* (pp. 68–73). Washington, D.C.: American Psychological Association.

Sparrow, S. S., Balla, D. A., & Cicchetti, D. V. (1984). *Vineland adaptive behavior scales, interview edition, survey form manual.* Circle Pines, MN: American Guidance Service.

Stone, W. L., Coonrod, E. E., & Ousley, O. Y. (2000). Brief report: Screening tool for autism in two-year-olds (STAT): Development and preliminary data. *Journal of Autism and Developmental Disorders, 30*, 607–612.

Stone, W. L., & Hogan, K. L. (1993). A structured parent interview for identifying young children with autism. *Journal of Autism and Developmental Disorders, 23*, 639–652.

Szatmari, P., Bryson, S. E., Streiner, D. L., Wilson, F., Archer, L., & Ryerse, C. (2000). Two-year outcome of preschool children with autism or Asperger's syndrome. *American Journal of Psychiatry, 157*, 1980–1987.

Szymanski, L., & King, B. H. (1999). Practice parameters for the assessment and treatment of children, adolescents, and adults with mental retardation and comorbid mental disorders. *Journal of the American Academy of Child and Adolescent Psychiatry, 38, Supplement*, 5S–31S.

Thomas, G. E. (1996). *Teaching students with mental retardation: A life goal curriculum planning approach.* Englewood Cliffs, NJ: Merrill.

Thorndike, R. L., Hagen, E. P., & Sattler, J. M. (1986). *Guide for administering and scoring for the Stanford-Binet intelligence scale* (4th ed.). Chicago: Riverside Publishing.

Towbin, K. F. (1997). Pervasive developmental disorder not otherwise specified. In D. J. Cohen & F. R. Volkmar (Eds.), *Handbook of autism and pervasive developmental disorders* (2nd ed.; pp.123–147). New York: Wiley.

Treffert, D. A. (1988). The idiot savant: A review of the syndrome. *American Journal of Psychiatry, 145*, 563–572.

Van Acker, R. (1997). Rett's syndrome: A pervasive developmental disorder. In D. J. Cohen & F. R. Volkmar (Eds.), *Handbook of autism and pervasive developmental disorders* (2nd ed.; pp. 60–93). New York: Wiley.

Volkmar, F. R. (2001). Pharmacological interventions in autism: Theoretical and practical issues. *Journal of Clinical Child Psychology, 30*, 80–87.

Volkmar, F., Klin, A., Marans, W., & Cohen, D. J. (1997). Childhood disintegrative disorder. In D. J. Cohen & F. R. Volkmar (Eds.), *Handbook of autism and pervasive developmental disorders* (2nd ed.; pp. 47–59). New York: Wiley.

Wechsler, D. (1991). *Manual for the Wechsler intelligence scale for children-third edition.* San Antonio: The Psychological Corporation.

Wilhelm, H., & Lovaas, O. I. (1976). Stimulus overselectivity: A common feature in autism and mental retardation. *American Journal of Mental Deficiency, 81*, 26–31.

24

School-Related Issues in Child Abuse and Neglect

Rochelle F. Hanson
Daniel W. Smith
Adrienne Fricker-Elhai
Medical University of South Carolina

Child maltreatment, which typically includes sexual abuse, physical abuse, neglect, and emotional abuse, is highly prevalent in our society. Over the past two decades, a great deal of research and public attention has been focused on trying to determine the prevalence of maltreatment, ways to identify potential perpetrators, strategies to prevent or reduce the risk of child abuse, and interventions for children who have suffered abuse. School psychologists and educators are in a unique position to identify children who may be at risk and/or have experienced child abuse. They can also play an important role in ameliorating the potentially damaging long-term effects of child maltreatment. Since most children attend school (with the exception of home-schooled children) during the majority of their waking hours, educators and school psychologists probably spend more time with children than any other adult in their lives. As a result, educators and school psychologists share the responsibility for ensuring the safety and well-being of children and are forced into the sometimes unwelcome role of identifying and intervening in the lives of children who experience child abuse. The purpose of this chapter is to provide information on child maltreatment so that educators and school psychologists can become more fully aware of the scope and magnitude of child maltreatment. Hopefully, this information will serve as a useful resource and will assist educators and school psychologists in identifying children who experience maltreatment, perhaps prevent children from being abused, and enable educators and school psychologists to refer children for appropriate services. The first section of the chapter focuses on prevalence of child maltreatment, followed by a discussion on the effects associated with the different types of child abuse. The third section provides an overview of school-based abuse prevention programs, followed by a discussion on issues related to the mandated reporting of child maltreatment.

PREVALENCE OF CHILD MALTREATMENT

It is quite difficult to obtain an accurate rate for the prevalence of child maltreatment, and it is important to underscore the point that any prevalence rate is likely to be an underestimate. There are three primary reasons for this difficulty: (1) a reliance on cases reported to the police or child protection agencies; (2) a tendency for some researchers and agencies to combine across types of child maltreatment, making it difficult to determine separate prevalence rates for physical abuse, sexual abuse, or neglect; and (3) differences in definitions of child maltreatment.

Child Sexual Abuse (CSA)

Prevalence rates provided by agencies, such as child protection or law enforcement, are based on reported cases. The reality, however, is that only a small percentage of sexual abuse cases are ever reported (Kilpatrick, Edmunds, & Seymour, 1992), and this is even more true for CSA cases (Hanson, Resnick, Saunders, Kilpatrick, & Best, 1999). Thus, these rates are likely to be underestimates of the true prevalence of CSA. To compound the problem further, some child protection agencies report rates based on the family as a unit, rather than the number of children within the family who experienced CSA, yielding a lower prevalence rate (McCurdy & Daro, 1994).

In addition to problems with the source of the report, underestimates of CSA are likely because of the fact that few children actually disclose their sexual abuse; thus, many cases remain undetected (Smith et al., 2000). Reasons for not reporting CSA include fear of not being believed, fear of being punished, and/or feelings of shame (Roesler & Wind, 1994; Sauzier, 1989). Relatedly, because of the typical patterns of disclosure observed among sexually abused children, it is likely that some "true" cases of CSA are unfounded by child protection agencies. More specifically, Sorenson and Snow (1991) demonstrated that it is not uncommon for children initially to deny their abuse and then make a tentative disclosure (i.e., "testing the waters"), before ever making a full disclosure. Additionally, recantation of the abuse is not unusual. Although neither initial denial, tentative disclosures, nor recantation indicate that the abuse did not occur, these cases are likely to be unfounded by child protection. Since this disclosure pattern is not uncommon, it contributes to an underestimate of CSA.

In addition to these problems associated with disclosure, differences in the definitions used by researchers and child protection and police agencies also contribute to the difficulties in arriving at a reliable, valid prevalence rate. For example, some research groups combine all child sexual abuse into one overall category, whereas others differentiate between contact (e.g., molestation, penetration assaults) and noncontact (e.g., exposure to pornography, exhibitionism) sexual abuse. These two different strategies for classifying sexual abuse undoubtedly contribute to different prevalence rates. One other definitional issue concerns the age of the victim versus the perpetrator. One of the most commonly used definitions for sexual abuse requires that the perpetrator be at least 5 years older than the victim (Browne & Finkelhor, 1986), thus eliminating abuse by peers as a form of CSA. However, since not everyone relies on this age differential, there is variability in the prevalence rates, depending on how the ages of the victim and perpetrator are defined.

Despite these limitations, national surveys probably provide the best information on prevalence rates because they are able to obtain information on cases that may not have been reported to the police and/or other agencies. For example, Boney-McCoy and Finkelhor (1995) conducted telephone interviews with a nationally representative probability sample of 2,000 youths between 10 and 16 years of age. They found that 15.3% of girls and 5.9% of boys reported having experienced attempted and completed sexual abuse. In addition, 1.7% of girls and 16.2% of boys reported attempted and completed violence to genitals that was separate from sexual abuse reports. In the National Survey of Adolescents (NSA), telephone interviews were conducted with 4,023 youth between the ages of 12 and 17. Detailed information was obtained on history of victimization, delinquency, substance use, and mental health problems, specifically posttraumatic stress disorder (PTSD) and depression (Kilpatrick & Saunders, 1999). In the NSA, a total of 326 adolescents, or 8.1% of the sample, reported having experienced at least one sexual assault prior to the interview. Almost one third of these sexual assaults (32.5%) involved perpetrators who were friends, and 23.2% of perpetrators were strangers. Other types of perpetrators included fathers, stepfathers, brothers or stepbrothers, sisters or stepsisters, grandparents, other adult relatives, other child relatives, neighbors, co-workers, other children, or other adults. Particularly noteworthy was the fact that the second most frequent location for the sexual assault was the victim's school (i.e., the victim's house or neighborhood was the most frequent location, and a friend's house was the third most frequently cited location for the sexual assault). What these data indicate is that sexual assaults by peers that occur in school settings may be more common than previously thought. The stereotype that most CSA cases involve an adult stranger sexually assaulting children appears to be invalid. It is also important to note that the vast majority of sexual assault cases were never reported to police or other authorities (85.7%). However, 13% of cases were reported to police, 5.8% to child protective services, 5% to school authorities, and 1.3% to other authorities (Kilpatrick & Saunders, 1999).

In the National Women's Study (NWS), 8.5% of the 4,008 women who completed a telephone survey reported that they had experienced a completed rape before age 18 (Saunders, Kilpatrick, Hanson, Resnick, & Walker, 1999), with 59.8% of these rapes occurring before age 13. Taken together, these studies underscore the multitude of children who experience sexual abuse and may be at risk for mental health difficulties in their lifetime.

Child Physical Abuse

Research on child physical abuse is also plagued by definitional issues. Physical punishment is a well-accepted form of discipline in our society. In fact, in a national study conducted in 1985, more than 90% of parents reported that they had used spanking as a way of disciplining their young children (Gelles, & Straus, 1988; Straus & Gelles, 1990; Straus, Gelles, & Steinmetz, 1980; Straus, 1994), and the vast majority of adults (approximately 80%) endorsed the use of spanking (Lehman, 1989; Straus et al., 1980; Straus, 1994). As a consequence, it is often difficult to determine when the line between physical punishment and physical abuse is crossed. Most states have statutes that define specific actions that exceed the boundaries of corporal punishment and fall into the realm of physical abuse. In general, physical abuse usually refers to actions that leave a mark or bruise on the child. As a consequence, parents who engage in excessive corporal punishment could be in danger of allegations of physical abuse.

A related issue concerning physical abuse is that children do not always define their caregivers' actions as abusive. Thus, if prevalence rates for physical abuse are based on children's reports, rates are likely to be underestimates. One way to address this concern is the use of behaviorally specific questions to define physical abuse, rather than reliance on the child's perceptions. In other words, rather than asking children if they have been physically abused, they are instead asked if anyone has ever hit them in such a way as to leave a mark or bruise.

In the National Women's Study described above, 2.6% of the 4,008 respondents reported experiencing severe physical assaults in childhood (Duncan, Saunders, Kilpatrick, Hanson, Resnick, 1996). Data from the NSA, which included the nationally representative sample of youth ages 11–17, indicated that 9.9% of the adolescents reported that they had experienced physically abusive punishment by someone in a caregiving role, and 12.5% adolescents reported a physical assault. The physical assaults were perpetuated by someone other than a caregiver and included incidents in which a weapon was used and/or the victim thought he would be killed or seriously injured (Kilpatrick & Saunders, 1999).

Neglect

In contrast to prevalence rates of physical and sexual abuse, which have been examined in a variety of samples using several different survey methods, at present the prevalence of neglect may be estimated only from official records. No large-scale studies examining either community rates or national estimates have been conducted thus far, apart from those based on officially reported cases. As noted above, reliance on statistics generated from official reports is undesirable because of the high likelihood that such figures significantly underestimate the actual prevalence rates and that cases of maltreatment reported to child protection agencies may not be representative of all cases (e.g., cases involving racial and ethnic minorities and families from lower socioeconomic strata may be more likely to be reported). One of the principal difficulties in gathering data regarding the prevalence of neglect in the general population is that researchers cannot agree on the best definition of neglect or the most effective method of assessing for history of neglect. Complicating these issues are the considerable overlap between neglect and poverty and the many different subtypes of neglect that have been proposed (e.g., physical, medical, educational, etc.). Until there is greater consensus regarding the behaviors (and contexts for behaviors) that constitute neglect, and until reliable methods for measuring such behaviors are developed, it is unlikely that our knowledge regarding the prevalence of neglect will move beyond what is revealed by official records.

According to the most recent data from the National Child Abuse and Neglect Data System (NCANDS; U.S. Department of Health and Human Services, 2001), which compiles official state records and extrapolates national prevalence figures, neglect is the most common form of maltreatment experienced by children. Approximately 482,000 of the 826,000 children (58.4%) who experienced child maltreatment during 1999 were victims of neglect. This corresponds roughly to 6.5 per 1,000 children in the general population who experienced some form of parental neglect. Medical and physical neglect were the most common subtypes reported. Neglect appeared to be a particularly significant problem among children 0–3 years old, who had the highest incidence rates. Neglect occurred with nearly equal frequency to both genders. Few would argue that these data are useful. However, it is disconcerting that although neglect appears to be the most prevalent form of maltreatment experienced in the United States, we have very little reliable information beyond official records regarding its prevalence and correlates.

SEQUELAE/EFFECTS OF CHILD ABUSE

Sexual Abuse

Considerable research in the area of child sexual abuse has indicated that its effects are widespread and multifaceted. What is evident from the extant research is that no single symptom characterizes all sexually abused children, nor is there an identified pattern or cluster of symptoms that can be used to identify definitively a child as a sexual abuse victim. CSA has been found to be associated with myriad psychosocial difficulties including depression, sexualized behaviors, aggression, anxiety, dissociation, and posttraumatic stress disorder (PTSD) (Beitchman, Zucker, Hood, daCosta, & Akman, 1991; Beitchman et al., 1992). In their review of research on CSA, Kendall-Tackett, Williams, and Finkelhor (1993) found that two specific behaviors differentiated sexually abused children from their nonabused, clinical counterparts: sexualized behaviors (Friedrich et al., 2001) and PTSD (e.g., Deblinger, McLeer, & Henry, 1990; Deblinger, McLeer, Atkins, Ralphe, & Foa, 1989; Wolfe, Gentile, & Wolfe, 1989). Of particular interest in this review were the findings that not all sexually abused children developed symptoms, at least not at the time of assessment. Kendall-Tackett and colleagues (1993) noted that between one fourth and one half of children were *asymptomatic* at the time of assessment. Although the authors point out that this absence of reported symptoms could be because of the use of insensitive measures, the fact that abuse–related symptoms are gradual, or that symptom onset may be delayed, it is important to entertain the notion that not all children will display noticeable effects. This does not mean that the abuse did not occur, or that the child was unaffected. It just means that the symptoms may not be obvious or readily apparent to others.

As discussed by Kendall-Tackett and colleagues (1993), it is also important to recognize that there may be developmental differences in children's responses to sexual abuse. For example, preschoolers are more likely to show anxiety symptoms, nightmares, PTSD, internalizing and externalizing behaviors, and sexual acting out; school-age children are more likely to experience fears, aggression, and school problems. Adolescents are more prone toward depression, withdrawal, suicidal or self-injurious behaviors, somatic complaints, illegal acts, substance abuse, and running away.

Although it is not possible to identify a cluster of symptoms common to all or even most sexually abused children, researchers have identified certain abuse-related characteristics that increase the likelihood or risk of adverse psychological outcomes (Kendall-Tackett et al., 1993). For example, studies have been fairly consistent in finding that threats, the use of force, weapons, and penetration increased the risk for problems, such as PTSD (Wolfe, Sas, & Wekerle, 1994). The relationship of the perpetrator to the victim also affects outcome, with increased symptoms found in victims who were abused by a close family member (Beitchman et al., 1992). A greater frequency and longer duration of abuse, lack of maternal support at the time of disclosure, and the victim's negative outlook or coping style were other variables found to be associated with increased symptomatology (Kendall-Tackett et al., 1993). Additionally, children who experience multiple types of abuse (i.e., sexual, physical abuse, neglect) are at increased risk for the development of mental health problems. When it comes to child maltreatment, it is not surprising that more is definitely worse.

In sum, research has clearly indicated that children who experience sexual abuse are a diverse group, with no discernible pattern of symptoms common to even most children. Furthermore, symptoms may differ across developmental levels, some children may not evidence any symptoms, and the response to sexual abuse may be gradual or delayed. Findings also indicate that there may be certain characteristics related to the assault that increase the likelihood of adverse academic, social, and mental health outcomes.

Physical Abuse

Studies examining the sequelae of physical abuse report associations with aggression, externalizing behavior problems (Conaway & Hansen, 1989; Kolko, 2002; Kolko, 1992; Swenson & Kolko, 1998), poor social competence (e.g., Egeland, 1991; Kaufman & Cicchetti, 1989), anxiety symptoms such as fear and PTSD (e.g., Deblinger et al., 1989; Famularo, Fenton, & Kinscherff, 1993; Kiser, Heston, Millsap, & Pruitt, 1991; Pelcovitz, Kaplan, Goldenberg, & Mandel, 1994), depression and suicidality (Boney-McCoy & Finkelhor, 1995; Finzi et al., 2001; Kaplan, et al., 1999), developmental delays (e.g., Cicchetti, 1989; Crittenden & Ainsworth, 1989; Pianta, Egeland, & Erickson, 1989; Herrenkohl, Herrenkohl, Egolf, & Wu, 1991), deficits in relationship skills, and cognitive/neuropsychological deficits (e.g., Burke, Crenshaw, Green, Schlosser, & Strocchia-Rivera, 1989; Vondra, Barnett, & Cicchetti, 1989). Physical abuse has also been associated with delinquent behavior, including alcohol use, drug abuse, property offenses, and criminal arrests (Kaplan, Pelcovitz, & Labruna, 1999; Kolko, Moser, & Weldy, 1990). Retrospective data from clinical (e.g., Surrey, Swett, Michaels, & Levin, 1990) and community samples (e.g., Duncan et al., 1996) indicate that child physical abuse is associated with an increased risk for substance abuse, major depression, and PTSD in adulthood.

With respect to academic performance, studies have indicated that physically abused children evidence poorer adjustment in school, are more likely to repeat a grade, and obtain lower mean grades compared to their nonabused counterparts (e.g., Eckenrode, Laird, & Doris, 1993; Kinard, 1999; Leiter & Johnson, 1994, 1997). These differences between abused and nonabused children are evidenced even after controlling for socioeconomic factors, such as poverty, parents' educational levels, race, or gender.

Neglect

Research examining short-term effects of neglect has typically looked at children within specific, developmentally critical contexts: the mother–child relationship, interactions with peers, and school. Much of the research examining mother–child interactions in neglectful families has been conducted within the attachment theory model (Bowlby, 1980). The attachment model states that an individual's capacity to form meaningful personal relationships has its roots in early parent–child bonding, and that compromised attachment in early childhood is likely to compromise an individual's healthy psychosocial development. Most studies in this area have demonstrated that severe neglect is associated with behaviors reflecting insecure attachment, such as low levels of overt affection toward, more behavioral avoidance of, and fewer initiations of play with caregivers (Egeland & Sroufe, 1981; see reviews by Crittenden & Ainsworth, 1989, and Crouch & Milner, 1993). Thus, there does seem to be evidence that the experience of childhood neglect has a negative impact on early mother–child interactions.

Other studies have examined social outcomes in neglected children. For example, young neglected children have been described as withdrawn and having particular difficulty initiating social interactions with peers (Hoffman-Plotkin & Twentyman, 1984). Increased aggression has also been observed among children identified as neglected (e.g., Hoffman-Plotkin & Twentyman, 1984). Further, Frodi and Smetana (1984) demonstrated that neglected toddlers were less aware of other children's emotions than comparison controls; however, this effect may have been because of the lower overall intelligence of the neglected group. Finally, other studies of "abused and neglected" children indicate poor social adjustment among maltreated children (e.g., Aber & Allen, 1987; Aber, Allen, Carlson, & Cicchetti, 1989), but the absence of a separate neglect group makes it difficult to determine the independent contribution of neglect to such outcomes. Overall, the extant data, although sparse, suggest that neglected children are at greater risk for social and peer problems than their non-neglected peers.

A large number of studies examining short-term sequelae of child neglect focus on intellectual and school performance. Several studies have indicated that neglected preschoolers have cognitive deficits (e.g., Egeland, Sroufe, & Erickson, 1983; Frodi & Smetana, 1984; Herrenkohl et al., 1991; Hoffman-Plotkin & Twentyman, 1984) compared to nonmaltreated comparison groups. Others have demonstrated academic deficiencies among neglected school-age children. Eckenrode and colleagues (Eckenrode et al., 1993; Kendall-Tackett & Eckenrode, 1996), for example, demonstrated that neglected children in grades K–12 had academic records worse than both nonmaltreated comparison controls and children who were victims of physical and/or sexual abuse. Similarly, two studies (Kurtz, Gaudin, Howing, & Wodarski, 1993; Wodarski, Kurtz, Gaudin & Howing, 1990) comparing physically abused, neglected, and nonmaltreated school-age children revealed severe academic deficits among neglected children that did not considerably improve over time. These studies strongly suggest that child neglect has serious consequences for academic achievement.

Apart from a handful of studies suggesting that neglected children may be more aggressive than nonmaltreated peers (Hoffman-Plotkin & Twentyman, 1984) or have greater problems with self-esteem (Egeland et al., 1983) and impulsiveness (Rohrbeck & Twentyman, 1986), the literature is nearly silent on the psychological symptoms that are associated with child neglect. This is in sharp contrast to the literature addressing the short-term effects of physical and sexual abuse (e.g., Beitchman et al., 1991; Kendall-Tackett et al., 1993).

Taken together, the literature on the short-term sequelae of child neglect indicate that children affected by neglect are at increased risk for mother–child interaction problems, social and peer problems, and academic failure. Each of these problems has been linked, either theoretically or empirically, to long-term adjustment problems. Attachment theory (Main, Kaplan, & Cassidy, 1985) holds that poor mother–child interactions lay the groundwork for problematic adult relationships. Family conflict has been shown to predict several negative outcomes, including delinquency and substance abuse (Elliott, Huizinga, & Menard, 1989). Social and peer problems have been linked with a variety of negative long-term outcomes, including psychiatric disorders (e.g., Cowen, Pederson, Babigian, Izzo, & Trost, 1973). Finally, academic failure has also been shown to be a risk factor for delinquency and other problems (Elliott et al., 1989). However, despite the clear long-term implications of the immediate sequelae of childhood neglect, and despite the explicit prescription contained within the developmental–ecological framework to consider the impact of childhood events across the entire life span, studies examining the long-term correlates of child neglect remain sparse.

In a series of studies, for example, Widom and colleagues (Perez & Widom, 1994; Rivera & Widom, 1990; Widom, 1989; Widom, Ireland, & Glynn, 1995) identified a large sample of substantiated/validated cases of child abuse and neglect that had occurred before age 11 and conducted a prospective, case file review of later local, state, and federal records of juvenile/adult criminal behavior. Abused and neglected children ($n = 908$) had higher rates of arrest as juveniles (26% vs. 17%) and as adults (29% vs. 21%) than the matched comparison control group($n = 667$). One obvious limitation of this work is that cases of abuse and neglect were combined, eliminating the ability to examine separately the effects of childhood neglect on juvenile and adult criminal behavior. However, in a separate study, Perez and Widom (1994) assessed the effects of type of maltreatment (physical abuse, sexual abuse, and neglect) on long-term intellectual outcomes. A sample of adults who were abused or neglected in childhood were compared to a matched control group on intelligence, reading ability, and academic history. Adults with a history of neglect had the poorest intellectual and academic outcomes. Specifically, those with a neglect history had significantly lower IQ scores and reading scores than the comparison controls, whereas physically abused individuals differed only on intelligence, and sexually abused individuals did not differ from controls in either intelligence or reading ability. No relationship between childhood abuse and neglect and subsequent alcohol problems was found for the overall sample. However, childhood neglect was associated with a greater number of alcohol-related symptoms (Widom et al., 1995).

When studies do differentiate across abuse types, the sequelae of neglect appear to differ from sexual or physical abuse (e.g., Perez & Widom, 1994; Widom et al., 1995). Neglected children seem to be at increased risk for academic difficulties and problems with alcohol. The limited number of studies that have been conducted with adults suggest that these academic or psychosocial difficulties may persist into late adolescence or adulthood. However, additional research that examines the independent effects of childhood neglect is clearly needed.

Multiple Types of Child Abuse

A perusal of the research literature reveals an interesting phenomenon: most researchers investigate a single type of abuse (i.e., either physical OR sexual abuse OR neglect), meaning that they may exclude those children who experience more than one type of maltreatment from their studies or fail to adequately screen for all types of maltreatment. Related to the first point, researchers have demonstrated that many children experience multiple types of victimization. As discussed by Chaffin and Hanson (2000), studies using clinical samples (e.g., Deblinger et al., 1989; Gayford, 1975; Lewis, Lovely, Yeager & Femina, 1989) suggest that there may be a high rate of co–occurrence among sexual abuse, physical abuse, witnessing violence, and other trauma.

With respect to the second point, it is possible that the behaviors or symptoms observed in children could be due to multiple victimizations, rather than the particular type of abuse being examined. Alternatively, some researchers and agency personnel more broadly refer to child "maltreatment" or "abuse." The use of this umbrella term is also problematic because it eliminates the possibility of determining whether there may be unique correlates or effects associated with a particular type of child maltreatment. The ideal solution, then, would be to screen for all types of maltreatment and provide information for each separate type, as well as various combinations. When this has been done, not surprisingly, the general finding is that "more is worse." As discussed by Chaffin and Hanson (2000), children who experience multiple types of maltreatment evidence more frequent and severe symptoms and behavior problems than children who experience only one type of maltreatment. In the National Women's Study, described previously, victims of both childhood physical and sexual assault evidenced higher rates of PTSD and major depression than victims of either type of assault alone (Hanson et al., 2001). In addition, children who experience multiple types of maltreatment are at an increased risk for being revictimized as children and adults (Boney–McCoy & Finkelhor, 1995; Wyatt, Guthrie, & Notgrass, 1992). To make the picture even more bleak, children who experience prior abuse are also more likely to develop PTSD following a subsequent traumatic event (e.g., Bremner, Southwick, Johnson, Yehuda, & Charney, 1993; Boney-McCoy & Finkelhor, 1995; Zaidi & Foy, 1994). These data indicate that, contrary to popular belief, children do not habituate or become desensitized by exposure to repeated trauma. Instead, they become even more vulnerable.

Summary

As indicated by this review, child maltreatment of all forms is highly prevalent in our society. The effects of child abuse are widespread, ranging across the full spectrum of behavioral and emotional problems. It is not surprising that these types of problems have the potential to affect school performance adversely. It is thus critically important for school psychologists and school personnel to be fully aware of the scope and magnitude of child maltreatment. One of the ways that schools have tried to address child abuse is through the provision of school-based abuse prevention programs. The next section of the chapter provides an overview of these types of programs.

SCHOOL-BASED CHILD ABUSE PREVENTION PROGRAMS

Prevalence of Abuse Prevention Programs

School-based abuse prevention programs, aimed at reducing the risk of child victimization, were introduced to the school curriculum in the 1970s, with the majority of programs initiated between 1980 and 1985 (Kohl, 1993). These programs initially focused on stranger abductions and sexual assaults by strangers. Over time the programs have included information regarding other types of child victimization perpetrated by adults, and some programs include information about bullying from peers. Although school-based abuse prevention programs are offered at all age levels (i.e., preschool to high school), the majority of programs are offered in elementary school and serve from 1,500 to 12,000 students yearly (Kohl, 1993). Research suggests that the majority of elementary schools offer abuse prevention programs (Breen, Daro, & Romano,

1991). A national survey of 10 to 16 year olds indicated that two thirds of the adolescents had been exposed to some type of abuse prevention programs in their schools (Finkelhor & Dzuiba-Leatherman, 1995).

Curriculum of Programs

While school-based abuse prevention programs do not have uniform curriculums and modes of instruction (Kohl, 1993), most programs teach similar concepts and skills. Finkelhor and Dzuiba-Leatherman (1995) conducted a nationwide survey and asked children what they remembered about their school prevention programs. The most common topics included in the prevention programs were kidnaping (95%), good touch/bad touch, to yell when attacked, child sexual abuse and incest, that abuse is not the child's fault, confusing touches, and bullies (63%) (Finkelhor & Dzuiba-Leatherman, 1995). Kohl's (1993) survey of 126 prevention programs found similar results, with self-esteem, saying no, appropriate and inappropriate touch, personal safety, body integrity, resisting sexual abuse, and establishing a support system as the most frequently included concepts and skills in programs. The preventative skills typically taught included verbal strategies to resist an attacker, increase assertiveness, and decrease compliance with the perpetrator; and to disclose to adults (Finkelhor & Dzuiba-Leatherman, 1995; Ko & Cosden, 2001; Kohl, 1993).

Almost three fourths of the children reported that the abuse prevention program was presented on more than 1 day; about half said that they practiced skills in class (e.g., yelling "no"); and half reported that they discussed the program at home with their parents (Finkelhor'& Dzuiba-Leatherman, 1995). Research suggests that multiday training and in-class practice is liked the most by students and that in-class practice is associated with a greater likelihood of children using the skills outside of the classroom setting (Finkelhor & Dzuiba-Leatherman, 1995).

Outcome of Programs

Despite the widespread nature of school-based abuse prevention programs, few studies have been conducted to assess their effectiveness in the actual prevention of abuse. However, research has indicated that children who have been exposed to a prevention program have more knowledge about abuse concepts than children who have not been exposed (Dhooper & Schneider, 1995; Hazzard, 1993; Finkelhor, Asdigian, Dzuiba-Leatherman, 1995; Kolko, Moser, Litz, & Hughes, 1987) and that prevention-exposed youth continue to report greater knowledge up to 1 year after the program (Hazzard, 1993; Rispens, Aleman, & Goudena, 1997). Other research has suggested that long-term retention of abuse information occurs only after multiple exposures to school-based abuse prevention programs (Finkelhor et al., 1995).

Although children presented with prevention programs appear to learn more about abuse concepts, there has been little research assessing the effectiveness of this knowledge in preventing abuse. Further, of the evidence available, there is little to no support suggesting that prevention programs actually decrease risk for abuse or harm sustained. A national survey of two thousand 10 to 16 year olds found that, while youth exposed to prevention programs were more likely to use the prevention strategies taught in the programs and were more likely to feel that their actions were helpful, they were not less likely to be abused (Finkelhor et al., 1995; Finkelhor & Dzuiba-Leatherman, 1995). Another study (Ko & Cosden, 2001) that assessed high school students' retrospective reports of exposure to prevention programs found no difference in use of strategies between those exposed and not exposed to prevention programs in elementary and middle school. However, contrary to Finkelhor and colleagues (1995), Ko & Cosden found that fewer prevention-exposed youth reported being physically abused (15%

vs. 32% of nonexposed youth), although they found no difference in reports of sexual abuse (Ko & Cosden, 2001).

Disadvantages of Programs

Many school-based abuse prevention programs originally focused on attacks or abductions from strangers, instead of abuse from family members or other adults known to the child. There has been some speculation that programs may be more or less effective depending on the type of assault that occurs to the child. For instance, prevention programs that focus primarily on attacks from strangers and strategies presumed to decrease harm from strangers may not be as helpful to children abused by adults known to them, such as family members. In their study of 137 high school students, Ko and Cosden (2001) found that, while 62% of children attacked by strangers felt that the prevention program information was useful in avoiding or reducing abuse, only 34% of the children who were abused by known offenders felt the same way.

School-based abuse prevention programs have also been criticized for increasing anxiety and oppositional behavior in children toward nonperpetrating adults. In fact, there is some evidence that there may be a slight increase in children's anxiety about being abused after exposure to a prevention program. Finkelhor and Dzuiba-Leatherman (1995) found that about half of the children in their study reported a slight increase in worries about being abused (53%) and less than 10% reported a great increase in worries. About a fifth of parents reported an increase in their children's worry and anxiety after being exposed to a prevention program. The authors suggested that the nature and duration of the children's anxiety should be examined before determining that the prevention programs are detrimental to children. While there is some evidence that prevention programs increase children's worry about being abused, there is little evidence that it increases noncompliance to legitimate adult requests (Finkelhor & Dzuiba-Leatherman, 1995).

One other concern related to school-based prevention programs is that they do not, typically, take into account the fact that some of the child participants will have experienced a sexual assault. In other words, these programs emphasize self-protective measures and provide education, but they do not acknowledge that this information could be confusing, disturbing, and, possibly, misinterpreted by children who have already been sexually victimized. For example, telling a child to practice abstinence as a way to avoid HIV or STDs certainly makes sense from a prevention and safety perspective. However, if a child has already experienced sexual abuse, this type of information can be highly distressing and confusing. Thus, based on the fact that a substantial number of children do experience sexual abuse, it is critical for sex education programs to incorporate this information into their curriculums.

ISSUES RELATED TO MANDATED REPORTING

Legal Standards

In the late 1960s, all states passed laws requiring that physicians report cases of nonaccidental physical injury to proper authorities, such as a child protective service agency or law enforcement (U.S. Department of Health and Human Services, 2001). In the following years, the types of reportable maltreatment have been expanded to include sexual abuse, neglect, emotional abuse, and sexual exploitation. Also, in addition to physicians, other individuals have been included in reporting laws, often on the basis of their professional activities. Such individuals are termed *mandated reporters*. Designation as a mandated reporter typically compels an individual to report any situation in which he or she believes, or has reason to suspect, that a child has been the victim of some form of child maltreatment. Laws do not typically require that a mandated reporter have clear evidence or proof that a child has been maltreated. Investigation by designated authorities is deemed necessary to make such a determination. The main reasons for requiring only the suspicion of abuse as the criterion for reporting are (1) to attempt to maximize the identification of maltreated children, and (2) to relieve the reporter of any investigatory obligations. Specific language pertaining to the standard of suspicion varies from state to state, and educational professionals are strongly encouraged to become familiar with the actual wording of the pertinent laws within their state. As of the end of 2000, in approximately 18 states statutes dictated that all adults were deemed mandated reporters. Other states identify specific professions or those who engage in specified activities to be mandated reporters. Teachers, school personnel, and psychologists are included as mandated reporters in every such list. Thus, in all 50 states, school personnel are required to report actual and suspected child maltreatment.

Mandatory reporting laws also typically include guidance regarding how to make a report, to whom suspected maltreatment should be reported, exceptions to the requirement to report, and penalties for failure to report. States vary considerably regarding most of these issues, especially the procedures for reporting. Exceptions to mandated reporting requirements, when present, are most often made for maltreatment discovered within the context of an attorney-client or a clergy-penitent relationship (as long as the attorney or clergy member was acting in his or her professional capacity at the time that the information that aroused suspicion was obtained). No state recognizes any exceptions to mandated reporting requirements that involve teachers or most other school personnel (some states may recognize the psychologist-client relationship as an exception).

Virtually all states have established punishment for mandated reporters who fail to make a report. To be sanctioned, a mandated reporter typically must "knowingly," "willfully," "intentionally," or "negligently" fail to report suspected maltreatment, again depending on the particular state statute. The penalties for such violations are most commonly misdemeanors and fines. Several states, however, subject the individual to civil liability for any damages that may have resulted from his or her failure to make the report. Finally, all states provide at least some form of legal immunity for people who report suspected abuse or neglect in accordance with reporting laws. Sometimes the immunity is global (that is, it applies to all reporters regardless of circumstances), and in other cases the immunity applies only to mandated reporters or those making reports "in good faith." Legal immunity protects mandated reporters from civil or criminal penalties that they might be subject to in contexts other than reporting suspected child maltreatment (e.g., suits for defamation of character). Again, school psychologists and education professionals are urged to familiarize themselves with pertinent standards for their locality.

Reporting Practices in Education Settings

Research has indicated that, despite the legal requirement to report suspected child maltreatment, school personnel do not always report suspicious cases to authorities (Abrahams, Casey, & Daro, 1992; Bavolek, 1983; National Center on Child Abuse and Neglect, 1988). This finding has been attributed to several different factors, including poor knowledge of mandated reporting statutes, lack of knowledge regarding appropriate reporting practices, lack of faith in the utility or value of making a report, fear of retaliation from parents or families, and confusion over definitions of abuse and neglect. Although some older research documented low teacher confidence in their knowledge of mandated reporting laws (e.g., Bavolek, 1983; McIntyre, 1987), more recent studies have generally found that the great majority of school teachers and personnel are aware of reporting statutes and recognize how their professional behavior can be affected by them (Crenshaw, Crenshaw, & Lichtenberg, 1995; Shoop & Firestone, 1988; Zellman, 1990).

With respect to knowledge of appropriate reporting practices, data are mixed. In two studies (Hinson & Fossey, 2000; Shoop & Firestone, 1988), many teachers reported confusion regarding the best methods of making child abuse reports, which may influence their likelihood of reporting abuse or neglect. Other data, however, indicate that even when school personnel are not confident of reporting procedures, this lack of information does not interfere with their reporting behavior (Crenshaw et al., 1995). In response to concern over complying with reporting laws, many schools and districts are developing and disseminating policies for the management of abuse reports (Tower, 1992). Some of these require "front line" personnel (e.g., teachers, nurses, etc.) to report suspected abuse to principals or administrators, who then contact appropriate authorities. The legality of such policies requires careful examination. In some states (e.g., Georgia), the law was changed to allow such "chain of command" reports. However, in other states, it is not clear that such reports to administrators discharge the teacher's legal mandate to report to appropriate authorities. This can place teachers in a very difficult bind. In order to obey the law they must make a report; however, if they make a report, they violate school policy and expose themselves to work sanctions.

Data also indicate that school personnel fear that their reports are not taken seriously by child protection workers or that the child protection system will not protect the child. Although one study (Crenshaw et al., 1995) did not find this variable to be related to reporting behavior in hypothetical scenarios, considerable anecdotal data suggest that it may affect teachers' attitudes toward making reports. This may be particularly true when teachers are less confident regarding whether to initiate a report. Similarly, some empirical data suggest that fear of retaliation from parents inhibits reporting behavior (Hinson & Fossey, 2000). This may be because of the school personnel's ignorance of legal immunity provisions for mandated reporters. In Crenshaw and colleagues' (1995) sample of generally well-informed education personnel, anecdotal evidence did suggest that fear of retaliation was a salient factor, but it was not related to reporting behavior in the statistical analyses.

The variable most consistently associated with the failure of school personnel to report cases of suspected child maltreatment is knowledge of abuse definitions and symptoms. Data do appear to support the notion that understanding definitions and recognition of problem behaviors as abuse related is associated with educators' decisions to report suspected maltreatment, at least in hypothetical scenarios (Crenshaw et al., 1995; O'Toole, Webster, O'Toole, & Lucal, 1999). When cases involve child disclosures of maltreatment or other unambiguous indicators that limit teachers' needs to exercise their personal judgment, reports are more likely to be made (Bavolek, 1983; Crenshaw et al., 1995).

Taken together, these data suggest a somewhat muddled picture. Whereas teachers and school personnel are designated as mandated reporters throughout the United States (and in many other countries as well), it is evident that, in some circumstances, child maltreatment that is suspected by educators goes unreported. More training in recognizing abuse-related behaviors and understanding state definitions of abuse and neglect seem to be warranted for educators, and indeed, surveys indicate strong support for such training among school personnel (Abrahams et al., 1992).

CONCLUSIONS

The purpose of this chapter was to provide information on the prevalence and effects of child maltreatment to increase knowledge and awareness for educators and school psychologists. As stated at the outset, children spend the majority of their waking hours in school settings.

Educators and psychologists are thus in the unique and, sometimes, unenviable position of being the ones responsible for protecting and ensuring the safety of the children in their care. In some instances, teachers may be the first source of an abuse disclosure for a child. It is thus incumbent on teachers to be fully aware and knowledgeable about issues related to child maltreatment. The proliferation of school-based abuse prevention programs, as well as school-based mental health clinics, underscores the awareness that children are in need of information and treatment services within the school setting. Studies on the effectiveness of school-based prevention programs have been mixed but, nonetheless, appear to indicate that some valuable information and preventive strategies are learned by at least some children. If even one instance of abuse is prevented or the effects of abuse can be ameliorated, then these programs are useful. Future programs need to be developed to address other types of child maltreatment, including physical abuse, neglect, and domestic violence. In addition, parents and teachers would benefit from presentations and ongoing trainings that address issues related to child maltreatment. It is not surprising that increased knowledge, awareness, and collaborative relationships among teachers, parents, school administrators, and mental health treatment providers offer the best chance of preventing abuse and/or reducing the risk of long-term difficulties.

REFERENCES

Aber, J. L., & Allen, J. P. (1987). The effects of maltreatment on young children's socioemotional development: An attachment theory perspective. *Developmental Psychology, 23*, 406–414.

Aber, J. L., Allen, J. P., Carlson, V., & Cicchetti, D. (1989). The effects of maltreatment on development during early childhood: Recent studies and their theoretical clinical and policy implications. In D. Cicchetti & V. Carlson (Eds.), *Child maltreatment: Theory and research on the causes and consequences of child abuse and neglect* (pp. 579–619). New York: Cambridge University Press.

Abrahams, N., Casey, K., & Daro, D. (1992). Teachers' knowledge, attitudes, and beliefs about child abuse and its prevention. *Child Abuse and Neglect, 16*, 229–238.

Bavolek, S. J. (1983). Why aren't school personnel reporting child abuse in Wisconsin? *Teacher Education and Special Education, 6*, 33–38.

Beitchman, J., Zucker, K., Hood, J., daCosta, G., & Akman, D. (1991). A review of the short-term effects of child sexual abuse. *Child Abuse and Neglect, 15*, 537–556.

Beitchman, J., Zucker, K., Hood, J., daCosta, G., Akman, D., & Cassavia, E. (1992). A review of the long-term effects of child sexual abuse. *Child Abuse and Neglect, 16*, 101–118.

Boney-McCoy, S., & Finkelhor, D. (1995). Psychosocial sequelae of violent victimization in a national youth sample. *Journal of Consulting and Clinical Psychology, 63*, 726–736.

Bowlby, J. (1980). Attachment and loss: Loss, sadness, and depression. New York: Basic Books.

Breen, M., Daro, D., & Romano, N. (1991). Prevention services and child abuse: A comparison of services availability in the nation and Michigan. Chicago: National Committee to Prevent Child Abuse.

Bremner, J. D., Southwick, S. M., Johnson, D. R., Yehuda, R., & Charney, D. S. (1993). Childhood physical abuse and combat-related posttraumatic stress disorder in Vietnam veterans. *American Journal of Psychiatry, 150*(2), 235–239.

Browne, A., & Finkelhor, D. (1986). Impact of child sexual abuse: A review of the research. *Psychological Bulletin, 99*, 66–77.

Burke, A. E., Crenshaw, D. A., Green, J., Schlosser, M. A., & Strocchia-Rivera, L. (1989). Influence of verbal ability on the expression of aggression in physically abused children. *Journal of the American Academy of Child Psychiatry, 28*, 215–218.

Chaffin, M., & Hanson, R. F. (2000). The multiply traumatized Child. In R. M. Reece (Ed.), *The treatment of child abuse* (pp. 271–288). Baltimore, MD: Johns Hopkins University Press.

Cicchetti, D. (1989). How research on child maltreatment has informed the study of child development: Perspectives from developmental psychopathology. In D. Cicchetti & V. Carlson (Eds.), *Child maltreatment: Theory and research on the causes and consequences of child abuse and neglect* (pp. 377–431). New York: Cambridge University Press.

Conaway, L. P., & Hansen, D. J. (1989). Social behavior of physically abused and neglected children: A critical review. *Clinical Psychology Review, 9*, 627–652.

Cowen, E. L., Pederson, A., Babigian, H., Izzo, L. D., & Trost, M. (1973). Long-term follow-up of early detected vulnerable children. *Journal of Consulting & Clinical Psychology, 41*, 438–446.

Crenshaw, W. B., Crenshaw, L. M., & Lichtenberg, J. W. (1995). When educators confront child abuse: An analysis of the decision to report. *Child Abuse and Neglect, 19*, 1095–1113.

Crittenden, P. M., & Ainsworth, M. D. S. (1989). Child maltreatment and attachment theory. In D. Cicchetti & V. Carlson (Eds.), *Child maltreatment: Theory and research on the causes and consequences of child abuse and neglect* (pp. 432–463) New York: Cambridge University Press.

Crouch, J. L, & Milner, J. S. (1993). Effects of child neglect on children. *Criminal Justice and Behavior, 20*, 49–65.

Deblinger, E., McLeer, S. V., Atkins, M., Ralphe, D., & Foa, E. (1989). Posttraumatic stress in sexually abused children, physically abused, and non-abused children. *Child Abuse and Neglect, 13*, 403–408.

Deblinger, E., McLeer, S. V., & Henry, D. (1990). Cognitive behavioral treatment for sexually abused children suffering post-traumatic stress: Preliminary findings. *Journal of the American Academy of Child and Adolescent Psychiatry, 29*, 747–752.

Dhooper, S. S., & Schneider, P. L. (1995). Evaluation of a school based child abuse prevention program. *Research on Social Work and Practice, 5*, 36–46.

Duncan, R. D., Saunders, B. E., Kilpatrick, D. G., Hanson, R. F., & Resnick, H. S. (1996). Childhood physical assault as a risk factor for PTSD, depression and substance abuse: Findings from a national survey. *American Orthopsychiatric Association, 66*(3), 437–448.

Eckenrode, J., Laird, M., & Doris, J. (1993). School performance and disciplinary problems among abused and neglected children. *Developmental Psychology, 29*(1), 53–62.

Egeland, B. (1991). A longitudinal study of high-risk families: Issues and findings. In R. H. Starr Jr. & D. A. Wolfe (Eds.), *The effects of child abuse and neglect* (pp. 33–56). New York: Guilford.

Egeland, B., & Sroufe, L. A. (1981). Developmental sequelae of maltreatment in infancy. *New Directions for Child Development, 11*, 77–92.

Egeland, B., Sroufe, L. A., & Erickson, M. (1983). The developmental consequences of different patterns of maltreatment. *Child Abuse & Neglect, 7*, 459–469.

Elliott, D. S., Huizinga, D., & Menard, S. (1989). Multiple problem youth: Delinquency, substance use and mental health problems. New York: Springer-Verlag.

Famularo, R., Fenton, T., & Kinscherff, R. (1993). Child maltreatment and the development of posttraumatic stress disorder. *American Journal of the Diseases of Children, 147*, 755–760.

Finkelhor, D., Asdigian, N., & Dzuiba-Leatherman, J. (1995). The effectiveness of victimization prevention instruction: An evaluation of children's responses to actual threats and assaults. *Child Abuse & Neglect, 19*, 141–153.

Finkelhor, D., & Dzuiba-Leatherman, J. (1995). Victimization prevention programs: A national survey of children's exposure and reactions. *Child Abuse and Neglect, 19*, 129–139.

Finzi, R., Ran, A., Shnit, D., Har-Even, D., Tyano, S., & Weizman, A. (2001). Depressive symptoms and suicidality in physically abused children. *American Journal of Orthopsychiatry, 71*, 98–107.

Friedrich, W. N., Fisher, J. L., Dittner, A., Acton, R., Berliner, L., Butler, J., Damon, L., Davies, W. H., Gray, A. & Wright, J. (2001). Child sexual behavior inventory: Normative, psychiatric and sexual abuse comparisons. *Child Maltreatment Journal of the American Professional Society on the Abuse of Children, 6*, 37–49.

Frodi, A., & Smetana, J. (1984). Abused, neglected, and nonmaltreated preschoolers' ability to discriminate emotions in others: The effects of IQ. *Child Abuse and Neglect, 8*, 459–465.

Gayford, J. J. (1975). Wife battering: A preliminary survey of 100 cases. *British Medical Journal, 1*, 194–197.

Gelles, R. J., & Straus, M. A. (1988). *Intimate violence*. New York: Simon & Schuster.

Hanson, R. F., Resnick, H. S., Saunders, B. E., Kilpatrick, D. G., & Best, C. (1999). Factors related to the reporting of childhood sexual assault. *Child Abuse & Neglect, 23*, 559–569.

Hanson, R. F., Saunders, B. E., Kilpatrick, D. G., Resnick, H. S., Crouch, J., & Duncan, R. (2001). The impact of childhood rape and/or aggravated assault on adult mental health.

American Journal of Orthopsychiatry, 71, 108–119.

Hazzard, A. (1993). Psychoeducational groups to teach children sexual abuse prevention skills. *Journal of Child and Adolescent Group Therapy, 3*, 13–23.

Herrenkohl, R. C., Herrenkohl, E. C., Egolf, B. P., & Wu, P. (1991). The developmental consequences of child abuse: The Lehigh longitudinal study. In R. H. Starr & D. A. Wolfe (Eds.), *The effects of child abuse and neglect* (pp. 57–81). New York: Guilford.

Hinson, J., & Fossey, R. (2000). Child abuse: What teachers in the '90s know, think, and do. *Journal of Education for Students Placed at Risk, 5*, 251–266.

Hoffman-Plotkin, D., & Twentyman, C. T. (1984). A multimodal assessment of behavioral and cognitive deficits in abused and neglected preschoolers. *Child Development, 55*, 794–802.

Kaplan, S. J., Pelcovitz, D., & Labruna, V. (1999). Child and adolescent abuse and neglect research: A review of the past 10 years. Part I: Physical and emotional neglect. *Journal of the American Academy of Child and Adolescent Psychiatry, 38*(10), 1214–1222.

Kaplan, S. J., Pelcovitz, D., Salzinger, S., Mandel, F., Weiner, M., & Labruna, V. (1999). Adolescent physical abuse and risk for suicidal behaviors. *Journal of Interpersonal Violence, 14*, 976–988.

Kaufman, J., & Cicchetti, D. (1989). Effects of maltreatment on school-age children's socioemotional development: Assessments in day-camp setting. *Developmental Psychology, 25*, 516–524.

Kendall-Tackett, K. A., & Eckenrode, J. (1996). The effects of neglect on academic achievement and disciplinary problems: A developmental approach. *Child Abuse & Neglect, 20*, 161–169.

Kendall-Tackett, K., Williams, L., & Finkelhor, D. (1993). Impact of sexual abuse on children: A review and synthesis of recent empirical studies. *Psychological Bulletin, 113*, 164–180.

Kilpatrick, D. G., Edmunds, C. N., & Seymour, A. K. (1992). *Rape in America: A report to the nation*. Arlington, VA: National Victim Center.

Kilpatrick, D. G., & Saunders, D. G. (1999, June). *Prevalence and consequences of child victimization: Results from the National Survey of Adolescents-Final Report* (Grant No. 93-IJ-CX-0023). Washington D. C.: U.S. Department of Justice, Office of Justice Programs, National Institute of Justice.

Kinard, E. M. (1999). Psychosocial resources and academic performance in abused children. *Children & Youth Services Review, 21*(5), 351–376.

Kiser, L. J., Heston, J., Millsap, P. A., & Pruitt, D. B. (1991). Physical and sexual abuse in childhood: Relationship with post-traumatic stress disorder. *Journal of the American Academy of Child and Adolescent Child Psychiatry, 30*, 776–783.

Ko, S. F., & Cosden, M. A. (2001). Do elementary school-based child abuse prevention programs work? A high-school follow-up. *Psychology in the Schools, 38*, 57–66.

Kohl, J. (1993). School-based child sexual abuse prevention programs. *Journal of Family Violence, 8*, 137–150.

Kolko, D. J. (1992). Characteristics of child victims of physical violence. *Journal of Interpersonal Violence, 7*, 244–276.

Kolko, D. J. (2002). Child physical abuse. In: J. E. B. Myers, L. Berliner, J. Briere, C. T. Hendrix, C. Jenny, & T. Reid (Eds.), *The APSAC handbook of child maltreatment* (2nd ed., pp. 21–54). Thousand Oaks, CA: Sage.

Kolko, D. J., Moser, J T., Litz, J., & Hughes, J. (1987). Promoting awareness and prevention of child sexual victimization using the red flag/green flag program: An evaluation with follow-up. *Journal of Family Violence, 2*, 11–35.

Kolko, D. J., Moser, J., T., & Weldy, S. R. (1990). Medical/health histories and physical evaluation of physically and sexually abused child psychiatric patients: A controlled study. *Journal of Family Violence, 5*(4), 249–267.

Kurtz, P. D., Gaudin, J. M., Howing, P. T., & Wodarski, J. S. (1993). The consequences of physical abuse and neglect on the school age child: Mediating factors. *Children and Youth Services Review, 15*, 85–104.

Lehman, B. A. (1989, March). Spanking teaches the wrong lesson. *Boston Globe, 13*, p. 27.

Leiter, J., & Johnson, M. (1994). Child maltreatment and school performance. *American Journal of Education, 102*, 154–189.

Leiter, J., & Johnson, M. (1997). Child maltreatment and school performance declines: An event-history analysis. *American Educational Research Journal, 34*, 563–589.

Lewis, D. O., Lovely, R., Yeager, C., & Femina, D. (1989). Toward a theory of the genesis of violence: A follow-up study of delinquents. *Journal of the American Academy of Child and Adolescent Psychiatry, 28*, 431–436.

Main, M., Kaplan, N., & Cassidy, J. (1985). Security in infancy, childhood, and adulthood: A move to the level of representation. In I. Bretherton & E. Waters (Eds.), *Growing points in attachment theory and research: Monographs of the Society for Research in Child Development* (pp. 66–104). Chicago: University of Chicago Press.

McCurdy, D., & Daro, D. (1994). *Current trends in child abuse reporting and fatalities: The results of the 1993 annual fifty state survey*. Chicago, IL: National Committee to Prevent Child Abuse, National Center on Child Abuse Prevention Research.

McIntyre, T. C. (1987).Teacher awareness of child abuse and neglect. *Child Abuse and Neglect, 11*, 133–135.

National Center on Child Abuse and Neglect. (1988). *Study findings: Study of national incidence and prevalence of child abuse and neglect: 1988*. Washington, D.C.: U.S. Government Printing Office.

O'Toole, R., Webster, S. W., O'Toole, A. W., & Lucal, B. (1999). Teachers' recognition and reporting of child abuse: A factorial survey. *Child Abuse and Neglect, 23*, 1083–1101.

Pelcovitz, D., Kaplan, S., Goldenberg, B., & Mandel, F. (1994). Post-traumatic stress disorder in physically abused adolescents. *Journal of the American Academy of Child & Adolescent Psychiatry, 33*, 305–312.

Perez, C. M., & Widom, C. S. (1994). Childhood victimization and long-term intellectual and academic outcomes. *Child Abuse & Neglect, 18*, 617–633.

Pianta, R., Egeland, B., & Erickson, M. F. (1989). The antecedents of maltreatment: Results of the mother-child interaction research project. In D. Cicchetti & V. Carlson (Eds.), *Child maltreatment: Theory and research on the causes and consequences of child abuse and neglect* (pp. 203–253). New York: Cambridge University Press.

Rispens, J., Aleman, A., & Goudena, P. P. (1997). Prevention of child sexual abuse victimization: A meta-analysis of school programs. *Child Abuse & Neglect, 21*, 975–987.

Rivera, B., & Widom, C. S. (1990). Childhood victimization and violent offending. *Violence & Victims, 5*, 19–35.

Roesler, T. A., & Wind, T. W. (1994). Telling the secret: Adult women describe their disclosures of incest. *Journal of Interpersonal Violence, 9*, 327–338.

Rohrbeck, C., & Twentyman, C. T. (1986). Multimodal assessment of impulsiveness in abusing, neglecting, and nonmaltreating mothers and their preschool children. *Journal of Consulting and Clinical Psychology, 54*, 231–236.

Saunders, B. E., Kilpatrick, D. G., Hanson, R. F., Resnick, H. S., & Walker, M. E. (1999). Prevalence, case characteristics, and long-term psychological correlates of child rape among women: A national survey. *Child Maltreatment, 4*, 187–200.

Sauzier, M. (1989). Disclosure of child sexual abuse: For better or for worse. *Psychiatric Clinics of North America, 12*, 455–469.

Shoop, R. J., & Firestone, L. M. (1988). Mandatory reporting of suspected child abuse: Do teachers obey the law? *West's Education Law Reporter, 46*, 1115–1122.

Smith, D. W., Letourneau, E. J., Saunders, B. E., Kilpatrick, D. G., Resnick, H. S., & Best, C. L. (2000). Delay in disclosure of child rape: Results from a national survey. *Child Abuse & Neglect, 24*, 273–287.

Sorenson, T., & Snow, B. (1991). How children tell: The process of disclosure in child sexual abuse. *Child Welfare League of America, LXX*, 3–15.

Straus, M. A. (1994). *Beating the devil out of them: Corporal punishment in American families*: San Francisco: Jossey-Bass.

Straus, M. A., & Gelles, R. J. (Eds.). (1990). *Physical violence in American families: Risk factors and adaptations to violence in 8,145 families*. New Brunswick, NJ: Transaction Publishers.

Straus, M. A., Gelles, R. J., & Steinmetz, S. K. (1980). *Behind closed doors: Violence in the American family, 48*, 465–480.

Surrey, S., Swett, C., Michaels, A., & Levin, S. (1990). Reported history of physical and sexual abuse and severity of symptomatology in women psychiatric outpatients. *American Journal of Orthopsychiatry, 60*, 412–417.

Swenson, C. C., & Kolko, D. J. (1998). Long-term management of the developmental consequences of child physical abuse. In R. R. Reece (Ed.), *Treatment of child abuse: Common ground for mental health, medical, and legal practitioners* (pp. 135–154). Baltimore: Johns Hopkins University Press.

Tower, C. C. (1992). *The role of educators in the prevention and treatment of child abuse and neglect*. Washington, D.C.: U.S. Government Printing Office.

U.S. Department of Health and Human Services, Administration on Children, Youth, and Families. (2001). *Child maltreatment 1999*. Washington, D.C.: U.S. Government Printing Office.

Vondra, J. A., Barnett, D., & Cicchetti, D. (1989). Perceived and actual competence among maltreated and comparison school children. *Development and Psychopathology, 1*, 237–255.

Widom, C. S. (1989). Child abuse, neglect, and adult behavior: Research design and findings on criminality, violence and child abuse. *American Journal of Orthopsychiatry, 59*, 355–367.

Widom, C. S., Ireland, T., & Glynn, P. J. (1995). Alcohol-abuse in abused and neglected children followed-up: Are they at increased risk? *Journal of Studies on Alcohol*, 207–217.

Wodarski, J. S., Kurtz, P. D., Gaudin, J. M., & Howing, P. T. (1990). Maltreatment and the school-age child: Major academic, socioemotional and adaptive outcomes. *Social Work, 35*, 506–513.

Wolfe, V. V., Gentile, C., & Wolfe, D. A. (1989). The impact of sexual abuse on children: A PTSD formulation. *Behavior Therapy, 20*, 215–228.

Wolfe, D., Sas, L., & Wekerle, C. (1994). Factors associated with the development of posttraumatic stress disorder among child victims of sexual assault. *Child Abuse and Neglect, 18*, 37–50.

Wyatt, G. E., Guthrie, D., & Notgrass, C. M. (1992). Differential effects of women's child sexual abuse and subsequent sexual revictimization. *Journal of Consulting & Clinical Psychology, 60*(2), 167–173.

Zaidi, L. Y., & Foy, D. W. (1994). Childhood abuse experiences and combat-related PTSD. *Journal of Traumatic Stress, 7*(1), 33–42.

Zellman, G. L. (1990). Linking schools and social services: The case of child abuse reporting. *Educational Evaluation and Policy Analysis, 12*, 41–55.

25

Elimination Disorders

Edward R. Christophersen
Children's Mercy Hospital

Patrick C. Friman
Father Flanagan's Boys' Home

INTRODUCTION

This chapter discusses the primary elimination disorders that afflict children in school, enuresis and encopresis. Although the descriptor *school aged* has traditionally referred to children age 6 years and older, there has been an inexorably increasing emphasis on academic training in preschool coupled with increasing enrollment over the past few decades. Thus, it seems appropriate to include problems relevant to preschoolers in a chapter for a book on pediatric psychology in school settings. Correspondingly, the chapter also discusses toileting refusal, a category of problems sometimes exhibited by children between the ages of 3 and 5 years. Although the defining clinical features of these disorders are biological, the optimal conceptual orientation is biobehavioral (Friman & Jones, 1998; Houts, 1991; Levine, 1982; Mellon & Houts, 1995; Mellon & McGrath, 2000). The reader should note that page limitations for chapters in this book necessarily limit coverage. There are vast literatures on enuresis and encopresis and we are not able to equitably credit the many able investigators who have worked on these problems. In lieu of that, we refer readers to comprehensive reviews of the literature that exhaustively cite primary sources and that we cite liberally throughout this chapter (especially Christophersen & Purvis, 2001; Friman & Jones, 1998; Houts, 1991; McGrath, Mellon, & Murphy, 2000; Mellon & Houts, 1995; Mellon & McGrath, 2000).

For much of the last century, the prevailing interpretations of elimination disorders were psychological. Initially they were perceived as involving volitional acts occurring as a function of character defect and treatment tended to be punitive. A cultural residue of this early characterological perspective remains; accidents are still often attributed to traits such as laziness and stubbornness and many children are punished for urinary and fecal accidents. Toward the middle of this century, a psychopathological perspective superseded the characterological perspective by shifting emphasis away from volition and toward variables such as aberrant family and psycho dynamics. This perspective has proven no more tenable than the characterological perspective.

Although it may reduce the likelihood of punishment, it also increases the possibility of stigma and it has not generated any effective treatments. During the past two decades the strictly psychological perspective shifted to a model that incorporates physiological and environmental as well as psychological variables resulting in the biobehavioral perspective mentioned above.

Although it may seem superfluous to include extensive information on physiology in a chapter destined for use by nonmedical professionals (e.g., psychologists), the biobehavioral perspective on incontinence requires inclusion of that information. Furthermore, the emerging model of pediatric school psychology is heavily influenced if not primarily guided by a biobehavioral perspective. Therefore, we employ the biobehavioral perspective in our discussion of the major topics of this chapter: toileting refusal, encopresis, and enuresis. A section is devoted to each topic and each section is organized into the following subsections: definitional criteria, relevant physiology, prevalence, etiology, evaluation, and treatment. The enuresis component primarily involves nocturnal enuresis but also includes a small section on diurnal enuresis. Our intent is to provide school-based practitioners and scientists with current information on each of these topics with a guide to effective treatment plans as the overarching goal.

An important reason for including a chapter on elimination disorders in a book on school settings is that early referral leads to early appropriate evaluation and management. Unfortunately, professional contact with child incontinence can be delayed by parental reluctance to report it prior to applying home-based remedies, most of which involve the passage of extensive time. Because of the high probability of detection of incontinence occurring in a school setting, teachers or school-based psychologists may often be the first professionals to encounter the problem. In order to address threats to public health posed by public incontinence (see for example, Berk & Friman, 1990) and those to the physical and social well-being of the incontinent school-based child (Friman & Jones, 1998), it is critical for school professionals to be fully informed about elimination disorders.

TOILETING REFUSAL

Definitional Criteria

A toileting problem that often precedes, and almost as often evolves into, functional encopresis (fully described below) has variously been referred to as toileting refusal or stool withholding. This typically occurs in children 3 to 5 years of age, so it would only be relevant to children in preschool and kindergarten. Often these children are not actually having bowel movements in their clothing because they will ask their parent or alternative caregiver for a diaper or a pull up and promptly relieve themselves in the garment.

Because the *Diagnostic and Statistical Manual of Mental Disorders* (DSM-IV; American Psychiatric Association, 1994) states that the child must be at least 48 months of age to be diagnosed with encopresis, many of these children are not, strictly speaking, encopretic. However, there is no other DSM-IV diagnosis that describes children displaying these symptoms. Toileting refusal is also not included in the *DSM for Primary Care—Child and Adolescent Version* (American Academy of Pediatrics, 1994).

Relevant Physiology

There are no known organic conditions that predispose a child to toileting refusal. While constipation is present in the majority of children who exhibit toileting refusal, the etiology of the constipation varies from child to child. There is also the question of whether constipation predisposes a child to toileting refusal or toileting refusal leads to constipation.

Prevalence

Taubman (1997), in a prospective study of 482 children, reported that 22% experienced at least 1 month of stool toileting refusal. Taubman also reported that there was an association between the presence of a younger sibling and parental inability to set limits for the child and stool toileting refusal.

Etiology

Blum, Taubman, and Osborne (1997) suggested that a variety of factors could be related to toileting refusal including early toilet training, excessive parent–child conflict, irrational fears or anxieties around toileting, a difficult temperament, and hard or painful stools as a result of chronic constipation or an anal fissure. No published studies have actually examined these various factors; however, as indicated above, there are several reports that children with toileting refusal often have histories of constipation and/or painful defecation (Blum et al., 1997; Luxem, Christophersen, Purvis, & Baer, 1997; Taubman, 1997). Toileting refusal does not appear to be caused by diagnosable behavioral conditions. In the Blum and colleagues (1997) study that included 54 children (27 with toileting refusal and 27 matched controls), the children with stool toileting refusal were not found to have more behavior problems than matched children who were toilet trained. This is consistent with the findings of Friman, Mathews, Finney, Christophersen, and Leibowitz (1988) for children with encopresis. One plausible possibility is learning history. Children with stool toileting refusal have typically tried to have a bowel movement on the adult size toilet and either were unable to or did so with some degree of discomfort.

Evaluation

The psychologist whose child client has an elimination disorder—and even for children with toileting refusal—should go no further with treatment until a medical evaluation has been conducted. The vast majority of cases of toileting refusal involve only behavior, but there is still a possibility of a biological problem (e.g., constipation).

In the initial evaluation of a child with toileting refusal by the psychologist, a standardized behavior rating scale, completed by the parents and, if the child attends a preschool or a day-care center, by the teacher or day-care provider, can provide helpful information. If the child has problems with compliance or exhibits disruptive behaviors, then the compliance or disruptive behaviors may need to be addressed either prior to addressing the toileting refusal or at the same time.

A detailed toileting history is important to identify the extent to which the child has been bothered by constipation. Because the term *constipation* has not been a commonly accepted definition, the clinician usually has to ask questions about the frequency and consistency of the child's bowel movements. Simply asking if there is a history of constipation is usually not productive. The symptoms commonly associated with constipation include hard, pebbly stools, large stools, infrequent stools (less than 1 stool every 3 days), and stools that are difficult to pass.

Treatment

Christophersen and Mortweet (2001) suggested that, for children who are already refusing to defecate in the adult toilet, the first step is to make certain that their stools are soft and formed. This can usually be accomplished over a period of a couple of weeks by suggesting changes in diet, use of medication, or both. The dietary changes include the addition of more dietary fiber to moisten and soften the stools, and, in cases where the child is consuming an excess of dairy products, reducing the number and amount of diary products that are offered or are available (Davidson, 1958). A small amount of mineral oil (1 ml/kg of weight) mixed in with 7-Up, Sprite, or other liquid is usually sufficient to soften stool.

If the child whose stools are soft and formed is still reluctant to defecate in the toilet, the child's physician can recommend the use of glycerin rectal suppositories for a period up to one week. The suppositories, when given just prior to a meal (the meal closest to when the child typically has a bowel movement), help to produce a movement. Several bowel movements in the toilet, without discomfort, may diminish the learned aversive properties of appropriate toileting.

By treating toileting refusal at an early age, the clinician may be able to avoid later episodes of encopresis. Many parents of children who present with encopresis will report that their children had problems with constipation, toileting refusal, or both, at an earlier age. It is interesting to note that the first research paper that documented normal bowel habits in children did not appear in the literature until 1984 (Weaver & Steiner). It reported that the average 1-year-old child has 1 or 2 stools per day and that, by 4 years of age, the majority of children have 1 stool a day, although it is not unusual for 4 year olds to have 2 stools per day. Constipation would be considered if stool frequency is fewer than three times per week (Loening-Baucke, 1996).

Luxem and colleagues (1997), using a combination of bowel cleanout procedure (typically enemas), high-fiber foods, mineral oil therapy, and positive reinforcement appropriate toileting, reported that the 11 children they treated were accident free and having at least 1 bowel movement every 2 days during 5 consecutive days of follow-up conducted 3 to 4 months after treatment. Parents reported general satisfaction with the treatment.

ENCOPRESIS

Definitional Criteria

The definition of encopresis from the *DSM-IV* (American Psychiatric Association, 1994) lists four criteria for encopresis: (1) repeated passage of feces into inappropriate places whether involuntary or intentional; (2) at least 1 such event a month for at least 3 months; (3) chronological age is at least 4 years (or equivalent developmental level); and, (4) the behavior is not due exclusively to the direct physiological effects of a substance or a general medical condition except through a mechanism involving constipation. The *DSM-IV* describes two types, primary—in which the child has never had fecal continence—and secondary—in which incontinence returns after at least 6 months of continence. Nocturnal encopresis does occur but is rare (Walker, Kenning, & Faust-Campanile, 1989).

Prevalence

Approximately 3% of the general pediatric population have encopresis (Levine, 1975). About 80% of encopretic children seen by primary care physicians present with a history of fecal retention and/or constipation.

Relevant Physiology

The large intestine or colon is the distal end of the alimentary tract that is sequentially composed of the esophagus, stomach, biliary tract, and the intestines (small and large). The colon has three major functions, storage of, fluid absorption from, and evacuation of waste. Extended storage and planned evacuation of fecal waste into an appropriate location are the defining features of fecal continence. Evacuation is achieved through a motor function called peristalsis, involving a wavelike motion of the walls of the colon. Retrograde peristalsis in the ascending colon keeps liquid fecal waste in contact with the absorptive walls of the colon, resulting in gradual solidification of the waste, which begins to move forward as it takes on mass. Movement occurs over an extended period and is potentiated by external events. Examples of these events include gross motor activity, resulting in the orthocolic reflex, and eating, resulting in the gastrocolic reflex.

Most of the time the rectum contains little or no fecal matter, but when colonic movement leads to contraction of the sigmoid colon, feces are propelled into the rectum and its distension stimulates sensory receptors in the rectal mucosa and in the muscles of the pelvic floor. Two muscle-based "switching systems," the internal and external sphincters, regulate fecal progression from that point. The internal sphincter is involuntary and opens only through the stimulation generated by the process described above. As fecal mass distends the rectum, the child can manipulate the external sphincter using three muscle groups (thoracic diaphragm, abdominal musculature, levator ani) to start or stop defecation (these muscle groups are also used to start or stop urination—described more fully in the enuresis section). Thus, as with the achievement of urinary continence, fecal continence requires appropriate responses to stimulation generated by a waste-receiving organ system. In very general terms, the purpose of fecal toilet training is to acquaint the child with the proprioceptive feedback from the colon and to coordinate the relaxing of the external anal sphincter with sitting on a toilet (Friman & Jones, 1998; Weinstock & Clouse, 1987).

Etiology

The fecal eliminational process is profoundly affected by diet and behavior. For example, the motility of the colon is easily reduced either involuntarily due to insufficient bulk or roughage or too many bland foods in the diet, or voluntarily due to toileting refusal. Reduced motility results in excess quantities of moisture being drawn off the fecal mass, making it dryer than normal and reducing colonic motility even further. This pattern can lead to a regressive cycle where the retention of feces decreases motility, leading to further retention of feces, and this cycle is a primary cause of constipation and fecal incontinence. Not surprisingly, the vast majority of children with encopresis have histories of constipation (Friman & Jones, 1998; Levine, 1982).

Precisely establishing the etiology for this constipation/soiling cycle is a difficult assignment. There are, however, several behavioral/dietary factors with a known causative role. These include (1) insufficient roughage or bulk; (2) a bland diet, too high in dairy products and cheeses, which results in reduced colonic motility; (3) insufficient oral intake of fluids, which allows the normal reabsorption of water from the colon to dehydrate the feces too much, or dehydration stemming from many activities that increase loss of fluids from sweating; (4) fecal retention by the child; (5) medications (such as some drugs used to control seizures or attention deficit hyperactivity disorder and narcotics used to control pain) that may have a side effect of promoting constipation; and (6) the child's emotional state. Any of these factors, singly or in some combination, can result in constipation-like symptoms or actual constipation. Loening-Baucke, Cruikshank, and Savage (1987) found that the persistence of encopresis at 6-month and 12-month follow-up was not related to social competence, but was significantly related to the inability to defecate and the inability to relax the external anal sphincter during defecation attempts.

When a child with a history of uncomfortable or painful bowel movements feels the urge to defecate, he or she may associate that urge with sensations previously followed by a painful or uncomfortable bowel movement. In an attempt to prevent a recurrence of the painful bowel movement, the child may voluntarily retain feces, thus exacerbating the problem. If constipation is extended, the child may become lethargic, which in turn reduces activity level, leading to an additional decrease in colonic motility, and the constipation is perpetuated. Also, more severe constipation may result in a decreased appetite. The child may develop a fecal impaction, which is a large blockage caused by the collection of hard dry stool. Not infrequently, these children will experience seepage around the fecal mass, producing what has been termed *paradoxical diarrhea*. Although the child is actually constipated, he or she appears to have diarrhea. Some parents will attempt to treat this type of "diarrhea" with the over-the-counter antidiarrheal agents, which only worsen the problem.

Evaluation

Our "go no further with treatment until the child has received a medical evaluation" rule is important for all elimination problems discussed in this chapter, but it may be most important for the approach to encopresis. Forgoing the possibility of organic disease (discussed below), there is still the very serious problem of excessive waste accumulating in an organ with a finite amount of space. An unfortunately all-too-frequent presenting problem in medical clinics is an encopretic child who has been in extended therapy with a nonmedical professional whose initial evaluation did not include referral for a medical evaluation and whose treatment did not address known causes of encopresis (e.g., diet, behavior, constipation). As a result, the children's colonic systems can become painfully and dangerously distended, sometimes to the point of being life threatening (e.g., McGuire, Rothenberg, & Tyler, 1983).

Levine (1975) reported on 102 children with encopresis who were seen in a general pediatric outpatient clinic. Of these children, 81 were found to have stool impaction at the time of the first visit. Of these 81 children, 39 were treated for constipation in infancy. The physician will typically take a thorough medical, dietary, and bowel history. In addition, an abdominal examination and rectal examination is often necessary to check for either large amounts of stool or very dry stool in the rectal vault and to check for poor sphincter tone. Approximately 70% of constipation can be determined on physical exam and detection can be increased to above 90% with a KUB (x-ray of kidneys, ureter, and bladder) (Barr, Levine, Wilkinson, & Mulvihill, 1979). This latter method is also helpful with children who refuse a rectal exam or who are obese (Loening-Bauke, 1996).

Some medical conditions (e.g., Hirschsprung's disease), if identified, may preclude referral to a behavioral practitioner. Levine (1981) provided an excellent tabular comparison for the clinician to use in differentiating encopresis from Hirschsprung's disease (the most common organic cause for bowel dysfunction that is present from birth on). Additionally, the absence of weight gain in a child who is below the growth curve for weight may be suggestive of one of the variety of malabsorption syndromes that are known to be present in a small percentage of children.

Despite the emphasis on diet and behavior here and in many other parts of the relevant literature, some psychologists and psychiatrists persist in viewing encopresis as a psychological problem. A growing body of research undermines the plausibility of that view, however. At least three studies have examined the incidence of behavioral disorders in children who present with encopresis (Friman et al., 1988; Gabel, Hegedus, Wald, Chandra, & Chaponis, 1986; Loening-Baucke et al., 1987). All three concluded that, although some children with encopresis also have behavioral problems, the incidence is simply not high enough to suggest a causal relationship between the two conditions. Thus, targeting psychological problems in order to obtain fecal continence would seem imprudent from the perspective of the scientific literature. Rather, the encopresis and the emotional/psychological problems may have to be dealt with separately.

The actual presenting symptoms would determine how these problems were addressed. For example, noncompliant encopretic children should receive some form of instructional control training prior to or along with treatment for encopresis (cf., Stark, Spirito, Lewis, & Hart, 1990).

Treatment

Encopresis (with Constipation). The first treatment-based break with characterological (punish) and psychopathological (psychotherapy) perspectives on encopresis was provided by Murray Davidson who described what has come to be called the pediatric approach to retentive encopresis (Davidson, 1958; Davidson, Kugler, and Bauer, 1963). The regimen involved starting a child on a daily dose of mineral oil (which acts both as a stool softener and as a lubricant) and increasing the dosage until regular bowel functioning was established. The mineral oil regimen was often accompanied by reductions in dairy products (which slow colonic motility) and increases in fruits and vegetables (which increase colonic motility). The initial evaluation study produced a high rate of success (90%) (Davidson et al., 1963).

Over the past 20 years, several descriptive and controlled experimental studies have supported incorporating Davidson's pediatric regimen into a multicomponent approach to treatment of chronic retentive encopresis (Christophersen & Purvis, 2001; Friman & Jones, 1998; McGrath et al., 2000). The first component can be addressed within the evaluation. Specifically, the entire elimination process including its disordered manifestations should be "demystified" (Levine, 1982). The belief, born of the characterological and psychopathological perspective on encopresis, that bowel retention and bowel accidents are generally associated with personality development, and specifically with such characteristics as stubbornness, immaturity, or laziness, can result in parents shaming and blaming their children into the bathroom. But a disordered process of elimination such as encopresis should no more be a target for censure and blame than should a disordered process of respiration, digestion, or motor movement. As indicated above, the literature does not support the association between behavioral profiles and bowel habits (Friman et al., 1988; Gabel et al., 1986; Loening-Baucke et al., 1987). On the contrary, this literature recommends that parents avoid blaming the child and suggests that they restructure toileting conditions in order to increase the likelihood of proper elimination. Second, if there is a fecal impaction it should be removed with enemas and/or laxatives. Third, the child should sit on the toilet for about 5 minutes 1 or 2 times a day. Fourth, the parents should promote proper toileting with encouragement and not with coercion. Additionally, they should not reserve all their praise and affection for proper elimination; a child should be praised just for sitting on the toilet. Fifth, a stool softener such as mineral oil or glycerin suppositories should be used in order to ease the passage of hard stools. Sixth, dietary fiber should be increased in the child's diet. Seventh, in order to increase and maintain motility in the child's colon, the child's activity levels and fluid intake should be increased. Eighth, during toileting episodes the child's feet should be on a flat surface (e.g., Stool). Foot placement is crucial to the "Valsalva maneuver" (grunting push necessary to produce a bowel movement). And finally, the child should be rewarded for all bowel movements in the toilet (Christophersen & Purvis, 2001; Friman & Jones, 1998; McGrath et al., 2000).

An occasionally voiced concern with this comprehensive direct treatment approach is that treating only the symptoms of encopresis may produce behavioral or psychological side effects (e.g., "symptom substitution"). Levine, Mazonson, and Bakow (1980) demonstrated that, although encopresis may have psychological implications, it is a specific disease entity that can be treated without fear of symptom substitution. Their study used a behavioral inventory to compare (before and after treatment and at 3-year follow-up) a group of encopretic children who were cured with a group who were not cured to determine whether any significant symptom substitution occurred in children cured of encopresis. They concluded that successful treatment was not accompanied by any problematic behavioral side effects and their findings were subsequently replicated by research using even more rigorous methods (e.g., Young, Brennen, Baker, & Baker, 1995).

The literature on this comprehensive approach (or variations thereof) has progressed sufficiently to lead to group trials. For example, in a study of 58 children with encopresis, 60% were completely continent after 5 months and those that did not achieve full continence averaged a 90% decrease in accidents (Lowery, Srour, Whitehead, & Schuster, 1985). In a more recent study Cox, Sutphen, Borowitz, Kovatchev, and Ling (1998) reported on a comparison of three treatment conditions: (1) medical care (including enemas for disimpaction and laxatives to promote frequent bowel movements); (2) enhanced toilet training—a comprehensive approach very similar that described above (using reinforcement and scheduling to promote response to defecation urges and instruction and modeling to promote appropriate straining, along with laxatives and enemas; and (3) biofeedback (directed at relaxing the external anal sphincter during attempted defection, along with toilet training, laxatives, and enemas). At 3 months after treatment, the enhanced toilet training group significantly benefited more children than the other two treatments with fewer treatment sessions and lower costs.

The multiple successes of the comprehensive approach to treatment have led to evaluation of group treatment. In the initial evaluation, 18 encopretic children between the ages of 4 and 11 years and their parents were seen in groups of 3 to 5 families for 6 sessions. Noteworthy is that all of these children had previously failed a medical regimen (cf., Davidson, 1958; Davidson et al., 1963). The sessions in this trial focused on a much-expanded regimen very similar to that described above. Soiling accidents decreased by 84% across the groups and these results were maintained or improved at 6 months' follow-up (Stark, Owens-Stively, Spirito, Lewis, & Guevremont, 1990). Additionally, the results were subsequently replicated in a much larger group (Stark et al., 1997).

An aid for treatment of resistant cases is biofeedback training (mentioned in the Cox et al. study above). For those children with very limited awareness of rectal distension and/or with abnormal defecation dynamics, biofeedback has been successfully used to increase awareness and retrain bowel habits (e.g., Loening-Baucke, 1990; Wald, Chandra, Gabel, & Chiponis, 1987). These findings on biofeedback should be viewed with some caution, however, because a recent trial was not supportive. Van der Plas, Benninga, Redekop, Taminiau, and Buller (1996) evaluated the use of biofeedback in the treatment of encopresis using two randomly assigned groups of encopretic children. Both groups received dietary and toilet advice, enemas, oral laxatives, and anorectal manometry. The biofeedback group also received five biofeedback-training sessions. The results did not indicate that biofeedback training had an additive effect on the success rate. These results, however, do not bear on biofeedback procedures used alone or with highly treatment resistant children. It is also possible that the comprehensive regimens we have described are so successful that ceiling effects are established, making it difficult for the addition of biofeedback to produce a statistically detectable change.

Encopresis (without Constipation). Treatment of nonretentive encopresis is not well established, thus recommending an optimal course of treatment is premature. Perhaps the best approach would begin with a comprehensive psychological evaluation that includes behavioral assessment techniques. Virtually all investigators who have described this subsample of children report emotional and behavioral problems and treatment resistance (e.g., Landman & Rappaport, 1985), and it is possible that some of these children's soiling is related to modifiable aspects of their social ecology. Some investigators have employed versions of the approach outlined above and included supportive verbal therapy (Landman & Rappaport, 1985) or they have specifically taught parents how to manage their children's misbehavior (Stark et al.,

1990). Clearly the various problems, other than soiling, exhibited by this subsample require some form of treatment (but the soiling itself needs direct treatment too).

NOCTURNAL ENURESIS

Definitional Criteria

The current criteria for enuresis (nocturnal and diurnal) from *DSM-IV* (American Psychiatric Association, 1994) are: (1) repeated urination into bed or clothing; (2) at least 2 occurrences per week for at least 3 months or a sufficient number of occurrences to cause clinically significant distress; (3) chronological age of 5 or, for children with developmental delays, a mental age of at least 5; (4) not due exclusively to the direct effects of a substance (e.g., diuretics) or a general medical condition (e.g., diabetes).

There are three subtypes of enuresis—nocturnal only, diurnal only, and mixed nocturnal and diurnal. There are two courses, primary and secondary. The primary course includes children who have never established continence and the secondary course involves children who, after establishing continence, resume having accidents.

Relevant Physiology and Related Skills

The bladder is the primary organ in a complex set of physiological systems that govern urination. A comprehensive review of these systems is far beyond the scope of this chapter (for more thorough discussions see Muellner, 1951; Vincent, 1974). Optimal bladder training requires detection of bladder filling and either urination in an appropriate location or retentive contraction of pelvic floor muscles (Friman & Jones, 1998; Mellon, Scott, Haynes, Schmidt, & Houts, 1997).

In very general terms, the voluntary components of the bladder system can be used to initiate the involuntary components to achieve urination or continence. Establishing nocturnal continence involves a sequence of continence skills including awareness of urgency, initiating urination, inhibiting actual and impending urination while awake and inhibiting actual and impending urination while asleep. Mastery of continence skills requires abundant practice, especially for enuretic children.

Prevalence

Even the most conservative research-based estimates show enuresis is a very common problem. The National Health Examination Survey reported as many as 25% of boys and 15% of girls were enuretic at age 6 with as many as 8% of boys and 4% of girls still enuretic at age 12 (Gross & Dornbusch, 1983; see also Foxman, Valdez, & Brook, 1986). Prevalence studies from outside the United States indicate at least 7% of all 8-year-old children wet their beds with an approximate 2-to-1 ratio of boys over girls (Verhulst et al., 1985). Estimates of the percentage of primary cases begin at 80% to 90% (Friman & Jones, 1998; Mellon & Houts, 1995).

Etiology

Enuresis has a variable clinical presentation, which makes establishing its precise etiology a difficult assignment. Not only are its initiating causes and maintaining variables also variable and often different from child to child, they can actually differ within the same child at different points in time (Friman & Jones, 1998). The etiological variables that have received the most scientific investigation are family history, maturation, functional bladder capacity, sleep dynamics, physical pathology, psychopathology, and nocturnal polyuria.

Family History. The research on family history shows that the probability of enuresis increases as a function of closeness or number of blood relations with a positive history (Friman & Jones, 1998; Kaffman & Elizur, 1977). It is possible that families convey tolerant attitudes toward bed wetting and not enuretic "genes," but even in settings where family custom plays a minimal role in child development, there is a high correlation between family history and enuresis (Kaffman & Elizur, 1977).

Maturation. The possibility of a genetic connection suggests a biologic factor one plausible candidate for which is maturational lag. For example, children with decreased developmental scores at the ages of 1 and 3 years are significantly more likely to be enuretic than children with higher scores (Fergusson, Horwood & Sannon, 1986). There is also an inverse relationship between birth weight and enuresis at any age. Enuretic children tend to lag slightly behind their nonenuretic peers in Tanner sexual maturation scores, bone growth, and height (Gross & Dornbusch, 1983). The increased prevalence of enuresis in boys also suggests maturation lag because boys generally have a slower rate of development than girls throughout childhood and adolescence. Finally, enuretic children exhibit a 15% annual spontaneous remission rate, which is consistent with the notion that they are lagging behind in the acquisition of continence, a developmental milestone for all children (Forsythe & Redmond, 1974). Despite the apparent maturational lag in many (perhaps most) enuretic children, their scores on standardized intellectual tests are in the average range. Thus the maturational lag appears more anatomical and/or physiological than intellectual and its cardinal expression is delayed bladder control (Friman & Jones, 1998; Gross & Dornbusch, 1983).

Functional Bladder Capacity (FBC). FBC refers to voiding capacity as distinguished from true bladder capacity (TBC), which refers to bladder structure (Troup & Hodgson, 1971). FBC is established in various ways, examples of which include the higher volume in either of the first 2 voidings after ingestion of a specified water load (e.g., 30 ml/kg body weight), the average of all voidings in 24 hours, or the average of all voidings in 1 week. The FBC of enuretic children is generally lower than that of their nonenuretic siblings and peers but their TBC is about the same. Overall the research on FBC suggests many enuretic children urinate more frequently with lesser volume than their nonenuretic peers and siblings. Their urinary pattern has been compared to that found in infants and very young children (Friman & Jones, 1998).

Sleep Dynamics. By definition nocturnal enuresis is a sleep problem. It is also regarded as a parasomnia by most sleep researchers, as a manifestation of sleep disturbance by some sleep researchers, and as an outcome of deep sleep by most parents (Friman & Jones, 1998). Still, sleep dynamics have not been established as a cause of enuresis. Wetting episodes occur in all stages of nonrapid eye movement (NREM) sleep and the probability of their occurrence appears to be a function of the amount of time spent in each stage. Enuretic episodes also rarely occur during REM sleep, therefore thematically related dreams (e.g., dreaming of urinating) may be a result rather than a cause of wetting.

A final issue pertaining to sleep involves whether enuretic children are more difficult to awaken than their nonenuretic peers. Generally, findings from most studies are mixed and marred by experimental limitations (e.g., sleep stages not established). A recent study with 15 enuretic boys and 18 controls addressed this problem by employing sleep EEGs and auditory tones delivered via earphones. During 512 arousal attempts enuretic children awoke 8.5% of the time compared to 39.6% of the time for controls (Gellis, 1994). Thus, the common parental complaint about bed-wetting children who are difficult to awaken may have an empirical basis.

Physical Pathology. There are numerous well-known potential physiopathologic causes of enuresis. These include urinary tract infection, urinary tract anomaly, bladder instability, occult spina bifida, epilepsy, diabetes mellitus, and sleep apnea. Most of these causes can be ruled out by complete history, physical exam, and urinalysis. When unanswered questions remain, other more elaborate laboratory examinations such as voiding cystourethrogram or polysomnographic evaluation are available (Friman & Jones, 1998; Gross & Dornbusch, 1983).

Psychopathology. Although remnants of the once prominent (if not dominant) position that enuresis was a function of underlying psychopathology remain, the majority position appears to be that psychopathology is not a causal variable for primary enuresis. To the extent there are increased behavior problems, they are more likely a result of than a cause of enuresis (e.g., Friman, Handwerk, Swearer, McGinnis, & Warzak, 1998; Friman & Jones, 1998). Moreover, recent longitudinal research showing that maturational variables were predictive of enuresis also showed that psychosocial variables such as emotional disposition were not (Fergusson et al., 1986). A possible exception to the above involves increased emotional problems in children with secondary enuresis. First, as noted above in the physiology section, continence involves skilled practice, and necessary skills can be lost, regained, and lost again. Thus secondary enuresis, by itself, does not indicate presence of emotional problems, but major life stressors (e.g., loss of parent, moving, academic failure, etc.) may result in various types of temporary skill loss, including continence skills (Friman & Jones, 1998).

Nocturnal Polyuria. The presence of antidiuretic hormone (ADH) or arginine vasopression causes the kidneys to increase the concentration of urine (by increasing reabsorption of free water in the renal-collecting duct). Theoretically, serum ADH levels increase at night and thereby protect sleep from urinary urgency and facilitate nocturnal continence. Recent research has shown that a subset of enuretic children do not exhibit the normal diurnal rhythm of ADH secretion and perhaps wet their beds as a result of increased urine production while sleeping (e.g., Norgaard, Pedersen, & Djurhuus, 1985). Earlier (and subsequent) related research showed that desmopressin (DDAVP), an intranasally administered vasopressin analogue, reduced nocturnal enuretic episodes in children (e.g., Dimson, 1977; and see DDAVP under the section Treatment below). Whether the effectiveness of DDAVP is due to restoration of insufficient nocturnal ADH or is merely the result of decreased urine volume (due to increased concentration) and thus not a primary causal variable is still unknown (Houts, 1991). In fact, support for decreased nocturnal ADH as a primary causal variable is still quite limited, for several reasons. The sample sizes in the related studies were small (e.g., Norgaard et al., 1985). Fewer than one fourth of treated bed-wetting children achieve short-term dryness (Moffat, Harlos, Kirshen, Burd, 1993). Not all children with known urine concentrating problems wet the bed (e.g., only 50% of children with sickle cell anemia are enuretic). Lastly, lower ADH is not linked in any empirical way to why children do not awaken to full bladders, and not all persons (children included) awaken to a full bladder or wet their bed because they do not awaken. As indicated above, nocturnal enuresis is multiply determined and abnormality in nocturnal ADH secretion is but one of several possible causal contributors.

Evaluation

As with toileting refusal and encopresis, the initial stage of an enuresis evaluation should contain a "go no further" maxim. That is, once the history has been obtained and preliminary information about enuresis has been shared with the parents and child, the psychologist should go no further with direct treatment until a medical examination has been conducted. As indicated in the etiology section, a number of pathophysiological variables can cause enuresis and, although these are rare, they are a possibility and must be ruled out medically before a primary treatment plan is implemented. This emphasis on initial medical examination should not be construed as undermining the role of the psychologist. The medical examination is but one of a number of components necessary for effective management of enuresis, most of which could (and typically would) be implemented by the school-based psychologist. Effective management involves direct and indirect components and the medical examination merely precedes the direct components. There are, however, important indirect components that can be pursued immediately. For example, the parents and child will most likely have contended unsuccessfully with enuresis for some time and thus it is likely to seem beyond their control. Additionally, because a residue of characterological and psychopathological interpretations of enuresis still remain in western culture, it is possible the parents and the child will have misinterpreted the problem. In the initial encounter the psychologist can introduce optimism about management and disabuse parents and child of antiquated notions about enuresis that sometimes lead to blaming or shaming the child.

While taking the history, the psychologist should include questions derived from the subsections above on defining characteristics (e.g., primary vs. secondary) and etiological factors mentioned above (e.g., family history of enuresis, disease history, mental health history, etc.). Some screening for mental health problems should be included (e.g., behavior checklists, related inquiry). As indicated earlier, mental health problems do not appear to have a direct forward causal relationship with enuresis (i.e., they are much more likely to be caused than they are to cause enuresis). However, if the child presents with mental health problems, these should be addressed in the ultimate treatment plan.

In addition to addressing medical and psychological complications, the evaluation should also address three other very important topics. First, the psychologist should probe all aspects of the child's life to determine sources of punishment for wetting and take steps to neutralize them. Warning parents away from punishment can do this directly and educating them that the incontinence is beyond their child's immediate control can do it indirectly. Second, the psychologist should assess the motivational level and availability of social resources for the parents. If the parent is minimally motivated and/or has few social resources (e.g., single working parent), the number of treatment components he or she will be able to implement may be limited. Third, the psychologist should assess the motivation of the child. As is seen in the treatment section, optimal treatment plans involve multiple components and require compliance from the child for completion of most steps. An unmotivated or noncompliant child would be difficult to treat with any method known to cure enuresis. Fortunately, enuresis itself usually contributes to the afflicted child's motivation. As the quantity of pleasant experiences missed (e.g., sleepovers, camp) and unpleasant experiences encountered (e.g., wetness, social detection, embarrassment) accumulate, motivation naturally increases.

Treatment

Medication.

1. *Tricyclic antidepressants.* Historically, tricyclic antidepressants were the drugs of choice for treatment of enuresis and imipramine was the most frequently prescribed drug treatment (Blackwell & Currah, 1973; Foxman et al., 1986; Stephenson, 1979). The mechanism by which imipramine reduces bed wetting is still, for the most part, unknown (Stephenson, 1979). Most experts now agree its antidepressant and sleep effects are not the significant mechanisms

leading to a decrease in wetting. A review and synthesis of the research on mechanisms is beyond the scope of this chapter. It is important to know, however, that imipramine somehow reduces premature contractions of the bladder following partial filling and thereby increases functional bladder capacity (Stephenson, 1979).

Imipramine, in doses between 25 and 75 mg given at bedtime, produces initial reductions in wetting in a majority of children, often within the first week of treatment (Blackwell & Currah, 1973). The primary therapeutic gain from imipramine, however, appears to be the respite from wetting obtained while the child is on the drug. Reviews of both short- and long-term studies show enuresis usually recurs when tricyclic therapeutic agents are withdrawn. The permanent cure produced with imipramine is reported to be 25% (ranging from 5% to 40%) (Blackwell & Currah, 1973; Houts, Berman, & Abramson, 1994). But no study we found factored in the annual spontaneous remission rate of 15% and doing so could reduce this already low figure considerably.

More importantly, use of imipramine does not teach continence skills. In fact, by diminishing bladder contractions it reduces opportunities for learning sensory awareness of those contractions and practicing needed responses. This reduced opportunity to learn may account for the high relapse rate following termination of the medication and for reports showing that drug regimens can impair subsequent continence skill training programs (Houts, Peterson, Liebert, 1984). Finally, imipramine can cause several untoward side effects ranging in severity from excessive sweating, irritability, nausea, and vomiting to convulsions, collapse, coma, and death (e.g., Cohen, 1975).

Given its low cure rate and high relapse rates, side effects, potential to diminish skill development, and potential toxicity, imipramine should not be used as a primary treatment for enuresis. But, because its effects are seen so quickly (when they occur), it can be a valuable adjunct to treatment, especially when other methods are failing and a dry night is needed to heighten motivation or when a child plans to attend camp or a sleepover (Friman & Jones, 1998).

2. *Antidiuretics.* As described in the section on nocturnal polyuria, Norgaard and colleagues reported on a small number of enuretic children who had abnormal circadian patterns of plasma vasopressin concentration (e.g., Norgaard et al., 1985). As a result of these reports and because of its known antidiuretic properties, DDAVP rapidly became a popular treatment for enuresis and it may now have displaced the tricyclics as the most prescribed treatment. DDAVP concentrates urine, thereby decreasing urine volume and intravesical pressure, which makes bladder neck descent and bladder contraction less probable and nocturnal continence more probable. DDAVP also has far fewer side effects than imipramine (e.g., Moffatt et al., 1993; Norgaard et al., 1985).

Research on DDAVP has yielded mixed results and a recent review indicated that fewer than 25% of children become fully dry on the drug and, similar to tricyclics, its effects appear to last only as long as the drug is taken and are less likely to occur in younger children or children who have frequent accidents (Moffatt et al., 1993; see also Houts et al., 1994). Additionally, DDAVP is also very expensive. Finally, because DDAVP reduces urine output it also reduces opportunities to practice continence skills. Nonetheless, its effects are as immediate as imipramine but with fewer side effects and thus DDAVP may be preferable to imipramine as an adjunct to treatment.

Behavioral Treatment Behavioral treatment requires more effort than drug treatment but it is safer, in terms of side effects, and more effective, in terms of higher cessation rates and lower relapse rates. Behavioral treatment is superior to drug treatment because the drugs used for enuresis cause changes in body chemistry and corresponding physiology that are impermanent—they last only as long as the drugs are in the system. Behavioral treatment, however, trains skills that are necessary for continence and they outlast the implementation of the methods employed to teach them in all children and are permanent in most. The following section describes the most commonly used behavioral treatments for enuresis.

1. *Urine alarm.* The alarm works using a moisture sensitive switching system, the closing of which rings the alarm. Numerous safe, efficient, and effective alarms are available, many of which attach directly to the child's pajamas and thus increase the child's access to alarm feedback. The mechanism of action in alarm treatment was initially described as classical conditioning with the alarm as the unconditioned stimulus, bladder distention the conditioned stimulus, and waking as the conditioned response. The alarm may also involve negative reinforcement obtained when child awakens to the alarm, stops urinating and either completes urination in the toilet or holds his or her urine until a more convenient time. Cures are obtained slowly and during the first few weeks of alarm use the child often awakens only after voiding completely. Reports of controlled comparative trials show the alarm is superior to imipramine, DDAVP, and other skill-based methods. In fact, the literature has consistently described the urine alarm as the single most effective treatment for enuresis with its success rate is higher (approximately 75%) and its relapse rate lower (approximately 41%) than any other drug or skill-based treatment (e.g., Friman & Jones, 1998; Mellon & McGrath, 2000).

2. *Retention control training (RCT).* The emergence of RCT followed the observation that many enuretic children had reduced functional bladder capacity (Starfield, 1967). RCT expands functional bladder capacity by requiring children to drink extra fluids (e.g., 16 oz of water or juice) and delay urination as long as possible (Starfield, 1967; Starfield & Mellits, 1968). To assess progress, an enuretic child's parents should set up a weekly game where the child urinates in an appropriate container and tries to produce more urine than in previous weeks. RCT is successful in as many as 50% of cases (Starfield & Mellits, 1968), but it is not as effective as the urine alarm. This lesser effectiveness is not surprising because RCT does not train nocturnal skills directly. It directly trains volume control skills during the day, which indirectly affects nocturnal continence skills.

3. *Stream interruption exercises.* Kegel exercises involve purposeful manipulation of the muscles necessary to prematurely terminate urination or contraction of the muscles of the pelvic floor (Kegel, 1951). Originally developed for stress incontinence in women, a version of these exercises, stream interruption, has been used in enuresis treatment packages for years (Friman & Jones, 1998). For children, stream interruption requires initiating and terminating urine flow at least once a day during a urinary episode. The use of stream interruption exercises in the treatment of enuresis is logical from a physiological perspective, because, as indicated in the physiology section, terminating an actual or impending urinary episode involves the same muscle systems. Thus regular practice could increase a child's capacity to retain urine longer and expedite attainment of continence. A recent study of Kegel exercises, however, showed their regular practice eliminated enuresis in 47 of 79 children with diurnal enuresis. Stream interruption was used to train the appropriate muscle contractions, but dry contraction composed the exercise and it was held for 5 to 10 seconds, followed by a 5-second rest, 10 times on 3 separate occasions a day (Schneider, King, & Surwit, 1994). Of the 52 children who also wet at night, nocturnal episodes were eliminated in 18 and improved in 9 children. Thus Kegel exercises may have a functional role in enuresis treatment.

4. *Waking schedule.* This treatment component involves waking the children and guiding them to the bathroom for urination. Results obtained are attributed to a change in arousal, increased access to the reinforcing properties of dry nights, and urinary urge in lighter stages of sleep (Bollard & Nettlebeck, 1982; Friman & Jones, 1998). In a representative study using a staggered waking schedule, four of nine children reduced their accidents to less than twice

a week, suggesting a waking schedule may improve but is unlikely to cure enuresis (Creer & Davis, 1975). A less effortful schedule involves waking the children just before the parents go to bed and systematically fading the schedule by waking them one-half hour earlier on nights following several successive dry nights (Bollard & Nettlebeck, 1982).

5. *Reward systems.* Reward systems may not cure enuresis but they can sustain a child's motivation to participate in treatment, especially when the system rewards success in small steps (Friman & Jones, 1998; Jenson & Sloane, 1979). An example involves a dot-to-dot drawing and a grab bag. The child identifies an affordable and desirable prize and the parent draws (or traces) a picture of it using a dot-to-dot format with every third or fourth dot bigger than the rest. The child then connects two dots for each dry night and when the line reaches a larger dot, he or she earns access to a grab bag with small rewards (e.g., small toys, edibles, money, privileges, special time with parents). When all the dots are connected, the child earns the prize.

6. *Responsibility training.* All of the skill-based components mentioned above are designed to promote a mature voiding repertoire in the child. To be consistent with this design, the child should be treated in a way that promotes maturation. For example, he or she should not be left in diapers at night. The child should be assigned household responsibilities associated with his or her accidents. In younger children this may merely mean bringing their sheets to the laundry basket. In older children, however, it may mean actually laundering the sheets. These responsibilities should not be presented as a punishment but as a correlate of increased responsibility and a demonstration of the parent's confidence in and respect for their maturing child.

Cognitive Therapy In the treatment subsections above, we have emphasized "treatments that work." In the history of enuresis, there have been numerous treatments that did not work. These include a variety of ancient (often horrific) treatments (e.g., sacral burning), punishment, fluid restrictions, and traditional psychotherapy (Friman & Jones, 1998; Houts, 1991, 2000). None of these treatments has been supported by empirical research. Cognitive therapy, a version of psychotherapy, however, competed favorably with conditioning treatment in a comparative trial a decade ago (Ronen, Wozner, & Rahav, 1992). In our view, these findings should be viewed with great caution and should not guide practice, for several reasons. First, a decade has come and gone and the findings still have not been independently replicated, despite the ease of their application. Second, they are dramatically inconsistent with over 50 years of research showing the routine success of behavioral approaches and routine failure of purely psychological (e.g., cognitive) approaches to treatment of enuresis (e.g., Friman & Jones, 1998; Houts, 1991, 2000; Mellon & McGrath, 2000). Third, the authors made no attempt to explain how a purely cognitive approach could so powerfully influence a problem that has such a fundamentally biological basis. Fourth and finally, the original study is flawed methodologically in several ways (see Houts, 2000, for thorough critique).

Very possibly enuresis is accompanied by cognitive problems (e.g., thinking errors, flawed heuristics, etc.) but, as indicated above, there is no empirically derived evidence these are causal nor is there evidence to suggest treating such problems (rather than the enuresis) would lead to continence. In light of the absolute failure to establish continence by reasoning with bed-wetting children, the extraordinary number of successful attempts to establish it through conditioning during the past 50 years, and the relatively well-developed picture of the physiology of micturation, it appears there is no cogent conceptually derived evidence either. Essentially, it appears the Ronen and colleagues (1992) study is an anomaly and scientific anomalies should not guide practice.

Optimal Treatment Plans Historically, the choice of treatment for enuresis was governed more by the desire to establish continence than by concern for the child's health and well-being. Fortunately, health care for enuretic children has evolved substantially since that time. Nonetheless, the sustained reliance on drugs as a primary treatment, the abiding parental use of punishment, and the often excessive restriction on fluid intake still places the health and well-being of many enuretic children at risk. The treatments most likely to cure enuresis with minimal risk to child health are those that specifically teach continence skills and decades of behavioral research have generated several skill-based treatment components.

Initially, the psychologist should inform the child and parents that numerous other children, many probably in the child's neighborhood and school, also have enuresis. Then with the child in attendance, the psychologist should tell the parents to avoid blaming or shaming the child for wetting then obtain the child's cooperation in treatment and work with the child and family on a treatment plan. The initial choice of components should be based on the provider's assessment of child readiness, child and parent willingness, and family resources. The components in the plan can be "titrated" over time in accord with family resources and motivation until continence is obtained. So, for example, a 2-parent, 1-wage-earner, middle-income family with a motivated 10-year-old bed-wetting child and at least 1 motivated parent could be given a waking schedule, a motivational system, and the alarm on the initial visit. Over the course of one or two additional visits, other skill-based treatment components could be added as needed along with a small prescription of (DDAVP or imipramine) for sleepovers or campouts. Families with fewer resources and less motivation would be given fewer components. So, for example, a 1-parent, low-income family with a motivated 10-year-old child and a nonmotivated parent could be given urine retention and stream interruption. The chances for cure, other things being equal, are lower in the second case than in the first, but they are still higher than if no treatment were used. Furthermore, the active involvement of the child may lead to increased involvement by the parent, at which point the provider could add more components.

DIURNAL ENURESIS

Although we placed our discussion of diurnal enuresis, after nocturnal enuresis, it may be a much more important concern in the school setting for multiple reasons. First, by definition nocturnal enuresis cannot occur at school whereas diurnal enuresis not only can but also often does. Second, having an accident at school is a highly distressing experience for the incontinent child. In a survey of 20 childhood fears, "wetting pants in class" was third behind "losing a parent" and "going blind" (Allantoic, King, & Fray, 1989). Third, there are public health considerations, especially in young children. For example, the increase in the prevalence of infectious disease (e.g., hepatitis) seen in day-care settings and preschools over the past few decades has been partially attributed to the spread of bacteria through child incontinence (Berk & Friman, 1990).

Definitional Criteria and Prevalence

The research on diurnal and mixed enuresis is much smaller (and the problems occur less frequently) and thus virtually all aspects of this problem are less understood. In fact, the *DSM-IV* criteria notwithstanding, no widely accepted definitional criteria exist for diurnal enuresis. Prevalence estimates for diurnal and mixed enuresis for both boys and girls at ages 6 and 7 years range between 1/2% to 2% (Blomfield & Douglas, 1956; also see Berk & Friman, 1990; Friman & Jones, 1998).

Etiology

The pathophysiological etiology of diurnal enuresis can be grouped into bacteriuria (much more likely in girls), disease (e.g., diabetes), anatomical abnormalities (e.g., nephropathy), and functional abnormalities (e.g., unstable bladder). Although these conditions all may require behavioral interventions as part of a comprehensive treatment plan, the initial and primary management is medical. The class of diurnal enuresis for which primary management is behavioral (after all medical issues have been addressed or ruled out) has various labels (e.g., day time dribbling; nonneurogenic neuorgenic bladder) and the one we prefer to use is urge incontinence (Meadow, 1990).

A key variable in urge incontinence is (similar to routine toilet training) awareness of bladder distension and incipient or actual bladder neck descent (see section on physiology of bladder). This distension and/or descent gives rise to postural changes and limb movements suggestive of urinary urgency. The function of these movements appears to be maintenance of bladder neck ascent. For example, when children scissor their legs or compress their thighs, the movements produce upward pressure in the perineal region that lifts the bladder neck and forestalls urination (Fielding, 1982; also see Muellner, 1951; Vincent, 1974). These movements and their function are paradoxical, however, in that children are often unaware of them and of urinary urgency. So, when parents advise their children to go the bathroom, based on observation of the movements, the children may appear unaware of need. Routine aspects of parental teaching can be applied to help the child make the necessary connections, initially between body movements and need, and ultimately between bladder contraction and need, and thus enable to complete or forestall urination based on a plan.

A major factor inhibiting attainment of the awareness needed for continence is limited bladder capacity (Fielding, 1982; Friman & Jones, 1998). This limitation is primarily due to either functional capacity variables (as with nocturnal enuresis) or partial emptying. Children with these problems have poor control over their pelvic floor musculature and/or immature (oversensitive to filling) bladders. Behavior problems (e.g., noncompliance) may also have a role in the limited attainment of continence.

Treatment

There are few published studies on behavioral treatment of diurnal enuresis. A notable one used the nocturnal urine alarm to heighten awareness of urge and train continence skills (Halliday, Meadow, & Berg, 1987). Two thirds of the 44 children in the study became dry on the alarm, although no individualized treatment plans or data were reported. A subsequent controlled case study of a 15-year-old girl ruled out medical variables and used an ecological assessment to show awareness and detection variables were causal. The assessments revealed accidents occurred only at home, never in school. Thus it appeared that in an environment with a high probability of punitive responses following detection, awareness and therefore continence was increased. Following implementation of alarm treatment at home, complete continence was attained and maintained at long-term follow-up (Friman & Vollmer, 1995). Recent advances in the technology of urine alarms enhance their potential as a primary treatment for diurnal enuresis even further. Various alarm makers now provide an alarm that vibrates rather than emits noise, resulting in private but not public detection of accidents.

Another recent study targeted increased control of pelvic floor musculature by training 79 day-wetting children to practice Kegel exercises at least 3 times a day (Schneider et al., 1994). The intervention eliminated accidents in 44 children and reduced them in another 9.

Optimal approach

The optimal approach to diurnal enuresis involves comprehensive assessment (medical and psychological). Medical conditions need to be ruled out initially and psychological complications need to be addressed prior to behavioral intervention. Treatment should then focus on known causes of wetting that can be remediated behaviorally. These include limited awareness and pelvic floor insufficiency. Although motivational systems have not been reported, it is difficult to argue how they could impair progress. In the event of behavioral resistance (non compliance, opposition) treatment should initially be directed toward variables related to it.

CONCLUSIONS

Eliminations disorders involve a complex interplay between a child's gastrointestinal and/or genital-urinary systems and a variety of environmental events. Although the expression of the disorders is primarily medical, biobehavioral approaches to evaluation and treatment are optimal. The medical expression and the emphasis on biology in the biobehavioral approach obligates the school-based psychologist to become knowledgeable about normal eliminational physiological functioning. As we have indicated several times earlier, prior to implementing a treatment plan the psychologist should refer incontinent children for a medical evaluation.

There has been a long-standing cultural bias against incontinent children and it continues to this day. Part of its basis could involve the contingencies of survival. Human waste when not properly disposed of is a threat to health and thus revulsion is a response that may have an evolutionary basis. But the bias is also due in no small way to the perpetuated misattributions of incontinence to character flaws (e.g., laziness) and over interpretations of it as an indicator of underlying psychopathology. The school-based psychologist can begin treatment indirectly by addressing these sources of bias when and where they are encountered.

It is also likely that cases encountered by school-based psychologists have a history of failed attempts at resolution by child and parent. Another way to begin treatment indirectly is to inform both of the many effective treatment methods available. It is no exaggeration to say that biobehavioral treatments for elimination disorders represent one of the most notable successes of pediatric behavior therapy in the 20th century. Despite this achievement, many cases remain unmanaged, mismanaged, or overmedicated. By expanding detection and treatment of elimination problems in school settings, psychologists will simultaneously be reducing the number of these problematic cases and increasing the success of the biobehavioral approach to child elimination disorders.

REFERENCES

Allantoic, T. H., King, N. J., & Fray, R. (1989). Fears in children and adolescents: Reliability and generalizability across gender, age, and nationality. *Behavior Research and Therapy, 27*, 19–26.

American Academy of Pediatrics. (1994). *Diagnostic and statistical manual for primary care—Child and adolescent version*. Elk Grove Village, IL: American Academy of Pediatrics.

American Psychiatric Association. (1994). *Diagnostic and statistical manual of mental disorders* (4th ed.). Washington, D.C.: American Psychiatric Association.

Barr, R. G., Levine, M. D., Wilkinson, R. H., & Mulvihill, D. (1979). Chronic and occult stool retention: A clinical tool for its evaluation in school aged children. *Clinical Pediatrics, 18*, 674–686.

Berk, L. B., & Friman, P. C. (1990). Epidemiologic aspects of toilet training. *Clinical Pediatrics, 29*, 278–282.

Blackwell, B., & Currah, J. (1973). The psychopharmacology of nocturnal enuresis. In I. Kolvin, R. C. MacKeith, & S. R. Meadow (Eds.), *Bladder control and enuresis* (pp. 231–257). Philadelphia: Lippincott.

Blomfield, J. M., & Douglas, J. W. B. (1956). Bed-wetting: Prevalence among child aged four to seven years. *Lancet, I*, 850–852.

Blum, N. J., Taubman, B., & Osborne, M. D. (1997). Behavioral characteristics of children with stool toileting refusal. *Pediatrics, 99*, 50–53.

Bollard, J., & Nettlebeck, T. (1982). A component analysis of dry-bed training for treatment of bed-wetting. *Behavior Research & Therapy, 20*, 383–390.

Christophersen, E. R., & Mortweet, S. L. (2001). *Treatments that work with children: Empirically supported strategies for managing childhood problems*. Washington, D.C.: APA Books.

Christophersen, E. R., & Purvis, P. C. (2001). Toileting problems in children. In C. E. Walker & M. C. Roberts (Eds.), *The handbook of clinical child psychology* (3rd ed. pp. 453–469). New York: John Wiley and Sons.

Cohen, M. W. (1975). Enuresis. *Pediatric Clinics of North America, 22*, 545–560.

Cox, D. J., Sutphen, J., Borowitz, S., Kovatchev, B., & Ling, W. (1998). Contribution of behavior therapy and biofeedback to laxative therapy in the treatment of pediatric encopresis. *Annals of Behavioral Medicine, 20*(2), 70–76.

Creer, T. L., & Davis, M. H. (1975). Using a staggered waking procedure with enuretic children in an institutional setting. *Journal of Behavior Therapy & Experimental Psychiatry, 6*, 23–25.

Davidson, M. (1958). Constipation and fecal incontinence. *Pediatric Clinics of North America, 5*, 749–757.

Davidson, M., Kugler, M. M., & Bauer, C. H. (1963). Diagnosis and management in children with severe and protracted constipation and obstipation. *Journal of Pediatrics, 62*, 261–275.

Dimson, S. B. (1977). Desmopressin as a treatment for enuresis. *Lancet, 1*, 1260.

Fergusson, D. M., Horwood, L. J., & Sannon, F. T. (1986). Factors related to the age of attainment of nocturnal bladder control: An 8-year longitudinal study. *Pediatrics, 78*, 884–890.

Fielding, D. (1982). An analysis of the behavior of day- and night-wetting children: Towards a model of micturition control. *Behavior Research and Therapy, 49*, 49–60.

Forsythe, W., & Redmond, A. (1974). Enuresis and spontaneous cure rate study of 1129 enuretics. *Archives of Diseases in Children, 49*, 259–269.

Foxman B., Valdez R. B., & Brook, R. H. (1986). Childhood enuresis: Prevalence, perceived impact, and prescribed treatments. *Pediatrics, 77*, 482–487.

Friman, P. C., Handwerk, M. L., Swearer, S. M., McGinnis, C., & Warzak, W. J. (1998). Do children with primary nocturnal enuresis have clinically significant behavior problems? *Archives of Pediatrics and Adolescent Medicine, 152*, 537–539.

Friman, P. C., & Jones, K. M. (1998). Elimination disorders in children. In S. Watson & F. Gresham (Eds.), *Handbook of child behavior therapy* (pp. 239–260). New York: Plenum.

Friman, P. C., Mathews, J. R., Finney, J. W., Christophersen, E. R., & Leibowitz, J. M. (1988). Do children with encopresis have clinically significant behavior problems? *Pediatrics, 82*, 407–409.

Friman, P. C., & Vollmer, D. (1995). Successful use of the nocturnal urine alarm for diurnal enuresis. *Journal of Applied Behavior Analysis, 28*, 89–90.

Gabel, S., Hegedus, A. M., Wald, A., Chandra, R., & Chaponis, D. (1986). Prevalence of behavior problems and mental health utilization among encopretic children. *Journal of Developmental and Behavioral pediatrics, 7*, 293–297.

Gellis, S. S. (1994). Are enuretics truly hard to arouse? *Pediatric Notes, 18*, 113.

Gross, R. T., & Dornbusch, S. M. (1983). Enuresis. In M. D. Levine, W. B. Carey, A. C. Crocker, & R. T. Gross (Eds.), *Developmental behavioral pediatrics* (pp. 575–586). Philadelphia: Saunders.

Halliday, S., Meadow, S. R., & Berg, I. (1987). Successful management of daytime enuresis using alarm procedures: A randomly controlled trial. *Archives of Diseases in Children, 62*, 132–137.

Houts, A. C. (1991). Nocturnal enuresis as a biobehavioral problem. *Behavior Therapy, 22*, 133–151.

Houts, A. C. (2000). Commentary: Treatments for enuresis: Criteria, mechanisms, and health care policy. *Journal of Pediatric Pschology, 25*, 219–224.

Houts, A. C., Berman, J. S., & Abramson, H. (1994). Effectiveness of psychological and pharmacological treatments for nocturnal enuresis. *Journal of Consulting and Clinical Psychology, 62*, 737–745.

Houts, A. C., Peterson, J. K., & Liebert, R. M. (1984). The effects of prior imipramine treatment on the results of conditioning therapy with enuresis. *Journal of Pediatric Psychology, 9*, 505–508.

Jenson, W. R., & Sloane, H. N. (1979). Chart moves and grab bags: A simple contingency management. *Journal of Applied Behavior Analysis, 12*, 334.

Kaffman, M., & Elizur, E. (1977). Infants who become enuretics: A longitudinal study of 161 Kibbutz children. *Monographs of the Society for Research on Child Development, 42*, 2–12.

Kegel, A. H. (1951). Physiologic therapy for urinary stress incontinence. *Journal of the American Medical Association, 146*, 915–917.

Landman, G. B., & Rappaport, L. (1985). Pediatric management of severe treatment-resistant encopresis. *Development and Behavioral Pediatrics, 6*, 349–351.

Levine, M. D. (1975). Children with encopresis: A descriptive analysis. *Pediatrics, 56*, 407–409.

Levine, M. D. (1981). The schoolchild with encopresis. *Pediatrics in Review, 2*, 285–291.

Levine, M. D. (1982). Encopresis: Its potentiation, evaluation, and alleviation. *Pediatric Clinics of North America, 29*, 315–330.

Levine, M. D., Mazonson, P., & Bakow, H. (1980). Behavioral symptom substitution in children cured of encopresis. *American Journal of Diseases in Childhood, 134*, 663–667.

Loening-Baucke, V. A. (1990). Modulation of abnormal defecation dynamics by biofeedback treatment in chronically constipated children with encopresis. *Journal of Pediatrics, 116*, 214–221.

Loening-Baucke, V. (1996). Encopresis and soiling. *The Pediatric Clinics of North America 43*, 279–298.

Loening-Baucke, V. A., Cruikshank, B., & Savage, C. (1987). Defecation dynamics and behavior profiles in encopretic children. *Pediatrics, 80*, 672–679.

Lowery, S., Srour, J., Whitehead, W. E., & Schuster, M. M. (1985). Habit training as treatment of encopresis secondary to chronic constipation. *Journal of Pediatric Gastroenterology and Nutrition, 4*, 397–401.

Luxem, M. C., Christophersen, E. R., Purvis, P. C., & Baer, D. M. (1997). Behavioral-medical treatment of pediatric toileting refusal. *Journal of Development and Behavioral Pediatrics, 18*, 34–41.

McGrath, M. L., Mellon, M. W., & Murphy, L. (2000). Empirically supported treatments in pediatric psychology: Constipation and encopresis. *Journal of Pediatric Psychology, 25,* 225–254.

McGuire, T., Rothenberg, M., & Tyler, D. (1983). Profound shock following interventions for chronic untreated stool retention. *Clinical Pediatrics, 23*, 459–461.

Meadow, S. R. (1990). Day wetting. *Pediatric Nephrology, 4*, 178–184.

Mellon, M. W., & Houts, A. C. (1995). Elimination disorders. In R. T. Ammerman & M. Hersen (Eds.). *Handbook of child behavior therapy in the psychiatric setting* (pp. 341–366). New York: Wiley.

Mellon, M. W., & McGrath, M. L. (2000). Empirically supported treatments in pediatric psychology: Nocturnal enuresis. *Journal of Pediatric Psychology, 25,* 193–214.

Mellon, M. W., Scott, M. A., Haynes, K. B., Schmidt, D. F., & Houts, A. C. (1997). *EMG recording of pelvic floor conditioning in nocturnal enuresis during urine alarm treatment: A preliminary study*. Paper presented at the Sixth Florida Conference on Child Health Psychology, University of Florida, Gainesville, Florida.

Moffatt, M. E. K., Harlos, S., Kirshen, A. J., & Burd, L. (1993). Desmopressin acetate and nocturnal enuresis: How much do we know? *Pediatrics, 92*, 420–425.

Muellner, S. R. (1951). The physiology of micturition. *The Journal of Urology, 65*, 805–813.

Norgaard, J. P., Pedersen, E. B., & Djurhuus, J. C. (1985). Diurnal antidiuretic hormone levels in enuretics. *Journal of Urology, 134*, 1029–1031.

Ronen, T., Wozner, Y., & Rahav, G. (1992). Cognitive intervention in enuresis. *Child and Family Behavior Therapy, 14*, 1–14.

Schneider, M. S., King, L. R., & Surwit, R. S. (1994). Kegel exercises and childhood incontinence: A new role for an old treatment. *The Journal of Pediatrics, 124*, 91–92.

Starfield, B. (1967). Functional bladder capacity in enuretic and nonenuretic children. *Journal of Pediatrics, 70*, 777–782.

Starfield, B., & Mellits, E. D. (1968). Increases in functional bladder capacity and improvements in enuresis. *Journal of Pediatrics, 72*, 483–487.

Stark, L. J., Opipari, L. C., Donaldson, D. L., Danovsky, M. R., Rasile, D. A., & DelSanto, A. F. (1997). Evaluation of a standard protocol for rententive encopresis: A replication. *Journal of Pediatric Psychology, 22*, 619–633.

Stark, L., Owens-Stively, J., Spirito, A., Lewis, A., & Guevremont, D. (1990). Group behavioral treatment of retentive encopresis. *Journal of Pediatric Psychology, 15*, 659–671.

Stark, L. J., Spirito, A., Lewis, A. V., & Hart, K. J. (1990). Encopresis: Behavioral parameters associated with children who fail medical management. *Child Psychiatry and Human Development, 20*, 169–179.

Stephenson, J. D. (1979). Physiological and pharmacological basis for the chemotherapy of enuresis. *Psychological Medicine, 9*, 249–263.

Taubman, B. (1997). Toilet training and toileting refusal for stool only: A prospective study. *Pediatrics, 99*, 54–58.

Troup, C. W., & Hodgson, N. B. (1971). Nocturnal functional bladder capacity in enuretic children. *Journal of Urology, 105*, 129–132.

Van der Plas, R. N., Benninga, M. A., Redekop, W. K., Taminiau, J. A., & Buller, H. A. (1996). Randomized trial of biofeedback training for encopresis. *Archives of Diseases in Children, 75*, 367–374.

Verhulst, F. C., van der Lee, J. H., Akkeruis, G. W., Sanders-Woudstra, J. A. R., Timmer, F. C., & Donkhorst, I. D. (1985). The prevalence of nocturnal enuresis: Do DSM-III criteria need to be changed? A brief research report. *Journal of Child Psychology and Psychiatry, 26*, 989–993.

Vincent, S. A. (1974). Mechanical, electrical and other aspects of enuresis. In J. H. Johnston & W. Goodwin (Eds.). *Reviews in pediatric urology* (pp. 280–313). New York: Elsevier.

Wald, A., Chandra, R., Gabel, S., & Chiponis, D. (1987). Evaluation of biofeedback in childhood encopresis. *Journal of Pediatric Gastroenterology and Nutrition, 5*, 346–351.

Walker, C. E., Kenning, M., & Faust-Campanile, J. (1989). Enuresis and encopresis. In E. J. Mash & R. A. Barkley (Eds.). *Treatment of childhood disorders* (pp. 423–448). New York: Guilford.

Weaver, L. T., & Steiner, H. (1984). The bowel habit of young children. *Archives of Diseases in Childhood, 59,* 649–652.

Weinstock, L. B., & Clouse, R. E. (1987). A focused overview of gastrointestinal physiology. *Annals of Behavioral Medicine, 9,* 3–6.

Young, M. H., Brennen, L. C., Baker, R. D., & Baker, S. S. (1995). Functional encopresis: Symptom reduction and behavioral improvement. *Developmental and Behavioral Pediatrics, 16,* 226–232.

PART V: Health Issues Related to Development

26

Neonatology and Prematurity

Glen P. Aylward
Southern Illinois University School of Medicine

Psychologists who work in school settings are increasingly involved in the assessment and care of children who were born prematurely (<37 weeks gestational age) and those who have experienced potential insult to their central nervous systems (CNS) during the pre-, peri- or postnatal periods (Aylward, 1997a). Such involvement may occur in early childhood-related assessments or later, when the child encounters problems in school performance. A prime reason for the intensified focus on these children is the fact that many more now survive because of innovative medical procedures such as assisted ventilation in the delivery room, use of surfactant to facilitate respiration in immature lungs, and administration of prenatal and postnatal steroids to enhance lung maturation (Hack & Fanaroff, 1999). However, while many of these medical advances have had a positive impact on mortality, neurodevelopmental morbidity and later psychoeducational outcome have not necessarily improved (Bregman, 1998).

Although the prevalence of major handicap (severe mental retardation, cerebral palsy, epilepsy, sensorineural dysfunctions) in low-birth-weight babies has leveled off at approximately 15%, high frequency/low severity dysfunctions (learning disabilities, attention deficit hyperactivity disorders, borderline mental retardation, and behavior disorders) appear to be increasing (Botting, Powls, Cooke & Marlow, 1998). This suggests that the nature of impairment may be changing. Children born at medical/biologic risk who sustain major handicaps or high frequency/low severity dysfunctions will place increasing demands on school systems for evaluations, interventions, and liaison with medical professionals. Besides infants born prematurely, those exposed prenatally to drugs (Azuma & Chasnoff, 1993), hypoxic-ischemic encephalopathy (Robertson & Finer, 1988), or various innovative medical treatments such as indomethacin (Ment et al., 1996), extracorporeal membrane oxygenation (ECMO; Ikle et al.,

1999), or surfactant (Bregman & Kimberlin, 1993) may be at increased risk for school problems.

In general, there is a gradient of sequelae in children with decreasing birth weights: the smaller the baby, the greater the likelihood of later problems. Low-birth-weight (LBW) babies (<2500 g.; 5.5 lbs) have a 6%–8% incidence of major handicap, very-low-birth weight (VLBW) babies (<1500 g.; 3.3 lbs) have a 14%–17% incidence, while extremely low-birth-weight (ELBW) babies (<1000 g.; 2.2 lbs) have a 20% rate of major handicaps (Hack & Fanaroff, 1999). In comparison, major handicaps occur in 5% of the full-term population. Estimates of the less severe dysfunctions are not as well established, although it is estimated that 50% to 60% of children born at very low birth weight will require special education services, 20% will necessitate self-contained learning disabilities placement, and 16% will repeat at least one grade.

Babies born prematurely comprise 11% of births (Paneth, 1995) whereas low-birth-weight babies make up only 7.4%. Therefore, although the *percentage* of LBW babies having sequelae is greater than fullterms, in *real numbers*, there are more full-term babies who have disabilities. Moreover, with the limit of viability now at 23 to 24 weeks of gestation, and increasing survival of infants with birth weights in the 500 g to 750 g range, there is a need to consider both birth weight and gestational age. Prior to the 1990s, birth weight was the primary benchmark because of inaccuracy in obstetrical estimation or postnatal assessment. With refinement of ultrasound techniques, estimation of gestational age has become more precise, and gestational age is a strong determinant of organ system maturation and viability. Sole use of a birth weight cutoff as the prime descriptor is confounded because it could include: (1) extremely preterm infants who are average for gestational age (AGA), (2) less preterm infants who are small for gestational age (SGA; <3rd or 10th percentile, depending on cutoff used), or (3) older preterm or full-term infants who are extremely SGA (Touwen, 1986). Small-for-gestational-age babies often have better survival rates than their AGA counterparts; conversely, they often have higher developmental morbidity. This is particularly the case in SGA preterm babies (Bos, Einspieler, & Prechtl, 2001). Moreover, use of gestational age tends to increase homogeneity of biologic risks at birth.

It is difficult to accurately determine probabilities of later outcomes for premature infants or those at biologic risk because the literature is not consistent in that regard. This is because of differences in medical interventions employed in a given neonatal intensive care unit (NICU), diversity in study populations, confounding and mediating variables (e.g., environment), and the type of outcome measured (neurodevelopmental, cognitive, behavioral, academic, health) (Aylward, 2002). For example, the incidence of cerebral palsy can vary fourfold between different NICUs and the rate of severe intraventricular hemorrhage (IVH) can vary by two to three times, depending on the neonatal center (Synnes, Chien, Peliowski, Baboolal & Lee, 2001).

Hence, there is no simple prediction algorithm for an individual infant or a specific group of infants. The baby's admission status (how sick he or she was), medical response to intervention, and sequelae at discharge (her or his need for oxygen, chronic illness) must be considered. Various risk scores and neonatal admission severity scores for physiologic status and intensity of therapeutic intervention have been developed (e.g., Brazy, Eckerman, Oehler, Goldstein & O'Rand, 1991; Korner et al., 1993; Richardson, Gray, McCormick, Workman-Daniels, & Goldmann, 1993). These are often helpful in clarifying an infant's medical course and the likelihood of sequelae. The major sources of morbidity in the neonatal period are intracranial events, pulmonary immaturity, and infections (McCormick, 1989); therefore, severe ultrasound abnormality (e.g., grades III or IV intraventricular hemorrhage [IVH], periventricular leukomalacia [PVL], periventricular hemorrhagic infarction [PVI]—discussed subsequently), septicemia, necrotizing enterocolitis, chronic lung disease (oxygen dependence ≥36 weeks conceptional age) and bronchopulmonary dysplasia (BPD), apnea of prematurity, and indicators of asphyxia such as seizures are indicators for increased risk. The infants' medical status postdischarge is important, as subsequent hospitalizations are associated with lower verbal, visual-perceptual, and visual-motor scores, and less positive teacher ratings (Zelkowitz, Papageorgiou & Allard, 1994). Nutritional adequacy is also a crucial postnatal influence because of the developing brain's need for folic acid, iron, vitamins, and other nutrients.

More recently, there has been increased emphasis on a broader, multidimensional conceptualization of outcome and health, including functional and health-related quality of life (HRQL; McCormick, 1997; Vohr & Msall, 1997). HRQL and actual health status are two major outcome considerations that will have a major impact on a child's school success. The emerging consensus is that children at early biologic risk subsequently have poorer health, related restrictions in ability to engage in usual childhood activities, slower physical growth, and poorer social–emotional development. For example, a very premature infant with lung disease has a high likelihood of bronchopulmonary dysplasia, which, in turn, increases the risk of reactive airway disease or asthma. This chronic illness would then pose a myriad of potential obstacles to development and later school performance. Moreover, there is a 25%–58% readmission rate in VLBW babies (4 times greater than fullterms), a high posthospital discharge death rate, and increased occurrence of reactive airway disease, sudden infant death syndrome, gastrointestional reflux, hernias, and poor postnatal growth.

REPRESENTATIVE CONTEMPORARY STUDIES ON PREMATURE INFANTS

The focus of contemporary research and follow-up studies is on smaller preterm infants. The Case Western Reserve/Rainbow Children's Cohort (Taylor, Klein, Minich & Hack, 2000) contained three groups of infants: those <750 g, 750–1499 g, and term babies. At age 7 years, those born at <750 g had more health problems, lower body weight and smaller head circumference, more attention deficit hyperactivity disorder (ADHD) and behavior problems, and lower cognitive and achievement scores than the other two groups. Of the <750 g children, 45% required special education services, as did 25% of those in the 750–1499 g range, and 14% of term infants. This suggests a significant difference even among the two VLBW preterm groups with regard to sequelae. Medical complications had a stronger association with perceptual motor function; social variables were more influential on verbal and behavioral outcome. Moreover, when higher neonatal risk was combined with VLBW, cognitive impairment increased five-fold, whereas special education rates tripled.

The NICHD Neonatal Research Network (Vohr et al., 2000) included 1,151 ELBW (401–1000 g) infants from 12 centers, evaluated at 18–22 months of age (mean birth weight 796 g; gestational age 26 weeks). Of these, 25% had an abnormal neurologic evaluation (17% with cerebral palsy), 37% had a Bayley Scales of Infant Development-II Mental Developmental Index <70, 29% obtained a BSID-II Psychomotor Developmental Index <70, and 9%–11% had vision and hearing impairment. Similar to the Case Western cohort, medical conditions such as chronic lung disease, grades III and IV intraventricular hemorrhage, necrotizing enterocolitis, septicemia, and use of steroids were morbidity factors.

In a sample of <800 g infants born in Vancouver and followed to school age, (Whitfield, Eckstein-Grunau & Holsti, 1997), 47% were found to have learning disabilities, 14% severe mental retardation, and 13% had borderline intelligence (IQ). Conversely, 26% were *not* disabled. In another large, longitudinal sample of more than 9,000 children, Resnick and colleagues (1998) reported that perinatal variables (birth weight, transport, medical condition, ventilation) were associated with physical impairment, sensory impairment, and moderate and profound mental retardation. Sociodemographic variables (gender, mother's marital status, race, education, family income) were associated with emotional handicaps and speech/language impairment, whereas both arrays of background variables were predictive of mild mental retardation and specific learning disabilities.

Taken together, these representative studies suggest that there are different relationships between specific background variables and outcomes. Medical/biologic variables have strong associations with severe impairments, as well as visual motor/visual perceptual, neuromotor, and attention problems. Verbal, cognitive, and emotional behaviors are strongly determined by environmental or combined medical/environmental factors. Moreover, approximately 50% of VLBW babies will have "normal" outcome, while 26%–37% of ELBW infants will be "normal," the percentage falling corresponding to decreasing birth weight. There also appears to be a progressively greater incidence of impairment with increasing age at time of assessment, probably due to enhanced ability to detect more subtle problems.

ENVIRONMENTAL AND BIOLOGIC RISK

Risk refers to factors that have a potentially negative impact on the infant's development. Tjossem (1976) delineated three categories of risk: established, biological, and environmental. The latter two are particularly important in terms of premature infants. Established risks are medical disorders of a known etiology whose compromised developmental outcome is well documented (e.g., Down syndrome and other genetic disorders). Biological risks include exposure to potentially noxious prenatal, perinatal, or postnatal events such as intraventricular hemorrhage, hypoxic-ischemic encephalopathy, or LBW. Environmental risks encompass the quality of the mother–infant interaction, opportunities for developmental/cognitive stimulation, and health care. It is documented that adverse environmental factors such as low socioeconomic status and poor social support can place a child at risk for compromised outcome. Because relationships between social class, perinatal complications, and cognitive development are complex and intertwined, many children are exposed to both biologic and environmental risk (Thompson et al., 1997); this combination is sometimes referred to as "double jeopardy" or "double hazard" (Escalona, 1982; Parker, Greer, & Zuckerman, 1988). In these cases, nonoptimal biologic and environmental risks work synergistically to negatively affect later function (Aylward, 1990, 1992). However, there is a ceiling effect in which a severe degree of biologic risk will minimize environmental influences. Stated differently, the smallest and sickest infants are least responsive to environmental influences (Aylward, 1996).

Environmental Risk

Socioeconomic status (SES) is typically represented by maternal education and occupational status. However, it is an insufficient marker for environmental quality. Social support includes tangible components (e.g., housing) and intangible components (attitudes, encouragement). The environment involves both *process* and *status* features. The former are more proximal aspects of the environment that are experienced most directly (e.g. mother–infant interaction); the latter are distal and broader, involving environmental aspects that are experienced more indirectly (social class, location of residence). Environmental effects become increasingly apparent between 18 and 36 months, with 24 month being an age that is cited frequently (Murphy, Nichter, & Liden, 1982). Process or proximal environmental variables are more predictive of subsequent outcome early on; status or distal factors are more predictive at school age or later (Aylward, 1990, 1992, 1996). The components of environmental risk are complex and may include family risk (social support, parent–child interaction, stressful events, organization) and social class risk (SES, parental education) (Bendersky & Lewis, 1994). Moreover, to complicate matters further, certain aspects of the environment mediate the effects of other environmental variables on outcome, this varying by the age of the child. For example, in a recent study, environmental risks (unemployment, high family density, depression in parent, stressful life events) influenced outcome at 1 to 3 years, poverty (family income) exerted influence at 2 and 3 years, and neighborhood affluence influenced development at 3 years (Kato-Klebanov, Brooks-Gunn, McCarton, & McCormick, 1998). IQ scores in disadvantaged families typically are .5 to 1 standard deviation below average (8–16 points). In several studies (e.g., Hunt, Cooper & Tooley, 1988) medical/biologic factors were found to determine whether a developmental problem occurred, but environmental factors had a tempering or exacerbating effect on the degree of problem. However, Breslau, Chilcout, Del Dotto, Andreski, & Brown (1996) reported a gradient between birth weight and IQ in a LBW group: even when controlling for maternal IQ and social class, there was a linear relationship between IQ and birth weight.

Appreciation of the mechanisms underlying the interaction of environmental and biologic risks has increased over the last several decades. The "continuum of reproductive casualty" (Pasamanick & Knobloch, 1961) was biologically based, wherein the severity of developmental problems (cerebral palsy, epilepsy, mental retardation, behavioral disorders, and learning problems) was directly attributable to the degree of perinatal complications. More serious conditions such as cerebral palsy would be associated with more obstetric and perinatal complications than would a milder disorder such as a learning disability. Data from the Kauai Longitudinal Project (Werner, 1986) and other studies discounted this model. Negative components of the environment have a synergistic or additive effect on infants who are biologically vulnerable vis-à-vis the transactional (Sameroff & Chandler, 1975) or "risk-route" models (Aylward & Kenny, 1979). These models assume that a degree of plasticity is inherent in both the child and the environment. The child is constantly reorganizing and self-righting, and the environment can facilitate or impede resiliency, leading to the "continuum of caretaking casualty." As a result, environment and resilience processes (Masten, 2001) must be considered as part of the mix when psychologists work with children born prematurely, particularly when they reach school age.

Biologic Risk

There are several terms often encountered by psychologists who work with children who have been at biologic risk. *Hypoxemia* is a reduction of oxygen in the blood (brain hypoxia is a reduction of oxygen to brain tissue). *Ischemia* is defined as reduced blood flow to the brain, and *asphyxia* is a disturbed exchange of oxygen and carbon dioxide due to an interruption in respiration, which results in hypoxemia, hypercarbia (increased carbon dioxide), and acidemia (decreased blood pH). Asphyxia is accompanied by multisystem organ dysfunction (cardiovascular, gastrointestinal, pulmonary, and renal). *Hypoxic-ischemic encephalopathy* (HIE) refers to a deprivation of oxygen to the brain due to the combined effects of hypoxemia and ischemia. *Anoxia* refers to a complete lack of oxygen.

Asphyxia has traditionally been indexed as a low Apgar score (range 0–10, based on heart rate, respiratory effort, reflex irritability, muscle tone, and color). However, Apgar scores have been misused and are not necessarily predictive of subsequent outcome. A low 1-minute Apgar score does not correlate with later outcome (American Academy of Pediatrics, 1996; Aylward, 1993), and even a low 5-minute score has limited utility, but may be more useful if *change* between 1 and 5 minutes is considered. Apgar scores should be considered indicative of the infant's condition during and immediately after birth, and not much else. In fact, normal Apgar scores are found in 75% of children who later have cerebral palsy. Therefore, psychologists working in school settings should not automatically consider low Apgar scores as the cause of intellectual or academic problems in the children they serve. However, asphyxia is the precipitating event for HIE, and perinatal HIE is the major biologic risk for neurodevelopmental morbidity in the neonatal period (Volpe, 1998).

In full-term infants, HIE causes cell death in the cerebral cortex, diencephalon, brain stem, and cerebellum. Injury to the basal ganglia and thalamus also occurs. Moderate and severe HIE in term babies is associated with a high incidence of cognitive and motor dysfunction, including microcephaly, mental retardation, epilepsy, and cerebral palsy. Mild HIE lasts less than 24 hours and the infant displays hyperalertness, uninhibited reflexes, irritability and jitteriness; later cognitive and academic problems are minimal. Moderate HIE is characterized by lethargy, stupor, hypotonia, depressed primitive reflexes, seizures, and decreased movements. This lasts for approximately 1 week, and 20%–40% of these infants will have sequelae. Severe HIE involves coma, flaccid tone, seizures, increased intracranial pressure, and suppressed brainstem function; virtually all survivors have significant cognitive and psychoeducational sequelae.

HIE in the preterm infant causes cell death deeper within the brain, namely, in the white matter behind and to the side of the lateral ventricles (*periventricular leukomalacia)*; there is less effect on grey matter in preterm than in full-term infants. This type of insult is more often associated with spasticity, neurosensory, and motor problems than with cognitive deficits per se. *Periventricular/intraventricular hemorrhage* (PVH/IVH) involves bleeding into the subependymal germinal matrix (site of cell proliferation) and this occurs in 35%–45% of infants less than 32 weeks gestational age. IVH is graded (I-IV), based on amount of blood in the ventricles and degree of distention, with grades III and IV being considered severe. Grade IV IVH is thought to not be on a continuum and reflects *periventricular hemorrhagic infarction* (PVI). This disorder involves death of periventricular white matter, is large and asymmetric, and involves frontal-parieto-occipital regions, with alterations in hemispheric connectivity. The risk of disability at preschool and school age increases, directly in relation to the grade of IVH: 5%–10% with Grade I, 15%–20% with Grade II, 35%–50% with Grade III, and greater than 90% with Grade IV will have school problems.

REPRESENTATIVE STUDY OF THE RELATIONSHIP BETWEEN BIOLOGIC AND ENVIRONMENTAL RISK

The Infant Health and Development Program (IHDP; Infant Health and Development Program, 1990) was an 8-site randomized clinical trial of LBW/preterm infants from 985 families (1/3 intervention, 2/3 control). The average level of maternal education was high school or less. Pediatric, educational, and family support services were provided in the intervention model and interventions began at hospital discharge and continued for 3 years. These consisted of home visits, parent groups, enrollment at child development centers, and other family support. Assessments were made from 40 weeks through 3 years; long-term follow-up extended to 5 and 8 years as well.

At 1 year there were no differences between the intervention and control groups; by 2 years, a 9.75 IQ point difference was found, favoring the intervention group, and at 3 years the difference was 9.31 points. However, when the LBW group was subdivided into: (1) heavier LBW (2001–2500 g), and (2) lighter LBW (<2001 g), differences between intervention and control groups varied. At age 3 years, heavier LBW intervention babies had a 14.3 IQ point advantage over controls, while in the lighter LBW children, the difference was 7.1 points. By age 5 years, heavier LBW children had a 3.7 point advantage, while lighter LBW children had a 1.5 point disadvantage; at 8 years, differences between intervention and controls was 4.4

and –1.2 IQ points, for heavy and light LBW groups, respectively (Brooks-Gunn et al., 1994; McCarton, Brooks-Gunn, & Wallace, 1997; McCormick, McCarton, Brooks-Gunn, Belt, & Gross, 1998).

The IHDP study was considered representative because of the combined biologic and environmental risk status of the participating children. The findings underscore the fact that environmental factors may have a tempering effect, but biologic risks (i.e., birth weight <2001 g) determine "ceilings" or minimize effects of intervention. Although the environmental enrichment had an influence while it was in effect (i.e., 3 years and younger), biologic influences may have once again reemerged as the primary influence once the protective environmental supports were withdrawn. Moreover, infants whose mothers had <12 years of education were more likely to benefit from the intervention than children of mothers having a college education, suggesting some type of "threshold" effect.

MECHANISMS OF EARLY CENTRAL NERVOUS SYSTEM DAMAGE

Given the concept of biologic risk and the number of children exposed to this who subsequently have school problems, it is important for psychologists to appreciate *how* damage to the developing nervous system translates into later cognitive and academic dysfunction. Impairments resulting from damage to the functionally uncommitted brain of the infant and child qualitatively and quantitatively differ from those caused by damage to the committed brain of the adolescent and adult. There are two schools of thought in that regard. The major premise of the Kennard principle (Kennard, 1942) is that brain lesions acquired early in life produce fewer deficits than similar lesions sustained in later life. Therefore, the degree of impairment resulting from brain damage is considered proportional to the age at which the damage occurred. Conversely, the Dobbing hypothesis (Dobbing & Smart, 1974) holds that brain damage during CNS development has its greatest impact on cell populations or processes that show the greatest rate of development at the time of the insult. For example, if an insult occurs during cell proliferation, this would result in decreased cell numbers in certain layers within the brain. If the damage was incurred later when cell differentiation occurred, the end result would be alteration of cell size or function (architecture). In actuality, both interpretations are accurate. If damage occurs too early it will disrupt brain development sequences; later damage will disrupt areas that had been "dedicated" to specific functions. Damage during infancy and early childhood therefore may prove less devastating than damage during the fetal/neonatal period or in the more mature brain (preschool level). Timing, duration, and type of insult will influence residual cognitive and learning deficits. Different measures used to assess outcome will yield different results and there is a strong correlation between dendritic aborization and behavioral recovery (Kolb, 1989).

As mentioned previously, hypoxia and ischemia are considered to be the major determinant of developmental morbidity in the neonatal period (Hill & Volpe, 1989; Volpe, 1998). The consequences of HIE are due to a neurotoxic cascade in which the excitatory amino acid, glutamate, is released, binds to receptors, hyperexcites the cell, and depletes it of energy. There is an influx of calcium into the cell, and this, coupled with continued excitation, causes "death by calcium" (Dammann & Leviton, 1999). Essentially, there is necrosis (cell swells, ruptures/bursts and its contents cause inflammation to adjacent cells) and apoptosis (shrinkage of the cell, similar to programmed cell death). The second wave of damage occurs with reperfusion, where free radicals (outer orbital electron is unpaired) and nitric oxide cause more injury, and granulocytes plug microvessals. The situation is further compounded by several developmental components in the preterm infant: (1) immature blood-brain barriers, (2) incomplete myelination, and (3) suboptimal levels of endogenous cell neuroprotectors (called neurotrophins or oligotrophins).

This course of events produces white matter damage. There is also ample evidence to suggest that maternal infections during pregnancy will release proinflammatory cytokines that will prompt premature labor and also produce white matter damage in the premature infant, as indicated above (Perlman, 1998). In fact, the combination of maternal infection and HIE increases the rate of cerebral palsy 70-fold in full-term infants.

This translates into a problem in prediction of outcome for professionals working with children who have been born at biologic risk. The same insult may have a different pattern of damage, depending on the gradient of (1) necrosis, (2) necrosis and apoptosis, and (3) apoptosis as one moves away from the focal site of injury. Perinatal histories alone will raise probabilities of compromised outcome, but prediction is enhanced with the inclusion of serial assessments of the child and environment. Therefore, pre- and perinatal damage may prevent normal development or destroy some portion of the brain. Subtle metabolic and chemical changes occur, which may add to insult, actually cause dysfunction, or interfere with recovery. This leads to variability in later deficits in infants who have sustained the same apparent CNS insult. Moreover, the hippocampus is particularly vulnerable, with deficits in episodic memory being a frequent outcome.

Development depends on experience, behavior, and brain maturation (synaptic aborization, pruning, increased metabolic capacity). Peak dendritic/axonal growth occurs from 20 weeks to 2 years, synapse formation from 25 weeks to 3 years, and pruning from 2 to 14 years. It is established that experience can influence the genesis and survival of neurons and glial cells. Input from the environment can modify existing circuitry or create novel circuitry (Black, Jones, Nelson, & Greenough, 1998; Greenough & Black, 1999). In a "use it or lose it" scenario, input can maintain prewired synapses, called "experience-expectant synapses," or lack of input could cause axons to be overpruned or produce apoptosis. Similarly, experience-dependent synapses are idiosyncratic to the child's experience but can result in new synaptic connections; these are not limited to infancy and can extend through adulthood (Greenough & Black, 1999). Hence, initially there is synaptic overproduction, the purpose being to capture and incorporate experience into the synaptic architecture of the brain; however, synapses also continue to develop throughout life, and in fact there is recent evidence for continued neurogenesis in the hippocampus as well (Gould, 1999).

Therefore, prediction of later outcome in preschool or school-age children is difficult because of a host of factors: neural reorganization, behavioral compensation, recovery from illness, variability in residual damage (necrosis and apoptosis mentioned above), the deficits not emerging at time of testing (e.g., Golgi type 2 interneurons required for higher order processes), environmental effects, and intervening insults/illness. Moreover, abnormal findings, particularly in the preschool and early-school-age range, could be due to maturational delay (suggesting "catch-up"), neural dysfunction, motor deficits, an artifact of external variables (testing concerns, test used, irritability), or some combination of the above.

CLINICAL APPLICATIONS

The logical question is how do the issues outlined in the previous sections of this chapter translate into applications for pediatric psychologists working in the schools. Essentially, there are two levels of involvement: (1) evaluation and intervention for early childhood education, typically involving preschool and early-school-age children, and (2) assessment and intervention with older children and adolescents as they progress in their academic careers. There also are two groups of children who will require services. Children with major handicaps will necessitate multidisciplinary, long-term efforts of physicians, psychologists, occupational and physical therapists, and other allied professionals. Alternative technologies, accessibility, identification and emphasis on strengths, and consideration of functional issues are particular areas of focus. Because of the magnitude of these disorders (which typically are due to established or severe biologic risks), these children most likely will be identified at earlier ages, by physicians or early intervention programs.

The second group of children who will require services includes those with high frequency/low severity dysfunctions (ADHD, learning disabilities, borderline intelligence, neuropsychological deficits, behavioral problems). These children have more subtle, "hidden impairments" that are defined at later ages when problems become more apparent because of increasing demands for performance that involves these deficits. Although there sometimes will continue to be a need for interdisciplinary collaboration, interventions more typically will be in the psychoeducational realm.

With respect to testing of preschool and early-school-age children, it can be very difficult to obtain cooperation. This is even more problematic in NICU graduates who are lower functioning. It is difficult to distinguish "cannot" from "will not," and some children will refuse to perform a task simply because they find it difficult and are sensitized and frustrated by their lack of ability. However, there is emerging evidence that children who are uncooperative and untestable in the preschool-age range have poorer outcomes at school age (Langkamp & Brazy, 1999). Therefore, serial testing and close monitoring of these children are necessary.

With respect to clinical application, it is helpful to summarize functions with a high probability of deficit in children born prematurely or at biologic risk and provide suggestions as how to best evaluate these areas of function. The following is a summary of deficits frequently noted in outcome studies of premature infants that have particular relevance in school settings. These potential deficits are based on group data and do not reflect individual outcomes:

- High incidence of low average IQ scores on standardized IQ tests; higher prevalence of borderline IQ.
- Relative weaknesses in executive functions (organization, planning, problem solving, abstracting).
- Frequent learning disabilities in mathematics and reading (particularly reading comprehension).
- ADHD.
- Nonverbal learning disabilities.
- Auditory processing disorders.
- Problems in behavior, social skills.
- Memory deficits (visual, auditory).
- Weaknesses in fine motor speed.

(See Levy-Shiff, Einat, Mogilner, Lerman & Krikler, 1994; Rickards, Kelly, Doyle, & Callanan, 2001; Taylor, Hack, & Klein, 1998; Taylor, Klein, Schatschneider, & Hack, 1998.) Moreover, the relative contributions of birth status and environmental factors vary, according to the outcome measured and time of measurement. Health concerns and their potential contribution to school problems must also be considered.

Given this array of potential disorders, assessment should include but also extend beyond basic IQ and achievement testing. More specific tests that measure (1) attention and executive function, (2) language (phonological processing, comprehension of instructions, speeded naming, higher order functions), (3) sensorimotor functions (fingertip tapping, visuomotor precision, fine motor speed), (4) visuospatial processes (design copying, visual closure), and (5) memory and learning (list learning, narrative memory, delayed recall, consideration of both rote/episodic and semantic/strategic visual and verbal information) are necessary. The NEPSY (Korkman, Kirk, & Kemp, 1997), Wide Range Assessment of Memory and Learning

(WRAML; Sheslow & Adams, 1990), Clinical Evaluation of Language Fundamentals-3 (CELF-3; Semel, Wiig, & Secord, 1995), Gordon Diagnostic System (Gordon, 1983; or other continuous performance tasks), as well as broad-band (e.g., Child Behavior Checklist; Achenbach, 1991) or narrow-band ADHD rating scales are useful. It is recommended that evaluations be tailored to the individual child, depending on the types of concerns that are raised.

Younger children may also be given the NEPSY, although the richness of clinical information may be limited at younger ages. Other tests that are appropriate for younger children include the Kaufmann Assessment Battery for Children (K-ABC; Kaufman & Kaufman, 1983), Differential Abilities Scale (DAS; Elliott, 1990), Wechsler Preschool and Primary Scale of Intelligence-Revised (WPPSI-R; Wechsler, 1989), the Bayley Scales of Infant Development-II (BSID-II; Bayley, 1993), and the McCarthy Scales of Children's Abilities (MSCA; McCarthy, 1972). A neuropsychological approach is recommended in the interpretation of data obtained from these instruments (Aylward, 1997a). As in the case with older children, assessment of verbal functions and behavior is also important. Some authors suggest that the Stanford-Binet-IV (Thorndike, Hagen, & Sattler, 1986) may be of limited utility in assessment of cognitive outcomes of children born VLBW because of exclusion of subtests on which the child received a score of zero in the calculation of a composite score and because of a high test floor and low sensitivity (Eckstein-Grunau, Whitfield, & Petrie, 2000; Saylor, Boyce, & Peagler, 2000).

Finally, it is important to identify cognitive, neuromotor, and functional deficits early, particularly in light of the possibility that prematurity and its effects act through the association with health, cognitive and neuromotor function, to explain behavioral and other problems at school age (e.g., Nadeau, Boivin, Tessier, Lefebvre, & Robaey, 2001). More specifically, the link in developmental pathways between extremely preterm birth and internalizing and externalizing behavioral problems is indirect; preterm birth contributes to child maladjustment via its impact on health, intellectual, and neuromotor development. Behavioral attention/hyperactivity problems and possibly other concerns surface as the result of the mediating effects of both neuromotor and cognitive delays (e.g., language, executive function) that arise as sequelae of prematurity. The associative chain that is presumed to occur holds that prematurity-> specific deficits in cognitive/neuromotor function-> behavioral and other problems. This would be analogous to the aforementioned associative chain in which prematurity/LBW would affect physical health (e.g., bronchopulmonary dysplasia), which, in turn, would cause restriction in activity (e.g., reactive upper airway disease) and thereby impede development (Hack, 1999). Adverse environmental effects could also contribute to compromised behavior in a synergistic fashion (Girouard, Baillargeon, Tremblay, Glorieux & Lefebvre, 1998; Harvey, O'Callaghan & Mohay, 1999; Nadeau et al., 2001).

It also appears that neuromotor, cognitive, and health disabilities do not lead to the same problematic behavioral outcomes. In a recent study (Nadeau et al., 2001), neuromotor deficits, because of their resultant functional limitations in social situations, are thought to cause the child to be more cautious in peer interactions and lead to peer rejection. Cognitive problems (disruptions in executive function, sequential memory, or global intelligence) are more strongly associated with deficits in attention and hyperactivity. There is neurobiologic evidence to suggest a CNS basis for these differences: for example, neonatal white matter damage is associated with cerebral palsy, while intellectual and attention deficits are related to subplate neuronal damage (Volpe, 1996).

In summary, the spectrum of sequelae found in children who were born prematurely or at biologic risk does not necessarily differ dramatically from the array of problems routinely seen in the general school-age population. What is different, however, is the greater percentage of children having these problems, the specific deficit profiles, and the interactive effects of biologic risk, environment, and outcome. Without doubt, these children will be major consumers of psychological services provided in the schools.

REFERENCES

Achenbach, T. M. (1991). *Manual for the child behavior checklist 4–18 and 1991 profile*. Burlington: University of Vermont Department of Psychiatry.

American Academy of Pediatrics, Committee on Fetus and Newborn. (1996). Use and abuse of the Apgar score. *Pediatrics, 98*, 141–142.

Aylward, G. P. (1990). Environmental influences on the developmental outcome of children at risk. *Infants and Young Children, 2*, 1–9.

Aylward, G. P. (1992). The relationship between environmental risk and developmental outcome. *Journal of Developmental and Behavioral Pediatrics, 13*, 222–229.

Aylward, G. P. (1993). Perinatal asphyxia: Effects of biologic and environmental risks. *Clinics in Perinatology, 20*, 433–449.

Aylward, G. P. (1996). Environmental risk, intervention, and developmental outcome. *Ambulatory Child Health, 2*, 161–170.

Aylward, G. P. (1997a). *Infant and early childhood neuropsychology*. New York: Plenum.

Aylward, G. P. (1997b). Conceptual issues in developmental screening and assessment. *Journal of Developmental and Behavioral Pediatrics, 18*, 340–349.

Aylward, G. P. (2002). Methodologic issues in outcome studies of at-risk infants. *Journal of Pediatric Psychology, 27*, 37–45.

Aylward, G. P., & Kenny, T. J. (1979). Developmental follow-up: Inherent problems and a conceptual model. *Journal of Pediatric Psychology, 4*, 331–343.

Azuma, S. D., & Chasnoff, I. J. (1993). Outcome of children prenatally exposed to cocaine and other drugs: A path analysis of three-year data. *Pediatrics, 92*, 396–402.

Bayley, N. (1993). *Bayley scales of infant development* (2nd ed.). San Antonio, TX: The Psychological Corporation.

Bendersky, M., & Lewis, M. (1994). Environmental risk, biological risk, and developmental outcome. *Developmental Psychology, 30*, 484–494.

Black, J. E., Jones, T. A., Nelson, C. A., & Greenough, W. T. (1998). Neuronal plasticity and the developing brain. In N. E. Alessi, J. J. Coyle, S. I. Hanesin, & S. Eth (Eds.), *Handbook of child and adolescent psychiatry* (pp. 31–52). New York: Wiley.

Botting, N., Powls, A., Cooke, R. W., & Marlow, N. (1998). Cognitive and educational outcome of very low birthweight children in early adolescence. *Developmental Medicine and Child Neurology, 40*, 652–660.

Bos, A. F., Einspieler, C., & Prechtl, H. F. R. (2001). Intrauterine growth retardation, general movements, and neurodevelopmental outcome: A review. *Developmental Medicine and Child Neurology, 43*, 61–68.

Brazy, J. E., Eckerman, C. O., Oehler, J. M., Goldstein, R. F., & O'Rand, M. A. (1991). Nursery neurobiologic risk score: Important factors in predicting outcome in very low birth weight infants. *Journal of Pediatrics, 118*, 783–792.

Bregman, J. (1998). Developmental outcome in very low birthweight infants. Current status and future trends. *Pediatric Clinics of North America, 45*, 673–690.

Bregman, J., & Kimberlin, L. V. (1993). Developmental outcome in extremely premature infants. Impact of surfactant. *Pediatric Clinics of North America, 40*, 937–953.

Breslau, N., Chilcout, H., Del Dotto, J. E., Andreski, P., & Brown, G. G. (1996). Low birth weight: Behavioral sequelae at six years of age. *Biological Psychiatry, 40*, 389–397.

Brooks-Gunn, J., McCarton, C. M., and Casey, P. H., (1994). Early intervention in low-birthweight premature infants. Results through age 5 years from the Infant Health and Development Program. *Journal of the American Medical Association, 272*, 1257–1262.

Dammann, O., & Leviton, A. (1999). Brain damage in preterm newborns: Might enhancement of developmentally regulated endogenous protection open a door for prevention? *Pediatrics, 104*, 541–550.

Dobbing, J., & Smart, J. L. (1974). Vulnerability of developing brain and behavior. *British Medical Journal, 30*, 164–168.

Eckstein-Grunau, R., Whitfield, M., & Petrie, J. (2000). Predicting IQ of biologically "at risk" children from age 3 to school entry: Sensitivity and specificity of the Stanford-Binet Intelligence Scale-IV. *Journal of Developmental and Behavioral Pediatrics, 21*, 401–407.

Elliott, C. D. (1990). *Differential abilities scale. Administration manual.* San Antonio, TX: The Psychological Corporation.

Escalona, S. K. (1982). Babies at double hazard: Early development of infants at biologic and social risk. *Pediatrics, 70*, 670–676.

Girouard, P. C., Baillargeon, R. H., Tremblay, R. E., Glorieux, J., & Lefebvre, F. (1998). Developmental pathways leading to externalizing behaviors in 5 year olds born before 29 weeks of gestation. *Journal of Developmental and Behavioral Pediatrics, 19*, 244–253.

Gordon, M. (1983). *The Gordon diagnostic system.* Boulder, CO: Gordon Systems.

Gould, E. (1999). Neurogenesis in adulthood: A possible role in learning. *Trends in Cognitive Sciences, 3*, 186–192.

Greenough, W. T., & Black, J. R. (1999). Experience, neural plasticity and psychological development. In N. A. Fox, L. A. Leavitt, & J. G. Warhol (Eds.), *The role of early experience in infant development* (pp. 29–40). Skillman, NJ: Johnson Pediatric Institute.

Hack, M. (1999). Consideration of the use of health status, functional outcome, and quality of life to monitor neonatal intensive care. *Pediatrics, 103*, 319–328.

Hack, M., & Fanaroff, A. A. (1999). Outcomes of children of extremely low birthweight and gestational age in the 1990's. *Early Human Development, 53*, 193–218.

Harvey, J. M., O'Callaghan, M. T., & Mohay, H. (1999). Executive function of children with extremely low birth weight: A case control study. *Developmental Medicine and Child Neurology, 41*, 292–297.

Hill, A., & Volpe, J. J. (1989). Perinatal asphyxia: Clinical aspects. *Clinics in Perinatology, 16*, 435–457.

Hunt, J. V., Cooper, B. A. B., & Tooley, W. H. (1988). Very low birth weight infants at 8 and 11 years of age: Role of neonatal illness and family status. *Pediatrics, 82*, 596–603.

Ikle, L., Ikle, D. N., Moreland, S. G., Fashaw, L. M., Waas, N., & Rosenberg, A. R. (1999). Survivors of neonatal extracorporeal membrane oxygenation at school age: unusual findings on intelligence testing. *Developmental Medicine and Child Neurology, 41*, 307–310.

Infant Health and Development Program. (1990). Enhancing the outcomes of low birth weight, premature infants: A multisite, randomized trial. *Journal of the American Medical Association, 263*, 3035–3042.

Kato-Klebanov, P., Brooks-Gunn, J., McCarton, C., & McCormick, M. (1998). The contribution of neighborhood and family income to developmental test scores over the first three years of life. *Child Development, 69*, 1420–1436.

Kaufmann, A. S., & Kaufmann, N. (1983). *Kaufmann assessment battery for children.* Circle Pines, MN: American Guidance Service.

Kennard, M. A. (1942). Cortical reorganization of motor function: Studies on series of monkeys of different ages from infancy to maturity. *Archives of Neurology and Psychiatry, 47*, 227–240.

Kolb, B. (1989). Brain development, plasticity and behavior. *American Psychologist, 44*, 1203–1212.

Korkman, M., Kirk, U., & Kemp, S. (1997). *NEPSY.* San Antonio, TX: The Psychological Corporation.

Korner, A. F., Stevenson, D. K., Kraemer, H. C., Spiker, D., Scott, D. T., Constantinou, J., & Dimiceli, S. (1993). Prediction of the development of low birth weight preterm infants by a new Neonatal Medical Index. *Journal of Developmental and Behavioral Pediatrics, 14*, 106–111.

Langkamp, D. L., & Brazy, J. E. (1999). Risk for later school problems in preterm infants who do not cooperate for preschool developmental testing. *Journal of Pediatrics, 135*, 756–760.

Levy-Shiff, R., Einat, G., Mogilner, M. B., Lerman, M., & Krikler, R. (1994). Biological and environmental correlates of developmental outcome of prematurely born infants in early adolescence. *Journal of Pediatric Psychology, 19*, 63–78.

Masten, A. S. (2001). Ordinary magic. Resilience processes in development. *American Psychologist, 56*, 227–238.

McCarthy, D. A. (1972). *Manual of the McCarthy scales of children's abilities.* New York: The Psychological Corporation.

McCarton, C. M., Brooks-Gunn, J., & Wallace, I. F. (1997). Results at age 8 years of early intervention for low birth-weight premature infants: The Infant Health and Development Program. *Journal of the American Medical Association, 277*, 126–132.

McCormick, M. C. (1989). Long-term follow-up of infants discharged from neonatal intensive care units. *Journal of the American Medical Association, 261*, 1767–1772.

McCormick, M. C. (1997). The outcome of very low birth weight infants: Are we asking the right questions? *Pediatrics, 99*, 869–876.

McCormick, M. C., McCarton, C., Brooks-Gunn, J., Belt, P., & Gross, R. T. (1998). The infant health and development program: Interim summary. *Journal of Developmental and Behavioral Pediatrics, 19*, 359–370.

Ment, L. R., Vohr, B., Oh, W., Scott, D. T., Allan, W. C., Westerveld, M., Duncan, C. C., Ehrenkranz, R. A., Katz, K. H., Schneider, K. C., & Makuch, R. W. (1996). Neurodevelopmental outcome at 36 months' corrected age of preterm infants in the multicenter indomethacin intraventricular hemorrhage prevention trial. *Pediatrics, 98*, 714–718.

Msall, M. E., Di Gaudio, K. M., & Duffy, L. C. (1993). Use of functional assessment I children with developmental disabilities. *Physical Medicine Rehabilitation Clinics of North America, 4*, 517–527.

Murphy, T. F., Nichter, C. A., & Liden, C. B. (1982). Developmental outcome of the high-risk infant: A review of methodological issues. *Seminars in Perinatology, 6*, 353–364.

Nadeau, L., Boivin, M., Tessier, R., Lefebvre, F., & Robaey, P. (2001). Mediators of behavioral problems in 7-year-old children born after 24 to 28 weeks of gestation. *Journal of Developmental and Behavioral Pediatrics, 22*, 1–10.

Paneth, N.S. (1995). The problem of low birth weight. In *The future of children: Low birth weight* (pp. 11–34). Los Altos, CA: Packard Foundation.

Parker, S., Greer, S., & Zuckerman, B. (1988). Double jeopardy: The impact of poverty on early child development. *Pediatric Clinics of North America, 35*, 1227–1240.

Pasamanick, B., & Knobloch, H. (1961). Epidemiologic studies on the complications of pregnancy and the birth process. In G. Caplan (Ed.), *Prevention of mental disorders in children*. New York: Basic Books.

Perlman, J. M. (1998). White matter injury in the preterm infant: An important determinant of abnormal neurodevelopmental ourcome. *Early Human Development, 53*, 99–120.

Resnick, M. B., Gomatam, S. V., Carter, R. L., Ariet, M., Roth, J., Kilgore, K. L., Bucciarelli, R. L., Mahan, C. S., Curran, J. S., & Eitzman, D. V. (1998). Educational disabilities of neonatal intensive care graduates. *Pediatrics, 102*, 308–316.

Richards, A. L., Kelly, E. A., Doyle, L. W., & Callanan, C. (2001). Cognition, academic progress, behavior and self concept at 14 years of very low birth weight children. *Journal of Developmental and Behavioral Pediatrics, 22*, 11–18.

Richardson, D. K., Gray, J. E., McCormick, M. C., Workman-Daniels, K., & Goldmann, D. A. (1993). Score for acute neonatal physiology (SNAP): A physiologic severity index for neonatal intensive care. *Pediatrics, 91*, 617–623.

Robertson, C. M. T., & Finer, N. N. (1988). Educational readiness of term neonatal encephalopathy. *Journal of Developmental and Behavioral Pediatrics, 9*, 298–306.

Sameroff, A. J., & Chandler, M. J. (1975). Reproductive risk and the continuum of caretaking casualty. In F. D. Horowitz (Ed.), *Review of child development research. Vol. 4.* (pp. 187–244). Chicago: University of Chicago Press.

Saylor, C.F., Boyce, G. C., & Peagler, S. M. (2000). Brief report: Cautions against using the Stanford-Binet IV to classify high risk preschoolers. *Journal of Pediatric Psychology, 25*, 179–183.

Semel, E., Wiig, E. H., & Secord, W. A. (1995). *CELF-3: Clinical evaluation of language fundamentals. Examiner's manual.* (3rd ed.). San Antonio, TX: The Psychological Corporation.

Sheslow, D., & Adams, W. (1990). *Wide range assessment of memory and learning. Administration manual.* Wilmington, DE: Jastek Associates.

Synnes, A. R., Chien, L. Y., Peliowski, A., Baboolal, R., & Lee, S. C. (2001). Variations in intraventricular hemorrhage incidence rates among Canadian neonatal intensive care units. *Journal of Pediatrics, 138*, 525–531.

Taylor, H. G., Hack, M., & Klein, N. K. (1998). Attention deficit in children with <750 gm birth weight. *Developmental Neuropsychology, 4*, 21–34.

Taylor, H. G., Klein, N., Minich, N. M., & Hack, M. (2000). Middle-school-age outcomes in children with very low birthweight. *Child Development, 71*, 1495–1511.

Taylor, G. H., Klein, N., Schatschneider, N., & Hack, M. (1998). Predictors of early school age outcomes in very low birth weight children. *Journal of Developmental and Behavioral Pediatrics, 19*, 235–243.

Thompson, R. J., Gustafson, K. E., Oehler, J. M., Catlett, A. T., Brazy, J. E., & Goldstein, R. F. (1997). Developmental outcome of very low birth weight infants at four years of age as a function of biological risk and psychosocial risk. *Journal of Developmental and Behavioral Pediatrics, 18*, 91–96.

Thorndike, R. L., Hagen, E. P., & Sattler, J. M. (1986). *Guide for administering and scoring the fourth edition Stanford-Binet Intelligence Scale.* Chicago: Riverside Publishing.

Tjossem, T. (1976). *Intervention strategies for high risk infants and young children.* Baltimore: University Park Press.

Touwen, B. C. L. (1986). Very low birth weight infants. *European Journal of Pediatrics, 145*, 460.

Vohr, B. R., & Msall, M. (1997). Neuropsychological and functional outcomes of very low birth weight infants. *Seminars in Perinatology, 21*, 202–220.

Vohr, B. R., Wright, L., Dusick, A. M., Mele, L., Verter, J., Steichen, J. J., Simon, N. P., Wilson D. C., Broyles, S., Bauer, C. R., Delaney-Black, V., Youlton, K. A., Fleisher, B. E., Papile, L., & Kaplan, M. (2000). Neurodevelopmental and functional outcomes of extremely low birth weight infants in the National Institute of Child health and Human Development neonatal research network, 1993–1994. *Pediatrics, 105*, 1216–1226.

Volpe, J. J. (1996). Subplate neurons-missing link in brain injury of the premature infant? *Pediatrics, 97*, 112–113.

Volpe, J. J. (1998). Neurologic outcome of prematurity. *Archives of Neurology, 55*, 297–300.

Wechsler, D. (1989). *Wechsler preschool and primary scale of intelligence-R.* San Antonio, TX: The Psychological Corporation.

Werner, E. E. (1986). A longitudinal study of perinatal risk. In D. C. Farran & J. D. McKinney (Eds.), *Risk in intellectual and psychosocial development* (pp. 3–27). New York: Academic Press.

Whitfield, M. F., Eckstein-Grunau, R. V., & Holsti, L. (1997). Extremely premature ($\leq$ 800g) school children: Multiple areas of hidden disability. *Archives of Disease in Children, 77*, F85–F90.

Zelkowitz, P., Papageorgiou, A., & Allard, M. (1994). Relationship of rehospitalization to cognitive and behavioral outcomes in very low birth weight and normal birth weight children. *Journal of Developmental and Behavioral Pediatrics, 15*, 179–185.

27

Adolescent Health-Related Issues

Jan L. Wallander
Karen M. Eggert
Katrina K. Gilbert
University of Alabama at Birmingham

The term *adolescence* is derived from the Latin verb meaning "to grow to maturity" (Branwhite, 2000). Conceptually, this encompasses biological maturation as well as cognitive and psychosocial changes. Historically, the cognitive and psychosocial changes have been greatly influenced by the social context of the times. Before the Industrial Revolutions in the United States and Europe, adolescence was mainly perceived as the biological changes associated with puberty, therefore being of short duration; this is still the prominent view in agrarian cultures today. However, since the 1900s, technological societies have been redefining adolescence. Not only is puberty beginning at an earlier age as a result of better health care and nutrition (Petersen & Leffert, 1995), but the social framework of modern society requires that adolescence be a time that defines the gap between sexual maturity and adulthood. In this rather large gap, preparation to accept adult responsibilities takes place (Thompson, 1999).

In this chapter we discuss how developmental transitions provide risks and opportunities for adolescents (Schulenberg, Maggs, & Hurrelmann, 1997). Although developmental changes are positive over the adolescent years, the rates for problem behaviors threatening healthy development also increase during this time. We focus on the most salient threats to health and development in adolescence in this chapter, namely injury, violence, depression and suicide, substance use, sexual activity, and chronic illness. We conclude with a call for comprehensive school-based prevention programs. First, however, we provide an overview of development during adolescence.

ADOLESCENT DEVELOPMENT

The biological changes associated with the onset of puberty initiate adolescence (Branwhite, 2000). Modern society defines adolescence as a period of transition and change that lasts approximately a decade. We summarize in Table 27.1 the key developments that occur biologically,

TABLE 27.1
Summary of Adolescent Development

	Biological Changes	*Cognitive Changes*	*Social Changes*
Early Adolescence	–Growth spurt –Skin, voice, and body hair changes –Increases in body fat –Development of secondary sex characteristics	–Abstract and logical thinking, hypothesis testing emerge –Firmer grasp on cause-effect relationships	–Increased interest in opposite sex –Adjustment to independence and self-reliance
Middle Adolescence	–Secondary sex characteristics continue to develop –High levels of androgen secretion increasing desire for sexual stimulation leading to sexual maturation	–Emotional and intellectual capacity increase –Abstract and logical thinking, hypothesis testing increase –Autonomous functioning	–Seeks "distinctiveness" and develops preferences –Peer relationships are given greater significance
Late Adolescence	–Physically mature	–Have established self-identity and bolstered self-esteem –Adult-like cognitions are present	–Plan for future –Establish more intimate relationships

cognitively, and socially at three stages of adolescence. These stages are used for convenience and are not intended as clear demarcations.

Early adolescence extends from approximately 10 to 13 years of age and is dominated by pubertal development. However, it is important to note that there is a wide variability in age of puberty onset. Puberty may begin as early as 8 years for females and 9.5 years in males, or as late as 13 years in females and 13.5 years in males (Gondoli, 1999). There are average differences also between races, for example with African American youth initiating puberty earlier in life than White youth.

In this early stage, the adolescent grows taller, experiences skin, voice, and body hair changes, as well as increased body fat and development of secondary sex characteristics. Body image becomes an important issue. Emotional swings are common secondary to hormonal changes (Thompson, 1999). In addition to these individual biological changes, the transition from elementary to middle school requires psychosocial and educational adjustments. This is also the stage in which a marked increase in interest in the opposite sex begins. Therefore, understanding the responsibilities and consequences of sexual behaviors becomes of paramount importance.

This stage corresponds to Piaget's formal operations, indicated by a greater capacity for abstract thinking, hypothesis testing, and logic (Petersen & Leffert, 1995). As a result, adolescents can think into the future and are capable of reflective thinking (Keating, 1980). Adolescents are more prepared to process information and have a better capacity to retain information that will help them solve problems efficiently, leading to a better understanding of how the world works and a firmer grasp on logic and cause-effect relationships.

Social cognitions begin to take on an egocentric perspective; that is, the adolescent believes his experience is unique as well as that others are as preoccupied with him as he is with himself

(Santrock, 1997). The adjustment to independence and self-reliance brings the challenge of negotiating relationships with adults and clarifying roles in respect of one's position with peers. This facilitates self-reliance, self-control, and the capacity for independent decision making (Crockett & Petersen, 1993) and supports development of autonomy. Parent–child conflicts increase in early adolescence, peaking with pubertal change (Petersen & Leffert, 1995).

Middle adolescence extends from approximately 14 to 16 years of age. The individual seeks to exhibit "distinctiveness" in his or her lifestyle and preferences for hairstyles, clothing, and music. However, one adolescent's preferences are generally similar to those of his or her peers. Problem-solving abilities become more adult-like. Whereas ability to assess possible risks and consequences continues to increase, an adolescent at this stage typically underestimate's her personal risk for negative outcomes. The continuing cognitive changes have been attributed to two biological changes: continued brain growth and puberty. Another explanation is "changes in socialization" brought about academically and socially by new and varied social experiences (Petersen & Leffert, 1995).

During middle adolescence, peer and family relationships usually change. Like other developmental transitions, changes in relationships originate in the interaction of physical maturational processes, cultural influences and expectations, and personal values and goals (Schulenberg et al., 1997). Although friends exert a great deal of influence on the developing adolescent at this point, the family remains a strong influence.

The parent relationship is important for coping successfully with the developmental tasks of adolescents (Hendry, Shucksmith, & Philip 1995). Adolescents indicate being less self-conscious and better able to concentrate at home than in other settings (Csikszentmihalyi & Larson, 1984). Because parents serve as role models and teenagers learn by observation and modeling, parenting styles and childrearing patterns have an important influence on adolescents' social and emotional development. For many adolescents, relationships with parents are perceived as accepting and comfortable (Thiede-Call & Mortimer, 2001). Consequently, many adolescents are responsive to their parents and favor their parent's ideologies.

However, as the adolescent's emotional and intellectual capabilities increase they also strive to loosen ties to their parents. The adolescent becomes adventuresome, marking the beginning of finding one's relationship to others and greater significance is given to peer relationships. In contrast to the activity-based relationships of childhood that are easily changed by shifts in interests or access to one another, adolescent friendships emerge as more stable, intimate, and affectively oriented attachments that occupy increasing amounts of an adolescent's time and exist with little parental oversight or interference (Brown, Dolcini, & Leventhal, 1997). It is the peer group that forms a vital and often useful avenue by which adolescents make the transition from the family to the wider world (Heaven, 1994). Peers become companions and providers of advice, support, and feedback. They are used as a reference for developing lifestyles and values and often provide emotional support as adolescents disengage partially from their families.

Late adolescence ranges from approximately 17 to 21 years of age. This is the stage of planning for a career, establishing more intimate relationships, and taking on adult responsibilities (Petersen & Leffert, 1995). This is a time also for exploring different occupations, religious beliefs, political views, and sexual identities (Thompson, 1999). Biological changes are relatively small. More adult-like cognitions are present and the psychosocial development of the earlier years has ideally established a healthy, strong self-identity bolstered by increased self-esteem. The journey from dependence as a child is ending in autonomy. Ideally, relationships with parents have been maintained but revised, and relationships with peers are becoming stable and reciprocal based on shared values and experiences.

Success at this stage is defined by the ability to competently take on adult roles and responsibilities and to be a positive contributor to society (Petersen & Leffert, 1995). The end of adolescence, unlike the beginning, however, is not biologically defined; rather, it is defined in cultural and socioeconomic terms (Branwhite, 2000). Subjectively therefore, adulthood is achieved when the individual accepts responsibility for one's self, makes independent decisions, and becomes financially independent. More objectively, however, adulthood achievement is marked by having a stable residence, having completed school, settled into a career, and committed to a long-term love relationship (Arnett, 2000). This obviously may take further years beyond age 21, raising the possibility that another transition stage needs to be negotiated in the 20s (Arnett, 2000).

The next several sections address selected problems that are the leading causes of morbidity and mortality in this age period and may negatively impact adolescent health and development. Table 27.2 presents the prevalence of various specific health-risk behaviors, based on data from

TABLE 27.2
Percentage of Students Grades 9–12 Who Report Health-Risk Behaviors in the Past 30 Days*

Substance use	
Alcohol	50.0
Tobacco	32.8
Marijuana	26.7
Cocaine	4.0
Heroin (in lifetime)	2.4
Methamphetamine (in lifetime)	9.1
Inhalants	4.2
Steroids (in lifetime)	3.7
Sexual Behavior	
Sexually active	39.9
No condom use, sexually active	42.0
Taking birth control pills	16.2
Pregnant/gotten someone else pregnant	6.3
Alcohol or drug use at last sexual intercourse	24.8
Behaviors that contribute to unintentional injuries	
Rarely or never worn seat belts	16.4
Bicycle riding without helmets	70.8
Motorcycle riding without helmets	23.9
Treated for unintentional injury (in last 12 mos.)	32.7
Suicidal Ideation and Suicide Attempts	
Sad/hopeless enough to stop usual activities for ≥2 wks (in last 12 mos.)	28.3
Seriously considered suicide (in last 12 mos.)	19.3
Made a specific suicidal plan (in last 12 mos.)	14.5
≥1 suicidal attempt (in last 12 mos.)	8.3
Violence/Aggressive Behaviors	
Carried a gun	4.9
Carried a weapon	17.3
Involved in ≥1 physical fight (in last 12 mos.)	35.7
Hit, slapped, physically hurt by boyfriend/girlfriend (in last 12 mos.)	8.8
Forced sexual intercourse (in lifetime)	8.8

Notes: From *Youth Risk Behavior Survey* (CDC, 1999); *unless other time period is indicated.

the recurring Youth Risk Behavior Survey of 9th- through 12th-grade students nationwide (Centers for Disease Control and Prevention (CDC), 1999).

INJURY AND VIOLENCE

Injury and violence are the most important threats to the health of school children. The two leading causes of death among 15–19 year olds are unintentional injury and homicide, and these account for about 60% of all deaths among 10–24 year olds (CDC, 1998). In comparison, the leading causes of death in the 5–9-year-old-age range are injuries sustained as a passenger in a motor vehicle or as a pedestrian or from fire or burns (Tuchfarber, Zins, & Jason, 1997). About 13 million children are injured severely enough each year to require medical attention and 50,000 are permanently disabled (CDC, 1995). The CDC further reported that 7,200 unintentional injury deaths occurred among children under age 15 years, and an additional 1,600 deaths resulted from intentional injury (i.e., homicide and suicide) in 1991. While the statistics on the impact of injury and violence meld to some extent, they are different problems and require different attention.

Intentional injury resulting from violence, of which homicide is the most severe outcome, has escalated in recent times. For example, the homicide rates of youth ages 14–17 increased by 172% from 1985 to 1994 (Fox, 1996). However, about the same proportion of youth is committing violent acts today as in 1980 and the frequency of offending is quite comparable over this period (Elliott, 1994). The increase in youth homicide primarily is attributable to an increase in the lethality, not to the frequency of violent acts (Murray, Guerra, & Williams, 1997). The availability of firearms is the major culprit in this state of affairs. Death rate in adolescents from firearms is expected to have surpassed that of motor crashes by 2003, becoming their leading cause of death.

There are many theories of the etiology of violence, representing widely differing paradigms. Most prevention efforts have been risk-focused, where presumed earlier steps in a sequence toward violent behavior are addressed (e.g., violence in the family, aggressive behavior in preschool). Interventions during the elementary school years, however, are diverse. Some are predominantly child centered and skill based, addressing the skills and competencies directly through instructional interventions. Other programs address these skills indirectly by educating teachers and parents about how to manage children's behavior and enhance relationships. Although some programs have demonstrated modest gains in targeted competencies, others have been less successful, and results have been discouraging in the most disadvantaged urban settings. Research has not suggested a single best approach to elementary school intervention to reduce violence (cf. Murray et al., 1997; Tolan & Guerra, 1994).

In adolescence, prevention efforts are less common in favor of targeted interventions for those already displaying violent behavior. Such programs are usually implemented within the legal system, but also at alternative schools, rather than the regular education program. Another strategy has been to change the organization of schools or the school climate. It is well documented that certain characteristics of schools are associated with high delinquency rates, including violence, namely large school size, absence of individual attention, ability grouping and negative labeling, low teacher expectations, lack of structure, and inconsistent treatment by school staff (cf. Dryfoos, 1990). Gottfredson, Gottfredson, and Hybl (1993) demonstrated in several studies that improvements in school climate are associated with decreases in delinquency, and presumably violence, following systematic efforts at altering the school climate.

Although intentional injury because of violence has received a great deal of attention over the past couple of years related to extremely rare, albeit high-impact incidences of group homicides at school, it remains that *unintentional injury* is a much more extensive threat to the health of young people during the school years. Prevention and competence-enhancement approaches can help children and their parents focus on (1) increasing skills that encourage the development of positive, health-enhancing behaviors (e.g., defensive driving, anger control skills), (2) eliminating or reducing health-compromising actions (e.g., driving after drinking, diving in shallow waters), and (3) altering the environment so they are more supportive of these activities (Tuchfarber et al., 1997). Numerous factors that lead to unintentional injury are under the control of young people and they can be changed. However, injury prevention cannot solely be directed toward the young person, but also must involve parents because they are important mediators of adolescents' environments.

Several strategies are being used to prevent unintentional injury (cf. Tuchfarber et al., 1997). Environmental or passive change methods are those that once implemented work automatically (e.g., setting water heater temperature at a lower level to prevent burns). Legislative methods often undergird environmental methods by mandating some methods to be adopted to prevent injury (e.g., motorcycle helmet use). Education methods involve the provision of information about safety issues for the purpose of motivating change (e.g., drinking and driving).

Schools usually do not initiate environmental or legislative methods, but may be one location where these are implemented. Rather, schools can be actively involved in reducing unintentional injury primarily through educational efforts. Unfortunately, although educational methods, particularly one-shot attempts, may produce some short-term benefits, change is usually not observed through long periods (Geddis & Pettengel, 1982). When expanded and implemented programmatically and broadly across the school setting, however, schools can become effective places for injury prevention (Tuchfarber et al., 1997).

It seems obvious that given the impact of unintentional injury, schools, being the universal environment for young people, need to be involved in prevention efforts. In adolescence, this should primarily target motor vehicle use because it is the foremost cause of death and disability in this age range and it is a high-frequency behavior. More specific behaviors that would need to be targeted include, among others, safe driving and riding, use of safety restraints, and avoidance of alcohol and other substances in connection with driving. If implemented universally, effective efforts will have a notable effect on injury rates in adolescence. However, at present we lack the empirical base for designing effective school-based programs in this area. Research therefore is needed into effective ways of achieving this.

DEPRESSION AND SUICIDE

Various mental health problems can be experienced in adolescence. However, a particular concern is depression because it is among the most prevalent mental health problems at this time and because it is associated with other health threats in adolescence, for example, suicidal behavior and substance use. Depression is a mental state marked by three main groups of symptoms: a sad mood, vegetative features, and psychomotor symptoms (American Psychiatric Association, 2000). The sad mood may consist of feelings of worthlessness because of negative self-evaluation and excessive guilt often accompanied by feelings of emptiness, irritability, and/or boredom. Vegetative features can include loss of interest in daily activities, insomnia or increased need for sleep, decreased energy, inability to concentrate or make decisions, decreased or increased appetite, and decreased sex drive. Psychomotor symptoms can be seen in the form of agitation or slowed speech and body movement.

Considerable evidence shows that the rate of depression in adolescents has been increasing in recent years (cf. Compas, Conner, & Wadsworth, 1997). One fifth to one half of adolescents are experiencing significant symptoms of depression at any given point in time (Seiffge-Krenke, 1998). CDC (1999) reported that 28% of high school students reported feeling sad or hopeless enough in the last year to stop usual activities for at least 2 weeks. The prevalence of adolescents experiencing a major depressive disorder is 5%–10% (Luthar, Burack, Cicchetti, & Weisz, 1997).

There are gender and racial differences in depression. Females are at greater risk for depression than are males from onset of puberty (Call & Mortimer, 2001). Moreover, females are two times more likely to attempt suicide; however, males are four times more likely to die from a suicide attempt (Blau & Gullotta, 1996) because they choose more lethal methods than females (e.g., guns vs. drug overdoses) (Seiffge-Krenke, 1998). These gender differences are maintained across races even though there are racial differences in depression and suicide. Hispanics reported more depression, suicidal ideation, and suicidal attempts than African Americans, and African American in turn reported more of these behaviors than Whites (CDC, 1999; Compas et al., 1997).

Depression has an impact on adolescents in several pervasive ways. The depression impairs ability to function normally at school, at home, and in social settings, which may interfere with mastery of important developmental tasks (Compas et al., 1997). Sustained and/or recurrent depression may hinder an adolescent's ability to do his or her best academically, to fulfill his or her functional role in the family, and to interact normally with his or her peers. Depression also is strongly associated with delinquency and substance abuse (Loeber, Farrington, Stouthamer-Loeber, & Van-Kammen, 1998).

Additionally, depression is a major risk factor in adolescent suicide. Suicide behaviors span the range from ideation to repeated attempts. Table 27.2 shows that among high school students, about 1 in 5 has had serious thoughts of suicide and 1 in 10 has made an attempt at suicide in the past year. There is a sharp increase in depression by middle adolescence (Compas et al., 1997) and suicide is the third leading cause of death in 13–19 year olds (CDC, 1998). At the same time, it is important to note that suicidal behaviors can occur without a depressed mood.

There is no single cause of depression (Luthar et al., 1997). Depression is hypothesized to be a culmination of biological, cognitive, social, and contextual factors. These factors interact with each other in a transactional model of depression. Biological factors are genetics (e.g., increased risk of depression for other family members) and neurotransmitter anomalies (e.g., decreased serotonin levels), as well as endocrine dysregulation (e.g., thyroid irregularities). Cognitive factors that impact depression include an attributional style (i.e., a tendency to assign blame to the self for bad events and attribute the cause of good events to external sources) that results in low-self esteem and feelings of hopelessness about the future. Social factors include poorer quality friendships and general decreased social competence in depressed compared to nondepressed youth. Contextual factors associated with increased rates of depression include poverty, maternal depression, dysfunctional parent–child relationships, and parental discord (Compas et al., 1997; Johnson, 1986).

Blau and Gullotta (1996) identified risk factors for suicide behavior in adolescents. Depression is the best predictor for suicide, but another prominent risk factor is substance abuse. Of those who complete a suicide, 70% also abuse alcohol and/or illicit drugs. Poverty, delinquency, overt conflicts with parents, parental discord, and having a sibling with an emotional disorder also increase the risk of suicide. An immediate crisis, like an embarrassment or humiliation, an intense conflict with a peer, pregnancy, a romantic breakup, or an academic or athletic disappointment, also increases the risk of suicide. Additionally, the suicide attempt of an acquaintance; death, illness, or injury of a loved one; separation; divorce or remarriage of parent(s); or a change in residence have been associated with suicide. Of those who commit suicide, 60% have stated intent to do so (Blau & Gullotta, 1996).

Because depression and suicidal behavior are serious mental health problems, which schools are rarely equipped to address in indicated ways, the major role of school personnel will be to identify the problem, refer to mental health professionals, and provide support (e.g., temporary adjustments in academic expectations). Adolescents with depression require outpatient individual intervention usually over numerous weeks. Indicated interventions include cognitive-behavioral or cognitive therapy and antidepressant medication. Inpatient intervention may be indicated during severe episodes.

SUBSTANCE USE: ALCOHOL, TOBACCO, AND ILLICIT DRUGS

Alcohol and illicit drug use are health-damaging behaviors that are implicated in all three leading causes of mortality and disability in adolescence: unintentional injury and especially motor vehicle crashes, homicide, and suicide (Chassin, Presson, Sherman, & McConnell, 1995; U.S. Congress, Office of Technology Assessment, 1991). Alcohol and drug use have a major impact on a variety of developmental processes as well, such as academic motivation and achievement, vocational planning, development of life goals, and mental health. Consistent alcohol and illicit drug use is known to affect many organ systems in the human body over time, such as the brain, stomach, pancreas, and kidneys, impairing health. Tobacco use also is implicated in several causes of mortality and morbidity across the life span. Primary among these is lung cancer, which is one of the leading causes of premature death in the U.S. population, but tobacco use is also strongly linked to cardiovascular disease.

It has been well established that the vast majority of adult smokers initiated this behavior in adolescence (Chassin, Presson, Sherman, & Edwards, 1990). Alcohol, tobacco, and/or illicit substance use commonly develop in adolescents from multiple and varying etiological pathways. There is no single cause, of course, nor a necessary one. Rather, multiple determinants interact in any given case. However, the accumulated research points to salient risk factors that are associated with substance use. Table 27.3 lists risk factors that Dryfoos (1990) concluded as having been supported in at least several empirical studies.

Schools can play a major role in addressing these problems. There have been numerous efforts at preventing initiation of and reducing alcohol, tobacco, and illicit drug use in young people through programs implemented in the schools (e.g., Botvin, Baker, Dusenbury, Tortu, & Botvin, 1990; Botvin, Baker, Dusenbury, Botvin, & Diaz, 1995; Ellickson & Bell, 1990; Pentz et al., 1989; Pentz et al., 1990; Shope, Kloska, Dielman, & Maharg, 1994). Numerous descriptive reviews (e.g., Botvin & Botvin, 1992; Hansen, 1992, 1993; Mrazek & Haggerty, 1994; Perry & Kelder, 1992) as well as empirical meta-analyses (Bangert-Drowns, 1988; Bruvold, 1990, 1993; Bruvold & Rundall, 1988; Hansen, Rose, & Dryfoos, 1993; Rundall & Bruvold, 1988; Tobler, 1986, 1992, 1994; Tobler & Stratton, 1997) of this literature uniformly conclude that certain types of school-based prevention programs can achieve measurable reductions in adolescent substance use. Most importantly, some studies show that measurable reduction in adolescent alcohol, tobacco, and illicit drug use can be sustained through high school and into young adulthood.

It is well known now what contributes to the success of school-based prevention programs. Structure and intensity is important. Intensive programs, implementation across school grades, including booster sessions, and involvement of the families and the community are important. As Tobler and Statton (1997) illuminated in their meta-analysis, program content and process is also extremely important. They classified 120 programs as being either noninteractive or interactive.

Noninteractive programs relied primarily on didactic presentation of knowledge by a leader, often a teacher. Although a few noninteractive programs included drug refusal skills training, this was uniformly present in the interactive programs. However, what especially defined the *interactive programs* was their emphasis on a social process including adolescent group work, deliberation, and learning, which was absent in the noninteractive programs. Interactive

TABLE 27.3
Risk Factors for Substance Use Identified by Dryfoos (1990)

Substance Behavior
Early initiation
Lack of belief that use will harm
Psychological
Truancy
Conduct problems
Early delinquency
Nonconformity
Independent minded
Depression
Family
Lack of parental support
Parental substance use
Social-community
Low resistance to peer influence
Peer substance use
Low attendance at religious institution
Urban, high-density residence
Education
Low expectations for education
Low achievement in middle school
Alternative/vocational school enrollment

programs were further divided into social influence and comprehensive life skills programs. Social influence programs are highly focused drug refusal programs, whereas the comprehensive life skills programs subsume all components of the social influence programs but added components that were not related solely to the use of drugs. This included communication, assertiveness, decision/problem solving, and coping skills as well as increasing self-esteem.

Tobler and Stratton (1997) found that the collection of interactive programs had a substantially larger median effect size, 8 to 10 times that of the noninteractive programs. The interactive programs were equally effective with alcohol, tobacco, and marijuana use, whereas the noninteractive programs were equally ineffective across types of substances. The comprehensive life skills programs were slightly more successful than social influence programs, suggesting an added benefit from targeting a broader range of skills. Through further analyses, Tobler and Stratton (1997) could infer that attitudes inconsistent with substance use resulting from the interactive programs were largely responsible for their positive effects. Attitudes were generally not changed in the noninteractive programs.

Tobler and Stratton (1997) concluded that the observed effect size of approximately .20 for the interactive programs (compared to .02 for noninteractive) equals a success rate of 9.5%. This was deemed clinically significant in particular when the mean delivery intensity was just 10 hours. This success rate is larger than many observed for well-established public health prevention efforts. For example, a 9.5% impact was compared to the 3.5% success rate reported for aspirin on heart attacks in the Physician's Health Study, which led to immediate and widespread public health recommendations.

Of the numerous substance use prevention programs incorporating an interactive process and comprehensive life skills, Botvin and colleagues' efforts remain the most thoroughly evaluated. Botvin's program (Botvin, Baker, Botvin, Filazzola, & Millman, 1984) was initially implemented over 15 class periods in 7th grade, but 10 additional intervention sessions were provided in 8th grade and 5 in 9th grade. The main focus was on (1) teaching information and skills for resisting social influences to use substances and (2) promoting generic personal and social skills that lead to the development of characteristics associated with decreased risk for substance use.

More specifically, the intervention was designed to teach students cognitive, emotional, and social skills for building a constructive sense of self, managing feelings, communication skills, developing personal relationships, and asserting rights. It was also designed to teach skills and knowledge specifically related to resisting advertising pressure and social influences to use alcohol, tobacco, and illicit drugs through goal setting, problem solving, negotiation, refusal, and help seeking. These skills were taught using a combination of techniques including demonstration, behavioral rehearsal, feedback, and reinforcement, and behavioral assignments for out-of-class practice.

Efficacy of this program has been demonstrated where schools enrolling 5,954 7th-grade students were randomly assigned to either of two versions of the experimental intervention (differing primarily in terms of leader training and feedback) or a control condition. The latter followed a traditional health education curriculum. Botvin and colleagues have published at least 10 evaluations of program efficacy, showing initial reductions of up to 50%–70% in alcohol, tobacco, and marijuana use at a 7th-grade posttest. A follow-up evaluation 6 years after initial implementation, involving 4,466 12th-grade students, showed that substance use resistance had eroded only slightly, now at 44% (Botvin et al., 1995). Although the intervention had targeted alcohol, tobacco, and marijuana use, follow-up evaluations also found effects on the use of hashish, heroin, PCP, and inhalants, but not on cocaine in the 12th grade.

SEXUAL ACTIVITY

Sexual activity among adolescents has increased dramatically since the 1970s. Approximately 10% of youth are sexually active by age 13, but by age 15 one third of males and one fourth of females have had sexual intercourse. The majority of males become sexually active by age 16, whereas the majority of females have had intercourse by age 17 (Sells & Blum, 1996). Initiating sexual intercourse at an earlier age has a cumulative impact on the frequency of sexual activity and number of sex partners (CDC, 1999). Adolescents who begin to date earlier have more dates involving sexual experience, have more sexual partners, and greater levels of sexual activity during late adolescence and young adulthood. This increase in sexual intercourse at younger ages and in sex partners puts many youth at risk for pregnancy and for contracting sexually transmitted diseases (STDs) including exposure to human immunodeficiency virus (HIV).

During adolescence many factors influence a young person's decision to engage in sexual activity with others. Puberty coincides with the onset of sexual awareness (Heaven, 1994). The adolescent female experiences her first menstruation and the adolescent male experiences his first ejaculation. These are major psychological events for adolescents that herald the end of childhood. In this transition toward adulthood, the adolescent, who is already engaged in identity formation, must also come to terms with his or her own sexuality (Heaven, 1994).

Family and friends influence adolescent sexuality. The family sets the social context within which an adolescent will learn about sexuality (Miller & Moore, 1990). For instance, because of decreased parental supervision in single-parent homes, daughters from these families are more likely to engage in sexual activity at younger ages than their peers from two-parent homes. Single parents who are dating may model sexual behavior (Gunatilake, 1998). Factors such as the adolescent sexual experience of the mother, the educational level of parents, the sexual activity of older siblings, communication within the family, and parental attitude and value toward adolescent sexual intercourse all influence adolescent sexual behavior (Heaven, 1994).

Peer group influences also strongly affect sexual behaviors. Adolescent perceptions of the sexual norms, expectations, and behaviors of peers predict adolescent sexual behavior (Heaven, 1994). A longitudinal peer network study reported that their closest friends influenced sexual behavior of females; girls who were virgins when the study began were more likely to have intercourse if they had sexually experienced friends (Gunatilake, 1998). Although there are strong similarities between sexual behaviors of peers, the congruence may not reflect peer pressure; rather, adolescents tend to acquire friends with similar sexual behavior (Billy & Udry, 1985). Friends may provide a powerful motivation to engage in or avoid sexual situations depending on friendship norms (Brooks-Gunn & Paikoff, 1997).

Aside from any moral issues that may surround sexual activity in adolescence, this puts the adolescent at risk for pregnancy and STDs. Adolescents in the United States continue to have the highest teen birth (and STDs) rate of any industrialized nation. The Alan Guttmacher Institute (1994) reported that among sexually experienced adolescents, 9% of 14 year olds, 18% of 15–17 year olds, and 22% of 18–19 year olds become pregnant each year. About one half of these pregnancies result in a live birth. Adolescent childbearing has numerous adverse implications, including increased health and developmental risk to the offspring (Ketterlinus, Henderson, & Lamb, 1990; Rosenthal, Muram, Tolley, & McAlpine, 1993), interruption or discontinuation of the adolescent's education (Upchurch & McCarthy, 1990), reduced employment opportunities (Hayes, 1987; Hofferth & Moore, 1979), and unstable or nonexistent marriages (Sagrestano & Paikoff, 1997).

Because adolescence is a time of sexual curiosity, experimentation, and risk taking, adolescents have the highest risk of exposure to STDs of any age, with about 3.8 million adolescents acquiring an STD every year (Gunatilake, 1998). Once adolescents have begun sexual activity, their use of barrier contraception (e.g., condoms) becomes important for preventing STDs (Cates & Berman, 1999). Although there has been an increase in contraceptive use over the past decade, this increase has not kept pace with the numbers of adolescents who engage in sexual intercourse. Of the 40% of sexually active adolescents in the United States, 42% are not using condoms (CDC, 1999). Drug and alcohol abuse and inaccurate perceptions of STD risk decreases an adolescent's likelihood to use condoms (Cates & Berman, 1999). Cates and Berman (1999) identified four factors making adolescents more likely to use condoms: (1) concern about acquiring HIV, (2) believing that condoms prevent HIV transmission, (3) not being embarrassed about using or asking a partner to use a condom, and (4) having the opportunity to talk to a physician about condoms.

Adolescents usually make their decisions about sex in social situations, where time is limited and when they are sexually aroused (Brooks-Gunn & Paikoff, 1997). It is crucial for adolescents to learn to exercise control over sexual situations by anticipating, planning, and maintaining control over their choices. This is achieved when adolescents recognize and understand the links between behavioral choices and sexual outcomes.

Schools face difficult choices in how programmatically to address the issues around sexual development of students. Their approach needs to reflect the values and priorities of the communities they serve. Schools to varying degrees can provide sexual development education, but may restrict this to the biological facts and leave out the important psychosocial aspects of sexual development. On the other hand, some schools provide sexual health care as part of school-based clinics (e.g., Gullotta, Noyes, & Blau, 1996).

Numerous school-based programs to foster young people making informed choices about how to manage their developing sexuality have been tested. Several of these programs report change in the areas of increased knowledge and positive attitudes, postponing the onset of sexual intercourse, increased intentions to use condoms, increased use of contraception, fewer partners, and/or decreased pregnancy rates (cf. American School Health Association, 1998; Moore, Sugland, Blumenthal, Glei, & Snyder, 1995; Oakley, Fullerton, & Holland, 1995; Sagrestano & Paikoff, 1997).

Because of the young age at which adolescents may initiate sexual activity, primary prevention targeting preadolescents is one important approach for reducing pregnancy and STD, in adolescence. Illustrative of this approach, Howard and McCabe (1990, 1992) developed the Postponing Sexual Involvement Program to provide information and decision-making skills to 8th graders to resist peer pressure to have sex. One component of the program provided basic factual information, decision-making skills, and information about proper use of contraceptives. Nurses and counselors administered this component over five class periods.

A second component was designed to develop skills to deal with social and peer pressures to engage in sexual activity by helping participants to (1) understand the societal pressures that influence teen sexual behavior, (2) learn where to go for information regarding sexuality, (3) understand their personal rights in relationships, (4) deal assertively with pressure situations, and (5) postpone sexual involvement (Howard & Mitchell, 1990). Older teen leaders, who served as positive role models for sexual abstinence, presented this component.

Follow-up data were collected yearly through 12th grade with medical records to verify reported pregnancies (Howard & McCabe, 1990, 1992). Program participants were found to be significantly more likely to postpone sexual involvement than participants in a comparison condition receiving only factual information. For those who did initiate sexual intercourse during the program year, program participants reported having sex fewer times and being more likely to use contraceptives than those in the comparison group. This was also reflected in the decreased rate of pregnancy in the former compared to the latter. Among those youth sexually active prior to the program, however, there were no change in sexual involvement or pregnancy rates.

CHRONIC ILLNESS

A chronic illness is defined as a disease interfering in daily life for more than 3 months in a year or resulting in hospitalization for more than 1 month in a year, or believed at the time of diagnosis to be likely to do either (Pless & Pinkerton, 1975). This includes numerous specific illnesses (see Section III of this volume). Between 10%–20% of the childhood population meet this definition (Newacheck & Halfon, 1998); however, most experience physiologically rather benign conditions. Only 1%–2% of the total childhood population has severe conditions. With the exception of allergies and asthma, which affect 10%–15% of the total childhood population (Taylor & Newacheck, 1992), most specific chronic illnesses (e.g., leukemia, cystic fibrosis, sickle cell disease) affect fewer than 1 young person in 1,000 (Newacheck & Halfon, 1998).

With medical and technological advances most children and adolescents survive chronic illnesses and live well into adulthood. Therefore issues of their psychosocial well-being and development have come to the forefront. Although there are studies that present exceptions, the weight of the evidence, especially from large-scale epidemiological surveys (e.g., Cadman, Boyle, Szatmari, & Offord, 1987) and a meta-analysis (Lavigne & Faier-Routman, 1992), suggest that adolescents who have a chronic illness are at increased risk for experiencing reduced well-being and hinders to their development (Wallander & Thompson, 1995; Wallander & Varni, 1998).

A chronic illness can become an important issue in adolescence because of the developmental tasks that need to be negotiated during this period (Wallander & Varni, 1995). Emancipation from parental attachment, development of attitudes and styles of behavior in social and sexual domains, emergence of a more complete self-concept, and formation of vocational plans can be negatively affected because of a chronic disease, although biological development is rarely affected. Aside from the potentially stifling effect of just being different at a time when fitting in with the peer group is paramount, most chronic illnesses necessarily hinder independence. The adolescent with a chronic illness will have to depend at least to some extent on a parent and/or health professional for the management of his illness. Examples are following the demanding diabetes treatment regimen (see Toung-human, this volume) and obtaining transportation when confined to a wheelchair due to spina bifida or being unable to obtain a driver's permit due to seizure disorder (see Williams, this volume).

The actual psychosocial impact of a chronic illness in adolescence will depend on numerous factors. Wallander and Varni (1995, 1998) proposed a model that is commonly used to conceptualize these factors into a risk and resilience framework. Exposure to stressful events both related and unrelated to the illness may be the most important risk factor, whereas parameters of the illness (e.g, severity) appear less salient for the adolescent's well-being. Personal strengths such as having effective coping strategies, maternal adjustment, and family and peer support are examples of factors that can decrease the impact of the chronic illness. More detailed discussion of this research appears in chapters in Section III, this volume.

There are at least two aspects to the role of the school for adolescents with a chronic illness. Some adolescents with a chronic illness qualify for special program considerations under the federal Individuals with Disabilities Education Act (IDEA). Various adaptations may be indicated in the educational program (e.g., resources help, Transition Plan) and day-to-day experience in school (e.g., schedule classes close by to ease ambulation) depending on the individual's needs. It is important to realize that, while possibly not qualifying under IDEA, students with some chronic illnesses experience more subtle, sometimes varying, cognitive deficits, which can affect academic achievement (see Section III). Insulin-dependent diabetes and brain tumor are examples that can have this effect.

The other role is to support the particular developmental needs of the adolescent with a chronic illness, through various informal and individualized efforts. For example, it may be important alleviate the teachers' concerns about the physical health and even medical emergency needs that may arise through education and establishment of standard procedures. Classmates of the adolescent may have similar concerns, but they may be more focused on how to relate to a peer that is different in some respects. These types of issues may have been most formally addressed regarding students with cancer returning to the school after a significant absence associated with the initial treatment (Katz, Varni, Rubenstein, Blew & Hubert, 1992; Varni, Katz, Colegrove, & Dolgin, 1993). Here, a school reintegration program has been implemented involving the student with the illness and a health professional, addressing these issues directly with and soliciting support for the returning student from teachers and classmates. As this approach has been used primarily with younger students, it would have to be adapted to the particular developmental needs and educational structures experienced by adolescents with a chronic illness.

A CALL FOR COMPREHENSIVE, DEVELOPMENTALLY BASED PREVENTION EFFORTS

It will be an overwhelming task for schools to try to address each one of the threats to adolescent health discussed herein. However, adopting an integrated framework for doing this will facilitate this effort and likely make it more effective. We propose that recognizing the central role of social and emotional competence in healthy human development will enhance progress. A major task of childhood is to develop the competencies necessary for personal well-being, physical health, and social contributions throughout life. As a society, however, we are sadly recognizing that we can no longer rely exclusively on family and kin relations to support this development (Hamburg, 1989). Schools have therefore become widely acknowledged as the major setting outside the family in which activities should be undertaken to actively promote the development of a range of competencies, including social–emotional competencies.

Initially, promoting social–emotional learning in schools through explicit interventions was intended to support personal growth (e.g, self-esteem) and prosocial engagement (e.g., getting along), and indirectly academic achievement. Over the past two decades, however, a major impetus for school-based social–emotional learning has been to prevent young people from engaging in health-damaging behaviors, such as substance use, violence, and risky sexual activity. In fact some of the most successful school-based health promotion programs already described in this chapter focus in part on the development of social–emotional competencies (e.g., Botvin et al., 1984; Howard & McCabe, 1990).

Social competence and emotional competence, both independently and in combination, are terms that have had a range of meanings (Payton et al., 2000). We construe social–emotional competencies as involving the capacity to effectively manage and coordinate one's affect, cognitions, and behavior in response to environmental demands and to achieve positive developmental outcomes (the Consortium on the School-based Promotion of Social Competence, 1994). It comprises a set of core skills and attitudes related to the capacity to recognize and manage emotions, appreciate the perspectives of others, establish prosocial goals and solve problems, cope with aversive emotions and distressing experiences, and use a variety of interpersonal skills to manage environmental demands effectively and ethically (cf. Payton et al., 2000; Saarni, 1999). Contemporary social–emotional learning programs have as their aims to educate students so that they are motivated to learn and achieve academically; engage in positive, safe, healthy practices; are socially skilled and have positive relationships with peers and adults; contribute responsibly and ethically to their peer group, family, school, and community; and acquire a basic set of skills, work habits, and values as a foundation for a lifetime of meaningful work (Elias et al., 1997). These competencies are intended to be generally applicable across various life situations.

However, these competencies cannot develop effectively without an environment that supports using these adaptive behaviors and achieving the positive developmental outcomes. Coordinated school–family-community partnerships must be created to support competence enhancement. There are three critical environmental conditions for children to develop social–emotional competence (Hawkins & Catalano, 1990): they must have multiple opportunities for meaningful positive involvements when they can use these skills; those with whom they interact must clearly and consistently reinforce competent behavioral performance; and clear family, school, and community norms must exist that support positive behavioral development. Attempting only to enhance personal competencies results in but short-term and limited improvements in the participants.

Contemporary school-based social–emotional learning programs typically target multiple outcomes, are multiyear in duration, coordinate school-based efforts with those in families and the larger community, and include environmental supports so that children have opportunities to practice positive behaviors and receive consistent reinforcement. Thus, effective programs have been found to include multiple program design, coordination, implementation, and evaluation features (Payton et al., 2000). Researchers have developed and evaluated a variety of programs designed to accomplish these goals. Other resources contain descriptions and comparisons of various social–emotional learning programs (e.g., USDHHS, 1997). We urge the further implementation of these types of programs with comprehensive evaluation of their impact on adolescent health in the multiple important domains discussed in this chapter and elsewhere in this volume.

REFERENCES

Alan Guttmacher Institute. (1994). *Sex and America's teenagers*. New York: Alan Guttmacher Institute.

American Psychiatric Association. (2000). *DSM-IV-TR: Diagnostic and statistical manual of mental disorders* (4th ed.). Washington, D.C.: American Psychiatric Association.

American School Health Association. (1998). *School health: Findings from evaluated programs* (2nd ed.). Washington, D.C.: U.S. Department of Health and Human Services.

Arnett, J. J. (2000). Emerging adulthood: A theory of development from the late teens through the twenties. *American Psychologist, 55*, 469–480.

Bangert-Drowns, R. L. (1988). The effects of school-based substance abuse education: A meta-analysis. *Journal of Drug Education, 18*, 243–264.

Billy, J. O. G., & Udry, J. F. (1985). The influence of male and female best friends on adolescent sexual behavior. *Adolescence, 20*, 21–32.

Blau, G. M., & Gullotta, T. P. (1996). *Adolescent dysfunctional behavior*. Thousand Oaks, CA: Sage.

Botvin, G. J., Baker, E., Botvin, E. M., Filazzola, A. D., & Millman, R. B. (1984). Prevention of alcohol misuse through the development of personal and social competence: A pilot study. *Journal of Studies on Alcohol, 45*, 550–552.

Botvin, G. J., Baker, E., Dusenbury, L., Botvin, E. M., & Diaz, T. (1995). Long-term follow-up results of a randomized drug abuse prevention trial in a White middle-class population. *Journal of the American Medical Association, 273*, 1106–1112.

Botvin, G. J., Baker, E., Dusenbury, L., Tortu, S., & Botvin, E. M. (1990). Preventing adolescent drug abuse through a multimodal cognitive-behavioral approach: Results of a 3-year study. *Journal of Consulting and Clinical Psychology, 58*, 437–446.

Botvin, G. J., & Botvin, E. M. (1992). School-based and community-based prevention approaches. In J. Lowinson, P. Ruiz, & R. Millman (Eds.), *Comprehensive textbook of substance abuse* (pp. 910–927). Baltimore, MD: Williams & Wilkins.

Branwhite, T. (2000). *Helping adolescents in school*. Westport, CT: Praeger.

Brooks-Gunn, J., & Paikoff, R. (1997). Sexuality and developmental transitions during adolescence. In J. Schulenberg, J. L. Maggs, & K. Hurrelman (Eds.), *Health risks and developmental transitions during adolescence* (pp. 190–219). Melbourne, Australia: Cambridge University Press.

Brown, B., Dolcini, M., & Leventhal, A. (1997). Transformations in peer relationships at adolescence: Implications for health-related behavior. In J. Schulenberg, J. L. Maggs, & K. Hurrelman (Eds.), *Health risks and developmental transitions during adolescence* (pp. 161–189). Melbourne, Australia: Cambridge University Press.

Bruvold, W. H. (1990). A meta-analysis of the California school based risk reduction program. *Journal of Drug Education, 20*, 139–152.

Bruvold, W. H. (1993). A meta-analysis of adolescent smoking prevention programs. *American Journal of Public Health, 83*, 872–880.

Bruvold, W. H., & Rundall, T. G. (1988). A meta-analysis and theoretical review of school based tobacco and alcohol intervention programs. *Psychology and Health, 2*, 53–78.

Cadman, D., Boyle, M., Szatmari, P., & Offord, D. R. (1987). Chronic illness, disability, and mental and social well-being: Findings of the Ontario Child Health Study. *Pediatrics, 79*, 805–813.

Call, K. T., & Mortimer, J. T. (2001). *Arenas of comfort in adolescence: A study of adjustment in context*. Mahway, NJ: Lawrence Erlbaum Associates.

Cates, W. Jr., & Berman, S. M. (1999). Prevention of sexually transmitted diseases other than human immunodeficiency virus. In A. J. Goreczny & M. Herson (Eds.), *Handbook of pediatric and adolescent health psychology*. Boston, MA: Allyn & Bacon.

Centers for Disease Control. (1998). *Leading causes of death reports* [Online]. Retrieved October 20, 2001, available: http://webapp.cdc.gov/sasweb/ncipc/leadcaus.html

Centers for Disease Control. (1999). *Youth risk behavior surveillance system* [Online]. Retrieved October 20, 2001, available: http://www.cdc.gov/nccdphp/dash/yrbs/

Centers for Disease Control and Prevention. (1995). Health-related quality-of-life measures—United States, 1993. *MMWR, 44*(11), 195–200.

Chassin, L., Presson, C. C., Sherman, S. J., & Edwards, D. A. (1990). The natural history of cigarette smoking: Predicting young-adult smoking outcomes from adolescent smoking patterns. *Health Psychology, 9*, 701–716.

Chassin, L., Presson, C. C., Sherman, S. J., & McConnell, A. R. (1995). Adolescent health issues. In M. C. Roberts (Ed.), *Handbook of pediatric psychology* (pp. 723–740). New York: Guilford.

Compas, B. E., Conner, J., & Wadsworth, M. (1997). Prevention of depression. In R. P. Weissburg, T. P. Gullotta, R. L. Hampton, B. A. Ryan, & G. R. Adams (Eds.), *Healthy children 2010: Enhancing children's wellness* (pp. 129–174). Thousand Oaks, CA: Sage.

Consortium on the School-based Promotion of Social Competence (1994). The school-based promotion of social competence: Theory, research, practice, and policy. In R. J. Haggerty, L. R., Sherrod, N. Germezy, & M. Rutter (Eds.), *Stress, risk, and resilience in children and adolescence: Processes, mechanisms, and interventions* (pp. 268–316). New York: Cambridge University Press.

Crockett, L. J., & Petersen, A. C. (1993). Adolescent development: Health risks and opportunities for health promotion. In S. G. Millstein, A. C. Petersen, & E. O. Nightingale (Eds.), *Promoting the health of adolescents: New directions for the twenty-first century* (pp. 13–37). New York: Oxford University Press.

Csikszentmihalyi, M., & Larson, R. (1984). *Being adolescent: Conflict and growth in the teenage years*. New York: Basic Books.

Dryfoos, J. G. (1990). *Adolescents at risk: Prevalence and prevention.* New York: Oxford University Press.

Elias, M. J., Zins, J. E., Weissberg, R. P., Frey, K. S., Greenberg, M. T., Haynes, N. M., Kessler, R., Schwab-Stone, M. E., & Shriver, T. P. (1997). *Promoting social and emotional learning: Guidelines for educators*. Alexandria, VA: Association for Supervision and Curriculum Development.

Ellickson, P. L., & Bell, R. M. (1990). Drug prevention in junior high: A multi-site longitudinal test. *Science, 247*, 1299–1305.

Elliott, D. S. (1994). *Youth violence: An overview.* Boulder, CO: Center for the Study and Prevention of Violence.

Fox, J. A. (1996). *Trends in juvenile violence.* Washington, D.C.: U.S. Bureau of Justice Statistics.

Geddis, D. C., & Pettengel, R. (1982). Parent education: Its effect on the way children are transported in cars. *New Zealand Medical Journal, 95*, 314–316.

Gondoli, D. M. (1999). Adolescent development and health. In T. L. Whitman, T. V. Merluzzi, & R. D. White (Eds.), *Life-span perspectives on health and illness*. Mahwah, NJ: Lawrence Erlbaum Associates.

Gottfredson, D. C., Gottfredson, G. D., & Hybl, L. G. (1993). Managing adolescent behavior: A multi-year, multi-school experiment. *American Educational Research Journal, 30*, 179–216.

Gullotta, T. P., Noyes, L., & Blau, G. M. (1996). School-based health and social service centers. In G. M. Blau & T. P. Gullotta (Eds.), *Adolescent dysfunctional behavior* (pp. 267–283). Thousand Oaks, CA: Sage.

Gunatilake, S. (1998). Recognizing and preventing sexually transmitted diseases among adolescents. In A. Henderson, S. Champlin, & W. Evashwick (Eds.), *Promoting teen health: Linking schools, health organizations, and community*. Thousand Oaks, CA: Sage. Publications.

Hamburg, B. A. (1989). Research on child and adolescent mental disorders. *Science, 246*, 738.

Hansen, W. B. (1992). School-based substance abuse prevention: A review of the state of the art in curriculum, 1980–1990. *Health Education Research, 7*, 403–430.

Hansen, W. B. (1993). School-based alcohol prevention programs. *Alcohol Health and Research World, 17*, 54–60.

Hansen, W. B., Rose, L. A., & Dryfoos, J. G. (1993). *Causal factors, interventions and policy considerations in school-based substance abuse prevention.* Report submitted to the U.S. Congress, Office of Technology Assessment, Washington, DC.

Hawkins, J. D., & Catalano, R. F. (1990). Broadening the vision of education: Schools as health promoting environments. *Journal of School Health, 60*, 178–181.

Hayes, C. D. (1987). *Risking the future: Adolescent sexuality, pregnancy, and childbearing (Vol. 1).* Washington, D.C.: National Academy Press.

Heaven, P. C. L. (1994). *Contemporary adolescence: A social psychological approach.* Melbourne, Australia: MacMillan Education.

Hendry, L., Shucksmith, J., & Philip, K. (1995). *Educating for health: School and community approaches with adolescents*. London: Cassell.

Hofferth, S. L., & Moore, K. A. (1979). Early childbearing and later economic well-being. *American Sociological Review, 44*, 784–815.

Howard, M., & McCabe, J. A. (1990). Helping teenagers postpone sexual involvement. *Family Planning Perspectives, 22*, 21–26.

Howard, M., & McCabe, J. A. (1992). An information skills approach for younger teens: Postponing sexual involvement program. In B. C. Miller, J. J. Card, R. L. Paikoff, & J. L. Petersen (Eds.), *Preventing adolescent pregnancy* (pp. 83–109). Newbury Park, CA: Sage.

Howard, M., & Mitchell, M. E. (1990). *Postponing sexual involvement: An educational series for preteens*. Atlanta, GA: Grady Memorial Hospital, Emory/Grady Teen Services Program.

Johnson, J. H. (1986). *Life events as stressors in childhood and adolescence*. Newbury Park, CA: Sage.

Katz, E. R., Varni, J. W., Rubenstein, C. L., Blew, A., & Hubert, N. (1992). Teacher, parent, and child evaluative ratings of a school reintegration integration for children with newly diagnosed cancer. *Chidren's Health Care, 21*, 69–75.

Keating, D. P. (1980). Thinking processes in adolescence. In J. Adelson (Ed.), *Handbook of adolescent psychology* (pp. 211–246). New York: Wiley.

Ketterlinus, R. D., Henderson, S. H., & Lamb, M. E. (1990). Maternal age, sociodemographics, prenatal health and behavior: Influences on neonatal risk status. *Journal of Adolescent Health Care, 11*, 423–431.

Lavigne, J. V., & Faier-Routman, J. (1992). Psychological adjustment to pediatric physical disorders: A meta-analytic review. *Journal of Pediatric Psychology, 17*, 133–157.

Loeber, R., Farrington, D. P., Stouthamer-Loeber, M., & Van-Kammen, W. B. (1998). *Antisocial behavior and mental health problems: Explanatory factors in childhood and adolescence*. Mahwah, NJ: Lawrence Erlbaum Associates.

Luthar, S. S., Burack, J. A., Cicchetti, D., & Weisz, J. R. (1997). *Developmental psychopathology: Perspectives on adjustment, risk and disorder*. Cambridge: Cambridge University Press.

Miller, B. C., & Moore, K. A. (1990). Adolescent sexual behavior, pregnancy, and parenting: Research through the 1980's. *Journal of Marriage and Family, 52*, 1025–1044.

Moore, K. A., Sugland, B. W., Blumenthal, C., Glei, D., & Snyder, N. (1995). *Adolescent pregnancy prevention programs: Interventions and evaluations*. Washington, D.C.: Child Trends.

Mrazek, P. J., & Haggerty, R. J. (1994). *Reducing risks for mental disorders: Frontiers for preventive intervention research*. Washington, D.C.: National Academy Press.

Murray, M. E., Guerra, N. G., & Williams, K. R. (1997). Violence prevention for the 21st Century. In R. P. Weissberg, T. P. Gullotta, R. L. Hampton, B. A. Ryan, & G. R. Adams (Eds.), *Healthy children 2010: Enhancing children's wellness* (pp. 105–128). Thousand Oaks, CA: Sage.

Newacheck, P. W., & Halfon, N. (1998). Prevalence and impact of disabling chronic conditions in childhood. *American Journal of Public Health, 88*, 610–617.

Oakley, A., Fullerton, D., & Holland, J. (1995). Behavioural interventions for HIV/AIDS prevention. *AIDS, 9*, 479–486.

Payton, J. W., Wardlaw, D. M., Graczyk, P. A., Bloodworth, M. R., Tompsett, C. J., & Weissberg, R. P. (2000). Social and emotional learning: A framework for promoting mental health and reducing risk behavior in children and youth. *Journal of School Health, 70*, 179–185.

Pentz, M. A., Dwyer, J. H., MacKinnon, D. P., Flay, B. R., Hansen, W. B., Wang, E. Y., & Johnson, C. A. (1989). A multicommunity trial for primary prevention of adolescent drug abuse. *Journal of the American Medical Association, 261*, 3259–3266.

Pentz, M. A., Trebow, E. A., Hansen, W. B., MacKinnon, D. P., Dwyer, J. H., Johnson, C. A., Flay, B. R., Daniels, S., & Cormack, C. C. (1990). Effects of program implementation on adolescent drug use behavior: The Midwestern Prevention Project (MPP). *Evaluation Review, 14*, 264–289.

Perry, C. L., & Kelder, S. H. (1992). Models for effective prevention. *Journal of Adolescent Health, 13*, 355–363.

Petersen, A. C., & Leffert, N. (1995). What is special about adolescence? In M. Rutter (Ed.), *Psychosocial disturbances in young people: Challenges for prevention* (pp. 3–36). New York: Cambridge University Press.

Pless, I. B., & Pinkerton, P. (1975). *Chronic childhood disorder: Promoting patterns of adjustment*. Chicago: Year Book Medical Publishers.

Rosenthal, T. L., Muram, D., Tolley, E. A., & McAlpine, J. (1993). Teenage pregnancy: A small comparison group of known mothers. *Journal of Sex Education & Therapy, 19*, 246–250.

Rundall, T. G., & Bruvold, W. H. (1988). A meta-analysis of school-based smoking and alcohol use prevention programs. *Health Education Quarterly, 15*, 317–334.

Saarni, C. (1999). *The development of emotional competence*. New York: Guilford.

Sagrestano, L. M., & Paikoff, R. L. (1997). Preventing high-risk sexual behavior, sexually transmitted diseases, and pregnancy among adolescents. In R. P. Weissberg, T. P. Gullotta, R. L. Hampton, B. A. Ryan, & G. R. Adams (Eds.), *Healthy children 2010: Enhancing children's wellness* (pp. 76–104). Thousand Oaks, CA: Sage.

Santrock, J. W. (1997). *Life-span development* (6th ed.). Dubuque, IA: Brown & Benchmark Publishers.

Schulenberg, J., Maggs, J. L., & Hurrelmann, K. (1997). *Health risks and developmental transitions during adolescence*. Cambridge, UK: Cambridge University Press.

Seiffge-Krenke, I. (1998). *Stress, coping, and relationships in adolescence*. Mahwah, NJ: Lawrence Erlbaum Associates.

Sells, W. C., & Blum, R. W. (1996). Current trends in adolescent health. In R. DiClemente, W. B. Hansen, & L. B. Ponton (Eds.), *Handbook of adolescent risk behavior* (pp. 5–29). New York: Plenum.

Shope, J. T., Kloska, D. D., Dielman, T. E., & Maharg, R. (1994). Longitudinal evaluation of an enhanced alcohol mis-use prevention study (AMPS) curriculum for grades six-eight. *Journal of School Health, 64*, 160–166.

Taylor, W. R., & Newacheck, P. W. (1992). Impact of childhood asthma on health. *Pediatrics, 90*, 657–662.

Thiede-Call, K., & Mortimer, J. T. (2001). *Arenas of comfort in adolescence: A study of adjustment in context*. Mahwah, NJ: Lawrence Erlbaum Associates.

Thompson, R. A. (1999). The individual child: Temperament, emotion, self, and personality. In M. H. Bornstein & M. E. Lamb (Eds.), *Developmental psychology: An advanced textbook* (4th ed.; pp. 377–409). Mahwah, NJ: Lawrence Erlbaum Associates.

Tobler, N. S. (1986). Meta-analysis of 143 adolescent drug prevention programs: Quantitative outcome results of program participants compared to a control or comparison group. *Journal of Drug Issues, 16*, 537–567.

Tobler, N. S. (1992). Drug prevention programs can work: Research findings. *Journal of Addictive Diseases, 11*, 1–28.
Tobler, N. S. (1994). *Meta-analysis of adolescent drug prevention programs.* Doctoral dissertation submitted to the State University of New York, Albany, School of Social Welfare.
Tobler, N. S., & Stratton, H. H. (1997). Effectiveness of school-based drug prevention programs: A meta-analysis of the research. *Journal of Primary Prevention, 18*, 71–128.
Tolan, P. H., & Guerra, N. G. (1994). *What works in reducing adolescent violence: An empirical review of the field.* Boulder, CO: Center for the Study and Prevention of Violence.
Tuchfarber, B. S., Zins, J. E., & Jason, L. A. (1997). Prevention and control of injuries. In R. P. Weissberg, T. P. Gullotta, R. L. Hampton, B. A. Ryan, & G. R. Adams (Eds.), *Healthy children 2010: Enhancing children's wellness* (pp. 250–277). Thousand Oaks, CA: Sage.
United States Congress, Office of Technology Assessment, & Adolescent Health. (1991). *Summary and policy options. Vol. 1.* Washington, D.C.: U.S. Government Printing Office, Publication OTA-H-468.
United States Department of Health and Human Services (USDHHS). (1997). Youth risk behavior surveillance—United States, 1997. *Morbidity and Mortality Weekly Report, 47.*
Upchurch, D. M., & McCarthy, J. (1990). The timing of a first birth and high school completion. *American Sociological Reviews, 55*, 224–234.
Varni, J. W., Katz, E. R., Colegrove, J. R., & Dolgin, M. (1993). The impact of social skills training on the adjustment of children with newly diagnosed cancer. *Journal of Pediatric Psychology, 18*, 751–767.
Wallander, J. L., & Thompson, R. J. Jr. (1995). Psychosocial adjustment of children with chronic physical conditions. In M. C. Roberts (Ed.), *Handbook of pediatric psychology* (pp. 124–141). New York: Guilford.
Wallander, J. L., & Varni, J. W. (1995). Appraisal, coping, and adjustment in adolescents with a physical disorder. In J. L. Wallander & L. J. Siegel (Eds.), *Adolescent health problems: Behavioral perspectives*. New York: Guilford.
Wallander, J. L., & Varni, J. W. (1998). Effects of pediatric chronic physical disorders on child and family adjustment. *Journal of Child Psychology and Psychiatry, 39*, 29–46.

PART VI: Interventions Within School Settings

28

Behavioral Approaches to Intervention in Educational Settings

Thomas R. Kratochwill
Erin Cowell
Kelly Feeney
Lisa Hagermoser Sannetti
University of Wisconsin–Madison

INTRODUCTION

Children spend the majority of their time in school settings, where they may experience many challenging academic and behavioral problems. Some problematic behavior that children experience is situation specific and is likely to occur only in school settings. For example, a teacher may report a student's inattentive behavior as problematic in the classroom whereas the child's parents may not report this concern at home. School settings therefore represent essential environments for the implementation of a wide range of interventions.

Behavioral approaches to intervention—the focus of this chapter—have a long history of application and implementation within educational settings (Kratochwill & Bijou, 1987). There are two main reasons for this history. First, behavioral approaches have been extremely successful in producing positive outcomes for students in school settings; the empirical research literature supports the use of many interventions for a wide range of academic and challenging behaviors (e.g., Christophersen & Mortweet, 2001; Kendall, 2000; Shapiro, 1987). Moreover, many behavioral treatments, especially when used in combination or in "packages," have been reviewed by strict criteria and identified as "evidence-based" by task forces of national organizations (e.g., Chambless & Ollendick, 2001; Kratochwill & Stoiber, 2000; Stoiber & Kratochwill, 2000). Second, although many behavioral procedures can be implemented by psychologists who directly intervene with the student, many treatments described in this chapter can be implemented through mediators (teachers, parents, other school staff) who are able to play an active role in the treatment process, but who may not necessarily have extensive training in their theoretical base and application.[1]

The purpose of this chapter is to provide an overview of behavioral treatment techniques that can be implemented in educational settings.[2] Clearly, it is impossible to review in one chapter the empirical literature on behavioral interventions used in educational settings as there are numerous books devoted to the topic. Therefore, we provide a general review of some fundamental principles that form the theoretical base of behavioral treatment techniques. As behavioral techniques have been applied to increasingly complex problems, many individuals may lose sight of the basic theoretical and foundation principles on which the treatments are based. This situation has become especially apparent when multiple behavioral procedures are packaged (multiple techniques across multiple theoretical models) and applied to complex and challenging problems. There is little doubt that the practice of behavioral treatments has become technique oriented (a recognition of this movement was long ago recognized in the field; see Azrin, 1977). Thus, examples of behavioral interventions are provided throughout the chapter to demonstrate relevance of the basic behavioral principles in educational settings.

THEORETICAL FOUNDATIONS

Behavioral approaches have evolved from diverse theoretical roots. Three major areas of learning theory have shaped contemporary behavior therapy approaches, including classical conditioning, operant conditioning, and modeling or observational learning (Kratochwill & Bijou, 1987; see Kadzin, 1978, for more detailed coverage of the theoretical origins of behavioral approaches). Many of the cognitive behavioral approaches have also evolved from social learning theory, which evolved to take a largely cognitive focus.

Classical Conditioning

Pavlov's Work

The Russian physiologist Ivan Pavlov's (1849–1936) early interests were in the biological processes of digestion. In Pavlov's classic experiment, he observed that dogs salivated with the presentation of food. He called the food an *unconditioned stimulus (UCS)* and the salivation an *unconditioned response (UR)*. He also noticed that dogs salivated in response to other sights, odors, and sounds immediately preceding the presentation of food. For example, by itself, the sight of a food dish or the sound of a metronome ringing did not elicit the salivatory response. Therefore, these stimuli are considered to be *neutral stimuli*. However, when repeatedly paired with the presentation of food, these once neutral stimuli elicit salivation. They are now considered *conditioned stimuli*. The neural connection between the unconditioned stimulus and the unconditioned response is an unlearned or reflexive stimulus response connection (S-R connection). This learned response is called a *conditioned reflex*. Pavlov's dogs had "learned" that these sights and sounds signaled the appearance of food (see Fig. 28.1).

Features of Classical Conditioning. Pavlov presented several principles of classical conditioning that are relevant to the design of behavioral treatment programs. These include stimulus generalization, discrimination, and extinction.

Stimulus generalization refers to the process by which the conditioned response transfers to other stimuli that are similar to the original conditioned stimulus. Stimulus generalization often explains the transfer of a response from one situation to another. Pavlov found that once a dog learned to salivate to a particular tone, it would also salivate to similar tones. As the tone becomes less similar to the original, the dog salivates less. This event demonstrates two facts about generalization. First, once conditioning to a stimulus occurs, its effectiveness is not

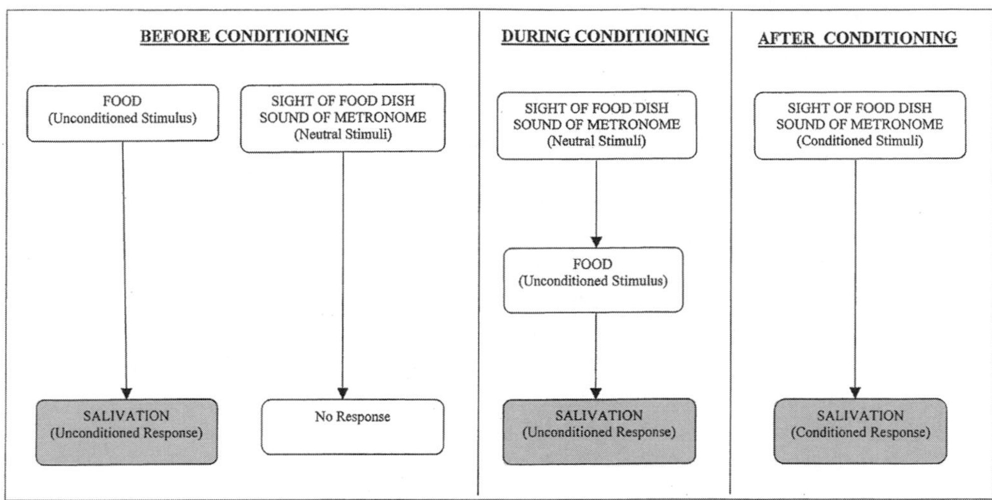

FIG. 28.1. Classical conditioning paradigm.

restricted to that stimulus. Second, as a stimulus becomes less similar to the one originally used, its ability to produce a response decreases accordingly. The process of stimulus generalization can also be seen in the way a first-grade youngster, terrified by a stern teacher, transfers that fear or anxiety to other features about school: teachers, books, or the school building itself.

Discrimination refers to the process by which one learns *not* to respond to similar stimuli in the same way. Generalization between two stimuli can be abolished if the response to one is reinforced while the response to the other is extinguished. For example, if a dog's food is always followed by a particular tone, but not similar sounding tones, the dog will gradually stop salivating to similar sounding tones. Again, we can draw important applied implications. Children might have difficulty learning to read if they cannot tell the difference between circles and curved lines, or horizontal from vertical lines. They then could not (or at least not consistently) discriminate the letters *v* from *u* or *b* from *d*, which could lead to reading problems. Similar discrimination challenges exist for young learners confronted with pairs of numbers such as 21 and 12, or 25 and 52. Learning to make discriminations of form is a critical component of successful learning.

Extinction refers to the gradual reduction of frequency or intensity of a learned response. In his experiments, Pavlov found that by presenting the sound of the metronome alone, eventually he could eliminate the conditioned response. In other words, if over time there is no food accompanying the metronome, the dog will stop salivating in the presence of the metronome only. For example, in a school setting a teacher may ignore students who do not raise their hands before speaking. Over time, the students will decrease the number of times they speak without raising their hands.

Behavioral learning theory has been used to explain the development of a number of childhood disorders and problems (see Mash & Barkley, 1996). For example, the childhood disorder Posttraumatic Stress Disorder (PTSD) is said to develop, in part, through classical conditioning (Fletcher, 1996). Although learning theories (both classical and operant) have been criticized for not explaining the complex phenomena surrounding the development of PTSD, the theories have helped researchers to formulate behavioral treatment procedures, such as flooding, for this disorder (see Saigh, Yasik, Sack, & Koplewicz, 1999).

Operant Conditioning

Skinner's Views

Although Skinner initially made his impact during the 1930s when the classical conditioning of Pavlov was popular and influential, he demonstrated that the environment had a much greater influence on learning and behavior than Pavlov's theories suggested. In his explanation of *operant conditioning*, Skinner argued that the environment (e.g., parents, teachers, peers) influences our behavior by either reinforcing or eliminating it. According to this view, behavior is a causal chain of three links: (1) an operation performed on the organism from without—a girl comes to school without breakfast; (2) some inner condition—she gets hungry; and (3) a kind of behavior—she exhibits listless behavior in the classroom. The basic work on operant conditioning has developed into the behavioral field known as *applied behavior analysis* where operant principles and procedures are used in treatment of a wide range of concerns.

Reinforcement

Skinner considered reinforcement a key element in explaining how and why learning occurred. The *principle of reinforcement* refers to an increase in the frequency of a response when certain consequences immediately follow it. The consequence that follows behavior must be contingent on the behavior. A contingent event that increases the frequency of behavior is referred to as a reinforcer (Kazdin, 2001). In other words, a reinforcer is a *stimulus event* that, if it occurs in the proper temporal relation with a response, tends to maintain or increase the strength of a response, a stimulus-response connection, or a stimulus-stimulus connection.

In our discussion of applied behavior analysis, it is important to distinguish between the basic principles of behavior and various behavior change procedures. Reinforcement is a *principle of behavior* in that it describes a functional relationship between behavior and controlling variables. In contrast, a *behavior change procedure* is a method used to put the principle into practice. Praise, for example, is a procedure that may be a powerful reinforcer. If one praises a student's correct responses immediately and the student increases correct responses, praise can be identified as a behavior change procedure that functions as a reinforcer.

The operant model attempts to link reinforcement to response as follows:

`antecedents–response–reinforcement`

The antecedents represent the range of environmental stimuli acting on an individual at a given time. They influence the likelihood that a behavior or response will occur. Often we are unaware of the nature of the antecedents. Therefore, if we focus on what is observable (the response) and reinforce it, the environment (i.e., teachers, parents) then controls the behavior. For example, when a teacher praises a student for raising his or her hand to answer a question, the student is more likely to engage in this appropriate behavior in the future.

The Nature of Reinforcement

There are two types of reinforcement, *positive reinforcement* and *negative reinforcement*. Positive reinforcement strengthens behavior through a contingent relationship with a satisfying consequence (Schloss & Smith, 1998). For example, students may complete an academic task because doing so results in teacher and/or parent praise. Techniques based on positive reinforcement have been well developed and empirically validated over many problem behaviors and situations (Maag & Kotlash, 1994). Negative reinforcement will strengthen behavior through a contingent relationship involving the removal or avoidance of various dissatisfying events (Schloss & Smith, 1998). For example, doing homework may result in the avoidance of teacher and parent reprimands. In other words, completing homework can be negatively reinforced by avoiding a reprimand.

It is important to note that both positive and negative reinforcement are not things, but effects. These effects function to increase behavior. "Therefore, the statement made by some, 'I've tried positive reinforcement and it doesn't work,' is oxymoronic because, by definition, if a consequence did not function to increase behavior, then it was not a reinforcer" (Maag, 2001, p. 178).

Types of Reinforcers

Skinner developed two categories of reinforcers, primary and secondary. *Primary reinforcers* are those that effect behavior without the necessity of learning (e.g., food, water, sex). In this sense, they are natural reinforcers, because they satisfy a biological need of an organism. *Secondary reinforcers* are those that acquire reinforcing power because individuals learn they are associated with primary reinforcers. For example, a student who behaves appropriately on a field trip could be given a token. He or she could then be given the opportunity to trade in a certain number of tokens for a prize. Over time, the tokens will gradually acquire reinforcing potential of their own.

Secondary reinforcers can be grouped into three major categories (Alberto & Troutman, 1986) *Social reinforcers*, which typically include attention, can be verbal or nonverbal. Usually social reinforcers are verbal, either used alone, "Paul, I am really proud of you for completing your assignments," or in combination with some other form of reinforcement, "Paul, you can act as class monitor because of the way you behaved in gym." Nonverbal social reinforcers may include, for example, facial expression, contact, proximity, and privileges. *Activity reinforcers,* also known as the Premack principle, are high-preference activities that are used to increase a student's willingness to participate in low-preference activities (Schloss & Smith, 1998). For example, a pediatric psychologist notices at recess that several students who dislike math class, seem to enjoy playing basketball. Playing basketball could be an effective reinforcer for these students once they have completed math worksheets. *Generalized reinforcers*, a form of secondary reinforcers, are those that acquire reinforcing power because they have accompanied several primary reinforcers. Money belongs to this category because it leads to the possession of food, liquids, and an infinite number of other things that individuals find reinforcing.

Schedules of Reinforcement

A continuous schedule of reinforcement allows a student to be reinforced every time he or she displays an appropriate behavior. While initially beneficial, the student may satiate, rendering the reinforcement ineffective. In addition, continuous reinforcement does not promote generalization or maintenance of appropriate behavior. On the other hand, *intermittent reinforcement* refers to when only some occurrences of a response are reinforced. The appropriate behavior continues because the student is unable to predict when it will be reinforced. Two kinds of intermittent reinforcement can be identified: interval and ratio reinforcement. *Interval reinforcement* is reinforcement that occurs after a certain amount of time. For example, a teacher may be directed to reinforce a student every two minutes for doing work. *Ratio reinforcement* is reinforcement that occurs after a specific number of responses. For example, a teacher may be advised that one of his or her students completes four math problems before playing a game. Both types of intermittent reinforcement can be varied with different

	RATIO SCHEDULES	INTERVAL SCHEDULES
FIXED SCHEDULES	**Fixed ratio** reinforcement schedules are those that depend on a specific number of responses. For example, as part of a treatment program a teacher may require his or her students to complete 30 workbook problems before they can engage in a more pleasurable activity.	**Fixed interval** reinforcement schedules are those in which a response results in reinforcement after a specific length of time. For example, reinforcement occurs every 20 seconds. Responses made during the 20-second interval are not reinforced. Teachers occasionally fall into a pattern in which they have students work independently, and then ask for responses 10 or 15 minutes into the work period. It is possible that students may learn this pattern and start to work just before the teacher is due to call on them. This pattern of behavior suggests a point of treatment for the consulting psychologist.
VARIABLE SCHEDULES	**Variable ratio** schedules are those in which the number of responses needed for reinforcement differs from one reinforcement to the next. Require responses may vary, and the child never knows which response will be reinforced. For example, a teacher may be directed to not only reinforce completed projects, but also reinforce them during various stages of progress and record what has been done.	**Variable interval** schedules are those in which reinforcement again depends on time and a response, but the time between reinforcements varies. Rather than waiting for 10-15 minutes, as in the above example, teachers may be directed to ask for responses at different times: immediately, later, and in the middle of class.

FIG. 28.2. Four types of partial reinforcement schedules.

reinforcement schedules, whereby reinforcement can appear after any time interval or number of responses.

Four classes of reinforcement schedules can be identified and are depicted in Fig. 28.2. Several conclusions can be drawn from this analysis of reinforcement schedules. First, *continuous reinforcement* produces a high level of response only as long as reinforcement persists. Second, *intermittent reinforcement* may take longer for results to be seen, but is more likely to have long-term effects. Third, *ratio schedules* can be used to generate a high level of responding but may become monotonous and hinder performance. For example, fixed ratios are common in educational settings; teachers reinforce students for papers, projects, and examinations. However, after students respond and receive reinforcement, behavior drops off sharply and learning efficiency declines (Skinner, 1953). Finally, *interval schedules* produce the most stable behavior.

Effective Reinforcers

It is not always easy to identify positive reinforcers, because what one student reacts to positively may have the opposite effect on another student. For example, adolescents can show considerable variation in their reactions to teacher attention. While many students may be positively reinforced by teacher attention, others may wish to escape from or avoid it. The varied reactions depend on a student's reinforcement history. When reinforcement does not produce a desired result, it may not be due to faulty reinforcement principles but rather to inappropriate reinforcers.

Suggestions for Use

Positive reinforcement is a powerful principle and can be applied in educational settings. However, it is important to make certain that students are not too dependent on the reinforcement provided, because the ultimate goal is for them to be reinforced by the natural environment. For example, a student who has been encouraged to use appropriate social skills through positive reinforcement, such as tokens, will hopefully be reinforced by positive peer interactions.

This process of reducing dependence on reinforcers is called *thinning*. Effective use of thinning will result in the following benefits: a more constant rate of responding with appropriate behavior (e.g., students consistently follow classroom rules); a lessened anticipation of reinforcement (e.g., students learn not to rely on outside reinforcement); a shift of control to typical classroom procedures, such as occasional praise (e.g., students gradually acquire a sense of satisfaction from their own classroom successes); and maintenance of appropriate behavior over longer periods of time.

Punishment

Punishment can be defined as "the presentation of an aversive event or the removal of a positive event following a response that decreases the frequency of that response" (Kazdin, 2001, p.144). Punishment, like reinforcement, is defined by its functional effect on behavior.

Categories of Punishment

There are three general categories of punishment: the presentation of aversive events, the withdrawal of positive consequences, and consequences based on activity. The most commonly recognized form of punishment involves presenting something aversive following an individual's performance or response. This stimulus is called an *aversive stimulus*. For example, a teacher may scold a child who misbehaves in class. If the event presented (e.g., scolding) reduced the frequency of the behavior, it would be functionally defined as punishment. (If scolding the child did not serve to reduce the inappropriate behavior but rather increased the behavior, it would be considered a reinforcer, not punishment.) Verbal statements such as reprimands commonly function as punishment but may lose their effectiveness over extended applications.

Withdrawal of positive consequences can also serve to reduce the frequency of some behaviors and thus serve as punishment. In the previous example, the child who misbehaves may not be able to go outside for recess. The two major forms of withdrawal of positive consequences are time-out from reinforcement and response cost. *Time-out from positive reinforcement* refers to the removal of all positive reinforcers for some time period. Time-out is often ineffective because not all sources of reinforcement are removed. For example, a student sent to the hallway for a time-out period may actually receive considerable attention from peers who happen to be walking by. Time-out also may not be effective if a student engages in inappropriate behavior to avoid participating in an activity that requires skills he or she does not have or in which he or she is not proficient. Brief time-out has been found to be effective but has some disadvantages in educational settings. First, there is a tendency for teachers and others to use time-out as the sole method of discipline. During these periods, the child is often excluded from learning activities. There also is the danger that teachers might revert to longer and longer time-out periods with no real benefit to the student.

Response cost involves a loss of a positive reinforcer and, unlike time-out, does not involve a period during which positive events are unavailable. Response cost most often involves a fine or penalty of some sort. For example, students given access to some reinforcer, such as free play, for a specified period of time may have that time taken away for inappropriate behavior.

Like time-out, response cost should be used with positive procedures. Indeed, response cost depends on positive events being present to work effectively.

Another class of punishment techniques is based on *aversiveness following some response* or consequences based on activity. For example, requiring a person to do something that involves effort or work may reduce the response and therefore serve as punishment. Overcorrection is a procedure that is included in this category and involves a penalty for some inappropriate behavior that includes two procedures. First, restitution is involved, because the person corrects the effects of some negative action. For example, a student who breaks another student's pencil could be required to replace it. Second, positive practice is included; this procedure consists of repeatedly practicing an appropriate behavior. A student may be required to demonstrate the correct use of a pencil, by writing, for example. Of course, not all behaviors that a teacher is trying to reduce would be handled with both components of overcorrection.

Dimensions of Punishment

Studying the psychological mechanisms underlying punishment, researchers have identified several key elements that influence its effectiveness (Kazdin, 2001).

Schedule of Punishment. Generally, punishment is more effective when it is delivered consistently, rather than intermittently. However, when punishment is discontinued, it is more likely that an inappropriate behavior will reappear if punishment has been applied continuously rather than intermittently. A teacher who reprimands a student for some rule infraction would be advised to use the reprimand each time the problem behavior occurs. Nevertheless, once a behavior has been suppressed, the punishment procedure should be used intermittently to keep it from reappearing.

Intensity of Punishment. It was once believed that increasing the intensity of punishment increases its effectiveness. However, this is not the case. If punishment is to be considered, mild forms should be used (see further discussion of this issue later).

Source of Reinforcement. Punishment is usually enhanced when the sources of reinforcement that maintain the behavior are removed. It is important to recognize that behavior (both positive and negative) is maintained by various reinforcement contingencies. Therefore, punishment will be more effective when a certain behavior is not reinforced at the same time that punishment contingencies are involved. For example, when a teacher tries to use punishment in the classroom, it is common for a student's peers to reinforce the child's inappropriate behavior through laughing or clapping. Punishment would be expected to be less effective when peers reinforce the child for inappropriate behavior.

Timing of Reinforcement. Most student behavior consists of a series of actions that make up a response class, or group of behaviors. Punishment is usually more effective when it is delivered early in a sequence of behaviors that form a response group. Consider the student who throws spit wads in the classroom. The act of throwing spit wads is actually made up of a series of actions that lead to the final act of throwing. Punishment early in the sequence leading to the act of throwing will be more effective in breaking up the chain of a problematic behavior.

Delay of Punishment. The longer the interval between behavior and punishment, the less effective the punishment will be. If the interval between the behavior and punishment is lengthy, the unwanted behavior may be reinforced by something or someone else in the environment. By the time the child is disciplined, he or she may have received the attention of peers, who may laugh, give the "thumbs up" signal, or provide some other form of support that reinforces misbehavior.

Also, punishment becomes more effective if students know exactly why a punishment contingency is being used. In addition to clarifying why a student is receiving a consequence, consistency is important: if a contingency is invoked once, it must be used each time the problematic behavior appears. Otherwise, students may become confused and continue to exhibit the challenging behavior.

Variation of Punishment. Although punishment usually consists of a contingency applied after some behavior, varying the punishment that follows a behavior can actually enhance the effects (Kazdin, 2001). It is possible that some type of adaptation to the repeated effects of the same punishment occurs (e.g., always verbally reprimanding a child will become less effective over repeated applications). It important to keep in mind that variation of punishment techniques does not imply combining several aversive events. Doing so might be objectionable on ethical and practical grounds.

Reinforcement of Alternative Behaviors. There are at least two important points that must be considered in any use of punishment techniques (Kazdin, 2001). First, aversive events of relatively weak intensity can effectively suppress behavior if reinforcement also is provided for an alternative positive response. Second, punishment usually teaches a person what not to do, rather than what to do, which leaves the development of desirable behaviors to chance. Thus, it is important that the treatment agent, such as a teacher follow-up with positive reinforcement and focus his or her attention on teaching positive behaviors to increase the effectiveness of punishment, replace the negative behaviors, and reduce the negative side effects of using aversive strategies.

Two generalizations about punishment should be considered. First, punishment is highly effective when properly used. When it is effective, punishment will be used less rather than more frequently because the desired outcome is to reduce the inappropriate behavior (Maag, 2001). Second, there is little doubt that the side effects of punishment, most of which are undesirable, accompany punishment that is routine, and possibly even unplanned.

Generally, procedures that reinforce appropriate behavior are preferred over those that use punishment for inappropriate behavior. Punishment only serves to restrict a child's inappropriate behavior and does not teach positive replacement behaviors. Therefore, the use of positive procedures should be a goal in child treatment. Often punishment is appealing because it is easy to administer, it frequently works for a short period of time, and it may give adults a feeling of having established control. Not only can punishment destroy rapport with students if excessively used, but it can also lead to a "negative reinforcement trap" (Patterson, 1982). This is a phenomenon in which teachers are negatively reinforced for punishing students and can actually result in increased use of punishment in the classroom.

In analyzing punishment and its alternatives, Alberto and Troutman (1986) offered a sequential hierarchy with four levels as a means of reducing inappropriate behavior (see Fig. 28.3). This hierarchy begins at Level I with the least restrictive and least aversive methods and gradually progresses to Level IV methods that are more restrictive and aversive. The best professional practice dictates beginning with Level I and moving to a higher level only when a child's behavior does not improve in a reasonable time period and when other positive procedures have been tried.

Level I Strategies

These procedures are designated as the preferred option, because in applying them, treatment agents use positive techniques. They are based on the idea of *differential reinforcement*; that is, they rely on reinforcement to strengthen one set of behaviors over another. *Differential reinforcement of low rates of behavior* provides reinforcement anytime an individual's response

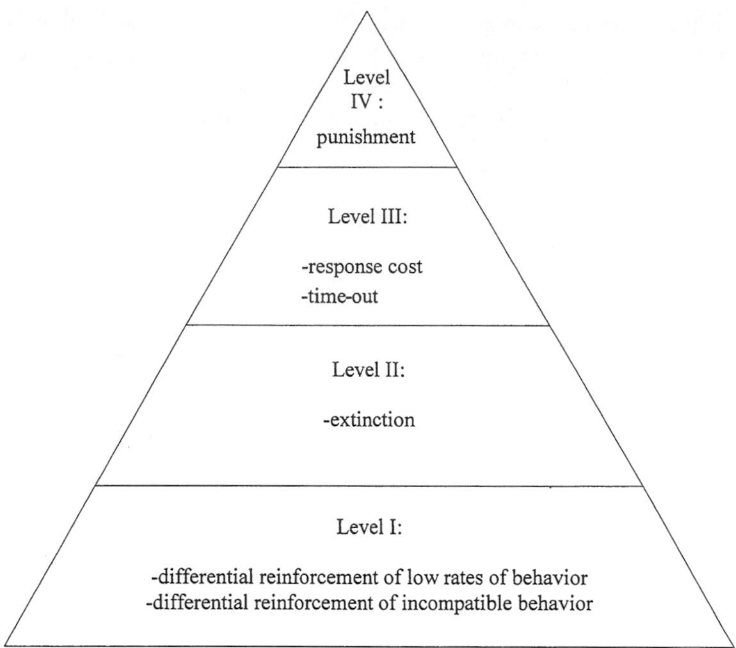

FIG. 28.3. Four levels of punishment Strategies.

level is below a predetermined criterion for a particular period. For example, when using differential reinforcement to eliminate a student's talking out behavior, a teacher would first select a specific length of time during which the student should remain silent. When the student successfully stays silent for the specified length of time, the teacher would offer praise and time to work on a pleasurable activity. The teacher would then gradually increase the time period for remaining silent. *Differential reinforcement of incompatible behavior* involves reinforcing an incompatible behavior. For example, a teacher may decide to reinforce silent reading; talking out is incompatible with silent reading.

Level II Strategies

The strategies in this category are intended to reduce misbehavior by *withholding reinforcement*. As Alberto and Troutman (1986) noted, teachers use extinction, the removal of positive consequences that maintain behavior, to reduce inappropriate behavior. An example of extinction is a teacher ignoring a student's talking-out behavior, thereby removing the positive reinforcer of teacher attention. Extinction is best used in conjunction with positive reinforcement of appropriate behavior. Again, it is important to keep in mind what reinforces or does not reinforce a particular student.

The effects of extinction may not be immediate because students may demonstrate a phenomenon called *resistance to extinction*. Teachers may also encounter increased rates of misbehavior before the effects of extinction become noticeable. Even after the misbehavior disappears, it may occasionally surface once again, a phenomenon called *spontaneous recovery*. If this event should occur, ignoring the behavior should cause it to disappear rapidly.

Level III Strategies

Level III strategies involve the use of punishment techniques, ranging from less severe to more severe. In the first of the suggested strategies, *response cost*, a teacher attempts to reduce behavior by removing a reinforcer (Alberto & Troutman, 1986). A response-cost technique proven to be effective combines a token reinforcement system with response cost. Students not only can earn tokens toward something desirable, but also can lose tokens by misbehaving. A student who talks out acquires tokens by periods of silence but also loses tokens by inappropriate talking.

The second of the Level III strategies entails the use of *time-out procedures*, in which students are denied reinforcement for a specific period of time. There are two basic time-out procedures. The first procedure is *nonseclusionary time-out* where the student remains in the classroom but is barred from normal reinforcement. For example, using the directive, "Put your head on your desk for the next five minutes," may prevent the student from receiving reinforcement from both teachers and classmates. The second procedure, *seclusionary time-out*, occurs when the student is removed from an activity or from the classroom itself. A teacher may resort to this technique by seating a student alone in a remote corner of the room for some specified period. Putting a student in a separate room is a technique usually reserved for special situations and must be used with sensitivity and caution.

In using time-out procedures, it is important to consider the function of a student's inappropriate behavior before resorting to time-out procedures. It is possible that a student engages in inappropriate behavior to avoid a task that he or she does not have the skills to complete. As simply stated by Martens, Witt, Daly, and Vollmer (1999), "if students do not find ongoing classroom activities enjoyable, time away from these activities, contingent upon misbehavior, is not likely to be perceived as aversive" (p. 642). In addition, it is important to ensure that the location of time-out does not offer reinforcers that a student may seek out. For example, a student who wishes to escape math class may talk out of turn so that he or she is sent to the hallway. While in the hallway, other students may walk by, thus reinforcing the inappropriate classroom behavior.

Level IV Strategies

This level involves the use of aversive stimuli in what is most frequently regarded as punishment. Considering the previous discussion of punishment, the psychologist must make sure to use least restrictive procedures over more restrictive procedures.

FUNCTIONAL ASSESSMENT

One of the biggest challenges involved in managing problem behaviors is selecting the most effective intervention. Although the purpose of the chapter is not to feature behavioral assessment techniques and procedures, one assessment approach, functional assessment, helps the psychologist link assessment to treatment. Traditionally, behavioral assessment of childhood problems has focused on identifying the topography, or form, of the behavior (Kratochwill et al., 1999). Operant learning theory, however, is based on functionalism, a philosophy of science that rejects the analysis of behavior based on topography because it fails to address the controlling functions of behavior (Skinner, 1953, 1974). Classroom behavioral interventions may not be effective if treatments are selected and implemented without considering the behavioral function (Gresham, Watson, & Skinner, 2001). As noted previously, a time-out procedure may be effective for a student who engages in loud and disruptive behavior to gain peer attention, but it may be ineffective for a student who is disruptive because he or she wishes to avoid a difficult task.

The purpose of functional behavioral assessment (FBA) is to identify and assess functions of behavior by gathering information about antecedents, behaviors, and consequences.

Once behavioral functions have been identified, the information is used to design and implement interventions that serve to decrease problem behaviors and increase positive behaviors. Not only have many behavioral analysts considered functional behavioral assessment to be "best practices" (Gresham et al., 2001), but the Individuals with Disabilities Education Act (IDEA) Amendments of 1997 (Public Law 105–117) requires the use of FBA for children with disabilities prior to any disciplinary action. A variety of functional assessment procedures and techniques have recently appeared in the professional literature. Most of the FBA procedures follow a multistep process leading to the design and evaluation of a treatment program (Doggett, Edwards, Moore, Tingstrom, & Wilczynski, 2001; Schill, Kratochwill, & Gardner, 1996; Stoiber & Kratochwill, in press).

The first step in FBA is identifying target behavior(s) and concerns and gathering information under natural conditions in which the problem behavior is occurring. Indirect FBA methods involve gathering information from historical records, interviews, rating scales, and checklists. Direct observation of antecedents, behaviors, and consequences in naturalistic settings is used to confirm the information collected through indirect FBA methods. Event-based, interval-based, time-based, and permanent product recording methods are typically used during direct observations. The direct and indirect information gathered can be used in generating hypotheses about the antecedent and consequence events that may be maintaining a student's problem behaviors but typically are not sufficient for the selection of interventions (Schill et al., 1996).

The second step in the functional analysis approach to treating problem behavior is forming hypothesis statements regarding the variables that maintain problem behavior. Within a behavior analysis framework, problem behavior is said to be maintained by one or more of the following classes of reinforcement: (1) social attention/communication, (2) access to materials or activities, (3) escape or avoidance of demand conditions, or (4) internal stimulation (automatic or sensory reinforcement) (McComas & Mace, 2000). A wider range of hypotheses for the functions of behavior have been presented by Stoiber and Kratochwill (in press). Behavioral hypothesis statements should be based on information from earlier assessments; they should specify variables that are testable, measurable, and can be manipulated by teachers or other treatment agents; and they should be written for target behaviors as well as desired alternative behaviors (Gresham & Noell, 1998) including the development of social competencies (Stoiber & Kratochwill, in press). Consider the following examples of some hypotheses: "Ryan shows off and disrupts the class during a science lesson to gain peer and teacher attention. Ryan would complete his lesson if he worked with a peer tutor during science independent seatwork." "Susan throws her pencils around the room and shouts in a loud voice when the teacher assigns math worksheets to avoid completing an easy task. Susan would complete the assigned work if the difficulty level of the worksheets was increased."

The third step of FBA is to test the hypotheses by isolating the influence of particular variables on a student's challenging behavior. Simulations of naturally occurring conditions are arranged that control for extraneous variables. More specifically, conditions are such that the variable being tested is directly manipulated and all other variables are held constant. Two conditions are needed to test hypotheses: *control* and *test*.

In the control condition, the environment is designed to decrease the probability of the problem behavior occurring. In addition, no consequences are provided for the target problem. For example, a student is given frequent access to preferred activities or attention, and no demands on the student are presented. Test conditions involve isolation and examination of variables hypothesized to influence the occurrence of the behavior (McComas & Mace, 2000). In this condition, positive or negative reinforcement is used, given the occurrence of the target behavior. Test conditions where the problem behavior occurs most frequently are considered to be the variable(s) that maintains the challenging behavior.

After manipulating the variables that are presumed to control behavior and identifying the maintaining variable(s) for the problem behavior, selection and implementation of the most appropriate intervention begins. Examples of commonly used applied behavior analysis interventions presented previously are extinction, alternative reinforcement, and antecedent interventions. Extinction involves terminating the response—reinforcer contingency. For example, for Ryan, the student who engages in disruptive behavior to gain teacher attention, attention is no longer provided as a response to this behavior. Alternative reinforcement refers to reinforcement provided for behaviors other than problem behaviors. For instance, a teacher may decide to reinforce Ryan's socially appropriate behavior, or reinforce him contingent upon the omission of disruptive behavior for a certain period of time. Antecedent interventions involve controlling environmental events that occur prior to problem behavior and that serve to maintain the problem behavior. For example, a teacher may give Ryan individualized attention immediately before science class in an attempt to quell his need for her attention during independent seatwork.

Once the most appropriate intervention(s) have been selected and implemented, it is important to evaluate the effectiveness of the intervention. Ongoing data collection allows teachers and other school professionals to assess the effects of the intervention objectively, facilitates the integrity of the intervention, and provides for the systematic fading of reinforcement. A variety of single-participant designs can be used to assess the outcomes of treatment designed from the functional assessment (see Hayes, Barlow, & Nelson-Gray, 1999, for an overview of designs).

The homework intervention training program for parents developed and evaluated by Rhoades and Kratochwill (1998) illustrates a number of behavioral principles that were packaged and implemented for four children who had difficulty completing homework assignments. The intervention involved a series of five individual parent consultation training sessions to teach the use of specific homework interventions including a structured home study time (see Table 28.1). The homework intervention program involved an adapted version of a group intervention program developed by Olympia, Jensen, and Neville (1990) titled *Do It Yourself Homework Manual: A Sanity Savior for Parents* and was combined with a manual for homework interventions developed by Sonna (1990), *The Homework Solution: Getting Kids to Do Their Homework*.

The training program was embedded within a problem-solving consultation model (see Bergan & Kratochwill, 1990) and the process is illustrated in Table 28.1. The consultation process consisted of problem identification, problem analysis, plan implementation, and treatment evaluation. The training sessions were held with individual parents or parent sets in the student's school. The focus of the intervention was on teaching specific skills, designing individualized homework interventions, reviewing progress, and problem-solving issues that emerged during the sessions. The training sessions emphasized the use of regular study times, positive reinforcement, and home-school communication. The training involved didactic instruction, skill practice, and skills in defining problems with workable solutions. The specific components of the training program are presented in Table 28.2. It can be observed that there were five meetings with different components of the interventions as well as assignments made during each of these sessions.

An evaluation of the program included data on student work completion and accuracy, which were collected throughout the duration of the school year. Rhoades and Kratochwill (1998) found a clinically and socially significant change in both work completion rates of students rising to within the normal range of peers in the classroom. Moreover, accuracy of work completion remained high over the duration of the program. Again, the program illustrates the combined package of behavioral techniques to produce socially significant and meaningful change in an academic area of concern with students in educational settings.

TABLE 28.1
Conceptual Integration of the Behavioral Consultation Process with Training Content

Process Variables	*Content Variables*
Problem identification	Home-school communication • Teacher survey and interview • Parent survey and interview • Student outcome data
Problem analysis	Environment management • Work time • Work setting • Organizational strategies • Time management
Plan implementation	Behavior management • Goal setting/monitoring • Intentional feedback • Logical consequencing • Contracting/motivating Home-school communication • Monthly phone calls • Assignment notebook Parent training • Self-instruction • Professional consultation • Skill application • Evaluation • Problem solving • Role plays • Didactic instruction
Treatment evaluation	Posttraining assessment • Student outcome data • Parent outcome data 4-week follow-up assessment • Student outcome data • Parent outcome data

Source: Table 2 (p. 251) from Rhoades, M. M., & Kratochwill, T. R. (1998). Parent training and consultation: An analysis of a homework intervention program. *School Psychology Quarterly, 13*, 241–264.

SOCIAL LEARNING AND COGNITIVE APPROACHES

Bandura initiated a program of theory and research that led to the development of social learning theory (see Bandura, Ross, & Ross, 1963, for a foundational study in the field). Social cognitive learning theory suggests that our behavior is influenced by the information we process from observing other people, things, and events. Although some scholars now consider Bandura

TABLE 28.2
Outline of Homework Intervention Training

MEETING 1	
I	**Introduction and Overview**
Content:	Program Overview
	Discuss dual-parent support and plan ways to share readings and information.
	Present *Homework Solution* book.
	Introduce homework log.
II	**Problem Identification and Analysis**
Content:	Identify areas of concern based on student work completion and accuracy data, teacher interview information, parent interview information, and completed parent questionnaires.
	Preview next week.
Assignments:	Complete homework log.
	Complete weekly evaluation (bring both to next meeting).
	Read manual (first 12 pages, efficacy of homework and the study environment).
	Reading on study periods (Ch. 5).
	Obtain a timer.
MEETING 2	*Designing a Homework Environment and Initiating Study Periods*
Content:	Review homework log.
	Review and graph teacher data, plan for parent to graph data with child.
	Discuss assigned readings.
	Clarify fading supervision and home note.
	Select homework environment.
	Review Chapter 5 together.
	Establish study periods and discuss use of letters to child, involving all family members, different study times/grade, scheduling and posting times, separate timers, breaks for questions, availability for supervision, family meeting, contacts.
	Review and preview next week.
Assignments:	Complete homework log.
	Present data graph and graph data with student.
	Complete weekly evaluations (bring both to next meeting).
	Read Chapter 6.
	Initiate study periods.
MEETING 3	*Maintaining Effective Study Periods and Interfacing with School*
Content:	Review homework log and graphing.
	Review and graph new data.
	Problem solve.
	Review manual.
	Discuss home note and teacher conference goals.
	Reconsider use of contracts.
	Prepare for teacher conference.
	Review and preview next week (incentives).
Assignments:	Complete homework log.
	Complete weekly evaluation (bring both to next meeting).
	Graph data with student.
	Continue study periods.
	Respond to problems as planned.
	Initiate teacher conference.
	Conduct conference as planned.
	Plan home-school communication (bring notes from conference to next meeting).

(Continued)

TABLE 28.2
(Continued)

MEETING 4	*Behavior Management Techniques and Homework Incentive Programs*
Content:	Review homework log and graph data. Complete new HPC Ratings. Review parent-teacher meeting. Plan response to problems. Teach reinforcement techniques. Review manual. Plan incentive strategies. Review and preview next week (communication and evaluation).
Assignments:	Complete homework log. Continue study periods. Complete weekly evaluations (bring both to next meeting). Read manual. Graph data with student. Initiate incentive plan.
MEETING 5	*Maintaining Effective Intervention and Program Evaluation.*
Content:	Review homework log and graph data. Review total program. Communication patterns. Complete evaluation forms. Plan for continued communication.
Assignments:	Telephone consultant biweekly. Continue study periods. Continue incentive program.

Source: Table 2 (pp. 252–253) from Rhoades, M. M., & Kratochwill, T. R. (1998). Parent training and consultation: An analysis of a homework intervention program. *School Psychology Quarterly, 13*, 241–264.

and those who embrace his theory to be cognitive theorists, his theory has strong behavioral foundations.

Modeling Approaches

Considerable evidence exists that observational learning occurs even if imitation and its consequent reinforcement do not take place. Children in all cultures learn and develop by observing experienced people engaging in culturally important activities. In this way, teachers and parents help students to adapt to new situations, aid them in their problem-solving attempts, and guide them to accept responsibility for their behavior (Rogoff, 1990). Observational learning has particular relevance for the design of treatment programs in educational settings because children not only follow adult directives regarding behavior, but also model adult behavior. Thus, teachers can be a potent force in shaping the behavior of their students with the behavior they demonstrate in school. Moreover, peers are a potent source of influence in the behavior they model in social and academic competency domains. Bandura notes three results of observing others' behaviors. First, the observer may acquire new responses. Second, observation of models may strengthen or weaken existing responses. Third, the observation of models may cause the reappearance of responses that were apparently forgotten. Children who witness undesirable behavior that is either rewarded or unpunished may also engage in undesirable behavior; the reverse also is true. Classroom intervention implications are apparent: positive, consistent teacher behavior may contribute to a positive classroom environment.

An Explanation of Modeling as a Therapeutic Procedure

Modeling behavior can be described as one person's observation of another person's behavior and the subsequent acquisition of that behavior, without necessarily performing the response (Bandura, 1977, 1986). Four important processes are involved in observational learning:

1. *Attention*. Mere exposure to a model does not ensure acquisition of behavior. An observer must attend to and recognize the distinctive features of the model's response. The modeling conditions also must incorporate features such as attractiveness in the model and reinforcement of the model's behavior. Children who recognize these characteristics in adults will attend to the important features of the adult's presentation. Children are attracted to the compelling features of desirable models.
2. *Retention*. Reproduction of the desired behavior implies that a child symbolically retains the observed behavior. Bandura noted that "symbolic coding" helps to explain lengthy retention of observed behavior. For example, a child codes, classifies, and reorganizes the model's responses into personally meaningful units, thus aiding retention. What does this mean? As a child observes an adult, he or she must also form some type of image or mental schema that corresponds to what the adult is actually doing. (Note: the child cannot form this mental picture unless they attend.) The task of the adult model is to urge the child, either covertly or overtly (or both), to form this image while the adult is instructing.
3. *Motor reproduction processes*. Bandura noted that symbolic coding produces internal models of the environment that guides the observer's future behavior. The cognitive guidance of behavior is crucial because it explains how modeled activities are acquired without performance. But cognitive activity is not autonomous: stimulus and reinforcement control its nature and occurrence. What are the applied and therapeutic implications of this point? After observing and urging children to form an image of the task's solution, they should demonstrate the solution as soon as possible. The pediatric psychologist can then reinforce correct behavior and alter any incorrect responses. The psychologist should not be satisfied with "show and tell"; he or she must reproduce the necessary behavior so that all of learning's mechanisms are used: stimulus–cognition–reinforcement.
4. *Motivational processes*. Although an observer acquires and retains the ability to perform modeled behavior, there will be no overt performance unless conditions are favorable. For example, if reinforcement previously accompanied similar behavior, the individual tends to repeat it. But vicarious reinforcement (observing a model being reinforced) and self-reinforcement (satisfaction with one's own behavior) are also powerful motivational procedures.

Bandura introduces a distinction here that helps to distinguish social learning theory from operant conditioning. Reinforcement acts on our students' *motivation* to behave, and not on the behavior itself. In this way, Bandura believes that the resulting learning is stronger and longer lasting than that produced by reinforcing behavior alone.

Self-Efficacy

Social cognitive learning results from the interactions among behavior, environmental variables, cognitive processing, and personal factors (Schunk, 1989). These factors, especially the environment (in the form of modeling or the feedback from others), influence feelings of competency on a particular task or skill. Such feelings of competency, called self-efficacy, develop from information conveyed by the following four sources (Bandura, 1981, 1986):

1. *Enactive mastery experiences.* Children (and adults) acquire personal and effective information from what they do; they learn from firsthand experience how successful they are in mastering various environments.
2. *Vicarious experience.* Watching "similar others" perform, the child can persuade himself or herself that he or she can probably do the action as well; the reverse is also true.
3. *Verbal persuasion.* Persuasion can lead children into believing that they can overcome their difficulties and improve their performance.
4. *Emotional arousal.* Stressful situations constitute a source of personal information. If children project images of themselves as inept and fearful in certain situations, then they enhance the possibility of that behavior. But if an admired model demonstrates "coolness under fire," that behavior reduces their tendency toward debilitating emotional behavior.

Receiving data from these sources enables the child to judge the extent of his or her self-efficacy; that is, success raises the sense of self-efficacy, while failure diminishes it. As a respected model, adult evaluations carry significant weight and can have a powerful effect on a child's feelings of competency. When a teacher says, "Of course you can do it, Kevin," he or she is providing verbal persuasion. Teachers should then follow through on this encouragement by ensuring that the student's performance accomplishment meets both the teacher's and student's expectations.

Teacher instructional techniques also are important. Research has consistently shown that when students are taught how to go about a task—that is, when they are given strategy training—their performance improves (e.g., Paris, Cross, & Lipson, 1984). This performance improvement in turn influences student self-efficacy—students' beliefs that they know what they are doing improves their control over a situation.

Social cognitive learning theory offers pertinent suggestions for understanding children's behavior, particularly by demonstrating the modeling power of an adult's behavior and the importance of self-efficacy to learning. The principles of social learning theory have been used to treat children's problems as well as to teach adults skills to intervene with their children's problems. Next we feature an application of modeling to teaching parents to treat their children.

Videotape Modeling Treatment Programs

Although a large number of treatment programs have been developed based on social learning theory, the one devised by Carolyn Webster-Stratton and her associates (see Webster-Stratton, 1996) has been deemed especially efficacious. Her approach emphasizes an intervention through parent mediators and is most commonly identified as "parent training." The rationale for focusing on parents is that they play such an important role in mediating problematic behavior. For example, based on the work of Patterson (1982, 1986), it has been determined that children experiencing externalizing problems such as conduct problems and oppositional-defiant disorders often demonstrate certain coercive behaviors and avoid parental negative comments by escalating their own negative behaviors. In short, a spiral of increasingly aversive parent–child interactions can occur. Nevertheless, the focus of treatment has been on parents wherein they are taught skills to intervene directly with their children. Videotape modeling was deemed a cost-effective and widely disseminated methodology for training parents, and much of Webster-Stratton and her associates' research (Webster-Stratton, 1998) is based on this technology.

Webster-Stratton and her associates have developed a number of specific intervention programs featuring parent-mediated videotape interventions. Table 28.3 provides an overview of

TABLE 28.3
Overview of Videotape Interventions

Interventions	*Skills Targeted*	*Person Trained*	*Setting Targeted*
Parenting skills training (BASIC)	Parenting skills • Play, involvement • Praise, rewards • Limit setting • Discipline	Parent	Home
Interpersonal skills training (ADVANCE)	Interpersonal skills • Problem solving • Anger management • Communication • Depression control • Giving and receiving support	Parent	Home, work, community
Academic skills training (PARTNERS 1)	Academic skills • Academic stimulation • Learning routine after school • Homework support • Reading • Limit setting • Involvement at school • Teacher conferences	Parent	Home-school connection
Child skills training (KIDVID)	Social skills • Friendship • Teamwork • Cooperation, helping • Communication Problem solving • Anger management • Steps 1–7 Classroom behavior • Quiet hand up • Compliance • Listening • Stop—look—think—check • Concentrating	Child	Home and school
Teacher training (PARTNERS 2)	Classroom management skills Promoting parent involvement	Teacher	School

Source: Webster-Stratton, C. (1996). Early intervention with videotape modeling: Programs for families of children with oppostional defiant disorder or conduct disorder. In E. D. Hibbs and P. S. Jensen (Eds.), *Psychosocial treatments for child and adolescent disorders: Empirically-based strategies for clinical practice* (pp. 435–474). Washington, D.C.: American Psychological Association.

five programs that she and her associates have implemented. The programs focus on working with young children who are experiencing externalizing type behavior problems including, for example, oppositional defiant disorder and conduct disorder. Although it is beyond the scope of the current chapter to provide a detailed review of the research in this area, the program of Webster-Stratton and her associates (e.g., Webster-Stratton, 1996; Webster-Stratton & Hammond, 1997) is very clearly an evidence-based approach to intervention with children experiencing a wide range of externalizing type behavior problems (see Christophersen & Mortweet, 2001).

Classroom Applications

Bandura's ideas have particular relevance for interventions in classrooms, especially as they furnish information about the characteristics of desirable models and the personal features of students, notably their self-efficacy. As previously mentioned, certain characteristics of models seem to relate positively to observational learning. The behavior of those who have achieved status and distinction undoubtedly has produced successful consequences, thus suggesting a high functional value for observers. The model's behavior, then, also furnishes information about the probable consequences of similar behavior by the observer. Thus, model characteristics attract observers not only because the models have achieved status, even adulation (as in the example of rock stars), but also because their behavior has resulted in rewards, such as money and power.

Bandura (1981) expressed concern about the development of self-knowledge, particularly the notion of self-efficacy, which "is concerned with judgments about how well one can organize and execute courses of action required to deal with prospective situations that contain many ambiguous, unpredictable, and often stressful, elements" (p. 201). Estimates of self-efficacy affect choices of activities and situations; children avoid situations that they fear will exceed their abilities, but confidently perform those activities that they think they can handle. Self-efficacy estimates also affect the quality of behavior and persistence in difficult tasks.

Schools offer an excellent opportunity for the development of self-efficacy; consequently, treatment practices should reflect this reality (Bandura, 1997). That is, materials and methods should be evaluated not only for academic skills and knowledge, but also for what they can accomplish in enhancing students' perceptions of themselves and social relationships. Patrick (1997) noted that social cognitive research has identified that many of the same social cognitive factors are important for both the regulation of academic work and social relationships.

Case Example

Social cognitive learning methods have been used to treat children's internalizing problems and anxiety disorders (e.g., Carlson, Figueroa, & Lahey, 1986; Morris & Kratochwill, 1983; Ollendick & King, 1998). The following case study illustrates the application of a cognitive treatment for Tim, an 11–year-old boy who has been identified as fearful of speaking in class. Whenever he knows that he will be required to speak in class, he trembles and his stomach becomes so nauseous that he doesn't want to go to class. Instead, Tim's teachers find him in the nurse's office. Tim reports being afraid that everything he might say in class will be wrong. He feels as if all of his peers are judging him and will call him "stupid" if he makes a mistake.

Tim is experiencing severe anxiety that is interfering with his functioning and academic performance at school. His perceptions of himself and of his peers are distorted and are causing him to engage in maladaptive behavior. To decrease Tim's anxiety related to speaking in class, a cognitive-behavioral based intervention may help him to change his distorted pattern of thinking. One such therapeutic intervention is described by Kendall, Chu, Pimentel, and Choudhury (2000).

Kendall and colleagues' (2000) cognitive-behavioral therapy program for anxious children involves four areas of skill training. The first area involves teaching children to develop an "awareness of bodily reactions to feelings and those physical symptoms specific to anxiety" (Kendall et al., 2000, p. 255). Using our case example, Tim would be taught to identify and monitor the physical sensations that accompany his anxiety in addition to progressive muscle relaxation techniques to decrease these physical sensations. Whenever Tim experienced a physical sensation that was indicative of anxiety, he would be encouraged to use relaxation techniques (see King, Hamilton, Ollendick, 1988, for further information regarding relaxation procedures).

The second area of skill training involves the "recognition and evaluation of 'self talk,' or what the child thinks and says to him or herself when anxious" (Kendall et al., 2000, p. 255). Tim would be taught to identify and examine his distorted thoughts. Kendall and associates (2000) suggested using cartoons with empty thought bubbles that a child can fill in, with assistance, to illustrate both "anxiety-provoking and anxiety-reducing (coping) thoughts for the characters" (p. 264). Tim's pediatric psychologist might ask him questions that challenge his current pattern of thinking, such as how he knows that his peers will call him "stupid" or how he knows that what he says in class will be wrong. These questions would assist Tim in developing alternative and more adaptive self-talk to place in his character bubbles. Gradually, Tim would be able to replace his distortions with this new adaptive self-talk. Kendall and associates (2000) cautioned that even when a child seems to be able to develop "coping thoughts" he or she may have not internalized them, thus resulting in a lack of change in anxiety symptoms. To increase the internalization process, Tim might be given an assignment to ask his friends or teachers what they would think if he made a mistake while speaking in class.

The third area of skill training entails the use of "problem-solving skills, including modifying anxious self-talk and developing plans for coping" (Kendall et al., 2000, p. 255). Tim would be taught that he has control over his thoughts and over his level of anxiety about speaking in the classroom. The psychologist would begin with an example of a problem event that did not make Tim feel fearful. Together, they would develop and explore different solutions to the problem, evaluate each solution, and then determine which solution to use. If Tim expressed any cognitive distortions during this process, in particular distortions that lead to anxiety, the psychologist would address them, thereby increasing Tim's awareness of the relationship between his thoughts and feelings. Tim and the psychologist would apply these same analytical techniques to his stressful situation of speaking in class. Kendall and colleagues (2000) also emphasized the use of relaxation techniques, learned previously, during this stage (see D'Zurilla & Goldfried, 1971, and D'Zurilla & Nezu, 1999, for further information on problem-solving processes).

The fourth and final area of skill training involves self-evaluation and reward. Kendall and colleagues (2000) noted that children with anxiety problems often have difficulty evaluating themselves accurately and/or set extremely high standards for success. Therefore, the psychologist would help Tim set appropriate and realistic goals for working with his anxiety. Tim would be taught to evaluate his success in terms of a continuum, rather than as "all or nothing." The psychologist would help him construct a list of rewards for his efforts, such as self-praise or time engaging in an enjoyable activity. More importantly though to avoid discouragement, Tim's therapist would need to convey that all of the skills that Tim is trying to learn take practice and time to learn.

With the assistance of his psychologist, Tim would be able to learn the skills in each of the areas described in Kendall and colleagues' (2000) cognitive behavioral therapy program for children exhibiting anxiety. Many of the behavioral procedures described in this chapter, such as modeling and positive reinforcement, can also be used to help increase the acquisition of these four areas of skills.

BEHAVIORAL INTERVENTIONS FOR PEDIATRIC PROBLEMS

Interventions for Pediatric Obesity

The prevalence of obesity in children and adolescents has increased over the last two decades (Jelalian & Saelens, 1999). Nearly 14% of children and 12% of adolescents are overweight as defined by criteria of body mass index (BMI) greater than or equal to 95th percentile (Jelalian & Saelens, 1999). Obese youth are at risk for overweight status in adulthood (Whitaker, Wright, Pepe, Seidel, & Dietz, 1997), negative self-perceptions, body image disturbance, and difficulty with peer relationships (Friedman & Brownell, 1995). The risks associated with obesity in children and adolescents indicate the importance of effective weight management intervention.

Well-established, evidence-based treatments exist for pediatric obesity in children between the ages of 8 and 12 years with no concurrent medical or psychological concerns or treatments. Decreases of approximately 5%–20% in percent overweight have been achieved through a comprehensive behavioral treatment, including self-monitoring, stimulus control, behavioral contracting and therapist phone contact, targeting eating, and physical activity (e.g., Epstein, Wing, Steranchak, Dickson, & Michelson, 1980). This treatment is superior to wait-list control or nutrition education alone in achieving short-term weight loss in children. Studies that targeted children and their parents for weight loss and that combined dietary and lifestyle changes resulted in superior long-term—more than two years from the end of treatment—weight loss (Epstein, McCurley, Wing, & Valoski, 1990; Epstein, Valoski, Wing, & McCurley, 1994).

There are also "promising interventions" for the treatment of adolescent (12–18 years) obesity (Jelalian & Saelens, 1999). These interventions demonstrated short-term treatment efficacy and include the common element of behavioral modification of diet (e.g., Brownell, Kelman, & Stunkard, 1983; Mellin, Slinkard, & Irwin, 1987). It is evident that the literature on weight loss in adolescence is less developed than the literature on weight loss in childhood and more well-designed studies are needed to develop well-established treatments for adolescent obesity.

Interventions for Recurrent Abdominal Pain

Frequent gastrointestinal symptoms can interfere with a child's social and academic functioning. Whether somatic or physiologically based, conditions such as constipation, cramping, bloating, and nausea can impede a chlid's abilitiy to concentrate, learn, and in some cases, attend school. One of the more prevalent gastrointestinal disorders, recurrent abdominal pain (RAP), affects 10%–15% of children in school (e.g., Apley, 1975; Faull & Nicol, 1986; Zuckerman, Stevenson, & Bailey, 1987). RAP is marked by sharp, sudden pain that is present at least three times during a period of three or more months, and causes a child's functioning to be altered (Janicke & Finney, 1999). Potential causes of RAP, such as poor coping skills (Walker, Garber, & Greene, 1994), increases in levels of anxiety and stress (Robinson, Alverez, & Dodge, 1990; Stone & Barbero, 1970), and modeling behavior (Bennett-Osborne, Hatcher, & Richtsmeier, 1988; Robinson et al., 1990), illustrate the psychosomatic characteristics of the disorder and, therefore, the necessity of psychological intervention.

There are evidence-based interventions that can be used by pediatric psychologists and other professionals to treat RAP. Of the nine studies reviewed by Janicke and Finney (1999) the most effective intervention for RAP was cognitive behavioral therapy (CBT), meeting the guidelines for a "probably efficacious" treatment under criteria by the Task Force for Empirically Supported Interventions. The CBT studies included the use of self-monitoring, relaxation techniques, various reinforcement procedures, and parent-training. In general, children who received CBT reported a decrease in or cessation of pain symptoms (see Finney, Lemanek, Cataldo, Katz, & Fuqua, 1989; Linton, 1986; Sanders et al., 1989, Sanders, Shepherd,

Cleghorn, & Woolford, 1994). More research, including the replication of these existing studies, is needed to further establish empirically supported treatments for RAP. Nevertheless, it has been suggested that RAP interventions may also serve as interventions for other analogous and reoccurring medical conditions affecting school-age children (Janicke & Finney, 1999).

Interventions for Painful Medical Procedures

A major focus of pediatric behavioral medicine research and practice in the past two decades has been the development of interventions to help children cope with the stress of undergoing painful medical procedures. Powers (1999) reviewed studies that have demonstrated that cognitive behavioral therapy (CBT) reduces the distress of children undergoing routine immunizations (e.g., Blount et al., 1992), treatment for burn injuries (e.g. Elliott & Olson, 1983), dental treatments (Stokes, Stark, & Allen, 1990), and for children with cancer undergoing a variety of painful medical procedures (e.g. Jay, Elliott, Katz, & Siegel, 1987).

The most common components of CBT include breathing exercises and other forms of relaxation and distraction (e.g., counting aloud, progressive muscle relaxation), imagery and other cognitive coping skills such as positive self statements, filmed modeling typically showing a peer model, reinforcement for using coping skills and lying still, and behavioral rehearsal using modeling and role play. In addition, active coaching—encouraging the child to engage in coping skills—by a psychologist, parent, or medical staff during the medical procedure has also been used consistently in CBT (Powers, 1999).

Over the course of 10 years, Jay and colleagues demonstrated the superiority of a package of CBT interventions to baseline conditions (Jay, Elliott, Ozolins, Olson & Pruitt, 1985): Valium at a dose of 0.3 mg/kg given orally before the medical procedure (Jay et al., 1987): and watching cartoons for the 30 minutes before the medical procedure (Jay et al., 1987). In these studies, CBT reduced the level of distress experienced by the child. In addition, Jay and colleagues (1987) found that children who received CBT gave lower pain ratings and had lower pulse rates than children in the attention-control condition. Jay, Elliott, Woody, and Siegel (1991) also found decreases in self-reported pain and pulse rate after CBT.

COGNITIVE SELF-CONTROL TECHNIQUES

A major objective in working with children is to have them accept responsibility for their own behavior, that is, exercise "self-control." Kazdin (2001) offered the following definition: "Self-control usually refers to those behaviors that a person deliberately undertakes to achieve self-selected outcomes" (p. 303). In aiding children to acquire this skill, it is important that they know precisely what behavior produced reinforcement in a given instance. Children should be encouraged to talk about why they were or were not reinforced, thus aiding them to understand their behavior. For example, once a teacher has made a student aware of the inappropriateness of some behavior and he or she is willing to cooperate, have the student note, with help at first, the frequency of their misbehaviors—a kind of self-recording device. Conversely, a student can record the number of times that he or she was helpful to one of his or her fellow students while trying to increase prosocial behavior.

Next, the child can be involved in the management of reinforcement. For instance, the child can help decide what reinforcers should be used, when reinforcers should be given, what constitutes misbehavior, and how much each instance of misbehavior should cost him or her. In this way, responsibility slowly shifts from the teacher to the student. For example, the child can be asked to select some activity that they would like to participate in and the criteria for the reinforcement.

Teaching Students Self-Control

Some children learn to regulate their own behavior during their early years within the family. Many children, however, can benefit from learning some strategies to help them control their own behavior in social and learning settings. In recent years, psychologists have developed programs that teachers and other professionals can use to help children in their psychosocial development (e.g., Esveldt-Dawson & Kazdin, 1982; Kendall, 2000; Shapiro & Cole, 1994; Workman, 1982). There are three components that can be used to teach students self-control: (1) self-assessment, or self-analysis; (2) self-monitoring; and (3) self-reinforcement.

Self-assessment requires that children examine their own behavior or thinking and determine whether they have performed some behavior or thought process. To foster this examination, for example, teachers might ask students if they have been completing math assignments. It is important that children have some idea or standard that they can use in self-assessment. Remember that all students do not routinely set self-standards, and therefore it is often necessary to teach these skills.

Self-monitoring is a procedure in which students record their performance. Interestingly, the very act of recording some action has been shown to change performance. For example, if teachers encourage kind or positive statements from students when they interact with peers, self-monitoring the frequency of such statements is likely to increase the occurrence of these behaviors. Research has shown that self-monitoring can increase academic performance, but may not be sufficient in itself to sustain any improvement (e.g., Piersel & Kratochwill, 1979).

Self-reinforcement refers to students' giving themselves something following successful completion of the activity being monitored that increases the behavior. Self-reinforcement can be a very potent strategy for increasing the occurrence of a student's performance. For example, students can be taught to praise themselves or arrange some pleasant activity as a self-reward, which then acts to sustain performance.

Several advantages of using self-control strategies can be identified. First, self-control strategies allow children to manage their own behavior in the absence of the teacher or other adults. Second, self-control strategies can help children develop responsibility for their own behavior. Third, self-control strategies can help improve the chances that children's behavior will transfer (generalize—see next section) to other settings with other individuals. Although some children appear to regulate their behavior quite well without formal attempts to teach this skill, others may need additional assistance to do so. Teaching self-control strategies to these children can increase both their sense of self-efficacy and their sense of responsibility.

MAINTAINING AND GENERALIZING BEHAVIOR CHANGES

Techniques to Maintain Behavior

Once a child's behavior has changed, it is important to *maintain* the desirable behavior over time. It is also important for students to demonstrate the appropriate behavior in other settings, known as *generalization*. For example, after a student's talking-out behavior has been successfully reduced during history class, a teacher also wants that student to talk out less in English and science class. Likewise, a social competency taught in school should be displayed in social situations outside the school context.

Strategies for Facilitating Generalization

Behavioral researchers have developed a technology that can be used to help students generalize their academic and social behavior. Building on some of the classic work of Stokes and Baer (1977), White and his associates (1988) presented a review and update of the strategies for facilitating generalization. The procedures specified below come from the behavior analytic tradition but have clear application to all the theoretical approaches presented in this chapter. The following 12 strategies are presented within the context of how a teacher-consultee would use the techniques in the classroom:

1. *Teach and hope*. In this traditional strategy, the therapist provides regular instruction and hopes that the child's behavior will generalize. For example, a teacher-consultee introduces some new vocabulary words in class, emphasizing their meaning in the hope that most students will remember their meaning. Some children may remember, while others will not. "Teach and hope" does not use any special techniques to facilitate generalization and is common in many instructional plans. The subsequent procedures are more proactive than this strategy.

2. *Teach in the natural setting*. The intervention is conducted directly in at least one setting in which the skill or knowledge will actually be used. Generalization is then assessed in other, nonintervention settings. For example, the teacher might ask parents to teach new vocabulary words at home after they are taught in the classroom. Effective teachers use this tactic quite often.

3. *Teach sequentially*. This strategy is an extension of the previous strategy, in which the intervention is conducted in one setting and generalization is assessed in other settings. If necessary, teaching is conducted sequentially in more and more settings, until generalization to all the desired settings is observed. For example, a teacher interested in teaching social skills might schedule the teaching of the skill in school, at home, and on the playground.

4. *Introduce students to natural maintaining contingencies*. In this strategy, the therapist ensures that the student experiences the natural consequences of a new skill, by (1) teaching a functional skill that is likely to be reinforced outside of the instructional setting; (2) teaching to a level of proficiency that makes the skill truly useful; (3) making sure that the learner actually experiences the natural consequences; and (4) teaching the child to seek reinforcement outside of the instruction. A teacher may consider using academic content that will be useful to students outside the classroom, such as teaching words that they will likely use when interacting with peers and adults.

5. *Use indiscriminable contingencies*. Sometimes natural consequences cannot be expected to facilitate and maintain generalization. In such cases it may be necessary to use artificial consequences. It is best if the child is not able to discern precisely when those consequences will be available. For example, when teaching social skills to preschoolers, a teacher might praise the children after progressively greater delays rather than after each skill is demonstrated, as would be the strategy during initial teaching.

6. *Train students to generalize*. With this strategy, the child is reinforced only for performing some generalized instance of a new skill. Performance of a previously reinforced version of the skill is no longer reinforced. For example, students could be taught the names of various shapes. Reinforcement would then be provided when students named shapes that had not been taught previously in the classroom.

7. *Program common stimuli*. The therapist can select a salient, but not necessarily task-related, stimulus from the situation to which generalization is desired and include that stimulus in the teaching program. For example, students might be taught skills in the presence of their peers. These skills would then be expected to be available in other settings when the peers were present.

8. *Use sufficient exemplars*. This strategy entails the sequential addition of stimuli to the intervention program until generalization to all related stimuli occurs. Different skills may require a different number of examples to ensure generalization, and teachers should make this determination based on a student's performance.

9. *Use multiple exemplars*. Using this technique means presenting, at the same time, several examples of the stimulus class to which generalization is desired. The teacher who uses multiple examples of a concept or skill will increase the chances that a student will use the skill outside a classroom setting.

10. *Conduct general case programming*. To use this strategy, the therapist must conduct a careful analysis of both the skill and the environment to which generalization is desired. Thereafter, the therapist selects and teaches stimuli in the presence of which the skill should be used, stimuli in the presence of which the skill should not be used, and stimuli that should not affect skill use but could inappropriately do so. For example, in teaching high school students to use a stick shift in a driver education class, it would be useful to analyze the range of stick shift options found in most cars and trucks and teach this universe of options. One could then anticipate that good generalization to most cars in the community would occur.

11. *Teach loosely*. By "teaching loosely" we mean that the intervention should be implemented through various formats, so as to avoid a ritualized, highly structured, invariant program that inhibits generalization. For example, teaching that involves a variety of settings, materials, and reinforcers will help facilitate generalization.

12. *Mediate generalization*. This tactic involves intervening with a strategy or other procedure to help the student remember when to generalize, or at least when to reduce the differences between the teaching and generalization settings. For example, children can be taught to self-monitor their own behavior across settings (see next section).

SYSTEMS LEVEL INTERVENTIONS: SCHOOL-WIDE BEHAVIORAL SUPPORT

Many of the behavioral approaches described thus far can be expanded from the single student context and incorporated into a system of school-wide positive behavioral support. School-wide positive behavioral support is a multilayered approach designed to maximize social and learning outcomes while preventing problem behavior for all students (Sugai & Horner, 1999). Figure 28.4 presents the model that Sugai and Horner (1999) used to match the various student needs to behavioral supports. The behavioral supports of each layer address different aspects of the school community. The four layers include: (1) *school-wide procedures* that affect all students, staff, and settings, (2) *classroom procedures* for teachers and their students during instructional time, (3) *nonclassroom procedures* for students and staff in settings such as hallways, parking lots, and the like, and (4) *individual student procedures* for students who present significant behavioral challenges.

School-wide Discipline Systems

The majority of behavior concerns within a school are addressed in this phase, which includes all guidelines, procedures, and so on that affect students, school settings, and staff members. Several features common to successful school-wide discipline systems have been identified (Sugai & Horner, 1999). The first element is a statement of purpose or mission. For example, it is essential that the school administration convey to the student body the overarching academic and behavioral expectations that will guide more specific school-wide procedures and routines. Another element of a school-wide discipline system is a well-developed and positively stated set of behavioral expectations and exemplars as well as procedures for teaching them. For

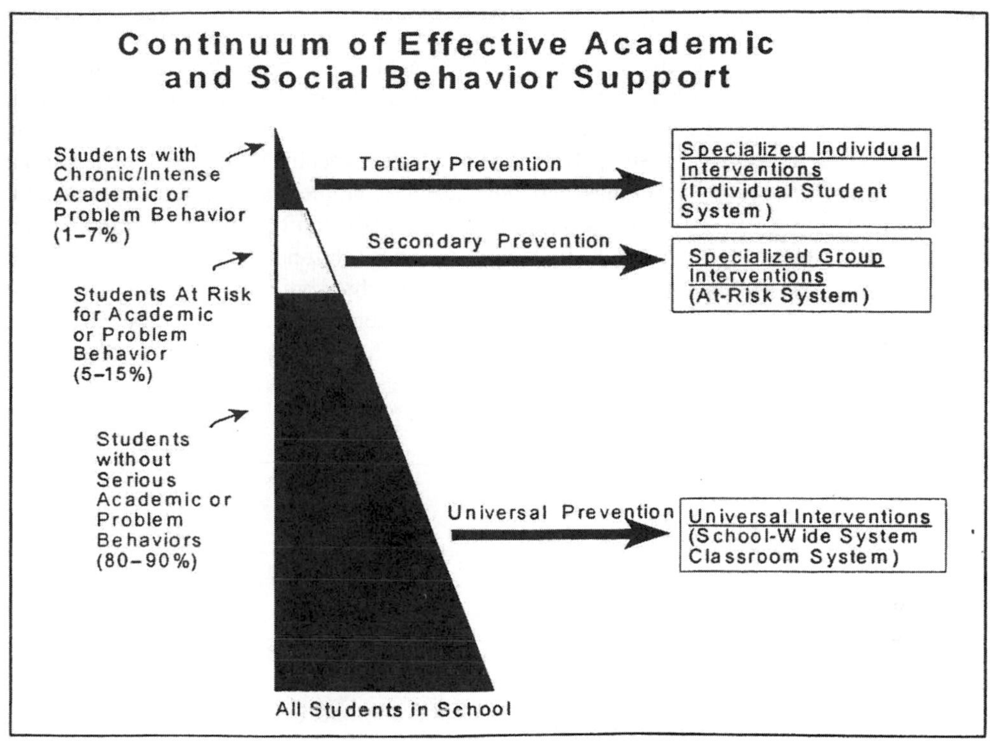

FIG. 28.4. School-wide behavior support.

example, "a show-and-tell model of teaching school-wide expectations can be effective for a large number of children (e.g., 80–90% of school enrollment)" (Sugai & Horner, 1999, p. 12). In addition, the behavior that teachers and administrators demonstrate in school can greatly influence the behavior of students, as noted previously in this chapter. Next, there should be a wide range of methods for encouraging adherence to behavioral expectations and discouraging rule violations. Meeting these objectives may depend on the use of various reinforcement and punishment techniques. Finally, staff should monitor and record student behavior to inform teachers' decision making.

Classroom Setting Systems

Many of the classroom behavioral support approaches parallel the features of school-wide support systems. For example, it is important for teachers to establish and directly teach their classroom rules, expectations, and routines in a positive manner. In addition, teachers have the ability to: (1) help shape their students' behavior through modeling appropriate behavior, (2) increase appropriate behavior and decrease inappropriate behavior through reinforcement and punishment techniques, and (3) record behavior patterns in their classrooms to inform further intervention approaches. In addition, teachers must also be sure to organize their classrooms in ways that enhance their instruction and curriculum. For example, poorly designed seating arrangements or congested traffic patterns can increase inappropriate behavior in the classroom. By taking into account the arrangement of student's desks and other stations within the room, many behavior problems can be prevented.

Nonclassroom Setting Systems

A different set of behavioral expectations and management challenges apply to settings outside of the classroom such as hallways, cafeterias, restrooms, parking lots, and so on. Unlike the classroom, these settings are characterized by a high number of student-to-student interactions with minimal adult supervision. Students must be taught how specific school-wide expectations apply in various nonclassroom settings, and they must have ample opportunities to practice the expected routines and behaviors. Nonclassroom settings also require a more explicit approach to behavior management. For example, if elementary school staff noticed significant problems in the morning when children are waiting to be let into the school building, they would meet and develop a strategy for teachers to overtly remind all students of the behavioral expectations during this time period. Additionally, teachers or staff that waited with the children in the morning could be instructed to interact actively and positively with appropriately behaving students.

Individual Student Support Systems

Occasionally, students' behaviors are unresponsive to school- and classroom-wide systems. In such instances, more comprehensive, intense, and individualized support systems must be developed (Sugai & Horner, 1999). Individualized systems of support often include a team-based approach to problem solving in which a teacher may work with parents and other teachers to identify and operationally define the problem behavior and intervene as early as possible. Also incorporated in these systems are the behavioral approaches described throughout this chapter including efforts to generalize and maintain behavior changes. It is important to note that individualized support systems must have an overt link to school-wide academic and behavioral expectations. Finally, attempts are made to involve both family and community resources to provide a comprehensive system of care.

Many aspects of the school-wide positive behavioral support systems described earlier are not uncommon. However, traditional discipline systems, which may include school handbooks or codes of conduct that describe behavioral expectations at various levels, are often ineffective and unsustainable. Therefore, the real challenge lies not in identifying and developing new strategies, but rather in delivering and maintaining these strategies in schools (Sugai & Horner, 1999). By combining theories from organizational behavior management with the behavioral intervention approaches described throughout this chapter, school-wide behavioral support systems can be created and implemented. School-wide behavioral support systems aim to create an environment in which general procedures and routines encourage the implementation of evidence-based, behavioral support practices at various levels within the school setting to maximize student outcomes.

CONCLUSIONS

Children of school age spend more time in school than in most structured environments outside the home. They also have their most consistent and extensive contact with teachers who influence their behaviors directly and on an ongoing basis (Maag, 2001). Given this situation, it is important that pediatric psychologists become familiar with behavioral approaches and interventions in the school setting to promote the development of appropriate academic and interpersonal skills among their students. In using these interventions, it is important that pediatric psychologists carefully select the most effective and least intrusive interventions, while keeping in mind the individual needs of students. Increasingly, evidence-based treatments are appearing in the literature that can guide the selection of interventions for a wide range of child concerns in educational settings.

Although it is apparent that behavioral approaches have much to offer in educational settings, there are three barriers that may impede the implementation of behavioral approaches in schools. First, many educators lack information about the value of behavioral strategies. Second, despite appreciating the benefits of behavioral techniques, some individuals may lack the knowledge of basic principles and applied skills or knowledge to implement them. Finally, current societal contingencies (e.g., the structural organization of schools) may impede the implementation of behavioral techniques. By working to overcome these challenges, most behavioral researchers and pediatric practitioners feel confident about the future of their theory, both in its viability and in its application.

NOTES

[1] In this chapter we have chosen to use the term *pediatric psychologist* to refer to the primary change agent for the child and adolescent. We realize especially in education settings that the change agent is often a teacher, parent, or care provider who works with the psychologist to provide educational and/or psychological services to the child. In such cases, the professional serves as "consultant" and the adult as a mediator or consultee (see Bergan & Kratochwill, 1990).

[2] We do not review the extensive literature on behavioral assessment methods and techniques. The interested reader is referred to some other sources for detailed coverage of behavioral assessment in educational settings (Kratochwill, Sheridan, Carlson, & Lasecki, 1999; Shernoff & Kratochwill, in press).

AUTHOR NOTES

Portions of this chapter are an extension of a chapter by the first author and his associates from the text *Educational Psychology Educational Psychology* (Elliott, Kratochwill, Littlefield Cook, & Travers, 2000).

The authors express appreciation to Karen O'Connell and Lois Triemstra for their helpful contribution to completion of this work.

REFERENCES

Alberto, P., & Troutman, A. (1986). *Applied behavioral analysis for teachers*. Columbus, OH: Merrill.

Apley, J. (1975). *The child with abdominal pain* (2nd ed.). Oxford: Blackwell Scientific.

Azrin, N. H. (1977). A strategy for applied research: Learning based but outcome oriented. *American Psychologist, 32*, 140–149.

Bandura, A. (1977). *Social learning theory*. Englewood Cliffs, NJ: Prentice-Hall.

Bandura, A. (1981). Self-referent thought: A developmental analysis of self-efficacy. In J. Flavell & L. Ross (Eds.), *Social cognitive development*. New York: Cambridge University Press.

Bandura, A. (1986). *Social foundations of thought and action: A social-cognitive theory*. Englewood Cliffs, NJ: Prentice-Hall.

Bandura, A. (1997). *Self-efficacy: The exercise of control*. New York: Freeman.

Bandura, A., Ross, D., & Ross, S. (1963). Imitation of film-mediated aggressive models. *Journal of Abnormal and Social Psychology, 66*, 3–11.

Bennett-Osborne, R., Hatcher, J. W., & Richtsmeier, A. J. (1988). The role of social modeling in unexplained pediatric pain. *Journal of Pediatric Psychology, 14*, 43–61.

Bergan, J. R., & Kratochwill, T. R. (1990). *Behavioral consultation and therapy*. New York: Plenum Press.

Blount, R. L., Bachanas, P. J., Powers, S. W., Cotter, M. W., Franklin, A., Chaplin, W., Mayfield, J., Henderson, M., & Blount, S. D. (1992). Training children to cope and parents to coach them during routine immunizations: Effects on child, parent, and staff behaviors. *Behavior Therapy, 23,* 689–705.

Breen, M. J., & Fielder, C. R. (Eds.) (1996). *Behavioral approach to assessment of youth with emotional/behavioral disorders: A handbook for school-based practitioners*. Austin, TX: Pro-Ed.

Brownell, K. D., Kelman, J. H., & Stunkard, A. J. (1983). Treatment of obese children with and without their mothers: Changes in weight and blood pressure. *Pediatrics, 71*, 515–523.

Carlson, C. L., Figueroa, R. G., & Lahey, B. B. (1986). Behavior therapy for childhood anxiety disorders. In R. Gittelman (Ed.), *Anxiety disorders of childhood* (pp. 204–232). New York: Guilford.

Craighead, L. W., Craighead, W. E., Kazdin, A. E., & Mahoney, M. J. (1994). *Cognitive and behavioral interventions: An empirical approach to mental health problems*. Boston: Allyn & Bacon.

Chambless, D. L., & Ollendick, T. H. (2001). Empirically supported psychological interventions: Controversies and evidence. *Annual Review of Psychology, 52*, 685–716.

Christophersen, E. R., & Mortweet, S. L. (2001). *Treatments that work with children: Empirically-supported strategies for managing childhood problems*. Washington, D.C.: American Psychological Association.

Cone, J. D. (1997). Issues in functional analysis in behavioral assessment. *Behavior Research and Therapy, 35*, 259–275.

Doggett, R. A., Edwards, R. P., Moore, J. W., Tingstrom, D. H., & Wilczynski, S. M. (2001). An approach to functional assessment in general education classroom settings. *School Psychology Review, 30*, 313–328.

D'Zurilla, T. J., & Goldfried, M. R. (1971). Problem-solving and behavior modification. *Journal of Abnormal Psychology, 78*, 107–126.

D'Zurilla, T. J., & Nezu, A. M. (1999). *Problem solving therapy: A social competence approach to clinical intervention* (2nd ed.). New York: Springer.

Elliott, C. H., & Olson, R. A. (1983). The management of children's distress in response to painful medical treatment for burn injuries. *Behavioral Research and Therapy, 21*, 675–683.

Elliott, S. N., Kratochwill, T. R., Littlefield Cook, J., & Travers, J. F. (2000). *Educational psychology: Effective teaching effective learning* (3rd ed.). New York: McGraw-Hill.

Epstein, L. H., McCurley, J., Wing, R. R., & Valoski, A. (1990). Five-year follow-up of family-based behavioral treatments for childhood obesity. *Journal of Consulting and Clinical Psychology, 58*, 661–664.

Epstein, L. H., Valoski, A., Wing, R. R., & McCurley, J. (1994). Ten-year outcomes of behavioral family-based treatment of childhood obesity. *Health Psychology, 13*, 373–383.

Epstein, L. H., Wing, R. R., Steranchak, L., Dickson, B., & Michelson, J. (1980). Comparison of family-based behavior modification and nutrition education for childhood obesity. *Journal of Pediatric Psychology, 5*, 25–36.

Esveldt-Dawson, K., & Kazdin, A. E. (1982). *How to use self-control*. Lawrence, KS: H & H Enterprises.

Faull, C., & Nicol, A. R. (1986). Abdominal pain in six-year-olds: An epidemiological study in a new town. *Journal of Child Psychology and Psychiatry, 27*, 251–260.

Finney, J. W., Lemanek, K. L., Cataldo, M. F., Katz, H. P., & Fuqua, R. W. (1989). Pediatric psychology in primary health care: Brief targeted therapy for recurrent abdominal pain. *Behavior Therapy, 20*, 283–291.

Fletcher, K. E. (1996). Childhood posttraumatic stress disorder. In E. J. Mash & R. A. Barkley (Eds.), *Child psychopathology* (pp. 242–276). New York: Guilford.

Friedman, M. A., & Brownell, K. D. (1995). Psychological correlates of obesity: Moving to the next research generation. *Psychological Bulletin, 117*, 3–20.

Gresham, F. M., & Noell, G. H. (1998). Functional analysis assessment as a cornerstone for noncategorical special education. In D. Reschly, W. Tilly, & J. Grimes (Eds.), *Functional and noncategorical identification and intervention in special education* (pp. 39–64). Des Moines: Iowa Department of Education.

Gresham, F. M., Watson, T. S., & Skinner, C. H. (2001). Functional behavioral assessment: Principles, procedures and future directions. *School Psychology Review, 30*, 156–172.

Hayes, S. C., Barlow, D. H., & Nelson-Gray, R. O. (1999). *The scientist practitioner: Research and accountability in the age of managed care* (2nd ed.). Boston, MA: Allyn & Bacon.

Hibbs, E. D., & Jensen, P. S. (Eds.). (1997). *Psychosocial treatments for child and adolescents disorders: Empirically based strategies for clinical practice* (3rd ed.). Washington, D.C.: American Psychological Association.

Janicke, D. M., & Finney, J. W. (1999). Empirically supported treatments in pediatric psychology: Recurrent abdominal pain. *Journal of Pediatric Psychology, 24*, 115–127.

Jay, S. M., Elliott, C. H., Katz, E., & Siegel, S. E. (1987). Cognitive-behavioral and pharmacologic interventions for children's distress during painful medical procedures. *Journal of Consulting and Clinical Psychology, 55*, 860–865.

Jay, S. M., Elliott, C. H., Ozolins, M., Olson, R. A., & Pruitt, S. D. (1985). Behavioral management of children's distress during painful medical procedures. *Behavioral Research and Therapy, 23*, 513–520.

Jay, S. M., Elliott, C. H., Woody, P. D., & Siegel, S. (1991). An investigation of cognitive-behavior therapy combined with oral Valium for children undergoing medical procedures, *Health Psychology, 10*, 317–322.

Jelalian, E., & Saelens, B. E. (1999). Empirically supported treatments in pediatric psychology: Pediatric obesity. *Journal of Pediatric Psychology, 24*, 223–248.

Kazdin, A. E. (1978). *History of behavior modification: Experimental foundations of contemporary research*. Baltimore, MD: University Park Press.

Kazdin, A. E. (1981). *From behavior science to behavior modification*. New York: McGraw-Hill.

Kazdin, A. E. (2001). *Behavior modification in applied settings* (6th ed.). Belmont, CA: Wadsworth Thomson Learning.

Kendall, P. E. (2000). *Child and adolescent therapy: Cognitive-behavioral procedures* (2nd ed.). New York: Guilford.

Kendall, P. C., Chu, B. C., Pimentel, S. S., & Choudhury, M. (2000). Treating anxiety disorders in youth. In P. C. Kendall (Ed.), *Child and adolescent therapy: Cognitive behavioral procedures* (2nd ed.; pp. 235–287). New York: Guilford.

King, N. J., Hamilton, D. I., & Ollendick, T. H. (1988). *Children's phobias: A behavioral perspective*. London: Wiley.

Kratochwill, T. R., & Bijou, S. W. (1987). The impact of behaviorism on educational psychology. In J. A. Glover & R. R. Ronning (Eds.), *Historical foundations of educational psychology* (pp. 131–157). New York: Plenum.

Kratochwill, T. R., Sheridan, S. M., Carlson, J., & Lasecki, K. L. (1999). Advances in behavioral assessment. In C. R. Reynolds & T. B. Gutkin (Eds.), *The handbook of school psychology* (pp. 350–382). New York: John Wiley & Sons.

Kratochwill, T. R., & Stoiber, K. C. (2000). Empirically supported interventions: Conceptual and practical issues—Part II. *School Psychology Quarterly, 15*, 233–253.

Linton, S. J. (1986). A case study of the behavioural treatment of chronic stomach pain in a child. *Behaviour Change, 3*, 70–73.

Maag, J. W. (2001). Rewarded by punishment: Reflections on the disuse of positive reinforcement in schools. *Counsel for Exceptional Children, 67*, 173–186.

Maag, J. W., & Kotlash, J. (1994). Review of stress inoculation training with children and adolescents: Issues and recommendations. *Behavior Modification, 18*, 443–469.

Martens, B. K., Witt, J. C., Daly, E. J. III, & Vollmer, T. R. (1999). Behavior analysis: Theory and practice in education settings. In C. R. Reynolds and T. B. Gutkin (Eds.), *The handbook of school psychology* (3rd ed.; pp. 638–663). New York: Wiley.

Mash E. J., & Barkley, R. A. (1996). *Child psychopathology*. New York: Guilford.

McComas, J. J., & Mace, F. C. (2000). Theory and practice in conducting functional analysis. In E. S. Shapiro & T. R. Kratochwill (Eds.), *Behavioral assessment in schools: Theory, research, and clinical foundations* (2nd ed.; pp.78–103). New York: Guilford.

Mellin, L. M., Slinkard, L. A., & Irwin, C. E. (1987). Adolescent obesity intervention: Validation of the SHAPEDOWN program. *Journal of the American Dietetic Association, 87*, 333–338.

Morris, R. J., & Kratochwill, T. R. (1983). *Treating children's fears and phobias: A behavioral approach*. New York: Pergamon.

Ollendick, T. H., & King, N. J. (1998). Empirically-supported treatment for children with phobic and anxiety disorders: Current status. *Journal of Clinical and Child Psychology, 27*, 156–167.

Olympia, D. M., Jenson, W. R., & Neville, M. R. (1990). *Do it yourself homework manual: A sanity saver for parents*. (Available from W. Jenson, 327 MBH, University of Utah, SLC, UT 84105.)

Paris, S., Cross, D., & Lipson, M. (1984). Informed strategies for learning: A program to improve children's reading awareness and comprehension. *Journal of Educational Psychology, 76*, 1239–1252.

Patrick, H. (1997). Social self-regulation: Exploring the relations between children's social relationships, academic self-regulation, and school performance. *Educational Psychologist, 32*, 209–220.

Patterson, G. R. (1982). *Coercive family process*. Eugene, OR: Castalia Publishing Co.

Patterson, G. R. (1986). Performance models for antisocial boys. *American Psychologist, 41*, 432–444.

Piersel, W., & Kratochwill, T. R. (1979). Self-observation and behavior change: Applications to academic and adjustment problems through behavioral consultation. *Journal of School Psychology, 17*, 151–161.

Powers, S. W. (1999). Empirically supported treatments in pediatric psychology: Procedure-related pain. *Journal of Pediatric Psychology, 24*, 131–145.

Rhoades, M. M., & Kratochwill, T. R. (1998). Parent training and consultation: An analysis of a coursework intervention program. *School Psychology Quarterly, 13*, 241–264.

Robinson, J. O., Alverez, J. H., & Dodge, J. A. (1990). Life events and family history in children with recurrent abdominal pain. *Journal of Psychosomatic Research, 34*, 171–181.

Rogoff, B. (1990). *Apprenticeship in thinking*. New York: Oxford.

Saigh, P. A., Yasik, A., Sack, W., & Koplewicz, H. (1999). Child-adolescent posttraumatic stress disorder: Prevalence, comorbidity, and risk factors. In P. A. Saigh & J. D. Bremmer (Eds.), *Posttraumatic stress disorder: A comprehensive text* (pp. 19–43). Needham Heights, MA: Allyn & Bacon.

Sanders, M. R., Rebgetz, M., Morrison, M., Bor, W., Gordon, A., Dadds, M., & Shepherd, R. W. (1989). Cognitive-behavioral treatment of recurrent nonspecific abdominal pain in children: An analysis of generalization, maintenance, and side effects. *Journal of Consulting and Clinical Psychology, 57*, 294–300.

Sanders, M. R., Shepherd, R. W., Cleghorn, G., & Woolford, H. (1994). The treatment of recurrent abdominal pain in children: A controlled comparison of cognitive-behavioral family interventions and standard pediatric care. *Journal of Consulting and Clinical Psychology, 62*, 306–314.

Schill, M. T., Kratochwill, T. R., & Gardner, W. I. (1996). Conducting a functional analysis of behavior. In M. J. Breen & C. R. Fiedler (Eds.), *Behavioral approach to assessment of youth with emotional/behavioral disorders: A handbook for school-based practitioners* (pp. 83–179). Austin, TX: Pro-Ed.

Schloss, P. J., & Smith, M. A. (1998). *Applied behavior analysis in the classroom* (2nd ed.). Boston: Allyn & Bacon.

Schunk, D. (1989). Self-efficacy and cognitive skill learning. In C. Ames & R. Ames (Eds.), *Research on motivation in education: Vol. 3. Goals and cognition* (pp. 111–142). San Diego, CA: Academic Press.

Schunk, D., Hanson, A., & Cox, P. (1987). Peer model attributes and children's achievement behaviors. *Journal of Educational Psychology, 79*, 54–61.

Selinske, J. E., Greer, R. D., & Lodhi, S. (1991). A functional analysis of the comprehensive application of behavior analyses to schooling. *Journal of Applied Behavior Analysis, 24*, 107–117.

Shapiro, E. S. (1987). Intervention research methodology in school psychology. *School Psychology Review, 16*, 290–305.

Shapiro, E. S., & Cole, C. L. (1994). *Behavior change in the classroom: Self-management interventions.* New York: Guilford.

Shapiro, E. S., & Kratochwill, T. R. (2001). *Conducting school based assessments of child and adolescent behavior* (pp. 78–120). New York: Guilford.

Shernoff, E. S., & Kratochwill, T. R. (in press). In M. Hersen, S. N. Haynes, & E. M. Heiby (Eds.), *The handbook of psychological assessment, volume: Behavioral assessment* (pp. XX). New York: Wiley.

Skinner, B. F. (1953). *Science and human nature*. New York: Macmillan.

Skinner, B. F. (1968). *The technology of teaching*. New York: Appleton-Century-Crofts.

Skinner, B. F. (1974). *About behaviorism*. New York: Vintage Books.

Skinner, B. F. (1986, March). Some thoughts about the future. *Journal of the Experimental Analysis of Behavior, 22*, 229–235.

Sonna, L. A. (1990). *The homework solution: Getting kids to do their homework.* Charlotte, VT: Williamson Publishing Co.

Stoiber, K. C., & Kratochwill, T. R. (2000). Empirically supported interventions and school psychology: Rationale and methodological issues—Part II. *School Psychology Quarterly, 15*, 75–105.

Stoiber, K. C., & Kratochwill, T. R. (in press). *Functional assessment and intervention systems*. San Antonio, TX: The Psychological Corporation.

Stokes, T. F., & Baer, D. M. (1977). An implicit knowledge of generalization. *Journal of Applied Behavior Analysis, 11*, 285–303.

Stokes, T. F., Stark, L. J., & Allen, K. D. (1990). Therapeutic consultation in pediatric dentistry. In A. M. Gross & R. S. Drabman (Eds.), *Handbook of clinical behavioral pediatrics* (pp. 279–289). New York: Plenum.

Stone, R. T., & Barbero, G. J. (1970). Recurrent abdominal pain in childhood. *Pediatrics, 45*, 732–738.

Sugai, G., & Horner, R. (1999). Discipline and behavioral support: Practices, pitfalls, and promises. *Effective School Practices, 17*, 10–22.

Sulzer-Azaroff, B., & Mayer, G. R. (1991). *Behavior analysis for lasting change*. San Francisco: Holt, Rinehart & Winston, Inc.

Walker, L. S., Garber, J., & Greene, J. W. (1994). Somatic complaints in pediatric patients: A prospective study of the role of negative life events, child social and academic competence, and parental somatic symptoms. *Journal of Consulting and Clinical Psychology, 62*, 1213–1221.

Webster-Stratton, C. (1996). Early intervention with videotape modeling: Programs for families of children with oppostional defiant disorder or conduct disorder. In E. D. Hibbs and P. S. Jensen (Eds.), *Psychosocial treatments for child and adolescent disorders: Empirically-based strategies for clinical practice* (pp. 435–474). Washington, D.C.: American Psychological Association.

Webster-Stratton, C. (1998). Preventing conduct problems in Head Start children: Strengthening parenting competencies. *Journal of Consulting and Clinical Psychology, 66*, 715–730.

Webster-Stratton, C., & Hammond, M. (1990). Predictors of treatment outcome in parent training for families with conduct problem children. *Behavior Therapy, 21*, 319–337.

Webster-Stratton, C., & Hammond, M. (1997). Treating children with early-onset conduct problems: A comparison of child and parent training interventions. *Journal of Consulting and Clinical Psychology, 65*, 93–109.

Webster-Stratton, C., Hollinsworth, T., & Kolpacoff, M. (1989). The long-term effectiveness and clinical significance of three cost-effective training programs for families with conduct problem children. *Journal of Consulting and Clinical Psychology, 7*, 550–553.

Webster-Stratton, C., Kolpacoff, M., & Hollinsworth, T. (1988). Self-administered videotape therapy for families with conduct problem children: Comparison with two cost-effective treatments and a control group. *Journal of Consulting and Clinical Psychology, 56*, 558–566.

Whitaker, R. C., Wright, J. A., Pepe, M. S., Seidel, K. D., & Dietz, W. H. (1997). Predicting obesity in young adulthood from childhood and parental obesity. *New England Journal of Medicine, 337*, 869–873.

White, O. R., & Associates. (1988). Review and analysis of strategies for generalization. In N. G. Haring (Ed.), *Generalization for students with severe handicaps: Strategies and solutions* (pp. 15–51). Seattle: University of Washington Press.

Workman, E. A. (1982). *Teaching behavioral self-control to students*. Austin, TX: Pro-Ed.

Zuckerman, H., Stevenson, J., & Bailey, V. (1987). Stomach-aches and headaches in a community sample of pre-school children. *Pediatrics, 79*, 677–682.

29

Group and Psychoeducational Approaches

Karen Callan Stoiber
University of Wisconsin–Milwaukee

Gregory A. Waas
Northern Illinois University

INTRODUCTION

As the 21st century unfolds, children and adolescents are facing new and diverse threats to their mental health and psychosocial well-being, including increased exposure to violent community crime, lethal weapons, school violence, in utero cocaine and crack, and single-parent family life (Centers for Disease Control and Prevention, 1998). Other aspects of the lives of youth will likely remain much the same as we begin the 21st century. For example, many children will continue to experience poverty, be victims of abusive relationships, lack social skills, engage in early sexual activity, join gangs, abuse drugs and alcohol, and drop out of school. All of these issues can potentially produce heightened levels of disruptive behavior, anxiety, depression, stress, risk-taking behavior, and emotional vulnerability among students attending our nation's schools (Doll, 1996; Garbarino, 1999). Recent data indicate that approximately one fifth of all school-age youth suffer developmental, emotional, or problem behaviors requiring psychosocial intervention (Kazdin & Johnson, 1994).

Although the severity and extent of problems that some youth experience may suggest the need for community-based mental health services, the majority of students' mental health and social behavioral concerns can be addressed through school-based services. Thus, the overwhelming mental health and health care needs of children, adolescents, and families as well as the fact that many students arrive at school lacking a capacity to benefit from the learning environment, present a combined and compelling argument for group and psychoeducational therapeutic approaches in our schools. Group and psychoeducational service delivery models are not only efficient, but also offer an essential and unique structure for prevention and intervention (Stoiber & Kratochwill, 1998).

The purposes of this chapter are to provide (1) an overview of general considerations for conducting groups, (2) highlight special considerations for conducting group interventions and psychoeducational approaches in school contexts, and (3) review selected group interventions shown to have empirical support. In addition to these three major goals, we discuss the role of consultation in conducting group intervention, the need to evaluate group interventions within the context of evidence-based practices (Kratochwill & Stoiber, 2000a, 2000b; Spirito, 1999; Stoiber & Kratochwill, 2000, 2002), and future directions for group intervention and psychoeducational practices. Although evaluation research on group prevention and intervention generally support the effectiveness of group approaches, the evidence base endorsing group interventions is not unequivocal (Ang & Hughes, 2002; Arnold & Hughes, 1999; Miller, Brehm, & Whitehouse, 1998; Nastasi, 2000) and continual focused research and program evaluation is needed.

PRACTICAL AND THEORETICAL CONSIDERATIONS FOR IMPLEMENTING GROUP APPROACHES

Similar to other forms of therapeutic work, group intervention and psychoeducational approaches in the schools require ongoing planning, monitoring, and evaluating of the therapeutic or preventative process. The primary goal of group prevention, intervention, and psychoeducational activities is to improve or alter affective, cognitive, and/or behavioral functioning of children and/or families (Stoiber & Kratochwill, 1998). In general, prevention-focused activities seek to reduce the incidence of psychological and/or behavioral problems through introducing proactive and resistance-oriented initiatives prior to the development of serious concerns, risk-taking behaviors, or other behavioral problems (Durlak, 1997). An example of a prevention program is a classroom-based curriculum that attempts to reduce early sexual activity, gang behavior, and substance abuse by targeting students along a wide potential risk continuum. In contrast, intervention groups focus on individuals for which a problem has already been detected or diagnosed. Hence, participants of a group intervention usually share a similar mental health issue, psychological problem, or behavioral disorder, such as depression, substance abuse, or the loss of a significant person (Stoiber & Kratochwill, 1998).

Group Participant Considerations

One of the first questions that school psychologists and other clinicians should consider when planning a group intervention is: What reasons and evidence exist to support conducting a group intervention rather than an individual-based intervention? This question should help delineate initial decision making about the purpose and advantages of group prevention and intervention efforts. A response to this question also requires a thoughtful analysis of the group participants—including type and severity of the problem, capacity to work in a group, and one's social and emotional stability, especially related to receiving feedback from other group members. Similar to individual therapy, group intervention typically targets particular affective, social, and/or behavioral concerns. In addition, whether conducting individual or group intervention, best practices suggest that adequate assessment procedures should be used for developing intervention plans (Elliott, Witt, Kratochwill, & Stoiber, 2002; Stoiber & Kratochwill, 2002). The practice of using assessment procedures to conceptualize intervention planning is consistent with models of intervention that are based on psychopathology as well as those based on wellness or the development of social competencies (Stoiber & Kratochwill, 2002, in press).

By using procedures that link assessment to intervention, the interventionist is able to evaluate important considerations and conceptualize intervention plans based on the severity of the presenting concern, client needs, focus of the intervention (e.g., child, parent–child dyad, family), and available resources. Although factors such as severity of the problem occur on a continuum, individuals who demonstrate severe psychosocial problems or require intense intervention strategies are not considered good candidates for group intervention. Individuals who exhibit particular problems that can interfere with group participation and processing, such as attention deficit hyperactivity disorder (ADHD) or severe antisocial characteristics, also may not be well matched to group intervention. Semrud-Clikeman (1995) aptly noted children with severe aggressive and impulsive behaviors, autistic characteristics, language deficits, thought disorders, or severe withdrawal may be poor candidates for many groups. In addition, those individuals experiencing heightened crises or loses (e.g., death of a parent or sibling) may require individualized attention, at least initially, which is not available in groups. It is critical that each individual group member has the capacity to function in a group as a group participant (e.g., can take turns, listen to others, wait to voice needs, cope in a group) and to contribute to the group's goal of producing positive outcomes in participants. Thus, an additional and important consideration when choosing a group approach rather than individual therapy is the individual's readiness and capacity to function as group members. Because of the critical influence that each individual group member has on the success of the group intervention, this issue is discussed in further detail later in the chapter.

Group Facilitator Considerations

Consideration needs to be given to skills and knowledge base of the group facilitator when determining whether to conduct group intervention as opposed to individual therapy. Group intervention, like individual therapy, is challenging work. Inherent in intervention groups is a planned process of psychosocial interaction between the group facilitator and the group members. The skills required of group facilitators are diverse in type and developmental in form. Group facilitators need to come to the task of implementing groups with well-developed capacities in the areas of empathy, listening, collaboration, confronting, and interpreting. In addition, group facilitation involves various "multitasking" demands and skills. As noted by Stoiber and Kratochwill (1998):

> Although similar competencies are needed for individual counseling and therapy, knowledge and skill in their use is more complex when one needs continually to focus and re-focus attention on affective, emotional, and behavioral indicators across several individuals. The group facilitator should monitor the development and progress of each group participant, which frames what and how questions are asked and processed, guides observations, and informs when and how to proceed. An ongoing, conscious effort to attend to all group participants is extremely demanding work. Similar to other areas of mental health competence, group facilitation develops with deliberate reflective practice, explicit skill refinement, continuous monitoring, and careful supervision. (p. 5)

School psychologists and other mental health providers must evaluate their own competence in dealing with and responding to the complex nature of implementing groups so that they do not go beyond their professional skill and knowledge base. Although group intervention is a common form of therapy in schools, it can produce adverse effects if facilitators enter into the process with naïve notions about the dynamics and mechanisms involved in conducting groups (Ang & Hughes, 2002; Arnold & Hughes, 1999; Kazdin, 1997).

THE SCHOOL CONTEXT: SPECIAL CONSIDERATIONS

Schools are viewed as key sites for group prevention and intervention for at least three reasons. First, the literature on the mental health needs of school-age children is replete with examples documenting the interrelationships among physical, academic, social, and behavioral functioning (e.g., Adelman & Taylor, 1998; Stoiber & Good, 1998). The high numbers of students experiencing difficulties coupled with the connection between students' academic functioning and social–behavioral functioning provides strong support for attending to the multiple aspects of children's development in the context of school-based group intervention. Several researchers have demonstrated that group interventions that focus on improving students' social–emotional and behavioral functioning leads to improvements in the academic areas (Conduct Problems Prevention Research Group [CPPRG] 1999a, 1999b; Shechtman, Gilat, Fos, & Flasher, 1996). A second reason for providing school-based intervention and prevention groups centers on accessibility and acceptability issues. Both children and parents are more likely to avail themselves to school-based services as compared to community-based or clinic-based mental health services because schools connote a less stigmatizing environment. Thus, there is a greater likelihood of follow-through for mental health services provided in the school setting. Third, groups are a natural context within which children function in the school. Schools are considered to be a strategic position for conducting group prevention and intervention because groups can be formed naturally and utilized readily. For example, violence reduction or social competence enhancement programs such as the Fast Track Program (CPPRG, 1999b) that targets entire classes of children are uniquely well suited to classroom contexts.

In sum, schools are considered viable and critical sites for group prevention and intervention for at least three reasons: (1) children are increasingly exposed to psychosocial risks and these risks are interconnected and frequently involve academic performance, (2) schools are more accessible and children and families are responsive to school-based interventions, and (3) groups are formed naturally in school and classroom settings. Despite the evidence and logistics supporting school-based prevention and intervention groups, there are "systems" level and school ecology issues requiring attention. Any group leader or facilitator, when planning a therapeutic group in a school setting, needs to consider the organizational context in which the group is going to occur. The school setting is a complex culture unto itself (Sarason, 1982; Stoiber & Kratochwill, 2000). We next describe both facilitative features and potential challenges to successful group intervention that relate to the ecology of schools.

Ecological Issues and Elements

Facilitative Features. One of the key advantages of conducting school-based therapeutic groups is that they provide an opportunity to develop goals and objectives for therapy that maximize ecological validity. By conducting groups in the school milieu, where many of the child's difficulties are manifested, the group leader can consult closely with teachers and observe the student in critical settings (e.g., classroom, lunch, playground). Information collected through these procedures can then be used to carefully match treatment objectives and tactics with the child's needs (Bierman, Miller, & Stabb, 1987; Elliott et al., 2002; Stoiber & Kratochwill, 2002).

During treatment itself, school-based therapists have easy access to pertinent information about the child's progress. Therapists can monitor children's use of newly learned skills, easily conduct ongoing assessments of children's behavior change, and even engage in observations and coaching outside of the group intervention setting. Therapists working in schools also are well positioned to coordinate interventions between the child's school and home. This type of consultation, sometimes referred to as conjoint behavioral consultation (Sheridan, 1997; Sheridan, Kratochwill, & Bergan, 1996), may involve simple progress reports between school and home or may involve more comprehensive coordination of therapy goals with class and home-based assignments.

Potential Challenges. Although there are several advantages to conducting groups in a school setting, such an approach presents a number of potential challenges to the group facilitator as well. For example, consideration should be given to how the intervention group will be perceived by teachers and administrators. If the group intervention is viewed positively, teachers and administrators will be willing to accommodate missed class time, and they will be eager to contribute to the child's treatment in any way possible. It is extremely useful, therefore, for group leaders to inform teachers and administrators about the potential value of the group activities. Teachers can often serve as important facilitators of group activities by encouraging children to utilize newly learned skills, monitor children's behavior, and provide positive feedback to group participants.

Conducting groups in a school setting often means that children in the groups will be acquainted with each other. This propinquity factor can hold both advantages and disadvantages for the group participants. For example, because children may see each other on a daily basis outside of the group, the positive interactions they engage in during group may evolve into lasting friendships (e.g., Waas & Graczyk, 1998). Group members can also provide each other assistance in implementing group homework assignments. For example, group members may cue each other to use newly learned skills or provide social support during periods of stress. However, if children have a great deal of animosity toward each other through previous interactions, or develop hostility during group sessions, the group process may be disrupted and treatment goals jeopardized.

Confidentiality also is a major concern when conducting groups in a school setting. Children may fear being honest during group activities in the presence of fellow classmates who could reveal sensitive information to nongroup members. Children may have similar concerns about the group leader sharing information with teachers and parents. Group leaders need to be cognizant of these concerns and take active steps to address them. Establishing clear rules about the confidentiality of group interactions can help prevent inappropriate sharing of information with nongroup members and promote an atmosphere of openness and honesty within the group.

The sharing of information by the group leader with teachers and parents is an especially sensitive issue. As has already been noted, it is therapeutically useful to involve teachers and parents in the therapy process when feasible, but it is also important to maintain the confidence of group members so that they are fully engaged and unrestrained in the group. An open and clear discussion of the types of information that both will and will not be shared with teachers and parents (e.g., general information about group activities will be shared but personal information about individuals will not be shared) can reduce children's concerns about these issues.

Children might also be concerned about possible stigmatizing effects of participating in a therapy group (Waas & Anderson, 1991). Because children in the same class are often aware of each other's schedule, it is likely that a child's participation in a therapy group will not be kept completely private. Some therapists encourage students to adopt a group name (e.g., "The Friendship Group" or "Keeping Cool Group") as one way of ameliorating possible stigmatizing effects. Another strategy that has considerable empirical support, especially for groups involving youth with externalizing behaviors, is to include nonreferred students in the group (Ang & Hughes, 2002; Arnold & Hughes, 1999).

Group Features and Elements

The particular characteristics of any given therapy group will be influenced by a number of factors: orientation of the group leader, focus of the group, age, motivation level, and problem severity of the participants, environmental constraints, and so on. Nevertheless, there are several common issues that a therapist needs to consider when conducting group interventions in a school context. Some of these, of course, are similar to those encountered when conducting groups outside of schools, and some are unique to the school setting.

Composition. The issue of group composition is relevant to any therapy group, but it takes on added importance when working with children who may have preexisting relationships outside the group, as is frequently the case with school-based groups. When determining group membership, it is useful to include only those children who have potential for contributing to group cohesiveness and are not likely to exhibit behaviors that are so deviant as to be disruptive to group functioning (George & Dustin, 1988; Semrud-Clikeman, 1995).

Rose and Edelson (1987) suggested that each member of the group should be able to identify at least one other member who is similar in level of social skills, social background, or presenting problem. Group cohesiveness will be maximized by children who share commonalties with each other and who are attracted to the group leader and their fellow group members (George & Dustin, 1988). Conversely, the inclusion of children who are actively antagonistic toward other members of the group will likely undermine group cohesiveness and should, therefore, be avoided.

In a narrative review of social skills groups for children and adolescents with aggression problems, Arnold and Hughes (1999) demonstrated that the composition of participants in the group can affect intervention outcomes in unexpected ways. Specifically, Arnold and Hughes presented research evidence showing that grouping deviant aggressive youth in interventions without incorporating nondeviant peers may produce unintended, harmful results. In other research by Hughes and colleagues (Cavell & Hughes, 2000), at-risk children who participated in a problem-solving skills training program were shown to develop attitudes more aligned with aggression than at-risk youth who did not participate in the problem-solving skills intervention. Finally, in a recent meta-analysis by Ang and Hughes (2002), results indicated that social skills training interventions delivered in the context wherein some participants were appropriate, prosocial peers showed greater benefits than skills training groups comprised exclusively of antisocial and/or aggressive youth. Taken together, the results by Hughes and her colleagues add to the growing literature indicating the benefit associated with incorporating appropriate peers when conducting group interventions with troubled youth. The inclusion of prosocial youth in group interventions may not always be feasible and may present concerns or issues for the positive peer members, but nonetheless, can produce better outcomes for the youth requiring treatment services.

Group Size. Closely related to the issue of group composition is the question of group size. Significant variability exists in the treatment literature regarding the number of children included in therapy groups, with 3 to 10 children most often included. In some circumstances larger groups may have advantages over smaller groups in that there is greater opportunity for positive modeling within the group, a greater chance that each member of the group will identify with a fellow member, and more children with whom each member can practice newly learned skills.

Although larger groups carry with them some advantages, they also have a number of risks associated with them. For example, as group membership increases, the therapist will find it more difficult to provide individual attention to each child. Planning activities that are therapeutically relevant and engaging to all children in the group will be more difficult. In larger groups it will be easier for some children to be "off task," disruptive, or passive. One procedure for minimizing the disadvantages associated with larger groups is to recruit a cotherapist or assistant to help plan and implement group activities. The use of a cofacilitator also holds considerable advantage because therapeutic tasks can be split and thus more easily monitored (e.g., one facilitator is responsible for implementing the intervention activities while the other has responsibility for monitoring how group participants are responding to the activities).

Group Structure and Development. An extensive body of literature exists on the stages of development in group therapy (e.g., Corey, 2000; Rogers, 1972; Yalom, 1995; Siepker & Kandaras, 1985). Although a detailed review of this literature is beyond the purview of this chapter, it is important for group leaders to be aware of the typical stages a group goes through during the therapy process. Corey (2000), for example, identified four general stages of group development. In Stage 1, group members define rules, goals, and expectations, begin the process of establishing trust and identity with the group, and establish norms of behavior. For groups conducted in a school setting, this stage may involve such tasks as setting the schedule for group meetings, establishing rules for the group, and completing activities designed to encourage group cohesiveness and trust among group members.

During Stage 2, group members work through feelings of resistance and anxiety. In school settings, resistance may be related to feelings of being singled out, fears of stigmatization, doubts about confidentiality, and class disruption. During Stage 3, the group moves into a period of cohesiveness and productivity. School-based groups often focus on specific objectives that match participants' needs and provide a structure for therapy sessions (e.g., anger control, social skills, coping with loss).

During this stage extra care should be taken to ensure the active involvement of all group members in each therapy session (Braswell, Kendall, Braith, Carey, & Vye, 1985). Frequently, this requires the group leader to assign roles to all members of the group during activities (e.g., while two members are role playing, two others are serving as judges). The use of behavioral programs, such as token economies and response-cost procedures, have also been used successfully to promote group members' participation (e.g., Bierman et al., 1987).

Finally, during Stage 4, participants review the gains they have made during the group and prepare for termination and possible after care. In schools, termination may be related to issues outside of therapy, such as school or schedule changes and end of the year (Semrud-Clikeman, 1995). After-care planning may involve helping to plan the child's schedule for the following year, meeting with teachers to familiarize them with the academic and behavioral needs of the child, and consulting with counselors, social workers or psychologists to provide continuity of care.

Scheduling Issues. Conducting therapy groups within a school setting necessarily involves grappling with a variety of complex scheduling issues. For example, the length of most children's groups range from 30 to 90 minutes, with younger children typically meeting for shorter periods of time and older children able to meet for longer periods. However, within a school setting, the therapist must also consider the children's schedule of other school activities. It may be, for example, that group meetings will need to be held within a single class period so as to minimize disruption to the children's class schedule.

A second scheduling issue is when groups will meet. Ideally, groups should meet on a regular basis, but teachers may object to children missing the same academic class each week. It may be necessary, therefore, to identify nonacademic periods such as study hall, recess, or lunch for meetings or to establish a rotating meeting schedule. Closely related to when groups will meet is where they will meet. Schools frequently operate under severe space shortages, and this may make finding an appropriate space for group therapy difficult. Groups should be conducted in an area that is free from distraction, allows for a variety of group activities, and provides privacy to group members. If a designated group therapy room is not available, school groups have been held in vacant offices, art and music rooms, or other rooms not being used during the period of the group.

Many of the scheduling issues must be resolved through consultation with teachers, parents, and administrators. For example, permission for a student to attend group will be needed from the child's parent. Teachers will need to be consulted about their students being absent from class and how missed assignments will be made up. Administrators will need to be consulted to find appropriate space in which to conduct the group. Clearly, conducting groups within the school necessarily involves understanding the school milieu and gaining the support of other professionals within the school.

OVERVIEW OF COMMON SCHOOL-BASED GROUP INTERVENTIONS

There is a wide diversity of group interventions that are conducted in educational settings. These range from nondirective experiential type groups to support groups for students experiencing stressful life events (e.g., divorce, loss), and highly structured groups focusing on specific social, emotional, behavioral, or educational concerns (e.g., social skills, depression, inclusion). In addition, there exist a variety of prevention programs that target such concerns as substance abuse, early adolescent pregnancy, and school violence. The search for group prevention and intervention programs shown to produce intended and positive outcomes is driven by the adverse health and mental health consequences many children and family endure when appropriate treatment is not rendered.

Many group programs are supported by published results demonstrating improved social, behavioral, and/or academic results. Unfortunately, much of the literature pertaining to group intervention programs has not incorporated rigorous outcome measurement procedures. In this section, we provide a brief overview of three types of group intervention (i.e., programs that target social skill development, resilience promotion, and depression) commonly conducted in the school setting that have received a reasonably high level of empirical support. The interested reader is referred to several excellent comprehensive volumes that describe additional school-based group interventions such as the *Handbook of Group Intervention for Children and Families* (Stoiber & Kratochwill, 1998), *Handbook of Child and Adolescent Treatment Manuals* (LeCroy, 1994), *Preventing School Problems—Promoting School Success: Strategies and Programs That Work* (Minke & Bear, 2000), *Theory and Practice of Group Counseling* (Corey, 2000), and *Successful Prevention Programs for Children and Adolescents* (Durlak, 1997).

Social Skills Development

One of the most common targets of group intervention with elementary-age students is social skill development (Elliott et al., 2002). The popularity of this type of intervention is understandable given that a wide body of research suggests that the development of effective social skills is critical to children establishing and maintaining positive peer relationships (e.g., Merrell & Gimpel, 1998). Failure to establish positive social relationships with peers places a child at risk for a variety of concurrent and future adjustment difficulties (Kupersmidt, Coie, & Dodge, 1990).

Interventions designed to build children's social skills are particularly appropriate for a school setting. It is in the school milieu that many peer relationship difficulties emerge. Thus, the implementation of social skills interventions within the school context allows for close proximity to the settings in which the child is having difficulty (e.g., playground, specific classes). This proximity permits an "authentic social development setting" as well as a careful match between problem areas and treatment objectives. The inclusion of social skills programs at school also allows for the involvement of actual peers in the treatment process, participation of significant others, such as teachers, to facilitate interventions, and it likely increases the probability of transference of newly learned skills from the therapy room to the playground and classroom (Waas & Graczyk, 1998).

Some of the most common social skills taught in treatment intervention studies with school-age children include the following: social problem-solving skills, self-management skills, anger management skills, empathy training, and social perspective taking (Elias et al., 1997; Greenberg, Kusche, Cook, & Quamma, 1995). Most programs emphasizing the development of social skills combine many of the above areas, and some programs incorporate extensive attention to subskills or components. For example, programs that teach self-management strategies or self-monitoring strategies often include self-evaluation and self-reinforcement (Cone, 1999; Shapiro & Cole, 1994). Most typically, these skills are taught through a social-learning or social problem-solving methodology, and numerous handbooks and manuals that utilize this approach are available to the interested reader (e.g., Cartledge & Milburn, 1995; Elliott & Gresham, 1991; Shure, 1992; Rathvon, 1999). Teaching children social problem solving and thinking skills is frequently part of programs for treating aggression, antisocial behavior, and conduct problems (CCPRG, 1999a, 1999b).

A number of comprehensive reviews and meta-analyses have examined the effectiveness of group interventions that target the development of social skills through structured activities emphasizing social cognition and social problem solving (e.g., Bear, Webster-Stratton, Furlong, & Rhee, 2000; Larson, 1998; Waas & Graczyk, 1998). One of the major problems that has plagued the implementation of social skills training programs is that most programs have failed to demonstrate maintenance and generalization of taught skills outside of the training setting (see Bear et al., 2000; Beelmann, Pfingsten, & Losel, 1994; Mathur, Kavale, Quinn, Forness, & Rutherford, 1998). Another problem is that the research design used to evaluate program effects often incorporate only self-report measures of social problem-solving skills or behavior and/or do not incorporate comparison groups (e.g., Flanagan, Povall, Dellino, & Byrne, 1998). Although many programs report positive results based on self report procedures, there are very few studies that have incorporated research designs and empirical methods consistent with expectations for demonstrating evidence-based practices, which emphasize multimethod, multisource, and multitype (e.g., behavioral observations, teacher ratings, parent ratings, self-monitoring, etc.) of measured outcomes (Stoiber & Kratochwill, 2002; in press). In light of limitations in the current knowledge base on social skills programs, it is recommended that outcome evaluation procedures that provide ongoing monitoring and feedback should accompany the implementation of social skills programs whenever possible (Stoiber & Kratochwill, 2002). In addition, it should be noted that research supports the use of "active" decision making, cognitive processing, and learning opportunities over approaches based on passive "lecture" or "discussion" (Gottfredson, 1997). Finally, program implementation should be matched as much as possible to the actual settings and circumstances wherein the child will typically use the targeted social skills. For example, if the child demonstrates difficulties with aggressive behavior on the playground, then attempts to implement the group intervention with groups of children on the playground should be part of the program. Similarly, social skills programs should be implemented and monitored at the classroom level when the specific behavior of concern involves classroom behavior (e.g., participating appropriately during large and small classroom-based groups), so that direct application opportunities for relevant skills are available.

Teaching Social Skills. Following a careful assessment of children's social skill deficits (e.g., Elliott et al., 2002; Merrell & Gimpel, 1998; Shapiro & Kratochwill, 2000), clinicians utilizing this approach focus on developing children's understanding of skill concepts, promoting skill performance, and fostering skill maintenance (e.g., Cartledge & Milburn, 1995; Ladd & Mize, 1983). Conducting therapy in groups when intervening with children who exhibit poor social skills is particularly appropriate. The group format allows children to practice newly learned skills with actual peers and begin the process of building more positive relationships with classmates (Waas & Graczyk, 1998).

The first step in teaching social skills is introducing the skill concept and increasing the group members' motivation for learning the skill. For children exhibiting social skill deficits, this often involves pointing out the causal connection between inappropriate behavior (e.g., aggression) and the negative consequences they experience (e.g., loneliness). It is also useful to highlight the benefits (e.g., friendships, improved grades) of learning better social skills (Kazdin, 1988).

During the skill-building stage of training, a variety of modeling procedures are utilized to provide children behavioral cues about how to perform the skill. Through these procedures a child learns the target skill by watching others perform the component behaviors of the skill under various conditions (Elliott & Gresham, 1993). For example, the group leader might perform the target skill initially, and then group members would take turns attempting to implement the skill while giving and receiving feedback on skill performance.

Children's understanding and mastery of the skill is developed further by having group members identify relevant and irrelevant attributes of the skill concept and generating both positive and negative exemplars of the skill. For example, in a group working on making appropriate requests for assistance, children might be asked to think of both positive and negative examples of assistantship bids. They might then take turns role playing the positive and negative suggestions and observe the natural consequences of each example. Such role playing can be incorporated into game-like activities as well. The use of such embellishments as a game board, dice, and points can be effective at maintaining children's interest and motivation.

The central component of a social-learning approach to skill training is the promotion of skill performance through guided rehearsal, structured feedback, reinforcement, and practice (Cartledge & Milburn, 1995; Ladd & Mize, 1983). As with learning the skill concept, each group member should be involved actively in all phases of the skill performance stage. Not only will such involvement enhance motivation and peer relations within the group (Waas & Graczyk, 1998), but the use of peers during role playing and feedback activities will maximize the modeling effect of these exercises.

Guided rehearsal is a structured form of role playing in which a particular skill, such as entering an ongoing activity or making a social bid to play with a peer, is rehearsed under the supervision of the group leader. The group leader coaches children on the sequence of behaviors required for performing the skill successfully. Group members will often participate in several role-playing exercises designed to give them practice with a diversity of conditions. Role plays may initially be well planned or even scripted to ensure that children perform the targeted social skill successfully. As children gain experience performing the skill, however, role plays should become increasingly improvised, realistic, and challenging (Elliott & Gresham, 1993). As children become more at-ease with role playing, they can take on the role of coach for each other.

An extension of such structured skill rehearsal is practicing new skills under less structured, less closely supervised conditions (Cartledge & Milburn, 1995; Ladd & Mize, 1983). The group setting provides an ideal context in which such a transition can take place. For example, Bierman and Furman (1984) coached children in self-expression (e.g., sharing information about self and feelings), questioning (e.g., asking others about themselves and feelings), and leadership bids (e.g., giving advice, invitations). Children then practiced the skills by making videotapes of each other using the target skills. Other researchers have made extensive use of games to ensure that children practice skills in a wide variety of circumstances (Yu, Harris, Solovitz, & Franklin, 1986).

Structured feedback involves providing children with constructive analysis of their performance of the social skill being practiced. Initially, feedback is provided by the group facilitator. As the group progresses, other children can also provide important feedback about a group member's use of a particular skill. The use of peers to provide such feedback ensures the active involvement of all group participants, promotes the commentator's understanding of the target skill, and provides the recipient with relevant feedback from his or her actual peers.

A second form of feedback involves the tangible reinforcement for successful skill performance. Bierman et al. (1987) used a token reinforcement procedure to increase prosocial behavior among elementary-age group members. Whenever a child was observed using a targeted skill, the group facilitator praised the performance, labeled the skill, and placed a token in a cup with the child's name on it. At the end of each session, children were allowed to exchange their tokens for a snack. Bierman et al. (1987) reported that children involved in the reinforcement conditions exhibited improved and sustained positive peer interactions.

Another way to enhance the power of such interventions and increase the likelihood that children will use newly learned skills in the naturalistic environment is to encourage children to share actual incidents in their lives. Edelson and Rose (1982), for example, began each group session by having children describe recent problematic encounters with peers outside the therapy session and critique their own performance in that situation. These actual situations served as the focus for group training activities, which included brainstorming of alternative solutions, response selection, modeling of responses, rehearsal, coaching, and group feedback. The use of homework assignments is also common in social skills groups to promote skill generalization (see, for example, Elliott & Gresham, 1991; Elliott et al., 2002).

Resilience-Building Programs

Increased awareness of the scope of risk-taking behaviors being engaged in by many school-age children and adolescents has presented an obvious need for prevention and intervention programs aimed at promoting resilience behaviors. Recent estimates suggest that as many as 25% of youth between 10 and 17 years of age are highly vulnerable, and another approximately 25% are moderately vulnerable to engage in one or multiple risk-taking behaviors, including early sexual activity and adolescent pregnancy, substance abuse, school dropout, and delinquency, gangs, and violent behavior (Dryfoos, 1993; Hawkins et al., 1998; Kazdin, 1994). Our knowledge of the many unfortunate consequences that are linked to risk-taking behaviors such as heightened levels of poverty and crime behavior, and lower educational attainment and job status, has provided a compelling argument for making prevention-oriented interventions a priority for schools (Nastasi, 2000; Stoiber & Good, 1998).

In general, there are two types of group-based programs for preventing risk behavior and promoting resilience: (1) small-group programs that target students at risk for problem behavior and emphasize social relationship components not available in individual or large-group interventions, and (2) classroom-based programs where all children engage in lessons and activities. Some programs, such as Fast Track (CPPRG, 1999a, 1999b) are multicomponent interventions that combine classroom-based prevention and small-group intervention approaches. Another example of a multicomponent resiliency program is an antibullying behavior project conducted in Norway by Olweus (1999). This project incorporated classroom-based curricula and school-wide application (e.g., playground, lunchroom) components, including (1) establishing clear rules against bullying; (2) using various forms of media to inform teachers, parents, and children about what bullying looks and feels like and how to counteract it; (3) conducting class meetings to discuss bullying and clarify sanctions and norms against it; and (4) promoting teacher responsibility and involvement in countering bullying through their use of sanction and reward systems and construction of a positive, safe school climate. Olweus reported impressive results of approximately a 50% reduction in bullying in addition to decreases in vandalism, theft, and truancy at treatment schools. Unfortunately, no data are available on applications/replications of Olweus's model with students attending U.S. schools or on long-term outcomes or continued effects.

The most effective resilience programs aimed at reaching high-risk populations of students (cf., Catalano, Arthur, Hawkins, Berglund, & Olson, 1998; CPPRG, 1999a, 1999b; Loeber, Farrington, & Waschbusch, 1998) are those that share the following characteristics:

1. Attempt to alter predispositions to risk-taking behaviors early before the problem begins or becomes severe (e.g., reach adolescents before they begin drinking or engage in sexual activity).
2. Incorporate multiple components and strategies that target a cluster of risk-taking behaviors (e.g., delinquency, school dropout, and early sexual activity).
3. Integrate comprehensive and broad-based intervention strategies, including the involvement of parents and families whenever feasible.
4. Promote active involvement and interactive techniques, such as role plays, perspective taking, and behavioral rehearsal.
5. Emphasize decision-making skills, motivation, and social competence to help children and adolescents make healthy choices and realize the potential long-term negative consequences of risk-taking behavior.
6. Provide realistic expectations grounded in developmentally as well as ethnic and culturally sensitive approaches that are matched to the characteristics of the targeted population.

In addition to these characteristics, Dryfoos (1993) in her review of more than 100 programs designed to address risk-taking behaviors among adolescents noted that interventions demonstrating the strongest empirical data had two important components. First, successful programs placed an emphasis on individuals having the opportunity to develop a positive relationship with at least one adult role model. This adult may function as an advocate or a mentor for the adolescent in providing social support and helping the adolescent make sound decisions. Second, the most successful programs were those that reached beyond school boundaries and incorporated multiagency and community-wide service delivery. Although it is beyond the scope of this chapter to discuss ethnic and cultural diversity issues that should be considered when implementing groups aimed at preventing risk behavior, obviously consideration of the particular needs of group participants because of cultural and ethnic background is essential for establishing effective prevention programs (Kratochwill & Stoiber, 2000b; Stoiber & Kratochwill, 2002). The following section illustrates features of some of the most effective group intervention approaches for altering high-risk behavior.

Resistance-Skills Programs. An assumption of programs emphasizing resistance skills is that adolescents do NOT want to engage in the risk-taking behaviors such as smoking, drinking, sexual intercourse, or gang behaviors but lack the confidence or persuasiveness to resist peer influences. Resistance-skills programs teach participants to resist social influences, through the use of "refusal skills," "social resistance skills," or "resistance-skills" approaches. The term *resistance-skills training* will be used in this chapter to describe approaches based on social learning theory. Put simply, resistance-skills training attempts to help students recognize situations or scenarios where they are more likely to experience peer pressure to engage in risk-taking behaviors. Another component of resistance-skills programs is to increase students' awareness of actual levels of risk-taking behavior among peers in their school, as well as develop realistic estimates for other children and adolescents at the community, state, or national level. For example, students will be asked to estimate how many students at their grade and age level are sexually active, and then provide students with accurate data based on recent surveys. Typically students who engage in risk-taking behaviors overestimate the prevalence of smoking, drug use, sexual activity, teen pregnancy, and so on in their peers. Thus this approach is designed to correct normative impressions (Botvin & Griffin, 2000).

The primary goal of resistance-skills training is to develop knowledge, confidence, and persuasive countering skills in students so that they can handle peer pressure. Participants are shown and taught specific assertion and communication skills, using interactive strategies such as media-triggered role plays, peer modeling, rehearsal, and peer coaching. Studies have examined the effects of resistance-skills-based curriculum on postponing or deterring adolescent sexual activity, smoking, alcohol, and marijuana use. The most effective resistance-skills programs (cf., Alan Guttmacher Institute [AGI], 1994; Robinson, Watkins-Ferrell, Davis-Scott, & Ruch-Ross, 1993; Stoiber, Anderson, & Schowalter, 1998) include five discrete, yet integrated components: (1) provides a group-orientation based on social learning or social influence theory and recognizes the impact of peers and other social influences on risk-taking behavior; (2) offers opportunities to explore types of social pressures and to develop assertive responses to them; (3) uses real-life, media-based, or experiential type activities to point out potential risks; (4) emphasizes group support and social norms to help develop knowledge-based norms; and (5) incorporates communication and decision-making activities to increase confidence and skill in using them when needed.

Support for resistance-skills programs comes from research demonstrating that this approach can reduce smoking by 30–50% (Donaldson, Graham, & Hansen, 1994; Sussman, Dent, Stacy, & Sun, 1993) and decrease pregnancy rates by approximately 50% (Paine-Andrews et al., 1996) when compared to control groups. Less data are available on the effects of resistance-skills programs on alcohol or marijuana use; however, the majority of studies (63%) conducted from 1980 to 1990 have indicated positive results in reducing drug use behavior (Hansen, 1992). At this time it is unclear whether such effects are maintained at long-term follow-up, as several long-range (1 to 3 years) follow-up studies have indicated that effects decay over time and that booster sessions are likely necessary to maintain positive effects (Botvin & Griffin, 2000).

It should be noted that not all group interventions based on skills-resistance programs have demonstrated positive or intended effects. For example, one of the most popular classroom-based programs based on social influence is Drug Abuse Resistance Education (Project D.A.R.E.) despite its limited evidence base. A distinguishing characteristic of D.A.R.E. is that trained, uniformed police officers typically teach the drug prevention curriculum to children in the fifth or sixth grade. Most of the outcome studies on the D.A.R.E. program have limited empirical significance because of poor research design characteristics (e.g., posttest only, nonrandom assignment of participants, poor measurement procedures, faulty data analysis) and a focus on only short-term effects (Rosenbaum & Hanson, 1998). Rosenbaum and Hanson astutely noted that the stronger the research design used to evaluate D.A.R.E., the lesser degree of impact has been documented. Several reasons have been advanced to explain the poor results for the D.A.R.E. program, including instructional methods are less interactive than successful programs, students may "tune-out" authority figures, and over emphasis on knowledge-based components (Hansen & McNeal, 1997).

Similarly, it should be noted that those adolescent pregnancy prevention programs that only focus on educational component programs or that emphasize brief classroom-based informational sessions and abstinence ("just say no") have not altered adolescent behavior effectively (AGI, 1994; DiClemente, 1993). Thus, in addition to understanding "what works" in group interventions that target at-risk behaviors, it is important to understand which, when, and why intervention approaches have not been shown to produce intended effects. Unfortunately, our knowledge of program components that fail to produce expected outcomes is limited by the tendency of both authors and journals not to publish studies yielding negative results or no significant effects (Kratochwill, Stoiber, & Gutkin, 2001).

Competency-Based Programs. Research has demonstrated that some of the most effective group intervention programs focus on the development of targeted competencies or resilient behaviors (Botvin & Griffin, 2000; St. Lawrence et al., 1995). Similar to social skills programs, a competence enhancement approach teaches personal self-management skills, decision-making skills, and social coping skills. The basis for skills-oriented or competency-based intervention approaches stems from indications that adolescents who tend to lack social problem solving or future-directed thinking are more prone to aggression and/or risk-taking behaviors. Competence enhancement approaches differ from resistance-skills programs in that competence approaches acknowledge the possibility that some students may *want* to use drugs, be sexually active, or join gangs. Thus, competence enhancement approaches combine education with cognitive-behavioral or behavioral skills. In addition, competency-based or enhancement programs are distinguished by their incorporation of several proven risk-reduction strategies, such as dyadic or triadic role-play practice situations wherein the group facilitator provides feedback, reinforcement, and suggestions; panel discussions by "cool" individuals such as a Rap Team that discloses their HIV status and fears to the group; group sharing of strategies for escaping risky situations; and extended demonstrations, behavioral practice, and rehearsal of resistance techniques (e.g., St. Lawrence et al., 1995).

Competency-based programs also often include broad-based resiliency approaches that target clusters of risk-taking and other problem behaviors (e.g., substance use, gang behavior, and early sexual activity) as opposed to targeting only one behavior. Each group session typically targets specific competencies such as personal goal setting, values clarification, communication and social assertion, conflict resolution, social coping, peer negotiation, social support and empowerment, and problem-solving and critical thinking steps—that are considered to be linked to resilient or appropriate social behavior. The objectives and group activities for specific sessions correspond to the competencies being emphasized and one or more sessions may be devoted to a particular competence (e.g., conflict resolution, personal goal setting).

Research has suggested that competence enhancement approaches may be far reaching in that they promote improved outcomes on several problem behaviors as well as other important school behaviors, including academic achievement and attendance (Rathvon, 1999; Stoiber, Hughes, & Young, 2000). For example, a comparison of a 12-session classroom-based resiliency program to a 12-session confidence-building activity-based intervention (i.e., known as "ropes and courses") by Stoiber and colleagues (2000) found that the sixth-grade urban students in the competency program reported significantly less sexual activity, gang-affiliated behavior, and delinquency behavior. In addition, positive effects were shown for reducing the number of suspensions for students who participated in the competency-based prevention program compared to a control group of sixth-grade students.

Combining Classroom-Based Proactive and Small-Group Intervention Strategies. The Families and Schools Together (Fast Track; CPPRG, 1999a, 1999b) is an intervention program that targets young children showing antisocial and conduct problems using combined small-group and classroom-based approaches and multiple intervention targets (see Table 29.1). The Fast Track program is based on research indicating that children who begin showing conduct problems in early childhood are at risk for becoming "life-course-persistent offenders." In addition, Fast Track is based on a developmental framework that suggests high-risk children should be identified early and provided with intervention that helps them develop the kind of competencies needed to move them along more adaptive developmental trajectories. Although the Fast Track intervention program is initiated when children are in first grade, the

TABLE 29.1
Overview and Description of Fast Track Program Components

Component	*Description*
Universal Classroom Component	
PATHS curriculum (Kusche & Greenberg, 1994; Bierman, Greenberg, & CPPRG, 1996)	Classroom-based curriculum, lessons included: 1. Skills for emotional understanding and communication 2. Friendship skills 3. Self-control skills 4. Social problem-solving skills
"Enrichment Programs" with High-risk Sample	
Parent groups (Forehand & McMahon, 1981; Webster-Stratton, 1989; Burgoyne, Hawkins, & Catalano, 1991; Hawkins et al., 1988; McMahon, Slough, & CPPRG, 1996)	Family coordinators and coleaders led 1-hour parent groups. The curriculum included: 1. Establishing a positive family–school relationship and supporting child adjustment to school 2. Building parental self-control 3. Promoting developmentally appropriate expectations for the child's behavior 4. Improving parenting skills to improve parent–child interaction and decrease disruptive behavior
Child social skills training groups (Bierman et al., 1996)	Children identified as high risk met in 1-hour "friendship groups" of 5–6 students led by Fast Track Educational Coordinators. Sessions provided an opportunity to review and practice emotional understanding and communication, friendship building, self-control, and social problem solving.
Parent–child sharing time (McMahon et al., 1996)	Parent–child pairs participated in positive cooperative activities and practiced positive parenting skills with staff support during 30-minute sessions.
Home visits (Wasik, Bryant, & Lyons, 1990)	Family coordinators conducted home visits approximately every other week to: 1. Develop trusting relationships with the entire family system 2. Promote generalization of parenting skills to home 3. Promote parental support for child's school adjustment 4. Promote parental problem solving, coping, and goal setting A problem-solving approach was used to promote parental empowerment and self-efficacy.
Child peer pairing	Paraprofessional tutors conducted 30-minute play sessions with classroom peer partners and high-risk children to help promote generalization of friendship skills to the classroom.
Academic tutoring (Wallach & Wallach, 1976)	Paraprofessional tutors also provided academic tutoring to build reading skills.

long-range goal of this program is to reduce adolescent pregnancy, substance abuse, risky sexual practices, and social/emotional disorders by providing long-term, combined classroom-based and small-group approaches (CPPRG, 1999a, 1999b). Fast Track was designed to incorporate an ongoing school context component that extends from Grade 1 to Grade 10. The initial effectiveness of the Fast Track intervention, which is reviewed below, has focused on altering key child and family risk factors and improving social competence in Grade 1 children.

As can be seen in Table 29.1, the Fast Track program incorporates a universal-level classroom program plus small-group social skills training, parent training groups, and small therapeutic play groups. It also includes academic tutoring and home visiting. Fast Track builds on the success of a classroom intervention known as the PATHS [Promoting Alternative THinking Strategies] (Kusche & Greenberg, 1994) curriculum, which emphasizes social problem solving and social/emotional competence. Teachers are trained to implement this curriculum and all children receive two or three weekly lessons using the PATHS curriculum from first through fifth grade. In addition to PATHS, behaviorally disruptive "high-risk" children are identified by teachers during kindergarten (i.e., those scoring in the upper 10% on problem behavior checklists) and receive additional small-group and individual-based interventions. For example, high-risk target children attend "friendship groups" and participate in parent–child group intervention programs that draw on approaches previously shown to be effective (Burgoyne, Hawkins, & Catalano, 1991; Hawkins et al., 1988; Forehand & McMahon, 1981; Webster-Stratton, 1989).

The Fast Track program was evaluated using a multisite, randomized design with a no-intervention control group. Based on results shown for children at the end of Grade 1, the Fast Track program is considered an exemplary, evidence-based intervention program (see Lewis-Snyder, Stoiber, & Kratochwill, 2002, for a comprehensive evaluation of the evidence base to support Fast Track using the School Psychology Task Force criteria). Significant moderate positive effects based on peer ratings and observer ratings were found when comparing the 198 classrooms where teachers taught the PATHS curriculum to 180 control classrooms. Specifically, Grade 1 participants (especially boys) were rated by their peers as less aggressive and less hyperactive-disruptive, and intervention classrooms were rated by observers as having a more positive climate when compared to control classrooms.

Evaluations of the multicomponent approach on the targeted behaviorally disruptive, high-risk subgroup of children also showed significant positive results compared to the control subgroup of target children. The sample of Fast Track high-risk children showed significantly better social skills (i.e., spent more time in positive peer interaction and were more socially accepted), emotional regulation (i.e., emotion recognition, emotion coping, social problem solving, aggressive retaliation), and were rated by unbiased raters, teachers, and their parents as less aggressive-disruptive. Evidence was also reported to show that high-risk project participants spent less time per week in special education. In addition, moderate positive effects were found for parent participants. Fast Track parents rated themselves as engaging in less physical punishment, having greater parenting satisfaction, and increased warmth/positive involvement toward their child and the school. Teachers agreed that the project parents were more involved in their child's schooling.

In sum, initial reports of Fast Track suggest that intervention practices that combine classroom-based prevention strategies with more intense small-group interventions for selected high-risk students is an effective approach for improving social–behavioral, emotional, and academic outcomes for children and families. In particular, an evaluation of Fast Track provides evidence that matching the type of intervention components to intervention needs can produce important benefits in reducing the challenging behaviors and special education services for high-risk children. Future evaluations of Fast Track will be important to determine whether long-term outcomes are documented and maintained, especially with regard to preventing adolescent risk-taking behavior.

Depressive Disorders

The prevalence of depressive disorders among school-age children is increasingly being recognized as a significant psychoeducational problem. It has been estimated that between 5% and 7% of fourth- through seventh-grade children experience a depressive disorder at any given time. It is believed that this prevalence rate is higher among older children and adolescents (Stark, 1990). Because these disorders can interfere with a child's social, emotional, and academic functioning, interest has grown in school-based interventions for these at-risk children.

A detailed description of the etiology of depression and current models of depression is beyond the purview of this chapter. However, the reader is referred to several excellent sources for a more in-depth discussion of these issues (e.g., Barlow, 1993; Lewis & Miller, 1990; Reynolds & Johnston, 1994). In recent years, a well-articulated intervention program based on a cognitive-behavioral model has been developed for the treatment of depressive disorders in children (e.g., Stark, 1990; Stark et al., 1998; Stark & Kendall, 1996). This approach has been widely used in school settings and has received extensive empirical support (Reynolds & Coates, 1986; Kahn, Kehle, Jenson, & Clark, 1990; Stark, Reynolds, & Kaslow, 1987). Because depressive disorders often affect children's cognitions, affect, and behavior, the cognitive-behavioral approach to treating depression incorporates a wide variety of interventions. These include activities to enhance problem-solving skills, alter dysphoric mood, modify maladaptive cognitions, improve social skills, and teach self-evaluation skills.

Depression-Altering Strategies. According to Stark and colleagues (1998), problem-solving training should be conducted throughout the treatment program. This training is done opportunistically by having the group facilitator model effective problem solving and encourage children to use these strategies for problems that arise in their lives and in the group itself. Children also are taught a formal method of problem solving based on Kendall's (1981) work with impulsive children. Through modeling, coaching, practice, and feedback, children are taught to define the problem, motivate themselves to face the problem, generate alternative solutions, consider likely consequences, identify the best solution, and evaluate the result.

Intervening with dysphoric mood involves modifying both cognitions and behaviors. Extensive group work is devoted to teaching children about emotions and the relationship between thoughts, feelings, and behaviors. These activities take the form of games such as emotional vocabulary, emotion charades, and emotion password. For example, during an emotion vocabulary game, children might use a deck of cards that has the name of an emotion on each card. Players take turns drawing a card from the deck and then describe how the emotion feels and what was happening the last time they felt the emotion.

A variation of the game involves having children act out the expression of the emotion while other members of the group guess the emotion. Activity scheduling also is used to alter dysphoric mood; children identify mood-enhancing activities, such as listening to a favorite song, taking a bike ride, or talking on the phone, and then assist in planning their participation in these activities. In addition, deep muscle relaxation can be taught to children as a coping strategy they can use when confronted with excessive anxiety.

Cognitive restructuring procedures are used to correct habitual errors in information processing and depressogenic automatic thoughts. For example, "What's the Evidence?" is a technique used to help children critically examine automatic thoughts and the negative schemata that underlie them. In this procedure, children (with the guidance of the group leader) help each other identify the underlying assumptions that underlie their automatic thoughts. Children then establish what evidence would be necessary to either support or refute the negative assumptions. The group then evaluates the available evidence and makes plans for collecting additional evidence if needed. In the procedure "What's Another Way to Look at It?" the group generates alternative and more adaptive interpretations of an event. Children then evaluate systematically the supporting evidence for the different interpretations.

Behavioral experiments also are designed and implemented in the group as a way of objectively assessing maladaptive automatic thoughts and interpretations. With all of these procedures, a high level of group leader skill is required to promote children's understanding of their automatic thoughts, generate alternatives to these thoughts, and carry out behavioral assignments and experiments. Conducting such groups in a school context may allow the therapist to provide children in-vivo coaching and reinforcement. Consultation with other school personnel (e.g., teachers, aides) may also facilitate the extension of these activities to the playground and classroom.

Children experiencing depressive disorders frequently exhibit a variety of social skill deficits as well. Stark and colleagues (1998) reported that the group format allows the leader to assess for social skill deficits among group members and provides a venue in which social skills can be taught. With children exhibiting depressive disorders, teaching assertiveness skills is frequently the focus of social skills training. These include such skills as appropriate expression of feelings, providing and accepting feedback, listening skills, refusing unreasonable requests, negotiation, and asking for assistance.

Finally, self-evaluation training is also incorporated into group activities. A central characteristic of the attributional style of depressed individuals is that they tend to be overly negative in their self-evaluations. In the group intervention developed by Stark and colleagues (1998), children are taught to recognize their positive attributes and to evaluate themselves more positively. Children's standards for self-evaluation are assessed by the My Standards Questionnaire-Revised (Stark, 1990), and self monitoring and cognitive restructuring (e.g., "What's the evidence?") procedures are utilized to help children adopt more appropriate standards. Children are also assisted in setting appropriate goals for future personal development.

EXTENDING THE GROUP: THE ROLE OF CONSULTATION

The importance of consultation among teachers, administrators, parents, school psychologists, and other health service professionals has long been recognized (Gutkin & Curtis, 1999). Although several different models of consultation have been developed over the years, an early definition of consultation still provides an informative overview of this indirect type of intervention. According to Medway (1979), consultation involves "collaborative problem-solving between a mental health specialist (the consultant) and one or more persons (the consultees) who are responsible for providing some form of psychological assistance to another (the client)" (p. 276). This type of collaborative problem solving is especially relevant as schools embrace group prevention approaches because the *agents of change* may shift to the teacher or parent.

Within the context of school-based small-group therapy, consultation most often involves ongoing interaction between the group leader and a child's teacher and/or parent, with the aim of facilitating the generalization of skills learned in group therapy to the classroom, playground, and home. When conducting a social skills group, for example, a group leader may work with the classroom teacher to provide opportunities for the child to practice newly learned skills in a naturalistic setting. A therapist working with depressed children may consult with teachers to increase a child's positive attributions about his or her academic performance or encourage children's involvement with peers.

An ecobehavioral or problem-solving approach to consultation (Gutkin & Curtis, 1999; Bergan, 1977) has received wide support for addressing these types of problems. This approach typically involves the mental health professional and teacher engaging in a systematic problem-solving sequence of problem identification, problem analysis, intervention development, plan implementation, and treatment evaluation. Engaging in such problem solving with the child's teacher to identify, plan, and implement relevant interventions helps to ensure the social validity of group therapy goals (cf., Gresham & Lopez, 1996; Stoiber & Kratochwill, 2002). A similar problem-solving process is used in conjoint behavioral consultation in which both the child's teacher and parents participate in the planning and implementation of interventions for the child (e.g., Sheridan et al., 1996).

Group leaders may wish to pursue other consultative interventions with school personnel and parents as well. For example, a mental-health model of consultation might be utilized to address a teacher's lack of objectivity or knowledge about a child (Caplan & Caplan, 1993). A systems approach might also be used to achieve organizational changes that promote competence and resilience among all children (e.g., CPPRG, 1999b; Curtis & Stollar, 1996). Finally, consultative practices make sense when the goal is to attempt to enhance student, teacher, and/or environmental features of the classroom through classroom-based approaches (which may involve training the teacher in prevention and/or intervention procedures) before rendering intensive therapy or remediation.

CONCLUSIONS

The challenge of responding to the diverse and critical needs of children requires that school psychologists and other school-based mental health professionals receive training and develop competence in designing, implementing, monitoring, and evaluating group interventions. Significant progress has been made in recent years in developing a knowledge base of evidence-based interventions (EBIs) for serving children through therapeutic and prevention-oriented groups (Ang & Hughes, 2002; Cavell & Hughes, 2000; Nathan & Gorman, 1998; Spirito, 1999; Stoiber & Kratochwill, 2000; Stoiber, 2002). For example, considerable data have accrued to support the notion that the benefits of social skills group approaches are maximized when approaches reflect the developmental and social needs of participants, when implemented in environments that closely match the environments where they are used, and when positive peer models are included. Perhaps one of the most remarkable advances affecting group therapeutic approaches in schools has been the prevention movement (Zins, Elias, Greenberg, & Pruett, 2000). Rather than waiting for children to become antisocial, delinquent, or substance abusers, schools and school-based mental health providers have awakened to the advantage of promoting preventive interventions (Durlak, 1997; Stoiber & Kratochwill, 1998). Recent research has demonstrated that comprehensive approaches that place an emphasis on social resistance and personal competence are capable of reducing risk-taking behaviors. In contrast, several studies indicate that programs that emphasize only brief educational or resistance-oriented ("just say no") strategies tend to be less effective and may not produce intended results.

Although much of the research has suggested promising results for school-based group intervention approaches, more rigorous investigations are sorely needed. In particular, very little is known about which group intervention components or procedures are essential to bring about desired changes. Also, evaluations of group interventions in schools with urban, low-income, and culturally diverse populations of students needs to occur. Most group prevention and intervention approaches have been evaluated with primarily White, middle-class populations; thus, it is unclear whether and how group intervention programs might need to be altered to achieve positive outcomes with diverse student populations. Finally, it is considered critical for school professionals who conduct group interventions to develop a knowledge base of "what works," in "which contexts" with "what populations" of children and families (Stoiber,

2002). If school mental health professionals are to advocate effectively for the children and families they serve, they must herald the task of promoting, implementing, and disseminating evidence-based group intervention practices.

REFERENCES

Adelman, H. S., & Taylor, L. (1998). Reframing mental health in schools and expanding school reform. *Educational Psychologist, 33*, 135–152.

Alan Guttmacher Institute (AGI). (1994). *Sex and America's teenagers.* New York: Alan Guttmacher Institute.

Ang, R. P., & Hughes, J. N. (2002). Differential benefits of skills training with antisocial youth based on group composition: A meta-analytic investigation. *School Psychology Review, 31*, 164–185.

Arnold, M. E., & Hughes, J. N. (1999). First do no harm: Adverse effects of grouping deviant youth for skills training. *Journal of School Psychology, 37*, 99–115.

Barlow, D. H. (1993). *Clinical handbook of psychological disorders: A step by step treatment manual.* New York: Guilford.

Bear, G. C., Webster-Stratton, C., Furlong, M. J., & Rhee, S. (2000). Preventing aggression and violence. In K. M. Minke & G. C. Bear (Eds.), *Preventing school problems—promoting school success* (pp. 1–70). Bethesda, MD: NASP.

Beelmann, A., Pfingsten, U., & Losel, F. (1994). Effects of training social competence in children: A meta-analysis of recent evaluation studies. *Journal of Clinical Child Psychology, 23*, 260–271.

Bergan, J. R. (1977). *Behavioral consultation.* Columbus, OH: Merrill.

Bierman, K. L., & Furman, W. (1984). The effects of social skills training and peer involvement on the social adjustment of preadolescents. *Child Development, 55*, 151–162.

Bierman, K. L., Greenberg, M. T., & Conduct Problems Prevention Research Group. (1996). Social skills training in the Fast Track program. In R. D. Peters & R. J. McMahon (Eds). *Preventing childhood disorders, substance abuse, and delinquency* (pp. 65–89). Thousand Oaks, CA: Sage.

Bierman, K. L., Miller, C. M., & Stabb, S. (1987). Improving the social behavior and peer acceptance of rejected boys: Effects of social skill training with instructions and prohibitions. *Journal of Consulting and Clinical Psychology, 55*, 194–200.

Botvin, G. J., & Griffin, K. W. (2000). Preventing substance use and abuse. In K. M. Minke & G. C. Bear (Eds.), *Preventing school problems—promoting school success* (pp. 259–298). Bethesda, MD: NASP.

Braswell, L. N., Kendall, P. C., Braith, J., Carey, M. P., & Vye, C. S. (1985). "Involvement" in cognitive-behavioral therapy with children: Process and its relationship to outcome. *Cognitive Therapy and Research, 9*, 611–630.

Burgoyne, K., Hawkins, D., & Catalano, R. (1991). *How to help your child succeed in school.* Seattle, WA: Developmental Research and Programs.

Caplan, G., & Caplan, R. B. (1993). *Mental health consultation and collaboration.* San Francisco: Jossey-Bass.

Cartledge, G., & Milburn, J. F. (Eds.). (1995). *Teaching social skills to children* (3rd ed.). New York: Pergamon.

Catalano, R. R., Arthur, M. W., Hawkins, J. D., Berglund, L., & Olson, J. J. (1998). Comprehensive community- and school-based interventions to prevent antisocial behavior. In R. Loeber & D. P. Farrington (Eds.), *Serious & violent juvenile offenders: Risk factors and successful interventions* (pp. 197–247). Thougsand Oaks, CA: Sage.

Cavell, T. A., & Hughes, J. N. (2000). Secondary prevention as context for studying change processes in aggressive children. *Journal of School Psychology, 38*, 199–235.

Centers for Disease Control and Prevention. (1998). Youth Risk Behavior Surveillance—United States, 1997. (SS No. 3). *Morbidity & Mortality Weekly Report, 47*, 1–89.

Conduct Problems Prevention Research Group. (1999a). Initial impact of the Fast Track prevention trial for conduct problems: I. The high-risk sample. *Journal of Consulting and Clinical Psychology, 67*, 631–647.

Conduct Problems Prevention Research Group. (1999b). Initial impact of the Fast Track prevention trial for conduct problems: II. Classroom effects. *Journal of Consulting and Clinical Psychology, 67*, 648–657.

Cone, J. D. (1999). Introduction to the special section on self-monitoring: A major assessment method in clinical psychology. *Psychological Assessment, 11*, 411–414.

Corey, G. (2000). *Theory and practice of group counseling* (5th ed.). Pacific Grove, CA: Brooks/Cole.

Curtis, M. J., & Stollar, S. A. (1996). Applying principles and practices of organizational change to school reform. *School Psychology Review, 25*, 409–417.

DiClemente, R. J. (1993). Preventing HIV/AIDS among adolescents: Schools as agents of behavior change. *Journal of the American Medical Association, 270*, 760–762.

Doll, B. (1996). Prevalence of psychiatric disorders in children and youth: An agenda for advocacy by school psychology. *School Psychology Quarterly, 11*, 20–46.

Donaldson, S. I., Graham, J. W., & Hansen, W. B. (1994). Testing the generalizability of intervening mechanism theories: Understanding the effects of adolescent drug use prevention interventions. *Journal of Behavioral Medicine, 17*, 195–216.

Dryfoos, J. G. (1993). Common components of successful interventions with high-risk youth. In N. J. Bell & R. W. Bell (Eds.), *Adolescent risk taking* (pp. 131–147). Newbury Park, CA: Sage.

Durlak, J. A. (1997). *Successful prevention programs for children and adolescents.* New York: Plenum.

Edelson, J. L., & Rose, S. D. (1982). Investigations into the efficacy of short-term group social skills training for socially isolated children. *Child Behavior Therapy, 3*, 1–16.

Elias, M. J., Zins, J. E., Weissberg, R. P., Frey, K. S., Greenberg, M. T., Haynes, N. M., Kessler, R., Schwab-Stone, M. E., & Shriver, T. P. (1997). *Promoting social and emotional learning: Guidelines for educators.* Alexandria, VA: Association for Supervision and Curriculum Development.

Elliott, S. N., & Gresham, F. M. (1991). *Social skills intervention guide.* Circle Pines, MN: American Guidance Service.

Elliott, S. N., & Gresham, F. M. (1993). Social skills interventions for children. *Behavior Modification, 17*, 287–313.

Elliott, S. N., Witt, J. C., Kratochwill, T. R., & Stoiber, K. C. (2002). Selecting and evaluating classroom interventions. In M. Shinn, G. Stoner, & H. Walker (Eds.), *Interventions for academic and behavior problems II: Preventive and remedial approaches* (pp. 243–294). Washington, D.C.: NASP.

Flanagan, R., Povall, L., Dellino, M., & Byrne, L. (1998). A comparison of problem solving with and without rational emotive behavior therapy to improve children's social skills. *Journal of Rational-Emotive and Cognitive-Behavior Therapy, 16*, 125–134.

Forehand, R., & McMahon, R. J. (1981). *Helping the noncompliant child: A clinician's guide to parent training.* New York: Guilford.

Garbarino, J. (1999). *Lost boys: Why our sons turn violent and how we can save them.* New York: Free Press.

George, R. L., & Dustin, D. (1988). *Group counseling theory and practice.* Englewood Cliffs, NJ: Prentice-Hall.

Gottfredson, D. C. (1997). School-based crime prevention. In L. W. Sherman, D. C. Gottfredson, D. MacKenzie, J. Eck, P. Reuter, & S. Bushway (Eds.), *Preventing crime: What works, what doesn't, what's promising: A report to the United States Congress.* Washington, D.C.: Department of Justice.

Greenberg, M. T., Kusche, C. A., Cook, E. T., & Quamma, J. P. (1995). Promoting emotional competence in school-aged children: The effects of the PATHS curriculum. *Development & Psychopathology, 7*, 117–136.

Gresham, G. M., & Lopez, M. F. (1996). Social validation: A unifying concept for school-based consultation research and practice. *School Psychology, 11*, 204–227

Gutkin, T. B., & Curtis, M. J. (1999). School-based consultation theory and practice: The art and science of indirect service delivery. In C. R. Reynolds & T. B. Gutkin (Eds.), *Handbook of school psychology* (3rd ed., pp. 598–638). New York: Wiley.

Hansen, W. B. (1992). School-based substance abuse prevention: A review of the state of the art in curriculum, 1980–1990. *Health Education Research: Theory & Practice, 7*, 403–430.

Hansen, W. B., & McNeal, R. B. (1997). How D.A.R.E. works: An examination of program effects on mediating variables. *Health Education & Behavior, 24*, 165–176.

Hawkins, J. D., Catalano, R. F., Brown, E. O., Vadasy, P. F., Roberts, C., Fitzmahan, D., Starkman, N., & Ransdell, M. (1988). *Preparing for the drug (free) years: A family activity book.* Seattle, WA: Comprehensive Health Education Foundation.

Hawkins, J. D., Herenkohl, T., Farrington, D. P., Brewer, D., Catalano, R. E., & Harachi, T. W. (1998). A review of predictors of youth violence. In R. Loeber & D. P. Farrington (Eds.), *Serious & violent juvenile offenders: Risk factors and successful interventions* (pp. 106–146). Thousand Oaks, CA: Sage.

Kahn, J. S., Kehle, T. J., Jenson, W. R., & Clark, E. (1990). Comparison of cognitive-behavioral, relaxation, and self-modeling interventions for depresion among middle-school students. *School Psychology Review, 19*, 196–211.

Kazdin, A. E. (1988). *Child psychotherapy.* New York: Pergamon.

Kazdin, A. E. (1994). Antisocial behavior and conduct disorder. In L. W. Craighead & W. E. Craighead (Eds.), *Cognitive and behavioral interventions: An empirical approach to mental health problems* (pp. 267–299). Boston: Allyn & Bacon.

Kazdin, A. E. (1997). A model for developing effective treatments: Progression and interplay of theory, research, and practice. *Journal of Clinical Child Psychology, 26*, 114–129.

Kazdin, A. E., & Johnson, B. (1994). Advances in psychotherapy for children and adolescents: Interrelations of adjustment, development, and intervention. *Journal of School Psychology, 32*, 217–246.

Kratochwill, T. R., & Stoiber, K. C. (2000a). Empirically supported interventions and school psychology: Conceptual and practical issues: Part II. *School Psychology Quarterly, 15*, 233–253.

Kratochwill, T. R., & Stoiber, K. C. (2000b). Uncovering critical research agendas for school psychology: Conceptual dimensions and future directions. *School Psychology Review, 29*, 591–603.

Kratochwill, T. R., Stoiber, K. C., & Gutkin, T. B. (2001). Empirically supported interventions in school psychology: The role of negative results in outcome research. *Psychology in the Schools, 37*, 399–413.

Kupersmidt, J. B., Coie, J. D., & Dodge, K. A. (1990). The role of poor peer relationships in the development of disorder. In S. R. Asher & J. D. Coie (Eds.), *Peer rejection in childhood* (pp. 274–305). New York: Cambridge University Press.

Kusche, C. A., & Greenberg, M. T. (1994). *The PATHS curriculum.* Seattle, WA: Developmental Research and Programs.

Ladd, G. W., & Mize, J. (1983). A cognitive-social learning model of social-skill training. *Psychological Review, 90*, 127–157.

Larson, J. (1998). Managing student aggression in high schools: Implications for practice. *Psychology in the Schools, 35*, 283–295.

LeCroy, C. W. (Ed.). (1994). *Handbook of child and adolescent treatment manuals.* New York : Lexington Books.

Lewis, M., & Miller, S. M. (Eds.). (1990). *Handbook of developmental psychopathology.* New York: Plenum.

Lewis-Snyder, G., Stoiber, K. C., & Kratochwill, T. R. (2002). Evidence-based interventions in school psychology. An illustration of task force coding criteria using group-based research design. *School Psychology Quarterly, 17*, pp. 423–465.

Loeber, R., Farrington, D. P., & Waschbusch, D. A. (1998). Serious and violent juvenile offenders. In R. Loeber & D. P. Farrington (Eds.), *Serious & violent juvenile offenders: Risk factors and successful interventions* (pp. 13–29). Thousand Oaks, CA: Sage.

Mathur, S. R., Kavale, K. A., Quinn, M. M., Forness, S. R., & Rutherford, R. B. (1998). Social skills interventions with students with emotional and behavioral problems: A quantitative synthesis of single-subject research. *Behavioral Disorders, 23*, 193–201.

McMahon, R. J., Slough, N., & Conduct Problems Prevention Research Group. (1996). Family-based intervention in the Fast Track program. In R. D. Peters & R. J. McMahon (Eds.), *Preventing childhood disorders, substance abuse, and delinquency* (pp. 99–110). Thousand Oaks, CA: Sage.

Medway, F. J. (1979). How effective is school consultation: A review of recent research. *Journal of School Psychology, 17*, 275–282.

Merrell, K. W., & Gimpel, G. A. (1998). *Social skills of children and adolescents: Conceptualization, assessment, treatment.* Mahwah, NJ: Lawrence Erlbaum Associates.

Miller, G. E., Brehm, K., & Whitehouse, S. (1998). Reconceptualizing school-based prevention for antisocial behavior within a resiliency framework. *School Psychology Review, 27*, 364–379.

Minke, K. M., & Bear, G. C. (Eds.). (2000). *Preventing school problems—promoting school success.* Bethesda, MD: NASP.

Nastasi, B. (2000). School psychologists as health-care providers in the 21st century: Conceptual framework, professional identity, and professional practice. *School Psychology Review, 29*, 540–554.

Nathan, P. E., & Gorman, J. M. (Eds.). (1998). *A guide to treatments that work.* New York: Oxford University Press.

Olweus, D. (1999). *Bully prevention program.* Boulder, CO: Institute of Behavioral Science.

Paine-Andrews, A., Vincent, M. L., Fawcett, S. B., Campuzano, M. K., Harris, K. J., Lewis, R. K., Williams, E. L., & Fisher, J. L. (1996). Replicating a community initiative for preventing adolescent pregnancy: From South Carolina to Kansas. *Family and Community Health, 19*, 14–30.

Parker, J. G., & Asher, S. R. (1993). Friendship and friendship quality in middle childhood: Links with peer group acceptance and feelings of loneliness and social dissatisfaction. *Developmental Psychology, 29*, 611–621.

Rathvon, N. (1999). *Effective school interventions: Strategies for enhancing academic achievement and social competence.* New York: Guilford.

Reynolds, W. M., & Coates, K. I. (1986). A comparison of cognitive-behavioral therapy and relaxation training for the treatment of depression in adolescents. *Journal of Consulting and Clinical Psychology, 54*, 653–660.

Reynolds, W. M., & Johnston, H. F. (Eds.). (1994). *Handbook of depression in children and adolescents.* New York: Plenum.

Robinson, W. L., Watkins-Ferrell, P., Davis-Scott, P., & Ruch-Ross, H. S. (1993). Preventing teenage pregnancy. In D. S. Glenwick & L. A. Jason (Eds.), *Promoting health and mental health in children, youth, and families* (pp. 99–124). New York: Springer.

Rogers, C. R. (1972). The process of the basic encounter group. In R. C. Diedrich & H. A. Dye (Eds.). *Group procedures* (pp. 185–211). Boston: Houghton-Mifflin.

Rose, S. D., & Edelson, J. L. (1987). *Working with children and adolescents in groups.* San Francisco: Jossey-Bass.

Rosenbaum, D. P., & Hanson, G. S. (1998). Assessing the effects of school-based drug education: A six-year multilevel analysis of Project D.A.R.E. *Journal of Research in Crime & Delinquency, 35*, 381–412.

Sarason, S. B. (1982). *The culture of the school and the problem of change.* Boston: Allyn and Bacon.

Schechtman, Z., Gilat, I., Fos, L., & Flasher, A. (1996). Brief group therapy with low-achieving elementary school children. *Journal of Counseling Psychology, 43*, 376–382.

Schiffer, M. (1984). *Children's group therapy.* New York: Free Press.

Semrud-Clikeman, M. (1995). *Child and adolescent therapy.* New York: Allyn & Bacon.

Shapiro, E. S., & Cole, C. L. (1994). *Behavior change in the classroom: Self-management interventions.* New York: Guilford.

Shapiro, E. S., & Kratochwill, T. R. (Eds.). (2000). *Conducting school-based assessments of child and adolescent behavior.* New York: Guilford.

Sheridan, S. M. (1997). Conceptual and empirical bases of conjoint behavioral consultation. *School Psychology Quarterly, 12*, 119–133.

Sheridan, S. M., Kratochwill, T. R., & Bergan, J. R. (1996). *Conjoint behavioral consultation: A procedural manual.* New York: Plenum.

Shure, M. B. (1992). *I can problem solve: An interpersonal cognitive problem-solving program: Intermediate elementary grades.* Champaign, IL: Research Press.

Siepker, B. B., & Kandaras, C. S. (1985). *Group therapy with children and adolescents.* New York: Human Sciences Press.

Soldz, S., & McCullough, L. (Eds.). (2000). *Reconciling empirical knowledge and clinical experience: The art and science of psychotherapy.* Washington, D.C.: American Psychological Association.

Spirito, A. (Ed.). (1999). Empirically supported treatments in pediatric psychology. *Journal of Pediatric Psychology, 24*, 87–174.

Stark, K. D. (1990). *The treatment of depression during childhood: A school-based program.* New York: Guilford.

Stark, K. D., & Kendall, P. C. (1996). *Treating depressed children: Therapist manual for "Action."* Ardmore, PA: Workbook Publishing.

Stark, K. D., Reynolds, W. M., & Kaslow, N. J. (1987). A comparison of the relative efficacy of self-control therapy and a behavioral problem-solving therapy for depression in children. *Journal of Abnormal Child Psychology, 15*, 91–113.

Stark, K. D., Swearer, S., Sommer, D., Hickey, B. B., Napolitano, S., Kurowski, C., Dempsey, M. (1998). School-based group treatment for depressive disorders in children. In K. C. Stoiber & T. R. Kratochwill (Eds.), *Handbook of group intervention for children and families* (pp. 68–99). New York: Allyn & Bacon.

St. Lawrence, J. S., Brasfield, T. L., Jefferson, K. W., Alleyne, E., O'Bannon, R. E., & Shirley, A. (1995). Cognitive-behavioral intervention to reduce African American adolescents' risk for HIV infection. *Journal of Consulting and Clinical Psychology, 63*, 221–237.

Stoiber, K. C. (2002). Revisiting efforts on constructing a knowledge base of evidence based intervention within school psychology. *School Psychology Quarterly, 17.*

Stoiber, K. C., Anderson, A. J., & Schowalter, D. S. (1998). Group prevention and intervention with pregnant and parenting adolescents. In K. C. Stoiber & T. R. Kratochwill (Eds.), *Handbook of group intervention for children and families* (pp. 280–306). Boston: Allyn & Bacon.

Stoiber, K. C., & Good, B. (1998). Risk and resilience factors linked to problem behavior among urban, culturally diverse adolescents. *School Psychology Review, 27*, 380–397.

Stoiber, K. C., Hughes, B., & Young, K. (August, 2000). *The effects of a resiliency-focused prevention program on urban middle school students' risk-taking behavior.* Paper presented at the annual meeting of the American Psychological Association, Boston, MA.

Stoiber, K. C., & Kratochwill, T. R. (Eds.). (1998). *Handbook of group intervention for children and families.* Boston: Allyn & Bacon.

Stoiber, K. C., & Kratochwill, T. R. (2000). Empirically supported interventions in schools: Conceptual and methodological issues—Part I. *School Psychology Quarterly, 15*, 75–105.

Stoiber, K. C., & Kratochwill, T. R. (2002a). *Outcomes: Planning, monitoring, evaluating.* San Antonio: Psychological Corporation.

Stoiber, K. C., & Kratochwill, T. R. (2002b). Evidence-based interventions in school psychology: Conceptual foundations of the procedural and coding manual of Division 16 and the Society for the Study of School Psychology Task Force. *School Psychology Quarterly, 17*, pp. 341–389.

Stoiber, K. C., & Kratochwill, T. R. (in press). *Functional assessment and intervention system.* San Antonio: Psychological Corporation.

Sussman, S., Dent, C. W., Stacy, A. W., & Sun, P. (1993). Project towards no tobacco use: 1-year behavior outcomes. *American Journal of Public Health, 83*, 1245–1250.

Waas, G. A., & Anderson, G. P. (1991). Outcome expectancy and treatment acceptability: Perceptions of school-based interventions. *Professional Psychology: Research & Practice, 22*, 149–154.

Waas, G. A., & Graczyk, P. A. (1998). Group interventions for the peer-rejected child. In K. C. Stoiber & T. R. Kratochwill (Eds.), *Handbook of group intervention for children and families* (pp. 141–158). New York: Allyn & Bacon.

Wallach, M. A., & Wallach, L. (1976). *Teaching all children to read.* Chicago: University of Chicago Press.

Wasik, B. H., Bryant, D. M., & Lyons, C. M. (1990). *Home-visiting: Procedures for helping families.* Newbury Park, CA: Sage.

Webster-Stratton, C. (1989). *The parents and children series.* Eugene, OR: Castalia.

Yalom, I. D. (1995). *The theory and practice of group psychotherapy* (4th ed.). New York: Basic Books.

Yu, P., Harris, G. E., Solovitz, B. L., Franklin, J. L. (1986). A social problem-solving intervention for children at high risk for later psychopathology. *Journal of Clinical Child Psychology, 15*, 30–40.

Zins, J. E., Elias, M. J., Greenberg, M. T., & Pruett, M. K. (2000). Promoting quality implementation in prevention programs. *Journal of Educational and Psychological Consultation, 11*, 173–174.

30

Pharmacological Approaches

George J. DuPaul
Jennifer M. Coniglio
Michelle R. Nebrig
Lehigh University

INTRODUCTION

Children and adolescents can experience a variety of health difficulties that may warrant treatment. Approximately 21% of children and adolescents in the United States are diagnosable with one or more psychiatric disorders (Shaffer et al., 1996). Similarly, between 10–15% of children are afflicted with chronic illnesses or other health conditions at some point in their development (Tarnowski & Brown, 2000). One of the most common methods for treating these physical and mental health conditions is pharmacotherapy. Psychotropic medications are increasingly prescribed to treat behavior and emotional disorders in children (Brown & Sawyer, 1998). Furthermore, the effectiveness of medication has been studied widely for the treatment of a variety of disorders. For example, the most widely studied treatment for attention deficit hyperactivity disorder (ADHD) is a stimulant medication, methylphenidate (Barkley, 1998).

Given the popularity of pharmacotherapy in treating childhood disorders, it is important for professionals working in or with the schools to be cognizant of medication effects on school performance. Children and adolescents in the United States spend a significant percentage of their time (i.e., at least 6 hr per day) in school settings. Medications, particularly those with psychotropic properties, can have a significant impact on key areas of functioning, such as cognitive, affective, social, and academic behaviors. Thus, school-based personnel and consultants to the schools should be involved in assessing pharmacotherapeutic outcomes. The school is an ideal setting for assessing medication effects, because multiple sources of information are available, including teachers, peers, and the children themselves, as well as archival data (e.g., performance on academic tasks and tests).

A variety of medications have been used to treat childhood health disorders. Some of the major classes of medications, the illnesses they treat, and their cognitive/behavioral effects are

TABLE 30.1
Pharmacotherapeutic Effects on Childhood Disorders

Class of Medication	*Disorders Treated*	*Possible Cognitive and/or Behavioral Effects*
Anabolic hormones (insulin)	Insulin-dependent diabetes mellitus	Direct effects unknown
Analgesics (opioid and nonopioid)	Headache, minor injuries, juvenile rheumatoid arthritis, and severe pain	Mood changes, sedation, concentration difficulties (opioid analgesics)
Antidiuretics (desmopressin)	Nocturnal enuresis	None known
Antineoplastics and biological agents	Cancer	Fatigue; possible long-term effects on attention, language skills, and academic achievement
Bronchodilators and nonbronchodilators	Asthma and allergic disorders	Generally, no adverse effects; however, corticosteroids may be associated with depressive symptoms, anxiety, and memory deficits (at high doses and when administered orally)
Antiepileptics	Seizure disorders	Possible effects on visual-motor functioning and memory
Antidepressants	ADHD, enuresis	Sedation
Antipsychotics	Schizophrenia, aggressive behavior	Sedation; possible cognitive impairment at higher doses
CNS Stimulants	ADHD	Positive effects on attention, impulse control, and, possibly, academic productivity

ADHD = attention deficit hyperactivity disorder; CNS = central nervous system.

listed in Table 30.1. Not surprisingly, psychotropic medications used to manage emotional and behavioral disorders have significant effects on behavioral, academic, and cognitive functioning. It is important to note, however, that some medications (e.g., antineoplastics) prescribed to ameliorate symptoms of physical illnesses can have unintended adverse effects on school performance and child behavior. Examples of the potential effects of medication on child functioning are provided later in the chapter.

The purpose of this chapter is to help mental health and educational professionals understand the possible effects of pharmacotherapy on school functioning and to promote the use of reliable, valid, and practical methods for monitoring medication effects in school settings. Pharmacological effects on key domains of functioning (e.g., cognitive abilities) that are important to school success are reviewed. Methods that could be used for school-based medication monitoring will be described. Important logistical issues that need to be considered in implementing medication evaluations in the schools also will be discussed. A case study will be used to exemplify critical aspects of school-based medication assessment. It is beyond the purview of this chapter to provide a comprehensive review of medications used to treat child disorders, and readers are referred to more comprehensive texts for this purpose (e.g., Phelps, Brown, & Power, 2002; Werry & Aman, 1999).

PHARMACOLOGICAL EFFECTS ON SELECTED DOMAINS OF FUNCTIONING

This section will cover the major classes of medication related to common childhood illnesses and disorders (see Table 30.1). Where available, relevant literature concerning domains of functioning pertinent to school performance for each class of medication will be covered. These domains include cognitive, academic, behavioral and attention, mood and emotions, social competence, and physiological effects (i.e., target symptoms and adverse effects).

Anabolic Hormones

Insulin is a major anabolic hormone that regulates use and storage of nutrient fuels in the body. A deficiency of insulin leads to diabetes mellitus, requiring insulin therapy to supplement the body's natural supply (Hirsch, 1998). There is a dearth of research attesting to the direct effects of insulin therapy on children's cognition, although there are a number of complications associated with high (hyperglycemia) and low (hypoglycemia) insulin levels, all of which can affect body systems, such as the central nervous system (CNS) in young children (Rovet & Fernandez, 1999). In adults, diabetes has been shown to have both transient and permanent effects on the brain, and these are associated with a variety of neuropsychological sequelae (Holmes, 1990). Therefore, constant monitoring of insulin levels in children is important not only for its impact on metabolism, but also to prevent any neuropsychological damage.

Analgesics

Analgesics include a number of pharmacological agents used in the management of pediatric pain resulting from surgery, burns, or illness-related pain from, for example, vaso-occlusive episodes in sickle cell disease. Nonopioid (nonnarcotic) analgesics refer to the most commonly used substances like acetaminophen to reduce pain associated with headache, otitis media, or minor injuries. In contrast, nonsteroidal anti-inflammatory medications are used to relieve pain associated with inflammation (i.e., juvenile rheumatoid arthritis) and include acetylsalicylic acid (aspirin), ibuprofen, and tolmetin (Robieux, 1993). Frequent side effects include stomach upset, while long-term use is associated with potential damage to the kidneys and stomach lining; however, no research indicates adverse effects on other domains of functioning.

Finally, opiod (narcotic) analgesics are used for the management of severe pain and include meperidine (Demerol), nalbuphine (Nubain), morphine, hydromorphone, acetaminophen with codeine, methadone, and buprenorphine. These agents bind to opiate receptors located in the CNS and medulla to reduce pain, and have been associated with acute adverse physiological effects, such as constipation, urinary retention, nausea/vomiting, lethargy, and respiratory depression (Cole, Sprinkle, Smith, & Buchanan, 1986). Changes in mood, such as dysphoria or euphoria, have also been noted. Medications like morphine, meperidine, and codeine also have been associated with sedation, difficulties in concentration, and *mental clouding* in children (Yaster & Deshpande, 1988). However, current and previous reviews of the literature have been unable to locate studies of any additional cognitive effects of these medications (Handler & DuPaul, 1999), and long-term effects of the medication with children are unknown (DuPaul & Kyle, 1995).

Antidiuretics

The etiology of enuresis has been associated with a variety of psychosocial and biological factors; but, recently, researchers have proposed that nocturnal enuresis is the result of decreased production of the antidiuretic hormone at night resulting in overproduction of urine

(Moffatt, 1997). Therefore, a vasopressin analogue known as desmopressin acetate (DDVAP) has been introduced as a treatment to decrease the volume of urine produced. Adverse effects of DDVAP are minimal, and its safety has been established in patients requiring long-term therapy (Spencer, Wilens, & Biederman, 1995).

Antineoplastics and Biological Agents

Pharmacological treatment of cancer in children includes a combination of antineoplastic medications (i.e., alkylating agents, intercalating agents, mitotic inhibitors and plant alkaloids, antimetabolites, and enzymes) and biological agents (i.e., interferons, interleukins, and various growth factors; Chan & Erlichman, 1993). The goal of these chemotherapies is to eliminate cancer cells; but, intratreal in the process, they also lower blood cell counts. This often leaves children fatigued, and this may deleteriously affect school performance (Armstrong & Horn, 1995).

The effects of chemotherapy in children must be monitored to assess possible learning difficulties, especially over the course of several years. Handler and DuPaul (1999) compiled the latest research on systemic or intratrecal chemotherapy on children's cognitive and academic abilities and found mixed results. Chemotherapy appears to impair the mental abilities and academic achievement in children less than 4 years old, but may not affect these functions postdiagnosis in children older than 4 years (Brown et al., 1992, 1993, 1996). However, results from longitudinal studies suggest that the effects of chemotherapy on attention, language skills (Brown et al., 1992), memory (Mulhern et al., 1988), and verbal and nonverbal mental abilities (Brown et al., 1998), as well as on arithmetic (Brown et al., 1992), reading, and spelling achievement (Brown et al., 1996), may become evident several years after treatment has terminated.

Bronchodilators/Nonbronchodilators, Including Antihistamines

Effective medications for the management of asthma include various bronchodilator antiasthma agents (i.e., β-adrenergic agonists, theophylline, and anticholinergics) and nonbronchodilator antiasthma medications (i.e., cromolyn sodium and corticosteriods). Furthermore, asthma and allergies are often treated through the use of antihistamines. For the most part, the effects of these medications cause minor changes in cognition that have little impact on children's learning (Bender, 1999).

β-adrenergic agonists include albuterol (trade names: Alupent, Proventil, and Ventolin), metaproterenol, and tolterol and provide quick relief of asthma symptoms by acting directly on the bronchial muscles to open narrowed airways (Bender, 1999). One effect of these medications is increased skeletal muscle tremor and pulse rate (Lonnerholm, Foucard, & Lindstrom, 1984). Although fine motor tremors of short-term duration have been documented in other studies, there have been no adverse effects on general motor performance, including tests of response speed, visual-motor control, and speed and dexterity; nor have these medications had adverse effects on complex perceptual-motor tasks, verbal learning and memory, visual memory, mental speed and efficiency, or sustained attention (e.g., Mazer, Figueroa-Rosario, & Bender, 1990).

Two other types of bronchodilator medications include anticholinergics (i.e., atropine sulfate and ipratropium bromide) that relax smooth muscles in the respiratory tract and theophylline that acts as a CNS stimulant to reduce bronchial hyperresponsiveness. Studies conducted to determine the adverse effects of anticholinergics in children could not be located. In contrast, several studies exist regarding the effects of theophylline in children. Although there is evidence for individual differences in measures of attention among children receiving theophylline, in general, research does not indicate that this medication has any adverse effects on cognition or behavior, verbal memory, or on standardized achievement tests of reading and mathematics (Bender, 1999).

Nonbronchodilators include corticosteroids (prednisone, cortisol, beclomethasone dipropionate, and methylprednisolone; trade names: Beclovent, Vanceril, Azmacort, and Flovent), which are anti-inflammatory agents that prevent and/or inhibit inflammation of airways, and cromolyn sodium that also acts an anti-inflammatory agent by reducing the airway and pulmonary response to irritant stimuli (i.e., specific pollen, food, cold air, or exercise; Celano & Geller, 1993). Prednisone has been associated with decreases in verbal and visual memory 8 hr after administration, but effects seem to dissipate within 48 hr (Bender, Lerner, & Polland, 1991). Children receiving high doses, compared with low doses of prednisone, also reported significantly more depressive symptoms and anxiety; but no dose-related changes emerged on measures of attention, overactivity, impulsivity, or motor control (Bender, 1999). Alternatively, cromolyn sodium (trade name Intal) is known to be a particularly safe medication with few physical or behavioral adverse effects (Bender, 1999).

Antihistamines are used to treat symptoms of chronic cough and rhinitis in children with and without asthma. Shanon et al. (1993) found no adverse effects on laboratory tests of attention or visual memory for children receiving allergy medications, nor have adverse effects been found on reading comprehension (McLoughlin, Nall, & Berla, 1990). In general, however, there is remarkably little research on traditional or nonsedating antihistamines (Bender, 1999).

Antiepileptics

Antiepileptic drugs (AEDs), sometimes referred to as anticonvulsants, are used in the management of seizure disorders in children and adolescents. The most common AEDs include sodium valproate (or valproic acid), carbamazepine (CBZ), phenytoin (PHT), and phenobarbital, which is actually a type of barbiturate. Studies of newer drugs are also underway. For example, clobazam is a benzodiazepine that has been found as effective as standard monotherapy with CBZ or PHT in the management of seizure disorders in children (Canadian Study Group for Childhood Epilepsy, 1999).

Despite numerous studies, the relationship between AEDs and children's functioning has not been fully elucidated for two reasons. First, AED studies have been plagued by methodological problems, such as lack of double-blind protocols and premature conclusions drawn from improper statistical analyses (Vermeulen & Aldenkamp, 1995). Second, it is difficult to discern whether effects on cognitive and behavioral functioning are the result of seizure type, underlying neurological etiology, or the effects of the type and dosage of the AEDs (Mandelbaum & Burack, 1997). In general, however, monotherapy (one medication) is superior to polytherapy (several medications), and adverse effects of drugs are normalized when drug serum levels are sufficiently controlled and when prescribed within the assumed therapeutic range (Vining, Carpenter, & Aman, 1999).

Although there is a paucity of well-controlled studies, valproate is labeled by some as a preferred drug in managing common childhood seizure disorders (Legarda, Booth, Fennell, & Maria, 1996). Valproic acid has shown either no change or improvement on intelligence as measured by the Wechsler Intelligence Scale for Children Full-Scale IQ, performance IQ, and verbal IQ (Chen, Kang, & So, 1996). Furthermore, Mandelbaum and Burack (1997) found that children taking valproic acid had higher cognitive composite scores after 12 months than subjects on either carbomazepine or ethosuximide. Aman, Werry, Paxton, and Turbott (1987) found that valproic acid had adverse effects on simple psychomotor tasks, but no adverse effects of valproic acid were found on the Bender Gestalt visual-motor test (Chen et al., 1996). With regard to behavior, Berg, Butler, Ellis, and Foster (1993) found that children receiving valproic acid demonstrated minor behavior difficulties at 1 month, but these effects did not persist. Stores, Williams, Styles, and Zaiwalla (1992) reported some decrease in attention and concentration in 63 children with epilepsy treated with valproic acid.

Like valproic acid, the use of carbomazepine (Tegretol) is associated with no change in intelligence (Chen et al., 1996), but adverse effects have been reported on simple psychomotor tasks (MacPhee, McPhail, Butler, & Brodie, 1986). Berg et al. (1993) found minor behavioral difficulties associated with carbomazepine did not persist after 1 month, but other studies have found adverse effects in children treated with carbomazepine, including emotional lability, overactivity, insomnia, drowsiness, and agitation (Herranz, Armijo, & Arteaga, 1988).

Cognitive effects of phenytoin (Dilantin) include deficits in visual-motor functioning, attention, and problem solving (Trimble, 1990). Phenytoin can also be associated with lethargy and emotional lability (Herranz et al., 1988).

Possible cognitive effects of phenobarbital, which increase with dose, include either no change (Chen et al., 1996) or decreased performance (Farwell et al., 1990) on intelligence tests, impaired memory (Camfield et al., 1979), and increased auditory evoked potentials (Chen et al., 1996). Riva and Devoti (1996) found that discontinuation of phenobarbital leads to significant improvement in some tests of performance, memory, and attention. Adverse behavioral effects of phenobarbital include irritability, hyperactivity, emotional lability, oppositional behavior, dysthymic symptoms, and lethargy (Camfield et al., 1979; Herranz et al., 1988). Preliminary studies have indicated that phenobarbital can impair long-term reading achievement if given to toddlers with febrile seizures (Sulzbacher, Farwell, Temkin, Lu, & Hirtz, 1999).

Antidepressants

Antidepressants can be divided into several classes, including tricyclics (tricyclic antidepressants [TCAs]), selective serotonin reuptake inhibitors (SSRIs), monoamine oxidase inhibitors (MAOIs), and atypical antidepressants. Because an MAOI can have severe adverse effects, its use is not widely advocated with children, and therefore will not be covered here.

The tricyclics include amitriptyline (Elavil), nortriptyline (Pamelor), imipramine (Tofranil), desipramine (Norpramin), and clomipramine (Anafranil). Although tricyclics are primarily used to ameliorate the symptoms of depression, they have been used to treat ADHD (Biederman, 1998), enuresis (Moffatt, 1997), and as adjunctive treatments in pain management (Rogers, 1989).

A meta-analysis of all available placebo-controlled trials of TCAs in depressed youth (Hazell, O'Connell, Heathcote, Robertson, & Henry, 1995) and a recent review of the TCA literature (Ambrosini, 2000) both concluded that the difference between active treatment and placebo is too small in pediatric populations to be clinically significant. Results of published studies consistently indicate that TCAs are not efficacious in treating children or adolescents with major depressive disorder. The use of TCAs with anxiety disorders does not lead to significant improvement for most children and adolescents (for review, see Birmaher, Yelovich, & Renaud, 1998). Alternatively, placebo-controlled studies of TCAs as a treatment for ADHD have been consistently positive, with most children exhibiting symptomatic improvement (Spencer, Biederman, & Wilens, 1998). A common adverse effect of TCAs is sedation, which may impede a child's overall function at school (Brown & Sawyer, 1998); but, overall, there is a paucity of data on the cognitive and learning effects of these medications. One exception is a study by Aman (1980) that concluded TCAs neither impaired nor improved the functioning on laboratory tests of short-term memory or cognitive functioning.

The SSRIs include fluoxetine (Prozac), paroxetine (Paxil), sertraline (Zoloft), and fluvoxamine (Luvox). Like TCAs, the literature on SSRIs includes minimal, double-blind, placebo-controlled studies of the medication effects in children and adolescents. Of the two fluoxetine

(Prozac) studies in youth with depression, only Emslie et al. (1997) found those receiving fluoxetine compared with placebo were *much* or *very much* improved on weekly clinician ratings of treatment. In contrast, although Simeon, Dinicola, Ferguson, and Copping (1990) found a significant improvement by 3 weeks of treatment, response to fluoxetine was not superior to placebo. A third double-blind, placebo-controlled study of the response of youth with depression used an SSRI-like medication called venlafaxine (Effexor). Although the venlafaxine + therapy group showed a significant improvement over time based on self-report and parent report, the response was not superior to the placebo + therapy group (Mandoki, Tapia, Tapia, Sumner, & Parker, 1997).

SSRIs have also been studied in the treatment of anxiety disorders and externalizing behavior disorders in children and adolescents (Biederman, 1998; Birmaher et al., 1998). Fluoxetine has been suggested as a treatment to reduce the symptoms of obsessive-compulsive disorder in preadolescents (see, e.g., Geller, Biederman, Reed, Spencer, & Wilens, 1995), and also seems to reduce symptoms associated with selective mutism and social phobia (Black & Udhe, 1994), as well as ADHD (Spencer et al., 1998). However, further research is needed because Geller et al. (1995) have reported motoric activity, anxiety, agitation, insomnia, lethargy, and decreased appetite resulting from SSRI use.

Atypical antidepressants, such as bupropion (Wellbutrin), have been shown to reduce the symptoms of ADHD (Barrickman et al., 1995), to improve memory performance (Clay, Gualtieri, Evans, & Gullion, 1988), and to increase attention to classroom tasks (Nebrig, DuPaul, & Showalter, 2001) in children with ADHD. However, adverse effects—including agitation, confusion, irritability, and decreased seizure threshold (Dager & Herich, 1990)—are associated with bupropion, warranting further research to establish its safety and utility.

Antipsychotics/Neuroleptics

Antipsychotic medications, such as haloperidol (Haldol), clozapine (Clozaril), thioridazine (Mellaril), chlorpromazine (Thorazine), and molindone (Moban), have been used in the management of childhood psychoses (including childhood schizophrenia) and in managing aggressive behavior in children. Several studies have documented the efficacy of antipsychotic agents in suppressing the aggressive behavior of individuals, including children and adolescents with mental retardation, autism, overactivity, and conduct disorders (for review, see Campbell & Cueva, 1995a,b). In addition, antipsychotic drugs have been demonstrated effective in reducing behaviors, such as social withdrawal, overactivity, stereotypies, and fidgetiness associated with autism (Poling, Gadow, & Cleary, 1991).

Antipsychotic medications are frequently utilized to reduce children's symptoms of Tourette's disorder (e.g., Shapiro, Shapiro, Young, & Feinberg, 1988). Despite the positive effects of antipsychotics in these areas, they do have troublesome adverse side effects. Sedation is a frequent side effect that may cause impairments in social relationships in addition to learning problems (Whitaker & Rao, 1992). Although the results of early studies of the effects of antipsychotics on cognition are somewhat equivocal, it appears that the adverse side effects on cognition and behavior are dose related, with higher doses impairing learning and school performance (Brown & Sawyer, 1998).

Stimulants

CNS stimulants are frequently used in the management of ADHD and conduct disorder. Stimulants include methylpenidate (Ritalin, Concerta, and Metadate), dextroamphetamine (Dexedrine), dextroamphetamine sacharate/sulfate (Adderall), and pemoline (Cylert). Methylphenidate is the most commonly used stimulant medication (Barkley, 1998).

Stimulants can result in the temporary improvement of several domains of functioning. Research demonstrates that stimulants enhance children's performance on laboratory tasks of cognitive functioning, such as paired associate learning, short- and long-term recall, picture recognition, and stimulus identification. Furthermore, stimulants show salutary effects on tasks that require vigilance and sustained attention, and improvement has been documented on tasks related to inhibitory control, and perceptual and motoric functioning (for reviews, see Barkley, DuPaul, & Connor, 1999; Brown & Sawyer, 1998; Rapport & Kelly, 1991). A few studies have indicated that these improvements persist over the long-term (Aggarwal & Lillystone, 2000). There is also some limited evidence that stimulants enhance higher order cognitive functioning, such as phonological word processing (Malone, Kershner, & Seigel, 1988), receptive language capacity, and auditory processing skills (Keith & Engineer, 1991).

Perusal of the academic achievement literature indicates that stimulant medications seem to exert their primary effects on academic efficiency (i.e., increased amount and accuracy of work) rather than on achievement, as measured by standardized achievement tests (Brown & Borden, 1989; Brown & Sawyer, 1998). Researchers have found that methylphenidate results in enhanced academic efficiency (Rapport & Kelly, 1991), increased problem-solving attempts on reading and math tasks (Elia, Welsh, Gullotta, & Rapoport, 1993), and greater percentage of correct answers on a reading task (Elia et al., 1993). Dextroamphetamine has been associated with increased problem-solving attempts on reading and math tasks, but it also has resulted in an increased percentage of correct answers on both reading and math tasks (Elia et al., 1993). Finally, parents and teachers report that children receiving stimulants show a marked improvement in their school work (Rapport, Denney, DuPaul, & Gardner, 1994).

Stimulants also exert beneficial influences on children's behavioral self-regulation, compliance with adult commands, and ability to modulate motor behavior in structured settings (DuPaul, Barkley, & Connor, 1998). Data suggest that children's behavior when receiving stimulants can be normalized to that of their peers (Rapport et al., 1994). Stimulants also have been associated with reduced nonphysical, physical, and verbal aggression in the classroom (Brown & Sawyer, 1998).

Adverse effects of stimulants have been documented, including eating and sleeping difficulties. Less frequently, some children may develop tics or have an increase in tics, particularly when there is a positive family history for tic disorders (DuPaul, Barkley, & Connor, 1998). Therefore, regular monitoring of salutary and adverse medication effects is recommended. Rapport et al. (1994) have identified that improvement in behavior, academic efficiency, and attention is idiosyncratic and dose-dependent. Therefore, dosage is an important determinant of a stimulant's effect on children's functioning. At overly high doses, adverse effects on cognition (e.g., overfocused behavior) and attribution are possible (Brown & Sawyer, 1998).

MEASURING PHARMACOLOGICAL EFFECTS ON SCHOOL PERFORMANCE

In addition to cognitive and academic effects, thorough evaluation of medication outcomes should include behavior rating scales and direct observation to enhance the utility and validity of conclusions based on clinic measures alone (DuPaul & Kyle, 1995; Rapport, Chung, Shore, Denney, & Isaacs, 2000). For this reason, clinicians are encouraged to develop monitoring protocols designed to address the specific needs of a child across a number of domains. Thus, we will briefly review measures and procedures as a function of the domain(s) purportedly affected by medication as reported in the literature. Additional sources (e.g., Aman & Pearson, 1999; Brown & Sawyer, 1998; Shapiro & Kratochwill, 2000) offer extensive reviews of these and other instruments that may be useful in medication evaluations.

Cognition and Memory

Clinic-based evaluations of a child's medication response may include annual assessment of cognitive functioning, including standardized ability tests, such as the Wechsler scales of intellectual ability (e.g., Wechsler, 1991) or screeners of cognitive ability (e.g., Peabody Picture Vocabulary Test; Dunn & Dunn 1981). Intellectual ability tests have been widely used to monitor the long-term effects of medication in children (see review by Handler & DuPaul, 1999). Most of these standardized assessments may not be administered within 1 year of a previous administration, and therefore do not lend themselves to the more frequent assessment of medication effects or for consideration of dose changes.

Given the administration limitations of these instruments, more dynamic screenings of cognitive ability are desirable and could be administered on a more frequent basis in school settings (Hyman et al., 1998). None of these screening measures can serve as a comprehensive cognitive assessment, but may reflect components of an individual's idiosyncratic response to medication over shorter trial periods, including effects on attention and concentration. Such tasks could include measures of auditory memory, such as percentage retention of a list of words read, and a modified digit recall task (with new numbers each week; Hyman et al., 1998).

Academic Performance

Standardized achievement tests (e.g., Woodcock Johnson Test of Academic Achievement-Revised; Woodcock & Johnson, 1990) have been utilized to assess long-term medication effects in children, but many studies have concluded that frequently used medications have no effect on these measures (Brown & Sawyer, 1998). Like standardized cognitive ability assessments, the need for short-term assessment of changes and lengthy time required for standardized achievement tests to detect changes make the use of these instruments inefficient (Brown & Sawyer, 1998). In addition, norm-referenced measures are not necessarily a reflection of children's progress in their classroom curriculum (Shapiro, 1996).

To combat the potential pitfalls of standardized tests for academic monitoring, curriculum-based assessments have been recommended and provide greater ecological validity (Brown & Sawyer, 1998; Handler & DuPaul, 1999) and ease of integration within the school. Curriculum-based assessments comprise a variety of methodologies and directly assesses specific academic subskills or general skills through standardized procedures (for a review, see Shapiro, 1996). These assessments are not norm-referenced, but typically come directly from the child's curriculum and are usually derived from short, timed samples of performance that can be compared across administrations (Shapiro, 1996). Thus, a child's performance is evaluated over time rather than against a normative reference group. In addition to strict curriculum-based assessment, proportion completed and percentage accuracy of independent seat-work have been used to measure school-relevant medication effects (e.g., Rapport et al., 2000). An indirect means by which to monitor the effects of medication on academic success is via informant report (e.g., Academic Performance Rating Scale; DuPaul et al., 1991).

Behavior and Attention

There are a variety of measures created for completion by school personnel that offer an economical and efficient means to evaluate behavior (including infrequently occurring behaviors) over a wide range of settings and times in school (for reviews, see Aman & Pearson, 1999; Brown & Sawyer, 1998; Shapiro & Kratochwill, 1999). Many scales offer adequate normative data and sound psychometric properties, are clinically relevant, and are sensitive to the effects of pharmacological treatment (Aman & Pearson, 1999). Caveats are warranted when using any rating scales, such as leniency or severity of raters, or basing ratings on the most recent episodes of behavior, instead of the general functioning over a specified period of time. These measures are also prone to practice effects, rater error, and halo effects (Aman & Pearson 1999). Normative rating scales do not, in isolation, evaluate adaptive behavior and may not always be appropriate measures for children with a chronic illness (e.g., Perrin, Stein, & Drotar, 1991). Despite these concerns, a number of rating scales have been found in the literature to assess and monitor various medication effects.

Broad-band rating scales offer a general look at a child's global functioning as assessed by the teacher and/or parent. They may or may not tap into specific domains affected by a medication, but provide screening information in a number of areas. Broad-band scales may be limited by their length (i.e., more than 100 items) and their potential insensitivity to repeated short-term monitoring. Alternatively, these longer questionnaires may be useful for long-term monitoring of medication outcomes. Examples of broad-band questionnaires include the Teacher Report Form (Achenbach, 1991a), Child Behavior Checklist (Achenbach, 1991b), and Behavioral Assessment System for Children (Reynolds & Kamphaus, 1992).

When concerned with the primary or adverse side effects of medication on specific behaviors (e.g., attention, concentration, and motor activity), narrow-band rating scales can be used. Examples of brief, narrow-band scales include the IOWA Conners Rating Scale (Loney & Milich, 1982), ACTeRS scale (Ullmann, Sleator, & Sprague, 1997), ADHD Rating Scale-IV (DuPaul, Power, Anastopoulos, & Reid, 1998), and School Situations Questionnaire (Barkley, 1981, 1990).

Direct observation of school behavior provides an objective means by which to delineate a child's behavior (Shapiro & Kratochwill, 1999). Medication evaluations in school commonly utilize partial interval recording (instead of event, duration, latency recording, or momentary time sampling), balancing comprehensive inclusion of a variety of behavioral categories yet allowing for a representative sample of behavior over a short time. Observation coding systems that are sensitive to medication effects include the Classroom Observation Code (Abikoff & Gettelman, 1985) and Restricted Academic Task (Barkley, Fischer, Newby, & Breen, 1988). In addition, Rapport and colleagues (2000) have found that relatively simple direct observations of on- and off-task behaviors in the classroom, setting were sensitive to the effects of stimulant medication. In conjunction with other measures, academic seat-work time was observed in the child's classroom, and the percentage of intervals with on-task behavior (objectively defined) were reported as a measure of attention. This method is applicable across ages and activities.

Functional assessment has been an important addition to understanding better the effects of stimulant medication in the school setting. For example, Northup and colleagues (1995) conducted functional assessments in classrooms of children receiving methylphenidate to document its effects better in relation to classroom variables, such as teacher or peer attention conditions. Peer confederates and classroom teachers were instructed to ignore or interact with students receiving medication, and behavior was directly observed with interval recording procedures, similar to the procedures described previously. This procedure may complement information obtained through rating scales and direct observations, because it illuminates better the relative effects of medication versus environmental variables.

Social/Peer Relationships

Teacher-completed questionnaires, such as the Social Skills Rating System (Gresham & Elliott, 1990) or the School Social Behavior Scales (Merrell, 1993), consider specific behaviors and interactions related to social situations. The utility of these rating scales for assessing dose-related medication outcomes has not been examined. The Code for Observing Social Activity (Gadow, 1993) is a 15-second partial interval technique that has been utilized in medication trials to obtain information on appropriate and inappropriate social behaviors both within and outside of the classroom (e.g., the lunchroom or playground).

Mood and Emotions

Self-report scales are often used to assess changes in the internal states of children from the effects of medication and are easily administered within school and clinic settings. Scales used for this purpose include the Reynolds Children's Manifest Anxiety Scale (Reynolds & Richmonds, 1985), State-Trait Anxiety Inventory for Children, Children's Depression Inventory (Kovacs, 1992), and Reynolds Adolescent Depression Scale (Reynolds, 1987).

Physiological and Side Effects

Assessment of physiological effects across home and school settings can be optimized by using objective measures that allow for different demands and evident behaviors across environments. For example, the Stimulant Drug Side Effects Rating Scale (Barkley, 1998) offers a relatively simple means by which parents and teachers can rate the most common adverse side effects of a medication, including methylphenidate, clonidine, and Adderall. Many experts (e.g., Aman & Pearson, 1999; Hyman et al., 1998) endorse the use of customized scales. An instrument can be tailor-made to include the principal target symptoms and behaviors gained through teacher consultation; information directly from the *Physician's Desk Reference*; and relevant items from existing scales, including low-frequency but significant behaviors (Hyman et al., 1998). Improved ecological validity and a wider range of clinically significant behaviors are traded for standardization, normative data, and known psychometric properties.

Multimethod Assessment

Comprehensive evaluation of medication effects requires the use of multiple assessment methods and sources of information. For example, the American Academy of Child and Adolescent Psychiatry (1997) recommends that to best assess medication response among children with ADHD, multiple outcome measures, including information from teachers, are essential. Each of the assessment measures described previously has inherent strengths and weaknesses. For example, rating scales provide quantification of the frequency, duration, or severity of problem behaviors that can be compared with normative data. Alternatively, behavior questionnaires are limited by the subjectivity and potential biases of the person completing the measure. Thus, one of the major advantages of a multimethod assessment protocol is that a system of checks and balances is implemented, wherein the strengths of one assessment method can offset the limitations of another. Given the importance of making accurate decisions about medication response and dosage, multiple methods are particularly necessary when evaluating pharmacotherapy in children.

LOGISTICAL ISSUES IN SCHOOL-BASED MEDICATION MONITORING

Obtaining School Input

The first step in any medication monitoring process is a meeting of the important school members (e.g., teacher, nurse, principal, school counselor, and school psychologist), the pediatric psychologist, and parent to discuss confidentiality and the physician's intent to treat (Gadow &

Nolan, 1993; Gadow, Nolan, Paolicelli, & Sprafkin, 1991). During this meeting, permission to exchange information must be obtained via written parent consent, and the potential roles of team members in assisting with information collection are negotiated. Most school districts have generic forms for authorization to receive/release information that can be modified to accommodate the details of a child's specific monitoring program.

Teachers and school personnel can play an integral role in assisting families and physicians in determining children's responses to medication, especially when single subject ($n = 1$) designs are utilized (e.g., Kent, Camfield, & Camfield, 1999). Unfortunately, despite the potential wealth of information and insight offered by teachers regarding medication monitoring, teachers are rarely, if ever, invited to participate in the assessment or monitoring process. Many special education teachers have direct experience with students receiving medication, but few have direct communication with their students' physicians or any formal training in drug therapy (Jerome, Gordon, & Hustler, 1994).

Facilitating Accuracy and Accountability. As the person responsible for accurately administering medication, the school nurse plays a critical role in ensuring adherence to the medication regimen during school hours. The nurse could also be responsible for documenting any adverse side effects of medication reported by the child and/or persons observing the child (i.e., teachers and parents). Despite the important role of the school nurse in a medication evaluation, there is a shortage of these professionals available in the schools. According to Lear, Montgomery, Schlitt, and Rickett (1996), only approximately 40,000 nurses with credentials ranging from licensed practical nurses to master's-level nurse practitioners are working in the 82,000 public schools across the United States. This shortage represents a concern for medication monitoring, given that some medications (i.e., bronchodilators that must be inhaled or anabolic hormones that must be injected) must be carefully administered at precise dosages under the supervision of a trained professional with a medical background.

Facilitating teachers' continued and accurate participation in the monitoring process is of utmost importance. Teacher knowledge about treatment effectiveness is related to acceptability of behavioral interventions (e.g., Von Brock & Elliott, 1987), and acceptability is associated with treatment integrity (e.g., Ehrhardt, Barnett, Lentz, Stollar, & Reifin, 1996). Unfortunately, teacher knowledge about pharmacological treatment in children may be limited (e.g., Jerome, et al., 1994), but it is an important component in facilitating teacher participation. There is a dearth of research regarding the relationship between teacher knowledge, acceptability of pharmacological treatments, and integrity of monitoring procedures.

Preparing School Staff. Despite the underinvestigation of this area, teacher knowledge and education regarding the rationale for and process involved in monitoring medication effects are integral to accountability for data collection. School staff should be well-informed and given opportunities to ask questions about their involvement in the process, provided the information shared remains within the limits of confidentiality protecting the child. Teachers and school staff will require information regarding the realistic impact of a medication, especially when there is the potential for behavioral adverse side effects. They should also be apprised of the potential variability of medication effects, depending on setting, demands, and other factors.

School professionals need to be aware of the rationale for and practical implications of various methodologies, such as a double-blind medication trial. It is imperative that the school-based team be fully informed regarding the need for adjustment of dosage levels and how their input will affect this decision-making process. School officials may be realistically concerned about uncertainty of a child's current medication dose in a blind trial in the event of an emergency. Some medication studies have safely maintained double-blind status in the school by providing the child's current dose in a sealed envelope, which is made available to the school nurse in case of emergency (e.g., Hyman et al., 1998). Offering appropriate education to the school will facilitate communication, and help increase mutual understanding and accountability of monitoring procedures.

Data Collection

When planning a medication evaluation, psychologists must be sensitive to the demands already existing in the school, and allow for a reasonable compromise between the ideal and the practical. Because medications affect various domains differently, even at the same dose, a multifaceted approach to understand the medication's comprehensive impact is necessary (DuPaul, Barkley, & Connor, 1998). Possible measures could be presented to the school team, and expectations for data collection and timelines for communication can be agreed on.

For example, if a child is receiving medication that has known effects on the domains of attention, short-term memory, work completion, and social skills, a weekly monitoring schedule completed via school personnel could address these specific areas, as well as potential physical adverse side effects. For the case of an elementary school student, frequent, brief assessments of these areas are desired. Conversely, a middle- or high-school student may be monitored less frequently but could have additional areas of need (e.g., mood disturbance) that should be evaluated.

The team could agree on a short individualized menu of about 10–15 questions, considering isolated behaviors and potential adverse side effects, to be completed weekly by the teacher or selected teachers for middle- and high-school students. Another option would be the completion of a published rating scale of related behaviors (e.g., one of the Conners' scales) at regular intervals, offering a within-subject comparison of medication effects, as well as comparisons with normative data.

Next, the child's short-term auditory memory could be monitored through brief, weekly administrations of a modified digit span task administered by designated school staff. Through communication with the classroom teacher, a child's acquisition of reading and mathematics skills can be monitored through weekly curriculum-based assessment probes. Direct observations of classroom and social behavior could be completed by the school counselor for 10 minutes of academic time and 10 minutes of recess time twice per week utilizing one of the observation codes described previously. Finally, a standardized measure of social skills could be completed weekly by the teacher. Any anecdotal information noted by the teacher would also be encouraged. Materials for collecting these data are provided to the school team, and on agreed-upon intervals, these results are then compiled and forwarded to the psychologist.

This protocol offers a general approach to monitoring a child's medication at a single dose. A more detailed description of a school-based stimulant medication assessment protocol, for example, can be found elsewhere (e.g., Gadow & Nolan, 1993).

Presenting the Information

Medication evaluation data must be formatted in a meaningful way for use by the prescribing physician or treatment team. This presentation should include feedback from the parent or other caregivers (e.g., nurse) regarding the child's actual adherence to the prescribed treatment regimen. The presentation format may vary, ranging from raw data, to graphs or brief descriptions, or to short reports. Although they may be less familiar with single-subject ($n = 1$) designs, both physicians and parents may find this methodology extremely valuable (e.g., Kent et al., 1999). The frequency with which information is shared with the physician will dictate the schedule for contact with schools, but frequent communication (e.g., weekly) is typically preferred, particularly during initial stages of dosage titration.

CASE STUDY

Earl was a 13-year-old boy diagnosed with ADHD-Combined Type, who was referred by his parents and middle-school math teacher for a medication evaluation. Earl was experiencing difficulty sustaining attention and concentration in several of his classes, resulting in inconsistent and often inaccurate completion of classwork and homework assignments. Because he was often unable to complete the assignments in a timely manner, he received low grades. In addition, there was concern from the parents and teacher about Earl's "forgetfulness" during daily activities and of lesser concern, his inability to suppress verbal and motoric behaviors (i.e., talking in class and fidgeting). According to parent report, Earl had not responded to medication trials of either Ritalin or Adderall, and a collaborative decision was made between Earl, his parents, and his psychiatrist to evaluate Earl's response to the novel antidepressant, bupropion (trade name: Wellbutrin). A double-blind, placebo-controlled design was used across the 10-week evaluation period. A pharmacist prepared identical opaque capsules of lactose powder (placebo) or 75 mg of bupropion to be administered twice daily, depending on the week. A weekly pill count and medication-monitoring sheet (dated and signed by either the parent or school nurse) helped to ensure medication integrity.

Because of Earl's reported difficulties in math and because of the ease of collecting quantifiable data, math class was chosen as the target for data collection. At least twice weekly, a school psychologist would unobtrusively observe Earl in his classroom to determine the percentage of intervals during which Earl's behavior was considered to be on- or off-task. At the end of the observation, the observer photocopied Earl's seat-work assignment, which was later graded for the percentage of problems completed and the percentage of problems accurate. Earl's weekly grades on assignments and tests also were collected from the teacher.

To determine if the medication had any impact on overall ADHD symptomatology, the parents and math teacher completed a weekly ADHD Rating Scale-IV (DuPaul et al., 1998). Also, Earl and his parents collaboratively filled out a weekly side-effects checklist (a 10-item Likert scale based on the extent to which the common adverse side-effects of bupropion were present).

Results indicated that bupropion was effective in reducing Earl's symptoms of hyperactivity/impulsivity, as reported by both the parents and teacher on the ADHD Rating Scale-IV. Similarly, the parents noted a dramatic decrease in inattentive symptoms. Teacher ratings showed evidence of a decrease in inattentive symptoms, although these were still in the clinically significant range. Direct observation data revealed that the bupropion, compared with placebo, resulted in high levels of on-task behavior during independent seat-work assignments. There also was a concomitant increase in the number of problems Earl completed during his assignments. However, his level of accuracy did not increase, and the medication did not appear to result in increased levels of on-task behavior during teacher lecture periods. There was no significant difference in Earl's grades between bupropion and placebo phases. Finally, the side-effects checklist indicated that Earl did not experience any adverse side effects.

Provided with these data in the form of a brief written report, Earl and his parents met with the psychiatrist to determine the next course of action. All were pleased with the objective data, which showed general, albeit moderate, improvement in the areas of concern. A collaborative decision was made to increase the dosage of the medication and to continue with monthly collection of parent rating scale and adverse side-effects data to ensure maintenance of desired effects.

CONCLUSIONS

Pharmacotherapy is one of the most popular and effective methods to manage a variety of childhood physical and mental disorders. Medications can have both intended and unintended effects on several critical areas of child functioning. Because pharmacological effects can impact school performance, it is important to consider methods for assessing medication outcomes in this setting. This chapter provided a brief review of research examining medication effects on cognitive, affective, behavioral, and academic functionings. Methods to assess performance in these areas and logistical issues to consider when conducting school-based medication evaluations were delineated. It is clear that school and health professionals must work in close collaboration to optimize pharmacotherapeutic effects and to minimize any deleterious impact on children's educational, behavioral, and social functioning.

REFERENCES

Aggarwal, A., & Lillystone, D. (2000). A follow-up study of objective measures in children with attention deficit hyperactivity disorder. *Journal of Paediatric Child Health, 36*, 134–138.

Abikoff, H., & Gettelman, R. (1985). Classroom observation code: A modification of the Stony Brook Code. *Psychopharmacology Bulletin, 21*, 902–909.

Achenbach, T. M. (1991a). *Manual for the TRF and 1991 profile*. Burlington, VT: University of Vermont, Department of Psychiatry.

Achenbach, T. M. (1991b). *Manual for the CBCL and 1991 profile*. Burlington, VT: University of Vermont, Department of Psychiatry.

Aman, M. G. (1980). Psychotropic drugs and learning problems—A selective review. *Journal of Learning Disabilities, 13*, 87–97.

Aman, M. G., & Pearson, D. A. (1999). Monitoring and measuring drug effects. II. Behavioral, emotional and cognitive effects. In J. S. Werry & M. G. Aman (Eds.), *Practitioner's guide to psychoactive drugs for children and adolescents* (2nd ed., pp. 99–164). New York: Plenum Medical Book Library.

Aman, M. G., Werry, J. S., Paxton, J. W., & Turbott, S. H. (1987). Effect of sodium valproate on psychomotor performance in children as a function of dose, fluctuations in concentration, and diagnosis. *Epilepsia, 28*, 115–126.

Ambrosini, P. J. (2000). A review of pharmacotherapy of major depression in children and adolescents. *Psychiatric Services, 41*, 627–633.

American Academy of Child and Adolescent Psychiatry (1997). Practice parameters for the assessment and treatment of children, adolescents, and adults with attention-deficit/hyperactivity disorder. *Journal of the American Academy of Child and Adolescent Psychiatry, 36(Suppl.)*, 85S–121S.

Armstrong, R. D., & Horn, M. (1995). Educational issues in childhood cancer. *School Psychology Quarterly, 10*, 292–304.

Barkley, R. A. (1981). *Hyperactive children: A handbook for diagnosis and treatment.* New York: Guilford Press.

Barkley, R. A. (1990). *Attention-deficit hyperactivity disorder: A handbook for diagnosis and treatment.* New York: The Guilford Press.

Barkley, R. A. (1998). *Attention-deficit hyperactivity disorder: A handbook for diagnosis and treatment* (2nd ed.). New York: The Guilford Press.

Barkley, R. A., DuPaul, G. J., & Connor, D. F. (1999). Stimulants. In J. S. Werry & M. G. Aman (Eds.), *Practitioner's guide to psychoactive drugs for children and adolescents* (2nd ed.). New York: Plenum.

Barkley, R. A., Fischer, M., Newby, R. F., & Breen, M. J. (1988). Development of a multimethod clinical protocol for assessing stimulant drug response in children with attention deficit disorder. *Journal of Clinical Child Psychology, 17*, 14–24.

Barrickman, L. L., Perry, P. J., Alle, A. J., Kuperman, S., Arndt, S. V., Hermann, K. J., & Schumacher, E. (1995). Bupropion versus methylphenidate in the treatment of attention-deficit hyperactivity disorder. *Journal of the American Academy of Child and Adolescent Psychiatry, 34*, 649–657.

Bender, B. G. (1999). Learning disorders associated with asthma and allergies. *School Psychology Review, 28*, 204–214.

Bender, B. G., Lerner, J. A., & Poland, J. E. (1991). Association between corticosteriods and psychologic change in hospitalized asthmatic children. *Annals of Allergy, 66*, 414–419.

Berg, I., Butler, A., Ellis, M., & Foster, J. (1993). Psychiatric aspects of epilepsy in childhood treated with carbamazepine, phenytoin, or sodium valproate: A random trial. *Developmental Medicine and Child Neurology, 35*, 149–157.

Biederman, J. (1998). Attention-deficit/hyperactivity disorder: A life-span perspective. *Journal of Clinical Psychiatry, 59*(Suppl. 7), 4–16.

Birmaher, B., Yelovich, A. K., & Renaud, J. (1998). Pharmacologic treatment for children and adolescents with anxiety disorders. *Child and Adolescent Psychopharmacology, 45*, 1187–1204.

Black, B., & Udhe, T. W. (1994). Treatment of elective mutism with fluoxetine: A double-blind, placebo-controlled study. *Journal of the American Academy of Child and Adolescent Psychiatry, 33*, 1000–1006.

Brown, R. T., & Borden, K. A. (1989). Neuropsychological effects of stimulant medication on children's learning and behavior. In C. R. Reynolds & E. Fletcher-Janzen (Eds.), *Handbook of clinical child neuropsychology* (pp. 443–474). New York: Plenum.

Brown, R. T., & Madan-Swain, A. (1993). Cognitive, neuropsychological, and academic sequelae in children with leukemia. *Journal of Learning Disabilities, 26*, 74–90.

Brown, R. T., Madan-Swain, A., Pais, R., Lambert, R. G., Sexson, S., & Ragab, A. (1992). Chemotherapy for acute lymphocytic leukemia: Cognitive and academic sequelae. *Journal of Pediatrics, 121*, 885–889.

Brown, R. T., Madan-Swain, A., Walco, G. A., Cherrick, I., Ievers, C. E., Conte, P. M., Vega, R., Bell, B., & Lauer, S. J. (1998). Cognitive and academic late effects among children previously treated for acute lymphocytic leukemia receiving chemotherapy as CNS prophylaxis. *Journal of Pediatric Psychology, 23*, 333–340.

Brown, R. T., & Sawyer, M. G. (1998). *Medications for school-age children: Effects on learning and behavior.* New York: Guilford.

Brown, R. T., Sawyer, M. B., Antoniou, G., Toogood, I., Rice, M., Thompson, N., & Madan-Swain, A. (1996). A three-year follow-up of the intellectual and academic functioning of children receiving central nervous system prophylactic chemotherapy for leukemia. *Developmental and Behavioral Pediatrics, 17*, 392–398.

Camfield, C. S., Chaplin, S., Doyle, A. B., Shapiro, S. H., Cummings, C., & Camfield, P. R. (1979). Side effects of phenobarbital in toddlers: Behavioral and cognitive aspects. *Journal of Pediatrics, 95*, 361–365.

Campbell, M., & Cueva, J. E. (1995a). Psychopharmacology in child and adolescent psychiatry: A review of the past seven years. Part I. *Journal of the American Academy of Child and Adolescent Psychiatry, 34*, 1124–1132.

Campbell, M., & Cueva, J. E. (1995b). Psychopharmacology in child and adolescent psychiatry: A review of the past seven years. Part II. *Journal of the American Academy of Child and Adolescent Psychiatry, 34*, 1262–272.

Canadian Study Group for Childhood Epilepsy. (1999). The cognitive and behavioural effects of clobazam and standard monotherapy are comparable. *Epilepsy Research, 33*, 133–143.

Celano, M. P., & Geller, R. J. (1993). Learning, school performance, and children with asthma: How much at risk? *Journal of Learning Disabilities, 26*, 23–32.

Chan, H. S., & Erlichman, C. (1993). Cancer chemotherapy in pediatric malignancies. In I. C. Radde & S. M. MacLeod (Eds.), *Pediatric pharmacology and therapeutics* (pp. 515–528). St. Louis: C. V. Mosby.

Chen, Y. K., Kang, W. M., & So, W. C. M. (1996). Comparison of antiepileptic drugs on cognitive function in newly diagnosed epileptic children: A psychometric and neurophysiological study. *Epilepsia, 37*, 81–86.

Clay, T. H., Gualtieri, C. T., Evans, R. W., & Gullion, C. M. (1988). Clinical and neuropsychological effects of the novel antidepressant bupropion. *Psychopharmacology Bulletin, 24*, 143–148.

Cole, T. B., Sprinkle, R. J., Smith, S. J., & Buchanan, G. R. (1986). Intravenous narcotic therapy for children with severe sickle cell pain crisis. *American Journal of Diseases of Children, 140*, 1255–1259.

Dager, S. R., & Herich, A. J. (1990). A case of bupropion-associated delirium. *Journal of Clinical Psychiatry, 51*, 307–308.

Dunn, L. M., & Dunn, L. M. (1981). *Peabody Picture Vocabulary Test.* Circle Pines, MN: American Guidance Service.

DuPaul, G. J., Barkley, R. A., & Connor, D. F. (1998). Stimulants. In R. A. Barkley (Ed.), *Attention deficit hyperactivity disorder: A handbook for diagnosis and treatment* (pp. 510–551). New York: Guilford.

DuPaul, G. J., & Kyle, K. K. (1995). Pediatric pharmacology and psychopharmacology. In M. C. Roberts (Ed.), *Handbook of pediatric psychology* (2nd ed., pp. 741–758). New York: Guilford.

DuPaul, G. J., Power, T. J., Anastopoulos, A. D., & Reid, R. (1998). *ADHD Rating Scale-IV.* New York: Guilford Press.

DuPaul, G. J., Rapport, M. D., & Perriello, L. M. (1991). Teacher ratings of academic skills: The development of the academic performance rating scale. *School Psychology Review, 20*, 284–300.

Ehrhardt, K. E., Barnett, D. W., Lentz, F. E., Stollar, S. A., & Reifin, L. H. (1996). Innovative methodology in ecological consultation: Use of scripts to promote treatment acceptability and integrity. *School Psychology Quarterly, 11*, 149–168.

Elia, J., Welsh, P. A., Gullotta, C. S., & Rapoport, J. L. (1993). Classroom academic performance: Improvement with both methylphenidate and dextroamphetamine in ADHD boys. *Journal of Child Psychology and Psychiatry, 34*, 785–804.

Emslie, G. J., Rush, A. J., Weinberg, W. A., Kowatch, R. A., Hughes, C. W., Carmody, T., & Rintelmann, J. (1997). A double-blind, randomized, placebo-controlled trial of fluoxetine in children and adolescents with depression. *Archives of General Psychiatry, 54*, 1031–1037.

Farwell, J. R., Lee, Y. J., Hirtz, D. B., Sulzbacher, S. I., Ellenberg, J., H., & Nelson, K. B. (1990). Phenobarbital for febrile seizures—Effects on intelligence and on seizure recurrence. *New England Journal of Medicine, 322*, 364–369.

Gadow, K. D. (1993). A school-based medication evaluation program. In J. L. Matson (Ed.), *Handbook of hyperactivity in children* (pp. 186– 219). Needham Heights, MA: Allyn and Bacon.

Gadow, K. D., & Nolan, E. E. (1993). Practical considerations in conducting school-based medication evaluations for children with hyperactivity. *Journal of Emotional and Behavioral Disorders, 1*, 118–126.

Gadow, K. D., Nolan, E. E., Paolicelli, L. M., & Sprafkin, J. (1991). A procedure for assessing the effects of methylphenidate on hyperactive children in public school settings. *Journal of Clinical Child Psychology, 20*, 268–276.

Geller, D. A., Biederman, J., Reed, E. D., Spencer, T., & Wilens, T. E. (1995). Similarities in response to fluoxetine in the treatment of children and adolescents with obsessive-compulsive disorder. *Journal of the American Academy of Child and Adolescent Psychiatry, 34*, 36–44.

Gresham, F. M., & Elliott, S. N. (1990). *The social skills rating system*. Circle Pines, MN: American Guidance.

Handler, M. W., & DuPaul, G. J. (1999). Pharmacological issues and iatrogenic effects on learning. In R. T. Brown (Ed.), *Cognitive aspects of chronic illness in children* (pp. 355–385). New York: Guilford.

Hazell, P., O'Connell, D., Heathcote, D., Robertson, J., & Henry, D. (1995). Efficacy of tricyclic drugs in treating child and adolescent depression: A meta-analysis. *British Medical Journal, 310*, 897–901.

Herranz, J. L., Armijo, J. A., & Arteaga, R. (1988). Clinical side effects of phenobarbital, primidone, phenytoin, carbamazepine, and valproate during monotherapy in children. *Epilepsia, 29*, 794–804.

Hirsch, I. B. (1998). Intensive treatment of type I diabetes: Prevention and treatment of diabetes and its complications. *Medical Clinics of North America, 82*, 689–719.

Holmes, C. S. (1990). Neuropsychological sequelae of acute and chronic blood glucose disruption in adults with insulin-dependent diabetes. In C. Holmes (Ed.), *Neuropsychological and behavioral aspects of diabetes* (pp. 122–154). New York: Springer-Verlag.

Hyman, I. A., Wojtowicz, A., Lee, K. D., Haffner, M. E., Fiorellio, C. A., Storlazzi, J. J., & Rosenfield, J. (1998). School-based methylphenidate placebo protocols: Methods and practical issues. *Journal of Learning Disabilities, 31*, 581–594.

Jerome, L., Gordon, M., & Hustler, P. (1994). A comparison of American and Canadian teachers' knowledge and attitudes towards attention deficit hyperactivity disorder (ADHD). *Canadian Journal of Psychiatry, 39*, 563 567.

Keith, R. W., & Engineer, P. (1991). Effects of methylphenidate on the auditory processing of children with attention deficit-hyperactivity disorder. *Journal of Learning Disabilities, 24*, 630–636.

Kent, M. A., Camfield, C. S., & Camfield, P. R. (1999). Double-blind methylphenidate trials: Practical, useful, and highly endorsed by families. *Archives of Pediatric and Adolescent Medicine, 153*, 1292–1296.

Kovacs, M. (1992). *Children's Depression Inventory*. Los Angeles: Multi-Health Systems.

Lear, J. G., Montgomery, L. L., Schlitt, J. J., & Rickett, K. D. (1996). Key issues affecting school-based health centers and Medicaid. *Journal of School Health, 66*, 83–88.

Legarda, S. B., Booth, M. P., Fennell, E. B., & Maria, B. L. (1996). Altered cognitive functioning in children with idiopathic epilepsy receiving valproate monotherapy. *Journal of Child Neurology, 11*, 321–330.

Loney, J., & Milich, R. (1982). Hyperactivity, inattention, and aggression in clinical practice. In M. Wolraich & D. K. Routh (Eds.), *Advances in developmental and behavioral pediatrics* (Vol. 3, pp. 113–147). Greenwich, CT: JAI Press.

Lonnerholm, G., Foucard, T., & Lindstrom, B. (1984). Dose, plasma concentration, and effect or oral terbutaline in long-term treatment of childhood asthma. *Journal of Allergy and Clinical Immunology, 73*, 508–515.

MacPhee, G. J. A., MacPhail, E. M., Butler, E., & Brodie, M. J. (1986). Controlled evaluation of a supplementary dose of carbamazepine on psychomotor function in epileptic patients. *European Journal of Clinical Pharmacology, 31*, 195–199.

Malone, M. A., Kershner, J. R., & Seigel, L. (1988). The effects of methylphenidate on levels of processing and laterality in children with attention deficit disorder. *Journal of Abnormal Child Psychology, 16*, 379–395.

Mandelbaum, D. E., & Burack, G. D. (1997). The effect of seizure type and medication on cognitive and behavioral functioning in children with idiopathic epilepsy. *Developmental Medicine & Child Neurology, 30*, 731–735.

Mandoki, M. G., Tapia, M. R., Tapia, M. A., Sumner, G. S., & Parker, J. L. (1997). Venlafaxine in the treatment of children and adolescents with major depression. *Psychopharmacology Bulletin, 33*, 149–154.

Mazer, B., Figueroa-Rosario, W., & Bender, B. (1990). The effect of albuterol aerosol on fine-motor performance in children with chronic asthma. *Journal of Allergy and Clinical Immunology, 86*, 243–248.

McLoughlin, J. A., Nall, M., & Berla, E. (1990). Effect of allergy medication on children's reading comprehension. *Allergy Proceedings, 11*, 225–228.

Merrell, K. W. (1993). *School Social Behavior Scales.* Austin, TX: PRO-ED.

Moffatt, M. E. (1997). Nocturnal enuresis: A review of the efficacy of treatment and practical advice for clinicians. *Developmental and Behavioral Pediatrics, 18*, 49–56.

Mulhern, R. K., Wasserman, A. L., Fairclough, D., & Ochs, J. (1988). Memory function in disease-free survivors of childhood acute lymphocytic leukemia given CNS prophylaxis with or without 1,800 cGy cranial irradiation. *Journal of Clinical Oncology, 6*, 315–320.

Nebrig, M. R., DuPaul, G. J., & Showalter, J. (2001). The effects of bupropion hydrochloride on the classroom performance of students with attention-deficit/hyperactivity disorder. Manuscript submitted for publication, Lehigh University.

Northup, J., Broussard, C., Jones, K., George, T., Vollmer, T. R., & Herring, T. (1995). The differential effects of teacher and peer attention on the disruptive classroom behavior of three children with a diagnosis of attention deficit hyperactivity disorder. *Journal of Applied Behavior Analysis, 28,* 227–228.

Perrin, E. C., Stein, R. E. K., & Drotar, D. (1991). Cautions in using the child behavior checklist: Observations based on research about children with chronic illnesses. *Journal of Pediatric Psychology, 16*, 411–421.

Phelps, L., Brown, R. T., & Power, T. J. (2002). *Pediatric psychopharmacology: Combining medical and psychosocial interventions*. Washington, DC: American Psychological Association.

Poling, A., Gadow, K. D., & Cleary, J. (1991). *Drug therapy for behavior disorders: An introduction.* New York: Pergamon.

Rapport, M. D., Chung, K. M., Shore, G., Denney, C. B., & Isaacs, P. (2000). Upgrading the science and technology of assessment and diagnosis: Laboratory and clinic-based assessment of children with ADHD. *Journal of Clinical Child Psychology, 29*, 555–568.

Rapport, M. D., Denney, C., DuPaul, G. J., & Gardner, M. J. (1994). Attention deficit disorder and methylphenidate: Normalization rates, clinical effectiveness, and response prediction in 76 children. *Journal of the American Academy of Child and Adolescent Psychiatry, 54*, 334–341.

Rapport, M. D., & Kelly, K. L. (1991). Psychostimulant effects on learning and cognitive function in children with attention deficit hyperactivity disorder: Findings and implications. In J. L. Matson (Ed.), *Hyperactivity in children: A handbook* (pp. 97–136). New York: Pergamon Press.

Reynolds, C. R., & Kamphaus, R. W. (1992). *Behavior assessment system for children.* Circle Pines, MN: American Guidance Service.

Reynolds, C. R., & Richmond, B. O. (1985). *Revised Children's Manifest Anxiety Scale Manual.* Los Angeles, CA: Western Psychological Services.

Reynolds, W. M. (1987). *Professional Manual for the Reynolds Adolescent Depression Scale.* Los Angeles, CA: Western Psychological Services.

Riva, D., & Devoti, M. (1996). Discontinuation of phenobarbital in children: Effects on neurocognitive behavior. *Pediatric Neurology, 14*, 36–40.

Robieux, I. C. (1993). Treatment of pain in infants and children: The role of pharmacology. In I. C. Radde & S. M. MacLeod (Eds.), *Pediatric pharmacology and therapeutics* (pp. 499–513). St. Louis: C. V. Mosby.

Rogers, A. G. (1989). Use of amitriptyline for phantom limb pain in younger children. *Journal of Pain Symptom Management, 4*, 96.

Rovet, J., & Fernandez, C. (1999). Insulin-dependent diabetes mellitus. In R. T. Brown (Ed.)., *Cognitive aspects of chronic illness in children* (pp. 142–171). New York: Guilford.

Shaffer, D., Fisher, P., Dulcan, M. K., Davies, M., Piacentini, J., Schwab-Stone, M. E., Lahey, B. B., Bourdon, K., Jensen, P. S., Bird, H. R., Canino, G., & Regier, D. A. (1996). The NIMHD Diagnostic Interview Schedule for Children Version 2.3 (DISC-2.3): Description, acceptability, prevalence rates, and performance in the MECA Study (Methods for the Epidemiology of Child and Adolescent Mental Disorders Study). *Journal of the American Academy of Child and Adolescent Psychiatry, 35*, 865–877.

Shanon, A., Feldman, W., Leikin, L., Pong, A. J., Peterson, R., & Williams, V. (1993). Comparison of CNS adverse effects between astemizole and chlorpheniramine in children: A randomized, double-blind study. *Developmental Pharmacology and Therapeutics, 20*, 239–246.

Shapiro, E., Shapiro, A. K., Young, J. G., & Feinberg, T. E. (1988). *Gilles de la Tourette syndrome.* New York: Raven Press.

Shapiro, E. S. (1996). *Academic skills problems.* New York: Guilford Press.

Shapiro, E. S., & Kratochwill, T. R. (2000). *Conducting school-based assessments of child and adolescent behavior.* New York: Guilford Press.

Simeon, J. G., Dinicola, V. G., Ferguson, H. B., & Copping, W. (1990). Adolescent depression: A placebo-controlled fluoxetine treatment study and follow-up. *Progress in Neuropsychopharmacology and Biologic Psychiatry, 14*, 791–795.

Spencer, T. J., Biederman, J., & Wilens, T. (1998). Pharmacotherapy of ADHD with antidepressants. In R. Barkley (Ed.), *Attention deficit hyperactivity disorder: A handbook for diagnosis and treatment* (2nd ed., pp. 552–563). New York: Guilford Press.

Spencer, T., Wilens, T., & Biederman, J. (1995). Psychotropic medication for children and adolescents. *Child & Adolescent Psychiatric Clinics of North America, 4*, 97–122.

Stores, D. L., Williams, P. L., Styles, E., & Zaiwalla, Z. (1992). Psychological effects of sodium valproate and carbamazepine in epilepsy. *Archives of Disease in Children, 67*, 1330–1337.

Sulzbacher, S., Farwell, J. R., Temkin, N., Lu, A. S., & Hirtz, D. B. (1999). Late cognitive effects of early treatment with phenobarbital. *Clinical Pediatrics, 38*, 387–394.

Tarnowski, K. J., & Brown, R. T. (2000). Psychological aspects of pediatric disorders. In M. Hersen & R. T. Ammerman (Eds.), *Advanced abnormal child psychology* (2nd ed., pp. 131–152). Mahwah, NJ: Lawrence Erlbaum.

Trimble, M. R. (1990). Antiepileptic drugs, cognitive function, and behaviour in children: Evidence from recent studies. *Epilepsia, 31*(Suppl. 4), 30–34.

Ullmann, R. K., Sleator, E. K., & Sprague, R. L. (1997). *ACTeRS Teacher and Parent Forms Manual* (2nd ed.). Champaign, IL: MetriTech, Inc.

Vermeulen, J., & Aldenkamp, A. P. (1995). Cognitive side-effects of chronic antiepileptic drug treatment: A review of 25 years of research. *Epilepsy Research, 22*, 65–95.

Vining, E. P. G., Carpenter, R. O., & Aman, M. G. (1999). Antiepileptics (anticonvulsants). In J. S. Werry & M. G. Aman (Eds.), *Practitioner's guide to psychoactive drugs for children and adolescents* (2nd ed., pp. 355–385). New York: Plenum.

Von Brock, M. B., & Elliott, S. N. (1987). Influence of treatment effectiveness information on the acceptability of classroom interventions. *Journal of School Psychology, 25*, 131–144.

Wechsler, D. (1991). *Wechsler Intelligence Scale for Children* (3rd ed.). New York: The Psychological Corporation.

Werry, J. S., & Aman, M. G. (1999). *Practitioner's guide to psychoactive drugs for children and adolescents* (2nd ed.). New York: Plenum.

Whitaker, A., & Rao, U. (1992). Neuroleptics in pediatric psychiatry. In D. Shaffer (Ed.), *The psychiatric clinics of North America* (Vol. 15, pp. 243–276). Philadelphia: Saunders.

Woodcock, R. W., & Johnson, M. B. (1990). *Woodcock-Johnson Psychoeducational Battery. Revised.* Allen, TX: Teaching Resources.

Yaster, M., & Deshpande, J. K. (1988). Management of pediatric pain with opioid analgesics. *Journal of Pediatrics, 113*, 421–429.

31

Consultation With School Personnel

Susan M. Sheridan
Richard J. Cowan
University of Nebraska–Lincoln

INTRODUCTION

Consultation services in school settings is gaining increased recognition in research, training and practice, and is expanding to include a variety of related professionals as consultants (e.g., special educators, counseling psychologists, community psychologists, speech pathologists; Gutkin & Curtis, 1999). There also appears to be a trend in increased consultation between medical professionals (e.g., general physicians, pediatricians, psychiatrists) and school personnel. Whereas the term *consultation* may have broad meanings across educational, medical, and psychological practice, one common feature is that consultation generally consists of two or more people working together to address concerns regarding a third-party client (Sheridan & Kratochwill, 1991). As applied to school settings, consultation is defined as collaborative problem-solving between a professional *consultant* (e.g., psychologist, medical expert) and one or more persons (or *consultees*; e.g., parents, educators) who are responsible for providing some form of educational and/or psychological assistance to a *child-client* (adapted from Medway, 1979). This definition represents consultation as conceptualized in this chapter.

The purpose of this chapter is to introduce school-based consultation as a viable feature of pediatric and psychological services. The salient features of consultation will be presented, including theoretical foundations, models, and stages. Benefits of consultation, research findings, and considerations for conducting consultation in school settings will also be explored.

Models of School-based Consultation

Three models have been particularly influential within the field of school-based consultation: (1) behavioral consultation (BC; Bergan & Kratochwill, 1990), (2) mental health consultation (MHC; Caplan, 1970), and (3) organizational consultation (Maher, Illback, & Zins, 1984). BC, which is based on behavioral theory and applied behavior analysis, has received the most empirical and clinical attention in the field (Bramlett & Murphy, 1998; Sheridan, Welch, & Orme, 1996). BC is procedurally operationalized through a four-stage, problem-solving model, including problem identification, problem analysis, treatment implementation, and treatment evaluation (see later section). Conjoint behavioral consultation (CBC; Sheridan, Kratochwill, & Bergan, 1996) is a conceptual and procedural expansion of BC, in which parents are actively and meaningfully involved with school personnel and other service providers throughout the consultation process (e.g., Sheridan, Eagle, Cowan, & Mickelson, 2001).

Mental health consultation is grounded on psychoanalytic theory—focusing primarily on helping consultees gain insight into how personal feelings and behaviors that may be contributing to the presenting problem(s) (Caplan, 1970)—has been operationalized via two approaches: (1) teacher-centered consultation (primarily emphasizing the teacher's feelings, attitudes, and skills in relation to identified concerns) and (2) child-centered consultation (focusing primarily on specific academic or behavioral concerns related to a child or group of children; adapted from Bramlett & Murphy, 1998). Organizational consultation is concerned with systems-level change. The primary focus in organizational consultation is on broad-based organizational assessment and intervention, rather than individual child-centered services. Compared with BC and MHC, organizational consultation has received the least amount of empirical and clinical attention within school settings (Bramlett & Murphy, 1998; Gutkin & Curtis, 1999).

The Role of Indirect Services and Ecological Theory in Consultation Practice

In traditional psychological and medical practice, the psychologist or medical expert works directly with the client to problem-solve or provide treatment. Alternatively, in school-based consultation, the psychologist or medical expert works primarily with other professionals or caregivers (i.e., teachers, support staff) and parents who (1) have frequent, direct contact with the child-client (i.e., student); and (2) ultimately implement an applied intervention (i.e., consultees act as treatment agents within the consultation framework). Given their pivotal role in the consultation process, parent and teacher expertise and support are necessary conditions for consultation, and for the child to receive the services he/she needs to achieve success across settings. The indirect service-delivery model operates on the premise of two primary goals: (1) the short-term goal of resolving the student's presenting problem (i.e., a remedial approach) and (2) the long-term goal of improving the consultees' problem-solving skills (i.e., a preventive approach; Bramlett & Murphy, 1998).

Ecological theory provides a useful conceptual framework for school-based consultation. Ecological theory conceptualizes behavior and development as a "mutual accommodation" between an individual and the individual's environment (Sheridan & Gutkin, 2001). Bronfenbrenner (1977) maintains that each individual is an inseparable part of a small social system and that an individual's development occurs within the context of four interrelated systems within the greater ecological environment: microsystem, mesosystem, exosystem, and macrosystem. A child's microsystem is defined as the relationship between the child and his/her immediate environment (e.g., home, school). A mesosystem is comprised of the interrelation between the major systems (and settings) in a child's life (e.g., the interaction between home, school, and other treatment settings). In ecological theory, an exosystem is defined as influences from settings in which the child is not directly included, but that affect that child in his/her immediate setting (e.g., a teacher's personal life). Finally, the macrosystem is concerned with the overall cultural and subcultural patterns (e.g., the effects of political influences and societal norms and values on an individual child's life). Consultation is concerned primarily with the mesosystemic patterns and relationships influencing development (Conoley, 1987; Hansen, 1986; Sheridan, Kratochwill, & Bergan 1996), and focuses analysis and intervention at this level.

Because parents and teachers have a strong presence in the home and school environments, and because of their expertise about, influence over, and relationship with the child-client, they are the primary consultees (and treatment agents) in school-based consultation. Gutkin and Conoley (1990) refer to the premise of working with parents and teachers to promote behavioral change as *The Paradox of School Psychology*, stating that, "to serve children effectively school psychologists must first and foremost concentrate their attention and professional expertise on adults" (p. 203). That is, in school-based consultation, the primary focus is working with parents and teachers who ultimately interact with and provide intervention for the child. Alternatively, in traditional psychological practice, direct services with the identified client is the norm, and working with significant others is considered supplementary to one-on-one interactions between the psychologist and client. These considerations have implications for school psychologists, clinical and counseling psychologists, medical experts, and other professionals alike.

Because school-based consultation implies by name the inclusion of teachers, educators, and other school-based personnel, it may be easy to direct limited attention to the significant role parents can play in the consultation process. There are several benefits of working with parents. Parent participation in school-based services and activities is related to increased student achievement, better attendance, better study habits, fewer discipline problems, regular homework habits, greater similarity between the home and school systems, and more positive attitudes toward school (Christenson & Sheridan, 2001). Furthermore, including parents as resources in educational problem-solving may have benefits for educators faced with demanding schedules and often-limited resources.

Additional benefits of including parents in school-based services are evident. Research has clearly demonstrated the efficacy of models utilizing parents and teachers as joint consultees (Colton & Sheridan, 1998; Ray & Watson, 2001; Sheridan, 1997; Sheridan et al., 2001; Weiner, Sheridan, & Jenson, 1998). Furthermore, continuity among programs across multiple settings, enhanced maintenance and generalization of consultation goals, and constant monitoring of intervention side effects have been noted (Galloway & Sheridan, 1994; Sheridan, Kratochwill, & Elliott, 1990). It is the belief of these authors that consultants should strive to include parents in consultation practice whenever possible.

Participant Roles in Consultation

By definition and design, consultation in school settings and with school personnel requires interdisciplinary communication and partnering. Optimal conditions for such partnerships occur when participants assume close working relationships, wherein all parties have specified and joint rights, roles, and responsibilities (Welch & Sheridan, 1995).

In school-based consultation, the teacher-professional (consultee) has important roles related to the classroom context and a child's functioning within that context. Teacher consultees are generally responsible for sharing information about the target child, collecting information, contributing ideas for intervention plans, and monitoring effects of the intervention in the natural setting of the classroom (Sheridan & Kratochwill, 1991). Specifically, teachers can share expertise about a particular classroom within which the target child must function, describe academic/behavioral concerns, report the child's behavioral functioning in school environment, assist in the determination of consultation priorities and goals, collect naturalistic data, implement plan strategies at school, and collect data to ascertain efficacy of the intervention in addressing primary concerns.

Parents of children who are the focus of consultation also have important roles in problem-solving. Parent roles include sharing expertise about the child from historical, developmental, and cross-setting perspectives; describing behavioral, social, and emotional concerns as they present in multiple contexts; and reporting behaviors that occur at home and in other settings.

Similar to teacher consultees, parents can help determine consultation priorities and goals, collect data in naturalistic settings, implement specific plan strategies at home, and monitor the effectiveness of the intervention plan.

Consultants have unique and essential roles in consultation, particularly when the issues to be discussed present complex or challenging circumstances. They share expertise about unique conditions that are presented (e.g., medical, developmental, psychiatric issues) and their expected effects on the child's functioning. Furthermore, they are generally responsible for guiding the problem-solving process from initial identification of a concern to its resolution or management (Sheridan & Kratochwill, 1991). They assist consultees to focus on salient issues, explore conditions surrounding a primary concern, form hypotheses about behavioral function, generate alternative intervention options, establish specific and effective plan strategies, and evaluate treatment outcomes. Importantly, they also provide support and assistance throughout the consultation and plan implementation process through formal (e.g., provision of materials and resources, demonstration or training related to interventions) and informal means (e.g., phone calls, visits to the school, offers for assistance).

Relationships Among Participants in Consultation

Consultation is an interpersonal endeavor. It involves human interaction among individuals in an ongoing relationship. There are certain characteristics of consultative relationships that, when realized, can maximize the success of the team's functioning. These are listed in Table 31.1 and described herein.

The relational status in the consultation interaction is *coordinate and interdependent*, meaning that participants' roles are complementary, and each member has equal opportunity in the decision-making process. This recognizes the benefits of the unique contributions of each individual, and that expertise is unique and not necessarily identical. Decisions are made when team members collectively identify the most appropriate, effective, and reasonable alternative given the range of possibilities and resources available. There is joint responsibility for the child's success, and for the establishment and maintenance of a cooperative consultation relationship. This is contrasted with a hierarchical relationship in which one party attempts to control or dictate the actions of the others. Most authors now agree that coordinate, coequal status in consultation is most conducive for constructive and successful interactions (Brown, Pryzwansky, & Schulte, 1995; Gutkin & Curtis, 1999; Sheridan & Kratochwill, 1991).

Consistent with the coordinate relational status in consultation is the *prerogative of consultees to reject consultants' recommendations*. Recognition of this inherent aspect of the process is critical for consultants who enter systems with the intent of imparting expertise and expecting complete acceptance and compliance with intervention requirements. Several variables affect a consultee's willingness to accept an intervention, including features of the

TABLE 31.1
Characteristics of Relationships in Consultation

- Relationships are coordinate and interdependent.
- All participants are active in identifying priorities, exploring options, and making decisions.
- Participation is voluntary.
- Participants have the right to reject suggestions.
- Maintenance of a positive interdisciplinary relationship is a priority.
- The relationship occurs in a context with the child at center.

school and classroom systems; theoretical orientation of the consultee; skills, knowledge, or materials necessary to implement the intervention; and perceived effectiveness of the treatment plan (Witt, Martens, & Elliott, 1984). Respect for these unique perspectives and realities is a critical element in the consultation relationship.

The *active involvement of all participants* is generally considered important in the consultative relationship. This is based on the premise that such involvement will increase ownership and commitment to identifying, analyzing, and resolving concerns. Early research has demonstrated that consultee implementation of interventions developed in consultation is directly related to the degree of consultee involvement in problem-solving (Reinking, Livesay, & Kohl, 1978).

A primary assumption in consultation relationships is that participants are involved *voluntarily*. In some circumstances, a consultee (e.g., teacher, school administrator) approaches a consultant (e.g., medical or pediatric specialist) and requests assistance with a particular concern. In other cases, specialists working with a child or family recognize the importance of sharing and obtaining information with and from school personnel. Regardless of the direction of referral, it is imperative that such interactions occur, and that they do so without coercion or undue pressure. It is the experience of these authors that school personnel welcome overtures made by specialists who are working with a specific child or family when they are collegial, constructive, and sensitive to the unique systemic features of schools.

Participant interest in problem-solving is but one essential element to maximize success in consultation. Maintenance of a *positive interdisciplinary relationship* is also a priority. Effective consultation requires more than simply coming together and sharing ideas and information. To promote benefits to the child in terms of effective cross-system services, identifying and prioritizing ongoing means by which individuals can work together and continue problem-solving on behalf of the child are necessary. Personal needs, goals, and agendas are put aside to allow the needs and goals of the group (i.e., to identify, implement, and evaluate services for the target child) to take precedence. All parties must believe in the worth of the interprofessional relationship, and expend time and energy necessary for its maintenance.

A final consideration is the recognition that consultation relationships occur in a context with the *child at center* (Christenson & Sheridan, 2001). Although time may be spent sharing facts and expertise, primary attention is always given to the benefits and outcomes to the child-client. To be successful, interventions or management plans must be developed based on the specific needs and contexts within which the specific child resides. Consultative interventions are useful only to the extent to which they are responsive to needs within the naturalistic context (i.e., within the particular school, classroom, family unit).

OVERARCHING BENEFITS AND GOALS OF CONSULTATION IN SCHOOL SETTINGS

There are numerous benefits and goals associated with consultation, particularly when practiced across settings in an interdisciplinary fashion. Table 31.2 outlines several benefits to clients and participants in the consultation process. When conducted in school settings, the goals of consultation are threefold: to share information among primary individuals in a child's life, to assist in addressing concerns or problems experienced by the child, and to identify and coordinate multiple services needed by children and families.

Consultation as Information-Sharing

In consultatitive forms of interaction, individuals with a range of skills, knowledge, and expertise come together to share information relevant to a situation. Ideally, the sharing of information is bidirectional, with pediatric or health-related information shared by appropriate medical

TABLE 31.2
Benefits of Interdisciplinary Consultation-Based Services

- Improved performance (e.g., behavioral competence, skill development) for targets of consultation (i.e., clients).
- Enhanced communication and coordination among medical/community professionals and educational personnel.
- Continuity in programs and approaches across multiple contexts.
- Shared ownership and commitment to educational goals.
- Increased understanding and conceptualization of the complexities of a child and his/her situation.
- Pooling of resources across home and school increases the:
  –range and quality of solutions,
  –diversity in expertise and resources, and
  –integrity of educational programs.

personnel, academic and behavioral information shared by school staff, and developmental and personal information (as appropriate) shared by parents. Sharing information in this manner is beneficial for many reasons. First, it allows for comprehensive and functional data to be communicated among the primary individuals who share responsibility for a child. When questions remain about aspects of the child's functioning, it provides a mechanism by which more data can be collected over distal temporal and contextual bases. In this way, the holistic nature and needs of the child are kept central.

Information-sharing among professionals and parents is also beneficial in that the diversity of expertise and resources available to address target concerns is maximized. By virtue of unique backgrounds, training, and experiences, the various participants in consultation hold differing perspectives and ideas. Pooling such information magnifies the range and quality of services available to a child. No one individual is expert in all knowledge and skill domains necessary to fully support a child with developmental, medical, or learning challenges. In a similar vein, children present their difficulties in unique ways in different settings (i.e., what is demonstrated in a school setting may not be exhibited in a clinic setting and vice versa). Knowledge of the perspectives and skills of the various members may help determine the most appropriate or relevant individual to provide specialized services (Neill, 1997).

Third, information-sharing among pediatric and school professionals enhances the skills, knowledge, and behaviors of all parties (i.e., family members, school personnel, medical personnel, child). For example, characteristics of a child's medical or psychological condition may likely affect his/her academic, social, and/or behavioral functioning at school and home. Information about characteristics of the disorder, behavioral expectancies, medication issues, and necessary precautions is extremely important for all service providers and caregivers to understand. Likewise, school personnel, such as teachers and aides, can share important information about the classroom or school structure, academic or social-behavioral expectations, observations of performance, and changes in behavior or temperament.

Related to sharing relevant information about a child and his/her situation, a fourth benefit of information-sharing is that it increases knowledge about systems. Interdisciplinary consultation recognizes at its core that a child is part of several interrelated systems. Consultation theory posits that these ecological contexts are interlocking, such that events, expectations, and contingencies that occur in one system affect all other systems. Unfortunately, oftentimes these systems do not communicate or interact on behalf of the child, and although perhaps equally interested in the child's welfare, they may often work at cross-purposes, or at least inefficiently, with each other. Consultation can improve relationships among change agents, promote continued problem-solving over time, and lend to efficient intervention in the advent of new or related problems.

Consultation as Problem-Solving

Among the hallmark goals of consultation is the goal to address problems or concerns as they present themselves in specific contexts. By virtue of the diverse expertise available in consultative relationships, many sources of information and opportunities for problem-solving are available. The structure inherent in behavioral consultation (see discussion later) provides an opportunity to address concerns in an organized and systematic way. Clarity in goals, objectives, and procedures for assessment, intervention, and evaluation are the cornerstone of BC. Furthermore, the data-based, decision-making process allows for ongoing monitoring of intervention effects and ensures that concerns are addressed in an effective manner.

In consultation, teams of individuals work together to identify and prioritize the primary issues in need of attention and intervention. Individuals from across the child's primary contexts (i.e., school, home, health/mental health systems) together explore behavioral, medical, academic, and social-emotional issues. This joint effort allows for a greater conceptualization and understanding of the child in his/her multiple systems. Furthermore, the onus of responsibility for problem-solving is not placed on any one individual (e.g., medical staff, teacher), but rather is shared among all parties. Together, the unique knowledge and expertise brought to the consultation dialogue contribute to the identification of an appropriate plan and relevant strategies. Thus, shared ownership for problem definition and solution are promulgated through the BC process.

Among the problem-solving objectives of consultation is the importance of enhancing improved functioning across the multiple naturalistic settings within which a child functions. Ultimately, it is the effectiveness with which a child manages his/her behaviors at school, home, and other environments that is of primary significance. By bringing together key individuals responsible for these environments (i.e., teachers, parents, health/mental health providers), consultants promote consistent programming, systematic evaluation, and routine follow-up of interventions in natural settings. Thus, generalization and maintenance of solutions are inherent, not tangential, to consultative problem-solving.

Effective problem-solving requires unique expertise that concerns both the substantive issues of which consultation addresses, as well as the process by which concerns are identified, prioritized, and addressed. That is, effective problem-solving consultation entails content and process expertise (Welch & Sheridan, 1995). Content expertise concerns the issues being addressed by the consultation team, such as information about a child's medical history, psychiatric disorder, or academic functioning. Evidence-based information about course, etiology, and interventions for identified disorders is an example of important content expertise necessary for effective problem-solving. Knowledge about the consultation process is also necessary for effective practice. This includes expertise in identifying concerns, exploring environmental conditions, conducting functional assessments, pooling intervention ideas, developing effective plan strategies, assessing acceptability of treatments, monitoring integrity of implementation, and evaluating outcomes of interventions. The ability to blend content and process expertise appears to be important for effective consultation (Sheridan, Kratochwill, & Bergan, 1996; Welch & Sheridan, 1995).

Consultation as Coordination of Services

Coordination across school, medical, and other settings provides an effective and efficient means of service delivery (U.S. Department of Education/American Educational Research Association, 1995). Virtually all serious problems are multidetermined (Schoenwald &

Henggeler, 1997). Characteristics of the family, peer group, individual, neighborhood, and school system can be predictive of serious childhood psychopathology (Henggeler, 1991). Bringing together individuals who represent these systems in consultative problem-solving recognizes the need to address concerns across and not only within settings in a coordinated manner (Sheridan, Kratochwill & Bergan, 1996).

There are many benefits of a coordinated approach in multisystemic consultation. Importantly, bringing all primary players together to discuss issues, needs, and resources establishes patterns of communication within and across systems that may have been nonexistent. Such communication can serve to increase understanding about the multiple systems involved with a child and family, provide important avenues for dialogue about programs and services, and allow for ongoing feedback and renewal of treatment or management plans.

Implicit in the notion of coordinated services is the provision of a common plan of intervention across the multiple service providers (e.g., teachers, medical professionals, parents). Common approaches to addressing behavioral, social-emotional, or academic concerns can promote generalization and maintenance of intervention effects across settings (Galloway & Sheridan, 1994). Continuity among change agents also maximizes consistency and clarity in program objectives, procedures, and outcomes (Sheridan, Kratochwill, & Bergan, 1996).

RESEARCH IN CONSULTATION

Research in consultation has tended to focus on one of two areas of emphasis: behavioral outcome studies and consumer satisfaction studies. Behavioral outcome research has received the greatest amount of attention in the consultation literature and has resulted in promising conclusions. In an early meta-analysis considering MHC, BC, and organizational consultation, Medway and Updyke (1985) concluded that, on average, consultees indicated improvements greater than 71%, compared with controls (i.e., untreated groups), and clients showed improvements greater than 66% of controls. This study found no differences in terms of effectiveness among the three models, and represented one of the first consultation outcome studies to consider outcome variables as assessed by multiple raters (i.e., consultees and consultants). In a more recent review of outcome research, Sheridan, Welch, and Orme (1996) reported that, over a 10-year period (1985–1995), BC had received the most empirical attention (46% of the articles reviewed for their analysis), with 89% of these studies reporting positive outcomes, 11% neutral, and no negative results reported. MHC represented 11% of the studies, with 57% of these studies reporting positive outcomes, 43% neutral, and no negative results reported. Finally, organizational development consultation represented only 4% of the articles reviewed, with less promising outcomes. Combined, these research reviews indicate consultation to be an effective means for providing services for clients across settings and demonstrate positive outcomes for children and other identified clients.

BC and its derivatives continue to receive the most attention in the consultation research literature (Bramlett & Murphy, 1998; Gutkin & Curtis, 1999), and has demonstrated to be more rigorous in experimental methodology than research in other consultation models (Sheridan, Welch, & Orme, 1996). In a seminal study reporting the results of a 5-year research project involving teacher-only BC, Kratochwill, Elliott, and Busse (1995) reported that, for 23 cases, the average effect size for behavioral change was 0.95 (range = −0.55–2.90), which is considered quite effective (Cohen, 1992). In another large-scale study reporting the results of a 4-year research project involving parents and teachers as joint consultees, Sheridan et al. (2001) reported that, for 55 cases, the average effect size was 1.10 (range = −3.6–7.08; *SD* = 1.07). These data indicated approximately equal effect sizes across settings, with home-based targets yielding an average effect size of 1.08 ($SD = 0.82$), and school-based targets yielding an average effect size of 1.11 ($SD = 1.24$).

In school-based consultation, the social significance, acceptability, and importance of the targeted behavior and treatment plan are assessed by the consultees throughout the various phases of consultation, which likely affects treatment integrity (the extent to which the intervention is implemented as intended; Yeaton & Sechrest, 1981) and outcome (Witt & Elliott, 1985). These variables are related to what Wolf (1978) termed social validity, which may be defined as the subjective value judgment regarding the validation of the goals, procedures, and effects of interventions. Consultees determine social validity based on their conclusions about the goals, procedures, and outcomes of consultation. There is a need for more research investigating consumer satisfaction with and acceptability of consultation services (Sheridan, Welch, & Orme, 1996).

To date, the primary focus of many field-based research studies has been client outcomes, with consumer satisfaction and acceptability serving as secondary variables. In one major study, Kratochwill, Elliott, and Busse (1995) measured teacher *acceptability of treatments* implemented in school settings using a 15-item, 6-point Likert scale. They reported relatively high scores on the measure (mean score = 80.3; total possible score = 90; range of individual item scores = 4.9–5.6). Sheridan et al. (2001) reported multiple measures of social validity as assessed by parents and teachers. Among them, consumer perceptions regarding the *acceptability of the consultation process* was measured using a 15-item, 6-point Likert scale (with 6 being the highest possible rating), indicating relatively high scores for parents (average = 5.44; $SD = 0.52$) and teachers (average = 5.45; $SD = 0.60$). Sheridan et al. also reported parent and teacher perceptions of *treatment efficacy* using a 7-item, 6-point Likert-scale instrument (6 being the highest possible rating). On this instrument, parents reported an average perceived efficacy score of 4.71 ($SD = 0.95$), and teachers reported an average perceived efficacy score of 4.30 ($SD = 1.3$). Whereas these studies represent meaningful contributions to the field, a review of the literature reveals that more research is clearly needed assessing data from multiple settings (e.g., home, school), multiple sources (e.g., parents, teachers), and multiple measures. Furthermore, more research is needed assessing multiple outcome indices (e.g., behavioral outcome data, consumer satisfaction data, treatment acceptability, and consultation process acceptability data) and investigating the relationship among such variables in consultation (Sheridan et al., 2001).

STAGES OF BC AND CBC

BC (Bergan & Kratochwill, 1990) and its derivative, CBC (Sheridan, Kratochwill, & Bergan, 1996), are comprised of four general stages (i.e., problem identification, problem analysis, treatment implementation, and treatment evaluation), three of which (i.e., problem identification, analysis, and evaluation) are operationalized via structured interviews between the consultee(s) and consultant. These stages of consultation are generally described as linear; however, in practice, BC is a dynamic process in which there may overlap and/or the process may become cyclical in nature to meet the individual needs of the child-client and consultation team (Bergan & Kratochwill, 1990; Sheridan, Kratochwill, & Bergan, 1996). The stages of BC and CBC are nearly identical, the primary difference being that the home system is considered in addition to the school system throughout the CBC process. Following is a discussion of each stage of BC, including specific objectives for each progressive phase. Table 31.3 provides a summary of the stages and objectives of the model. For additional resources and interview outlines, the interested reader is referred to Kratochwill and Bergan (1990) and Sheridan, Kratochwill, & Bergan (1996).

TABLE 31.3
Stages and Objectives in Behavioral Consultation

I. Problem Identification
   A. Define the problem(s) in behavioral terms.
   B. Provide a tentative identification of antecedent, sequential, and consequent conditions that may be maintaining the behavior.
   C. Provide a tentative strength of the behavior (e.g., frequency, intensity, or duration).
   D. Establish a procedure for baseline data collection, including specification of what, how, and by whom it is to be recorded.

II. Problem Analysis
   A. Evaluate and obtain agreement on the sufficiency and adequacy of baseline data.
   B. Discuss and reach an agreement on a goal for behavior change.
   C. Conduct a functional assessment (i.e., discuss antecedent, sequential, and consequent conditions of the behavior).
   D. Design an intervention plan, including the specification of conditions to be changed and the practical guidelines regarding treatment implementation.
   E. Reaffirm record-keeping procedures.

III. Treatment Implementation
   A. Determine whether the consultee(s) have the necessary skills to implement the plan effectively, providing assistance and training as needed.
   B. Monitor data collection procedures and determine whether the plan is proceeding as designed.
   C. Determine whether any changes or revisions in the treatment plan are necessary.
   D. Continue with data collection.

IV. Treatment Evaluation
   A. Determine whether the consultation goals have been obtained.
   B. Evaluate the overall effectiveness of the treatment plan.
   C. Discuss strategies and tactics regarding the continuation, modification, or termination of the treatment plan.
   D. Schedule additional meetings if necessary, or terminate consultation.

Note. Adapted from "Behavioral Consultation in Educational Settings," by S. M. Sheridan and T. R. Kratochwill, 1991. In J. W. Lloyd, N. N. Singh, & A. C. Repp (Eds.), *The Regular Education Initiative: Alternative Perspectives on Concepts, Issues, and Models* (p. 197), Sycamore, IL: Sycamore Publishing. Copyright 1991 by Sycamore Publishing. Adapted with permission.

Problem Identification

The primary goals of the problem identification stage are to identify the most salient target concern or issue to be addressed in consultation, and to collect pretreatment data on its topography (e.g., frequency, severity) and function. Along with assessment methods (e.g., direct observation, record reviews, and behavioral rating scales), this stage includes a structured behavioral interview (Problem Identification Interview; Kratochwill & Bergan, 1990). During the interview, the consultation team convenes to address the following objectives: (1) define the target problem(s) in behavioral terms; (2) identify tentative surrounding (i.e., antecedent, consequential, and sequential) conditions hypothesized to maintain the behavior; (3) provide a tentative strength of the behavior; (4) discuss and reach a goal for behavior change; and (5) establish a procedure for and begin baseline data collection. The baseline data collection procedures established during problem identification will continue throughout consultation to promote data-based decision making.

Target Behavior Specification. There are several factors to consider during target behavior selection and specification (Bergan & Kratochwill, 1990; Kratochwill, 1985; Sheridan, Kratochwill, & Bergan, 1996). Specifically, it is beneficial to narrow down behavioral *clusters* into behaviors that may be clearly operationalized and monitored (e.g., the difference between describing a child-client as "a defiant student" and describing him as "a student who fails to complete his independent seatwork, especially during math"). Additionally, it is generally more feasible to select one target behavior at a time. Behaviors that are (1) physically dangerous to the student and/or others, and/or (2) likely to result in behavior change that is maintained in an environment beyond the time of specific intervention (e.g., self-help or problem-solving skills) are often prioritized. It is desirable that the target behavior be selected and agreed on by all team members; be deemed problematic for the child-client; and be recognized as worthy of attention and expenditure of valuable resources.

During operationalization, behaviors are specified in concrete, observable, objective terms. Among many guidelines for target behavior specification, Maag (1999) recommends the *stranger test* (i.e., Could the target behavior definition be used by a complete stranger to monitor a specific behavior?). This test speaks to the importance of clarity and specificity in delineating the target behavior to ensure that (1) consultation members are describing and monitoring the same target behavior, and (2) independent observers who may be employed in research or practice are measuring the appropriate behaviors.

Data Collection Considerations. The development of reliable, valid data collection procedures is a critical endeavor, because data collection will continue throughout consultation, thus promoting and guiding a data-based problem-solving process (Sheridan, Cowan, & Eagle, 2001). Data collection requires the consultation team to consider several relevant questions (Bergan & Kratochwill, 1990): What kinds of data shall be recorded? How shall it be recorded? How long shall data collection last? Where shall it take place? The answers to the "how" and "what" questions stem in part from considering the type of concern (e.g., medical, behavioral, academic) being addressed through behavioral consultation. It is recommended that data be collected from multiple sources (e.g., parents, resource teachers, support staff), using multiple methods (e.g., behavioral checklists, permanent products), representing multiple settings (e.g., classroom, playground, home). Multi- source, method, and setting data collection provides both depth and breadth of information to assess performance and overall behavioral outcomes across settings, from the perspective of multiple individuals (Gresham & Noell, 1993).

For school-based target behaviors that are academic in nature (e.g., reading fluency), data collection procedures typically entail curriculum based measurement (CBM), work samples, and/or observational measures of client performance. According to Shinn (1998), CBM is "a set of standard simple, short-duration fluency measures of reading, spelling, written expression, and mathematics computation . . . that measure 'vital signs' of student achievement in important areas of basic skills or literacy" (p. 1). CBM entails taking curriculum-related probes and assessing (1) the typical approach of the target student to a specific task, and (2) the types of errors being made by the student. A comparison group is achieved by assessing several "average students" within the target setting on a specific set of tasks from which a "local performance norm" is derived. The performance of the target student is then compared with this local norm sample to determine areas of relative strengths and needs.

Less complex data collection procedures include work samples and observations of student performance. Work samples are one form of "permanent products," a term frequently used in school settings that refers to items generated through the natural course of an environment that may be utilized as a means of performance assessment (e.g., homework assignments, written essays, grades, etc.). These data are among the most reliable, and are considered less taxing of time and staff resources. A less formal approach than curriculum-based assessment is the direct observation of a particular student's approach to a specific academic task. Error analyses can be conducted to ascertain the types of mistakes made or faulty algorithms used by students. Direct observation of academic tasks is similar to observations utilized for behavioral concerns (see section below) and may be used to monitor academic performance over time for one particular student.

For behavioral performance concerns targeted in consultation (e.g., physical aggression, off-task behavior, noncompliance), the consultation team may select from a range of data collection procedures. Event recording involves tallying or recording the number of times a specific behavior is emitted within a specific time period. In duration recording, an observer records latency, duration, or other temporal aspect of a behavior (e.g., the time it takes for a student to begin working on her math assignment). Momentary time sampling requires the observation of the occurrence or nonoccurrence of a behavior at some predetermined time (e.g., observing whether a student is pulling her hair out or biting her nails at the end of each 10-min interval). In interval recording, an observation period is broken down into discrete, equal intervals, and a behavior is recorded if it occurs at all (partial interval) or throughout (whole interval) that interval for a specified time interval (e.g., observing whether or a not a student is engaged in his classroom assignment during a 15-sec interval over the course of a 10-min period). For detailed information regarding data collection systems, the interested reader is referred to Maag (1999), Martin and Pear (1999), and Kazdin (1982). Such observation systems may provide valuable information to parents, medical experts, and others regarding the effects of a medical intervention (e.g., medication) on a child's behaviors (Northup & Gulley, 2001).

Together, the consultant and consultees must consider the amount of time each type of data collection procedure is likely to require, and assess the cost-benefit relationship with regard to the type and quality of data likely to be yielded by each approach. They then determine which method is likely to (1) provide enough information to guide the consultation team through data-based decisions, and (2) be employed easily and reliably by the teacher or other consultee in the classroom.

Problem Analysis

Problem analysis is the second stage of BC. The goals of problem analysis are to develop hypotheses related to the function of the target behavior and identify appropriate intervention strategies. The problem analysis stage is put into operation via a structured interview (Problem Analysis Interview, or PAI; Kratochwill & Bergan, 1990). At the interview, the team reconvenes to achieve the following related objectives: (1) evaluate and obtain agreement on the baseline data; (2) conduct an ecological analysis of the behavior; (3) design an intervention plan, including specification of conditions to be changed and the practical guidelines regarding treatment implementation; and (4) reaffirm data collection procedures. The problem analysis stage of consultation primarily consists of two phases: the analysis phase and the plan design phase.

Analysis Phase. During the analysis phase, the team collaboratively explores setting specific antecedent, consequent, and sequential conditions surrounding the target behavior to form hypotheses about which condition(s) might be causing and/or maintaining the behavior. Antecedent conditions are events that precede the occurrence of a behavior (e.g., the student typically does not complete assignments because she becomes distracted when instructions are delivered). Setting events are antecedents that are temporally or contextually removed from the behavior (e.g., lack of adequate sleep may result in a student becoming tired and distractible at school the next day). Consequent conditions are events that result from a target behavior and may be reinforcing or punitive in nature. In a school setting, the function of undesirable behavior is often to escape a task, avoid work, gain attention from others, or attain sensory stimulation (Gresham, Watson, & Skinner, 2001). For example, it may be the case that a student receives more reinforcement from talking with specific peers than she does through completing her classroom assignments. In this case, minimizing the peer attention (e.g., separating the child from her favorite peers) and allowing for interaction to occur contingent on work completion may result in increased academic engagement and work completion. Finally, sequential conditions are common patterns across problematic behaviors (e.g., a teacher may notice that the student is particularly distractible and inattentive on the Monday's immediately following weekends she spends with her father away from home). For comprehensive information regarding functional assessment and analysis, the interested reader is referred to Watson, Gresham, and Skinner (2001); O'Neill et al. (1997); and Tilly, Knoster, and Ikeda (2001).

In the analysis phase, team members are faced with the task of ascertaining whether a child's difficulties result from a skill deficit (i.e., the student lacks the requisite skills to perform a behavior or task) or a performance deficit (i.e., the child has the skill but is unable to produce a desired behavior because of environmental factors). Such analyses, when conducted appropriately, yield important treatment information, because different intervention components are utilized to address either skills deficits (e.g., skills training with modeling, with opportunities for practice and feedback) or performance deficits (e.g., environmental manipulation to preclude a specific antecedent or consequent event from causing, maintaining, or precluding a specific behavior). Information gleaned from the conditions and/or the skills analyses may be readily used by the consultation team to design a child-specific intervention plan.

Plan Design Phase. There are several variables to consider when designing an intervention to be implemented by the consultee(s). First, the plan should be based on empirically validated principles. As a scientist-practitioner, it is the consultant's responsibility to ensure that treatment components are derived from evidence-based procedures validated for similar behaviors, similar contexts, or similar functions. Second, the plan should be reasonable (i.e., not overly complex, readily applicable to the target setting), manageable, and acceptable (Sheridan, Kratochwill, & Bergan, 1996). Treatment acceptability—defined as the judgments about treatment procedures by consumers of treatment as to whether treatment is fair, reasonable, and/or intrusive (Kazdin, 1980)—has received much attention in the consultation literature. It is generally assumed that if consultees find an intervention to be unacceptable in terms of their time, resources, or other practical and theoretical aspects, it is likely that treatment integrity (the degree to which an intervention is delivered as intended; Yeaton & Sechrest, 1981) will suffer. Witt and Elliott (1985) hypothesize that treatment acceptability leads to treatment integrity, which in turn is directly related to consultation outcomes. Gutkin and Curtis (1999) recommend that consultants and consultees work together to design and implement plans that are acceptable in terms of criteria that are both objective (i.e., based on evidence-based practice) and subjective (i.e., is acceptable to the consultees). A review of the treatment integrity and acceptability research and practice literature is beyond the scope of this chapter. The interested reader is referred to Gresham (1989, 1996) for a thorough discussion regarding how to monitor and improve treatment integrity, and Eckert and Hintze (2000) for a review of the treatment acceptability literature.

Treatment Implementation

During this stage of BC, the consultee(s) implements the treatment plan developed through the functional assessment and PAI. Although there is no structured meeting associated with this stage of consultation, the consultation team remains in constant contact to monitor treatment integrity, assess any unintentional side effects, and assess the initial efficacy of the treatment plan. The primary objective of this stage of consultation is to maximize the likelihood that the plan will produce the desired effects (Sheridan, Kratochwill, & Bergan, 1996). During intervention implementation, the consultant is advised to remain in constant contact with consultees to: (1) monitor their needs; (2) provide sufficient knowledge and support; (3) reinforce their efforts in plan implementation; and (4) monitor and guide them should an alteration to the plan be necessary. More complex interventions may require additional supports (i.e., additional staff) and/or individualized consultee training (i.e., providing education, modeling, and allowing the consultees to practice before intervention; Gutkin & Curtis, 1999) to maximize treatment integrity and outcome.

Treatment Evaluation

The goals of treatment evaluation are to evaluate the data collected over the course of consultation (i.e., baseline, treatment implementation), determine if consultation goals have been attained, and assess the need for modification or continuation of the treatment plan. A structured interview (the Treatment Evaluation Interview; TEI; Kratochwill & Bergan, 1990) is associated with this stage. The specific objectives of this interview are to: (1) evaluate treatment data to determine whether the goals of consultation have been met; (2) evaluate the overall effectiveness of the treatment plan; (3) discuss strategies and tactics regarding the continuation, modification, or termination of the treatment plan; and (4) discuss strategies for maintenance and generalization of the treatment gains. This stage of consultation assesses whether the hypotheses generated through data analysis were valid, and evaluates whether or not the plan responded to those conditions hypothesized to maintain the target behavior.

Like all stages of consultation, treatment evaluation is a process unique to the needs of the child-client and team members. Treatment evaluation may entail one meeting, one meeting plus telephone contact(s), or several meetings spread out over time until a mutually determined set of consultation and behavioral goals are met. In cases where no progress is made, the consultation team may recycle through the consultation process to more thoroughly analyze the target behavior, and develop an alternative treatment plan based on either a significant alteration of the original plan or another hypothesis regarding the cause for the behavior. In cases where some progress has been made, yet behavioral goals were not completely met, the consultation team may opt to make minor adjustments to the plan to maximize the potential for success (e.g., adjust the dosage or schedule of a medication, change the available reinforcer items to maintain motivation and progress). In cases where the goal has been met, the team may either (1) continue with implementation as is, or (2) discuss specific strategies for maintenance (e.g., increasing the behavioral goal required for reinforcement, gradually fading the intervention) and generalization (e.g., transferring the intervention procedures to a setting not originally targeted for intervention). Regardless of the next step in the consultation process, it should be a collaborative decision, with all team members across settings supporting and assisting one another until termination is mutually determined.

CONSULTATION WITHIN THE SCHOOL CONTEXT

Problem-solving in consultation entails more than identifying a target concern and implementing chosen interventions. Contextual features of applied consultation and intervention (e.g., interpersonal climate, adult/peer relations, expectations for staff and students, values among service providers) are some of the intangible aspects of service delivery worthy of consideration. Furthermore, consideration of a school's culture and entry into the school system invokes important considerations.

School Culture

A school's culture is a pool of information related to virtually every aspect of its environment. It includes the importance value placed on various activities, expected procedures of operation, and appropriate behaviors among individuals within the school environment.

Culture is comprised of a set of variables that include attitudes, values, norms, beliefs, role expectations, and customs that are transmitted to group members (Gollnick & Chinn, 1990). It influences how an individual in that setting thinks, feels, and behaves; it serves to maintain stability in that environment and is often difficult to alter by individuals within or external to the system (Welch & Sheridan, 1995). The culture of a school is essential to understand as it permeates the beliefs, expectations, and experiences of teachers and administrators. Problem-solving strategies or instructional or behavioral modifications for an individual student may be perceived as unrealistic or inappropriate, depending on the degree to which they fit within the norms of the particular school environment.

Consulting in school settings presents unique challenges because of the systemic and organizataional features of schools in general. Historically, one of the most salient barriers to consultation in school settings and among school personnel has been the organizational issue of lack of time (Idol-Maestas & Ritter, 1985). Teachers are responsible for delivering instruction in their classrooms for several consecutive hours per day, often with little time away from students or only brief periods dedicated for planning. Teachers' work is defined by the time spent with students, and whole group instruction is the primary instructional format (Elmore, 1987). Other pragmatic difficulties encountered in school settings include large caseloads and classrooms, scheduling problems, and competing and overwhelming responsibilities. Such issues are of paramount importance when considering the nature and complexity of requests made of teachers. As already reviewed, the time required for implementation and complexity of an intervention influence its acceptability by treatment agents, which may affect the degree to which it is delivered in the natural setting (cf. Witt & Elliott, 1985).

Entry Considerations

Some of the aforementioned concerns about school systems and cultural and contextual features therein can be addressed through appropriate entry practices. *Entry* refers to "the consultant's crossing of organizational boundaries into a system or work setting" (Brown et al., 1995, p. 107). Two distinct aspects of entry are relevant. Formal entry requires consultants to gain sanction for consultation activities by persons in administrative or authority positions within the setting (e.g., school principals). There are also informal aspects of entry, requiring consultants' activities and roles to be accepted by consultees (e.g., teachers, other school personnel, parents).

Several authors have discussed issues surrounding formal entry extensively (e.g., Conoley & Conoley, 1992; Dougherty, 2000; Gallesich, 1982). The processes surrounding entry are critical to the success of consultation and should not be underestimated. Dougherty (2000) identified four phases of entry, including exploring needs, contracting, physically entering the setting, and psychologically entering the setting. A formal discussion of expectations regarding roles (for the consultant, consultees, and system/organization) and activities (including active involvement, information-sharing, data collection, and evaluation) is essential. A verbal or written contract is often useful as it outlines specific details of the relationship, including fees, responsibilities, time limits, accepted activities, issues of confidentiality, and other parameters of consultation (Conoley & Conoley, 1992).

Informal acceptance of consultation services is perhaps the most critical feature of the relationship. During the time that consultants and consultees begin their working relationship, issues of trust, cooperation, or reluctance to share information may be salient (Gallesich, 1982). The transition from formal entry to informal acceptance is a normal and expected process, because it affords consultees opportunities to evaluate the consultant's skills and operating style, and to assess possible risks of consultation. Because consultees participate voluntarily and may or may not be committed to a long-term consultative relationship, the effective consultant begins relationship-building early on in the consultation process by establishing trust, rapport, and a shared perspective of the nature of the consultation process (a process similar to, but not the same as, the therapist–client relationship). Furthermore, Gutkin and Curtis (1999) recommend that the school consultant: (1) maintain professional confidence with regard to both the consultees and the child-client; (2) encourage and reinforce active consultee participation; and (3) actively support the consultee(s) throughout the consultation process. Without consultee support, consultation is not possible; effective entry is achieved when the consultant takes the time to establish rapport, demonstrate respect, and build mutual trust. Challenges associated with informal acceptance also may be minimized through ongoing interaction, contact, and opportunities to develop an interpersonal connection outside of the consultation interaction.

Brown et al. (1995) summarize the issues surrounding the critical entry stage aptly: "Entry... is not a single step, but an ongoing process that has both formal and informal components. Successful entry is characterized by a progressively deeper understanding of the organization on the part of the consultant, increased trust and acceptance of the consultant by members of the consultee organizations, and a clear, mutual understanding of the objectives, methods, and procedural details of consultation by both parties" (p. 111).

CONCLUSIONS

School-based consultation is a vehicle through which consultants (i.e., medical professionals, psychologists) can work together with parents and educators to promote cross-setting information-sharing, problem-solving, and coordination of services. The use of consultation in schools can achieve several goals, including (1) the short-term goal of resolving the student's presenting difficulties (i.e., remedial intervention), and (2) the long-term goals of preventing future similar challenges and improving the consultees' problem-solving skills (i.e., a preventive approach). The purpose of this chapter is to provide an impetus for professionals in various pediatric settings to utilize this service-delivery model within schools.

By considering consultation through the lens of ecological theory, the importance of relationships among the significant adults in a child's life is evident. Evidence-based, structured consultation procedures provide a technology by which these key adults (e.g., pediatric specialists, parents, teachers) can come together to share information and expertise, address presenting concerns, and coordinate services for children and families. By recognizing and understanding unique issues presented in school contexts and engaging in important entry practices, consultants can be positioned to offer important and effective indirect services in the natural settings within which their clients function.

ACKNOWLEDGMENTS

Preparation of this chapter was supported in part by Grants 325H980126 and 325D990010 awarded to the first author by the U.S. Department of Education, Office of Special Education and Rehabilitative Services. The opinions expressed herein belong to the authors and do not reflect those of the granting agency.

REFERENCES

Bergan, J. R., & Kratochwill, T. R. (1990). *Behavioral consultation and therapy*. New York: Plenum.

Bramlett, R. K., & Murphy, J. J. (1998). School psychology perspectives on consultation: Key contributions to the field. *Journal of Educational and Psychological Consultation, 9*, 29–55.

Bronfenbrenner, U. (1977). Toward an experimental ecology of human development. *American Psychologist, 32*, 513–529.

Brown, D., Pryzwansky, W. B., & Schulte, A. C. (1995). *Psychological consultation: Introduction to theory and practice* (3rd ed.). Boston: Allyn and Bacon.

Caplan, G. (1970). *The theory and practice of mental health consultation*. New York: Basic Books.

Christenson, S. L., & Sheridan, S. M. (2001). *Schools and families: Creating essential connections for learning*. New York: Guilford Press.

Cohen, J. (1992). A power primer. *Psychological Bulletin, 112*, 155–159.

Colton D. L., & Sheridan, S. M. (1998). Conjoint behavioral consultation and social skills training: Enhancing the play behaviors of boys with attention deficit hyperactivity disorder. *Journal of Educational and Psychological Consultation, 9*, 3–28.

Conoley, J. C. (1987). Schools and families: Theoretical and practical bridges. *Professional School Psychology, 2*, 191–203.

Conoley, J. C., & Conoley, C. W. (1992). *School consultation practice and training* (2nd ed.). Boston: Allyn and Bacon.

Dougherty, A. M. (2000). *Psychological consultation and collaboration in school and community settings* (3rd ed.). Belmont, CA: Wadsworth/Thomson Learning.

Eckert, T. L., & Hintze, J. M. (2000). Behavioral conceptualizations and applications of treatment acceptability: Issues related to service delivery and research methodology. *School Psychology Quarterly, 15*, 123–148.

Elmore, R. F. (1987). Reform and the culture of authority in schools. *Educational Administration Quarterly, 23*(4), 60–78.

Gallesich, J. (1982). *The profession and practice of consultation*. San Francisco: Jossey Bass.

Galloway, J., & Sheridan, S. M. (1994). Implementing scientific practices through case studies: Examples using home-school interventions and consultation. *Journal of School Psychology, 32*, 385–413.

Gollnick, D. M., & Chinn, P. C. (1990). *Multicultural education in a pluralistic society* (3rd ed.), Columbus, OH: Merrill.

Gresham, F. M. (1989). Assessment of treatment integrity in school consultation and prereferral intervention. *School Psychology Review, 18*, 37–50.

Gresham, F. M. (1996). Treatment integrity in single-subject research. In R. D. Franklin, D. B. Allison, & B. S. Gorman (Eds.), *Design and analysis of single-case research* (pp. 93–117). Mahweh, NJ: Lawrence Erlbaum.

Gresham, F. M., & Noell, G. H. (1993). Documenting the effectiveness of consultation outcomes. In J. E. Zins & T. R. Kratochwill (Eds.), *Handbook of consultation services for children: Applications in educational and clinical settings* (pp. 249–273). San Francisco, CA: Jossey-Bass.

Gresham, F. M., Watson, T. S., & Skinner, C. H. (2001). Functional behavioral assessment: Principles, procedures, and future directions. *School Psychology Review, 30*, 156–172.

Gutkin, T. B., & Conoley, J. C. (1990). Reconceptualizing school psychology from a service delivery perspective: Implications for practice, training, and research. *Journal of School Psychology, 28*, 203–223.

Gutkin, T. B., & Curtis, M. (1999). School based consultation theory and practice: The art and science of indirect service delivery. In C. R. Reynolds & T. B. Gutkin (Eds.), *Handbook of school psychology* (3rd *ed.*, pp. 598–637). New York: Wiley.

Hansen, D. A. (1986). Family-school articulations: The effects of interaction rule mismatch. *American Educational Research Journal, 23*, 643–659.

Henggeler, S. W. (1991). Multidimensional causal models of delinquent behavior. In R. Cohen & Y. A. Siegel (Eds.), *Context and development* (pp. 211–231). Hillsdale, NJ: Lawrence Erlbaum.

Idol-Maestas, L., & Ritter, S. (1985). A follow-up study of resource/consulting teachers: Factors that facilitate and inhibit teacher consultation. *Teacher Education and Special Education, 8*, 121–131.

Kazdin, A. E. (1980). Acceptability of alternative treatments for deviant child behavior. *Journal of Applied Behavior Analysis, 13*, 259–273.

Kazdin, A. E. (1982). *Single-case research designs: Methods for clinical and applied settings*. New York: Oxford University Press.

Kratochwill, T. R. (1985). Case study research in school psychology. *School Psychology Review, 14*, 204–215.

Kratochwill, T. R., & Bergan, J. R. (1990). *Behavioral consultation in applied settings: An individual guide*. New York: Plenum.

Kratochwill, T. R., Elliott, S. N., & Busse, R. T. (1995). Behavioral consultation: A five-year evaluation of consultant and client outcomes. *School Psychology Quarterly, 10*, 87–117.

Maag, J. W. (1999). Behavior management: From theoretical implications to practical applications. San Diego, CA: Singular Publications.

Maher, C. A., Illback, R. J., & Zins, J. E. (1984). *Organizational psychology in the schools: A handbook for professionals*. Springfield, IL: Thomas.

Martin, G., & Pear, J. (1999). *Behavior modification: What it is and how to do it.* Upper Saddle River, NJ: Prentice Hall.

Medway, F. J. (1979). How effective is school consultation: A review of recent research. *Journal of School Psychology, 17*, 275–282.

Medway, F. J., & Updyke, J. F. (1985). Meta-analysis of consultation outcome studies. *American Journal of Community Psychology, 13*, 489–504.

Neill, T. K. (1997). Integrating services for children with severe emotional disabilities through coordination. In R. J. Illback, C. T. Cobb, & H. M. Joseph (Eds.), *Integrated services for children and families: Opportunities for psychological practice* (pp. 157–190). New York: APA Books.

Northup, J., & Gulley, V. (2001). Some contributions of functional analysis to the assessment of behaviors associated with attention deficit hyperactivity disorder and the effects of stimulant medication. *School Psychology Review, 30*, 227–238.

O'Neill, R. E., Horner, R. H., Albin, R. W., Sprague, J. R., Storey, K., & Newton, J. S. (1997). Functional assessment and program development for problem behavior: A practical handbook (2nd ed.). Pacific Grove, CA: Brooks/Cole.

Ray, K. P. & Watson, T. S. (2001). Analysis of the effects of temporally distant events on school behavior. *School Psychology Quarterly, 16*, 324–342.

Reinking, R. J., Livesay, G., & Kohl, M. (1978). The effects of consultation style on consultee productivity. *American Journal of Community Psychology, 6*, 283–290.

Schoenwald, S. K., & Henggeler, S. W. (1997). Combining effective treatment strategies with family-preservation models of service delivery. In R. J. Illback, C. T. Cobb, & H. M. Joseph (Eds.), *Integrated services for children and families: Opportunities for psychological practice* (pp. 121–136). New York: APA Books.

Sheridan, S. M. (1997). Conceptual and empirical bases of conjoint behavioral consultation. *School Psychology Quarterly, 12*, 119–133.

Sheridan, S. M., Cowan, R. J., & Eagle, J. W. (2001). Partnering with parents in educational programming for students with special needs. In C. F. Telzrow & M. Tankersley (Eds.), *IDEA amendments of 1997: Practice guidelines for school-based teams* (pp. 307–350). Bethesda, MD: National Association of School Psychologists.

Sheridan, S. M., Eagle, J. W., Cowan, R. J., & Michelson, W. (2001). The effects of conjoint behavioral consultation in inclusionary settings: Results of a four-year investigation. *Journal of School Psychology, 39*, 361–385.

Sheridan, S. M., & Gutkin, T. B. (2000). The ecology of school psychology: Examining and changing out paradigm for the 21st century. *School Psychology Review, 29*, 485–502.

Sheridan, S. M., & Kratochwill, T. R. (1991). Behavioral consultation in educational settings. In J. W. Lloyd, A. C. Repp, & N. N. Singh (Eds.), *The regular education initiative: Alternative perspectives on concepts, issues, and methods* (pp. 193–210). Sycamore, IL: Sycamore Publishing Co.

Sheridan, S. M., Kratochwill, T. R., & Bergan, J. R. (1996). *Conjoint behavioral consultation: A procedural manual.* New York: Plenum.

Sheridan, S. M., Kratochwill, T. R., & Elliott, S. N. (1990). Behavioral consultation with parents and teachers: Delivering treatment for socially withdrawn children at home and school. *School Psychology Review, 19*, 33–52.

Sheridan, S. M., Welch, M., & Orme, S. (1996). Is consultation effective? A review of outcome research. *Remedial and Special Education, 17*, 341–354.

Shinn, M. R. (Ed.). (1998). *Advanced applications of curriculum-based measurement.* New York: Guilford.

Tilly W. D., III, Knoster, T. P., & Ikeda, M. J. (2001). Functional behavioral assessment: Strategies for positive behavior support. In C. F. Telzrow & M. Tankersley (Eds.), *IDEA amendments of 1997: Practice guidelines for school-based teams* (pp. 151–198). Bethesda, MD: National Association of School Psychologists.

U.S. Department of Education/American Educational Research Association (1995). *School-linked comprehensive services for children and families: What we know and what we need to know.* Washington, DC: Author.

Watson, T. S., Gresham, F. M., & Skinner, C. (Guest Eds.). (2001). Issues and procedures for implementing functional behavior assessments in schools [Special issue]. *School Psychology Review, 30*(2), 153–304.

Weiner, R. K., Sheridan, S. M., & Jenson, W. R. (1998). The effects of conjoint behavioral consultation and a structured homework program on math completion and accuracy in junior high school students. *School Psychology Quarterly, 13*, 281–309.

Welch, M., & Sheridan, S. M. (1995). *Educational partnerships: Serving students at risk.* San Antonio, TX: Harcourt Brace.

Witt, J. C., & Elliott, S. N. (1985). Acceptability of classroom intervention strategies. In T. R. Kratochwill (Ed.), *Advances in school psychology* (Vol. 4, pp. 251–288). Hillsdale, NJ: Lawrence Erlbaum.

Witt, J. E., Martens, B. K., & Elliott, S. N. (1984). Assessing the acceptability of behavioral interventions used in classrooms. *Psychology in the Schools, 20*, 510–517.

Wolf, M. M. (1978). Social validity: The case for subjective measurement or how applied behavior analysis is finding its heart. *Journal of Applied Behavior Analysis, 11*, 203–214.

Yeaton, W. H., & Sechrest, L. (1981). Critical dimensions in the choice and maintenance of successful treatment: Strength, integrity, and effectiveness. *Journal of Consulting and Clinical Psychology, 49*, 156–167.

32

Consultation With Caregivers and Families

Cindy Carlson
Thomas Kubiszyn
Laura Guli
University of Texas at Austin

INTRODUCTION

Pediatric illness, both chronic and acute, has an impact that extends well beyond the biological symptoms associated with the illness that are experienced by the child. Because children live within a broad social–ecological context that includes the family, school, peer group, neighborhood, and larger community, childhood illness affects all persons with whom they have contact. Once diagnosed with a pediatric illness, children and families become embedded in an additional system: health care. The rules, organizing principles, goals, and beliefs of each of these systems differ. Simply managing the medical aspects of the child's illness successfully across such diverse systems is a challenge for caregivers, not to mention their concern about the psychosocial aspects of the child's adaptation to his/her illness in these various social environments. Moreover, the distinctive properties of each social system will influence the meaning and response that is given to the child's illness, which, in turn, impact the child's coping and adaptation.

The family is the most significant and pervasive influence on a child's development. The degree to which the family is functioning well significantly enables or constrains the developing child. Research is replete with data to support the conclusion that stress impairs functioning. Caregivers and family members of a chronically ill child will each, to a greater or lesser degree, experience stress related to the child's illness. Medical management of the child's disease may be physically, emotionally, and financially draining for caregivers and other family members. Families have different beliefs around pain and illness that may influence the degree to which they can be open about a child's illness and seek support related to it. The developmental age of the ill child and siblings will further impact family coping and adaptation. Regardless of the stress associated with chronic or acute childhood illness, family relations will be affected by this para-normative event in the family. For better or worse, parenting quality and teamwork, marital relations, sibling relations, and relations with extended family members will all be influenced by the presence of a chronically ill child in the family. All family roles are likely to be affected. Research studies consistently find that family functioning both directly influences children's adjustment to childhood illness and mediates family stress associated with chronic childhood disease (Wallander & Thompson, 1995).

Pediatric illnesses frequently impact the normal development of the child and may impact the child's rate and ability to learn in school. Helping family members understand the developmental and learning effects of a particular disease is an important role for the pediatric psychologist in the school setting or the school psychologist functioning with a pediatric orientation. Because it is generally viewed to be the responsibility of parents to keep schools informed about the needs of their children, psychologists can help caregivers clearly communicate the needs of their child to the school and help schools be responsive to the stress of pediatric illness on the family. It is at the nexus of the child-family-school-health care system that pediatric psychology consultation occurs with caregivers and families. It is the purpose of this chapter to describe that process.

Several premises guide the chapter. The first is the importance of integrated services to children (e.g., Kubiszyn, 1999). The second is the usefulness of family systems theory and a social–ecological model for understanding coping and adaptation in childhood chronic illness. The third is the value of consultation as a therapeutic intervention with caregivers and families who are affected by pediatric illness and its particular fit with the norms of the school and health care system. The final premise is the necessity of considering family consultation to include systems consultation with the school and health care systems. This chapter will examine guiding models for consulting with caregivers and families, the impact of childhood chronic illness on the family context, the value of family consultation as a therapeutic intervention, the consultation process, empirical support for parent and family consultation, and special issues related to particular childhood illnesses.

FRAMEWORKS FOR FAMILY CONSULTATION RELATED TO CHILDHOOD ILLNESS

There are several useful frameworks for thinking about consultation with families and caregivers who are responsible or impacted by childhood illness. These include systems theory, social–ecological model, biopsychosocial model, and models of family adaptation and coping. Each provides a useful way of conceptualizing the interlocking systemic influences related to the experience of childhood illness within the family and larger social system. No particular model has adequate empirical support to compel singular adoption of that framework (Kazak, Segal-Andrews, & Johnson, 1995).

Systems Theory

General Systems Theory proposes that a system is a set of objects together with their mutual interactions that are actively interrelated and operate in some sense as a bounded unit (Von Bertalanffy, 1956, cited by Broderick, 1993). Two key properties emerge from this definition: active interrelatedness of the elements and boundary. Active interrelatedness of the elements implies that all elements in a system are impacted in some way by a change in any single element. Also critical to systems theory is a focus on the interaction among the elements in contrast to a focus on any individual element. Applied to the family as a system, the focus of assessment and intervention then would be the interactions and relationships between family members and not any single member, such as the ill child, or any particular dyad, such as the mother–child relationship.

Boundary is another key element of systems theory. Boundaries in systems theory are defined as the invisible rules that regulate the exchange of information across system elements and subsystems. Boundaries protect the differentiated functioning of the family within the larger social context and the differentiated functioning of elements and subsystems within the family system. Information exchange between family members is critical to coordinated functioning; however, too much information or inappropriate information across family members may create stress and compromise functioning. In the case of the family with an ill child, for example, caregivers must balance the need for the ill child and siblings to have enough information about the illness, provided at their developmental level, to cope; however, excessive sharing of information about financial strain related to the illness may worry the ill child and/or siblings and compromise their accomplishment of appropriate developmental tasks. In general, clear boundaries and roles are considered a bench mark of the well-functioning family system.

Other key elements of a systems perspective include hierarchy, reciprocal causality, and goal attainment. All living systems are organized for a purpose. The goal of the family system is commonly viewed to be the survival and development of its members. Complex social systems, such as families and schools, must differentiate their organization into hierarchically nested subsystems to accomplish the goals of the system. The nuclear family commonly includes the subsystems of parent/caregiver, spouse/partner, and child/sibling. Optimally, adult family members in the parent/caregiver hierarchy have adequate power to protect and socialize children. Critical to well-functioning families is a clear hierarchy and boundaries to protect subsystem roles. A final element of systems theory is the concept of reciprocal causality. In contrast to linear causality where X is viewed to cause Y, a systems perspective argues for the reciprocal influence of X and Y on one another. A linear, child focus in the case of anorexia, for example, would view the eating disorder as a sign of individual psychopathology, whereas a family systems perspective would identify the family transactional patterns that maintain the anorexia (e.g., Minuchin, Rosman, & Baker, 1978).

According to Minuchin (1974), a schema of the family as a system operating within specific social contexts over time has three components. The first is that the family is an open system whose structure transforms in response to demands from the sociocultural milieu. Second, as family members develop, structure must adapt to better meet their changing needs. Third, family adaptation to external and internal circumstances is necessary to maintain continuity and enhance the psychosocial growth of family members.

Systems theory applied to families with a chronically ill child argues that all members of the family will be influenced by and will influence one another in their adaptation and coping related to the disease. An important element of family adaptation and coping will be the establishment of clear roles, boundaries, organization, and power regarding the demands placed on the family by the child's illness. The medical management demands placed on a family with a seriously ill child, for example, may require the augmentation of the parental/caregiver subsystem with other family members. A concern of the family systems consultant would be the clarity of rules, roles, and hierarchy required for a smooth-functioning caregiver team with multiple members. Finally, a systems perspective assumes that the family must continuously adapt and change, yet maintain continuity of patterns and routines, in the face of the demands related to normal development, as well as the unique pressures associated with a child's illness.

Biopsychological Model

Family systems theory is extended more directly to the family with a chronically ill member in the biopsychosocial model (Engel, 1977, cited by Kazak et al., 1995). This model acknowledges the interdependent and mutually influencing relationships among biological, psychological, individual, family, and community subsystems. This model asserts that symptoms associated with illness may be exacerbated or eased depending on the social and emotional functionings of these interrelated systems. From the biopsychosocial perspective, the child's medical problems are intrinsically linked with the structure and organization of the family and the school. Medical family therapy is a treatment modality consistent with the biopsychosocial model (McDaniel, 1995). The medical family therapist takes a family systems intervention approach to helping the family and school cope more adaptively with the child's illness. (The distinction between family consultation and family therapy will be addressed later in this chapter.)

Social–Ecological Model

Also complementary to systems theory, the social–ecological model examines relationships between the individual and the settings or contexts in which they actively engage (Bronfenbrenner, 1979). Specifically, the developing child is viewed is residing within nested concentric spheres of influence. The microsystem level, represented by the family, is defined as the social context in which the child is directly embedded. The mesosystem level includes social systems in which the child actively participates, such as school, peer group, church, and health care system. The mesosystem is further embedded within the exosystem. The child does not directly participate in exosystem settings, but may be indirectly influenced by them because these include the social settings that may influence members of the micro- and mesosystems (e.g. employment environment). Finally, all nested systems are embedded in the larger macrosystem that identifies influences from the larger cultural milieu, such as culture and ethnicity, urban/rural. The social–ecological model argues that each system level is constrained by the qualities of the system in which it is embedded. This model further proposes that children's development is fostered when settings share similar values and rules for the child, as well as when settings are in active communication with one another. An expert discussion of the social–ecological framework applied to the family with a chronically ill child appears in Kazak et al. (1995).

Family Adaptation and Coping Models

Several models of family adaptation and coping with illness have been developed and are briefly described in Quittner and DiGirolamo (1988). The models include the Double ABCX Model, Varni-Wallander Model, and the Transactional Stress and Coping Model. A major impetus for the development of these models was the conclusion reached across research studies that, although chronic childhood illness places children and families at risk for psychological disorder, the effects are variable with most families coping successfully. The important question is, what are the predicting and mediating variables that affect more adaptive coping?

The Double ABCX Model (McCubbin & Patterson, 1982; Patterson, 1988; both cited in Quittner & DiGirolamo, 1988) posits that the childhood illness is the stressor or crisis that places extra demands on the family. The family's ability to meet the demands is mediated by the meaning they ascribe to the event and the resources they have available. The Varni-Wallander Risk and Resilience Model (Varni & Wallander, 1988; Wallander & Varni, 1989; both cited in Quittner & DiGirolamo, 1988) similarly proposes the severity of the child's illness, life stresses and daily hassles pose risk factors that will increase the probability of psychological adjustment problems in the family. The causal link is mediated by resistance factors, such as temperament, cognitive appraisals, coping behaviors, and social–ecological support. The Transactional Stress and Coping Model (Thompson, Gustafson, Hamlett, & Spock, cited in Quittner & DiGirolamo, 1988) proposes similar components to the other models, but argues that their importance will vary with the type of childhood disorder.

A recent review of the stress and coping models in pediatric psychology concluded there is currently little evidence that stressful life events are strong predictors of family adaptation to childhood illness and disability (Quittner & DiGirolamo, 1998). In part this conclusion is a function of the general ways in which stress has been measured. When measurement focuses on stressors that are specific to the context of the child's illness, and that reflect the specific daily tasks faced by the family in the care of the child, the link between stress, coping, and the psychological and physical well-being among family members is stronger.

Studies have consistently found that family environment mediates the link between stress and coping (Quittner & DiGirolamo, 1998). When family members' self-report higher levels of cohesion and expressiveness, and lower levels of conflict on the Family Environment Scale (Moos & Moos, 1981) or optimal levels of cohesion and adaptability on the Family Adaptability and Cohesion Evaluation Scale III (Olson, Portner, & Lavee, 1985), these are associated with better outcomes related to coping with a child's chronic illness. Outcomes include adherence to the treatment regimen, as well as better physical and mental health of parents.

In contrast with the consistent role of family environment in mediating family stress and coping with chronic childhood illness, studies examining the benefits of social support have produced inconsistent findings. Kazak (1989) reported on her program of research on social support networks among families with a chronically ill child compared with matched controls. She found similar findings across several studies. Families with a medically involved child have smaller, more dense social networks, and this higher density was related to increased parental distress. Specifically, distress experienced was related to ongoing interactions with medical, educational, and social service systems.

Taken together, research related to parent and caregiver distress when rearing a child with a chronic illness or disability argues strongly for a focus in family consultation on both processes within the family and the across relevant social systems in which the family is involved.

THE CHRONICALLY ILL CHILD IN THE FAMILY

Having a child with a chronic illness, serious acute disorder, physical handicap, or terminal condition is recognized as stressful for all subsystems of the family: parental, marital, and sibling. Several excellent reviews have been written on the effects of childhood chronic illness on the family system (Kazak, 1989; Quittner & DiGirolamo, 1998), and the mediating effects of parent and family adjustment on the child's adaptation to chronic conditions (Wallander & Thompson, 1995). This chapter section provides a summary of findings.

Parenting

Research generally finds that parents with a chronically ill or disabled child, and particularly mothers, report elevated levels of parenting stress compared with control families. This is particularly true for stress related to managing the child's behavior and for childhood disabilities involving sensory impairment. Parents raising children with autism, deafness, failure to thrive, and cystic fibrosis have reported higher parenting stress. In addition, most studies find higher rates of psychological distress, as measured by reported physical and emotional symptoms, among parents with chronically ill children, compared with matched controls. In particular, mothers caring for disabled or chronically ill children report 40–50% more symptoms, and especially depression, compared with community controls. In an alarming statistic, one study found 64% of mothers and 43% of fathers reported clinically significant levels of depression after the diagnosis of cystic fibrosis in a child (Quittner, DiGirolano, et al., 1992, cited in Quittner & DiGirolano, 1998). Parenting stress and coping are inversely related in families of children with developmental disabilities (Bramlett, Hall, Barnett, & Rowell, 1995).

One noteworthy exception to the pattern of parents' reported stress and psychological distress related to rearing a chronically ill or disabled child is found for parents of children with cancer. Parents of children diagnosed with cancer report much lower rates of depression (mothers 13% and fathers 8%; Dahlquist et al., 1993, cited in Quittner & DiGirolano, 1998). Childhood cancer typically involves multiple stages of response and coping: anxiety with diagnosis; several years of aggressive treatment; and hope of a remission and cure (Kupst et al., 1984, cited in Quittner & DiGirolano, 1998). It is presumed that childhood cancer presents caregivers with a different set of challenges at each stage and thus differs from coping with a condition that is chronic and unremitting. Communication among family members, for example, may be compromised in the wish to avoid the inevitability of death (Drotar, 1975).

Caregiving is, in fact, recommended as a framework for understanding the demands on parents of a chronically ill child. For example, a salient variable in maternal depression appears to be worry over the long-term care demands of a child who is dependent not only in childhood, but also anticipated to be dependent on parental care in adulthood (Kazak et al., 1995). An additional stressor affecting parental caregiver demands is the increased use of home care versus institutional care in medicine. This is a good example of the social–ecological model in which macrosystem changes in social policy impact the family microsystem of the chronically ill or disabled child.

Research also supports a relationship between children's adjustment to their chronic illness and parental stress (Wallander & Thompson, 1995). In a series of longitudinal studies by Thompson and colleagues, maternal anxiety was associated with mother-reported child internalizing and externalizing behavior problems. Unfortunately, the methodological confound of maternal reports for the child's behavior may indicate the relationship is an artifact of response bias.

Marital Relationship

Research studies find that parents of children with a chronic illness or disability are more likely to experience marital distress than parents of nondisabled children. Moreover, rates of reported marital distress are high. In one study, 43–63% of parents with a chronically ill child reported significant marital distress, compared with 22% in a comparison control sample (Quittner, 1991, cited in Quittner & DiGirodano, 1998). Less well understood is the source of marital relationship distress. It is hypothesized that caregiver demands, unequal division of labor, and barriers to rest and recreation may be relevant; however, additional research is clearly needed to clarify the sources of marital distress.

Siblings

Having a sibling with a chronic illness or disability is expected to both directly and indirectly impact siblings (Kazak et al., 1995). Early research found siblings to be at higher risk for adjustment disorders, compared with matched control families. Unfortunately, there are so few recent and methodologically sound studies examining the impact of a chronic illness on siblings that treatment recommendations are premature.

Summary

It should be clear from the preceding discussion that the family with a chronically ill or disabled child is at greater risk for parenting stress, psychological and physical symptoms among parents, and marital relationship dissatisfaction compared with families with nondisabled children. Moreover, quality of family relationships is the most consistent mediator of stress and coping among families with a chronic childhood illness. Thus, it is imperative to consider assessment and intervention with the family to be a critical component of the medical management of pediatric illness.

FAMILY CONSULTATION

Consultation is broadly defined as any service provided by a professional or specialist. More specifically, consultation may be distinguished by several characteristics: (1) it is a helping or problem-solving process that occurs between a professional help-giver (the consultant) and a help-seeker (the consultee) who has responsibility for the welfare of another person (the client); (2) it is voluntary, collaborative, time-limited, and competence-oriented; (3) the goal is to resolve the presenting concern of the consultee; and (4) the consultee benefits from the relationship in such a way that future concerns regarding the client may be handled more sensitively (Kazak, Simms, & Rourke, 2002; Meyers, Parsons, & Martin, 1979). Gerald Caplan makes the distinction between client-centered case consultation, consultee-centered case consultation, program-centered administrative consultation, and consultee-centered administrative consultation (Caplan & Caplan, 1999). This chapter is primarily concerned with family consultation as consultee-centered case consultation and secondarily concerned with family-oriented, program-centered administrative consultation. Thus, in this chapter, most frequently we are referring to the pediatric or school psychologist as the consultant who assists the family (the consultee) in its socioecological milieu with concerns related to adaptation and coping with a chronically ill or disabled child. In the process of establishing successful consultation relationships within the school and/or health care systems, the pediatric and school psychologists may find that they are requested to provide program-centered administrative consultation directed toward improving the ability of the system to respond to the needs of families with a chronically ill or disabled child or a client-centered case consultation with the physician regarding relevant family issues.

Family consultation in pediatric psychology (Kazak et al., 2002; Wynne, McDaniel, & Weber, 1987) and school psychology (Carlson & Hickman, 1992) is embedded in systems theory. In assessing the concerns of the family, the systems-oriented family consultant will focus on the expressed needs of the family as these reflect not only stressors in family relationships, but also problems within and between the systems in the larger social–ecological milieu of the family. Thus, consultation with a family with a medically involved child is seldom limited to the family unit. Rather, the focus of assessment and problem-solving frequently must expand to the key therapeutic relational systems involved with the child. Beyond the caregiver/family system, these commonly include the health care and school systems, and may also include community service and extended family systems. When two or more relational systems become the focus of the consultation, it may be more appropriately termed *systems consultation* (Wynne et al., 1987).

Consultation vs. Therapy

With a common foundation in systems theory, the distinction between family consultation and family therapy is easily blurred, yet important. Wynne et al. (1987) argue that family consultation, rather than family therapy, is the most appropriate and strategic framework for working with families when a family member has an identified physical illness or disability. This is because a referral for family therapy commonly implies that the family "caused" the illness or problem. In contrast, family consultation is a collaborative relationship in which the family with the consultant agrees on an agenda and course of action that will be taken together.

The course of action may be family therapy; however, this is seldom the optimal place to begin. Wynne et al. provide a useful illustration with a pediatric neurology case of a systems-oriented family consultation that included the following stages: (1) family consultation to determine the needs of the family; (2) a systems consultation with the medical team and the family to clarify roles, responsibilities, and communication; (3) family therapy to deal with family members' guilt and grief related to the child's illness; (4) a systems consultation with the school as family–school relationship difficulties emerged; and (5) marital therapy as parents begin to acknowledge the strain placed on their marriage by the illness. These authors argue strongly that intervention with families with a chronically ill child should begin as a time-limited consultation, but remain open to the necessity to expand professional availability to include broader services. Thus, family consultation may involve family therapy and systems consultation at various stages of the consultation process.

Family-Oriented Program Consultation

Up to this point, family consultation has been discussed as case or consultee centered, that is, focused on problem-solving with a particular family and child. Family consultation may also be program centered. In a program-centered administrative consultation, the consultant is invited by an administrator to help with a current problem of program development or organization policies (Caplan & Caplan, 1999). After an evaluation of the problem, the psychology consultant may recommend changes in procedures or policies or the development of new programs to benefit staff and/or caregivers of children with a chronic illness or disability.

Psychoeducational workshops, for example, are often an appropriate component of family consultation that fits well with the norms of both the school and medical settings. This format is cost-effective and permits the consultant to share valuable expertise with a group of families who may be invited because they are coping with a similar childhood disorder. Psychoeducational workshops may also be an effective means to join families together in a continuing supportive network. Finally, psychoeducational workshops may be the most comfortable help-seeking format for many caregivers, especially fathers, and open the door to fuller use of professional services. Family consultation may also include the development and evaluation of programs designed to facilitate the coping of teachers and families with childhood chronic illness and disability. Although not limited in scope to descriptions of programs for families with chronically ill or disabled children, an excellent resource is *Model Programs in Child and Family Mental Health* (Roberts, 1996).

Family Consultation Process

The process of consultation has been described in the pediatric psychology literature (e.g., Hamlett & Stabler, 1995; Kazak et al., 2002), the school psychology and counselor literature (e.g., Caplan & Caplan, 1999; Meyers et al., 1979; Strother & Jacobs, 1986), and the family medicine literature (e.g., Wynne et al., 1987). Although models of consultation may differ, in general, the process of consultation across a sequence of stages is similar. These stages include the following: (1) referral; (2) initial meeting/assessment; (3) collaborative problem-solving; and (4) evaluation, follow-up, and termination. The family systems-oriented consultant will approach each stage of the consultation process with a view to the larger eco-systemic context, the relational processes within and between relevant social systems, and an emphasis on strengths and competencies. Finally, the consultation literature, regardless of model of practice, emphasizes that consultation is primarily an interpersonal influence process that demands interpersonal skill at all stages. Key interpersonal processes that have been identified for family consultation in pediatric psychology are the following: joining with the family;

focusing on systemic problem-solving; identifying competence underlying the problem; and collaborating with the family at each step of the process (Kazak et al., 2002).

Referral. The referral in a family consultation related to a child's chronic health or disability is likely to originate from a source that is not the family. The referral may come from personnel involved with the child in the school setting or the health care setting who are either experiencing difficulty with the child or the family, or who may be making a referral on behalf of the family who is requesting assistance in coping with their chronically ill child and his or her siblings. Obviously, the source of the referral, the nature of the referral, and the degree to which the family desires the consultation are relevant. Thus, the first stage of family consultation requires a determination of the following questions: Who is the referring party? What do they want to see happen? What is their view of the problem? What is their view of the family's view of the problem? What type of help do they think the family would like to receive? How do they see that they can be helpful? How would they like to be involved? Some final issues to clarify in the referral stage are the desired outcome, who will be responsible for the outcome, and in what form should the outcome be communicated to the referral source.

The answers to these questions are likely to vary, depending on the model of consultation being implemented. Hamlett and Stabler (1995) identify several theoretical models of consultation that vary in degree of contact between the consultant, the family, and the referring teacher or physician. In the resource consultation model, the consultant provides feedback to the referring party in writing. The psychologist may or may not actually interview or work with the family. In the process-educative model, the consultant advises/educates the referring party on how to better work with the family. Again, the psychologist may or may not actually meet or work directly with the family. In the collaborative model, which is most common in school settings, the psychologist and the referring party interact with each other and with the family to alleviate the presenting concerns.

As noted by Hamlett and Stabler (1995), ethical responsibilities should be carefully considered at the outset of a family consultation. It may be less clear in a family consultation that originates from outside the family exactly who is the client and what are the boundaries of confidentiality. When a physician requests family consultation with the primary goal of regimen compliance, for example, is the consultee the physician or the parents in the family. Issues of confidentiality are particularly important if the consultant is practicing within the school or medical setting, and notes regarding the consultation are subject to review by staff within the setting. Compared with the well-established guidelines for handling confidentiality in family therapy (e.g., Huber & Baruth, 1987), the applicability of these rules to a systems-oriented family consultation is largely unexplored in the literature.

Initial Meeting/Assessment. Clarification of the referral informs hypotheses about the nature of the complaints for which family consultation is being sought (Kazak et al., 2002). The focus of the initial consultation meeting with the family is (1) a systems-oriented assessment of the complaint; (2) acknowledgment of the family's perspective, concerns, and level of cooperation; (3) identification of the outcomes desired by the family; (4) clarification of roles and responsibilities; and (5) collaboration in planning the steps to achieve the desired outcome. The systems-oriented family consultant will be particularly attuned to family relationship dynamics related to the presenting concern and the detection of isomorphic patterns across the family and other social systems (Fishman, 1993). As noted by Fishman, when intervention involves working at the interfaces of the family with other social systems, it is important to determine whether certain structural patterns evident in the family are being carried into their relationship with other contexts and vice versa. For example, if a parent, teacher, and medical social worker, each in separate settings, are all using a similar strategy for gaining regimen compliance from an adolescent with diabetes, and all are failing, the family consultant would focus on the isomorphic pattern of interaction across settings.

Collaborative Problem-Solving. A hallmark of family consultation is collaborative problem-solving. Collaboration may be defined as a cooperative process of planning and problem-solving. Key steps in collaborative problem-solving with the family, as well as the family in meetings with other relevant systems, include introduction, finding facts, blocking blame, checking for consensus, decision and action, and follow-up (Weiss & Edwards, 1992). In the introduction, it is important to clarify the purpose of the initial meeting or consultation and relevant rules, such as everyone's point of view is important. Finding facts refers to hearing the thoughts, feelings, and perspective of each family member regarding their perceived needs and/or concerns. The consultant may probe for information regarding both the historical and contemporary systemic context of the problem. A collaborative problem-solving orientation to consultation seeks to block blame among family members or between systems. The consultant may acknowledge the family member's blaming perspective, but seeks to reframe or normalize it. If unsuccessful, the consultant may actively block blame or establish rules for the consultation process. An important difference in family consultation versus family therapy is coming to a consensus on a plan of action related to the family's concern. The action plan may involve additional meetings with the consultant; meetings between the consultant, family, and other systems; or only an additional follow-up meeting to determine the success of the plan. A variation on the collaborative problem-solving approach is the collaborative solution-oriented approach (Carlson & Hickman, 1992; Carlson, Hickman, & Horton, 1992).

Evaluation, Followup, Termination. It is important that family consultants evaluate the efficacy of their intervention with the family. This is most frequently accomplished in practice informally through a follow-up meeting with the family. Collecting follow-up data with a satisfaction questionnaire is also advisable. Optimally, school-based family consultation by a psychologist would be subject to a single-subject case design evaluation, because the efficacy of the systems-oriented family consultation model has not been evaluated (Marsh & Johnson, 1997).

EMPIRICAL SUPPORT FOR PARENT AND FAMILY CONSULTATION

Increasingly, the profession of psychology demands empirical support for proposed interventions. Unfortunately, we discovered few studies that directly examined the efficacy of parent or family consultation with families with a chronically ill or disabled child. There is a small body of literature that finds parent and family consultation services to be effective in medical settings, parent consultation to be an effective mode of intervention delivery for a variety of general childhood problems in the school setting, and there are a number of government reports that include parent consultation as a component of statewide services, but provide no data evaluating the efficacy of this program.

Parent Consultation in the Medical Setting

Several studies exist that provide at least preliminary evidence of the effectiveness of parent and family consultation in the pediatric setting. Parental consultation successfully reduced the anxiety levels of parents after ultrasound diagnosis of fetal surgical malformation (Kemp, Davenport, & Pernet, 1998). Family consultation was also used successfully as one component of a multicomponent intervention designed to help families of children with asthma (Evans et al., 1999) and assist families with a child who had been sexually abused (Grosz, Kempe, &

Kelly, 2000). In a review of empirical studies on consultation and collaboration in pediatric psychology, Drotar (1995) cited several studies finding positive outcomes associated with parent and family consultation services. These included high ratings by parents of general consultation services for a variety of emotional, behavioral, and developmental problems (Finney et al., 1991; Kanoy & Schroeder, 1985, cited in Drotar, 1995), and positive parent report about the efficacy of behavior management consultation (Charlop et al., 1987, cited in Drotar, 1995). Pediatric psychologists in a medical setting delivered the consultation services to families.

Parent Consultation in the School Setting

A recent review of empirically based parent consultation literature in the school setting found that parent consultation was an effective mode of intervention for a variety of social–emotional, behavioral, and academic difficulties in elementary and middle school-age children (Guli, 2001). All studies used behavioral competency-based training within the consultation framework. Childhood problems included school phobia (Gresham & Nagle, 1981), tic disorder (Pray, Kramer, & Lindskog, 1986), child noncompliance (Gmeinder & Kratochwill, 1998; Rotto & Kratochwill, 1994), parent–adolescent conflict (Doll & Kratochwill, 1994), and homework completion (Loitz & Kratochwill, 1995; Rhoades & Kratochwill, 1998).

The Conjoint Behavioral Consultation (CBC) model (Sheridan & Kratochwill, 1992; see also Sheridan, this volume), in particular, has been shown to be an effective means of delivering parent consultation in schools. CBC is a conceptual framework for home-school collaboration in which parents and teachers are joint consultees. Advantages of this approach include the identification of contextually based issues, consistency across settings, and creation of constructive partnerships between school and home systems (Sheridan & Kratochwill, 1992). The CBC model has been demonstrated to be effective in the development of social skills in children with attention deficit hyperactivity disorder (Colton & Sheridan, 1998), eliminating a child's irrational fear of sleeping in his bedroom (Sheridan & Colton, 1994), eliminating social withdrawal (Sheridan, Kratochwill, & Elliott, 1990), and improving homework completion (Galloway & Sheridan, 1994; Weiner, Sheridan, & Jenson, 1998). CBC was rated the most acceptable consultation approach by parents and teachers for academic, behavioral, and social–emotional problems when compared with teacher-only and parent-only consultations (Freer & Watson, 1999).

Methodological Strengths and Weaknesses. School-related parent consultation studies have both methodological strengths and limitations (Guli, 2001). All studies cited previously demonstrated significant key outcomes. Key outcomes included a change in parent behavior, attitudes or knowledge, as well as a change in the child's behavior. All studies also met acceptable criteria regarding implementation fidelity, clinical evidence of change, and use of multiple sources for the assessment of key outcomes. It should be noted, however, that the majority of studies measuring the effectiveness of parent consultation used single-participant and mixed designs versus between-group designs. The evidence base for parent consultation, therefore, would be strengthened with the inclusion of between-group research designs.

Several other methodological limitations weaken the evidence base for parent consultation (Guli, 2001). Parent consultation studies have been conducted primarily with middle-class White parents and their children in elementary and middle schools. The failure of many studies to identify and evaluate separately specific treatment components makes it difficult to determine the unique contribution of parent or family consultation to key outcomes. Parent consultation studies generally lacked follow-up data and reliable outcome measures. Moreover, no studies have examined the efficacy in the school setting of parent or family consultation with families with a chronically ill or disabled child.

State-Funded Initiatives

Although lacking in methodologically rigorous empirical investigation, several federal and state-funded outreach projects report use of parent consultation as a way to educate and assist parents of children with developmental disabilitiess. Many state projects provide consultative services to parents of deaf-blind children and report a change in parent knowledge and/or attitudes (e.g., Georgia State Department of Education, 1995). In another example, Golden (1995) described the Parent Consultation Center (PCC), housed in an elementary school, as an alternative to referral for family therapy. The PCC, which was available to parents at the end of the work day, used a short-term, behaviorally oriented approach to help parents solve problems with their children. The PCC has preliminary evidence of success.

Summary

There is limited empirical data that support the efficacy of parent and family consultation as an intervention for children's school-related social, emotional, and psychological problems in either the school-based consultation or pediatric psychology literature. Despite a considerable body of literature espousing its value (e.g., Kazak et al., 1995; Wynne et al., 1987), there were few studies located that evaluated the efficacy of family systems consultation in pediatric psychology or school psychology. Clearly, this is a relevant gap in our knowledge and practice with this at-risk population.

LEGAL, ETHICAL, AND PROFESSIONAL ISSUES

Elsewhere in this volume Rae addresses legal and ethical issues that pediatric psychologists should be aware of when they practice in school settings, and Spirito addresses relevant training issues for pediatric psychologists interested in school practice. Pediatric psychologists who wish to practice family consultation within any of the models we have reviewed will need to be aware of all these issues and an array of unique legal, ethical, and professional issues attendant to multisystemic family consultation.

Pediatric psychologists know that practice within the complex health care system and especially the hospital setting can be challenging. The complex system of the school can be no less of a challenge. Family therapists and consultants also know that working with the family system presents challenges beyond those that characterize individual or even intervention with couples. Psychologists who interface with all three systems face unique and varied ethical, legal, and regulatory challenges beyond those that apply to consultation within school or medical settings alone, or independent practice. Because space limitations preclude an exhaustive review of these issues, we will address a sample of the unique challenges that pediatric psychologists face when they practice at the nexus of pediatric psychology, family consultation, and the school setting.

Risk Reduction

The potential complexity of the ethical, legal, and professional entanglements that can confront multisystemic family consultants may be intimidating and overwhelming. Our intent, however, is to encourage rather than to deter pediatric psychologists interested in this emerging practice arena. So, we begin our brief review of potential challenges with two suggestions to consultants to reduce ethical and legal exposure offered by Brown, Pryzwansky, and Schulte (2001). A broader review of legal and ethical principles that apply to the practice of consultation, in general, can also be found in Brown et al. (2001). An excellent guide to the legal, ethical, and professional issues in the practice of marriage and family therapy is provided by Huber and Baruth (1987).

Brown et al. (2001) recommend adherence to the American Psychological Association's (APA's) *Ethical Principles of Psychologists and Code of Conduct* (APA, 1992) as the consultant's first line of defense against ethical breaches and potential legal action. Although the *Ethical Principles* were established to protect the consumer, adherence to these rules of conduct is also an important defense against ethical and legal entanglements. Failure to do so can place psychologists at risk for both sanctions from ethics committees and lawsuits.

Equally important, according to Brown et al. (2001), is that the consultant's practice conform to the standards for practice established by a professional group. They note, however, that there are no such standards for consultants (Lowman, 1985, reported in Brown et al., 2001). Without standards for consultation practice, multisystemic family consultants should engage in practices that would be deemed acceptable by other family, pediatric, and school psychologists and avoid practices that are unlikely to be supported by these colleagues. This suggestion is offered in the hope of reducing legal risk for those who do choose to venture into this important but emerging and complex practice arena.

Competence, Confidentiality, and Multisystemic Family Consultation

To illustrate the breadth and depth of the complexities associated with ethical consultation practice in the multisystemic arena, we will consider how the ethical principles of competence and confidentiality interface with this practice venue. Several other principles articulated in the APA's *Ethical Principles* (APA, 1992) also can inform practice in this emerging practice arena.

Competence. Fundamental to multisystemic practice is the issue of competence. The APA's *Ethical Principles* (APA, 1992) require that psychologists recognize the limitations of their expertise and provide only those services and techniques for which they are qualified by training and experience. Thus, the question for pediatric psychologists interested in practicing family consultation in school settings is whether one possesses the training and experience to do so. This is a difficult call in any emerging practice area because training and practice standards are not yet articulated.

The APA's *Ethical Principles* (APA, 1992) recognize the unique challenges posed by emerging practice arenas. The code states, "In those emerging areas where recognized standards for preparation and training do not yet exist psychologists nevertheless take reasonable steps to ensure the competence of their work to protect patients, clients, students, and research participants from harm (p. 1600)." Brown et al. (2001) recommend "consultation with others is an appropriate and ethical way to determine competence to function and improve competence if skills are needed..."(p. 285).

Some psychologists (e.g., school psychologists) possess competencies in school practice, and consultation training is generally a core component of the curriculum. Other psychologists possess competencies in psychological treatment of chronic and serious medical disorders (e.g., pediatric psychologists). Still other psychologists may possess competency in family therapy and consultation with families. Yet others may possess competencies in consultation, school practice, and practice with chronic and serious medical disorders. Still others may possess none of these competencies. The APA's *Ethical Principles* (APA, 1992) seem to suggest that those pediatric psychologists with competency in school practice and family consultation would be best suited for multisystemic family consultation. To reduce risk, psychologists who lack this unique mix of competencies should consider obtaining needed competencies or consider practice in line with the alternatives we have outlined herein.

School Practice Competency. School psychologists may possess competencies in school practice that health care psychologists without such specialty training may lack (Talley & Short, 1994). This is not to suggest that specialty training in school psychology is prerequisite for pediatric psychologists to practice ethically and competently in delivering family consultation services in the schools. Nevertheless, the pediatric psychologist should be able to demonstrate competency in school practice to engage in multisystemic family consultation. Such competency may be obtained through appropriate school-related training and experience. As an alternative, the health care psychologist without school practice competency may be able to ethically consult in the schools by seeking supervision and consultation regarding school practice issues from a school psychologist or other psychologist with school practice competency (Kubiszyn, 1999).

Competency in Treating Chronic and Severe Medical Conditions. Psychologists trained in hospital or other health care settings may have competencies in the treatment and management of medical disorders that school psychologists and other psychologists may lack (Kubiszyn, 1999). Just as developing school practice competency is necessary for pediatric psychologists to practice in schools, school psychologists should also develop competency in delivering psychological services for serious and chronic medical disorders before practicing with this population in schools or other settings. Competencies in psychological intervention for medical disorders may be obtained through appropriate training and supervised experience. Alternatively, school psychologists may practice with this population by seeking supervision and consultation from a pediatric psychologist or other psychologist with appropriate competencies (Kubiszyn, 1999).

Competency in Consultation. Psychologists trained in consultation have competencies that psychologists who are not systematically trained in consultation will lack. Developing competency in consultation as an intervention is no less important than developing competency in school practice and practice with chronic and serious medical disorders. Competency in consultation also can be obtained through appropriate training and supervised experience, or psychologists may seek supervision and consultation from a psychologist with consultation competency. Training in consultation as an intervention process, however, does not ensure that the consultant has the appropriate knowledge or expertise to consult with a particular type of consultee, such as the family.

Competency in Family Consultation. Family systems therapists argue that working with the complex multimember family system as a unit requires appropriate training. Many helping professionals consider that they may apply the same theories, diagnostic measures, and intervention strategies that are appropriate for an intervention with an individual family member. Family systems interventions have a unique body of theory and knowledge base that is necessary to master before engaging in family (versus parent or caregiver) consultation. As family systems theorists espouse, the family as a whole is not the sum of the parts. Related to the issue of competence, this chapter has proposed that consultation with a family with a chronically medical condition may involve multiple stages and forms of intervention. Just as a consultant should not engage in family consultation without appropriate training, neither should he or she provide broader professional services to the family, such as family therapy, without appropriate training and supervision.

Confidentiality

Ensuring confidentiality of records and disclosures may be especially problematic when pediatric psychologists interface with families and schools. Because collaboration across the family, school, and the health care systems often requires information-sharing across systems and providers, special threats to confidentiality can emerge beyond those that are typical in a health care, school, or independent practice setting alone. In addition to myriad health-related professionals often involved in the care of a chronically or seriously ill child, an array of school-based professionals are added to the mix when the family consultation involves the school system. These individuals can include the administrator, teacher or teachers, school psychologist, counselor or social worker, paraprofessionals (i.e., teacher aides), and as many therapists as may be needed to care for the child in the school setting.

Pediatric psychologists are accustomed to striving to ensure the confidentiality of the client/patient, and are increasingly aware of how complex and difficult this can be when the family is involved in treatment. When health care and school systems also are involved in the child's treatment, issues of confidentiality exponentially increase to include not only multiple individuals, but also the processes of these multiple systems. In other words, because multiple systems are involved, it is not only the confidentiality of the child/patient and the family that may be breached, but breaches may also occur at the systemic level. Ethical complaints and lawsuits may be initiated by any of the systems involved in multisystemic family consultation.

Because involvement of pediatric psychologists with the school system as a result of family consultation is in its infancy, there exists little in the way of established policy and procedure to guide the clinician in this area. To protect patient confidentiality (and is the patient the child, the family, or both?), procedural safeguards will need to be developed to ensure that written, informed consent is obtained by and from all concerned parties. Yet obtaining this written consent will need to be done in a way that does not obstruct the timely exchange of information that will be necessary for all systems to be responsive to the needs of the family and the patient (Kubiszyn, 1999).

The APA's *Ethical Principles* (1992) again offer guidance. As interpreted by Brown et al. (2001), the APA's *Ethical Principles* indicate that consultants should discuss the limits of confidentiality with all consultees at the outset of the consulting relationship. In addition, Brown et al. encourage consultants to also discuss the "foreseeable uses of the information generated through their services" (APA, 1992, p. 1606). In family-oriented, multisystemic, multistage consultation, this can be a considerable challenge. For example, information revealed in confidence to a consultant by a health care provider or school staff about the patient or family may be unintentionally revealed to another system, or may have to be revealed if the consultant is later required to testify in a child custody, criminal, or malpractice case. Similarly, information that a child or family member reveals may also have to be revealed in such cases. Clearly, this is a complex area and pediatric psychologists considering multisystemic consultation should afford thoughtful consideration to this issue.

Professional Issues

Beyond this sampling of important legal and ethical issues, a number of professional practice issues should be considered by prospective multisystemic family consultants. These issues can present challenging barriers to effective collaboration and consultation across the three systems. We will limit this discussion to professional training and practice policies, and turf and guild issues that can interfere with effective family consultation within the school setting.

Training and Practice Issues. Professional education programs are typically discipline-specific and often do not encourage cross-disciplinary contact and responsibility. Where consultation is encouraged, it is often expert consultation, wherein the consultant takes over diagnostic and treatment responsibilities for a case (Caplan & Caplan, 1999). Universally accepted cross-disciplinary training, practice, and consultation models do not exist, and there is often little common vocabulary across disciplines.

To combat these training barriers, multidisciplinary team approaches to diagnosis and intervention have been encouraged in recent years. Although well-intended, these models vary in their effectiveness. Team members may have different outcome goals that result from their differing training and values (Koeske, Koeske, & Mallinger, 1993; McDaniel, 1995; McDaniel, Campbell, & Seaburn, 1990). Differences in values and goals may be exacerbated when clinicians are not interested in interacting with and learning from each other and are more interested in focusing on their own, or solely on their professions' clinical issues and decisions. Cultural sensitivity and competence in consultation also should be considered if collaborative consultative practice is to be accepted and effective, particularly in low-income ethnically mixed populations (Abe-Kim & Takeuchi, 1996; Isaacs & Benjamin, 1991).

Turf and Guild Issues. Turf and guild issues and concerns also can interfere with family consultation in schools. Representatives from a wide range of disciplines now practice in the schools. Indeed, schools appear to be approaching "one stop shopping centers" for services (Dryfoos, 1994). All these providers are interested in helping students. Staff from diverse disciplines may have unique perspectives on what needs to be done, to whom, how, when and where. Moreover, staff from the various disciplines must be able to justify their roles and existence.

The large number of professionals now working in the school setting invites both actual and perceived turf violations. Health, mental health, and other service delivery fields can overlap significantly in the services they provide. Counseling, for example, may be provided by psychologists, school psychologists, nurses and nurse practitioners, social workers, mental health or substance abuse counselors, school guidance counselors, and other school staff, including some paraprofessionals. When a pediatric psychologist engages in consultation with a family regarding school issues, which of these providers, or which subset, is to be contacted? Because turf and guild issues are widespread across disciplines, similar quandaries are likely to arise in deciding who to contact regarding instructional, administrative, or health-related issues in the school setting.

With a large number of professionals providing services and competing for limited resources within the school setting, it follows that turf conflicts will occur. Furthermore, these natural conflicts can be inflamed by emotional or politically driven rhetoric. Because of the inevitability of turf violations, it appears unlikely that resolution of these issues can occur in the absence of informed, reasoned, and dedicated negotiation and conflict resolution policies and procedures. Unfortunately, very little has been written about this process, and relevant research is almost nonexistent (Noblit & Cobb, 1997).

SUMMARY AND CONCLUSIONS

Families with a chronically ill or disabled child face enormous stressors. Serious physical and mental illness in a family member challenges the family financially, emotionally, physically, and psychologically. Family roles and routines must be altered to adapt to the ill child. At the core of the family experience is grief and chronic loss, the objective burden of caregiving, the complexities of the service delivery, and educational systems. Yet research finds that healthy family relationships are the best mediator of the stress created by a chronically ill child in the family. The purpose of family consultation is to enhance family relationships and the socioenvironmental support of these relationships, such that adaptive coping can ensue.

This chapter has proposed that family consultation is optimally conceptualized as a multistage, multisystemic, collaborative, problem-solving process between the psychologist and the family around issues related to the developmental needs of the chronically ill or disabled child and the family. Research and theory provide helpful guidelines for the process of consultation, systems-oriented family intervention, and a family systems orientation in pediatric psychology. Unfortunately, there are few practice guidelines or empirical studies to guide the psychologist in conducting a pediatric psychology family consultation in the school setting. This chapter has attempted to identify helpful resources to the family consultant from the related areas of school consultation, family therapy, and pediatric psychology to provide guidance in this new area of specialized practice while acknowledging that the professional roads are just being paved.

REFERENCES

Abe-Kim, J. S., & Takeuchi, D. T. (1996). Cultural competence and quality of care: Issues for mental health service delivery in managed care. *Clinical Psychology: Science and Practice, 3*, 273–295.

American Psychological Association. [APA]. (1992). *Ethical principles of psychologists and code of conduct.* Washington, DC: Author.

Bramlett, R. K., Hall, J. D., Barnett, D. W., & Rowell, R. K. (1995). Child developmental/educational status in kindergarten and family coping as predictors of parenting stress: Issues for parent consultation. *Journal of Psychoeducational Assessment, 13*, 157–166.

Broderick, C. B. (1993). *Understanding family process: Basics of family systems theory.* Newbury Park, CA: Sage Publications.

Bronfenbrenner, U. (1979). *The ecology of human development.* Cambridge, MA: Harvard University Press.

Brown, D., Pryzwansky, W. B., & Schulte, A. C. (2001). *Psychological consultation: Introduction to theory and practice.* Boston: Allyn & Bacon.

Caplan, G., & Caplan, R. B. (1999). *Mental health consultation and collaboration.* Prospect Heights, IL: Waveland Press.

Carlson, C. I., & Hickman, J. (1992). Family consultation in schools in special services. *Special Services in the Schools, 6*(3/4), 83–112.

Carlson, C. I., Hickman, J., & Horton, C. B. (1992). From blame to solutions: Solution-oriented family-school consultation. In S. L. Christenson & J. C. Conoley (Eds.), *Home-school collaboration* (pp. 193–214). Silver Spring, MD: National Association of School Psychologists.

Colton, D. L., & Sheridan, S. M. (1998). Conjoint behavioral consultation and social skills training: Enhancing the play behaviors of boys with attention deficit hyperactivity disorder. *Journal of Educational and Psychological Consultation, 9*, 3–28.

Doll, B., & Kratochwill, T. R. (1994). Treatment of parent-adolescent conflict through behavioral technology training: A case study. *Journal of Educational and Psychological Consultation, 3*, 281–300.

Drotar, D. (1975). Death in the pediatric hospital: Psychological consultation with medical and nursing staff. *Journal of Clinical Child Psychology, 4*, 33–35.

Drotar, D. (1995). *Consulting with pediatricians: Psychological perspectives.* New York: Plenum Press.

Dryfoos, J. G. (1994). *Full-service schools*, San Francisco: Jossey Bass.

Evans, R., LeBailly, S., Gordon, K. K., Sawyer, A., Christoffel, K. K., & Pearce, B. (1999). Restructuring asthma care in a hospital setting to improve outcomes. *Chest, 116(4)*, 210S–216S.

Fishman, H. C. (1993). *Intensive structural therapy: Treating families in their social context.* New York: Basic Books.

Freer, P., & Watson, T. S. (1999). A comparison of parent and teacher acceptability ratings of behavioral and conjoint behavioral consultation. *School Psychology Review, 28*, 672–684.

Galloway, J., & Sheridan, S. M. (1994). Implementing scientific practices through case studies: Examples using home-school interventions and consultation. *Journal of School Psychology, 32*, 385–413.

Georgia State Department of Education, Atlanta. (1995). *Georgia Deaf-Blind Project [IEE29025]. Final Report, 1992–1995.* State and Multi-State Projects for Children with Deaf-Blindness. Atlanta, GA: Author.

Gmeinder, K. L., & Kratochwill, T. R., (1998). Short-term, home-based intervention for child noncompliance using behavioral consultation and a self-help manual. *Journal of Educational and Psychological Consultation, 9*, 91–117.

Golden, L. (1995). The parent consultation center: A time-limited behaviorally-oriented approach. In M. Dougherty (Ed.), *Case studies in human services consultation.* Pacific Grove, CA: Brooks/Cole Publishing, Inc.

Gresham, F. M., & Nagle, R. J. (1981). Treating school phobia using behavioral consultation: A case study. *School Psychology Review, 10*, 104–107.

Grosz, C. A., Kempe, R.S., & Kelly, M. (2000). Extrafamilial sexual abuse: Treatment for child victims and their families. *Child Abuse and Neglect, 24*, 9–23.

Guli, L. (2001, August). Evidence based parent consultation in school psychology. In C. Carlson & S. Christenson (co-chairs), *Evidence supported parent and family interventions in school psychology*. Symposium conducted at the annual meeting of the American Psychological Assocation, San Francisco.

Hamlett, K. W., & Stabler, B. (1995). The developmental progress of pediatric psychology consultation. In M. C. Roberts (Ed.), *The handbook of pediatric psychology* (2nd ed., pp. 39–54). New York: Guilford Press.

Huber, C. H., & Baruth, L. G. (1987). *Ethical, legal and professional issues in the practice of marriage and family therapy*. Columbus, OH: Merrill Publishing Co.

Isaacs, M. R., & Benjamin, M. P. (1991). *Towards a culturally competent system of care: Vol. II. Programs which utilize culturally competent principles*. Washington, DC: CASSP Technical Assistance Center, Georgetown University Child Development Center.

Kazak, A. E. (1989). Families of chronically ill children: A systems and social-ecological model of adaptation and challenges. *Journal of Consulting and Clinical Psychology*, *57*, 25–30.

Kazak, A. E., Segal-Andrews, A. M., & Johnson, K. (1995). Pediatric psychology research and practice: A family/systems approach. In M. C. Roberts (Ed.), *The handbook of pediatric psychology* (2nd ed., pp. 84–104). New York: Guilford Press.

Kazak, A. E., Simms, S., & Rourke, M. T. (2002). Family systems practice in pediatric psychology. *Journal of Pediatric Psychology*, *27*, 133–143.

Kemp, J., Davenport, M., & Pernet, A. (1998). Antenatally diagnosed surgical anomalies: The psychological effect of parental antenatal counseling. *Journal of Pediatric Surgery, 33*(9), 1376–1379.

Koeske, G. F., Koeske, R. D., & Mallinger, J. (1993). Perceptions of professional competence: Cross-disciplinary ratings of psychologists, social workers, and psychiatrists. *American Journal of Orthopsychiatry*, *63*, 45–54.

Kubiszyn, T. (1999). Integrating health and mental health services in schools: Psychologists collaborating with primary care providers. *Clinical Psychology Review, 19*(2), 179–198.

Loitz, P. A., & Kratochwill, T. R. (1995). Parent consultation: Evaluation of a self-help manual for children's homework problems. *School Psychology International, 16*, 389–396.

Marsh, D. T., & Johnson, D. L. (1997). The family experience of mental illness: Implications for intervention. *Professional Psychology: Research and Practice, 28*, 229–237.

McDaniel, S. H. (1995). Collaboration between psychologists & family physicians: Implementing the biopsychosocial model. *Professional Psychology: Research & Practice, 26*, 117–122.

McDaniel, S. H., Campbell, T. L., & Seaburn, D. (1990). *Family-oriented primary care: A manual for medical providers.* New York: Springer-Verlag.

Meyers, J., Parsons, R. D., & Martin, R. (1979). *Mental health consultation in the schools*. San Francisco: Jossey-Bass.

Minuchin, S. (1974). Families and family therapy. Cambridge, MA: Harvard University Press.

Minuchin, S., Rosman, B. L., & Baker, L. (1978). *Psychosomatic families: Treating anorexia nervosa in context.* Cambridge, MA: Harvard University Press.

Moos, R., & Moos, B. (1981). *Family environment scale manual.* Palo Alto, CA: Consulting Psychologists Press.

Noblit, G. W., & Cobb, C. C. (1997). Organizing for effective integrated services. In R. J. Illback, C. C. Cobb, & H. M. Joseph, Jr. (Eds.), Integrated services for children and families: Opportunities for psychological practice (pp. 191–220). Washington, DC: American Psychological Association.

Olson, D., Portner, J., & Lavee, Y. (1985). *FACES III manual*. Unpublished manual. Available from D. H. Olson, Family Social Science, University of Minnesota, 290 McNeal Hall, St. Paul, MN 55108.

Pray, B., Kramer, J. & Lindskog, R. (1986). Assessment and treatment of tic behavior: A review and case study. *School Psychology Review, 15*, 418–429.

Quittner, A. L., & DiGirolamo, A. M. (1998). Family adaptation to childhood disability and illness. In R. T. Ammerman & J. V. Campo (Eds.), *Handbook of pediatric psychology and psychiatry, Vol. II: Disease, injury, and illness* (pp. 70–102). Boston: Allya & Bacon.

Rhoades, M., & Kratochwill, T. (1998). Parent training and consultation: An analysis of a homework intervention program. *School Psychology Quarterly, 13*, 241–264.

Roberts, M. (Ed.). (1996). *Model programs in child and family mental health.* Mahwah, NJ: Lawrence Erlbaum Associates.

Rotto, P. C., & Kratochwill, T. R. (1994). Behavioral consultation with parents: Using competency-based training to modify child noncompliance. *School Psychology Review, 23*, 669–693.

Sheridan, S. M., & Colton, D. L. (1994). Conjoint behavioral consultation: A review and case study. *Journal of Educational and Psychological Consultation, 5*, 211–228.

Sheridan, S. M., & Kratochwill, T. R. (1992). Behavioral parent-teacher consultation: Conceptual and research considerations. *Journal of School Psychology, 30*, 117–139.

Sheridan, S. M., Kratochwill, T. R., & Elliott, S. N. (1990). Behavioral consultation with parents and teachers: Delivering treatment for socially withdrawn children at home and school. *School Psychology Review, 19*, 33–52.

Strother, J., & Jacobs, E. (1986). Parent consultation: A practical approach. *The School Counselor, 33*, 292–296.

Talley, R. T., & Short, R. J. (1994). (Summer, 1994). A wake-up call to school psychologists from school psychologists. *The School Psychologist, 48*, 1–3, 15.

Wallander, J. L., & Thompson, R. J. Jr. (1995). Psychosocial adjustment of children with chronic physical conditions. In M. C. Roberts (Ed.), *The handbook of pediatric psychology* (2nd ed., pp. 124–141). New York: Guilford Press.

Weiner, R. K, Sheridan, S. M., & Jenson, W. R. (1998). The effects of conjoint behavioral consultation and a structured homework program on math completion and accuracy in junior high students. *School Psychology Quarterly, 13*, 281–309.

Weiss, H. M., & Edwards, M. E. (1992), The family-school collaboration project: Systemic interventions for school improvement. In S. L. Christenson & J. C. Conoley (Eds.), *Home-school collaboration* (pp. 467–486). Silver Spring, MD: National Association of School Psychologists.

Wynne, L. C., McDaniel, S. H., & Weber, T. T. (1987). Professional politics and the concepts of family therapy, family consultation, and systems consultation. *Family Process, 26*, 153–166.

33

School and Social Reintegration After a Serious Illness or Injury

Avi Madan-Swain
University of Alabama–Birmingham

Ernest R. Katz
Children's Hospital Los Angeles and the Keck School of Medicine, University of Southern California

Jason LaGory
Sparks Clinics, University of Alabama–Birmingham

INTRODUCTION

Dramatic medical advances in the treatment of chronic illness and injury in children and adolescents have increased both the life expectancy and functional capability of these youth. With improvement in disease management and survival, new problems have emerged in the reintegration of these young people into school settings. Factors associated with the school reentry process have been delineated in the literature (Madan-Swain, Fredrick, & Wallander, 1999). These factors include the direct effect of the illness or its treatment on the central nervous system (CNS), functional independence, school participation, as well as intrapersonal psychological resources, peer social support, and familial and cultural resources.

Youth with chronic illnesses, as well as those who have sustained an injury, need to return to prediagnosis activities and environments, particularly school, as soon as medically feasible to promote optimal adjustment, rehabilitation, and psychosocial well-being (Katz, 1980; Katz, Kellerman, Rigler, Williams, & Siegel, 1977). To maximize attendance and thereby facilitate educational and social growth, students with health care concerns will need minor coordinated environmental and instructional modifications within the regular classroom (e.g., shortened school day, frequent breaks because of fatigue, increased time to complete assignments/tests, decreased amount of classwork and homework assignments; Madan-Swain et al., 1999; Sexson & Madan-Swain, 1993, 1995).

Some children and adolescents—particularly those experiencing intensive treatments, progressive medical complications, and those at the end stage of their illness—will require more individualized educational assistance to maintain their involvement in school and continue developing to the best of their potential (Katz & Ingle-Nelson, 1989; Madan-Swain et al., 1999).

These youth are entitled to a complete range of assistive interventions through the federal Individuals with Disabilities Education Act (1990) and are typically served through special education departments under the category Other Health Impaired. After meeting eligibility criteria, an individualized educational plan (IEP) is developed specifying educational goals and objectives, and the means for realizing each goal (e.g., type of special education services). The child's IEP is agreed on by the parents (and older adolescents themselves), school, school district personnel, and the medical team. Clearly, the process of reintegrating the child or adolescent into school after a prolonged absence and monitoring adequate attendance and achievement requires intensive cooperative efforts among health care providers, school personnel, the child or adolescent, and the family (Madan-Swain et al., 1999).

This chapter will review literature regarding the potential impact a chronic illness may have on the child or adolescent's school attendance and performance. Based on the available literature, factors associated with school adjustment are examined, along with the tasks to be accomplished during each of the three school reentry phases. Finally, suggestions for future research directions in the field of school reentry are presented.

IMPACT OF CHRONIC ILLNESS

Epidemiological Studies

Increased risk for school performance difficulties in children with chronic illness has been well documented (Madan-Swain et al., 1999). One of the earliest and most comprehensive studies examining the educational consequences of physical illness in school-age children was the Isle of Wight study (Rutter, Tizard, & Whitmore, 1970), whose purpose was to examine both direct and indirect consequences of chronic illness. The sample included two groups of children: those with brain-related medical conditions and those without documented brain-related medical conditions. Findings from this investigation were interpreted to suggest that the intellectual and academic difficulties experienced by children with brain-related illnesses were likely the direct consequence of the medical illness, whereas the school-related difficulties experienced by children with non-brain-related illnesses are more likely the indirect consequences of the medical condition (e.g., absenteeism).

Similarly, results from the Ontario Child Health Study, another large-scale epidemiological investigation examining school performance of children with chronic illness, revealed that almost half of the children classified as having both a chronic illness and a disability had repeated a grade or were receiving remedial educational services, relative to 15% of children diagnosed with a chronic illness but without a disability, and 12% of healthy children (Cadman, Boyle, Szatmari, & Offord, 1987). A subsequent epidemiological study (Gortmaker, Walker, Weitzman, & Sobel, 1990) examining the psychological risk in children with physical illness revealed that children with chronic health conditions were at significantly higher risk for grade failure and special education placement relative to their healthy peers. However, children with chronic illness were not at increased risk for suspension or expulsion. Findings from both these investigations are limited because of their reliance on subjective reports from parents regarding school performance, the lack of objective measures to assess academic achievement (e.g., school records, standardized achievement testing), and the lack of specificity pertaining to brain involvement.

Clinical Studies

Interest in studying the school performance of adolescents with chronic illness is reflected in the growing literature in this area. For example, Howe, Feinstein, Reiss, Molock, and Berger (1993) evaluated school performance, using standard achievement tests among three groups of adolescents: those diagnosed with brain-related chronic physical illness (e.g., cerebral palsy), those diagnosed with non-brain-related chronic illness (e.g., cystic fibrosis), and a healthy comparison group. Results indicated that both groups of chronically ill adolescents scored significantly below the healthy comparison group on school achievement. Furthermore, adolescents with brain-related illnesses scored significantly lower than the healthy group in mathematics, reading, and general knowledge, whereas the adolescents with the non-brain-related illnesses scored significantly lower than the healthy peers only in mathematics.

In a similar investigation, Fowler, Johnson, and Atkinson (1985) examined school functioning through utilization of objective school data for a large sample of children diagnosed with a variety of chronic health conditions. Children with chronic health conditions scored significantly lower than their healthy counterparts, although their scores were well within the average range. In addition, approximately one fourth of the chronic illness sample had repeated a grade, and nearly one third were receiving special education services. Children with seizure disorders, sickle cell disease (SCD), and spina bifida were especially at risk for repeating a grade, poor scores on standardized achievement tests, and special education placement. Race and socioeconomic background were found to account for a considerable amount of variance in achievement scores for the chronic illness group.

In the development of generic and illness-specific measures of health-related quality of life, Varni, Burwinkle, Katz, Meeske, and Dickerson (2002) evaluated 220 children and adolescents with cancer along with 337 parents. School and social functioning were two dimensions of the core quality-of-life measures used, and the authors compared the ratings of children with cancer, their parents, and a large healthy community comparison group. Patients and their parents reported significantly more school and social difficulties than did the normal population, a finding that was maintained even for children off-treatment for an extended period of time. Children with brain tumors had the poorest school and social outcomes of any oncology groups studied. These results suggest that children with cancer are at greater risk for poor school performance than healthy peers, an effect that continues well beyond diagnosis and treatment. These findings are consistent with data from long-term cancer survivors indicating a significantly higher rate of poor educational and vocational outcomes than sibling controls or community samples (Chen et al., 1998; Hayes et al., 1992).

Summary

Taken together, the results from the epidemiological and clinical investigations clearly indicate that some children and adolescents with chronic illness are at increased risk for school problems. This risk is particularly apparent in children who experience cognitive impairment as a direct consequence of the illness, such as those with SCD who suffer strokes and young people with brain tumors, or as a consequence of treatment, such as cranial irradiation or chemotherapy to control leukemia. The locus and extent of direct brain damage through disease (e.g., brain tumor), treatment (e.g., leukemia), or traumatic brain injury (TBI) will generally correlate to the level of school and functional impairment by the child (Aicardi, 1998).

Although some children with chronic illnesses do not experience specific cognitive impairment, they may still fail to maximize their psychoeducational potential relative to their healthy peers (Madan-Swain et al., 1999; Sexson & Madan-Swain, 1993, 1995). This may be explained best by mediating processes (such as absenteeism); emotional difficulties reflected in depression or anxiety, temporary illness, or treatment-related effects (such as problems with attention, fatigue, and lethargy); and functional limitations on activity. In addition, attitudes of parents and school personnel toward the school reentry process also may contribute to school and social adjustment difficulties (Katz, 1980).

FACTORS ASSOCIATED WITH SCHOOL ADJUSTMENT

Given the considerable evidence of increased risk for school problems in children with chronic illness, we now examine factors that contribute to school reentry. First, we examine the neurocognitive sequelae of the illness and the iatrogenic CNS effects of the treatment, and subsequent absenteeism. We specifically examine the learning, academic, and behavioral problems of children diagnosed with chronic illnesses that follow a constant (e.g., spina bifida, TBI), progressive (e.g., juvenile insulin-dependent diabetes mellitus), or relapsing (e.g., epilepsy, SCD, childhood cancer) course, with emphasis on brain-related chronic illnesses or injuries. Second, we examine the impact of individual psychological adjustment, familial and cultural adaptation, and peer social relationships and support on the school reentry process.

Disease-Related Neurocognitive Sequelae

Within the past several years, there has been a growing body of research examining the neurocognitive profile of children diagnosed with insulin-dependent diabetes mellitus. Verbal deficits—including word knowledge, general store of information, and verbal fluency—have been noted in the literature (Kovacs, Ryan, & Obrosky, 1994). There is some evidence to suggest an association between verbal deficits and later disease onset, suggesting that various brain regions may have different critical periods of vulnerability related to the effects of diabetes mellitus (Rovet, Ehrlich, Czuchta, & Akler, 1993). Although earlier investigations indicated an association between visuospatial deficits and earlier onset of diabetes mellitus, recent studies indicate no change in visuospatial abilities over time (Rovet & Fernandes, 1999). Comparing multiple aspects of attentional processing in children with diabetes to comparison controls, Rovet and Alvarez (1997) found that selective attention was weaker in all children with diabetes, whereas focused attention was weaker only in children with early disease onset, or seizures from hypoglycemia. The effects of diabetes on memory are generally mixed, but studies indicate that children with disease onset before age five and those who experience severe hypoglycemia or hyperglycemia evidence weakness in initially coding novel verbal or visual information, whereas recall of semantically meaningful information is unaffected (Rovet & Fernandes, 1999).

Diabetes is associated with generally poorer scholastic performance (Sansbury, Brown, & Meachum, 1997), as well as with underachievement in reading or spelling and arithmetic, and a greater need for special education and remedial help (Rovet & Fernandes, 1999). Peer difficulties are more likely to emerge during adolescence when teenagers are required to adhere to a strict medical regimen while they struggle with the typical developmental tasks that are characteristic of adolescence.

Spina bifida is a malformation of the CNS and, consequently, there is potential risk for neurocognitive sequelae in children with this condition. Spina bifida follows a constant course and may be physically incapacitating. A comprehensive review of the neuropsychological functioning of children with spina bifida and/or hydrocephalus reveals that whereas verbal abilities are generally intact, these children evidence difficulty with tasks involving visuospatial and tactile perception; rapid, precise, or sequenced movement; and "executive control" functions. In addition, various academic areas are affected, including arithmetic calculation, spelling, and reading comprehension (Wills, 1993).

Prospective longitudinal studies of intellectual recovery after sustaining a TBI indicates a decline of 2, 9, and 13 Full Scale IQ points 1-year after sustaining a mild, moderate, or severe injury respectively (Jaffe et al., 1993). Attentional deficits are common during the early stages of recovery, but long-term studies indicate persisting impairment on measures of psychomotor speed, divided attention, focused attention, shifting attention, and sustained attention

(Ewing-Cobb & Bloom, 1999). Memory is the most significant area of neuropsychological deficit after TBI (Ewing-Cobb & Bloom, 1999). This difficulty may result in slow yet steady decline in academic performance over time. Thus, as their peers advance in knowledge, the child or adolescent with a TBI may not. Another common problem is that many children with TBI appear physically normal, but experience executive difficulties that are not necessarily detectable on routine examinations. With increasing severity of injury, children exhibit corresponding deficits in adaptive problem-solving skills, memory, speed of processing, language, perceptual-motor skills, intelligence, and academic performance relative to peers (Dalby & Obrzut, 1991; Jaffe et al., 1993).

Epilepsy and SCD are brain-related diseases that follow a relapsing course. Epilepsy is considered by many to be the most prevalent chronic neurological disorder in children, and has been implicated as the cause of impaired cognitive, academic, behavioral, and emotional functioning. It appears that epilepsy may disrupt learning by a number of mechanisms ranging from variations in ability to sustain attention to incoming information to more permanent reduction of information-processing capacity (Hiemenz, Hynd, & Jimenez, 1999). Available literature suggests that even after controlling for IQ, children diagnosed with epilepsy are at greater risk for experiencing school difficulties relative to their healthy peers. Academic difficulties are greatest in arithmetic, spelling, reading comprehension, and word recognition (Gourley, 1990). Boys with epilepsy may be more likely to underachieve at school and be more impaired with respect to reading skills (Stedman, Van Heyningen, & Lindsey, 1982). This is consistent with the findings noted in the Isle of Wight study (Rutter et al., 1970), which indicated that more than twice as many children diagnosed with epilepsy evidenced serious reading comprehension problems relative to a group of children without seizure disorders.

There is a growing body of literature attesting to the fact that children with SCD are at significant risk for cognitive impairments (Brown, Armstrong, & Eckman, 1993). Children with SCD but without any overt symptoms of cerebral vascular accident (stroke) have lower intellectual functioning and greater neuropsychological deficits compared with sibling controls (e.g., Brown, Buchanan, et al., 1993; Wasserman, Wilimas, Fairclough, Mulhern, & Wang, 1991). Programmatic research conducted by Brown, Buchanan, et al. (1993) has demonstrated associations among neuropsychological functions, socioeconomic background, and hemoglobin, suggesting that deficits in cognitive functioning in part may be attributable to social class and to the possible etiological effects of reduced oxygen delivery.

Approximately 7–17% of children with SCD (HbSS type, the homozygous condition known as sickle cell anemia) sustain a cerebral vascular accident, a condition frequently resulting in learning impairments, including impairments in intellectual functioning, attention, visual-motor integration, and academic achievement (Brown et al., 2000). Findings from the multisite Cooperative Study of Sickle Cell Disease (Armstrong et al., 1996) indicated that children with a clinical stroke as revealed on magnetic resonance imaging (MRI) showed the highest frequency of neurocognitive deficits, including impairments in intellectual functioning, language abilities, visual-motor and visuospatial processing, sequential memory, and academic achievement. Children with silent infarcts did not show problems as severe or pervasive as those who demonstrated overt cerebral vascular accident's, although they did perform more poorly on visual-motor speed, arithmetic, and vocabulary than those with no MRI abnormality. These findings have recently been reiterated in an investigation by Brown et al. (2000).

Iatrogenic Treatment Effects

Children with chronic illness also may require treatments for their illness that may have iatrogenic effects on cognitive functioning and, hence, on school achievement. Iatrogenic effects may range from mental status changes associated with particular pharmacological agents and treatments (e.g., difficulties with attention and concentration secondary to steroids) or prophylactic therapies, including cranial radiation or intrathecal chemotherapy used to prevent infiltration of neoplasms into the CNS.

There is considerable evidence documenting the iatrogenic effects of treatment for childhood cancer. Children with leukemia receive CNS prophylactic treatment to prevent the infiltration of leukemic cells into the CNS. Although this protocol has increased the rate of survival, in some cases, it has had deleterious effects on neurocognitive functioning (Raymond-Speden, Tripp, Lawrence, & Holdaway, 2000). Several reviews of existing studies show evidence of iatrogenic effects of CNS prophylaxis, particularly cranial irradiation in patients diagnosed with leukemia (Eiser & Tillmann, 2001; Fletcher & Copeland, 1988; Madan-Swain & Brown, 1991). More recently, evidence suggests intrathecal chemotherapy may have deleterious effects even in the absence of radiation therapy (Eiser & Tillmann, 2001). Documented neurocognitive deficits after completion of medical therapy include impairment on tasks of higher order functioning and diagnosable learning disabilities in reading and mathematics (Brown et al., 1992, 1996, 1998).

Youth diagnosed with brain tumors also are treated with high-dose cranial radiation and chemotherapy, and similar deleterious CNS effects have been reported (Glauser & Packer, 1991). Moreover, there is some evidence that the extent of the radiation therapy (i.e., focal vs. whole brain) in patients with brain tumors may be associated with the degree of neurocognitive difficulties (Kun, Mulhern, & Crisco, 1983; Ris, Packer, Goldwein, Jones-Wallace, & Boyett, 2001; Taylor et al., 1998). The most common neurocognitive sequelae is in the area of nonverbal abilities, attention, and concentration (Fletcher & Copeland, 1988), short-term memory, speed of processing, visual-motor coordination, and sequencing ability (Cousens, Ungerer, Crawford, & Stevens, 1991).

In summary, children with diagnosable learning problems, either preexisting or subsequent to the onset of the chronic illness, are at greater risk for school reentry problems (Katz et al, 1977). In particular, obvious CNS involvement related to the disease or injury itself (e.g., TBI) or as a result of toxicities associated with medical treatments (e.g., leukemia treatment) may result in documented learning difficulties that require special education placement. Prolonged or brief absences—such as in the case of children diagnosed with asthma, Crohn's disease, or SCD—may significantly impact school performance. Children who were only marginally academically successful before the onset of the illness may be more vulnerable to educational difficulties associated with intermittent school absences (Katz, 1980). Additionally, academic deficits are most likely to be manifested in academic skill areas that build on previous knowledge (Chekryn, Deegan, & Reid, 1987). Although the majority of the children with chronic illnesses will be able to return to their regular classrooms with minimal modifications, many will sustain delays and need to catch up on missed work, resulting in anxiety, and possibly complicating both attendance and functioning in school.

Absenteeism

Attending school is important to children's academic, social, and emotional development. It is a highly normative experience. Yet children and adolescents with chronic illness can potentially miss a large amount of school because of illness exacerbation, minor illnesses or health problems, adverse treatment side effects, hospitalizations, and outpatient clinic appointments. Therefore, school attendance is frequently used as a measure of disease-related functional capacity of children and adolescents with chronic illness (Cook, Schaller, & Krischer, 1985; Fowler et al., 1985; Weitzman & Siegel, 1992).

Studies of children and adolescents with chronic illness consistently have shown higher rates of school absence for these youth than for children without a chronic illness (Cook et al., 1985; Fowler et al., 1985; Weitzman et al., 1986). However, there is variability in the literature regarding the rates and patterns of absenteeism across chronic illnesses that likely reflects the variable manifestations and course of these medical conditions. Relative to their healthy peers, children diagnosed with asthma have higher absenteeism rates, characterized by frequent brief absences. This trend, however, seems to diminish with increasing age (Parcel et al., 1979). Rates of absenteeism that are four times higher than that of the general school-age population have been found for children with cancer (Stehbens et al., 1983). However, in contrast to children diagnosed with asthma, the pattern of school attendance in children diagnosed with cancer is characterized by one long period of absence at the time of diagnosis and initiation of treatment, followed by regular short absences for follow-up treatment or monitoring of progress (Charlton et al., 1991).

Absenteeism rates for children with cystic fibrosis and SCD have been among the highest, with children missing an equivalent of nearly 1 month each school year (Fowler et al., 1985). Even among children with SCD, in which disease severity in some cases can be mild, absence rates are high (Thompson & Gustafson, 1996), presumably related to low-grade pain experiences. Although children with insulin-dependent diabetes mellitus have fewer absences than for other chronic illnesses (Fowler et al., 1985), they typically have more absences than their healthy peers (Ryan, Longstreet, & Morrow, 1985).

Numerous factors have been associated with absenteeism in children with chronic illness. Medical factors include the course of the illness (i.e., constant, progressive, or relapsing), onset (i.e., acute or chronic), degree of incapacitation and physical restrictions (Fowler et al., 1985), and the type of treatment (e.g., CNS chemotherapy; Cairns, Klopovich, Hearne, & Lansky, 1982). Demographic factors associated with lower rates of school attendance include parental education (Charlton et al., 1991; Cook et al., 1985), gender (i.e., female; Cairns et al., 1982; Charlton et al., 1991; Fowler et al., 1985), and birth position (Cairns et al., 1982). Psychosocial factors associated with increased absenteeism include parental reluctance to allow the ill child to return to school even when medically approved; difficulties coordinating communication between hospital, home, and school; and lack of support and understanding from school personnel (Bessel, 2001; Katz, 1980; Katz et al., 1977; Katz, Rubenstein, Hubert, & Blew, 1988; Lansky, Lowman, Vata, & Gyulay, 1975).

Intraindividual Psychological Adjustment

The child's emotional response to an illness also may impact school functioning. Clearly, psychosocial and emotional factors play an important role in school functioning for children with chronic illness by affecting attendance and influencing the child's ability to engage effectively in the academic process or social milieu while at school. Prolonged absences with little peer contact create social discomfort for the child or adolescent with a chronic illness (Bessel, 2001). Illness-related stress, psychological distress, concerns about peer reactions to physical changes, and the lack of confidence in both physical and academic abilities may contribute to the child's willingness to attend school and to perform well when in school. Frequently, these issues are developmentally related. Peers in elementary school may be concerned that the disease is contagious, whereas adolescent peers are likely to avoid interaction because of fears associating with someone who is different (Davis, 1989). Anxiety over returning to school results when a child or, particularly, an adolescent is confronted with major physical changes, such as hair loss secondary to chemotherapy, disfigurement associated with burns, or amputation necessitated by trauma or diseases (Blakeney, 1994). Physical limitations hindering full participation in the regular school curriculum may contribute to difficulties interacting with peers and ultimately hamper return to school. Students' concerns about physical appearance frequently result in seeking mental health services (Henning & Fritz, 1983). Interestingly, although the fear of peer rejection regarding physical changes is paramount before the return to school, most youth ultimately find that the fundamental social and emotional support for their return to school comes from classmates who have been educated about their particular disease (Chekryn et al., 1987).

A fairly complicated emotional obstacle to school reentry is that of school phobia or separation anxiety. An incidence of school refusal five times that found in the general population has been reported among chronically ill children (Henning & Fritz, 1983). Lansky and colleagues (1975) also found an increased incidence of school phobia in youth 10 years or older who were diagnosed with cancer. Psychosocial regression was significant in all age groups. Parents endorsed feelings of vulnerability, and the children were reported to foster separation anxiety associated with school avoidance. The symptom onset was often insidious with physical complaints initially leading to parent-sanctioned school absences and ultimately to school refusal.

Peer Social Support

Children with chronic illness are at risk for peer difficulties because of negative reactions to their physical changes and from the disruption of social contact brought about by the illness. Any major physical change threatens the child's body image, and ultimately self-esteem, potentially causing discomfort in peer relations. Adolescents, in particular, express specific concerns about the changes in their appearance, fears of peer ridicule or teasing, and discomfort in discussing the illness with classmates and teachers. This is particularly salient with adolescents diagnosed with gastrointestinal diseases, such as Crohn's disease. Although the literature generally indicates that the majority of youth who have experienced a severe injury, such as burns, achieve satisfactory psychological adaptation to their illness (Blakeney, 1994; Blakeney, Herndon, Desai, Beard, and Wales-Sears, 1988), a small segment of this population does not fare as well. In fact, Tarnowski, Rasnake, Linscheid, and Mullick (1989) found clinically significant behavioral problems for children with chronic illnesses, as measured by parental ratings.

Social support has been found to serve as a protective factor in adaptation to chronic illness (Thompson & Gustafson, 1996). Wallander and Varni (1989) examined the unique contribution of family and peer support with children diagnosed with a variety of chronic illnesses, including Type I diabetes mellitus, spina bifida, juvenile rheumatoid arthritis, cerebral palsy, and chronic obesity. Results from this investigation indicates that children with high levels of both family and peer social support evidenced significantly lower levels of internalizing and externalizing behavior problems than children with social support from only one of these sources. These findings were interpreted to suggest that children with chronic conditions can potentially benefit from efforts to improve social support in school by means as social skills training. Varni, Katz, Colgrove, and Dolgin (1994) studied the association between various types of social support and psychological adjustment in thirty school-age children with cancer. Perceived classmate social support was the most consistent predictor of adaptation, providing evidence for the essential function of the school's social environment. This group also conducted a randomized trial of a social skills intervention program for newly diagnosed children with cancer (Varni, Katz, Colgrove, & Dolgin, 1993). Their findings indicated that social skills training was associated with higher perceived classmate and teacher social support, and better overall psychological adjustment.

Familial and Cultural Resources

School performance and adjustment is generally facilitated in families and cultures that place a high emphasis on education and educational pursuits (Hernandez & Charney, 1998). Established families and communities are generally better able to meet the educational needs of their children in providing a consistent and supportive environment for learning than are immigrant families. Helping immigrant families in their acculturation process and acclimation to life in this country, and helping them gain mastery in the systems and processes associated with their child's education have been useful strategies for enhancing educational outcomes of immigrant children (Fuligni, 1997).

Healthy children from immigrant families face many potential challenges to their educational success (Hernandez & Charney, 1998). Coming from homes in which English is not the primary spoken language, children and their parents may not have the ability to communicate easily or directly with school personnel. Parents from many foreign countries do not understand the culture of schools, and that it is acceptable for parents to request services for their child even when they may not be first offered such services. Immigrant families tend to settle in large urban areas that may have troubled school districts that cannot easily meet the needs of healthy immigrant children. When a serious illness is added into the mix of adjustment issues facing an immigrant family, difficulties in communication with school personnel to obtain specialized support or services for their child can easily be overwhelming (Katz et al., 1988).

Special attention needs to be given to ethnic minority families with a chronically ill child or adolescent. Most of these families have the added burden of learning how to adapt to the dominant English culture. Caregivers have difficulty learning how to negotiate both the medical and school system for a number of reasons. First, their resources, both financial and social, are limited. Second, language barriers put them at a disadvantage in identifying potential community resources. For some of these families, it is simpler to homeschool the ill child or adolescent than try to get him/her back into the school setting. Therefore, the importance of school needs to be stressed so that families understand it is critical to their child's overall adjustment and quality of life. Conversely, having a child with a chronic illness may also be viewed as a benefit. Hospital personnel serve a liaison for connecting the family with community resources, including school resources, for all family members (e.g., securing necessary special education services for siblings of chronically ill children or adolescents).

PHASES OF SCHOOL REENTRY

Meeting the educational needs of children with a chronic illness requires cooperative and coordinated efforts among the medical treatment team, school personnel (including teachers, classmates, administrators, school psychologists, and counselors), and the children and their families. The groups are integral components to "school reentry," particularly after diagnosis, or after a prolonged absence. Successful school reentry is focused on meeting the unique needs of the individual child or adolescent, ensuring continuing academic and social skill development by appropriately modifying the school environment, and assisting parents to be effective advocates for their children.

Although there is a burgeoning body of clinical literature describing the school reentry process for various populations of children with chronic disease, there are scant empirical data available. Typically, school reentry studies have a number of methodological shortcomings, including small sample sizes, lack of control groups, limited use of objective outcome measures, and anecdotal rather than empirical data analyses (e.g., Sandford, Falk-Palec, & Spears, 1999; Staley, Anderson, Greenhalgh, & Warden, 1999). Nonetheless, findings from a few data-driven studies focusing on children or adolescents diagnosed with cancer do provide a framework to guide comprehensive integrated school reentry efforts. For example, findings from the school investigation by Katz and colleagues (1988) indicate that, compared with pretest measures, youth diagnosed with cancer who received a structured intervention program exhibited fewer parent-reported internalizing problems, and according to classroom teachers were socially better adjusted relative to the comparison control group.

School reentry programs typically share the common goal of preparing the chronically ill children, the family, and school personnel for transition back into the typical routine of attending school (Davis, 1989; Katz et al., 1988; Lefebvre & Arndt, 1988). These programs serve to establish a formal liaison function between various systems. Programs vary in terms of the formality and structure of services provided, but the underlying premises are the same (Blakeney, 1994; Katz et al., 1988; Katz, Varni, Rubenstein, Blew, & Hubert, 1992). Three major phases of the school reentry process have been identified, each with its own unique challenges, roles, and responsibilities of the various groups of individuals involved. *Phase 1* begins soon after diagnosis and includes hospitalization, initiation of community links, and the development of a school reentry plan. This phase focuses on assessing the child's school behavior and parents' involvement with the school before the illness, arranging interim educational programs like hospital and homebound instruction before school return, and educating peers. *Phase 2* includes contact and education of school personnel by the medical and liaison team, focusing on the provision of information regarding the child's illness and treatment (e.g., scheduling medical treatments and their adverse side effects), planning for absences, anticipating psychosocial adjustment issues (e.g., reaction of school personnel and other children to the child), and developing a plan for educational accommodations or special education services (i.e., creating the IEP). Emphasis during this phase is placed on preparing the teacher and classmates for the child's imminent reentry. *Phase 3*, the final phase, is for follow-up contact with school personnel and parents. This phase occurs after the child returns to school and continues as needed to provide essential ongoing monitoring to ensure that the child or adolescent is indeed attending school.

PHASE 1: INITIAL HOSPITALIZATION, HOMEBOUND INSTRUCTION, AND PLANS FOR REENTRY

During the initial hospitalization, the medical team plays a primary role to both the child and the family by stressing the importance of returning to school. The medical team must convey the message that while the illness or accident is a disruption to life, which for some youth will require new ways of performing activities (e.g., having to move at a slower pace than prior to their illness), with time and practice, in most instances they will be able to resume premorbid activities. Educating parents to the psychosocial importance of school must be clearly communicated, especially when working with diverse ethnic minority populations.

With the parents' permission, a member of the treatment team should contact the child's school to notify school personnel of the child's status, obtain information regarding the child's premorbid academic and social functioning, and elicit any concerns from the school's perspective. It is important to obtain premorbid learning and social data. As soon as the child or adolescent is medically stable, school instruction is incorporated into the child's daily inpatient treatment program. Hospital-based school programs vary greatly in terms of how educational instruction is provided. In some hospital settings, children receive individual instruction if they are physically or emotionally unable to attend school in a classroom setting. If hospitals do not have school programs, then schoolwork can be forwarded from the school and a parent or staff member can function as a teacher.

Homebound Instruction

Very often after the onset of an illness or an acute injury, the child will not be medically ready to return to school for a period of time. This will be true if a child is recovering from surgery, is receiving intensive chemotherapy and is severely immunosuppressed, or is requiring a period of convalescence and rehabilitation. Homebound school programs are mandated by federal and state laws to continue a child's school program at home until the child is medically able to return to school. Families will very often need assistance requesting this service from their local school districts, and will need a letter from the attending physician that formalizes the need for home services.

Larger school districts will usually have specially trained homebound teachers ready to be dispatched to a child's home, whereas smaller districts might not have teachers immediately available. The quality and sophistication of home teachers can vary tremendously, and care needs to be given to the "fit" between a particular home teacher and the child she/he is assigned to teach. Non-English speaking families will need assistance negotiating the teaching sessions and schedule with a home teacher that may speak their language. Variability also exists between school districts as to the number of hours of home teaching they will provide, from a minimum of 1 hr per week to a few hours per day. A recent study by Bessel (2001) indicated that many families have been dissatisfied with the quality and quantity of home teaching their ill child received before returning to school. To be effective, the homebound teacher should work to maintain the child's academic performance with that of his/her classmates in the regular classroom to facilitate a smooth reentry. The homebound teacher will ideally have ongoing contact with the regular teacher to coordinate the individualized program and participate in the reentry preparation when the child is ready to return to school.

Return to School

When a child's medical condition stabilizes and his/her physician gives approval for returning to school, parents may be reluctant to allow the child with a chronic illness or injury back to school for a variety of reasons. Parents may not agree with the medical team when it is determined the child or adolescent is physically ready to return to school, because they may want to protect their child from potential hurt, ridicule, and/or rejection by other children. Parents are susceptible to their own emotions and feelings of guilt and may become too protective and overly responsive to their child's physical complaints or expressions of anxiety related to rejection and ridicule. Understanding the importance of the child's integration, parents may provide support by also contacting the child's school, keeping the teacher and classmates informed of medical progress, and encouraging mutual communication between the ill or injured child and peers (Davis, 1989; Lefebvre & Arndt, 1988). In addition, for those youth who will require homebound instruction, the home teacher should be contacted so that he/she may be incorporated into the school reentry process.

With the family's consent, the child's teacher or school counselor should inform the class about their classmate's chronic illness or injury. Communication with the hospitalized child may be encouraged through cards, electronic mail, phone calls, weekly newsletters, class meetings conducted with a speakerphone to include the classmate, audiotaped class discussions of a high-interest topic with comments from the teacher to include the classmate, and, when possible, visits from classmates to the hospital. If peers stay in close contact, the chronically ill child may find it easier to return to school and as a result be less likely to experience anxiety related to school reentry (Sexson & Madan-Swain, 1995).

School reentry is critical. Even adolescents who have withdrawn from school prematurely before the injury should be expected to become involved in some structured educational or vocational program. Most importantly, the adolescent cannot be allowed to withdraw into the safety of isolation, receiving no new information, feedback from others, or social support. If adolescents, particularly those who have sustained physical changes, are allowed to withdraw, they may experience the daily isolation as confirmation that they are, in fact, incompetent and physically unattractive.

PHASE 2: CONTACT AND EDUCATION OF SCHOOL PERSONNEL

Teachers and School Personnel

The extent to which school personnel can successfully facilitate the reentry process will be partially determined by the attitudes of school personnel (Sexson & Madan-Swain, 1995). It is likely that many teachers lack the necessary information or experience with chronic illnesses and are susceptible to all the fears, anxieties, and failings of the general public. Having a child with a serious chronic illness or injury returning to their classroom is a new experience for most teachers. Limited knowledge about the disease, preconceived notions about certain disorders, and the vulnerability communicated by the change in a child's appearance or energy level may cause teachers to arrive at the premature or erroneous conclusion that the child is likely to die (Ross, 1984). Teachers may be overwhelmed, unsure of how to approach the child, and uncomfortable in seeking information from the parents who are already stressed from the illness experience and unable to deal with their own anxieties about the situation. Lacking this information, teachers may be overly sympathetic and reluctant to challenge the student to his or her potential (Ross, 1984). Conversely, teachers may be unable to recognize true limitations, thus exerting unrealistic expectations that may lead to frustration and discouragement. Teachers also may worry that they will be unable to handle the medical issues that could arise (Blakeney, 1994). These fears may cause the teacher to be increasingly more protective, overreacting to even minor complaints, isolating the child, decreasing the child's self-confidence, limiting peer acceptance, and as a result, further hampering the child's normalization process (Ross, 1984).

To provide a reinforcing classroom in which students are successful, teachers need specific information regarding the illness or injury and its possible impact on school performance and general development (Nessim & Katz, 2000). This allows the teacher to adapt instruction to ensure that the child is successful. Classroom presentations to peers will help demystify the illness or accident, facilitating open communication and peer social support that will likely result in a more reinforcing environment for the child (Katz et al., 1988). Initially, teacher verbal reinforcement should be provided to the chronically ill child reentering the classroom simply for returning to school and for participating in classroom activities. This reinforcement should be delivered at a rapid pace at the beginning of each instructional session (Zanily, Dagged, & Pestine, 1995). In addition, teachers need to analyze the function of behaviors in which the child is likely to engage on returning to the classroom. Many of these behaviors may actually reinforce school avoidance, like requiring the ill child to sit in a designated place or making a fuss over the ill child's special needs that will likely elicit negative peer reactions (e.g., Iwata, Dorsey, Slifer, Bauman, & Richman, 1994). Avoidance may also be reinforced if the child is required to perform tasks that are academically too difficult, either because of missed instruction or the cognitive difficulties associated with the illness, or because of adverse side effects of treatments, such as fatigue.

Educational Assessment and Programming

It is inappropriate to rely on a one-time assessment to determine the academic functioning level and educational needs of children diagnosed with chronic illness. Repeated assessments are needed to determine whether abilities that typically emerge developmentally are negatively impacted by the injury or disease and/or subsequent treatments delivered at an early age. The assessment should include psychoeducational testing to be completed annually by a clinical or pediatric psychologist, a neuropsychologist, or a school psychologist who is employed by the school system, as well as criterion-referenced assessment completed by the classroom teacher. The assessment tools selected for the psychoeducational evaluation are critical. Typically, global measures of intellectual and cognitive functioning are not likely to be adequate indicators of the needs of children who have experienced CNS disease effects and treatment of TBI. Instead, the assessment battery should include neurocognitive measures of processing speed, cognitive flexibility, attention and concentration, language, memory, visuospatial and visual-motor abilities. This will allow the development of an educational plan that targets weaknesses, but also builds on areas of strength. Teachers need to be aware that the child may have difficulty with the development of skills, and for this reason the educational program should strengthen those skills present at the time of treatment and foster the development of strategies to aid in the acquisition of later skills. Based on the nature of the deficits, educational plans should adequately facilitate the child's learning.

One important consideration for young children is to ensure that they become competent readers. Most children need systematic instruction in reading so that they may become competent readers. If children are frequently absent during this instruction, they are likely to have difficulty learning to read, which will quickly compound exponentially unless addressed. One specific method is to identify portable, systematic reading instruction that may be easily implemented both with the hospital and homebound instruction.

In addition to instructional program consideration, children should be allowed to use technology as an aid or to adapt procedures as needed. For example, children may use tape recorders to capture lectures and other oral instructions, word processors to produce work that would otherwise be handwritten, and calculators to perform calculations used in the application of mathematical concepts. Equally important is the consideration of the removal of time constraints and writing requirements in test taking.

Educational programs need to accommodate children's frequent absences because of hospitalizations, dual homebound/school based schooling during treatment, and, when necessary, environmental adaptations for children requiring wheelchairs or walking devices. Adjustment in school rules may need to be made regarding the wearing of particular garments (e.g., allowing hats for those students who have lost their hair secondary to medical treatment) and the provision of access to a quiet area for rest when children become fatigued during periods of low blood counts or pain crises (Armstrong & Horn, 1995).

Although some children with chronic illness may have prolonged absences from school, for most, the pattern of school absences is multiple brief absences that accumulate over the school year. This pattern often leaves the child behind in schoolwork with few available educational resources. Resource teachers on campus and tutors can help children and adolescents bridge the repeated gaps associated with absences, but such programs require considerable coordination to ensure continuity of instruction and social interactions.

Children and adolescents who have specific cognitive deficits associated with their illness, injury, or treatment may need very specialized educational interventions that have been termed *cognitive remediation* (Butler & Namerow, 1988; Butler & Rizzi, 1995). These interventions identify the specific underlying cognitive deficit rather than merely the academic weakness that a particular child may be experiencing and attempts to help the child develop the underlying skills that can facilitate academic success. In addition to focusing on strengthening attention and concentration skills, which are often weak in children with acquired cognitive impairments, interventions that include learning strategies (e.g., getting ready to learn) and social-cognitive problem-solving show great promise.

Classroom Presentation

To ease the transition back into the classroom, members from the medical team may visit the school and present information regarding the chronic illness. The child is generally given the opportunity to provide expert information during the presentation to encourage peers to communicate directly with the child or adolescent if they have questions, but may elect not to do so if this poses a discomfort for the chronically ill child (Nessim & Katz, 1999). Anecdotal literature on reentry presentations for children who have sustained burn injuries illustrates content areas that may typically be addressed in the presentation (Blakeney, 1994), including injury etiology, hospital care, physical implications, and use of special procedures or equipment (e.g., splints, masks, pressure garments). Although the words and methods selected to communicate vary with the target audience, the content remains the same. The format may be adapted for classroom presentations on other chronic illnesses and injury (Nessim & Katz, 1999).

Parental Support

If the school provides a reinforcing environment for the child's return, the parents' behavior encouraging the child's returning to school, reinforced by school personnel, will ensure that the transition will proceed more smoothly. One way to reinforce the parents' efforts is to provide frequent positive communication about the school reentry process. For the first few days, it may be necessary to phone the parents several times during the day to assure them that the reentry is progressing well and to reassure them that the child is experiencing no adjustment difficulties. Over time, the frequency of the contacts may fade as the parents view the success of their child's return to the classroom.

For children and teenagers who are returning to school with significant learning difficulties and in need of special education services, parents will need to learn how to become educational advocates for their children throughout their school experience. Parents need to learn about their child's rights to programs and services, how to ensure that their child is progressing properly, and what resources they may access (e.g., parent advocacy groups) if the school is not meeting its obligations to the child. These skills are especially important to non-English-speaking families that may need referrals to community educational advocacy organizations (e.g., Flood, 1999).

PHASE 3: FOLLOW-UP CONTACT

Central to this phase is continued communication among the family, school personnel, and medical team. Even after the child returns to school, it is important that school personnel remain in close contact with an identified medical team member so that school-related concerns can be easily discussed. Such communication allows the school to inform the medical team of increasing absences and to seek information regarding how to address the issue. The medical team can assist with the development of decision-rules that are acceptable to the school and family. These rules can be used to determine when a child may stay home from school and when attendance is mandatory. Because the decision-rules may change depending on the course of the illness, continual contact must be maintained, particularly for children diagnosed with relapsing illnesses (e.g., Crohn's disease).

For children receiving special education services, the annual IEP meeting conducted by the school to review the child or adolescent's progress and educational needs can help ensure that the child with special health care needs does not fall through the cracks of the school. The medical liaison will likely need to provide follow-up. One should consider writing into the IEP the requirement that the health care team be consulted on an annual basis to determine if the child's medical needs have changed and to obtain their input into the child's ongoing educational program. The annual IEP meeting can become an automatic time for parents to consult with the medical team and review how the child is progressing at school and if all of the child's needs are being adequately met.

CONCLUSIONS AND FUTURE DIRECTIONS

School reentry is a dynamic, ongoing process that requires continuous cooperation and commitment among the medical team, family, and school from initial hospitalization through follow-up contact. Regardless of whether the chronic illness follows a constant, progressive, or relapsing course, the child's return to school poses a significant stressor. Yet, reentry to school is imperative. With the importance of school reentry comes a need to establish a scientific basis for enhancing this process. Several questions must be considered in an effort to facilitate school reentry.

1. To what extent is the reentry process disease specific? Whereas there are a few programs that have been evaluated and published addressing school reentry for children with specific illnesses, such as cancer (Katz et al., 1988) and burns (Blakeney, 1994), further work is needed to extend these efforts to other chronic conditions. On the one hand, school reentry can appear to be a relatively generic challenge. Thus, it is possible that these existing illness-specific programs could be applied to other illnesses with only minor modification. However, this type of generalizability of reentry programs is an empirical question warranting the evaluation of a generic school reentry program across various chronic illnesses. Finding common approaches across illnesses would be helpful. Alternatively, some types of illnesses may require differential attention to reentry issues, which may be need to be evaluated.
2. If the school reentry process is not disease specific, does it vary according disease parameters? This should be delineated initially through a qualitative analysis, and then empirically validated on a larger scale using objective data from several sources (e.g., medical team, parents, child or adolescent, and teacher). For example, relapsing illnesses, such as asthma and SCD, require ongoing adjustments from all parties. As a specific example, the school would need to modify attendance policies so that the child who must miss large numbers of school days is not retained simply because of the number of absences. Alternatively, a child or adolescent who has sustained a TBI may have a long follow-up reentry phase, because recovery may initially be slow, but once a child with this illness is in school, attendance should not be an issue.
3. Regardless of whether the process is disease specific, typology specific, or generic to all diseases, what is the impact of the developmental stage of the child or adolescent? Development would likely interact with reentry phase and type of illness. Thus far, this three-way interaction has been all but ignored. The needs of children reentering school will vary according to their developmental stage. For example, although peers are important at all stages, they play a critical role during adolescence. At this stage, school becomes an important arena for experimenting with different social roles and exploring one's evolving sexuality. Having a chronic illness can readily interfere with these important socialization processes during adolescence. To achieve truly successful school re-entry requires attention to these developmental issues.
4. Develop a predictive model of successful reentry based on Wallander and Varni's (1989) risk/resistance framework and test its ability to successfully predict children at risk who can be targeted for early intervention.
5. Develop specific educational advocacy training programs for parents to ensure that they can provide ongoing supervision of their child's medical program. These programs should be tailored to specific cultural and linguistic issues relevant to specific subpopulations or parents.

6. Develop and evaluate specific educational curriculum methods and materials that can help remediate cognitive deficits associated with sequelae of the disease, treatment, or injury.

In conclusion, the questions are complex and the research designed to answer them will have to consider their interactive nature. In this chapter, we delineated a three-phase reentry process that may be applied to children and adolescents diagnosed with a chronic illness. As data are gathered, it may be necessary to revise aspects of the proposed three-phase reentry process and embed it within a theoretical framework, such as the risk/resistance model (Wallander & Varni, 1989).

REFERENCES

Aicardi, J. (1998). *Diseases of the nervous system in childhood* (2nd ed.). London: MacKeith Press.

Armstrong, F. D., & Horn, M. (1995). Educational issues in childhood cancer. *School Psychology Quarterly, 10*, 292–304.

Armstrong, F. D., Thompson, R. J., Wang, W., Zimmerman, R., Pegelow, C., Miller, S., Moser, F., Bello, J., Hurtig, A., & Vass, K. (1996). Cognitive functioning and brain magnetic resonance imaging in children with sickle cell disease. Neuropsychology of the Cooperative Study of Sickle Cell Disease: Multicenter Study. *Pediatrics, 97*, 864–870.

Bessel, A. G. (2001). Children surviving cancer: Psychosocial adjustment, quality of life, and school experiences. *Exceptional Children, 67*, 345–359.

Blakeney, P. (1994). School reintegration. In K. J. Tarnowski (Ed.), *Behavioral aspects of pediatric burns* (pp. 217–239). New York: Plenum Press.

Blakeney, P., Herndon, D., Desai, M., Beard, S., & Wales-Sears, P. (1988). Long-term psychological adjustment following burn injury. *Journal of Burn Care and Rehabilitation, 9*, 661–665.

Brown, R. T., Armstrong, F. D., & Eckman, J. R. (1993). Neurocognitive aspects of pediatric sickle-cell disease. *Journal of Learning Disabilities, 26*, 33–45.

Brown, R. T., Buchanan, I., Doepke, K., Eckman, J. R., Baldwin, K., Goonan, B., & Schoenherr, S. (1993). Cognitive and academic functioning in children with sickle-cell disease. *Journal of Clinical Child Psychology, 22*, 207–218.

Brown, R. T., Davis, P. C., Lambert, R., Hsu, L., Hopkins, K., & Eckman, J, (2000). Neurocognitive functioning and magnetic resonance imaging in children with sickle cell disease. *Journal of Pediatric Psychology, 25*, 503–513.

Brown, R. T., Madan-Swain, A., Pais, R., Lambert, R. G., Sexson, S. B., & Ragab, A. (1992). Chemotherapy for acute lymphocytic leukemia: Cognitive and academic sequelae. *Journal of Pediatrics, 121*, 885–889.

Brown, R. T., Madan-Swain, A., Walco, G. A., Cherrick, I., Ievers, C. E., Conte, P. M., Vega, R., Bell, B., & Lauer, S. J. (1998). Cognitive and academic late effects among children previously treated for acute lymphocytic leukemia receiving chemotherapy as CNS prophylaxis. *Journal of Pediatric Psychology, 23*, 333–340.

Brown, R. T., Sawyer, M. B., Antoniou, G., Toogood, I., Rice, M., Thompson, N., & Madan-Swain, A. (1996). A 3-year follow-up of the intellectual and academic functioning of children receiving central nervous system prophylactic chemotherapy for leukemia. *Journal of Developmental and Behavioral Pediatrics, 17*, 392–398.

Butler, R. W., & Namerow, N. S. (1988). Cognitive retraining in brain injury rehabilitation: A critical review. *Journal of Neurological Rehabilitation, 2*, 97–101.

Butler, R. W., & Rizzi, L. P. (1995). The remediation of attentional deficits secondary to treatment for childhood cancer: Progress notes. *Society of Pediatric Psychology, 19*, 5–13.

Cadman, D., Boyle, M., Szatmari, P., & Offord, D. R. (1987). Chronic illness, disability, and mental and social well-being: Findings of the Ontario Child Health Study. *Pediatrics, 79*, 805–813.

Cairns, N. U., Klopovich, P., Hearne, E., & Lansky, S. B. (1982). School attendance of children with cancer. *Journal of School Health, 52*, 152–155.

Charlton, A., Larcombe, I. J., Meller, S. T., Morris-Jones, P. H., Mott, M. G., Potton, M. W., Tranmer, M. D., & Walker, J. J. P. (1991). Absence from school related to cancer and other chronic conditions. *Archives of Diseases in Childhood, 66*, 217–1222.

Chen, E., Zeltzer, L. K., Bentler, P. M., Byrne, J., Nicholson, H. S., Meadows, A. T., Mills, J. L., Haupt, R., Fears, T. R., & Robison, L. L. (1998). Pathways linking treatment intensity and psychosocial outcomes among adult survivors of childhood leukemia. *Journal of Health Psychology, 3*, 23–38.

Chekryn, J., Deegan, M., & Reid, J. (1987). Impact on teachers when a child with cancer returns to school. *Children's Health Care, 15*, 161–165.

Cook, B. A., Schaller, K., & Krischer, J. P. (1985). School absence among children with chronic illness. *Journal of School Health, 55*, 265–267.

Cousens, P., Ungerer, J. A., Crawford, J. A., & Stevens, M. (1991). Cognitive effect of childhood leukemia therapy: A case for four specific deficits. *Journal of Pediatric Psychology, 16*, 475–488.

Dalby, P. R., & Obrzut, J. E. (1991). Epidemiological characteristics and sequelae of closed head injured children and adolescents: A review. *Developmental Neuropsychology, 7*, 35–68.

Davis, K. G. (1989). Educational needs of the terminally ill student. *Issues in Comprehensive Pediatric Nursing, 12*, 235–245.

Eiser, C., & Tillmann, V. (2001). Learning difficulties in children treated for acute lymphoblastic leukemia. *Pediatric Rehabilitation, 4*, 105–118.

Ewing-Cobb, L., & Bloom, D. R. (1999). Traumatic brain injury. In R. T. Brown (Ed.), *Cognitive aspects of chronic illness in children.* New York: Guilford Press.

Fletcher, J. M., & Copeland, D. R. (1988). Neurobehavioral effects of central nervous system prophylactic treatment of cancer in children. *Journal of Clinical and Experimental Neuropsychology, 10*, 495–538.

Flood, G. (1999). *Advocacy training: A look towards the future of pediatric cancer patients and their families.* Unpublished doctoral dissertation, Pepperdine University, Graduate School of Education and Psychology, Culver City, CA.

Fowler, M. G., Johnson, M. P., & Atkinson, S. S. (1985). School achievement and absence in children with chronic health conditions. *Journal of Pediatrics, 106*, 683–687.

Fuligni, A. J. (1997). The academic achievement of adolescents from immigrant families: The roles of family background, attitude, and behavior. *Child Development, 68*, 351–363.

Glauser, T. A., & Packer, R. J. (1991). Cognitive deficits in long-term survivors of childhood brain tumors. *Child's Nervous System, 7*, 2–12.

Gortmaker, S. L., Walker, D. K., Weitzman, M., & Sobel, A. M. (1990). Chronic conditions, socioeconomic risks and behavioral problems in children and adolescents. *Pediatrics, 85*, 267–276.

Gourley, R. (1990). Educational Policies. *Epilepsia, 31*(4), 59–60.

Hayes, D. M., Landsverk, J., Sallan, S. E., Hewett, K. D., Patenaude, A. F., Schoonover, D., Zilber, S. L., Ruccione, K., & Siegel, S. E. (1992). Educational, occupational, and insurance status of childhood cancer survivors in their fourth and fifth decades of life. *Journal of Clinical Oncology, 10*, 1397–1406.

Henning, J., & Fritz, G. K. (1983). School reentry in childhood cancer. *Psychosomatics, 24*, 261–269.

Hernandez, D. J., & Charney, E. (1998). *From generation to generation: The health and well-being of children in immigrant families.* Washington, DC: National Academy Press.

Hiemenz, J. R., Hynd, G. W., & Jimenez, M. (1999). Seizure disorders. In R.T. Brown (Ed.), *Cognitive aspects of chronic illness in children.* New York: Guilford Press.

Howe, G. W., Feinstein, C., Reiss, D., Molock, S., & Berger, K. (1993). Adolescent adjustment to chronic physical disorders: I. Comparing neurological and non-neurological conditions. *Journal of Child Psychology and Psychiatry, 14*, 1153–1171.

Individuals with Disabilities Education Act. (1990). Public Law-101–456. *Reauthorization of Public Law 94–142.* Washington, DC: U.S. Government Printing Office.

Iwata, B. A., Dorsey, M. F., Slifer, K. J., Bauman, K. E., & Richman, G. S. (1994). Towards a functional analysis of self-injury. *Journal of Applied Behavior Analysis, 27*, 197–209.

Jaffe, K. M., Fay, G. C., Polissar, N. L., Martin, K. M., Shurtleff, H., Rivara, J. B., & Winn, H. R. (1993). Severity of pediatric traumatic brain injury and neurobehavioral recovery at one year—A cohort study. *Archives of Physical Medicine and Rehabilitation,74*, 587–595.

Katz, E. R. (1980). Illness impact and social reintegration. In J. Kellerman (Ed.), *Psychological aspects of cancer in children.* (pp. 14–46). Springfield, IL: Thomas.

Katz, E. R., & Ingle-Nelson, M. J. (1989). School and the seriously ill child. In B. B. Martin (Ed.), *Pediatric hospice care: What helps.* Los Angeles, CA: Children's Hospital Los Angeles.

Katz, E. R., Kellerman, J., Rigler, D., Williams, K. O., & Siegel, S. E. (1977). School intervention with pediatric cancer patients. *Journal of Pediatric Psychology, 2*, 72–76.

Katz, E. R., Rubenstein, C. L., Hubert, N. C., & Blew, A. (1988). School and social reintegration of children with cancer. *Journal of Psychosocial Oncology, 6*, 123–140.

Katz, E. R., Varni, J. W., Rubenstein, C. L., Blew, A., & Hubert, N. (1992). Teacher, parent, and child evaluative ratings of school reintegration intervention for children with newly diagnosed cancer. *Children's Health Care, 21*, 69–75.

Kovacs, M., Ryan, C., & Obrosky, D. (1994). Verbal intellectual and verbal memory performance of youths with childhood-onset insulin dependent diabetes mellitus: A longitudinal study. *Developmental Psychology, 28*, 676–684.

Kun, L. E., Mulhern, R. K., & Crisco, J. J. (1983). Quality of life in children treated for brain tumors: Intellectual, emotional, and academic function. *Journal of Neurosurgery, 58*, 1–6.

Lansky, S. B., Lowman, J. T., Vata, T., & Gyulay, J. (1975). School phobia in children with malignant neoplasms. *American Journal of Diseases of Children, 129*, 42–46.

Lefebvre, A. M., & Arndt, E. M. (1988). Working with facially disfigured children: A challenge in prevention. *Canadian Journal of Psychiatry, 33*, 453–458.

Madan-Swain, A., & Brown, R. T. (1991). Cognitive and psychosocial sequelae for children with acute lymphocytic leukemia and their families. *Clinical Psychology Review, 11*, 267–294.

Madan-Swain, A., Fredrick, L. D., & Wallander, J. L. (1999). Returning to school after a serious illness or injury. In R. T. Brown (Ed.), *Cognitive aspects of chronic illness in children.* New York: Guilford Press.

Nessim, S., & Katz, E. R. (2000). *CanSurvive teacher guide for kids with cancer.* Los Angeles: CanSurvive.

Parcel, G. S., Gilman, S. C., Nader, P. R., & Bunce, H. (1979). A comparison of absenteeism rates of elementary school children with asthma and nonasthmatic schoolmates. *Pediatrics, 64*, 878–881.

Raymond-Speden, E., Tripp, G., Lawrence, B., & Holdaway, D. (2000). Intellectual, neuropsychological, and academic functioning in long-term survivors of leukemia. *Journal of Pediatric Psychology, 25*, 59–68.

Ris, M. D., Packer, R., Goldwein, J., Jones-Wallace, D., & Boyett, J. M. (2001). Intellectual outcome after reduced-dose radiation therapy plus adjuvant chemotherapy for medulloblastoma: A children's cancer study group study. *Journal of Clinical Oncology, 19*, 3470–3476.

Ross, J. W. (1984). Resolving nonmedical obstacles to successful school reentry for children with cancer. *Journal of School Health, 54*, 84–86.

Rovet, J. F., & Alvarez, M. (1997). Attentional functioning in children and adolescents with IDDM. *Diabetes Care, 46*, 14.

Rovet, J. F., Ehrlich, R. M., Czuchta, D., & Akler, M. (1993). Psychoeducational characteristics of children and adolescents with insulin-dependent diabetes mellitus. *Journal of Learning Disabilities, 26*, 7–22.

Rovet, J. F., & Fernandes, C. (1999). Insulin-dependent diabetes mellitus. In R. T. Brown (Ed.), *Cognitive aspects of chronic illness in children.* New York: Guilford Press.

Rutter, M., Tizard, J., & Whitmore, K. (1970). *Education, health, and behavior.* London: Longsman, Green.

Ryan, C. M., Longstreet, C., & Morrow, L. A. (1985). The effects of diabetes mellitus on the school attendance and school achievement of adolescents. *Child: Care, Health, and Development, 11*, 229–240.

Sandford, P., Falk-Palec, D., & Spears, K. (1999). Return to school after spinal cord injury. *Archives of Physical & Medical Rehabilitation, 80*, 885–88.

Sansbury, L. Brown, R. T., & Meachum, L. (1997). Predictors of cognitive functioning in children and adolescents with insulin-dependent diabetes mellitus: A preliminary investigation. *Children's Health Care, 26*, 197–210.

Sexson, S. B., & Madan-Swain, A. (1993). School reentry for the child with chronic illness. *Journal of Learning Disabilities, 26*, 115–125.

Sexson, S. B., & Madan-Swain, A. (1995). The chronically ill child in the school. *School Psychology Quarterly, 10*, 359–368.

Staley, M., Anderson, L., Greenhalgh, D., & Warden, G. (1999). Return to school as an outcome measure after a burn injury. *Journal of Burn Care & Rehabilitation, 20*, 91–94.

Stedman, J., Van Heyningen, R., & Lindsey, J. (1982). Educational underachievement and epilepsy: A study of children from normal schools admitted to a special hospital for epilepsy. *Early Childhood Development Care, 9*, 5–82.

Stehbens, J. A., Kisker, C. T., & Wilson, B. K. (1983). School behavior and attendance during the first year of treatment for childhood cancer. *Psychology in the Schools, 20*, 223–228.

Tarnowski, K. J., Rasnake, L. K., Linscheid, T. R., & Mullick, J. A. (1989). Behavioral adjustment of pediatric burn victims. *Journal of Pediatric Psychology, 14*, 607–615.

Taylor, B. V., Buckner, J. C., Cascino, T. L., O'Fallon, J. R., Schaefer, P. L., Dinapoli, R. P., & Schomberg, P. (1998). Effects of radiation and chemotherapy on cognitive function in patients with high-grade glioma. *Journal of Clinical Oncology, 16*, 2195–2201.

Thompson, R. J., Jr., & Gustafson, K.F. (1996). *Adaptation to chronic childhood illness*. Washington, DC: American Psychological Association.

Varni, J. W., Burwinkle, T. M., Katz, E. R., Meeske, K., & Dickerson, P. (2002). The PedsQL in pediatric cancer: Reliability and validity of the Pediatric Quality of Life Inventory Generic Core Scales, Multidimensional Fatigue Scale, & Cancer Module. *Cancer, 94*(7), 2090–2106.

Varni, J. W., Katz, E. R., Colgrove, R., & Dolgin, M. J. (1993). The impact of social skills training on the adjustment of children with newly diagnosed cancer. *Journal of Pediatric Psychology, 18*, 751–767.

Varni, J. W., Katz, E. R., Colgrove, R., & Dolgin, M. J. (1994). Perceived social support and adjustment of children with newly diagnosed cancer. *Journal of Developmental and Behavioral Pediatrics, 15*, 20–26.

Wallander, J. L., & Varni, J. W. (1989). Social support and adjustment in chronically ill and handicapped children. *American Journal of Community Psychology, 17*, 185–201.

Wasserman, A. L., Wilimas, J. A., Fairclough, D. L., Mulhern, R. K., & Wang, W. (1991). Subtle neuropsychological deficits in children with sickle-cell disease. *American Journal of Pediatric Hematology/Oncology, 13*, 14–20.

Weitzman, M., & Siegel, D. M. (1992). What we have not learned from what we know from excessive school absence and school drop-out. *Journal of Developmental & Behavioral Pediatrics, 13*, 55–58.

Weitzman, M., Walker, D. K., & Gortmaker, S. (1986). Chronic illness, psychosocial problems, and school absences. *Clinical Pediatrics, 25*, 137–141.

Wills, K. E. (1993). Neuropsychological functioning in children with spina bifida and/or hydrocephalus. *Journal of Clinical Child Psychiatry, 22*, 247–265.

Zanily, L., Dagged, J., & Pestine, H. (1995). The influence of the pace of teacher attention on preschool children's engagement. *Behavior Modification, 19*, 339–356.

PART VII: Special Topics

34

Peer Relations

Annette M. La Greca
Karen J. Bearman
Hannah Moore
University of Miami

INTRODUCTION

Peer relations and close friendships play extremely important roles in youngsters' social and emotional development. By the early school years, children spend most of their daytime hours in school or play settings with classmates and friends (Ellis, Rogoff, & Cromer, 1981). This trend continues, and accelerates, through adolescence. In fact, research has documented the developmentally unique social behaviors that develop in the context of children's peer interactions (see Asher & Coie, 1990; Hartup, 1983, 1996; La Greca & Prinstein, 1999).

Despite the many positive functions of youngsters' peer relations, they can also represent a source of stress. Substantial evidence indicates that children who experience interpersonal difficulties during elementary school display internalizing difficulties, such as depression, anxiety, and loneliness (Asher & Wheeler, 1985; La Greca & Stone, 1993; Strauss, Lahey, Frick, Frame, & Hynd, 1988). Over time, problematic peer relations may contribute to serious mental health and academic problems. For example, children who are actively rejected by their classmates have more mental health problems during late adolescence and early adulthood than their more accepted peers (Cowen, Pederson, Babijian, Izzo, & Trost, 1973), and drop out of high school at much higher rates than their classmates (Kupersmidt & Coie, 1990). Findings such as these underscore the critical role of peer relations in social and emotional adjustment.

As a result, it is essential that professionals working in the schools pay close attention to children's and adolescents' peer relations and friendships. This is especially true when a child or adolescent has a chronic disease or a physically handicapping condition. Peers represent a significant source of emotional support that can buffer the negative impact of stressors, such as adjusting to a chronic disease or coping with a difficult medical treatment (e.g., La Greca et al., 1995; Varni, Babani, Wallander, Roc, & Frasier, 1989). On the other hand, children and adolescents with a complicated, chronic, or time-consuming treatment are often very concerned about the social impact of their condition, and the possible disruption of their friendships. Thus, youngsters with pediatric problems may need special assistance in developing and maintaining peer relationships and friendship ties.

With these issues in mind, the present chapter will examine the peer relations of youth with pediatric conditions. It is organized into several sections. The first provides a developmental overview of children's and adolescents' peer relations and friendships. The next main section reviews relevant research in the area of peer relations and child health—specifically with respect to social competence, psychosocial adjustment, disease management, and the reduction of health-risk behaviors. The implications of existing findings for practice within the schools are described. The last section of the chapter briefly highlights general directions for future research and intervention.

THE DEVELOPMENTAL CONTEXT OF YOUNGSTERS' PEER RELATIONS

Elementary School Years

Children's peer relations have been most widely studied during the elementary school years (approximately ages 6–12 years). During this period, children typically spend the school day in self-contained classrooms with a set group of classmates, although some children interact with peers in special educational settings (e.g., services for youth with disabilities, enhancement activities for gifted children). After school and on weekends, many children are involved in organized activities with peers (e.g., sports, dance, scouts), as well as in unstructured play activities with friends and neighborhood youth. In these social contexts, two aspects of children's peer relations become highly salient: their *peer status* and their close *friendships*.

Peer status (or peer acceptance) refers to the extent to which a child is liked or accepted by the peer group. In contrast, peer friendships refer to close, supportive ties with one or more peers, and these friendships may occur within or outside the classroom (Furman & Robbins, 1985). Children's peer groups and friendships serve different emotional needs. Peer group acceptance provides children with a sense of belonging or social inclusion, whereas friendships provide children with a sense of intimacy, companionship, and self-esteem (Furman & Robbins, 1985). Thus, peer acceptance and peer friendships are related, but distinct aspects of children's peer relations. Both are critical for emotional health and development.

Peer Acceptance. With respect to peer acceptance, it is important to distinguish between children who are accepted and those who are rejected by peers (e.g., Coie, Dodge, & Coppotelli, 1982; Coie, Dodge, & Kupersmidt, 1990). *Popular* children are well liked and have few detractors. Popular children's acceptance from peers most likely reflects their positive social skills and personal competencies, such as being helpful and considerate, and having good athletic and academic abilities (e.g., Coie et al., 1982, 1990; Dodge, Coie, & Brakke, 1982; Hartup, 1983).

In contrast, children who are *rejected* by peers are widely disliked and lack friends or supporters; these children have the most interpersonal, emotional, and academic difficulties. For example, rejected children often display academic problems (Green, Forehand, Beck, & Vosk, 1980; Stone & La Greca, 1990), and report symptoms of depression, loneliness, and social anxiety (Asher & Wheeler, 1985; La Greca & Stone, 1993). Moreover, rejected children are often aggressive, disruptive, or inattentive, and may have limited social skills (see Coie et al., 1990).

Children who are *neglected* by peers (also known as "social isolates") are neither liked nor disliked; they go unnoticed by their peers. Neglected children do not usually display behavior problems, but may be withdrawn (Coie & Dodge, 1988; Dodge et al., 1982) or socially anxious (La Greca & Stone, 1993). Although not as problematic as rejected youth, neglected children may have difficulty developing supportive friendship ties, given their low sociability and low rates of social interactions with peers.

Some of the research reviewed in subsequent sections of this chapter has examined the peer acceptance of youth with chronic or life-threatening diseases, because there is concern that illness may jeopardize children's peer acceptance. In elementary school settings, children who are neglected or rejected by peers bear close monitoring, and this is especially the case with children who also have a chronic disease or another pediatric condition. Children who are disliked may need help developing better peer relations; for example, interventions may be needed to increase these children's positive interaction skills, or to modify the aversive or annoying behaviors (or other personal characteristics) that contribute to peers' dislike (see La Greca, 1993; La Greca & Prinstein, 1999). Children who are neglected, or who lack friends and playmates, may need assistance in developing friendship ties.

Friendships. The ability to form and maintain supportive dyadic friendships also represents a critical social adaptation task (Parker & Asher, 1993a). Much of children's social lives revolve around dyadic or small group interactions with their same-aged friends (Parker & Asher, 1993b).

Research suggests that most children have close friends in school. For example, in a study of third to fifth graders (Parker & Asher, 1993a), 78% had at least one reciprocal "best friend" in the classroom, and 55% of the children had a "very best friend." Girls were more likely to have a best friend than boys (82% vs. 74%, respectively); girls also had significantly more best friends than boys. Children who have *at least one* close friendship appear to fare better emotionally than those who lack such personal ties (Parker & Asher, 1993a).

A variety of factors contribute to children's friendship selection. One is social proximity; that is, children are likely to choose peers from their classroom, scouts group, or immediate neighborhood as friends (Hartup, 1983). Children also choose as friends others who are similar to themselves (e.g., same age, same gender), who share common interests (e.g., play sports, listen to music), and who are fun to be with (Hartup, 1996; Parker & Asher, 1993b).

In addition, the *quality* of children's friendships is important. Friends provide emotional support and are children's primary source of companionship (Berndt, 1989; Cauce, Reid, Landesman, & Gonzales, 1990; Furman & Buhrmester, 1985; Reid, Landesman, Treder, & Jaccard, 1989). However, friendships can also vary tremendously in the amount and type of support they provide, the degree to which conflict is present, and their level of reciprocity (Parker & Asher, 1993b). Furthermore, girls often report more intimate and supportive relationships with their friends than do boys. This may reflect boys' tendency to associate with peers in large groups that are often centered on sports and outdoor games, whereas girls are typically involved in dyads or small groups that spend time in conversation and quiet activities (e.g., Lever, 1976; Thorne, 1986).

In general, the number and quality of children's close friendships are important for children's mental health. Because close, supportive friendships can help children manage the stress of a chronic illness, or life-threatening disease, school personnel and mental health professionals should pay attention to whether or not a child has close friends (both inside and outside the classroom). It will also be important to understand the *qualitative* features of these friendships. Helping children to develop more positive, supportive friendship ties may be an important goal for intervention.

Adolescence

During adolescence, peer relations take on increasing prominence and complexity. Most adolescents have a rich network of peers that includes their best friends, other close friends, larger friendship groups or cliques, social crowds, and even romantic relationships (Furman, 1989; Urberg, Degirmencioglu, Tolson, & Halliday-Scher, 1995). Some terms that are useful for understanding adolescents' peer relations include peer crowds, cliques, and dyads. *Peer crowds* are reputation-based peer groups; that is, a large collective of similarly stereotyped individuals who may or may not spend much time together. *Cliques* typically are a small number of adolescents who spend time together; and *dyads* refer to pairs of friends or romantic partners (Brown, 1989, pp. 189–190).

Peer Crowds. To the extent that crowds reflect adolescents' peer status and reputation, they are an outgrowth of the social status groups observed in elementary school. Peer crowd affiliation reflects the primary attitudes or behaviors by which an adolescent is known to peers (Brown, 1989).

Specific adolescent peer crowds may vary with age, with some changes occurring between middle school and high school (O'Brien & Bierman, 1987), and also may vary with a particular school or neighborhood (Brown, 1989). Nevertheless, remarkable cross-setting consistencies have been observed. The most common peer crowds include: populars, brains, jocks, druggies or burnouts, loners, nonconformists or alternatives, and special interest groups (e.g., drama, dance; Brown & Clausen, 1986; Mosbach & Leventhal, 1988; Urberg, 1992). Some adolescents identify with more than one group, and many do not identify with any group or consider themselves to be "average."

Peer crowds vary in obvious and not-so-obvious ways. For instance, "brains" typically are smart, do well in school, and value academic activities; however, they also tend to be low in their levels of sexual activity, smoking, alcohol and drug use (e.g., La Greca, Prinstein, & Fetter, 2001; Mosbach & Leventhal, 1988). "Jocks" typically are involved in athletic activities or competitive sports but are less likely to smoke or use drugs than other teens. Thus, an adolescent's peer crowd may "say something" about the adolescent's behavior and reputation, and also about health-risk behaviors.

From a developmental perspective, the significance of peer crowds is that they contribute to adolescents' reputation and identity, and provide a sense of belonging. Peer crowd membership also may determine the pool of individuals from which adolescents meet and select friends. Finally, peer crowd affiliation may influence behavior, in that an adolescent who wishes to be a part of a particular crowd may feel compelled to maintain behaviors that are compatible with the crowd's reputation. For example, adolescents who affiliate with the "burnouts" may smoke or drink alcohol to "fit in" with others. Thus, from a health perspective, it becomes extremely important to understand the kind of peer crowd with which an adolescent identifies, especially when the adolescent has a chronic disease. An adolescent with diabetes who affiliates with the "jock" or "brain" peer crowds may be more likely to get support for a healthy lifestyle than one who affiliates with the "alternative" or "burnout" crowds.

Peer Rejection or Victimization Experiences. There is a paucity of data on peer rejection among adolescents, even though it is an area of concern. During adolescence, fitting in with one's peers becomes a major priority for most teens (Bowker, Sippola, & Bukowski, 1996). In this context, peer rejection may be particularly stressful. Bowker et al. (1996) found that peer rejection experiences accounted for more than 50% of the "peer-related hassles" reported by seventh graders. In addition, Parkhurst and Asher (1992) found that many seventh and eighth graders were "victimized" and pushed around by peers in school, and that this type of rejection was associated with subjective distress.

Others have studied aversive exchanges among adolescents. Vernberg, Ewell, Beery, Freeman, and Abwender (1995) surveyed 130 middle school students, and found that 73% of them reported at least one aversive exchange (i.e., teased, hit, threatened, or excluded by peers) during the prior 3 months. Many adolescents did not talk to anyone about these events, and when they did, they were more likely to disclose this information to a friend, classmate, or sibling than to an adult. This suggests that parents and other concerned adults (such as school personnel) may be completely unaware of these aversive exchanges. Furthermore, adolescents who reported more verbal and physical harassment or peer exclusion endorsed more loneliness, especially if they did not discuss these events with anyone else.

Prospective studies further indicate that aversive exchanges with peers lead to feelings of internal distress. In one study, peer rejection experiences at the beginning of the school year predicted adolescents' feelings of social anxiety later in the school year (Vernberg, Abwender, Ewell, & Beery, 1992). In addition, large-scale longitudinal investigations of bullying among Scandinavian youth (Olweus, 1993) have found that adolescents who are bullied frequently during early adolescence are likely to report low self-esteem and symptoms of anxiety as adults.

In summary, although peer rejection and victimization (i.e., harassment, exclusion) have not received much empirical attention, they appear to be common occurrences and represent a significant source of subjective distress for many adolescents. Because adolescents are not likely to talk about aversive peer exchanges with other adults, they may go undetected and underreported. Adolescents who have a medical condition, especially one that has some physical manifestation, may be concerned about teasing and harassment from peers (see La Greca, 1990), and need support and assistance.

Friendships. Peer friendships are particularly salient during adolescence. Adolescents spend more time talking to peers than in any other activity and also describe themselves as happiest when talking to friends (Berndt, 1982). Adolescents' interactions with friends primarily occur in dyads (friendship pairs, romantic partners) or in cliques. Cliques are friendship-based groupings that vary in size (usually 5–8 members), density (the degree to which each person regards others in the clique as friends), and "tightness" (the extent to which they are closed or open to outsiders; Brown, 1989; Urberg et al., 1995). Cliques constitute the primary base for adolescents' peer interactions (Brown, 1989) and typically contain specific dyadic pairings (e.g., best friends; Urberg et al., 1995).

An important determinant of adolescents' friendships is similarity or "homophily"; that is, adolescents *select* as friends others who share similar attributes and characteristics, and are also *influenced* by the behaviors and attitudes of the friends they choose. In addition to similarities in age, sex, and race, similarities in specific interests, school attitudes, achievement, orientation to the contemporary peer culture, and substance use are important factors in adolescents' friendship choices (Berndt, 1982; Brown, 1989; Hartup, 1996). Once friendships are established, mutual socialization further enhances the similarities between friends (Hartup, 1996; Kandel, 1978). Furthermore, cross-sex friendships become increasingly common during adolescence (Bukowski, Gauze, Hoza, & Newcomb, 1993; Kuttler, La Greca, & Prinstein, 1999), and adolescents with cross-sex friendships appear to be better integrated into the peer network at school (Degirmencioglu & Urberg, 1996).

Many of the qualities observed in children's friendships (companionship, aid, validation and caring, trust) are important for adolescents (Berndt, 1982). However, a defining feature of adolescents' friendships is their *intimacy* (i.e., sharing of personal, private thoughts and feelings; knowledge of intimate details about one another). Close friendships become increasingly more intimate during adolescence (Berndt, 1982). In addition, girls report more intimacy in their friendships than boys (Berndt, 1982), which may reflect girls' preference for "exclusive" relationships (Elder & Hallinan, 1978; Waldrop & Halverson, 1975). In contrast, boys appear to be more flexible and open in their friendship choices (Urberg et al., 1995).

Having an intimate friendship during adolescence has psychological benefits (e.g., enhances self-esteem; reduces anxieties, loneliness). For example, Vernberg (1990) found that less contact with friends, less closeness with a best friend, and greater peer rejection experiences over the course of 6 months contributed to increases in adolescents' depressive affect. In other studies, support from close friends has been positively associated with school involvement and achievement (Berndt & Keefe, 1992; Cauce, 1986), self-esteem and psychosocial adjustment (e.g., Buhrmester, 1990; Compas, Slavin, Wagner, & Cannatta, 1986), and peer popularity (Cauce, 1986).

For adolescents with health problems, the presence of a mutual best friend in school may help such adolescents to cope more effectively with stresses that may result either from normal adolescent life circumstances, or the additional burden of managing a serious health condition. School personnel might encourage adolescents to involve their best friends in disease management and coping. This issue is discussed further in this chapter.

PEER RELATIONS: AN IMPORTANT CONSIDERATION FOR PEDIATRIC POPULATIONS

Despite the importance of peers and friendships for all youth, including those with medical conditions, the peer relations of youth with pediatric problems have not been well studied (see La Greca, 1990, 1992). In this chapter section, we review some of the key ways that peer relations have been examined in pediatric psychology research. Specifically, we review several areas of research and their implications for school settings: (1) the association between pediatric conditions and youngsters' social adjustment, (2) the role of peers/close friends as a source of support for youth with pediatric conditions, (3) friends' influence on treatment adherence, and (4) peers/friends' impact on healthy behaviors (e.g., exercise) and health-risk behaviors (e.g., smoking, drinking, etc.).

The Social Adjustment of Youth With Pediatric Conditions

Many children and adolescents express concern or worry about their peer relations. For example, Brown, Clausen, and Eicher (1986) found that the most common stressors reported by youngsters 10–18 years of age were "fear of negative evaluations from others" and "fights with or rejection by a friend." These concerns can be especially prominent for youth with a chronic pediatric condition (Wolman, Resnick, Harris, & Blum, 1994). Nevertheless, in general, children with chronic disease do not appear to have more social difficulties than their healthy peers. This literature can best be divided into studies of youth with and without cognitive impairments associated with their pediatric condition.

No Cognitive Impairments. The most extensive work on the peer relations of youth with chronic pediatric conditions has come from Noll and colleagues (e.g., Noll, Bukowski, Davies, Koontz, & Kalkarni, 1993; Noll, Bukowski, Rogosch, LeRoy, & Kulkarni, 1990; Noll, LeRoy, Bukowski, Rogosch, & Kulkarni, 1991; Noll et al., 1996, 1999). These investigators have used child, peer, teacher, and parent reports to examine various aspects of children's social adjustment, such as popularity, social acceptance, and loneliness.

Specifically, in the first of a series of studies, children with cancer were compared with matched classroom controls on measures such as popularity, friendship, and social reputation (Noll et al., 1990). Based on peers' ratings, the children with cancer were seen as less sociable, less prone toward leadership, and more socially isolated and withdrawn than controls. However, two follow-up studies (Noll et al., 1991, 1993) found no differences between the two groups of children in terms of their general social acceptance, self-concept, and loneliness, even though the children with cancer were perceived to have more illness and to be more socially isolated than their classmates. When teacher reports were included as a measure of social reputation, children with cancer were nominated more often for sociability-leadership roles and less often for aggressive-disruptive roles. More recent work has shown that children with cancer were remarkably similar to controls in terms of their emotional functioning and social adjustment (Noll et al., 1999).

Work with children who have asthma suggests that their peer relations are comparable with their classmates, even though peers perceive these youth as being sicker and missing more school (Graetz & Shute, 1995). However, those with more severe asthma (e.g., more hospitalizations) were perceived as less preferred as playmates and as being more sensitive-isolated; these children also reported more loneliness than did children with less severe asthma. Some preliminary work suggests that adolescents with asthma may have higher than average levels of social anxiety, suggesting a high degree of worry or concern about peer relations (Bearman, La Greca, Glickman, & Kuttler, 2001).

In a study of children with sickle cell disease (SCD), gender appeared to be an important determinant of peers' perceptions of the affected child's social competence (Noll et al., 1996). Girls with SCD were perceived by peers as being less sociable and less well accepted than comparison girls, whereas boys with SCD were perceived as being less aggressive than comparison boys.

Together, these studies provide limited support for the notion that chronic disease has a negative impact on youngsters' peer relations or friendships. Nevertheless, the findings do identify considerable variability in the peer relations of children and adolescents' with chronic disease, and youth who have more severe illness may be more socially affected than other youth.

In view of these findings, it would be useful for school personnel to know how to identify youth with chronic pediatric conditions, and to be able to monitor their health and school adjustment on a regular basis. Children and adolescents who miss a substantial amount of school because of hospitalizations may be especially important to monitor and assist in their social adaptation.

Cognitive Impairments. Pediatric conditions that are associated with cognitive impairments present a special challenge to social relations. Cognitive impairments occur with a variety of chronic conditions and treatments, and may range from mild learning disabilities to significant impairment (e.g., mental retardation). Chronic health conditions that are associated with cognitive difficulties include cerebral palsy, spina bifida, epilepsy, congenital heart disease, SCD, and human immunodeficiency virus (HIV) infection (Armstrong, Seidel, & Swales, 1993; Brouwers, Belman & Epstein, 1991; DeMaso, Beardslee, Silbert, & Fyler, 1990; Fabian & Peters, 1984; Gammal et al., 1988; Huttnelocher, Moohr, Johns, & Brown, 1984; Nassau & Drotar, 1997; Shepherd & Hosking, 1989; Wiznitzer et al., 1990). Cancers that involve brain tissue also can produce central nervous system (CNS) complications (Nassau & Drotar, 1997).

Studies suggest that children with CNS-related health conditions may have trouble developing age-appropriate peer relations. Nassau and Drotar (1997) suggest that this linkage may be from: (1) cognitive impairments, such as below average intelligence or specific cognitive deficits (e.g., memory or attention problems) associated with CNS-related conditions that interfere with social understanding and affect peer relations (Dodge & Price, 1994); (2) varying degrees of physical handicap (e.g., braces or wheelchairs) that limit children's ability to participate in age-appropriate peer activities (La Greca, 1990) and lead to social isolation or peer rejection; and (3) limited opportunities for peer involvement for those who attend special education classes or participate in rehabilitation settings.

Available evidence highlights problems in peer relations among children and adolescents with CNS-related conditions (see Nassau & Drotar, 1997). For example, studies have found that youth with CNS-related conditions—such as spina bifida, cerebral palsy, and other chronic physical disorders—are rated as less socially competent than comparison control youth or normative samples (Ammerman, Van Hasselt, Hersen, & Moore, 1989; Apter et al., 1991; Wallander, Feldman, & Varni, 1989; Wallander, Hubert, & Varni, 1988; Wallander, Varni, Babini, Banis, & Wilcox, 1988). When peer-based sociometric ratings have been used (Center & Ward, 1984), children with spina bifida have been found to be less socially accepted than their classmates. In addition, research suggests that children who survive brain tumors have more social problems, fewer friends (Vannatta, Gartstein, Short, & Noll, 1998), and are viewed as more sensitive and isolated than their healthy classmates (Noll, Ris, Davies, Bukowski, & Koontz, 1992; Vannatta et al., 1998).

In addition, HIV-infected children with encephalopathy have been found to display less adaptive and appropriate behavior than those without encephalopathy (Moss, Wolters, Brouwers, Hendricks, & Pizzo, 1996). The social stigma associated with HIV infection also may contribute to problems in children's social functioning.

In summary, available evidence suggests that youngsters with physical conditions that involve cognitive difficulties are at risk for problems in their peer relations and friendships. In their extensive review, the balance of studies cited by Nassau and Drotar (1997) support this observation.

Implications for School Settings

Although pediatric conditions do not necessarily have a negative impact on most youngsters' peer relations, many children and adolescents express concern about this possibility. As a result, it may be important for school personnel to help children and adolescents communicate with teachers and peers about their disease or condition. In some circumstances, self-disclosure can be helpful, but this should not be done indiscriminately. For youth with CNS-related difficulties, schools can be tremendously useful in helping children and adolescents to adapt to the social demands of school. Some suggestions for intervention are summarized herein.

Self-disclosure of difficult or traumatic experiences has been associated with improved physiological health (e.g., Greenberg & Stone, 1992; Pennebaker & Beall, 1986). For children and adolescents, sharing intimate concerns, fears, and worries with peers is an essential part of friendships (La Greca, 1990). Children and adolescents who do not have close friends for confidants may be missing a valuable mechanism for coping with their chronic illness. For example, Sherman, Bonanno, Wiener, and Battles (2000) found that children with HIV+ status who disclosed their diagnosis to friends had a significantly larger increase in CD4% (a sign of improved immune functioning) than children who had not disclosed their status to friends.

School personnel can help children and adolescents to find appropriate ways to disclose disease information, while at the same time recognizing the potential social barriers that can arise when integrating children and adolescents with pediatric conditions into school settings. Studies have found that "educating" classmates about a child's medical condition may be helpful under some, but not all, circumstances. For example, Guite, Walker, Smith, and Garber (2000) found that when classmates were told that a child has somatic symptoms (recurrent abdominal pain) and these symptoms were illustrated as medically based, this information had little or no impact on the likeability of the child. Thus, disclosure did not appear to put children with recurrent abdominal pain at a social disadvantage (La Greca & Bearman, 2000). Similar findings have been obtained for adolescents with cancer (Gray & Rodrigue, 2001).

In contrast, when a child has a visible or stigmatizing condition (e.g., obesity, burns, physical handicap), giving the child's classmates a medical explanation for the child's condition may *negatively* influence children's attitudes or receptivity, instead of easing the transition into the classroom (Bell & Morgan, 2000; Morgan, Bieberich, Walker, & Schwerdtfeger, 1998). Thus, La Greca and Bearman (2000) suggest alternative ideas for enhancing children's receptivity in the classroom. For example, providing information to classmates about the child's skills (e.g., sports, academics) may help to compensate for stigmatizing conditions. In addition, peer-pairing and close friendships might be used to enhance a child's school integration. Overall peer likeability may not matter if children with medical conditions have supportive, close friendships (La Greca & Bearman, 2000).

For youth with cognitive impairments, more specific guidance may be needed to ensure that children are well integrated into appropriate social networks at school, and that they are not left out. Such youth may benefit from social skills training programs that explicitly teach age-appropriate social skills and ways to develop and maintain friendships (see La Greca & Prinstein, 1999).

Friends as a Source of Support for Chronic or Life-Threatening Pediatric Conditions

For youth with chronic or life-threatening conditions, social support is believed to be important for their disease adjustment and treatment management (e.g., Burroughs, Harris, Pontious, & Santiago, 1997; La Greca et al., 1995; Varni et al., 1989). Children and adolescents with pediatric conditions face a challenging array of stressors, including distress about their medical condition, teasing from peers, restrictions on activities, difficult or painful medical interventions, and chronic or demanding treatment regimens (Vessey, Swanson, & Hagedorn, 1995). In this context, support from friends may help to buffer stress reactions among children and adolescents with pediatric conditions, and thus may facilitate their psychosocial adaptation.

Psychosocial Adaptation. Several studies have addressed the role of friends in facilitating the psychosocial adaptation of youth with chronic or life-threatening pediatric conditions. Specifically, Wallander and Varni (1989) examined the contributions of family and friend support for children diagnosed with a variety of chronic illnesses. Children who reported high levels of both family and friend support exhibited lower levels of internalizing and externalizing behavior problems than children with support from only one source. Furthermore, Varni and colleagues (1989) demonstrated that perceptions of friend support predicted psychological adaptation among adolescents with diabetes whereas family support predicted adaptation in childhood. Their findings suggested that friend support may become increasingly important during the adolescent years for youth with chronic illnesses.

In subsequent studies, Varni, Setoguchi, Rappaport, and Talbot (1992) found that, among children with congenital and acquired limb deficiencies, higher perceived classmate support was predictive of lower levels of depressive symptoms, lower trait anxiety, and higher self-esteem. Similarly, Varni, Katz, Colegrove, and Dolgin (1994) also found that, among children with cancer, higher perceived classmate support predicted fewer symptoms of depression and anxiety, and lower levels of internalizing and externalizing behavior problems. Overall, these studies suggest that classmates and friends are very important for the psychosocial adaptation of youth with chronic and life-threatening conditions.

Studies of distinct and complementary roles of family and friend support for diabetes management have revealed that family members provide different types of disease-specific support. For example, La Greca and colleagues (1995) examined both family and friend support for adolescents with Type 1 diabetes and found that friends provided more emotional and companionship support than family members. Moreover, Bearman and La Greca (2002) found that adolescents' friends provided more frequent emotional support than support for many other routine aspects of care. In addition, adolescents perceived their friends' behaviors in certain areas of diabetes to be very supportive, with one such area being emotional support. Such findings suggest that friends' support is typically focused on emotional needs (e.g., acceptance, understanding) and companionship for youth with chronic disease.

Gender differences in friends' support have also emerged, with girls reporting more disease-specific support from close friends than boys (e.g., Bearman & La Greca, 2002; La Greca et al., 1995). Thus far, however, very little attention has been directed to possible ethnic differences in friendship support. Some preliminary data suggest that Black males with diabetes receive less disease-specific support from their friends than do Black girls, or Hispanic boys and girls (Bearman, La Greca, Patino, & Delamater, 2001), although further study of this issue would be desirable.

Implications for School Settings. School provides the opportunity for ongoing socialization and social support, and helps to normalize a difficult and stressful experience (Varni, Katz, Colegrove, & Dolgin, 1993; Varni et al., 1994). To facilitate the long-term adjustment to a chronic illness, children are encouraged to return to school and engage in social experiences as soon as medically possible (e.g., Katz, Varni, Rubenstein, Blew, & Hubert, 1992). However, some classmates may be nonsupportive, or may engage in potentially hurtful behaviors, such as teasing and name-calling (Varni et al., 1994). In a descriptive analysis of youth in school settings, Lightfoot, Wright, and Sloper (1999) illustrated that friends of youngsters with an illness or disability may help them deal with bullying and curiosity, crisis tasks, ongoing physical care, keeping up with school work, and keeping in touch with classmates during school absences. These findings suggest that promoting children's support from friends in the school setting is critical, and one strategy for accomplishing this is through formal "school re-entry" programs.

Successful school re-entry focuses on addressing the unique needs of the individual child or adolescent, with an emphasis on academic and social skills (Madan-Swain, Fredrick, & Wallander, 1999) and on promoting social support from parents, teachers, and classmates. Several strategies have been suggested for strengthening social support from classmates in schools. For example, social skills training may enhance the self-efficacy and social competence of children with pediatric conditions, ultimately fostering positive social interactions (Varni et al., 1994), and leading to greater perceived support from classmates and close friends.

As a specific example of this approach, Varni and colleagues (1993) developed a social skills intervention for children newly diagnosed with cancer. The intervention was organized into three individual 60-min sessions and two booster sessions, and included social-cognitive problem-solving training, assertiveness instruction, and coping with teasing and name-calling resulting from changes in physical appearance. A detailed treatment manual was developed that included videotape modeling, relaxation, and homework assignments; the assignments included activities for children and parents to promote generalization of the skills to the home and school settings. Compared with children receiving "standard care," children in the social skills group reported greater classmate and teacher support at follow-up. Additionally, parents of the children in the social skills group reported a decrease in their children's internalizing and externalizing behavior problems and an increase in school competence.

The success of this program for improving social support and psychological adjustment for children and adolescents with pediatric conditions illustrates the importance and feasibility of strengthening friend support. Such interventions could be conducted in the school setting, directly involving teachers and classmates. With the collaborative efforts of health professionals, teachers, parents, and friends, children and adolescents with chronic illnesses may be able to continue "normal" social and academic activities without significant disruption (Varni et al., 1993).

Peers' Influence on Treatment Adherence

Nonadherence to medical regimens is believed to contribute to increased morbidity, mortality, and health care utilization and costs (Rapoff, 1998). Disease management may be burdensome, especially for youth with complex disease maintenance regimens (e.g., diabetes, cystic fibrosis) and for older children who are increasingly responsible for their own disease management (La Greca, Follansbee, & Skyler, 1990). In particular, Rapoff (1998) has described adolescents as having poor adherence to medical regimens, such as cancer, cystic fibrosis, diabetes, and renal disease. If youth with chronic illnesses perceive that self-care behaviors (e.g., dietary and exercise restrictions) are supported and encouraged by their friends, they may be more likely to perform these behaviors when in the company of peers. In this manner, adolescents' friends may play important roles in their disease management.

Although friends may have a positive affect on youngsters' treatment adherence, children and adolescents also may disregard their self-care so as not to call attention to themselves or appear "different" from peers (Schuman & LaGreca, 1999). For example, Christian and D'Auria (1997) found that adolescents with cystic fibrosis reported not adhering to their treatment regimens for fear of being seen as different or of losing a romantic partner. La Greca and Hanna (1983) also found that, for youth with diabetes, social barriers played a role in poor regimen adherence and problems with metabolic control. Specifically, children and adolescents reported that social interference represented a barrier to dietary adherence and blood glucose testing, mainly because youth with diabetes did not want to appear different or less socially competent than their friends (La Greca & Hanna, 1983). In an attempt to facilitate adherence, schools may be able to improve integration of children and adolescents with pediatric conditions in a way that would prevent them from feeling different or left out by peers.

For adolescents with diabetes, friends have been identified as providing more frequent support for certain aspects of the diabetes regimen (e.g., exercise and helping out with reactions) than others (e.g., insulin injections and meals; Bearman & La Greca, 2002; La Greca et al., 1995). Furthermore, adolescents perceive friends' behaviors in certain areas (e.g., meals) to be more supportive than behaviors in other areas of management (e.g., insulin injections, blood testing; Bearman & La Greca, 2002). Such findings suggest the importance of identifying specific areas of disease management in which friends can be most supportive. This information would help to provide a focus for intervention programs designed to enhance friends' support of treatment management.

School Interventions

Because peers play an important role in adherence, recognizing potential social barriers and enhancing friend support for children and adolescents with pediatric conditions are useful strategies for promoting positive health practices. Friendship support for treatment management may be enhanced in the school setting through peer group interventions. For example, Greco, Pendley, McDonell, and Reeves (2001) developed a group program for adolescents with diabetes and their best friends. This four-session intervention was structured to encourage friends to become involved with adolescents' diabetes management. Each session included a review of homework, instruction on a particular topic, a game or exercise to practice the new concepts, and a homework assignment for the following week. The sessions covered topics such as descriptive information about diabetes, reflective listening skills and problem-solving, the ways friends could be supportive and provide assistance with diabetes care, and stress management skills. After completing the intervention, adolescents and their friends reported higher levels of diabetes knowledge and support, and a higher ratio of friend to family support; and parents rated their adolescents as having less diabetes-related conflict (Greco et al., 2001).

Other strategies for enhancing friendship support among youngsters with pediatric conditions might include encouraging their close friends to maintain contact with them during hospitalizations (Sexson & Madan-Swain, 1995). Teachers, parents, and health professionals may need to make sure that children's and adolescents' close friendship ties are not disrupted during periods of extended treatment or hospitalization.

The Role of Peers in the Promotion of Health Behaviors

Peers not only affect children with *current* medical conditions, but also can have an impact on youngsters' *future* medical conditions by influencing health-related behaviors such as smoking, alcohol and drug use, diet, exercise, sexual behavior, and risky behaviors leading to injury. Together, these six behaviors are greatly responsible for the most serious mortality and morbidity-related health problems in the United States: heart disease, cancer, stroke, motor vehicle accidents, accidental deaths, HIV, other STDs, and teen pregnancy. According to the Centers for Disease Control and Prevention (CDC, 2000a, p. 1), "these behaviors usually are established in youth; persist into adulthood; are interrelated; and are preventable."

Children and adolescents' health behaviors are influenced both by the health behaviors of their closest friends and by perceptions of the behaviors and attitudes of the larger peer group. Close friends tend be similar in their health behaviors and these similarities increase with age. Tolson and Urberg (1993) found that adolescent best friends were more similar in their health behaviors than in their attitudes, family relationships, or school activities. Children and adolescents are also influenced by perceived pressures from the larger peer group. Newman (1984) describes peer pressure as pressure to project a desirable image, rather than pressure for specific behaviors. These image-based pressures include pressure to appear independent, pressure for recognition, pressure to appear grown up, and pressure to have fun. Many health-related behaviors, such as smoking, drug and alcohol use, and sexual and risk-taking behaviors, may be perceived as easy ways to project these desired images.

Membership in a peer crowd is one way for adolescents to establish and maintain a strong identity during a time when they are questioning and exploring who they are. Members of adolescent peer crowds tend to be very similar in behaviors. As discussed previously, this similarity increases through a bidirectional influence: adolescents associate with similar peers through the process of selection and grow more similar to these peers through processes of socialization. Peer influence does not always negatively affect health behaviors; Clasen and Brown (1985) found that peer pressure may also discourage unhealthy behaviors and encourage healthy ones.

Understanding how peers influence the development of health behaviors is extremely important, but has been understudied. Most of the research in this area has examined the impact of peers on the initiation, continuation, and cessation of smoking behaviors.

Smoking. Researchers have examined adolescent smoking for several reasons: (1) tobacco use is the chief preventable cause of premature aging and death in the United States; (2) nearly all first-time tobacco use and two thirds of new habitual tobacco use takes place in adolescence; (3) once smoking becomes habitual, it is extremely difficult to quit; and (4) cigarette smoking is often a gateway drug that leads to alcohol and drug use (Elders, 1994; Jessor & Jessor, 1977; National Center for Chronic Disease Prevention and Health Promotion, 2000).

The consensus of this research is that peer smoking is the single best predictor of adolescent smoking (Flay, d'Avernas, Best, Kersell, & Ryan, 1983; Petraitis, Flay, & Miller, 1995).

However, the tendency for adolescents to form friendships based on shared characteristics has made it difficult to isolate the effect of peer influence on smoking behaviors. For example, it is well known that adolescents who affiliate with the Burnout crowd are more likely to smoke, but it is not clear whether selection or socialization processes are primarily responsible for these similarities (La Greca, et al., 2001; Moshbach & Leventhal, 1988; Sussman, et al., 1994). To control for the effects of selection, many researchers have used longitudinal designs to examine changes on smoking behavior over time.

Using these methodologies, researchers have found strong evidence of both selection and socialization processes. Ary and Biglan (1988) found that peers were instrumental in the maintenance of smoking behaviors and increases from triers to habitual smokers. In one longitudinal study, the smoking behaviors of best friends was the only consistent and significant factor in predicting adolescent smoking progression to a more advanced level of acquisition (Wang, Fitzhugh, Eddy, Fu, & Turner, 1997). Nonsmoking adolescents with at least one smoking friend are more likely to become smokers than nonsmokers who associate only with other nonsmokers (Ennett & Bauman, 1994). Researchers have found developmental differences in susceptibility to peer influence; early adolescence appears to be a particularly vulnerable time, particularly for boys (Urberg, Cheng, & Shyu, 1991).

Based on these findings, it seems imperative that schools incorporate antismoking messages into their curriculum very early and teach students alternative ways of fitting into a group. For example, involvement in sports or academics are good ways to gain membership in groups that discourage cigarette smoking. Because peers are also instrumental in the maintenance of smoking behaviors, it is important to teach refusal skills to teens who smoke, because they are much more likely than other adolescents to be offered cigarettes (Ary & Biglan, 1988). Adolescents who want to quit smoking may need to develop new interests to make new, nonsmoking friends.

Research on school-based interventions has found that a social influence resistance model is the most effective approach to reducing youth smoking. Such models focus on building skills to recognize and resist negative influences, communication skills, decision-making skills, and assertiveness training (Institute of Medicine, 1994).

Alcohol and Drug Use. Though alcohol consumption in the United States has declined in recent years, adolescents are drinking more at younger ages than ever before (Williams & Perry, 1998). A *1997 Monitoring the Future* study found that 54% of eighth graders, 72% of tenth graders, and 82% of twelfth graders reported having consumed "more than a few sips" of alcohol (Johnston, O'Malley, & Bachman, 1998). Adolescent alcohol use is associated with increases in a variety of risky behaviors, including sexual risk behavior and drunk driving (O'Malley et al., 1998). In addition, early adolescent alcohol use puts adolescents at risk for later alcohol abuse, even when genetic factors are controlled for, and significantly increases the chances that adolescents will try illegal drugs (Grant & Dawson, 1997; Kandel, 1980; O'Malley et al., 1998). These sobering statistics have turned attention in recent years to the socialization factors associated with alcohol and drug use.

Several recent longitudinal studies have found clear evidence of a strong peer influence on alcohol and drug use. Wills and Cleary (1999) found more support for socialization than selection factors in the rate of change of substance use in middle schoolers. Two other large, longitudinal studies of adolescent alcohol use found similar results (Curran, Stice, & Chassin, 1997; Sieving, Perry, & Williams, 2000). Thus, unlike cigarette use that has both strong peer selection and peer socialization processes, alcohol use escalates primarily through peer socialization processes. Further research is needed to clarify the roles of gender, ethnicity, and individual differences in these processes (Farrell & Danish, 1993; Santor, Messervey, & Kusumakar, 2000).

The strong evidence for socialization effects on adolescent alcohol use has led to the development of school and community-based interventions that heavily target peer influence. One such intervention, Project Norland, has had some success in delaying the onset of alcohol use in middle school (Williams & Perry, 1998). School-based intervention techniques in Project Norland include interactive techniques, with peer leaders or role plays; normative education programs designed to change students' misconceptions about the prevalence of underage drinking; resistance skills training, leadership skills training, and media-savvy training. Preliminary results show significant reductions in the onset and prevalence of alcohol use among young adolescents (Williams & Perry, 1998).

Sexual Risk Behaviors. High-risk sexual behavior includes lack of condom use, frequent sexual intercourse, and having sex with multiple partners, partners from high-risk groups (e.g., intravenous drug users, homosexual men, prostitutes), or partners of unknown status (Goedert, 1987). High-risk sexual behaviors are strongly related to other health-risk behaviors, such as cigarette, alcohol, and drug use, and are associated with friends' engagement in problem behaviors (Biglan et al., 1990; Metzler, Noell, Biglan, Ary, & Smolkowski, 1994). Romer et al. (1994) found that perceived peer sexual behavior was associated with the rate at which sexual behavior progressed with age and with the degree to which condom use was maintained with age. However, there is a need for longitudinal studies of selection and socialization factors in similarities between peers' sexual behaviors.

There is some evidence of gender and ethnic differences in the influence of peers on sexual behavior. Leland and Barth (1992) found that females perceived larger proportions of their peers as sexually active, were more likely to have used oral contraceptives instead of condoms, were less likely to have used protection during first intercourse, and were less likely to always use protection. Billy and Undry (1985a, 1985b) found that the sexual behavior of male and female best friends influenced the sexual behavior of White girls, but there were no influence effects for White boys or for Black girls and boys. Similarly, Nathanson and Becker (1986) found that White girls, but not Black girls, were influenced by the perceived contraceptive use of same-sex friends. In a sample of Black adolescents, St. Lawrence, Brasfield, Jefferson, Alyene, and Shirley (1994) found that those with less perceived social support reported higher sexual risk behaviors. These results suggest that effective intervention strategies may differ by gender and ethnicity. For example, interventions targeted to females should emphasize realistic appraisals of peer sexual activity and the importance of condom use for effective prevention of STDs.

Diet and Exercise. The percentage of children and adolescents who are defined as overweight has more than doubled since the early 1970's (National Center for Chronic Disease Prevention and Health Promotion, 2001a). Childhood obesity is a public health concern both because of its immediate impact on physical health and because it places the child at risk for myriad health problems associated with adult obesity (Kanders, 1995). Physical inactivity and poor diet together account for at least 300,000 deaths in the United States each year (McGinnis & Foege, 1993).

Peer influence on childhood and adolescent obesity can be harmful or beneficial. Children with obesity are often victims of peer teasing and rejection, which can lead to the development of psychological and social difficulties on top of their medical difficulties (Baum & Forehand, 1984; Strauss, Smith, Frame, & Forehand, 1985). Positive peer relationships may promote physical activity by boosting the mood and physical self-esteem of adolescents (Smith, 1999). One effective school-based obesity prevention program used older children as peer counselors (Foster, Wadden, & Brownell, 1985). Other programs encourage students to participate in physical activities together, such as walking to school (National Center for Chronic Disease Prevention and Health Promotion, 2001b).

Although the percentage of children and adolescents who are overweight has dramatically increased in recent years, there has also been an increase in the numbers of children and adolescents whose efforts to reduce their weight lead to serious health problems, such as potentially fatal eating disorders (Fairburn, Hay, & Welch, 1993). Peers serve as a subculture that may enhance or diminish cultural pressures for thinness and engaging in weight loss strategies through modeling, verbal reinforcement, and teasing (Paxton, 1996). Although most of the literature examines these processes among adolescent girls, peer feedback also influences the body images and body-changing methods of adolescent boys (Ricciardelli, McCabe, & Banfield, 2000). Adolescent girls who perceive that their peers go on diets are more likely to go on diets themselves (Huon, Lim, & Gunewardene, 2000; Huon & Walton, 1999). The body image concerns, dietary restraints, and extreme weight-loss behaviors of adolescent girls are most similar within friendship cliques, suggesting that this is the most effective level for intervention (Paxton, Schutz, Wertheim, & Muir, 1999).

Summary of Suggestions for School Interventions. The Centers for Disease Control and Prevention recommend that schools incorporate health behavior information and skills into a sequential, comprehensive health education curriculum that begins in preschool and continues through secondary school (CDC, 2000b). Research suggests that such programs can be highly effective in reducing health risk behavior. For example, one such program reduced by 37% the onset of smoking in seventh graders (National Center for Chronic Disease Prevention and Health Promotion, 2001b).

Understanding the precise mechanisms and levels of peer influence on health behaviors can lead to the development and implementation of targeted, more effective interventions. For example, the impact of peers on alcohol and drug use is mainly through socialization, so effective interventions might focus on teaching children and adolescents refusal and moderation skills. In contrast, the influence of peers on cigarette smoking has both selection and socialization components. Interventions should discourage children and adolescents who do not smoke from associating with smokers, whereas those who do smoke should be taught strong refusal skills. Interventions must also consider the level of peer influence for a particular health behavior. For example, diet and exercise behaviors are most similar within peer cliques, so effective interventions should target adolescents within the same clique. In contrast, smoking influence occurs at the peer crowd level and effective interventions must either target entire peer crowds or, perhaps more realistically, attempt to draw individuals away from these crowds.

CONCLUSIONS

In summary, in this chapter, we have reviewed key developmental aspects of children's and adolescents' peer relations and friendships, with special attention to youth with chronic pediatric conditions. In general, the resilience of youth affected by medical conditions is remarkable, and the findings suggest that most youth with pediatric conditions have peer relations and friendships that are comparable with those of their peers. Nevertheless, youth with visible and physically handicapping conditions and those with associated cognitive impairments may have an especially difficult time in social contexts. Special efforts to help such youth in the school setting are needed.

One important aspect of friendships is the emotional support they provide. Social support from friends appears to be critical for youth with chronic pediatric conditions. Involving youngsters' close friends in their disease management and making sure that friendships are not disrupted when children miss school or have an extended leave of absence from illness are ways that health care professionals and school personnel can facilitate the social adjustment and disease adaptation of youth with pediatric conditions.

Another key theme of the chapter, most relevant to adolescents, is the importance of peer relations and peer crowd affiliations for health behaviors. Peer crowds provide a context for encouraging health-risk or health-promoting behaviors. Given that proper diet, exercise, and restraint from using various substances (e.g., tobacco, alcohol, drugs) are especially important for adolescents with pediatric conditions, understanding these adolescents' social contexts becomes a critical task for health care professionals and school personnel.

In view of the aforementioned themes and the findings reviewed in this chapter, future research efforts are needed that examine in a detailed manner the social challenges associated with children's and adolescents' pediatric conditions in the school setting. Much of the existing research has been done with children and adolescents who are seen in tertiary health care settings; it would be of interest to extend this work to the primary contexts in which children and youth spend their time on a daily basis.

Further attention might also be directed toward developing pediatric interventions that are feasible to implement in school settings. Intervention programs that focus on issues such as school reentry, enhancing peer support and close friendships, and teaching peers how to accept those who are different, are especially appropriate for the interface between "pediatric psychology" and "schools." It is hoped that the ideas and information provided in this chapter will provide an impetus to psychologists working in school settings with youth who have health-related problems.

REFERENCES

Ammerman, R. T., Van Hasselt, V. B., Hersen, M., & Moore, L. E. (1989). Assessment of social skills in visually impaired adolescents and their parents. *Behavioral Assessment, 11*, 327–351.

Apter, A., Aviv, A., Kaminer, Y., Weizman, A., Lerman, P., & Tyano, S. (1991). Behavioral profile and social competence in temporal lobe epilepsy of adolescence. *Journal of the American Academy of Child and Adolescent Psychiatry, 30*, 887–892.

Armstrong, F. D., Seidel, J. F., & Swales, T. P. (1993). Pediatric HIV infection: A neuropsychological and educational challenge. *Journal of Learning Disabilities, 26*, 92–103.

Ary, D. V., & Biglan, A. (1988). Longitudinal changes in adolescent cigarette smoking behavior: Onset and cessation. *Journal of Behavioral Medicine, 11*, 361–382.

Asher, S. R., & Coie, J. D. (1990) (Eds.), *Peer rejection in childhood*. New York: Cambridge University Press.

Asher, S. R., & Wheeler, V. A. (1985). Children's loneliness: A comparison of rejected and neglected peer status. *Journal of Consulting and Clinical Psychology, 53*, 500–505.

Baum, C. G., & Forehand, R. (1984). Social factors associated with adolescent obesity. *Journal of Pediatric Psychology, 9*, 293–302.

Bearman, K. J., & La Greca, A. M. (2002). Assessing friend support of adolescents' diabetes care: The Diabetes Social Support Questionnaire—Friends Version. *Journal of Pediatric Psychology, 27*, 417–428.

Bearman, K. J., La Greca, A. M., Glickman, A. R., & Kuttler, A. F. (2001, March). *Adolescents with asthma: Are they at risk for social problems*? Poster presented at the Eighth Florida Conference on Child Health Psychology, Gainesville, FL.

Bearman, K. J., La Greca, A. M., Patino, A. M., & Delamater, A. (2001). *The role of peer support in multicultural adolescents' diabetes care*. Presented at the 109th Annual American Psychological Association Convention, San Francisco, CA.

Bell, S. K., & Morgan, S. B. (2000). Children's attitudes and behavioral intentions toward a peer presented as obese: Does a medical explanation for the obesity make a difference? *Journal of Pediatric Psychology, 25*, 137–146.

Berndt, T. J. (1982). The features and effects of friendship in early adolescence. *Child Development, 53*, 1447–1460.

Berndt, T. J. (1989). Obtaining support from friends during childhood and adolescence. In D. Belle (Ed.), *Children's social networks and social supports* (pp. 308–331). New York: John Wiley.

Berndt, T. J., & Keefe, K (1992). Friends' influence on adolescents' perceptions of themselves in school. In D. H., Schunk, & J. L. Meece (Eds.), *Students perceptions in the classroom* (pp. 51–73). Hillsdale, NJ: Erlbaum.

Biglan, A., Metzler, C. W., Wirt, R., Ary, D., Noell, J., Ochs, L., French, C., & Hood, D. (1990). Social and behavioral factors associated with high-risk sexual behavior among adolescents. *Journal of Behavioral Medicine, 13*, 245–261.

Billy, J. O. G., & Udry, J. R. (1985a). The influence of male and female best friends on adolescent sexual behavior. *Adolescence, 20*, 21–32.

Billy, J. O. G., & Udry, J. R. (1985b). Patterns of adolescent friendship and effects on sexual behavior. *Social Psychology Quarterly, 48*, 27–41.

Bowker, A., Sippola, L. K., & Bukowski, W. (1996, March). *Coping with daily hassles in the peer group during early adolescence*. Paper presented at the biennial meeting of the Society for Research in Adolescence, Boston, MA.

Brouwers, P., Belman, A. L., & Epstein, L. G. (1991). Central nervous system involvement: Manifestations and evaluation. In P. A. Pizzo & C. M. Wilfert (Eds.), *Pediatric AIDS: The challenge of HIV infection in infants, children, and adolescents* (pp. 318–335). Baltimore, MD: Williams & Wilkins.

Brown, B. B. (1989). The role of peer groups in adolescents' adjustment to secondary school. In T. J. Berndt and G. W. Ladd (Eds.), *Peer relationships in child development* (pp. 188–215). New York: John Wiley and Sons.

Brown, B. B., & Clausen, D. R. (1986, March). *Developmental changes in adolescents' conceptions of peer groups*. Paper presented at the biennial meeting of the Society for Research in Adolescence, Madison, WI.

Brown, B., Clausen, D., & Eicher, S. (1986). Perceptions of peer pressure, peer conformity dispositions, and self-reported behavior among adolescents. *Developmental Psychology, 22*, 521–530.

Buhrmester, D. (1990). Intimacy of friendship, interpersonal competence, and adjustment during preadolescence and adolescence. *Child Development, 61*, 1101–1111.

Bukowski, W. M., Gauze, C., Hoza, B., & Newcomb, A. F. (1993). Differences and consistency between same-sex and other-sex peer relationships during early adolescence. *Developmental Psychology, 29*, 255–263.

Burroughs, T. E., Harris, M. A., Pontious, S. L., & Santiago, J. V. (1997). Research on social support in adolescents with IDDM: A critical review. *Diabetes Educator, 23*, 438–448.

Cauce, A. M. (1986). Social networks and social competence: Exploring the effects of early adolescent friendships. *American Journal of Community Psychology, 14*, 607–628.

Cauce, A. M., Reid, M., Landesman, S., & Gonzales, N. (1990). Social support in young children: Measurement, structure, and behavioral impact. In B. R. Sarason, I. G. Sarason, & G. R. Pierce (Eds.), *Social support: An interactional view* (pp. 64–94). New York: John C. Wiley and Sons.

Center, Y., Ward, J. (1984). Integration of mildly handicapped cerebral palsied children into regular schools. *Exceptional Child, 31*, 104–113.

Centers for Disease Control [CDC] National Center for Chronic Disease Prevention and Health Promotion. (2000a). *Risk behaviors overview* [On-line]. Available: www.cdc.gov/nccdphp/dash/risk/htm

Centers for Disease Control [CDC] National Center for Chronic Disease Prevention and Health Promotion. (2000b). *Guidelines for school health programs to promote lifelong healthy eating* [On-line]. Available: www.cdc.gov/nccdphp/dash/nutguide.htm

Christian, B. J., & D'Auria, J. P. (1997). The child's eye: Memories of growing up with cystic fibrosis. *Journal of Pediatric Nursing, 12*, 3–12.

Clasen, D. R., & Brown, B. B. (1985). The multidimensionality of peer pressure. *Journal of Youth and Adolescence, 14*, 451–468.

Coie, J. D., & Dodge, K. A. (1988). Multiple sources of data on social behavior and social status in the school: A cross-age comparison. *Child Development, 59*, 815–829.

Coie, J. D., Dodge K. A., & Coppotelli, H. (1982). Dimensions and types of social status: A cross-age perspective. *Developmental Psychology, 18*, 557–570.

Coie, J. D., Dodge K. A., & Kupersmidt, J. B. (1990). Peer group behavior and social status. In S. R. Asher & J. D. Coie (Eds.), *Peer rejection in childhood* (pp. 17–59). Cambridge: Cambridge University Press.

Compas, B. E., Slavin, L. A., Wagner, B. A., & Cannatta, K. (1986). Relationship of life events and social support with psychological dysfunction among adolescents. *Journal of Youth and Adolescence, 15*, 205–221.

Cowen, E. L., Pederson, A., Babijian, H., Izzo, L. D., & Trost, M. A. (1973). Long-term follow-up of early detected vulnerable children. *Journal of Consulting and Clinical Psychology, 41*, 438–446.

Curran, P. J., Stice, E., & Chassin, L. (1997). The relation between adolescent alcohol use and peer alcohol use: A longitudinal random coefficients model. *Journal of Consulting and Clinical Psychology, 65*, 130–140.

Degirmencioglu, S. M., & Urberg, K. A. (1996, March). *Cross-gender friendships in adolescence: Who chooses the "other"?* Paper presented at the biennial meeting of the Society for Research in Adolescence, Boston, MA.

DeMaso, D. R., Beardslee, W. R., Silbert, A. R., & Fyler, D. C. (1990). Psychological functioning in children with cyanotic heart defects. *Journal of Developmental and Behavioral Pediatrics, 11*, 289–294.

Dodge, K. A., Coie, J., & Brakke, N. (1982). Behavioral patterns of socially rejected and neglected pre-adolescents: The roles of social approach and aggression. *Journal of Abnormal Child Psychology, 10*, 389–409.

Dodge, K. A., & Price, J. M. (1994). On the relation between social information processing and socially competent behavior in early school-aged children. *Child Development, 65*, 1385–1397.

Elder, D., & Hallinan, M. (1978). Sex differences in children's friendships. *American Sociological Review, 43*, 237–250.

Elders, M. J. (1994). *Preventing tobacco use among young people: A report of the Surgeon General* (RR-4). Atlanta, GA: Centers for Disease Control and Prevention.

Ellis, S., Rogoff, B., & Cromer, C. C. (1981). Age segregation in children's social interactions. *Developmental Psychology, 17*, 399–407.

Ennett, S. T., & Bauman, K. E. (1994). The contrition of influence and selection to adolescent peer group homogeneity: The case of adolescent cigarette smoking. *Journal of Personality and Social Psychology, 67*, 653–663.

Fabian, R. H., & Peters, B. H. (1984). Neurological complications of hemoglobin SC disease. *Archives of Neurology, 41*, 289–292.

Fairburn, C. G., Hay, P. J., & Welch, S. L. (1993). Binge eating and bulimia nervosa: Distribution and determinants. In C. G. Fairburn & G. T. Wilson (Eds.), *Binge eating: Nature assessment, and treatment* (pp. 317–360). New York: Guilford Press.

Farrell, A. D., & Danish, S. T. (1993). Peer drug associations: causes or consequences of adolescents' drug use? *Journal of Consulting and Clinical Psychology, 61*, 327–334.

Flay, B., d'Avernas, J., Best, J. A., Kersell, M., & Ryan, M. (1983). Cigarette smoking: Why young people do it and ways of preventing it. In P. McGreath & P. Firestone (Eds.), *Pediatric and adolescent behavior medicine.* New York: Springer-Verlag.

Furman, W. (1989). The development of children's social networks. In D. Belle (Ed.), *Children's social networks and social supports* (pp. 151–172). New York: Academic Press.

Furman, W., & Buhrmester, D. (1985). Children's perceptions of the personal relationships in their social networks. *Developmental Psychology, 21*, 1016–1024.

Furman, W., & Robbins, P. (1985). What's the point: Issues in the selection of treatment objectives. In B. H. Schneider, K. H. Rubin, & J. E. Ledingham (Eds.), *Children's peer relations: Issues in assessment and intervention* (pp. 41–56). New York: Springer-Verlag.

Gammal, T. E., Adams, R. J., Nichols, F. T., McKie, V., Milner, P., McKie, K., & Brooks, B. S. (1988). Investigation of cerebrovascular disease in sickle cell patients with MRI and CT. *American Journal of Neuroradiology, 7*, 1043–1049.

Goedert, J. J. (1987). What is safe sex? Suggested standards linked to testing for human immunodeficiency virus. *New England Journal of Medicine, 316*, 1339–1342.

Graetz, B., & Shute, R. (1995). Assessment of peer relationships in children with asthma. *Journal of Pediatric Psychology, 20*, 205–216.

Grant, B. F. & Dawson, D. A. (1997). Age at onset of alcohol use and its association with DSM-IV alcohol abuse and dependence: Results from the National Longitudinal Alcohol Epidemiological Survey. *Journal of Substance Abuse, 9*, 103–110.

Gray, C. C., & Rodrigue, J. R. (2001). Brief report: Perceptions of young adolescents about a hypothetical new peer with cancer: An analog study. *Journal of Pediatric Psychology, 26*, 247–252.

Greco, P., Pendley, J. S., McDonell, K., & Reeves, G. (2001). A peer group intervention for adolescents with type 1 diabetes and their best friends. *Journal of Pediatric Psychology, 26*, 485–490.

Green, K. D., Forehand, R., Beck, S. J., & Vosk, B. (1980). An assessment of the relationship among measures of children's social competence and children's academic achievement. *Child Development, 51*, 1149–1156.

Greenberg, M. A., & Stone, A. A. (1992). Emotional disclosure about traumas and its relation to health: Effects of previous disclosure and traumatic severity. *Journal of Personality and Social Psychology, 63*, 75–84.

Guite, J. W., Walker, L. S., Smith, C. A., & Garber, J. (2000). Children's perceptions of peers with somatic symptoms: The impact of gender, stress, and illness. *Journal of Pediatric Psychology, 25*, 125–136.

Hartup, W. W. (1983). Peer relations. In P. H. Mussen (Series Ed.) & E. M. Hetherington (Volume Ed.), *Handbook of child psychology: Vol. 4. Socialization, personality, and social development* (4th ed., pp. 103–196). New York: Wiley.

Hartup, W. W. (1996). The company they keep: Friendships and their developmental significance. *Child Development, 67*, 1–13.

Huon, G. F., Lim, J., & Gunewardene, A. (2000). Social influences and female adolescent dieting. *Journal of Adolescence, 23*, 229–232.

Huon, G. F., & Walton, C. J. (2000). Initiation of dieting among adolescent females. *International Journal of Eating Disorders, 28,* 226–230.

Huttenlocher, P. R., Moohr, J. W., Johns, L., & Brown, F. D. (1984). Cerebral blood flow in sickle cell cerebrovascular disease. *Pediatrics, 73*, 615–621.

Institute of Medicine. (1994). *Growing up tobacco free: Preventing nicotine addiction in children and youth.* Washington, DC: National Academy Press.

Jessor, R., & Jessor, S. (1977). *Problem behavior and psycho-social development: A longitudinal study of youth.* New York: Academic Press.

Johnston, L. D., O'Malley, P. M., & Bachman, J. G. (1998). *National survey results on drug use from the Monitoring the Future Study, 1975–1997: Volume I, Secondary School Students.* DHHS Publication No. (NIH) 98-4345. Rockville, MD: National Institute on Drug Abuse.

Kandel, D. (1978). Homophily, selection, and socialization in adolescent friendships. *American Journal of Sociology, 84*, 427–436.

Kandel, D. B. (1980). Drug and drinking behavior among youth. *Annual Review of Sociology, 6*, 235–285.

Kanders, B. S. (1995). Pediatric obesity. In P. R. Thomas (Ed.), *Weighing the options: Criteria for evaluating weight-management programs* (pp. 210–233). Washington, DC.: National Academic Press.

Katz, E. R., Varni, J. W., Rubenstein, C. L., Blew, A., & Hubert, N. (1992). Teacher, parent, and child evaluate ratings of a school reintegration integration for children with newly diagnosed cancer. *Children's Health Care, 21*, 61–75.

Kupersmidt, J. B., & Coie, J. D. (1990). Preadolescent peer status, aggression, and school adjustment as predictors of externalizing problems in adolescence. *Child Development, 61*, 1350–1362.

Kuttler, A. F., La Greca, A. M., & Prinstein, M. J. (1999). Friendship qualities and social-emotional functioning of adolescents with close, cross-sex friendships. *Journal of Research on Adolescence, 9*, 339–366.

La Greca, A. M. (1990). Social consequences of pediatric conditions: Fertile area for future investigation and intervention? *Journal of Pediatric Psychology, 15*, 285–307.

La Greca, A. M. (1992). Peer influences in pediatric chronic illness: An update. *Journal of Pediatric Psychology, 17*, 775–784.

La Greca, A. M. (1993). Children's social skills training: Where do we go from here? *Journal of Clinical Child Psychology, 22*, 288–298.

La Greca, A. M., Auslander, W. F., Greco, P., Spetter, D., Fisher, E. B., & Santiago, J. V. (1995). I get by with a little help from my family and friends: Adolescents' support for diabetes care. *Journal of Pediatric Psychology, 20*, 449–476.

La Greca, A. M., & Bearman, K. J. (2000). Commentary: Children with pediatric conditions: Can peers' impressions be managed? And what about their friends? *Journal of Pediatric Psychology, 25*, 147–149.

La Greca, A. M., Follansbee, D., & Skyler, J. S. (1990). Developmental and behavioral aspects of diabetes management in youngsters. *Children's Health Care, 19*, 132–139.

La Greca, A. M., & Hanna, N. (1983). Diabetes related health beliefs in children and their mothers: Implications for treatment. *Diabetes, 32(Suppl. 1)*, 66.

La Greca, A. M., & Prinstein, M. J. (1999). Peer group. In W. K. Silverman & T. H. Ollendick (Eds.), *Developmental issues in the clinical treatment of children* (pp. 171–198). Needham Heights, MA: Allyn & Bacon.

La Greca, A. M., Prinstein, M. J., & Fetter, M. D. (2001). Adolescent peer crowd affiliation: Linkages with health-risk behaviors and close friendships. *Journal of Pediatric Psychology, 26*, 131–143.

La Greca, A. M., & Stone, W. L. (1993). The Social Anxiety Scale for Children-Revised: Factor structure and concurrent validity. *Journal of Clinical Child Psychology, 22*, 17–27.

Leland, N. L., & Barth, R. P. (1992). Gender differences in knowledge, intentions, and behaviors concerning pregnancy and sexually transmitted disease prevention among adolescents. *Journal of Adolescent Health, 13*, 589–599.

Lever, J. (1976). Sec differences in the games children play. *Social Problems, 23*, 478–487.

Lightfoot, J., Wright, S., & Sloper, P. (1999). Supporting pupils in mainstream school with an illness or disability: Young people's views. *Child: Care, Health, and Development, 25*, 267–283.

Madan-Swain, A., Fredrick, L., & Wallander, J. L. (1999). Returning to school after a serious illness or injury. In R. T. Brown (Ed.), *Cognitive aspects of chronic illness in children.* (pp. 312–332). New York: Guilford Press.

McGinnis, J. M., & Foege, W. H. (1993). Actual causes of death in the United States. *Journal of the American Medical Association, 270*, 2207–2212.

Metzler, C. W., Noell, J., Biglan, A., Ary, D., & Smolkowski, K. (1994). The social context for risky sexual behavior among adolescents. *Journal of Behavioral Medicine, 17*, 419–438.

Morgan, S. B., Bieberich, A. A., Walker, M., & Schwerdtfeger, H. (1998). Children's willingness to share activities with a physically handicapped peer: Am I more willing than my classmates? *Journal of Pediatric Psychology, 23*, 367–375.

Mosbach, P., & Leventhal, H. (1988). Peer group identity and smoking: Implications for intervention. *Journal of Abnormal Psychology, 97*, 238–245.

Moss, H. A., Wolters, P. L., Brouwers, P., Hendricks, M. L., & Pizzo, P. A. (1996). Impaired of expressive behavior in pediatric HIV-infected patients with evidence of CNS disease. *Journal of Pediatric Psychology, 21*, 379–400.

Nassau, J. H., & Drotar, D. (1997). Social competence among children with central nervous system-related chronic health conditions: A review. *Journal of Pediatric Psychology, 22*, 771–793.

Nathanson, C. A., & Becker, M. H. (1986). Family and peer influence on obtaining a method of contraception. *Journal of Marriage and Family, 48*, 513–525.

National Center for Chronic Disease Prevention and Health Promotion (2000). *Tobacco information and prevention source (TIPS): Overview* [On-line]. Available: http://www.cdc.gov/tobacco/issue.htm

National Center for Chronic Disease Prevention and Health Promotion (2001a). *Obesity and overweight: A public health epidemic* [On-line]. Available: www.cdc.gov/nccdphp/dnpa/obesity/epidemic.htm

National Center for Chronic Disease Prevention and Health Promotion (2001b). *Kids walk-to-school: A guide to promoting walking to school* [On-line]. Available: www.cdc.gov/nccdphp/dnpa/kidswalk/index.htm

Newman, I. M. (1984). Capturing the energy of peer pressure: Insights from a longitudinal study of adolescent cigarette smoking. *Journal of School Health, 54*, 146–148.

Noll, R. B., Bukowski, W. M., Davies, W. H., Koontz, K., & Kulkarni, R. (1993). Adjustment in the peer system of adolescents with cancer: A two-year study. *Journal of Pediatric Psychology, 18*, 351–364.

Noll, R. B., Bukowski, W. M., Rogosch, F. A., LeRoy, S., & Kulkarni, R. (1990). Social interactions between children with cancer and their peers: Teacher ratings. *Journal of Pediatric Psychology, 15*, 43–56.

Noll, R. B., Gartstein, M. A., Vannatta, K., Correll, J., Bukowski, W. M., Davies, & W. H. (1999). Social, emotional, and behavioral functioning of children with cancer. *Pediatrics, 103*, 71–78.

Noll, R. B., LeRoy, S., Bukowski, W. M., Rogosch, F. A., & Kulkarni, R. (1991). Peer relationships and adjustment of children with cancer. *Journal of Pediatric Psychology, 16*, 307–326.

Noll, R. B., Ris, M. D., Davies, W. H., Bukowski, W. M., & Koontz, K. (1992). Social interactions between children with cancer or sickle cell disease and their peers: Teacher ratings. *Journal of Developmental and Behavioral Pediatrics, 13*, 187–193.

Noll, R. B., Vannatta, K., Koontz, K., Kalinyak, K., Bukowski, W. M., & Davies, W. H. (1996). Peer relationships and emotional well-being of youngsters with sickle cell disease. *Child Development, 67*, 423–436.

O'Brien, S. F., & Bierman, K. L. (1987, April). *Conceptions and perceived influence of peer groups: Interviews with preadolescents and adolescents*. Paper presented at the biennial meeting of the Society for Research in Child Development, Boston, MA.

Olweus, D. (1993). *Bullying at school: What we know and what we can do*. Oxford, UK: Blackwell.

Parker, J. G., & Asher, S. R. (1993a). Friendship and friendship quality in middle childhood: Links with peer group acceptance and feelings of loneliness and social dissatisfaction. *Developmental Psychology, 29*, 611–621.

Parker, J. G., & Asher, S. R. (1993b). Beyond group acceptance: Friendship and friendship quality as distinct dimensions of peer adjustment. In W. H. Jones & D. Perlman (Eds.), *Advances in personal relationships* (Vol. 4, pp. 261–294). London: Kingsley.

Parkhurst, J. T., & Asher, S. R. (1992). Peer rejection in middles childhood: Subgroup differences in behavior, loneliness, and interpersonal concerns. *Developmental Psychology, 28*, 231–241.

Paxton, S. J. (1996). Prevention implications of peer influences on body image dissatisfaction and disturbed eating in adolescent girls. *Eating Disorders: The Journal of Treatment and Prevention, 4*, 334–337.

Paxton, S. J., Schutz, H. K., Wertheim, E. H., & Muir, S. L. (1999). Friendship clique and peer influences on body image concerns, dietary, restraint, extreme weight-loss behaviors, and binge eating in adolescent girls. *Journal of Abnormal Psychology, 108*, 255–266.

Pennebaker, J., & Beall, S. (1986). Confronting a traumatic event: Toward an understanding of inhibition and disease. *Journal of Abnormal Psychology, 95*, 274–281.

Petraitis, J. Flay, B. R., & Miller, T. Q. (1995). Reviewing theories of adolescent substance use: Organizing pieces of the puzzle. *Psychological Bulletin, 117*, 67–86.

Rapoff, M. A. (1998). Adherence issues among adolescents with chronic disease. In: S. A. Shumaker & E. B. Schron (Eds.), *The Handbook of Health and Behavior Change* (pp. 377–408). New York: Springer Publishing Company, Inc.

Reid, M., Landesman, S., Treder, R., & Jaccard, J. (1989). "My family and friends." 6 to 12 year old children's perceptions of social support. *Child Development, 60*, 896–910.

Ricciardelli, L. A., McCabe, M. P., & Banfield, S. (2000). Body image and body change methods in adolescent boys: Role of parents, friends, and the media. *Journal of Psychosomatic Research, 49*, 189–197.

Romer, D., Black, M., Ricardo, I., Feigelman, S., Kaljee, L., Galbraith, J., Nesbit, R., Hornik, R. C., & Stanton, B. (1994). Social influences on the sexual risk behavior of youth at risk for HIV exposure. *American Journal of Public Health, 84*, 977–982.

Santor, D. A., Messervey, D., & Kusumakar, V. (2000). Measuring peer pressure, popularity, conformity in adolescent boys and girls: Predicting school performance, sexual attitudes, and substance abuse. *Journal of Youth and Adolescence, 29*, 163–182.

Schuman, W. B., & La Greca, A. M. (1999). Social correlates of chronic illness. In R. T. Brown (Ed.), *Cognitive aspects of chronic illness in children.* (pp. 289–311). New York: Guilford Press.

Sexson, S. B., & Madan-Swain, A. (1995). The chronically ill child in the school. *School Psychology Quarterly, 10*, 359–368.

Shepherd, C., & Hosking, G. (1989). Epilepsy in school children with intellectual impairments in Sheffield: The size and nature of the problem and the implications for service provision. *Journal of Mental Deficiency Research, 33*, 511–514.

Sherman, B. F., Bonanno, G. A., Wiener, L. S., & Battles, H. B. (2000). When children tell their friends they have AIDS: Possible consequences for psychological well-being and disease progression. *Psychosomatic Medicine, 62*, 238–247.

Sieving, R. E., Perry, C. L., & Williams, C. L. (2000). Do friendships change behaviors or do behaviors change friendships? Examining paths of influence in young adolescents' alcohol use. *Journal of Adolescent Health, 26*, 27–37.

Smith, A. L. (1999). Perceptions of peer relationships and physical activity participation in early adolescence. *Journal of Sport and Exercise Psychology, 21*, 329–350.

St. Lawrence, J. S., Brasfield, T. L., Jefferson, K. W., Allyene, E., & Shirley, A. (1994). Social support as a factor in African-American adolescents' sexual risk behavior. *Journal of Adolescent Research, 9*, 292–310.

Stone, W. L., & La Greca, A. M. (1990). The social status of children with learning disabilities: A reexamination. *Journal of Learning Disabilities, 23*, 32–37.

Strauss, C. C., Lahey, B. B., Frick, P., Frame, C. L., & Hynd, G. (1988). Peer social status of children with anxiety disorders. *Journal of Consulting and Clinical Psychology, 56*, 137–141.

Strauss, C. C., Smith, K., Frame, C., & Forehand, R. (1985). Personal and interpersonal characteristics associated with childhood obesity. *Journal of Pediatric Psychology, 10*, 337–343.

Sussman, S., Dent, C. W., McAdams, L. A., Stacy, A. W., Burton, D., & Flay, B. R. (1994). Group self-identification and adolescent cigarette smoking: A one year prospective study. *Journal of Abnormal Psychology, 103*, 576–580.

Thorne, B. (1986). Girls and boys together . . . but mostly apart: Gender arrangements in elementary schools. In W. W. Hartup & Z. Rubin (Eds.), *Relationships and development* (pp. 167–184). Hillsdale, NJ: Lawrence Erlbaum.

Tolson, J. M., & Urberg, K. A. (1993). Similarity between adolescent best friends. *Journal of Adolescent Research, 8*, 274–288.

Urberg, K. A. (1992). Locus of peer influence: Social crowd and best friend. *Journal of Youth and Adolescence, 21*, 439–450.

Urberg, K. A., Cheng, C. H., & Shyu, S. J. (1991). Grade changes in peer influence on adolescent cigarette smoking: A comparison of 2 measures. *Addictive Behaviors, 16*, 21–28.

Urberg, K. A., Degirmencioglu, S. M., Tolson, J. M., & Halliday-Scher, K. (1995). The structure of adolescent peer networks. *Developmental Psychology, 31*, 540–554.

Vannatta, K., Gartstein, M. A., Short, A., & Noll, R. B. (1998). A controlled study of peer relationships of children surviving brain tumors: Teacher, peer, and self-ratings. *Journal of Pediatric Psychology, 23*, 279–288.

Varni, J. W., Babani, L., Wallander, J. L., Roc, T. F., & Frasier, S. D. (1989). Social support and self-esteem effects on psychological adjustment in children and adolescents with insulin-dependent diabetes mellitus. *Child and Family Behavior Therapy, 11*, 1–17.

Varni, J. W., Katz, E. R., Colegrove, R., & Dolgin, M. (1993). The impact of social skills training on the adjustment of children with newly diagnosed cancer. *Journal of Pediatric Psychology, 18*, 751–767.

Varni, J. W., Katz, E. R., Colegrove, R., & Dolgin, M. (1994). Perceived social support and adjustment of children with newly diagnosed cancer. *Journal of Developmental and Behavioral Pediatrics, 15*, 20–26.

Varni, J. W., Setoguchi, Y., Rappaport, L. R., & Talbot, D. (1992). Psychological adjustment and perceived social support in children with congenital/acquired limb deficiencies. *Journal of Behavioral Medicine, 15*, 31–44.

Vernberg, E. M. (1990). Psychological adjustment and experiences with peers during early adolescence: Reciprocal, incidental, or unidirectional relationships? *Journal of Abnormal Child Psychology, 18*, 187–198.

Vernberg, E. M., Abwender, D. A., Ewell, K. K., & Beery, S. H. (1992). Social anxiety and peer relationships in early adolescence: A prospective analysis. *Journal of Clinical Child Psychology, 21*, 189–196.

Vernberg, E. M., Ewell, K. K., Beery, S. H., Freeman, C. M., & Abwender, D. A. (1995). Aversive exchanges with peers during early adolescence: Is disclosure helpful? *Child Psychiatry and Human Development, 26*, 43–59.

Vessey, J. A., Swanson, M. N., & Hagedorn, M. I. (1995). Teasing: Who says names can never hurt you? *Pediatric Nursing, 21*, 297–302.

Waldrop, M. F., & Halverson, C. F. (1975). Intensive and extensive peer behavior: Longitudinal and cross-sectional analyses. *Child Development, 46*, 19–26.

Wallander, J. L., Feldman, W. S., & Varni, J. W. (1989). Physical status and psychosocial adjustment in children with spina bifida. *Journal of Pediatric Psychology, 14*, 89–102.

Wallander, J. L., Hubert, N. C., & Varni, J. W. (1988). Child and maternal temperament characteristics, goodness of fit, and adjustment in physically handicapped children. *Journal of Clinical Child Psychology, 17*, 336–344.

Wallander, J. L., & Varni, J. W. (1989). Social support and adjustment in chronically ill and handicapped children. *American Journal of Community Psychology, 17*, 185–201.

Wallander, J. L., Varni, J. W., Babini, L., Banis, H. T., DeHaan, C. B., & Wilcox, K. T. (1989). Disability parameters, chronic strain, and adaptation of physically handicapped children and their mothers. *Journal of Pediatric Psychology, 14*, 23–42.

Wallander, J. L., Varni, J. W., Babini, L., Banis, H. T., & Wilcox, K. T. (1988). Children with chronic physical disorders: Maternal reports of their psychological adjustment. *Journal of Pediatric Psychology, 13*, 197–212.

Wang, M. Q., Fitzhugh, E. C., Eddy, J. M., Fu, Q., & Turner, L. (1997). Social influences on adolescents' smoking progress: A longitudinal analysis. *American Journal of Health Behavior, 21*, 111–117.
Williams, C. L., & Perry, C. L. (1998). Lessons from the Norland Project: Preventing alcohol problems during adolescence. *Alcohol Health and Research World, 22*, 107–116.
Wills, T. A., & Cleary, S. D. (1999). Peer and adolescent substance use among 6th–9th graders: Latent growth analysis of influence versus selection mechanisms. *Health Psychology, 18*, 453–463.
Wiznitzer, M., Ruggieri, P. M., Masaryk, T. J., Ross, J. S., Modic, M. T., & Berman, B. (1990). Diagnosis of cerebrovascular disease in sickle cell anemia by magnetic resonance angiography. *Journal of Pediatrics, 117*, 551–555.
Wolman, C., Resnick, M. D., Harris, L. J., & Blum, R. W. (1994). Emotional well-being among adolescents with and without chronic conditions. *Journal of Adolescent Health, 15*, 199–204.

35

Solid Organ Transplantation

James R. Rodrigue
Regino P. Gonzalez-Peralta
Max R. Langham, Jr.
University of Florida

INTRODUCTION

Children waiting for or receiving organ transplantation face many physical, emotional, social, developmental, and cognitive challenges. For most children, transplantation follows a progressive and debilitating physical health condition. They are confronted first with numerous demands associated with managing their chronic illness and then the anxiety and uncertainty of transplantation. Transplantation provides renewed hope and improved quality of life for most children, yet it simultaneously introduces new challenges to its young recipients. Throughout this process, children and their families must navigate a complex web of transplantation—from initial evaluation to long-term recovery.

Several types of solid organ transplants are now routinely performed in children: kidney, liver, heart, lung, small intestine, and combined organs. The expanding scope of solid organ transplantation necessitates that all pediatric psychologists, and especially those employed in school settings, become familiar with the medical, psychological, social, and developmental sequelae that children may experience throughout the transplant process. Therefore, the broad purpose of this chapter is to consider clinical issues that are relevant to organ transplantation in children. More specifically, we will examine: (1) the incidence, medical indications, and outcomes for solid organ transplantation in children; (2) the psychological assessment of the child throughout the transplant process; and (3) common targets of psychological intervention in this population. Throughout the chapter, we will highlight the key areas in which pediatric psychologists can make substantive clinical and scientific contributions to enhancing the lives of pediatric transplant patients and their families.

PEDIATRIC TRANSPLANTATION: INCIDENCE, MEDICAL INDICATIONS, AND OUTCOMES

According to data from the U.S. Scientific Registry of Transplant Recipients, there were 1,582 pediatric (i.e., under 18 years of age) transplant recipients in the United States in 2000. This represents a 26% increase from 12 years earlier (1,253 pediatric transplant recipients in 1989). Unfortunately, although pediatric patients generally have shorter waiting times when compared with adults, the number of pediatric patients wait-listed for transplantation has increased by 144% in the last decade. For comparison purposes, the number of adult transplant recipients increased by 69% during the last 10 years, whereas the number of adult patients wait-listed has increased an astounding 233%. The number of pediatric patients waitlisted for and receiving transplantation in 2000 is broken down by organ type in Fig. 35.1.

The increasing gap between the number of donor organs and the number of patients awaiting transplantation has been the focus of intense educational, scientific, and political efforts to raise organ donation rates (Howard, 2001; Radecki & Jaccard, 1997). For pediatric patients, the discrepancy is not as dramatic as it is for adults; however, 242 pediatric patients died while on the waiting list in 2000. This represents an increase of 31% over pediatric deaths on the waiting list in 1990. Moreover, the death rate for very young children (i.e., less than 1 year of age) is much higher than those for older children or adults. In recent years, the sharp increase in living organ donation has benefited children (Live Organ Donor Consensus Group, 2000). In 1999, for instance, 29% of all pediatric transplants were from living organ donation—predominantly kidney and liver donations (UNOS, 2000). The increase in living donation and the availability of new surgical techniques that benefit children (e.g., splitting a liver for transplantation into more than one person) have been essential advances for children since both the percentage and the actual number of pediatric cadaveric donors have decreased substantially over the last decade.

The medical conditions that lead to transplantation and patient survival rates, of course, vary by organ type. Primary indications for transplantation and overall survival rates in children are broken down by organ type and presented in Table 35.1. The following sections provide a brief description of the most common types of pediatric transplantation, their indications, and

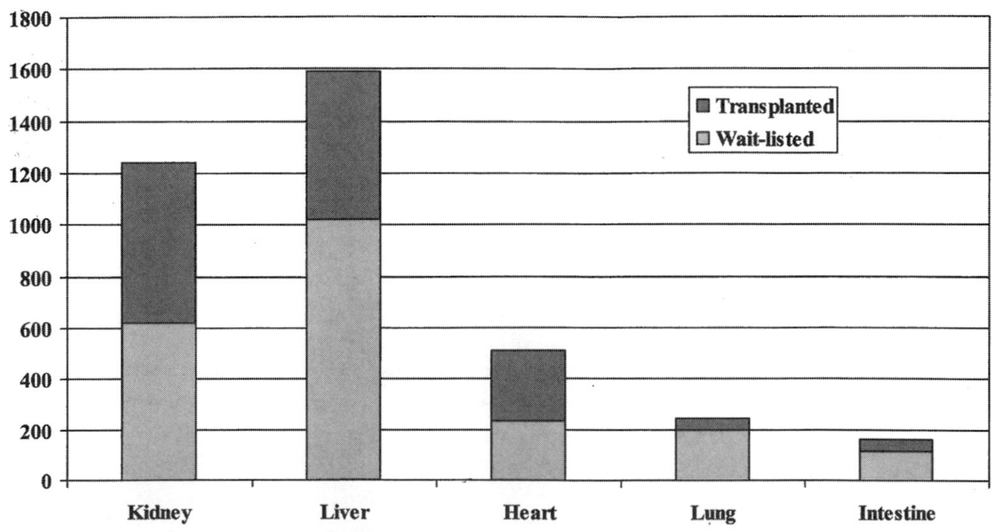

FIG. 35.1. Number of pediatric patients transplanted and wait-listed at year end, 2000.

TABLE 35.1
Primary Indications for Pediatric Transplantation and 1-, 3-, and 5-Year Patient Survival Rates[a]

Indications for Transplant		Survival Rates[b] 1 Year	3 Years	5 Years
Kidney transplantation	CD	98%	96%	94%
	LD	99%	97%	96%
Glomerulonephritis				
Chronic pyelonephritis				
Hereditary (e.g., polycystic kidneys, Alport's syndrome)				
Metabolic				
Obstructive uropathy				
Tumors				
Congenital				
Liver transplantation	CD	88%	83%	81%
Cholestatic liver disease				
Metabolic liver disease				
Fulminant liver failure				
Malignancy				
Chronic active hepatitis				
Miscellaneous (e.g., Budd-Chiari syndrome, cystic fibrosis, trauma)				
Heart transplantation		85%	72%	66%
Hypoplastic left heart syndrome				
End-stage cardiomyopathy				
Miscellaneous (e.g., obstructive cardiac tumors, unresectable ventricular diverticula)				
Lung transplantation		81%	54%	43%
End-stage lung parenchymal diseases				
Cystic fibrosis				
Congenital disorders (e.g., surfactant protein disorders, diaphragmatic hernia)				
Pulmonary fibrosis				
Primary pulmonary hypertension				

CD = cadaveric donor; LD = living donor.
[a]The list of indications is not exhaustive, but rather highlights the more common conditions leading to transplantation in children.
[b]United Network for Organ Sharing, 2000.

associated outcomes. Readers who wish to pursue more detailed descriptions of the medical and surgical aspects of specific types of organ transplantation in children are referred to other excellent sources (Ginns, Cosimi, & Morris, 1999; Stewart, Abecassis, & Kaufman, 2000).

Kidney Transplantation

Kidney transplantation is the treatment of choice for virtually all causes of end-stage renal disease. The vast majority of children undergoing kidney transplantation are school-age; 20% are 6–10 years of age, whereas 65% are 11–17 years old. Indications for kidney transplantation in children are primarily those associated with glomerulonephritis, chronic pyelonephritis, and hereditary conditions (e.g., polycystic kidneys). Children with these conditions will eventually require dialysis (either hemodialysis or peritoneal), but transplantation may serve a preemptive function to avoid clinical deterioration or allow for the discontinuation of dialysis. It is critical to emphasize, however, that some patients will cycle through dialysis and transplantation—for instance, initial dialysis followed by transplantation, then loss of the graft several years later, more dialysis, and another transplant. This is especially true for recipients of cadaver kidneys, because the graft survival time for those is considerably less than that for kidneys from a living donor (UNOS, 2000).

Medical management of children with end-stage renal disease is focused largely on preventing growth retardation, malnutrition, anemia, and renal osteodystrophy (Hanna, Foreman, & Chan, 1991). Growth problems can develop secondary to the age of onset and duration of kidney disease, glomerulofiltration rate, malnutrition, anemia, chronic acidosis, and uremia. Enteral feedings via nasogastric tube or gastronomy are used for children who are significantly malnourished. Although adults with end-stage renal disease are usually on a protein-restricted diet, children often receive additional protein and growth hormones. Additionally, erythropoietin, oral iron, a low phosphate diet, phosphate binders, and vitamin D supplements may be prescribed during the pretransplant management phase.

As noted in Table 35.1, patient survival rates are excellent for kidney transplantation. Indeed, successful transplantation offers improved survival rates compared to dialysis. For instance, the death rates for children on dialysis are 3.8 per 1,000 patient years, compared with 0.4 per 1,000 patient years for pediatric transplant recipients (U.S. Renal Data System, 1998). Primary causes of death after transplantation include infection (e.g., varicella/zoster), cardiovascular disease, hemorrhage, and malignancies (Tejani et al., 1994). Regarding morbidity outcomes, most children are readmitted to the hospital at least once, with rejection episodes, infection, urological complications, and dehydration as the primary reasons for hospital readmission (Almond et al., 1992).

The growth trajectory of children receiving kidney transplantation is an important outcome. Most children with end-stage renal disease have experienced some growth deficits, with an average height deficit of about two standard deviations below the mean (Tejani, Cortes, & Sullivan, 1996). In a series of studies, Tejani and colleagues (Tejani, Fine, Alexander, Harmon, & Stablein, 1993; Tejani & Sullivan, 1993; Tejani et al., 1996) have consistently determined that age and degree of height deficit at the time of transplantation are the two best predictors of posttransplant growth. Specifically, children most likely to experience catch-up growth after transplant are those under 6 years of age and those with minimal growth retardation at time of transplantation.

Cognitive functioning and quality of life are two additional endpoints that have been of interest to researchers and clinicians. Without proper intervention, malfunction of the kidneys leads to retention of urea and this can cause problems with concentration, attention, memory, alertness, and perceptual-motor coordination in children (Stewart, Kennard, Waller, & Fixler, 1994). For these patients, dialysis is inevitable. Research on the cognitive effects of dialysis and kidney transplantation is scarce and limited by a number of methodological problems (Bock et al., 1989; Brouhard et al., 2000; Fennell et al., 1990a, 1990b; Fennell, Fennell, Mings, & Morris, 1988; Fennell, Rasbury, Fennell, & Morris, 1984; Mendley & Zelko, 1999). This research, nevertheless, suggests cognitive deficits (e.g., verbal and nonverbal reasoning, visual-motor integration, memory) for children on dialysis and minimal to no cognitive deficits after kidney transplantation. Some of the findings indicate that children who receive transplantation either show cognitive improvement (e.g., mental processing speed and sustained attention) from pretransplant assessments or outperform children with kidney disease who have not yet undergone transplantation. Longer disease duration, longer time on dialysis, and more severe kidney dysfunction before and after transplantation may increase the risk of cognitive problems in childhood.

Surprisingly, there have been few systematic studies focused on identifying the quality of life outcomes or psychological functioning of child and adolescent kidney transplant recipients. Most existing reports are anecdotal or largely qualitative and the psychological implications raised in these reports, although perhaps still valid, were considered in the context of the state of transplantation and medical management during that time period (e.g., Bernstein, 1977; Gulledge, Busztu, & Montague, 1983). Several major pharmacological, medical, and surgical advances have occurred in recent years, and the degree to which quality of life outcomes have been impacted by these new developments has not been scientifically examined. Some researchers have found a high incidence of internalizing disorders among children on dialysis (Fukunishi & Kudo, 1995; Garralda, Jameson, Reynolds, & Postlethwaite, 1988), and the presence of internalizing and externalizing behavioral difficulties in children who have undergone transplantation (Douglas, Hulson, & Trompeter, 1998; Fukunishi & Kudo, 1995). However, a variety of methodological problems in these studies and the lack of replication in other transplant centers underscores the need to interpret these findings with caution.

Liver Transplantation

Unlike kidney transplantation, the majority (>60%) of pediatric cadaveric liver transplant recipients are of preschool age or younger. For children who receive living-related liver transplantation, about 80% are under 5 years of age. The most common indications for liver transplantation in children are cholestatic (e.g., biliary atresia, sclerosing cholangitis, Alagille's syndrome) and metabolic (e.g., α_1-antitrypsin deficiency, Wilson's disease, glycogen storage disease) liver diseases. During the pretransplant waiting period, optimizing nutritional status is a primary focus of treatment, because a malnourished child is at much higher risk for morbidity and mortality before and after transplantation. Fat malabsorption and protein energy malnutrition are common during the pretransplant waiting period. Consequently, children awaiting liver transplantation may receive nasograstric feedings at night or parenteral nutrition. Other complications seen during the pretransplant period include variceal bleeding, cholangitis, and bacterial peritonitis.

Hepatic artery thrombosis has historically been a major complication after transplantation, and it is one of the primary reasons for retransplantation and death in children. However, recent improvements in surgical techniques have significantly reduced the incidence of this serious complication. Other short- and long-term medical complications after liver transplantation include bowel perforation, primary nonfunction, bile duct problems, hepatorenal syndrome, rejection, nephrotoxicity, neurotoxicity, hyperlipidemia, and lymphorproliferative disease. These complications are serious and can lead to substantial morbidity and/or death in young children.

Monitoring of growth and development throughout the transplant spectrum is also very important for these children. According to a recent comprehensive report (SPLIT Research Group, 2001), the mean height and weight deficit for children at the time of transplant is about 1.4 and .6 standard deviations, respectively, below normal. Children less than 5 years of age are at substantially greater risk for height deficits than adolescents. Normal weight for age and catch-up growth can be expected for most children after transplantation, although this depends on several variables, including age at time of transplantation, diagnosis, and nutritional status both before and after transplantation (McDiarmid et al., 1999; SPLIT Research Group, 2001).

Children with liver disease are at risk for cognitive problems because a poorly functioning or obstructed liver is unable to sufficiently break down or excrete substances that are toxic to the nervous system. For instance, when the liver cannot adequately break down ammonia, encephalopathy may result. Children may have symptoms of disorientation, confusion, and memory problems. Similarly, children with Wilson's disease may experience significant neurological difficulties, because the liver is not able to excrete substances that accumulate in the brain. Severe malnutrition and vitamin E deficiency, with associated neurological sequelae, are also common among children with liver disease.

Stewart and her colleagues (e.g., Kennard et al., 1999; Stewart, Campbell, McCallon, Waller, & Andrews, 1992; Stewart et al., 1988, 1991) have conducted the most comprehensive series of investigations focused on the cognitive functioning of children who receive liver transplantation. Intellectual functioning for these children has generally been found to be in the average to low average range, with minimal to no real improvement in IQ scores several years after transplantation. When compared with children with cystic fibrosis, children who received liver transplantation showed deficits in learning and memory, visuospatial skills, abstract reasoning skills, and motor function. Their series of studies indicate that children with early onset of symptoms and growth delays are at highest risk for broad cognitive impairment. These children may also be at risk for unidentified learning disabilities. For instance, Kennard et al. (1999) found that only 5 of the 13 liver transplant recipients who had intellectual-achievement score discrepancies indicative of learning disability actually received special education services.

Regarding psychological functioning after liver transplantation, study findings are mixed. Earlier research found evidence of low social functioning before transplantation (Hoffmann, Rodrigue, Andres, & Novak, 1995), with improved social competence and behavioral adjustment after transplantation (Stewart et al., 1989; Zitelli et al., 1988). However, more recent research has suggested that social deficits and posttraumatic stress responses may persist well after liver transplantation in some segments of this population (e.g., DeBolt, Stewart, Kennard, Petrik, & Andrews, 1995; Tornqvist et al., 1999; Walker, Harris, Baker, Kelly, & Houghton, 1999). Little is known about the incidence of such internalizing factors as depression or anxiety in this patient population.

Heart Transplantation

In 1984, surgeons at Loma Linda University performed the first successful heart transplant in a 4-day-old infant with hypoplastic left heart syndrome, a congenital heart defect with a guarded prognosis (Bailey et al., 1986). Today, pediatric heart transplants account for about 12% of all heart transplants performed in the United States, with half of these occurring in children less than 5 years of age. More than one third of all pediatric heart transplants have been done during the child's first year of life. Complex congenital heart disease (e.g., including hypoplastic left heart syndrome) and end-stage cardiomyopathy are the primary indications for heart transplantation in children. It has been estimated that, because of the extreme shortage of donor hearts, 15–20% of pediatric patients needing heart transplantation will die of congestive heart failure or multiorgan failure while waiting (Vricella & Bailey, 1999). However, once a suitable donor has been found and transplant surgery is completed, attention shifts to the identification and management of early complications, including seizures, hyperperfusion syndrome, renal failure, and infections. Possible long-term complications include hypertension, graft vasculopathy, arrhythmias, renal failure, and neoplastic diseases.

A recent report from the Registry of the International Society for Heart and Lung Transplantation (Boucek et al., 2001) shows that survival statistics for pediatric heart transplantation have improved in recent years. Older children and adolescents have survival rates that are nearly identical to those of adults, with children less than a year old having the worst survival rates. The half-life for pediatric patient survival after heart transplantation is about 12 years.

As with other solid organ transplant types, heart transplantation provides opportunity for return to normal growth for many children (Boucek et al., 2001). However, the velocity of linear growth appears to increase primarily for children under 5 years of age, with mean height values near the 40th percentile for age. These children also show substantial weight gain. Unfortunately, most adolescents fail to demonstrate any significant increase in height after heart transplantation, although they do grow in weight. The implications of this problem in proportional growth for adolescents are not yet known.

The cognitive functioning of children both before and after heart transplantation has been reviewed recently (Todaro, Fennell, Sears, Rodrigue, & Roche, 2000). Children with heart disease requiring transplantation may experience low cardiac output, cardiac arrhythmias, and acute anoxic effects, which all may impair cognitive development and functioning. Of course, any interruption in the flow of oxygenated blood to the brain can produce brain injury or affect brain development, especially during the first few years of life. Moreover, open-heart surgeries, deep hypothermic circulatory arrest procedures, and long duration on the cardiopulmonary bypass pump before transplantation may lead to increased risk of cerebral complications (Bellinger et al., 1991; Dickson & Sambrooks, 1979; Miller, Mamourian, Tesman, & Baylen, 1994). Despite estimates that about 20% of pediatric heart transplant patients experience neurological problems (Baum et al., 1993; Martin et al., 1992), there are surprisingly few studies examining the cognitive status of children before or after heart transplantation (e.g., Baum et al., 1993; Trimm, 1991; Wray, Long, Radley-Smith, & Yacoub, 2001; Wray, Pot-Mees, Zeitlin, Radley-Smith, & Yacoub, 1994; Wray & Yacoub, 1991). The available research indicates that the cognitive development of pediatric heart transplant recipients may not be impaired relative to children with congenital heart disease who have not undergone transplantation. Scores on standardized measures of cognitive functioning have generally been in the low average to average range, and there is some evidence to suggest that children with postsurgical infection and/or rejection episodes may be at higher risk for cognitive difficulties.

Although some researchers note that pediatric heart transplant recipients enjoy normal quality of life (e.g., Boucek et al., 2001), there are few published studies using validated quality-of-life measures that substantiate such claims. In the report of the International Society for Heart and Lung Transplantation, it is noted that 95% of pediatric patients reported no activity limitations 3 years after heart transplantation. These data are certainly encouraging, but they reflect only one aspect (i.e., physical functioning) of the more comprehensive construct of quality of life. In one large-scale study of children after heart transplantation, Uzark et al. (1992) found that 93% of the children over 8 years of age were attending school and participating in extracurricular activities. They also found that social competence, behavior problems, and depression were rather common in this population. Similar findings of increased risk among pediatric heart transplant recipients have been reported by some research teams (Serrano-Ikkos, Lask, Whitehead, Rees, & Graham, 1999; Wray et al., 1994, 2001), but not others (Demaso, Twente, Spratt, & O'Brien, 1995).

Lung Transplantation

The success of lung transplantation in adults has led to a recent increased use of this intervention in children and adolescents. In 2000, 43 pediatric lung transplants were performed in the United States, compared with only nine in 1990. The primary indications for lung transplantation vary as a function of child age (Boucek et al., 2001). For instance, for infants, congenital lung abnormality is the most common indication. For children under 11 years of age, there is no one disease that leads to transplantation above all others. However, more than two thirds of adolescents who undergo lung transplantation have cystic fibrosis as their primary diagnosis. Although most children with cystic fibrosis live well into adulthood with medical therapy, a small percentage of them eventually become refractory to medical therapy and may need lung transplantation for longer term survival. For such patients, frequent hospitalizations, progressive weight loss, and worsening gas exchange may be indications for pediatric lung transplantation.

Once listed, most children will wait longer than a year for lung transplantation and about 20–25% will die while waiting. Consequently, children are typically listed for transplantation when their life expectancy is about 12–24 months. The child's nutritional status may require supplemental enteric feedings during this time period, and active participation in physical therapy and pulmonary rehabilitation is usually expected to optimize functional status. After transplantation, children may be required to participate in a cardiopulmonary reconditioning program. Common morbidities after transplantation include hypertension and diabetes. Also, about one half of pediatric lung transplant recipients will be readmitted to the hospital within the first year. The mortality rate is highest during the first year after transplantation, with the primary causes being graft failure, infection, hemorrhage, rejection, and cardiovascular complications. After the first year, rejection and brochiolitis obliterans are the leading causes of death (Boucek et al., 2001).

Unlike with other transplant types, the cognitive functioning, psychological adjustment, and quality of life of children receiving lung transplantation have not been the focus of study. Considering the possible neuropsychological complications associated with use of corticosteroids, chronic hypoxia, and compromised nutritional status among patients with lung diseases requiring transplantation (e.g., Crews, Jefferson, Broshek, Barth, & Robbins, 2000), the cognitive status of children should be examined. For instance, Wong, Mallory, Goldstein, Goyal, and Yamada (1999), in a review of 135 pediatric lung transplant recipients, found that 45% of the patients experienced one or more neurological complications, with seizures being the most common complication. Regarding psychological functioning, children being evaluated for lung transplantation appear to be coping well with their medical status and report few symptoms of psychological distress (Thompson, DiGirolamo, & Mallory, 1996). However, nothing is known about their psychological status or quality of life after transplantation.

PSYCHOLOGICAL ASSESSMENT AND INTERVENTION THROUGHOUT THE TRANSPLANT PROCESS

It is widely recognized that living with chronic health conditions and their treatments during childhood and adolescence can be enormously stressful for youths and their families. When one adds the complexities of organ transplantation to chronic health conditions, it can be argued that the associated stress increases exponentially. In addition to their usual physical limitations and medical treatments, children and their parents must drive great distances or relocate to a tertiary care transplant center, establish new relationships with health care providers, undergo comprehensive evaluation, miss extensive amounts of school and work, face financial hardships, and cope with increased isolation. Consequently, all pediatric transplant centers use social workers, psychologists, and/or psychiatrists to provide both evaluation and intervention services for pediatric transplant patients and their families. In some instances, transplant programs have one or more identified pediatric psychologists as part of their team. In the absence of designated transplant psychologists, many programs use existing pediatric psychology consultation services on an as-needed basis.

Transplant programs are characterized by their interdisciplinary nature, comprised usually of specialty pediatricians, pediatric surgeons, nurse coordinators, social workers, and psychologists. Because children who pursue transplantation often live great distances from the transplant center, other community-based health professionals may be active members of the health care team as well. School teachers, school psychologists, counselors, developmental specialists, extended family members, and others may have played essential roles in the lives of children with chronic health conditions before referral for transplantation. Therefore, the coordination of transplantation in the context of such community-based care and services, both before and after transplant surgery, requires close collaboration among all health and service providers from time of referral to long-term posttransplant recovery.

A child referred for transplant consideration will undergo a comprehensive, multiday evaluation, on either an inpatient or an outpatient basis, to determine medical and surgical suitability for transplantation. Standard components of such evaluations include a detailed medical history and physical examination, several laboratory tests, radiographic tests, vaccinations as appropriate, and various consultations with pediatric subspecialists, psychologists, social workers, and nutritionists. In many instances, this evaluation process may represent the first meeting between the child, his/her family, and the pediatric psychologist.

The purpose and scope of the pretransplant psychological evaluation will depend on individual transplant program policies, the developmental level of the child, the physical health status of the child, and time constraints. However, unlike the psychological evaluations conducted with adult transplant candidates, it is rarely the case that psychological or behavioral health factors alone preclude children from being listed for transplantation. Consequently, such evaluations are designed to assess the relative behavioral health strengths and limitations of the child and his/her family system and to determine the need and timing of appropriate psychological interventions. They generally involve a comprehensive assessment of the child and family system across multiple domains of functioning (Streisand & Tercyak, 2001). A review of available medical records and clinical interviews with the transplant candidate (if age appropriate), primary caregivers, other family members, health providers, and educators are standard components of most assessments. When time permits and the conditions are appropriate (e.g., current health status of the child, assessment setting, etc.), formal testing may be conducted at the time of evaluation or scheduled for a later date. The major domains of functioning that are of primary importance to the psychologist evaluating the pediatric transplant patient are listed in Table 35.2.

Physical Health History and Quality of Life

An important step in preparing for the psychological evaluation is to conduct a thorough review of the child's available medical records and to discuss the child's physical health history with the transplant physician and nurse coordinator. The information gathered will enhance the psychologist's understanding of the medical context in which the transplant evaluation is occurring and will highlight any psychosocial issues that may need particular attention or assessment. Obtaining this information in advance of the initial clinical evaluation will help the child and caregivers see that the psychologist is an integrated member of the transplant team who is knowledgeable about the child's relevant health history. The assessment can also be conducted more efficiently with appropriate background medical information.

Since determining the timing of transplant listing and surgery is a critical objective of the overall pretransplant evaluation, pediatric psychologists can provide valuable information about the child's current level of health-related quality of life. An assessment of current functional status, particularly in light of past medical history and future prognosis, may prove useful in decisions about how quickly to proceed to transplant listing. Also, because one of the goals of transplantation is to improve quality of life, assessment at this time in the evaluation process serves as an important baseline index to which posttransplant quality of life scores can be compared. When the age of the child permits (i.e., at least 10 years old), it is highly recommended that quality of life measures be obtained from both the child and the parents. Ideally, both illness-specific and generic indices of quality of life should be assessed, although there are relatively few validated measures that are appropriate for children (Rodrigue, Geffken, & Streisand, 2000). At the University of Florida, we have administered the Child Health Questionnaire (Landgraf, Abetz & Ware, 1996) to obtain assessments of the physical and psychological health status of children. This instrument provides useful clinical

TABLE 35.2
Assessment Domains and Strategies of the Pediatric Transplant Candidate Psychological Evaluation

Domain	*Strategies*
Physical Health History and Quality of Life	Medical chart review Clinical interview with child, primary caregivers, and health providers Checklists (e.g., Child Health Questionnaire)
Development	Clinical interview with primary caregivers, educators, and health providers Testing (e.g., Bayley Scales of Infant Development, Child Development Inventory)
Cognitive Functioning	Consultation with educators and developmental specialists Review of educational records and prior testing Testing (e.g., Bayley Scales of Infant Development, Wechsler Intelligence Scales, Stanford-Binet Intelligence Scale, Differential Ability Scale, Wide Range Assessment of Memory and Learning)
Academic Achievement	Consultation with educators and developmental specialists Review of educational records and prior testing Testing (e.g., Wechsler Individual Achievement Test, Woodcock-Johnson Psych-Educational Battery)
Psychological Adaptation and Coping	Clinical interview with child, primary caregivers, and health providers Review of previous psychological records Child-completed checklists (e.g., Child Depression Inventory, State-Trait Anxiety Inventory for Children, Kidcope) Parent-completed behavior checklists (e.g., Child Behavior Checklist, Conners Parent Rating Scale)
Adherence	Clinical interview with child, primary caregivers, and health providers Medical chart review
Family	Clinical interview with child and primary caregivers Testing (e.g., Family Adaptability and Cohesion Evaluation Scales, Family Environment Scale, Parent-Adolescent Communication Scale, Pediatric Inventory for Parents, Caregiver Strain Index)

information about global health, role and social limitations caused by physical, emotional, or behavioral difficulties, self-esteem, behavioral problems, and family adaptation. More disease-specific instruments, although available for use with certain children who may eventually need transplantation (e.g., cystic fibrosis), have not been developed for pediatric transplant patients.

Development, Cognitive Functioning, and Academic Achievement

End-stage diseases and their treatments, organ transplantation, and immunosuppressive medications produce an impressive range of possible developmental, cognitive, and academic manifestations and complications. This is not that surprising when one considers the complexities of the integrated human organ system and the fact that impairment in one organ may affect other organ systems and, consequently, various aspects of cognitive and developmental functioning. Several excellent reviews focusing on the cognitive and developmental aspects of transplantation have recently been published (Hobbs & Sexson, 1993; Stewart & Kennard, 1999; Stewart et al., 1994; Streisand & Tercyak, 2001; Todaro et al., 2000; Wijdicks, 1999).

As noted in Table 35.3, problems in cognitive functioning may develop as a function of the underlying disease processes that initially caused organ failure, child's stage of development and maturation, psychosocial factors that are secondary to illness parameters, pretransplant

TABLE 35.3
Mechanisms for Development of Cognitive Problems in Pediatric Transplant Patients

Mechanism	*Examples*
Underlying disease processes	Inability to detoxify or remove toxins Cyanosis Cerebrovascular injury Low cardiac output Hypoxia Hypoxemia Uremia Hyperparathyroidism Micronutrient deficits Vitamin E deficiency Hyperammonemia Stroke Diffuse encephalopathy
Psychosocial	Inability to participate in normative age-appropriate activities to stimulate cognition School absences Frequent hospitalizations Social isolation Nonadherence Substance abuse
Development/maturation	Interference with dendretic growth and/or myelination Malnutrition Growth deficits Delayed motor development Curtailed head growth
Pretransplant treatment regimen	Dialysis Open-heart surgery Long duration on cardiopulmonary bypass pump Numerous medications
Transplant surgery	Anesthesia duration and complications Invasive surgical procedures
Posttransplant factors	Immunosuppressant medications Corticosteroids Rejection episodes Frequent hospitalizations Retransplantation Infections

treatment regimen, transplant surgery, and medications designed to suppress the immune system and prevent organ rejection. Not only can each one of these sets of variables independently impact cognitive functioning in children, but also their combined effects on the intellectual, memory, and academic systems have the potential to be very substantial. It is imperative that pediatric psychologists, especially those practicing in schools, understand the subtle and more overt cognitive sequelae associated with organ failure and transplantation to best evaluate and assist pediatric transplant patients.

Evaluations of cognitive functioning and academic achievement should be considered part of standard care for pediatric transplant patients, but few programs systematically conduct such evaluations. Moreover, serial assessments are necessary to ascertain the nature of any changes in development, memory, cognitive abilities, and academic performance and to implement appropriate developmental services for preschoolers or effective educational curricula for school-age children. These assessments can be conducted by either the transplant psychologist or the school psychologist, but it is imperative that test results, educational programming, and medication or treatment changes be shared between the transplant program and the school to attend to the child's needs in the most integrated manner.

Children in either the pre- or posttransplant period may be eligible for modified educational services under Section 504 of the Rehabilitation Act of 1973. Section 504, which defines disability more broadly than those categories typically associated with the Individuals with Disabilities Education Act (IDEA), prohibits discrimination against qualified persons with disabilities. Use of Section 504 should always be considered when a child returns to school after a serious illness, has a chronic health condition, or has experienced extended hospitalization or a major medical event (e.g., transplantation). Thus, a child with heart disease, who has missed school because of illness and hospitalization and who has a history of learning problems, language impairment, or physical disability may qualify for services under Section 504, whether or not special educational services were provided previously under the IDEA. Clearly, in light of recent developmental, cognitive, and achievement findings, Section 504 has important implications for many children either waiting for or who have received organ transplantation. Furthermore, Section 504 requires periodic reevaluations of children, although the time frame for such evaluations is not specified. The IDEA mandates reevaluations at least every 3 years. However, the nature of the pediatric transplant treatment and medication regimen is such that repeat evaluations of development, cognitive functioning, and/or academic achievement should be conducted every 9–12 months.

Psychological Adaptation and Coping

All health care providers involved in transplantation recognize that the child's successful psychological adaptation to chronic illness and transplantation is an essential measure of clinical outcome. The changing demands of illness, effects of treatment, and the child's transition through various stages of development make the assessment of psychological adaptation and coping resources very challenging for the pediatric psychologist. For very young children, attachment may be compromised by multiple separations and/or parental overprotectiveness. For preschool and school-age children, problems in body image development, behavioral functioning, and development of peer relationships may be affected. For older children and adolescents, self-esteem issues, affective disturbance, and assimilation of the transplanted organ may be the focus of assessment.

Although there is a considerable body of research on the psychological adjustment of children with chronic illness (e.g., Roberts, in press), very little research has examined the psychological functioning of children throughout the organ transplant process specifically. Our clinical experiences, however, tell us that the psychological status and coping resources of children should be assessed repeatedly throughout all phases of transplantation. Evaluation for transplantation often introduces the child to an entirely new team of health professionals. The unfamiliarity with the transplant clinics and health care team may precipitate distress in young children. Transplant evaluation may also heighten anxiety about the severity of illness and the possibility of death, separation worries, and body image concerns. We usually obtain an assessment of behavioral functioning, depression, anxiety, and preferred coping strategies at this time to help us determine whether psychological intervention is immediately warranted. Also, the child's understanding of transplantation and its extant requirements is usually assessed at this time and examined in the context of the child's developmental level. Any misperceptions about the transplant process, the origin of the donated organ, and medication issues can be addressed early in the transplant process.

Once listed for transplantation, the waiting period can be very emotionally challenging for children and adolescents. Feelings of sadness, anxiety, guilt, helplessness, and hopelessness may appear, but are usually transient in nature. Nevertheless, regular check-ups with the pediatric psychologist during this period of waiting allows for the assessment of any changes in behavioral or psychological functioning since the pretransplant evaluation. Some children may require very extended hospitalizations during this time period, which may precipitate intense feelings of isolation, in addition to affective disturbance. Pain frequency, intensity, and coping strategies are also important to assess at this time. Some children may experience multiple medical procedures that lead to significant physical discomfort, and pain assessments may be useful in guiding the development and implementation of appropriate interventions.

As previously noted, little is known about the long-term psychological adjustment of children after transplantation. Nevertheless, virtually all authors who have written about the psychological ramifications of transplantation during childhood and adolescence stress the importance of psychological follow-up assessments in the months and years after transplantation. It is unlikely that this is a routine practice in most pediatric transplant programs, although we would argue that it become a standard component of the aftercare program for transplant recipients. Considerable diligence is apparent in the monitoring and assessment of the transplanted organ, and the psychological adaptation of its host should be monitored with equal fervor.

For many children with chronic conditions leading to transplantation, participation in school activities is frequently disrupted. This disruption has the potential to negatively impact academic achievement, social development, and psychological adaptation. The specific nature and course of school reentry, therefore, has been a critical focus in the literature on children with chronic health conditions (Madan-Swain, Fredrick, & Wallander, 1999). However, it is important to emphasize that, in the case of transplantation, there is likely to be not one single point of school reentry, but multiple disruptions in school attendance followed by several reentries. Although the relative impact of multiple disruptions in school attendance and extended absences has not yet been studied in the context of pediatric transplantation, our clinical experience suggests that school refusal, concerns about peer reactions to their physical appearance, and separation anxiety are common in children and young adolescents awaiting and receiving transplantation.

Efforts to facilitate the school reentry process require close collaboration between the transplant team and school psychologist. At the University of Florida, for instance, the transplant psychologist often meets with the child, parents, and school personnel before reentry to discuss the importance of and benefits derived from returning to school. At this time, information about the child's medical condition, medications, and any psychoeducational findings can be shared and their implications for curriculum planning discussed. This type of meeting also provides an opportunity for child and/or parental concerns to be raised and discussed. Finally, a detailed plan for future psychoeducational assessment and programming is outlined. For many children, their classmates are informed about the nature of the child's condition and medical experience, using developmentally appropriate language and activities or materials. The child may be introduced as an "expert" on their medical condition and transplantation and may be coached on how to respond to their peers' questions.

Adherence

Concerns about poor adherence to the posttransplant regimens are prominent in the minds of all pediatric transplant professionals, with good reason. The consequences of poor adherence to the complex medication regimen and dietary restrictions can result in loss of the transplanted organ, retransplantation, and/or death (Sigfusson et al., 1997). In addition, there are potential societal costs (e.g., impact on public willingness to be organ donors), financial costs (e.g., expense of rehospitalizations, health care of second organ failure, retransplantation), and ethical dilemmas (e.g., should retransplantation be an option?) associated with graft loss secondary to nonadherence. The rate of nonadherence after transplantation is really unknown, but it is suspected to be about 30–75% among adolescents (Serrano-Ikkos, Lask, Whitehead, & Eisler, 1998; Wolff, Strecker, Vester, Latta, & Ehrich, 1998). Actual rates, of course, vary according to how nonadherence is defined by researchers. Clinically, nonadherence typically includes not filling prescriptions at all or in a timely manner, not completing a prescribed medication regimen, deviations in the dose and/or frequency of medications taken, not attending scheduled clinic visits, not following diet and/or activity restrictions, and not maintaining a healthy lifestyle (e.g., tobacco or alcohol use).

Assessment of adherence behaviors should be conducted by the pediatric psychologist at the time of initial evaluation. Comprehensive review of medical records, telephone interviews with the child's health care providers and pharmacists, and clinical interviews with the parents and child are minimally necessary. The transplant team typically wants to know what the likelihood is of nonadherence after transplantation, due in large part to the severe consequences noted previously. It is important to recognize, however, that such predictions are difficult, if not impossible, to make with a high degree of certainty for several reasons. First, adherence must occur across a broad array of behaviors and nonadherence in one domain does not necessarily equate with nonadherence in other domains. Second, there are multiple intrapersonal, interpersonal, and systems variables that may either facilitate good adherence behaviors or make nonadherence more likely, and some of these variables are difficult to assess. They include, in part, the nature of the relationship between the child, family, and health care team, perceptions about the benefits and limitations of the treatment regimen, the quality of the parent–child relationship, the cognitive and memory functioning of the child, the presence of psychopathology or affective distress, the complexity of the treatment regimen, the family's financial resources to carry out the treatment regimen as prescribed, and treatment sideeffects. Third, there are reasons why we can expect the correspondence between pre- and posttransplant adherence to be less than perfect (Dew et al., 2001). Changes in the medical regimen, behavioral and psychological functioning, physical functioning, reasons for or understanding of certain behaviors, and evaluators make predicting posttransplant nonadherence from pretransplant factors very challenging.

Typically, the most pressing adherence-related concern after transplantation is whether children and adolescents are taking their immunosuppressant medications, essential for ensuring optimal graft functioning and, ultimately, patient survival. Adherence to these medications, therefore, is an important consideration during the pretransplant evaluation, as well as in the long-term follow-up assessments of the patient and family. Immunosuppressant medications that are used with children include cyclosporine A, cyclosporine microemulsion, tacrolimus, muromonab-CD3, azathioprine, mycophenolate mofetil, daclizumab, and sirolimus, among others. Immunosuppressant medications have historically been administered in combination with corticosteroids (e.g., prednisone). However, more recent advances in immunosuppressant medications and related outcome data yield some enthusiasm for the use of low-dose steroid

TABLE 35.4
Possible Complications and Adverse Side Effects of Immunosuppression Medications and Corticosteroids

Medication Type	*Possible Complications/Side Effects*	
Immunosuppressants	Nephrotoxicity	Hypertension
	Neurological (e.g., tremor, headache, convulsions)	Hepatotoxicity
		Gingival hyperplasia
	Metabolic disturbances (e.g., hyperkalemia, hyperglycemia, hyperlipidemia, hypomagnesemia)	Tremor
		Excessive hair growth
		Facial dysmorphism
		Skin cancer
	Opportunistic infection	Nausea
	Diarrhea	Confusion
	Vomiting	Anxiety
	Delirium	Hallucinations
	Restlessness	Disorientation
	Insomnia	Depression
Corticosteroids	Sodium and fluid retention	Potassium loss
	Muscle weakness or loss of muscle mass	Growth retardation
		Diabetes
	Reduced rate of wound healing	Weight gain/obesity
	Bone fractures and disease	Hyperlipidemia
	Cushingoid features (e.g., moon face, acne, altered hair distribution, truncal obesity)	Abdominal distension
		Peptic ulceration
		Hypertension
	Headaches	Thin fragile skin
	Increased sweating	Convulsions
	Decreased carbohydrate tolerance	Mood changes
	Menstrual irregularities	Vertigo
	Delirium	Euphoria
	Mania	Insomnia
	Irritability	Tremor

regimens or steroid-withdrawal protocols in children (Superina, Acal, Bilik, & Zaki, 1993; Vricella & Bailey, 1999).

Although the immunosuppressant agents and steroids are necessary to prevent rejection of the transplanted organ, there are many adverse effects associated with their use, either alone or in combination. Possible adverse effects of immunosuppressant medications and steroids are highlighted in Table 35.4. In addition to these medications, children and adolescents may be prescribed several other medications after transplant to optimize the health benefits of transplantation. These medications may include antihypertensives, diuretics, anticoagulants, antibiotics, antifungals, and vitamins. Some health providers have noted that the extensive medication regimen, which may include a dozen pills daily, highlights the reality that transplant recipients have exchanged one chronic health condition for another (Sexson & Rubenow, 1992).

Adherence represents another domain in which a close working relationship between the transplant team and the school psychologist can be substantially beneficial for the child. In addition to playing a central role in monitoring adherence behaviors of children, school psychologists and teachers can be instrumental in helping to identify possible barriers to adherence, teaching self-management strategies to children, prompting adherence behaviors, and alerting the transplant team to adherence-related problems before they become health-compromising or life-threatening.

Family Functioning

Any psychological evaluation of a child needing transplantation should be done in the broader context of the family system. There are many reasons to broaden the assessment to include the parents, siblings, and other extended family members. Of primary importance is the consistent finding that pediatric transplantation places significant stress on the family system (Rodrigue et al., 1997; Stewart et al., 1993; Tarbell & Kosmach, 1998). The demands of the child's illness and transplantation often lead to role transitions within the family, financial strains, caregiver burden, adjustment difficulties among siblings, and occupational changes. A family's attempts to maintain normal stability or equilibrium is seriously challenged throughout the transplant process, and there is evidence that stress even *increases* in the months after transplantation (Rodrigue et al., 1997).

The association between parental distress and child psychological functioning (e.g., Wallander & Thompson, 1995) further highlights the need to assess how mothers and fathers are coping with and adjusting to the rigors of transplantation. The degree of caregiver burden, the presence of any significant affective distress, histories of substance use or abuse, and the nature of any preexisting psychopathology all are important targets of evaluation, especially at the time of initial consideration for transplantation. Situations in which parents are unable to provide adequate support, emotionally or instrumentally, and supervision raise concerns about the child's psychological adaptation and adherence behaviors (Beck et al., 1980; Uzark et al., 1992). Conversely, families in which parents are well-adjusted, have a loving and stable marriage, have adequate coping resources, and are flexible in responding to the illness and treatment demands portends a greater likelihood of optimal psychological functioning in the child.

As noted previously, living organ donation has increased dramatically in recent years. It is now possible for individuals to donate a kidney and parts of their liver, lung, and pancreas to others. Kidney donation is by far the most common, but there has been a sharp increase in liver donation by parents to their young children. This has important implications for the assessment and treatment of families, because both the child recipient and the parent donor are simultaneously hospitalized and recovering from surgery, thus potentially placing even greater stress on the family system. Shifts in family responsibilities and roles can be expected during this time period and may cause some degree of instability in the absence of an extended network of support. Clearly, the role of extended family members and other support systems in helping the family must be evaluated as well.

CONCLUSIONS

The range of possible psychological issues embedded within the transplant continuum is quite expansive. The pediatric psychologist should play an active role in the ongoing assessment of quality of life, developmental progress, cognitive functioning, academic achievement, behavioral and psychological adaptations, adherence behaviors, and family functioning. We recommend that the child transplant candidate meet with the psychologist during the pretransplant evaluation process, at which time a comprehensive assessment can be completed. Subsequent, and more limited, evaluations should occur regularly (i.e., every 6 months), while the child is listed for transplantation and in the first 2 years after transplantation. Annual psychological evaluations should be sufficient in subsequent years. The recommended timing and sequence of such evaluations are listed in Table 35.5. Throughout this process, the pediatric psychologist

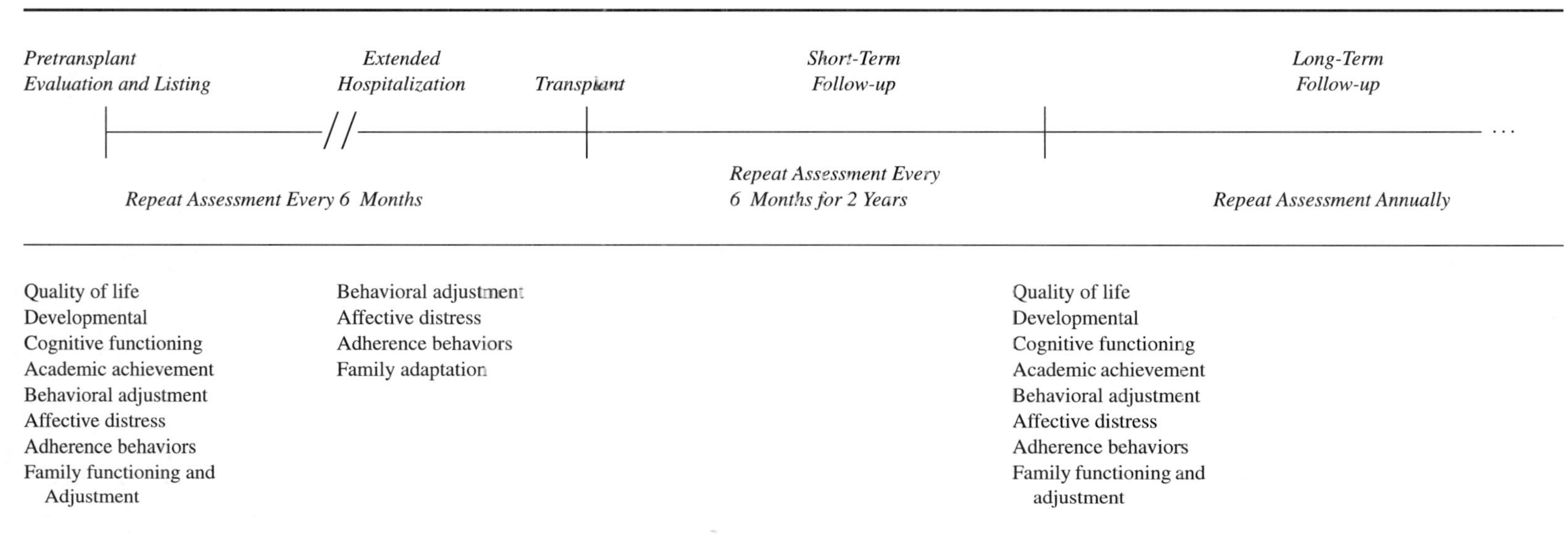

TABLE 35.5
Continuum of Child Psychological Assessment Throughout the Transplant Process

Pretransplant Evaluation and Listing	*Extended Hospitalization*	*Transplant*	*Short-Term Follow-up*	*Long-Term Follow-up*
Repeat Assessment Every 6 Months			*Repeat Assessment Every 6 Months for 2 Years*	*Repeat Assessment Annually*
Quality of life Developmental Cognitive functioning Academic achievement Behavioral adjustment Affective distress Adherence behaviors Family functioning and Adjustment	Behavioral adjustment Affective distress Adherence behaviors Family adaptation		Quality of life Developmental Cognitive functioning Academic achievement Behavioral adjustment Affective distress Adherence behaviors Family functioning and adjustment	

and transplant team should maintain close collaboration with the child's school psychologist to share evaluation findings and consult regarding appropriate educational programming and psychosocial interventions.

REFERENCES

Almond, P. S., Matas, A. J., Gillingham, K., Moss, A., Mauer, M., Chavers, B., Nevins, T., Kashtan, C., Dunn, D., & Payne, W. (1992). Pediatric renal transplants results with sequential immunosuppression. *Transplantation, 53*, 46–51.

Auchincloss, H., & Sachs, D. H. (1998). Xenogeneic transplantation. *Annual Review of Immunology, 16*, 433–470.

Bailey, L. L., Nehlsen-Cannarella, S. L., Doroshow, R. W., Jacobson, J. G., Martin R. D., Allard, M. W., Hyde, M. R., Dang-Bui, R. H., & Petry, E. L. (1986). Cardiac allotransplantation in newborns as therapy for hypoplastic left heart syndrome. *New England Journal of Medicine. 315*, 949–951.

Baum, M., Chinnock, R., Ashwal, S., Peverini, R., Trimm, F., & Bailey, L. (1993). Growth and neurodevelopmental outcome of infants undergoing heart transplantation. *Journal of Heart and Lung Transplantation, 12*, S211–S217.

Beck, D. E., Fennell, R. S., Yost, R. L., Robinson, J. D., Geary, D., & Richards, G. A. (1980). Evaluation of an educational program on compliance with medication regiments in pediatric patients with renal transplants. *Journal of Pediatrics, 96*, 1094–1097.

Bellinger, D. C., Wernovsky, G., Rappaport, L. A., Mayer, J. A., Castaneda, A. R., Farrell, D. M., Wessel, D. L., Lang, P., Hickey, P. R., Joans, R. A., & Newburger, J. W. (1991). Cognitive development of children following early repair of transposition of the great arteries using deep hypothermic circulatory arrest. *Pediatrics, 87*, 701–707.

Bernstein, D. M. (1977). Psychiatric assessment of the adjustment of transplanted children. In R. G. Simmons, S. D. Klein, & R. L. Simmons (Eds.), *Gift of life: The social and psychological impact of organ transplantation* (pp. 119–147). New York: Wiley.

Bock, G. H., Conners, C. K., Ruley, J., Samango-Sprouse, C. A., Conry, J. A., Weiss, I., Eng, G., Johnson, E. L., & David, C. T. (1989). Disturbances of brain maturation and neurodevelopment during chronic renal failure in infancy. *Journal of Pediatrics*, 114, 231–238.

Boucek, M. M., Faro, A., Novick, R. J., Bennett, L. E., Keck, B. M., & Hosenpud, J. D. (2001). The Registry of the International Society for Heart and Lung Transplantation: Fourth official pediatric report—2000. *Journal of Heart and Lung Transplantation, 20*, 39–52.

Brouhard, B. H., Donaldson, L. A., Lawry, K. W., McGowan, K. R. B., Drotar, D., Davis, I., Rose, S., & Tejani, A. (2000). Cognitive functioning in children on dialysis and post-transplantation. *Pediatric Transplantation, 4*, 261–267.

Crews, W. D., Jefferson, A. L., Broshek, D. K., Barth, J. T., & Robbins, M. K. (2000). Neuropsychological sequelae in a series of patients with end-stage cystic fibrosis: Lung transplant evaluation. *Archives of Clinical Neuropsychology, 15*, 59–77.

DeBolt, A. J., Stewart, S. M., Kennard, B. D., Petrik, K., & Andrews, W. S. (1995). A survey of psychosocial adaptation in long-term survivors of pediatric liver transplants. *Children's Health Care, 24*, 79–96.

Demaso, D. R., Twente, A. W., Spratt & E. G., & O'Brien, P. (1995). Impact of psychological functioning, medical severity, and family functioning in pediatric heart transplantation. *Journal of Heart and Lung Transplantation, 14*, 1102–1108.

Dew, M. A., Dunbar-Jacob, J., Switzer, G. E, DiMartini, A. F., Stilley, C., & Kormos, R. L. (2001). Adherence to the medical regimen in transplantation. In J. R. Rodrigue (Ed.), *Biopsychosocial perspectives on transplantation* (pp. 93–124). New York: Kluwer Academic/Plenum Publishers.

Dickson, D. F., & Sambrooks, J. E. (1979). Intellectual performance in children after circulatory arrest with profound hypothermia in infancy. *Archives of Disease in Childhood, 54*, 1–6.

Douglas, J. E., Hulson, B., & Trompeter, R. S. (1998). Psycho-social outcome of parents and young children after renal transplantation. *Child Care Health and Development, 24*, 73–83.

Fennell, E. B., Fennell, R. S., Mings, E., & Morris, M. K. (1988). The effects of various modes of therapy for end-stage renal disease on cognitive performance in a pediatric population: A preliminary report. *International Journal of Pediatric Nephrology, 7*, 107–112.

Fennell, R. S., Fennell, E. B., Carter, R. L., Mings, E. L., Klausner, A. B., & Hurst, J. R. (1990a). Association between renal function and cognition in childhood chronic renal failure. *Pediatric Nephrology, 4*, 16–20.

Fennell, R. S., Fennell, E. B., Carter, R. L., Mings, E. L., Klausner, A. B., & Hurst, J. R. (1990b). A longitudinal study of the cognitive function of children with renal failure. *Pediatric Nephrology, 4*, 11–14.

Fennell, R. S., Rasbury, W. C., Fennell, E. B., & Morris, M. K. (1984). Effects of kidney transplantation on cognitive performance in a pediatric population. *Pediatrics, 74*, 273–278.

Fukunishi, I., & Kudo, H. (1995). Psychiatric problems of pediatric end-stage renal failure. *General Hospital Psychiatry, 17*, 32–36.

Garralda, M. E., Jameson, R. A., Reynolds, J. M., & Postlethwaite, R. J. (1988). Psychiatric adjustment in children with chronic renal failure. *Journal of Child Psychology and Psychiatry, 29*, 79–90.

Ginns, L. C., Cosimi, A. B., & Morris, P. J. (Eds.). (1999). *Transplantation.* Malden, MA: Blackwell Science, Inc.

Gulledge, A. D., Busztu, C., & Montague, D. K. (1983). Psychosocial aspects of renal transplantation. *Urological Clinics of North America, 10*, 327–335.

Hanna, J. D., Foreman, J. W., & Chan, J. C. M. (1991). Chronic renal insufficiency in infants and children. *Clinical Pediatrics, 30*, 365–384.

Hobbs, S. A., & Sexson, S. B. (1993). Cognitive development and learning in the pediatric organ transplant recipient. *Journal of Learning Disabilities, 26*, 104–113.

Hoffmann, R. G., Rodrigue, J. R., Andres, J. M., & Novak, D. A. (1995). Moderating effects of family functioning on the social adjustment of children with liver disease. *Children's Health Care, 24*, 107–117.

Howard, R. J. (2001). Organ donation: Social policy, ethical, and legislative issues. In J. R. Rodrigue (Ed.), *Biopsychosocial perspectives on transplantation* (pp. 39–58) New York: Kluwer/Plenum Press.

Kennard, B. D., Stewart, S. M., Phelan-McAuliffe, D., Waller, D. A., Bannister, M., Fioravani, V., & Andrews, W. S. (1999). Academic outcome in long-term-term survivors of pediatric liver transplantation. *Journal of Developmental and Behavioral Pediatrics, 20*, 17–23.

Landgraf, J. M., Abetz, L., & Ware, J. E. (1996). *The Child Health Questionnaire (CHQ) user's manual.* Boston, MA: The Health Institute, New England Medical Center.

Live Organ Donor Consensus Group. (2000). Consensus statement on the live organ donor. *Journal of the American Medical Association, 284*, 2919–2926.

Madan-Swain, A., Fredrick, L. D., & Wallander, J. L. (1999). Returning to school after a serious illness or injury. In R. T. Brown (Ed.), *Cognitive aspects of chronic illness in children* (pp. 312–332). New York: Guilford.

Martin, A. B., Bricker, J. T., Fishman, M., Frazier, O. H., Price, J. K., Radovancevic, B., Louis, P. T., Cabalka, A. K., Gelb, B. D., & Towbin, J. A. (1992). Neurologic complications of heart transplantation in children. *Journal of Heart and Lung Transplantation, 11*, 933–942.

McDiarmid, S. V., Gornbein, J. A., DeSilva, P. J., Goss, J. A., Vargas, J. H., Martin, M. G., Ament, M. E., & Busuttil, R. W. (1999). Factors affecting growth after pediatric transplantation. *Transplantation, 67*, 404–411.

Mendley, S. R., & Zelko, F. A. (1999). Improvement in specific aspects of neurocognitive performance in children after renal transplantation. *Kidney International, 56*, 318–323.

Miller, O., Mamourian, A. C., Tesman, J. R., & Baylen, B. G. (1994). Long-term MRI changes in brain after pediatric open heart surgery. *Journal of Child Neurology, 9*, 390–397.

Radecki, C. M., & Jaccard, J. (1997). Psychological aspects of organ donation: A critical review and synthesis of individual and next-of-kin donation decisions. *Health Psychology, 16*, 183–195.

Roberts, M. C. (Ed.). (in press). *Handbook of pediatric psychology* (3rd ed.). New York: Guilford

Rodrigue, J. R., Geffken, G. R., & Streisand, R. M. (2000). *Child health assessment: A handbook of measurement techniques.* Needham Heights, MA: Allyn & Bacon.

Rodrigue, J. R., MacNaughton, K., Hoffmann, R. G., Graham-Pole, J., Andres, J. M., Novak, D. A., & Fennell, R. S. (1997). Transplantation in children: A longitudinal assessment of mothers' stress, coping, and perceptions of family functioning. *Psychosomatics, 38*, 478–486.

Serrano-Ikkos, E., Lask, B., Whitehead, B., & Eisler, I. (1998). Incomplete adherence after pediatric heart and heart-lung transplantation. *Journal of Heart and Lung Transplantation, 17*, 1177–1183.

Serrano-Ikkos, E., Lask, B., Whitehead, B., Rees, P., & Graham, P. (1999). Heart or heart-lung transplantation: Psychosocial outcome. *Pediatric Transplantation, 3*, p. 301–308.

Sexson, S., & Rubenow, J. (1992). *Psychiatric aspects of organ transplantation: Transplants in children and adolescents.* New York: Oxford University Press.

Sigfusson, G., Fricker, F. J., Bernstein, D., Addonizio, L. J., Baum, D., Hsu, D. T., Chin, C., Miller, S. A., Boyle, G. J., Miller, J., Lawrence, K. S., Douglas, J. F., Griffith, B. P., Reitz, B. A., Michler, R. E., Rose, E. A., & Webber, S. A. (1997). Long-term survivors of pediatric heart transplantation: A multicenter report of sixty-eight children who have survived longer than five years. *Journal of Pediatrics, 130*, 862–871.

Stewart, F. P., Abecassis, M. M., & Kaufman, D. B. (eds.). (2000). *Organ transplantation.* Georgetown, TX: Landes Bioscience.

Stewart, S. M., Campbell, R., McCallon, D., Waller, D. A., & Andrews, W. S. (1992). Cognitive patterns in school-age children with end-stage liver disease. *Journal of Developmental and Behavioral Pediatrics, 13*, 331–338.

Stewart, S. M., Hiltebeitel, C., Nici, J., Waller, D. A., Uauy, R., & Andrews, W. S. (1991). Neuropsychological outcome of pediatric liver transplantation. *Pediatrics, 87*, 367–376.

Stewart, S. M., & Kennard, B. D. (1999). Organ transplantation. In R. T. Brown (Ed.), *Cognitive aspects of chronic illness in children* (pp. 220–237). New York: Guilford Press.

Stewart, S. M., Kennard, B. D., De Bolt, A., Petrik, K., Waller, D. A., & Andrews, W. S. (1993). Adaptation of siblings of children awaiting transplantation. *Children's Health Care, 22*, 205–215.

Stewart, S. M., Kennard, B. D., Waller, D. A., & Fixler, D. (1994). Cognitive function in children who receive organ transplantation. *Health Psychology, 13*, 3–13.

Stewart, S. M., Uauy, R., Kennard, B. D., Benser, M., Waller, D., & Andrews, W. S. (1988). Mental development and growth in children with chronic liver disease of early and late onset. *Pediatrics, 82*, 167–172.

Stewart, S. M., Uauy, R., Waller, D. A., Kennard, B. D., Benser, M., & Andrews, W. S. (1989). Mental and motor development, social competence, and growth one year after successful pediatric liver transplantation. *Journal of Pediatrics, 114*, 574–581.

Streisand, R. M., & Tercyak, K. P. (2001). Evaluating the pediatric transplant patient: General considerations. In J. R. Rodrigue (Ed.), *Biopsychosocial perspectives on transplantation* (pp. 71–92). New York: Kluwer Academic/Plenum Publishers.

Studies of Pediatric Liver Transplantation [SPLIT]. Research Group. (2001). Studies of Pediatric Liver Transplantation Research Group (SPLIT): Year 2000 outcomes. *Transplantation, 72*, 463–476.

Superina, R., Acal, L., Bilik, R., & Zaki, A. (1993). Growth in children after liver transplantation on cyclosporine alone or in combination with low-dose azathioprine. *Transplant Proceedings, 25*, 2580.

Tarbell, E. E., & Kosmach, B. (1998). Parental psychosocial outcomes in pediatric liver and/or intestinal transplantation: Pretransplantation and the early postoperative period. Liver *Transplantation and Surgery, 4*, 378–387.

Tejani, A., Cortes, L., & Sullivan, E. K. (1996). A longitudinal study of the natural history of growth post-transplantation. *Kidney International, 49*(Suppl. 53), S103–S108.

Tejani, A., Fine, R., Alexander, S., Harmon, W., & Stablein, D. (1993). Factors predictive of sustained growth in children after renal transplantation. *Journal of Pediatrics, 122*, 397–402.

Tejani, A., & Sullivan, K. (1993). Long-term follow-up growth in children post-transplantation. *Kidney International, 44*(Suppl. 43), S56–S58.

Tejani, A., Sullivan, E. K., Alexander, S., Fine, R., Harmon, W., & Lilienfeld, D. (1994). Posttransplant deaths and factors that influence the mortality rate in North American children. *Transplantation, 57*, 547–553.

Thompson, S. M., DiGirolamo, A. M., & Mallory, G. B. (1996). Psychological adjustment of pediatric lung transplantation candidates and their parents. *Journal of Clinical Psychology in Medical Settings, 3*, 303–317.

Todaro, J. F., Fennell, E. B., Sears, S. F., Rodrigue, J. R., & Roche, A. K. (2000). A review of cognitive and psychological outcomes in pediatric heart transplant recipients. *Journal of Pediatric Psychology, 25*, 567–576.

Tornqvist, J., Van Broeck, N., Finkenauer, C., Rosati, R., Schwering, K. L., Hayez, J. Y., Janssen, M., & Otte, J. B. (1999). Long-term psychosocial adjustment following pediatric liver transplantation. *Pediatric Transplantation, 3*, 115–125.

Trimm, F. (1991). Physiologic and psychological growth and development in pediatric heart transplant recipients. *Journal of Heart and Lung Transplantation, 10*, 848–855.

United Network for Organ Sharing. [UNOS]. (2000). *2000 Annual Report of the U.S. Scientific Registry for Transplant Recipients and the Organ Procurement and Transplantation Network: Transplant Data: 1990–1999.* U.S. Department of Health and Human Services, Health Resources and Services Administration, Office of Special Programs, Division of Transplantation, Rockville, MD.

United States Renal Data System (1998). *USRDS 1998 Annual Report.* Bethesda, MD: National Institutes of Health, National Institute of Diabetes and Digestive and Kidney Disease.

Uzark, K. C., Sauer, S. N., Lawrence, K. S., Miller, J., Adonizio, L., & Crowley, D. C. (1992). The psychological impact of pediatric heart transplantation. *Journal of Heart and Lung Transplantation, 11*, 11602–1167.

Vricella, L. A., & Bailey, L. L. (1999). Heart transplantation in children. In L. C. Ginns, A. B. Cosimi, & P. J. Morris (Eds.), *Transplantation* (pp. 474–489). Malden, MA: Blackwell Science, Inc.

Walker, A. M., Harris, G., Baker, A., Kelly, D., & Houghton, J. (1999). Post-traumatic stress responses following liver transplantation in older children. *Journal of Child Psychology and Psychiatry, 40*, 363–374.

Wallander, J. L., & Thompson, R. J. (1995). Psychosocial adjustment of children with chronic physical conditions. In M. C. Roberts (Ed.), *Handbook of pediatric psychology* (2nd ed.; pp. 124–141). New York: Guilford.

Wijdicks, E. F. M. (Ed.). (1999). *Neurologic complications in organ transplant recipients.* Boston, MA: Butterworth-Heinemann.

Wolff, G., Strecker, K., Vester, U., Latta, K., & Ehrich, J. H. (1998). Non-compliance following renal transplantation in children and adolescents. *Pediatric Nephrology, 12*, 703–708.

Wong, M., Mallory, G. B., Jr., Goldstein, J., Goyal, M., & Yamada, K. A. (1999). Neurologic complications of pediatric lung transplantation. *Neurology, 53*, 1542–1 549.

Wray, J., Long, T., Radley-Smith, R., & Yacoub, M. (2001). Returning to school after heart or heart-lung transplantation: How well do children adjust? *Transplantation, 72*, 100–106.

Wray, J., Pot-Mees, C., Zeitlin, H., Radley-Smith, R., & Yacoub, M. (1994). Cognitive function and behavioral status in pediatric heart and heart-lung transplant recipients: The Harefield Experience. *British Medical Journal. 309*, 837–841.

Wray, J., & Yacoub, M. (1991). Psychosocial evaluation of children after open heart surgery versus cardiac transplantation. In M. Yacoub & J. R. Pepper (Eds.), *Annals of cardiac surgery* (pp. 50–55). London: Current Science Publications.

Zitelli, B. J., Miller, J. W., Gartner, C., Malatack, J. J., Urbach, A. H., Belle, S. H., Williams, L., Kirkpatrick, B., & Starzl, T. E. (1988). Changes in life-style after liver transplantation. *Pediatrics, 82*, 173–180.

PART VIII: Professional Issues

36

Training in the Delivery of Pediatric Psychology Services in School Systems

Celia Lescano
Wendy Plante
Anthony Spirito
Rhode Island Hospital and Brown Medical School

INTRODUCTION

This chapter describes the training background most useful to provide pediatric psychology services in school settings. The chapter is designed for school psychologists who wish to receive additional training in pediatric psychology and persons trained in pediatric psychology who are employed by schools to provide pediatric psychology services. Ten topic areas are reviewed including: Lifespan Developmental Psychology and Psychopathology; Disease Process and Medical Management; Child, Adolescent, and Family Assessment; Prevention and Health Promotion; Intervention Strategies; Consultation/Liaison and the Role of Multiple Disciplines in Service Delivery Systems; Research Methods and Systems Evaluation; Professional, Ethical, and Legal Issues; Social Issues Affecting Children, Adolescents, and Families; and Issues of Diversity. These recommendations have been adapted from a document prepared by a task force of the Society of Pediatric Psychology (SPP), which provided training recommendations for pediatric psychology (for details, see Spirito et al., 2001). Organization of the chapter is based on a framework proposed by Roberts and colleagues (1998) to define clinical training guidelines for services to children and adolescents.

There are several important points to consider when reading this chapter. First, one premise of the SPP Task Force report is that clinical child psychology training is the foundation for developing skills in pediatric psychology. Thus, adequate training in traditional clinical child psychology is assumed. Pediatric psychologists, however, provide not only general psychological treatments, but, in addition, need to receive training regarding health and illness. Second, these training recommendations represent an ideal course of study representing a broad area of training. Trainees will not be able to participate in all of these experiences. Exposure to all of these areas is recommended. However, to develop an area of expertise, concentrated training in one or two specific areas is advocated throughout the SPP document (Spirito et al., 2001). This training may occur at any level, including graduate school, internship, and postdoctoral fellowship. Third, there is an emphasis on providing services in primary care as well as obtaining interdisciplinary training. Providing pediatric psychology services in the schools is consistent with this approach to training. Finally, given the breadth of training described, it is important that trainees adhere to the ethical principles of psychologists and only practice within their area of competence.

In each section, the first paragraph(s) describes the importance of the topic area, and the latter paragraph(s) outlines ways in which the trainee might receive training in the topic area. Many of the sections (e.g., life span developmental psychology) are key to all aspects of psychology training. In such cases, we have tried to provide examples specific to conducting psychological services in schools. These are not offered as mandatory experiences necessary to obtain competency in pediatric psychology, but merely as several suggested experiences. There will be other routes to obtaining these competencies. The reader will note that the large majority of this training will occur outside of the school system, primarily in medical settings.

LIFE SPAN DEVELOPMENTAL PSYCHOLOGY AND PSYCHOPATHOLOGY

Life span development includes a focus on infants, preschool-age children, school-age children, adolescents, adults, and elderly persons within their ecological (family, school, community) and cultural contexts. Knowledge of typical development and behavior is essential for understanding children and their contexts, determining the presence of abnormal development and behavior, and designing appropriate effective treatments (Roberts et al., 1998, p. 295). Developmental issues specific to the practice of pediatric psychology in schools include the influence of disease process and/or prescribed medical regimens on emotional, social, motor, academic and behavioral development, as well as on physiological maturation.

Directed readings, seminars, or lectures highlighting the influence of health-related issues on developmental processes would provide background knowledge to the psychology trainee interested in working in schools. Observations of and supervised clinical activities with children at various developmental levels in health care settings are the types of experiences that may serve to consolidate background knowledge into practice.

Life span developmental psychopathology refers to emotional, behavioral, developmental, and learning disorders, occurring from infancy through old age, viewed within the context of developmental and sociocultural processes (Roberts et al., 1998, p. 295). When applied to pediatric psychology, developmental psychopathology specifically refers to the effects of illness on the manifestation of psychopathology and vice versa. Children with chronic illness demonstrate an array of emotional and behavioral responses to their diseases, ranging from resilient adaptation and positive coping behaviors to significant psychopathology. Because children with chronic illness may be at heightened risk for emotional and behavioral symptoms, knowledge of psychopathology is essential. Knowledge of psychopathology is also necessary to make a differential diagnosis between psychological conditions and health-related symptoms. Through training in life span developmental psychopathology, psychologists can also identify children with health-related issues that may place them at risk for problems of adaptation in school settings, thereby promoting positive adaptation, emotional well being, and academic achievement.

Psychology trainees interested in working in school settings should make use of directed readings, seminars, or lectures highlighting the effects of psychopathology and learning problems on children with acute and chronic illness, as well as more general health-related issues. Trainees should also observe and engage in supervised clinical activities with children in health care settings who have different types of emotional and behavioral disturbances. This type of training will prepare them for managing children with conjoint health and emotional/behavioral disturbances in schools.

Supervised clinical cases across age groups in which developmental issues are exemplified are also encouraged. For example, in chronic illness, typical developmental processes affecting peer relations and autonomy from parents may affect adherence to medical regimens. Additionally, supervised experience in differentiating emotional distress within normal limits vs. psychopathology in children with acute and chronic medical conditions is essential.

DISEASE PROCESS AND MEDICAL MANAGEMENT

Psychologists working with children with chronic illness must have a working knowledge of various medical conditions. In addition, they need to understand the adverse cognitive, academic, and behavioral effects of common nonpsychotropic medications (e.g., steroids) and other medical interventions. Although this is necessary for many activities in which pediatric school-based psychologists are engaged, it is particularly relevant for their key role in assisting in the school reentry of children with serious medical disorders. Having an appropriate level of medical knowledge is necessary to anticipate potential psychological issues for particular students, design interventions related to these factors, and consult effectively with physicians and other school personnel. A sufficient working knowledge of the terminology relevant to various aspects of disease process and treatment is necessary to communicate with the providers caring for students, as well as with family caregivers who often rapidly become knowledgeable about the specifics of their own child's illness. Familiarity with relevant medical issues is also applicable to the design of health-related prevention programs.

The familiarity with disease and treatment required for the practice of pediatric psychology in school settings will most easily be obtained through training in medical settings. Background medical information can be provided to trainees in the form of coursework, seminars, readings, and lectures on various diseases, disease processes, and medical treatment. Additionally, reviews in specialty medical journals and continuing education and pediatric grand rounds offered in most major medical centers on advances in the understanding and treatment of various childhood disorders can often provide up-to-date information at an appropriate level for the psychology trainee. For the advanced trainee, opportunities to learn about disease and treatment issues are available through attendance at pediatric bedside rounds, medical procedures, and specific teaching rounds (e.g., walking rounds, tumor boards). Rotations through primary care, community health clinics, and specialty clinics will also allow trainees to gain first-hand knowledge of various pediatric conditions, their treatments, and associated psychosocial implications.

CHILD, ADOLESCENT, AND FAMILY ASSESSMENT

All psychologists who work with children, whether they work in school settings or not, are first trained in the traditional areas of assessment in child psychology. Training in intelligence, behavioral, and personality assessment is the foundation needed to perform thorough evaluations. At the same time, assessment of the sociocultural context must be considered in all comprehensive assessments. Sociocultural factors may include social support, school environment, community resources, cultural influences, and peer relationships. Finally, training in family assessment is important despite the fact that access to families for assessment is often limited because of practical constraints of the school setting. In addition, assessment of the extended family may also raise concerns regarding confidentiality. The psychologist working in the schools must be trained to assess children of varying ages and to be cognizant of diversity, which may affect the results of the assessment. Awareness of the systems within which the child functions is also critical for an accurate assessment (Roberts et al., 1998).

In addition to the considerations described previously, which dictate that psychologists must be proficient in cognitive, personality, and behavioral assessment of the healthy child, there are a number of special circumstances relevant to pediatric psychology which need to be covered in training. First, there are variations to the assessment protocol that must be taken into account when evaluating children with chronic illness (Kupst, 1999). The psychologist working in schools must consider behavioral factors related to illness that may affect the validity of the assessment. Training must include an awareness that assessment tools with norms appropriate to children with chronic illness are to be used whenever possible. Such measures help the evaluator to differentiate the symptoms associated with disease and/or medical treatment, those secondary to poor adjustment, and those indicative of psychological dysfunction. Exposure to the most appropriate selection of instruments to assess chronically ill children is a necessary part of training and can be accomplished through practica.

Second, psychologists providing services in schools should be well versed in assessment of general family functioning as it affects adaptation to illness (Wodrich, Swerdlik, Chenneville, & Landau, 1999). Psychologists also need to have a working knowledge of the interaction between individual adaptive functioning (e.g., social support and coping) and family functioning. For example, it is important to determine whether a family is able to provide the necessary support to a child with a medical condition. A necessary part of training is supervised experience in family interview techniques that identify both family strengths, such as problem-solving abilities, and deficits in assisting the child in coping with health-related stresses.

Third, there are other important factors that affect behavior among chronically ill children. These include children's adherence to medications, health beliefs, and quality of life. Psychology trainees interested in pediatric psychology should therefore gain familiarity with how both individual and family processes affect a child's adaptation to illness and the demands of medical regimens because of their potential effect on school functioning. Seminars, lectures, and coursework are potential means to gain knowledge about how to thoroughly assess coping, adaptation, and behavioral health. Supervised training in the selection of instruments, both generic and disease-specific, for screening and a more thorough assessment of coping, adaptation, and behavioral health is an important component of training.

Fourth, other health-related concerns are commonly seen in the general school population. Identification, referral, and brief intervention for students affected by obesity and cigarette and other substance use are potentially important areas for intervention. Important areas for prevention include injury, poor nutrition, sedentary lifestyles, and risky sexual behavior, including HIV risk. Therefore, another aspect of training involves an understanding of how to assess, in a developmentally appropriate fashion, health-risk behaviors to identify the most appropriate health promotion intervention.

Finally, writing assessment reports and providing feedback to school personnel regarding health-related issues are important. School personnel are not likely to have much experience with health-related issues. Consequently, learning how to inform and educate school personnel regarding these issues is another part of training specific to the provision of pediatric psychology services within school systems. For example, it is important to convey to school personnel that diversity is not only reflected in cultural and ethnic factors, but also in health conditions (e.g., physical and sensory disabilities).

PREVENTION AND HEALTH PROMOTION

Prevention and health promotion interventions are fundamental to improving quality of life and avoiding serious problems before they arise. It is essential to reduce the incidence and prevalence of disorders by strengthening protective variables and reducing risk variables (Roberts et al., 1998, p. 298).

An important role for pediatric psychologists working in schools is promoting healthy lifestyles and preventing health-risk behaviors in both healthy and chronically ill children (Kolbe, Collins, & Cortese, 1997; Power, 2000; Wurtele, 1995). Particularly important is the promotion of exercise and a healthy diet to prevent childhood obesity and associated sequelae such as hypertension and Type 2 diabetes. For example, psychologists working in school settings might collaborate with physical education teachers, health teachers, and food service staff to implement appropriate behavioral interventions for increasing exercise and healthy food choices within the school setting (Kolbe et al., 1997). For adolescents, prevention efforts are geared toward reducing unprotected sex, smoking, substance abuse, and other high-risk health behaviors. Additionally, pediatric psychologists working in schools should be knowledgeable of physical and familial factors that may place children at risk for disease later in adulthood (e.g., environmental tobacco exposure) and take steps to mitigate these risk factors in childhood.

Given the increased risks for psychosocial problems in children with chronic illness, pediatric psychologists should use preventive interventions whenever possible to mitigate the potential development of negative emotional sequelae in these children, including intervening with and providing psychoeducation to classmates. Pediatric psychologists should also work in conjunction with pediatric health care providers and school personnel to identify and intervene with families at risk for domestic violence, child abuse, or neglect.

Trainees can learn about the science of prevention and principles of behavior change as they pertain to healthy development and prevention of disease in adulthood through didactic coursework, formal readings, or seminars. Trainees should attend seminars on screening and identification of children who are at risk for or experiencing abuse and neglect. Supervised experience in promoting healthy lifestyles/prevention in the areas of safety, nutrition, weight management, exercise, and safe sex behaviors should be obtained. Training should also include experience in addressing family risk factors, such as family violence and sexual and physical abuse, and individual risk factors, such as substance use (including nicotine).

INTERVENTION STRATEGIES

For the psychologist interested in working in schools settings, familiarity with interventions that account for developmental processes and social contexts, along with their empirical foundations, is recommended in the following areas: individual child-adolescent interventions, parent interventions, family interventions, and school and community interventions (Roberts et al., 1998 p. 296).

Trainees interested in working within school settings should receive training in theory-driven, empirically supported treatments for a variety of childhood problems. Because most of the empirically supported treatments to date are behavioral or cognitive-behavioral in nature, adequate training in individual and family-based behavioral intervention strategies should be provided. Exposure to and experience with other treatment approaches that have less empirical support, but that are promising, are also important. The unique challenges of conducting child therapy in school settings (e.g., maintaining therapy confidentiality while collaborating with school personnel) must be covered in training.

Pediatric psychologists must have a working knowledge of the child's disease status, and psychological interventions should be understood within the context of the child's medical condition and treatment. Specific interventions developed for nonmedical problems (e.g., parent training for child disruptive behavior or behavioral modification programs implemented by teachers) must be modified when co-occurring with a medical condition (e.g., cancer). Pediatric psychologists need to have a basic working knowledge of pediatric psychopharmacology, including potential concerns and differences in efficacy of various psychotropics when administered to children with health conditions (Kubiszyn, 1994; Power, DuPaul, & Shapiro, 1995).

Training in interventions applied in the school setting is necessary for assisting students with adherence to medical regimens and with pain management and disease-related symptoms that may interfere with academic and social functioning. Training should include information on and experience with stress/anxiety management, which may be used to treat anxiety secondary to reentry to school, and medical crisis counseling, such as assisting in adaptation to a recent diagnosis of a medical condition.

Other areas of intervention should also be covered. These include, family therapy to assist families in managing the impact of illness on child and family lifestyle, assistance for children with parents with a chronic or terminal illness, therapy to discuss end-of-life decisions made by both children and their family members, and bereavement counseling for issues related to death of a child or death of a child's family member. Providing psychological support to school personnel and classmates who interact with children and their families at all stages of illness is another area of importance for psychologists working in schools.

Information on empirically supported treatments relevant to pediatric psychology can be obtained through coursework and directed readings. For example, the empirically supported treatment series in the *Journal of Pediatric Psychology* (Volume 24, issue numbers 2, 3, 4, and 6; Volume 25, issue number 1) reviews data-based interventions for enuresis, encopresis, recurrent abdominal pain, disease-related pain, headaches, obesity, cancer, asthma, and diabetes. Additionally, trainees can learn about basic psychopharmacology through coursework, seminars, lectures, and readings. Trainees can obtain clinical experience through observation of clinical supervisors (in vivo or via videotape) conducting interventions for children with medical conditions, their families, and their peers.

CONSULTATION/LIAISON AND THE ROLE OF MULTIPLE DISCIPLINES IN SERVICE DELIVERY SYSTEMS

The psychologist working in the school setting consults to both school personnel and, with the increased emphasis on providing health care in primary care settings, to both community physicians and specialists or their designates, as well as medical center-based physicians. They might educate pediatric care providers about school environments, policies influencing educational practice, and approaches to treating educational and social problems. Likewise, the psychologist can educate school personnel about hospital and clinic settings, the medical model, the pediatrician's role as child advocate, and the time and monetary constraints of working in medical settings (Power, DuPaul, & Shapiro, 1995).

To provide the services described, training experiences in consultation/liaison should be conducted in a number of different settings, including schools, rehabilitation centers for children with disabilities, pediatric-medical hospitals, and office practices. Interaction with professionals from a variety of disciplines should be encouraged (e.g., social work, psychiatry, physical therapy, occupational therapy, speech and language therapy, education, and pediatrics). Given the rapidly changing health care system, service delivery in the future demands adaptability. Consequently, training should not focus solely on a single approach, setting, or discipline.

Understanding of consultation models and the ability to complete brief, focused consultations to both medical and allied health staff, and school personnel is a particularly important skill for psychologists. Effective oral and written communication is a key to consultation success in medical and school settings. Formal readings or seminars on consultation-liaison models as applied to pediatric psychology will be helpful in this respect. Trainees also benefit from observing their supervisors providing consultation. Later in training, supervised experience providing consultation to health care professionals through participation on a consultation/liaison service, in both inpatient and outpatient settings, is encouraged.

Psychologists also educate and consult to nonmedical professionals, such as teachers and counselors, regarding pediatric disease and its sequelae. For example, school staff may need to learn how to work with specialized medical equipment (e.g., feeding tubes or respiratory aides) and how to help children who use them, especially with regard to questions and teasing from classmates (Power, McGoey, Heathfield, & Blum, 1999). To that end, trainees should receive supervised experience in consultation to nonmedical settings, such as schools regarding psychological sequelae of children with medical problems. Psychologists should learn how to teach the principles of learning, development, and behavioral health to health care professionals and school personnel, as well as how to train these professionals in the integration of behavioral science into health care and school settings. This can be accomplished through observation of faculty presentations to medical students or pediatricians, as well as supervised experience in consulting with parent groups on various issues related to child development and behavior.

Because children and adolescents served by health care systems often require evaluation by multiple disciplines, it is important for psychologists to understand the role of primary care physicians and their relationship to subspecialists in the care of children's health problems. Trainees should participate in seminars, lectures, and readings on the roles and hierarchy of different disciplines and service systems in various health care settings. Later in training, the trainee can receive supervised experience in consultation to community-based pediatricians on common childhood problems. Participating in multidisciplinary staffings, team meetings, and teaching rounds, as well as hospital administration and department meetings will also sensitize the trainee to important issues related to multidisciplinary collaboration. Supervised experience regarding systems issues within the delivery of health care (e.g., communicating with attending physicians before providing a specific intervention to a patient, coordinating treatment team meetings) will also serve as a valuable follow-up to didactics on health care systems.

Managing collaboration with the multiple systems and subsystems involved in the child's care also requires good communication skills and some knowledge of common medical terms. The trainee can accomplish this, in part, through supervised experience in providing lectures on psychological factors in health and illness to medical students, pediatric residents during their primary care or psychiatry rotation, other health care professionals, and school personnel.

Equally important for the trainee is to understand family perspectives on the services the families receive and to learn skills to promote family-professional collaboration. This is an especially important role for the psychologist when caregivers themselves are struggling to understand the roles of the various providers. Trainees might learn about multidisciplinary services from a family's perspective by following a family through an entire evaluation in a multidisciplinary clinic and discussing the process with attending physicians and supervisors.

RESEARCH METHODS AND SYSTEMS EVALUATION

Psychologists need to be able to evaluate critically the quality of research in the field of pediatric psychology to apply research findings to their clinical work (Nastasi, 2000). In addition, psychologists working with pediatric populations in schools are in a unique position to contribute to research on the interplay between pediatric conditions and children's academic and social functioning (Power et al., 1995) and the efficacy of pediatric-focused prevention and intervention programs in schools. For these reasons, an empirical orientation should be integrated throughout all aspects of professional training for psychologists intending to work in school settings.

Coursework and seminars should focus on experimental design, advanced statistics, and clinical trials. Exposure to health-related outcome measures of disease severity, quality of life, and aspects of functional status that are relevant to the school setting, such as academic achievement and social functioning, should be included. Psychologists in school settings will also benefit from learning how to conduct program evaluation to assess the efficacy of school-based health promotion services for children. During training, opportunities are needed to conduct clinical research, including analogue, observational, cross-sectional, prospective, as well as controlled treatment outcome research in school settings. Collaboration with investigators outside the school system on ongoing projects may allow psychologists in schools greater participation in research and exposure to the ways in which research questions in pediatric psychology may be applied to school settings. Therefore, during training, exposure to interdisciplinary research projects, that involve coordination of the research design with other disciplines, will be valuable.

The low incidence of certain diseases in a particular school population will likely result in insufficient sample sizes for testing many empirical questions at a single site using between-groups research designs. Therefore, it will be important for research training to include a focus on experimentally controlled single-subject research designs, such as reversal and multiple baseline designs, that allow for empirically valid research at a single site with a small number of participants (Power et al., 1999). Opportunities to design qualitative research, as well as single-subject designs that may be applied in instances in which there are small samples, may also be useful training experiences for psychologists intending to investigate pediatric issues in school settings.

Psychologists working in the school setting should also develop skills in grantsmanship (Power, 2000). This is particularly important given that some schools do not provide funded time for psychologists to be involved in health care initiatives within the school setting. Federal and state agencies and private and national foundations have funds appropriated for developing innovative school-based programs. Therefore, research training should include exposure to the grant writing process by reading grants already submitted and funded, reading critiques written in response to submitted applications, and working with mentors who have been successful in obtaining research funding.

Familiarity with biomedical research concepts and terminology may be relevant to research training for those wishing to conduct pediatric psychology research in the schools. The ways in which cultural diversity and developmental issues affect research design also should be integrated into research training. Similarly, psychologists in schools will benefit from knowledge of the unique systems issues involved in conducting research in school settings (e.g., eliciting permission from school boards where applicable, working with school personnel who are being asked to provide data, and presenting research findings to school personnel).

PROFESSIONAL, ETHICAL, AND LEGAL ISSUES

Psychologists working in schools must be aware of the ethical issues and pertinent state and national legislation pertaining to child abuse reporting, duty to protect and to warn, custody evaluations, confidentiality of child and parent reports, limits of privileged communication, children's and parents' potential right to agree to or refuse treatment, informed consent or assent (child, adolescent, parent), best interest of the child, and civil commitment (Roberts, 1998).

When providing services to children and families affected by health issues and interfacing with the health care system, additional professional, ethical, and legal issues are likely to arise. For example, in making decisions about medical care, it is important to understand the rights of the parent vs. those of the child. Psychologists need to be cognizant of the complexity of serving the best interests of the child while at the same time attending to the needs and wishes of the family and the concerns of relevant school and health care personnel. When consulting with school personnel and health care providers, special ethical issues may arise regarding confidentiality, privileged communication, protection of research participants, and parental consent and refusal of medical treatment for their child (Rae, Worchel, & Brunnquell, 1995). In addition, for psychologists who reside in states that allow school-based mental health professionals to bill Medicaid and private insurance for services, ethical problems related to provision of third-party reimbursement, including confidentiality of records, providing justification for reimbursement of particular therapeutic approaches, and decision-making that weighs the best interest of the children and the limits of their insurance coverage will be relevant.

Trainees may learn about important ethical and legal issues specific to pediatric psychology through seminars, lectures, and directed readings. For example, materials published by professional organizations, including the SPP, the Society of Developmental and Behavioral Pediatrics, and the National Association of School Psychologists often address ethical and professional issues of interest to pediatric psychology. Attendance at medical rounds, particularly those that focus on ethical issues related to medical practice and hospital policies, may be relevant for trainees planning to provide school-based pediatric psychology services.

During initial periods of training, observation of supervisors providing information to school personnel and other health care professionals will help the trainee to develop an understanding of issues of confidentiality and privilege. Later in training, it will be valuable to obtain supervised experience in establishing the limits of confidentiality unique to health care and school settings; in managing cases in which parental vs. child rights and privilege are a significant concern; and in providing information obtained at school to other health care professionals, both orally and in written form, outside the school. It will be important for the trainee to develop an understanding of any differences in the ways in which ethical and legal guidelines for communication, confidentiality, and decision making differ across medical and educational contexts, including those settings in which managed care and insurance companies are relevant. Through supervision, trainees can become more adept at considering options for resolving differences in ethical and professional obligations that may arise when interfacing between the school system and the health care system.

As advances in medical diagnostic procedures (e.g., genetic testing) and treatments (e.g., organ transplantation, gene therapies) are made, new ethical dilemmas will arise. Also, new technology—such as closed-circuit televisions, speakerphones, and the Internet—allow alternative modes of communication that might be quite convenient for children with chronic illness in maintaining contact with their peers or receiving treatment services from school-based psychologists. Psychologists working with children who are medically ill in schools will need to remain updated on these new technologies and their ethical and legal implications to provide the best services to these children.

SOCIAL ISSUES AFFECTING CHILDREN, ADOLESCENTS, AND FAMILIES

Exposure to abuse, neglect, and other traumatic events; separation and loss; poverty; discrimination; and problems in access to health care resources, as well as health disparities, can result in negative consequences for children's physical and psychological well-being. Therefore, these issues are worthy of the attention of both pediatric and school psychologists regardless of the settings in which they are used. Psychologists working in school settings have a unique opportunity to identify children who are at risk for being adversely affected by such social circumstances. By identifying and providing early intervention services for children at risk for behavioral and health problems, psychologists can help to ensure more favorable outcomes. In addition, through intervention programming, psychologists in schools may play an important role in preventing the negative consequences of adverse social circumstances for children already affected by physical and psychological conditions.

An additional role for psychologists providing pediatric psychological services in the school is to serve as advocates at the individual, local, state, and national levels for children, especially regarding the provision of health care and educational accommodations (Hart & Jacobi, 1992). On a local level, psychologists providing pediatric psychology services in the schools may choose to focus their advocacy efforts on the mobilization of community response programs or the integration of community resources into existing school efforts to impact child health (Power et al., 1999).

Training should include readings, seminars, and conferences on social issues that affect health care delivery and the impact of various health care delivery systems on the well-being of children and families. At the trainee level, there are opportunities to begin involvement within local, state, and national professional associations, including the American Psychological Association (APA) and the American Academy of Pediatrics. Publications and newsletters published by national organizations—such as APA, SPP, the Society of Developmental and Behavioral Pediatrics, and local and state psychological associations—can provide information about the types of advocacy activities in which psychologists, and, in particular, pediatric psychologists, engage. Opportunities may exist through practica and internships to observe and assist school-based pediatric psychologists in such advocacy efforts. Clinical supervision of assessment and intervention with children with medical involvement should provide the trainee with insight into the impact of social stressors and societal conditions on physical and psychological functioning of children and guidance in considering the advocacy role that psychologists can play on an individual level.

ISSUES OF DIVERSITY

Psychologists need to appreciate broad sociocultural perspectives with regard to beliefs, values, expectations, and social status of the children and families as they relate to the following: cultural norms in the determination of psychopathology, interactions between providers or teachers and the patients/students and their families, the match between the children's and the families' view of problems and the provider's treatment theory and methods, service delivery systems and agencies, the children's and families' level of acculturation, and the development of ethnic identity. Particular attention should be given to differences in sexual orientation, gender roles, disability, socioeconomic status, religious preferences, and family structure (e.g., blended and one-parent families; Roberts et al., 1998, p. 297). Diversity yields a wide range of perspectives on the nature of health and mental health in children and families.

Pediatric psychologists working in schools need to be aware of the cultural and ethnic context in which medical and psychological care is delivered to children and families (Nastasi, 2000). Pediatric psychology training should enhance clinicians' sensitivity to ethnic, cultural, and religious factors that affect health beliefs, medical treatment, and relationships among families, health care professionals, and school personnel. Also, pediatric psychologists should incorporate factors related to patients' cultural background and religious beliefs into intervention programs, and their work with patients and families coping with stressful medical situations, including terminal illness.

Pediatric psychologists need to be cognizant of the problem of access to health care and disparities in health outcomes among certain minority and ethnic groups. Also important is understanding non-mainstream health practices influenced by a family's cultural or religious beliefs, the association between spirituality and health, and how cultural beliefs affect recommendations to seek and comply with medical care. Cultural beliefs may also impact parents' expectations for scholastic achievement in their children, especially in the context of an illness.

It is important for pediatric psychologists to be sensitive to issues related to sexual orientation in the families with whom they work. This issue becomes particularly important for psychologists working in schools, because adolescence is a time when confusion and distress over concerns with sexual identity can occur. In addition to their own awareness of diversity issues in the context of providing services to children and their families, psychologists working in schools often need to help school personnel and other pediatric health care providers to address these issues in their patient/student care activities. Health care providers and school personnel may fail to address these issues because of lack of information or their own discomfort regarding issues of diversity and its impact on health and illness.

Formal coursework and readings on diversity should include training on cultural beliefs relevant to health and illness, and should address issues of sexual orientation and its potential impact on adjustment and coping with health-related problems. The growing literature on the effects of religious beliefs on mental and physical health should be presented in courses or seminars and as a part of clinical supervision. Understanding of community resources, particularly those that are outside of the health care and educational system, such as religious organizations, ethnic community centers, and the use of language translators that may facilitate or impede treatment with diverse populations, is important. Trainees should receive supervised clinical experience with patients of diverse ethnic/cultural backgrounds and different sexual orientations in health care and educational settings.

CONCLUSIONS

This chapter has attempted to adapt the SPP's recommendations for the training of pediatric psychologists providing psychological services in school settings. We hope that school psychology trainees will use this chapter as a means of identifying coursework, seminars, and experiences in preparing to provide these services. In addition, the suggestions may also be helpful to pediatric psychology trainees interested in working within educational settings. School psychology training programs might also find the suggestions outlined here helpful as they develop training sequences and coursework for their students interested in developing expertise in pediatric psychology, whereas clinical psychology training programs should be encouraged to develop ways to make school experiences available for trainees in pediatric psychology. We recognize that these training guidelines are comprehensive and likely not entirely possible at the graduate school level, given all of the other requirements necessary for training as school and pediatric psychologists. There are currently a few graduate programs throughout the country that combine graduate school training in school and pediatric psychology. These programs have been successful in combining the disciplines while only adding a few additional credit hours beyond the regular doctoral requirements. However, because of the relative scarcity of such programs, the training described in this chapter will most likely be obtained at the postdoctoral level. Alternatively, psychologists may have to construct experiences in pediatric and school psychology by finding mentors who work in medical and school settings after obtaining training in their primary discipline and while established in their careers. The next decade will see the burgeoning of pediatric psychology in schools, and this has the potential for improving the availability of services for children, increasing access to care, and diminishing health disparities.

REFERENCES

Hart, P., & Jacobi, M. (1992). From gatekeeper to advocate: Transforming the role of the school counselor. New York: College Board.

Kolbe, L. J., Collins, J., & Cortese, P. (1997). Building the capacity of schools to improve the health of the nation. *American Psychologist, 52*(3), 256–265.

Kubiszyn, T. (1994). Pediatric psychopharmacology and prescription privileges: Implications and opportunities for school psychologists. *School Psychology Quarterly, 9*, 26–40.

Kupst, M. J. (1999). Assessment of psychoeducational and emotional functioning. In R. T. Brown (Ed.), *Cognitive aspects of chronic illness in children* (pp. 25–44). New York: The Guilford Press.

Nastasi, B. K. (2000). School psychologists as health-care providers in the 21st century: Conceptual framework, professional identity, and professional practice. *School Psychology Review, 29*, 540–554.

Power, T. J. (2000). Commentary—The school psychologist as a community-focused, public health professional: Emerging challenges and implications for training. *School Psychology Review, 29*(4), 557–559.

Power, T. J., DuPaul, G. J., & Shapiro, E. S. (1995). Pediatric school psychology: The emergence of a subspecialty. *School Psychology Review, 24*(2), 244–257.

Power, T. J., McGoey, K. E., Healthfield, L. T., & Blum, N. J. (1999). Managing and preventing chronic health problems in children and youth: School psychology's expanded mission. *School Psychology Review, 28*(2), 251–263.

Rae, W. A., Worchel, F. F., & Brunnquell, D. (1995). Ethical and legal issues in pediatric psychology. In M. C. Roberts (Ed.), *Handbook of pediatric psychology* (2nd ed., pp. 19–38). New York: The Guilford Press.

Roberts, M. C. (1998). Innovations on specialty training: The clinical child psychology program at the University of Konsas. *Professional Psychology: Research and Practical, 29*, 394–397.

Roberts, M., Carlson, C., Erickson, M., Friedman, R., LaGreca, A., Lemanek, K., Russ, S., Schroeder, C., Vargas, L., & Wohlford, P. (1998). A model for training psychologists to provide services for children and adolescents. *Professional Psychology: Research and Practice, 29*, 293–299.

Spirito, A., Brown, R., D'Angelo, E., Delamater, A., Rodrigue, J., & Siegel, L. (2003). *Society of Pediatric Psychology Task Force Report: Recommendations for the training of pediatric psychologists. Journal of Pediatric Psychology, 28*, 85–98.

Wodrich, D. L., Swerdlik, M. E., Chenneville, T., & Landau, S. (1999). HIV/AIDS among children and adolescents: Implications for the changing role of *school psychologists. School Psychology Review, 28*(2), 228–241.

Wurtele, S. K. (1995). Health promotion. In M. C. Roberts (Ed.), *Handbook of pediatric psychology* (2nd ed., pp. 200–218). New York: The Guilford Press.

37

Clinical Opportunities for the Pediatric Psychologist Within the School Setting

Deborah L. Anderson
Lloyd A. Taylor
Alexandra Boeving
Medical University of South Carolina

INTRODUCTION

The current climate of managed health care services and the seemingly insurmountable challenge of obtaining third-party payments for services rendered by health care providers within the medical setting have placed pediatric psychologists under ever-increasing pressure to provide time-limited, problem-focused, and evidenced-based psychological services to children. One means of meeting this challenge is to provide psychological services in school-based settings. This chapter will focus on the diverse roles and clinical opportunities that are potentially available to pediatric psychologists wishing to extend their practice to school settings. These roles extend beyond traditional services provided by psychologists within the school setting (i.e., providing mandated assessment and intervention treatment for children with disabilities). We will discuss three novel domains within the school setting, where pediatric psychology has the opportunity to make significant contributions to the mental and academic health of school-age children. These areas include (1) providing primary mental health care, (2) meeting the psychological and social needs of children with chronic medical conditions, and (3) developing and implementing evidenced-based research programs in the school setting.

PRIMARY MENTAL HEALTH CARE OF SCHOOL-AGE CHILDREN

Over the last decade, as a result of significant changes in the health care system from the advent of managed care services, modern-day pediatricians are frequently faced with the challenge of treating larger numbers of patients with varying illnesses in shorter amounts of time (Wodrich & Landau, 1999). In a recent study that examined the prevalence of different conditions within the primary care setting, Kronke and Mangelsdorff (1989) demonstrated that 30–75% of patients seen by primary care physicians experience symptoms not attributable to physical illnesses (i.e., fatigue, sadness, irritability, gastrointestinal symptoms, and headaches). Estimates of the prevalence of various behavior problems and/or mental health conditions (i.e., attention-deficit hyperactivity disorder [ADHD], conduct disorder, oppositional defiant disorder) treated within the pediatric setting range from 9% to 38% (Brown et al., 2001). A large proportion of the modern-day pediatrician's clinical practice is devoted to the management and care of mental health conditions and behavior disorders rather than exclusively to the treatment of physical illness.

Although pediatricians are trained intensively in the management and care of physical illness, their training in the treatment and care of childhood mental health conditions and behavior problems may be variable across pediatric training programs. The lack of standardized training among pediatricians in the realm of behavioral health, coupled with the logistical demands of their practices, often hamper the pediatrician's ability to manage children effectively who are seen in their office because of psychosocial and psychological conditions. For example, pediatricians typically receive minimal training in the area of psychological problems and disorders of childhood, whereas pediatric psychologists routinely devote between 5 and 7 years of training toward developing expertise in the assessment and treatment of these conditions. In addition, logistical demands of pediatric practice differ significantly from those found within the context of pediatric psychology. Although the typical length of a visit to the pediatrician's office ranges from 10 to 15 min, the length of time required to effectively manage behavior problems and teach appropriate parenting skills ranges from six to eight 50-min therapy sessions with appropriate follow-up contact as needed. Differences in both the extent of training devoted to behavioral problems, as well as the demands of pediatric practices, place pediatricians in the tenuous position of being challenged by managing difficult behavioral and emotional problems commonly experienced by their young patients.

Another burden placed on today's pediatricians is acquiring an adequate understanding of legislation aimed at assisting children with various mental and/or psychosocial conditions so as to enable intervention with school placement issues in accordance with the federal mandates. Currently, there exist numerous laws that advocate for the educational needs of children with mental health conditions (i.e., children who qualify for special education needs and service entitlements because of a mental health condition). These laws must be readily understood, implemented, and enforced by health care providers treating these children. Expecting pediatricians to remain abreast of these ever-changing legislative demands and also to find the time necessary to dedicate to the cause of advocating for these children within the educational setting is unrealistic; even pediatricians with the best of intentions are hard pressed to find sufficient time in their busy practices to manage these legislative nuances effectively.

The aforementioned training and logistical issues that pediatricians commonly experience, along with the burgeoning number of traditional mental health and psychosocial cases treated within the pediatric primary care setting (cf., Brown et al., 2001), provide support for employing pediatric psychologists within the school setting in an attempt to address these needs and conditions. Pediatric psychologists enjoy the unique position of bridging the gap between traditional medicine and child psychology. Trained specifically in the assessment, management, and maintenance of mental health disorders of childhood, pediatric psychologists have the clinical skills and expertise required to manage children who are experiencing various mental health conditions and/or disorders and are currently cared for within the context of the pediatrician's office. The use of school-based treatment to assess, manage, and treat psychological difficulties within the context that children spend most of their time is a model solution to the aforementioned difficulties experienced in the pediatrician's office. Working within the school setting would also be ideal for pediatric psychologists, because it would allow the treating professional to understand the contextual demands placed on their patients. Treating these children within the context of the school would enable the pediatric psychologist to communicate effectively with school administrators, parents, teachers, and pediatricians to advocate for the optimal treatment for special needs children. Finally, employing pediatric psychologists within the school setting would enhance the likelihood that children would be seen and treated within a timely fashion and that parents would participate in the treatment.

There are numerous additional clinical issues/problems that could be effectively managed within the school setting by pediatric psychologists, rather than within the pediatric health care setting. Assessment of psychopathology (i.e., mental health disorders of childhood), clinical intervention, and parent training are only a few examples of interventions that could be managed within the school setting by pediatric psychologists. Addressing these issues and/or conditions in the school will facilitate their management and care, and will simultaneously alleviate the burden of case management currently found within pediatric health care settings. For example, providing clinical intervention in the school setting to youth diagnosed with conduct disorder will enable the pediatric psychologists to implement in vivo behavioral management strategies tailored to meet the specific system demands of the school setting as they relate to this condition. School-based clinical intervention will also increase the likelihood that treatment will occur because of diminished problems with adherence.

In addition to addressing ongoing clinical issues within the school setting, pediatric psychologists working in the school setting will be able to provide training programs and workshops to school officials regarding proper administration of various behavioral techniques aimed at addressing behavior difficulties (i.e., oppositional defiant disorder, conduct disorder, ADHD) and thereby improve the child's ability to function socially as well as academically. The presence of the pediatric psychologist within the school will additionally enhance the continuity of care and the consistency of application of various behavioral strategies, thereby increasing their efficacy in the classroom setting. It is far more likely that this level of intervention could occur within the school setting, compared with the pediatrician's office due to the previously mentioned logistical demands found in the pediatric setting. By employing pediatric psychologists within the school system, the mental health treatment and care of children become immeasurably more efficient.

Aside from the implementation of behavior strategies and management of these strategies in the school setting, a consistent presence of a pediatric psychologist in the school would augment the opportunities to provide preventative intervention. Issues such as alcohol and/or substance abuse, school bullying, reintegration issues for childhood survivors of physical illnesses, bereavement, and management of various psychiatric conditions found in children could be addressed through daily interactions between school officials and pediatric psychologists.

CHILDREN WITH CHRONIC MEDICAL CONDITIONS

Another important arena for the pediatric psychologist working within the school system involves children with chronic medical conditions. Children with chronic illnesses and survivors of pediatric illness are at risk for significant social, emotional, behavioral, and academic difficulties (Wallander & Thompson, 1995). Reintegration into school after a chronic illness or prolonged absence is often a significant challenge for children. Typically, clinical psychologists not directly associated with the school that the child attends are asked to address reintegration problems in time-limited sessions with the child, peers, and school officials. Often, reintegration difficulties are disease-specific (i.e., frequent coughing for patients with cystic fibrosis, blood sugar management for children with diabetes, gastrointestinal difficulties for children with Crohns disease), and frequently create social problems and significant stress for children with chronic conditions. Devoid of professional intervention, these children are forced to manage difficult social nuances themselves. A common solution to these problems is to educate peers of these children about the medical condition before reintegration (Madan-Swain et al., 1999). However, brief psychoeducation attempts may fail to assist the child with a chronic condition in his/her daily work with peer groups. The routine presence of a pediatric psychologist within the school system would greatly reduce the burden and stressors placed on childhood survivors of physical illnesses/conditions, because these children would have a familiar in-house professional and support system to assist them with navigation of social difficulties resulting from their physical illness.

A primary goal for the chronically ill child is to adjust to the demands related to the tasks of childhood, as well as to manage the demands of illness and the treatment regimen. The pediatric psychologist has a vital role in facilitating this balance. Aspects of this role include consulting with the school and hospital staff, assessing for potential cognitive or emotional difficulties, working with the child and family, and intervening at the level of the school setting. It is important for the pediatric psychologist to work closely with school personnel (i.e., teachers and guidance counselors) to identify problems that the child may be experiencing. Teachers spend a great deal of time with the child throughout the day, and are thus an excellent source of information and collaboration for the psychologist. Certain aspects of the child's functioning that require monitoring include the presence of depression or anxiety, as well as quality of life. Communication with the child's teacher is essential to obtain an adequate assessment of the child's functioning. It is often helpful for the pediatric psychologist to observe in-classroom behavior as well to obtain an assessment of the child's functioning in a full spectrum of activities.

After assessing for functioning difficulties, intervention opportunities with the child can include problem solving, educational intervention strategies, and coping interventions. The pediatric psychologist can work with the child to identify areas of emotional and social distress, and facilitate the identification of strategies to ameliorate this distress. Additionally, there is often a lack of children's understanding of diagnosis-specific information that has been given to them by their health care providers or caregiver (which may be related to anxiety). The pediatric psychologist's role can include educational interventions that engage the child at a developmentally appropriate level regarding his or her illness and medical treatment. Finally, coping interventions can serve to increase the child's repertoire of strategies with which to approach stressful situations.

Childhood chronic illness does not merely impact the child; rather, it is an event that affects the child's entire family system (Kazak & Nachman, 1991). In intervening with the childhood chronic illness population, it is essential to enlist the aid of caregiver and family members in optimizing the child's benefits from intervention efforts. Parents have been demonstrated as integral to their children's self-regulatory skills when in duress (e.g. during hospitalization, or procedural pain, such as a needle prick). Visualization, guided imagery, and progressive muscle relaxation are easily learned by parents, and can provide a common focus for parent and child during painful medical procedures. Conducting a comprehensive functional analysis will delineate target symptoms to which the pediatric psychologist may tailor intervention efforts (which will obviously reduce total time from treatment onset to symptom alleviation). The psychologist can then train family members in assisting children with learned techniques and establishing an appropriate home environment to facilitate the child's gains from intervention. Additionally, the pediatric psychologist should work with the family to facilitate open communication and appropriately positive attitudes about the child's illness, because these are characteristics of family functioning that reliably predict positive child adjustment outcomes.

Intervening with the ill child includes not only the family, but also necessitates targeting the child's school and hospital settings. The school environment does not merely serve an educational purpose for the child, but is a primary source of social interaction as well. It is thus important for the child to be an active participant in the school environment when medically possible, and for the transitions from hospitalization and home-based care to school to be conducted with minimal distress. The pediatric psychologist can provide services that target multiple aspects of the school-based functioning, including the child's reintegration into the school setting and consultation regarding homebound education and other mandatory services provided to the child by the school system.

School reintegration programs are very important in assisting with the child's social and educational transition back to school (Madan-Swain et al., 1999). It is important for the child's classmates and school staff to receive education about the child's illness in efforts to prevent teasing about symptoms or treatment sequelae (e.g., loss of hair in children receiving chemotherapy), educable fears (e.g., questions of contagion), and activities that classmates may perceive as special privileges (e.g., children with diabetes being allowed to eat snacks more frequently than healthy peers). Additionally, pediatric psychologists need to focus on the child's emotional responses to returning to school, as well as areas of academic difficulty. Psychologists can serve as liaisons and advocates for children and families within the school system in obtaining needed services (as indicated by child assessment). These services can include individualized educational plans, accessible classrooms for children with physical disabilities, and specific attention to learning disabilities that may be associated with the child's illness and treatment.

Pediatric psychologists also consult with families and schools on the appropriateness of homebound education. If necessary for medical reasons, children have the legal right to receive state-funded education in their home environment. This is an important service and essential for facilitating educational gains for children who are currently unable to attend school. However, it is not uncommon for children who have sustained illnesses also to have been on homebound education to develop an anxiety response regarding returning to school. An important role for pediatric psychologists is to intervene with the child in this transition, as well as to consult with the caregiver regarding the timing of the child's return to school. It is developmentally optimal for children to be in social settings with their peers, and thus a primary goal is for ill children to resume functioning in a school environment as quickly as is medically feasible.

Along with the school system, the hospital is another organization in which the chronically ill child and family routinely function. An important role of the pediatric psychologist is to serve as a liaison between the family, school, and medical team. Coordinating efforts across these system levels will increase the efficacy of applied interventions (via maintaining consistency of intervention components). Additionally, by serving as a system liaison, the psychologist can facilitate accurate communication between families, schools, and the treatment team. In utilizing this approach, problems experienced at any level of the system are identified and solved more efficiently, and thus the child's needs (medically and psychologically) are increasingly met. This can be an important role for pediatric psychologists in school settings.

DEVELOPING AND IMPLEMENTING EVIDENCED-BASED RESEARCH PROGRAMS

It is clear that the school environment offers substantial clinical opportunities for the pediatric psychologist, including assessment and intervention with youngsters exhibiting behavioral problems typically addressed in the pediatric primary care clinic. However, the role of the pediatric psychologist working in the school setting would extend beyond providing clinical services to individual students. Instead, the school environment offers the pediatric psychologist the opportunity to contribute to the understanding of mental health aspects of childhood problems and difficulties specific to the school environment. These problems include issues such as absenteeism, disciplinary referrals, and grade retention and dropout. School dropout is one of the most pressing school-related difficulties facing educators today (Mattison, 2000).

Through the development of empirically based research programs, pediatric psychologists working within the school system have the opportunity to impact significantly the number of students who are absent, suspended, expelled, and/or retained, and ultimately, the number of students who fail to complete school before earning a high school diploma.

Absenteeism has generally been attributed to either school refusal or truancy. These categories are considered as distinct, because youngsters with school refusal often have been diagnosed with either an anxiety disorder, such as separation anxiety or school phobia (Last & Strauss, 1990), or with a depressive disorder (Bernstein & Garfinkel, 1986), whereas students who are truant typically exhibit conduct disorder (Berg, 1996). However, these reports are based largely on clinical anecdotes. There is little empirical information on the cognitive, personality, or family characteristics of youngsters who are frequently absent from school or on the longitudinal course of frequent school absenteeism. Not only does the pediatric psychologist functioning within the school setting have the opportunity to intervene on an individual basis with youngsters who are frequently absent from school, but the pediatric psychologist also is in an ideal position to obtain more information about risk factors for chronic absenteeism through carefully designed empirical studies. The results of such research will contribute substantially to our ability to design evidence-based interventions to address this problem effectively.

Issues related to disciplinary referrals, including suspension and expulsion, have only recently been investigated in the literature. In their study of more than 10,000 midwestern middle school students, Skiba, Peterson, and Williams (1997) conclude that disciplinary referrals were a frequent occurrence in middle school and were most commonly the result of noncompliant or disrespectful behavior. Disciplinary referrals were more frequent among minority boys of low socioeconomic status and those who had been classified as emotionally disabled. In a separate study of suspended middle and high school students, it was found that suspended students exhibited elevated levels of externalizing behavior problems (Morgan-D'Atrio, Northup, LaFleur, & Spera, 1996). To date, there is no outcome research examining the efficacy of suspension. Likewise, research on students who have been expelled is sparse. In their investigation of 158 students ranging from kindergartners to twelfth graders who had been expelled, Morrison and D'Incau (1997) found that risk factors for expulsion included poor academic performance, frequent absenteeism from school, and a prior history of disciplinary referrals and suspensions. Again, no outcome research can be found demonstrating effective interventions for these students, providing yet another opportunity for the pediatric psychologist functioning within the school system to make a substantial contribution to our understanding of how to assist these youngsters most effectively.

Finally, the issue of grade retention, and subsequently higher levels of dropout, is a serious social and educational problem that typically leads to negative consequences for both the individual and society. Students who are retained are more likely to drop out of high school before graduation than students who are not retained (Ensminger & Slusarick, 1992; Jimerson, 1999; Roderick, 1994, 1995; Rumberger, 1995). By the time they enter the ninth grade, half of all children in the United States will have failed at least one grade or will have dropped out of school entirely (Jimerson, 1999). Recent research indicates that compared with their classmates who have not failed a grade, students who are retained are more likely to drop out of high school by age 19, less likely to earn a diploma by age 20, and less likely to enroll in a postsecondary education program. Retained students who have been followed into their early 20's earn significantly lower wages than do their counterparts who are routinely promoted. In addition, their employers rate them as less competent. Even when compared with a group of low-achieving students who had never been held back, the retained students still performed more poorly in all of these areas. Therefore, grade retention represents another area of importance for investigation by the pediatric psychologist employed within the school setting. Future research hopefully has the potential to impact school dropout rates positively.

Research has been fundamental in the identification of factors, such as grade retention, that predict increased risk of school dropout; however, there is far less information available about effective intervention strategies. We currently know much more about who drops out of school than we do about what components make for a viable intervention program or what designates a program as successful in reducing the rates of school dropout. In this regard, a number of dropout prevention programs have been developed and implemented, although very few incorporate systematic outcome measures or systematic evaluation of their program and its components.

The school setting affords the pediatric psychologist an opportunity not only to develop programs aimed at ameliorating existing problems, but also to implement programs that promote healthy behaviors among children. These programs typically target behaviors demonstrated through empirical investigation to compromise both current and future health status of children. The recent advent of programs aimed at reducing smoking behaviors among youth serve as just one example of such prevention programs. There are multiple roles for the pediatric psychologist in smoking cessation programs, including providing education about the health risks of smoking, debunking myths about smoking prevalence among family members and peers, assisting children in identifying social pressures to smoke, and developing strategies to resist these peer pressures. Outcome evaluation has indicated moderate success of school-based curriculums in smoking prevention. Pediatric psychologists have the opportunity to make substantial contributions in school settings through health promotion programs.

The pediatric psychologist who works within the school setting is in an ideal position to design and implement a scientifically based program that serves as a model of how to help students at-risk for dropping out of school to succeed in school and beyond by tapping into readily available community resources and guiding them in working collaboratively. This research opportunity for the psychologist working in the school offers the unique opportunity of not only impacting the individual student, but also through research enriching and extending the school completion interventions that are currently available for use.

CONCLUSIONS

Children attending school have multiple needs that are by no means limited to the academic realm. Pediatric psychologists are in a unique position to address directly many of these needs when they are employed directly by the school system. In addition to serving in the traditional role of completing routine assessment and intervention of students with learning disabilities, the pediatric psychologist is well equipped to manage mental health conditions and behavior disorders currently addressed in the primary care setting. Moreover, the extensive training and background of the pediatric psychologist renders them particularly capable of providing clinical services (i.e., assessment, interventions, serving as a liaison between school personnel, medical team, and family) to children within the school setting. Finally, the school environment offers substantial opportunity for the pediatric psychologist to extend empirical knowledge of how best to develop and implement behavioral programs aimed at improving chronic school-related problems, such as absenteeism, disciplinary referrals, grade retention, and school dropout. For the psychologist with a strong interest in pediatrics and the appropriate training and experience, the school environment is a rich and rewarding possibility for employment.

REFERENCES

Berg, I. (1996). School avoidance, school phobia, and truancy. In M. Lewis (Ed.), *Child and adolescent psychiatry: A comprehensive textbook* (2nd ed., pp. 1104–1109). Baltimore, MD: Williams & Williams.

Bernstein, G. A., & Garfinkel, B. D. (1986). School phobia: the overlap of affective and anxiety disorders. *Journal of the American Academy of Child and Adolescent Psychiatry, 25*, 235–241.

Brown, R., Freeman, W., Perrin, W., Perrin, J., Stein, M., Amler, R., Feldman, H., Pierce, K., & Wolraich, M. (2001). Prevalence and assessment of attention-deficit/hyperactivity disorder in primary care settings. *Pediatrics, 17*(3), 1–11.

Ensminger, M., & Slusarick, A. (1992). Paths to high school graduation or dropout: A longitudinal study of a first grade cohort. *Sociology of Education, 65*(2), 95–113.

Jimerson, S. R. (1999). On the failure of failure: Examining the association between early grade retention and education and employment outcomes during late adolescence. *Journal of School Psychology, 37*(3), 243–272.

Kazak, A. E., & Nachman, G. S. (1991). Family research on childhood chronic illness: Pediatric oncology as an example. *Journal of Family Psychology, 4*(4), 462–483.

Kroenke, K., Mangelsdorff, A. D. (1989). Common symptoms in ambulatory care: Incidence, evaluation, therapy, and outcome. *American Journal of Medicine, 86*, 262–266.

Last, C. G., & Strauss, C. C. (1990). School refusal in anxiety-disordered children and adolescents. *Journal of the American Academy of Child & Adolescent Psychiatry, 29*, 31–35.

Madan-Swain, A., Fredrick, L. D., & Wallander, J. L. (1999). Returning to school after a serious illness or injury. In R. T. Brown (Ed.), *Cognitive aspects of chronic illness in children.* (pp. 312–332). New York: Guilford Press.

Mattison, R. E. (2000). School consultation: A review of research on issues unique to the school environment. *Journal of the American Academy of Child & Adolescent Psychiatry, 39*(4), 402–412.

Morgan-D'Atrio, C., Northup, J., LaFleur, L., & Spera, S., (1996). Toward prescriptive alternatives to suspensions: A preliminary evaluation. *Behavior Disorders, 21*, 190–200.

Morrison, G. M., & D'Incau, B. (1997). The web of zero-tolerance: Characteristics of students who are recommended for expulsion from school. *Education and Treatment of the Child, 20*, 316–335.

Roderick, M. (1994). Grade retention and school dropout: Investigating the association. *American Educational Research Journal, 31*, 729–759.

Roderick, M. (1995). Grade retention and school dropout. Policy debate and research questions. *The Research Bulletin, 15*, 88–92.

Rumberger, R. (1995). Dropping out of middle school: A multilevel analysis of students and schools. *American Educational Research Journal, 32*(3), 583–625.

Skiba, R. J., Peterson, R. L., & Williams. T. (1997). Office referrals and suspension: Disciplinary interventions in middle school. *Education and Treatment of the Child, 20*, 295–315.

Wallander, J. L., & Thompson, R. J., Jr. (1995). Psychosocial adjustment of children with chronic physical conditions. In M.C. Roberts (Ed.), *Handbook of pediatric psychology* (2nd ed., pp. 124–141). New York: Guilford Press.

Wodrich, D., & Landau, S. (1999). School psychologists: Strategic allies in the contemporary practice of primary care pediatrics. *Clinical Pediatrics, 38*, 597–606.

38

Ethical and Legal Issues for Pediatric Psychology and School Psychology

William A. Rae
Constance J. Fournier
Texas A&M University

INTRODUCTION

Pediatric psychologists and school psychologists are more alike than they are different. Each profession has typical setting and specific training standards, yet ethical and legal issues have much in common. Both have prescribed ethical standards of conduct. The *Ethical Principles of Psychologists and Code of Conduct* by the American Psychological Association (APA, 2002) is applicable to both pediatric psychologists and school psychologists. In addition, school psychologists are provided additional guidance from the *Professional Conduct Manual* by the National Association of School Psychologists (NASP, 2000), which contains both the "Principles for Professional Ethics" and "Guidelines for the Provision of School Psychological Services." Both professional groups are also bound by the *Standards for Educational and Psychological Testing* (APA, AERA, & NCME, 1998) regarding the administration or interpretation of psychological tests. Legal issues are also similar, because both professions practice with children, which requires awareness of their special legal standing as minors.

There are several general ethical principles that pediatric psychologists and school psychologists must consider in more depth because of their practice with children. First, psychologists should practice inside of their areas of competence. This is probably the most important principle that pediatric psychologists should address when dealing with patients with educational issues or school psychologists should address when dealing with students with medical issues. Second, psychologists must adjust their interventions to the needs of any special population with whom they work. The pediatric psychologist and school psychologist must be sensitive to the cultural, ethnic, gender, religious, and socioeconomic status differences of patients or students, as well as educational diversity that may impact assessment, intervention, or consultation activities. Third, psychologists must also be concerned with the welfare and rights of their clients. They should treat any student or patient with respect and promote their well-being and welfare. This principle includes such factors as promoting confidentiality, fairness, and autonomy during their professional interactions. Within the scope of helping the child, the pediatric psychologist and school psychologist may have many other "clients" (e.g., parents, teachers, nurses) whose welfare and rights need to be respected. Finally, psychologists should be honest and straightforward in their dealings with their students and patients during assessment, consultation, and intervention activities. School psychologists and pediatric psychologists must also be aware of their own values and biases, and should communicate these in a straightforward way to clients.

Although it is beyond the scope of this chapter to delve into detailed examination of these two professions, exploring commonalties and differences as they pertain to ethical and legal issues may be helpful. In this chapter, general information about both professions will be presented. Common interests and concerns will be discussed, as well as issues that tend to differentiate the two professions within the purview of ethical and legal issues for the pediatric psychologist dealing with school issues and for the school psychologist dealing with health issues. Finally, recommendations regarding how to maintain ethical and legal practices with the common goal to serve the needs of children will be discussed.

COMMON ELEMENTS FOR PEDIATRIC PSYCHOLOGY AND SCHOOL PSYCHOLOGY

By their very names, pediatric psychologists and school psychologists announce the essence of their professional practice—the care of children in a particular practice setting. In this section, discussion of common elements of the two professions provides a foundation for the later discussion of legal and ethical issues.

Child Focus

Both school psychology and pediatric psychology serve children, either directly or indirectly. Direct services can include assessment and intervention. Both the school psychologist and the pediatric psychologist can provide a similar range of services that can include, but are not limited to: intellectual, educational, and socioemotional assessment; individual, group, and family therapy; and specific intervention to meet a specific need, such as social skills training. Indirect services include systems consultation and services to those who are directly responsible to the child. The "client" of the indirect service will vary according to setting. The school psychologist most typically provides indirect services for school personnel (e.g., teachers, principals), and the pediatric psychologist most typically provides services for health care professionals (e.g., pediatricians, nurses).

Developmental Focus

School psychologists and pediatric psychologists have an orientation of viewing problems as developmental adaptations rather than a psychopathological process. Often, both the pediatric psychologist and school psychologist see a child's behavior as a variant of normal development, or alternately as a way of coping with a deviant situation. Both the pediatric psychologist and school psychologist tend to see a variety of children, most who are "normal," except for some specific issue such as a learning disability or a chronic illness. This can be different than other disciplines—such as clinical child psychology or child psychiatry—where the focus and the caseload are typically with children who have significant psychopathology.

Institutional Practice

Both the pediatric psychologist and school psychologist typically work within a larger institution (e.g., hospital, clinic, school). The pediatric psychologist and school psychologist typically use a systemic orientation within the institution. There is also a similar understanding that interventions are most effective if coordinated across the institutional hierarchies of their home institution. These settings place unique demands on the professional practice of psychology. In particular, there are institutional demands that may conflict with the welfare of students or patients, yet cannot be ignored.

Multidisciplinary Focus

Both the pediatric psychologist and school psychologist work with colleagues from other disciplines. This can be within both formal and informal contexts. In schools, teams such as the Individual Education Plan (IEP) committee or a behavioral assessment team will have designated roles for the school psychologist. In the health care setting, teams such as a transplant team or multidisciplinary assessment team will often include the pediatric psychologist. Informal interactions for both pediatric psychologists and school psychologists occur with a variety of professionals, such as administrators or physicians and in a variety of ways (e.g., telephone conversation, meeting in the hallway). Both the pediatric psychologist and school psychologist work with common support professionals, such as the occupational therapist, speech pathologist, and physical therapist. Whatever the setting, the pediatric psychologist and school psychologist often serve as translator, interpreting assessment information to colleagues, and utilizing other discipline information to specifically benefit the child. Furthermore, the psychologist often will assist in how to incorporate the suggestions of the multidisciplinary team into plans of action, such as the treatment plan or IEP goals.

Assessment Expertise

Both the pediatric psychologist and school psychologist assess children and adolescents. Assessment can serve many purposes. The rationale for assessment is similar for both the school psychologist and pediatric psychologist. Typically, both assess where the child is currently (baseline) to assist in the determination of appropriate interventions. Assessment can be used to review the effect of intervention and can assist in examining institutional impact as well. Tools for assessment will be the same or similar for the most part; however, there may be pieces of assessment that are germane to the setting (e.g., the school psychologist may incorporate social rating scales, and the pediatric psychologist may use a pain scale.) Both the pediatric psychologist and school psychologist utilize a diagnostic-prescriptive orientation toward children and adolescents; both diagnose cases having complex social, emotional, intellectual, and physical problems. Both generate practical recommendations that follow from the child's diagnosed problem.

Consultation Expertise

Both pediatric psychologists and school psychologists utilize consultation as a primary intervention strategy focus (Conoley & Conoley, 1992; Drotar, 1995). Effective intervention often must go beyond the individual and reach into the institution. Whether working with those most involved with the child (such as the nurse or the teacher) or with those who can provide less direct but no less vital intervention (such as administrators), consultation is an important tool for both the pediatric psychologist and school psychologist.

Intervention Expertise

Pediatric psychologists and school psychologists use appropriate, empirically supported approaches to intervention with children or adolescents within their respective school or health care institution. Both the pediatric psychologist and school psychologist develop interventions for the individual child, the child's family, and adults caring for the child (e.g., teacher, principal, physician, nurse), or for the institution where the psychologist practices (e.g., school, hospital). This can take the form of individually based interventions (e.g., individual psychotherapy) or more systemic interventions (e.g., develop a behavior modification plan for a classroom). Intervention is often brief, solution-focused, and, most often, behavioral.

Prevention Orientation

Both the pediatric psychologist and school psychologist have as part of their training and as their general orientation a prevention focus. Primary prevention, that is, providing intervention to avoid problems from starting is important to both school and pediatric psychologists. From programs involving social skills training to playground and safety belt use, prevention and early intervention are themes seen throughout the respective bodies of literature (e.g., Meyers & Nastasi, 1999; Roberts & McNeal, 1995).

PEDIATRIC PSYCHOLOGISTS WORKING WITH EDUCATIONAL ISSUES

One basic ethical concern for pediatric psychologists assessing, consulting, or intervening with children who have significant educational problems involves the question of competence. Pediatric psychologists receive little training in academic assessment, academic intervention, and consultation issues in school settings (Spirito et al., in press). At the same time, pediatric psychologists commonly work with children who have a range of educational disabilities, some obvious, some less so. Typically, the pediatric psychologist will know this first hand through the interview with the parent or the child. Sometimes the information will come through a report generated by other professionals. At times, the information may be conveyed, either through oversight, or sometimes by a parent deliberately withholding information to receive an "unbiased" opinion. The pediatric psychologist must consider what kind of assessment is needed for the child. Pediatric psychologists may use a standard battery of psychological tests to provide information (e.g., cognitive, academic, personality), but often the focus of the assessment does not address educational issues directly. Although having a typical battery is often helpful, the child may not be able to perform optimally because of learning disabilities, and/or may have recently been assessed using similar or identical instruments and procedures. This latter situation can occur for several reasons, including limited parent and child knowledge of the assessments conducted in the school setting, and/or not understanding how assessments can have similar or identical procedures.

Pediatric psychologists often are unfamiliar with the culture of schools. Schools have customs, language, and procedures that may be unfamiliar to a psychologist outside the school system. Schools often use acronyms to describe various programs or procedures in the educational system (e.g., IEP) that may not be well-known to pediatric psychologists. In the same way, pediatric psychologists often do not know about the appropriate legal mandates surrounding assessment, intervention, and consultation in the schools. Schools are subject to numerous Federal and state laws. Typically, once a referral is made for assessment in a school, there is a limited amount of time allotted between the referral and the meeting to develop the

IEP. Although both health care and educational settings work on tight timelines, schools are perhaps more vulnerable because of restrictive legal mandates. These institutional differences can contribute to confusion, misunderstanding, and working at cross-purposes for all involved in the care of the child. Additional information about legal issues in the schools is available elsewhere (e.g., Reschly & Bersoff, 1999; Sales, Krauss, Sacken, & Overcast, 1999).

Assessment: Practical Considerations

Pediatric psychologists often have limited knowledge about Federal and state regulations, statutes, case law, and other administrative mandates that can profoundly affect how assessments are performed in educational settings. Pertinent Federal statutes include Individuals with Disabilities Education Act (IDEA), the Rehabilitation Act of 1973 (Public Law 93-122 or "Section 504"), and the Family Educational Rights and Privacy Act (FERPA). Practitioners must consider that, in addition to Federal guidelines, individual states implement the Federal mandates according to their own idiosyncratic rules (Woody, La Voie, & Epps, 1992). Furthermore, most public school statutory law is enacted at the state level (Jacob-Timm & Hartshorne, 1998). As it is beyond the scope of this chapter to review in detail laws as they pertain to assessment (see Rae & Fournier, 2001), a summary is provided herein.

Most of the required regulations concerning assessment are contained in the IDEA. The original act called the Education for all Handicapped Children Act (Public Law 94-142) included Protection in Evaluation Procedures, which required assessment of the student's underlying strengths and needs. Under these regulations, assessment is used to determine if a student could be qualified for special services and to determine the best placement if the student was found to be eligible (National Council on Disability, 1996). Additional standards for assessment were developed in Public Law 99-457 mandating multidisciplinary evaluation and procedures for measuring progress, as well as allowing for the provision of services to the preschool-age population. In 1997, IDEA was renewed, with assessment procedures added for students with behavioral concerns (i.e., functional assessment). Functional assessment is intended to investigate the environmental and social context of behaviors as an important part of the assessment of the student. Examining patterns of strengths, needs, and influences of the setting helps to direct intervention and placement for the student. Although currently required for students with behavioral disorders, functional assessment may become an essential part of all assessment for special education services in the years to come.

The parameters of IDEA can have a profound impact on pediatric psychologists because of the special requirements for nondiscriminatory assessment. First, the assessment must include multiple sources of information. Pediatric psychologists often do not have access to school personnel and, as a result, are at a disadvantage if trying to write a useful report for educational purposes. Second, the assessment process must be timely. Timely evaluation refers to the legal requirements that evaluation must be completed within a prescribed period of time from the initiation of the referral. Third, the testing tools must be reliable and valid for the unique population for which they are used. Although pediatric psychologists should address the adaptive and accommodation needs of the students, they might not be aware of specialized educational tests and common adaptations used in an educational setting. Finally, the child must meet the specific legal criteria needed for certification in a particular special education category. Pediatric psychologists are not always aware of the special education categories or the specific criteria needed to certify the child in that category for their particular state.

In addition to IDEA, in 1973 Public Law 93-122 produced what is commonly called Section 504. This law provides for equal access to programs and services, as well as forbidding discrimination of persons with disabilities solely on their disability. Although the law was not originally developed for school settings, there is increasing use of Section 504 for school-age children (Jacob-Timm & Hartshorne, 1998). In particular, many school systems are choosing to serve children under Section 504 mandates if they do not qualify for services under IDEA. This suggests that the children served by Section 504 must already be assessed to have a disability. With Section 504, there are not the legal protections and due process available in IDEA. As such, it is generally believed that providing services under IDEA is a first choice, and Section 504 can be used as a second choice, or in some cases, an additional choice. Pediatric psychologists may not be aware that Section 504 can be a useful tool in helping to get a child with a disability specific educational services.

In 1974, FERPA was enacted. This law provides for parents, and in some cases for the students themselves, to inspect and possibly to challenge school records. There are several aspects of this act that have been addressed in case law that have an impact on pediatric psychologists even though the act is most applicable to educational agencies. For example, if the pediatric psychologist's report is used as a part of the educational assessment, that report is subject to FERPA, even though it was generated outside of the school setting. Therefore, this law may create ethical dilemmas for the pediatric psychologist, especially in regard to securing confidentiality, test materials, and maintenance of records. In the same way, pediatric psychologists usually consider raw test data and test protocols as confidential material. Under FERPA case law, the parents have the right to examine this information. It must be made available by the pediatric psychologist if requested by the parents. This holds true even if the pediatric psychologist keeps the materials in a file separate from the student's cumulative folder (John K. and Mary K. v. Board of Education for School District #65, Cook County, 1987; Parents Against Abuse in Schools v. Williamsport Area School District, 1991). Case law can also dictate the conditions in which assessment procedures can be used or the type of assessment (Guadalupe Organization, Inc. v. Tempe Elementary School District, 1972; California Association of School Psychologists v. Superintendent of Public Education, 1994). Case law has even prescribed assessment procedures for ethnic populations (Larry P. v. Riles, 1972). Obviously, pediatric psychologists who are not knowledgeable of the legal regulations required in the school setting are at a distinct disadvantage to complete a competent evaluation.

Schools often do not accept assessment reports by pediatric psychologists for one of several reasons. First, the reports are often not relevant to the legal requirements of the school. For example, the pediatric psychologist might report that a child has a specific learning disability, but the psychologist has not used the relevant state-mandated inclusion criteria, and/or the psychologist has not used psychometric instruments approved by the state. Second, the reports might not have relevant and/or useful recommendations for the educational setting. For example, the pediatric psychologist might not know how to translate the test results into meaningful modifications or accommodation strategies for the classroom. In the same way, because they may not be aware of the resources available in the school district, the recommendations provided by pediatric psychologists might be unrealistic or unaffordable to the school district (e.g., a full-time aide in a self-contained classroom). Furthermore, any specific programmatic recommendation must come from the IEP committee that has the legal mandate for making this type of recommendation. Thus, the pediatric psychologist must carefully consider the nature and scope of recommendations intended for the school setting. In practice, it is generally better of describe the setting (e.g., a placement with a low student-to-teacher ratio and where there are few transitions) than prescribe a specific placement (e.g., self-contained classroom). In the same vein, although recommendations regarding specific educational goals and objectives should be left to the IEP committee, general modifications and accommodations can be included (e.g., the child may benefit from use of larger print size in reading).

Intervention: Practical Considerations

Pediatric psychologists interfacing with school settings must first determine to whom the intervention should be directed. Initially, the child would appear to be the prime candidate for the intervention, but in actual practice pediatric psychologists often direct interventions to others in the child's environment. For example, for the young child who is oppositional and defiant, the target for intervention is likely to include the parents. In the school setting, the target could be the teacher as well, particularly when considering classroom and instruction management. If the target of the intervention does not agree, then working around this can be challenging. Although the pediatric psychologist would readily have access to parents, the pediatric psychologist might not have access to school and thus would not be able to conduct an intervention with teachers or other school personnel. In fact, to interface with schools, pediatric psychologists must have consent from the child's parents. Even when permission is given, pediatric psychologists may still not have access to schools; legal restrictions in some states do not allow any practitioners access to a particular school unless they are certified as a "school psychologist."

Pediatric psychologists usually generate their own treatment plan directed toward the needs of the child. In contrast, school psychologists work within the purview of the IEP; the treatment plan for the school psychologist is a collaborative agreement among the members of the IEP committee. Direct intervention can encompass a wide range of activities for the psychologist in the school setting. Interventions can also be indirect, which can include parent training, adjustment of curriculum in the school setting, or introduction of additional resources, such as bibliotherapy or a school-wide social skills program. Certain interventions might also be restricted in school settings, such as the use of adversive-based interventions (Jacob Timms, 1996). The access to resources must also be considered. Certain types of interventions, such as conducting family therapy, may not be available because training and expertise of available school personnel precludes this or because of the lack of access to the child's parents. Another consideration is that interventions in the school setting need to take into account the educational needs of the child. The pediatric psychologist may not be sensitive to the school's available resources rendering the intervention worthless.

School psychologists rarely make recommendations that impact the child in the medical setting, but pediatric psychologists make recommendations that can and do impact the child in the school setting. There are several possible reasons for this. One possibility is the mystique of the medical profession who is respected and rarely challenged by school personnel. For example, few school personnel would challenge a physician's diagnosis of attention deficit hyperactivity disorder. Pediatric psychologists also may have a presumed higher status, because many school psychologists are at the master's or specialist level instead of the doctoral level. On the other hand, it is recognized that educational recommendations from pediatric psychologists often are not generated. First, educational evaluations for children in health care settings may be a low priority. Second, the pediatric psychologist may not be interested in or trained to make educational recommendations

Consultation: Practical Considerations

Pediatric psychologists are specifically trained to consult with physicians, nurses, and other health care personnel (Drotar, 1995). Unlike school psychologists who are able to consult with teachers over the course of an entire school year, pediatric psychologists often are only able to consult with health care providers over a much shorter period of time because children move in and out of the health care system. In addition, health care providers (e.g., physicians, nurses) only have contact with a child for a few days at a time, unlike teachers who are involved with a child for an entire year of sustained contact. Consultation services by pediatric psychologists are often not funded directly and, as a result, consults are done quickly. In contrast to school psychologists, pediatric psychologists frequently consult with parents. Within the consulting relationship, there is always a question about who actually is the "customer" of the consultation. Care must be taken that the needs of the child are balanced with the institutional needs of the school setting. In most cases, school psychologists consult with teachers, but less frequently consult with parents because of availability issues.

SCHOOL PSYCHOLOGISTS WORKING WITH MEDICAL ISSUES

Akin to the problem with pediatric psychologists in school settings, a prime ethical concern for school psychologists assessing, consulting, or intervening with children who have medical problems involves the question of competence. It is commonplace for school psychologists to work with children and adolescents who have medical or health-related conditions. In fact, there are trends toward greater collaboration with primary care providers; growth of school-based health centers; increased involvement in the collaborative treatment of chronic and serious medical disorders; and the integration of health, mental health, social, and community services in schools (Kubiszyn, 1999). From the common cold to multiple hospitalizations for chronic illnesses or with the death of a child from accident or illness, the school psychologist must work with a range of medically related problems. For example, the school psychologist must consider whether or not a child scheduled for assessment should be evaluated if she or he has a functional medical problem that can interfere with test performance. From common illnesses to medication effects of treatment of a chronic health condition, the school psychologist must determine if the medical condition will interfere with performance. In addition, there is the legally mandated timetable for assessment that can complicate the school psychologist's decision. The child's ability to produce representative performances across assessment foci must be considered. With other types of medical problems, school psychologists face other challenges. When a child is receiving ongoing medical treatment, the school psychologist may or may not have knowledge of the course of the illness, the course of treatment, or the impact of the illness and/or treatment on physical, psychosocial, or cognitive processes. It should be noted that this is an essential part of the training of pediatric psychologists (Spirito et al., in press). To make an informed decision, the school psychologist must rely on training, and access to available resources (such as journal articles and books), and personnel (such as the school nurse, the child's parents, and the child). Although medical reports might be available, these reports are written for medical personnel. These reports are filled with medical terminology, unfamiliar abbreviations, and have little, if any, relevance to school functioning. The pediatric psychologist typically has more in-depth training in medical illness, access up-to-date medical information, and access to personnel (often the "curbside" consultation) that can assist in better understanding of the impact of the illness.

School personnel are often not informed when a child has a serious medical condition. There are several reasons this occurs. Parents may be focused on the medical aspects that can be life-threatening, rather than addressing the more mundane school issues. The parents may also be assuming that the school personnel know what is occurring. The parent may also assume that school personnel understand the nature of the disease or illness, as well as the course of treatment. Parents may assume that school personnel can understand the implications of the illness or disease and its associated treatment on the child's education. Finally, the nature of the illness and its treatment may not allow time for information to be shared.

When school psychologists do interact with medical personnel and the medical "system," they often do not understand the rules of the medical culture (Drotar, 1995). This can lead to difficulty in interdisciplinary collaboration in that school psychologists may not appreciate the subtle "turf issues" for medical professionals. Physicians, nurses, and other health care personnel believe that they know best what would constitute proper medical care for the child. They can sometimes see a well-intentioned school psychologist as intervening inappropriately in the medical domain of the child. In the same way, school psychologists can also believe that, although well-intentioned, medical personnel do not understand important issues regarding the child's school environment or the child's educational needs. A subtle competition can occur between school psychologists and medical personnel about who is best able to help the child.

School psychologists are not always knowledgeable about the customs, language, and practices in medical situations. In contrast to the diagnoses made by medical personnel (e.g., physical disabilities, psychiatric illness, medical conditions), school psychologists tend to diagnose problems related to special education categories (e.g., learning disability) or those associated with emotional adjustment. In addition, school psychologists often have a behavioral and/or systemic orientation to conceptualizing cases whereas medical personnel often conceptualize cases in terms of medical or biological processes. Obviously, recommendations also have a similar bias. Finally, school psychologists may not be able to move within time parameters required in medical settings. Often assessment, consultation, and intervention are expedited at a pace that is quicker in medical settings as compared with school settings. School psychologists should familiarize themselves with ethical concerns in health care settings (see Rae, Worchel, & Brunnquell, 1995).

Assessment: Practical Considerations

Any assessment of children with medical and emotional disabilities requires extraordinary attention to the special vulnerabilities of these children. It is also exacerbated by the complicated and chronic nature of these conditions requiring a qualitative and developmental approach to assessment (Rae & Fournier, 2001). In addition, assessment of children by a school psychologist most likely will take place in a school where the psychologist might have conflicting roles. These role conflicts might include being an employee of the school district, an advocate for the child, and a supportive helping professional for parents. For example, school administrators might have a vested interest in a particular assessment outcome (e.g., labeling a child as "autistic"), because additional funding may become available to the school district. This role conflict is very similar for the hospital administrator who would compel a pediatric psychologist to diagnose a child with an insurance-reimbursable DSM-IV diagnosis.

School psychologists assessing children always must consider the rights, welfare, and best interests of all parties involved (Knauss, 2001). Ethical mandates require honesty in evaluations, but professional judgments can be influenced by institutional requirements for expedience. School psychologists can be constrained by the educational system when they write assessment reports. Because of the various requirements of Federal and state guidelines and laws, school psychologists can write a legally safe report, but one that may not provide useful information to address the referral question. In this regard, the welfare of the students might be compromised.

Because physicians usually diagnose "Other Health-Impaired" students, school psychologists may have a limited role in the assessment of these children. At the same time, school psychologists are almost always involved in the development and implementation of recommendations for these children. In addition, school psychologists often have responsibility as part of an interdisciplinary team to diagnose other disorders that often require interface with medical personnel (e.g., attention deficit hyperactivity disorder). This fact requires school psychologists to become very knowledgeable about a range of medical disorders often seen in schools (Phelps, 1998). It also requires school psychologists to interact with medical personnel to understand the nature and extent of the medical disorder. In the same way, school psychologists should know that pediatric psychologists often have access to a range of tests specifically designed for particular medical populations (e.g., cerebral palsy) or specialized tests that may be unavailable to the school psychologist (e.g., neuropsychological tests). To ensure that the most competent assessment is undertaken with the goal of benefiting the student, school psychologists and pediatric psychologists should consult with each other about who can provide the most appropriate assessment of these children and adolescents.

Intervention: Practical Considerations

Children with medical problems require special consideration to the nature of their medical problem when planning an intervention. Obviously, this situation requires individualized interventions tailored to the special needs of that child. At the same time, school psychologists working with children who have medical needs may extend focus from individual approaches to intervention (e.g., individual psychotherapy) to more institutional approaches (e.g., classroom intervention). School psychologists are trained in systemic interventions and also have to pay particular attention to the unique needs of the particular child.

When children have significant medical problems and have to miss a significant amount of school because of extended hospitalizations, incapacitating medical treatments or lack of mobility, those children may require specialized interventions to integrate them back into school (e.g., Worchel-Prevatt et al., 1998). In the same way, school-based health centers are also an emerging practice area (Carlson, Tharinger, Bricklin, DeMers, & Paavola, 1996). Finally, school psychologists have had to negotiate emerging health care problems (e.g., AIDS) in the schools. This type of situation provokes serious ethical considerations, such as confidentiality vs. need to know (Peter, 1998). In every instance, the overriding ethical principle for school psychologists considering any intervention should be the best interest and welfare of the child.

Consultation: Practical Considerations

School psychologists are specifically trained in consultation with teachers and other school personnel. Because the child is in a school setting, school psychologists are able to consult with teachers and others involved in the child's education over the course of the entire school year. If the child is in the same school over a period of years (e.g., a 3-year middle school), then there can be longitudinal consultation as well. In contrast to pediatric psychologists, school psychologists infrequently consult with parents. It is difficult for school psychologists to consult with school staff about medically related problems of students when they lack specific knowledge about the medical conditions. School psychologists must always work for the welfare of the child and/or the consultee; they should be aware that a dual relationship with the school, the child, and the consultee may exist (Conoley & Conoley, 1992). As a consultant, the school psychologist must keep in mind that other school personnel (e.g., teachers) may not be aware and are not bound by the specific ethical guidelines for professional psychologists (Riccio & Hughes, 2001). As a result, the school psychologist as consultant should help the consultee understand ethical principles, such as confidentiality, informed consent, and welfare of the student before proceeding with the consultation.

GENERAL ETHICAL AND LEGAL ISSUES

Confidentiality

Ensuring confidentiality of personal information within a school or health care setting gleaned from an assessment, consultation, and intervention is a primary obligation for both school psychologists and pediatric psychologists (APA, 2002). If confidentiality was not maintained, patients and students would be reluctant to divulge any personal information whatsoever; it is the hallmark of trust for any therapeutic relationship (Everstine et al., 1980). At the same time, maintaining confidentiality for children is different than maintaining confidentiality for adults. Children do not expect strict confidentiality, because parents, teachers, and doctors are often knowledgeable about intimate aspects of their private lives unknown to others. In contrast, teenagers require more assurances of confidentiality, because they are often suspicious of intentions and motives of adults (Rae, 2001).

The limits of confidentiality are often a problem for psychologists working in a health care or school setting because of the conflicting expectations for the client (e.g., student, patient), parent, setting stakeholders (e.g., teacher, physician), and the institution (e.g., school, clinic, hospital). Before undertaking a clinical activity, the school psychologist or pediatric psychologist should attempt to clarify any potential differences in understanding of confidentiality issues for those involved. Even when this is clarified, it is recognized that each individual or institution might have different expectations of the limits of privacy. For example, a physician might expect to be informed of private information (e.g., trouble with the law) obtained during an individual therapy session that has little relevance to the child's medical condition, but may impact on adherence to medical regimen. Exactly who controls the information and to whom it is shared must be discussed with the individuals and institutional representatives before the clinical activity occurs. It is important that the parents and child have the final decision about the limits of confidentiality. It is also recognized that, over time, confidentiality expectations might change. For example, the adolescent may not want teachers to know about medication management of an illness. If these changes occur, the school psychologist or pediatric psychologist should redefine his or her role to all parties involved. The situation is exacerbated by the fact that, in schools, the integrity in professional relationships may be difficult to maintain; the community nature of the schools can also lead to dual relationship conflicts (Riccio & Hughes, 2001).

Confidentiality should be discussed before any assessment or intervention activity. Parents and older children should acknowledge in writing their mutual understanding of confidentiality although this is not always done in schools or health care settings. This would include the fact that no written or oral information would be communicated to anyone without the parent's written approval. The circumstances when confidentiality would be broken either by statue (e.g., abuse) or by ethical principle (e.g., danger to self or others) should also be delineated. In contrast, confidentiality is usually not obtained for consultation in schools and health care institutions. Students and patients have given tacit consent to consultation activities by being in the institution. Both pediatric psychologists and school psychologists are allowed to obtain or administer appropriate professional consultations as a way of providing appropriate professional care, but they should reveal only that information that is relevant to the consultation and avoid revealing unnecessary private information.

There are several legal considerations in regard to confidentiality. The pediatric psychologist and school psychologist should be willing to consult with legal and professional colleagues, and be knowledgeable of all local, state, Federal, and case law requirements (Gustafson & McNamara, 1987). For example, reporting suspicion of abuse is legally required in all states, although the abuse may not always be reported because of the concern of negative impact on the child (National Research Council, 1993; Rae & Worchel, 1991). In the same way, many states mandate breaking confidentiality without the client's consent to disclose information to protect the child from harm to self or others. The pediatric psychologist or school psychologist must assess the potential of danger and disclose information only to appropriate public authorities, professional workers, the potential victim, and/or the parents as prescribed by law. In this situation, the psychologist must evaluate the risk of imminent and serious harm being inflicted. If a child or adolescent has threatened and is capable of committing suicide or homicide, it is clear that confidentiality should be broken. On the other hand, in schools and health care settings, the decision to break confidentiality can be effected by the psychologist's values and biases. The school psychologist or pediatric psychologist must decide if there is imminent and/or serious harm as defined by his or her value system. Pediatric psychologists have illustrated these value differences when judging risky adolescent behaviors in such areas as substance use, sexual behavior, and suicidal behavior that are effected by intensity, frequency, and duration of the behavior (Rae, Sullivan, Razo, George, & Ramirez, 2002). The pediatric psychologist and school psychologist should discuss their values and beliefs during the initial stages of professional contact.

Another key confidentiality issue for the psychologist is balancing the *right* vs. the *need* to obtain confidential information. Parents have both the right and the need to know confidential information. In fact, parents have the legal right to information about their minor children in most circumstances. In contrast, in the health care and/or school setting, the right and the need to know become blurred. For example, if a child has been assessed to have a learning disability in reading, the child may be eligible for special education services. In the school setting, the need to know about this information extends to all that have a responsibility for teaching the child. In fact, not knowing about a disability compromises legally mandated modifications and accommodations that might be required to assist the child's learning. Others less involved in direct teaching, such as the bus driver, would typically have no need to know about this. In the medical setting, knowledge about the learning disability could be helpful to the physician and the pediatric psychologist, but is not needed by those not involved with indirect care, such as a lab technician. In contrast, for a child in the school who has a medical condition, such as Type I diabetes, the need to know is more comprehensive. Not only will those with direct teaching responsibility need to know, so will those involved with daily activities, such as the playground supervisor. To do less compromises the child's safety and welfare. The same would hold true in the medical setting, with the need to know extended into indirect care personnel as well.

Ethical principles state that psychologists must document the services they perform and should maintain accurate, current, and pertinent records of services. In addition, they should maintain appropriate confidentiality in the creating, storing, accessing, transferring, and disposition of records (APA, 2002). In schools, written information is typically kept in a central location, with procedures for access, such as signatures as well written rationale for access. In health care settings, the procedures vary widely and can range from access limited by the pediatric psychologist in a private file to the written information being part of the medical record. Any documentation (e.g., progress notes, IEP report, assessment report, letters) should only include information that is germane to the purposes of that documentation. This situation often creates a dilemma for the pediatric psychologist and school psychologist who want to document thoroughly and accurately, but also wants to be sensitive to the potentially harmful effects to the child of revealing this information. In disseminating confidential information about a child, information should be limited to that which is required to assist with educational intervention in the schools and/or medical care in the health care setting. In practice, pediatric psychologists arguably may have more difficulty with this requirement, because their reports are likely to include more sensitive details and may involve confidential information about others besides the child that are necessary for understanding a clinical issue. For example, although information about parent martial status may be beneficial for the pediatric psychologist to develop psychological interventions, it is less likely to have direct bearing on the development of educational interventions. Information that involves parents or other caregivers must either be restricted, or must be specifically released. In the same way, there might be information related to a child's medical condition (e.g., parent health status) that is included in the pediatric psychologist's report that does not need to be communicated with the school. The same rationale holds true for the educational report generated by a school psychologist.

Although educational information may be less problematic as it is more typically solely about the child, information that is not germane to the specific request for information should not be included. For example, a school psychologist's report that includes information about other children in a group therapy would be inappropriate for release.

One issue that emerges between schools and health care facilities is the question of when it is appropriate for the pediatric psychologist and school psychologist to share verbal information. Obviously, information about a specific case should not be discussed without appropriate releases obtained. School psychologists and pediatric psychologists can be itinerant, that is, not practicing in a set office with set times. The school psychologist often has responsibility for more than one school, thus is "on the road" frequently. Furthermore, within each school, the locale of practice is changed. The school psychologist may be observing in any number of locations, including classrooms, playgrounds, and the lunchroom. Meeting places can include classrooms, offices, and/or any space that is available. Even planned time in one locale can be changed by ongoing circumstances. Like the school psychologist, the pediatric psychologist faces similar locale problems. Although there may be a designated office, consultations often are conducted in hospital rooms. Planned time in one locale can be changed by emergencies. Thus, the sharing of information face to face can be challenging and is most often performed by telephone.

A second aspect of sharing information comes through reports. Both the pediatric psychologist and school psychologist write reports in an ethically responsible manner. Their reports will contain similar elements, such as background information, behavioral observations, assessment results, interpretation, and recommendations. In addition, the reports will conform to institutional standards. Despite these similarities, these reports may or may not be helpful in alternative settings because of several factors. First, each institutional setting requires psychological reports to be performed for a specific purpose. The school psychologist typically writes reports to be used in eligibility determinations (e.g., severely emotionally disturbed, learning disabled, mentally retarded). In contrast, the pediatric psychologist typically is writing reports that are addressing a focal referral question that will vary dependent on the source of referral. A second reason the reports may not bridge well between the two settings is the audience of the report. Although both the school psychologist and the pediatric psychologist will be writing to a multidisciplinary audience, the typical training of the report recipients will vary. School personnel have predominantly educationally focused training, and the medical personnel tend have medically focused training. Whereas this appears to be blatantly obvious difference, there are also subtleties that must be considered. Both disciplines must write reports in a manner that parents, who may or may not have educational and/or medical training, can understand. Additionally, the report must be useful to the intended purpose; however, the report may be required in another setting. For example, the child recently diagnosed with Type I diabetes, an understanding of learning disabilities (available from the school report) would enhance the pediatric psychologist's input in designing the appropriate level of the child's involvement in the medical regimen. Conversely, understanding the psychosocial impact and recommended interventions would be helpful to the school psychologist in consulting with the classroom teacher.

Consent and Assent

Pediatric psychologists and school psychologists may not be familiar with informed consent requirements in school settings and in health care settings, respectively. In health care settings, parents or guardians must give consent to have a minor child assessed or treated. In school settings, parents or guardians also give consent, but if the parents refuse, the assessment or intervention can take place after a due process procedure as prescribed by state and Federal laws.

When assessing or treating in a school setting, psychologists should explain the potential risks and benefits of any assessment or intervention to parents and children. At the same time, fully informing children is difficult because they have an age-appropriate lack of experience and diminished capabilities to make an informed decision. Informed consent with children and parents involves four elements. First, participants must be competent to make a decision about assessment and/or intervention. Psychologists should inform children in a manner commensurate with their psychological capabilities, seek their assent, and consider the child's preferences and best interests. Unfortunately, pediatric psychologists do not always attempt the assessment of competence (Rae & Worchel, 1991). At the same time, the psychologist should assess the child's stage of cognitive development (Koocher & Keith-Spiegel, 1990). Weithorn (1984) has postulated that minors aged 14 years and above appear to be equally competent to consent to treatment when compared with adults. Assent issues become more complicated when dealing with life-threatening illnesses (Kunin, 1997).

Second, participation must be voluntary. In both school and health care settings, refusal for assessment or intervention is not usually tolerated. Although there is an institutional need to complete the assessment or intervention, the psychologist should attempt to develop an atmosphere where coercion is kept to a minimum. In fact, it can be argued that, to be effective, an assessment and/or intervention needs to be voluntary; coercion is unlikely to yield a positive result. In actual fact, once the parents or guardians have consented, the minor's wishes are usually irrelevant from a legal standpoint. On the other hand, a minor has the legal right to consent to certain kinds of assessments (e.g., suicide) or interventions (e.g., drug abuse counseling), depending on the laws of the particular state in which the child or adolescent resides. In most states, children or adolescents can also consent to psychological services if they have been legally designated as an emancipated minor. In the same way, a minor can obtain emergency psychological services if the minor has diminished capacity or is in danger to self or others.

Third, participants must be knowledgeable about the assessment or intervention. The psychologist should fully explain all elements of the assessment or intervention in a way that is understandable and unambiguous. Again, it is incumbent on the psychologist to answer questions and to avoid apparent misunderstandings. In actual practice, this is often not done with children or adolescents. Finally, the consent must be appropriately documented. Because of regulations of health care settings, pediatric psychologists usually have little trouble with this requirement. When a child enters a health care setting (e.g., hospital), parents have already given a blanket permission to perform a range of expected interventions on a child. In school settings, the consent is much more tacit, except for psychological assessments where legally mandated written consent is required.

On the other hand, obtaining informed assent might not be possible for some children. There may be circumstances in which the child is assessed or treated regardless of his or her assent. This occurs in both health care settings and schools. In these circumstances, sensitivity to the dignity of the child must be a major concern of the psychologist. For example, if the child does not want to participate in an assessment, it is important that the psychologist provide a positive experience where he or she experiences success; there must be opportunity for the child to show strengths and skills, rather than only weaknesses.

Research Issues

Pediatric psychologists and school psychologists may be interested in conducting research in schools or health care settings, but may be unfamiliar with the logistical, ethical, and legal issues involved. Most of the relevant ethical considerations are delineated in the *Ethical Principles of Psychologists and Code of Conduct* (APA, 2002), because this code is most applicable to research for psychologists in educational and health care settings. The Belmont Report (OPRR, 1979) describes basic ethical principles in research, including respect for persons, beneficence, and justice and preeminent Federal guidelines outline ethical procedures in research (OPRR, 1991).

From the beginning of a research project, a sound research plan is crucial to conducting an ethical study. If an ethical quandary exists, the researcher should consult with peers, institutional review boards, appropriate authorities, and colleagues who have expertise working with the special population being studied (e.g., children with disabilities). Psychological research should yield some benefit to research participants, researchers, funding agencies, and society (Sieber, 2000). Researchers might be prone to overestimate benefits to "win over" potential participants or to justify a risky intervention. The researcher also should be cognizant of the degree of risk inherent in the research being planned. Research participants should be fully informed as to the nature and extent of any potential risk. Research should have a favorable risk/benefit ratio that is related to the general ethical principle of beneficence. Most research in psychology entails minimal or no risk; it almost never involves any physical risk. Because of this comparatively lower risk, psychologists might minimize the negative impact of an unpleasant emotional experience. Psychologists must be aware when their status might inadvertently influence the participant during the informed consent process. For example, an authoritative researcher encouraging their inclusion might inappropriately influence children and parents to participate.

When performing research, great care should be taken to protect children's rights and welfare. It must be demonstrated that the researcher is cognizant of the special vulnerabilities of children and take care to address them. Because of the easy availability of children as research participants, schools or hospitals have the potential to be inadvertently misused. Children have a compromised capacity for free consent, while in the dependent setting of a school or hospital. Children do not have appropriate judgment or mental capacity to make an informed decision about research participation. In addition, children with disabilities common to school settings (e.g., learning disabilities, mental retardation, emotional disturbance) or health care settings (e.g., mental incapacity, medication cognitive effects) may have additional difficulty understanding the concepts of risk and benefit. Because of this diminished capacity, we have previously argued that children should not be participants in any psychosocial research that has potential for even minimal risk (Rae & Fournier, 1986).

The Institutional Review Board must approve any research project, but this may not be available in school districts. Often, schools have a much more informal process of approving research and in those cases the psychologist must educate those involved about the research and what special considerations must be taken into account. It is at this point that participants are recruited and informed consent obtained. Informed consent must be provided voluntarily and without coercion. Prospective participants must be given the option to decline participation or withdraw at any time, even after they have provided consent. For consent to be voluntary, prospective participants should understand the benefits and risks of participation, all relevant aspects of the research, and the consequences of declining participation—all of which should have been included on the consent form. A more detailed description of this process is described elsewhere (Jacob-Timm & Hartshorne, 1998; Rae & Sullivan, 2003).

RECOMMENDATIONS FOR MAINTAINING ETHICAL AND LEGAL STANDARDS

First and foremost, pediatric psychologists and school psychologists must be aware of their own limitations and not practice outside the bounds of their competence. Pediatric psychologists and school psychologists may not always have skills appropriate for professional functioning in each other's domain. It requires a vigilant self-awareness to continue to monitor one's own level of skill proficiency in a new professional area. A psychologist should also be aware of his or her bias and values that could effect ethical decision-making. Another important component of appropriate professional functioning is the ability to understand the institutional culture with which one is working. For example, the pediatric psychologist should know school settings, and the school psychologist should know health care settings if each is going to function competently. This would include knowing the unique ethical and legal standards of each setting and how they apply to people in those settings. Before interacting with school settings, pediatric psychologists should study a general text about the field of school psychology (e.g., Reynolds & Gutkin, 1999); in the same way, school psychologists should study a general text about the field of pediatric psychology (e.g., Roberts, 1995).

Empirically supported or evidenced-based interventions must be considered as the standard of care (Stoiber & Kratochwill, 2001). When interventions are applied, the psychologist must understand the unique constraints for each setting. For example, school systems will likely need to consider if there is an IEP involved, and medical settings must consider if the intervention is appropriate to the setting. Although it may seem appropriate to consider a particular intervention, there are serious legal and ethical ramifications of doing this without considering what is realistic within settings. If there is an ethical or legal question, it is incumbent on the pediatric psychologist or school psychologist to consult with colleagues. In this regard, pediatric psychologists should consult with school psychologists and visa versa to keep communication flowing between the two professional groups. Although the complexity will most likely create "ethical tugs" (Jacob-Timms, 1999), both groups will benefit from the interaction.

School psychologists and pediatric psychologists are more alike than they are different. Because of the foci of their practices, they work toward the best interest and welfare of children they serve. Knowing the commonalties and distinctions of legal and ethical practice will not only assist in better understanding of each other's discipline, this understanding can ultimately better serve the interests of children and their families.

REFERENCES

American Psychological Association [APA]. (2002). Ethical principles of psychologists and code of conduct. *American Psychologist, 57*, 1060–1073.

American Psychological Association [APA], American Educational Research Association [AERA], & the National Council on Measurement in Education [NCME]. (1998). *Standards for educational and psychological testing.* Washington, DC: Author.

California Association of School Psychologists v. Superintendent of Public Instruction, 21 IDELR 130 (N.D. Cal. 1994).

Carlson, C. I., Tharinger, D. J., Bricklin, P. M., DeMers, S. T., & Paavola, J. C. (1996). Health care reform and psychological practice in schools. *Professional Psychology: Research and Practice, 27*, 14–23.

Conoley, J. C., & Conoley, C. W. (1992). *School consultation: Practice and training* (2nd ed.). New York: Macmillan.

Drotar, D. (1995). *Consulting with pediatricians: Psychological perspectives.* New York: Plenum.

Everstine, L., Everstine, D. S., Heymann, G. M., True, R. H., Frey, D. H., Johnson, H. G., & Seiden, R. H. (1980). Privacy and confidentiality in psychotherapy. *American Psychologist, 35*, 828–840.

Guadaupe Organization, Inc. v. Tempe School District No. 3, Civ. No. 71-435 (D. Ariz., 1972).

Gustafson, K. E., & McNamara, J. R. (1987). Confidentiality with minor clients: Issues and guidelines for therapists. *Professional Psychology: Research and Practice, 18*, 503–508.

Jacob-Timm, S. (1996). Ethical and legal issues associated with the use of aversives in the public schools: The SIBIS controversy. *School Psychology Review, 25*, 184–198.

Jacob-Timm, S. (1999). Ethically challenging situations encountered by school psychologists. *Psychology in the Schools, 36*, 205–217.

Jacob-Timm, S., & Hartshorne, T. S. (1998). *Ethics and law for school psychologists* (3rd ed.). New York: Wiley.

John K. and Mary K. v. Board of Education for School District #65, Cook County, 504 N.E.2d 797 (Ill.App. 1 Dist. 1987).

Koocher, G. P., & Keith-Spiegel, P. C. (1990). *Children, ethics, and the law: Professional issues and cases*. Lincoln, NE: University of Nebraska Press.

Knauss, L. K. (2001). Ethical issues in psychological assessment in school settings. *Journal of Personality Assessment, 77*, 231–241.

Kubiszyn, T. (1999). Integrating health and mental health services in schools: Psychologists collaborating with primary care providers. *Clinical Psychology Review, 19*, 179–198.

Kunin, H. (1997). Ethical issues in pediatric life-threatening illness: Dilemmas of consent, assent, and communication. *Ethics and Behavior, 7*, 43–57.

Larry P. v. Riles, 343 F.Supp. 1306 (D.C. N.D. Cal., 1972), *aff'd.*, 502f.2d 963 (9th Cir. 1974), further proceedings, 495 F.Supp. 926 (D.C. N.D. Cal., 1979), *aff'd.*, 502 F.2d 693 (9th Cir. 1984).

Meyers, J., & Nastasi, B. K. (1999). Primary prevention in school settings. In C. R. Reynolds & T. B. Gutkin (Eds.), *Handbook of school psychology* (3rd ed., pp. 764–799). New York: Wiley.

National Association of School Psychologists [NASP]. (2000). *Professional conduct manual*. Bethesda, MD: Author.

National Council on Disability. (1996). *Improving the implementation of the individuals with disabilities education act: Making schools work for all of America's children*. Washington, DC: Author.

National Research Council. (1993). *Understanding child abuse and neglect*. Washington, DC: National Academy Press.

Office for Protection from Research Risks [OPRR], Protection of Human Subjects. National Commission for the Protection of Human Subjects of Biomedical and Behavioral Research. (1979). *The Belmont Report: Ethical principles and guidelines for the protection of human subjects of research* (GPO 887–809). Washington, DC: U.S. Government Printing Office.

Office for Protection from Research Risks [OPRR], Protection of Human Subjects. (1991, June 18). Protection of human subjects: Title 45, Code of Federal Regulations, Part 46 (GPO 1992 O-307-551). *OPRR Reports*, pp. 4–17.

Parents Against Abuse in Schools (PAAS) v. Williamsport Area School District, 594 A.2d 796 (Pa. Commw. Ct. 1991).

Peter, M. (1998). Psychology, AIDS, and ethics: A discussion of selected practice issues. In R. M. Anderson, T. L. Needels, & H. V. Hall (Eds.), *Avoiding ethical misconduct in psychology specialty areas* (pp. 159–165). Springfield, IL: Charles C Thomas.

Phelps, L. (Ed.). (1998). *Health-related disorders in children and adolescents*. Washington, DC: American Psychological Association.

Rae, W. A. (2001). Common teen-parent problems. In C. E. Walker & M. C. Roberts (Eds.), *Handbook of clinical child psychology* (3rd ed., pp. 621–637). New York: Wiley.

Rae, W. A., & Fournier, C. J. (1986). Ethical issues in pediatric research: Preserving psychosocial care in scientific inquiry. *Children's Health Care, 14*, 242–248.

Rae, W. A., & Fournier, C. J. (2001). Ethical and legal issues in assessment of children with special needs. In R. J. Simeonsson & S. L. Rosenthal (Eds.), *Psychological and developmental assessment: Children with disabilities and chronic conditions* (pp. 359–376). New York: Guilford.

Rae, W. A., & Sullivan, J. R. (2003). Ethical considerations in clinical psychology research. In M. C. Roberts & S. S. Ilardi (Eds.), *Handbook of research methods in clinical psychology* (pp. 52–70). Malden, MA: Blackwell.

Rae, W. A., Sullivan, J. R., Razo, N. P., George, C. A., & Ramirez, E. (2002). Adolescent health risk behavior: When do pediatric psychologists break confidentiality? *Journal of Pediatric Psychology, 27*, 541–549.

Rae, W. A., & Worchel, F. F. (1991). Ethical beliefs and behaviors of pediatric psychologists: A survey. *Journal of Pediatric Psychology, 16*, 727–745.

Rae, W. A., Worchel, F. F., & Brunnquell, D. (1995). Ethical and legal issues in pediatric psychology. In M. C. Roberts (Ed.), *Handbook of pediatric psychology* (2nd ed., pp. 19–36). New York: Guilford.

Reynolds, C. R., & Gutkin, T. B. (Eds.). (1999). *Handbook of school psychology* (3rd ed.). New York: Wiley.

Reschly, D. J., & Bersoff, D. N. (1999). Law and school psychology. In C. R. Reynolds & T. B. Gutkin (Eds.), *Handbook of school psychology* (3rd ed., pp. 1077–1112). New York: Wiley.

Riccio, C. A., & Hughes, J. N. (2001). Established and emerging models of psychological services in school settings. In J. N. Hughes, A. M. La Greca, & J. C. Conoley (Eds.), *Handbook of psychological services for children and adolescents* (pp. 63–87). New York: Oxford.

Roberts, M. C. (Ed.). (1995). *Handbook of pediatric psychology* (2nd ed.). New York: Guilford.

Roberts, M. C., & McNeal, R. E. (1995). Historical and conceptual foundations of pediatric psychology. In M. C. Roberts (Ed.), *Handbook of pediatric psychology* (2nd ed., pp. 3–18). New York: Guilford.

Sales, B. D., Krauss, D. A., Sacken, D. M., & Overcast, T. D. (1999). The legal rights of students. In C. R. Reynolds & T. B. Gutkin (Eds.), *Handbook of school psychology* (3rd ed., pp. 1113–1144). New York: Wiley.

Sieber, J. E. (2000). Research planning: Basic ethical decision-making. In B. D. Sales & S. Folkman (Eds.), *Ethics in research with human participants* (pp. 13–26). Washington, DC: American Psychological Association.

Spirito, A., Brown, R. T., D'Angelo, E., Delamater, A., Rodrigue, J., & Siegel, L. (in press). Training pediatric psychologists for the 21st century. In M. C. Roberts (Ed.), *Handbook of pediatric psychology* (3rd eds.). New York: Guilford.

Stoiber, K. C., & Kratochwill, T. R. (2001). Evidence-based intervention programs: Rethinking, refining, and renaming the new standing section of *School Psychology Quarterly*. *School Psychology Quarterly, 16*, 1–8.

Weithorn, L. A. (1984). Children's capacities in legal contexts. In N. D. Reppucci, L. A. Weithorn, E. P. Mulvey, & J. Monahan (Eds.), *Children, mental health, and law* (pp. 25–55). Beverly Hills, CA: Sage.

Woody, R. H., LaVoie, J. C., & Epps, S. (1992). *School psychology: A developmental and social systems approach.* Boston: Allyn and Bacon.

Worchel-Prevatt, F., Heffer, R. W., Prevatt, B. C., Miner, J., Young-Saleme, T., Horgan, D., Lopez, M. A., Rae, W. A., & Frankel, L. (1998). A school reentry program for chronically ill children. *Journal of School Psychology, 36*(3), 261–279.

Author Index

Numbers in *italics* indicate pages with complete bibliographic information.

B

C

D

E

F

G

H

I

K

M

O

P

Q

R

S

T

U

V

W

X

Y

Z

Subject Index

A

B

C

D

F

I

J

K

L

M

N

O

P

Q

R

S

T